THE BOOK OF
ANSWERS

FROM THE PUBLISHERS OF
THE GUINNESS BOOK OF RECORDS

GUINNESS BOOKS

Published by GBR Educational Ltd, a division of Guinness
Publishing Ltd, 33 London Road, Enfield, Middlesex EN2
6DJ, England.

'Guinness' is a registered trademark of Guinness Publishing
Ltd.

British Library Cataloguing in Publication Data

Guinness book of answers. – 6th ed.
  1. Curiosities and wonders
  032′.02   AG243

  ISBN 0–85112–857–2

Acknowledgements
The publishers would particularly like to thank the following
for their help in preparing this edition:

David Symes, Peter Johnson, Christine Hughes, Anna
Pavord, Frederico Magnano Spoleto SJ, Béatrice Frei,
Richard Laws, David Roberts, Bernadette Bidwell,
Hortense Michelob, Morton D. Tipple, John Catchpole,
Tim Furniss, Yvonne Burgess, Alan Hamp.

Typeset, printed and bound in Great Britain by
William Clowes Limited, Beccles and London

Contents

4   Contents

The Calendar

Days of the week

ENGLISH	LATIN	SAXON
Sunday	Dies Solis	Sun's Day
Monday	Dies Lunae	Moon's Day
Tuesday	Dies Martis	Tiu's Day
Wednesday	Dies Mercurii	Woden's Day
Thursday	Dies Jovis	Thor's Day
Friday	Dies Veneris	Frigg's Day
Saturday	Dies Saturni	Saeternes' Day

Tiu was the Anglo-Saxon counterpart of the Nordic Tyr, son of Odin, God of War, who came closest to Mars (Greek, Ares) son of the Roman God Jupiter (Greek, Zeus). Woden was the Anglo-Saxon counterpart of Odin, Nordic dispenser of victory, who came closest to Mercury (Greek, Hermes), the Roman messenger of victory. Thor was the Nordic God of Thunder, eldest son of Odin and nearest to the Roman Jupiter (Greek, Zeus), who was armed with thunder and lightning. Frigg (or Freyja), wife of Odin, was the Nordic Goddess of Love, and equivalent to Venus (Greek, Aphrodite), Goddess of Love in Roman mythology. Thus four of the middle days of the week are named after a mythological husband and wife and their two sons.

The seasons

The four seasons in the northern hemisphere are astronomically speaking:

Spring from the vernal equinox (20 Mar.) to summer solstice (21 June till AD 2000).

Summer from the summer solstice (21 June) to the autumnal equinox (22 Sept. in 1988).

Autumn (or Fall in USA) from the autumnal equinox (22 Sept.) to the winter solstice (21 Dec. or 22 Dec.).

Winter from the winter solstice (21 Dec.) to the vernal equinox (20 Mar. in 1988).

In the southern hemisphere, of course, autumn corresponds to spring, winter to summer, spring to autumn and summer to winter.

The solstices (from Latin *sol*, sun; *stitium*, standing) are the two times in the year when the sun is farthest from the equator and appears to be still. The equinoxes (from Latin *aequus*, equal; *nox*, night) are the two times in the year when day and night are of equal length when the sun crosses the equator.

The longest day (day with the longest interval between sunrise and sunset) is the day on which the *solstice* falls and in the northern hemisphere occurs on 21 June, or more rarely on 22 June.

Old style (Julian) and new style (Gregorian) dates

The Julian Calendar, introduced by Julius Caesar in 46 BC, on the advice of the Egyptian astronomer Sosigenes, was in use throughout Europe until 1582 when Pope Gregory XIII ordained that 5 Oct. should be called 15 Oct. The discrepancy occurred because of the Augustinian ruling of AD 4 that every fourth year shall be of 366 days and hence include a Leap Day.

Countries switched from the Old Style (Julian) to the New Style (Gregorian) system as follows:

1582	Italy, France, Portugal, Spain
1583	Flanders, Holland, Prussia, Switzerland, and the Roman Catholic states in Germany
1586	Poland
1587	Hungary
1600	Scotland (except St Kilda till 1912)
1700	Denmark and the Protestant states in Germany
1700–40	Sweden (by gradual process)
1752	England and Wales, Ireland and the Colonies, including North America (11-day lag)
1872	Japan (12-day lag)
1912	China (13-day lag)
1915	Bulgaria (13-day lag)
1917	Turkey and the USSR (13-day lag)
1919	Romania and Yugoslavia (13-day lag)
1923	Greece (13-day lag)

LEAP YEAR

Leap years occur in every year the number of which is divisible by four, e.g. 1980, except centennial years, e.g. 1700, 1800, or 1900, which are treated as common or non-leap years *unless* the number of the *century* is divisible by four, e.g. 1600 was a leap year and 2000 will be a leap year.

The whole process is one of compensation for over-retrenchment of the discrepancy between the calendar year of 365 days and the mean solar year of 365·24219878 days. The date when it will be necessary to suppress a further leap year, sometimes assumed to be AD 4000, AD 8000, etc., is not in fact yet clearly specifiable, owing to minute variations in the earth-sun relationship.

The word 'leap' derives from the Old Norse *hlaupár*, indicating a leap in the sense of a jump. The origin probably derives from the observation that in a bissextile (i.e. leap) year any fixed day festival falls on the next day of the week but one to that on which it fell in the preceding year, and not on the next day of the week as happens in common years.

The term bissextile derives literally from a double (bis) day inserted after the sixth (sextile) day before the calends of March. Thus the Julian calendar compensated (albeit inaccurately) for the discrepancy between its year and the mean solar year.

EASTER DAY

Easter, the Sunday on which the resurrection of Christ is celebrated in the Christian world is, unlike Christmas which is fixed, a 'moveable feast'.

The celebration of Easter is believed to have begun in about AD 68. The English word Easter probably derives from *Eostre*, a Saxon goddess whose festival was celebrated about the time of the vernal equinox.

EASTER DAYS AND LEAP YEARS 1980–2000
(Years in bold type are leap years)

1980	6 Apr.	1987	19 Apr.	1994	3 Apr.
1981	19 Apr.	**1988**	3 Apr.	1995	16 Apr.
1982	11 Apr.	1989	26 Mar.	**1996**	7 Apr.
1983	3 Apr.	1990	15 Apr.	1997	30 Mar.
1984	22 Apr.	1991	31 Mar.	1998	12 Apr.
1985	7 Apr.	**1992**	19 Apr.	1999	4 Apr.
1986	30 Mar.	1993	11 Apr.	**2000**	23 Apr.

The date of Easter has been a matter of constant dispute between the eastern and western Christian churches. Much of the calendar of the Christian religion revolves around the date upon which, in any given year, Easter falls and repercussions extend in Christian countries into civil life.

The United Nations in 1949 considered the establishment of a perpetual world calendar, which would automatically and incidentally have fixed Easter, but the proposals were shelved indefinitely in 1956.

The Vatican Council in Rome in October 1963 approved the resolution to fix the date of Easter, subject to the agreement of other Christian churches, by 2058 votes to nine against.

The boldest scheme for calendar reform, which is winning increasing support, is that the year should be divided into four quarters of thirteen weeks, with each day of the year being assigned a fixed day of the week. By this scheme it is thought likely that Easter would always fall on Sunday, 8 Apr. For this calendar to conform with the mean solar year, a 'blank day' would be required each year in addition to the intercalary day in a leap year.

Jewish Calendar 5757–48

Jewish Month				AM, 5747				AM, 5748	
Tishri	1st	..	..	1986 October	4	..	..	1987 September	24
Marcheshvan	1st	..	..	November	3	..	..	October	24
Kislev	1st	..	..	December	3	..	..	November	22
Tevet	1st	..	..	1987 January	2	..	..	December	22
Shevet	1st	..	..	January	31	..	..	1988 January	20
Adar	1st	..	..	March	2	..	..	February	19
Ve-Adar	1st	..	..			..	..		
Nisan	1st	..	..	March	31	..	..	March	19
Iyar	1st	..	..	April	30	..	..	April	18
Sivan	1st	..	..	May	29	..	..	May	17
Tammuz	1st	..	..	June	28	..	..	June	16
Av	1st	..	..	July	27	..	..	July	15
Elil	1st	..	..	August	26	..	..	August	14

Islamic Calendar

The Islamic Calendar is a lunar reckoning from the year of the *hegira*, AD 622, when Mohammed travelled from Mecca to Medina. It runs in cycles of 30 years, of which the 2nd, 5th, 7th, 10th, 13th, 16th, 18th, 21st, 24th, 26th, and 29th are leap years; 1406 is the 26th year of the cycle. Common years have 354 days, leap years 355, the extra day being added to the last month, Zu'lhijjah. Except for this case, the 12 months beginning with Muharram have alternately 30 and 29 days.

Hijrah year	Muslim New Year	First day of Ramadan	Festival of Breaking the Fast	Festival of Sacrifice
1405 AH	26 September 1984	20 May 1985	19 June 1985	26 August, 1985
1406 AH	15 September 1985	9 May 1986	8 June 1986	15 August 1986
1407 AH	5 September 1986	29 April 1987	29 May 1987	5 August 1987
1408 AH	25 August 1987	17 April 1988	17 May 1988	24 July 1988
1409 AH	13 August 1988	6 April 1989	6 May 1989	13 July 1989
1410 AH	3 August 1989	27 March 1990	26 April 1990	3 July 1990
1411 AH	23 July 1990	16 March 1991	15 April 1991	22 June 1991
1412 AH	12 July 1991	4 March 1992	3 April 1992	10 June 1992
1413 AH	1 July 1992	22 February 1993	24 March 1993	31 May 1993
1414 AH	20 June 1993	11 February 1994	13 March 1994	20 May 1994
1415 AH	9 June 1994	31 January 1995	2 March 1995	9 May 1995
1416 AH	30 May 1995	21 January 1996	20 February 1996	28 April 1996
1417 AH	18 May 1996	9 January 1997	8 February 1997	17 April 1997
1418 AH	8 May 1997	30 December 1997	29 January 1998	7 April 1998
1419 AH	27 April 1998	19 December 1998	18 January 1999	27 March 1999
1420 AH	16 April 1999	8 December 1999	7 January 2000	15 March 2000

Names of Islamic months

1	Muharram (New Year)	4	Rabia II	7	Rajab	10	Shawwai
2	Safar	5	Jumada I	8	Shaban	11	Zu'lkadah
3	Rabia I	6	Jumada II	9	Ramadan*	12	Zu'lhijjah

* The date on which Ramadan begins may vary from the calendar date. It actually starts only after the new moon is sighted from the Naval Observatory in Cairo.

Chinese Calendar

The Chinese New Year begins at the first new moon after the sun enters Aquarius, meaning that the day will fall between 21 January and 19 February of the modern (Gregorian) calendar.

Bat	Ox	Tiger	Hare (Rabbit)	Dragon	Snake	Horse	Sheep (Goat)	Monkey	Rooster	Dog	Pig
1960	1961	1962	1963	1964	1965	1966	1967	1968	1969	1970	1971
1972	1973	1974	1975	1976	1977	1978	1979	1980	1981	1982	1983
1984	1985	1986	1987	1988	1989	1990	1991	1992	1993	1994	1995

Eight-year calendar

1987	M	T	W	T	F	S	S	M	T	W	T	F	S	S	M	T	W	T	F	S	S	M	T	W	T	F	S	S	M	T	W	T	F	S	S	M	T
January				1	2	3	4	5	6	7	8	9	10	11	12	13	14	15	16	17	18	19	20	21	22	23	24	25	26	27	28	29	30	31			
February							1	2	3	4	5	6	7	8	9	10	11	12	13	14	15	16	17	18	19	20	21	22	23	24	25	26	27	28			
March							1	2	3	4	5	6	7	8	9	10	11	12	13	14	15	16	17	18	19	20	21	22	23	24	25	26	27	28	29	30	31
April			1	2	3	4	5	6	7	8	9	10	11	12	13	14	15	16	17	18	19	20	21	22	23	24	25	26	27	28	29	30					
May					1	2	3	4	5	6	7	8	9	10	11	12	13	14	15	16	17	18	19	20	21	22	23	24	25	26	27	28	29	30	31		
June	1	2	3	4	5	6	7	8	9	10	11	12	13	14	15	16	17	18	19	20	21	22	23	24	25	26	27	28	29	30							
July			1	2	3	4	5	6	7	8	9	10	11	12	13	14	15	16	17	18	19	20	21	22	23	24	25	26	27	28	29	30	31				
August						1	2	3	4	5	6	7	8	9	10	11	12	13	14	15	16	17	18	19	20	21	22	23	24	25	26	27	28	29	30	31	
September			1	2	3	4	5	6	7	8	9	10	11	12	13	14	15	16	17	18	19	20	21	22	23	24	25	26	27	28	29	30					
October				1	2	3	4	5	6	7	8	9	10	11	12	13	14	15	16	17	18	19	20	21	22	23	24	25	26	27	28	29	30	31			
November							1	2	3	4	5	6	7	8	9	10	11	12	13	14	15	16	17	18	19	20	21	22	23	24	25	26	27	28	29	30	
December	1	2	3	4	5	6	7	8	9	10	11	12	13	14	15	16	17	28	19	20	21	22	23	24	25	26	27	28	29	30	31						

1988	M	T	W	T	F	S	S	M	T	W	T	F	S	S	M	T	W	T	F	S	S	M	T	W	T	F	S	S	M	T	W	T	F	S	S	M	T
January					1	2	3	4	5	6	7	8	9	10	11	12	13	14	15	16	17	18	19	20	21	22	23	24	25	26	27	28	29	30	31		
February	1	2	3	4	5	6	7	8	9	10	11	12	13	14	15	16	17	18	19	20	21	22	23	24	25	26	27	28	29								
March	1	2	3	4	5	6	7	8	9	10	11	12	13	14	15	16	17	18	19	20	21	22	23	24	25	26	27	28	29	30	31						
April					1	2	3	4	5	6	7	8	9	10	11	12	13	14	15	16	17	18	19	20	21	22	23	24	25	26	27	28	29	30			
May							1	2	3	4	5	6	7	8	9	10	11	12	13	14	15	16	17	18	19	20	21	22	23	24	25	26	27	28	29	30	31
June			1	2	3	4	5	6	7	8	9	10	11	12	13	14	15	16	17	18	19	20	21	22	23	24	25	26	27	28	29	30					
July			1	2	3	4	5	6	7	8	9	10	11	12	13	14	15	16	17	18	19	20	21	22	23	24	25	26	27	28	29	30	31				
August	1	2	3	4	5	6	7	8	9	10	11	12	13	14	15	16	17	18	19	20	21	22	23	24	25	26	27	28	29	30	31						
September			1	2	3	4	5	6	7	8	9	10	11	12	13	14	15	16	17	18	19	20	21	22	23	24	25	26	27	28	29	30					
October						1	2	3	4	5	6	7	8	9	10	11	12	13	14	15	16	17	18	19	20	21	22	23	24	25	26	27	28	29	30	31	
November			1	2	3	4	5	6	7	8	9	10	11	12	13	14	15	16	17	18	19	20	21	22	23	24	25	26	27	28	29	30					
December				1	2	3	4	5	6	7	8	9	10	11	12	13	14	15	16	17	18	19	20	21	22	23	24	25	26	27	28	29	30	31			

1989	M	T	W	T	F	S	S	M	T	W	T	F	S	S	M	T	W	T	F	S	S	M	T	W	T	F	S	S	M	T	W	T	F	S	S	M	T
January							1	2	3	4	5	6	7	8	9	10	11	12	13	14	15	16	17	18	19	20	21	22	23	24	25	26	27	28	29	30	31
February			1	2	3	4	5	6	7	8	9	10	11	12	13	14	15	16	17	18	19	20	21	22	23	24	25	26	27	28							
March			1	2	3	4	5	6	7	8	9	10	11	12	13	14	15	16	17	18	19	20	21	22	23	24	25	26	27	28	29	30	31				
April						1	2	3	4	5	6	7	8	9	10	11	12	13	14	15	16	17	18	19	20	21	22	23	24	25	26	27	28	29	30		
May	1	2	3	4	5	6	7	8	9	10	11	12	13	14	15	16	17	18	19	20	21	22	23	24	25	26	27	28	29	30	31						
June				1	2	3	4	5	6	7	8	9	10	11	12	13	14	15	16	17	18	19	20	21	22	23	24	25	26	27	28	29	30				
July						1	2	3	4	5	6	7	8	9	10	11	12	13	14	15	16	17	18	19	20	21	22	23	24	25	26	27	28	29	30	31	
August		1	2	3	4	5	6	7	8	9	10	11	12	13	14	15	16	17	18	19	20	21	22	23	24	25	26	27	28	29	30	31					
September					1	2	3	4	5	6	7	8	9	10	11	12	13	14	15	16	17	18	19	20	21	22	23	24	25	26	27	28	29	30			
October							1	2	3	4	5	6	7	8	9	10	11	12	13	14	15	16	17	18	19	20	21	22	23	24	25	26	27	28	29	30	31
November			1	2	3	4	5	6	7	8	9	10	11	12	13	14	15	16	17	18	19	20	21	22	23	24	25	26	27	28	29	30					
December					1	2	3	4	5	6	7	8	9	10	11	12	13	14	15	16	17	18	19	20	21	22	23	24	25	26	27	28	29	30	31		

1990	M	T	W	T	F	S	S	M	T	W	T	F	S	S	M	T	W	T	F	S	S	M	T	W	T	F	S	S	M	T	W	T	F	S	S	M	T
January	1	2	3	4	5	6	7	8	9	10	11	12	13	14	15	16	17	18	19	20	21	22	23	24	25	26	27	28	29	30	31						
February				1	2	3	4	5	6	7	8	9	10	11	12	13	14	15	16	17	18	19	20	21	22	23	24	25	26	27	28						
March				1	2	3	4	5	6	7	8	9	10	11	12	13	14	15	16	17	18	19	20	21	22	23	24	25	26	27	28	29	30	31			
April							1	2	3	4	5	6	7	8	9	10	11	12	13	14	15	16	17	18	19	20	21	22	23	24	25	26	27	28	29	30	
May		1	2	3	4	5	6	7	8	9	10	11	12	13	14	15	16	17	18	19	20	21	22	23	24	25	26	27	28	29	30	31					
June					1	2	3	4	5	6	7	8	9	10	11	12	13	14	15	16	17	18	19	20	21	22	23	24	25	26	27	28	29	30			
July							1	2	3	4	5	6	7	8	9	10	11	12	13	14	15	16	17	18	19	20	21	22	23	24	25	26	27	28	29	30	31
August			1	2	3	4	5	6	7	8	9	10	11	12	13	14	15	16	17	18	19	20	21	22	23	24	25	26	27	28	29	30	31				
September						1	2	3	4	5	6	7	8	9	10	11	12	13	14	15	16	17	18	19	20	21	22	23	24	25	26	27	28	29	30		
October	1	2	3	4	5	6	7	8	9	10	11	12	13	14	15	16	17	18	19	20	21	22	23	24	25	26	27	28	29	30	31						
November				1	2	3	4	5	6	7	8	9	10	11	12	13	14	15	16	17	18	19	20	21	22	23	24	25	26	27	28	29	30				
December						1	2	3	4	5	6	7	8	9	10	11	12	13	14	15	16	17	18	19	20	21	22	23	24	25	26	27	28	29	30	31	

1991	M	T	W	T	F	S	S	M	T	W	T	F	S	S	M	T	W	T	F	S	S	M	T	W	T	F	S	S	M	T	W	T	F	S	S	M	T
January		1	2	3	4	5	6	7	8	9	10	11	12	13	14	15	16	17	18	19	20	21	22	23	24	25	26	27	28	29	30	31					
February					1	2	3	4	5	6	7	8	9	10	11	12	13	14	15	16	17	18	19	20	21	22	22	23	25	26	27	28					
March					1	2	3	4	5	6	7	8	9	10	11	12	13	14	15	16	17	18	19	20	21	22	23	24	25	26	27	28	29	30	31		
April	1	2	3	4	5	6	7	8	9	10	11	12	13	14	15	16	17	18	19	20	21	22	23	24	25	26	27	28	29	30							
May			1	2	3	4	5	6	7	8	9	10	11	12	13	14	15	16	17	18	19	20	21	22	23	24	25	26	27	28	29	30	31				
June						1	2	3	4	5	6	7	8	9	10	11	12	13	14	15	16	17	18	19	20	21	22	23	24	25	26	27	28	29	30		
July	1	2	3	4	5	6	7	8	9	10	11	12	13	14	15	16	17	18	19	20	21	22	23	24	25	26	27	28	29	30	31						
August				1	2	3	4	5	6	7	8	9	10	11	12	13	14	15	16	17	18	19	20	21	22	23	24	25	26	27	28	29	30	31			
September							1	2	3	4	5	6	7	8	9	10	11	12	13	14	15	16	17	18	19	20	21	22	23	24	25	26	27	28	29	30	
October		1	2	3	4	5	6	7	8	9	10	11	12	13	14	15	16	17	18	19	20	21	22	23	24	25	26	27	28	29	30	31					
November					1	2	3	4	5	6	7	8	9	10	11	12	13	14	15	16	17	18	19	20	21	22	23	24	25	26	27	28	29	30			
December							1	2	3	4	5	6	7	8	9	10	11	12	13	14	15	16	17	18	19	20	21	22	23	24	25	26	27	28	29	30	31

1992	M	T	W	T	F	S	S	M	T	W	T	F	S	S	M	T	W	T	F	S	S	M	T	W	T	F	S	S	M	T	W	T	F	S	S	M	T
January			1	2	3	4	5	6	7	8	9	10	11	12	13	14	15	16	17	18	19	20	21	22	23	24	25	26	27	28	29	30	31				
February						1	2	3	4	5	6	7	8	9	10	11	12	13	14	15	16	17	18	19	20	21	22	23	24	25	26	27	28	29			
March							1	2	3	4	5	6	7	8	9	10	11	12	13	14	15	16	17	18	19	20	21	22	23	24	25	26	27	28	29	30	31
April			1	2	3	4	5	6	7	8	9	10	11	12	13	14	15	16	17	18	19	20	21	22	23	24	25	26	27	28	29	30					
May					1	2	3	4	5	6	7	8	9	10	11	12	13	14	15	16	17	18	19	20	21	22	23	24	25	26	27	28	29	30	31		
June	1	2	3	4	5	6	7	8	9	10	11	12	13	14	15	16	17	18	19	20	21	22	23	24	25	26	27	28	29	30							
July			1	2	3	4	5	6	7	8	9	10	11	12	13	14	15	16	17	18	19	20	21	22	23	24	25	26	27	28	29	30	31				
August						1	2	3	4	5	6	7	8	9	10	11	12	13	14	15	16	17	18	19	20	21	22	23	24	25	26	27	28	29	30	31	
September		1	2	3	4	5	6	7	8	9	10	11	12	13	14	15	16	17	18	19	20	21	22	23	24	25	26	27	28	29	30						
October				1	2	3	4	5	6	7	8	9	10	11	12	13	14	15	16	17	18	19	20	21	22	23	24	25	26	27	28	29	30	31			
November							1	2	3	4	5	6	7	8	9	10	11	12	13	14	15	16	17	18	18	20	21	22	23	24	25	26	27	28	29	30	
December		1	2	3	4	5	6	7	8	9	10	11	12	13	14	15	16	17	18	19	20	21	22	23	24	25	26	27	28	29	30	31					

1993	M	T	W	T	F	S	S	M	T	W	T	F	S	S	M	T	W	T	F	S	S	M	T	W	T	F	S	S	M	T	W	T	F	S	S	M	T
January					1	2	3	4	5	6	7	8	9	10	11	12	13	14	15	16	17	18	19	20	21	22	23	24	25	26	27	28	29	30	31		
February	1	2	3	4	5	6	7	8	9	10	11	12	13	14	15	16	17	18	19	20	21	22	23	24	25	26	27	28									
March	1	2	3	4	5	6	7	8	9	10	11	12	13	14	15	16	17	18	19	20	21	22	23	24	25	26	27	28	29	30	31						
April				1	2	3	4	5	6	7	8	9	10	11	12	13	14	15	16	17	18	19	20	21	22	23	24	25	26	27	28	29	30				
May						1	2	3	4	5	6	7	8	9	10	11	12	13	14	15	16	17	18	19	20	21	22	23	24	25	26	27	28	29	30	31	
June		1	2	3	4	5	6	7	8	9	10	11	12	13	14	15	16	17	18	19	20	21	22	23	24	25	26	27	28	29	30						
July				1	2	3	4	5	6	7	8	9	10	11	12	13	14	15	16	17	18	19	20	21	22	23	24	25	26	27	28	29	30	31			
August							1	2	3	4	5	6	7	8	9	10	11	12	13	14	15	16	17	18	19	21	21	22	23	24	25	26	27	28	29	30	31
September			1	2	3	4	5	6	7	8	9	10	11	12	13	14	15	16	17	18	19	20	21	22	23	24	25	26	27	28	29	30					
October					1	2	3	4	5	6	7	8	9	10	11	12	13	14	15	16	17	18	19	20	21	22	23	24	25	26	27	28	29	30	31		
November	1	2	3	4	5	6	7	8	9	10	11	12	13	14	15	16	17	18	19	20	21	22	23	24	25	26	27	28	29	30							
December			1	2	3	4	5	6	7	8	9	10	11	12	13	14	15	16	17	18	19	20	21	22	23	24	25	26	27	28	29	30	31				

1994	M	T	W	T	F	S	S	M	T	W	T	F	S	S	M	T	W	T	F	S	S	M	T	W	T	F	S	S	M	T	W	T	F	S	S	M	T
January						1	2	3	4	5	6	7	8	9	10	11	12	13	14	15	16	17	18	19	20	21	22	23	24	25	26	27	28	29	30	31	
February		1	2	3	4	5	6	7	8	9	10	11	12	13	14	15	16	17	18	19	20	21	22	23	24	25	26	27	28								
March		1	2	3	4	5	6	7	8	9	10	11	12	13	14	15	16	17	18	19	20	21	22	23	24	25	26	27	28	29	30	31					
April					1	2	3	4	5	6	7	8	9	10	11	12	13	14	15	16	17	18	19	20	21	22	23	24	25	26	27	28	29	30			
May							1	2	3	4	5	6	7	8	9	10	11	12	13	14	15	16	17	18	19	20	21	22	23	24	25	26	27	28	29	30	31
June			1	2	3	4	5	6	7	8	9	10	11	12	13	14	15	16	17	18	19	20	21	22	23	24	25	26	27	28	29	30					
July					1	2	3	4	5	6	7	8	9	10	11	12	13	14	15	16	17	18	19	20	21	22	23	24	25	26	27	28	29	30	31		
August	1	2	3	4	5	6	7	8	9	10	11	12	13	14	15	16	17	18	19	20	21	22	23	24	25	26	27	28	29	30	31						
September				1	2	3	4	5	6	7	8	9	10	11	12	13	14	15	16	17	18	19	20	21	22	23	24	25	26	27	28	29	30				
October						1	2	3	4	5	6	7	8	9	10	11	12	13	14	15	16	17	18	19	20	21	22	23	24	25	26	27	28	29	30	31	
November		1	2	3	4	5	6	7	8	9	10	11	12	13	14	15	16	17	18	19	20	21	22	23	24	25	26	27	28	29	30						
December				1	2	3	4	5	6	7	8	9	10	11	12	13	14	15	16	17	18	19	20	21	22	23	24	25	26	27	28	29	30	31			

THE ZODIAC

The zodiac (from the Greek *zōdiakos kyklos*, circle of animals) is an unscientific and astrological system devised in Mesopotamia *c.* 3000 BC.

The zodiac is an imaginary belt of pictorial constellations which lie as a backdrop quite arbitrarily 8 degrees on either side of the annual path or ecliptic of the sun. It is divided into twelve sections each of 30 degrees. Each has been allocated a name from the constellation which at one time coincided with that sector. The present lack of coincidence of the zodiacal sectors with the constellations from which they are named, has been caused mainly by the lack of proper allowance for leap days. The old order is nonetheless adhered to.

The traditional 'signs' are:
Aries, the Ram 21 Mar.–19 Apr.
Taurus, the Bull 20 Apr.–20 May
Gemini, the Twins 21 May–21 June
Cancer, the Crab 22 June–22 July
Leo, the Lion 23 July–22 Aug.
Virgo, the Virgin 23 Aug.–22 Sept.
Libra, the Balance 23 Sept.–23 Oct.
Scorpio, the Scorpion 24 Oct.–21 Nov.
Sagittarius, the Archer 22 Nov.–21 Dec.
Capricornus, the Goat 22 Dec.–19 Jan.
Aquarius, the Water Carrier 20 Jan.–18 Feb.
Pisces, the Fishes 19 Feb.–20 Mar.

STANDARD TIME

Until the last quarter of last century the time kept was a local affair, or, in the smaller countries, based on the time kept in the capital city. But the spread of railways across the vaster countries caused great time-keeping confusion to the various railway companies and their passengers. In 1880 Greenwich Mean Time (GMT) became the legal time in the British Isles and by 1884 the movement to establish international time zones was successful.

The world, for this purpose, is divided into 24 zones, or segments, each of 15° of longitude, with twelve that, being to the east, are fast on Greenwich time, and twelve that, being to the west, are slow on Greenwich time, due to the West-to-East rotation of the Earth.

Each zone is $7\frac{1}{2}$° on either side of its central meridian. The International Date Line – with some variations due to the convenience of political geography – runs down the 180° meridian. Sunday becomes Saturday when crossing the date line travelling eastward while Sunday becomes Monday when travelling west.

A very few countries or divisions of countries do not adhere to the Greenwich system at all and in others no zoning system is used, i.e. the whole nation, despite spanning more than one of the 24 segments, elects to keep the same time. Yet a third group (e.g. India) uses differences of half an hour.

Europe has three zones, part keeping GMT, others mid-European time (i.e. GMT + 1) and the remainder east European time (GMT + 2).

In the United States there are four zones: Eastern, Central, Mountain and Pacific, and these are 5, 6, 7 and 8 hours respectively slow on Greenwich.

The authoritative and complete reference, where the method of time keeping in every place in the world can be found, is *The Nautical Almanac*, published annually by HMSO.

WATCHES AT SEA

A watch at sea is four hours except the period between 4 p.m. and 8 p.m., which is, in the Royal Navy, divided into two short watches termed the first dog watch and the last dog watch. The word dog is here a corruption of 'dodge'. The object of these is to prevent the same men always being on duty during the same hours each day.

Midnight–4 a.m.	Middle Watch
4 a.m.–8 a.m.	Morning Watch
8 a.m.–noon	Forenoon Watch
noon–4 p.m.	Afternoon Watch
4 p.m.–6 p.m.	First Dog Watch
6 p.m.–8 p.m.	*Last Dog Watch
8 p.m.–Midnight	First Watch

* Called Second Dog in Merchant Navy.

Time is marked by bells – one stroke for each half-hour elapsed during a watch which thus ends on 8 bells or 4 bells for a dog watch. The New Year is brought in with 16 bells.

SUNRISE, SUNSET AND TWILIGHT

The Nautical Almanac gives the GMT of sunrise and sunset for each two degrees of latitude for every third day in the year. The sunrise is the instant when the rim of the sun appears above the horizon, and the sunset when the last segment disappears below the horizon. But because of the Earth's atmosphere, the transition from day to night and vice versa is a gradual process, the length of which varies according to the declination of the sun and the latitude of the observer. The intermediate stages are called twilight.

There are three sorts of twilight:

Civil twilight. This occurs when the centre of the sun is 6° below the horizon. Before this moment in the morning and after it in the evening ordinary outdoor activities are impossible without artificial light.

Nautical twilight. This occurs when the sun is 12° below the horizon. Before this time in the morning and after it in the evening the sea horizon is invisible.

Astronomical twilight. This is the moment when the centre of the sun is 18° below the horizon. Before this time in the morning or after it in the evening there is a complete absence of sunlight.

Time Zones and Relative Times

The surface of the earth is divided into 24 time zones. Each zone represents 15° of longitude or one hour of time. The passage of time follows the path of the sun moving in a westerly direction so that countries to the east of London and the Greenwich Meridian are ahead of Greenwich Mean Time (GMT) and countries to the west are behind.

All times given are based on noon in London but there may be inconsistencies of one or two hours in some cities caused by the seasonal use of daylight saving.

WEDDING ANNIVERSARIES

The choice of object or material attached to specific anniversaries is in no sense 'official'. The list below is a combination of commercial and traditional usage.

First/Cotton	Fourteenth/Ivory
Second/Paper	Fifteenth/Crystal
Third/Leather	Twentieth/China
Fourth/Fruit, flowers	Twenty-fifth/Silver
Fifth/Wooden	Thirtieth/Pearl
Sixth/Sugar	Thirty-fifth/Coral
Seventh/Wool, copper	Fortieth/Ruby
Eighth/Bronze, pottery	Forty-fifth/Sapphire
Ninth/Pottery, willow	Fiftieth/Golden
Tenth/Tin	Fifty-fifth/Emerald
Eleventh/Steel	Sixtieth/Diamond
Twelfth/Silk, linen	Seventieth/Platinum
Thirteenth/Lace	

Birthstones

Month	Stone
January	Garnet
February	Amethyst
March	Bloodstone or Aquamarine
April	Diamond
May	Emerald
June	Pearl, Moonstone or Alexandrite
July	Ruby
August	Sardonyx or Peridot
September	Sapphire
October	Opal or Tourmaline
November	Topaz
December	Turquoise or Zircon

When it is 12 noon in London the time in other cities of the world is:

City	Time	City	Time	City	Time
Accra	Noon	Darwin	9.30 p.m.	Nicosia	2 p.m.
Abu Dhabi	4 p.m.	Delhi	5.30 p.m.	Oslo	1 p.m.
Adelaide	9.30 p.m.	Djakarta	8 p.m.	Ottawa	7 a.m.
Algiers	1 p.m.	Dubai	4 p.m.	Panama City	7 a.m.
Amman	2 p.m.	Dublin	Noon	Paris	1 p.m.
Amsterdam	1 p.m.	Frankfurt	1 p.m.	Peking	8 p.m.
Ankara	2 p.m.	Geneva	1 p.m.	Perth	8 p.m.
Athens	2 p.m.	Gibraltar	1 p.m.	Prague	1 p.m.
Auckland	Midnight	Helsinki	2 p.m.	Quebec	7 a.m.
Baghdad	3 p.m.	Hobart	10 p.m.	Rangoon	6.30 p.m.
Bahrain	3 p.m.	Hong Kong	8 p.m.	Rawalpindi	5 p.m.
Bangkok	7 p.m.	Istanbul	2 p.m.	Reyjavik	Noon
Beirut	2 p.m.	Jerusalem	2 p.m.	Rio de Janeiro	9 a.m.
Belgrade	1 p.m.	Johannesburg	2 p.m.	Riyadh	3 p.m.
Berlin	1 p.m.	Karachi	5 p.m.	Rome	1 p.m.
Berne	1 p.m.	Kuala Lumpur	8 p.m.	San Francisco	4 a.m.
Bogota	8 a.m.	Kuwait	3 p.m.	Santiago	8 a.m.
Bombay	5.30 p.m.	Lagos	1 p.m.	Seoul	9 p.m.
Bonn	1 p.m.	Leningrad	3 p.m.	Singapore	7.30 p.m.
Brisbane	10 p.m.	Lima	7 a.m.	Sofia	2 p.m.
Brussels	1 p.m.	Lisbon	1 p.m.	Stockholm	1 p.m.
Bucharest	2 p.m.	Luxemburg	1 p.m.	Sydney	10 p.m.
Budapest	1 p.m.	Madras	5.30 p.m.	Taipei	8 p.m.
Buenos Aires	9 a.m.	Madrid	1 p.m.	Tehran	3.30 p.m.
Cairo	2 p.m.	Manila	8 p.m.	Tokyo	9 p.m.
Calcutta	5.30 p.m.	Melbourne	10 p.m.	Toronto	7 a.m.
Canberra	10 p.m.	Mexico City	6 a.m.	Tunis	1 p.m.
Cape Town	2 p.m.	Monrovia	11 a.m.	Vancouver	4 a.m.
Caracas	8 a.m.	Montevideo	8.30 a.m.	Vienna	1 p.m.
Chicago	6 a.m.	Montreal	7 a.m.	Warsaw	1 p.m.
Colombo	5.30 p.m.	Moscow	3 p.m.	Washington	7 a.m.
Copenhagen	1 p.m.	Nairobi	3 p.m.	Wellington	Midnight
Damascus	2 p.m.	New York	7 a.m.	Winnipeg	6 a.m.

Chronology of World Events

Wherever possible, the day and month are given for each entry;
otherwise they are listed after the dated entries for each relevant year.

c. 250 000 to	Paleolithic activity in Central America, Middle East,
c. 10 000 BC	Africa and Europe.
c. 9000 BC	Neolothic activity in Middle East; the domestication of animals and cultivation of crops.
c. 8000 BC	Cave paintings in France and Spain.
c. 7500 BC	Dog is domesticated.
c. 6800 BC	The first houses and towns (Jericho).
c. 6000 BC	Occupation of Crete.
	Rock paintings in N. America.
c. 4800 BC	Settlement in Upper Tigris valley.
	Settlement near Nile Delta.
c. 4200 BC	Start of Sumerian civilization.
4100 BC	Many settlements in Fertile Crescent in Middle East.
c. 4000 BC	Neolithic farmers arrive in Britain.
c. 3500 BC	Writing invented.
c. 3300 BC	First use of wheels for traction in Sumeria.
c. 3200 BC	Beginnings of Bronze Age in Middle East.
3100 BC	Egypt united under 1st Dynasty.
c. 2900 BC	Biblical Flood or Deluge.
	Indus Valley civilization formed.
c. 2750 BC	Founding of Troy.
2686 BC	First Pyramid built.
2575 BC	Great Pyramid at Giza.
2550 BC	Sphinx erected at Giza.
c. 2500 BC	Development of Chinese civilization.
c. 2145 BC	Silbury Hill, Wiltshire, built.
c. 2000 BC	Spread of Bronze Age 'Beaker People' from Spain to Europe.
c. 1900 BC	Wheel-made pottery in China.
c. 1800 BC	Use of horses in war.
1792 BC	Babylonia Empire founded.
c. 1600 BC	Stonehenge finished.
c. 1557 BC	Shang Dynasty founded in China.
1250/40 BC	Trojan War.
1235 BC	Exodus of Israelites from Egypt.
	Laws of Moses.
1195 BC	Battle of Jericho.
1122 BC	Foundation of Chow Dynasty in China.
1010 BC	David becomes King of Judah.
c. 900 BC	Rise of Assyria.
850 BC	Probable birthdate of Homer.
776 BC	First Olympiad in Greece.
753 BC	Founding of Rome by Romulus.
551 BC	Confucius born.
c. 500 BC	Iron Age people arrive in Britain.
495 BC	Sophocles born.
c. 490/400 BC	Beginnings of Maya civilization in Central America.
490 BC	Battle of Marathon.
480 BC	Persia invades Greece: the battle of Thermopylae.
	Buddha dies.
c. 460 BC	Birth of Hippocrates.
448 BC	Parthenon built.
435 BC	Pelopennesian War begins.
428 BC	Plato born.
404 BC	Athens falls to Sparta: end of Pelopennesian War.
399 BC	Socrates dies.
390 BC	Rome sacked by Gauls.
384 BC	Aristotle born.
323 BC	Alexander the Great dies.
275 BC	Celts settle in Yorkshire.
265 BC	First Punic War.
225/214 BC	Great Wall of China built.
218 BC	Hannibal crosses the Alps.
206 BC	Han Dynasty founded.
c. 200 BC	Chinese invent technique for casting iron.
102 BC	Julius Caesar born.
c. 100 BC	Use of water power to grind corn in Rome.
87 BC	Chinese record a comet, probably Halley's.
55 BC	Caesar lands in Britain.
46 BC	Introduction of Julian Calendar (present-day system).
44 BC	Assassination of Julius Caesar.
30 BC	Deaths of Cleopatra and Mark Anthony.
27 BC	Roman Empire declared under Augustus.
12 BC	First noted appearance in West of Halley's Comet.
4 BC	Most probable date of birth of Jesus Christ.

AD		
27		John the Baptist executed by Herod.
30		Death of Jesus Christ.
33		St Stephen, First Christian martyr, stoned.
37		Nero born.
43		Roman invasion of Britain.
		Paul begins his missions.
65		St Paul executed in Rome.
		Buddhism reaches China.
73		End of Masada siege.

79		Vesuvius erupts; Pompeii destroyed.
82		Romans penetrate to Scotland.
105		Paper invented in China.
122/8		Building of Hadrian's Wall.
132/5		Destruction of Jews as a nation by Romans.
139		Ptolomy makes accurate calculations of planetary movements.
192		Han Dynasty comes to an end.
c. 200		Goths found empire around Black Sea.
303		Persecution of Christians by Romans.
c. 310		St Alban, first British Christian martyr, dies.
312		Battle of Milvian Bridge won by Constantine.
316		Tsin Dynasty established in S. China.
317		Han Hun Dynasty established in N. China.
325		Council of Nicea.
330		Constantinople new, Christian, capital of Roman Empire.
341		Franks invade Gaul.
376/400		Goths and Vandals invade Roman Empire.
400		Attila born.
406		Roman legions leave Britain.
410		Visigoths led by Alaric sack Rome.
449		Beginnings of Saxon settlement in Britain, under Hengist.
451/2		Depredations of Attila in W. Europe.
453		Attila dies.
482		Emperor Justinian born.
c. 500		Possible victories of King Arthur over Anglo-Saxons.
c. 500		Beginnings of Japanese nation and culture.
525		St Benedict founds the monastery of Monte Cassino, and lays down his 'Rule' for monastic life.
534		Justinian Codex of Laws.
c. 550		Probable invention of gunpowder by Chinese.
		Mayan civilization builds Tikal.
552		Buddhism introduced to Japan.
563		St Columba founds Iona.
570		Mohammed born.
c. 590		Hindu arithmetic with place notations and use of symbol zero.
596		St Augustine sent to England (Kent).
604		Ethelbert builds first church of St Paul in London.
622		Mohammed flees from Medina and founds Islamic faith: his followers become Muslims.
628		Mecca becomes holy city.
632		Mohammed dies.
633		Koran compiled from Mohammed's revelations.
635		St Aidan founds monastery at Lindisfarne.
639		Lhasa becomes stronghold of Buddhism. Tibetan monasteries are built.
642		Destruction of the great library of Alexandria.
660		Ship and treasure burial at Sutton Hoo, Suffolk.
664		Synod of Whitby.
673		'Greek fire' invented and used in the defence of Constantinople.
689		Charles Martel born.
c. 700		Lindisfarne Gospels written.
		Beowulf composed.
731		Bede's Ecclesiastical History completed.
732		Battle of Tours, beginning Charles Martel's successful campaign to drive the Saracens out of France.
735		Bede dies.
741		Charles Martel dies.
742		Charlemagne born.
762		City of Baghdad founded.
776		Charlemagne begins his successful campaign against the Saxons.
c. 785		Offa's Dyke built.
786		Haroun el Rashid's court at Baghdad flourishes. The Thousand and One Nights recorded in state archives.
787		First Viking raid on England.
793		Vikings sack Lindisfarne.
c. 799		Book of Kells produced at Iona.
800	25 Dec.	Charlemagne crowned Emperor.
		The Athanasian Creed.
811		Paper currency first used in China.
817		Division of Carolingian Empire.
821		Chinese conquer Tibet.
835		First reference to a printed book (in China).
837		First carrier pigeon service (in Arab Empire).
843		Partition of Carolingian Empire.
		Scotland first united under MacAlpin.
846		Chola Empire in India.
847		Vikings colonize Iceland.
850		Capture of Kiev begins Varangian Empire of the Ros and, whence, Russia.
		Beginnings of algebra in Islamic Empire.
		First Viking settlement in Britain on Isle of Thanet.
853		Olaf the White (of Norway) subdues Vikings and Danes in Ireland and makes Dublin his capital.
860		Book of Artifices the earliest book on mechanical science, in Arabic.

871		Alfred becomes King of Wessex.
872		First hospital (in Cairo).
878		Alfred of Wessex defeats Danes at Edington.
888	13 Jan.	Death of Charles the Fat is followed by end of Carolingian Empire.
889		Angkor Wat, Cambodia, begun.
899		Death of Alfred.
914		Edward the Elder begins conquest of the Danelaw.
929	28 Sep.	Death of St Wenceslas.
930		The Althing (general court), the oldest parliament in the world, established in Iceland.
937		Scots defeated by Athelstan at Brunanburh.
942/945		Edmund conquers Danish England.
956		Windmills first described (in Persia); also horse racing.
962		Otto crowned as Holy Roman Emperor.
972		University founded in Cairo.
973		Edgar crowned at Bath as (First) King of all England.
978		First teaching hospital completed in Baghdad.
979		Ethelred becomes King of England.
980		Vikings renew raids on England.
982		North/South war in Vietnam.
		Eric the Red colonizes Greenland for Vikings.
984		Earliest dated astrolabe (Persian).
		New Mayan Empire founded.
990		Foundation of Orthodox Church in Russia.
991		Danes defeat English at Battle of Maldon.
999		Election of first French Pope (Silvester II).
1003		Leif Ericsson's voyage to N. America; discovers 'Wineland' (Nova Scotia).
1009		Danes invade England and attack London.
1010		*Tale of Genji*, first psychological novel in literature (Japanese).
1014		Svein of Denmark conquers England.
1016		Cnut becomes King of England.
1020		Floating magnet for navigation mentioned (Chinese).
1030		Chinese use movable wooden characters (type) for printing.
1040		Arabs introduce Hindu (so called 'Arabic') numerals in mathematical calculations.
1042		Edward the Confessor becomes King of England.
1045		Refounding of University of Constantinople.
1063		'Leaning Tower' and Campanile at Pisa started.
1066	14 Oct.	At the Battle of Hastings, Harold is defeated by William of Normandy.
	25 Dec.	William crowned King of England.
1071		Turks destroy Byzantine forces at Manzikert.
1086		Domesday Book completed.
1095		First Crusade.
1119		Knights Templar founded.
1147		Second Crusade.
1154		Henry II becomes King of England.
1170		Thomas à Becket murdered in Canterbury Cathedral.
1189		Third Crusade joined by Richard I of England.
1204		Fourth Crusade captures Constantinople.
1212		Most of Spain conquered by Christians.
1215		Magna Carta.
1220		Genghis Khan conquers Central Asia.
1242		Alexander Nevsky's victory over Teutonic Knights.
1265		First English Parliament meets.
1284		Edward I conquers Wales.
1314		Battle of Bannockburn secures Scottish independence.
1321		Dante dies.
1338		Beginning of 100 Years War between England and France.
1346		Battle of Crécy.
1348		The Black Death reaches Europe from Asia.
1349		Black Death in Britain kills up to half of the population.
1362		English replaces French as official language in Parliament and in the Courts.
1368(-1644)		Ming Dynasty in China.
1380		Victories of Timur (Tamburlaine) in Central Asia.
1381		Wat Tyler leads Peasants' Revolt.
1399		Henry IV becomes first Lancastrian King of England.
1400		Chaucer dies.
1415		Battle of Agincourt.
1431		Joan of Arc burned at the stake.
1453		End of 100 Years War.
		Turks seize Constantinople, ending Byzantine Empire.
1455		Gutenberg's 42-line Bible printed from movable type.
		Beginning of the Wars of the Roses (York and Lancaster).
1476		Caxton's printing press at Westminster.
1481		Beginnings of Inquisition in Spain.
1485		Battle of Bosworth; Henry VII claims throne: beginning of Tudor monarchy.
1492		Columbus discovers West Indies.
1494		The Pope divides the unexplored part of the world between Spain and Portugal.
1497-8		Vasco da Gama reaches India.
1513		Balboa discovers Pacific Ocean (by crossing Panama Isthmus).
		Battle of Flodden.
1517	17 Oct.	Luther nails his 95 theses to a church door in Wittenburg (beginning of the Reformation).
1519-20		Magellan's expedition completes circumnavigation of the world.
1519		Death of Leonardo da Vinci.
1520	4 June	Field of The Cloth of Gold meeting between Henry VIII and Francis I.
1521		Mexico conquered by Cortez.
1524		Peasants' Revolt in Germany.
1527	6 May	The Sack of Rome by German soldiers.
1531		Henry VIII becomes Head of Church of England.
1532		Conquest of Peru by Pizzarro.
1533		Birth of Elizabeth I.
1534		Execution of Sir Thomas More.
1545-63		The Council of Trent.
1547		Henry VIII dies.
1549		First prayer book in English.
1553		Northumberland's plot for Lady Jane Grey to become Queen fails and Mary I becomes Queen.
1555	25 Sept.	Peace of Augsberg.
		Tobacco introduced to Europe from America.
1558		Accession of Queen Elizabeth I.
1564		Shakespeare born.
		Michelangelo dies.
1568		Bottled beer invented.
1571		Battle of Lepanto; Turks defeated by Don Juan of Austria.
1576	27 Aug.	Titian dies.
1580		Akbar the Great is Emperor of India.
1580	30 Nov.	Francis Drake returns from circumnavigating the world in the *Golden Hind*.
1584		Death of Ivan the Terrible.
1587	8 Feb.	Mary Queen of Scots executed.
	19 Apr.	Sir Frances Drake 'singes the King of Spain's beard' by sacking Cadiz.
1588	23 July-8 Aug.	Defeat of Spanish Armada.
1590		Invention of a microscope.
1598	15 Apr.	Edict of Nantes grants toleration to Protestants in France.
1600		East India Company formed.
1602		Dutch East India Company founded.
1603		James VI of Scotland accedes to throne on death of Elizabeth I; becomes James I of England and Scotland.
1605	5 Nov.	Gunpowder Plot to blow up House of Lords discovered.
1607		Foundation of Jamestown, Virginia, as an English colony.
1608		Quebec founded as French settlement.
1610	3 Aug.	Hudson's Bay discovered.
1611		*Authorised Version of the Holy Bible* published.
1613		Michael Romanov elected Tsar of Russia and founds the House of Romanov.
1616	23 Apr.	Shakespeare and Cervantes die.
		Galileo threatened by Inquisition to stop teaching Copernican system (that the Earth goes round the sun).
1618		Beginning of the Thirty Years War.
1619		Harvey discovers the circulation of the blood.
1620	6 Sept.	Pilgrim Fathers leave Plymouth for New England in the *Mayflower*.
1621		Drainage of Lowlands in Netherlands begun.
1625		Charles I becomes King of England.
1629		Charles I orders Parliament to be dissolved and assumes personal rule.
1633		Dutch settle in Connecticut.
1636		Harvard University founded.
1640	3 Nov.	Long Parliament meets.
1642	22 Aug.	Civil War in England begins.
1643		Louis XIV becomes King of France.
1644		Battle of Marston Moor; Cromwell defeats Royalists.
1646		Charles I surrenders to Scots.
1648		Second Civil War in England begins.
1649	30 Jan.	Execution of Charles I.
	19 May	England declared to be a Commonwealth, under Oliver Cromwell as Protector.
1650		Air pump invented.
1652	30 June	First Anglo–Dutch War.
		Dutch found Cape Town.
1654		Union of Scotland and Ireland.
1658	3 Sept.	Oliver Cromwell dies.

1660		Long Parliament dissolved; Charles II restored to English throne.
1664		New York annexed to British.
1665		The Plague in Britain.
		Second Anglo–Dutch War begins.
1666	2–6 Sept.	Great Fire of London.
		Plague in London at its height.
1669	4 Oct.	Rembrandt dies.
1678		Titus Oates' 'Popish Plot'.
1679		Habeus Corpus Act passed.
1685		Duke of Monmouth's rebellion crushed at Battle of Sedgemoor.
		Louis XIV revokes Edict of Nantes.
1687		Newton's theory of gravitation.
1688		William of Orange lands in England.
		James II flees to France.
1689		Declaration of Rights in England.
		William and Mary become King and Queen.
1690	1 July	William III defeats James II at the Battle of the Boyne.
1692	13 Feb.	Massacre of Glencoe.
1693		National Debt established.
1694		Bank of England founded.
1698		First Eddystone lighthouse built.
1700		Great Northern War, between Baltic Powers, begins.
1701	12 June	Act of Settlement establishes House of Hanover to English Throne.
		War of Spanish Succession begins.
1703		Peter the Great founds St Petersburg.
1704	2 Aug.	Battle of Blenheim.
1705		Newcomen's steam engine.
1707		Union of England and Scotland establishes Great Britain.
1712		Last execution for witchcraft in England.
1713		Peace of Utrecht.
1715		First Jacobite rising defeated.
1716		Septennial Act extends life of parliament from 3 to 7 years.
1720		'South Sea Bubble' bursts, ruining thousands of speculators.
		Fahrenheit invents mercury thermometer.
1723		Christopher Wren dies.
1724		Kant born.
1726		First circulating library opens in Edinburgh.
1732		Covent Garden Theatre opened in London.
1733		Kay's Flying Shuttle for weaving.
1740		Frederick II (The Great) becomes King of Prussia.
1741		War of Austrian Succession.
1746	16 Apr.	Final defeat of Jacobites at Culloden.
1750		J. S. Bach dies.
1751		First volume of Encyclopédie published in France.
1752		Britain adopts Gregorian Calendar.
1753		British Museum founded.
1755	1 Nov.	Lisbon earthquake kills 30 000.
		Samuel Johnson's Dictionary published.
1756	27 Jan.	Wolfgang Amadeus Mozart born.
		Outbreak of the Seven Years War. The Black Hole of Calcutta.
1759	25 Jan.	Robert Burns born.
	18 Sept.	General Wolfe takes Quebec.
		Brindley's Canal between Manchester and Worsley marks beginning of canal transport in England.
1762		Harrison's chronometer for sea navigation wins Board of Longitude's prize for accuracy.
1763	10 Feb.	End of Seven Years War.
1764		Hargreaves invents Spinning Jenny.
1766	17 Feb	Malthus born.
1767	May	Britain taxes imports in American colonies.
1768	1 May	Duke of Wellington born.
		Royal Academy founded.
		Arkwright invents spinning frame.
1769		Cugnot's steam road carriage.
1770	28 Apr.	Cook lands at Botany Bay.
	17 Dec.	Beethoven born.
1771	14 May	Robert Owen born.
		Galvain discovers electric nature of nervous impulse.
1772	5 Aug.	First partition of Poland.
		Rutherford discovers nitrogen.
1773	16 Dec.	Boston Tea Party.
		First cast iron bridge commenced at Coalbrookdale.
1774	5 Sept.	Philadelphia Congress of American Colonies.
	13 Dec.	Dr Johnson dies.
		Priestley discovers oxygen.
1775	19 Apr.	War of American Independence starts.
	23 Apr.	J. M. W. Turner born.
	16 Dec.	Jane Austen born.
		James Watt's steam engine.
1776	11 June	John Constable born.
	4 July	American Declaration of Independence.
1777		Torpedo invented.

1778	30 May	Voltaire dies.
1779		Crompton's spinning mule.
1780	8 June	Gordon riots.
1781	9 June	George Stephenson born.
	19 Oct.	Cornwallis surrenders at Yorktown.
1783	3 Sept.	Peace of Versailles recognizes independence of USA.
		First paddle steamboat.
1784	28 Feb.	Wesley founds Methodism.
		Cavendish discovers components of water (hydrogen and oxygen).
1785		Steam engine used to drive cotton spinning machinery.
1787		First ascent of Mont Blanc.
1788	1 Jan.	The Times begins publication.
	22 Jan.	Lord Byron born.
	2 Aug.	Gainsborough dies.
1789	14 July	Sack of Bastille by Paris mob; beginning of French Revolution.
		Volta propounds nature of electricity.
1790	17 Apr.	Benjamin Franklin dies.
1791	3 Sept.	France becomes constitutional monarchy.
	22 Sept.	Michael Faraday born.
	5 Dec.	Mozart dies.
		Thomas Paine publishes Rights of Man.
1792	4 Aug.	Shelley born.
		Dollar coinage introduced in USA.
1793	21 Jan.	Louis XVI executed.
		Whitney invents cotton gin.
1794	5 Apr.	Danton executed.
	28 July	Robespierre executed.
		Abolition of slavery in French colonies.
1795	19 May	Boswell dies.
		Mungo Park explores River Niger.
	31 Oct.	Keats born.
1796	31 July	Burns dies.
		Jenner uses smallpox vaccine.
1797	31 Jan.	Schubert born.
		British naval mutinies at Spithead and Nore.
1798	1 Aug.	Battle of the Nile.
		Lithography invented.
1799	20 May	Balzac born.
	7 June	Pushkin born.
	14 Dec.	George Washington dies.
1800	14 June	Battle of Marengo.
1801	1 Jan.	Union of England and Ireland.
	2 Apr.	Battle of Copenhagen.
		First London horse-drawn trams.
1802	26 Feb.	Victor Hugo born.
1803	30 Apr.	Louisiana Purchase.
		Dalton propounds atom theory of chemistry.
1804	12 Feb.	Kant dies.
	2 Dec.	Napoleon crowned Napoleon I in Paris.
1805	20 Oct.	Battle of Trafalgar, Nelson killed.
	2 Dec.	Battle of Austerlitz.
1806	9 Apr.	Brunel born.
	6 Aug.	End of Holy Roman Empire.
	14 Oct.	Battle of Jena.
1807	4 July	Garibaldi born.
	7 July	Treaty of Tilsit.
1809	5 Jan.	Sir John Moore killed at Battle of Corunna.
	12 Feb.	Lincoln born.
	31 May	Haydn dies.
	5/6 July	Battle of Wagram.
	28 July	Battle of Talavera.
		Gas light in London streets.
1810	22 Feb.	Chopin born.
	8 June	Schumann born.
	6 Aug.	Tennyson born.
	10 Aug.	Cavour born.
1811	2 Feb.	George (IV) becomes Prince Regent.
	18 July	Thackeray born.
	22 Oct.	Liszt born.
1812	7 Feb.	Dickens born.
	7 May	Browning born.
	19 July	US declares war on Britain.
	19 Oct.	Napoleon retreats from Moscow.
1813	19 Mar.	Livingstone born.
	22 May	Wagner born.
	10 Oct.	Verdi born.
	16 Oct.	Battle of Leipzig.
1814	11 Apr.	Napoleon exiled to Elba.
	29 Oct.	Bakunin born.
1815	1 Mar.	Napoleon lands in France.
	1 Apr.	Bismarck born.
	18 June	Battle of Waterloo.
		Davy invents miners' lamp.
		US Navy's Fulton, first steam warship.
1816	21 Apr.	Charlotte Brontë born.
	17 July	Sheridan dies.

1817	18 July	Jane Austen dies.
		Ricardo's *Principles of Political Economy* published.
1818	5 May	Karl Marx born.
	24 Dec.	Turgenev born.
		First steamship *Savannah* crosses Atlantic in 26 days.
1819	24 May	Queen Victoria born.
	31 May	Walt Whitman born.
	19 Aug.	James Watt dies.
	16 Aug.	Peterloo massacre.
	26 Aug.	Albert (Prince Consort) born.
1820	29 Jan.	George III dies.
	23 Feb.	Cato Street Conspiracy.
	12 May	Florence Nightingale born.
	26 Sept.	Engels born.
		First iron steamship.
1821	23 Feb.	Keats dies.
	6 Mar.	Greek War of Independence.
	9 Apr.	Baudelaire born.
	5 May	Napoleon dies.
	30 Oct.	Dostoievsky born.
		Independence of Mexico and Peru.
1822	8 July	Shelley dies.
		Royal Academy of Music founded.
		Independence of Brazil.
1823	2 Dec.	Monroe doctrine.
		Babbage's calculating machine.
		Mackintosh's waterproof fabric.
1824	26 June	Lord Kelvin born.
1825	26 Dec.	Decembrist uprising in Russia.
		Independence of Bolivia and Uruguay.
		Stockton and Darlington Railway opened.
1826	4 July	Jefferson dies.
		Royal Zoological Society founded.
		University College, London, founded.
		First railway tunnel in England.
1827	26 Mar.	Beethoven dies.
	20 Oct.	Battle of Navarino.
		Ohm's Law formulated.
1828	20 Mar.	Ibsen born.
	28 Aug.	Tolstoy born.
	19 Nov.	Schubert dies.
		Beginnings of organic chemistry.
1829	29 May	Humphrey Davy dies.
	9 Aug.	First steam locomotive in USA.
		Metropolitan Police force founded by Peel.
		Stephenson's *Rocket* wins Liverpool and Manchester railway competition.
1830		Royal Geographic Society founded.
1831	14 Nov.	Hegel dies.
		British Association for Advancement of Science founded.
1832	27 Jan.	Lewis Carroll born.
	22 Mar.	Goethe dies.
	21 Sept.	Walter Scott dies.
		Reform Act extends Franchise.
1833	7 May	Brahms born.
	21 Oct.	Nobel born.
		Oxford Movement founded.
		First state grant for education in Britain.
1834	18 Mar.	Tolpuddle Martyrs sentenced to transportation.
	1 Aug.	Abolition of slavery in British Empire.
		Braille invented.
1835	30 Nov.	'Mark Twain' (Samuel Clemens) born.
		Colt's revolver patented.
1836	10 June	Ampère dies.
	18 Nov.	W. S. Gilbert born.
1837	10 Feb.	Pushkin dies.
		Pitman invents his shorthand.
		Morse invents telegraph.
1838		First typecasting machine invented.
1839	19 Jan.	Cezanne born.
	27 July	Anglo–Chinese Opium War begins.
		Fox-Talbot produces photographic negative.
		Daguerre perfects 'daguerreotype'.
1840	10 Jan.	Penny Post introduced in Britain by Rowland Hill.
	2 Apr.	Zola born.
	7 May	Tchaikovsky born.
	2 June	Thomas Hardy born.
	14 Nov.	Monet and Rodin born.
1841	26 Jan.	Hong Kong becomes British colony.
	3 May	New Zealand becomes British colony.
	8 Sept.	Dvorak born.
		Carbon–zinc battery invented.
1842	23 Mar.	Stendhal dies.
	30 Mar.	Ether used as anaesthetic in USA.
	9 Aug.	Canada/US border defined.
1843	15 Apr.	Henry James born.
	15 June	Grieg born.
		Thames railway tunnel completed.

1844	14 May	Morse transmits first message on US telegraph.
	15 Oct.	Nietzsche born.
		Co-operative Society formed.
1845	1 Mar.	Texas annexed by USA.
		Engels publishes *The Condition of the Working Classes in England*.
1846	26 May	Repeal of the Corn Laws.
	4 Nov.	Mendelssohn dies.
		Nitroglycerine prepared.
		Gun-cotton invented.
		First sewing machine patented in USA.
1847		Californian gold rush.
1848	8 Dec.	Gauguin born.
		Marx and Engels publish *Communist Manifesto*.
1849	22 Jan.	Strindberg born.
	17 Oct.	Chopin dies.
		Reinforced concrete first made.
1850	23 Apr.	Wordsworth dies.
	17 Aug.	Balzac dies.
	13 Nov.	Robert Louis Stevenson born.
		Second Law of Thermodynamics propounded.
1851	19 Dec.	J. M. W. Turner dies.
		The Great Exhibition, Hyde Park.
		The Singer sewing machine introduced.
1852	24 Sept.	Duke of Wellington dies.
		Niagara Falls suspension bridge built.
1853	5 July	Cecil Rhodes born.
	17 Dec.	Van Gogh born.
1854	14 Sept.	Crimean War begins.
	20 Oct.	Rimbaud born.
	25 Oct.	Battle of Balaclava.
	2 Dec.	Battle of Inkerman.
	8 Dec.	Dogma of Immaculate Conception declared article of faith by Pius IX.
1855	23 Feb.	Charlotte Brontë dies.
	11 Sept.	Fall of Sebastapol.
		Livingstone discovers Victoria Falls.
1856	29 Jan.	Queen Victoria institutes Victoria Cross.
	17 Feb.	Heine dies.
	26 July	George Bernard Shaw born.
	29 July	Schumann dies.
		Bessemer's steel smelting process.
1857	10 May	Indian Mutiny.
	2 June	Elgar born.
		Otis invents first safety elevator (lift).
		Transatlantic cable is laid (finished 1866).
1858	2 Aug.	East India company powers transferred to British Crown.
	23 Dec.	Puccini born.
		Covent Garden Opera House built.
1859	6 May	A. von Humboldt dies.
	22 May	Conan Doyle born.
		Charles Darwin publishes *The Origin of Species by Natural Selection*.
		SS *Great Eastern* completed.
1860	17 Jan.	Chekhov born.
	7 July	Mahler born.
	26 Oct.	Garibaldi proclaims Victor Emmanuel King of Italy.
	4 Nov.	Lincoln elected US President.
		Atomic weights of elements defined.
1861	12 Apr.	American Civil War begins.
		Pasteur develops germ theory of disease.
		Open-hearth process for producing steel developed.
1862	22 Aug.	Debussy born.
	17 Sept.	Lincoln declares all slaves to be free, 1 Jan 1863.
1863	17 Jan.	Lloyd George born.
	1–3 July	Confederate Army defeated at Gettysburg.
1864	May	Sherman 'marches through Georgia'.
	28 Oct.	Toulouse-Lautrec born.
		Pasteur invents pasteurization (for wine)
		Whitehead's torpedo.
		Metropolitan Railway, London, opened.
1865	15 Apr.	Lincoln assassinated.
	26 May	End of American Civil War.
	30 Dec.	Kipling born.
		Lister founds antiseptic surgery, using carbolic acid.
1866	21 Sept.	H. G. Wells born.
		Mendel establishes laws of heredity.
		Nobel invents dynamite.
		Queensberry Rules for Boxing codified.
		Translatlantic cable completed.
1867	29 Mar.	Canada becomes a dominion.
	27 May	Arnold Bennett born.
	14 Aug.	Galsworthy born.
	31 Aug.	Baudelaire dies.
		Marx publishes *Das Kapital*, Vol 1.
		Paris World Fair.
		Reform Act extends vote to working men.
1868	14 Mar.	Maxim Gorki born.
		Westinghouse brake invented.

1868	14 Mar.	First professional US baseball club founded (Cincinnati Red Stockings).
1869	9 Mar.	Berlioz dies.
	8 June	Frank Lloyd Wright born.
	17 Nov.	Suez Canal opened.
		Margarine invented.
1870	9 Apr.	Lenin born.
	9 June	Dickens dies.
	19 July	Franco–Prussian War begins.
	19 Sept.	Siege of Paris begins.
		Diamonds discovered in Orange Free State, South Africa.
		Standard Oil Company founded by J. D. Rockefeller.
1871	18 Jan.	William I of Prussia declared German Emperor at Versailles.
	28 Jan.	Paris falls, France signs armistice with Germany.
	15 Mar.	Paris Commune begins.
	28 May	Defeat of Paris Commune.
	10 June	Proust born.
	10 Nov.	Meeting of Stanley and Livingstone.
1872	19 Mar.	Diaghilev born.
	18 May	Bertrand Russell born.
		Edison's telegraph.
		New York/Brooklyn Bridge opened.
1873	1 Apr.	Rachmaninov born.
		Remington typewriter.
		Beginnings of colour photography.
1874	25 Jan.	Somerset Maugham born.
	29 May	Chesterton born.
	13 Sept.	Schoenberg born.
	30 Nov.	Winston Churchill born.
		First Impressionist Exhibition, Paris.
		Lawn tennis invented.
1875	14 Jan.	Albert Schweitzer born.
	22 Feb.	Corot dies.
	7 Mar.	Ravel born.
	4 Dec.	Rilke born.
		Theosophical Society founded in New York.
		London's main drainage system completed.
1876		Bell invents telephone.
		US Baseball League founded.
1877	1 Jan.	Queen Victoria proclaimed Empress of India.
		First public telephone.
		First Wimbledon Tennis Championship: winner Spencer Gore.
		Trotsky born.
1878		Swan's carbon filament electric lamp.
		David Hughes invents microphone.
		Edison invents phonograph (gramophone).
1879	12 Jan.	British–Zulu War.
	21 Dec.	Stalin born.
		Siemens shows first electric railway in Berlin.
1880	18 May	Flaubert dies.
		Parcel post introduced in UK.
		First girls high schools in UK.
		Jacob Epstein born.
1881	9 Feb.	Dostoievsky dies.
	25 Oct.	Picasso born.
		Canadian Pacific Railway founded.
1882	30 Jan.	Franklyn D. Roosevelt born.
	19 Apr.	Charles Darwin dies.
	6 May	Phoenix Park murders.
	5 June	Stravinsky born.
		Daimler builds petrol engine.
1883	3 Jan.	Attlee born.
	18 Feb.	Wagner dies.
	14 Mar.	Karl Marx dies.
	16 Apr.	Kruger becomes President of S. African Republic.
	19 July	Mussolini born.
		First skyscraper, Chicago.
1884	8 May	Harry S. Truman born.
		Parsons makes first practical steam turbine.
		Maxim's machine gun.
		Reform Act extends vote to nearly all men.
1885	26 Jan.	Death of General Gordon at Khartoum.
	22 May	Victor Hugo dies.
		Daimler invents internal combustion engine; Benz builds engine for motor car.
1886	31 July	Liszt dies.
		Gas mantle invented.
		Niagara Falls hydroelectric scheme started.
1887	31 Oct.	Chiang Kai-shek born.
1888		AC electric motor invented.
		Dunlop's pneumatic tyre.
		Football League founded.
		Lawn Tennis Association founded.
1889	20 Apr.	Hitler born.
	12 Dec.	Browning dies.
		Cordite invented.
		Eastman produces celluloid-roll film.
1890	22 Nov.	de Gaulle born.
		Van Gogh dies.
		Forth Bridge completed.
		First steel-framed building (Chicago).
1891		Trans-Siberian Railway begun.
1892	6 Oct.	Tennyson dies.
		Discovery of viscose to make artificial silk.
		First automatic telephone switchboard.
1893	6 Nov.	Tchaikovsky dies.
		Benz's four wheeled car.
		Zip fastener invented.
1894	15 Oct.	Dreyfus arrested in France.
	3 Dec.	Robert Louis Stevenson dies.
1895	28 Sept.	Pasteur dies.
		Discovery of X-rays.
		Cinematograph invented.
		Marconi's wireless telegraphy.
		Engels dies.
1896	10 Dec.	Nobel dies.
		Nobel prizes established.
		Langley makes successful flights in flying machine.
		Marconi successfully experiments with radio.
1897	3 Apr.	Brahms dies.
		Monotype typesetting machine.
		Klondike Gold Rush.
1898	19 May	Gladstone dies.
	31 July	Bismarck dies.
		Curies discover radium.
1899	3 Oct.	Boer War starts.
		Magnetic recording of sound devised.
		London Borough Councils established.
1900	1 May	Relief of Mafeking.
	13 June	Boxer Rebellion in China.
		Planck formulates quantum theory.
		First Zeppelin completed.
1901	1 Jan.	Commonwealth of Australia proclaimed.
	22 Jan.	Queen Victoria dies.
		Trans-Siberian railway opened.
1902	26 Mar.	Cecil Rhodes dies.
	31 May	End of Boer War.
		Discovery of hormones.
1903	6–9 July	Beginning of *Entente Cordiale* arises out of Edward VII's visit to France.
	17 Dec.	Wright Brothers make first flight in petrol-powered aeroplane.
1904	4 Feb.	Outbreak of Russo–Japanese War.
	4 May	Work on Panama Canal begins.
	2 July	Chekhov dies.
		Invention of photoelectric cell.
		Invention of radio valve.
1905	22 Jan.	'Bloody Sunday' massacre in St Petersburg.
		Einstein postulates his first theory of relativity.
1906	23 May	Ibsen dies.
	1 June	Simplon Tunnel opened.
		Commencement of Zuider Zee drainage.
		Launching of HMS *Dreadnought*.
1907	4 Sept.	Greig dies.
		Boy Scout Movement founded.
		Bakelite invented.
1908	20 Aug.	Congo annexed from Leopold II by Belgians.
		Ammonia synthesized (basis for artificial fertilizers).
		Cellophane invented.
1909	1 Jan.	Old-age pensions payable to over-70s.
	6 Apr.	Peary reaches North Pole.
		First Model 'T' Ford car.
		Bleriot crosses English Channel in monoplane.
1910	6 May	On death of Edward VII, George V accedes to the throne.
	1 July	South Africa becomes a dominion.
	13 Aug.	Florence Nightingale dies.
	10 Nov.	Tolstoy dies.
1911	15 May	Parliament Bill passed to reduce power of Lords.
	16 Oct.	Revolution in China.
	26 Oct.	Chinese Republic proclaimed.
	15 Dec.	Amundsen reaches South Pole.
		Agadir crisis in Morocco.
1912	18 Jan.	Scott reaches South Pole.
	15 Apr.	*Titanic* disaster.
	14 May	Strindberg dies.
	15 July	National Health Insurance Act passed.
		Stainless steel invented.
		First Balkan War.
1913	3 Feb.	Second Balkan War.
		Henry Ford introduces assembly-line technique with conveyor belts.
1914	28 June	Archduke Ferdinand assassinated at Saravejo.
	28 July	Austria–Hungary declares war on Serbia.
	1 Aug.	Germany declares war on Russia.
	3 Aug.	Germany declares war on France.
	4 Aug.	Britain declares war on Germany.

1914	15 Aug.	Panama Canal opened.
	23 Aug.	Battle of Mons.
	5 Sept.	Battle of the Marne.
	30 Oct	First battle of Ypres.
1915	22 Apr.	Second battle of Ypres; Germans first use poison gas.
	7 May	*Lusitania* sunk by Germans.
	23 May	Italy declares war on Austria–Hungary.
		Einstein's General Theory of Relativity.
1916	21 Feb.	Battle of Verdun.
	24 Apr.	'Easter Rebellion' in Dublin.
	31 May	Battle of Jutland.
	1 July	Battle of the Somme begins.
	7 July	Lloyd George forms coalition government.
		First tanks used in war.
1917	8 Mar.	'February' revolution in Russia.
	16 Mar.	Tsar Nicholas II abdicates.
	6 Apr.	USA declares war on Germany.
	9 Apr.	Battle of Vimy Ridge.
	15 Sept.	Russian republic proclaimed by Kerensky.
	2 Nov.	Balfour declaration on Palestine for Jewish Home-land.
	7 Nov.	October revolution in Russia; Bolsheviks led by Lenin against Kerensky.
	8 Nov.	Lenin and Trotsky become leaders in Russia.
	5 Dec.	Armistice signed between Russia and Germany at Brest-Litovsk.
1918	8 Jan.	Woodrow Wilson propounds Fourteen Points for World Peace.
	3 Mar.	Treaty of Brest-Litovsk.
	21 Mar.	Second battle of the Somme.
	1 Apr.	RAF formed out of RAC.
	11 Nov.	Armistice signed between Allies and Germany. Women over 30 gain vote.
1919	18 Jan.	Peace Conference at Versailles begins.
	14 Feb.	Woodrow Wilson presents League of Nations Cove-nant to Peace Conference (adopted 25 March).
	23 Feb.	Mussolini founds Fascist Party.
	15 June	Alcock and Brown fly Atlantic.
	28 June	Germans sign Peace Treaty at Versailles.
	7 Nov.	Lady Astor becomes first woman MP to take her seat.
1920	10 Jan.	League of Nations officially founded.
	16 Jan.	Prohibition in USA.
	14 Oct.	Degrees open to women at Oxford for first time.
		First public broadcasting station opened in Britain.
1921	8 Mar.	French occupy Ruhr.
	6 Dec.	Peace treaty sets up Irish Free State.
		Chinese Communist Party formed.
1922	14 Apr.	Irish Civil War begins.
	10 Oct.	Turkish–Greek war ends.
	28 Oct.	Mussolini marches on Rome; forms Fascist govern-ment.
	1 Nov.	Turkish republic proclaimed.
	15 Nov.	Proust dies.
	Nov.	Tutankhamen's tomb discovered.
		Insulin isolated and used in treatment of diabetes.
		First BBC radio broadcasts.
1923	1 Jan.	Union of Soviet Socialist Republics (USSR) estab-lished.
	11 Jan.	French and Belgian troops occupy Rhur.
	18 July	Women given equality in divorce suits.
	1 Sept.	Earthquake in Japan devastates Tokyo and Yoko-hama.
	29 Sept.	Turkish Republic proclaimed under Kemal.
	8–9 Nov.	Hitler fails to take power in 'Beer Hall Putsch' in Munich.
		First FA Cup to be played at Wembley.
1924	21 Jan.	Lenin dies.
	22 Jan.	First Labour Government under Ramsay Mac-Donald.
		'Fonofilm' talking pictures developed.
1925	12 Mar.	Sun Yat Sen dies.
	1 Dec.	Locarno treaties signed in London.
		Vol. I of Hitler's *Mein Kampf* published.
1926	21 Apr.	Queen Elizabeth II born.
	3–12 May	General Strike in Britain.
	5 Dec.	Monet dies.
		Baird demonstrates television in Soho.
1927	20–21 May	Lindbergh flies New York to Paris, solo, in 37 hours.
	27 Dec.	Stalin assumes power and Trotsky expelled from Communist Party.
		Vol. II of Hitler's *Mein Kampf* published.
1928	7 May	Women get right to vote at 21.
	27 Aug.	Kellogg–Briand peace pact signed by 65 states.
	15 Oct.	*Graf Zeppelin* crosses Atlantic.
		Fleming discovers penicillin.
		First Five-Year Plan in Russia.
1929	29 Aug.	Diaghilev dies.
	28 Oct.	Wall Street crash.
	30 Nov.	Byrd flies over South Pole.
1930	12 Mar.	Mahatma Gandhi's civil disturbance campaign in India.

1930	30 June	Allied troops leave Rhineland.
	7 Oct.	Airship R101 crashes.
		Perspex invented.
1931	21 Sept.	Britain abandons Gold Standard.
		Japanese invade Manchuria.
		Cyclotron ('atom smasher') devised.
1932	2 Feb.	Geneva disarmament conference.
	9 Mar.	Sydney Harbour bridge opened.
	8 Nov.	F. D. Roosevelt elected US President.
1933	30 Jan.	Hitler becomes German Chancellor.
	27 Feb.	Reichstag fire.
	1 Apr.	Persecution of Jews begins in Germany.
1934	26 Mar.	Driving tests first introduced in Britain.
	25 July	Dollfuss murdered.
	19 July	Hitler becomes *Führer*.
	26 Sept.	*Queen Mary* launched.
		Long march of Chinese Communists.
		Stalin begins purge of opponents.
1935	12 Mar.	30-mph speed limit introduced in built-up areas.
	2 Oct.	War between Italy and Abyssinia.
		Tape-recorder invented.
		Radar invented by Watson Watt.
		Nuremberg Laws passed by Hitler to remove civil rights from Jews.
1936	15 Jan.	Edward VIII accedes upon death of George V.
	7 Mar.	Germany occupies Rhineland.
	18 July	Spanish Civil War begins.
	July	Jarrow Crusade.
	2 Nov.	First TV broadcasts by BBC from Alexandra Palace.
	10 Dec.	Edward VIII abdicates in favour of George VI (Dec. 12).
	12 Dec.	China forced to declare war on Japan.
1937	27 Apr.	Germany and Italy supporting Spanish rebels destroy Guernica.
	28 May	Neville Chamberlain becomes Prime Minister.
	26 June	Duke of Windsor marries Wallis Simpson.
	29 Dec.	Irish Free State becomes Eire.
		Whittle's first jet engine.
		Nylon stockings first made.
1938	11 Mar.	Germans enter and annex Austria.
	27 Sept.	*Queen Elizabeth* launched.
	29 Sept.	Munich Agreement.
	10 Oct.	Germans occupy Sudetenland.
		New York World Fair.
1939	16 Mar.	Slovakia annexed by Germans, completing occupa-tion of Czechoslovakia.
	28 Mar.	End of Spanish Civil War.
	7 Apr.	Italy invades Albania.
	25 May	Anglo–Polish Treaty signed.
	23 Aug.	Nazi–Soviet non-aggression pact.
	1 Sept.	Germany invades Poland.
	3 Sept.	Britain and France declare war on Germany.
	13 Dec.	Battle of River Plate.
		DDT invented.
		Polythene invented.
1940	9 Apr.	Germany invades Denmark and Norway.
	10 May	Churchill forms coalition government.
	29 May	Dunkirk evacuation begins.
	10 June	Italy declares war on France and Britain.
	22 June	France concludes armistice with Germany.
	10 July	Battle of Britain begins.
	21 Aug.	Trotsky killed.
	29 Dec.	London severely damaged by incendiary bombing.
1941	11 Mar.	Lend–Lease Bill signed between Britain and USA.
	11 Apr.	Blitz on Coventry.
	10 May	London's heaviest air raid.
	22 June	Germany invades Russia.
	7 Dec.	Japanese bomb Pearl Harbor.
	8 Dec.	Britain and USA declare war on Japan.
	11 Dec.	USA declares war on Germany and Italy.
		'Manhattan project' begun to develop atomic bomb.
		Terylene invented.
1942	15 Feb.	Singapore surrenders.
	4–8 May	Battle of Coral Sea.
	3–7 June	Battle of Midway.
	7 Aug.	US forces land on Guadalcanal.
	26 Aug.	Germans reach Stalingrad.
	23 Oct.	Battle of El Alamein.
	2 Dec.	Fermi splits the atom.
1943	30 Jan.	German army destroyed at Stalingrad.
	12 May	German army surrenders in N. Africa.
	10 July	Allies invade Sicily.
	26 July	Mussolini overthrown.
	7 Sept.	Italy surrenders to Allies.
	28 Nov.	Meeting in Teheran between Churchill, Stalin and Roosevelt.
		Streptomycin discovered.
		First programmable electronic computer developed in the UK.

1944	6 June	D-day invasion in Normandy.
	12 June	First flying bomb (V1) drops on London.
	20 June	Bomb plot to assassinate Hitler fails.
	1 Aug.	Warsaw rising begins.
	25 Aug.	de Gaulle enters Paris with Allies.
	8 Sept.	First V2 rocket falls on England.
	17 Sept.	Battles of Arnhem and Eindhoven.
	16 Dec.	German counter-offensive (Battle of the Bulge).
1945	4 Feb.	Yalta Conference.
	14 Feb.	Dresden bombed.
	1 Apr.	US invasion of Okinawa.
	12 Apr.	Roosevelt dies.
	20 Apr.	Russians reach Berlin.
	28 Apr.	Mussolini killed.
	30 Apr.	Hitler commits suicide.
	8 May	End of war against Germany (VE Day).
	27 July	Attlee becomes Prime Minister.
	6 Aug.	First atomic bomb dropped on Hiroshima.
	9 Aug.	Second atomic bomb dropped on Nagasaki.
	14 Aug.	Japan surrenders to Allies and ends Second World War (VJ Day).
1946	10 Jan.	UN Assembly opens in London.
	18 Apr.	League of Nations dissolved.
	30 June	Bikini atom bomb exploded.
	21 July	Bread rationing in Britain.
	30 Sept.	Nuremburg Trials end.
	6 Nov.	National Health Act comes into effect.
		Xerography invented.
1947	1 Jan.	Coal industry nationalized.
	1 Apr.	School leaving age raised to 15.
	5 June	Marshall Aid propounded.
	15 Aug.	India and Pakistan become separate states.
	20 Nov.	Princess Elizabeth marries Philip Mountbatten.
		First supersonic air flight.
1948	1 Jan.	British Railways nationalized.
	30 Jan.	Mahatma Gandhi assassinated.
	17 Mar.	Brussels Treaty signed.
	14 May	New state of Israel founded.
	1 July	Berlin Airlift begins.
	3 Nov.	Truman elected President of USA.
		Transistor invented.
1949	15 Mar.	Clothes rationing ends.
	4 Apr.	North Atlantic Treaty signed.
	2 June	*Apartheid* programme begins in S. Africa.
	24 Aug.	North Atlantic Treaty effective.
	1 Oct.	Communist People's Republic of China proclaimed under Mao Tse-Tung.
1950	9 Jan.	Colombo Plan for Asiatic states.
	26 May	Petrol rationing ends.
	25 June	Korean War begins.
	2 Nov.	Bernard Shaw dies.
		Kon-Tiki Expedition.
1951	18 Apr.	Schuman Plan signed.
	25 Oct.	Conservatives returned to power in UK.
		Festival of Britain.
		Electric power first produced from atomic energy (in USA).
		Cinerama invented.
1952	6 Feb.	George VI dies; Queen Elizabeth II accedes to throne.
	26 Feb.	Britain's first atomic bomb announced.
	6 July	Last tram runs in London.
	20 Oct.	Mau Mau disturbances in Kenya; emergency proclaimed.
	4 Nov.	Eisenhower becomes US President.
	6 Nov.	US explodes first hydrogen bomb.
		First contraceptive tablets made.
1953	6 Mar.	Stalin dies.
	29 May	Hillary and Tenzing climb Mount Everest.
	2 June	Coronation of Queen Elizabeth II.
	27 July	Korean war armistice signed.
	2 Aug.	USSR explodes hydrogen bomb.
1954	1 Mar.	US hydrogen bomb test at Bikini.
	18 Apr.	Nasser becomes Premier of Egypt.
	7 May	Dien Bien Phu falls to Communist Vietnamese.
	20 July	Indo-China armistice.
	8 Oct.	Hanoi occupied by Communists.
	3 Nov.	Terrorist activity in Algeria.
		Solar battery developed.
1955	5 Apr.	Churchill resigns; is succeeded by Eden.
	18 Apr.	Einstein dies.
	9 May	West Germany admitted to NATO.
	2 Sept.	Commercial television (ITV) starts.
	21 Nov.	Emergency declared in Cyprus.
		Salk vaccine against polio developed.
		Warsaw Pact signed between Russian and Communist satellite countries.
1956	17 Apr.	Premium Bonds first issued.
	23 May	Nuclear-generated electric power started from Calder Hall.
		Nasser nationalizes Suez Canal.

1956	25 Sept.	Transatlantic telephone service in operation.
	4 Nov.	Hungarian revolt against communists crushed by Soviet forces in Budapest.
	5 Nov.	Anglo–French airborne troops land at Port Said, Suez.
	7 Nov.	Ceasefire accepted by Egypt.
1957	9 Jan.	Eden resigns; Macmillan becomes Prime Minister (Jan. 10).
	25 Mar.	Common Market treaty signed by Belgium, France, West Germany, Italy, Luxemburg and Holland.
	15 May	First British hydrogen bomb exploded.
	4 Sept.	Wolfenden report on prostitution and homosexuality.
	4 Oct.	*Sputnik I* launched successfully by USSR.
	3 Nov.	*Sputnik II* containing a dog launched by USSR.
1958	31 Jan.	US launches *Explorer I* satellite.
	25 Feb.	Campaign for Nuclear Disarmament launched in UK.
	27 Mar.	Kruschev succeeds Bulganin as Soviet Prime Minister.
	28 Oct.	Pope John XXIII elected.
	21 Dec.	de Gaulle elected President of France.
		Stereo gramophone recordings introduced.
		First parking meters in London.
		Subscriber trunk dialling of telephones.
1959	1 Jan.	Batista government overthrown in Cuba by Castro.
	16 Feb.	Castro becomes Premier of Cuba.
	9 June	First atomic-powered submarine launched in US.
	25 July	Hovercraft crosses English channel in 2 hours.
	4 Oct.	*Lunik III* photographs moon.
	29 Nov.	European Free Trade Association (EFTA) treaty ratified by Britain, Norway, Sweden, Portugal, Switzerland, Austria and Denmark.
		Synthetic diamonds first manufactured.
1960	29 Feb.	Agadir earthquake in Morocco.
	27 Mar.	Sharpeville shootings in South Africa.
	25 Aug.	Split between Russia and China.
	9 Nov.	John F. Kennedy elected President of USA.
		Heart pacemaker developed.
1961	12 Apr.	Yuri Gagarin of USSR becomes first man in space.
	5 May	Alan Shepard of USA becomes second man in space.
	31 May	South Africa leaves the Commonwealth.
	13 Aug.	E. Germany seals off border and (Aug. 17–18) builds 'Berlin Wall'.
	17 Sept.	CND demonstrations in Trafalgar Square; over 1300 arrests.
	18 Dec.	UN forces restore order in Congo.
		Structure of DNA established.
1962	1 July	Algeria becomes independent.
	10 July	*Telstar* satellite launched.
	1 Sept.	Iranian earthquake disaster.
	11 Oct.	Vatican Council opens.
	22 Oct.–20 Nov.	Soviet missile installations in Cuba provoke US blockade and Cuban crisis.
1963	29 Jan.	Britain refused entry into Common Market.
	Jan.–Feb.	Coldest months in Britain since 1740.
	16 June	V. Tereshkova first woman in space (USSR).
	4 June	Profumo resigns from Parliament after scandal.
	26 July	Skopje earthquake.
	5 Aug.	Britain, USSR and USA sign nuclear test-ban treaty.
	8 Aug.	Great Train Robbery on Glasgow–London mail train.
	22 Nov.	President Kennedy assassinated by Lee H. Oswald in Dallas. Lyndon B. Johnson sworn in as President of USA.
1964	12 June	Nelson Mandela sentenced to life imprisonment in S. Africa.
	2 July	US Civil Rights Act ratified.
	4 Sept.	World's longest bridge (Verrazano Narrows) opened.
	16 Oct.	China explodes atomic bomb.
	16 Oct.	Wilson becomes Prime Minister.
		Britain grants licences for North Sea oil drilling.
1965	8 Mar.	US Marines land in South Vietnam.
	18 Mar.	USSR cosmonaut leaves spacecraft and floats in space.
	9 Apr.	India–Pakistan war begins.
	8 June	US forces in action in S. Vietnam.
	30 June	India–Pakistan armistice signed.
	21 Sept.	BP strikes oil in North Sea.
	11 Nov.	Rhodesia Declaration of Independence.
		Beatles awarded MBE.
1966	3 Feb.	Russian *Luna 9* lands on moon.
	23 Mar.	Meeting of Archbishop of Canterbury and Pope in Rome.
	31 Mar.	Labour wins General Election.
	10 Apr.	Evelyn Waugh dies.
	26 May	Guyana becomes independent.
	30 July	England wins World Cup at football.
	6 Sept.	Verwoerd assassinated in S. Africa.
	21 Oct.	Aberfan disaster.
		Cultural Revolution in China begins.
1967	4 Jan.	Donald Campbell killed attempting water speed record.

1967	18 Mar.	*Torrey Canyon* disaster.
	19 Apr.	Adenauer dies.
	5 June	Six-day War between Israel and Arab nations.
	17 June	China detonates her first H-bomb.
	20 Sept.	*QE2* launched.
	8 Oct.	Drink-and-Drive laws come into force in UK.
	3 Dec.	First human heart transplant.
1968	27 Mar.	Yuri Gagarin dies.
	4 Apr.	Martin Luther King assassinated.
	5–6 June	Robert Kennedy shot and dies.
	10 June	NHS prescription charges introduced.
	16 Sept.	Two-tier postal charges introduced.
	8 Nov.	Nixon elected President of USA.
1969	2 Mar.	First flight of *Concorde*.
	28 Apr.	de Gaulle resigns.
	12 May	Voting age lowered to 18.
	21 July	First landing on Moon by Armstrong and Aldrin.
	14 Nov.	Colour programmes begin on BBC1 and ITV.
	16–18 Dec.	House of Commons votes for abolition of death penalty.
1970	3 Feb.	Bertrand Russell dies.
	2 Mar.	Rhodesia becomes a republic.
	10 June	Conservatives win General Election.
	21 Jul.	Brazil wins World Cup.
	29 Sept.	Nasser dies.
	24 Oct.	Allende elected President of Chile.
	9 Nov.	de Gaulle dies.
1972	30 Jan.	'Bloody Sunday' in N. Ireland.
	16 June	'Watergate' scandal begins in USA.
	4 Aug.	Amin orders expulsion of British Asians in Uganda.
	10 Oct.	Betjeman becomes Poet Laureate.
	13 Oct.	Bank rate abolished.
1973	1 Jan.	Britain, Ireland, Denmark become members of EEC.
	22 Jan.	Lyndon Johnson dies.
	26 Mar.	Noel Coward dies.
	29 Mar.	Last US soldiers leave Vietnam.
	1 Apr.	VAT introduced in Britain.
	14 May	*Skylab* launched.
	2 Sept.	J.R.R. Tolkien dies.
	6 Oct.	Arab–Israeli War starts.
1974	28 Feb.	General Election in UK produces no clear majority.
	4 Mar.	Labour government formed after resignation of Edward Heath.
	1 June	Flixborough chemical-works explosion.
	1 July	Peron dies.
	8 Aug.	Nixon resigns.
	20 Aug.	Gerald Ford new President of USA.
	30 Oct.	Muhammad Ali regains World Heavyweight Title.
1975	4 Feb.	Mrs Thatcher becomes leader of Conservative Party.
	25 Feb.	Bulganin dies.
	5 Apr.	Chiang Kai-shek dies.
	30 Apr.	End of Vietnamese War.
	9 June	First live radio broadcast of House of Commons sitting.
	8 Aug.	Shostakovich dies.
	3 Nov.	First flow of N. Sea oil (official).
	29 Dec.	Sex Discrimination and Equal Pay Acts come into force.
1976	8 Jan.	Chou En-Lai dies.
	5 Apr.	Wilson resigns; Callaghan becomes Prime Minister.
	24 June	Vietnam reunified.
	9 Sept.	Mao Tse-Tung dies.
	1 Nov.	Jimmy Carter elected President of USA.
	4 Dec.	Benjamin Britten dies.
1977	27 Mar.	Tenerife aircraft disaster: 577 killed.
	20 May	Last run of Orient Express, Paris–Istanbul.
	1 July	Expiry of SEATO treaty.
	12 Sept.	Death of Stephen Biko in S. Africa.
	25 Sept.	Laker's Skytrain service to USA begins.
	29 Dec.	Charlie Chaplin dies.
1978	16 Mar.	Aldo Moro kidnapped.
	1 May	First May Day (Bank Holiday) in Britain.
	25 July	World's first 'test-tube' baby born in Oldham.
	22 Aug.	Kenyatta dies.
	26 Aug.	John Paul I elected Pope.
	28 Sept.	Pope John Paul I dies.
	15 Oct.	Polish John Paul II elected first non-Italian pope for 450 years.
	8 Dec.	Golda Meir dies.

1979	1 Feb.	Ayatollah Khomeini returns to Iran from exile.
	28 Mar.	Radiation leak at Three Mile Island nuclear power plant in USA.
	4 Apr.	Ex-President Bhutto of Pakistan executed.
	4 May	Margaret Thatcher becomes first woman Prime Minister of Britain.
	18 June	Presidents Carter and Brezhnev sign SALT II treaty.
	27 Aug.	Mountbatten killed by bomb explosion in his boat.
	29 Sept.	Pope visits Ireland for first time.
	27 Dec.	Soviet forces intervene in Afghanistan.
1980	7 Jan.	Mrs Gandhi's Congress Party wins Indian General Election.
	15 Apr.	Sartre dies.
	28 Apr.	Alfred Hitchcock dies.
	30 Apr.	Iranian Embassy siege in London.
	4 May	Tito dies.
	18 May	Eruption of Mt St Helens, USA.
	22 Sept.	Gulf War between Iran and Iraq starts.
	4 Nov.	Reagan elected President of USA.
	7 Dec.	John Lennon killed in New York.
1981	12 Feb.	Murdoch purchases *The Times*.
	6 Mar.	Social Democratic Party officially launched.
	30 Mar.	Reagan shot and wounded in Washington.
	12 Apr.	US shuttle *Columbia* launched.
	13 May	Pope shot and wounded.
	29 July	Wedding of Prince Charles and Lady Diana Spencer.
	16 Sept.	Liberal–SDP Alliance announced.
1982	2 Apr.	Argentina invades Falkland Islands.
	11 Apr.	Trans-Globe expedition reaches North Pole, completing first circumnavigation of globe via both Poles.
	2 May	*General Belgrano* sunk in S. Atlantic.
	14 June	Cessation of hostilities agreed in Falkland Islands between Britain and Argentina.
	11 Oct.	*Mary Rose* raised.
	12 Nov.	Andropov becomes USSR president.
1983	30 Aug.	Korean Airways airliner shot down by USSR.
	2 Oct.	Kinnock elected Leader of Labour Party.
	14 Nov.	First Cruise missiles arrive at Greenham Common.
	17 Dec.	IRA bomb explosion outside Harrods.
1984	9 Feb.	Andropov dies; succeeded by Chernenko as USSR President.
	12 Oct.	IRA bomb explosion at Grand Hotel, Brighton.
	31 Oct.	Indira Gandhi assassinated by Sikh bodyguards; succeeded by her son, Rajiv.
	6 Nov.	Reagan elected for second term.
	3 Dec.	Bhopal, Indian pesticides factory gas disaster.
	19 Dec.	Anglo–Chinese agreement on Hong Kong signed.
1985	23 Jan.	House of Lords televised for first time.
	4 Feb.	Border between Spain and Gibraltar re-opened.
	15 Feb.	House of Commons majority banning all experiments on human embryos.
	10 Mar.	Chernenko dies; Gorbachev new President of USSR.
	24 May	Bangladesh tidal wave drowns thousands.
	29 May	38 killed in football rioting at Heysel Stadium, Brussels.
	13 July	Live Aid pop concerts in Britain and America raise £50 million for famine relief in Africa.
	9 Sept.	Huge earthquake in Mexico.
	19 Nov.	Summit meeting between Reagan and Gorbachev
1986	28 Jan.	*Challenger* space shuttle explodes on takeoff killing all on board.
	7 Feb.	President Duvalier flees Haiti for France.
	25 Feb.	Cory Aquino assumes power in Philippines.
	28 Feb.	Olaf Palme, Swedish premier, assassinated.
	1 Apr.	Oil prices slump to less than $10 a barrel.
	15 Apr.	US planes bomb Tripoli and Benghazi in Libya.
	28 Apr.	Chernobyl nuclear power plant fire causes disaster and widespread radiation.
	24 July	Commonwealth Games boycotted by 32 teams for British opposition to sanctions against S. Africa.
1987	6 Jan.	US Congressional hearing opens in Washington D.C. on the 'Irangate' affair.
	4 Feb.	USA win back the America's Cup in Australia.
	11 June	British General Election results in third consecutive Conservative victory.
	3 July	Richard Branson completes first transatlantic crossing in hot-air balloon.

The Earth

Introduction

Mass, density and volume

The Earth, including its atmosphere, has a mass estimated in 1979 to be 5 880 000 000 000 000 000 000 tons *5·974 × 10²¹ tonnes* and has a density 5·515 times that of water to an accuracy of 0·06%. The volume of the Earth has been estimated at 259 875 300 000 miles³ *1 083 207 000 000 km³*.

Dimensions

Its equatorial circumference is 24 901·47 miles *40 075,03 km* with a polar or meridianal circumference of 24 859·75 miles *40 007,89 km* indicating that the Earth is not a true sphere but flattened at the poles and hence an ellipsoid. The Earth also has a slight ellipticity at the equator since its long axis (about longitude 37°) is 174 yd *159 m* greater than the short axis. Artificial satellite measurements have also revealed further departures from this biaxial ellipsoid form in minor protuberances and depressions varying between extremes of 244 ft *74 m* in the area of Papua New Guinea and a depression of 354 ft *108 m* south of Sri Lanka (formerly Ceylon) in the Indian Ocean. The equatorial diameter of the Earth is 7926·385 miles *12 756,280 km* and the polar diameter 7 899·809 miles *12 713,510 km*.

Land and sea surfaces

The estimated total surface area of the Earth is 196 937 400 miles² *510 065 600 km²* of which the sea or hydrosphere covers five sevenths or more accurately 70·92 per cent and the land or lithosphere two sevenths or 29·08 per cent. The mean depth of the hydrosphere is 11 660 ft *3554 m*. The total volume of the oceans is 308 400 000 miles³ or *1 285 600 000 km³*, or 0·022 per cent by weight of the whole earth, viz. 1·3 × 10¹⁸ tons.

The oceans and seas

The strictest interpretations permit only three oceans – The Pacific, Atlantic and Indian. The so-called Seven Seas would require the three undisputed oceans to be divided by the equator into North and South and the addition of the Arctic Sea. The term Antarctic Ocean is not recognized by the International Hydrographic Bureau.

The Continents

There is ever increasing evidence that the Earth's land surface once comprised a single primaeval land mass, now called Pangaea, and that this split during the Upper Cretaceous period (65 000 000 to 100 000 000 years ago) into two super-continents, called Laurasia in the North and Gondwanaland in the South. The Earth's land surface embraces seven continents, each with their attendant islands. Europe, Africa and Asia, though politically distinct, physically form one land mass known as Afro-Eurasia. Central America is often included in North America (Canada, the USA and Greenland). Europe includes all the USSR territory west of the Ural Mountains. Oceania embraces Australasia (Australia and New Zealand) and the non-Asian Pacific Islands.

Glossary

abyssal Pertaining to the depths of the oceans.
affluent A tributary stream flowing into a larger stream or river.
aiguille Sharp point or pinnacle of rock.

alluvial fan Fan-shaped area of sediment deposited as a river enters a plain and slows down.
alluvium Sand, mud, silt, etc., carried by a river and deposited as the river slows down.
altitude Height above sea level.
archipelago A group of islands.
arête A sharp ridge between two *cirques*.
artesian well Well that taps water held in a permeable layer of rock, sandwiched between two impermeable layers of rock in a basin. The rim of the permeable section of the basin is higher than the level of the well, so the water contained in the permeable layer pushes the water up out of the well.
atoll A ring of coral islands or coral reefs.
avalanche A mass of snow and ice that slides down a mountainside because of its own weight.

bar Shingle and sand deposited in a line or ridge across a bay or mouth of a river.
barchan Crescent-shaped sand dune, the shape being due to the constant effect of the wind.
bayou Swampy creek leading off a river, found in flat land.
bergschrund Gap between the upper edge of a glacier and the rock wall in a *cirque*.
bight A large bay.
bill A small peninsula.
bluff A vertical cliff, standing out prominently from the surrounding countryside.
bog Area of wet spongy ground consisting of waterlogged and decaying moss and other plants.
bore A tidal wave running up a river estuary.
boulder clay Rocks and gravel dragged along by the base of a glacier and deposited when the glacier recedes.
bourne A stream that only flows intermittently.
bund A term used in the Indian subcontinent for an artificial embankment.
bush Scrubland not cleared for cultivation.
butte A flat-topped hill, often with steep sides.

cairn A man-made heap of stones.
caldera A crater flanked by steep cliffs. It is usually formed by the top of a volcano that has subsided.
canal A man-made waterway, either for transport or irrigation.
canyon A river-cut gorge, often of great depth, with steep sides.
cape A piece of land projecting into the sea.
cascade Small waterfall.
cataract Large waterfall.
cave Underground opening reached from the surface or from the sea.
cavern A cave.
chaparral Dry scrubland, particularly in the south-eastern US.
chimney A vertical crack in a rock face.
cirque A rounded basin in a mountainside, formed by the action of a glacier.
cliff Steep face of rock.
col A high valley across a mountain range or line of hills.
coombe A short valley into the side of a hill.
concordant coastline A submerged coastline consisting of drowned valleys and lines of islands, all running parallel with an inland range of mountains or hills.
confluence Point at which two rivers converge.
continent A single large landmass.
continental drift The movement of landmasses on the molten rock that makes up the earth's interior.
continental shelf The offshore seabed, down to a depth of 600 ft *200 metres*.
contour Line joining all points at the same height.
coral The exoskeleton of a small marine animal. They live in colonies, and when each animal dies the calcium-rich exoskeleton remains. As generation succeeds generation, masses of coral build up into reefs, atolls, etc.
coral reef A line of coral rocks at or just below the surface of the sea.

cordillera Parallel lines of mountains.
corrasion Mechanical erosion of rocks by the action of other rocks, gravel, etc., in a river or by wind-borne sand.
corrosion Chemical erosion of rocks.
cove A small bay.
crater Hollow at the top of a volcanic cone, or the depression caused by the impact of a meteorite.
crevasse A vertical crack in a glacier or ice sheet.
cuesta A ridge or hill formed by sloping rock strata.
cwm A *cirque*.

dale An open valley.
deep A marine valley or trench, considerably deeper than the surrounding seabed.
delta Deposits of alluvium in a fan shape, formed where a river flows into the sea or a lake.
desert Area with very low rainfall in which little if any vegetation grows.
discordant coastline An irregular coastline in which the mountains, valleys and inlets are at right-angles to the coast.
drowned valley Valley that has been submerged by a rise in the sea level or by the land sinking.
drumlin Small hump-backed hill formed by the action of a glacier. Swarms of drumlins are exposed as ice sheets recede.
dune A wind-formed accumulation of sand.
dust bowl Dry region that has been badly managed agriculturally, such that the topsoil has been removed by wind erosion.
dyke Vertical sheet of rock which cuts across the bedding or structural planes of the host rock.

earthquake Series of shock waves generated from a single point within the earth's mantle or crust.
epicentre Point on the earth's surface above the point at which the shock waves of an earthquake are generated.
equator Imaginary circle around the Earth's surface, midway between the poles.
equinox Time when the sun appears vertically overhead at noon at the equator; about 21 March and 21 September.
erg Part of the Sahara desert covered with sand.
erosion Removal or wearing away of the land surface by natural means.
estuary The mouth of a river, and the stretch immediately up-river of the mouth, that is tidal.
étang A shallow lake among coastal sand-dunes.

fall line The line showing where a number of rivers leave an upland area for a lowland area, in each case passing over a waterfall or series of waterfalls.
fathom Unit of depth at sea; 6 ft *1·83 m*.
fell Bare hill.
fen Marshy land in which peat is formed.
fiord Glaciated steep-sided valley that runs into the sea and is subsequently flooded. They are typified by a great depth of water in the main body of the fiord, with a shallower bar across the mouth.
firth A narrow inlet in the sea coast in Scotland; either an estuary or a fiord.
flood plain Plain on either side of a river formed by alluvial deposits left when the river floods and then recedes again.
fold A vertical bend in the rock strata, formed by compression within the earth's crust.
forest Large area of land, extensively covered with trees.
frost hollow Hollow into which cold air sinks from the surrounding slopes. The hollow is therefore more liable to suffer frost than the surrounding land.

garrigue Form of scrub found in dry limestone areas around the Mediterranean.
geyser A hot spring of such depth that steam periodically forms, erupting from the mouth of the spring in a fountain of steam and hot water.

glacier Mass of ice, formed due to great weight of snow, that slowly moves down a valley towards the sea.

glen Long narrow steep-sided valley in Scotland.

gorge A deep narrow rugged valley with near vertical walls.

grassland Large area where the rainfall is greater than that of a desert but not enough to support a forest.

great circle A circle on the earth's surface whose centre is the earth's centre.

gulf A large bay.

gully A narrow steep-sided channel formed by water erosion.

hammada Bare rocky desert found in the Sahara.

hanging valley Glaciated valley entering a main valley part-way up the valley side.

headland Isolated cliff projecting into the sea.

hot spring Spring whose water is heated by hot volcanic rocks.

iceberg Massive lump of ice which has broken off the end of a glacier or ice sheet and floats in the sea.

ice floe Floating sheet of ice that has detached from an ice shelf.

ice sheet Mass of ice and snow covering a land mass.

ice shelf Mass of ice and snow floating on the sea.

inlet Opening into the sea or lake coast.

inselberg An isolated hill in a relatively flat area.

irrigation Artificial supply of water to a crop-producing area.

island Mass of land surrounded by water. It may occur in a river, a lake, a sea or an ocean.

islet A small island.

isthmus A narrow neck of land connecting two land masses.

jebel A mountain range.

jungle A misnomer for tropical monsoon forest.

karst Type of limestone scenery produced by water erosion of limestone and dolomite rock. It is characterized by sinks, underground rivers and caves, and other erosion features.

kettle hole A hollow in the outwash plain of a glacier, formed where an ice block melts.

key (or cay) Small island or sandbank in the Caribbean.

knick point Point at which the slope of a river changes.

knoll Small rounded hill

kyle A channel of water or strait in Scotland.

lagoon Expanse of water that has been separated from the sea by a narrow strip of land.

lake Expanse of water entirely surrounded by land.

landslide A mass of soil, mud and rock that slides down a mountainside or cliff-slope because of its own weight.

latitude A degree of latitude (°) is the angular distance of a point on the surface of the earth, north or south of the equator, taken from the centre of the earth. A line of latitude is the line joining all points with the same degree of latitude, i.e. it is a circle with the axis of the earth between the two poles at its centre.

lava fountain Fountain of molten lava ejected from a volcano.

lava plateau Plateau formed from a flat sheet of volcanic rock.

levee River-bank formed during flooding of the river. As the river water spreads out, alluvium is deposited, the greatest quantity being along the line of the river bank.

littoral That part of the seashore between high and low tide.

load Solid material carried by a river, ranging from boulders to fine silt.

loch An inlet of the sea, a fiord or a lake in Scotland.

longitude The angular distance between one of the earth's meridians and the standard or Greenwich meridian.

longshore drift Movement of sand and shingle along the shore due to the action of the waves as

they advance and retreat obliquely along the shore.

lough An inlet of the sea, a fiord or a lake in Ireland.

lunar day Time between successive crossings of a meridian by the moon; about 24 hours 50 minutes.

lunar month Time between two successive new moons, i.e. the time the moon takes to travel around the earth once; 29½ days.

maelstrom A large whirlpool.

magnetic pole Point at which the earth's magnetic flux is strongest. The magnetic poles do not coincide with the true poles; furthermore they move slightly with time.

mangrove swamp A tropical coastal swamp typified by the extensive growth of mangroves, whose long tangled roots drop from the trunks and branches of the mangroves.

maquis Low scrub growing on rocky soil in the mediterranean area.

marsh Low-lying soft wet land.

massif A block of mountains which only breaks up into separate peaks towards the various summits.

meander A wide curve or loop in a river. These often link up in a series of meanders.

meridian Half a great circle on the earth's surface, finishing at each pole and cutting the equator at right-angles, i.e. a line of longitude.

mesa A table-land with steep sides.

meteorite A solid lump of rock which enters the atmosphere from space and is large enough such that it does not burn up in the atmosphere but reaches the earth's surface.

midnight sun Appearance of the sun throughout the day and night. This occurs in latitudes close to the poles at times around the solstices.

monadnock An isolated hill or rock, left when the surrounding rock has been eroded more rapidly.

monsoon forest Tropical forest found where the monsoon climate is prevalent. Because of the dry season between monsoons, it is not so dense as tropical equatorial forest.

moor Area of high rolling land covered in grass, heather and bracken, often with marshy areas.

moraine Rock and other debris transported by a glacier. Terminal moraines are formed at the ends of glaciers; lateral moraines are formed at the sides of glaciers; median moraines are formed in the middle of glaciers where two glaciers meet and unite.

mountain Mass of high land projecting well above the level of the surrounding land.

muskeg A mossy swamp in northern Canada.

neap tide Small tidal difference between high and low tide, caused when the sun and moon are out of phase.

névé Granular snow, formed as snow is gradually impacted. Eventually *névé* forms the ice of a glacier.

nunatak Mountain peak projecting through an ice sheet.

oasis Area in a desert in which water occurs, giving rise to fertile land and allowing cultivation.

ocean A very large area of seawater, divided off by or surrounding the continents.

outwash Alluvium carried from the end of a glacier by the melting ice.

outwash plain Plain formed by the outwash of a glacier.

oxbow lake A lake formed when a river cuts off one of its meanders, leaving a crescent-shaped or horseshoe-shaped lake.

pack ice Ice floes that have been forced together to form an almost continuous sheet.

pampas Grasslands between the Andes and the Atlantic in South America.

pass A gap through a mountain range that is relatively easily traversable.

pediment Sloping plain that leads up to a mountain range.

percolation Descent of water through porous rock.

permafrost Ground that is always frozen solid.

piedmont Pertaining to the foot of a mountain or mountain range.

plain Extensive area of flat or gently rolling land.

plateau Extensive area of flat or gently rolling land that is raised above the level of the surrounding land.

plug Vertical core of solidified lava at the centre of a volcanic cone.

polder Area in the Netherlands that has been reclaimed from the sea.

pole One end of the earth's axis; it remains stationary while all other points on earth rotate round the axis.

pot-hole A hole worn down through solid rock by the swirling action of water or water and accompanying debris.

prairie Flat or rolling plains, largely grasslands, that occupy the central areas of North America east of the Rockies.

profile The profile of a river is a cross-section of its total length, showing the various slopes and changes of slope.

promontory A headland.

puy A French term for an isolated cone of a long-extinct volcano.

quagmire Soft wet ground which shakes when walked on.

quicksand Loose sand in a dense suspension in water. Although it may look solid, its properties are those of a liquid.

race A rapid marine current caused by the tides.

rainbow An arc formed of the colours of the spectrum. It is caused by raindrops refracting the sunlight.

ravine Small steep-sided valley, usually caused by water erosion.

reef Line of rocks just below the surface of the sea.

reg Area of the Sahara desert consisting of gravel and small rocks, but no sand.

ria An inlet of the sea, formed from a drowned, i.e. submerged, river valley.

rift Valley formed by the sinking of a section of land between two parallel faults.

river capture Process by which one river erodes a larger and larger valley, eventually cutting into the valley of another river and 'capturing' its waters.

river terrace Flat land on either side of a river, left when a river erodes a channel well below the level of its flood plain.

roads (roadstead) Large area of deepwater anchorage for ships, usually well protected from bad weather.

run-off Rainfall which pours over the ground surface and into streams and rivers.

salt dome Mass of salt that has been forced up through layers of rock until it lies relatively close to the earth's surface.

salt lake A lake in a hot dry climate that has only a limited outlet or no outlet at all. As water evaporates, the concentration of salt in the water increases.

salt marsh Area of marsh that is flooded by seawater at high tides.

salt pan An area of salt water that has evaporated completely, leaving behind a deposit of salt.

sandbank Line or bank of sand just below the surface of the sea or of a river.

savanna Area of grassland with few trees, found to the north and south of the equatorial areas. There is a wet and a dry season each year, limiting the growth of trees.

scarp (escarpment) A steep slope, often forming the steeper slope of a cuesta.

scree Broken rocks at the foot of a rocky slope. They are broken off by the action of weathering and tumble down the slope.

sea level Mean level between high and low tides.

shoal Area of sandbanks.

sidereal day The interval of time for a star to describe a circle around the pole star.

sierra Long mountain range, usually very jagged.

sill A slab of igneous rock, forced when molten between two layers of sedimentary rock and subsequently exposed by erosion.

snowdrift Bank or mass of snow that has been deposited in the one place by the wind.

snowfield Permanent mass of snow.

snowline On a high land, the level above which snow is permanently present.

solar day The interval of time between the sun appearing in the meridian of any one place.

solstice The time when the sun appears vertically overhead at its most northerly or southerly point; about 21 June and 22 December.

sound A narrow inlet of the sea.

source The point at which a river begins – a spring, lake, etc.

spit A long narrow strip of shingle or sand, attached at one end to a land mass, projecting into the sea or across an estuary.

spring A flow of water up through the ground and out at a particular point. It can be permanent or intermittent.

spring tide Great tidal difference between high and low tide, caused when the sun and moon are in phase.

stack An isolated pillar of rock off the coast, caused by erosion.

steppes Flat grasslands, from central Europe to eastern Russia and on into south-west Siberia.

strait A narrow stretch of sea connecting two large expanses of sea or ocean.

subtropical The region between the tropics and temperate regions.

swamp Low marshland that is permanently wet.

swash Flow of water up a beach after a wave has broken.

taiga Vast belt of coniferous forests in the northern hemisphere, particularly Siberia.

tarn A mountain lake, often occupying a *cirque*.

temperate The region between subtropical regions and polar circles, excluding the continental and eastern coastal regions of the northern hemisphere.

tide Rise and fall of the surface of the sea, caused by the gravitational pull of the moon. The gravitational pull of the sun also influences the tides.

tombolo A bar joining an island to the mainland.

trench A long deep submarine valley.

tributary A river which flows into another river rather than into a lake or the sea.

Tropic of Cancer Latitude 23°N. The position at which the sun appears vertically overhead at midday on the 21 June solstice.

Tropic of Capricorn Latitude 23°S. The position at which the sun appears vertically overhead at midday on the 22 December solstice.

tropics Region between the Tropics of Cancer and Capricorn.

truncated spur A spur that has at some time been foreshortened by the action of a glacier.

tsunami A tidal wave caused by an earthquake under the sea's surface.

tundra Area in the northern hemisphere, north of the coniferous forest belt, typified by the absence of trees. The ground is covered by mosses, lichens and a few other plants that can survive the long harsh winters and short cool summers.

undertow The undercurrent after a wave has broken on a beach.

volcanic ash Particles of lava ejected by a volcano and often falling over a wide area.

volcano Vent or fissure in the earth's crust through which molten magma can force its way to the surface.

wadi A watercourse in the desert. It is usually dry but can contain water after the occasional rainstorms.

waterfall Abrupt fall of water in the course of a river.

water gap Gap in a ridge or line of hills, cut by a river.

watershed The dividing line, running along high land, between the tributaries feeding into two separate river systems.

water table The surface which the pores in the rock are fully saturated with water.

well A hole dug from ground level to below the surface of the water table.

whirlpool A circular eddy of water, formed by the interaction of two or more currents.

year Time taken for the earth to complete one revolution about the sun.

zenith Point vertically above the ground.

Oceans

Ocean with adjacent seas	Area in millions (miles²)	Area in millions (km²)	Percentage of world area	Greatest depth (ft)	Greatest depth (m)	Greatest depth location	Average depth (ft)	Average depth (m)
Pacific	69·96	179,80	35·52	35 840	10 924	Mariana Trench	13 740	4188
Atlantic	41·11	106,48	20·88	31 037	9460	Puerto Rico Trench	12 257	3736
Indian	28·59	74,06	14·52	24 744	7542	Java Trench	12 703	3872
Total	139·66	360,34	70·92					

If the adjacent seas are detached and the Arctic Sea regarded as an ocean, the oceanic areas may be listed thus:

	Area (miles²)	Area (km²)	Percentage of sea area
Pacific	64 190 000	166 240 000	46·0
Atlantic	33 420 000	86 560 000	23·9
Indian	28 350 000	73 430 000	20·3
Arctic	5 110 000	13 230 000	3·7
Other Seas	8 600 000	22 280 000	6·1
	139 670 000	361 740 000	100·0

Ocean depths are zoned by oceanographers as bathyl (down to 6560 ft or *2000 m*); abyssal (between 6560 ft and 19 685 ft *2000 m and 6000 m*) and hadal (below 19 685 ft *6000 m*).

Seas

Principal seas	Area (miles²)	Area (km²)	Average depth (ft)	Average depth (m)
1. South China*	1 148 500	2 974 600	4000	1200
2. Caribbean Sea	1 063 000	2 753 000	8000	2400
3. Mediterranean Sea	966 750	2 503 000	4875	1485
4. Bering Sea	875 750	2 268 180	4700	1400
5. Gulf of Mexico	595 750	1 542 985	5000	1500
6. Sea of Okhotsk	589 800	1 527 570	2750	840
7. East China Sea	482 300	1 249 150	600	180
8. Hudson Bay	475 800	1 232 300	400	120
9. Sea of Japan	389 000	1 007 500	4500	1370
10. Andaman Sea	308 000	797 700	2850	865
11. North Sea	222 125	575 300	300	90
12. Black Sea	178 375	461 980	3600	1100
13. Red Sea	169 000	437 700	1610	490
14. Baltic Sea	163 000	422 160	190	55
15. Persian Gulf†	92 200	238 790	80	24
16. Gulf of St Lawrence	91 800	237 760	400	120
17. Gulf of California	62 530	162 000	2660	810
18. English Channel	34 700	89 900	177	54
19. Irish Sea	34 200	88 550	197	60
20. Bass Strait	28 950	75 000	230	70

* The Malayan Sea, which embraces the South China Sea and the Straits of Malacca (3 144 000 miles² *8 142 000 km²*), is not now an entity accepted by the International Hydrographic Bureau.

† Also referred to as the Arabian Gulf.

Deep-sea trenches

Length (miles)	Length (km)	Name	Deepest point	Depth (ft)	Depth (m)
1400	2250	Mariana Trench,* W Pacific	Challenger Deep†	35 840	10 924
1600	2575	Tonga-Kermadec Trench,‡ S Pacific	Vityaz 11 (Tonga)	35 598	10 850
1400	2250	Kuril-Kamchatka Trench,* W Pacific		34 587	10 542
825	1325	Philippine Trench, W Pacific	Galathea Deep	34 578	10 539
		Idzu-Bonin Trench (sometimes included in the Japan Trench, see below)		32 196	9810
200+	320+	New Hebrides Trench, S Pacific	North Trench	30 080	9165
400	640	Solomon or New Britain Trench, S Pacific		29 988	9140
500	800	Puerto Rico Trench, W Atlantic	Milwaukee Deep	28 374	8648
350	560	Yap Trench,* W Pacific		27 976	8527
1000	1600	Japan Trench,* W Pacific		27 591	8412
600	965	South Sandwich Trench, S Atlantic	Meteor Deep	27 112	8263
2000	3200	Aleutian Trench, N Pacific		26 574	8100
2200	3540	Peru-Chile (Atacama) Trench, E Pacific	Bartholomew Deep	26 454	8064
		Palau Trench (sometimes included in the Yap Trench)		26 420	8050
600	965	Romanche Trench, N-S Atlantic		25 800	7864
1400	2250	Java (Sunda) Trench, Indian Ocean	Planet Deep	25 344	7725
600	965	Cayman Trench, Caribbean		24 720	7535
650	1040	Nansei Shotó (Ryukyu) Trench, W Pacific		24 630	7505
150	240	Banda Trench, Banda Sea		24 155	7360

* These four trenches are sometimes regarded as a single 4600 mile *7400 km* long system.
† Subsequent visits to the Challenger Deep since 1951 have produced claims for greater depths in this same longitude and latitude. In Mar. 1959 the USSR research ship Vityaz claimed 36 198 ft *11 033 m*, using echo-sounding only.
‡ Kermadec Trench is sometimes considered to be a separate feature. Depth 32 974 ft *10 047 m*.

The continents

Continent	Area in miles²	Area in km²	Greatest distance between extremities of land masses			
			North to South (miles)	North to South (km)	East to West (miles)	East to West (km)
Asia	16 988 000	43 998 000	4000	6435	4700	7560
America	16 185 000	41 918 000				
North America	8 305 000	21 510 000	4080	6565	3750	6035
Central America	1 060 000	2 745 000	820	1320	950	1530
South America	6 795 000	17 598 000	4500	7240	3200	5150
Africa	11 506 000	29 800 000	4400	7080	3750	6035
Antarctica	c. 5 500 000	c.13 600 000	—	—	2700*	4340
Europe†	3 745 000	9 699 000	1800	2900	2500	4000
Australia	2 941 526	7 618 493	1870	3000	2300	3700

* Greatest transit from coast to coast.
† Includes 2 151 000 miles² *5 571 000 km²* of USSR territory west of the Urals.

Peninsulas

	Area in miles²	Area in km²		Area in miles²	Area in km²
Arabia	1 250 000	3 250 000	Labrador	500 000	1 300 000
Southern India	800 000	2 072 000	Scandinavia	309 000	800 300
Alaska	580 000	1 500 000	Iberian Peninsula	225 500	584 000

Deserts

Name	Approx. area in miles²	Approx. area in km²	Territories
The Sahara	3 250 000	8 400 000	Algeria, Chad, Libya, Mali, Mauritania, Niger, Sudan, Tunisia, Egypt, Morocco. Embraces the Libyan Desert (600 000 miles² 1 550 000 km²) and the Nubian Desert (100 000 miles² 260 000 km²)
Australian Desert	600 000	1 550 000	Australia. Embraces the Great Sandy (or Warburton) (160 000 miles² 420 000 km²), Great Victoria (125 000 miles² 325 000 km²), Simpson (Arunta) (120 000 miles² 310 000 km²), Gibson (85 000 miles² 220 000 km²) and Sturt Deserts
Arabian Desert	500 000	1 300 000	Southern Arabia, Saudi Arabia, Yemen. Includes the Ar Rab'al Khali or Empty Quarter (250 000 miles² 647 500 km²), Syrian (125 000 miles² 325 000 km²) and An Nafud (50 000 miles² 129 500 km²) Deserts
The Gobi	400 000	1 040 000	Mongolia and China (Inner Mongolia)
Kalahari Desert	200 000	520 000	Botswana
Takla Makan	125 000	320 000	Sinkiang, China
Sonoran Desert	120 000	310 000	Arizona and California, USA and Mexico
Namib Desert	120 000	310 000	In SW Africa (Namibia)
Kara Kum*	105 000	270 000	Turkmenistan, USSR
Thar Desert	100 000	260 000	North-western India and Pakistan
Somali Desert	100 000	260 000	Somalia
Atacama Desert	70 000	180 000	Northern Chile
Kyzyl Kum*	70 000	180 000	Uzbekistan-Kazakhstan, USSR
Dasht-e Lut	20 000	52 000	Eastern Iran (sometimes called Iranian Desert)
Mojave Desert	13 500	35 000	Southern California, USA
Desierto de Sechura	10 000	26 000	North-west Peru

* Together known as the Turkestan Desert.

Mountains

Key to Ranges: H = Himalaya K = Karakoram KS = Kunlun Shan HK = Hindu Kush P = Pamir S = in Sikiang, China.

Subsidiary peaks or tops in the same mountain massif are italicized

Mountain	Height (ft)	Height (m)	Range	Date of First Ascent (if any)
Mount Everest [Qomolangma-feng (Chinese); Sagarmatha (Nepalese); Mi-ti gu-ti cha-pu long-na (Tibetan)]	29 028	8848	H	29 May 1953
Everest South Summit	*28 707*	*8750*	*H*	*26 May 1953*
K2 (Chogori)	28 250	8610	K	31 July 1954
Kangchenjunga	28 208	8597	H	25 May 1955
Lhotse	27 923	8511	H	18 May 1956
Subsidiary Peak	*27 591*	*8410*	*H*	*unclimbed*
Yalung Kang Kangchenjunga West	27 894	8502	H	14 May 1973
Kangchenjunga South Peak	27 848	8488	H	19 May 1978
Makalu I	27 824	8481	H	15 May 1955
Kangchenjunga Middle Peak	27 806	8475	H	22 May 1978
Lhotse Shar	27 504	8383	H	12 May 1970
Dhaulagiri I	26 795	8167	H	13 May 1960
Manaslu I (Kutang I)	26 760	8156	H	9 May 1956
Cho Oyu	26 750	8153	H	19 Oct 1954
Nanga Parbat (Diamir)	26 660	8124	H	3 July 1953
Annapurna I	26 546	8091	H	3 June 1950
Gasherbrum I (Hidden Peak)	26 470	8068	K	5 July 1958
Broad Peak I	26 400	8047	K	9 June 1957
Shishma Pangma (Gosainthan)	26 398	8046	H	2 May 1964
Gasherbrum II	26 360	8034	K	7 July 1956
Broad Peak Middle	*26 300*	*8016*	*K*	*28 July 1975*
Annapurna East	26 280	8010	H	29 Apr 1974
Makalu South-East	26 280	8010	H	Unclimbed
Broad Peak Central	26 246	8000	K	28 July 1975
Gasherbrum III	26 090	7952	K	11 Aug 1975
Annapurna II	26 041	7937	H	17 May 1960
Gasherbrum IV	26 000	7923	K	6 Aug 1958
Gyachung Kang	25 990	7921	H	10 Apr 1964
Nanga Parbat Vorgipfel	25 951	7910	H	11 July 1971
Kangbachen	25 925	7902	H	26 May 1974
Disteghil Sar	25 868	7884	K	9 June 1960
Nuptse	25 850	7879	H	16 May 1961
Himalchuli	25 801	7864	H	24 May 1960
Khinyang Chchish	25 762	7852	K	26 Aug 1971
Manaslu II (Peak 29) Dakuro, Dunapurna	25 705	7835	H	Oct 1970
Masherbrum East	25 660	7821	K	6 July 1960
Nanda Devi West	25 643	7816	H	29 Aug 1936
Nanga Parbat North	25 643	7816	H	Unclimbed
Chomo Lönzo	25 640	7815	H	30 Oct 1954
Ngojumba Ri I (Cho Oyu II)	25 610	7805	H	5 May 1965
Masherbrum West	*25 610*	*7805*	*K*	*unclimbed*
Rakaposhi	25 550	7788	K	25 June 1958
Batura Muztagh I	25 542	7785	K	30 July 1976
Zemu Gap Peak	25 526	7780	K	Unclimbed
Gasherbrum II East	*25 500*	*7772*	*K*	*unclimbed*
Kanjut Sar	25 460	7760	K	19 July 1959
Kamet	25 447	7756	H	21 June 1931
Namcha Barwa	25 445	7756	H	Unclimbed
Dhaulagiri II	25 429	7751	H	18 May 1971
Saltoro Kangri I	25 400	7741	K	24 July 1962
Batura Muztagh II	25 361	7730	K	1978
Gurla Mandhata	25 355	7728	H	Unclimbed
Ulugh Muztagh	25 340	7725	KS	Unclimbed
Qungur II (Kongur)	25 326	7719	P	12 July 1981
Dhaulagiri III	25 318	7715	H	23 Oct 1973
Jannu	25 294	7709	H	27 Apr 1962
Tirich Mir	25 282	7706	HK	21 July 1950
Saltoro Kangri II	25 280	7705	K	Unclimbed
Molamenqing	25 272	7703	H	Unclimbed

Mountain	Height (ft)	Height (m)	Range	Date of First Ascent (if any)
Disteghil Sar E	25 262	7700	K	Unclimbed
Trich Mir, East Peak	*25 236*	*7691*	*HK*	*25 July 1963*
Saser Kangri I	25 170	7672	K	5 June 1973
Chogolisa South West	25 148	7665	K	2 Aug 1975
Phola Gangchhen	25 135	7661	H	Unclimbed
Dhaulagiri IV	25 134	7661	H	9 May 1975
Shahkang Sham	25 131	7660		Unclimbed
Chogolisa North-East ('Bride Peak')	25 110	7653	K	4 Aug 1958
Trivor	25 098	7650	K	17 Aug 1960
Fang	25 088	7647	H	17 May 1980
Ngojumba Ri II	25 085	7646		24 Apr 1965
Makalu II (Kangshungtse)	25 066	7640	H	22 Oct 1954
Khinyang Chchish South	25 000	7620	K	Unclimbed
Shispare	24 997	7619	K	21 July 1974
Dhaulagiri V	24 993	7618	H	1 May 1975
Broad Peak North	*24 935*	*7600*	*K*	*unclimbed*
Amne Machin	24 974	7612	S	2 June 1960
Qungur I (Kongur Tiubie)	24 918	7595	P	16 Aug 1956
Peak 38 (Lhotse II)	24 898	7589	H	Unclimbed
Minya Konka	24 891	7587	S	28 Oct 1932
Annapurna III	24 787	7555	H	6 May 1961
Khula Kangri I	24 784	7554	H	Unclimbed
Changtse (North Peak)	24 780	7552	H	Unclimbed
Muztagh Ata	24 757	7546	P	Unclimbed
Skyang Kangri	24 751	7544	K	11 Aug 1976
Khula Kangri II	24 740	7541	H	Unclimbed
Khula Kangri III	24 710	7532	H	Unclimbed
Yalung Peak	24 710	7532	H	Unclimbed
Yukshin Gardas Sar	24 705	7530	K	Unclimbed
Mamostong Kangri	24 692	7526	K	Unclimbed
Annapurna IV	24 688	7525	H	30 May 1955
Khula Kangri IV	24 659	7516	H	Unclimbed
Saser Kangri II (K24)	24 649	7513	K	Unclimbed
Shartse	24 612	7502	H	23 May 1974

South America

The mountains of the Cordillera de los Andes are headed by Aconcagua at 22 834 ft *6960 m* (first climbed on 14 Jan. 1897), which has the distinction of being the highest mountain in the world outside the great ranges of Central Asia.

Name	Height (ft)	Height (m)	Country
1. Cerro Aconcagua	22 834	6960	Argentina
2. Ojos de Salado	22 588	6885	Argentina–Chile
3. Nevado de Pissis	22 244	6780	Argentina–Chile
4. Huascarán, Sur	22 205	6768	Peru
5. Llullaillaco	22 057	6723	Argentina–Chile
6. Mercadario	21 884	6670	Argentina–Chile
7. Huascarán Norte	21 834	6655	Peru
8. Yerupajá	21 765	6634	Peru
9. Nevados de Tres Crucés	21 720	6620	Argentina–Chile
10. Coropuna	21 696	6613	Peru
11. Nevado Incahuasi	21 657	6601	Argentina–Chile
12. Tupungato	21 490	6550	Argentina–Chile
13. Sajama	21 463	6542	Bolivia
14. Nevado Gonzalez	21 326	6500	Argentina
15. Cerro del Nacimiento	21 302	6493	Argentina
16. El Muerto	21 246	6476	Argentina–Chile
17. Illimani	21 200	6462	Bolivia
18. Ancohuma (Sorata N)	21 086	6427	Bolivia
19. Nevado Bonete	21 031	6410	Argentina
20. Cerro de Ramada	21 031	6410	Argentina

North and Central America

Mt McKinley (first ascent 1913) is the only peak in excess of 20 000 ft *6100 m* in the entire North American continent. It was first climbed on 7 June 1913. The native name is Denali.

Name	Height (ft)	Height (m)	Country
1. McKinley, South Peak	20 320	6194	Alaska
2. Logan	19 850	6050	Canada
3. Citlaltépetl (Orizaba)	18 700	5699	Mexico
4. St Elias	18 008	5489	Alaska–Canada
5. Popocatépetl	17 887	5452	Mexico
6. Foraker	17 400	5304	Alaska
7. Ixtaccihuatl	17 342	5286	Mexico
8. Lucania	17 150	5227	Alaska
9. King Peak	17 130	5221	Alaska
10. Blackburn	16 522	5036	Alaska
11. Steele	16 440	5011	Alaska
12. Bona	16 420	5005	Alaska
13. Sanford	16 207	4940	Alaska
14. Wood	15 879	4840	Canada

Note: Mt McKinley, North Peak, is 19 470 ft *5934 m*.

Africa

All the peaks listed in Zaïre and Uganda are in the Ruwenzori group.

Name	Height (ft)	Height (m)	Location
1. Kilimanjaro (Uhuru Point,* Kibo)	19 340	5894	Tanzania
Hans Meyer Peak, Mawenzi	*16 890*	5148	
Shira Peak	*13 139*	4005	
2. Mount Kenya (Batian)	17 058	5199	Kenya
3. Ngaliema (Mount Stanley) (Margherita Peak)	16 763	5109	Zaïre–Uganda
4. Duwoni or Mt Speke (Vittorio Emanuele Peak)	16 062	4896	Uganda
5. Mount Baker (Edward Peak)	15 889	4843	Uganda
6. Mount Emin (Umberto Peak)	15 741	4798	Zaïre
7. Mount Gessi (Iolanda Peak)	15 470	4715	Uganda
8. Mount Luigi di Savoia (Sella Peak)	15 179	4626	Uganda
9. Ras Dashan (Rasdajan)	15 158	4620	Semien Mts, Ethiopia
10. Humphreys Peak	15 021	4578	Uganda

* Formerly called Kaiser Wilhelm Spitze.

Highest European Alps

The highest point in Italian territory is a shoulder of the main summit of Mont Blanc (Monte Bianco) through which a 4760 m *15 616 ft* contour passes. The highest top exclusively in Italian territory is Picco Luigi Amedeo (4460 m *14 632 ft*) to the south of the main Mont Blanc peak, which is itself exclusively in French territory.

Subsidiary peaks or tops on the same massif have been omitted except in the case of Mont Blanc and Monte Rosa, where they have been indented in italic type.

Name	Height (m)	Height (ft)	Country	First Ascent
1. Mont Blanc	4807	15 771	France	1786
Monte Bianco di Courmayeur	4748	15 577	France	1877
2. Monte Rosa				
Dufourspitze	4634·0	15 203	Switzerland	1855
Nordend	4609	15 121	Swiss–Italian border	1861
Ostspitze	4596	15 078	Swiss–Italian border	1854
Zumstein Spitze	4563	14 970	Swiss–Italian border	1820
Signal Kuppe	4556	14 947	Swiss–Italian border	1842
3. Dom	4545·4	14 911	Switzerland	1858
4. Lyskamm (Liskamm)	4527·2	14 853	Swiss–Italian border	1861
5. Weisshorn	4505·5	14 780	Switzerland	1861
6. Täschhorn	4490·7	14 733	Switzerland	1862
7. Matterhorn	4475·5	14 683	Swiss–Italian border	1865
Le Mont Maudit (Mont Blanc)	4465	14 649	Italy–France	1878
Picco Luigi Amedeo (Mont Blanc)	4460	14 632	Italy	
8. La Dent Blanche	4356·6	14 293	Switzerland	1862
9. Nadelhorn	4327·0	14 196	Switzerland	1858
10. Le Grand Combin de Grafaneire	4314	14 153	Switzerland	1859
Dôme du Goûter (Mont Blanc)	4304	14 120	France	1784
11. Lenzspitze	4294	14 087	Switzerland	1870
12. Finsteraarhorn	4273·8	14 021	Switzerland	1829*

* Also reported climbed in 1812 but evidence lacking.

Note: In the *Dunlop Book* (1st Edition) this list was extended to include the 24 additional Alps over 4000 m 13 123 ft.

Europe

The Caucasus range, along the spine of which runs the traditional geographical boundary between Asia and Europe, includes the following peaks which are higher than Mont Blanc (15 771 ft *4807 m*).

Name	Height (ft)	Height (m)
1. El'brus, West Peak	18 481	5663
El'brus, East Peak	18 356	5595
2. Dykh Tau	17 070	5203
3. Shkhara	17 063	5201
4. Pik Shota Rustaveli	17 028	5190
5. Koshtantau	16 876	5144
6. Pik Pushkin	16 732	5100
7. Jangi Tau, West Peak	16 572	5051
Janga, East Peak	*16 529*	*5038*
8. Dzhangi Tau	16 565	5049
9. Kazbek	16 558	5047

Name	Height (ft)	Height (m)
10. Katyn Tau (Adish)	16 355	4985
11. Pik Rustaveli	16 272	4960
12. Mishirgi, West Peak	16 148	4922
Mishirgitau, East Peak	_16 135_	4917
13. Kunjum Mishirgi	16 011	4880
14. Gestola	15 944	4860
15. Tetnuld	15 921	4853

Antarctica

Areas of Eastern Antarctica remain unsurveyed. Immense areas of the ice cap around the Pole of Inaccessibility lie over 12 000 ft _3650 m_ above sea-level rising to 14 000 ft _4265 m_ in 82° 25′ S 65° 30′ E.

Name	Height (ft)	Height (m)
1. Vinson Massif	16 863	_5140_
2. Mt Tyree	16 289	_4965_
3. Mt Shinn	15 750*	_4800*_
4. Mt Gardner	15 387	_4690_
5. Mt Epperley	15 098	_4602_
6. Mt Kirkpatrick	14 799	_4511_
7. Mt Elizabeth	14 698	_4480_
8. Mt Markham	14 271	_4350_
9. Mt MacKellar	14 074	_4290_
10. Mt Kaplan	13 943	_4250_
11. Mt Sidley	13 850*	_4221*_
12. Mt Ostenso	13 713	_4180_
13. Mt Minto	13 648	_4160_
14. Mt Long Gables	13 615	_4150_
15. Mt Miller	13 600	_4145_
16. Mt Falla	13 500	_4115_
17. Mt Giovinetto	13 408	_4087_
18. Mt Lister	13 353	_4070_
19. Mt Fisher	13 340	_4066_
20. Mt Wade	13 330	_4063_
21. Mt Fridtjof Nansen	13 156	_4010_

* Volcanic as is Erebus 12 447 ft _3794 m._

Oceania

The nomenclature of New Guinean mountains remains extremely confused.

Name	Height (ft)	Height (m)	Location
1. Puncak Jayakusumu (formerly Peak Sukarno, Carstensz Pyramid)	16 023	_4884_	West Irian
Ngga Pulu	15 950	_4861_	West Irian
Sunday Peak	15 945	_4860_	West Irian
2. Oost Carstensz top	15 879	_4840_	West Irian
3. Peak Trikora (formerly Sukarno, formerly Wilhelmina)	15 518	_4730_	West Irian
4. Enggea (Idenburg top)	15 475	_4717_	West Irian
5. Peak Mandala (formerly Juliana)	15 223	_4640_	West Irian
6. Mt Wilhelm	15 091	_4600_	New Guinea
7. Peak Wisnumurti	15 075	_4595_	New Guinea
8. Point (unnamed)	14 271	_4350_	New Guinea
9. Mt Kubor	14 107	_4300_	New Guinea
10. Mt Leonard Darwin	13 891	_4234_	New Guinea
11. Mt Herbert	13 999	_4267_	New Guinea
12. *Mauna Kea	13 796	_4205_	Hawaii*
13. *Mauna Loa	13 680	_4170_	Hawaii*
14. Mt Bangeta	13 474	_4107_	New Guinea
15. Mt Kinabalu	13 454	_4101_	Sabah (Borneo)
16. Mt Sarawaket	13 451	_4100_	New Guinea
17. Mt Giluwe	13 385	_4088_	New Guinea
18. Mt Victoria	13 362	_4073_	Owen Stanley Range
19. Mt Hogan	13 123	_4000_	New Guinea

* Politically part of the USA since 21 Aug. 1959.
Note: The highest mountain in North Island, New Zealand is the volcano Ruapehu (9176 ft _2797 m_).
Mt Cook (12 349 ft _3764 m_) in South Island is the highest in New Zealand and is called Aorangi by the Maoris.
Australia's highest point is Mt Kosciusko (7316 ft _2230 m_) in the Snowy Mtns, New South Wales.

World's largest islands

All illustrations are to scale

	Area in miles²	Area in km²
* Australia	2 941 526	7 618 493

* Geographically regarded as a continental land mass, as are Antarctica, Afro-Eurasia, and America.

1. Greenland
   Area in miles²
   840 000
   Area in km²
   2 175 600
   Location
   Arctic Ocean

2. New Guinea
   Area in miles²
   300 000
   Area in km²
   777 000
   Location
   W Pacific

3. Borneo
   Area in miles²
   280 100
   Area in km²
   725 545
   Location
   Indian Ocean

4. Madagascar
   Area in miles²
   227 800
   Area in km²
   590 000
   Location
   Indian Ocean

7. Honshū
   Area in miles²
   88 031
   Area in km²
   228 000
   Location
   NW Pacific

10. Ellesmere Island
    Area in miles²
    75 767
    Area in km²
    196 236
    Location
    Arctic Ocean

13. Java
    Area in miles²
    48 763
    Area in km²
    126 295
    Location
    Indian Ocean

17. Luzon
    Area in miles²
    40 420
    Area in km²
    104 688
    Location
    W Pacific

21. Hokkaido
    Area in miles²
    30 077
    Area in km²
    77 900
    Location
    NW Pacific

5. Baffin Island
   Area in miles²
   183 810
   Area in km²
   476 065
   Location
   Arctic Ocean

8. Great Britain
   Area in miles²
   84 186
   Area in km²
   218 041
   Location
   North Atlantic

11. Celebes (Sulawesi)
    Area in miles²
    72 987
    Area in km²
    189 035
    Location
    Indian Ocean

14. North Island, New Zealand
    Area in miles²
    44 281
    Area in km²
    114 687
    Location
    SW Pacific

18. Iceland
    Area in miles²
    39 769
    Area in km²
    103 000
    Location
    North Atlantic

22. Hispaniola (Dominican Republic and Haiti)
    Area in miles²
    29 418
    Area in km²
    76 192
    Location
    Caribbean Sea

15. Cuba
    Area in miles²
    44 217
    Area in km²
    114 522
    Location
    Caribbean Sea

19. Mindanao
    Area in miles²
    36 381
    Area in km²
    94 226
    Location
    W Pacific

23. Sakhalin
    Area in miles²
    28 597
    Area in km²
    74 060
    Location
    NW Pacific

6. Sumatra
   Area in miles²
   182 860
   Area in km²
   473 600
   Location
   Indian Ocean

9. Victoria Island
   Area in miles²
   81 930
   Area in km²
   212 197
   Location
   Arctic Ocean

12. South Island, New Zealand
    Area in miles²
    58 093
    Area in km²
    150 460
    Location
    SW Pacific

16. Newfoundland
    Area in miles²
    43 359
    Area in km²
    112 300
    Location
    North-West Atlantic

20. Ireland (Northern Ireland and the Republic of Ireland)
    Area in miles²
    31 839
    Area in km²
    82 460
    Location
    North Atlantic

24. Tasmania
    Area in miles²
    26 215
    Area in km²
    67 900
    Location
    SW Pacific

25. Sri Lanka
    Area in miles² *Area in km²*   *Location*
    25 332   65 600   Indian Ocean

World's greatest mountain ranges

The greatest mountain system is the Himalaya–Karakoram–Hindu Kush–Pamir range with 104 peaks over 24 000 ft *7315 m*. The second greatest range is the Andes with 54 peaks over 20 000 ft *6096 m*.

Length (miles)	Length (km)	Name	Location	Culminating Peak	Height (ft)	Height (m)
4500	*7200*	Cordillera de Los Andes	W South America	Aconcagua	22 834	*6960*
3000	*4800*	Rocky Mountains	W North America	Mt Elbert (Colorado)‡	14 433	*4400*
2400	*3800*	Himalaya–Karakoram–Hindu Kush	S Central Asia	Mt Everest	29 028	*8848*
2250	*3600*	Great Dividing Range	E Australia	Kosciusko	7 310	*2228*
2200	*3500*	Trans-Antarctic Mts	Antarctica	Mt Kirkpatrick	14 860	*4529*
1900	*3000*	Brazilian Atlantic Coast Range	E Brazil	Pico de Bandeira	9 482	*2890*
1800	*2900*	West Sumatran–Javan Range	W Sumatra and Java	Kerintji	12 484	*3805*
1650*	*2650*	Aleutian Range	Alaska and NW Pacific	Shishaldin	9 387	*2861*
1400	*2250*	Tien Shan	S Central Asia	Pik Pobeda	24 406	*7439*
1250	*2000*	Central New Guinea Range	Irian Jaya–Papua/ N Guinea	Jayakusumu†	16 020	*4883*
1250	*2000*	Altai Mountains	Central Asia	Gora Belukha	14 783	*4505*
1250	*2010*	Uralskiy Khrebet	Russian SFSR	Gora Narodnaya	6 214	*1894*
1200	*1930*	Range in Kamchatka§	E Russian SFSR	Klyuchevskaya Sopka	15 910	*4850*
1200	*1930*	Atlas Mountains	NW Africa	Jebel Toubkal	13 665	*4165*
1000	*1610*	Verkhoyanskiy Khrebet	E Russian SFSR	Gora Mas Khaya	9 708	*2959*
1000	*1610*	Western Ghats	W India	Anai Madi	8 841	*2694*
950	*1530*	Sierra Madre Oriental	Mexico	Citlaltépetl (Orizaba)	18 700	*5699*
950	*1530*	Kūhhā-ye-Zāgros	Iran	Zard Kūh	14 921	*4547*
950	*1530*	Scandinavian Range	W Norway	Galdhopiggen	8 104	*2470*
900	*1450*	Ethiopian Highlands	Ethiopia	Ras Dashan	c. 15 100	c. *4600*
900	*1450*	Sierra Madre Occidental	Mexico	Nevado de Colima	13 993	*4265*
850	*1370*	Malagasy Range	Madagascar	Maromokotro	9 436	*2876*
800	*1290*	Drakensberg (edge of plateau)	SE Africa	Thabana Ntlenyana	11 425	*3482*
800	*1290*	Khrebet Cherskogo	E Russian SFSR	Gora Pobeda	10 325	*3147*
750	*1200*	Caucasus	Georgia, USSR	El'brus, West Peak	18 481	*5633*
700	*1130*	Alaska Range	Alaska, USA	Mt McKinley, South Peak	20 320	*6193*
700	*1130*	Assam–Burma Range	Assam–W Burma	Hkakabo Razi	19 296	*5881*
700	*1130*	Cascade Range	Northwest USA–Canada	Mt Rainier	14 410	*4392*
700	*1130*	Central Borneo Range	Central Borneo	Kinabalu	13 455	*4101*
700	*1130*	Tihāmat ash Shām	SW Arabia	Jebel Hadhar	12 336	*3760*
700	*1130*	Appennini	Italy	Corno Grande	9 617	*2931*
700	*1130*	Appalachians	Eastern USA–Canada	Mt Mitchell	6 684	*2037*
650	*1050*	Alpa	Central Europe	Mt Blanc	15 771	*4807*
600	*965*	Sierra Madre del Sur	Mexico	Teotepec	12 149	*3703*
600	*965*	Khrebet Kolymskiy (Gydan)	E Russian SFSR	—	7 290	*2221*

* Continuous mainland length (excluding islands) 450 miles *720 km*.
§ Comprises the Sredinnyy and Koryakskiy Krebets.
† Also known (before 1970) as Ngga Pulu, Mount Sukarno and Cartensz Pyramide.
‡ Mt Robson 12 872 ft *3954 m* is the highest mountain in the Canadian Rockies.

Volcanoes

It is estimated that there are about 850 active volcanoes of which 80 are submarine. Vulcanologists classify volcanoes as extinct, dormant or active (which includes rumbling, steaming or erupting). Areas of volcanoes and seismic activity are well defined, notably around the shores of the N Pacific and the eastern shores of the S Pacific, down the Mid-Atlantic range, the Africa Rift Valley and across from Greece and Turkey into Central Asia, the Himalayas and Meghalaya (Assam).

Cerro Aconcagua (22 834 ft *6960 m*), the highest Andean peak, is an extinct volcano, while Kilimanjaro (19 340 ft *5895 m*) in Africa, and Volcán Llullaillaco in Chile (22 057 ft *6723 m*) are classified as dormant. The highest point on the Equator lies on the shoulder of the dormant Cayambe (18 982 ft *5786 m*) in Ecuador on the 4875 m *15 994 ft* contour. Among the principal volcanoes active in recent times are:

Name	Height (ft)	Height (m)	Range or Location	Country	Date of Last Notified Eruption
Ojos del Salado	22 588	*6885*	Andes	Argentina–Chile	1981–Steams
Guallatiri	19 882	*6060*	Andes	Chile	1960
Cotopaxi	19 347	*5897*	Andes	Ecuador	1975
Lascar	18 507	*5641*	Andes	Chile	1968
Tupungatito	18 504	*5640*	Andes	Chile	1964
Popocatépetl	17 887	*5451*	Altiplano de Mexico	Mexico	1920–Steams
Sangay	17 159	*5230*	Andes	Ecuador	1976
Klyuchevskaya sopka	15 913	*4850*	Sredinnyy Khrebet (Kamchatka Peninsula)	USSR	1974
Purace	15 059	*4590*	Andes	Colombia	1977
Tajumulco	13 881	*4220*		Guatemala	Rumbles
Mauna Loa	13 680	*4170*	Hawaii	USA	1978
Tacaná	13 379	*4078*	Sierra Madre	Guatemala	Rumbles
Cameroon Mt	13 350	*4070*	(monarch)	Cameroon	1959
Erebus	12 450	*3795*	Ross I	Antarctica	1975
Rindjani	12 224	*3726*	Lombok	Indonesia	1966

Name	Height (ft)	Height (m)	Range or Location	Country	Date of Last Notified Eruption
Pico de Teide	12 198	*3718*	Tenerife, Canary Is	Spain	1909
Semeru	12 060	*3676*	Java	Indonesia	1976
Nyiragongo	11 385	*3470*	Virunga	Zaïre	1977
Koryakskaya	11 339	*3456*	Kamchatka Peninsula	USSR	1957
Irazu	11 325	*3452*	Cordillera Central	Costa Rica	1967
Slamat	11 247	*3428*	Java	Indonesia	1967
Mt Spurr	11 070	*3374*	Alaska Range	USA	1953
Mt Etna	10 853	*3308*	Sicily	Italy	1979

Other Notable Active Volcanoes

Name	Height (ft)	Height (m)	Range or Location	Country	Date of Last Notified Eruption
Lassen Peak	10 453	*3186*	Cascade Range, California	USA	1915
Mt St Helens	9 677	*2949*	Cascade Range, Washington	USA	1980
Tambora	9 351	*2850*	Sumbawa	Indonesia	1913
The Peak	6 760	*2060*	Tristan da Cunha	S Atlantic	1962
Mt Lamington	5 535	*1687*		Papua New Guinea	1951
Mt Pelée	4 800	*1463*		Martinique	1929–32
Hekla	4 747	*1447*		Iceland	1980
La Soufrière	c. 4 200	*1280*	St Vincent Island	Atlantic	1979
Vesuvius	4 198	*1280*	Bay of Naples	Italy	1944
Kilauea	4 077	*1240*	Hawaii	USA	1977
Faial	3 421	*1043*	Azores	Azores	1968
Stromboli	3 038	*926*	Island	Mediterranean	1975
Santoríni	1 960	*584*	Thera	Greece	1956
Vulcano	1 637	*499*	Lipari Islands	Mediterranean	1888–90
Parícutin	1 213	*370*		Mexico	1943
Surtsey	568	*173*	off SW Iceland	Iceland	1963–65
Anak Krakatau	510	*155*	Island	Indonesia	1960

Depressions and glaciers

World's deepest depressions		Maximum depth below sea level (ft)	(m)
Dead Sea, Jordan–Israel		1296	395
Turfan Depression, Sinkiang, China		505	153
Munkhafad el Qattâra (Qattâra Depression), Egypt		436	132
Poluostrov Mangyshlak, Kazakh SSR, USSR		433	131
Danakil Depression, Ethiopia		383	116
Death Valley, California, USA		282	86
Salton Sink, California, USA		235	71
Zapadnyy Chink Ustyurta, Kazakh SSR		230	70
Prikaspiyskaya Nizmennost', Russian SFSR and Kazakh SSR		220	67
Ozera Sarykamysh, Uzbek and Turkmen SSR		148	45
El Faiyûm, Egypt		147	44
Península Valdiés Lago Enriquillo, Dominican Republic		131	40

Note: Immense areas of West Antarctica would be below sea level if stripped of their ice sheet. The deepest estimated crypto-depression is the bed rock on the Hollick–Kenyon plateau beneath the Marie Byrd Land ice cap (84° 37′ S 110° W) at −8100 ft *2468 m*. The bed of Lake Baykal (USSR) is 4872 ft *1484 m* below sea-level and the bed of the Dead Sea is 2600 ft *792 m* below sea-level. The ground surface of large areas of Central Greenland under the overburden of ice up to 11 190 ft *341 m* thick are depressed to 1200 ft *365 m* below sea-level. The world's largest exposed depression is the Prikaspiyskaya Nizmennost' stretching the whole northern third of the Caspian Sea (which is itself 92 ft *28 m* below sea-level) up to 250 miles *400 km* inland. The Qattâra Depression extends for 340 miles *547 km* and is up to 80 miles *128 km* wide.

World's longest glaciers

miles	km	
c. 320	515	Lambert-Fisher Ice Passage, Antarctica (disc. 1956–7)
260	418	Novaya Zemlya, North Island, USSR (1160 miles² *3004 km²*)
225	362	Arctic Institute Ice Passage, Victoria Land, E Antarctica
180	289	Nimrod–Lennox–King Ice Passage, E Antarctica
150	241	Denman glacier, E Antarctica
140	225	Beardmore Glacier, E Antarctica (disc. 1908)
140	225	Recovery Glacier, W Antarctica
124	200	*Petermanns Gletscher, Knud Rasmussen Land, Greenland
120	193	Unnamed Glacier, SW Ross Ice Shelf, W Antarctica
115	185	Slessor Glacier, W Antarctica

* Petermanns Gletscher is the largest in the Northern hemisphere: it extends 24·8 miles *40 km* out to sea.

Other Notable Glaciers

Name	Location	Length (miles)	Length (km)	Area (miles²)	Area (km²)
Vatnajökull	Iceland	88	141	3400	8800
Malaspina Glacier	Alaska	26	41	1480	3830
Nabesna Glacier	Alaska	43½	70	770	1990
Fedtschenko	Pamirs	47	75	520	1346
Siachen Glacier	Karakoram	47	75	444	1150

Name	Location	Length (miles)	Length (km)	Area (miles²)	Area (km²)
Jostedalsbre	Norway	62	100	415	1075
Hispar-Biafo Ice Passage	Karakoram	76	122	125 240	323 620
Kangchenjunga	Himalaya	12	19	177	458
Tasman Glacier	New Zealand	18	29	53	137
Aletschgletscher	Alps	16·5	26·5	44	114

Quarayaq Glacier, Greenland, flows at a velocity of 20 to 24 m (*65 to 80 ft*) a day – this is the fastest major glacier.
Hassanabad Glacier, Karakoram advanced 15·3 miles *9,5 km* in 'several months' c. 1900.

Glaciated areas of the world

It is estimated that 6 020 000 miles² *15 600 000 km²* or about 10·4 per cent of the world's land surface is permanently covered with ice, thus:

	miles²	km²
South Polar Regions	5 250 000	13 597 000
North Polar Regions (inc Greenland with 695 500)	758 500	1 965 000
Alaska–Canada	22 700	58 800
Asia	14 600	37 800
South America	4 600	11 900
Europe	4 128	10 700
New Zealand	380	984
Africa	92	238

World's deepest caves

ft	m		
4773	1455	Reseau du Foillis, Haute Savoie	France
4334	1321	Reseau de la Pierre St. Martin, Haute Savoie	France
4200	1280	Snezhnaya, Caucasus	USSR
4002	1220	Sistema Huautla	Mexico
3930	1198	Gouffre Berger	France
3887	1185	Sima de Ukendi	Spain
3772	1150	Avenc B15, Pyrenees	Spain
3645	1111	Schneeloch, Salzburg	Austria
3602	1098	Sima G.E.S. Malaga	Spain
3359	1024	Lamprechtsofen	Austria
3339	1018	Reseau Felix Trombe	France
1010	308	Ogof Ffynnon Ddu, Powys	Wales
702	214	Giant's Hole – Oxlow Caverns, Derbyshire	England
587	179	Reyfad Pot, Fermanagh	Ireland, N
459	140	Carrowmore Cavern	Ireland, Republic

Note: The most extensive cave system is the Mammoth Cave system in Kentucky, USA, discovered in 1799 and in 1972 linked with the Flint Ridge system so making a combined mapped length of 213·3 miles *345 km*. The largest known cavern is the Sarawak Chamber, Lobang Nasip Bagus, Sarawak, surveyed in 1980, which has measurements of 2300 ft *700 m* in length, 980 ft *300 m* in average width and with a minimum height of 230 ft *70 m*.

World's greatest rivers

The importance of rivers still tends to be judged on their length rather than by the more significant factors – their basin areas and volume of flow. In this compilation all the world's river systems with a watercourse of a length of 1500 miles *2400 km* or more are listed with all three criteria where ascertainable.

Length (miles)	(km)	Name of Watercourse	Source	Course and Outflow	Basin Area (miles²)	(km²)	Mean Discharge Rate (ft³/s)	(m³/s)	Notes
1 4145	6670	Nile (Bahr-el-Nil)–White Nile (Bahr el Jabel)–Albert Nile–Victoria Nile–Victoria Nyanza–Kagera-Luvironza	Burundi: Luvironza branch of the Kagera, a feeder of the Victoria Nyanza	Through Tanzania (Kagera), Uganda (Victoria Nile and Albert Nile), Sudan (White Nile), Egypt to eastern Mediterranean	1 293 000	3 350 000	110 000	3120	Navigable length to first cataract (Aswan) 960 miles *1545 km*. UAR Irrigation Dept. states length as 4164 miles *6700 km*. Discharge 93 200 ft³/s *2600 m³/s* near Aswan. Delta is 9250 miles² *23 960 km²*
2 4007	6448	Amazon (Amazonas)	Peru: Lago Villafro, head of the Apurimac branch of the Ucayali, which joins the Marañon to form the Amazonas	Through Colombia to Equatorial Brazil (Solimões) to South Atlantic (Canal do Sul)	2 722 000	7 050 000	6 350 000	180 000	Total of 15 000 tributaries, ten over 1000 miles *1600 km* including Madeira (2100 miles *3380 km*). Navigable 2300 miles *3700 km* upstream. Delta extends 250 miles *400 km* inland
3 3710	5970	Mississippi-Missouri–Jefferson-Beaverhead–Red Rock	Beaverhead County, southern Montana, USA	Through N. Dakota, S. Dakota, Nebraska–Iowa, Missouri–Kansas, Illinois, Kentucky, Tennessee, Arkansas, Mississippi, Louisiana, South West Pass into Gulf of Mexico	1 245 000	3 224 000	650 000	18 400	Missouri is 2315 miles *3725 km* the Jefferson–Beaverhead–Red Rock is 217 miles *349 km*. Lower Mississippi is 1171 miles *1884 km*. Total Mississippi from Lake Itasca, Minn., is 2348 miles *3778 km*. Longest river in one country. Delta is 13 900 miles² *36 000 km²*
4 3442	5540	Yenisey-Angara-Selenga	Mongolia: Ideriin branch of Selenga (Selenge)	Through Buryat ASSR (Selenga feeder) into Ozero Baykal, thence *via* Angara to Yenisey confluence at Strelka to Kara Sea, northern USSR	996 000	2 580 000	670 000	19 000	Estuary 240 miles *386 km* long. Yenisey is 2200 miles *3540 km* long and has a basin of 792 000 miles² *2050 000 km²*. The length of the Angara is 1150 miles *1850 km*
5 3436	5530	Yangtze Kiang (Chang' Chiang)	Western China, Kunlun Shan Mts. (as Dre Che and T'ungt'ien)	Begins at T'ungt'ien, then Chinsha, through Yünnan Szechwan, Hupeh, Anhwei, Kiangsu, to Yellow Sea	756 000	1 960 000	770 000	21 800	Flood rate (1931) of 3 000 000 ft³/s *85 000 m³/s*. Estuary 120 miles *190 km* long

Length (miles) (km)	Name of Watercourse	Source	Course and Outflow	Basin Area (miles²) (km²)	Mean Discharge Rate (ft³/s) (m³/s)	Notes
6 3362 / 5410	Ob'-Irtysh	Mongolia: Kara (Black) Irtysh *via* northern China (Sin Kiang) feeder of Ozero Zaysan	Through Kazakhstan into Russian SFSR to Ob' confluence at Khanty Mansiysk, thence Ob' to Kara Sea, northern USSR	1 150 000 / 2 978 000	550 000 / 15 600	Estuary (Obskaya Guba) is 450 miles *725 km* long. Ob' is 2286 miles *3679 km* long, Irtysh 1840 miles *2960 km* long
7 3000 / 4830	Hwang Ho (Yellow River)	China: Tsaring-nor, Tsinghai Province	Through Kansu, Inner Mongolia, Honan, Shantung to Po Hai (Gulf of Chili), Yellow Sea, North Pacific	378 000 / 979 000	100 000 to 800 000 / 2800 to 22 650	Changed mouth by 250 miles *400 km* in 1852. Only last 25 miles *40 km* navigable. Longest river in one country in Asia
8 2920 / 4700	Zaïre (Congo)	Zambia–Zaïre border, as Lualaba	Through Zaïre as Lualaba along to Zaïre (Congo) border to N.W. Angola mouth into the South Atlantic	1 314 000 / 3 400 000	1 450 000 / 41 000	Navigable for 1075 miles *1730 km* from Kisangani to Kinshasa (formerly Léopoldville). Estuary 60 miles *96 km* long
9 2734 / 4400	Lena-Kirenga	USSR Hinterland of west central shores of Ozero Baykal as Kirenga	Northwards through Eastern Russia to Lapter Sea, Arctic Ocean	960 000 / 2 490 000	575 000 / 16 300	Lena Delta (17 375 miles² *45 000 km²*) extends 110 miles *177 km* inland, frozen 15 Oct. to 10 July. Second longest solely Russian river
10 2700 / 4345	Amur-Argun' (He lung Chiang)	Northern China in Khingan Ranges (as Argun')	North along Inner Mongolian–USSR and Manchuria–USSR border for 2326 miles *3743 km* to Tartar Strait, Sea of Okhotsk, North Pacific	787 000 / 2 038 000	438 000 / 12 400	Amur is 1771 miles *2850 km* long (711 600 basin and 388 000 flow): *China Handbook* claims total length to be 2903 miles *4670 km* of which only 575 miles *925 km* is exclusively in USSR territory
11 2635 / 4240	Mackenzie-Peace	Tatlatui Lake, Skeena Mts, Rockies, British Columbia, Canada (as River Finlay)	Flows as Finlay for 250 miles *400 km* to confluence with Peace. Thence 1050 miles *1690 km* to join Slave (258 miles *415 km*) which feeds Great Slave Lake whence flows Mackenzie (1077 miles *1733 km*) to Beaufort Sea	711 000 / 1 841 000	400 000 / 11 300	Peace 1195 miles *1923 km*
12 2600 / 4180	Mekong (Me Nam Kong)	Central Tibet (as Lants'ang), slopes of Dza-Nag-Lung-Mong, 16 700 ft *5000 m*	Flows into China, thence south to form Burma-Laotian and most of Thai-Laotian frontiers, thence through Cambodia to Vietnam into South China Sea	381 000 / 987 000	388 000 / 11 000	Max flood discharge 1 700 000 ft³/s *48 000 m³/s*
13 2600 / 4184	Niger	Guinea: Loma Mts near Sierra Leone border	Flows through Mali, Niger and along Benin border into Nigeria and Atlantic	730 000 / 1 890 000	415 000 / 11 750	Delta extends 80 miles *128 km* inland and 130 miles *200 km* in coastal length
14 2485 / 4000	Rió de la Plata-Paraná	Brazil: as Paranáiba. Flows south to eastern Paraguay border and into eastern Argentina	Emerges into confluence with River Uruguay to form Rio de la Plata, South Atlantic	1 600 000 / 4 145 000	970 000 / 27 500	After the 75 mile *120 km* long Delta estuary, the river shares the 210 mile *340 km* long estuary of the Uruguay called Rio de la Plata (River Plate)
15 2330 / 3750	Murray-Darling	Queensland, Australia: as the Culgoa continuation of the Condamine, which is an extension of the Balonne-branch of the Darling	Balonne (intermittent flow) crosses into New South Wales to join Darling, which itself joins the Murray on the New South Wales–Victoria border and flows west into Lake Alexandrina, in South Australia	408 000 / 1 059 000	14 000 / 400	Darling c. 1700 miles *2740 km* Murray 1609 miles *2590 km* or 1160 miles *1870 km*
16 2293 / 3690	Volga	USSR	Flows south and east in a great curve and empties in a delta into the north of the Caspian Sea	525 000 / 1 360 000	287 000 / 8200	Delta exceeds 175 miles *280 km* inland and arguably 280 miles *450 km*
17 2200 / 3540	Zambezi (Zambeze)	Zambia: north-west extremity, as Zambezi	Flows after 45 miles *72 km* across eastern Angola for 220 miles *354 km* and back into Zimbabwe (as Zambezi), later forming border with eastern end of Caprivi strip of Namibia, thence over Victoria Falls (Mosi-Oa-tunya) into Kariba Lake. Thereafter into Mozambique and out into southern Indian Ocean	514 000 / 1 330 000	250 000 / 7000	Navigable 380 miles *610 km* up to Quebrabasa Rapids and thereafter in stretches totalling another 1200 miles *1930 km*
2100 / 3380	Madeira–Mamoré–Grande (Guapay)	Bolivia: rises on the Beni near Illimani	Flows north and east into Brazil to join Amazon at the Ilha Tupinambaram	Tributary of No. 2	530 000 / 15 000	World's longest tributary, navigable for 663 miles *1070 km*
2000 / 3200	Purus (formerly Coxiuara)	Peru: as the Alto Purus	Flows north and east into Brazil to join Amazon below Beruri	Tributary of No. 2	— / —	World's second longest tributary. Navigable for 1600 miles *2575 km*. Pronounced meanders
18 1979 / 3185	Yukon-Teslin	North-west British Columbia, Canada, as the Teslin	Flows north into Yukon Territory and into west Alaska, USA, and thence into Bering Sea	330 000 / 855 000	— / —	Delta 85 miles *136 km* inland, navigable (shallow draft) for 1775 miles *2855 km*
19 1945 / 3130	St Lawrence	Head of St Louis River, Minn. USA	Flows into Lake Superior, thence Lakes Huron, Erie, Ontario to Gulf of St Lawrence and North Atlantic	532 000 / 1 378 000	360 000 / 10 200	Estuary 253 miles *407 km* long or 383 miles *616 km* to Anticosti Island. Discovered 1535 by Jacques Cartier
20 1885 / 3033	Rio Grande (Rio Bravo del Norte)	South-western Colorado, USA; San Juan Mts	Flows south through New Mexico, USA, and along Texas-Mexico border into Gulf of Mexico, Atlantic Ocean	172 000 / 445 000	3000 / 85	
21 1800 / 2900	Ganges–Brahmaputra	South-western Tibet as Matsang (Tsangpo)	Flows east 770 miles *1240 km* south, then west through Assam, north-eastern India, joins Ganges (as Jamuna) to flow into Bay of Bengal, Indian Ocean	626 000 / 1 620 000	1 360 000 / 38 500	Joint delta with Ganges extends 225 miles *360 km* across and 205 miles *330 km* inland. Area 30 800 mile² *80 000 km²* the world's largest. Navigable 800 miles *1290 km*
22 1800 / 2900	São Francisco	Brazil: Serra da Canastra	Flows north and east into South Atlantic	270 000 / 700 000	— / —	Navigable 148 miles *238 km*
23 1790 / 2880	Indus	Tibet: as Sengge	Flows west through Kashmir, into Pakistan and out into northern Arabian Sea	450 000 / 1 166 000	195 000 / 5500	Delta (area 3100 miles² *8000 km²*) extends 75 miles *120 km* inland

Length (miles)	(km)	Name of Watercourse	Source	Course and Outflow	Basin Area (miles²)	(km²)	Mean Discharge Rate (ft³/s)	(m³/s)	Notes
24 1770	2850	Danube	South-western Germany: Black Forest as Breg and Brigach	Flows (as Donau) east into Austria, along Czech–Hungarian border as Dunaj into Hungary (273 miles *440 km*) as Duna, to Yugoslavia as Dunav along Romania–Bulgaria border and through Romania as Dunărea to Romania–USSR border as Dunay, into the Black Sea	315 000	*815 000*	250 000	*7000*	Delta extends 60 miles *96 km* inland. Flows in territory of 8 countries
25 1750	*2810*	Salween (Nu Chiang)	Tibet in Tanglha range	Flows (as Nu) east and south into western China, into eastern Burma and along Thailand border and out into Gulf of Martaban, Andaman Sea	125 000	*325 000*	—	—	
26 = 1700	2740	Tigris–Euphrates (Shatt al-Arab)	Eastern Turkey as Murat	Flows west joining the Firat, thence into Syria as Al Furāt and south and east into Iraq joining Tigris flowing into Persian Gulf at Iran–Iraq border as Shatt al-Arab	430 000	*1 115 000*	50 000	*400* low *2700* high	
26 = 1700	2740	Tocantins	Brazil: near Brazilia as Paraná	Flows north to join Pará in the Estuary Báia de Marajó and the South Atlantic	350 000	*905 000*	360 000	*10 000*	Not properly regarded as an Amazon tributary. Estuary 275 miles *440 km* in length
26 = 1700	2740	Orinoco	South-eastern Venezuela	Flows north and west to Colombia border, thence north and east to north-eastern Venezuela and the Atlantic	400 000	*1 036 000*	—	—	
29 1650	2650	Si Kiang (Hsi-Chiang)	China: in Yünnan plateau as Nanp'an	Flows east as the Hungshui and later as the Hsün to emerge as the Hsi in the South China Sea, west of Hong Kong	232 300	*602 000*	—	—	Delta exceeds 90 miles *145 km* inland and includes the Pearl River or Chu
30 1616	2600	Kolyma	USSR: in Khrebet Suntarkhayata (as Kulu)	Flows north across Arctic Circle into eastern Siberian Sea	206 000	*534 000*	134 000	*3800*	
31 = 1600	2575	Amu-Dar'ya (Oxus)	Wakhan, Afghanistan, on the border with Sinkiang China	Flows west to form Tadzhik SSR–Afghan border as Pyandzh for 680 km *420 miles* and into Turkmen SSR as Amu-Dar'ya. Flows north and west into Aral'skoye More (Aral Sea)	179 500	*465 000*	—	—	
31 = 1600	2575	Nelson–Saskatchewan	Canada: Bow Lake, British Colombia	Flows north and east through Saskatchewan and into Manitoba through Cedar Lake into Lake Winnipeg and out through northern feeder as Nelson to Hudson Bay	414 000	*1 072 000*	80 000	*2250*	Saskatchewan 1205 miles *1940 km* in length
33 1575	2540	Ural	USSR: South-central Urals	Flows south and west into the Caspian Sea	84 900	*220 000*	—	—	
1500	*2410*	Japurá	South-west Colombia in Cordillera Oriental as the Caquetá	Flows east into Brazil as Japurá, thence forms a left bank tributary of the Amazon opposite Tefé	Tributary of No. 2				
34 1500	2410	Paraguay	Brazil: in the Mato Grosso as Paraguai	Flows south to touch first Bolivian then Paraguayan border, then across Paraguay and then on to form border with Argentina. Joins the Paraná south of Humaitá	440 000 Tributary of No. 14	*1 150 000*	—	—	

Other Rivers of 1000 miles *1600 km* or longer

Miles	km	Name and Location	Area of Basin (miles²)	(km²)
1450	2335	Arkansas, USA	Tributary of No. 3	
1450	2335	Colorado, USA	228 000	*590 000*
1420	2285	Dnepr (Dnieper), USSR	194 200	*503 000*
1400	2255	Rio Negro, Colombia–Brazil	Tributary of No. 2	
1360	2188	Orange (Oranje), South Africa	394 000	*1 020 000*
1343	2160	Olenek, USSR	95 000	*246 000*
1330	2140	Syr-Dar'ya, USSR	175 000	*453 000*
1306	2100	Ohio–Allegheny, USA	Tributary of No. 3	
1250	2010	Irrawaddy, China–Burma	166 000	*430 000*
1224	1969	Don, USSR	163 000	*422 000*
1210	1950	Columbia-Snake, Canada–USA	258 000	*668 000*
1180	1900	Indigirka–Khastakh, USSR	139 000	*360 000*
1150	1850	Sungari (or Sunghua), China	Tributary of No. 10	
1150	1850	Tigris, Turkey–Iraq	Included in No. 26	
1112	1790	Pechora, USSR	126 000	*326 000*
1018	1638	Red River, USA	Tributary of No. 3	
1000	1600	Churchill, Canada	150 000	*390 000*
1000	1600	Uruguay, Brazil–Uruguay–Argentina	Included in No. 14	
1000	1600	Pilcomayo, Bolivia–Argentina–Paraguay	Tributary of Paraguay and sub-tributary of Paraná	

Note: Some sources state that the Amazon tributary the Juruá is over 1133 miles *1823 km* long and the Lena tributary, the Vitim, is 1200 miles *1931 km* long.

Waterfalls

World's Greatest Waterfalls – By Height

	Name	Total Drop (ft)	(m)	River	Location
1.	Angel (highest fall – 2648 ft *807* m*)	3212	979	Carrao, an upper tributary of the Caroni	Venezuela
2.	Tugela (5 falls) (highest fall – 1350 ft *410 m*)	3110	947	Tugela	Natal, S. Africa
3.	Utigård (highest fall – 1970 ft *600 m*)	2625	800	Jostedal Glacier	Nesdale, Norway
4.	Mongefossen	2540	774	Monge	Mongebekk, Norway
5.	Yosemite (Upper Yosemite – 1430 ft *435 m*; Cascades in middle section – 675 ft *205 m*; Lower Yosemite – 320 ft *97 m*)	2425	739	Yosemite Creek, a tributary of the Merced	Yosemite Valley, Yosemite National Park, Cal., USA
6.	Østre Mardøla Foss (highest fall – 974 ft *296 m*)	2154	656	Mardals	Eikisdal, W. Norway
7.	Tyssestrengane (highest fall – 948 ft *289 m*)	2120	646	Tysso	Hardanger, Norway
8.	Kukenaam (or Cuquenán)	2000	610	Arabopó, upper tributary of the Caroni	Venezuela
9.	Sutherland (highest fall – 815 ft *248 m*)	1904	580	Arthur	nr. Milford Sound, Otago, S. Island, New Zealand
10.	Kile (or Kjellfossen) (highest fall – 490 ft *149 m*)†	1841	561	Naerö fjord feeder	nr. Gudvangen, Norway
11.	Takkakaw (highest fall – 1200 ft *365 m*)	1650	502	A tributary of the Yoho	Daly Glacier, British Columbia, Canada
12.	Ribbon	1612	491	Ribbon Fall Stream	3 miles west of Yosemite Falls, Yosemite National Park, Cal., USA
13.	King George VI	1600	487	Utshi, upper tributary of the Mazaruni	Guyana
14.	Roraima	1500	457	An upper tributary of the Mazaruni	Guyana
15.	Cleve-Garth	1476	449	—	New Zealand
16.	Kalambo	1400	426	S.E. feeder of Lake Tanganyika	Tanzania–Zambia
17.	Gavarnie	1384	421	Gave de Pau	Pyrénées Glaciers, France
18.	Glass	1325	403	Iguazú	Brazil
19.	Krimmler fälle (4 falls, upper fall 460 ft *140 m*)	1280	390	Krimml Glacier	Salzburg, Austria
20.	Lofoi	1259	383	—	Zaïre
21.	Silver Strand (Widow's Tears)	1170	356	Merced tributary	Yosemite National Park, Cal., USA

* There are other very high but seemingly unnamed waterfalls in this area.
† Some authorities would regard this as no more than a 'Bridal Veil' waterfall, *i.e.*, of such low volume that the fall atomizes.

World's Greatest Waterfalls – By Volume of Water

Name	Maximum Height (ft)	(m)	Width (ft)	(m)	Mean Annual Flow (ft³/s)	(m³/s)	Location
Boyoma (formerly Stanley) (7 cataracts)	200 (total)	60	2400(7th)	730	c.600 000	17 000	Zaïre River nr. Kisangani
Guaíra (or Salto dos Sete Quedas) ('Seven Falls')	374	114	15 900	4846	470 000*	13 000	Alto Paraná River, Brazil–Paraguay
Khône	70	21	35 000	10 670	400 000 to 420 000	11 000 to 12 000	Mekong River, Laos
Niagara:							
Horseshoe (Canadian)	160	48	2500	760	212 000 (Horseshoe – 94%)	6000	Niagara River, Lake Erie to Lake Ontario
American	167	50	1000	300	100 000	2800	Niagara River, Lake Erie to Lake Ontario
Paulo Afonso	192	58	—	—	100 000	2800	São Francisco River, Brazil
Urubu-punga	40	12	—	—	97 000	2700	São Francisco River, Brazil
Cataratas del Iguazú (Quedas do Iguaçu)	308	93	c. 13 000	c. 4000	61 660	1700	Alto Paraná River, Brazil
Patos–Maribondo	115	35	—	—	53 000	1500	Iguazú (or Iguaçu) River, Brazil–Argentina
Victoria (Mosi-oa-tunya):							Rio Grande, Brazil
Leaping Water	355	108	108	33			Zambezi River, Zambia
Main Fall	(maximum)		2694	821	38 430	1100	Zimbabwe
Rainbow Falls			1800	550			
Churchill (formerly Grand)	245	75	—	—	30 000 to 40 000	850 to 1100	Churchill (formerly Hamilton) River, Canada
Kaieteur (Köituök)	741	225	300 to 350	90 to 105	23 400	660	Potaro River, Guyana

* The peak flow has reached 1 750 000 ft³/s *50 000 m³/s*.

Lakes of the World

	Name	Country	Area (miles²)	(km²)	Length (miles)	(km)	Maximum Depth (ft)	(m)	Average Depth (ft)	(m)	Height of Surface above Sea-level (ft)	(m)
1.	Caspian Sea	USSR and Iran	143 550	371 800	760	1225	3215	980	675	205	−92	−28
2.	Superior	Canada and USA	31 800	82 350	350	560	1333	406	485	147	600·4	183
3.	Victoria Nyanza	Uganda, Tanzania, and Kenya	26 828	69 500	225	360	265	80	130	39	3720	1134
4.	Aral'skoye More (Aral Sea)	USSR	25 300	65 500	280	450	223	68	52	15,8	174	53
5.	Huron	Canada and USA	23 010	59 600	206	330	750	228	196	59	579	176
6.	Michigan	USA	22 400	58 000	307	494	923	281	275	83	579	176
7.	Tanganyika	Zaire, Tanzania, Zambia and Burundi	12 700	32 900	450	725	4708	1435	—	—	2534	772
8.	Great Bear	Canada	12 275	31 800	232	373	270	82	240	73	390	118
9.	Ozero Baykal	USSR	11 780	30 500	385	620	6365	1940	2300	700	1493	455
10.	Malawi (formerly Nyasa)	Tanzania, Malawi, and Mozambique	11 430	29 600	360	580	2226	678	895	272	1550	472
11.	Great Slave	Canada	10 980	28 500	298	480	535	163	240	73	512	156
12.	Erie	Canada and USA	9930	25 700	241	387	210	64	60	18,2	572	174

Name	Country	Area (miles²)	(km²)	Length (miles)	(km)	Maximum Depth (ft)	(m)	Average Depth (ft)	(m)	Height of Surface above Sea-level (ft)	(m)
13. Winnipeg	Canada	9464	24 500	266	428	120	36	50	15	713	217
14. Ontario	Canada and USA	7520	19 500	193	310	780	237	260	79	246	75
15. Ozero Ladozhskoye (Lake Ladoga)	USSR	6835	17 700	120	193	738	225	170	51	13	3,9
16. Ozero Balkhash	USSR	6720	17 400	300	482	85	26	—	—	1112	339
17. Lac Tchad (Chad)	Niger, Nigeria, Chad and Cameroon	6300*	16 300	130	209	13–24	3,9–7,3	5	1,5	787	240
18. Ozero Onezhskoye (Onega)	USSR	3710	9600	145	233	361	110	105	32	108	33
19. Eyre	Australia	3700†	9580	115	185	65	19,8	—	—	−39	−11,8
20. Lago Titicaca	Peru and Bolivia	3200	8300	130	209	913	278	328	100	12 506	3811
21. Athabasca	Canada	3120	8100	208	334	407	124	—	—	699	213
22. Saimaa complex‡	Finland	c.3100	c.8030	203	326	—	—	—	—	249	75
23. Lago de Nicaragua	Nicaragua	3089	8000	100	160	200	60	—	—	110	33

* Highly variable area between 4250 and 8500 miles² *11 000 and 22 000 km²*.
† Highly variable area between 3100 and 5800 miles² *8030 and 15 000 km²*.
‡ The Saimaa proper (The Lake of a Thousand Isles) is, excluding the islands, c. 500 miles² *1300 km²*.

Lakes under 3000 miles² *770 km²* but over 2000 miles² *5180 km²*

Area (miles²)	(km²)	Name	Country
2473	6400	Turkana (formerly Rudolf)	Kenya and Ethiopia
2465	6380	Reindeer	Canada
2355	6100	*Issyk Kul'	USSR
2230	5775	Torrens	Australia
2149	5565	Vänern	Sweden
2105	5450	Winnipegosis	Canada
2075	5375	Mobutu Sese Seko (formerly Albert)	Uganda and Zaire
2050	5300	Kariba (dammed)	Zimbabwe and Zambia

* Has a maximum depth of 2303 feet *700 m* and an average depth of 1050 ft *320 m*. The height of the surface above sea-level is 5279 ft *1600 m*.

Forests

What is a forest?
Put very simply, a forest is a large area of land covered by trees. It is the type of vegetation most likely to result from the process of ecological succession, assuming that soil and weather conditions permit it. This is because trees grow taller and live considerably longer than other plants and so become the dominant members of the plant community.

Forests can be classified on various principles, but they are commonly recognized as tropical rain forests, temperate deciduous forests and the coniferous forests of the northern hemisphere.

Tropical rain forests
Tropical rain forests can be subdivided into two distinct types, the equatorial rain forest and the monsoon forest.

Equatorial rain forest
Equatorial rain forests are found in the low-altitude areas of the equatorial regions, where rainfall is heavy, usually occurring every day, and there is no dry season. The forests are thus hot and wet, typified by a wide range of broad-leaved evergreen trees. However, because of the competition for survival, individual species of trees tend to be scattered.

Because of the luxuriant and rapid growth, many trees tend to grow to enormous heights in their attempts to get clear of the other vegetation and obtain enough light. Beneath this high canopy of leaves can be found many epiphytes – plants which grow on the branches and trunks of the trees and obtain their nourishment from the air, rotting bark and leaves and suchlike. Lianas are also common, climbing up other trees in their attempts to obtain enough light. Closer to the ground can be found a wide variety and profuse growth of shrubs and plants, while an equally wide range of mammals, snakes and insects can be found both on the ground and amongst the trees.

A huge amount of organic material is locked up in such a forest. However, the soils that support the trees and plants tend to be very poor. If the forest cover is removed, the few nutrients tend to be leached out of the soil and an unproductive infertile area results.

Typical trees found in equatorial rain forests are the tropical hardwoods such as mahogany, as well as the rubber tree.

The major such forests are found in the Amazon basin, the basin of the river Zaïre, and the East Indies.

Monsoon forest
Monsoon forest differs from equatorial rain forest in that there is a distinct dry season between the monsoonal wet seasons. Enough rain falls during the monsoons to support the broad-leaved forests, but leaves are shed during the dry seasons. The forests are not as dense as the equatorial rain forests, and there is not such a wide variety of species, teak being one of the best known species.

The major monsoon forests are found in south-east Asia in such countries as India, Burma, Malaysia, Thailand, etc.

Temperate deciduous forest
This is the natural type of vegetation of the temperate regions, typified by trees that shed their leaves during the winter.

The canopy of leaves is not nearly as dense as with the tropical forests, so trees are shorter and the light filtering through allows shrubs and plants to grow at ground level. Because of the annual fall of leaves, which subsequently rot down, the soils tend to be nutrient-rich.

The major areas of temperate deciduous forest are North America, Europe and eastern Asia. However, because these are also areas of population concentration, much of these forests have been modified by human intervention, and many areas have been cleared.

Typical species found in temperate deciduous forests are oak, ash, beech, chestnut and maple.

Northern coniferous forest
In terms of area, the coniferous forests of the northern hemisphere are the largest. They cover a huge swathe of North America, and an even larger area of northern Europe, Scandinavia and northern Asia. Fingers of forest also reach down into more southerly latitudes along the lines of mountains, e.g. the Rockies, and occur on other 'islands' of mountains such as Alps.

The trees do not shed their leaves at any one season but do so continuously. Growth, however, occurs only during the limited warm season of three or four months. The leaves have a number of adaptations to the climate, including a thick waxy skin and a small surface area, both designed to reduce water loss. The canopy of these forests is very dense, and the leaves that fall to the ground do not decompose readily. The soils therefore tend to be nutritionally very poor, there is little or no undergrowth, and wildlife is scarce.

There is little variety in the species of tree found in these forests, spruce, pine and fir being the most common types, providing the world with its supply of softwood timber and wood-pulp.

Thorn forest
Thorn forest is a particular type of forest, not as extensive as the types mentioned already, but covering large enough areas to warrant a mention. It occurs in tropical and subtropical areas which have low rainfall, and therefore consists of trees that can shed their leaves during the dry periods, e.g. acacia.

Perhaps the largest area of thorn forest is the *caatinga* of north-eastern Brazil which, in addition to thorn trees, contains a wide variety of cacti.

The importance of forests
Forests constitute an enormous reserve of organic material, with the added attraction that they are self-replenishing. However, trees take a long time to grow; commercial softwoods take a minimum of 25 years to reach a marketable size, while the time it takes a hardwood to reach maturity may well exceed 100 years. It is easy to see that rapid deforestation will remove areas of forest faster than they can be replaced. Furthermore, if some areas of forest, such as tropical rain forests, are completely destroyed rather than selectively cropped, then the poor soils remaining will never again support a mature forest.

The economic implications of deforestation are obvious. What is perhaps less well understood are the ecological implications. For example, photosynthesis converts carbon dioxide to oxygen. Industrial man produces more and more carbon dioxide each year as a result of factory emissions, car exhausts, etc. If we destroy forests at the same time, what effect will this have on the balance of oxygen and carbon dioxide in the air?

Forests are also an important part of the water cycle, preventing rapid run-off and erosion of the soil, and returning water to the air as water vapour from their leaves. What effect will deforestation have on the world's climatic zones?

Geology

Introduction

Rocks of the Earth's crust
These are grouped in three principal classes:

(1) Igneous rocks have been solidified from molten *Magma*. These are divided into extrusive rock, viz. lava and pumice, or intrusive rock, such as some granites or gabbro which is high in calcium and magnesium and low in silicon. It should be noted that extreme metamorphism can also produce granitic rocks from sediment.

(2) Sedimentary rocks are classically formed by the deposition of sediment in water, viz. conglomerates (e.g. gravel, shingle, pebbles), sandstones and shales (layered clay and claystone). Peat, lignite, bituminous coal and anthracite are the result of the deposition of organic matter. Gypsum, chalk and limestone are examples of chemical sedimentation.

(3) Metamorphic rocks were originally igneous or sedimentary but have been metamorphosed (transformed) by the agency of intense heat, pressure or the action of water. Gneiss is metamorphosed granite; marble is metamorphosed limestone; and slate is highly pressurised shale. Metamorphic rocks made cleavable by intense heat and pressure are known generically as schist. Their foliate characteristics are shared by both gneiss and slate.

Geochemical abundances of the elements

	Lithosphere* (Parts per Mill. ‰)	Hydrosphere (Parts per Mill. ‰)
Oxygen	466·0	857·0
Silicon	277·2	0·003 to 0·00002
Aluminium	81·3	0·00001
Iron	50·0	0·00001
Calcium	36·3	0·40
Sodium	28·3	10·50
Potassium	25·9	0·38
Magnesium	20·9	1·35
Titanium	4·4	—
Hydrogen	1·40	103·0
Manganese	0·95	0·000002
Phosphorus	0·70	0·00007
Fluorine	0·65	0·0013
Sulfur	0·26	0·88
Carbon	0·25	0·028
Zirconium	0·17	—
Chlorine	0·13	19·0
Rubidium	0·09	0·0001
Nitrogen	0·02	0·0005
Chromium	0·01	0·00000005

* Assessment based on igneous rock.

Geo-chronology
Christian teaching as enunciated by Archbishop Ussher in the 17th century dated the creation of the Earth as occurring in the year 4004 BC. Lord Kelvin (1824–1907) calculated in 1899 that the earth was of the order of possibly some hundreds of millions of years old. In 1905 Lord Rutherford suggested radioactive decay could be used as a measurement and in 1907 Boltwood showed that a sample of pre-Cambrian rock dated from 1640 million years before the present (BP) measured by the uranium-lead method.

Modern dating methods, using the duration of radioisotopic half-lives, include also the contrasts obtained from thorium-lead, potassium-argon, rubidium-strontium, rhenium-osmium, helium-uranium and in the recent range of up to 40 000 years BP carbon-14. Other methods include thermoluminescence since 1968 and racemisation of amino acids since 1972 which latter is dependent upon the change from optically active to inactive forms which decline varies with the elapse of time.

Glossary

ablation Removal of rock debris by wind action.
abrasion Wearing away of rock particles so that they get smaller; usually the action of particles rubbing together.
abstraction The absorption of one river by another.
acid rock Igneous rock with over 10% free quartz.
adobe A type of clay.
aeolian deposits Particles carried and deposited by the wind.
alluvial fan Sediment deposited by a river when there is a decrease in gradient.
alluvium Sands and gravels carried by rivers and deposited along the course of the river.
amber A type of resin.
amorphous Material having no regular arrangement.
anhedral Having no crystalline structure.
anticline Fold system in the form of an arch.
aquifer A strata of rock containing water.
arenaceous rocks Sedimentary sandstones, deposited by wind or water.
argillaceous rocks Sedimentary rocks deposited by water; usually marls, silts, shales, muds and clays.
artesian Aquifer between two impermeable strata, forming a basin such that a pressure head is generated.
ash Fine material formed by volcanic explosions.
asphalt Hydrocarbon, either solid or just fluid at normal temperatures.
asthenosphere The lowest part of the earth's crust.
automorphic Grains having a crystal structure.

ball clay Reworked china clay.
banket A conglomerate of quartz.
basalt Fine-grained basic igneous rock, sometimes with a glassy characteristic.
basic rock Igneous rock containing little or no quartz.
basin Large depression.
batholith An intrusive mass of igneous rock.
bauxite An aluminium ore of aluminium oxide, out of which the easily leached ions have been removed.
bedding plane Surface parallel to the surface of deposition. Some rocks split along bedding planes; others have less obvious physical characteristics such as changes of particle size.
biolith Rock of organic material, formed by organic processes.
bitumen Hydrocarbon mineral with a tarry texture, ranging from a viscous liquid to a solid.
black-band ironstone A sedimentary rock, formed principally from a form of coal and iron carbonate (siderite).
boghead coal Coal formed by algal and fungal material.
bort Anhedral diamonds in a granular mass.
boss Mass of igneous rock with steep contact surfaces with the surrounding rock.
boudinage Stretching of a rock layer to give a sausage-shaped structure.
boulder bed Sedimentary rock consisting of boulders together with fine-grained material.
breccia Sedimentary rock consisting of angular material of more than 0·08 in 2 mm diameter.
brown coal Another name for lignite; a coal containing a low carbon content.

carbonate A large group of minerals, all having the carbonate group bond, $-CO_3$, in common. They can be divided into sedimentary and non-sedimentary carbonates, limestone being the most common form of sedimentary carbonate.
carbonatite Magmatic rock consisting of calcium carbonate and occasionally other carbonates.
carstone A form of sandstone with a high proportion of limonite.

cassiterite Tin oxide ore.
cataclasis Mechanical break-up of rock.
caulk Barytes (barium sulphate).
celestite A strontium mineral found mainly in sedimentary rock.
ceylonite A spinel mineral.
chalcedony A silica-based mineral, found in many forms, some of which are semi-precious stone, e.g. agate, onyx, carnelian, jasper.
chalcocite Copper sulphide ore.
chalcopyrite One of the principal copper ores.
chalk Fine-grained white limestone, calcium carbonate.
charnockite Granular rock, mainly consisting of quartz, feldspar and hypersthene.
chernozem Black earth, with a high proportion of humus but a leached surface layer.
chert A form of silica, found as bands and nodules in sedimentary rocks.
chiastolite A form of aluminium silicate.
china clay Kaolin, formed by decomposition of feldspar in granite.
chlorite Green mineral consisting of talc units.
chondrites Stony meteorites.
chromite A chromium ore, containing iron.
chrysocolla A copper ore mineral, copper silicate.
chrysoprase A green chalcedony.
chrysotile A form of asbestos.
cinnabar Mercury sulphide, associated with volcanic activity.
citrine A yellow quartz.
clastic rock Fragments of rock, transported to a site of deposition and built up into a conglomerate.
clay A sedimentary rock with a fine particle structure and a soft plastic texture when wet.
cleat Jointing found in coal.
cleavage A flat plane of breakage, perhaps parallel to a crystal face.
cleavage plane Plane of fracture in a rock.
clint Ridge in limestone rock surface.
coal Stratified deposits of carbonaceous material, originally derived from vegetation, i.e. decayed vegetable matter.
cobble A rock particle, between 5 in 125 mm and 10 in 250 mm in diameter.
columnar structure Vertical columns or prisms, formed for example in lava and basalt, caused by the cooling of the rock.
competent Flow or flexion of a rock layer, in which it is not broken.
composite Igneous bodies which have more than one material in them, e.g. due to intrusion.
concretion Accumulations of sedimentary constituents in certain defined areas of rock, often around a nucleus.
conglomerate Rounded pebbles cemented together into one mass.
convergence Metamorphosis of two dissimilar rocks so that they become similar.
coral Organic skeletal material of dead aquatic animals.
corrasion Vertical erosion of a river bed by the river.
corundum Aluminium oxide, used as an abrasive and also found as gemstones, e.g. sapphire, ruby.
country rock Body of rock which encloses an intrusion by another rock, e.g. an igneous rock.
creep Gradual deformation of a rock by stress applied over a long time.
crystal Three-dimensional structure arising from the atomic structure of the substance. The symmetrical arrangement for a given substance means that the angles within the structure are constant for that substance.
culm Carboniferous rocks found in Devon and Cornwall.
cuprite Copper oxide, an important copper ore.

deflation Surface debris transported by the wind.
deformation Any change in a bed or strata after it has been formed.

dendritic Branching into a many-fingered appearance.

denudation Any process that results in a lowering of the land surface.

detritus Particles of minerals and rocks formed by weathering and erosion.

diamond A crystalline form of carbon. It has a cubic structure, distinguishing it from graphite.

diatomite The remains of unicellular plants called diatoms. It is a highly-absorbent powdery siliceous material.

diorite A coarse-grained igneous rock consisting of feldspar plus ferromagnesium minerals.

dog-tooth spar Calcite, crystallized into tooth-like forms.

dolerite An igneous rock similar to basalt.

dolomite Calcium magnesium carbonate, or limestone with a substantial proportion of magnesium carbonate.

dyke A sheet of igneous rock which cuts across the bedding or structural planes of the host rock.

earthquake Series of shock waves generated from a single point within the earth's mantle or crust.

elaterite An elastic or rubbery form of bitumen.

elvan A dyke of granite.

emerald A green form of beryl.

emery Fine granules of corundum and magnetite.

epicentre Point above the focus of an earthquake, on the earth's surface.

epidiorite A metamorphic granular rock derived from igneous rock and containing the minerals of diorite.

epidotes Group of rock-forming silicate minerals.

erratic A stone or boulder carried by a glacier some distance from its source.

evaporite Sediment left by the evaporation of salt water.

extrusive Igneous rock that has flowed out at the earth's surface.

fault A fracture plane in rock, along which displacement occurs.

feldspar Silicate minerals, in which the silicon ions are in part replaced with aluminium ions. Calcium, sodium and potassium feldspars exist, as do the rare barium feldspars.

feldspathoid Rock-forming silicates with sodium and/or potassium in the lattice structure. They never occur with quartz.

festoon bedding A type of cross-bedding.

fire clay Argillaceous fossil soil found with some coal seams.

flint A type of chert.

flowage Irreversible deformation, i.e. deforming a material beyond its elastic limit.

fluorite Calcium fluoride, found as veins in rocks.

fold A flexing of a rock strata.

fool's gold Iron pyrites.

fossil Impression of an animal or plant, or its skeletal remains, buried by natural processes and then preserved.

fracture A break in a direction that is not a cleavage plane.

fuchsite Mica mineral containing chromium.

fulgurite A branching tube of fused silica, caused by lightning striking sandy soil.

gabbro Coarse-grained igneous rock, equivalent to basalt and dolerite. It contains feldspar, pyroxene and olivine as the major constituents.

galena Lead sulphide, the most important lead ore.

gangue The material in which an ore deposit from the metal is not extracted.

gannister Arenaceous strata found beneath coal seams.

gas cap Collection of gas above an oil deposit.

gems Hard minerals, free from cleavages. Fragments are artificially cut and polished for decorative use.

garnet Semi-precious mineral with a wide range of colours, although red is the most commonly found.

geode A rock cavity containing crystals pointing inwards.

geosyncline Elongated basin, filled with sedimentary deposits. These deposits can then be deformed by orogenic forces.

glassy Non-crystalline rocks, caused for example by rapid cooling of molten material.

gneiss Banded rocks formed during metamorphosis. They are coarse-grained rocks.

granite Coarse-grained igneous rock, consisting essentially of quartz and feldspar and occurring as intrusive bodies in a variety of forms.

granule Rock particle of about 0·08–0·16 in *2–4 mm*.

graphite Soft black form of carbon.

gravel The same size particles as granules.

grike A cleft in a limestone pavement.

grit Arenaceous rock in which the particle shape is angular.

gull A fissure caused by cambering, which tapers downwards and is then filled with material from above.

gumbo A soil which, when wet, gives a sticky mud.

gypsum An evaporite calcium sulphate mineral found in clays and limestone.

hade A fault plane's angle to the vertical.

haematite An iron-oxide iron ore.

halite Common salt, left as an evaporite.

hardness Mineral property propounded by Mohs. It measures the ability to scratch, as follows:

10	Diamond	5	Apatite
9	Corundum	4	Fluorite
8	Topaz	3	Calcite
7	Quartz	2	Gypsum
6	Orthoclase	1	Talc

hard-pan Strongly cemented material occurring below the surface of some sediments as a result of groundwater action.

hemicrystalline Rocks containing both crystalline and glassy material.

hornfels Fine-grained granular rock formed by thermal metamorphosis.

hornstone Fine-grained volcanic ash.

horst Area thrown up between two parallel faults.

humus Organic material in soil.

Iceland spar Variety of calcite.

igneous One of the three major divisions of rocks. Generally they are crystalline, although glassy forms can be found. They are either extrusive, i.e. produced on the earth's surface as a result of volcanic action, or intrusive into other rocks, in which case they only appear on the earth's surface if the surrounding rock is eroded.

impervious Does not allow the passage of water.

impregnation In-filling of pores by mineral material, e.g oil.

inclusion A portion of one material totally enclosed within another.

incretion A cylindrical hollow concretion.

inlier Area of older rock surrounded by younger rock.

interbedded A layer of rock between two other layers.

intermediate rock Rock containing no more than 10% quartz plus a feldspar.

intrusion Igneous rock structure that has forced its way into pre-existing rock.

jade Gem stone of a hard compact aggregate.

jasper Red chert-like variety of chalcedony.

jet Homogeneous form of cannel coal or black lignite.

joint Fracture in a rock structure along which no movement can be observed.

kaolin The main constituent of china clay.

karst Type of limestone scenery produced by water erosion of limestone and dolomite rock. It is characterized by sinks, underground rivers and caves, and other erosion features, together with a red soil on the surface. If the soil is not present, then clints and grykes will be observed.

kieselguhr Diatomite.

kimberlite A brecciated peridotite containing mica and other minerals.

kyanite An aluminium silicate.

labradorite A type of feldspar.

lamination Thin layers of rock, each of them distinct.

landscape marble A type of limestone that, when sliced at right angles to the bedding plane, reveals patterns reminiscent of a landscape scene.

lapis lazuli A type of lazulite.

laterite An iron-oxide ore, out of which the easily-leached ions have been removed.

lava The mineral that flows out of volcanoes. It consists of molten silicates. In general they are basic, although acidic lava flows are known. Acidic lavas flow readily and tend to cover much larger areas, while basic lavas are more viscous.

leaching The removal of ions from a soil or rock by the through-flow of water.

lepidolite A type of mica.

lignite Brown coal, low in carbon content.

limestone A group of sedimentary rocks consisting of carbonates. Calcite and dolomite are the most important limestone rocks.

limonite A group of iron oxides and hydroxides.

lithifaction Formation of a large rock from small fragments.

loam Sand, silt and clay in equal proportions in a soil.

loess Deposits of wind-blown fine particles.

lustre The ability of minerals to reflect light.

magma The molten fluid within the earth's crust. Igneous rocks are formed from the magma, although various constituents of the magma will be lost during this process of consolidation.

magnesite Magnesium carbonate.

magnetite An iron ore consisting of ferric oxide.

malachite A carbonate ore of copper.

marble Metamorphosed limestone, usually with other compounds giving marble its recognizable appearance.

marl A mudstone with a high calcium content.

metamorphism The processes of heating, pressure and chemical action which cause rocks to change from one form to another in the earth's crust.

mica A large group of silica-based minerals, characterized by the fact that the crystal structure gives cleavage into flat flexible sheets.

migmatite A form of gneiss.

mineral A chemical, formed naturally, with a constant composition and structure.

mobile belt A part of the earth's crust in which metamorphosis, igneous activity and deformation occur.

monzonite Coarse igneous rock with a high feldspar content.

mud Wet clay soil in a near-liquid state.

mudstone A type of argillaceous rock, similar to shale, but without the property of splitting along bedding planes.

muscovite A type of mica.

natural gas Gaseous hydrocarbons found together with oil deposits.

neck A volcanic plug.

nodule A rounded concretion.

obsidian A type of rhyolite with a black glassy sheen to it.

oceanite A type of basalt.

oil Often called petroleum, oil is naturally occurring liquid hydrocarbon. It is invariably found in association with saline water and natural gas, and often with solid hydrocarbons.

oil shale A dark argillaceous rock. It does not contain liquid oil, but a solid organic material kerogen which gives oil on distillation.

olivine A group of silicates, containing ferrous iron and magnesium. They largely occur in igneous rocks.

onyx A type of banded chalcedony.

oolith A rounded lump of rock formed by accretion round a nucleus. Ooliths usually contain calcium minerals.

opal An amorphous type of silica, believed to have been derived from silica gel.

ore Mixture of the wanted mineral, the useless minerals and the surrounding rock.

orogeny The process or period of mountain building.

outlier A relatively small area of young rock, surrounded by older rock.

overburden Useless, soil, etc., found on top of a bed of useful mineral.

peat An early form of coal. It is a dark-brown to black mass of partially decomposed vegetation.

pebble Rock fragment of 0·2–2·3 in *5–60 mm* diameter.

pedalfer Leached soil in a region with high rainfall.

pegmatite Coarse-grained igneous rock, usually granitic. Very long crystals may be apparent.

peridot Gem-quality olivine.

permeability Ability of water to percolate through a rock.

pervious Water passes through a pervious rock via cracks, fissures, etc.

pitchblende Uranium oxide ore.

plug The solidified lava and other material left in the neck of a volcano. Often the surrounding material is subsequently eroded away.

plutonic Igneous material of a deep-seated origin, i.e. originating from the magma.

podsol Soil found in cool temperate humid zones, in which substantial leaching has occurred.

porous Water is held in or passes through a rock in cavities between the mineral grains.

pudding stone A conglomerate.

pumice One of the pyroclastic rocks thrown out of a volcano. It contains a high proportion of air space.

pyrite Iron sulphide.

pyroclastic rock This can either be liquid lava thrown out of the volcano, or solid lumps of surrounding rock broken up by the volcanic action.

quartz A silica mineral with three different forms. Sand is the most common. Low quartz is a crystalline form, occurring in a variety of colours. At 1063°F *573°C* low quartz gives rise to high quartz, but its natural occurrence is rare.

red bed Sedimentary rocks containing a high proportion of ferric minerals, giving them a reddish colour.

residual deposit Minerals left when part of a rock is dissolved or leached away.

rhyolite Fine-grained or glassy volcanic rock, rich in quartz.

rock A mass of mineral material, usually consisting of more than one mineral type.

rock crystal Clear form of quartz.

ruby A red transparent form of corundum.

rudaceous rock Sedimentary rocks deposited as detritus by water or air, and divided into conglomerates and breccias.

rutile Titanium oxide ore.

salt dome Under pressure salt behaves like a magma, and can be forced up through an overlying sediment as a salt dome.

sand A type of quartz, formed of fine particles. It can also be taken to mean any fine particles of 0·0025–0·08 in *0·0625–2 mm*.

sandstone Arenaceous rocks, consisting of fine grains cemented together by a variety of minerals.

sapphire A blue transparent form of corundum.

schist Metamorphosed rocks with the constituent minerals arranged in parallel.

scree Fragments formed by the weathering of rocks.

sedimentary rock Rock formed out of the material resulting from erosion and weathering, along with organic material. The principal sedimentary rocks are sandstone, limestone and shale.

shale A sedimentary rock composed of clay particles. The particles are orientated parallel to the bedding plane, giving the rock its characteristic fissility.

shingle Gravel or pebbles found on beaches.

silica Silicon dioxide, which can take a variety of forms, e.g. quartz, chalcedony, opal.

silicates The most prolific mineral group in the earth's crust. They are based on a silicon oxide structure, but a variety of other elements and ions can be substituted in this structure, particularly aluminium. The group includes the clays, the feldspars, the garnets, the micas, the silicas.

sill A sheet of igneous rock, lying along a bedding plane.

silt A type of argillaceous rock.

slate Argillaceous rock that has been metamorphosed. The slates all show cleavage, and may have new minerals showing up as marks or even crystals.

soapstone Any greasy rock, although usually applied to talc rocks.

soil The loose weathered material covering most of the earth's land surface.

spinel A group of minerals, including magnetite and chromite.

stalactite Calcium carbonate formed as a spike hanging down from the ceiling in a limestone cave.

stalagmite Calcium carbonate formed as a spike standing up from the floor in a limestone cave.

stock An intrusive mass of igneous rock, smaller than a batholith.

streak A mineral's colour when in a powdered state, e.g. formed by scratching it.

subsoil Partly weathered rock lying between the soil and the bedrock.

syenite A group of coarse-grained igneous rocks containing feldspars and feldspathoids.

talc Magnesium silicate, the softest common mineral.

tar pit Areas where asphalt or bitumen rises to the surface from an underground hydrocarbon source.

terra rossa Red clayey soil formed as a result of carbonates being leached out of limestone.

topaz A clear semi-precious form of aluminium silicate.

tor Piles of un-kaolinized granite blocks, left by differential weathering of the rock around them.

touchstone A very hard fine-grained black form of basalt or chart.

tripoli A type of diatomite.

tufa A calc tufa is a chalky deposit of calcium carbonate, found mainly in limestone.

tundra Soils produced under extremely cold conditions.

ultrabasic rock Igneous ferromagnesium rock, with little or no feldspar, quartz or feldspathoid in it.

ultramarine A type of feldspathoid.

valley fill Loose material filling or partly filling a valley.

vein A sheet of mineral which has intruded into a fissure or joint of a rock.

water table The upper limit of the groundwater saturation.

weathering The breaking down of stationary rocks by mechnical means, e.g. action of ice and the sun, and chemical means.

wind erosion Abrasive action of wind-driven particles of sand against stationary rocks.

wolframite A tungsten ore.

xenolith A inclusion of pre-existing rock in an igneous rock.

zeolite Group of silicates containing water of crystallization, and capable of reversible dehydration. They can act as powerful base exchangers.

zircon Zirconium silicate.

Geo-Chronology

For early phases of the Earth's history, radiometric dating is the main method of dating events. Before a thousand million years ago dates may err as much as 10 per cent. When fossils became abundant at the start of the Palaeozoic era, the sequence is best defined by those fossils in stratigraphic sequence and assigning radiometric dates to these. Then, by interpolation, a date can be put forward for a geological event, or for the bed in which a fossil has been found. The table below is based on revisions up to 1982 of the timescale put forward by the US Geological Survey of 1980. Myr = one million years ago.

The four main geological divisions, going backwards in time, are: The Cenozoic (Gk. *kainos*, new or recent, *zo-os*, living), the Mesozoic (Gk. *mesos*, middle), the Palaeozoic (Gk. *palaios*, ancient) and the Proterozoic (Gk. *protos*, first). The earliest known life forms, spherical microfossils, date back to 3400 Myr.

DATES OF STARTS OF PHASES IN THE GEOLOGICAL TIMESCALE
(Myr = 1 million years ago)

	Myr
Hadean era	est. 4450
Archean era	3800
Proterozoic era	
Early Proterozoic	2500
Middle Proterozoic	1600
Late Proterozoic	900
Paleozoic era	
Early Cambrian	
Georgian	570
Middle Cambrian	
Acadian	550
Late Cambrian	
Potsdamian	530
Early Ordovician	
Tremadocian	520
Arenigian	507
Llanvirnian	493
Llandeilian	476
Late Ordovician	
Caradocian	458
Ashgillian	447
Silurian	
Llandoverian	435
Wenlockian	430
Ludlovian	423
Downtonian	417
Early Devonian	
Gedinnian	410
Siegenian	399
Emsian	394
Middle Devonian	
Eifelian/Couvinian	389
Givetian	383
Late Devonian	
Frasnian	378
Famennian	370
Early Carboniferous	
Tournaisian	360
Visean	348
Late Carboniferous	
Namurian	335
Westphalian	316
Stephanian	306
Early Permian	
Sakmarian	290
Artinskian	278
Kungurian	268
Late Permian	
Kazanian	256
Tatarian	249
Mesozoic era	
Early Triassic	
Scythian	245
Middle Triassic	
Anisian	240
Ladinian	235
Late Triassic	
Karnian	230
Norian	225
Rhaetian	216
Early Jurassic	
Hettangian	208
Sinemurian	205
Pliensbachian	197
Toarcian	188
Aalenian	182
Middle Jurassic	
Bajocian	177
Bathonian	170
Late Jurassic	
Callovian	164
Oxfordian	159
Kimmeridgian	154
Tithonian	145
Early Cretaceous	
Berriasian	138
Valanginian	133
Hauterivian	126

Barremian	123
Aptian	120
Albian	114
Late Cretaceous	
Cenomanian	96
Turonian	92
Coniacian	89
Santonian	88
Campanian	84
Maastrichtian	72
Cenozoic era	
Tertiary period	
Early Paleocene	
Danian	67
Late Paleocene	
Thanetian	61
Early Eocene	
Ypresian	55
Middle Eocene	
Lutetian	50
Bartonian	45
Late Eocene	
Priabonian	41
Early Oligocene	
Rupelian	37
Late Oligocene	
Chattian	33
Early Miocene	
Aquitanian	25
Burdigalian	19·5
Middle Miocene	
Langhian	14·7
Serravallian	13·3
Late Miocene	
Tortonian	11·5
Messinian	6·7
Early Pliocene	
Zanclean, etc.	5·3
Late Pliocene	
Piacenzian	3·25
Quaternary period	
Early Pleistocene	1·8
Late Pleistocene	730 000 yr
Holocene	10 300 yr

Late Mammal Stages (Europe)

Late Pliocene	
Early Villafranchian	3·25 Myr
Late Villafranchian	2·60 Myr
Pleistocene	
Early Biharian	1·90 Myr (?1·80 Myr)
Middle Biharian	c. 1·5 Myr
Late Biharian	730 000 yr
Toringian	480 000 yr

Gemstones

Gemstones are minerals possessing a rarity and usually a hardness, colour or translucency which gives them strong aesthetic appeal. Diamond, emerald, ruby and sapphire used to be classed as 'precious stones' and all others as 'semi-precious'. This distinction is no longer generally applied. The principal gemstones in order of hardness are listed below with data in the following order: – name; birthstone (if any); chemical formula; classic colour; degree of hardness on Mohs' Scale 10–1; principal localities where found and brief notes on outstanding specimens. A metric carat is $\frac{1}{5}$th of a gram.

Diamond: (birthstone for April); C (pure crystalline isotope); fiery bluish-white; Mohs 10·0; S, SW and E Africa and India with alluvial deposits in Australia, Brazil, Congo, India, Indonesia, Liberia, Sierra Leone and USSR (Urals). Largest uncut: *Cullinan* 3106 carats (over 20 oz) by Capt M F Wells, Premier Mine, Pretoria, S Africa on 26 Jan. 1905. Cut by Jacob Asscher of Amsterdam 1909. Largest cut: *Cullinan I* or *Star of Africa* from the above in British Royal Sceptre at 530·2 carats. *Koh-i-nor* originally 186 now re-cut to 106 carats; also in

British Crown Jewels. The largest blue diamond is the 44·4 carat vivid blue *Hope Diamond* from Killur, Golconda, India *ante* 1642 in the Smithsonian Institution, Washington DC since November 1958. The rarest colour is blood red.

Diamonds can be produced by $1400°C$ $2500°F$ and 600 000 atmospheres. About 55 000 000 carats are mined annually with Antwerp the world's largest market with an annual turnover of £1000 million.

It takes an average 280 tons of diamond bearing ore to yield a 1 carat stone. The average diamond mined is 0·8 of a carat and less than 15% are used for jewellery (1 carat = 0·2 g).

Ruby: (birthstone for July); Al_2O_3 (red corundum with trace of chromic oxide); 9·0; Brazil, Burma, Sri Lanka, Thailand. Largest recorded gem ruby from Burma *ante* 1886 weighed 400 carats. Most valuable of all gems per carat.

Sapphire: (birthstone for September); Al_2O_3 (corundum); any colour but red, classically dark blue; 9·0; Australia, Burma, Sri Lanka, Kashmir, USA (Montana). Largest cut blue star: *Star of India*, 563·5 carats from Sri Lanka now in American Museum of Natural History, New York City. Largest star sapphire: 733 carat Black Star of Queensland from 1165 carat rough, found in 1934, owned by Kazanjian Foundation, Los Angeles.

Alexandrite: (birthstone for June, alternative to pearl); $Al_2[BeO_4]$ (chrysoberyl with chromium traces); green (daylight) but red (artificial light); 8·5; Brazil, Moravia, Sri Lanka, USSR (Urals), Zimbabwe.

Cat's Eye: $Al_2[BEO_4]$ (chrysoberyl) yellowish to brownish-green with narrow silken ray; 8·5.

Topaz: (birthstone for November); $Al_2SiO_4F_2$; tea coloured; 8·0; Australia, Brazil, Sri Lanka, Germany, Namibia, USSR. The largest recorded is one of 596 lb from Brazil.

Spinel: $MgAl_2O_4$ with trace of FE_2O_3; red; 8·0; mainly Burma, Sri Lanka, India and Thailand.

Emerald: (birthstone for May); $Al_2Be_3Si_6O_{18}$ (beryl); vivid green; 7·5–8·0; Austria, Colombia, Norway, USA (N Carolina), USSR (Urals), Zambia; largest recorded beryl prism (non-gem quality) 135 lb *61,2 kg* from Urals; largest beryl crystal 16 200 carats; Musó, Columbia. Devonshire stone of 1383·95 carats presented in 1831, is from same area.

Aquamarine: (birthstone for March); $Al_2Be_3Si_6O_{18}$ (beryl), pale limpid blue; 7·5–8·0; found in Brazil, Malagasy and USSR and elsewhere, including N. Ireland; largest recorded 243 lb *110 kg* near Marambaia, Brazil 1910.

Garnet: (birthstone for January); silicates of Al, Ca, Cr, Fe, Mg, Ti, V, Zr, purplish-red (Almandine, $Fe_3Al_2[SiO_4]_3$; 7·5–8·0; India, Sri Lanka, USA (Arizona); green (Demantoid, $Ca_3Fe_2[SiO_4]_3$); 6·5–7·0; USSR (Siberia and Urals); black (Malanite, $TiCa_3$ (Fe, Ti, Al)$_2$ $[SiO_4]_3$); 6·5.

Zircon: Zr (SiO_4); colourless but also blue and red-brown (hyacinth); 7·0–7·5; Australia (NSW), Burma, France, Norway, Sri Lanka, India, North America, Thailand, USSR (Siberia).

Tourmaline: (birthstone for October, alternative to opal); complex boro-silicate of Al, Mg alkalis; notably deep green, bluish green, deep red; 7·0–7·25; Brazil, Sri Lanka, USA, USSR (Siberia).

Rock Crystal: (birthstone for April, alternative to diamond); SiO_2; Colourless; 7·0; Brazil, Burma, France, Madagascar, Switzerland, USA (Arkansas). The largest recorded crystal ball is one of 106 lb *48 kg* from Burma now in the US National Museum, Washington DC.

Rose quartz: SiO_2; coarsely granular pale pink; 7·0; Bavaria, Brazil, Finland, Namibia, USA (Maine); USSR (Urals).

Cairngorm: (Smoky quartz); SiO_2; smoky yellow to brownish; 7·0; Brazil, Madagascar, Manchuria, Scotland (Cairngorm Mountains), Switzerland, USA (Colorado), USSR (Urals).

Amethyst: (birthstone for February); SiO_2; purple 7·0; Brazil, Sri Lanka, Germany, Madagascar, Uruguay, USSR (Urals).

Chrysoprase (Chalcedony form); (birthstone for May, alternative to emerald); SiO_2 with nickel hydroxide impurity; apple green (opaque); 6·5–7·0; Germany, USA.

Jade: Jadeite $Na(Al,Fe^{+3})Si_2O_6$; dark to leek green; 6·5–7·0; Burma, China, Tibet (pale green and less valuable form is nephrite, $Ca_2(Mg,Fe^{+2})_5Si_8O_{22}(OH)_2)$; China, Canada, New Zealand, USA.

Cornelian (Chalcedony form); often (wrongly) spelt carnelian; (birthstone for July, alternative to ruby); SiO_2 with ferric oxide impurity; blood red to yellowish-brown; 6·5–7·0; widespread, including Great Britain.

Agate (Striped chalcedony) SiO_2; opaque white to pale grey, blue; 6·6–7·0; variety is moss agate (milky white with moss like inclusions, often green); Brazil, Germany, India, Madagascar, Scotland.

Onyx: a black and white banded agate (see Agate).

Sardonyx: (birthstone for August, alternative to Peridot); a reddish-brown and white-banded agate (see Agate).

Jasper: (Chalcedony); SiO_2 with impurities; brown (manganese oxide), red (ferric oxide), yellow (hydrated ferric oxide); opaque; 6·5–7·0; Egypt, India.

Peridot (Green Olivine); (birthstone for August); $(Mg, Fe)_2[SiO_4]$ green; 6·5–7·0; Australia (Queensland); Brazil, Burma, Norway, St John's Island (Red Sea) now Zabargad Island, USA (Arizona).

Bloodstone or Blood Jasper: (Chalcedony): (birthstone for March, alternative to aquamarine); SiO_2; dark green with red spots (oxide of iron); 6·0–7·0.

Moonstone: (Feldspar): (birthstone for June, alternative to pearl); $K[AlSi_3O_8]$; white to bluish, iridescent; 6·0–6·5; Brazil, Burma, Sri Lanka.

Opal: (birthstone for October); $SiO_2.nH_2O$; rainbow colours on white background; other varieties include fire opal, water opal, black opal; 5·0–6·5; Australia, Mexico and formerly Hungary, USA. The largest recorded is one of 34 215 carats named *Desert Flame of Andamooka* found in Australia in 1969.

Turquoise: (birthstone for December); $CuAl_6[(OH)_8(PO_4)_4]5H_2O$; sky blue; 5·5–6·0; Egypt (Sinai Peninsula), Iran, Turkey, USA (California, Nevada, New Mexico, Texas).

Lapis Lazuli: (birthstone for September, alternative to sapphire); $(Na,Ca)_8[(S,Cl,SO_4)_2 (AlSiO_4)_6]$; deep azure blue, opaque; 5·5–5·75; Afghanistan, Chile, Tibet, USSR (Lake Baykal area).

Obsidian: (glassy lava); green or yellowish-brown; 5·0–5·5; volcanic areas.

Non-mineral gem material

Amber (organic): about $C_{40}H_{64}O_4$; honey yellow; clear; or paler yellow, cloudy; 2·0–2·5; Mainly Baltic and Sicily coasts. A variety is fly amber in which the body of an insect is encased.

Coral (polyps of *Coelenterata*): varied colourations including Blood or Red Coral; Australasia, Pacific and Indian Oceans.

Pearl: (birthstone for June); (secretions of molluscs, notably of the sea-water mussel genus *Pinctada* and the fresh-water mussel *Quadrula*); Western Pacific and Indian Oceans; largest recorded is the *Hope Pearl* weighing nearly 3 oz *85 g*, circumference 4½ in *114 mm*. A nacreous mass of 14 lb 2 oz *6,4 kg* from a giant clam (*Tridacna gigas*) was recovered in the Philippines in 1934 and is known as the 'Pearl of Allah'.

Earthquakes

It is estimated that each year there are some 500 000 detectable seismic or micro-seismic disturbances of which 100 000 can be felt and 1000 cause damage.

It was not until as recently as 1874 that subterranean slippage along overstressed faults became generally accepted as the cause of tectonic earthquakes. The collapse of caverns, or mine-workings, volcanic action, and also possibly the very rare event of a major meteoric impact can also cause tremors. The study of earthquakes is called seismology.

The two great seismic systems are the Alps-Himalaya great circle and the circum-Pacific belt. The foci below the epicentres are classified as shallow (<50 km deep), intermediate (50–200 km) and deep (200–700 km).

In 1954 the Gutenberg-Richter scale was introduced to compare the strengths of seismic shocks. The scale measures the magnitude Mw. $Mw = \frac{2}{3}[\log_{10}(2E \times 10^4) - 10\cdot7]$ where E is the energy released in dyne/cm. In 1977 the more satisfactory Kanamori scale, using the concept of seismic moment, devised by K-Aki (Japan) in 1966, was adopted. It measures the magnitude M_s. $M_s = \frac{2}{3}(\log_{10}E - 11\cdot8)$. The Lebu shock, south of Concepción, Chile on 22 May 1960 uniquely registered 9·5 on the Kanamori scale indicating an estimated energy of 10^{26} ergs. No earthquake has ever reached 9 in the Gutenberg-Richter scale. It has been estimated however that the Great Lisbon Earthquake of 1 Nov. 1755, 98 years before the invention of seismographs would have rated between $8\frac{3}{4}$ and 9. The death toll was 60 000.

HISTORIC EARTHQUAKES

The five earthquakes in which the known loss of life has exceeded 100 000 have been:

c. 1·1 m	E. Mediterranean	c. July 1201
830 000	Shensi Province, China	2 Feb. 1556
300 000	Calcutta, India	11 Oct. 1737
242 000*	Tangshan, China (8·2R)	27 July 1976
180 000	Kansu Province, China (landslides) (8·6R)	16 Dec. 1920
142 807	Kwanto Plain, Honshū, Japan (8·3R)	1 Sept. 1923

* Unaccountably reduced to this figure on 22 Nov. 1979 from 655 237 unannounced on 4 Jan. 1977.

The material damage done in the Kwanto Plain, which includes Tōkyō, was estimated at £1 000 000 000.

Other notable earthquakes during this century, with loss of life have been:

1906	Colombian coast (31 Jan) (8·6R; 8·8K)	
1906	San Francisco, USA (18 Apr.) (452) (8·3R)	
1908	Messina, Italy (28 Dec.) (80 000) (7·5R)	
1915	Avezzano, Italy (13 Jan.) (29 970)	
1932	Gansu Province, China (26 Dec.) (70 000) (7·6R)	
1935	Quetta, India (31 May) (60 000) (7·5R)	
1939	Erzincan, Turkey (27 Dec.) (30 000) (7·9R)	
1950	Assam, India (15 Aug.) (1500) (8·6R; 8·6K)	
1952	Kamchatka, USSR (4 Nov.) (8·5R; 9·0K)	
1957	Andreanol, Aleutian Is. USA (9 Mar) (8·3R; 9·1K)	
1960	Agadir, Morocco (29 Feb.) (12 000) (5·8R)	
1960	Lebu, Chile (22 May) (8·3R; 9·5K)	
1964	Anchorage, Alaska (28 Mar.) (131) (8·5R)	
1970	Northern Peru (31 May) (66 800) (7·7R)	
1971	Los Angeles (9 Feb.) (64) (6·5R)	
1972	Nicaragua (23 Dec.) (5000) (6·2R)	
1976	Guatemala (4 Feb.) (22 700) (7·5R)	
1976	Tangshan, China (27 July) (see above) (8·2R)	
1977	Buchárest, Romania (4 Mar.) (1541) (7·5R)	
1978	Tabas, N.E. Iran (16 Sept.) (25 000) (7·7R)	
1980	El Asnam, Algeria (10 Oct.) (2327) (7·5R)	
1980	Potenza, Italy (23 Nov.) (c. 3000) (6·8R)	
1982	North Yemen (13 Dec.) (2800) (6·0R)	
1983	Eastern Turkey (30 Oct.) (1233) (7·1R)	

R = Richter-Gutenberg scale   K = Kanamori scale

Attendant phenomena include:
(i) *Tsunami* (wrongly called tidal waves) or gravity waves which radiate in long, low oscillations from submarine disturbances at speeds of 450–490 mph *725–790 km/h*. The 1883 Krakatoa *tsunami* reached a height of 135 ft *41 m* and that off Valdez, Alaska in 1964 attained a height of 220 ft *67 m*. The word *tsu* (wild), *nami* (wave) is Japanese.
(ii) *Seiches* (a Swiss-French term of doubtful origin, pronounced sāsh). Seismic oscillations in landlocked water. Loch Lomond had a 2 ft *60 cm* seiche for 1 hr from the 1755 Lisbon 'quake.
(iii) *Fore and After Shocks*. These often occur before major 'quakes and may persist after these for months or years.

BRITISH EARTHQUAKES

The earliest British earthquake of which there is undisputable evidence was that of AD 974 felt over England. The earliest precisely recorded was that of 1 May 1048, in Worcester. British earthquakes of an intensity sufficient to have raised or moved the chair of the observer (Scale 8 on the locally used Davison's scale) have been recorded thus:

25 Apr.	1180	Nottinghamshire
15 Apr.	1185	Lincoln
1 June	1246	Canterbury, Kent
21 Dec.	1246	Wells
19 Feb.	1249	South Wales
11 Sept.	1275	Somerset
21 May	1382	Canterbury, Kent
28 Dec.	1480	Norfolk
26 Feb.	1575	York to Bristol
6 Apr.	1580*	London
30 Apr.	1736	Menstrie, Clackmannan
1 May	1736	Menstrie, Clackmannan
14 Nov.	1769†	Inverness
18 Nov.	1795	Derbyshire
13 Aug.	1816‡	Inverness
23 Oct.	1839	Comrie, Perth
30 July	1841	Comrie, Perth
6 Oct.	1863	Hereford
22 Apr.	1884§	Colchester
17 Dec.	1896	Hereford
18 Sept.	1901	Inverness
27 June	1906‖	Swansea
30 July	1926	Jersey
15 Aug.	1926	Hereford
7 June	1931	Dogger Bank (5·6R)
11 Feb.	1957	Midlands
26 Dec.	1979	Longtown, Cumbria
19 July	1984	W. Areas & Ireland (5·5R)

* About 6 p.m. First recorded fatality – an apprentice killed by masonry falling from Christ Church.
† 'Several people' reported killed. Parish register indicates not more than one. Date believed to be 14th.
‡ At 10.45 p.m. Heard in Aberdeen (83 miles *133 km*), felt in Glasgow (115 miles *185 km*). Strongest ever in Scotland.
§ At 9.18 a.m. Heard in Oxford (108 miles *174 km*), felt in Exeter and Ostend, Belgium (95 miles *152 km*). At least 3, possibly 5, killed. Strongest ever in British Isles at 6 on the Richter scale.
‖ At 9.45 a.m. Strongest in Wales. Felt over 37 800 miles² *98 000 km²*.

OTHER MAJOR NATURAL DISASTERS

Landslides caused by earthquakes in the Kansu Province of China on 16 Dec. 1920 killed 180 000 people.

The Peruvian snow avalanches at Huarás (13 Dec. 1941) and from Huascarán (10 Jan. 1962) killed 5000 and 3000 people respectively. The Huascarán alluvion flood triggered by the earthquake of 31 May 1970 wiped out 25 000.

Both floods and famines have wreaked a greater toll of human life than have earthquakes. The greatest river floods on record are those of the Hwang-ho, China. From September into October 1887 some 900 000 people were drowned. The flood of August 1931 is reputed to have drowned or killed 3 700 000. A typhoon flood at Haiphong in Viet Nam (formerly Indo-China) on 8 Oct. 1881 killed an estimated 300 000 people. The cyclone of 12–13 Nov. 1970 which struck the Ganges Delta Islands, Bangladesh drowned an estimated 1 000 000.

History's worst famines have occurred in Asia. In 1770 nearly one third of India's total population died with ten million dead in Bengal alone. It was revealed in May 1981 that the death toll from the northern Chinese famines of 1969–71 totalled some 20 000 000.

The Krakatoa eruptions of 26–28 Aug. 1883 killed 36 000 mostly due to a *tsunami*. The Mont Pelée volcanic eruption in Martinique on 8 May 1902 killed over 30 000.

Measuring earthquakes

The scales on which earthquakes are measured are logarithmic scales – a fact which is frequently forgotten by journalists and members of the public. It means that an earthquake of, say, magnitude 8 on the Richter scale is 10 times as powerful as an earthquake of magnitude 7. Similarly, an earthquake of magnitude 8 is not twice as powerful as one of magnitude 4; it is $10 \times 10 \times 10 \times 10$ as powerful.

RICHTER SCALE

The Richter scale is the scale of measurement that most members of the public are used to hearing about. It is in fact a measurement of an earthquake's magnitude, and as such would mean little to the layman. However it is possible to convert these readings of magnitude to a scale of intensity, i.e. an indication of the probable effects of an earthquake of a certain magnitude.

Magnitude	Probable effects
1	Detectable only by instruments.
2	Barely detectable, even near the epicentre.
4·5	Detectable within 20 miles *32 km* of the epicentre; possible slight damage within a small area.
6	Moderately destructive.
7	A major earthquake.
8	A great earthquake.

MERCALLI SCALE

The Modified Mercalli scale is an alternative, and more sophisticated, indication of the intensity of an earthquake.

Magnitude	Probable effects
1	Not felt by people. Doors may swing slightly.
2	Detected indoors by a few people. Hanging objects may swing.
3	Vibrations similar to those produced by a passing vehicle. Detected indoors by several people. A standing car may rock slightly.
4	Detected indoors by many people and outdoors by a few people. Crockery may clink. Parked cars may rock noticeably.
5	Detected indoors and outdoors by most people. Buildings tremble throughout. Trees and bushes shake slightly.
6	Detected indoors and outdoors by everyone. Many people frightened. Plaster cracks and some may fall.
7	General alarm. People find it difficult to stand. Bricks and stones are dislodged.
8	General fright. Considerable damage in buildings.
9	General panic. Ground cracks conspicuously. Some buildings collapse.
10	General panic. Ground cracks up to several inches. Landslides occur. Many buildings are destroyed.
11	General panic. Ground disturbances are many and widespread. Large sea waves develop. Few buildings remain standing.
12	General panic. Damage is total. Rivers are deflected. Surface waves are seen on the ground surface.

Meteorology

Glossary of terms

absolute humidity The amount of water vapour in a unit volume of air, usually given in g/m³.

advection fog A fog formed when damp air moves over a cool surface, such as the sea, and the air temperature falls below the dew point. Water vapour in the air condenses as a fog.

altocumulus cloud A mass of small rounded medium clouds, close together and sometimes joined.

altostratus cloud High sheet of cloud, sometimes thick enough to cover the sun or moon.

anabatic wind A type of wind found in mountainous and hilly areas. The sun warms the valley slopes, the air above the slopes is warmed and rises, and an anabatic wind blows as cooler air moves in under the rising air.

anticyclone An area of high atmospheric pressure. Winds around an anticyclone in the northern hemisphere circulate in a clockwise direction, in the southern hemisphere the opposite.

arid Dry; rainfall so slight as to support little or no vegetation.

atmospheric pressure Pressure due to the weight of the atmosphere.

backing A change of wind direction in an anticlockwise direction, i.e. back around the compass.

ball lightning A spherical glowing mass of energized air, usually about 1 ft *30 cm* in diameter. When it strikes an object it is immediately earthed, and so seems to disappear.

banner cloud Cloud formed on the leeward side of a hill or mountain, due to air rising up over the mountain and water vapour condensing in the reduced pressure found at that altitude.

bar A unit of pressure, equal to 750 mm of mercury at 0°C, or 10⁵ pascals.

barometer A device for measuring atmospheric pressure.

Beaufort scale Series of numbers, internationally agreed, indicating approximate scales of wind strength. (See associated article.)

blizzard A storm of powdery snow or ice accompanied by a very high wind. Visibility is very poor and much drifting occurs in the wind.

blood rain Rain coloured with dust particles, giving it a reddish-brown tinge.

blue moon A change in colour of the moon, caused by dust (from a volcanic eruption, for example) in the upper atmosphere diffracting its light.

Brocken spectre Magnified shadow of an observer in a mountainous area, cast on a cloud or bank of fog.

calm No perceptible movement of air.

cirrocumulus cloud High cloud in lines of small rounded masses, often so close together as to form a sheet.

cirrostratus cloud High veil of cloud that often forms a halo round the sun or moon.

cirrus cloud High cloud consisting of broken feathery patches.

climate Distinct pattern of weather found in one or a number of geographical zones, where the essential governing factors are the same.

cloud Mass of condensed water vapour, consisting either of minute droplets of water or particles of ice.

cloudburst Very heavy, and usually short-lived, rainstorm.

cold front The boundary between an advancing mass of cold air and a receding mass of warm air, the boundary being angled back over the advancing cold air. Heavy showers often accompany a cold front.

condensation The change of matter, from vapour to liquid.

continental climate A temperate climate in which warm dry summers alternate with cool or cold winters. The precipitation in winter often falls as snow.

convection Transmission of heat by movement of particles of the substance. As regards meteorology, it refers to the upward movement of warm air which has been heated by contact with the earth's surface.

convectional rain Rain resulting from damp air rising in a convection current. It passes the dew point, the water vapour condenses to cloud and rain results.

corona When the light from the sun or moon passes through a water droplet cloud, a ring of the colours of the rainbow (sometimes two rings) appears round the light source. The colour sequence is violet on the inside and red on the outside, and is due to diffraction.

cumulonimbus cloud A very large tall dark cloud with a low base, often wider at the apex than at the base. Typically, it produces thunderstorms.

cumulus cloud A tall cloud with a low base, not as large or dark as a cumulonimbus. It is often wider at its apex than its base.

cyclone An area of low pressure. In the tropics a cyclone can give rise to a violent storm with very strong winds and torrential rain.

deepening Increasing atmospheric pressure in a depression.

depression An area of low pressure, often referred to as a cyclone. it gives rise to unsettled wet weather, with winds radiating in an anti-clockwise direction from the centre of the area of low pressure in the northern hemisphere, and in a clockwise direction in the southern hemisphere.

dew Drops of water deposited on the earth's surface, plants, objects, etc., when air close to the earth's surface cools down at night to below its dew point.

dew point Temperature to which air has to be cooled before it becomes saturated with water vapour. The water vapour then condenses out as water droplets, forming dew or cloud.

doldrums Belt of low atmospheric pressure in the equatorial region, where the trade winds converge. The weather here is turbulent, the surface winds light and variable, the movement of air largely being upwards.

drizzle Rain consisting of very small droplets of less than 0·02 in *0·5 mm* diameter.

drought A long period of dry weather.

equatorial climate High temperatures (over 86°F *30°C*), high humidity and a daily pattern of weather change rather than an annual pattern.

false cirrus cloud Sections of cloud that break away from the top of a cumulonimbus cloud.

filling Increasing atmospheric pressure in the centre of a low pressure area.

Flachenblitz Unusual form of lightning which strikes upwards from the top of a cumulonimbus cloud into clear air.

fog Mass of air close to the ground that is cooled to below its dew point, forming tiny water droplets. Visibility is below 0·6 mile *1 kilometre*.

fogbow Rainbow in which the colours overlap, forming a white bow, due to the small size of the water droplets.

Föhn **wind** Dry warm wind that blows down a hill or mountain. Any moisture in the air is deposited as the air rises up the mountain. The air is then warmed as it descends to lower altitudes.

front A line or plane separating masses of warm and cold air and produced by movement of the two air masses across the earth's surface.

frost An air temperature at or below 32°F *0°C*. Any dew formed at such temperature will be deposited as particles of ice.

gale A very high wind, strictly speaking in excess of force 7 on the Beaufort scale.

glazed frost Covering of ice formed when rain falls in air temperature at or below 32°F *0°C*, or falls on to objects that are at or below 32°F *0°C*.

glory Halo seen around a Brocken spectre.

hail Ice particles, of about 0·2 in *5 mm* diameter but sometimes considerably in excess of this size, which fall when moist air rises rapidly in cumulonimbus clouds and freezes.

halo Ring of light around the sun or moon, caused by refraction of the light through ice crystals in high cloud. It is usually white, but can be red on the inside and bluish on the outside.

high An area of high atmospheric pressure, i.e. an anticyclone.

high cloud Clouds occurring in the range 19 700–39 400 ft *6000–12 000 metres*, or higher.

hill fog Low cloud covering high ground.

hoar frost Ice crystals deposited on the earth's surface and objects on or close to the earth's surface. It is formed when the dew point is at or below 32°F *0°C*.

hot desert climate Very high daily temperatures, up to 122°F *50°C*, with much cooler nights and very little rain at all.

humidity The amount of water vapour contained in the atmosphere.

hurricane A wind in excess of force 12 on the Beaufort scale. It can also refer to a tropical cyclone in the Caribbean and western North Atlantic.

isobar A line on a map joining all the points having equal atmospheric pressure.

isohyet A line on a map joining all those points that have equal amounts of rainfall over a given time.

isotherm A line on a map joining all the points having the same temperature at a given time.

jet stream A strong and persistent wind found at high altitudes, blowing from west to east.

land breeze A wind blows, usually during the night in coastal regions, from land out to sea. The land cools more rapidly than the sea at night, the air over the land also cools and flows seawards.

lenticular cloud An isolated cloud shaped like a convex lens, found over a hill or mountain.

lightning Development of static electricity due to the uprushing of air in a cumulonimbus thundercloud. Discharge of this static electricity causes the lightning flash.

low An area where the atmospheric pressure is markedly lower than the surrounding areas: a depression.

low cloud Clouds occurring below about 6600 ft *2000 metres*.

mackerel sky A sky filled with high cirrocumulus or cirrostratus clouds. These small round separate cloud masses are supposed to resemble the markings on a mackerel.

mare's tail cloud Thin wispy high cirrus clouds.

maritime climate A climate that is influenced by the seas, i.e. with cool summers and mild winters.

Mediterranean climate A hot dry summer alternates with a mild wet winter.

medium cloud Clouds occurring between about 6600 and 19 700 ft *2000 and 6000 metres*.

microclimate Climate found in a limited area. It is dependent on very local factors.

millibar The unit of pressure most used to measure atmospheric pressure. It is 1/1000 of a bar, i.e. 10² pascals.

mirage The refraction of light when layers of the atmosphere have sharply differing densities due to contrasting temperatures. An inferior mirage (the more common type) is when an object seems to be floating in a pool of water. A superior mirage is when an object near the horizon seems to float above its true position.

mist Mass of air close to the ground that is cooled to below its dew point, forming tiny water droplets. Visibility is between 3300 and 6600 ft *1000 and 2000 metres.*

mistral A cold persistent wind that blows from the north onto the shores of the northern Mediterranean. It is due to high pressure over central Europe and low pressure over the Mediterranean.

monsoon The wet stormy weather brought by south-easterly winds in south-east Asia between April and December. It is caused by warm wet south-easterly trade winds filling the low pressure created over the hot land mass. A second monsoon may occur later in the year if the reversing winds have to pass over any seas, e.g. south-east India and Sri Lanka.

monsoon climate This climate is characterized by a hot dry season and a cooler wet season when the monsoon rains arrive.

mountain climate Climate found in mountainous areas that differs from the climate of the surrounding lowland, approximating more to the climate found nearer the poles.

nacreous clouds Mother-of-pearl clouds occurring at very high altitudes over mountainous areas after sunset. They are lit by sunlight from below and can be visible from great distances.

nimbostratus cloud A low dark grey cloud with a flat base. It invariably brings persistent precipitation.

noctilucent cloud Bluish clouds that appear at very great altitudes – up to 600 miles *100 km.* They are not true clouds at all, but probably formed by cosmic dust.

occlusion The advance of a cold front of air on to a warm front of air, or vice versa, the warm air being lifted up by the cold air.

orographic rain Rain caused when advancing damp air is forced upward over hills, mountains or other high land. As it cools, its temperature falls below its dew point and rain falls.

parhelion A mock sun, or image of the sun, appearing to either side of the sun. It is equivalent to the halo, and is caused by light being refracted in ice crystals.

planetary winds System of winds and areas of stiller air that occurs on the earth's surface due to the heating effect of the sun and the rotation of the earth on its axis. The system moves north and south each year with the movement of the equatorial belt of low pressure.

polar climate Strictly speaking, a cold desert climate. Summer temperatures rarely rise above freezing point, while the winters are intensely cold. There is little precipitation; what does occur falls as snow.

precipitation Water which falls from the atmosphere on to the earth's surface. Depending on the circumstances, it can either occur as rain, hail, sleet, slush, snow, dew or frost.

prevailing wind The direction of the wind that tends to blow most frequently over a given area.

radiation fog On clear nights when there is little wind, warmth will be lost from the earth's surface by radiation. The air immediately above the earth's surface will be cooled and, if its temperature falls below its dew point, radiation fog will be formed.

rain Precipitation that falls as separate drops of water greater than 0·02 in *0·5 mm.*

rainbow An arc of colours seen when light falls on a belt of rain. It is caused by refraction and reflection of the light, so the sun must be behind the observer. A primary rainbow has violet on the inside and red on the outside. Occasionally a secondary rainbow is seen outside the primary rainbow; the colours are then reversed.

rainfall The total depth of precipitation of all kinds falling on a given place or area in a given time.

rain shadow An area that receives little rainfall due to the fact that it is in the lee of an area of high ground. Water in the air therefore falls as orographic rain over the high ground, and

relatively dry winds pass over the rain shadow.

relative humidity The ratio between the amount of water vapour in a volume of air at a fixed temperature and the amount of water vapour the same volume of air would hold at that temperature if it was saturated. It is expressed as a percentage.

ridge of high pressure An extended area of high pressure.

rime Layer of ice deposited on objects when the temperature is below freezing point and supercooled water droplets fall to earth.

roaring forties The westerly winds (and the regions they occupy) that blow between latitudes 40° and 50° S. They blow over the oceans with great persistence, and are associated with stormy weather.

Saint Elmo's fire Discharge of static electricity, seen as a luminous cloud, around the tips of tall objects sometimes during stormy weather.

scud Shreds of low cloud, often below the level of the main cloud mass, driven along relatively quickly by a strong wind.

sea breeze A wind that blows, usually during the day in coastal regions, from sea on to the land. The land heats up more rapidly during the day than the sea, and the air above it rises. Cooler air then moves in from off the sea to take its place.

sleet Precipitation consisting of a cold mixture of rain and snow.

smog An unpleasant mixture of fog and smoke or other industrial air-borne pollution.

snow Precipitation consisting of feathery crystals of water. It is formed at temperatures below freezing point.

squall A short-lived strong wind, lasting only for a minute or two and often coming from a different direction to the prevailing wind at the time. A short fierce rain shower may be associated with the squall.

stratocumulus cloud Rounded masses of medium or low cloud in a distinct and extensive layer.

stratus cloud Low cloud consisting of an unbroken uniform layer.

subpolar climate A short warm summer, but a bitterly cold windy winter. Permafrost is usual. Precipitation occurs in the winter as snow.

sun pillar A column of light above or below the sun when it is low on the horizon. It is caused by the reflection of light in ice crystals.

sunshine The visible light received from the sun. An indication of how sunny a place is is given by the number of hours of direct sunshine it receives in a day.

temperate maritime climate A warm damp summer alternates with a mild wet winter.

temperature inversion An increase of temperature with height (normally temperature decreases with height). It may be due to warm air rising in still conditions over relatively flat land, or due to cool air sinking down into valleys.

thaw The opposite of a freeze; the period when temperatures rise above freezing point and ice and snow melt to water.

thermal A rising current of warm air.

thunderbolt A misnomer for the effect of the intense heating effect of lightning striking. Such a strike may fuse materials, boil water instantaneously, blow masonry apart, etc.

thunderstorm A fierce storm typified by very strong upward currents of air. This produces very heavy showers of rain, sometimes with hail, due to the very rapid cooling of the air as it rises. The static electricity caused by these rapidly moving masses of air produces lightning, which in turn gives rise to thunder, due to the explosive effects of the electrical discharge.

tornado A whirlwind produced by intensely strong upward currents of air. The diameter of the whirlwind is usually less than 1600 ft *500 metres* and it travels in a straight line at speeds of about 10–40 mph *20–60 km per hour,* causing great damage.

trade winds Winds of great regularity which blow from the subtropical belts of high pressure to the equatorial belt of low pressure. Due to the rotation of the earth they blow from the north-

east in the northern hemisphere and from the south-east in the southern hemisphere.

tropical cyclone A small intense depression, occurring in the tropics, and producing very fierce storms.

trough of low pressure An extended area of low pressure.

turbulence At low altitudes this describes the irregular movement of air, with gusty winds and frequent changes of wind direction. At higher altitudes it describes ascending and descending movements of air, due to unequal heating by the earth's surface.

typhoon A tropical cyclone, particularly such a storm occurring in the China Sea.

veering A change of wind direction in a clockwise direction.

visibility The greatest distance which an object can be seen with the naked eye.

warm front The boundary between an advancing mass of warm air and the mass of cooler air over which it rises, the boundary being angled forward over the cold air. Rain usually precedes a warm front.

waterspout A tornado that occurs over water. Water and spray are sucked up by the rapidly spiralling winds, the spout often reaching a height of over 3300 ft *1 km.*

westerlies Westerly winds that blow in the region between the subtropical high pressure belts and the polar circles. In fact they blow from the south-west in the northern hemisphere and from the north-west in the southern hemisphere.

whirlwind A small local vertical column of rapidly rotating air, with an area of low pressure at the centre.

whiteout Conditions of dense falling snow in which physical features are totally obscured to sight.

wind A movement of air, usually parallel to the earth's surface.

BEAUFORT SCALE

A scale of numbers, designated Force 0 to Force 12, was originally devised by Commander Francis Beaufort (1774–1857) (later Rear-Admiral Sir Francis Beaufort, KCB, FRS) in 1805. Force numbers 13 to 17 were added in 1955 by the US Weather Bureau but are not in international use since they are regarded as impracticably precise.

Force No.	Descriptive term	Wind speed mph	knots
0	Calm	0–1	0–1
1	Light air	1–3	1–3
2	Light breeze	4–7	4–6
3	Gentle breeze	8–12	7–10
4	Moderate breeze	13–18	11–16
5	Fresh breeze	19–24	17–21
6	Strong breeze	25–31	22–27
7	Near gale	32–38	28–33
8	Gale	39–46	34–40
9	Strong gale	47–54	41–47
10	Storm	55–63	48–55
11	Violent storm	64–75	56–65
12	Hurricane	76–82	66–71
13	Hurricane	83–92	72–80
14	Hurricane	93–103	81–89
15	Hurricane	104–114	90–99
16	Hurricane	115–125	100–108
17	Hurricane	126–136	109–118

CONSTITUENTS OF AIR

Gas	Formula	% By volume
Invariable component gases of dry carbon dioxide-free air		
Nitrogen	N_2	78·110
Oxygen	O_2	20·953
Argon	A	0·934
Neon	Ne	0·001818
Helium	He	0·000524
Methane	CH_4	0·0002
Krypton	Kr	0·000114

Gas	Formula	% By volume
Hydrogen	H$_2$	0·00005
Nitrous Oxide	N$_2$O	0·00005
Xenon	Xe	0·0000087
		99·9997647 %
Variable components		
Water Vapour	H$_2$O	0 to 7·0*
Carbon dioxide	CO$_2$	0·01 to 0·10
		average 0·034
Ozone	O$_3$	0 to 0·000007
Contaminants		
Sulfur dioxide	SO$_2$	up to 0·0001
Nitrogen dioxide	NO$_2$	up to 0·000002
Ammonia	NH$_3$	trace
Carbon monoxide	CO	trace

* This percentage can be reached at a relative humidity of 100 per cent at a shade temperature of 40°C *104°F*

World and UK Meteorological Absolutes and Averages

Temperature: The world's overall average annual day side temperature is 59°F *15°C*. Highest shade (**world**): 136·4°F *58°C* Al'Aziziyah, Libya, 13 Sept. 1922. **UK:** 98·2°F *36,7°C* Rounds, Northants; Epsom, Surrey; Canterbury, Kent, 9 Aug. 1911. The hottest place (**world**) on annual average is Dallol, Ethiopia with 94°F *34,4°C* (1960–66) and in **UK** Penzance, Cornwall, and Isles of Scilly, both 52·7°F *11,5°C*. Annual Means: England 50·3°F *10,1°C*; Scotland 47·6°F *8,6°C*.
Lowest Screen (**world**): −128·6°F *−89,2°C* Vostok, Antarctica, 21 July 1983. **UK:** −17°F *−27,2°C* Braemar, Grampian, 11 Feb. 1895 and 9 Jan. 1982 (NB – Temperature of −23°F *−30,5°C* at Blackadder, Borders, in 1879 and of −20°F *−28,8°C* at Grantown-on-Spey, in 1955 were not standard exposures.) The coldest place (**world**) on annual average is the Pole of Cold, 150 miles *240 km* west of Vostok, Antarctica at −72°F *−57,8°C* and in the **UK** at Braemar, Aberdeen, Grampian 43·43°F *6,35°C* (1959–81).

Barometric Pressure: The world's average barometric pressure is 1013 mb. Highest (**world**): 1083·8 mb (32·00 in), Agata, Siberia, USSR, 31 Dec. 1968 and **UK**: 1054·7 mb (31·15 in) at Aberdeen, 31 Jan. 1902. Lowest (**world**): 870 mb (25·69 in), recorded at sea 300 miles *480 km* W of Guam, Pacific Ocean, 12 Oct. 1979 and **UK**: 925·5 mb (27·33 in), Ochtertyre, near Crieff, Tayside, 26 Jan. 1884.

Wind Strength: Highest sustained surface speed (**world**) 231 mph *371 km/h*, (200·6 knots) Mt Washington (6288 ft *1916 m*), New Hampshire, USA, 24 Apr. 1934. **UK**: 144 mph *231 km/h* (125 knots). Coire Cas ski lift (3525 ft *1074 m*) Cairngorm, Highland, 6 Mar. 1967. (NB – The 201 mph *175 kts* reading reported from Saxa Vord, Unst, Shetland, on 3 Mar. 1979 has *not* been accepted.) Windiest place (**world**): Commonwealth Bay, George V coast, Antarctica, several 200 mph *320 km/h* gales each year. **UK**: Fair Isle, Shetland annual average 20·7 mph *33,3 km/h*.

Rainfall: Highest (**world**) **Minute:** 1·23 in *31,2 mm* Unionville, Maryland, USA, 4 July 1956; **24 hr:** 73·62 in *1870 mm* Cilaos, La Réunion Island, Indian Ocean on 15–16 March 1952; **12 months:** 1041·78 in *26 461 mm* Cherrapunji, Assam, 1 Aug. 1860 to 31 July 1861. Highest (**UK**) **24 hrs:** 11·00 in *279 mm* Martinstown, Dorset, 18–19 July 1955; **Year:** 257·0 in *6527 mm* Sprinkling Tarn, Cumbria, in 1954. Wettest Place (**world**): Mt Wai-'ale'ale (5148 ft *1569 m*), Kauai I, Hawaiian Islands, annual average 451 in *11 455 mm* (1920–72). Most rainy days in a year (**world**) up to 350 on Mt. Wai-'ale'ale; **British Isles:** 309 at Ballynahinch, Galway, Ireland, in 1923.

Lowest (**world**) at places in the Desierto de Atacama of Chile, including Calama, where no rain has ever been recorded in the *c.* 400 years to 1971 since when there has been some rain. Lowest (**UK**) Year: 9·29 in *236 mm* Margate, Kent, in 1921. Longest Drought: 73 days from 4 March to 15 May 1893 at Mile End, Greater London.

Snowfall: Greatest (**world**) **Single Storm:** 189 in *4800 mm* Mt Shasta, California; **24 hr:** 76 in *1930 mm* Silver Lake, Colorado, 14–15 Apr. 1921; **Year:** 1224·5 in *31 102 mm* Paradise Ranger Station, Mt Rainier, Washington, USA, in 1971–2. **UK:** Annual days of snowfall vary between extremes of 40 in the Shetland Islands and 5 in Penzance, Cornwall. The gulleys on Ben Nevis (4406 ft *1342 m*) were snowless only 7 times in the 31 years 1933–64. An accumulated level of 60 in *1524 mm* was recorded in February 1947 in both Upper Teesdale and the Clwyd Hills of North Wales.

Sunshine: Maximum (**world**): in parts of the eastern Sahara the sun shines strongly enough to cast a shadow for 4300 hours in a year or 97 per cent of possible. **UK:** The highest percentage for a month is 78·3 per cent (382 hours) at Pendennis Castle, Falmouth, Cornwall, June 1925. Minimum (**world**): the longest periods of total darkness occur at the North Pole (over 9000 ft *2740 m* less altitude than South Pole) with 186 days. **UK:** the lowest monthly reading has been at Westminster, London, in Dec. 1890.

Cloud Classification

Genus (with abbreviation)	Ht of base (ft)	(m)	Temp at base level (°C)	Official description
Cirrus (Ci)	16 500 to 45 000	*5000 to 13 700*	−20 to −60	Detached clouds in the form of white delicate filaments, or white or mostly white patches or narrow bands. They have a fibrous (hair-like) appearance or a silky sheen, or both. They are the highest of the standard forms averaging 27 000 ft *8 250 m*.
Cirrocumulus (Cc)	16 500 to 45 000	*5000 to 13 700*	−20 to −60	Thin, white sheet or layer of cloud without shading, composed of very small elements in the form of grains, ripples, etc., merged or separate, and more or less regularly arranged.
Cirrostratus (Cs)	16 500 to 45 000	*5000 to 13 700*	−20 to −60	Transparent, whitish cloud veil of fibrous or smooth appearance, totally or partly covering the sky, and generally producing halo phenomena.
Altocumulus (Ac)	6500 to 23 000	*2000 to 7000*	+10 to −30	White or grey, or both white and grey, patch, sheet or layer of cloud, generally with shading, composed of laminae, rounded masses, rolls, etc. which are sometimes partly fibrous or diffuse, and which may or may not be merged.
Altostratus (As)	6500 to 23 000	*2000 to 7000*	+10 to −30	Greyish or bluish cloud sheet or layer of striated, fibrous or uniform appearance, totally or partly covering the sky, and having parts thin enough to reveal the sun at least vaguely.
Nimbostratus (Ns)	3000 to 10 000	*900 to 3000*	+10 to −15	Grey cloud layer, often dark, the appearance of which is rendered diffuse by more or less continually falling rain or snow which in most cases reaches the ground. It is thick enough throughout to blot out the sun. Low, ragged clouds frequently occur below the layer with which they may or may not merge.
Stratocumulus (Sc)	1500 to 6500	*460 to 2000*	+15 to −5	Grey or whitish, or both grey and whitish, patch, sheet or layer of cloud which almost always has dark parts, composed of tessellations, rounded masses, rolls, etc., which are non-fibrous (except for virga) and which may or may not be merged.
Stratus (St)	surface to 1500	*surface to 460*	+20 to −5	Generally grey cloud layer with a fairly low uniform base below 3500 ft *1050 m*, which may give drizzle, ice prisms or snow grains. When the sun is visible through the cloud its outline is clearly discernible. Stratus does not produce halo phenomena (except possibly at very low temperatures). Sometimes stratus appears in the form of ragged patches.
Cumulus (Cu)	1500 to 6500	*460 to 2000*	+15 to −5	Detached clouds, generally dense and with sharp outlines, developing vertically in the form of rising mounds, domes or towers, of which the bulging upper part often resembles a cauliflower. The sunlit parts of these clouds are mostly brilliant white; their bases are relative dark and nearly horizontal.
Cumulonimbus (Cb)	1500 to 6500	*460 to 2000*	+15 to −5	Heavy and dense cloud, with a considerable vertical extent, in the form of a mountain or huge towers up to 20 000 m *68 000 ft* in the tropics. At least part of its upper portion is usually smooth, or fibrous or striated, and nearly always flattened; this part often spreads out in the shape of an anvil or vast plume. Under the base of this cloud, which is often very dark, there are frequently low ragged clouds either merged with it or not, and precipitation, sometimes in the form of virga – (fallstreaks or trails or precipitation attached to the underside of clouds).

Note: The rare nacreous or mother-of-pearl formation sometimes attains an extreme height of 80 000 ft *24 000 m*.

The Earth's Atmospheric Layers

Troposphere
The realm of clouds, rain and snow in contact with the lithosphere (land) and hydrosphere (sea). The upper limit, known as the tropopause, is 17 km *11 miles* (58 000 ft) at the equator or 6–8 km *3·7–4·9 miles* (19 700–25 000 ft) at the Poles. In middle latitudes in high pressure conditions the limits may be extended between 13 km *8 miles* to 7 km *4 miles* in low pressure conditions. Aviation in the troposphere is affected by jet streams, strong, narrow air currents with velocities above 60 knots and by CAT (Clear Air Turbulence) which if violent can endanger aircraft.

Stratosphere
The second region of the atmosphere marked by a constant increase in temperature with altitude up to a maximum of $-3°C$ at about 50 km *30 miles* (160 000 ft).

Mesosphere
The third region of the atmosphere about 50 km *30 miles* (160 000 ft) marked by a rapid decrease in temperature with altitude to a minimum value even below $-113°C$ at about 85 km *55 miles* (290 000 ft) known as the mesopause.

Thermosphere
The fourth region of the atmosphere above the mesosphere characterized by an unremitting rise in temperature up to a night maximum during minimum solar activity of 225°C at about 230 km *140 miles* to above 1480°C in a day of maximum solar activity at 500 km *310 miles*. This region is sometimes termed the heterosphere because of the widely differing conditions in night and day and during solar calm and solar flare.

Exosphere
This is the fifth and final stage at 500 km *310 miles* in which the upper atmosphere becomes space and in which temperature no longer has the customary terrestrial meaning.

Note: The Appleton layer in the ionosphere at some 300 km is now referred to as the F_2 layer. The Heaviside layer at *c.* 100 km is now termed the E layer. They were named after the physicists Oliver Heaviside (1850–1925) and Sir Edward Appleton (1892–1965) and have importance in the reflection of radio waves.

Northern and Southern Lights

Polar lights are known as Aurora Borealis in the northern hemisphere and Aurora Australis in the southern hemisphere. These luminous phenomena are caused by electrical solar discharges between altitudes of 620 miles *1000 km* and 45 miles *72,5 km* and are usually visible only in the higher latitudes.

It is believed that in an auroral display some 100 million protons (hydrogen nuclei) strike each square centimetre of space in the exosphere or of atmosphere in the meso or thermospheres each second. Colours vary from yellow-green (attenuated oxygen), reddish (very low pressure oxygen), red below green (molecular nitrogen below ionized oxygen) or bluish (ionized nitrogen). Displays, which occur on every dark night in the year above 70°N or below 70°S (eg Northern Canada or Antarctica), vary in frequency with the 11-year sunspot cycle. Edinburgh may expect perhaps 25 displays a year against 7 in London, and Malta once a decade. The most striking recent displays over Britain occurred on 25 Jan. 1938 and 4–5 Sept. 1958. On 1 Sept. 1909, a display was reported from just above the equator at Singapore (1° 12′N) but is not uncritically accepted. In 1957 203 displays were recorded in the Shetland Islands (geometric Lat. 63°N).

Ice Ages

A new method of dating events over the past million years has been established and relies on the precision with which ice-age cycles follow variations in the Earth's position in space and the shape of its orbit. These are calculated by established astronomical methods, and are observed in the Milankovitch theory as climatic rhythms. These rhythms correspond with cycles of about 90 000 years (changes in orbital configuration), 41 000 years (axis tilt) and 23 000 and 19 000 years (axis wobble or precession of the equinoxes). Ocean bed cores provide evidence of the last magnetic reversal 730 000 years ago, and give an important dating monitor. From these one can correlate the climatic phases or 'core stages', evident from marine fossils, with the orbital variations, and arrive at a timescale.

Although the 90 000 year cycle became regular only 800 000 years ago a count of 28 ice ages between 3 250 000 years and the start of an ice age 649 000 years ago gives a mean average between each ice age of 92 900 years. Seven more ice ages to the present can thus be computed to the present day. In the table below the figures are rounded off.

Ice age number	Start (rounded)
29	650 000 yr
30	550 000 yr
31	475 000 yr
32	350 000 yr
33	280 000 yr
34	188 000 yr
35	72 000 yr
36	due soon

Astronomy

A guide to the scale of the Solar System and the Universe

If the Sun were reduced to the size of a beach ball of 1 ft *30,48 cm* in diameter, following on the same scale the nine planets would be represented *relatively* thus:
(1) Mercury = a grain of mustard seed 50 ft *15,2 m* away
(2) Venus = a pea 78 ft *23,7 m* away
(3) Earth = a pea 106 ft *32,3 m* away
    Moon = a grain of mustard seed 3½ in *8,5 cm* out from the Earth
(4) Mars = a currant 164 ft *49,9 m* away
(5) Jupiter = an orange 560 ft *170,6 m* away
(6) Saturn = a tangerine 1024 ft *312,1 m* away
(7) Uranus = a plum 2060 ft *627,8 m* away
(8) Neptune = a plum 3230 ft *984,5 m* away
(9) Pluto = a pinhead up to a mile *1,6 km* away.

The utter remoteness of the solar system from all other heavenly bodies is stressed by the fact that, still using this same scale of a 1 ft *30,48 cm* Sun, which for this purpose we shall place in the centre of London, the nearest stars, the triple Alpha Centauri system, would lie 5350 miles *8609,9 km* away, say near San Francisco with the largest member having a 2 ft *60,96 cm* diameter. Only the next six nearest stars in our Milky Way galaxy could, even on this scale, be accommodated on the Earth's surface.

Human imagination must boggle at distances greater than these, so it is necessary to switch to a much vaster scale of measurement.

Light travels at 186 282·397 miles/sec or *299 792,458 km/s* in vacuo. Thus, in the course of a tropical year (i.e. 365·242 198 78 mean solar days at January 0, 12 hours Ephemeris time in AD 1900) light will travel 5 878 499 814 000 miles or *9 460 528 405 000 km*. This distance has conveniently, since March 1888, been called a light year.

Light will thus travel to the Earth from the following heavenly bodies in the approximate times given:

From the Moon (reflected light)	1·25 sec
From the Sun (at perihelion)	8 min 27·3 sec
From Pluto (variable)	about 6 hrs
From nearest star (excepting the Sun)	4·28 yrs
From Rigel	900 yrs
From most distant star in the Milky Way	75 000 yrs
From nearest major extra-galactic body (Larger Magellanic cloud)	160 000 yrs
From Andromeda (limit of naked eye vision)	2 200 000 yrs
Limit of observable horizon (radio-located quasars)	c. 15 000 000 000 yrs

The stars

NUMBER OF STARS

There are 5776 stars visible to the naked eye. It is estimated that our own galaxy, the Milky Way galaxy, contains some 100 000 million (10^{11}) stars and that there are between 100 000 and 1 000 000 million (10^{11} to 10^{12}) galaxies in the detectable universe. This would indicate a total of 10^{22} to 10^{23} stars. The Milky Way galaxy is of a lens-shaped spiral form with a diameter of some 70 000 light years. The Sun is some 28 000 light years from the centre and hence the most distant star in our own galaxy is about 75 000 light years distant.

AGE OF STARS

Being combustible, stars have a limited life. The Sun, which is classified as a G2 Spectrum Yellow Dwarf, functions like a controlled hydrogen bomb, losing four million tons in mass each second. It has been estimated that it has more than 5 000 million years to burn. It is not yet possible to give a precise value for the age of the universe. However, the Earth is c. 4600 million years old, and the universe itself has most recently (Aug. 1978) been estimated to be between 13 500 and 15 500 million years old.

The planets

MERCURY

The closest of the planets to the Sun, Mercury, is never visible with the naked eye except when close to the horizon. Surface details were hard to see from Earth, even with powerful telescopes, but in 1974 the US probe Mariner 10 disclosed that the surface features are remarkably similar to those of the Moon, with mountains, valleys and craters. Mercury is virtually devoid of atmosphere, but it does have a weak but appreciable magnetic field.

VENUS

Venus, almost identical in size with the Earth, is surrounded by a cloud-laden atmosphere, so that its actual surface is never visible telescopically. Research with unmanned probes has shown that the mean surface temperature is 865°F *480°C*, that the atmospheric ground pressure is about 100 times that on Earth, and that the main atmospheric constituent is carbon dioxide; the clouds contain corrosive sulphuric acid. The US Pioneer Venus probe of Dec. 1978 revealed that Mount Maxwell is 12 000 m *39 370 ft* and winds of 640 km/h *400 mph* occur. Venus rotates very slowly in a retrograde direction (i.e. in a sense opposite to that of the Earth).

MARS

Mars was long thought to be the one planet in the Solar System, apart from Earth, to be capable of supporting life, but results from space-probes are not encouraging. Mariner 9 (1971–2) sent back thousands of high-quality pictures, showing that Mars is a world of mountains, valleys, craters and giant volcanoes;

one volcano, Olympus Mons, is some 15 miles high *over 24 000 m* and is crowned by a caldera 40 miles *64 km* in diameter. The Martian atmosphere is made up chiefly of carbon dioxide, and is very tenuous, with a ground pressure which is everywhere below ten millibars (cf. Earth's 1013 mb). The permanent polar caps are composed of ice. The Viking missions of 1976–7 disclosed no trace of organic material on Mars. The two dwarf satellites, Phobos and Deimos, were discovered by A. Hall in 1877; Mariner 9 pictures show that each is an irregular, crater-pitted lump of rocky material.

JUPITER

Jupiter is the largest planet in the Solar System. The outer layers are gaseous, composed of hydrogen and hydrogen compounds; it is now thought that most of the planet is liquid, and that hydrogen predominates. The famous Great Red Spot has proved to be a kind of whirling storm, as was shown by the close-range photographs sent back by the US probe Pioneer 10 and 11. Jupiter has a strong magnetic field, and is surrounded by zones of lethal radiation.

SATURN

Saturn is basically similar to Jupiter, but is less dense and is, of course, colder. The rings which surround Saturn are composed of pieces of material (probably ices, or at least ice-covered) moving round the planet in the manner of dwarf satellites; the ring-system is 169 000 miles *270 000 km* wide, but less than 5 miles *8 km* thick. There are three main rings; two bright (A and B) and one dusky (C). Rings A and B are separated by the Cassini Division. However, the flyby of Voyager 1, in November 1980, showed that the rings are much more complicated than had been thought; there are hundreds of 'grooves', and there are thin rings even inside the Cassini Division. The new rings F and E lie outside the main ring system; F is 'braided'. Of Saturn's satellites, Titan is the most important; its diameter is about 2700 miles *4350 km*, and Voyager established that it has a dense nitrogen atmosphere, with a ground pressure $1\frac{1}{2}$ times that of the Earth's air. Titan is permanently veiled by clouds; its surface may contain seas of liquid methane or even liquid nitrogen.

URANUS

Just visible to the naked eye, Uranus has the same low density as Jupiter and has a diameter nearly four times that of the Earth. Its axis is tilted at 98° compared with our 23°27′ which means that the night and day must at some points last up to 21 years each. In 1977, indirect researches showed that there are eight rings round Uranus – too faint to be detected visually from Earth.

NEPTUNE

Neptune is rather denser and *slightly* smaller than Uranus. It requires nearly 165 years to make one revolution of the Sun against the 84 years of Uranus. Its axial tilt at 28°48′ conforms more closely to those of the Earth (23°27′), Mars (25°12′), and Saturn (26°44′).

PLUTO

Discovered by systematic photography in 1930. The 248-year orbit of this faint planet with only 8 per cent of the volume of the Earth is so eccentric that at perihelion it came inside the orbit of Neptune on 21 Jan. 1979. The existence of a moon, Charon, was announced on 22 June 1978 by James W. Christy of the US Naval Observatory, Flagstaff, Arizona.

THE SUN

The Sun (for statistics see Solar System table) is a yellow dwarf star (spectrum classification G2) with a luminosity of 3×10^{27} candle power such that each square inch of the surface emits 1.53×10^6 candelas. Sun spots appear to be darker because they are 2700°F (1500°C) cooler than the surface temperature of 10 220°F (5660°C). These may measure up to 7×10^9 miles² *1·8 × 10^{10} km²* and have to be 5×10^8 miles² *1·3 × 10^9 km²* to be visible to the (*protected*) naked eye.

During 1957 a record 263 were noted. Solar prominences may flare out to 365 000 miles *588 000 km* from the Sun's surface.

Earth-Moon System

CREATION OF THE MOON

It was once believed that the Moon used to be part of the Earth, and that the original combined body broke in two as a result of tidal forces. This is not now believed to be the case. It may be that the Moon was once an independent body which was captured by the Earth; however, most authorities believe that it has always been associated with the Earth. Certainly the rocks brought back by the Apollo astronauts confirm that the age of the Moon is approximately the same as that of the Earth (c. 4600 million years).

CREATION OF THE EARTH

The long-popular theory that the Earth and other planets were globules thrown out from a molten Sun has long been discarded. Spectroscopic analysis has shown that the Sun consists of 98 per cent hydrogen and helium whereas the cores of planets are often a composite of heavy non-gaseous elements.

It is now thought that the planets including the Earth were formed by accretion from a cloud of material or 'solar nebula' which used to be associated with the Sun.

THE BRIGHTEST AND NEAREST STARS (EXCLUDING THE SUN)

Magnitude – a measure of stellar brightness such that the light of a star of any magnitude bears a ratio of 2·511 886 to that of the star of the next magnitude. Thus a fifth magnitude star is 2·511 886 times as bright, whilst one of the first magnitude is exactly 100 (or 2·511 886⁵) times as bright as a sixth magnitude star. In the case of such exceptionally bright bodies as Sirius, Venus, the Moon (magnitude −12·7) or the Sun (magnitude −26·8) the magnitude is expressed as a minus quantity. Such a value for the Sun is its 'apparent magnitude' (m_v) which is the brightness as seen from the Earth, but for comparison the intrinsic brightness needs to be known and this is defined as the 'absolute magnitude' (M_v), the magnitude that would be observed if the star was placed at a distance of ten parsecs. On this basis the magnitude of the Sun is reduced to +4·8 or a four billionfold reduction in brightness.

The absolute magnitude of a star is related to its apparent magnitude and its distance in parsecs (d) by means of the equation:

$$M_v = m_v + 5 - 5 \log_{10}(d)$$

Eclipses

An eclipse (derived from the Greek *ekleipsis* 'failing to appear') occurs when the sight of a celestial body is either obliterated or reduced by the intervention of a second body.

There are two main varieties of eclipse.
(i) Those when the eclipsing body passes between the observer on Earth and the eclipsed body. Such eclipses are those of the Sun by the Moon; occultations of various stars by the moon; transits of Venus or Mercury across the face of the Sun; and the eclipses of binary stars.
(ii) Those when the eclipsing body passes between the Sun and the eclipsed body. These can only affect planets or satellites which are not self-luminous. Such are eclipses of the Moon (by the Earth's shadow); and the eclipses of the satellites of Jupiter.

There is nothing in all the variety of natural phenomena that is quite so impressive as a total eclipse of the Sun.

Eclipses of the Sun (by the Moon) and of the Moon (by the Earth) have caused both wonder and sometimes terror since recorded history.

BRIGHTEST STARS

Name	Magnitude		Distance	
	Apparent	Absolute	Light years	Parsecs
Sirius	−1·46	+1·4	8·65	2·65
Canopus	−0·73	−4·6	200	60
Alpha Centauri	−0·29	+4·1	4·38	1·34
Arcturus	−0·06	−0·3	36	11
Vega	+0·04	+0·5	26	8·1
Capella	+0·08	−0·5	42	13
Rigel	+0·10	−7·0	900	275
Procyon	+0·35	+2·6	11·4	3·5
Achernar	+0·48	−2·5	127	39
Beta Centauri (Agena)	+0·60	−4·6	490	150
Altair	+0·77	+2·3	16	5·0
Betelgeuse	+0·85	−5·7	650	200
Aldebaran	+0·85	−0·7	65	21
Alpha Crucis	+0·90	−3·7	270	85
Spica	+0·96	−3·6	260	80
Antares	+1·08	−4·5	430	130
Pollux	+1·15	+1·0	35	10·7
Fomalhaut	+1·16	+1·9	23	7·0
Deneb	+1·25	−7·1	1500	500
Beta Crucis	+1·25	−5·1	530	160
Regulus	+1·35	−0·7	85	26
Adhara	+1·50	−4·4	490	150

NEAREST STARS

Name	Distance		Magnitude			
	Light Years	Parsecs	Apparent		Absolute	
Proxima Centauri	4·22	1·30	11·05		15·49	
Alpha Centauri	4·35	1·33	A −0·01 B 1·33		A 4·37 B 5·71	
Barnard's Star	5·98	1·83	9·54		13·22	
Wolf 359	7·75	2·38	13·53		16·65	
Lalande 21185	8·22	2·52	7·50		10·49	
Luyten 726−8*	8·43	2·58	A 12·52 B 13·02		A 15·46 B 15·96	
Sirius	8·65	2·65	A −1·46 B 8·68		A 1·42 B 11·56	
Ross 154	9·45	2·90	10·6		13·3	
Ross 248	10·4	3·18	12·29		14·77	
Epsilon Eridani	10·8	3·31	3·73		6·13	
Ross 128	10·9	3·36	11·10		13·47	
61 Cygni	11·1	3·40	A 5·22 B 6·03		A 7·56 B 8·37	
Epsilon Indi	11·2	3·44	4·68		7·00	
Luyten 789−6	11·2	3·45	12·18		14·49	
Groombridge 34	11·2	3·45	A 8·08 B 11·06		A 10·39 B 13·37	
Procyon	11·4	3·51	A 0·37 B 10·7		A 2·64 B 13·0	
Sigma 2398	11·6	3·55	A 8·90 B 9·69		A 11·15 B 11·94	
Lacaille 9352	11·7	3·58	7·36		9·59	
Giclas 51−15	11·7	3·60	14·81		17·03	
Tau Ceti	11·8	3·61	3·50		5·71	
Luyten's Star	12·3	3·76	9·82		11·94	
Luyten 725−32	12·5	3·83	12·04		14·12	
Lacaille 8760	12·5	3·85	6·67		8·74	
Kapteyn's Star	12·7	3·91	8·81		10·85	
Kruger 60	12·9	3·95	A 9·85 B 11·3		A 11·87 B 13·3	

* The B star companion is known as UV Ceti.

The element of rarity enhances the wonder of this event, which should on average only be seen from a given city or town once in about four hundred years. More specifically, Londoners saw no such eclipse between 20 March 1140 and 3 May 1715 – that is, about nineteen generations later. The next will be on 14 June 2151. The next total eclipse of the Sun visible from Great Britain will occur on 11 Aug. 1999 on the Cornish coast. Eclipses of the Sun are in fact commoner than those of the Moon but the area from which they can be seen is so much smaller that the number of possible spectators is infinitely smaller.

The places from which and the times at which solar eclipses have been seen have been worked out back as far as the year 4200 BC and can be worked out far into the future, with of course an increasing, but still slight, degree of inaccuracy. The precise date of actual historical events in the Assyrian, Chinese, Greek and Roman empires have been fixed or confirmed by eclipses. For example, the battle between the Lydians and the Medes, which is reported by Herodotus, can be fixed exactly as occurring on 28 May 585 BC, because a solar eclipse caused such awe that it stopped the fight. Modern astronomy has benefited from the study of ancient eclipses because they help to determine 'secular accelerations', that is, the progressive changes in celestial motions.

Solar Eclipses (i.e. of the Sun by the Moon)
Solar eclipses are of three sorts – Total, Partial and Annular. A *total* eclipse occurs when the Moon, which, of course, must be new, comes completely between the Sun's disc and the observer on Earth. The Moon's circular shadow – its umbra – with a maximum diameter of 170 miles *273 km.* sweeps across the face of the Earth from West to East. The maximum possible duration of totality for a stationary observer is 7 min 31 sec.

The dramatic events at the moment of totality are: sunlight vanishes in a few seconds; sudden darkness (but *not* as intense as that during a night even under a full moon); the brightest stars become visible; the Sun's corona is seen; there is a hush from the animal and bird world; cocks have been noted to crow when the light floods back.

The moon's partial shadow – its penumbra – which forms a much larger circle of about 2000 miles *3200 km* in diameter, causes a *partial* eclipse. Partial eclipses, of course, vary in their degree of completeness. There must be a minimum of two Solar eclipses each year.

An *annular* eclipse occurs when – owing to variations in the Sun's distance – the Moon's disc comes inside the Sun. In other words, the Moon's umbra stops short of the Earth's surface and an outer rim of the Sun surrounds the Moon. The maximum possible duration of containment is 12 min 24 sec.

Lunar Eclipses (i.e. of the Moon by the Earth's shadow)
Lunar eclipses are caused when the Moon – which, of course, must be full – passes through the shadow of the Earth and so loses its bright direct illumination by the Sun. A lunar eclipse is *partial* until the whole Moon passes into the Earth's umbra and so becomes *total*. After the Moon leaves the umbra it passes through the Earth's penumbra, which merely dims the moonlight so little that it is scarcely visible and is not even worth recording.

Other Observable Phenomena
I. During its movement across the sky the Moon may pass in front of a star, hiding or occulting it. Immersion takes place instantaneously, because the Moon has no atmosphere around its limb – in fact this was one of the earliest direct proofs of the Moon's lack of atmosphere. The emersion of the star is equally sudden. Planets may also be occulted, though in such cases both immersion and emersion are gradual because a planet presents an appreciable disk.
II. The two planets – Mercury and Venus – which are nearer the Sun than is the Earth, occasionally can be seen (with proper protection to the eyes) to pass slowly across the face of the Sun. These so-called Transits of Mercury occur on average about 14 times every century; Transits of Venus are far rarer with the last in 1882 and the next two on 8 June 2004 and 6 June 2012.
III. Some apparently single stars have been observed to vary sharply in brightness. They have been found in fact to be twin stars, revolving around each other and so eclipsing one another. Such stars are called *eclipsing binaries*, and the best-known examples are Algol and β Lyrae.

Comets

Comets are Solar System bodies moving in orbits about the Sun. Records go back to the 7th century BC. The speeds of the estimated 2 000 000 comets vary from only 700 mph in the outer reaches to 1 250 000 mph (*1100-2 million km/h*) when near the Sun. The periods of revolution vary, according to the ellipticity of orbit, from 3·3 years (Encke's comet) to millions of years as in the case of Delavan's Comet of 1914 which is not expected to return for 24 million years. Comet Wilson-Harrington, discovered in Nov. 1949, had a calculated period of only 2·3 years but has not since been sighted.

Comets are so tenuous to the point that 10 000 cubic miles *41 600 km³* of tail might embrace only a cubic inch of solid matter. Comets are not self luminous, hence only visible when in the inner part of the Solar System. They consist mainly of a head of dirty ice particles and a tail which always points more or less away from the Sun. In May 1910 the Earth probably passed through the tail of the famous Halley's Comet which returned on 9 Feb. 1986 (perihelion). Lexell's Comet of 1770 approached to within 1 200 000 km *750 000 miles*. The 35 megaton explosion 40 miles *64 km* north of Vanavara, Siberia on 30 June 1908, known as the Tunguska event, was concluded in July 1977 to have been caused by a cometary collision.

Telescopes

The prototype of modern refracting telescopes was that made in 1608 by the Dutchman Hans

Lippershey (or Lippersheim) after an accidental discovery of the magnifying power of spectacle lens when held apart. The principle of the reflecting telescope was expounded by the Scot, James Gregory in 1663 and the first successful reflector was built with a 5 cm *2 in* diameter mirror by Sir Isaac Newton for presentation to the Royal Society, London on 11 Jan. 1672.

The world's most powerful astronomical telescopes are now:

Diameter of Refractors (Lens)			Completion Date
Inches	cms		
40·0	*102*	Yerkes, Williams Bay, Wisconsin, USA	1897
36·0	*91*	Lick, Mt Hamilton, Cal., USA	1888
32·7	*83*	Paris Observatory, Meudon, France	1893
32·0	*81*	Astrophysical Observatory, Potsdam, Germany	1899

30·0	*76*	Nice Observatory, Nice, France	1880
30·0	*76*	Alleghany Observatory, Pittsburgh, Penn., USA	1914

Diameter of Reflectors (Mirror)			
Inches	cms		
236·2	*600*	Mount Semirodriki, Caucasus, USSR	1976
200·0	*508*	Hale, Mt Palomar, nr Pasadena, Cal., USA	1948
158·0	*401*	Kitt Peak Nat. Observatory, Tucson, Arizona, USA	1970
158·0	*401*	Cerro Tololo, Chile	1970
153·0	*389*	Siding Spring, Australia	1974
150·0	*381*	Mount Stromlo, Canberra, Australia	1972
150·0	*381*	La Cilla, Chile	1975
120·0	*305*	Lick, Mt Hamilton, Cal., USA	1959

107·0	*272*	McDonald Observatory, Fort Davis, Texas, USA	1968
104·0	*264*	Crimean Astrophysical Lab., Nauchny, USSR	1960
100·0	*254*	Hooker, Mt Wilson, Cal., USA	1917
98·0	*249*	Newton (Herstmonceux 1967) La Palma, Canary Is.	1983
88·0	*223*	Mauna Kea Observatory, Hawaii	1970

ELEMENTS OF THE PLANETARY ORBITS

Planet	Mean Distance From Sun miles km	Perihelion Distance miles km	Aphelion Distance miles km	Orbital Eccentricity	Orbital Inclination ° ′ ″	Sidereal Period days	Orbital Velocity Mean mph km/h	Maximum mph km/h	Minimum mph km/h
Mercury	35 983 100 *57 909 100*	28 584 000 *46 001 000*	43 382 000 *69 817 000*	0·205 630	7 00 15	87·9693	105 950 *170 500*	131 930 *212 310*	86 920 *139 890*
Venus	67 237 900 *108 208 900*	66 782 000 *107 475 000*	67 694 000 *108 943 000*	0·006 783	3 23 39	224·7008	78 340 *126 070*	78 870 *126 930*	77 810 *125 220*
Earth	92 955 800 *149 597 900*	91 402 000 *147 097 000*	94 510 000 *152 099 000*	0·016 718	— — —	365·2564	66 620 *107 220*	67 750 *109 030*	65 520 *105 450*
Mars	141 635 700 *227 940 500*	128 410 000 *206 656 000*	154 862 000 *249 226 000*	0·093 380	1 50 59	686·9797	53 860 *86 680*	59 270 *95 390*	49 150 *79 100*
Jupiter	483 634 000 *778 833 000*	460 280 000 *740 750 000*	506 990 000 *815 920 000*	0·048 286	1 18 16	4332·62	29 210 *47 000*	30 670 *49 360*	27 840 *44 810*
Saturn	886 683 000 *1 426 978 000*	837 000 000 *1 347 020 000*	936 370 000 *1 506 940 000*	0·056 037	2 29 21	10 759·06	21 560 *34 700*	22 820 *36 730*	20 400 *32 830*
Uranus	1 783 951 000 *2 870 991 000*	1 701 660 000 *2 738 560 000*	1 866 230 000 *3 003 400 000*	0·046 125	0 46 23	30 707·79	15 200 *24 460*	15 930 *25 630*	14 520 *23 370*
Neptune	2 794 350 000 *4 497 070 000*	2 766 270 000 *4 451 880 000*	2 822 430 000 *4 542 270 000*	0·010 050	1 46 20	60 199·63	12 150 *19 560*	12 270 *19 750*	12 030 *19 360*
Pluto	3 674 490 000 *5 913 510 000*	2 761 600 000 *4 444 400 000*	4 587 300 000 *7 382 600 000*	0·248 432	17 08 22	90 777·61	10 430 *16 790*	13 660 *21 980*	8 220 *13 230*

PHYSICAL PARAMETERS OF THE SUN AND PLANETS

Sun or Planet		Diameter miles	km	Equatorial Sidereal Rotation Period d h m s	Equatorial Inclination	Mass tons	kg	Density g/cm³	Escape Velocity mps	km/s
Sun		865 270	*1 392 520*	25 09 07	7° 15′	1·958 ×10²⁷	*1,989 × 10³⁰*	*1,407*	383·65	*617,43*
Mercury		3031	*4878*	58 15 30 34	0°	3·250 ×10²⁰	*3,302 × 10²³*	*5,433*	2·64	*4,25*
Venus		7520	*12 102*	*243 00 14	178°	4·792 ×10²¹	*4,869 × 10²⁴*	*5,246*	6·44	*10,36*
Earth	Equ.	7926	*12 756*	23 56 04·091	23° 27′	5·2880 ×10²¹	*5,974 × 10²⁴*	*5,515*	6·95	*11,19*
	Polar	7900	*12 714*							
Mars	Equ.	4221	*6794*	24 37 22·663	25° 12′	6·318 ×10²⁰	*6,419 × 10²³*	*3,934*	3·12	*5,03*
	Polar	4196	*6752*							
Jupiter	Equ.	88 780	*142 880*	9 50 30·003	3° 04′	1·869 ×10²⁴	*1,899 × 10²⁷*	*1,330*	37·42	*60,23*
	Polar	82 980	*133 540*							
Saturn	Equ.	74 880	*120 500*	10 14	26° 44′	5·596 ×10²³	*5,686 × 10²⁶*	*0,687*	22·42	*36,09*
	Polar	67 640	*10 860*							
Uranus	Equ.	31 950	*51 400**	16 10	97° 53′	8·602 ×10²²	*8,740 × 10²⁵*	*1,26*	13·28	*21,38*
	Polar	31 250	*50 300*							
Neptune	Equ.	30 200	*48 600*	18 26	28° 48′	1·013 ×10²³	*1,029 × 10²⁶*	*1,75*	14·82	*23,84*
	Polar	29 500	*47 500*							
Pluto		1860	*3000*	6 09 18	90°	1·46 ×10¹⁹	*1,49 × 10²²*	*0,93*	0·67	*1,08*

* Retrograde.

Sun or Planet	Surface Temperature °C	Equatorial Diameter	On Scale Earth = 1 Volume	Mass	Surface Gravity	Mean Apparent Magnitude	Number of Satellites
Sun	5660	109·16	1 305 000	332 946·0	27·88	−26·8	—
Mercury	−180 to +420	0·3824	0·0561	0·055 27	0·3771	0·0	0
Venus	462	0·9487	0·8568	0·815 00	0·9034	−4·4	0
Earth	−88 to +58	1·0000	1·0000	** 1·000 00	1·0000	—	1
Mars	−125 to +30	0·5326	0·1506	0·107 45	0·3795	−2·0	2
Jupiter	−108	11·20	1318	317·89	2·644	−2·6	16
Saturn	−133	9·45	764	95·18	1·139	+0·7	16
Uranus	−160	4·03	64	14·63	0·912	+5·5	5
Neptune	−160	3·81	54	17·22	1·200	+7·8	2
Pluto	−220	0·24	0·013	0·025	0·040	+15·0	1

** The Earth-Moon system weighs 1·012 30 Earth masses.

The Russian 600 cm *236·2 in* reflector is now the largest in the world; it may well remain so, as it is quite likely that future emphasis will be upon telescopes in space. The largest telescope in Great Britain was the 98 in *248 cm* reflector at the Royal Greenwich Observatory, Herstmonceux, known as the Isaac Newton Telescope of INT. However, this telescope was dismantled to be relocated on the island of La Palma in the Canary Isles in 1979 at the new La Palma Observatory.

RADIO TELESCOPE
The world's largest dish radio telescope is the non-steerable £3 750 000 ionospheric apparatus at Arecibo, Puerto Rico, completed in November 1963. It utilises a natural crater which is spanned by a dish 1000 ft *305 m* in diameter, covering an area of 18½ acres *7,28 ha*. Improvements and re-plating cost a further £4½ million in 1974.

RADIO ASTRONOMY
Radio astronomy became possible with the discovery in 1864 of radio waves by Dr M Loomis (USA). The earliest suggestion that extra-terrestrial radio waves might exist and be detected came from Thomas Edison (USA) who corresponded with Prof A E Kennelly on the subject on 2 Nov. 1890.

It was not until 1932 that Karl Guthe Jansky (1905–49) a US scientist of Czech descent first detected radio signals, from the Sagittarius constellation, at Holmdel, New Jersey. This 'cosmic static' was recorded on a 15-m wave length. The pioneer radio astronomer was Grote Reber (USA) (b. 1911) who built the world's first radio telescope, a 31 ft 5-in parabolic dish, in his back-yard at Wheaton, Illinois, in 1937. His first results were published in 1940.

Dr J S Hey (GB) discovered during war-time radar jamming research that sun spots emitted radio waves; that radio echoes come from meteor trails; and that the extra-galactic nebula Cygnus A was a discrete source of immense power.

In 1947 John G Bolton in Australia found that the Crab Nebula (M.1), a supernova remnant, is a strong radio source. Since then many more discrete sources have been found; some are supernova remnants in our Galaxy, while others are external galaxies and the mysterious, very remote quasars. Young science though it may be, radio astronomy is now of fundamental importance in our studies of the universe, and it has provided information which could never have been obtained in any other way.

Some milestones in astronomy

Aristotle (*c.* 385–325 BC) advanced the first argument against the flat Earth hypothesis. Eratosthenes of Cyrene (*c.* 285–203 BC) made the earliest estimate of the Earth's circumference in *c.* 230 BC. Ptolemy in *c.* AD 180 established the Ptolemic System, i.e. Earth was the centre of the universe.
Copernicus (1473–1543) established that both the Earth and Mars orbit the Sun.
Johannes Kepler published his first two laws of planetary motion in 1609: the third in 1619.
Galileo Galilei (1564–1642) harnessed in 1609 the use of the telescope and made astronomical observations with it. He was summonsed by the Roman Church to adjure his heresy that the Earth went round the Sun.
Christiaan Huygens (1629–95) built a 210 ft *64 m* long refractor. In 1665 he described Saturn's rings, later observing the markings on Mars.
In the 1670s Cassini recalculated the Sun's distance at 86 million miles *138 million km*.
In 1675 Rømer measured the velocity of light. His inspired answer, ignored for more than 100 years and not believed by himself, was 186 000 miles per sec *300 000 km per sec*. Sir Isaac Newton (1642–1727) published his *Principia* in 1687.
In 1705 Halley predicted the return of Halley's comet in 1758. This was confirmed in that year by Palitzsch.
Herschel discovered Uranus in 1781.
Giuseppe Piazzi observed the first asteroid in 1801, confirmed in 1802 and named *Ceres*.
Friedrich Bessel was one of the first to realise the vastness of our galaxy, measuring in 1835 *61 Cygni* to be 60 million million miles distant away.
The steady-state or continuous creation theory was postulated in 1948 by Professors H. Bondi and T. Gold but is now considered to be incorrect. Other theories of the universe currently under discussion are the evolutionary or 'big bang' theory, due to Abbé Lemaitre in 1927, and the oscillating theory of 1965 supported by Professor A. Sandage of the USA.

CHIRON
On 8 Nov. 1977 Charles Kowal at Palomar Observatory, California, discovered an exceptional object which may be about 500 miles *800 km* in diameter moving mainly between the orbits of Saturn and Uranus. It has been named Chiron. Its nature is still uncertain, and its size may have been over-estimated; it is thought to be rocky rather than icy, and may be classed as an exceptional asteroid.

CONSTELLATIONS
There are 31 accepted constellations in the northern and 52 in the southern hemispheres and 5 which appear at times in both hemispheres, making 88 in all. The International Astronomical Union completed the now accepted arc codification by 1945. The rectangular constellation Orion includes 15 stars above the 4th magnitude in its great quadrilateral – Rigel (bottom left, Mag. 0·08 variable), Betelgeuse (top right, Mag. 0·85 variable) and Bellatrix (top left, Mag. 1·64). For a complete list see *Guinness Book of Astronomy Facts and Feats*.

Meteorites

The term meteorite must now be confined to a fallen meteor, a meteoric mass of stone (aerolite) or nickel-iron (siderite). It is loosely and incorrectly used of a meteor or shooting star which is usually only the size of a pinhead. The existence of meteorites, owing to a religious bias, was first admitted as late as 26 Apr. 1803, after a shower of some 2500 aerolites fell around L'Aigle, near Paris, France.

The majority of meteorites inevitably fall into the sea (70·8 per cent of the Earth's surface) and are not recovered. Only eight meteorites exceeding ten tons have been located. All these are of the iron-nickel type. The largest recorded stone meteorite is the one which fell in the Kirin Province, Manchuria on 8 Mar. 1976 weighing 3894 lb *1766 kg*. The total number of strikes recorded since the mid-17th century is nearly 1700, including 22 in the British Isles.

World's largest meteorites

		Approximate tonnage
Hoba	nr Grootfontein, South West Africa	60
Tent (Abnighito)	Cape York, West Greenland	30·4
Bacuberito	Mexico	27
Mbosi	Tanganyika	26
Willamette (1902)	Oregon, USA	14
Chupaero	Chihuahua, Mexico	14
Campo de Cielo	Argentina	13
Morito	Chihuahua, Mexico	11

The largest recorded in other continents are:

Australia	Cranbourne	3·5
Asia	Sikhote-Alin, USSR	1·7
Europe	Magura, Czechoslovakia	1·5

The largest British Isles meteorites of the 22 recorded have been:

Country and Location	Date	Weight	
Ireland			
Adare, Limerick	10 Sept. 1813	65 lb (total 106 lb)	*29,5 kg (total 48 kg)*
England			
World Cottage, nr Scarborough, North Yorkshire	13 Dec. 1795	56 lb	*25,4 kg*
Barwell, Leicestershire	24 Dec. 1965	17⅜ lb (total 102 lb)	*7,8 kg (total 46,25 kg)*
Scotland			
Strathmore, Tayside	3 Dec. 1971	22¼ lb	*10,1 kg*

The twenty largest asteroids

Asteroid		Diameter miles	km	Rotation Period hours	Absolute Visual Magnitude V(1,0)*	Discoverer	Date
(1)	Ceres	637	*1025*	9·087	3·63	G Piazzi	1 Jan. 1801
(2)	Pallas	362	*583*	7·811	4·36	H W Olbers	28 Mar. 1802
(4)	Vesta	345	*555*	5·342	3·46	H W Olbers	29 Mar. 1807
(10)	Hygeia	275	*443*	18	5·64	A De Gasparis	12 Apr. 1849
(704)	Interamnia	210	*338*	8·723	6·37	V Cerulli	2 Oct. 1910
(511)	Davida	208	*335*	5·17	6·48	R S Dugan	30 May 1903
(65)	Cybele	193	*311*	6·07	7·07	E W Tempel	8 Mar. 1861
(52)	Europa	181	*291*	11·258	6·61	H Goldschmidt	4 Feb. 1858
(451)	Patentia	175	*281*	20	6·89	A Charlois	4 Dec. 1899
(31)	Euphrosyne	168	*270*	5·531	7·03	J Ferguson	1 Sept. 1854
(15)	Eunomia	162	*261*	6·081	5·50	A De Gasparis	29 July 1851
(324)	Bamberga	159	*256*	29·4	7·07	J Palisa	25 Feb. 1892
(107)	Camilla	157	*252*	4·56	7·18	N R Pogson	17 Nov. 1868
(87)	Sylvia	156	*251*	5·186	7·19	N R Pogson	16 May 1866
(45)	Eugenia	155	*250*	5·700	7·43	H Goldschmidt	27 Jun. 1857
(24)	Themis	155	*249*	8·369	7·21	A De Gasparis	5 Apr. 1853
(3)	Juno	155	*249*	7·213	5·65	K Harding	1 Sept. 1804
(16)	Psyche	155	*249*	4·303	6·21	A De Gasparis	17 Mar. 1852
(13)	Egeria	152	*245*	7·045	6·81	A De Gasparis	2 Nov. 1850
(165)	Loreley	142	*228*	?	7·40	C H F Peters	9 Aug. 1876

* Magnitude reduced to unit distance (one astronomical unit)
Note: the total mass of the asteroids is about 3×10^{18} tons 3×10^{21} *kg* or about one twenty-fifth of the mass of our Moon. The three largest asteroids account for over half of the total mass.

Wales
Beddgelert,
Gwynedd   21 Sept.   25½ oz   *723 g*
1949

Meteorite Craters
The most spectacular of all dry craters is the Coon Butte or Barringer crater near Canyon Diablo, Winslow, North Arizona, USA, discovered in 1891, which is now 575 ft *175 m* deep and 4150 ft *1265 m* in diameter. The next largest craters are Wolf's Creek, Western Australia

(3000 ft *914 m* diameter, 170 ft *52 m* deep) and a crater discovered in N Chile in 1965 (1476 ft *450 m* diameter, 100 ft *30 m* deep). The New Quebec (formerly Chubb) 'crater' in North Ungava, Canada, discovered in June 1943, is 1325 ft *404 m* deep and 2·2 miles *3,5 km* in diameter, but is now regarded as a water-filled vulcanoid.

Ancient and oblique meteoric scars are much less spectacular though of far greater dimensions. These phenomena are known as astroblemes (Gk *astron*, a star; *blemma*, a glance).

World's largest meteorite craters

Name of Astrobleme	Diameter miles	km
Vredefort Ring, South Africa (meteoric origin disputed, 1963)	24·8	*39,9*
Nordlinger Ries, Germany	15·5	*24,9*
Deep Bay, Saskatchewan, Canada (discovered 1956)	8·5	*13,6*
Lake Bosumtibi, Ghana	6·2	*9,9*
Serpent Mound, Ohio, USA	3·98	*6,4*
Wells Creek, Tennessee, USA	2·97	*4,7*
Al Umchaimin, Iraq	1·98	*3,1*

Metrology

In essence, measurement involves *comparison:* the measurement of a physical quantity entails comparing it with an agreed and clearly defined *standard.* The result is expressed in terms of a *unit,* which is the name for a standard, preceded by a number which is the *ratio* of the measured quantity of the appropriate fixed unit.

A *system of units* is centred on a small number of *base units.* These relate to the fundamental standards of length, mass and time, together with a few others to extend the system to a wider range of physical measurements, e.g. to electrical and optical quantities. There are also two geometrical units which belong to a class known as *supplementary units.*

These few base units can be combined to form a large number of *derived units.* For example, units of area, velocity and acceleration are formed from units of length and time. Thus very many different kinds of measurement can be made and recorded employing very few base units.

For convenience, *multiples* and *submultiples* of both base and derived units are frequently used, eg kilometres and millimetres.

Historically, several systems of units have evolved: in Britain, the imperial system; in the United States, the US customary units; and forms of the metric system (CGS for centimetre-gram-second and MKS for metre-kilogram-second), employed universally in science and generally in very many countries of the world.

The International System of Units (Système International d'Unités or SI) is a modern form of the metric system. It was finally agreed at the Eleventh General Conference of Weights and Measures in October 1960 and is now being widely adopted throughout the scientific world.

The imperial system

UNIT DEFINITION
The yard (yd). This is equal to 0·9144 metre exactly (Weights and Measures Act, 1963).

The pound (lb). This is equal to 0·453 592 37 kilogram exactly (Weights and Measures Act, 1963).

The gallon (gal). The space occupied by 10 pounds weight of distilled water of density 0·998 859 gram per millilitre weighed in air of density 0·001 217 gram per millilitre against weights of density 8·136 gram per millilitre (Weights and Measures Act, 1963). The definition of the gallon in the meaning of the 1963 Weights and Measures Act uses the 1901 definition of the litre [1 litre (1901) = 1·000 028 dm³].

OTHER UNITS OF LENGTH EMPLOYED

animal stature	the hand = 4 in. *NB* – a horse of 14 hands 3 in to the withers is often written 14·3 hands.
surveying	the link = 7·92 in or a hundreth part of a chain.
approximate	the span = 9 in (from the span of the hand).
biblical	the cubit = 18 in.
approximate	the pace = 30 in (from the stride).
nautical	the cable = 120 fathoms or 240 yd.
navigation	the UK nautical mile = 6080 ft at the Equator.
navigation	the International nautical mile (adopted also by the USA on 1 July 1954) = 6076·1 ft (0·99936 of a UK nautical mile).

The use of the metric system was legalized in the United Kingdom in 1897. The Halsbury Committee recommended the introduction of decimal currency in September 1963. The intention to switch to the metric system was declared on 24 May 1965 by the President of the Board of Trade 'within ten years'. The date for the official adoption of the metric system was announced on 1 Mar 1966 to be 'February 1971'. On Tuesday, 23 Mar 1976, the Government decided not to proceed with the second reading of the Weights and Measures (Metrication) Act.

The SI units

BASE UNITS

Quantity	Unit	Symbol	Definition
length	metre	m	the length of the path travelled by light in vacuum during a time interval of 1/299 792 458 of a second.
mass	kilogram	kg	the mass of the international prototype of the kilogram, which is in the custody of the Bureau International des Poids et Mésures (BIPM) at Sèvres near Paris, France.
time	second	s	the duration of 9 192 631 770 periods of the radiation corresponding to the transition between the two hyperfine levels of the ground state of the caesium-133 atom.
electric current	ampere	A	that constant current which, if maintained in two straight parallel conductors of infinite length of negligible circular cross-section, and placed 1 metre apart in vacuum, would produce between these conductors a force equal to 2×10^{-7} newton per metre of length.
thermodynamic temperature	kelvin	K	the fraction 1/273·15 of the thermodynamic temperature of the triple point of water. The triple point of water is the point where water, ice and water vapour are in equilibrium.

Quantity	Unit	Symbol	Definition
luminous intensity	candela	cd	the luminous intensity, in the perpendicular direction, of a surface of 1/600 000 square metre of a black body at the temperature of freezing platinum under a pressure of 101 325 pascals.
amount of substance	mole	mol	the amount of substance of a system which contains as many elementary entities as there are atoms in 0·012 kilogram of carbon-12.

SUPPLEMENTARY UNITS

plane angle	radian	rad	the plane angle between two radii of a circle which cut off on the circumference an arc equal in length to the radius.
solid angle	steradian	sr	the solid angle which having its vertex in the centre of a sphere, cuts off an area of the surface of the sphere equal to that of a square having sides of length equal to the radius of the sphere.

DERIVED UNITS

Quantity	Unit	Symbol	Expression in terms of other SI units
area	square metre	m^2	—
volume	cubic metre	m^3	—
velocity	metre per second	$m \cdot s^{-1}$	—
angular velocity	radian per second	$rad\ s^{-1}$	—
acceleration	metre per second squared	$m \cdot s^{-2}$	—
angular acceleration	radian per second squared	$rad\ s^{-2}$	—
frequency	hertz	Hz	s^{-1}
density	kilogram per cubic metre	$kg \cdot m^{-3}$	—
momentum	kilogram metre per second	$kg \cdot m \cdot s^{-1}$	—
angular momentum	kilogram metre squared per second	$kg \cdot m^2 \cdot s^{-1}$	—
moment of inertia	kilogram metre squared	$kg \cdot m^2$	—
force	newton	N	$kg \cdot m \cdot s^{-2}$
pressure, stress	pascal	Pa	$N \cdot m^{-2} = kg \cdot m^{-1} \cdot s^{-2}$
work, energy, quantity of heat	joule	J	$N \cdot m = kg \cdot m^2 \cdot s^{-2}$
power	watt	W	$J \cdot s^{-1} = kg \cdot m^2 \cdot s^{-3}$
surface tension	newton per metre	$N \cdot m^{-1}$	$kg \cdot s^{-2}$
dynamic viscosity	newton second per metre squared	$N \cdot s \cdot m^{-2}$	$kg \cdot m^{-1} \cdot s^{-1}$
kinematic viscosity	metre squared per second	$m^2 \cdot s^{-1}$	—
temperature	degree Celsius	°C	—
thermal coefficient of linear expansion	per degree Celsius, or per kelvin	$°C^{-1}, K^{-1}$	—
thermal conductivity	watt per metre degree C	$W \cdot m^{-1} \cdot °C^{-1}$	$kg \cdot m \cdot s^{-3} \cdot °C^{-1}$
heat capacity	joule per kelvin	$J \cdot K^{-1}$	$kg \cdot m^2 \cdot s^{-2} \cdot K^{-1}$
specific heat capacity	joule per kilogram kelvin	$J \cdot kg^{-1} \cdot K^{-1}$	$m^2 \cdot s^{-2} \cdot K^{-1}$
specific latent heat	joule per kilogram	$J\ kg^{-1}$	$m^2 \cdot s^{-2}$
electric charge	coulomb	C	$A \cdot s$
electromotive force, potential difference	volt	V	$W \cdot A^{-1} = kg \cdot m^2 \cdot s^{-3} \cdot A^{-1}$
electric resistance	ohm	Ω	$V \cdot A^{-1} = kg \cdot m^2 \cdot s^{-3} \cdot A^{-2}$
electric conductance	siemens	S	$A \cdot V^{-1} = kg^{-1} \cdot m^{-2} \cdot s^3 \cdot A^2$
electric capacitance	farad	F	$A \cdot s \cdot V^{-1} = kg^{-1} \cdot m^{-2} \cdot s^4 \cdot A^2$
inductance	henry	H	$V \cdot s \cdot A^{-1} = kg \cdot m^2 \cdot s^{-2} \cdot A^{-2}$
magnetic flux	weber	Wb	$V \cdot s = kg \cdot m^2 \cdot s^{-2} \cdot A^{-1}$
magnetic flux density	tesla	T	$Wb \cdot m^{-2} = kg \cdot s^{-2} \cdot A^{-1}$
magnetomotive force	ampere	A	—
luminous flux	lumen	lm	$cd \cdot sr$
illumination	lux	lx	$lm \cdot m^{-2} = cd \cdot sr \cdot m^{-2}$
radiation activity	becquerel	Bq	s^{-1}
radiation absorbed dose	gray	Gy	$J \cdot kg^{-1} = m^2 \cdot s^{-2}$

Metric and Imperial Units and Conversions (* = exact)

Column One	Equivalent	Column Two	To convert Col. 2 to Col. 1 Multiply by	To convert Col. 1 to Col. 2 Multiply by
Length				
inch (in)	—	centimetre (cm)	0·393 700 78	2·54*
foot (ft)	12 in	metre	3·280 840	0·304 8*
yard (yd)	3 ft	metre	1·093 61	0·914 4*
mile	1760 yd	kilometre (km)	0·621 371 1	1·609 344*
fathom	6 ft	metre	0·546 80	1·828 8*
chain	22 yd	metre	0·049 70	20·116 8*
UK nautical mile	6080 ft	kilometre	0·539 611 8	1·853 184*
International nautical mile	6076·1 ft	kilometre	0·539 956 8	1·852*
angstrom unit (Å)	10^{-10} m	nanometre	10	10^{-1}
Area				
square inch	—	square centimetre	0·155 00	6·451 6*
square foot	144 sq. in.	square metre	10·763 9	0·092 903*
square yard	9 sq. ft.	square metre	1·195 99	0·836 127*
acre	4840 sq. yd.	hectare (ha) ($10^4\ m^2$)	2·471 05	0·404 686*
square mile	640 acres	square kilometre	0·386 10	2·589 988*
Volume				
cubic inch	—	cubic centimetre	0·061 024	16·387 1*
cubic foot	1728 cu. in.	cubic metre	35·314 67	0·028 317*
cubic yard	27 cu. ft.	cubic metre	1·307 95	0·764 555*

Column One	Equivalent	Column Two	To convert Col. 2 to Col. 1 Multiply by	To convert Col. 1 to Col. 2 Multiply by
Capacity				
litre	100 centilitres	cubic centimetre or millilitre	0·001*	1000*
pint	4 gills	litre	1·759 753	0·568 261
UK gallon	8 pints or 277·4 in³	litre	0·219 969	4·546 092
barrel (for beer)	36 gallons	hectolitre	0·611 026	1·636 59
US gallon	0·832675 UK gallons	litre or dm³	0·264 172	3·785 412
US barrel (for petroleum)	42 US gallons	hectolitre	0·628 998	1·589 83
fluid ounce	0·05 pint	millilitre	0·035 195	28·413 074
Velocity				
feet per second (ft/s)	—	metres per second	3·280 840	0·304 8
miles per hour (m.p.h)	—	kilometres per hour	0·621 371	1·609 344
UK knot (1·00064 Int. knots)	nautical mile/hour	kilometres per hour	0·539 611 8	1·853 184
Acceleration				
foot per second per second (ft/s²)	—	metres per second per second (m/s²)	3·280 840	0·304 8*
Mass				
grain (gr)	a 1/480th of an oz troy	milligram (mg)	0·015 432 4	64·798 91
dram (dr)	27·3438 gr	gram	0·564 383	1·771 85
ounce (avoirdupois)	16 drams	gram	0·035 274 0	28·349 523 125
pound (avoirdupois)	16 ounces	kilogram	2·204 62*	0·453 592 37*
stone	14 pounds	kilogram	0·157 473 04	6·350 293 18*
quarter	28 pounds	kilogram	0·078 737 5	12·700 586 36*
hundredweight (cwt)	112 pounds	kilogram	0·019 684 1	50·802 345 44*
ton (long)	2240 pounds	tonne (= 1000 kg)	0·984 206 5	1·016 046 908 8

Note: A pound troy consists of 12 ounces troy each of 480 grains

Column One	Equivalent	Column Two	To convert Col. 2 to Col. 1	To convert Col. 1 to Col. 2
Density				
pounds per cubic inch	—	grams per cubic centimetre	0·036 127 2	27·679 9
pounds per cubic foot	—	kilograms per cubic metre	0·062 428 0	16·018 5
Force				
dyne (dyn)	10⁻⁵ newton	newton	10⁵	10⁻⁵
poundal (pdl)	—	newton	7·233 01	0·138 255
pound-force (lbf)	—	newton	0·224 809	4·448 22
tons-force	—	kilonewton (kN)	0·100 361	9·964 02
kilogram-force (kgf) (or kilopond)	—	newton	0·101 972	9·806 65
Energy (Work, Heat)				
erg	10⁻⁷ joule	joule	10⁷	10⁻⁷
horse-power (hp) (550 ft/lbf/s)	—	kilowatt (kW)	1·341 02	0·745 700
therm	—	mega joule (MJ)	0·009 478 17	105·506
kilowatt hour (kWh)	—	mega joule (MJ)	0·277 778	3·6
calorie (international)	—	joule	0·238 846*	4·186 8*
British thermal unit (Btu)	—	kilo-joule (kJ)	0·947 817	1·055 06
Pressure, Stress				
millibar (mbar or mb)	1000 dynes/cm²	Pa	0·01*	100*
standard atmosphere (atm)	760 torrs	kPa	0·009 869 2	101·325
pounds per square inch (psi)	—	Pa	0·000 145 038	6894·76
pounds per square inch (psi)	—	kilogram-force per cm²	14·223 3	0·070 307 0

Temperature

Degrees Celcius (Centigrade) converted to Degrees Fahrenheit
Multiply °C by 9/5 and add 32

Degrees C		Degrees F
37	=	98·6
50	=	122
100	=	212

Degrees Fahrenheit converted to Degrees Celcius (Centigrade)
Multiply °F by 5/9 after subtracting 32

Degrees F		Degrees C
−40	=	−40
32	=	0
59	=	15

Multiples and Sub-Multiples

In the metric system the following decimal multiples and sub-multiples are used:

Prefix	Symbol	British Equivalent	Factor
atto- (Danish *atten* = eighteen)	a	trillionth part (US quintillionth)	× 10⁻¹⁸
femto- (Danish *femten* = fifteen)	f	thousand billionth part (US quadrillionth)	× 10⁻¹⁵
pico- (L. *pico* = minuscule)	p	billionth part (US trillionth)	× 10⁻¹²
nano- (L. *nanus* = dwarf)	n	thousand millionth part (US billionth)	× 10⁻⁹
micro- (Gk. *mikros* = small)	μ	millionth part	× 10⁻⁶
milli- (L. *mille* = thousand)	m	thousandth part	× 10⁻³
centi- (L. *centum* = hundred)	c	hundredth part	× 10⁻²
deci- (L. *decimus* = tenth)	d	tenth part	× 10⁻¹
deca- (Gk. *deka* = ten)	da	tenfold	× 10
hecto- (Gk. *hekaton* = hundred)	h	hundredfold	× 10²
kilo- (Gk. *chilioi* = thousand)	k	thousandfold	× 10³
mega- (Gk. *megas* = large)	M	millionfold	× 10⁶
giga- (Gk. *gigas* = mighty)	G	thousand millionfold (US billion)	× 10⁹
tera- (Gk. *teras* = monster)	T	billionfold (US trillion)	× 10¹²
peta- (Gk. *penta* = five)	P	thousand billionfold (US quadrillion)	× 10¹⁵
exa- (Gk. *hexa* = six)	E	trillionfold (US quintillion)	× 10¹⁸

Weights and measures—miscellaneous information

Metric units

Length

10 ångström	=	1 nanometre
1000 nanometres	=	1 micrometre
1000 micrometres	=	1 millimetre
10 millimetres	=	1 centimetre
10 centimetres	=	1 decimetre
1000 millimetres	=	1 metre
100 centimetres	=	1 metre
10 decimetres	=	1 metre
10 metres	=	1 dekametre
10 dekametres	=	1 hectometre
10 hectometres	=	1 kilometre
1000 kilometres	=	1 megametre

Nautical

1852 metres	=	1 int. nautical mile

Area

100 sq millimetres	=	1 sq centimetre
100 sq centimetres	=	1 sq decimetre
100 sq decimetres	=	1 sq metre
100 sq metres	=	1 are
100 ares	=	1 hectare
100 hectares	=	1 sq kilometre

Weight (mass)

1000 milligrams	=	1 gram
10 grams	=	1 dekagram
10 dekagrams	=	1 hectogram
10 hectograms	=	1 kilogram
100 kilograms	=	1 quintal
1000 kilograms	=	1 tonne

Volume

1000 cu millimetres	=	1 cu centimetre
1000 cu centimetres	=	1 cu decimetre
1000 cu decimetres	=	1 cu metre
1000 cu metres	=	1 cu dekametre

Capacity

10 millilitres	=	1 centilitre
10 centilitres	=	1 decilitre
10 decilitres	=	1 litre
1 litre	=	1 cu decimetre
10 litres	=	1 dekalitre
10 dekalitres	=	1 hectolitre
10 hectolitres	=	1 kilolitre
1 kilolitre	=	1 cu metre

Length

12 inches	=	1 foot
3 feet	=	1 yard
$5\frac{1}{2}$ yards	=	1 rod, pole or perch
4 rods	=	1 chain
10 chains	=	1 furlong
5280 feet	=	1 mile
1760 yards	=	1 mile
8 furlongs	=	1 mile

Nautical

6 feet	=	1 fathom
100 fathoms	=	1 cable length
6080 feet	=	1 nautical mile

Water

1 litre		weighs 1 kilogram
1 cubic metre		weighs 1 tonne
1 UK gallon		weighs 10·022 lb
1 UK gallon salt water		weighs 10·3 lb

Imperial units

Speed

15 mph	=	22 feet per second
1 knot	=	1 nautical mph

Area

144 sq inches	=	1 sq foot
9 sq feet	=	1 sq yard
$304\frac{1}{4}$ sq yards	=	1 sq rod, pole or perch
40 sq rods	=	1 rood
4 roods	=	1 acre
4840 sq yards	=	1 acre
640 acres	=	1 sq mile

Weight (*avoirdupois*)

$437\frac{1}{2}$ grains	=	1 ounce
16 drams	=	1 ounce
16 ounces	=	1 pound
14 pounds	=	1 stone
28 pounds	=	1 quarter
4 quarters	=	1 hundredweight
20 hundredweights	=	1 ton

Volume

1728 cu inches	=	1 cu foot
27 cu feet	=	1 cu yard
5·8 cu feet	=	1 bulk barrel

Shipping

1 register ton	=	100 cubic feet

Capacity

8 fluid drachms	=	1 fluid ounce
5 fluid ounces	=	1 gill
4 gills	=	1 pint
2 pints	=	1 quart
4 quarts	=	1 gallon
2 gallons	=	1 peck
4 pecks	=	1 bushel
8 bushels	=	1 quarter
36 gallons	=	1 bulk barrel

Beer, wines and spirits

Proof spirit contains 57·03% pure alcohol by volume (at 50°F).

Proof strength in degrees = % of alcohol by volume (at 50°F) multiplied by 1·7535.

Beer

nip	=	$\frac{1}{4}$ pint
small	=	$\frac{1}{2}$ pint
large	=	1 pint
flagon	=	1 quart
anker	=	10 gallons
tun	=	216 gallons

Wines and spirits

tot (whisky)	=	$\frac{1}{6}$, $\frac{1}{5}$, $\frac{1}{4}$ or $\frac{1}{3}$ gill
noggin	=	1 gill
bottle	=	$1\frac{1}{3}$ pints

Champagne

2 bottles	=	1 magnum
4 bottles	=	1 jeroboam
20 bottles	=	1 nebuchadnezzar

Type sizes
Depth

$72\frac{1}{4}$ (approx)	=	1 inch
1 didot point	=	0·376 mm

Width
The normal unit is a pica em

1 pica em	=	12 points

Miscellaneous

Book sizes

Crown Quarto	=	246 × 189 mm
Crown Octavo	=	186 × 123 mm
Demy Quarto	=	276 × 219 mm
Demy Octavo	=	216 × 138 mm
Royal Quarto	=	312 × 237 mm
Royal Octavo	=	234 × 156 mm
A4	=	297 × 210 mm
A5	=	210 × 148 mm

Crops
UK (imperial) bushel of

wheat	=	60 lb
barley	=	50 lb
oats	=	39 lb
rye	=	56 lb
rice	=	45 lb
maize	=	56 lb
linseed	=	52 lb
potatoes	=	60 lb

US bushel:
as above except

barley	=	48 lb
linseed	=	56 lb
oats	=	32 lb

Bale (cotton):

US (net)	=	480 lb
Indian	=	392 lb

Energy

1000 British thermal units (Btu)	=	0·293 kW h
100 000 Btu	=	1 therm
1 UK horsepower	=	0·7457 kilowatt

Paper sizes

Large post	=	$16\frac{1}{2}$ × 21 in
		419·1 × 533·4 mm
Demy	=	$17\frac{1}{2}$ × 22 / in
		444·5 × 571·5 mm
Medium	=	18 × 23 in
		457·2 × 584·2 mm
Royal	=	20 × 25 in
		508 × 635 mm
Double crown	=	20 × 30 in
		508 × 762 mm

'A' Series (metric sizes)

A0	=	841 × 1189 mm
		$33\frac{1}{8}$ × $46\frac{3}{4}$ in
A1	=	594 × 841 mm
		$23\frac{3}{8}$ × $33\frac{1}{8}$
A2	=	420 × 594 mm
		$16\frac{1}{2}$ × $23\frac{3}{8}$ in
A3	=	297 × 420 mm
		$11\frac{3}{4}$ × $16\frac{1}{2}$ in
A4	=	210 × 297 mm
		$8\frac{1}{4}$ × $11\frac{3}{4}$ in
A5	=	148 × 210 mm
		$5\frac{7}{8}$ × $8\frac{1}{4}$ in

Petroleum

1 barrel	=	42 US gallons
	=	34·97 UK gallons
	=	0·159 cubic metre

Precious metals
24 carat implies pure metal.

1 metric carat	=	200 milligrams
1 troy (fine) ounce	=	480 grains

Millions and Billions

Some confusion has existed on the nomenclature of high numbers because of differing usage in various countries.

The position is that in the United Kingdom and in Germany it has been customary to advance by increments of a million thus:

million	$1\,000\,000(10^6)$
billion	$1\,000\,000\,000\,000(10^{12})$
trillion	$1\,000\,000\,000\,000\,000\,000(10^{18})$

In France and the United States it is the practice to advance in increments of a thousand thus:

million	$1\,000\,000(10^6)$
billion	$1\,000\,000\,000(10^9)$
trillion	$1\,000\,000\,000\,000(10^{12})$

Thus a US trillion is equal to a classic British billion.

Billion began to be used in Britain, in the US sense, as early as 1951 but the latest supplement to the Oxford English Dictionary, published in 1972, states that the older sense 'prevails'. In France one thousand million is described as a milliard which term is also permissibly used in Britain, as is the even more rare milliardth.

On 20 Dec. 1974 the then Prime Minister (J H Wilson) announced that HM Treasury would adhere to their practice of using the billion (made more prevalent by inflationary trends) in financial statistics in the sense of £1000 million. The word million has been in use since 1370 and a trillion was first mentioned c. 1484.

The higher degrees of numbers in use together with the date of their earliest usage and number of zeros are:

	First use	US	UK
quadrillion	(1674)	1×10^{15}	1×10^{24}
quintillion	(1674)	1×10^{18}	1×10^{30}
sextillion	(1690)	1×10^{21}	1×10^{36}
septillion	(1690)	1×10^{24}	1×10^{42}
octillion	(1690)	1×10^{27}	1×10^{48}
nonillion	(1828)	1×10^{30}	1×10^{54}
decillion	(1845)	1×10^{33}	1×10^{60}
vigintillion		1×10^{63}	1×10^{120}
centillion		1×10^{303}	1×10^{600}

International Clothing Sizes

The tables below should be used as approximate guides as actual sizes may vary according to manufacturers. **It is wise to check all measurements in centimetres.**

Ladies' coats and jackets

Belgium	38/34N	40/36N	42/38N	44/40N	46/42N	48/44N
France	38/34N	40/36N	42/38N	44/40N	46/42N	48/44N
Germany	34	36	38	40	42	44
Holland	34	36	38	40	42	44
Italy	36	38	40	42	44	46
Japan	7	9	11	13	15	17
Norway/Sweden/Denmark	36	38	40	42	44	46
Spain	40	42	44	46	48	50
UK	8/30	10/32	12/34	14/36	16/38	18/40
USA	6	8	10	12	14	16

Men's Suits and Overcoats

Belgium	46	48	50	52	54	56
France	46	48	50	52	54	56
Germany	46	48	50	52	54	56
Holland						
Italy	46	48	50	52	54	56
Norway/Sweden/Denmark	46	48	50	52	54	56
Spain	46	48	50	52	54	56
UK	46	48	50	52	54	56
USA	46	48	50	52	54	56

Men's Shirts

Belgium	36	37	38	39	40	41
France	36	37	38	39	40	41
Germany	36	37	38	39	40	41
Holland	36	37	38	39	40	41
Italy	36	37	38	39	40	41
Norway/Sweden/Denmark	36	37	38	39	40	41
Spain	36	37	38	39	40	41
UK	14	$14\frac{1}{2}$	15	$15\frac{1}{2}$	16	$16\frac{1}{2}$
USA	14	$14\frac{1}{2}$	15	$15\frac{1}{2}$	16	$16\frac{1}{2}$

Ladies' shoes

Belgium	36	37	38	39	40
France	36	37	38	39	40
Japan	22	23	24	25	
Norway/Sweden/Denmark	36	37	38	39	40
UK	3	4	5	6	7
USA	$4\frac{1}{2}$	$5\frac{1}{2}$	$6\frac{1}{2}$	$7\frac{1}{2}$	$8\frac{1}{2}$

Men's Shoes

Belgium	39	40	41	42	43
France	39	40	41	42	
Norway/Sweden/Denmark	40	41	42	43	44
UK	6	7	8	9	10
USA	$6\frac{1}{2}$	$7\frac{1}{2}$	$8\frac{1}{2}$	$9\frac{1}{2}$	$10\frac{1}{2}$

Mathematics

Glossary

abacus Apparatus used for counting.

acceleration Rate of change of velocity with time.

acute angle Angle of between 90° and 0°.

acute triangle All the interior angles are less than 90°.

addition To add together. One of the four fundamental operations of arithmetic.

algebra Study of the properties of numbers and quantities using letters and symbols.

alternate angles Angles on opposite sides of a transverse cutting two parallel lines, and on opposite sides of the parallel lines.

angle The amount of turn from one line to another.

annulus Area bounded by two concentric circles in a plane.

arc A straight or curved line joining two points; lines of a network. The arc of a circle is a specialized form of an arc.

area The size of a plane or curved surface.

arithmetic Calculations with definite numbers.

arithmetic mean The average.

arithmetic sequence Sequence of numbers in which consecutive terms are always separated by the same amount.

arrow diagrams These show the relation between sets of things.

arrowhead A quadrilateral with one concave angle and one line of symmetry.

associative An associative law states the irrelevance of the order in which operations are performed.

asymptote The asymptote of a curve is a straight line which approaches indefinitely close to the curve without ever meeting it.

average Usually taken to be the mean, but can be taken to be the median or mode.

axial symmetry Symmetry about an axis, i.e. the figure can be superimposed on itself by rotation or reflection in the line.

axiom Proposition presented without proof, in order to prove further propositions.

axis Reference lines on a graph, the x-axis in the horizontal plane, the y-axis in the vertical plane.

bar chart Information shown in a graphical form using columns (bars), the length of each column corresponding to the quantity it represents.

base Number of units grouped together in a number system before 1 occurs in the next position.

bearing The bearing of an object is the angle measured clockwise from north to the object.

binary system Number system using base two.

bisector A line cutting something into two equal parts.

brackets When three or more elements are combined by operations, brackets tell you which two elements you combine first.

chord A line joining two points on a circle.

circle The set of all points in a plane at a fixed distance (the radius) from a fixed point (the centre).

circular cone A cone whose base is a circle.

circumference The distance around a circle.

coefficient Coefficients are the numbers of each variable in a mathematical expression.

commutative An operation on a set is commutative when the result is unchanged by interchange of order of quantities.

complementary angles Two angles that add up to 90°.

complex number The sum of a real number and

the square root of a negative number.

concave Curved from the inside.

concentric Two circles with the same centre are concentric to one another.

cone A solid, usually having a circular base, which tapers to the top (the vertex).

congruent Having the same shape and size.

conic section Plane figure obtained as the intersection of a plane with a right circular cone.

constant An invariable quantity.

convex Curved from the outside.

coordinates A pair of numbers which describe a point's position on a graph with respect to two axes.

corresponding points Under a transformation, two points are corresponding if one is the object and the other its image.

cosecant (cosec) In a right-angled triangle, cosecant θ is the ratio of the hypotenuse to the side opposite the angle θ. It equals $1/\sin\theta$.

cosine (cos) In a right-angled triangle, cosine θ is the ratio of the side adjacent to the angle θ to the hypotenuse.

cotangent (cot) In a right-angled triangle, cotangent θ is the ratio of the side adjacent to the angle θ to the side opposite.

cube A regular solid with all its faces square and all its edges equal in length.

cuboid A solid having rectangles for all its faces.

cumulative frequency The sum of frequencies at or below a given value.

curve A geometrical structure derived from a straight line by a reversible transformation.

cylinder A prism with the shape of a circle along its length.

decimal fraction Fraction with a denominator of 10, 100, 1000, etc.

decimal system Number system using base 10.

degree Ninetieth part of a right angle.

deltoid Kite-shaped figure; a quadrilateral in which two pairs of neighbouring sides are equal.

denominator The bottom number in a fraction.

diagonal A straight line drawn from one vertex of a polygon or solid figure to another vertex.

diameter A chord which passes through the centre of a circle.

digit A single figure representing a number.

directed numbers Used to measure or count in two different directions.

distributive law This usually establishes a relation between addition and multiplication such that: $a(b + c) = ab + ac$

dividend The number being divided.

division The fourth fundamental operation of calculation; the inverse of multiplication.

divisor The number divided by.

domain The set of numbers mapped by a function.

ellipse The locus of points, the sum of whose distances from two fixed points (foci) is constant.

empty set A set with no elements.

equation A statement using the equals sign.

equilateral triangle A triangle with all three sides the same length.

equivalent fractions Fractions that can be cancelled to the same fraction.

Euler's formula For networks:
Nodes + Regions = Arcs + 2
For polyhedra:
Vertices + Faces = Edges + 2

even numbers Numbers that can be divided exactly by 2.

exponential function Function of the form:
$y = a^x$
a is a constant greater than zero and x is variable, either positive or negative.

face The flat side of a polyhedron.

factorial $n!$ (read as n factorial) is the product of the first n natural numbers:
$n! = 1 \times 2 \times 3 \ldots (n - 1) \times n$

factorize Formation of a product from a sum.

factors Those numbers which divide exactly into a number.

formula An equation showing the connection between related quantities.

fraction A number less than 1, represented as a denominator and a numerator.

frequency How many times an event has occurred.

frequency curve Graphical representation of distribution of accidental errors about an estimate of the unknown true value.

function Dependence of a quantity on one or more other variable quantities.

golden section A segment is divided in golden section if the ratio of the complete segment to the larger segment is equal to the ratio of the larger segment to the smaller segment.

gradient The gradient of a straight line is $\tan\theta$, where θ is the angle the line makes with the positive x-axis.

hemisphere Half a sphere.

highest common factor The largest integer which is a factor of two or more numbers.

histogram Frequency diagram in which the area of bars in a bar chart show the frequency, not the height of the bars.

horizontal At right angles to the vertical.

hyperbola The locus of two points for which the difference of their distance from two fixed points (the foci) is constant.

hypotenuse The side opposite the right angle in a right-angled triangle.

identical Exactly the same shape and size.

identical transformation A transformation in which all points coincide with their image points.

image The result when an object is transformed.

improper fraction Fraction in which the numerator is bigger than the denominator.

index form A number written as the power of another number.

indirect proof A proposition proved true by showing that its negation is false.

inequality A statement showing one quantity is not equal to another.

inflexion The point at which a curve changes from concave to convex.

integers The set of integers consists of the positive whole numbers, the negative whole numbers and zero.

interpolate Determination of an intermediary value of a function by means of a sequence of known values of the function.

intersect Curves and lines intersect if they touch or cross each other.

intersection The set of elements of two sets that contains only and all those elements that are in both sets.

inverse function See inverse mapping.

inverse mapping If a mapping f maps a point x on to its image y, the inverse mapping f^{-1} maps the point y back on to x.

irrational number A number that cannot be written as a fraction.

isometry A transformation in which all lengths are invariant.

isosceles triangle A triangle with two sides of equal length.

limit When the terms of an infinite sequence approach a definite value t such that, if we choose a quantity, we can always find a number A so that every term of the sequence after the Ath number differs from the definite value t by less than the selected small quantity, then the definite value t is said to be the limit of the sequence.

linear equation Equation of the first degree, containing an unknown raised at most to its first power.

locus Line or path of a set of points satisfying certain conditions.

logarithm The inverse of a power.

lowest common multiple The smallest number which contains two or more numbers as a factor.

mapping A relation in which there is only one image for each object.

matrix An array of coefficients of a system of linear equations in the shape of a rectangle.

mean The arithmetic mean of a set of numbers is the sum of those numbers divided by the size of the set. It is often called the average.

median That value in a set of numbers which

has an equal number of numbers greater and less than it.

member An element of a set.

method of least squares For a sequence of measurements, the sum of the squares of differences from a particular value is a minimum if that value is taken to be the arithmetic mean of the measurements.

mixed number A whole number with a fraction.

mode Most frequently occurring item in a sequence.

motif A shape that is repeated.

multiplication The third of the four fundamental calculating operations. It is the abbreviation of addition of equal summands.

natural numbers Counting numbers.

negative numbers Used to count in the opposite direction or sense to positive numbers. They allow subtraction to be performed without restriction.

net A plane shape which, when folded, yields a solid shape.

network A diagram of connected lines.

node The point at the beginning and end of every arc in a network.

nought The symbol that indicates zero.

null sequence A sequence whose limit is zero.

null set An empty set, with no members.

number A fundamental concept of mathematics; numerals, e.g. 1, 2, 3, etc., indicate numbers.

numerals Symbols used to represent numbers.

numerator The upper number in a fraction.

object The point or shape being transformed in a transformation.

obtuse angle An angle between 90° and 180°.

odd numbers Counting numbers that do not divide exactly by 2.

operation A method of combining elements in a set.

order (1) of a matrix. The size of the matrix.
(2) of a node. The number of arcs that meet at the node.

ordered pairs Pairs of numbers in which the order of the numbers in each pair is important. Coordinates are the most frequently encountered ordered pairs.

origin The point where the axes of a graph cross. It has the coordinates (0, 0).

parabola The locus of points equal distances from a fixed point and a fixed straight line.

parallel Two lines which lie in one and the same plane and do not intersect are parallel.

parallelogram A quadrilateral in which pairs of opposite sides are parallel.

Pascal's triangle An array of numbers, as follows:

```
              1
           1     1
        1     2     1
     1     3     3     1
  1     4     6     4     1
1     5    10    10     5     1
           etc.
```

Each number is the sum of the two numbers above it to the right and left. Each number is also equal to the sum of all the numbers in either diagonal, commencing with the number immediately above it to the left or right, Furthermore, each diagonal is an arithmetic sequence.

percentage A fraction with a denominator of 100.

perfect number A counting number which equals the sum of all its factors except itself.

perimeter The length of the boundary around the outside of a shape.

perpendicular At right angles. Not to be confused with vertical.

pi (π) The ratio of the circumference of a circle to its diameter. It is an irrational number; for day-to-day purposes it is approximated to either by 22/7 or 3·142.

pictogram Method of representing information using a motif.

pie chart Method of representing information in which a circle is divided into sectors such that the areas of the sectors represent the data.

plane One of the basic geometric elements of space. It has no thickness and extends forever in all directions in space. It is flat and thus needs at least three points to define it.

plane shape A shape that has all its points in one plane.

plane of symmetry A plane which divides a solid into two mirror images.

point The basic element of geometry. It has position but no magnitude.

polar coordinates Use of the distance from an origin and the angle from a fixed direction to establish the position of a point in a plane.

polygon A plane shape bounded by straight lines.

polyhedron A solid shape bounded by plane surfaces. These plane surfaces are all polygons.

polynomial Association of several expressions consisting of one term.

positive numbers Numbers greater than zero.

power A power is a product of equal factors, i.e. the result of multiplication using just one number.

prime number A number which has only two factors, itself and 1.

prism A polyhedron with the same shape along its length. It thus is bounded by parallelograms as lateral surfaces.

probability The measure of how likely an event is, indicated as a number between 0 and 1.

product The result of multiplying two or more numbers together.

proportion When corresponding pairs of two quantities are always in the same ratio they are in proportion.

pyramid A polyhedron with a polygon for its base and all the other faces meeting at a point called the apex.

Pythagoras' rule The square on the hypotenuse of a right-angled triangle is equal to the sum of the squares on the other two sides.

quadrant Rectangular coordinates in a plane are divided into four quadrants, each bounded by two mutually perpendicular coordinate axes.

quadratic equation An equation of the second degree, in which the unknown is at most raised to the second power, e.g.:
$$ax^2 + bx + c$$

quadrilateral A plane shape with four straight sides.

quotient The result of a division.

radius The distance from the centre of a circle to any point on the circumference.

ratio Comparison of two or more similar quantities, determined by the number of times one contains the others, integrally or fractionally.

rational integral Rational integral numbers are the integers.

rational number Numbers which can be written as a fraction $\frac{p}{q}$, where p and q are both integers.

real numbers All numbers that can be written as decimals.

reciprocal The multiplicative inverse of a number, e.g. the inverse of x is $\frac{1}{x}$.

rectangle A parallelogram with four right angles.

recurring decimal A decimal with digit or group of digits that is repeated endlessly.

re-entrant A polygon in which one of the angles is reflex.

reflex angle An angle between $180°$ and $360°$.

regular polygon A polygon with all its sides the same length and all its angles the same.

rhombus A parallelogram with four sides of equal length.

right angle An angle of $90°$.

right-angled triangle A triangle with one of its interior angles equal to $90°$.

root The nth root of a number x is the number y whose nth power equals x.

rotation A transformation in which every point turns through the same angle about the same centre.

rotational symmetry If every image point is mapped on to the object shape after a rotation, then the shape has rotational symmetry. The order of rotational symmetry is the number of possible rotations a shape can be given that yield rotational symmetry.

rounding Rounding off of decimal fractions is the omission, for convenience, of some of the non-zero digits.

scalar A pure numerical quantity, with no direction associated with it.

scalene triangle A triangle whose sides are all of different lengths.

secant (1) A straight line which intersects a circle at two points.
(2) sec. Sec θ is the ratio of hypotenuse to adjacent side to angle θ in a right-angled triangle. It is the reciprocal of $\cos \theta$.

sector A shape bounded by two radii of a circle and an arc of the circle.

segment A shape bounded by an arc of a circle and a chord of the circle.

semicircle A shape bounded by a diameter of a circle and the arc of the circle joining the two endpoints of the diameter.

set A collection of definite and distinguishable objects, either conceptual or concrete.

shear A transformation in which all points slide parallel to a fixed line or plane. The area of a sheared plane figure, or volume of a sheared solid shape, remains unchanged.

sign Signs used before numbers, $+$ indicating positive numbers and $-$ indicating negative numbers. (This use of $+$ and $-$ is *not* the same as when they are used to indicate operations.)

similar The same shape.

simultaneous equations Two equations that have the same solution.

sine (sin) Sin θ is the ratio of the opposite side to angle θ to the hypotenuse in a right-angled triangle.

sine rule If A, B and C are the sides of triangle and a, b and c are the angles, then $A:B:C = \sin a : \sin b : \sin c$. This can be used to solve a triangle if one side, the opposite angle and a further side or angle are known.

skew Two lines are skew to one another if they are neither parallel nor intersect.

solid A part of space enclosed by surfaces, either plane or curved.

sphere A set of points in space which are all the same distance (radius) from a fixed point (the centre).

square A quadrilateral with four equal sides and four right angles.

square numbers Squares of the natural numbers.

square root The square root of a number x is the number y whose square (2nd power) equals x, i.e. in this example:
$$\sqrt{x} = y$$

standard deviation The average measure of a number of errors or deviations, i.e. square root of the mean of the squares of deviations.

straight line One of the basic elements of plane geometry. It is uniquely determined by two points.

subset If all the elements of set M are also elements of set N, then set M is a subset of set N.

subtraction The second fundamental operation of arithmetic, meaning to take away. To make subtraction universally possible, negative numbers are necessary.

surd An irrational number.

tangent (1) A straight line with a point in common with a given curve. At the point the curve and the line have the same slope.
(2) tan. Tan θ is the ratio of the side opposite angle θ to the side adjacent to θ in a right-angled triangle.

tessellation Covering a plane with polygons to form a regular pattern.

topology The study of what happens to a shape if it is pulled and stretched as if on a sheet of elastic.

transformation A transformation is a rule which links a point in space with one or more other points in the same space.

translation A transformation in which a shape slides without turning.

trapezium A quadrilateral with one pair of sides parallel.

triangle Three points in a plane joined in pairs by straight lines.

trigonometry The calculation of elements of a triangle using the angular functions.

unicursal A curve drawn without going over the same arc twice and with the start and finish joined.

universal set All the elements being considered.

variable A quantity whose value can change.

vector A quantity with direction associated with it.

velocity Speed in a particular direction. Velocity is thus a vector.

Venn diagram A diagram used to show sets. The universal set is represented by a rectangle. Each set within it is represented by a circle.

vertex A corner of a shape or solid; a point where sides meet.

vertical The direction passing through the earth's centre.

volume The amount of space a solid occupies.

whole numbers The counting numbers and zero.

zero (1) The number which can be added to or subtracted from another number without the other number being altered.
(2) Used to show an empty place in a number with more than one digit.

Mathematical symbols

$=$	equal to
$\neq$	not equal to
$\equiv$	identically equal to; congruent
$>$	greater than
$<$	less than
$\not>$	not greater than
$\not<$	not less than
$\geq$	equal to or greater than
$\leq$	equal to or less than
$\simeq$	approximately equal to
$+$	plus
$-$	minus
$\pm$	plus or minus
$\times$	multiplication (times)
$\div$	divided by
$()[]\{\}$	brackets, square brackets, enveloping brackets
$\|\|$	parallel
$\#$	not parallel
$\#$	numbers to follow (USA)
$\%$	per cent(um) (hundred)
$\%_0$	per mille (thousand)
$\propto$	varies with
∞	infinity
$r!$ or $\underline{\lfloor r}$	factorial r
$\sqrt{}$	square root
$\sqrt[n]{}$	nth root
r^n	r to the power n
$\triangle$	triangle, finite difference or increment
$\sim$	difference
Σ	summation
$\int$	integration sign
$° ' ''$	degree, minute, second ($1° = 60'$, $1' = 60''$)
$\rightarrow$	appropriate limit of; tends to
$\therefore$	therefore
$\because$	because
$\Rightarrow$	implies that
$\Leftarrow$	is implied by
$\Leftrightarrow$	is equivalent to

MENSURATION

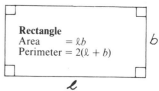

Rectangle
Area $= \ell b$
Perimeter $= 2(\ell + b)$

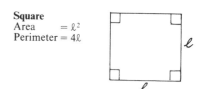

Square
Area $= \ell^2$
Perimeter $= 4\ell$

Parallelogram
Area $= bh$
Perimeter $= 2(a + b)$

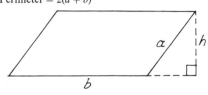

Triangle
Area $= \frac{1}{2} \cdot bh$
or $= \sqrt{[s(s - a)(s - b)(s - c)]}$
where $s = \dfrac{a + b + c}{2}$

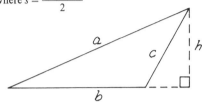

Trapezium
Area $= \frac{1}{2}(a + b)h$
i.e. $= \frac{1}{2}$ (sum of the parallel sides)
        $\times$ perp. distance between them

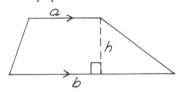

Note: "Square metres" and "Metres square" are not equivalent, e.g. 6 sq. m can refer to any shape, but 6 metres square only to a square. For this reason 'sq. m' or 'sq. km' and 'cu. m' or 'cu. cm' are preferred by some writers to m^2, km^2, m^3 and cm^3.

Rhombus
Area $= \frac{1}{2}(2a)(2b)$
i.e. $= \frac{1}{2}$ (product of the diagonals)
Perimeter $= 4\ell$

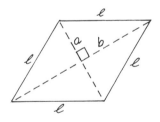

Circle
Circumference $= 2\pi r$ or πd
Area $= \pi r^2$

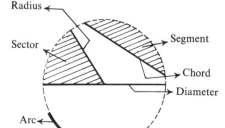

Radius
Sector
Segment
Chord
Diameter
Arc

Ring
Area $= \pi(R^2 - r^2)$
      $= \pi(R - r)(R + r)$

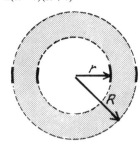

Rectangular block
Surface Area $= 2(\ell b + bh + h\ell)$
Volume $= \ell bh$
i.e. $=$ Area of the base $\times$ height
The volume of any solid whose sides are perpendicular to its base (or cross-section) and whose ends are parallel is always equal to the Area of the base $\times$ perpendicular height

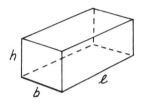

Pyramid
The volume of any pyramid (on a base of any shape) is always $= \frac{1}{3}$ (Volume of the surrounding solid)
Thus, the volume of a pyramid on a rectangular base $= \frac{1}{3}(\ell bh)$

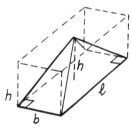

The volume of a pyramid within a triangular prism
$= \frac{1}{3}$ (Area of the triangular base $\times$ height)

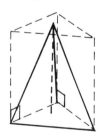

Cylinder
Curved Surface Area (C.S.A.) $= 2\pi rh$
Total Surface Area (T.S.A.) $= 2\pi r(h + r)$
Volume (for a closed cylinder) $= \pi r^2 h$

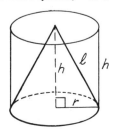

Cone
Curved Surface Area (C.S.A.) $= \pi rl$
where $l =$ slant height
Total Surface Area $= \pi r (l + r)$
Volume
   $= \frac{1}{3}$ (Volume of the surrounding cylinder)
   $= \frac{1}{3}\pi r^2 h$

Sphere
Surface Area $= 4\pi r^2$
Volume $= \frac{4}{3}\pi r^3$

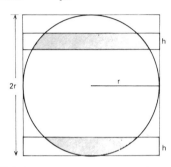

A little-known and interesting fact about the sphere is that the area of any zone of its curved surface lying between two parallel planes is exactly equal to the curved surface of the surrounding cylinder between the same two planes.

This applies to any belt of the sphere, or to a cap or to the whole sphere. It thus makes the calculation of what might appear to be a difficult area quite simple.
Thus, either shaded area of the sphere is equal to the curved surface area of a cylinder of radius a and height h, the height of the zone, i.e.
   $A = 2\pi rh$ and for the whole sphere
   $A = 2\pi r2r$
      $= 4\pi r^2$
which we already know to be the surface area of a sphere.

Ellipse
Area $= \pi ab$

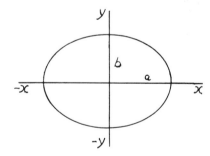

Parabola
Shaded area in the diagram $= \frac{1}{3}x_1 y_1$
i.e. one-third of the given rectangle

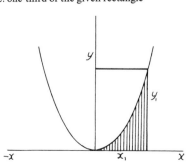

Area under any curve

(1) Trapezoidal Rule

$$\text{Area} = \left[\frac{y_1 + y_7}{2} + y_2 + y_3 + y_4 + y_5 + y_6\right]w$$

i.e. = [half the sum of the first and last ordinates + all the others]
    × the width of a strip

The area may be divided into any number of equal strips.

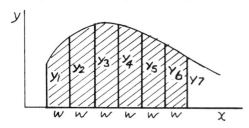

(2) Simpson's Rule

$$\text{Area} = \frac{w}{3}\left[y_1 + y_7 + 4(y_2 + y_4 + y_6) + 2(y_3 + y_5)\right]$$

i.e. = one-third of the width of a strip, multiplied by the sum of
    the first and last ordinates, + 4 times the even ordinates, + twice
    the remaining odd ordinates.

For this rule the area must be divided into an *even* number of strips
of equal width.

(3) Both the above rules give very good approximations, but the exact area
    is found by calculus provided the equation of the curve is known. Then:

$$\text{Area} = \int_{x_1}^{x_2} y\,dx$$

Important curves (conic sections, so called because they can all be obtained
by the intersection of a plane with a complete, or 'double' cone).

Circle
    General equation (centre at $-g, -f$)
    $x^2 + y^2 + 2gx + 2fy + c = 0$
    Basic equation (centre at the origin)
    $x^2 + y^2 = r^2$

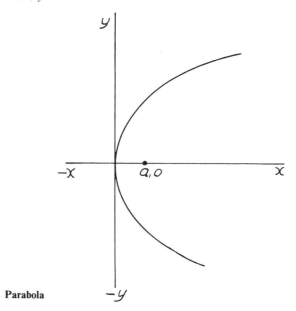

Parabola

Ellipse (*see previous page*)
    Basic equation (centre at the origin)
    $$\frac{x^2}{a^2} + \frac{y^2}{b^2} = 1$$

Parabola
    Basic equation [symmetrical about the *x*-axis, focus at $(a, 0)$]
    $$y^2 = 4ax$$

Hyperbola
    Basic equation (centre at the origin)
    $$\frac{x^2}{a^2} - \frac{y^2}{b^2} = 1$$

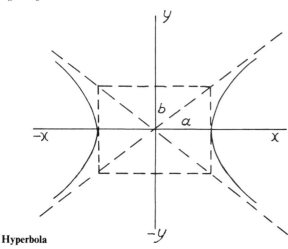

Hyperbola

Rectangular hyperbola (equal axes)
$x^2 - y^2 = a^2$

Rectangular hyperbola (referred to the axes of coordinates as asymptotes)
$xy = k^2$

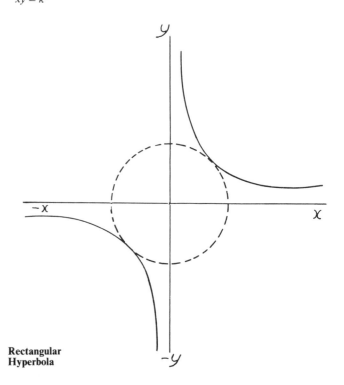

**Rectangular
Hyperbola**

Basic Algebra

$$x^a \times x^b = x^{a+b}$$
$$\frac{x^a}{x^b} = x^{a-b}$$
$$(x^a)^b \text{ or } (x^b)^a = x^{ab}$$
$$x^{-a} = \frac{1}{x^a}$$
$$x^{1/n} = \sqrt[n]{x}$$

Important identities
$$(x \pm y)^2 \equiv x^2 \pm 2xy + y^2$$
$$[A]^2 - [B]^2 \equiv (A - B)(A + B)$$
A difference of two squares
$$(x \pm y)^3 \equiv x^3 \pm 3x^2y + 3xy^2 \pm y^3$$
$$[A]^3 \pm [B]^3 \equiv (A \pm B)(A^2 \mp AB + B^2)$$
The sum or difference of two cubes

The solutions of the standard quadratic equation
$$ax^2 + bx + c = 0$$
are given by
$$x = \frac{-b \pm \sqrt{b^2 - 4ac}}{2a}$$

If b^2 is $> 4ac$ the roots are real and different
$\quad b^2$ is $= 4ac$ the roots are real and equal
$\quad b^2$ is $< 4ac$ the roots are imaginary (complex)
$\quad b$ is $= 0$ and c is $-ve$, the roots are real, equal and opposite
$\quad b$ is $= 0$ and c is $+ve$, the roots are imaginary (no real part)

If the roots are α and β, then $\alpha + \beta = -\dfrac{b}{a}$ and $\alpha\beta = \dfrac{c}{a}$

Logarithms
If N $= a^x$
then $\text{Log}_a N = x$ (i.e. Log N to the base 'a' $= x$)

$\text{Log } NM = \text{Log } N + \text{Log } M$ and $\text{Log}\dfrac{N}{M} = \text{Log } N - \text{Log } M$

To change the base of a logarithm:

$$\text{Log}_b N = \frac{\text{Log}_a N}{\text{Log}_a b} \quad \text{or} \quad \text{Log}_a N \times \text{Log}_b a$$

$$\text{Log } N^p = p \text{ Log } N \qquad \text{Log}_a b = \frac{1}{\text{Log}_b a}$$

$$\text{Log } \sqrt[n]{N} = \frac{1}{n} \text{Log } N$$

Basic Trigonometry

$$\text{Sin } C = \frac{AB}{AC}$$

$$\text{Cos } C = \frac{BC}{AC}$$

$$\text{Tan } C = \frac{AB}{BC}$$

$$\text{Cosec } \theta = \frac{1}{\text{Sin } \theta}$$

$$\text{Sec } \theta = \frac{1}{\text{Cos } \theta}$$

$$\text{Cot } \theta = \frac{1}{\text{Tan } \theta}$$

Trigonometrical equivalents of Pythagoras' Theorem (q.v.)
$$\text{Sin}^2 \theta + \text{Cos}^2 \theta = 1 \quad \text{Sec}^2\theta = 1 + \text{Tan}^2\theta \quad \text{Cosec}^2\theta = 1 + \text{Cot}^2\theta$$

Formulae for the solution of non-right-angled triangles:

Sine Rule
Given at least one side and the facing angle:
$$\frac{a}{\text{Sin } A} = \frac{b}{\text{Sin } B} = \frac{c}{\text{Sin } C} \quad (=2R)$$
where $R =$ radius of the circumcircle
Area of a triangle $= \frac{1}{2} ab \text{ Sin } C$

Cosine Rules
(1) Given two sides and the included angle (b, c and the angle A)
$$a^2 = b^2 + c^2 - 2bc \text{ Cos } A$$
(2) Given three sides
$$\text{Cos } A = \frac{b^2 + c^2 - a^2}{2bc}$$

Sines, cosines and tangents of angles greater than $90°$

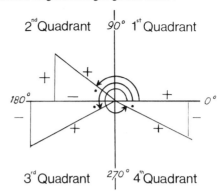

2nd quadrant
$90° < \theta < 180°$
$\text{Sin } \theta = \text{Sin } (180° - \theta)$
$\text{Cos } \theta = -\text{Cos } (180° - \theta)$
$\text{Tan } \theta = -\text{Tan } (180° - \theta)$

3rd quadrant
$180° < \theta < 270°$
$\text{Sin } \theta = -\text{Sin } (\theta - 180°)$
$\text{Cos } \theta = -\text{Cos } (\theta - 180°)$
$\text{Tan } \theta = \text{Tan } (\theta - 180°)$

4th quadrant
$270° < \theta < 360°$
$\text{Sin } \theta = -\text{Sin } (360° - \theta)$
$\text{Cos } \theta = \text{Cos } (360° - \theta)$
$\text{Tan } \theta = -\text{Tan } (360° - \theta)$

Radian measure
A radian is the angle subtended at the centre of a circle by a length of arc equal to the radius. Thus
$$1 \text{ radian} = \frac{180}{\pi} \text{ degrees}$$
or approx. $57.3°$
π radians $= 180°$

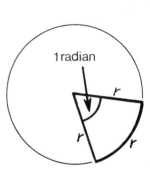

Length of an arc of a circle is given by:

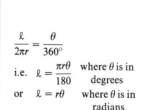

$$\frac{\ell}{2\pi r} = \frac{\theta}{360°}$$

i.e. $\ell = \dfrac{\pi r \theta}{180}$ where θ is in degrees

or $\ell = r\theta$ where θ is in radians

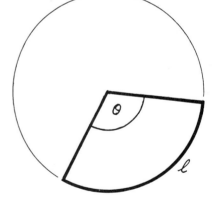

Area of the sector of a circle is given by:

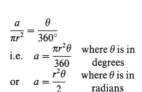

$$\frac{a}{\pi r^2} = \frac{\theta}{360°}$$

i.e. $a = \dfrac{\pi r^2 \theta}{360}$ where θ is in degrees

or $a = \dfrac{r^2 \theta}{2}$ where θ is in radians

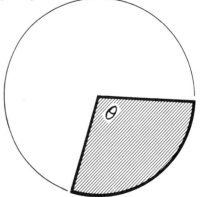

Pythagoras' Theorem

In the triangle ABC right-angled at B

$$AC^2 = AB^2 + BC^2$$

Four useful sets of whole-number values which fit the theorem are:

3, 4, 5   5, 12, 13
8, 15, 17   and 7, 24, 25

Such whole-number sets are sometimes called 'Pythagorean Triples'.

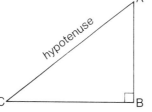

In words the theorem states that the area of the square drawn on the hypotenuse of a right-angled triangle is equal to the sum of the areas of the squares drawn on the other two sides.

Percentages

(1) $x\%$ of a number $(N) = \dfrac{x}{100} \times N$

(2) To find what percentage a quantity A is of a quantity B

$$\% = \frac{A}{B} \times 100$$

(3) To find the percentage increase or decrease of a quantity

$$\% \begin{cases} \text{Increase} \\ \text{Decrease} \end{cases} = \frac{\substack{\text{Actual increase} \\ \text{or decrease}}}{\text{Original amount}} \times 100$$

(4) To find the percentage profit or loss

$$\% \begin{cases} \text{Profit} \\ \text{Loss} \end{cases} = \frac{\substack{\text{Actual profit} \\ \text{or loss}}}{\text{Cost price}} \times 100$$

(5) To find 100% given that $x\% = N$

$$100\% = \frac{N}{x} \times 100$$

Note that percentages may not be added or subtracted unless they are percentages of the same quantity. Thus successive depreciations of 10% and 15% are not equivalent to a single depreciation of 25%.

Interest

Simple Interest (principal remains constant) $= \dfrac{PRT}{100}$

where P = principal (sum invested)
          R = rate $\%$ per annum
          T = time in years

Compound Interest (interest added to the principal each year)
$A = PR^n$
where A = Amount (i.e. Principal + Interest)

$R = 1 + \dfrac{r}{100}$ where r = rate $\%$ p.a.

n = number of years

Polygons (many-sided figures)

Sum of the interior angles $= (2n - 4) \times 90°$ where n = number of sides.

Each interior angle of a regular polygon $= \dfrac{(2n - 4) \times 90°}{n}$

$$\text{or} = 180° - \frac{360°}{n}$$

Sum of the exterior angles of any polygon $= 360°$, regardless of the number of sides.

Some important polygons

Triangle	3 sides	Octagon	8 sides
Quadrilateral	4 sides	Nonagon	9 sides
Pentagon	5 sides	Decagon	10 sides
Hexagon	6 sides	Dodecagon	12 sides
Heptagon	7 sides		

The area of any regular polygon of side 'a' $= \frac{1}{4} na^2 \mathrm{Cot}\, \dfrac{180°}{n}$

where n = the number of sides

The Regular Solids (Polyhedra)

There are 5 principal regular solids
The Tetrahedron (triangular pyramid)   4 faces

The Cube	6 faces
The Octahedron	8 faces
The Dodecahedron	12 faces
The Icosahedron	20 faces

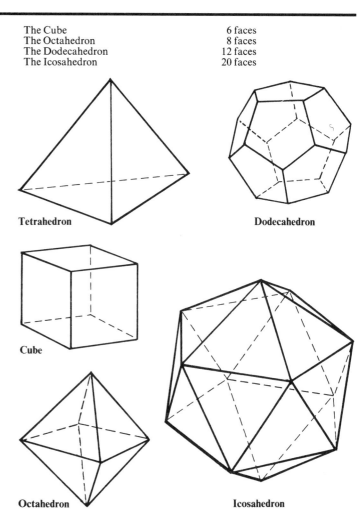

Tetrahedron   **Dodecahedron**

Cube

Octahedron   **Icosahedron**

In addition there are 4 much more complicated regular solids with star faces or vertices called the Kepler-Poinsot Polyhedra. They are

The Small Stellated Decahedron   The Great Dodecahedron
The Great Stellated Dodecahedron   The Great Icosahedron

The mathematician Euler made an interesting discovery about the relationship between the number of faces (F), vertices (V) and edges (E) of polyhedra. As far as is known, the equation $F + V - E = 2$ is true for all polyhedra except the two stellated ones mentioned above.

Furthermore, the same relationship is true for an area divided into any number of regions (R) by boundaries or arcs (A) which join at nodes (N).

Then $R + N - A = 2$

For the area shown,
$R = 8$ (the surrounding space
           counts as a region)
$N = 12 \quad A = 18$
Thus $R + N - A$
$= 8 + 12 - 18$
$= 2$

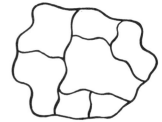

Incidentally, for such a region, or indeed any map, no more than 4 colours are necessary so that no two adjoining regions have the same colour.

NETWORKS
A series of nodes joined by arcs is called a network. A node is odd or even according to the number of arcs which are drawn from it. The network may represent a road or railway system, an electricity grid and so on. Such a system will be traversable (i.e. can be drawn without covering any arc twice or taking the pencil off the paper) if there are not more than 2 odd nodes. In which case the route must begin and end at an odd node. Here are two simplified networks, one of which is traversable and one is not. The latter was used by Euler to solve the famous Konigsberg Bridge problem.

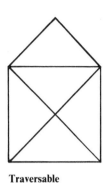

Traversable

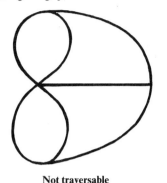

Not traversable

MATRICES
A matrix is an array of numbers, of rectangular shape, which presents information in a concise form. Matrices serve many purposes, and according to the circumstances they may be multiplied or added or subtracted.

Two matrices may be multiplied if there are the same number of ROWS in the second matrix as there are COLUMNS in the first, but they may only be added or subtracted if they have the same number of rows and columns. A 2×3 matrix is one with 2 rows and 3 columns. Thus a 2×3 matrix may be multiplied by a 3×4 or a 3×2 or a $3 \times n$ matrix where n is any number.

If $A = \begin{pmatrix} a & b \\ c & d \end{pmatrix}$ and $B = \begin{pmatrix} p & q \\ r & s \end{pmatrix}$

Then, $AB = \begin{pmatrix} a & b \\ c & d \end{pmatrix}\begin{pmatrix} p & q \\ r & s \end{pmatrix}$

$= \begin{pmatrix} ap + br & aq + bs \\ cp + dr & cq + ds \end{pmatrix}$

$A + B = \begin{pmatrix} a & b \\ c & d \end{pmatrix} + \begin{pmatrix} p & q \\ r & s \end{pmatrix}$

$= \begin{pmatrix} a + p & b + q \\ c + r & d + s \end{pmatrix}$

The Transformation Matrices change the position or shape of a geometrical figure, and sometimes both.
The following are the principal transformation matrices:

(1) Reflection in the x-axis $\begin{pmatrix} 1 & 0 \\ 0 & -1 \end{pmatrix}$

(2) Reflection in the y axis $\begin{pmatrix} -1 & 0 \\ 0 & 1 \end{pmatrix}$

(3) Reflection in the line $y = x$ $\begin{pmatrix} 0 & 1 \\ 1 & 0 \end{pmatrix}$

(4) Reflection in the line $y = -x$ $\begin{pmatrix} 0 & -1 \\ -1 & 0 \end{pmatrix}$

(5) Rotation through $90°$ about the origin in a $+ve$ (anticlockwise) direction $\begin{pmatrix} 0 & -1 \\ 1 & 0 \end{pmatrix}$

(6) Rotation through $180°$ ($+ve$ or $-ve$) $\begin{pmatrix} -1 & 0 \\ 0 & -1 \end{pmatrix}$

(7) $+ve$ rotation of $270°$ ($-ve$ rotation of $90°$) $\begin{pmatrix} 0 & 1 \\ -1 & 0 \end{pmatrix}$

(8) $+ve$ rotation about the origin through an angle θ $\begin{pmatrix} \cos\theta & -\sin\theta \\ \sin\theta & \cos\theta \end{pmatrix}$

(9) The *identity matrix* $\begin{pmatrix} 1 & 0 \\ 0 & 1 \end{pmatrix}$ leaves the elements of the multiplied matrix unchanged.

The following matrices change the shape of the figure.

(10) An enlargement, factor E $\begin{pmatrix} E & 0 \\ 0 & E \end{pmatrix}$ (e.g. if $E = 3$ the figure will have its linear dimensions trebled)

(11) A stretch, parallel to the x-axis, factor S $\begin{pmatrix} S & 0 \\ 0 & 1 \end{pmatrix}$

(12) A stretch, parallel to the y-axis, factor S $\begin{pmatrix} 1 & 0 \\ 0 & S \end{pmatrix}$

(13) A two-way stretch, parallel to the axes, factors S_1 and S_2 $\begin{pmatrix} S_1 & 0 \\ 0 & S_2 \end{pmatrix}$

(14) A shear, parallel to the x-axis $\begin{pmatrix} 1 & S \\ 0 & 1 \end{pmatrix}$

(15) A shear, parallel to the y-axis $\begin{pmatrix} 1 & 0 \\ S & 1 \end{pmatrix}$

The inverse of matrix A above (denoted by A^{-1}) is
$$\frac{1}{(ad - bc)}\begin{pmatrix} d & -b \\ -c & a \end{pmatrix}$$
The expression $(ad - bc)$ is called the determinant of the matrix

The value of the determinant of a matrix represents the ratio by which the area of the original figure has been changed. If the determinant is zero, all the points will be moved to lie on a line, and the matrix is said to be 'singular'.
If a matrix is multiplied by its inverse the result is the identity matrix.
A transformation which does not change either the shape or the size of a figure is called an isometric transformation.

NUMBER BASES
Our familiar denary system of calculating undoubtedly arose because we have 5 'digits' on each hand. Had we been created with 4 instead, we should have been just as happily working in the Octal scale. A denary number may be easily converted to any other base simply by repeated division by the new base, the remainders being recorded at each step, thus:
```
8)543₁₀
8)67 r 7
8)8  r 3
  1  r 0
```
Reading from the bottom up, 543_{10} is equivalent to 1037_8 (read 'one nought three seven base eight').

To convert a number in any other base into base 10, however, each digit must be given its appropriate place-value in the given base.

Thus, 1037_8
$= 1 \times 8^3 + 0 \times 8^2 + 3 \times 8^1 + 7$
$= 512 \quad + \quad 0 \quad + \quad 24 \quad + 7$
$= 543_{10}$

Base 2 or the binary scale is the most important non-denary base since it uses only the digits 0 and 1, and these can easily be related to the 'off' and 'on' of an electrical impulse and form the basis for the operation of electronic calculators and computers.

As before, a number may be converted to base 2 by repeated division.
Thus, to convert 217_{10}
```
2)217
2)108 r 1
2)54 r 0
2)27 r 0      i.e.    217₁₀ = 11011001₂
2)13 r 1
2) 6 r 1
2) 3 r 0
   1 r 1
```

The reverse process will be:
11011001_2
$= 1 \times 2^7 + 1 \times 2^6 + 0 \times 2^5 + 1 \times 2^4 + 1 \times 2^3$
$\quad + 0 \times 2^2 + 0 \times 2^1 + 1$
$= 128 + 64 + 0 + 16 + 8 + 0 + 0 + 1$
$= 217_{10}$

A denary-binary conversion table reveals some interesting points about binary numbers. Note the repetitive patterns in the columns of the successive numbers. Since odd numbers always end in 1 while even numbers end in 0, a number is doubled simply by adding a 0 (in the same way that a denary number is multiplied by 10 by adding a nought), and divided by 2, where possible, by removing a terminal 0. Denary numbers which are powers of 2 have a binary equivalent consisting of a 1 followed by the same number of zeros as the appropriate power of 2.

Denary	Binary		Denary fractions are rendered as negative powers of 2.
1	1		
2 (2^1)	10		
3	11		
4 (2^2)	100	Denary	Binary
5	101	0·5 (2^{-1})	0·1
6	110	0·25 (2^{-2})	0·01
7	111	0·125 (2^{-3})	0·001
8 (2^3)	1000	0·0625 (2^{-4})	0·0001
9	1001	0·03125 (2^{-5})	0·00001
10	1010	0·015625 (2^{-6})	0·000001

Denary	Binary
11	1011
12	1100
13	1101
14	1110
15	1111
16 (2^4)	10000

Thus, to convert a 'bicimal' to a decimal,

$$0 \cdot 1101_2 = 0.5 + 0.25 + 0 + 0.0625$$
$$= 0.8125$$

Converting from a decimal to a bicimal requires repeated *multiplication* of the *decimal part only* at each stage, the result being given by the whole-number parts read from the top. Thus, to convert 0·3 to a bicimal we proceed as follows:

0.3×2
$\overline{\textbf{0}\cdot6 \times 2}$
$\textbf{1}\cdot2 \times 2$
$\textbf{0}\cdot4 \times 4$
$\textbf{0}\cdot8 \times 2$
$\textbf{1}\cdot6 \times 2$
$\textbf{1}\cdot2$ and so on.

Reading the whole-numbers from the top we have: 0·010011. Clearly this could go on until we have the required number of bicimal places or the process comes to a stop.

The check shows that we have only an approximate equivalence.
$$0 \cdot 010011_2$$
$$= 0 + 0.25 + 0 + 0 + 0.03125 + 0.015625$$
$$= 0.296875_{10}$$

Some Important Series

Arithmetic progression (AP)
$$a, \quad a+d, \quad a+2d, \quad a+3d \ldots [a+(n-1)d]$$

Sum to n terms $= \dfrac{n}{2}[2a+(n-1)d]$

or $\qquad = \dfrac{n}{2}(a+l)$ where l = last term

Geometric series (GP)
$$a, \quad ar, \quad ar^2, \quad ar^3 \ldots ar^{n-1}$$

Sum to n terms $= a\dfrac{(1-r^n)}{1-r}$ if $r < 1$, or $\dfrac{a(r^n-1)}{r-1}$ if $r > 1$

When $r < 1$, the sum to infinity $S_\infty = \dfrac{a}{1-r}$

The sum of the first n natural (counting) numbers

$1 + 2 + 3 + 4 + \cdots n$ (i.e. an AP in which $a = 1$ and $d = 1$) $= \dfrac{n}{2}(n+1)$

The sum of the squares of the first n natural numbers

$$1^2 + 2^2 + 3^2 + 4^2 \ldots n^2 = \dfrac{n}{6}(n+1)(2n+1)$$

The sum of the cubes of the first n natural numbers

$$1^3 + 2^3 + 3^3 + 4^3 \ldots n^3 = \left[\dfrac{n}{2}(n+1)\right]^2$$

i.e. the square of the sum of the first n natural numbers.
The sum of the first n odd numbers
$1 + 3 + 5 + 7 \ldots$ to n terms $= n^2$
i.e. the square of the numbers of numbers.
The sum of the first n even numbers
$2 + 4 + 6 + 8 \ldots$ to n terms $= n(n+1)$
i.e. twice the sum of an equal number of natural numbers.

Factorial n If a number is multiplied by all the successive numbers between it and 1, this is called Factorial n, and is denoted by $\underline{n}$ or $n!$ Thus:
$$\underline{6} = 6.5.4.3.2.1$$
$$= 720$$

Exponential series
$$e^x = 1 + x + \dfrac{x^2}{\underline{2}} + \dfrac{x^3}{\underline{3}} + \dfrac{x^4}{\underline{4}} + \cdots \dfrac{x^n}{\underline{n}} + \cdots \infty \text{ for all values of } x$$

Hence, when $x = 1$
$$e = 1 + 1 + \dfrac{1}{\underline{2}} + \dfrac{1}{\underline{3}} + \dfrac{1}{\underline{4}} + \cdots \infty = 2 \cdot 71828$$

More generally,
$$e^{mx} = 1 + mx + \dfrac{(mx)^2}{\underline{2}} + \dfrac{(mx)^3}{\underline{3}} + \cdots \infty$$

If $m = \log_e a$
$$a^x = 1 + x \log_e a + \dfrac{(x \log_e a)^2}{\underline{2}} + \dfrac{(x \log_e a)^3}{\underline{3}} + \cdots \infty$$

Logarithmic series
$$\text{Log}_e(1 + x) = x - \dfrac{x^2}{2} + \dfrac{x^3}{3} - \dfrac{x^4}{4} \cdots (-1)^{n+1} \dfrac{x^n}{n} \text{ when } -1 < x \leqslant 1$$

$$\text{Log}_e(1 - x) = -\left[x + \dfrac{x^2}{2} + \dfrac{x^3}{3} + \dfrac{x^4}{4} + \cdots \right] \text{ when } -1 \leqslant x < 1$$

$$\text{Log}_e(n + 1) - \log_e n = 2\left[\dfrac{1}{2n+1} + \dfrac{1}{3(2n+1)^3} + \dfrac{1}{5(2n+1)^5} + \cdots \right]$$

Trigonometrical series
$$\text{Sin } \theta = \theta - \dfrac{\theta^3}{\underline{3}} + \dfrac{\theta^5}{\underline{5}} - \dfrac{\theta^7}{\underline{7}} + \cdots$$

$$\text{Cos } \theta = 1 - \dfrac{\theta^2}{\underline{2}} + \dfrac{\theta^4}{\underline{4}} - \dfrac{\theta^6}{\underline{6}} + \cdots$$

where θ is in radians

Trigonometrical series
$$\text{Sin } \theta = \theta - \dfrac{\theta^3}{3} + \dfrac{\theta^5}{5} - \dfrac{\theta^7}{7} + \cdots$$

$$\text{Cos } \theta = 1 - \dfrac{\theta^2}{2} + \dfrac{\theta^4}{4} - \dfrac{\theta^6}{6} + \cdots$$

where θ is in radians

Binomial theorem
$$(1 + x)^n = 1 + nx + \dfrac{n(n-1)}{1.2}x^2 + \dfrac{n(n-1)(n-2)}{1.2.3}x^3 + \cdots$$

If n is not a positive integer (whole number) the series is infinite and is only true if x is numerically < 1.
More generally,
$$(a + x)^n = a^n + {}_nC_1 a^{-1}x + {}_nC_2 a^{n-2}x^2 + \cdots {}_nC_r a^{n-r}x^r + \cdots x^n.$$

where ${}_nC_r = \dfrac{n(n-1)(n-2) \cdots (n-r+1)}{1.2.3 \ldots r}$

or $\qquad = \dfrac{\underline{n}}{\underline{r} \; \underline{n-r}}$

NUMBER PATTERNS

Rectangular numbers	Numbers which have a pair of factors (i.e. which are not prime) and can therefore be represented in the form of a rectangle.

Thus 6 = $\begin{smallmatrix} \cdot & \cdot & \cdot \\ \cdot & \cdot & \cdot \end{smallmatrix}$

Square numbers — Numbers with a pair of equal factors, and may therefore be represented as a square.

Thus 4 = $\begin{smallmatrix} \cdot & \cdot \\ \cdot & \cdot \end{smallmatrix}$ 9 = $\begin{smallmatrix} \cdot & \cdot & \cdot \\ \cdot & \cdot & \cdot \\ \cdot & \cdot & \cdot \end{smallmatrix}$

1 4 9 16 25 36 49 64 81 100 121 144 169 are the squares of the first 13 numbers.
Note that all square numbers are positive.

Triangular numbers — Numbers which can be formed into a series of equilateral triangles.

Thus   1   3   6   10   15

The most important number pattern, however, is
Pascal's Triangle
Although it was known long before Pascal (who died in 1662) he was the first to make ingenious and wide use of its properties. It forms the basis of probability theory and has applications to statistics, insurance and other fields.

The numbers in each row are formed by adding the numbers above and to each side of it.

The numbers in the rows so formed are then the coefficients of the terms in the Binomial Theorem referred to above.

Thus the numbers in the 4th row (1 3 3 1) are the coefficients in the expansion of $(a + x)^3$, while those in the 6th would be those in the expansion of $(a + x)^5$, i.e. 1 5 10 10 5 1.

Note that if the rows are added horizontally, the results are all successive powers of 2,

		Totals
1		$1 = 2^0$
1 1		$2 = 2^1$
1 2 1		$4 = 2^2$
1 3 3 1		$8 = 2^3$
1 4 6 4 1		$16 = 2^4$
1 5 10 10 5 1		$32 = 2^5$

Permutations and Combinations
The number of permutations of a set of items, i.e. the number of different *arrangements* of those items is denoted by ${}_nP_r$. The number of combinations of a set of items is the number of *groups* of those items (i.e. different arrangements do not count) and is denoted by ${}_nC_r$.

${}_nP_r$ means the number of permutations of n things taken r at a time.
${}_nP_n$ means the number of permutations of n things taken all at a time.

Thus $_nP_r = \dfrac{\underline{/n}}{\underline{/n-r}}$

$= n(n-1)(n-2)\ldots(n-r+1)$

and $_nP_n = \underline{/n}$, since $\underline{/0} = 1$

Note that $_nC_r = \dfrac{_nP_r}{\underline{/r}}$

$= \dfrac{\underline{/n}}{\underline{/r}\ \underline{/n-r}}$

i.e. the number of permutations of n things taken r at a time, divided by the number of permutations of all r things among themselves.

The Real Number System

The set of real numbers includes all the following:
(1) The natural or counting numbers.
(2) The integers (whole numbers) both positive and negative.
(3) The fractions.
All the above are called rational numbers since they can all be expressed as a ratio.
(4) The irrational numbers, i.e. those which cannot be expressed as a ratio. For example $\sqrt{10}$, $\sqrt[3]{7}$ and so on.
All the real numbers can be located on a number-line, and will in fact together form the solid line of geometry.

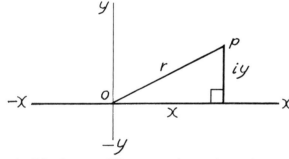

In addition we have the imaginary numbers e.g. $\sqrt{-1}$, $\sqrt{-3}$, which are part of the complex numbers. These are part real and part imaginary and are generally represented by the expression

$x + iy$ where $i = \sqrt{-1}$

Thus x is the real part and iy the imaginary part.

Complex numbers need to be located on a *plane*. This is done by an Argand diagram thus:

The point P (or the vector OP) represents the complex number $x + iy$. r is called the modulus and θ the amplitude (or 'argument') of the complex number, where:

$r = \sqrt{(x^2 + y^2)}$ and $\text{Tan}\ \theta = \dfrac{y}{x}$

Since $x = r\,\text{Cos}\,\theta$ and $y = r\,\text{Sin}\,\theta$ the complex number may also be rendered in the form $r(\text{Cos}\,\theta + i\,\text{Sin}\,\theta)$

SET SYMBOLS

{ }	the set of
$n\{A\}$	the number of elements in the set A
$\{x:\ \}$	the set of elements x such that
$\in$	is an element of
$\notin$	is not an element of
$\mathscr{E}$ (or $\mathscr{U}$)	the universal set
$\varnothing$	the empty (null set)
$\cup$	union
$\cap$	intersection
$\subset$	is a subset of
A'	the complement of the set A
PQ	the operation Q followed by the operation P
$f: x \mapsto y$	the function mapping the set X (the domain) into the set Y
f^{-1}	the inverse of the function f
$\mathbf{R}$	the set of all real numbers
$\mathbf{Z}$	the set of all integers
$\mathbf{Z}_+$	the set of all positive integers
$\mathbf{Q}$	the set of all rationals, e.g. $\frac{3}{4}$

The relationship between sets may be conveniently represented on a Venn diagram. If the various sets to be represented are shaded differently and the general principle is that *union* is represented by *everything* shaded and

intersection is represented by cross-hatched shading, quite complicated relationships may be easily clarified.

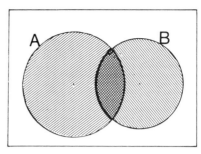

Thus $A \cup B$ = everything shaded and $A \cap B$ = cross-hatched shading and these two areas would contain the appropriate elements.

This illustrates that:
$A \subset B$ and $A \cap B = A$
and $A \cup B = B$

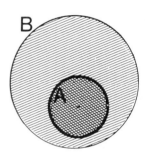

The shaded area represents A'

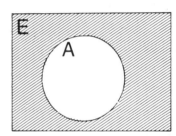

This shows that the elements in $A \cap B'$ will be found in the cross-hatched area. In this case the areas A and B' have been shaded.

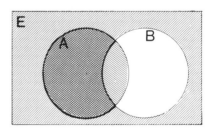

More complicated relationships between several sets may also be conveniently represented in this way, and the equivalence between apparently different relationships clearly illustrated.

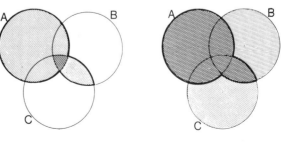

$A \cup (B \cap C)$
Everything shaded

$(A \cup B) \cap (A \cup C)$
Cross-hatched shading

Clearly these (bottom left) two are equivalent, but neither is equivalent to $(A \cup B) \cap C$ illustrated in the third diagram (below).

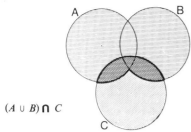

$(A \cup B) \cap C$

The reader should illustrate $A \cap (B \cup C)$, $(A \cap B) \cup (A \cap C)$ and $(A \cap B) \cup C$ in the same way.

BASIC CALCULUS

If y is any function of x, and Δy, Δx are corresponding increments of y and x, then the differential coefficient of y with respect to x

$$\left(\text{written } \frac{dy}{dx}\right) \text{ is defined as } \operatorname*{Lt}_{\Delta x \to 0} \frac{[f(x + \Delta x) - f(x)]}{\Delta x}$$

$\frac{dy}{dx}$ gives the gradient of a curve, i.e. it measures the rate of change of one variable with respect to another.

Thus, since velocity is the rate of change of distance with respect to time, it may be expressed in calculus terms as $\frac{ds}{dt}$ where s is the distance of a body from a fixed point and the equation of motion of the body is of the form $s = f(t)$.

Similarly, since acceleration is the rate of change of *velocity* with time, it may be expressed as $\frac{dv}{dt}$ or as $\frac{d^2s}{dt^2}$, i.e. as the second differential of s with respect to t. Acceleration may also be expressed as $v\frac{dv}{ds}$, i.e. as the velocity multiplied by the rate of change of velocity with distance. In general, if:
$y = ax^n$

then $\frac{dy}{dx} = nax^{n-1}$

Since $\frac{dy}{dx}$ gives the gradient of a curve it may be used to find the maximum and minimum values of a function. Thus if $y = f(x)$, then when $\frac{dy}{dx} = 0$, the tangents to the curve will be parallel to the x axis, and will indicate the positions of the critical values (the maximum or minimum) but without distinguishing them. However,

if $\frac{d^2y}{dx^2}$ is $+$ve   the critical value of x gives a *minimum* value of the function, while

if $\frac{d^2y}{dx^2}$ is $-$ve   the critical value gives a *maximum* value of the function, and

if $\frac{d^2y}{dx^2} = 0$,   and changes sign as x increases through the point, the curve is passing through a point of inflection

Minimum   Maximum   Point of inflection

Differential coefficient of a product
If $y = uv$ where u and v are functions of x, then
$$\frac{dy}{dx} = u\frac{dv}{dx} + v\frac{du}{dx}$$

Differential coefficient of a quotient
If $y = \frac{u}{v}$ where u and v are functions of x, then
$$\frac{dy}{dx} = \frac{v\frac{du}{dx} - u\frac{dv}{dx}}{v^2}$$

Integration
Integration is the reverse of differentiation. In general, $\int ax^n dx$ where a is a constant,

$$= \frac{ax^{n+1}}{n+1} + c \text{ where } c \text{ is constant.}$$

However, whereas in general differentiation is a straightforward process, integration may be difficult and require the knowledge of a number of standard results.

Integration may be used, among other things, for finding the area under a curve, the volume of revolution of a curve about an axis, and the length of the arc of a curve.

Thus, if the curve is represented by $y = f(x)$, then the area between it and the x-axis between the limits x_1 and x_2 is given by

$$A = \int_{x_1}^{x_2} y \, dx.$$

The volume of revolution about the x-axis between the same limits is given by

$$V = \pi \int_{x_1}^{x_2} y^2 \, dx$$

and the length of arc between the same limits is given by

$$L = \int_{x_1}^{x_2} \sqrt{1 + \left(\frac{dy}{dx}\right)^2} \, dx$$

Among the various processes used in integration an important one is *integration by parts*. If u and $\frac{dv}{dx}$ are functions of x, then

$$\int \left(u\frac{dv}{dx}\right) dx = uv - \int \left(v\frac{du}{dx}\right) dx$$

For convenience in memorizing this it may be abbreviated to

$$\int u \, dv = uv - \int v \, du$$

BASIC APPLIED MATHEMATICS
Newton's Laws of Motion were first published in his *Principia* in 1687.
(1) Every body continues in its state of rest, or of uniform motion in a straight line, unless it be compelled by external impressed forces to change that state.
(2) The rate of change of momentum is proportional to the impressed force, and takes place in the direction of the straight line in which the force acts.
(3) To every action there is an equal and opposite reaction.
Newton's famous Law of Gravitation states that
Every particle of matter attracts every other particle of matter with a force which varies directly as the product of the masses of the particles, and inversely as the square of the distance between them. This may be expressed as

$$F \propto \frac{m_1 m_2}{d^2}$$

Law 2 leads to the definition of a unit of force as that which, acting on a unit of mass, generates in it unit acceleration.

This leads to the fundamental equation
$F = ma$.

Basic equations of motion

$$s = \frac{(u + v)}{2} \qquad\qquad v^2 = u^2 + 2as$$

$$v = u + at \qquad\qquad s = ut + \tfrac{1}{2}at^2$$

where $u =$ initial velocity $v =$ final velocity
        $s =$ distance (space) $a =$ acceleration $t =$ time
For constant velocity,
Distance $=$ velocity $\times$ time.

Relative velocity
To find the velocity (and direction) of a body A relative to a body B, combine with the velocity of A a velocity equal and opposite to that of B.

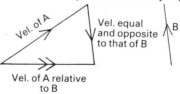

The sides of the triangle represent the velocities in magnitude and direction.

Thus to a person on a ship B, the ship A would *appear* to be moving in the direction (and at the speed) represented by the double-arrowed line.

Triangle of velocities
The triangle ABC shows how the track (i.e. the actual direction) and velocity relative to the ground (the ground speed) of an aircraft or boat may be found from the course set and the wind or current.

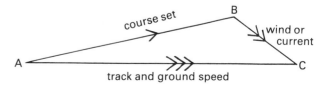

In vector terms, $\overrightarrow{AB} + \overrightarrow{BC} = \overrightarrow{AC}$

Note how, in the diagram, the sum of the arrows along AB + BC equals the number of arrows on AC.

Projectiles

For simple cases, in which air resistance is neglected (i.e. the horizontal component of the velocity is constant) and the vertical velocity is subject only to the force of gravity, the following results may be derived from the fundamental equations of motion:

(1) The time of flight

$$T = \frac{2u \sin \theta}{g}$$

(2) The time to the greatest height

$$= \frac{T}{2}$$

$$= \frac{u \sin \theta}{g}$$

(3) The greatest height attained

$$H = \frac{u^2 \sin^2 \theta}{2g}$$

(4) The range on a horizontal plane

$$R = \frac{u^2 \sin 2\theta}{g}$$

For a given velocity of projection u there are, in general, two possible angles of projection to obtain a given horizontal range. These directions will make equal angles with the vertical and horizontal respectively. For maximum range the angle makes $45°$ with the horizontal.

Note that
(1) the time taken for a body moving freely under gravity is the same to rise as it is to descend.
(2) the velocity at any point on its upward path is equal to that at the same point on its downward path, and that consequently . . .
(3) its velocity (and direction) on striking the ground at the same horizontal level are equal to that with which it was projected.

Impact of elastic bodies

If the bodies are smooth (e.g. two billiard balls) and only the forces between them are considered, then the following equations will determine the velocities and directions of the bodies after the impact.
(1) Momentum (i.e. product of the individual masses and velocities) along the line of centres after impact = momentum *in the same direction* before impact.
(2) The velocity of separation = the velocity of approach (also measured along the line of centres) multiplied by the coefficient of elasticity between the two bodies.

If the impact is oblique (and the bodies are smooth) the velocities at right-angles to the line of centres are unchanged.

If u_1 and u_2, m_1 and m_2 are the initial velocities and masses of the two spheres, and α, β the angles these velocities make with the line of centres, and v_1 and v_2 the components of velocities *along the line of centres* after impact, then the above statements are represented by the following equations:

(1) $m_1 v_1 + m_2 v_2 = m_1 u_1 \cos \alpha + m_2 u_2 \cos \beta$
(2) $v_2 \pm v_1 = e(u_1 \cos \alpha - u_2 \cos \beta)$

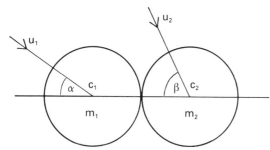

where e is the coefficient of elasticity between the two bodies. Note that in equation 2, v_1 and v_2 will be added or subtracted to get the 'velocity of separation' according to whether the bodies are considered to be going in the opposite or same direction respectively. The conditions of the problem will determine this for the 'velocity of approach'. In the example m_1 is 'catching up' on m_2 and therefore we take the difference in their velocities to obtain the velocity of approach.

Motion in a circle

If a body is moving in a circle with uniform speed, then its linear velocity v is given by the equation $v = r\omega$ where r is the radius of the circle, and ω is the angular velocity. The body will nevertheless have an acceleration (since a force is acting on it to make it move in a circle) but this will be directed *towards* the centre.

The acceleration will be $\dfrac{v^2}{r}$ or $r\omega^2$ and the force producing it will be $\dfrac{mv^2}{r}$ or $mr\omega^2$ where m is the mass of the body.

Note that if a body is whirled round on the end of a string there is no tendency for it to move outwards along the *radius* of the circle. If the string breaks it will instead move straight on along the *tangent* to the circle.

In the case of a train going round a curve the necessary force is provided by the flanges on the wheels, while in the case of a car going round a track it is provided by the friction between the wheels and the ground. By banking the rails or road the weight of the train or car may be made to provide the necessary force.

The required angle to prevent any tendency to skid is given by the equation

$$\tan \theta = \frac{v^2}{gr}$$

where θ is the angle made with the horizontal by the banking. It is the same angle by which a cyclist would lean over from the *vertical* when going round a corner.

Simple harmonic motion

If a particle moves so that its acceleration is directed towards a fixed point in its path, and is proportional to its distance from that point, it is said to move with simple harmonic motion.

The fundamental equation is $\dfrac{d^2 x}{dt^2} = -\omega^2 x$, and by integrating the corresponding equation $v\dfrac{dv}{dx} = -\omega^2 x$ the velocity at any displacement x is given by $v = \omega\sqrt{a^2 - x^2}$ where a is the maximum value of x.

By solving the first equation we find that
$$x = a \cos \omega t \quad \text{(if } t = 0 \text{ when } x = a\text{) or}$$
$$x = a \sin \omega t \quad \text{(if } t = 0 \text{ when } x = 0\text{)}$$

The period of the motion is given by $T = \dfrac{2\pi}{\omega}$

Some fundamental principles of **statics** (the study of the forces acting on bodies at rest, as opposed to **dynamics**, the study of bodies in motion) are:
(1) The *moment of a force* about a point is the product of the force and the perpendicular distance of the line of action of the force from the point.
(2) For a body to be at rest under a system of forces in one plane,
    (a) the algebraic sum of the resolved parts of the forces in any two directions which are not parallel must be zero, and
    (b) the algebraic sum of the moments of the forces about any point must be zero (i.e. clockwise moments = anticlockwise moments).
(3) For a system of particles of weights w_1, w_2, w_3 etc. whose distances from a fixed axis are x_1, x_2, x_3, etc., the position of the centre of gravity from that axis is given by $x = \dfrac{\sum wx}{\sum w}$ where $\sum wx$ is the sum of all the moments of all the particles about the axis, and $\sum w$ is the sum of all the weights of the particles.

From this, the centres of gravity of irregular shapes, or shapes with portions missing, can be found by the principles that

the Moment of the whole = the sum of the moments of the parts
and the Moment of the remainder = the moment of the whole − the sum of the moments of the parts removed

The positions of the centres of gravity of some important shapes are as follows:

(a) A triangle — at the intersection of the medians (i.e. the lines joining the vertices to the midpoints of the opposite sides) or at one-third of the length of the median from the base

(b) Square, rectangle, parallelogram, rhombus — at the intersection of the diagonals.

(c) Sector of a circle of angle 2θ radians — at a distance $\dfrac{2}{3}\dfrac{r \sin \theta}{\theta}$ from the centre along the line bisecting the sector, where r = the radius,

For a semi-circle — $\theta = \dfrac{\pi}{2}$, and the distance of the centre of gravity from the centre of the circle will $= \dfrac{4r}{3\pi}$

(d) A solid pyramid on any base — at a point one-quarter of the height of the pyramid above the base
(e) A hollow cone — at a point one-third of the height from the base
(f) A solid hemisphere — at a point along the axis distant $\dfrac{3r}{8}$ from the centre where r is the radius.

(g) A hollow hemisphere — at a point distant $\dfrac{r}{2}$ along the axis from the centre

[Note that this is the same as for the centre of gravity of the cylinder which would surround, or contain, the hemisphere].
(h) A solid, or hollow closed cylinder — Half-way along the axis.
(4) If a rigid body is in equilibrium under the action of three forces in a plane, the lines of action of these forces must either all be parallel, or must meet at a common point.

It must thus always be possible to draw a triangle to represent the forces.

(5) The Laws of Friction.
  (a) The direction of the frictional force is opposite to that in which the body tends to move.
  (b) The magnitude of the friction is, up to a certain point, exactly equal to the force tending to produce motion.
  (c) Only a certain amount of friction can be called into play. This is called 'limiting friction'.
  (d) The magnitude of the limiting friction for a given pair of surfaces bears a constant ratio to the normal (i.e. perpendicular) pressure between the surfaces. This ratio is denoted by μ and is called the Coefficient of Friction.
  (e) The amount of friction is independent of the areas and shape of the surfaces in contact provided the normal pressure remains unaltered.
  (f) When motion takes place, the friction still opposes the motion. It is independent of the velocity, and is proportional to the normal pressure, but is less than the limiting friction.

If F is the limiting friction (i.e. the force of friction when motion is about to occur), and R is the normal (perpendicular) force, then

$$F = \mu R \quad \text{where } \mu \text{ is the coefficient of friction}$$

The resultant of the forces F and R makes an angle (usually denoted by λ) with R, and thus

$$\tan \lambda = \frac{F}{R}$$
$$= \mu$$

λ is called the Angle of Friction.

These relationships are illustrated in the following diagrams:

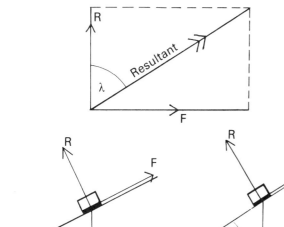

λ = Angle of Friction

If a body is placed on an inclined plane, then if the angle of the plane (α) is less than the angle of friction, it will not slide down.
  If the angle of the plane is equal to λ, the angle of friction, the body will be just on the point of sliding. If the angle of the plane is greater than the angle of friction the body will slide.

Fibonacci Numbers
Fibonacci Numbers were named in the 19th century after Leonardo Fibonacci of Pisa (b. *c.* 1170 d. *ante* 1240), who introduced Arabic figures 1 to 9 plus 0 in his *Liber abaci* in 1202. He earned the title of *Stupor mundi* (wonder of the world) from the Holy Roman Emperor. In 1225 he published a recursive sequence of his Arabic numbers 1, 1, 2, 3, 5, 8, 13, 21, 34, 55 etc. in which each number is the sum of the two preceding numbers. In the 19th century this sequence was found to occur in nature – the arrangement of leaf buds on a stem, animal horns, the genealogy of the male bee and spirals in sunflower heads and pine cones.

GLOSSARY OF COMPUTING TERMS

ALGOL	Computer language (ALGOrithmetic Language).
analog	Pertaining to data of continuously variable physical quantities.
artificial language	A programming language whose rules and syntax are specifically developed beforehand.
auxiliary storage	A storage device controlled by a computer but not part of it, e.g. tape, disc.
B	Abbreviation in programming language for 'binary'.
BASIC	A computer language, used in home computers.
binary	Number system using two digits: 0 and 1.
bit	Short for 'binary digit'. The smallest unit of information that can be recognized by a computer.
block	A sequence of bytes grouped together to provide a complete unit of information.
bps	Bits per second.

buffer	Temporary storage of data between devices of differing speeds.
bug	Fault or error in a computer program.
byte	Smallest group of bits which can be called up individually. A byte usually contains eight bits. Each byte corresponds to one character of data; a single letter, number or symbol. A unit of measurement for computer storage capacity.
capacity	The amount of information that can be stored by a computer, e.g. 48K equals 48 kilobytes of data.
channel	That which connects a computer to its peripheral devices.
character	Any symbol capable of being stored and processed by a computer.
chip	Small piece of silicon etched with impurities in a pattern to form a logical circuit or circuits.
circuit	Complete path of an electrical current.
clear	To erase the contents of a storage device by replacing the contents with blanks or zeros.
closed	(1) A switch is closed when turned on to allow the flow of current through it. (2) A file is closed when data cannot be read into it or written from it.
COBOL	Programming language for commercial data processing.
code	Instructions contained in a computer program.
coding	The process of writing program instructions.
command	Instructions to a program to perform some action or cause the execution of a certain program.
compatible	When two devices can work together without special hardware or software additions.
computer	Any device capable of accepting information, applying prescribed processes to the information, and supplying the results therefrom.
computer graphics	The processing and generation of visual information using a computer and a VDU.
console	A device that allows people to communicate directly with a computer.
CONTROL key	A keyboard key which, in conjunction with another key and both pressed at the same time, generates a function of the computer.
control panel	Part of the operator console that contains switches, lights and on/off buttons which control the computer system's various components.
control sequence	The sequence in which a program's instructions are carried out.
CP/M	Control Program for Microcomputers.
cps	Characters per second; the speed of operation of a character printer.
CPU	Central Processing Unit.
cursor	A small light pulse that traverses the VDU screen indicating where the next typed character will appear.
daisy wheel printer	Circular-element impact printer, printing one character at a time.
database	A collection of data arranged in files used for more than one purpose.
data processing	Operations performed on data to achieve a desired objective.
debug	To locate and correct errors and their sources in a computer program.
decode	To determine the meaning of information in a message by the reversal of previous coding.
digital	(1) Data in discreet quantities. (2) Pertaining to data in the form of digits.
disk	Computer memory device, either *hard* or *floppy*, in the shape of an audio record.
disk drive	Electromechanical device into which a disk is inserted to read or write information.
dot-matrix printer	A printing device that forms characters from a matrix of rows and columns of dots.
edit	To rearrange data or information.
enter	Computer keyboard key that is pressed at the end of each line to enter the contents of the line into the computer.
file	A collection of stored information, usually on disk or tape.
floppy disk	Made of non-rigid material.
hard copy	A printout on paper of computer output.
hardware	The physical components of a computer.
high-level language	A computer programming language permitting programs to be written without prior knowledge of the inner workings of a computer.
information	Data previously processed by a computer and produced as meaningful output.
input	Data fed into a computer for it to process.
interface	A boundary point where different elements of a system are linked together or between an operator and a computer system.
K	Represents 2^{10} or 1024. Usually represents a computer's byte capacity: e.g. 64K = 65,536 bytes of information. Short for kilobyte.
LED	Light Emitting Diode.
light pen	Small pen-like input device used with a VDU to select information or draw information etc.
liquid crystal display (LCD)	Video display type.

low-level languages	Symbolic programming languages coded at the same level of detail as machine code, and are translated in a ratio of one symbolic instruction to one machine code instruction.
machine code	The fundamental language of the computer, written in strips of binary Os and Is.
machine language	The binary code which a computer can immediately understand.
machine readable	Data recorded so that it can be read directly by the computer, e.g. data on tape or disk.
magnetic disk	Disk with magnetic surface on which data can be stored by selective magnetization of portions of the surface.
magnetic tape	Plastic tape with magnetic surface on which data can be stored by selective magnetization of portions of the surface.
mainframe	A large computer with a much greater capacity than that of a mini-computer.
malfunction	(Noun) Failure in a computer's hardware. (Verb) To operate incorrectly.
memory	That part of a computer system where data and instructions are stored.
menu	A list of options shown on a monitor screen or VDU during a computer program and from which the user must select an item. Such initial selection may subsequently present another menu.
merge	A process combining two or more sets of records with similarly ordered sets into one set that is arranged in the same order.
message	An item of data with a specific meaning transmitted through communication lines.
micro-computer	A computer whose processing unit is based on the microprocessor chip. Smaller than a mini-computer.
micro-processor	A complex chip that provides the CPU of a microcomputer system.
micro-program	Programs that are stored in RAM and are unalterable.
monitor	The screen of a VDU.
mouse	Hand-held object used to control the cursor on the monitor screen.
network	A system in which computers and terminals are so linked as to provide communications and data systems compatible with a user's needs.
NEW	A command in BASIC that clears the memory and allows the operator to start typing a new program.
node	Any terminal, station or communications computer in a computer network.
online	Under the direct control of the CPU, allowing data to be processed immediately.
online storage	Secondary storage devices, but under direct control of the CPU, so that it is immediately available when required.
open	(1) A file is open when data can be transferred in or out of it. (2) When a switch is open it is turned off.
open-ended system	Allows new programs, instructions, subroutines, modifications, terms or classifications without disturbing the original system.
open loop	An information system that does not allow for automatic error correction or data modification, and requires the operator to make such adjustments.
operand	An item on which an operation is performed.
operating system	A collection of routines used in overseeing the input, and output processing, of a computer program.
operation	The action specified by a single computer instruction.
operator	Someone who controls a computer or a computer-related device.
output	Data that has been processed and made available for use.
pack	(1) (Noun) Magnetic tape or disks or an assembly of such software. (2) (Verb) To compress data to conserve space in storage.
package	A self-contained collection of programs designed to serve a specific set of requirements.
page	A block or unit of fixed length of memory. A micro-computer page is normally 256 bytes.
PASCAL	A computer language which allows for different types of data.
password	A secret code of characters that a user must input to allow access to a computer system.
PEEK	A command that allows an operator to find out the contents of a specific location in a computer's memory.
peripherals	The mechanical and electric devices other than the computer which may be connected to it (terminals, VDU's, disk drives, printers, etc.)
portable program	One that can be used on more than one type of machine.
preprocessor	A program responsible for preparing data for further processing.
primary storage unit	The main memory unit of a digital computer.
printer	A peripheral output device which converts signals from a computer into hard copy on paper in readable form.
printout	Computer output printed on paper.
procedure	A computer program or routine.
processor	A microprocessor or central processor.

program	A set of instructions that a system follows to carry out tasks.
programming language	A communication system devised so that initial program writing in machine language binary code is obviated. (e.g. FORTRAN, BASIC, COBOL).
programming specifications	The precise steps to be taken to create a given application.
PROM	Programmable Read-Only Memory, a computer memory that can only be programmed once but not altered.
RAM	Random Access Memory. A memory device whereby any location in a memory system can be found as quickly as any other.
rated throughput	The maximum possible throughput of a computer.
raw data	Unprocessed data.
read head	A magnetic device that reads data from a storage tape or disk.
reader	Device able to transcribe data from an input medium.
readout	Processed information presented to the operator, usually on VDU, printer or plotter.
read/write head	A magnetic device that can read from or write into a storage medium.
real memory	A computer's actual memory which is directly addressable by CPU.
record	A collection of related data.
re-entry point	After a subroutine has been completed, the first instruction in the main program is addressed to the date being processed.
REM	A key word in BASIC used to announce the beginning of a comment.
remote station	Data terminal equipment used to communicate with a data processing system that is distant from the CPU.
resident	A program permanently stored in a computer's main memory or in a specific storage device.
resource sharing	The simultaneous use of computer facilities by several users (see time-sharing).
response time	Time taken by a system to respond to an operator's commands.
retrieval	The process by which a requested data item is located in a file and subsequently displayed or printed on the appropriate terminal commanded by the operator.
ROM	Read-Only Memory. Memory that contains fixed information that does not need to be changed. A computer can read out of ROM, but ROM cannot be changed, deleted or added to.
row	A horizontal arrangement of characters, numbers, bits or other expressions.
RPG	Report Program Generator. A business programming language.
RUN	A command in BASIC which causes a currently stored program to go into output function.
scrolling	An operation that allows display data of larger capacity than that which can appear on a specific display or VDU to be seen by 'rolling it upwards'. Input and output appear at the bottom of the screen and travel upwards as more lines of information are added. When the information reaches the top of the screen, it disappears to allow new material to be written in at the bottom of the screen.
secondary storage device	That which provides additional memory for a computer system (e.g. magnetic tape and disk storage units).
sequential file	The most straightforward method of file organization in which each record is written immediately after the previous one.
shared memory	A memory chip that can be accessed by two different CPUs.
shift register	A control signal where all the bits can be moved one place to the right or left by its activation.
silicon chip	A small piece of silicon on which complex miniaturized circuits are etched.
simulation	The process of representing one system by another.
skip	To ignore one or more instructions in a sequence of such instructions.
slave	Any device that is subject to the control of another.
soft copy	Output that appears on the screen of a VDU.
software	All the programs, computer languages and operations used to make a computer perform useful functions (see hardware).
software-compatible	Different makes or marks of computers are software-compatible if they can use the same machine language and, thus, can execute the same programs.
SOM	Start of Message
source program	High level programming language which must be translated into machine language before it can be used by a computer.
special symbol	Neither a letter nor a number (e.g. £, #).
station	Input or output point on a communication system.
storage capacity	Refers to the amount of information a system can store at any one time. A computer with 64K can store 65,5636 bytes in its inbuilt memory.
store	Transfer input data from the CPU to a memory device (tape or disk).
string	A group of characters stored in a computer.

STX Start-of-Text; usually a coded control character.

subprogram A section of a program that performs a specific function within it.

subroutine A set of instructions given a specific name that will be carried out when a main program calls for it.

syntax The set of rules in a programming language that specifies how the language symbols can be assembled to form meaningful statements.

system A group of interrelated units that can function together. The CPU controls the other units.

systems program A program for a computer (usually supplied with it) that allows the operator to use it easily and effectively. A collection of such programs constitutes the computer's operating system.

systems analyst A person who designs problems in data processing and indicates or writes directions for their solutions in data processing terms.

systems programmer A person who plans, generates, extends and controls the use of an operating system.

systems software The software supplied with the computer which make it perform effectively.

tape (See magnetic tape.)

tape drive Converts information stored on tape into signals that are sent to a computer, and receives information from the computer to be stored on tape.

terminal A point in a system where data can either enter or exist.

test The part of a message that contains the main body of information to be conveyed.

throughput 1. The rate at which information can be accurately transmitted when averaged out over a long period. 2. The time taken from an operation's beginning to its end.

time sharing A computer system that allows several users to be connected simultaneously to one computer.

track Concentric circles on a disk which store information. Each circle is a track.

transceiver A device that both transmits and receives data, often simultaneously.

translator A device that converts programs written in one language into another language.

up A computer system is up when it is available for use.

update To change, delete or add (or all three) data in a file or record.

user-friendly A computing system that provides for the capabilities and limitations of an operator: a system requiring little expertise to operate.

VDU Visual Display Unit.

verb An instruction to action in a programming language (e.g. READ, WRITE, PRINT).

visual display unit A peripheral device that displays information on a screen.

word processor A computer-based system or software package that allows an operator to input text into the system which can then be edited or reformatted at will before being printed out into hard copy.

Wordstar A popular brand of software package used in word processing.

write To transfer data from a computer to an output device.

zap To erase.

Chemistry

Glossary

ablation Degradation due to heat.

absolute temperature Temperature on the absolute scale is measured in kelvins (K), 1 K being equal to 1°C. Zero on the absolute scale is −273·16°C.

absorptiometer A device used to measure the absorption of light.

acetal A compound derived from an alcohol and an aldehyde or a ketone, with the general formula:

$$\begin{array}{c} R^2 \quad OR^4 \\ \diagdown \; / \\ C \\ / \; \diagdown \\ R^1 \quad OR^4 \end{array}$$

acetin An acetate derived from glycerol.

acetylation The introduction of one or more acetyl groups, $CH_3 \cdot CO—$, into organic compounds.

acid A substance able to form hydrogen ions when in solution, whether in water or in a non-aqueous solvent.

acid–base indicator An indicator that has a markedly different colour in acid and base solutions. The difference in colour is between the ionized and non-ionized form of the indicator.

actinides A group of radioactive elements, many of them artificially produced by irradiation: actinium, thorium, protactinium, uranium, neptunium, plutonium, americium, curium, berkelium, californium, einsteinium, fermium, mendelevium nobelium, lawrencium.

acyl Group left after the —OH group has been removed from carboxylic acid.

addition reaction Reaction by which unsaturated carbon bonds, e.g. $C\equiv C$, $C=C$ are saturated to give single bonds.

adhesive A substance which wets surfaces that are to be stuck together and then solidifies to form the actual joint.

adiabatic Process by which heat is neither added to nor allowed to leave a system.

adsorbate Substance which is adsorbed on to adsorbent.

adsorbent The substance that provides an absorption surface.

adsorption Process by which free atoms or molecules become attached to surface.

aerosol Fine particles of a solid suspended in air.

alcohol Organic compound in which hydroxyl —OH, group or groups are attached to carbon atoms.

aldehyde Organic compound in which a —CHO group is attached to a carbon atom.

aliphatic Organic compounds with carbon atoms arranged in chains rather than rings.

alkali Strictly speaking, a hydroxide of one of the alkali metals, although generally taken to mean a substance which gives a pH of greater than 7 in water.

alkanes Otherwise known as paraffins, these organic compounds have the general formula $C_nH_{2n}+_2$ and form the principal constituents of petroleum.

alkenes Aliphatic hydrocarbons containing one double $C=C$ bond. They have the general formula C_nH_{2n}.

alkyd resins Compounds used extensively in paints and other coatings. They are formed by condensation reactions between polybasic acids and polyhydric alcohols.

alkyls An aliphatic hydrocarbon with the final hydrogen atom removed.

allotropy An element existing in more than one physical form, e.g. carbon as diamond and graphite.

alloy A combination of two or more metals, or of metallic and non-metallic elements. The physical characteristics of this combination are metallic.

alum Potassium alum, $KAl(SO_4)_2 \cdot 12H_2O$, used in a variety of industrial processes including dyeing, paper manufacture, and waterproofing.

alumina Aluminium oxide, Al_2O_3.

aluminates Compounds containing an Al^{3+} ion in anions that are hydroxide or oxide based.

amalgam Compounds of a metal and mercury. They can be both liquid and solid.

amides Organic compounds based on ammonia. One or more of the hydrogen atoms in the ammonia molecule is substituted by organic acid groups:

$$\begin{array}{ll} R \cdot CO—N \diagup^H_{\diagdown H} & \text{primary} \\[2mm] R^1 \cdot CO—N \diagup^{R^2 \cdot CO}_{\diagdown H} & \text{secondary} \\[2mm] R^1 \cdot CO—N \diagup^{R^2 \cdot CO}_{\diagdown R^3 \cdot CO} & \text{tertiary} \end{array}$$

amines Organic compounds based on ammonia. One or more of the hydrogen atoms in the ammonia molecule is substituted by hydrocarbon groups. As with amides, primary, secondary and tertiary amines can be formed.

amino acids Organic compounds containing the amino group, —NH_2, and the carboxyl group, —COOH. Proteins are built up from amino acids.

ammonium A cation, $(NH_4)^+$, which behaves similarly to the alkali metal cations.

amphoteric Having both acid and basic properties.

aniline An important organic chemical used in the dye industry. Based on the benzene ring, its formula is $C_6H_5 \cdot NH_2$.

anisotropic Having different properties in different directions, e.g. an anisotropic crystal has different physical properties along different crystal axes.

annealing Reduction of the stresses within a metal by heating it and then cooling it in a controlled fashion.

aromatic Organic compounds based on the benzene ring, C_6H_6. The benzene ring is stable, even though the carbon atoms within it are unsaturated. It therefore undergoes substitution reactions rather than addition reactions.

aryls An aromatic hydrocarbon with a hydrogen atom removed.

asbestos A group of silicate minerals. The SiO_4 groups are linked together into chains, giving the characteristic fibrous texture.

atomic mass unit One-twelfth of the mass of carbon-12 atom. Approximately the mass of a proton or neutron.

atomic number The number of protons in the nucleus of an atom of the element.

atomic weight The average mass of atoms in an element, in atomic mass units.

Avogadro's number The number of particles in one mole of any pure substance is $L = 6.023 \times 10^{23}$.

azo dyes A group of dyes containing the group $-N{=}N-$ linking two aromatic groups.

base An aqueous solution of a compound which, with an acid, gives a salt and water only.

benzene C_6H_6. The six carbon atoms are arranged in a ring. The bonds between the carbon atoms have characteristics between single and double bonds; they are said to resonate between the two, and as such are stable.

benzyl The C_6H_5. CH_2- group.

Bessemer converter Large vessel in which pig iron is refined to steel. Air is blown through the molten mixture and impurities are oxidized and removed as slag.

Bimolecular reaction A reaction in which only two molecular types react together, e.g.:
$$2Cu + O_2 = 2CuO$$

biuret reaction A test for peptides and proteins, whereby the peptide linkage gives a pinkish colour with sodium hydroxide, NaOH, and copper sulphate, $CuSO_4$.

body-centred lattice A crystal structure in which atoms or molecules occur at the corners of each crystal cell and at the centre of the body of the crystal cell.

bond The link that holds atoms together in molecules and that is also the basis of crystal structure.

bond energy Energy involved in holding a bond together. When the bond is broken, this energy is released in a variety of forms.

borates Boric acid (H_3BO_3) salts.

borax A naturally-occurring source of boron, $Na_2(B_4O_5(OH)_4 . 8H_2O)$.

Bordeaux mixture Copper sulphate, $CuSO_4$, and calcium hydroxide, $Ca(OH)_2$, mixed in water. It is used as a fungicide.

brass An alloy of copper and zinc. Two principal forms of brass are made, one containing less than 30% zinc, the other between 30% and 40% zinc.

brine A solution of sodium chloride, NaCl.

bromates Salts with bromium oxy-anions. Commonly this is taken to mean the BrO_3^- oxyanion, but BrO^- and BrO_4^- oxy-anions are also found.

bromides Salts of HBr, hydrogen bromide, based on the bromide ion, Br^-.

bronze A group of alloys of copper and, originally, tin, often with smaller amounts of other elements. The term can now mean copper alloys with no tin, e.g. aluminium bronze.

buffer A mixture of acid, or alkali, and an associated salt, whose pH alters only gradually with addition of more acid or alkali. The salt acts as a supply of anions or cations, which combine with hydrogen or base ions.

butane The lowest member of the paraffin series, C_4H_{10}. It is widely used in cylinders and canisters as camping gas.

carboxylic acid Organic acid containing a carboxyl group, $-COOH$.

calcite A form of naturally-occurring calcium carbonate, $CaCO_3$, found as chalk, limestone and marble.

calcium carbonate The most commonly occurring salt of calcium, $CaCO_3$.

camphor $C_{10}H_{16}O$. Camphor occurs naturally, being extracted from the wood of the camphor tree. It is also manufactured.

carbohydrates General formula $C_xH_{2y}O_y$. Naturally-occurring compounds used as energy compounds, energy stores and for structural uses.

carbonates Salts of carbonic acid, H_2CO_3. The carbonate ion is CO_3^{2-} and forms a number of commercially-important salts, including calcium carbonate.

carbon dioxide CO_2. A product of respiration and a constituent of air. It represents the complete combustion of carbon.

carbon monoxide CO. Formed by the incomplete combustion of carbon. It is a toxic gas.

carotene $C_{40}H_{55}$. It occurs naturally in plants as one of the chief colouring pigments, and is also found in many animal tissues. It is a precursor of vitamin A.

cast iron A partly-refined form of iron containing 2–4% carbon. It is a brittle alloy.

catalyst A substance that speeds up the rate of a chemical reaction without being permanently chemically altered by the reaction.

cathode In electrolysis, this is the negative electrode.

cation A positively-charged ion, occurring in crystals, solutions and melts.

cellulose $(C_6H_{10}O_5)_n$. It is the principal structural component of cell walls, formed by the polymerization of glucose.

cement Common builders' cement, or Portland cement, consists of a mixture of calcium silicates, calcium aluminates and calcium sulphate. It is made by heating limestone and clay and grinding the product with gypsum. When mixed with water it hardens to a solid mass.

ceramic Hard high-melting point non-metallic inorganic materials, e.g. enamels, pottery, porcelain, abrasives.

chain reaction A process by which the product of one reaction takes part in a further reaction, the products of which take part in yet more reactions, etc.

chalk Naturally-occurring form of calcium carbonate, $CaCO_3$.

charcoal A form of carbon produced by the slow burning of wood in a shortage of air.

chlorates Chlorine oxy-acid salts, formed from the ClO^-, ClO_2^-, ClO_3^- and ClO_4^- ions.

chlorides Compounds containing the Cl^- ion.

chlorophyll A complex organic chemical colouring matter found in green plants. It is an essential constituent of the photosynthetic process, by which carbohydrates are produced in plants from carbon dioxide and water.

cholesterol $C_{27}H_{46}O$. A complex organic chemical based on the sterol ring structure. It is found in animals, particularly in membranes.

chromates Salts based on chromic acid, i.e. containing the CrO_4^{2-} and $Cr_2O_7^{2-}$ ions.

clay Naturally-occurring aluminosilicates consisting of $AlSiO_4$, together with $Mg(OH)_2$ and $Al(OH)_3$.

coenzymes Compounds necessary for the action of enzymes. They may be altered during the course of the reaction, but will be reformed during later reactions.

colloid Small particles, larger than atoms or molecules but too small to be seen by a light microscope, usually found in suspension or solution.

concrete The hardened material formed from mixing cement, sand or gravel, and water.

condensation reaction Reaction in which two molecules react together to give one product molecule plus water, H_2O.

conformation The shape a molecule has due to the positioning a group may have in relation to a bond. In complex organic molecules the conformation may affect physical properties.

copolymer A polymer resulting from the combination of two or more monomers.

covalent bond Two atoms linked by sharing two electrons, one electron originating from each atom.

crude oil A naturally-occurring mixture of hydrocarbons, often mixed with water, sulphur and other inorganic impurities.

crystal A solid particle with a regular geometric shape caused by the regular arrangement of atoms or ions or molecules.

crystallization Process by which crystals of a substance are removed from a solution by increasing the concentration above the saturation point.

cyanates Salts formed from the cyanate ion, NCO^-.

cyanides Salts formed from the cyanide ion, CN^-.

deliquescence Absorption of water by a solid to give a solution.

detergent A water-soluble surface-active agent which can wet surfaces and help to loosen oil and grease. Detergents invariably consist of a hydrophobic group that allows them to dissolve the oils and grease, and a hydrophilic group that promotes water-solubility.

dialysis Separation of mixtures by selective diffusion through a semipermeable membrane.

diamond Naturally-occurring crystalline form of carbon.

dicarboxylic acids Organic acids containing two carboxyl groups, $-COOH$.

dienes Organic chemicals with two carbon-carbon double bonds.

diffusion Movement of a gas or liquid caused by the random movement of its atoms or molecules.

diketones Organic compounds with two keto groups, $-CO-$.

dimer A polymer consisting of two molecules of a monomer.

distillation The separation of two liquids or a liquid from a solid by evaporation and recondensation.

doping The introduction of impurities into a crystal lattice, giving different electrical or other properties to the crystal.

double bond Two atoms sharing two pairs of electrons, i.e. two covalent bonds.

dry ice Solid CO_2.

EDTA Ethylenediaminetetra-acetic acid, it forms complexes with most elements.

efflorescence Formation of a powdery solid from crystals, by the loss of water of crystallization, or from liquids, by evaporation.

elastomer A material with elastic properties, e.g. rubber.

electrochemical series A series in which the elements are placed in decreasing order of oxidation potential. Among other things, an element higher up the series will displace from solution an element lower down the series.

electrolysis Decomposition of substance in solution by the passage of an electric current.

electrolyte A substance which, when in solution, dissociates into ions. It can thus act as an electric conductor.

electronegativity The degree to which an atom in a molecule attracts electrons to itself. In general, values of electronegativity decrease from right to left and from top to bottom of the periodic table of elements.

element A substance formed of atoms, all with the same atomic number.

emulsion A dispersed colloid of one liquid in another.

enantiomers Isomers that are mirror images of each other in the spatial arrangement of their constituent atoms.

endothermic reaction A reaction in which heat is absorbed.

enthalpy Symbol H. Thermodynamic function of a system equal to the sum of its internal energy and the product of its pressure and volume.

entropy Symbol S. The disorder of a system. The greater the disorder of a system, the greater the entropy.

enzyme A protein which catalyses one specific chemical reaction.

epimer A type of isomer which differs in the configuration around only one of a number of atoms.

epoxy Indicating a $C{-}O{-}C$ ring in the form:

$$\overset{\displaystyle O}{\overset{\displaystyle \diagup \diagdown}{C - C}}$$

equilibrium Any state in which the properties do not change with time, e.g. in a reversible reaction it is the stage at which the rate of the forward reaction equals the rate of the reverse reaction.

equivalent The weight of a substance that will combine with or displace eight parts by weight of oxygen.

ester Product of a condensation reaction between an organic acid and an alcohol.

ethane CH_3. CH_3, a naturally-occurring constituent of natural gas, as well as being extensively synthesized.

ethanoic acid CH_3. COOH, otherwise known as acetic acid.

ethanol CH_3CH_2OH, ethyl alcohol or merely alcohol. Although originally produced as result of fermentation, most ethanol is now synthesized.

ethene $CH_2=CH_2$, otherwise known as ethylene.

ether $(CH_3CH_2)_2O$, otherwise known as diethyl ether and diethyl oxide.

ethers Compounds with the general formula R^1-O-R^2, where R^1 and R^2 are alkyl or aryl groups.

ethyne $C_2H_2 \cdot HC \equiv CH$, otherwise known as acetylene.

eutectic A mixture of two substances which shows a clearly-defined melting point.

evaporation Conversion of a liquid to a vapour at a temperature below its boiling point.

fats Esters of fatty acids and glycerol with the general formula:

$$
\begin{array}{l}
CH_2 \cdot OOC \cdot R^1 \\
| \\
CH \cdot OOC \cdot R^2 \\
| \\
CH_2 \cdot OOC \cdot R^3
\end{array}
$$

R^1, R^2 and R^3 being the fatty acid residues.

fatty acids Organic acids consisting of an alkyl group attached to a carboxyl group, with the general formula $C_nH_{2n}O_2$.

Fehling's solution A solution of copper sulphate, sodium potassium tartrate and sodium hydroxide, used for testing for reducing sugars.

fermentation Use of microorganisms to break down substances and release, generally, useful products, e.g. fermentation of sugar by yeasts, yielding alcohol and carbon dioxide.

ferrates Oxy-anions of iron, incorporating the FeO_4^{2-} ion.

ferric compounds Compounds incorporating Fe(III) iron.

ferrous compounds Compounds incorporating Fe(II) iron.

flash point Temperature to which a substance must be heated before it can be ignited.

flavones Yellow pigments found in plants.

flocculation Coagulation of a colloid into larger particles.

flourescein $C_{20}H_{12}O_5$. A red crystalline substance that flouresces bright green.

flourides The salts of hydrogen flouride, HF.

flourocarbons A group of hydrocarbons in which hydrogen atoms are replaced by flourine atoms. They are widely used as refrigerants and as aerosols.

foams A dispersion of bubbles of gas in a liquid or solid.

fractional crystallization Separation of two or more substances by using changes in solubility with temperature. As the temperature is lowered, first one substance will crystallize out, then another, and so on.

fractional distillation Separation of two or more substances by evaporating the mixture, allowing the vapours to pass up a fractionating column and collecting the various fractions as they condense at different points up the column, depending on their volatility.

free radical An atom or group of atoms with unpaired electrons. It is therefore very reactive.

galvanizing The protection of steel by covering it with a thin layer of zinc.

gas Gases will expand spontaneously to fill a container. The intermolecular attractions are very weak and the constituent atoms or molecules show random movement.

gasification Conversion of a solid or liquid to a lower molecular weight gas. Usually applied to the conversion of hydrocarbon solids and liquids to fuel gases.

gasoline A mixture of various hydrocarbons used as motor fuel or aviation fuel.

gel A colloid suspension in which the particles are linked by a form of partial coagulation to form a jelly.

gelatin A protein made by boiling collegen in dilute acid.

glucose $C_6H_{12}O_6$, otherwise known as dextrose. It is the most common hexose sugar, found in plants and animals. It is the constituent monomer of cellulose, starch, glycogen, etc.

glue Proteins in a colloid mixture. It is prepared from animal waste containing collagen.

gluten Proteins from wheat dough.

glycerides The esters produced from glycerol. Depending on how many of the hydroxyl groups in the glycerol molecule combine with acid radicals, the glycerides are called mono-, di- or tri-glycerides.

glycerol Otherwise known as glycerin or 1,2,3-trihydroxypropane, with the structure:

$$
\begin{array}{l}
CH_2 \cdot OH \\
| \\
CH \cdot OH \\
| \\
CH_2 \cdot OH
\end{array}
$$

gram molecular volume Volume occupied by 1 mole of a substance in the gaseous state. At STP this equals 22·414 litres.

gram molecule A mole.

graphite A crystalline form of carbon, occurring naturally. It consists of flat sheets of hexagonal cells, which slip easily over each other, giving graphite its characteristic properties.

group In the periodic table of elements, a group is a vertical column of elements. A group will have distinct properties and characteristics in common.

haem A complex three-dimensional molecule with the formula $C_{34}H_{32}FeN_4O_4$. Haem is an important constituent of a number of active biochemicals, including haemoglobin. It has an iron atom at its centre which can act as an electron carrier, changing from the ferrous to the ferric state and back again.

haematite One of the iron ores, Fe_2O_3.

halogenation The addition or substitution of halogen atoms to a molecule.

halogens Group VII in the periodic table, consisting of flourine, chlorine, bromine, iodine and astatine.

hexanes A group of chemicals with the formula C_6H_{14}.

hexose A carbohydrate with a ring of six carbon atoms. Glucose is the most important of the hexoses.

hydration The addition of water to a substance, particularly to ions, e.g.:
$H^+ + H_2O = H_3O^+$

hydrocarbons Compounds of hydrogen and carbon.

hydrochloric acid An aqueous solution of hydrogen chloride, HCl.

hydrogenation A form of reduction in which hydrogen gas is used to add hydrogen to a compound.

hydrogen bond A weak bond between an electronegative atom, e.g. oxygen, and a hydrogen atom covalently bonded to another electronegative atom.

hydrolysis Reaction in which water combines with a compound.

hydroxylation Introduction of a hydroxyl group, OH^-, into a molecule.

imides Organic compounds containing the $-CO-NH-CO-$ group.

imines Organic compounds containing the $-NH-$ group. The nitrogen atom is not linked to a carbonyl group or hydrogen atom.

indicator Generally, an indicator shows the presence of a particular compound or group of compounds by a characteristic colour. More specifically, indicators are used to show precisely when the end-point in a titration has occurred.

indole An organic double-ring structure based on the formula C_8H_7N.

inorganic chemistry The chemistry of all elements other than carbon.

ion An atom or molecule that has lost or gained one or more electrons, thereby carrying a positive or negative charge.

isocyanates Organic compounds containing the group $-N=C=O$.

isomers Compounds with the same chemical formula, but existing in different three-dimensional structures due to differing orientation about certain atoms.

isomorphism Compounds having the same crystal structure.

isonitriles Organic compounds having the group $-N-C$. Otherwise known as isocyanides or carbylamines.

isotonic Solutions with the same osmotic pressure.

isotopes Atoms having the same number of protons but differing numbers of neutrons.

ketones Organic compounds with the general formula R^1-CO-R^2, where R^1 and R^2 are generally hydrocarbons.

lactose A disaccharide sugar with the formula $C_{12}H_{22}O_{11}$. It occurs in varying amounts in the milk of all animals.

lanthanides A series of metallic elements: lanthanum, cerium, praseodymium, neodymium, promethium, samarium, europium, gadolinium, terbium, dysprosium, holmium, erbium, thulium, ytterbium, lutetium.

lattice The regular three-dimensional arrangement of atoms in a crystal.

lime water Calcium hydroxide, $Ca(OH)_2$.

liquefied petroleum gas Hydrocarbon gases produced as a result of the refining of petroleum. Butane and propane are the two alternatives available, although neither are pure forms of the gas.

litmus Colouring obtained from lichens. It is used as an indicator to detect pH changes.

macromolecules Large molecules with molecular weight in excess of 10 000.

magnesium alloys A very light group of alloys.

manganates Salts containing the ion MnO_4^{2-}.

marble A form of calcium carbonate, $CaCO_3$.

mercaptans Otherwise known as thiols. A group of organic compounds containing the $-SH$ group linked to a carbon atom.

meta A prefix denoting the position of groups attached to the benzene ring. It means that the substituents are separated by one carbon atom, i.e. they occur at the 1,3 positions.

metal Elements that are malleable, lustrous, and conduct heat and electricity. They tend to form cations.

methane CH_4, otherwise known as marsh gas. It occurs naturally as a result of the decay of vegetable matter.

methanol CH_3OH, otherwise known as methyl alcohol.

methanal HCHO, otherwise known as formaldehyde.

methylation The addition of a methyl group, $-CH_3$, to an organic compound.

micelle A colloidal particle.

miscibility The ability of one substance to mix with another.

molarity The number of moles of a substance dissolved in 1 litre of solution.

mole Otherwise known as a gram molecule, it is the amount of substance that contains the same number of elementary entities (molecules, ions, atoms, etc.) as there are in 0·012 kg of carbon-12.

molecular weight Ratio of the mass per molecule of a substance to 1/12 of the mass of a carbon-12 atom.

molecule The smallest independent particle of a substance.

monotropy A substance that exists in only one stable crystalline form.

naphthalene $C_{10}H_8$. A double benzene ring structure.

natural gas A mixture of over 90% methane with other hydrocarbon gases, as well as nitrogen and carbon dioxide.

ninhydrin $C_9H_4O_3.H_2O$. It gives a blue colour on heating with amino acids and proteins and is therefore widely used as an indicator.

nitrates Salts of nitric acid, containing the ion NO_3^-.

nitric acid HNO_3. It has many important industrial uses, including the manufacture of fertilizers.

nitrides Compounds of nitrogen and other elements.

nitrites Salts of nitrous acid, containing the ion NO_2^-.

nitro compounds Group of aromatic compounds with the basic formula $R-NO_2$.

noble gases Inert group of gases: helium, neon,

argon, krypton, xenon, radon. Traces of all these gases are found in the atmosphere.

nylon A group of synthetic plastics and fibres, largely formed by condensation polymerization.

octanes Group of hydrocarbons with eight carbon atoms and the basic formula C_8H_{18}. The group falls in the alkane series, and the constituents are all found in crude oil.

optical activity The ability of certain substances to rotate the polarization plane of polarized light, due to the assymetry of the molecules.

organic Related to the compounds of carbon.

ortho A prefix denoting the position of groups attached to the benzene ring. It means that the substituents occur in the 1,2 positions.

oxidation Process by which the proportion of an electronegative constituent of a compound is increased. This invariably means the addition of oxygen to a compound.

oxide A compound containing oxygen and other element.

oximes Group of organic compounds containing $=N.OH$ linked to a carbon atom.

oxonium A positive ion with the basic formula R_3O^+, where R is hydrogen or an organic group, e.g. the hydroxonium ion H_3O^+.

ozone O_3. An allotrope of oxygen.

para A prefix denoting the position of groups attached to the benzene ring. It means that the substituents occur in 1,4 positions.

patina An oxide layer formed on metals and alloys.

pentanes Group of hydrocarbons with five carbon atoms and the basic formula C_5H_{12}. The constituents are all found in crude oil.

pentose A carbohydrate with a ring of five carbon atoms.

peptides Chains of two or more amino acids linked by a peptide linkage, $-CO-NH-$. Peptide chains are arranged in three-dimensional structures to form proteins.

period A period in the periodic table of elements is a horizontal series of elements, from an alkali metal to a noble gas.

periodic table Arrangement of elements in a table so that similarities between elements are emphasized.

permanganates A group of salts containing the MnO_4^- ion.

peroxides Derivatives of hydrogen peroxide, H_2O_2, containing linked pairs of oxygen atoms.

pewter An alloy of tin and lead.

pH The logarithm (base 10) of the reciprocal of the concentration of hydrogen ions in a solution, giving a measure of the acidity or alkalinity of a solution.

phenol $C_6H_5 \cdot OH$, an aromatic hydroxy compound.

phenolphthalein $C_{20}H_{14}O_4$. An aromatic compound used as an indicator.

phenyl The atomatic group C_6H_5-.

phosphates Salts based on the PO_4^{3-} and PO_7^{4-} ions.

phosphoric acid There are a number of oxy-acids of phosphorus, the best known being H_3PO_4. They are based on phosphorus (V).

phosphors Substances that phosphoresce.

phosphorus acid Oxy-acids of phosphorus (III), the best known being H_3PO_3.

pig iron Iron produced by a blast furnace, before it is cast to shape.

plastics Artificial organic polymers that can be moulded to shape.

polycarbonates A group of hard thermoplastics based on carbonic acid.

polyesters Polymers formed by condensation reactions between polybasic acids and polyhydric alcohols.

polymers A compound consisting of long-chain molecules made up of repeating molecular units.

polymorphism A substance existing in more than one crystalline form.

polysaccharides Carbohydrates formed by condensation reactions between monosaccharides.

precipitation Production of an insoluble compound in a solution by a chemical reaction.

propane $CH_3.CH_2.CH_3$. A constituent of natural gas.

proteins A large group of naturally-occurring organic compounds consisting of chains of amino acids folded into complex three-dimensional molecules.

radical Atom or molecule which has one or more free valencies.

rare earths Otherwise known as the lanthanide series of elements.

rectification Fractional distillation used to separate an organic liquid into its constituent parts.

redox Simultaneous oxidation and reduction occurring in one chemical reaction.

reduction Process by which the proportion of an electronegative constituent of a compound is decreased. This invariably means a reduction in the amount of oxygen in a compound or an addition of hydrogen.

resins A solid natural or synthetic polymer.

reversible reaction A reaction that can proceed in either direction. Such a reaction usually attains an equilibrium, depending on the concentrations of the reactants and the physical conditions.

ribose A pentose sugar, $C_5H_{10}O_5$, found in the nucleic acids.

rust The coating of $Fe_2O_3.H_2O$ found on iron.

salt Salt commonly refers to sodium chloride, NaCl. However, in chemistry it refers to the product of the reaction between a base and an acid.

sand A mixture of SiO_2 and other minerals, formed by the degradation of rocks.

saponification Hydrolysis of an ester using an alkali.

saturated compound A compound in which there are no double or triple bonds, only single bonds.

silica Silicon dioxide, SiO_2, one of the most common constituents of the earth's crust.

silicates At their simplest, silicates are compounds containing the SiO_4^{4-} ion. However, the term extends to cover a wide range of minerals based on the SiO_4 tetrahedral crystal structure.

silicones Organic polymers containing $-SiO-Si-$ linkages.

single bond A bond between two atoms involving two electrons in a single bonding orbital.

sintering Fusion of two or more substances by heating powders together under pressure at a temperature below their melting point.

soap The salt of a fatty acid.

solders Alloys used to join metals together. The solder melts at a temperature below that of the metals.

solution A single-phase homogeneous mixture of two or more compounds, one of them invariably being liquid (the solvent) in which the solute is dissolved.

standard temperature and pressure Abbreviated to STP, it indicates a temperature of 273·15 K and a pressure of 101·325 kPa.

starch A naturally-occurring polymer of glucose.

steel A group of alloys of iron and carbon, often with other elements added to give particular properties.

strength The strength of an acid or alkali indicates its ability to give hydroxonium ions, H_3O^+.

sublimation The change from solid to gaseous state without passing through a liquid state.

substitution A displacement reaction in which one atom or group in a molecule is replaced by another atom or group.

substrate The substance on which an enzyme acts.

sucrose A disaccharide carbohydrate with the formula $C_{12}H_{22}O_{11}$.

sugars Carbohydrates invariably based on six- or twelve-carbon atoms. They are crystalline, soluble in water and sweet to taste.

sulphates Salts based on the SO_4^{2-} ion.

sulphides Compounds of elements and sulphur, usually based on the S^{2-} ion.

sulphites Salts based on the SO_3^{2-} ion.

sulphuric acid A colourless liquid, H_2SO_4.

superphosphates A mixture of calcium hydrogen phosphate, $Ca(H_2PO_4)_2$, and calcium sulphate, $CaSO_4$. It is used as a fertilizer.

surface active agents Otherwise known as surfactants. Mainly organic substances which, when dissolved in water, reduce the surface tension.

2,4,5-T Otherwise known as 2,4,5-trichlorophenoxyacetic acid, $C_8H_5Cl_3O_3$. Widely used as a selective weedkiller.

tellurates Salts containing oxyanions of tellurium, i.e. TeO_6^{6-} and TeO_3^{2-} ions.

terpenes Volatile aromatic hydrocarbons with the formula $(C_5H_8)_n$. They are naturally occurring in the essential oils of many plants.

thermoplastics Plastics which can be softened by heating and then hardened by cooling many times.

thio- Containing sulphur.

tinning Coating the surface of iron with tin in order to prevent corrosion.

titration The determination of the amount of one substance needed to react with a fixed amount of another substance. The endpoint is determined by a change in property, e.g. change in colour.

toluene An aromatic compound, $C_6H_5 \cdot CH_3$.

transition elements A series of elements with an incomplete inner shell of electrons: scandium to zinc, yttrium to cadmium, and lanthanum to mercury.

triple bond A bond formed by three pairs of electrons shared between two atoms.

valency Another name for the oxidation state. It is the difference between the number of electrons attached to an atom of the free element and the number of electrons associated with an atom of the element in a compound.

van der Waals' bonds Weak forces between molecules due to electronic coupling, acting over short distances.

vapour pressure The pressure of a vapour produced by a solid or liquid. In a closed system a saturated vapour pressure will eventually be established, at which the vapour will be in equilibrium with the solid or liquid.

verdigris Copper carbonate, $CuCO_3$, coating on surface of copper or bronze, due to exposure to the atmosphere.

vinegar A dilute solution of ethanoic acid.

vinyl The $Ch_2=CH-$ group, otherwise known as ethenyl.

washing soda Sodium carbonate, $Na_2CO_3 \cdot 10H_2O$.

water Oxygen hydride, H_2O.

Inorganic chemistry

The nomenclature of chemistry is governed by the International Union of Pure and Applied Chemistry whose latest detailed and authoritative guidance was published in 1970 and was followed by a definitive interpretation by the Association of Science Education in 1972.

Because of the difficulties in trying to produce a systematic nomenclature which will adequately cover all aspects of inorganic chemistry, trivial names have not yet been completely discarded although, for example, the use of the familiar endings 'ous' and 'ic' to denote the lower and higher valency states of metal cations is to be discouraged in favour of the Stock System in which the oxidation number of the less electronegative constituent is indicated by Roman numerals in parentheses placed immediately after the name of the atom concerned, thus $FeCl_2$ is iron(II) chloride rather than ferrous chloride and $FeCl_3$ is iron(III) chloride rather than ferric chloride. For compounds consisting of simple molecules of known composition the stoichiometry determines the name using Greek or Roman multiplying affixes (see table below), thus P_4O_{10} is tetraphosphorus decaoxide. Trivial names for acids are still in use although such alchemical leftovers as 'Aquafortis' for nitric acid, 'Oil of Vitriol' for sulfuric acid, and 'Spirit of Salt' for hydrochloric acid have long (hopefully) been discarded.

Multiplying Affixes

$\frac{1}{2}$	hemi	8	octa	15	pentadeca
1	mono	9	nona (Latin)	16	hexadeca
$1\frac{1}{2}$	sesqui		ennea (Greek)	17	heptadeca
2	di	10	deca	18	octadeca
3	tri	11	undeca (Latin)	19	nonadeca
4	tetra		henadeca (Greek)	20	eicosa
5	penta	12	dodeca	24	tetracosa
6	hexa	13	trideca	30	triaconta
7	hepta	14	tetradeca	40	tetraconta

STABLE INORGANIC ACIDS OF THE NON-METALLIC ELEMENTS

Boron
boric acid (crystals) H_3BO_3

Arsenic
arsenious acid* H_3AsO_3
arsenic acid* H_3AsO_4

Bromine
hydrobromic acid (45%) HBr
hypobromous acid* $HBrO$
bromic acid* $HBrO_3$

Carbon
carbonic acid* H_2CO_3
carbolic acid (phenol) C_6H_5OH

Chlorine
hydrochloric acid (35%) HCl
hypochlorous acid* $HClO$
chlorous acid* $HClO_2$
chloric acid* $HClO_3$
perchloric acid (60%) $HClO_4$

Fluorine
hydrofluoric acid (40%) HF
fluoroboric acid (40%) HBF_4
fluorosilicic acid H_2SiF_6
fluorosulfonic acid (liquid) HSO_3F

Iodine
hydriodic acid (55%) HI
hypoiodic acid* HIO
iodic acid (crystals) HIO_3
periodic acid (crystals) HIO_4

Nitrogen
hyponitrous acid* $H_2N_2O_2$
nitrous acid* HNO_2
nitric acid (70%) HNO_3

Phosphorus
phosphinic acid (50%) H_3PO_2
(hypophosphorous acid)
phosphonic acid (crystals) H_3PO_3
(orthophosphorous acid)
diphosphonic acid (crystals) $H_4P_2O_5$
(pyrophosphorous acid)
diphosphoric acid (crystals) $H_4P_2O_6$
(hypophosphoric acid)
metaphosphoric acid (solid) $(HPO_3)_n$
orthophosphoric acid (85%) H_3PO_4
diphosphoric acid (crystals) $H_4P_2O_7$
(pyrophosphoric acid)

Selenium
selenious acid (crystals) H_2SeO_3
selenic acid (crystals) H_2SeO_4

Silicon
metasilicic acid (solid) $(H_2SiO_3)_n$
orthosilicic acid* H_4SiO_4

Sulfur
sulfurous acid* H_2SO_3
sulfuric acid (liquid) H_2SO_4
peroxomonosulfuric acid (crystals) H_2SO_5
(Caro's Acid)
dithionic acid* $H_2S_2O_6$
disulfuric acid (crystals) $H_2S_2O_7$
(pyrosulfuric acid)
peroxodisulfuric acid (crystals) $H_2S_2O_8$
(persulfuric acid)

Tellurium
tellurous acid (crystals) H_2TeO_3
orthotelluric acid (crystals) H_6TeO_6

---

* Stable only in aqueous solution
Values in parentheses indicate the concentration in aqueous solution of the usual commercial grades of the acid.

Organic chemistry

Organic chemistry is the chemistry of hydrocarbons and their derivatives. The original division between organic chemical compounds (meaning those occurring in the Animal and Plant Kingdoms) and inorganic chemical compounds (meaning those occurring in the mineral world) was made in 1675 by Lémery. This oversimplified division was upset when in 1828 Wöhler produced urea ($NH_2.CO.NH_2$) in an attempt to produce ammonium cyanate ($NH_4.CNO$) from inorganic sources and was ended with the synthesis of acetic acid (ethanoic acid) from its elements by Kolbe in 1845, and the synthesis of methane by Berthelot in 1856. Carbon has a valency number (from the Latin *valens* = worth) of 2 or 4, i.e. a combining power expressed in terms of the number of hydrogen atoms with which the atom of carbon can combine. In addition the carbon atom has the unique property of being able to join one to another to form chains, rings, double bonds and triple bonds.

Thus there are almost limitless numbers of organic compounds and since nearly four million are known then the transition to a strict system of nomenclature from the plethora of trivial names is an essential aim of the International Union of Pure and Applied Chemistry. When all the carbon valencies are utilized in bonding with other carbon or hydrogen atoms, with all the carbon linkages as single bonds, the hydrocarbons are said to be *saturated* and may be in the form of chains or rings. When the carbon atoms are joined together by double or triple bonds then these bonds are potentially available for completion of saturation and therefore such hydrocarbons are said to be *unsaturated*. Open chain compounds are called aliphatic from the Greek *aliphos*, fat, since the first compounds in this class to be studied were the so-called fatty acids.

Saturated hydrocarbons
Straight chain hydrocarbons necessarily conform to the formula C_nH_{2n+2} and are known collectively as **alkanes** or by their trivial name paraffins (form the Latin *parvum affinis*, small affinity, which refers to their low combining power with other substances). The first four alkanes retain their semi-trivial names:

CHEMFORM NO 1

methane (CH_4)   ethane (C_2H_6)

propane (C_3H_8)   butane (C_4H_{10})

The higher alkanes are named by utilizing the recommended multiplying affixes listed in the Inorganic Section to indicate the number of carbon atoms in the chain, i.e. C_5H_{12} is pentane, C_7H_{16} is heptane, and C_9H_{20} is nonane.

Ring compounds, in which the carbon atoms form a closed ring, are known as the **naphthene** family and of the formula C_nH_{2n}. They take their names from the corresponding alkanes by adding the prefix *cyclo-*, e.g.

CHEMFORM NO 2

cyclobutane (C_4H_8)   cyclopropane (C_3H_6)

cyclopentane (C_5H_{10})   cyclohexane (C_6H_{12})

Unsaturated hydrocarbons
Compounds with one double bond are of the structure type $> C = C <$ and are of the formula C_nH_{2n}. They are known as **alkenes** or by the trivial name olefins (from the Latin *oleum*, oil, *faceo* = to make). They are named after their alkane equivalents by substituting the ending *-ene* to the root of the name, although the old system was to substitute the ending *-ylene*, e.g.

CHEMFORM NO 3

ethene (ethylene) (C_2H_4)   propene (propylene) (C_3H_6)

The higher alkenes are similarly named:

C_4H_8 butene (butylene)
C_5H_{10} pentene (pentylene)
C_6H_{12} hexene (hexylene) et seq.

where the letter ending 'a' in buta, penta, hexa, etc. is dropped for ease of pronunciation. When more than one double bond is present the endings *diene*, *triene*, etc. are used with the positions of the double bonds being carefully noted, i.e. $CH_2 = CH - CH = CH_2$ is buta-1,3-diene.

Compounds with one triple bond are called **alkynes** or by their trivial name acetylenes (from the Latin *acetum* = vinegar) and are of the general formula C_nH_{2n-2}. The same rules for nomenclature are used with the ending *-yne* being added to the root of the name of the equivalent alkane. The first member of the group is named ethyne although the more common name acetylene still has a semi-trivial standing. Typical group members include:

CHEMFORM NO 4

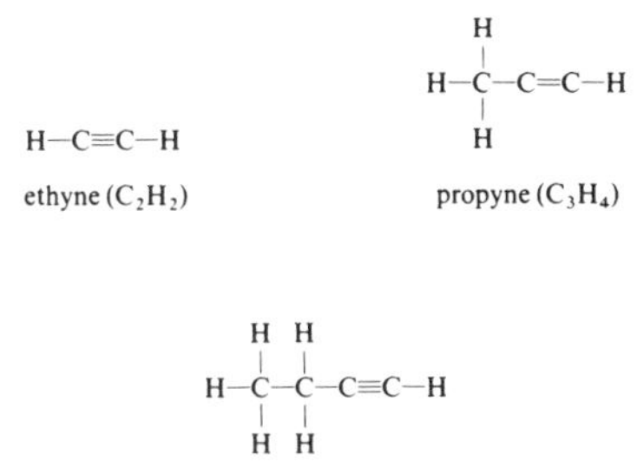

ethyne (C_2H_2) propyne (C_3H_4)

butyne (C_4H_6)

Aromatic hydrocarbons

Substances based on the hydrocarbon benzene C_6H_6 have the family name **aromatic** (from the Greek *aroma*, fragrant smell). They are characterized by the six membered ring represented as having alternating or conjugate double bonds as shown on the left below, although because the double bonds have no fixed positions it is usual to symbolize the structure as shown on the right:

CHEMFORM NO 5

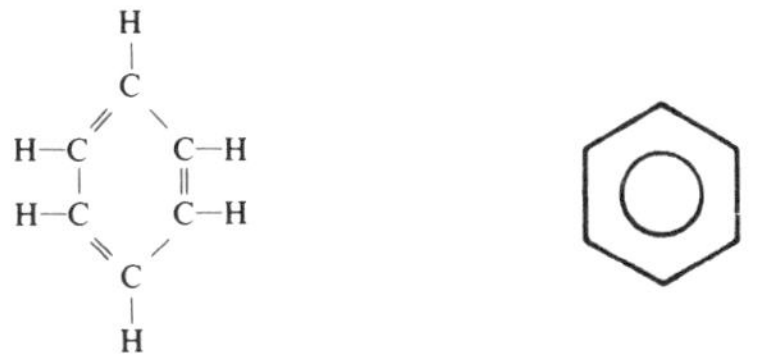

It is possible to produce multiple rings based on the benzene structure, e.g.

CHEMFORM NO 6

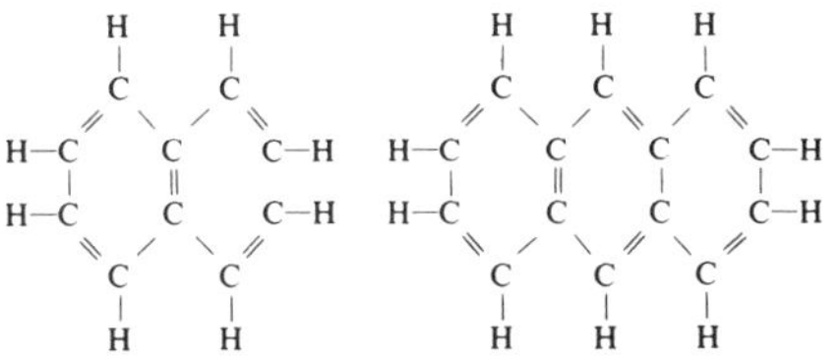

naphthalene ($C_{10}H_8$) anthracene ($C_{14}H_{10}$)

Organic radicals

Removal of a hydrogen atom from hydrocarbon molecules forms a radical which is named by replacing the suffix *-ane* by *-yl*, e.g.

$(CH_3)^-$ *methyl*; from Greek *methy*, wine, *hyle* = wood
$(C_2H_5)^-$ *ethyl*; from Greek *aither*, clean air (i.e. odourless)
$(C_3H_7)^-$ *propyl*; from Greek *pro*, before, and *peon*, fat, hence radical of fatty acid
$(C_4H_9)^-$ *butyl*, from Greek *butyrum* = butter (rancid smell)

Higher radicals are again based on the use of multiplying affixes, i.e. pentane becomes pentyl $(C_5H_{11})^-$ and hexane becomes hexyl $(C_6H_{13})^-$. These radicals are generically known as **alkyls** and being covalent they can be substituted for hydrogen in other molecules.

The general designation for radicals of aromatic hydrocarbons is **aryl** and the monovalent radical formed from benzene $(C_6H_5)^-$ is called *phenyl* and not *benzyl* which is reserved for the radical $(C_6H_5CH_2)^-$. The use of these radical names leads to a better description of a molecule's structure, i.e. the semi-trivial name toluene does not immediately convey an indication of molecular structure but its systematic equivalent methyl benzene indicates the replacement of one of the hydrogen atoms in the benzene ring by a methyl group.

Isomers and organic nomenclature

It is evident that except in the cases of the simplest organic molecules, it is possible to rearrange the positions of carbon atoms along the molecule skeleton (chain isomerism), or to a limited extent reposition double and triple bonds along the chain, or substitute radicals for hydrogen atoms at specific points along the chain (position isomerism).

In the case of the alkanes (paraffins) methane, ethane, and propane exist only as single molecular species, but butane exists in two – the normal straight chain (n) and a branched isomeric chain (iso), and pentane in three – normal, isomeric, and neopentane:

CHEMFORM NO 7

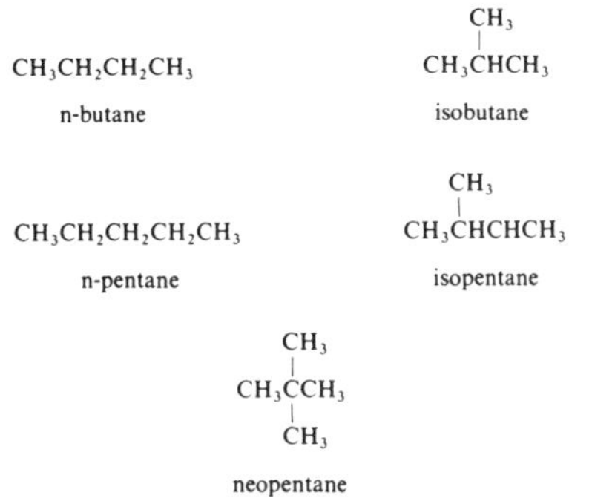

From then on there is a rapid increase with the alkane $C_{15}H_{32}$ exhibiting no less than 4347 possible isomeric states!

However in the IUPAC system of nomenclature the use of these prefixes becomes unnecessary since the longest possible chain is chosen as the *parent* chain and the positions of sites on the chain are indicated by numbers, the direction of numbering being so chosen as to give the lowest series of numbers for the *side* chains. Thus isobutane becomes 2-methyl propane (since the methyl radical is attached to the second carbon atom in the chain), isopentane becomes 2-methyl butane for the same reason, and neopentane becomes 2,2-dimethyl propane (since two of the methyl radicals are regarded as forming a 'chain' with the central carbon atom and the two other methyl radicals are both attached to the 'second' carbon atom). For single bonding the treatment of more complex molecules is a simple extension of this principle with apparent side chains being regarded as belonging to the parent chain where necessary, e.g. the structure below is 3-methyl hexane and *not* 2-propyl butane:

CHEMFORM NO 8

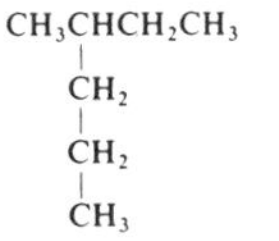

For alkenes (olefins) and alkynes (acetylenes) the chain is always numbered from the end closest to the double or triple bond and the positions of these bonds are also specified:

CHEMFORM NO 9A

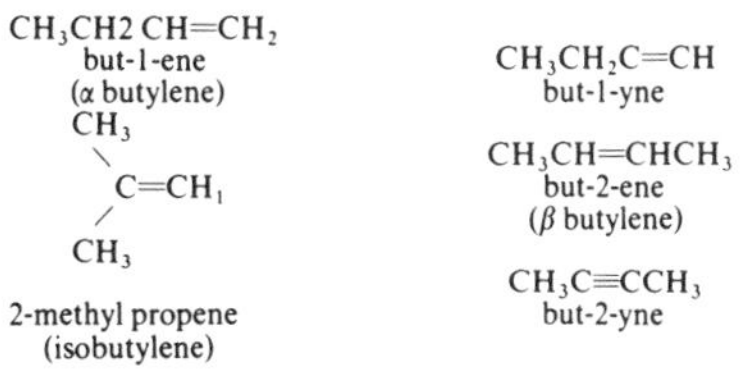

In compounds containing mixed bonds the double bond takes preference over triple bonds in numbering the chain and double and triple bonds take preference over single bonds in deciding the length of the parent chain.

When there is more than one type of radical attached to the parent chain then these are listed in strict alphabetical order without regard to the position on the chain, e.g. for the first five radicals the order will be: butyl, ethyl, methyl, pentyl, and propyl. The multiplying affixes used to indicate the total number of a particular type of radical are ignored in this sequence, e.g. ethyl still precedes dimethyl and triethyl before methyl.

For radicals the same rules apply and apart from the prefixes *normal*, *iso*, and *neo* discussed previously, the old system also includes *secondary* (*sec*) isomers (so called because two hydrogen atoms have been repositioned from the principal carbon atom and their bonds replaced by two of the carbon bonds) and *tertiary* (*tert*) isomers (so called because three hydrogen atoms have been repositioned). In the IUPAC system these prefixes are no longer required since the longest chain principle is applied and numbering specified from the carbon atom which has the free valency. In the examples of the propyl and butyl isomers listed below the names isopropyl and isobutyl are still retained on a semi-trivial basis:

CHEMFORM NO 9B

Trivial Name	Structure	IUPAC Name
n-propyl	$CH_3CH_2CH_2—$	propyl
iso-propyl	CH_3CHCH_3	1-methylethyl
n-butyl	$CH_3CH_2CH_2CH_2—$	butyl
iso-butyl	$(CH_3)_2CHCH_2—$	2-methylpropyl
sec-butyl	$CH_3CH_2CHCH_3$	1-methylpropyl
tert-butyl	$(CH_3)_3C—$	1,1-dimethylethyl

In the case of aromatic hydrocarbons, when two or more substituents are present in the benzene ring, the old nomenclature technique was to assign prefixes ortho, meta, and para to the name of the compound to indicate the differences in the positions of the radicals, i.e.

CHEMFORM NO 10

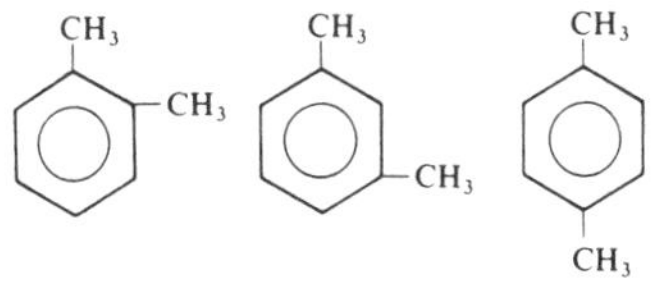

ortho (o) *meta* (m) *para* (p)

where ortho = neighbouring positions
meta = one position between the groups
para = opposite positions

In the IUPAC system these prefixes are again rendered unnecessary by simply numbering the benzene ring as shown below with the main functional group substituted usually assigned to position 1:

CHEMFORM NO 11

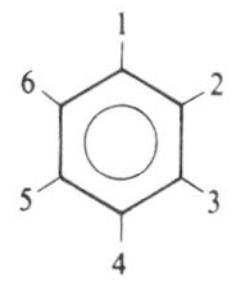

Thus a comparison of the different naming systems for the above examples clearly indicates the superiority of the IUPAC system:

Trivial Name	Semi-Trivial Name	IUPAC Name
o-xylene	o-dimethylbenzene	1,2,-dimethylbenzene
m-xylene	m-dimethylbenzene	1,3,-dimethylbenzene
p-xylene	p-dimethylbenzene	1,4-dimethylbenzene

Substitution radicals

(*a*) *Alcohols*. Replacement of hydrogen atoms by hydroxyl groups (OH) leads to the **alcohols**. If the hydroxyl radical is the *principal* group (see end of this section) then the alcohol molecule is named after the hydrocarbon base with the ending *-ol* substituted for the ending *-e*, e.g. methanol (methyl alcohol) CH_3OH and ethanol (ethyl alcohol) C_2H_5OH. However, with longer chains the position of the attachment has to be specified and this is achieved by selecting the longest chain containing the hydroxyl group and assigning the lowest possible number to this side chain hydroxyl radical using the suffix *-ol*, e.g.

CHEMFORM NO 11B

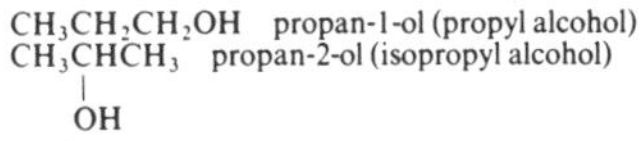

This simplified procedure can be extended to much more complex alcohols provided that the hydroxyl radical is the principal group. To represent a number of alcohols present in a single molecule the multiplying affixes are used to obtain the endings *-diol*, *-triol*, etc.

In the case of aromatic hydrocarbons the single hydroxyl attachment is known as *phenol* whilst multi-hydroxyl groups are named on the *benzene ... ol* system, even though the true aromatic alcohols are compounds containing the hydroxyl group in a side chain and may be regarded as aryl derivatives of the aliphatic alcohols, i.e. benzyl alcohol $C_6H_5CH_2OH$ is a true aromatic alcohol. Use of the new nomenclature gives a clearer understanding of molecular structure, e.g.

CHEMFORM NO 12

benzene-1,2-diol (catechol)

benzene-1,3-diol (resorcinol)

benzene-1,4-diol (quinol)

(*b*) *Ethers.* Derivatives of alcohols in which the hydrogen atoms in the hydroxyl groups are replaced by carbon are known as **ethers**. Thus $(C_6H_5)_2O$ is diphenyl ether and $CH_3.O.C_2H_5$ is ethylmethyl ether (using the rule that where there is no preference then the radicals are named alphabetically) but there is a tendency to treat the ether radical as a group (O.R) where 'R' is an alkyl radical part of the ether compound, so the above mixed radical compound would be methoxyethane since the group are known generically as **alkoxy** groups. Similarly $(C_2H_5)_2O$ becomes ethoxyethane rather than diethyl ether. When the two alkyl groups are the same the ether is said to be symmetrical or simple (i.e. ethoxyethane) but if the two alkyl groups are different the ether is said to be unsymmetrical or mixed (i.e. methoxyethane).

(*c*) *Aldehydes.* The substitution by the radical (CHO) leads to compounds known as the **aldehydes** although the suffix *carbaldehyde* is used if the carbon atom in the radical is not part of the base hydrocarbons, i.e. C_6H_5CHO is benzene carbaldehyde rather than its former name benzaldehyde. Where the carbon in the aldehyde is part of the original base hydrocarbon then the compound is named by substituting the ending *-al* for the hydrocarbon containing the same number of atoms in the parent group. Thus HCHO is methanal (formerly formaldehyde) and CH_3CHO is ethanal (formerly acetaldehyde).

(*d*) *Ketones.* Ketones are based on the double bonded (>CO) radical. The trivial naming technique is to add the name ketone to the ends of the names of the radicals connected by the bond, i.e. $(CH_3)_2CO$ is dimethyl ketone and $CH_3.CO.C_2H_5$ is ethyl methyl ketone. However the new recommended technique is to name the molecule after the longest structural chain by adding the ending *-one*. Thus dimethyl ketone or acetone is in reality propanone. For similar reasons ethyl methyl ketone becomes butanone, etc.

(*e*) *Acids.* The functional group (COOH) is known as carboxylic acid and is used as such if the carbon atom is not part of the main base hydrocarbon, e.g.

CHEMFORM NO 13

benzene carboxylic acid (benzoic acid)

benzene-1,2-dicarboxylic acid (phthalic acid)

However if the carbon atom is part of the base chain then the acid molecule is named by substituting the ending *-oic* to the name of the hydrocarbon containing the same number of carbon atoms, i.e.

HCOOH	methanoic acid (formic acid)
CH_3COOH	ethanoic acid (acetic acid)
CH_3CH_2COOH	propanoic acid
$CH_3CH_2CH_2COOH$	butanoic acid

(*f*) *Amines.* Amines are formed by substituting (NH_2) groups in place of hydrogen and the class name is added to the alkyl radical, i.e. CH_3NH_2 is methylamine. Further substitution can take place leading to dimethylamine $(CH_3)_2NH$ and even trimethylamine $(CH_3)_3N$. The aromatic amine $C_6H_5NH_2$ is phenylamine (aniline).

(*g*) *Principal Groups.* Since a large number of different radicals can attach to the base hydrocarbon it is important to produce an order of preference for listing these radicals. With a mixture of radicals the principal group is named as described above but the secondary groups are now named using prefixes to identify the type. Thus for hydroxy groups as secondary groups the ending *-ol* is dropped in favour of the prefix *hydroxy*. This occurs for many alcoholic compounds since this group is towards the bottom of the list. The carboxylic radical (COOH) heads the list and ethers, aldehydes, and ketones are intermediate.

Stereoisomerism
Where the carbon atoms are linked by double bonds, rotation of the kind exhibited by chain and position isomerism is not possible. In this case isomerism can occur geometrically. For example, dichloroethene which has a double bond may occur in a *cis* form (from the Latin *cis*, on the near side) which indicates that the chlorine atoms are on the same side of the molecule, and a *trans* form (from the Latin *trans*, on the far side) which indicates that the atoms are diagonally opposed across the double bond, i.e.

CHEMFORM NO 14

cis-dichloroethene

trans-dichloroethene

The third class of isomerism is optical isomerism. In this the molecule of one is in one form but the molecule of the other is laterally inverted as in a mirror image. Using the instrument known as a *polarimeter* it can be shown that one isomer has the effect of twisting the plane of light shone through it to the right while its

Common organic compounds

Common Name	Recommended Name	Formula
Acetaldehyde	Ethanal	$CH_3.CHO$
Acetic acid	Ethanoic acid	$CH_3.COOH$
Acetone	Propanone	$CH_3.CO.CH_3$
Acetylene	Ethyne	$CH{\equiv}CH$
Alcohol (ethyl)	Ethanol	$CH_3.CH_2OH$
Alcohol (wood)	Methanol	CH_3OH
Amyl acetate	Pentyl ethanoate	$CH_3.COO.C_5H_{11}$
Aniline	Phenylamine	$C_6H_5.NH_2$
Anthracene	no change	$C_{14}H_{10}$
Ascorbic acid (Vitamin C)	no change	$O.CO.C(OH){=}C(OH).CH.CHOH.CH_2OH$
Aspirin	Acetyl o-salicylic acid	$CH_3.COO.C_6H_4.COOH$
Aspirin (soluble)	Calcium salt of acetyl o-salicylic acid	$(CH_3.COO.C_6H_4.COO)_2Ca.2H_2O$
Benzaldehyde	Benzenecarbaldehyde	$C_6H_5.CHO$
Benzene	no change	C_6H_6
Benzoic acid	Benzenecarboxylic acid	$C_6H_5.COOH$
Bromoform	Tribromomethane	$CHBr_3$
Butane	no change	C_4H_{10}
Butylene	Butene	C_4H_8
Camphor	no change	$CO.CH_2CH[C(CH_3)_2].(CH_2)_2.C.CH_3$
Carbon tetrachloride	Tetrachloromethane	CCl_4
Celluloid	Poly(cellulose nitrate)	$[-C_6H_7O_2(OH)(ONO_2)_2-]_n$
Chloroform	Trichloromethane	$CHCl_3$
Citric acid	2-hydroxypropane-1,2,3-tricarboxylic acid	$(C(OH)(COOH)(CH_2.COOH)_2.H_2O$
Cyanogen	no change	$NC.CN$
Cyclohexane	no change	$CH_2.(CH_2)_4.CH_2$
Decane	no change	$C_{10}H_{22}$
Dimethylglyoxime	Butanedione dioxime	$(CH_3.C{=}N.OH)_2$
Diphenylamine	no change	$(C_6H_5)_2.NH$
Ethane	no change	C_2H_6
Ether (diethyl)	Ethoxyethane	$(CH_3.CH_2)_2O$
Ether (dimethyl)	Methoxymethane	$(CH_3)_2O$
Ethylene	Ethene	$CH_2{=}CH_2$
Ethyl mercaptan	Ethanethiol	$CH_3.CH_2SH$
Formaldehyde (Formalin)	Methanal	$H.CHO$
Formic acid	Methanoic acid	$H.COOH$
Fructose (Fruit Sugar)	no change	$O.CH_2(CHOH)_3C(OH).CH_2OH$
Glucose (Dextrose or Grape Sugar)	no change	$O.(CHOH)_4.CH.CH_2OH$
Glycerine (Glycerol)	Propane-1,2,3-triol	$CH_2OH.CHOH.CH_2OH$
Glycol	Ethane-1,2-diol	$CH_2OH.CH_2OH$
Heptane	no change	C_7H_{16}
Hexane	no change	C_6H_{14}
Indigo	Indigotin	$NH.C_6H_4.CO.C{=}C.CO.C_6H_4.NH$
Ketone, diethyl	Pentan-3-one	$(CH_3.CH_2)_2CO$
Ketone, ethylmethyl	Butanone	$CH_3.CO.CH_2.CH_3$
Lactic acid	2-hydroxypropanoic acid	$CH_3.CHOH.COOH$
Lactose (Milk Sugar)	no change	$C_{12}H_{22}O_{11}.H_2O$
Lead, tetraethyl	Tetraethyl lead (IV)	$(CH_3.CH_2)_4Pb$

Common Name	Recommended Name	Formula
Maltose (Malt Sugar)	no change	$C_{12}H_{22}O_{11}.H_2O$
Melamine	Tricyanodiamide	$NH_2.C=N.C(NH_2)=N.C(NH_2)=N$
Methane (Marsh Gas)	no change	CH_4
Mustard Gas	Dichlorodiethyl sulfide	$(ClCH_2.CH_2)_2S$
Naphthalene	no change	$C_{10}H_8$
Naphthol	Naphthalenol	$C_{10}H_7.OH$
Neoprene	Poly (2-chlorobuta-1,3-diene)	$[-CH_2.C(Cl)=CH.CH_2-]_n$
Nitroglycerine	Propane-1,2,3-triyl trinitrate	$(O_2N.O)_3C_3H_5$
Nonane	no change	C_9H_{20}
Nylon	no change	$[-CO.(CH_2)_4.CO.NH.(CH_2)_6.NH-]_n$
Octane	no change	C_8H_{18}
Oxalic acid	Ethanedioic acid	$(COOH)_2$
Pentane	no change	C_5H_{12}
Phenol (Carbolic Acid)	no change	$C_6H_5.OH$
Phenolphthalein	no change	$O.CO.C_6H_4.C(C_6H_4.OH)_2$
Phosgene	Carbonyl chloride	$COCl_2$
Phthalic acid	Benzene-1,2-dicarboxylic acid	$C_6H_4(COOH)_2$
Picric acid	2,4,6-trinitrophenol	$(NO_2)_3.C_6H_2.OH$
Polystyrene	Poly (phenylethene)	$[-CH(C_6H_5).CH_2-]_n$
PTFE (Polytetrafluoro-ethylene) (Teflon)	Poly (tetrafluoroethene)	$[-CF_2.CF_2-]_n$
Polythene	Poly (ethene)	$[-CH_2.CH_2-]_n$
PVC (Polyvinyl chloride)	Poly (chloroethene)	$[-CH_2.CHCl-]_n$
Propane	no change	C_3H_6
Propionic acid	Propanoic acid	$CH_3.CH_2.COOH$
Propylene	Propene	C_3H_6
Prussic acid	Hydrocyanic acid	$HN=CH.NC$
Pyridine	no change	C_6H_5N
Rayon	Regenerated cellulose	$S=C(OR).SNa(R=cellulose[C_6H_{10}O_5]_n)$
Rochelle Salt	Potassium sodium 2,3-dihydroxy butanedioate	$COOK.(CHOH)_2COONa.4H_2O$
Saccharin (soluble)	Sodium salt of o-sulfo-benzoicimide	$CO.C_6H_4.SO_2.NNa.2H_2O$
Salicylic acid	2-hydroxybenzenecarboxylic acid	$C_6H_4(OH).COOH$
Soap	Sodium or potassium salts of high molecular weight fatty acids such as palmitic acid (hexadecanoic acid) ($C_{15}H_{31}.COOH$) and stearic acid (octadecanoic acid) ($C_{17}H_{35}.COOH$)	$C_{15}H_{31}.COOR$ or $C_{17}H_{35}.COOR$ where $R=Na$ or K
Succinic acid	Butanedioic acid	$(CH_2.COOH)_2$
Sucrose (Cane Sugar or Beet Sugar)	no change	$C_{12}H_{22}O_{11}$
Tartaric acid	2,3-dihydroxybutanedioic acid	$(CHOH.COOH)_2$
Toluene	Methylbenzene	$C_6H_5.CH_3$
Trichloroethylene	Trichloroethene	$ClHC=CCl_2$
TNT (Trinitrotoluene)	Methyl-2,4,6-nitrobenzene	$(NO_2)_3.C_6H_2.CH_3$
Urea	Carbamide	$NH_2.CO.NH_2$
Valeric acid	Pentanoic acid	$CH_3.CH_2.CH_2.CH_2.COOH$
Xylene	Dimethylbenzene	$C_6H_4(CH_3)_2$

isomer twists it to the left. These optically active forms are known as the *d*-form (*dextro* or right rotating) and the *l*-form (*laevo* or left rotating). When the isomers are mixed in equal proportions the rotating effect is cancelled out to give an optically inactive or *racemic* form (from the Latin *racemus* = a bunch of grapes, because the mother liquid of fermented grape juice exhibits this characteristic). The practical importance of this phenomenon can be illustrated by the ability of yeast to convert *d*-grape sugar to alcohol and its powerlessness to affect the *l*-compound.

Carbohydrates

These are an important source of energy for living organisms as well as a means by which chemical energy can be stored. The name originally indicated the belief that compounds of this group could be represented as hydrates of carbon of general formula $C_x(H_2O)_y$ but it is now realized that many important carbohydrates do not have the required 2 to 1 hydrogen to oxygen ratio whilst other compounds which conform to this structure, such as methanal (formaldehyde) (HCHO) and ethanoic acid (acetic acid) (CH_3COOH) are obviously not of this group. Further, other carbohydrates contain sulfur and nitrogen as important constituents. Carbohydrates can be defined as polyhydroxy aldehydes or ketones or as a substance which yields these compounds on hydrolysis. Glucose and fructose (both of general formula $C_6H_{12}O_6$) are typical examples, respectively of an 'aldose' and a 'ketose', e.g.

CHEMFORM NO 15

glucose
$C_5H_{11}O_5.CHO$

fructose
$C_5H_{12}O_5.C=O$

Carbohydrates are defined by the number of carbon atoms in the molecule using the usual multiplying affixes, i.e. tetrose for 4 carbon atoms, pentose for 5, hexose for 6, etc. They are divided into two main groups known as sugars and polysaccharides, where the former is subdivided into monosaccharides of general formula $C_nH_{2n}O_n$ (where $n = 2$ to 10) which cannot be hydrolysed into smaller molecules, and oligosaccharides such as disaccharides ($C_{12}H_{22}O_{11}$), trisaccharides ($C_{18}H_{32}O_{16}$), and tetrasaccharides ($C_{24}H_{42}O_{21}$) which yield two, three, and four monosaccharide molecules respectively on hydrolysis.

The polysaccharides yield a large number of monosaccharides on hydrolysis and have molecular weights ranging from thousands to several million. The most widely spread polysaccharides are of the general formula $(C_6H_{10}O_5)_n$ and include *starch*, which occurs in all green plants and is obtained from maize, wheat, barley, rice and potatoes, and from which dextrins are produced by boiling with water under pressure; *glycogen*, which is the reserve carbohydrate of animals and is often known as 'animal starch'; and *cellulose*, the main constituent of the cell walls of plants.

Of the naturally-occurring sugars (which are all optically active), the most familiar monosaccharides are the dextrorotary (D+) aldohexose *glucose* (dextrose or grape sugar) and the laevorotary (D−) ketohexose *fructose* (laevulose or fruit sugar), both of formula $C_6H_{12}O_6$.

The most important disaccharides are those of the formula $C_{12}H_{22}O_{11}$ and include *sucrose* (cane sugar or beet sugar) obtained from sugar cane or sugar beet after chemical treatment; *maltose* (malt sugar) produced by the action of malt on starch; and *lactose* (milk sugar) which occurs naturally in the milk of all mammals.

Table of the 109 elements

Atomic Number	Symbol	Name of Element	Derived From	Discoverers	Year
1	H	Hydrogen	Greek, 'hydor genes' = water producer	H Cavendish (UK)	1766
2	He	Helium	Greek, 'helios' = sun	J N Lockyer (UK) and P-J-C Jannsen (France)	1868
3	Li	Lithium	Greek, 'lithos' = stone	J A Arfwedson (Sweden)	1817
4	Be	Beryllium	Greek, 'beryllion' = beryl	N-L Vauquelin (France)	1798
5	B	Boron	Persian, 'burah' = borax	L-J Gay Lussac and L-J Thenard (France) and H Davy (UK)	1808
6	C	Carbon	Latin, *carbo* = charcoal	Prehistoric	—
7	N	Nitrogen	Greek, 'nitron genes' = saltpetre producer	D Rutherford (UK)	1772
8	O	Oxygen	Greek, 'oxys genes' = acid producer	C W Scheele (Sweden) and J Priestley (UK) (pub. 1774)	*c.* 1772
9	F	Fluorine	Latin *fluo* = flow	H Moissan (France)	1886
10	Ne	Neon	Greek, 'neos' = new	W Ramsay and M W Travers (UK)	1898
11	Na	Sodium (Natrium)	English, soda	H Davy (UK)	1807
12	Mg	Magnesium	Magnesia, a district in Thessaly	H Davy (UK)	1808
13	Al	Aluminium	Latin, *alumen* = alum	H C Oerstedt (Denmark) and F Wöhler (Germany)	1825–7
14	Si	Silicon	Latin, *silex* = flint	J J Berzelius (Sweden)	1824
15	P	Phosphorus	Greek, 'phosphorus' = light bringing	H Brand (Germany)	1669
16	S	Sulfur (Note 1)	Sanskrit, 'solvere'; Latin, *sulfurum*	Prehistoric	—
17	Cl	Chlorine	Greek, 'chloros' = green	C W Scheele (Sweden)	1774
18	Ar	Argon	Greek, 'argos' = inactive	W Ramsay and Lord Rayleigh (UK)	1894
19	K	Potassium (Kalium)	English, potash	H Davy (UK)	1807
20	Ca	Calcium	Latin, *calx* = lime	H Davy (UK)	1808
21	Sc	Scandium	Scandinavia	L F Nilson (Sweden)	1879
22	Ti	Titanium	Latin, *Titanes* = sons of the earth	M H Klaproth (Germany)	1795
23	V	Vanadium	Vanadis, a name give to Freyja, the Norse goddess of beauty and youth	N G Sefström (Sweden)	1830
24	Cr	Chromium	Greek, 'chromos' = colour	N-L Vauquelin (France)	1798
25	Mn	Manganese	Latin, *magnes* = magnet	J G Gahn (Sweden)	1774
26	Fe	Iron (Ferrum)	Anglo-Saxon, *iren*	Earliest smelting	*c.*4000 BC
27	Co	Cobalt	German, *kobold* = goblin	G Brandt (Sweden)	1737
28	Ni	Nickel	German, abbreviation of *kupfernickel* (devil's 'copper') or niccolite	A F Cronstedt (Sweden)	1751
29	Cu	Copper (Cuprum)	Cyprus	Prehistoric (earliest known use)	*c.* 8000 BC
30	Zn	Zinc	German, *zink*	A S Marggraf (Germany)	1746
31	Ga	Gallium	Latin, *Gallia* = France	L de Boisbaudran (France)	1875
32	Ge	Germanium	Latin, *Germania* = Germany	C A Winkler (Germany)	1886
33	As	Arsenic	Latin, *arsenicum*	Albertus Magnus (Germany)	*c.* 1220
34	Se	Selenium	Greek, 'selene' = moon	J J Berzelius (Sweden)	1818
35	Br	Bromine	Greek 'bromos' = stench	A-J Balard (France)	1826
36	Kr	Krypton	Greek, 'kryptos' = hidden	W Ramsay and M W Travers (UK)	1898
37	Rb	Rubidium	Latin, *rubidus* = red	R W Bunsen and G R Kirchhoff (Germany)	1861
38	Sr	Strontium	Strontian, a village in Highland region, Scotland	W Cruikshank (UK)	1787
39	Y	Yttrium	Ytterby, in Sweden	J Gadolin (Finland)	1794
40	Zr	Zirconium	Persion, 'zargun' = gold coloured	M H Klaproth (Germany)	1789
41	Nb	Niobium	Latin, *Niobe*, daughter of Tantalus	C Hatchett (UK)	1801
42	Mo	Molybdenum	Greek, 'molybdos' = lead	P J Hjelm (Sweden)	1781
43	Tc	Technetium	Greek, 'technetos' = artificial	C Perrier (France) and E Segré (Italy/USA)	1937
44	Ru	Ruthenium	Ruthenia (The Ukraine, in USSR)	K K Klaus (Estonia/USSR)	1844
45	Rh	Rhodium	Greek, 'rhodon' = rose	W H Wollaston (UK)	1804
46	Pd	Palladium	The asteroid Pallas (discovered 1802)	W H Wollaston (UK)	1803
47	Ag	Silver (Argentum)	Anglo-Saxon, *seolfor*	Prehistoric (earliest silversmithery)	*c.*4000 BC
48	Cd	Cadmium	Greek, 'kadmeia' = calamine	F Stromeyer (Germany)	1817
49	In	Indium	Its indigo spectrum	F Reich and H T Richter (Germany)	1863
50	Sn	Tin (Stannum)	Anglo-Saxon, *tin*	Prehistoric (intentionally alloyed with Cu to make Bronze)	*c.* 3500 BC
51	Sb	Antimony (Stibium)	Lower Latin, *antimonium*	Near Historic	*c.* 1000 BC
52	Te	Tellurium	Latin, *tellus* = earth	F J Muller (Baron von Reichenstein) (Austria)	1783
53	I	Iodine	Greek, 'iodes' = violet	B Courtois (France)	1811
54	Xe	Xenon	Greek, 'xenos' = stranger	W Ramsay and M W Travers (UK)	1898
55	Cs	Caesium	Latin, *caesius* = bluish-grey	R W von Bunsen and G R Kirchoff (Germany)	1860
56	Ba	Barium	Greek, 'barys' = heavy	H Davy (UK)	1808
57	La	Lanthanum	Greek, 'lanthano' = conceal	C G Mosander (Sweden)	1839
58	Ce	Cerium	The asteroid Ceres (discovered 1801)	J J Berzelius and W Hisinger (Sweden); M H Klaproth (Germany)	1803
59	Pr	Praseodymium	Greek, 'prasios didymos' = green twin	C Auer von Welsbach (Austria)	1885
60	Nd	Neodymium	Greek, 'neos didymos' = new twin	C Auer von Welsbach (Austria)	1885
61	Pm	Promethium	Greek demi-god 'Prometheus' – the fire stealer	J Marinsky, L E Glendenin and C D Coryell (USA)	1945

Atomic Weight (Note 3)	Density at 20°C (unless otherwise stated) (g/cm³) (Note 4)	Melting Point °C (Note 5)	Boiling Point °C (Note 5)	Physical Description	Valency Number	Number of Nuclides
1·00794	0·0871 (solid at mp) 0·000 089 89 (gas at 0°C)	−259·192	−252·753	Colourless gas	1	3
4·00260	0·1908 (solid at mp) 0·000 178 5 (gas at 0°C)	−272·375 at 24·985 atm (Note 6)	−268·928	Colourless gas	0	7
6·941	0·5334	180·57	1344	Silvery-white metal	1	8
9·01218	1·846	1289	2476	Grey metal	2	9
10·811	2·297 (β Rhombohedral) 2·465 (α Rhombohedral) 2·396 (β Tetragonal)	2130	3865	Dark brown powder	3	11
12·011	2·266 (Graphite) 3·515 (Diamond)	3530 (Note 7)	3870	Colourless solid (diamond) or black solid (graphite)	2 or 4	13
14·0067	0·9426 (solid at mp) 0·001 250 (gas at 0°C)	−210·004	−195·806	Colourless gas	3 or 5	11
15·9994	1·359 (solid at mp) 0·001 429 (gas at 0°C)	−218·789	−182·962	Colourless gas	2	13
18·998 40	1·780 (solid at mp) 0·001 696 (gas at 0°C)	−219·669	−188·200	Pale greenish-yellow gas	1	13
20·179	1·434 (solid at mp) 0·000 899 9 (gas at 0°C)	−248·589	−246·048	Colourless gas	0	13
22·989 77	0·9688	97·819	884	Silvery-white metal	1	17
24·305	1·737	649	1097	Silvery-white metal	2	15
26·981 54	2·699	660·457	2525	Silvery-white metal	3	16
28·0855	2·329	1414	3225	Dark grey solid	4	16
30·973 76	1·825 (white) 2·361 (violet) 2·708 (black)	44·14 597 at 45 atm 606 at 48 atm	277 431 sublimes 453 sublimes	White to yellow, violet to red, or black solid	3 or 5	17
32·066	2·068 (rhombic)	115·21	444·674	Pale yellow solid	2, 4, or 6	16
35·453	2·038 (solid at mp) 0·003 214 (gas at 0°C)	−100·98	−33·99	Yellow-green gas	1, 3, 5, or 7	15
39·948	1·622 (solid at mp) 0·001 784 (gas at 0°C)	−189·352	−185·855	Colourless gas	0	15
39·0983	0·8591	63·65	760	Silvery-white metal	1	20
40·078	1·526	840	1493	Silvery-white metal	2	18
44·955 91	2·989	1541	2835	Metallic	3	14
47·88	4·504	1670	3360	Silvery metal	3 or 4	16
50·9415	6·119	1920	3425	Silvery-grey metal	2, 3, 4, or 5	15
51·9961	7·193	1860	2687	Silvery metal	2, 3, or 6	16
54·9380	7·472	1246	2065	Reddish-white metal	2, 3, 4, 6, or 7	14
55·847	7·874	1538	2865	Silvery-white metal	2 or 3	16
58·9332	8·834	1495	2900	Reddish-steel metal	2 or 3	12
58·69	8·905	1455	2885	Silvery-white metal	2 or 3	16
63·546	8·934	1084·88	2571	Reddish-bronze metal	1 or 2	17
65·39	7·140	419·58	908	Blue-white metal	2	23
69·723	5·912	29·772	2209	Grey metal	2 or 3	22
75·59	5·327	938·3	2835	Grey-white metal	4	22
74·9126	5·781	817 at 38 atm	603 sublimes	Steel-grey solid	3 or 5	22
78·96	4·810 (trigonal) 4·398 (α monoclinic) 4·352 (β monoclinic)	221·18	685	Greyish solid	2, 4, or 6	23
79·904	3·937 (solid at mp) 3·119 (liquid at 20°C)	−7·25	59·09	Red-brown liquid	1, 3, 5, or 7	23
83·80	2·801 (solid at mp) 0·003 749 (gas at 0°C)	−157·386	−153·35	Colourless gas	0	25
85·4678	1·534	39·29	688	Silvery-white metal	1	27
87·62	2·582	768	1387	Silvery-white metal	2	24
88·9059	4·468	1522	3300	Steel-grey metal	3	23
91·224	6·506	1855	4340	Steel-white metal	4	22
92·9064	8·595	2473	4860	Grey metal	3 or 5	23
95·94	10·22	2624	4680	Silvery metal	2, 3, 4, 5, or 6	22
(97·9072)	11·40	2180	4270	Silvery-grey metal	2, 3, 4, 6, or 7	21
101·07	12·37	2334	4310	Bluish-white metal	3, 4, 6, or 8	23
102·9055	12·42	1963	3705	Steel-blue metal	3 or 4	21
106·42	12·01	1555·3	2975	Silvery-white metal	2 or 4	24
107·8682	10·50	961·93	2167	Lustrous white metal	1	28
112·41	8·648	321·108	768	Blue-white metal	2	28
114·82	7·289	156·635	2076	Bluish-silvery metal	1 or 3	31
118·710	7·288	231·968	2608	Silvery-white metal	2 or 4	32
121·75	6·693	630·755	1589	Silvery metal	3 or 5	29
127·60	6·237	449·87	989	Silver-grey solid	2, 4, or 6	33
126·9045	4·947	113·6	185·3	Grey-black solid	1, 3, 5, or 7	32
131·29	3·410 (solid at mp) 0·005 897 (gas at 0°C)	−111·760	−108·1	Colourless gas	0	36
132·9054	1·896	28·5	671	Silvery-white metal	1	35
137·33	3·595	729	1827	Silvery-white metal	2	31
138·9055	6·145	921	3435	Metallic	3	29
140·12	6·688 (beta) 6·770 (gamma)	799	3465	Steel-grey metal	3 or 4	30
140·9077	6·772	934	3480	Silvery-white metal	3	25
144·24	7·006	1021	3025	Yellowish-white metal	3	28
(144·9128)	7·135	1042	3000	Metallic	3	24

Atomic Number	Symbol	Name of Element	Derived From	Discoverers	Year
62	Sm	Samarium	The mineral Samarskite, named after Col M Samarski, a Russian engineer	L de Boisbaudran (France)	1879
63	Eu	Europium	Europe	E A Demarçay (France)	1901
64	Gd	Gadolinium	Johan Gadolin (1760–1852)	J-C-G de Marignac (Switzerland)	1880
65	Tb	Terbium	Ytterby, in Sweden	C G Mosander (Sweden)	1843
66	Dy	Dysprosium	Greek, 'dysprositos' – hard to get at	L de Boisbaudran (France)	1886
67	Ho	Holmium	Holmia, a Latinised form of Stockholm	J-L Soret (France) and P T Cleve (Sweden)	1878–9
68	Er	Erbium	Ytterby, in Sweden	C G Mosander (Sweden)	1843
69	Tm	Thulium	Latin and Greek, 'Thule' = Northland	P T Cleve (Sweden)	1879
70	Yb	Ytterbium	Ytterby, in Sweden	J-C-G de Marignac (Switzerland)	1878
71	Lu	Lutetium	Lutetia, Roman name for the city of Paris	G Urbain (France)	1907
72	Hf	Hafnium	Hafnia = Copenhagen	D Coster (Netherlands) and G C de Hevesy (Hungary/Sweden)	1923
73	Ta	Tantalum	'Tantalus', a mythical Greek king	A G Ekeberg (Sweden)	1802
74	W	Tungsten (Wolfram)	Swedish, *tung sten* = heavy stone	J J de Elhuyar and F de Elhuyar (Spain)	1783
75	Re	Rhenium	Latin, *Rhenus* = the river Rhine	W Noddack, Fr I Tacke and O Berg (Germany)	1925
76	Os	Osmium	Greek, 'osme' = odour	S Tennant (UK)	1804
77	Ir	Iridium	Latin, *iris* = a rainbow	S Tennant (UK)	1804
78	Pt	Platinum	Spanish, *platina* = small silver	A de Ulloa (Spain)	1748
79	Au	Gold (Aurum)	Anglo-Saxon, *gold*	Prehistoric	—
80	Hg	Mercury (Hydrargyrum)	Assigned the alchemical sign of the Greek god 'Hermes' (Latin *Mercurius*), the divine patron of the occult sciences	Near Historic	*c.* 1600 BC
81	Tl	Thallium	Greek, 'thallos' = a budding twig	W Crookes (UK)	1861
82	Pb	Lead (Plumbum)	Anglo-Saxon, lead	Prehistoric	—
83	Bi	Bismuth	German, *weissmuth* = white matter	C-F Geoffroy (France)	1753
84	Po	Polonium	Poland	Mme M S Curie (Poland/France)	1898
85	At	Astatine	Greek, 'astos' = unstable	D R Corson (USA), K R Mackenzie (USA) and E Segrè (Italy/USA)	1940
86	RN	Radon	Latin, *radius* = ray	F E Dorn (Germany)	1900
87	Fr	Francium	France	Mlle M Perey (France)	1939
88	Ra	Radium	Latin, *radius* = ray	P Curie (France), Mme M S Curie (Poland/France) and M G Bemont (France)	1898
89	Ac	Actinium	Greek, 'aktinos', genitive of 'aktis' = a ray	A Debierne (France)	1899
90	Th	Thorium	Thor, the Norse god of thunder	J J Berzelius (Sweden)	1829
91	Pa	Protactinium	Greek, 'protos' = first, plus actinium	O Hahn (German) and Fr L Meitner (Austria); F Soddy and J A Cranston (UK)	1917
92	U	Uranium	The planet Uranus (discovered 1781)	M H Klaproth (Germany)	1789

Notes
1 The former spelling 'sulphur' is not recommended under International Union of Pure and Applied Chemistry rules on nomenclature.
2 Provisional International Union of Pure and Applied Chemistry names for elements 104 to 109.
3 A value in brackets is the atomic mass of the isotope with the longest known half-life (i.e. the period taken for its radioactivity to fall to half of its original value).

The transuranic elements (metallic)

Atomic Number	Symbol	Name of Element	Derived from	Year	Atomic Weight (Note 3)	Density at 20°C (g/cm³) (Note 4)	Melting Point °C (Note 5)	Boiling Point °C (Note 5)	Number of Nuclides
93	Np	Neptunium	The planet Neptune	1940	(237·0482)	20·47	637	4090	14
94	Pu	Plutonium	The planet Pluto	1940	(244·0642)	20·26	640	3330	15
95	Am	Americium	America	1944	(243·0614)	13·77	1176	2020	13
96	Cm	Curium	The Curies – Pierre (1859–1906) and Marie (1867–1934) of France	1944	(247·0703)	13·69	1340	3190	14
97	Bk	Berkelium	Berkeley, a town in California, USA	1949	(247·0703)	14·67	1050	710	11
98	Cf	Californium	California, USA	1950	(251·0796)	15·23	900	1470	18
99	Es	Einsteinium	Dr. Albert Einstein (1879–1955) (US citizen, b. Germany)	1953	(252·0828)	8·81	860	996	14
100	Fm	Fermium	Dr. Enrico Fermi (1901–54) of Italy	1953	(257·0951)	—	—	—	17
101	Md	Mendelevium	Dmitriy I Mendeleyev (1834–1907) (USSR)	1955	(258·0986)	—	—	—	11
102	No	Nobelium	Alfred B Nobel (1833–96) of Sweden	1958	(259·1009)	—	—	—	10
103	Lr	Lawrencium	Dr Ernest O Lawrence (1901–58)	1961	(260·1054)	—	—	—	8
104	Unq	Unnilquadium (Note 2)	Un-nil-quad (1–0–4)	1964 or 1969	(261·109)	—	—	—	9
105	Unp	Unnilpentium (Note 2)	Un-nil-pent (1–0–5)	1970	(262·114)	—	—	—	6
106	Unh	Unnilhexium (Note 2)	Un-nil-hex (1–0–6)	1974	(263·120)	—	—	—	4
107	Uns	Unnilseptium (Note 2)	Un-nil-sept (1–0–7)	1976	(262)	—	—	—	2 ?
108	Uno	Unniloctium (Note 2)	Un-nil-oct (1–0–8)	1984	(265)	—	—	—	3
109	Une	Unnilennium (Note 2)	Un-nil-enn (1–0–9)	1982	(266)	—	—	—	1

Atomic Weight (Note 3)	Density at 20°C (unless otherwise stated) (g/cm³) (Note 4)	Melting Point °C (Note 5)	Boiling Point °C (Note 5)	Physical Description	Valency Number	Number of Nuclides
150·36	7·517	1077	1794	Light-grey metal	2 or 3	26
151·96	5·243	822	1560	Steel-grey metal	2 or 3	24
157·25	7·899	1313	3270	Silvery-white metal	3	25
158·9254	8·228	1356	3230	Silvery metal	3	22
162·50	8·549	1412	2573	Metallic	3	26
164·9304	8·794	1474	2700	Silvery metal	3	25
167·26	9·064	1529	2815	Greyish-silver metal	3	27
168·9342	9·319	1545	1950	Metallic	2 or 3	28
173·04	6·967	817	1227	Silvery metal	2 or 3	28
174·967	9·839	1665	3400	Metallic	3	32
178·49	13·28	2230	4630	Steel-grey metal	4	31
180·9479	16·67	3020	5520	Silvery metal	3 or 5	28
183·85	19·26	3420	5730	Grey metal	2, 4, 5, or 6	30
186·207	21·01	3185	5610	Whitish-grey metal	1, 4, or 7	31
190·2	22·59	3100	5020	Grey-blue metal	2, 3, 4, 6, or 8	34
192·22	22·56	2447	4730	Silvery-white metal	3 or 4	33
195·08	21·45	1768·7	3835	Bluish-white metal	2 or 4	34
196·9665	19·29	1064·43	2860	Lustrous yellow metal	1 or 3	32
200·59	14·17 (solid at mp) 13·55 (liquid at 20°C)	−38·836	356·661	Silvery metallic liquid	1 or 2	33
204·383	11·87	304	1475	Blue-grey metal	1 or 3	29
207·2	11·35	327·502	1753	Steel-blue metal	2 or 4	32
208·9804	9·807	271·442	1566	Reddish-silvery metal	3 or 5	28
(208·9824)	9·155	254	948	Metallic	2, 3, or 4	27
(209·9871)	~7·0	302	377	Metallic	1, 3, 5, or 7	24
(222·0176)	~4·7 (solid at mp) 0·010 04 (gas at 0°C)	−64·9	−61·2	Colourless gas	0	29
(223·0197)	~2·8	24	657	Metallic	1	30
(226·0254)	5·50	707	1530	Silvery metal	2	25
(227·0278)	10·04	1050	3560	Metallic	3	24
232·0381	11·72	1760	4700	Grey metal	4	25
(231·0359)	15·41	1570	4490	Silvery metal	4 or 5	22
238·0289	19·05	1134	4160	Bluish-white metal	3, 4, 5, or 6	17

4 For the highly radioactive elements the density value has been calculated for the isotope with the longest known half-life.
5 All temperature values have been corrected to the International Practical Temperature Scale of 1968.
6 This value is the minimum pressure under which liquid helium can be solidified.
7 The melting point is for carbyne 6, the stable form of carbon above 3300°C. Recent evidence suggests that graphite is only metastable above 2300°C.

Nobel prizewinners in chemistry since 1950

1987 Donald J. Cram, US; Jean-Marie Lehn, French; Charles J. Pedersen, US
1986 Herbert A. Hauptman, US; Jerome Karle, US
1984 R. Bruce Merrifield, US
1983 Henry Taube, US
1982 Aaron Klug, S. African
1981 Kenichi Fukui, Japan; Roald Hoffmann, US
1980 Paul Berg, US; Walter Gilbert, US; Frederick Sanger, British
1979 Herbert C. Brown, US; George Wittig, German
1978 Peter Mitchell, British
1977 Ilya Prigogine, Belgian
1976 William N. Lipscomb, US
1975 John Cornforth, Austral.-Brit.; Vladimir Prelog, Yugo.-Switz.
1974 Paul J. Flory, US
1973 Ernst Otto Fischer, W. German; Geoffrey Wilkinson, British
1972 Christian B. Anfinsen, US; Stanford Moore, US; William H. Stein, US
1971 Gerhard Herzberg, Canadian
1970 Luis F. Leloir, Arg.
1969 Derek H. R. Barton, British; Odd Hassel, Norwegian
1968 Lars Onsager, US
1967 Manfred Eigen, German; Ronald G. W. Norrish, British; George Porter, British
1966 Robert S. Mulliken, US
1965 Robert B. Woodward, US
1964 Dorothy C. Hodgkin, British
1963 Giulio Natta, Italian; Karl Ziegler, German
1962 John C. Kendrew, British; Max F. Perutz, British
1961 Melvin Calvin, US
1960 Willard F. Libby, US
1959 Jaroslav Heyrovsky, Czech
1958 Frederick Sanger, British
1957 Sir Alexander R. Todd, British
1956 Sir Cyril N. Hinshelwood, British; Nikolai N. Semenov, USSR
1955 Vincent du Vigneaud, US
1954 Linus C. Pauling, US
1953 Hermann Staudinger, German
1952 Archer J. P. Martin, British; Richard L. M. Synge, British
1951 Edwin M. McMillan, US; Glen T. Seaborg, US
1950 Kurt Alder, German; Otto P. H. Diels, German

Periodic Table of Elements

IA	IIA	IIIB	IVB	VB	VIB	VIIB	VIII			IB	IIB	IIIA	IVA	VA	VIA	VIIA	O
s¹	s²	d¹	d²	d³	d⁴	d⁵	d⁶	d⁷	d⁸	d⁹	d¹⁰	p¹	p²	p³	p⁴	p⁵	p⁶
1 H																	2 He
3 Li	4 Be											5 B	6 C	7 N	8 O	9 F	10 Ne
11 Na	12 Mg			Transition metals								13 Al	14 Si	15 P	16 S	17 Cl	18 Ar
19 K	20 Ca	21 Sc	22 Ti	23 V	24 Cr	25 Mn	26 Fe	27 Co	28 Ni	29 Cu	30 Zn	31 Ga	32 Ge	33 As	34 Se	35 Br	36 Kr
37 Rb	38 Sr	39 Y	40 Zr	41 Nb	42 Mo	43 Tc	44 Ru	45 Rh	46 Pd	47 Ag	48 Cd	49 In	50 Sn	51 Sb	52 Te	53 I	54 Xe
55 Cs	56 Ba	57* La	72 Hf	73 Ta	74 W	75 Re	76 Os	77 Ir	78 Pt	79 Au	80 Hg	81 Tl	82 Pb	83 Bi	84 Po	85 At	86 Rn
87 Fr	88 Ra	89† Ac															

*Lanthanides	57 La	58 Ce	59 Pr	60 Nd	61 Pm	62 Sm	63 Eu	64 Gd	65 Tb	66 Dy	67 Ho	68 Er	69 Tm	70 Yb	71 Lu
†Actinides	89 Ac	90 Th	91 Pa	92 U	93 Np	94 Pu	95 Am	96 Cm	97 Bk	98 Cf	99 Es	100 Fm	101 Md	102 No	103 Lr

Physics

Glossary

Å Ångstrom, 0·1 nm.

absolute zero Lowest temperature theoretically possible, at which the random motion of the particles in a system is zero. It is equal to $-273\cdot15°C = 0\,K = -459\cdot67°F$.

absorption spectrum If light of a continuous frequency is passed through a medium into a spectroscope, dark regions appear in the spectrum, due to the absorption of light by the medium. The medium will absorb the wavelengths which it would normally emit if it were raised to a high enough temperature, i.e. the absorbed radiation excites atoms from the ground state to an excited state.

acceleration Rate of increase of velocity with time.

accelerator A large machine in which an electric field is used to increase the kinetic energy of charged particles such as electrons and protons by accelerating them. The stream of accelerated particles is guided into the desired path by a magnetic field.

acoustics The study and use of sound waves.

allotropy The existence of a substance in more than one form (allotropes), differing in physical rather than chemical properties.

alpha (α) particle A helium nucleus, consisting of two protons and two neutrons and carrying a positive charge.

alpha rays A stream of alpha particles, emitted by many radioactive substances. The alpha particles can be stopped by a piece of paper, i.e. they have a very low penetrating power.

alternating current An electric current that regularly reverses its direction in a circuit.

ammeter An instrument for measuring electric current.

ampere Symbol A. Unit of electric current.

anion A negatively charged ion.

anode Positive electrode.

antimatter Matter consisting of anti-particles. Anti-matter has never actually been detected.

Archimedes' principle A body floating in a fluid displaces a weight of fluid equal to its own weight.

atom Smallest particle of a pure element that can take part in a chemical reaction.

atomic mass unit Symbol u. One-twelfth of the mass of carbon-12 atom. Approximately the mass of a proton or neutron.

atomic number Symbol Z. Number of protons in the nucleus.

atomic weight Symbol A_r. The average mass of atoms in an element, in atomic mass units.

Avogadro's hypothesis Equal volumes of all gases measured at the same temperature and pressure contain the same number of molecules.

background radiation Low-intensity radiation resulting from bombardment of the earth by cosmic rays and from naturally occurring isotopes in soil, air, buildings, etc.

bar A unit of pressure equal to 10^5 pascals. The millibar is used by meteorologists.

barometer A device for measuring atmospheric pressure.

Becquerel rays Alpha, beta and gamma rays emitted by uranium compounds.

beta (β) particle An electron emitted by a radioisotope during beta decay.

beta rays A stream of beta particles, emitted by nuclei of certain radioisotopes. They can penetrate thin metal foil.

betatron An accelerator producing high-energy electrons. They are accelerated by means of magnetic induction.

black body A body that absorbs all radiation falling on it.

boiling point The temperature at which the saturated vapour pressure of a liquid equals the external pressure.

breeder reactor A nuclear reactor in which more fissile material is produced than is used.

Brownian movement Irregular movement of smoke particles, or of very small particles, e.g. pollen, in a liquid. It is due to molecular bombardment by moving molecules.

c The velocity of light; $2\cdot997 \times 10^8\,\mathrm{m\,s^{-1}}$.

calorimeter A device in which thermal measurements can be made.

candela Symbol cf. Unit of luminous intensity.

capacitance Symbol C. The ability of an isolated electrical conductor to store electrical charge.

capacitor A device containing one or more pairs of electrical conductors separated by insulators (the dielectric). It is used to store electrical charge.

capillarity The effect of surface tension on a liquid in a fine tube, causing the liquid to rise or fall in the tube.

cathode Negative electrode.

cathode ray tube Electrons from a heated cathode are projected on to a phosphor screen. The intensity and movement of the beam can be controlled, and the phosphor screen converts the kinetic energy of the electrons into a bright spot of light. This is the basis of a TV.

Celsius scale The official name of the centigrade temperature scale. The ice point is 0° and the boiling point 100°.

centrifugal force The inertial force directed radially outwards, in equilibrium with the applied centripetal force.

centripetal force A lateral force that makes a body move in a circular path. It is directed towards the centre of the circle.

CGS System of units based on the centimetre, gram and second. It has now been superseded by the more coherent SI system.

charge Symbol Q. The ability of some elementary particles, such as electrons and protons, to exert forces on one another. Like forces repel, unlike forces attract.

concave Curving inwards. Concave mirrors converge rays of light, concave lenses diverge them.

conductor A substance that offers a relatively low resistance to an electric current.

conservation of mass and energy In any system the sum of the mass and energy is always constant.

conservation of momentum In any system, the linear or angular momentum remains the same unless there is an external force acting on the system.

convection Transfer of heat in a fluid by movement of the fluid.

convex Curving outwards. A convex mirror diverges rays of light, a convex lens converges them.

cosmic rays Particle radiation reaching the earth from space.

cryogenics The study and production of very low temperatures.

curie Symbol Ci. The unit of activity of a radioactive substance. It corresponds to $3\cdot7 \times 10^{10}$ disintegrations per second, and is about equal to the activity of 1 g of radium.

current Symbol I. The rate of flow of electricity. The unit is the ampere.

cyclotron An accelerator in which the beam of charged particles follows a spiral path.

decay The breakdown of a radioactive nuclide into a daughter product by disintegration.

decibel A bel is a logarithmic unit for comparing two amounts of power. A decibel is one-tenth of a bel. One decibel represents an increase in intensity of about 26 per cent – about the smallest increase that the ear can detect. (The decibel is *not* a measure of loudness, as the sensitivity of the ear varies with frequency.)

densitometer Instrument for measuring the density of a substance.

density Symbol ρ. Mass per unit volume of a substance.

dielectric An insulator.

diffraction The phenomenon of waves appearing to travel round corners. It occurs when a wavefront meets a narrow slit or obstacle.

diffractometer An instrument used to measure the intensities of diffracted X-rays or neutron beams at different angles to each other.

diffusion Process by which substances mix due to the kinetic motions of the particles, be they atoms, molecules or groups of molecules.

diode An electronic device with only two electrodes.

direct current An electric current that flows in one direction only and is reasonably constant in magnitude.

discharge Passage of electric current through a gas-discharge tube, usually with luminous effects.

disintegration In which a nucleus emits particles, either after a collision or spontaneously.

dispersion The process by which a beam of white light is spread out to produce spectra.

Döppler effect Apparent change in frequency (of light or sound) when there is relative motion along a line between the source and the observer.

e The charge on an electron.

earth The electric potential of the earth is taken as being zero.

efficiency Symbol η. The ratio of the useful energy output of a machine to the energy input. A perfect machine would have an efficiency of 1.

Einstein's law $E = mc^2$, the law of equivalence of mass and energy, whereby a mass m has energy E, and vice versa.

elasticity The ability of a substance to return to its original size and shape after being deformed.

electric field strength Symbol E. The strength of an electric field at a given point, measured in volts per metre.

electric flux Symbol ψ. The quantity of electricity displaced across a given area in a dielectric, measured in coulombs.

electric potential Symbol V. The work done in bringing a unit positive charge from infinity to a point.

electrolyte A substance that conducts electricity in solution because of the presence of ions.

electron An elementary particle, found spinning around the nuclei of atoms. As free electrons they are responsible for electrical conduction.

electronics Nowadays, the study and use of electricity in semiconductors.

electronvolt Symbol eV. The energy acquired by an electron in falling freely through a potential difference of 1 volt.

elementary particle Any particle of matter that cannot be subdivided into smaller particles.

energy Symbol E. A measure of a systems capacity to do work.

enthalpy Symbol H. Thermodynamic function of a system equal to the sum of its internal energy and the product of its pressure and volume.

entropy Symbol S. The disorder of a system; the greater the disorder of a system, the greater the entropy.

evaporation Conversion of a liquid to a vapour at a temperature below the boiling point.

Fahrenheit scale Temperature scale on which the ice point is 32°F and the steam point is 212°F.

fallout Radioactive material that falls to earth after a nuclear explosion.

farad Symbol F. Unit of capacitance, in which a charge of 1 coulomb is acquired when 1 volt is applied.

ferromagnetism Solids that can be magnetized by weak magnetic fields, e.g. iron, cobalt, nickel.

fibre optics The study and use of the transmission of light by very fine flexible glass rods.

fission Splitting of a heavy nucleus into two or more fragments, normally accompanied by the emission of neutrons or gamma rays.

fluid A liquid or gas.

fluidics Study and use of jets of fluid in circuits to perform tasks usually carried out by electronic circuits.

fluorescence When electromagnetic radiation, e.g. X-rays, UV light, etc., strikes a fluorescent substance, radiation of a longer wavelength, e.g. light, is emitted.

flux The strength of a field of force through a specified area.

force Symbol F. Any action that tends to alter a body's state of rest or uniform motion.

free fall Downward motion in a gravitational field, unimpeded by any bouyancy effects.

freezing point The same as the melting point. The temperature at which both the solid and liquid phases of a substance can exist in equilibrium.

frequency Symbol v or f. The number of complete cycles or oscillations that occur in a unit of time.

fusion Change of state from liquid to solid at the melting point.

g Symbol for the acceleration due to free fall. On the earth it is $9.81 \, \mathrm{m \, s^{-2}}$.

gain The efficiency of an electronic system.

galvanometer An instrument for measuring or detecting electrical currents.

gamma (γ) rays Electromagnetic radiation emitted by certain radioactive substances. They can penetrate much greater distances than alpha and beta rays, and form the extreme short-wave end of the electromagnetic spectrum.

Geiger counter Device for detecting ionizing radiation, especially alpha particles. Because it can count the particles it can therefore measure the strength of radioactivity.

gravitation The attraction which all bodies have for one another.

h Symbol for Planck's constant.

half-life The time in which a radioactive substance decays to half its original quantity or half its original activity.

harmonic A simple multiple of a fundamental frequency.

heat That form of energy transferred between bodies as a result of differences in their temperature.

heat pump A device for extracting heat from large quantities of a substance, e.g. water, air, at a low temperature and supplying it at a higher temperature, e.g. to a building. Mechanical work must be performed for the pump to work.

hertz Symbol Hz. The unit of frequency; 1 cycle or oscillation per second.

holography A laser technique for producing stereoscopic images without cameras or lenses.

hydrodynamics The study and use of the motion of fluids.

hysteresis Lagging of effect behind cause when cause varies in amount, e.g. magnetic induction lagging behind an applied cycle of magnetic changes.

ice point The temperature at which ice and water are in equilibrium at standard pressure.

induction When an electrical conductor is moved so that it cuts the flux of a magnetic field, a potential difference is induced between the ends of the conductor.

inertia The tendency for a body to remain at rest or in a state of uniform motion in a straight line.

infrared rays Electromagnetic radiation (heat) emitted by hot bodies. It consists of radiation of longer wavelengths than the red end of the visible spectrum.

integrated circuit A complete circuit in a single package, usually in or on a single chip of silicon.

interference If light or sound waves of the same wavelength but from different sources cross over, areas of minimum and maximum intensity occur where the waves superimpose on each other.

ion Electrically charged atom, group of atoms, molecular or group of molecules.

isobar Line joining places with the same atmospheric pressure.

isotopes Atoms having the same number of protons but different numbers of neutrons.

joule Symbol J. Unit of energy; 1 newton moved through 1 metre in the direction of the applied force.

kelvin Symbol K. Unit of thermodynamic temperature; the temperature difference on the Kelvin and Celsius scale, where $1 \, \mathrm{K} = 1 \,°\mathrm{C}$.

kinetic energy Symbol T. Energy possessed by virtue of a body's motion.

laminar flow Steady flow in which a fluid moves in parallel layers (laminae), although the velocities of the fluid particles in each lamina are not necessarily equal.

laser Abbreviation for Light Amplification by Stimulated Emission of Radiation. A source of intense coherent radiation of a single wavelength in the infrared, visible and ultraviolet regions of the spectrum.

latent heat The quantity of heat released or absorbed when a substance changes phase at a fixed temperature.

lattice A regularly-repeated three-dimensional array of points that determines the positions of atoms or molecules in a crystalline structure.

lens A piece of transparent material, bounded by two regularly curved surfaces and designed to focus light to a fixed point.

light A narrow section of the electromagnetic spectrum.

longitudinal waves Waves in which displacement of the transmitting medium is in the same plane as the direction of travel, e.g. sound waves.

lumen Symbol lm. Unit of luminous flux, i.e. the rate of flow of radiant energy.

lux Symbol lx. Unit of illumination.

machine A device for doing work, in which a small effort is used to overcome a larger force or load.

Mach number Symbol M. Ratio of the relative velocity of a body in a fluid to the velocity of sound in the fluid. Mach 1 thus indicates the speed of sound.

magnetic bottle An arrangement of magnetic fields designed to contain a plasma.

magnetic field A field of force containing magnetic flux.

magnetism Attractive and repulsive forces due to the motion of electrons around the atoms in a substance.

magnifying power Ratio of the size of the image produced by an instrument to the size of the image as seen by the naked eye.

maser Abbreviation for Microwave Amplification by Stimulated Emission of Radiation. The microwave equivalent of a laser.

mass The quantity of matter in a body; the reluctance of a body to accelerate when acted on by a force. It is measured in grams.

mass number Symbol A. The number of nucleons in a nucleus.

mass spectrometer An instrument for measuring atomic masses of elements which can be formed into a beam of ions.

mechanics The study of motion and the equilibrium of bodies.

metrology The study of the accurate measurement of mass, length and time.

microscope An instrument, containing converging lenses, that produces an enlarged image of small objects.

microwave An electromagnetic wave with a wavelength between infrared radiation and radio waves.

mil One-thousandth of an inch.

mm HG Abbreviation for millimetres of mercury. A unit of pressure measured by the height in mm of a column of mercury supported by the pressure.

mole Symbol mol. The amount of substance that contains the same number of elementary entities (molecules, ions, atoms, etc.) as there are in $0.012 \, \mathrm{kg}$ of carbon-12.

moment A turning effect, equal to the magnitude of the force and the perpendicular distance from the line of action of the force to the axis.

momentum Symbol p. The product of the mass and the velocity of a body.

monochromatic radiation Radiation of one wavelength or, at worst, of a very narrow band of wavelengths.

motor A machine that converts electrical energy into mechanical energy.

neutron A constituent of the nucleus, with zero charge and about the same mass as the proton.

neutron number Symbol N. The number of neutrons present in the nucleus of an atom.

neutron star A massive star consisting largely of neutrons.

newton Symbol N. Unit of force that gives 1 kilogram an acceleration of 1 metre per second per second.

Newton's rings Circular interference fringes formed between a lens and a glass plate with which the lens is in contact.

NTP Abbreviation for normal temperature and pressure.

nuclear fusion A nuclear reaction in which light atomic nuclei combine to form a heavier atomic nucleus with the release of energy.

nuclear isomer Nuclei with the same mass number and atomic number but different radioactive properties.

nuclear magnetic resonance An effect observed when radio-frequency radiation is absorbed by matter. It is due to the spin of atomic nuclei developing characteristic magnetic moments.

nucleon Collective name for the constituents of the atomic nucleus, i.e. proton and neutron.

nucleus The most massive part of an atom, consisting of neutrons and protons held together by binding forces.

ohm Symbol Ω. Unit of resistance. The resistance between two points if an applied potential difference of 1 volt produces a current of 1 amp.

optics The study and use of light.

orbit A curved path described, for example, by a planet or comet around the sun or a particle such as an electron in a field of force such as that encountered around an atomic nucleus.

oscillation A vibration with a regular frequency; a movement backwards and forwards between two points with a regular frequency.

osmosis The use of a semipermeable membrane that allows certain kinds of molecule in a liquid to pass down a hydrostatic pressure gradient but that prevents the passage of other molecules.

parallax Apparent displacement of an object caused by an actual change of point of observation.

parity Symbol P. Parity invariance states that no distinction can be made between laws of physics for a right-handed system of coordinates and for a left-handed system of coordinates.

pascal Symbol Pa. Unit of pressure resulting from 1 newton acting uniformly over $1 \, \mathrm{m}^2$.

Pascal's principle Pressure applied at any point to a fluid at rest is transmitted without loss to all other parts of the fluid.

Pauli exclusion principle No two fermions can exist in identical quantum states, e.g. no two electrons in an atom can have the same quantum number.

pendulum A mass suspended from a fixed point that oscillates with a known and fixed period.

period Symbol T. Time occupied by one complete vibration or oscillation.

permeability Symbol μ. Ratio of magnetic flux density in a body to the external magnetic field strength inducing it.

phase The proportion of a period that has elapsed, taken from a fixed point in the cycle.

photoemission Release or emission of electrons due to bombardment of the substance by electromagnetic radiation, e.g. light.

piezoelectric effect Production of an electrical potential difference across a piece of crystal, e.g. quartz, when subjected to pressure.

pitch The frequency of a sound.

Planck's constant A universal constant, $h = 6.626 \times 10^{-34} \, \mathrm{J \, s}$.

Planck's law Electromagnetic radiation consists of small indivisible packets called photons or quanta whose energy $= hf$, where h is Planck's constant and f is the frequency of the radiation.

plasma Gas of positive ions and free electrons

with roughly equal positive and negative charges.

pneumatics Study and use of dynamic properties of gases.

polarization The restriction of particle displacement to a single plane. It can only occur in transverse waves, e.g. electromagnetic radiation.

pole Point towards which lines of magnetic flux converge.

positron Positive electron, the antiparticle of the electron.

potential difference The potential difference between two points is the work done per coulomb of positive electrical charge taken from one point to the other, measured in volts.

power Symbol P. Work done per second, measured in watts.

pressure Symbol p. Force per unit area, measured in pascals.

prism A refracting substance, such as glass, with two plane intersecting surfaces. It deviates a beam of light and disperses it into its constituent colours.

proton A positively-charged elementary particle about 1836 times as heavy as an electron. All atomic nuclei contain protons, and the hydrogen nucleus consists solely of one proton.

quantum mechanics A mathematical physical theory based on Planck's quantum theory and the probability of finding an elementary particle at any particular point.

quantum theory Theory based on Planck's idea of discrete quanta of electromagnetic radiation.

rad Unit of absorbed radiation equal to 0·01 joule per kilogram of absorbing material.

radiation Any energy propagated as rays, streams of particles or waves.

radioactivity Spontaneous disintegration of the nuclei of some isotopes of certain elements, with the emission of alpha or beta particles, sometimes together with gamma rays.

radiopaque Opaque to radiation, especially gamma rays and X-rays, e.g. bones are radiopaque to X-rays but other body tissues are not.

radio waves Electromagnetic radiation of radio frequency.

rectifier Electrical device that allows current to flow in only one direction and thus converts alternating to direct current.

reflection When light or sound strikes a surface between two different media, some is thrown back into the original medium.

refraction The change of direction a ray of light or sound wave undergoes when it passes from one medium to another.

relativity A theory developed by Einstein, confirming the unification of mass and energy, the former being a 'congealed' form of the latter.

resistance Symbol R. The ratio between the potential difference across a conductor and the current passing through it, measured in ohms.

resistivity Symbol ρ. Resistance per unit length of unit cross-sectional area of a conductor, measured in ohm-metres.

resonance Maximum response which occurs when a driving frequency applied to a system is equal to the natural frequency of the system.

rheology Study and use of the deformation and flow of matter.

saturated vapour A vapour in dynamic equilibrium with its liquid at a given temperature – it can hold no more substance in the gaseous phase at that temperature.

scattering Deflection of radiation by interaction with nuclei or electrons. Deflection of sound waves by a reflecting surface. Deflection of light waves by fine particles.

Schrödinger wave equation The basic equation of wave mechanics. It shows the behaviour of a particle moving in force field.

scintillation The emission of small flashes of light when radiation strikes certain substances.

second Symbol s. The basic unit of time in the SI units.

semiconductor A substance with a resistivity between that of conductors and insulators. Junctions between semiconductors form the basis of the modern electronics industry.

semipermeable membrane A membrane that allows the passage of certain molecules in a fluid while preventing the passage of other molecules.

shells Electrons moving round the atomic nucleus exist in different energy states. The sets of states corresponding to the same energy are called shells.

simple harmonic motion The periodic motion of a body subjected to a restoring force proportional to the displacement from the centre. The period of oscillation is independent of amplitude and the displacement varies sinusoidally with time.

sinusoidal Having a waveform the same as that of a sine function.

SI units Abbreviation for *Système International d'Unités*. An internationally-agreed coherent system of units based on the metre, kilogram and second.

solenoid A coil of wire with a greater length than diameter. When an electric current is passed through the wire it forms an electromagnet.

specific When applied to an extensive physical property, specific restricts the meaning to 'per unit mass' of the substance.

spectrometer An instrument for producing, recording or examining a spectrum of radiation.

spectrum A distribution of electromagnetic radiation. It is usually applied to the visible display of colours, but can be applied to any part of the range of electromagnetic radiation.

speed Rate of increase of distance travelled with time.

spin An electron travels round the atomic nucleus and as it does it spins on its own axis.

standard atmosphere Symbol atm. Unit of pressure equal to 101 325 pascals.

standard temperature and pressure A standard condition for the reduction of gas pressures and temperatures. It is equal to 0°C and 101 325 pascals.

steam point Temperature at which the liquid and vapour phases of water are in equilibrium at standard pressure, i.e. 100°C.

strain Change of shape and/or volume of a body due to applied forces.

stress Forces in equilibrium acting on a body and tending to produce strain.

superconductivity When many metals and alloys are cooled to near absolute zero (0 K, −273°C), their electrical resistance almost vanishes.

supercooling Slow and continuous cooling of liquids, taking them down below their normal freezing point.

superfluid A fluid, at a very low temperature, that has very high thermal conductivity and can flow through very fine channels without friction.

telescope An instrument for producing a magnified or intensified image of a distant object. Optical telescopes use lenses or lenses and mirrors; radio telescopes use electronic circuitry to amplify radio signals from distant sources.

temperature Symbol T. The hotness of a body that determines which direction heat flows when the body is in contact with other bodies.

thermodynamics The study and use of the interrelationships between heat and other forms of energy.

tone The quality of a musical sound, caused by the presence of harmonics.

transducer A device for converting a non-electrical variable into a proportionately variable electrical signal.

transformer A device, consisting of two electrical circuits magnetically coupled together such that an alternating voltage in one circuit is transformed into an alternating voltage (usually different) in the other.

transistor A semiconductor device in which a small base current or voltage can control or modulate a larger collector current or voltage.

transverse waves Waves in which displacement of the transmitting medium is perpendicular to the direction of travel, e.g. electromagnetic waves.

tribology The study of friction, lubrication and wear of surfaces.

triple point The temperature at which, for any substance, the three physical states of the substance can exist at equilibrium. For water this occurs at 0°C.

ultrasonics The study and use of frequencies beyond the limits of human hearing, i.e. above about 20 khz.

ultraviolet radiation Electromagnetic radiation lying beyond the violet end of the visible spectrum and before the X-ray region.

unified field theory Theory, yet to be developed, that seeks to link together the properties of gravitational, nuclear and electromagnetic fields.

vacuum Space or vessel devoid of matter or from which all air has been removed.

valence electrons Those electrons in the outermost shell of an atom that are involved in chemical changes.

vapour Substance in gaseous form but below its critical temperature. It can thus be liquefied merely by pressure, without the need for cooling.

vector A quantity that has direction as well as magnitude.

velocity Symbol v. Rate of increase of distance travelled by a body in a particular direction.

viscosity The ability of fluids to offer resistance to flow.

visible spectrum Visible electromagnetic radiation between 380 and 780 nm.

volt Symbol V. The potential difference between two points such that 1 joule of work is done by every coulomb of positive charge moved from one point to the other.

watt Symbol W. The unit of power resulting from the dissipation of 1 joule in 1 second.

wave A curve of an alternating quantity plotted against time, giving rise to a disturbance travelling through a medium.

wavelength Symbol λ. The distance between one vibrating particle in a wave train and the next particle that is vibrating in the same phase.

wave mechanics A form of quantum mechanics.

weight The pull of gravity on a body, measured in newtons.

work Symbol w or W. Work is carried out when a force moves its point of application. It is measured in joules, i.e. 1 newton moved through 1 metre.

X-rays Electromagnetic radiation lying between ultraviolet radiation and gamma rays.

Milestones in physics

Physics is very much concerned with fundamental particles – the building blocks out of which the Universe is constructed – and the forces which bind and regulate them. Many theories have been proposed from time to time to provide a better understanding of the vast number of facts and observations which have accumulated. The main development of physics is essentially a series of unifications of these theories.

1687 Sir Isaac Newton (1642–1727) produced the great unifying theory of **gravitation** which linked the falling apple with the force which keeps the stars and planets in their courses. This made available for further scientific investigation one of the basic universal forces of nature, the force of gravity. The gravitational force, F, between two bodies of masses, m_1, m_2, distance, r, apart is given by

$$F = G\frac{m_1 m_2}{r^2}$$

where G is a Universal constant. Though he first derived his inverse square law of gravity in the summer of 1666, at Woolsthorpe, Lincolnshire, Newton did not publish it until 1687 in his *Principia*.

By Newton's time there existed two rival theories to explain the passage of light from source to observer. One was the **particle theory** which maintained that light consists of vast numbers of minute particles ejected by the luminous body in all directions. Newton, who made so many brilliant advances in optics, favoured this theory. It accounted in a particularly simple way for the transmission of light through the vacuum of space, for its rectilinear propagation, and for the laws of reflection. The alternative was the **wave theory**, which assumed that light was transmitted by means of a wave motion. This would imply that light would bend round corners, but when it was discovered that the wavelength of the light was very small (about 1/2000th of a millimetre), it was realised that the effect would be small as is in fact observed. Light does not cast a perfectly sharp shadow. Further phenomena were discovered which demonstrated the wave nature of light and added support to that theory, e.g. interference and diffraction.

1820 Hans Christian Oersted (1777–1851) of Denmark discovered that the flow of electric current in a conductor would cause a nearby compass needle to be deflected.

1831 Michael Faraday (1791–1867) the English physicist, uncovered the principle of magnetic induction which led to the invention of the dynamo. He showed that a change in the magnetic field surrounding a conductor could cause a flow of electrical current.

1865 The unification between magnetism and electricity was brought to full flower by the Scottish physicist, James Clerk Maxwell (1831–79), in his great **electromagnetic theory**, which described every known kind of magnetic and electric behaviour. The set of equations named after him showed that electromagnetic waves travel at the velocity of light and confirmed that light is, in fact, an electromagnetic radiation. This provided further support for the wave theory of light.

1887 Heinrich Rudolph Hertz (1857–94), the German physicist, performed a classic experiment in which electromagnetic waves were produced and transmitted across the laboratory. This laid the foundation for radio transmission and provided ample vindication for Maxwell's theory.

As the 19th century drew to a close many of the problems of physics appeared to have been solved and there was a belief that, in principle, if all the observations and calculations could be made, the destiny of the Universe could be revealed in full detail. However, following on Hertz's experiment, a quick succession of phenomena presented themselves which threatened to destroy the orderly structure which had been so painstakingly built up over the preceding centuries.

1895 **X-rays** were discovered by Wilhelm Konrad von Röntgen (1845–1923) the German physicist. When experimenting with the passage of electrical discharges through gases, he noticed that fluorescent material near his apparatus glowed. He won the first Nobel prize for physics in 1901 for this work.

1896 Antoine Henri Becquerel (1852–1908), the French physicist, discovered that uranium salts, even in the dark, emit a radiation similar to Röntgen's X-rays and would fog a photographic plate. This was **radioactivity**.

1898 Marie Curie (1867–1934), of Poland, working with her French husband, Pierre, (1859–1906) announced the existence of two new chemical elements which powerfully emit radiation. She named the elements radium and polonium. The active phenomenon she gave the name radioactivity. She won the Nobel prize for physics in 1903 with Becquerel and her husband, and in 1911, for chemistry on her own.

Ernest Rutherford (1871–1937), New Zealand born British physicist and Frederick Soddy (1877–1956), British chemist, formulated a theory of radioactivity which forms the basis of our present understanding of the phenomenon. Three types of radioactivity were identified, α-rays, β-rays, and γ-rays. The γ-rays turned out to be like X-rays, more powerful than those of Röntgen. The β-rays were streams of fast moving electrons. The α-rays were found to consist of electrically charged particles being the nuclei of the element helium. The particles emitted from radioactive materials at such speed provided a means of investigating the structure of the atom itself, and enabled Rutherford to propose in 1911 a model of the atom which is the basis of our modern ideas of atomic structure.

A further important discovery which contributed to a revision of the ideas of classical physics was the **photoelectric effect**. It was observed that a polished zinc plate, when illuminated with ultra-violet light acquired a positive electric charge. In **1897** Joseph John Thomson (1856–1940), the British physicist, discovered the first of the fundamental particles, the **electron**, which is the basic unit of negative electricity. It became clear that the photoelectric effect was the result of electrons being knocked out of the metal surface by the incident light. It was further discovered that, firstly, the number of electrons emitted was greater for a greater intensity of light and, secondly, that their energy was related only to the wavelength of the light, being greater for shorter wavelengths. The first result was as expected but the second was a mystery.

MODERN PHYSICS

Modern physics could be said to have been born at the beginning of the 20th century, during the course of which a number of radical ideas have been formulated and developed into theories which have completely revolutionised the thinking in physics.

1900 The quantum theory was the first of these, put forward by the German physicist Max Karl Ernst Ludwig Planck (1858–1947). This arose out of yet another problem which had been insoluble up to that time. Calculations showed that the energy emitted from a hot body should be, at very short wavelengths, practically infinite: this was clearly not so. The calculations were satisfactory for radiation of longer wavelengths in that they agreed with experiment. To resolve this difficulty, Planck made the very novel suggestion that energy was radiated from the body, not in a continuous flow of waves as had been supposed up to then, but rather in distinct individual bundles. He called a bundle of energy a **quantum**. The energy of the quantum, E, is given by

$$E = \frac{hc}{\lambda}$$

where λ is the wavelength of the radiation, c is the velocity of light *in vacuo* and h is a fixed, universal constant called Planck's constant. On this theory, energy at the shorter wavelengths would require to be emitted in bigger bundles and thus there would be less of them available for emission in accordance with experimental results. Planck's constant is small and so quantum effects are also small, occurring only in the domain of atomic phenomena.

1905 Albert Einstein (1879–1955), a Swabian Jew, published his theory of the photoelectric effect and for which he was to win the Nobel prize in 1921. Einstein followed Planck's ideas and could see that the incident light must consist of a stream of quanta, that is, bundles of light, which came to be known as **photons**. A photon striking a metal surface is absorbed by an electron in it, the electron having more energy as a result. This causes it to jump from the surface, and since photons have greater energy at shorter wavelengths, so shorter wavelength light causes the emission of higher energy electrons. And, of course, the greater the intensity of the light the more quanta will be striking the surface and so more electrons will be emitted. Thus, the idea of the quantum enabled Einstein to account for the phenomena of the photoelectric effect and this was an early triumph for the new quantum theory which was to become a ground force in the subsequent developments in physics.

1905 This year also saw the publication of Einstein's **Special (or Restricted) Theory of Relativity**. It has been said that as a child he had wondered what would happen if it were possible to travel fast enough to catch a ray of light and that this led him some years later to formulate his celebrated theory. This theory arises from an apparent contradiction between two basic postulates:

1. The velocity of light *in vacuo* is a constant for all observers regardless of their state of motion relative to the light source.
2. The special principle of relativity which states that the laws of physics are the same for all observers in uniform motion relative to each other.

Imagine for a moment a train travelling with a uniform velocity v relative to the railway embankment, and a ray of light transmitted with velocity c along the embankment parallel, and in the direction of the train. For an observer in the train the velocity of the light should appear to be $c–v$: obviously less than c. But this violates the special principle of relativity above: the velocity of light must be the same for an observer on the embankment and an observer on the train. The reconciliation of these two apparently contradictory conclusions is the basis for the special theory and is achieved by surrendering the concepts of absolute time, absolute distance and of the absolute significance of simultaneity. From these ideas, fairly straightforward algebraic manipulation leads to equations which show that when a body is in uniform motion relative to an observer, the length of the body is diminished in the direction of travel and its mass is increased. The equations are:

$$l = l_o \sqrt{(1 - v^2/c^2)} \quad \text{and} \quad m = \sqrt{\frac{m_o}{(1 - v^2/c^2)}}$$

where l and m are the length and mass respectively of a body as seen by an observer, and moving at velocity v in the direction of its length relative to him. l_o is the velocity of the body at rest and m_o is its mass at rest.

Thus, if a 20 m rocket came past you in space at 149 896 km per sec (i.e. 0·5c) it would (if you could measure it) be only about 17 m long.

If two observers are moving at a constant velocity relative to each other, it appears to each that the other's clocks are slowed down and this is expressed in the equation:

$$t = t_o / \sqrt{(1 - v^2/c^2)}$$

where t is one observer's time as read by the other, and t_o is his own time as read by himself, v being the constant relative velocity of the two observers.

From the theory it can be shown that, at rest, a body possesses energy, E, given by

$$E = mc^2$$

Relativity theory thus confirms an important unification in physics between two of its very basic concepts: mass and energy with the former being a congealed form of the latter with a transmission constant being the speed of light (c) squared. This most famous of formulae was first published in Leipzig on 14 May 1907.

1911 Ernest Rutherford proposed a model of the atom which is the basis of our ideas of atomic structure to this day. He had from the first recognised the value of the fast moving α-particles emitted naturally from radioactive materials as probes for discovering the nature of the atom. He arranged for α-particles to bombard a thin gold foil and found that while many passed straight through a few were deflected at comparatively large angles, some even 'bouncing' back towards the source. He concluded from this that the mass of the atom was concentrated at its centre in a minute nucleus consisting of positively charged particles called **protons**. Around the nucleus and at a relatively large distance from it revolved the negatively charged electrons rather like a miniature solar system. The combined negative charges of the electrons exactly balanced the total positive charge of the nucleus. This important model of the atom suffered from a number of defects. One of these was that from Maxwell's electromagnetic theory the atom should produce light of all wavelengths whereas, in fact, atoms of each element emit light consisting of a number of definite wavelengths – a spectrum – which can be measured with great accuracy. The spectrum for each element is unique.

A further major difficulty was that the electrons, moving round the nucleus, should yield up their energy in the form of radiation and so would spiral into the nucleus bringing about the collapse of the atom. In fact, nothing of the sort occurs: under normal conditions an atom is a stable structure which does not emit radiation.

1913 The difficulties of the Rutherford atom were overcome by the Danish physicist, Niels Hendrik David Bohr (1885–1962) who proposed that electrons were permitted only in certain orbits but could jump from one permitted orbit to another. In so jumping the electron would gain or lose energy in the form of photons, whose wavelength followed from Planck's rule:

$$\lambda = \frac{hc}{E}$$

In this way the spectrum of light emitted, or absorbed, by an atom would relate to its individual structure. The theoretical basis to Bohr's work was confirmed by Einstein in 1917 and the Bohr theory went on successfully to explain other atomic phenomena. However, after many outstanding successes over a number of years, an increasing number of small but important discrepancies appeared with which the Bohr theory could not cope.

1919 Rutherford performed the first artificial nuclear disintegration when he bombarded nitrogen atoms with α-particles from radon-C. He demonstrated that protons were emitted as a result of the disintegration and this confirmed that the proton was, indeed, a nuclear particle.

1924 Louis-Victor de Broglie (1892–1976), French physicist, postulated that the dual wave-particle nature of light might be shown by other particles and particularly by electrons. The wavelength, λ, would be given by

$$\lambda = \frac{h}{mv}$$

where m is the mass of the particle, and v is its velocity. Electron waves were demonstrated experimentally in 1927 by C. J. Davisson (1881–1958) and L. H. Germer (b. 1896) of the USA. Subsequently, de Broglie's idea of matter waves was extended to other particles, protons, neutrons, etc. All matter has an associated wave character, but for the larger bodies of classical mechanics, the wavelengths are too small for their effects to be detectable.

1926 Erwin Schrödinger (1887–1961), a physicist from Vienna, took up the idea of de Broglie waves and applied them to the Bohr atom. The solutions to the resulting wave equation gave the allowed orbits or energy levels more accurately than the quantised orbits in the Bohr atom. Max Born (1882–1970), the German physicist, interpreted these solutions in terms of probability, i.e. they gave the probability of finding an electron in a given volume of space within the atom.

1927 The German physicist, Werner Karl Heisenberg (1901–76) formulated his celebrated Uncertainty Principle: this states that there is a definite limit to the accuracy with which certain pairs of measurements can be made. The more accurate one quantity is known, the less accurate is our knowledge of the other. Position and momentum is an example of such a pair of measurements. The more exactly we know the position of, say, an electron, the less will we know about its momentum. This can be expressed:

$$\Delta x . \Delta p \sim h$$

where Δx represents the uncertainty in position, Δp the uncertainty in momentum and h is Planck's constant. A further important example relates to time and energy: it is not possible to know how much energy E is possessed by a particle without allowing sufficient time t for the energy to be determined.

$$\Delta E . \Delta t \sim h$$

The uncertainty principle provides the main

THE FUNDAMENTAL PHYSICAL CONSTANTS

The constants are called 'fundamental' since they are used universally throughout all branches of science. Because of the unprecedented amount of new experimental and theoretical work being carried out, thorough revisions are now quite frequently published. Values are reported such that the figure in brackets following the last digit is the estimated uncertainty of that digit, e.g. the speed of light $c = 2 \cdot 99792458(1) \times 10^8 \, \text{m s}^{-1}$ could be written $c = (2 \cdot 99792458 \pm 0 \cdot 00000001) \times 10^8 \, \text{m s}^{-1}$. The unit $\text{m} \cdot \text{s}^{-1}$ represents m/s or metres per second.

	Quantity	Symbol	Value	Units
general constants	speed of light *in vacuo*	c	$2 \cdot 99792458(1) \times 10^8$	$\text{m} \cdot \text{s}^{-1}$
	elementary charge	e	$1 \cdot 6021892(46) \times 10^{-19}$	C
	Planck's constant	h	$6 \cdot 626176(36) \times 10^{-34}$	$\text{J} \cdot \text{s}$
		$\hbar = h/2\pi$	$1 \cdot 0545887(57) \times 10^{-34}$	$\text{J} \cdot \text{s}$
	gravitational constant	G	$6 \cdot 6720(41) \times 10^{-11}$	$\text{m}^3 \cdot \text{s}^{-2} \cdot \text{kg}^{-1}$
matter in bulk	Avogadro constant	N_A	$6 \cdot 022045(31) \times 10^{23}$	mol^{-1}
	atomic mass unit	$u = 1/N_A$	$1 \cdot 6605655(86) \times 10^{-27}$	kg
			$9 \cdot 315016(26) \times 10^2$	MeV
	faraday	$F = N_A e$	$9 \cdot 648456(27) \times 10^4$	$\text{C} \cdot \text{mol}^{-1}$
	normal volume of ideal gas	V_m	$2 \cdot 241383(70) \times 10^{-2}$	$\text{m}^3 \cdot \text{mol}^{-1}$
	gas constant	R	$8 \cdot 31441(26)$	$\text{J} \cdot \text{mol}^{-1} \cdot \text{K}^{-1}$
			$8 \cdot 20568(26) \times 10^{-5}$	$\text{m}^3 \cdot \text{atm} \cdot \text{mol}^{-1} \text{K}^{-1}$
	Boltzmann constant	$k = R/N_A$	$1 \cdot 380662(44) \times 10^{-23}$	$\text{J} \cdot \text{K}^{-1}$
electron	electron rest mass	m_e	$9 \cdot 109534(47) \times 10^{-31}$	kg
			$0 \cdot 5110034(14)$	MeV
	electron charge to mass ratio	e/m_e	$1 \cdot 7588047(49) \times 10^{11}$	$\text{C} \cdot \text{kg}^{-1}$
proton	proton rest mass	m_p	$1 \cdot 6726485(86) \times 10^{-27}$	kg
			$9 \cdot 382796(27) \times 10^2$	MeV
neutron	neutron rest mass	m_n	$1 \cdot 6749543(86) \times 10^{-27}$	kg
			$9 \cdot 395731(27) \times 10^2$	MeV
energy conversion	million electron volt unit	MeV	$1 \cdot 7826758(51) \times 10^{-30}$	kg
			$1 \cdot 6021892(46) \times 10^{-13}$	J

reason why the classical mechanics of Newton do not apply to atomic and subatomic phenomena.

1928 Paul Adrien Maurice Dirac (b. 1902), the Cambridge mathematician, introduced a theory of the electron which successfully brought together the ideas of quantum mechanics thus far developed with those of relativity. As a result of this, the important concept of electron spin previously advanced by Bohr became theoretically justified.

Dirac's equations revealed a negative quantity which led to the prediction of the existence of the antielectron, a particle identical to the electron, of the same mass but of opposite electric charge. This major idea, that there could exist **antimatter** in the universe composed of antiparticles arises from Dirac's bold prediction.

Heisenberg's uncertainty principle led to the idea of the instantaneous creation and annihilation of short-lived 'virtual' particles in the vicinity of stable particles. The basic uncertainty in the energy of a particle enables it to acquire a loan, as it were, of energy for a short time: the length of time, in fact, being inversely related to the amount of energy lent. Provided the loan is repaid in the time available, there is no violation of the law of conservation of energy. The action of forces could now be seen in terms of these 'virtual' particles, which behave as force-carriers travelling rapidly from one particle to the other. So, it comes about that particles, not in direct contact, respond each to the presence of the other.

1932 Ernest Orlando Lawrence (1901–58), an American physicist, developed the **cyclotron**. This was one of the first machines constructed for accelerating charged particles artificially to high velocities for research. The particles, which in the first instance were protons, were caused to move with ever increasing velocity in a spiral path by the suitable application of magnetic and electric fields. Lawrence was awarded the Nobel prize in 1939 for this work.

1932 Carl David Anderson (b. 1905), an American physicist of California, announced the discovery of the antielectron predicted a few years previously by Dirac. This was the first particle of antimatter to be discovered and he named it the **positron**.

1932 James Chadwick (1891–1974), the English physicist, discovered the **neutron**, a constituent of the atomic nucleus of zero charge and only slightly heavier than the proton.

1933 Wolfgang Pauli (1900–58) of Austria postulated the existence of the **neutrino**, a neutral particle of negligible mass in order to explain the fact that in β-emission in radioactivity, there was a rather greater loss of energy than could be otherwise explained.

In 1956 Fred Reines and Clyde Cowan in Los Alamos succeeded in detecting neutrinos (electron neutrinos). In 1962 Lederman and Melvin Schwarz of Columbia University demonstrated the existence of the other neutrino, the muon neutrino.

1934 Hideki Yukawa (b. 1907), the Japanese physicist, sought to explain the forces which held the particles in the nucleus together – the **strong force** – and called the force-carrying particles in this case **mesons**. The meson predicted by Yukawa, the **pion**, was discovered by Cecil F Powell of Bristol University in 1947.

1938 **Nuclear fission** was discovered by Otto Hahn (1879–1968) and Fritz Strassman (b. 1902) by bombarding uranium with neutrons, when trying to produce transuranic elements. They succeeded in producing elements lighter than uranium from the mineral of the periodic table. The incident neutron causes the target nucleus to split into two pieces of almost equal mass. Each of the fragments consists of protons and neutrons and an enormous amount of energy is released in the process. Enrico Fermi (1901–54) suggested that the neutrons released in fission could themselves induce further fission and that it should be possible to sustain a chain reaction.

1942 The first nuclear reactor, set up by Fermi in the University of Chicago, became critical.

1945 The first atomic explosion which was experimental took place in July followed by bombs dropped on Hiroshima and Nagasaki in August.

1952 The first hydrogen bomb was exploded in November. This derived its energy from the process of nuclear fusion in which two or more relatively light nuclei combined to form a heavier atomic nucleus releasing thereby a very considerable amount of energy. Considerable effort is being made to develop a fusion reactor and the main difficulty is the problem of containing the enormously high temperatures involved within the reactor for long enough to allow the reaction to proceed. In June 1954 the world's first nuclear powered generator produced electricity at Obnisk near Moscow, and in August 1956 the first large scale nuclear power generating station, Calder Hall, Cumberland (Cumbria), started up. It was officially opened by Her Majesty Queen Elizabeth II in October when power first flowed into the national grid.

By the 1950s a bewilderingly large number of apparently fundamental particles had been reported and their great number was becoming an embarrassment. Most particles then known fell into two classes: the **leptons** and the **hadrons** (see table below).

Hadrons are complex and there was evidence that they themselves possessed an internal structure. Certain of the unstable hadrons were found to take very much longer to decay than expected. These were called **strange** particles.

1953 Murray Gell-Mann (b. 1929) of the USA, introduced a concept he called **strangeness**, a quality akin in some ways to electric charge, which helped to account for the increased lifetimes of the strange particles. Aided by this idea, it was found that particles could be fitted into patterns according to the amount of strangeness they possessed. This led to the prediction of the existence of a rather unusual particle and it was a great triumph for these theories when in 1964 the omega-minus particle was discovered.

1963 From considerations of these patterns, Gell-Mann was led to the idea that the hadrons were composed of more basic particles called **quarks** (a name he borrowed from the writings of the Irish author, James Joyce). There were three kinds of quark, 'up', 'down' and 'strange' and, for each, a corresponding antiquark. These combined in only one of two ways to form either **baryons** or **mesons** as the table shows. Thus the proton can be pictured as consisting of three quarks – 2 up quarks and 1 down quark held together by force-carrying particles called **gluons**.

A free quark has not yet been detected and there is speculation that it never will. But there is experimental evidence suggesting their existence within baryons.

Current theory suggests that the gluons carry an enormously strong force called the **colour force**. This is much stronger than the strong nuclear force and permits quarks in the proton, for example, freedom of movement over a very short distance but increases with distance to hold them firmly within the proton.

1974 A particularly heavy particle, a hadron, was discovered and called the J or psi particle. Up to this time, the rules for building hadrons from quarks accounted in a complete and satisfying way for every known hadron and so it was that there appeared to be no room for the new particle. However, it could be explained by assuming it to be composed of a new quark together with its antiquark. This new, fourth quark called the charmed quark had been proposed in 1970 by Sheldon Lee Glashow (b. 1932) for other theoretical reasons. Charm, a property similar to strangeness, was first suggested in 1964 by Glashow on aesthetic grounds: there were two pairs of leptons so the up and down quark also formed a pair leaving the strange quark without a companion. Now, the charmed quark completed the team and also explained this new particle.

However, the charm in this psi particle cancelled out because of the charm/anti-charm combination. The search was then for a particle exhibiting 'naked' charm, a particle containing a charmed quark in combination with an up, down or strange quark.

1976 In May the D^0 meson was discovered by Gerson Goldhaber, co-discoverer of the psi particle, and Francoise Pierre at Stanford University. The D^0 particle consisted of a charmed quark and an anti-up quark.

The forces of physics

There are considered to be four basic forces in nature which differ very considerably in strength. These are listed here in ascending order of strength, together with a fifth, the superstrong colour force, the theory of which came into being in the early part of this decade. Its existence is a matter of speculation but it is offering a satisfying explanation of some phenomena at the very heart of matter.

	range	force-carrying particle	
gravity	very long	graviton, g	acts on all matter; weak within the atom
weak force	short, about 10^{-15} cm	W-meson	acts on all the basic particles, leptons and quarks: involved in radioactive processes.
electromagnetic force	very long	photon γ	acts on all charged particles: provides the basis to the reactions of chemistry and biology.
strong force	short, 10^{-13} cm	meson	acts on the hadrons, e.g. the proton and neutron, and is responsible for binding the nucleus together. Is involved in nuclear reactions.
colour force	short, 10^{-13} cm	gluon	acts on the quarks, allowing them freedom of movement within the hadron, e.g. proton, but holding them firmly within it.

The particles of physics

	Symbol	Anti-particle symbol	Mass MeV	Spin	Electric charge	Strangeness	Charm
THE QUANTA							
photon	γ		0	1	0		
graviton	g		0	2	0		

In addition to the quanta, there are thought to be only 2 families, the leptons and the quarks, which are elementary.

	Symbol	Anti-particle symbol	Mass MeV	Spin	Electric charge	Strangeness	Charm
THE LEPTONS							
electron	e^-	e^+	0·511003	$\frac{1}{2}$	-1	0	0
muon	μ^-	μ^+	105·659	$\frac{1}{2}$	-1	0	0
electron neutrino	v_e	v_e	0	$\frac{1}{2}$	0	0	0
muon neutrino	v_μ	v_μ	0	$\frac{1}{2}$	0	0	0
THE QUARKS							
up	u	u	100	$\frac{1}{2}$	$+\frac{2}{3}$	0	0
down	d	d	100	$\frac{1}{2}$	$-\frac{1}{3}$	0	0
strange	s	s	400	$\frac{1}{2}$	$\frac{1}{3}$	-1	0
charmed	c	c	1500	$\frac{1}{2}$	$+\frac{2}{3}$	0	$+1$

THE HADRONS
The other particles belong to the family of hadrons, and are constructed from the quarks: the baryons from 3 quarks and the mesons from 2. The following lists a few baryons and mesons.

	Symbol	Anti-particle symbol	Composition	Mass MeV	Spin	Electric charge	Strangeness	Charm
THE BARYONS								
proton	p^+	p^-	uud	938·280	$\frac{1}{2}$	$+1$	0	0
neutron	n^0	n^c	udd	939·573	$\frac{1}{2}$	0	0	0
omega minus	Ω^-	Ω^+	sss	1672·2	$\frac{3}{2}$	-1	-3	0
THE MESONS								
charged pion	π^+	n^-	ud	139·567	0	$+1$	0	0
neutral pion	π^0		uu or dd	134·963	0	0	0	0
neutral psi	ψ		cc	3097	1	0	0	0
neutral D	D^0	D^0	cu	1863·3	0	0	0	$+1$

In August, Wonyong Lee of Columbia University announced that a charmed antiproton had been detected, consisting of three antiquarks – up, down and charmed.

New particles were thus being discovered at this time with properties predicted by the charm theory.

1977 It was suggested that both quarks and leptons are combinations of more primitive fields known as preons. In November two very heavy Upsilon mesons with masses of 9400 MeV and 10 000 MeV were announced. These resonances indicated a massive new quark dubbed 'bottom' (symbol 'b').

Newton's laws of motion
These three self-evident principles were discovered experimentally before Newton's time but were first formulated by him.

Law 1. The law of inertia
A particle will either remain at rest or continue to move with uniform velocity unless acted upon by a force.

Law 2
The acceleration of a particle is directly proportional to the force producing it and inversely proportional to the mass of the particle.

Law 3. The law of action and reaction
Forces, the results of interactions of two bodies, always appear in pairs. In each pair the forces are equal in magnitude and opposite in direction.

Equations of motion
Where
u is the initial velocity of a body;
v is its final velocity after time t;
s is the distance it travels in this time;

a is the uniform acceleration it undergoes, then

$$v = u + at$$
$$s = ut + \tfrac{1}{2}at^2$$
$$v^2 = u^2 + 2as$$

Laws of Thermodynamics

Thermodynamics (Greek, *thermos*, hot; *dynamis*, power) is the quantitative treatment of the relation of heat to natural and mechanical forms of energy.

There are three Laws of Thermodynamics.

The **First Law**, derived from the principle of Conservation of Energy, may be stated 'Energy can neither be created nor destroyed, so that a given system can gain or lose energy only to the extent that it takes it from or passes it to its environment'. This is expressed as

$$E_f - E_i = \Delta$$

where E_i is the initial energy, E_f the final content of energy and Δ the change of energy. The impossibility of useful mechanical perpetual motion follows directly from this. The law applies only to systems of constant mass.

The **Second Law** concerns the concept of entropy (Gk. *en*, into; *tropos*, a changing) which is the relation between the temperature of and the heat content within any system. A large amount of lukewarm water may contain the same amount of heat as a little boiling water. The levelling out (equalising) of heat within a system (i.e. the pouring of a kettle of boiling water into a lukewarm bath) is said to increase the entropy of that system of two vessels. Any system, including the Universe, naturally tends to increase its entropy, i.e. to distribute its heat. If the Universe can be regarded as a closed system, it follows from the Law that it will have a finite end, i.e. when it has finally dissipated or unwound itself to the point that its entropy attains a maximal level – this is referred to as the 'Heat Death' of the Universe. From this it would also follow that the Universe must then have had a finite beginning for if it had had a creation an infinite time ago heat death would by now inevitably have set in. The second Law, published in Berlin in 1850 by Rudolf Clausius (1822–88) states 'Heat cannot of itself pass from a colder to a warmer body'. This is mathematically expressed by the inequality.

$$\Delta > 0$$

i.e. the change of entropy in any heat exchanging system and its surroundings taken together is always greater than zero.

The **Third Law** is not a general law but applies only to pure crystalline solids and states that at absolute zero the entropies of such substances are zero.

Celsius and Fahrenheit Compared

The two principal temperature scales are Celsius and Fahrenheit. The former was devised in 1743 by J P Christen (1683–1755) but is referred to by its present name because of the erroneous belief that it was invented by Anders Celsius (1701–44). The latter is named after Gabriel Daniel Fahrenheit (1686–1736), a German physicist.

To convert C to F, multiply the C reading by 9/5 and add 32.

To convert F to C, subtract 32 from the F reading and multiply by 5/9.

Useful comparisons are:

(1) Absolute Zero	=	$-273 \cdot 15°C$	$-459 \cdot 67°F$
(2) Point of Equality	=	$-40 \cdot 0°C$	$-40 \cdot 0°F$
(3) Zero Fahrenheit	=	$-17 \cdot 8°C$	$0 \cdot 0°F$
(4) Freezing Point of water	=	$0 \cdot 0°C$	$32 \cdot 0°F$
(5) Normal Human Blood Temperature	=	$36 \cdot 9°C$	$98 \cdot 4°F$
(6) 100 Degrees F	=	$37 \cdot 8°C$	$100 \cdot 0°F$
(7) Boiling Point of Water (at standard pressure)	=	$100 \cdot 0°C$	$212 \cdot 0°F$

Scientists in a non-meteorological context most frequently employ the Kelvin Scale in which kelvin (K) = fraction $1/273 \cdot 16$ of the triple point of water (where ice, water and water vapour are in equilibrium). Thus absolute zero is zero K, the ice-point of water ($0°C$ or $32°F$) is $273 \cdot 15 \, K$ and boiling point ($100°C$ or $212°F$) is $373 \cdot 15 \, K$.

NOBEL PRIZEWINNERS IN PHYSICS SINCE 1950

1987 Georg Bednorz, W. German; K. Alex Muller, Swiss.
1986 Ernest Ruska, W. German; Heinrich Rohrer, Swiss; Gerhard Binnig, W. German.
1985 Klaus von Klitzing, W. German
1984 Carlo Rubbia, Italian; Simon van der Meer, Dutch.
1983 Subrahmanyam Chandrasekhar, US; William A. Fowler, US.
1982 Kenneth G. Wilson, US.
1981 Nicolass Boembergen, Arthur Schlawlow, both US; Kai M. Siegbahn, Swedish.
1980 James W. Cronin, Val L. Fitch, both US.
1979 Steven Weinberg, Sheldon L. Glashow, both US; Abdus Salam, Pakistani.
1978 Pyotr Kapitsa, USSR; Arno Penzias, Robert Wilson, both US.
1977 John H. Van Vleck, Philip W. Anderson, both US; Nevill F. Mott, British.
1976 Burton Richter, US; Samuel C. C. Ting, US.
1975 James Rainwater, US; Ben Mottelson, US-Danish; Aage Bohr, Danish.
1974 Martin Ryle, British; Antony Hewish, British.
1973 Ivar Giaever, US; Leo Esaki, Japan; Brian D. Josephson, British.
1972 John Bardeen, US; Leon N. Cooper, US; John R. Schrieffer, US.
1971 Dennis Gabor, British.
1970 Louis Neel, French; Hannes Alfven, Swedish.
1969 Murray Gell-Mann, US.
1968 Luis W. Alvarez, US.
1967 Hans A. Bethe, US.
1966 Alfred Kastler, French.
1965 Richard P. Feynman, US; Julian S. Schwinger, US; Shinichiro Tomonaga, Japanese.
1964 Nikolai G. Basov, USSR; Aleksander M. Prochorov, USSR; Charles H. Townes, US.
1963 Maria Goeppert-Mayer, US; J. Hans D. Jensen, German; Eugene P. Wigner, US.
1962 Lev. D. Landau, USSR.
1961 Robert Hofstadter, US; Rudolf L. Mossbauer, German.
1960 Donald A. Glaser, US.
1959 Owen Chamberlain, US; Emilio G. Segre, US.
1958 Pavel Cherenkov, Ilya Frank, Igor Y. Tamm, all USSR.
1957 Tsung-dao Lee, Chen Ning Yang, both US.
1956 John Bardeen, US; Walter H. Brattain, US; William Shockley, US.
1955 Polykarp Kusch, US; Willis E. Lamb, US.
1954 Max Born, British; Walter Bothe, German.
1953 Frits Zernike, Dutch.
1952 Felix Bloch, US; Edward M. Purcell, US.
1951 Sir John D. Cockroft, British; Ernest T. S. Walton, Irish.
1950 Cecil F. Powell, British.

How Life Began

The beginnings of life

It is generally assumed by scientists who study the beginnings of life that its creation is a logical event, the result of conditions that existed on this planet more than 3 500 million years ago.

The raw materials and conditions for the creation of life must have been present at the time: temperature, humidity, chemicals, and the catalyst of violent electrical discharges, as in storms. After millions of years of the Earth's formation, the temperature of its atmosphere dropped to below $100°C$, and the vapour or humidity fell as rain, making lakes and seas in which were dissolved the chemicals from the rocks forming a rich solution, or 'primeval soup'. In this 'soup' life was created.

Due to ultra-violet ray bombardment from the Sun, intense volcanic activity and electrical storms, parts of this 'soup' were chemically changed into the components of living things: proteins and nucleic acids. How these two essentials combined is still a matter of conjecture, but they probably existed alongside each other for a long time before combining together.

The first living organisms derived from this combination were probably similar to viruses, but able to reproduce themselves in the environment in which they existed. The development to a cellular existence requires a membrane and this could have been constructed out of the phosphates in the 'soup', forming phospholipids, which are present in modern cell structure.

The first true cells probably resembled bacteria. These would obtain energy by breaking down the chemicals in the 'soup', probably by a kind of fermentation. As they evolved, they would extract energy from the phosphates around them, as do modern cells.

The next prerequisite for the development of living organisms was their ability to photosynthesise, the process by which carbon dioxide and water are chemically changed by the action of sunlight into glucose, releasing oxygen into the surrounding atmosphere. At first the rocks and minerals of the Earth absorbed the oxygen, forming the oxides we find in the Earth today, but gradually the oxygen became part of the atmosphere and with it ozone, the three-atom structure of oxygen. Ozone absorbs ultra-violet light, and protects the Earth's surface from these rays. Although ultra-violet rays were necessary in the first instance, they are lethal to living cells. Thus the screen of ozone in the atmosphere ameliorated conditions on the planet for life to evolve. This allowed increased photosynthesis by the organisms, leading to the evolution of more advanced plants and animals.

The first organisms to employ photosynthesis probably resembled the blue-green algae today found in ponds. The oldest-known fossils, dated as far back as 3,100 million years ago, resemble these algae, which have no separate nucleus. Eukaryotic cells (those possessing a separate nucleus) probably evolved 1 300 million years ago. Between the period of the discovery of the earliest fossils of 3 100 million years ago, and the period when fossils are abundant, the Cambrian period of 570 million years ago, little fossil evidence has been found to show us the development of life, but the Cambrian period has yielded more than 600 different organisms to show that life was, by then, truly established on this planet.

Biological classification

The founder of modern taxonomy is usually regarded as Carolus Linnaeus of Sweden. He drew up rules for botanists and zoologists for the assigning of names to both plants and animals. The binomial system was introduced by him in 1758 with the still standard hierarchy of class, order and genus.

International codes were established for nomenclature in botany in 1901; in Zoology in 1906 and for bacteria and viruses in 1948. The Linnaean binomial system is not employed for viruses. The 5-kingdom Schemes of Classification is as follows: Kingdom Procaryota, Kingdom Protista, Kingdom Fungi (see p. 85), The Plant Kingdom (see p. 85) and The Animal Kingdom (see p. 89).

Kingdom Procaryota

The organisms are characterized by an absence of distinct nuclei. Class Microtatobistes comprise viruses and the rickettsias, which are intermediate between viruses and bacteria in size and biochemistry.

Order Rickettsiales comprises some 60 species, four families, and were named after the virologist Howard T Ricketts (US) (1871–1910). No general classification of the 1000 plus viruses identified has yet been adopted. Eventual classification is expected to be based on the capsid (coat protein) symmetry in divisions between forms containing DNA (deoxyribonucleic acid) and RNA (ribonucleic acid). These infectious agents measure down to a minute 1.4×10^{-5} mm in diameter.

Bacterial unicellular micro-organisms, often spherical or rod-like, generally range from a micron in diameter to filaments several millimetres in length. They belong to the class Schizomycetes (Greek *Schizo* = I split;

Mykes = a fungus) in some 1500 species in ten orders.

Blue-green algae (Cyano phyta; Greek *Kyana* = corn-flower hence dark blue; *phyton* = a plant) have no motile flagellated cells and no sexual reproduction. Some 1500 species have been identified.

Kingdom Protista

This kingdom, first suggested by Ernst Haeckel in 1866, accommodates the mostly microscopic protozoa (Greek *protos* = first; *zoon* = an animal) of which some 30000 unicellular species have been described embracing flagellates (Latin *Flagellum*, diminutive of *flagrum* = a whip), ciliates (Latin *Ciliatus* = furnished with hairs), amoeba, ciliates and parasitic forms.

Algae possessing the nuclear mitochondrial and chloroplast membranes are also included among the protophyta in this kingdom.

The Plant World

Glossary

abscission The shedding of a leaf, fruit, flower, etc., by a plant.
absorption Taking up of water, solutes and other substances by both active and passive mechanisms. The taking up of radiant energy (from the sun) by pigments in plants.
achene A simple one-seeded indehiscent dry fruit.
acid rain Rain containing high levels of acidity caused by nitrogen and sulphur oxides – pollution from the burning of coal and oil.
active transport The transport of substances across a membrane, e.g. cell membrane, against a concentration gradient.
ADP Abbreviation for adenine diphosphate. The conversion of ADP to ATP is of central importance in the storage of light energy absorbed during photosynthesis.
adventitious Organs that arise in unexpected sites, e.g. leaves that grow roots.
aerial root A root that appears above soil level, usually hanging down in moist air.
aerobe Organism that can live only in the presence of oxygen.
aerobic respiration Respiration involving the oxidation of organic substrates and the associated absorption of free oxygen.
alcoholic fermentation Anaerobic respiration in which glucose is broken down to form ethanol and carbon dioxide. Carried out by yeasts.
algae Simple and diverse plant group. They are largely aquatic and many are unicellular.
alpine A regional community of plants found in high mountainous regions and on high plateaus.
alternation of generations The occurrence of an asexual and a sexual reproductive form during the life cycle of a plant.
amino acid These form the basic building blocks of proteins. About 20 commonly occur in proteins.
anaerobe An organism that can live in the absence of free oxygen.
anaerobic respiration This covers a number of chemical pathways by which chemical energy is obtained from various substrates without the use of free oxygen.
androdioecious Male and hermaphrodite flowers borne on separate plants.
androecium Male component of a flower, consisting of several stamens.

andromonoecious Male and hermaphrodite flowers carried on the same plant.
anemophily Wind pollination.
angiosperms The flowering plants.
annual Plant that germinates from seed, grows, flowers, produces seeds and then dies, all within a single year.
annual ring The ring of secondary xylem added to the wood of a tree in a single year.
anther The tip of the stamen that produces the pollen grains.
antheridium Male sex organ in lower plants.
aphids Insects that feed by sucking plant juices.
apomixis Asexual reproduction.
arboretum An area in which woody plants are grown.
asexual reproduction The formation of new individuals from the parent without the fusion of gametes.
ATP Abbreviation for adenosine triphosphate. It has one more phosphate grouping than ADP and it is the addition of this grouping that acts as an energy store.
auricle A small projection from the base of a leaf or petal.
auxin Plant growth substances that promote the elongation of shoots and roots.
axil The upper angle formed where the leaf or a similar organ joins the stem.

backcross Cross between an individual and one of its parents. Backcrossing is used to introduce desirable genes into a cultivated variety of a plant.
bacteria Microscopic unicellular plants with cell nuclear material not separated from the rest of the cell contents by a nuclear membrane.
bark All the tissues outside the vascular cambium in the stems and roots showing secondary growth.
benthos Plants that live on the seabed or a lake bed.
berry Many-seeded fleshy indehiscent fruit.
biennial A plant that takes two years to complete its life cycle, growing vegetatively in the first year, then flowering, seeding and dying in the second year.
binomial nomenclature System of naming plants using a generic name and a specific epithet. Developed by Linnaeus.
biochemistry Study and use of metabolism and metabolic chemicals.
biological control Control of pests by making

use of their natural predators.
blight Plant disease in which leaf damage is sudden and acute.
bloom A noticeable increase in the numbers of a species in the plankton. Usually refers to algae.
bolting Premature production of flowers and seeds.
bract Small leaflike structure that subtends a flower or inflorescence.
bracteole Small bract, typically on a flower stalk.
bud A short axis bearing a densely-packed series of leaf or flower primordia produced by an apical meristem.
budding Asexual reproduction in which a new individual is produced by an outgrowth of the parent.
bud grafting A bud and a small piece of bark is removed and inserted into a slit in the bark of the root-stock.
bulb A fleshy underground modified shoot, made up of swollen scale leaves or leaf bases. It is a perennating organ, allowing the plant to survive for many years.
bulbil Small bulb found on an aerial bud, functioning as a means of vegetative propagation.

callus Parenchymatous cells formed at the site of a wound.
calyx The sepals; the outer whorl of the perianth.
cambium A meristem that occurs parallel with the long axis of an organ. It is responsible for secondary growth.
canker Plant disease in which there is an area of necrosis which becomes surrounded by layers of callus tissue.
capillary action The effect of surface tension on a liquid in a fine tube, causing the liquid to rise up the tube. The supply of water throughout a plant is largely due to capillary action.
carbohydrates Contain carbon, hydrogen and oxygen, often in the formula $(CH_2O)_n$. They are energy storage molecules and form structural components.
carbon dioxide Makes up 0.03% of the air, and is converted to carbohydrates by photosynthesis.
carpel This carries and encloses the ovules in flowering plants. It consists of the ovary, style and stigma.
catkin Hanging unisexual inflorescence, designed for wind pollination.

cellulose A carbohydrate consisting solely of glucose units. It is present in plant cell walls as highly organized microfibrils.

chlorophyll The main class of photosynthetic pigment. They absorb red and blue light and reflect green light; hence the characteristic green colour of photosynthetic plants.

chloroplast Green bodies in plant cells, that contain photosynthetic pigment molecules.

chlorosis Condition in plants in which the chlorophyll levels drop, producing a yellow or pale unhealthy plant.

ciliate Describing a part of the plant fringed with hairs.

circadian rhythm A cycle in which physiological responses occur at 24-hourly intervals, e.g. opening and closing of stomata, change in position of leaves.

cladode A stem structure resembling a leaf, usually produced as an adaptation to dry conditions. The leaves will be reduced when a plant bears cladodes.

cleistogamy When flowers do not open to reveal the reproductive organs, thus preventing cross-pollination.

climacteric Rise in respiration rate in some fruits during ripening.

club root Fungal disease in which roots become swollen and malformed, causing wilting, yellowing and stunting.

coenocarpium Fruit that includes ovaries, floral parts and receptacles of a number of flowers on a fleshy axis.

collenchyma Long cells with thickened but non-lignified primary cell walls. A supporting tissue.

contractile root Specialized thickened root that pulls a rhizome, bulb, corm, etc., down into the soil.

coppicing Cutting trees back to ground level every 10–15 years. New shoots from the base are therefore encouraged and can be harvested when the coppice is next cut back.

cordate Heart-shaped, e.g. leaves.

corm Short swollen underground stem, acting as an organ of perennation and vegetative propagation.

corolla The petals.

corolla tube Fusion of the edges of the petals.

corona Crownlike out-growing of a corolla tube.

corymb Flat-topped cluster of flowers on lateral stalks of different lengths.

cotyledon The first leaf or leaves of the embryo in seed plants. In non-endosperm seeds they are used as food storage organs.

cross-pollination In which pollen from one individual is transferred to the stigma of another individual.

cultivar Variety or strain produced artificially and not found in the natural population.

cuticle Layer of cutin on the surface of aerial parts of a plant, broken only by stomata and lenticels. It acts to conserve water.

cutin Forms the waxy cuticle.

cutting A common form of artificial propagation whereby a portion of a living plant is detached and grown in soil or culture medium.

cymose Inflorescence in which apical tissues of the main and lateral stems differentiate into flowers.

cryptophyte Plant with perennating buds below ground or water.

2,4-D Abbreviation for 2,4-dichlorophenoxy-acetic acid, a synthetic auxin widely used in selective weedkillers.

damping off Disease of seedlings in which they rot at soil level and then die. Caused by crowded conditions and cold wet soil.

dark reactions Part of the photosynthetic process that is not light dependent. Stored energy in ATP is used to convert carbon dioxide to carbohydrate.

deciduous Woody perennial trees that shed their leaves before the winter or dry season.

decumbent A stem that lies along the ground.

deficiency disease Disease caused by lack of an essential nutrient, especially minerals.

definite growth A maximum size is reached, beyond which the plant can grow no more.

dehiscence The bursting open of certain plant organs at maturity, especially reproductive structures, to release their contents.

denitrification Loss of nitrate from the soil due to the action of denitrifying bacteria.

dentate A leaf margin that is toothed.

desert Regional community with low rainfall.

dichogamy Anthers and stigma maturing at different times on the same plant, thus reducing the chance of self-fertilization.

dicliny Male and female reproductive parts in different flowers.

dicotyledons Those angiosperms with embryos with two cotyledons. The group includes hardwood trees, shrubs and many herbaceous plants.

diffusion The movement of ions or molecules in solution down a concentration gradient. It is involved in, for example, transpiration and the uptake of carbon dioxide.

dioecious Male and female reproductive organs on different individuals, making cross-fertilization necessary and ensuring genetic variation.

DNA Abbreviation for deoxyribonucleic acid. The chemical constituent of genes. It determines the inherited characteristics of a plant.

dormancy An inactive phase of seeds, spores and buds, often in order to survive adverse conditions.

double fertilization In most flowering plants two male gametes participate in fertilization. One fuses with the female gamete to give the zygote which grows into the embryo, while the other fuses with the polar nuclei or definitive nucleus to give the endosperm.

double flower A flower with more than the usual number of petals, either due to the stamens or stamens and carpels forming petals.

drupe Fleshy indehiscent fruit with seed or seeds surrounded by woody tissue.

embryo Young plant after fertilization has taken place.

endocarp Innermost layer of the pericarp of an angiosperm fruit, outside the seeds. It can sometimes be woody.

endosperm Storage tissue in seeds of angiosperms.

entomophily Insect pollination.

enzyme A large protein molecule that can catalyse specific biochemical reactions.

epicalyx Calyx-like extra ring of floral appendages below the calyx, resembling a ring of sepals.

epicotyl Apical end of the axis of an embryo, immediately above the cotyledon or cotyledons. It grows into the embryo.

epidermis Outer layer of cells of a plant.

epigeal Germination of the seed in which the cotyledons are raised above the surface of the ground by elongation of the hypocotl, thus forming the first leaves.

epigyny Floral parts found above the ovary.

epiphyte Plant with no roots in the soil. It is usually supported by another plant, and gets its nutrients from the air, rain and organic material on the surface of the other plant.

etiolation When plants are grown in insufficient light they become pale and elongated as they grow towards what light there is.

eukaryotic Organisms with cells that have nuclei.

evergreen Woody perennial plants that keep their leaves throughout the year, shedding and replacing leaves on a continuous basis.

exocarp Outermost layer of an angiosperm fruit, usually forming a skin.

F_1 generation First filial generation obtained in breeding experiments.

F_2 generation Second filial generation, obtained by crossing the F_1 generation.

F_1 hybrid First filial generation produced by crossing two selected parental pure lines. They do not breed true.

fen Flat area of land originating from peaty marshes.

fermentation Anaerobic respiration of glucose and other organic substrates to obtain energy.

floral diagram Representation of flower structure. The whorls of floral parts are shown as a series of concentric circles.

floral formula Use of symbols, numbers and letters to record floral structure.

floret A small flower.

flower Sexual reproductive unit of angiosperms, consisting of perianth, androecium and gynoecium, all arising from the receptacle.

forest Community in which the dominant species are trees.

fragmentation Asexual reproduction in which the parent splits into two or more pieces which develop into new individuals.

frond Large leaf or leaflike structure.

fruit The ripened ovary of a flower, plus any accessory parts associated with it.

fungi Saprophytic, parasitic and symbiotic eukaryotic organisms, lacking chlorophyll, whose plant body is typically a mycelium.

gall Abnormal swelling or outgrowth on a plant caused by an attack by a parasite.

gamete A cell or nucleus that can undergo sexual fusion with another gamete to form a zygote, which in turn develops into a new individual.

gametophyte The generation in the life cycle of a plant that produces the gametes.

gamopetalous Petals fused along their margins forming a corolla tube.

gamosepalous Sepals that are fused to form a tubular calyx.

garigue Scrub woodland on limestone areas with low rainfall and thin soils.

gemma Multicellular structure for vegetative reproduction found in some mosses and liverworts.

gene Unit of inheritance.

genotype Genetic make-up of an organism, as opposed to its physical appearance.

genus A group of obviously homologous species.

germination Changes undergone by a reproductive body, e.g. zygote, spore, pollen, grain, seed, before and during the first signs of growth.

glabrous A surface that has no hairs.

glaucous Surfaces with a waxy blue-grey bloom on them.

gley Waterlogged soil lacking in oxygen.

glume Bracts subtending each spikelet in the flowers of grasses.

grafting Artificial means of propagation by which a segment of the plant to be propagated is attached to another plant so that their vascular tissues combine.

grassland Community in which grasses are the dominant group.

green manure Fast-growing crop grown at the end of the season and then ploughed or dug in, thus increasing the amount of organic matter in the soil.

growth ring Secondary xylem produced in a growing period in the stems and roots of many plants. When the stem or root is sliced across this ring is visible.

guard cells Pair of bow-shaped cells surrounding each stomatal pore and forming the stoma. The opening of the stoma is controlled by changes in the turgidity of the guard cells.

guttation Exudation from plants of water in liquid form.

gymnosperms Vascular plant with naked seeds borne on a sporophyll and not in an ovary.

gynandrous Stamens on the gynoecium.

gynodioecious Plants that bear female and hermaphrodite flowers on separate individuals.

gynoecium Female part of the angiosperm flower, consisting of one or more carpels.

gynomonoecious Plants that bear female and hermaphrodite flowers on the same individual.

halophyte Plant that can live in soil with a high salt concentration.

hardening The gradual exposure of plants to lower temperatures in order to increase their resistance to frost, prior to planting out.

hard seed A seed with a hard coat that is impervious to water.

hastate A leaf shaped like a three-lobed spear.

haustorium Organ produced by a parasite to absorb nutrients from the host plant.

heartwood Central part of secondary xylem in some woody plants. It is derived from the sapwood that has deteriorated with age.

heath A region of poor sandy soils exposed to strong winds.

helophyte Marsh plant with perennating buds

in the mud at the bottom of the lake.

hemicellulose Carbohydrate found in plant cell walls, often in association with cellulose. Unlike cellulose, it can be broken down by enzymes and thus used as a nutrient reserve.

hemicryptophyte Plants with perennating buds just below the soil surface.

herbaceous perennial Lives for many years, surviving each winter as an underground storage or perennating organ, the leaves and flowers dying back.

herbarium Dried pressed plants kept in a collection.

herbicide Chemical that kills plants.

hermaphrodite Male and female reproductive parts in the same flower.

hesperidium Berry with a leathery epicarp, e.g. citrus fruit.

heteroblastic development Progressive development in the form and size of successive organs such as leaves.

heterophylly Having two or more leaf types differing in morphology and function.

heterostyly Having two or more different arrangements of the reproductive parts in the flowers of a single species.

hilum Scar on the seed coat at the point of abscission.

hip Type of pseudocarp fruit.

homogamy The maturation of anthers and stigmas at the same time.

honey guide Dots or lines on petals that guide pollinating insects to the nectaries.

humus Soft moist organic matter in soil, derived from rotting plant and animal matter.

hybrid Individual produced by genetically distinct parents.

hybrid sterility Inability of some hybrids to produce gametes.

hydrophily Pollination by water transport of pollen grains.

hydrophyte Plant that is adapted to living in water or in waterlogged conditions.

hydroponics Growth of plants, for example in sand, to which nutrients are added in a liquid fertilizer.

hypha Branched filament of fungi. Many hyphae make up the mycelium of fungi.

hypocotl That part of the stem between the cotyledons and the radicle in the embryo.

hypogeal Seed germination in which the cotyledons remain below ground due to lack of growth of the hypocotl.

hypogyny Floral parts inserted below the ovary.

indefinite growth Unlimited growth, i.e. the plant or parts of the plant continue to grow throughout their lives.

indehiscent Fruit or fruiting body that does not open to disperse its seeds.

inflorescence A group of flowers borne on the same stalk.

insectivorous plant A plant that can obtain its nutrients by digesting insects and other tiny animals, in addition to photosynthesizing.

integument Protective envelope around the ovule of seed plants. Most gymnosperms have one integument, while most angiosperms have two.

keel The pair of fused lower petals in pea flowers.

key List of characteristics enabling rapid identification of species.

kingdom All organisms were at one time placed in the plant or animal kingdom. There is now a move to identify other kingdoms, e.g. for the fungi, unicellular organisms.

labellum Distinct lower three petals of an orchid.

lamina Flattened bladelike section of a leaf.

lanceolate Narrow; tapering at both ends.

layering Plant propagation in which runners or stolons are pegged down to the ground encouraging roots to form at that point.

leaching Washing out of minerals and other nutrients from the soil.

leaf Principal photosynthetic organ of green plants. It is formed as a lateral outgrowth from the stem, and consists of the lamina, petiole and leaf base.

leaf base Point of attachment of leaf to stem.

leaf fall Shedding of leaves due to abscission.

leaf spot Disease involving spots of dead tissue on the leaves.

legume A dry dehiscent fruit containing one or more seeds. It is also a general name for the plants in the family *Leguminosae* (pea family), whose fruit is a legume of one description or another.

lemma Lower of a pair of bracts beneath each flower in a grass.

lenticel Small pore containing loose cells in the periderm of plants. Gaseous exchange takes place through the lenticel.

lichen Plants composed of a fungus and algae in symbiotic relationships. The lichen is distinct from either of its constituents.

life cycle Various stages an organism passes through, from fertilized egg in one generation to fertilized egg in the next generation.

light Light from the sun forms the energy to drive the photosynthetic process.

light reactions Those reactions in the photosynthetic chain of reactions that are dependent on light.

lignin Carbohydrate polymer making up about a quarter of the wood of a tree.

liming Addition of lime to the soil to decrease the acidity of the soil and to improve the soil structure.

linear Leaves that are flat and parallel-sided.

lipid Water-insoluble fatty acids, consisting of carbon, hydrogen and oxygen plus some other elements. Their functions vary, but they can be for storage and as structural molecules.

lipoprotein Association of lipid and protein usually found in plant cell membranes.

lithophyte Plant that grows on rocky ground.

littoral The seashore between low and high tide.

loam Soil with even mixture of fine clay and coarser sand particles.

loess Fine yellowish soil, consisting of clay and silt particles.

macronutrient A chemical element required by a plant in relatively large amounts.

manure Animal excrement, perhaps mixed with other organic material, used to improve soil fertility.

maquis Stunted woodland in semi-arid areas that have been deforested.

meadow Moist grassland maintained by mowing.

meristem Region of a plant containing actively- or potentially actively-dividing cells.

mesocarp Middle layer of the pericarp of an angiosperm fruit. It may be absent.

mesophyte Plant with no adaptations to environmental extremes.

microflora Small plants found in a given area.

micronutrient Chemical element required in small quantities, i.e, a trace element.

midrib Vein running down the middle of a leaf.

mildew Fungal disease of plants in which the fungus is seen on the plant surface.

monadelphous Stamen filaments fused to form a tube.

monochasium Cymose inflorescence in which only one axillary bud develops into a lateral branch at each node.

monocotyledons Angiosperms possessing one cotyledon in the embryo. The group includes palms, grasses, orchids, lilies.

monoecious Female and male reproductive parts in separate floral structures on the same plant.

monopodial branching Secondary shoots or branches arise behind the main growing tip and remain subsidiary to the main stem.

moor Wet exposed land where soil water seeps away very slowly.

mosses Large group of the bryophyte division. Distinguished by filamentous or thalloid protonema which produces buds from which the familiar leafy moss plant develops.

mould Fungus that produces a velvety growth on the surface of its host.

mulch Organic material, e.g. grass cuttings, leaf mould, etc., spread on the ground to smother annual weeds.

multiple fruit Fleshy fruit incorporating the ovaries of many flowers and derived from a complete inflorescence.

mushroom Usually umbrella-like fruiting body arising from the underground hyphae of the fungal order *Agaricales* (edible mushrooms).

muskeg Peat bog in coniferous forest of N. America.

mycelium Loose mass of branching and interwoven fungal hyphae.

mycorrhiza Symbiotic relationship between a fungus and the roots of a plant.

nastic movement A plant response caused by an external stimulus. The stimulus acts merely as a trigger, and does not control the plant's response.

necrosis Death of part of a plant while the rest of the plant continues to live.

nectar Sugary solution secreted by the nectaries. Honey is made by bees from nectar.

nectaries Glands at the base of flower that secrete nectar in order to attract insect pollinators.

node Point on the plant stem at which one or more leaves develop.

nut A dry indehiscent fruit containing one seed. The pericarp is lignified and woody.

offset A sort of runner. A short shoot that develops from an axillary bud near the base of the stem and goes on to form a daughter plant.

ontogeny All the changes that occur during the life cycle of an organism.

opposite Pairs of leaves arising at each node.

ornithophily Bird pollination.

osmosis Passage of certain molecules in a solution, down a concentration gradient and across a semipermeable membrane that prevents the passage of other molecules. In plants it is usually water molecules that pass across the membrane, equalizing solute concentrations on either side of the membrane.

ovary Swollen basal part of the carpel in angiosperms. containing the ovule or ovules.

ovule Female gamete and its protective and nutritional tissues. It develops into the seed after fertilization.

palea Upper bract of the pair found beneath each floret in a grass inflorescence.

pampas S. American grassland.

panicle Racemose inflorescence in which the flowers are formed on stalks arising spirally or alternately from the main stem.

pappus Modified calyx consisting of a fine ring of hairs or teeth that persists after fertilization, aiding wind dispersal of the seeds.

parasitism Relationship between two organisms in which one is wholly dependent on the other, e.g. for food, shelter, etc.

parenchyma Unspecialized tissue in the plant, often forming a ground tissue in which other tissues are located.

parthenocarpy Production of a fruit without the process of fertilization.

pasture Moist grassland maintained by grazing.

peat Partially decomposed plant material, built up in poorly-drained areas.

pedalfer Acid soil from which soluble lime has been leached by rainfall.

pedicel Stalk attaching flowers to the main stem of the inflorescence.

pedocal Alkaline soil in which lime has built up in the surface layers.

pepo Berry with a hard exterior.

perennial A plant that lives for many years.

perianth The protective structure encircling the reproductive parts, consisting of the calyx and corolla or a ring of petals.

pericarp The wall of the fruit, derived from the ovary wall.

periderm Protective secondary tissue replacing the epidermis as the outer cellular layer of stems and roots.

perigyny Floral parts inserted on the receptacle at about the same level as the ovary.

permanent wilting point The point at which the amount of water in the soil is so low that a plant wilts and will not recover unless water is added to the soil.

petal A unit of the corolla, thought to be a modified leaf.

petiole Stalk that attaches the leaf lamina to the stem.

phanerophyte Plant with perennating buds on upright stems well above soil level.

phellem Compact protective tissue replacing the epidermis as the outer layer in plants with secondary growth.

phloem Vascular tissue in plants responsible for translocation of nutrients.

photic zone Surface waters of lakes and seas, in which light penetrates and which is inhabited by plankton.

photoperiodism Alternation of day and night, controlling the physiological mechanisms of many plants.

photorespiration Respiration that occurs in plants in the light.

photosynthesis Series of reactions in green plants in which light energy is used to drive reactions which convert carbon dioxide and water to carbohydrates and thence to other materials.

phycobiont Algal partner in a lichen.

phyllode Flattened petiole which performs the functions of a leaf.

phyllody Transformation of parts of a flower into leaflike structures.

pileus Cap of a mushroom or toadstool.

piliferous layer The absorbing region of the root epidermis. It is covered with root hairs.

pinna A first-order leaflet in a compound leaf.

pinnule Second-order leaflet in a compound leaf, i.e. each pinna is divided into a number of pinnules.

pistil A single carpel or group of carpels.

pith Region of parenchyma in the centre of many plant stems.

plankton Microorganisms floating in surface waters of seas and lakes.

plumule Embryonic shoot derived from the epicotyl.

podsol Acid infertile soil found in regions of heavy rainfall and long cold winters.

pollard To prune back a tree to the main trunk.

pollen The microspores, containing the male gamete, released in large numbers as a fine powder by gymnosperms and angiosperms.

pollen sac The chambers on the anther in which pollen is formed.

pollination Transfer of pollen from the male to the female parts in seed plants, i.e. from the anthers to the stigma.

pome A fleshy pseudocarp in which tissues develop from the receptacle and enclose the true fruit.

prickle Short pointed outgrowth from the epidermis.

primary growth Size increase due to cell division at apical meristems.

procumbent Plant that trails loosely along the ground.

prokaryotic Organisms in which the nuclear material is not separated from the rest of the cell contents.

proteins Large molecules consisting of carbon, hydrogen, nitrogen, oxygen and other elements. Plant proteins can largely be grouped as enzymes or structural and contractile proteins.

pruning Cutting back of some or all of the branches of woody plants, usually to promote growth in selected areas of the plant.

psuedocarp Fruit consisting of tissues other than those derived from the gynoecium.

raceme Inflorescence in which flowers are formed on individual pedicels on the main axis.

radicle Embryonic root, normally the first organ to emerge on germination.

receptacle The region at the end of the main axis of the flower, to which the floral parts are attached.

respiration The breakdown of food substances, utilizing molecular oxygen, in order to release energy.

rhizome Underground stem that acts as a means of vegetative propagation.

root Usually underground section of a plant involved with fixing the plant in position and absorbing water and nutrients. It can be used as a food storage organ.

root hair Projections from single cells in the root epidermis. They increase the surface area for absorption.

root nodule Lumpy growth that develops on the roots of leguminous plants as a result of symbiotic infections involved with nitrogen fixation.

rosette plant Plant with its leaves radiating outwards on the surface of the soil.

runner A creeping stem arising from an axillary bud, giving rise to new plants at the nodes.

rusts Fungal infections causing dark rust-coloured spots on the leaves or stem.

samara Achene with pericarp extended into a wing.

sap Liquid containing mineral salts and sugars dissolved in water, found in xylem and phloem vessels.

saprophyte Plant that feeds on dead and decaying organic material.

sapwood Outer functional part of the secondary xylem.

savanna Tropical grassland.

scape Leafless stem of a solitary flower or inflorescence.

schizocarp Dry fruit formed from two or more one-seeded carpels that divide into one-seeded units when mature.

scion Shoot or bud cut from one plant and grafted or budded on to another.

sclerenchyma Strengthening tissue.

seaweed Group of large algae found in the littoral zone and floating freely in the sea.

secondary growth Increase in diameter of a plant organ as a result of cell division in the cambium.

seed The structure that develops from the fertilized ovule in seed plants. It usually contains the embryo and a food store.

seedling A young plant.

self-incompatability Inability of gametes from the same plant to fertilize each other or form a viable embryo.

self-pollination Pollen transferred to the stigma of the same flower or flowers on the same plant.

seminal root Roots growing from the base of the stem and taking over from the radicle during early seedling growth.

sepal Individual unit of the calyx, usually green. They may be coloured and take over the function of petals.

sessile Unstalked.

shade plant Able to flourish in conditions of low light.

silicula Broad dry dehiscent fruit developed from two carpels fused together.

siliqua Longer than a silicula, but otherwise the same.

smut Fungal disease with a black spore mass on the host.

soil The surface layer of the earth's crust, consisting of water, air, living organisms, dead and decaying organisms and mineral particles.

spadix Racemose inflorescence in which the flowers are sessile and carried on a fleshy axis.

spathe Large bract enclosing a spadix.

species A single breeding group differentiated from other breeding groups by marked characteristics.

spike Racemose inflorescence in which the flowers are sessile and carried on an elongated axis.

spine Modified leaf or part of a leaf, forming a pointed structure.

spore Simple asexual unicellular reproductive unit.

stamen Male reproductive organ in flowering plants. Together the stamens make up the androecium and produce the pollen on the anthers.

starch Most common and important food reserve carbohydrate in plants.

stele The vascular cylinder responsible for transport of water and solutes in the stems and roots of vascular plants.

stem That part of the plant above ground that carries the leaves, buds and reproductive parts.

stigma The tip of the carpel that receives the pollen at the time of pollination and on which the pollen germinates.

stock Plant on to which shoots or buds are grafted.

stolon Long branch that bends over and touches the ground, at which point a new plant may develop.

stoma Pore in the epidermis of the aerial parts of a plant, especially the leaves, through which gaseous exchange occurs.

style That portion of the carpel between the ovary and stigma.

substrate Molecules on which enzymes act.

succulent A plant that conserves water by storing it in a swollen stem or leaves.

sucker A shoot that develops from the roots and that develops its own root system.

swamp Vegetation found in stagnant or slow-flowing water.

symbiosis Intimate relationship between two (or more) organisms, in which both benefit.

sympodial branching The apical bud dies at the end of one season and growth continues in the next season from the lateral bud immediately below.

syncarpous Gynoecium with fused carpels.

syngenesious Androecium with fused anthers.

2,4,5-T Selective weedkiller and defoliant.

tap-root A tough primary root, often penetrating deep into the soil. It can sometimes be a specialized food store.

taxis A directional movement of a whole plant in response to external stimuli.

tendril Modified inflorescence, branch or leaf of a climbing plant that can coil around objects to support the plant.

terra rossa Clayey soil, rich in lime, with a bright red colour from iron oxides.

testa Protective outer covering of a seed.

thallus Plant body undifferentiated into leaves, stem and roots.

thorn Modified reduced branch forming a pointed woody structure. It has a vascular structure within it.

tiller Shoot that grows from the base of the stem when the main stem has been cut back, as in coppicing.

toadstool Inedible fruiting body of fungi.

transpiration Loss of water by evaporation from a plant's surfaces, especially through the stoma. This water loss sucks up water through the rest of the plant, from the roots upwards.

trifoliate Compound leaf with three leaflets.

trimerous Arrangement, especially in monocotyledons, in which the floral parts in each whorl are inserted in threes or multiples of three.

tropism Directional growth of a plant in response to an external stimulus. It can be positive or negative.

tuber Swollen underground part of a stem or root, used for food storage and lasting only one year.

tundra Cold desert with frozen topsoil for most of the year and subsoil permanently frozen.

turgor Pressure of cell contents on cell walls, swelling them out, due to the cell taking in water by osmosis. Turgidity is the main effect that keeps non-woody plants erect.

umbel Racemose inflorescence in which flowers are borne on undivided stalks that arise from the main stem. The arrangement of these stalks is such that the flowers form a flat-topped plate or umbrella.

variegation Streaks of different colouring in a plant organ, especially leaves and petals.

vascular bundle A strand of primary vascular tissue, consisting largely of xylem and phloem.

vegetative reproduction Asexual reproduction in which specialized multicellular organs are formed and detached from the parent, generating new individuals.

vein Vascular bundle in a leaf.

venation The pattern of veins in a leaf.

vernalisation Promotion of flowering by exposing young plants to cold.

vernation Pattern of rolling and folding of leaves in a bud.

vivipary Young plants forming at the axils of flowers, or the germination of seeds on the parent plant before release.

weed Any plant growing where it is not wanted.

wilt Any plant disease causing inadequate water supply and thus wilting.

witches' broom Mass of twigs grown in response to an infection.

xylem Vascular tissue responsible for transporting water and solutes from the roots up to the leaves and other aerial parts. It constitutes the woody tissues.

zygote Product of the fusion of two gametes, before it undergoes subsequent cell division.

Kingdom Fungi

The fungus group of some 80 000 species because of dissimilarities to both plants and animals are now usually placed in a separate kingdom.

Sac fungi (Order Endomycetales) comprise yeasts (division mycota); moulds, mildews; truffles (class ascomycetes) and lichen (Order Lecanorales) which have both an algal and a fungal component.

Club fungi include smuts (Order Ustilaginales) so called because of black and dusty masses of spores; rusts (Order Uredinales) parasitic on vascular plants and hence destructive to agriculture; mushrooms (Order Agaricales); puff-balls (Order Lycoperdales and Order Sclerodermatales) and stinkhorns (Order Phallales).

The Plant Kingdom

Kingdom Plantae (Metaphyta) embraces mosses, liverworts, hornworts, whisk ferns, club mosses, horsetails, ferns, cycads, conifers and flowering plants in 11 divisions. These were listed together with their Greek or Latin derivatives on pp. 33–37 *Guinness Book of Answers* (2nd Edition). The most advanced clan among the vascular plants is Class Angiospermae.

Class Angiospermae (from Greek, *angeion* = receptacle; *sperma* = seed). The true flowering plants, of which there are more than 250 000 species. The Angiosperms have ovules enclosed within the ovary of a pistil (gynoecium) and the seeds are enclosed within the ripened ovary, which, when matured, becomes a fruit that may be single-seeded or many-seeded. The angiosperms usually have fibrous roots and soft herbaceous stem tissue. The leaves contain extensive mesophytic tissue (i.e. requiring only an average amount of moisture). The reproductive unit is the flower, which typically consists of a very short central axis bearing one or more apical megasporophylls, commonly called carpels, subtended by microsporophylls (termed stamens) and by two sets of sterile bract-like appendages collectively termed the perianth (composed of petals and sepals). In the simplest form of the flower, the ovules are borne along the inner margin of the megasporophyll – like peas in the pod. In all modern angiosperms the megasporophyll is closed and fused marginally, with the ovules in the loculus (cavity) thus formed. In this form, the carpel is termed the pistil and consists of the ovary (the ovule-containing organ) and its apical stigma (the pollen-receiving part). The microsporophylls are closed until maturity, when they open and their pollen is released. The pollen-producing part is the anther and the supporting stalk the filament. The fertilisation (which follows pollination) takes place entirely within the carpel of the flower. After the pollen grain (microgametophyte) reaches the receptive stigmatic surface of the pistil, a pollen tube is developed within, and into it moves the generative nucleus, which divides to form two male nuclei, each of which is a male gamete. Stimulated by the environment created in the stigma, the pollen tube grows through the wall of the pollen grain and into the tissue of the stigma and its style (i.e. the usually attenuated part of a pistil between the ovary and the stigma). This growth continues down the style until the tube penetrates the ovary. Growth continues and when the tube reaches the ovule it enters the micropyle (a pore at the tip of the ovule) or elsewhere through the integuments (i.e. the two outer layers of the ovule) and finally the female gametophyte (enclosed within the ovule). As pollen-tube growth progresses from stigma to female gametophyte it carries with it both male nuclei. On approach to the egg nucleus, within the female gametophyte, the two haploid male nuclei are released. One unites with the haploid egg nucleus and forms a diploid sporophyte, called the zygote, and the other unites with the polar nuclei to form a triploid endosperm nucleus. The zygote thus formed is a new generation, and becomes the embryo within the seed. The zygote (enclosed by a membrane) undergoes a series of divisions leading to wall formation (either transverse or longitudinal) separating the terminal cell from the basal cell. The terminal cell continues to divide to produce the axis or hypocotyl of the embryo, from which are later produced the cotyledons (Greek, *kotylēdōn* = cup-shaped hollow) or seed leaves (either one or two – see below under sub-classes). The basal cell divides to form a chain of cells that functions as a suspensor, and the lowest is attached to the embryo and ultimately gives rise to the root and root cap of the embryo. The endosperm nucleus, together with the embryo sac, multiplies to form the endosperm tissue of the seed. This tissue multiplies as the embryo develops, but the bulk of it is digested by the embryo. The angiosperms may be divided into two groups:

Sub-class Dicotyledonae
(Greek, *di* = two). The dicotyledons – over 200 000 species. This sub-class contains angiosperms in which the embryo has two cotyledons (seed leaves). The stems produce a secondary growth by successive cylinders of xylem tissue (Greek, *xylē* = wood), the wood element which, in angiosperms, contains vessels for water conduction and wood fibres for support. The veins of the leaves are typically arranged in a network, i.e. reticular venation. Leaves may be simple, with entire or toothed margins, or compound with leaflets arranged on either side of, or radiating from a petiole, or footstalk. The petals and sepals of the flowers number mostly four or five, or multiples of four or five, and the pollen grains are mostly tricolpate (with three furrows). This group may be sub-divided into 40 or more orders. There are several families of dicotyledons which appear to have no direct relationship with any other group. These include the Salicaceae (willows and poplars), Fagaceae (beeches and oaks), the Proteaceae and the Casuarinaceae.

Sub-class Monocotyledonae
(Greek, *monos* = one). The monocotyledons – about 50 000 species. The embryo has one cotyledon. The members of this sub-class have stems without any secondary thickening; the vascular strands are scattered through the stem and no cylinders of secondary xylem tissue are produced. The leaves have entire margins, the blades generally lack a petiole, and the veins are arranged in parallel form. The flower parts are always in multiples of three, and the sepals are often petal-like. The pollen grains are always monocolpate (i.e. with one furrow). This sub-class contains 15 orders, of which the Liliales (Lily order) is considered the most primitive, and the Orchidales (Orchid order) the most advanced. This sub-class also contains palms, grasses, and bamboos.

Fruit

Common name	Scientific name	Geographical origin	Date first described or known
Apple	*Malus pumila*	Southwestern Asia	Early times; Claudius 450 BC
Apricot	*Prunus armeniaca*	Central and western China	BC (Piling and Dioscoridês)
Avocado (Pear)	*Persea americana*	Mexico and Central America	Early Spanish explorers, Clusius 1601
Banana	*Musa sapientum*	Southern Asia	Intro: Africa 1st century AD, Canary Is 15th century
Cherry	*Prunus avium*	Europe (near Dardanelles)	Prehistoric times
Date	*Phoenix dactylifera*	unknown	Prehistoric times
Fig	*Ficus carica*	Syria westward to the Canary Is	c. 4000 BC (Egypt)
Grape	*Vitis vinifera*	around Caspian and Black Seas	c. 4000 BC
Grapefruit	*Citrus grandis*	Malay Archipelago and neighbouring islands	12th or 13th century
Lemon	*Citrus limon*	Southeastern Asia	11th–13th centuries
Lime	*Citrus aurantifolia*	Northern Burma	11th–13th centuries
Mandarin (Orange)	*Citrus reticulata*	China	220 BC in China; Europe 1805
Mango	*Mangifera indica*	Southeastern Asia	c. 16th century; Cult. India 4th or 5th century BC
Olive	*Olea europaea*	Syria to Greece	Prehistoric times
Orange	*Citrus sinensis*	China	2200 BC (Europe 15th century)
Papaya	*Carica papaya*	West Indian Islands or Mexican mainland	14th–15th centuries
Peach	*Prunus persica*	China?	300 BC (Greece)
Pear	*Pyrus communis*	Western Asia	Prehistoric times
Pineapple	*Ananas comosus*	Guadeloupe	c. 1493 (Columbus)
Plum	*Prunus domestica*	Western Asia	Possibly AD 100
Quince	*Cydonia oblonga*	Northern Iran	BC
Rhubarb	*Rheum rhaponticum*	Eastern Mediterranean lands and Asia Minor	2700 BC (China)
Water Melon	*Citrullus laratus*	Central Africa	c. 2000 BC (Egypt)

Vegetables

Common name	Scientific name	Geographical origin	Date first described or known
Asparagus	*Asparagus officinalis*	Eastern Mediterranean	*c.* 200 BC
Beetroot	*Beta vulgaris*	Mediterranean Area	2nd century BC
Broad Bean	*Vicia faba*	—	widely cultivated in prehistoric times
Broccoli	*Brassica oleracea* (variety *Italica*)	Eastern Mediterranean	1st century AD
Brussels Sprout	*Brassica oleracea* (variety *gemmifera*)	Northern Europe	1587 (Northern Europe)
Cabbage	*Brassica oleracea* (variety *capitata*)	Eastern Mediterranean lands and Asia Minor	*c.* 600 BC
Carrot	*Daucus carota*	Afghanistan	*c.* 500 BC
Cauliflower	*Brassica oleracea* (variety *botrytis*)	Eastern Mediterranean	6th century BC
Celery	*Apium graveolens*	Caucasus	*c.* 850 BC
Chive	*Allium schoenoprasum*	Eastern Mediterranean	*c.* 100 BC
Cucumber	*Cucumis sativus*	Northern India	2nd century BC (Egypt 1300 BC)
Egg plant	*Solanum melongena*	India, Assam, Burma	*c.* 450 AD (China)
Endive	*Cichorium endivia*	Eastern Mediterranean lands and Asia Minor	BC
Garden Pea	*Pisum sativum*	Central Asia	3000–2000 BC
Garlic	*Allium sativum*	Middle Asia	*c.* 900 BC (Homer)
Gherkin (W. Indian)	*Cucumis anguria*	Northern India	2nd century BC
Globe Artichoke	*Cynara scolymus*	Western and Central Mediterranean	*c.* 500 BC
Kale	*Brassica oleracea* (variety *acephala*)	Eastern Mediterranean lands and Asia Minor	*c.* 500 BC
Leek	*Allium porrum*	Middle Asia	*c.* 1000 BC
Lettuce	*Lactuca sativa*	Asia Minor, Iran and Turkistan	4500 BC (Egyptian tomb)
Marrow	*Cucurbita pepo*	America?	16th–17th century (Mexican sites 7000–5500 BC)
Musk Melon	*Cucumis melo*	Iran	2900 BC (Egypt)
Onion	*Allium cepa*	Middle Asia	*c.* 3000 BC (Egypt)
Parsnip	*Pastinaca sativa*	Caucasus	1st century BC
Pepper	*Capsicum frutescens*	Peru	Early burial sites, Peru; intro: Europe 1493
Potato	*Solanum tuberosum*	Southern Chile	*c.* 1530 Intro: Ireland 1565
Pumpkin	*Cucurbita maxima*	Northern Andean Argentina	1591
Radish	*Raphanus sativus*	Western Asia, Egypt	*c.* 3000 BC
Runner Bean	*Phaseolus vulgaris*	Central America	*c.* 1500 (known from Mexican sites 7000–5000 BC)
Soybean	*Soja max*	China	*c.* 2850 BC
Spinach	*Spinacia oleracea*	Iran	AD 647 in Nepal
Swede	*Brassica napobrassica*	Europe	1620
Sweet Corn	*Zea mays*	Andes	Cult. early times in America: intro: Europe after 1492
Tomato	*Lycopersicon esculentum*	Bolivia-Ecuador-Peru area	Italy *c.* 1550
Turnip	*Brassica rapa*	Greece	2000 BC

The Animal World

Glossary

abdomen The rear section of an arthropod, often divided into segments. Alternatively, in vertebrates, the body cavity in which are found the principal digestive organs.

abomasum The fourth chamber of a ruminant's stomach.

accommodation The adjustments to the eye by which an object is brought into focus.

acetyl choline A neurotransmitter chemical found in the nervous systems of both vertebrates and invertebrates.

acoelomate Animals lacking any form of coelom.

adipose tissue Fatty tissue occurring under the skin in mammals.

adrenaline Hormone secreted in many groups of higher animals. It prepares the body for 'fight and flight'. It is also found in the nervous system acting as a neurotransmitter.

afferent A nerve that passes information back to the central nervous system, i.e. a sensory nerve.

aggression Animal behaviour designed to frighten off another animal, usually of the same species, from a designated territory.

agonistic Behaviour associated with aggression, but actually involving little violence.

air sac Extension of a bird's respiratory system into other parts of the body. Expansion and contraction of these sacs with movement of the body speed up the movement of air in and out of the bird's lungs. The air sacs also cut down the bird's weight.

albinism Absence of pigments in the hair, skin and eyes.

alimentary canal The tube down which food passes, and in which it is broken down and digested.

alveolus An air sac at the end of a bronchiole in the lungs of reptiles and mammals. It is in the alveoli that gas exchange occurs between the air and the blood.

amino acid The constituent molecular 'building brick' of proteins.

amnion Membrane containing the embryo and the fluid in which it is bathed.

amphibia Animals that can live both in water and on land. They represent the first group of animals to develop two pairs of pentadactyl limbs.

antenna Jointed appendage found on the heads of many arthropods. It is usually sensory.

anticoagulent A chemical that prevents blood from clotting.

anus The final opening of the alimentary tract.

aorta Large blood vessel that carries blood from the heart to the body. It is found in the higher four-limbed animals.

arteriole Small artery linking an artery to the capillaries.

artery Blood vessel taking blood away from the heart.

articulation Movement of one part of a skeleton over another, often at a joint.

asexual reproduction Occurs only in the lower animals, e.g. the protozoa. It is a form of reproduction by budding.

assimilation Incorporation of the simple mole-cules resulting from digestion into more complex molecules.

atlas vertebra First vertebra, allowing free movement of the head.

autonomic nervous system Vertebrate nervous system concerned with controlling bodily functions. It consists of the sympathetic and parasympathetic nervous system.

axis vertebra The second vertebra. Its articulation with the atlas vertebra allows rotational movement of the head.

barb A hair-like structure attached to the shaft of a feather.

barbule One of the 'teeth' on the barb of a feather. The barbules interlock, linking the barbs together.

bilateral symmetry Arrangement of the body and organs of an animal in only one plane of symmetry.

bile Secretion of the liver in vertebrates. It is formed from the breakdown of blood cells, and helps in digestion of fats.

bivalves A group of molluscs in which the body is enclosed within a shell consisting of two hinged halves, or valves.

bladder A fluid- or gas-filled sac, often taken to mean the muscular sac into which urine drains from the kidneys.

blastula Early stage in the development of an animal embryo after fertilization.

blood Fluid that occupies the vascular system. It carries respiratory gases, digestive and excretory products and other biochemicals.

blubber Thick layer of subcutaneous fat found

in many marine mammals.

bone A form of tissue, rich in calcium, that forms the endoskeleton of the higher vertebrates.

brain The forward section of the nervous system. In invertebrates it consists of ganglia; in vertebrates it consists of an enlarged part of the neural tube.

bronchiole Tube leading to the alveoli in the lungs.

bronchus One of two tubes, each tube leading to one of the lungs in vertebrates.

buccal cavity The mouth cavity.

caecum An outgrowth of the alimentary canal.

canine tooth Pointed tooth found in mammals. It is used for gripping and tearing, and is prominant in carnivores.

capillary Fine blood vessels forming a network in vertebrate tissues. They carry respiratory gases, nutrients and waste products to and from the tissues.

carapace Shell of some crustaceans, e.g. crabs, and reptiles, e.g. tortoise.

carnassial teeth Modified molar and premolar teeth in many carnivores. They have sharp cutting edges for dealing with meat, bones, ligaments, etc.

carnivore Meat-eating animal.

carpals Bones found in the pentadactyl limb of the higher vertebrates.

cartilage Tough slippery flexible tissue, found in all vertebrates. It has skeletal functions; indeed, some of the lower vertebrates have skeletons consisting entirely of cartilage.

central nervous system That part of the nervous system which coordinates the activities of the other parts of the nervous system. It ranges in complexity from a simple series of paired ganglia to the brain and spinal cord of vertebrates.

chaeta A stiff bristle found on the body segments of worms.

chela Pincers found in arthropods.

chitin The polymeric chemical that comprises the exoskeleton of arthropods.

chordates Animals which have a notochord, either in the embryo or adult form.

chromatophore Cell containing pigment that is involved in colour changes.

chrysalis Pupal form of butterflies and moths.

cilium (plural cilia) A very fine hair, capable of independent movement. Unlike flagella, cilia are usually found in groups. They can only beat in one direction, and usually move in synchrony.

clitellum The 'saddle' of earthworms, involved in copulation.

cloaca Chamber into which the alimentary canal, the kidneys and the reproductive organs open.

coccyx Fused group of vertebrae at the base of the spine in tailless primates.

cocoon Protective covering around the eggs or larvae of many invertebrates.

coelenteron Body cavity in lower animals that functions as a digestive cavity. There is one opening, and the cavity itself is lined with two layers of cells.

coelom Body cavity in higher animals.

compound eye Simple eye found in crustaceans and insects. It is formed from hundreds of single light receptors, which build up a compound image.

cone Light-sensitive cell in the eyes of vertebrates. It detects colour and detail.

cranium The skull of vertebrates.

crop A section of the alimentary canal capable of being distended in order to store food.

deciduous teeth First set of teeth in mammals. These are shed to make way for the adult teeth.

demersal Inhabiting the sea or lake floor.

dental formula Expression of the arrangement of teeth in mammals. It indicates the number of incisors, canines, premolars and molars in one side of the upper and lower jaw.

dentine The main bulk of a tooth. It is served by blood vessels and covered with enamel.

diaphragm Dome of muscle separating the thoracic and abdominal cavities in mammals.

diastole The phase of the heart beat in which all the heart muscle is relaxed.

digestion Breakdown of foodstuffs into simple molecules that can be absorbed and used by the organism.

digit A finger or toe of the vertebrate pentadactyl limb.

dorsal The surface of an animal nearest to the notochord or spinal cord.

ear Vertebrate organ, primarily of balance but subsequently adapted as an organ of hearing.

ecdysis Moulting. The shedding of the exoskeleton in arthropods to allow for growth, or the shedding of the outer layer of skin in reptiles.

efferent Nerve that passes information from the central nervous system out to the tissues and organs of the body.

egg A structure containing the ovum and in which the embryo develops. It contains yolk, which nourishes the embryo during its development, and a number of membranes enclosing the contents, including an outer protective membrane, sometimes calcareous.

embryo Structure that develops from the zygote prior to birth or hatching.

enamel Hard white material that encases the exposed surface of a mammalian tooth.

endocrine gland Type of gland found in vertebrates and some invertebrates, in which the secretion passes into the blood stream and passes in this way to the organ or organs on which it acts.

endoskeleton A rigid and often articulated structure that lies within the body tissues. It provides support and shape, and often sites of attachment for muscles.

epiglottis Found in mammals, it is a cartilaginous flap that closes off the windpipe during the swallowing reflex.

excretion The elimination of waste chemicals from the body. This is *not* the same as defaecation.

exocrine gland A gland, found in vertebrates, in which the secretion is carried down a duct to the site of activity.

exoskeleton A rigid articulated structure that lies outside the body tissues. It provides protection, support and often sites of attachment for muscles.

faeces Remains of undigested food, bile, dead cells and bacteria, expelled through the anus.

fat body In amphibians the fat body consists solely of fat, and provides them with food reserves during hibernation. In insects it consists of fat, protein and other reserves, and provides nourishment during metamorphosis as well as during hibernation.

feather Birds have three types of feathers. Contour feathers have barbs and barbules that lock together; they are the feathers on the wings and tail associated with flight. Down feathers and filoplumes are fluffy feathers more important for heat retention.

fibrin A protein that forms a fibrous matrix as the basis of a blood clot.

filoplume Hairlike feathers scattered over the surface of a bird. They are important in heat retention.

fin The lateral fins of fishes are based on the pentadactyl limb, the two pectoral fins corresponding to fore limbs, the pelvic fins to the hind limbs. These, and the median and anal fin, are used for steering and balance. The caudal fin on the tail is used for propulsion.

flagellum A hairlike filament found on a cell surface. Its movement causes the cell, or the fluid around it, to move.

follicle A small sac or cavity.

gall bladder Storage organ for bile produced in the liver.

ganglion Mass of nervous tissue, rich in nerve cell bodies. In invertebrates, ganglia form the central nervous system.

gestation Time between conception, i.e. fertilization, and birth.

gill Respiratory organ in marine and freshwater animals. Each gill has a rich blood supply, promoting gas exchange between the blood and the surrounding water.

gizzard Part of the alimentary canal designed to break up hard foods.

gland Organ that secretes a specific chemical or group of chemicals, either into the bloodstream or into a specific site of activity.

glottis Opening of the larynx into the pharynx.

glycogen Storage compound in animals. It is a polymer of glucose.

gonad Organ which produces ova or sperm.

grey matter Region of the vertebrate brain that contains nerve cell bodies and synapses.

gut The alimentary canal.

haem The basis of many respiratory pigments, e.g. haemoglobin, as it can combine reversibly with oxygen.

haemocoel Body cavity containing the blood in arthropods and crustaceans.

hair Cornified threads produced by follicles in the skin of mammals. The colour is due to melanin pigment. The function of hair is largely heat retention.

hallux The often-vestigial digit on the inside of the rear limbs of the higher terrestrial vertebrates.

haltere A modified wing of flies that provides information on stability in flight.

heart Organ found in all vertebrates and many invertebrates that drives blood around the body unidirectionally.

herbivore Plant-eating animal.

heterocercal Fish in which the vertebral column extends into the tail fin. It is upturned, giving the fin a larger dorsal lobe than ventral lobe.

hibernation Period of time during winter when an animal becomes inactive and the basal metabolic rate drops, thus conserving energy.

hominid A primate in the family *Hominidae*, including early and modern man.

homiothermy Maintenance of the body temperature at a relatively constant temperature. Often referred to as being warm-blooded.

homocercal Fish in which the tail fin does not contain the vertebral column, but is supported merely with fin rays.

hormone Chemical secreted by endocrine glands. It is secreted into the bloodstream, which carries it to the organ it acts on, on which it usually has a specific and often regulatory effect.

ileum Section of the small intestine in mammals, immediately before the colon.

imago Sexually mature adult form of an insect.

implantation Attachment of a vertebrate fertilized ovum to the wall of the uterus.

impulse Passage of an electric current along a nerve fibre.

incisor Front teeth in mammals. They are sharp and are used for biting and gnawing off food.

instar The form adopted by an insect between moults.

insulin Important animal hormone responsible for the control of glucose levels in the blood.

intestine That part of alimentary canal in which food is digested and absorbed.

invertebrate Lacking a backbone or spinal column or notochord.

iris A ring of pigmented tissue which lies over the lens of the eye in invertebrates and cephalopods.

joint Point of contact between two body elements in invertebrates or between two bony or cartilaginous elements in vertebrates.

keel Large blade or projection from the sternum of bats and birds. It provides a large surface area for the attachment of the flight muscles.

keratin The structural protein found in horn, claws, beaks, nails, hair, etc., and in the outer cells of the epidermis of vertebrates.

kidney One of two excretory organs found in vertebrates.

labrum The upper 'lip' in insects that helps in feeding.

lactation Milk production. One of the chief characteristics of mammals.

lacteal Lymph vessels in vertebrates, involved in the absorption of digested fats in the intestine.

larva Form many animals take between hatching from the egg and metamorphosing into the adult, e.g. caterpillars, tadpole.

larynx Area of the throat that controls the

swallowing reflex and that contains the vocal chords.

lateral line System of receptors for the detection of vibration (sound) and movement, arranged in a line down each side of fish and some amphibians.

lens Transparent body in the eye designed to focus light on to the retina in vertebrates.

ligament Band of fibre holding two bones together at a vertebrate joint.

liver Largest internal organ found in vertebrates. It is responsible for the major metabolic functions.

lung Respiratory organ found in vertebrates.

lung book Respiratory organ found in some insects.

lymphatic system System of tubes containing lymph, found in vertebrates. It collects tissue fluid and returns it to the blood system, transports digested fats, and is involved in the immune system. Flow in the lymphatic system is effected by lymph hearts in some vertebrates, and by muscular and respiratory movements in mammals.

mammals Group of vertebrates characterized by being homiothermic, having hair on the skin, giving birth to well-developed young which have been nourished within the womb by a placenta and which are subsequently suckled at the mammary glands.

mammary gland Milk-producing gland found in all female mammals.

mandible Lower jaw in invertebrates.

mantle Folds of skin in molluscs which secretes the shell, if present, and protects the gills.

marsupium Pouch found on female marsupials. The mammary glands are found within the pouch, and the young finish their development there after birth.

maxilla Either a feeding appendage found in arthropods, or the upper jawbone of vertebrates.

meatus Passage leading from the outer ear to the eardrum.

median eye A third eye in the top of the head found in many invertebrates. It is formed from an outgrowth of the brain, and is represented vestigially in vertebrates by the pineal body.

medulla Central part of an organ.

medusa A jelly-fish. It is a motile form of a group of coelenterates.

melanin Pigment found in skin, hair, etc.

meninges Membranes surrounding the central nervous system of vertebrates and the spaces within it.

metacarpals Bones found in the pentadactyl limb of the higher vertebrates.

metameric segmentation Division of the body into a number of similar segments along its length.

metamorphosis Change from the larval to the adult stage. A process found in insects and amphibians.

metatarsals Bones found in the vertebrate pentadactyl limb. They are greatly elongated in running animals.

migration Movement of whole populations of animal species between two regions, often at roughly the same time each year.

mimicry Ability of one animal to resemble another, usually for the protection of the first animal.

mitral valve Heart valve of the higher vertebrates.

molar A chewing tooth occurring at the rear of the jaw in animals.

mucous membrane Surface membrane that secretes mucus.

mucus Slimy substance that does not dissolve in water.

muscle Contractile tissue that produces movement in invertebrates and vertebrates.

myelin sheath Membranous sheath around nerve fibres.

nasal cavity Cavity in the head of vertebrates containing the organs of smell.

nephridium Excretory organ in invertebrates.

nerve fibre The long thin unbranched section of a nerve cell that transmits the nerve messages over long distances within the body.

nerve net Simple form of nervous system found in the invertebrates.

neurone The chief nerve cell in the nervous system. It consists of a cell body, a number of finger-like dendrites which link up with other nerve cells, and one or more nerve fibres or axons which transport impulses over relatively long distances.

nidiculous Birds that hatch in an undeveloped state and need a lot of care.

nidifugous Birds that hatch in a well-developed state and are soon able to fend for themselves.

notochord A form of primitive cartilaginous spinal column. It is found in adult forms of the lower vertebrates, and in embryonic forms of the higher vertebrates.

nymph Immature form of some insects, in which the wings and reproductive organs are not fully developed.

ocellus A simple form of eye, consisting of a collection of light-sensitive cells, found in some invertebrates, especially insects. It is not capable of forming an image.

oesophagus The gullet. The tube by which food passes from the mouth to the digestive tract.

oestrous cycle The reproductive cycle of female mammals.

oestrus Period of the oestrous cycle when the female mammal is 'on heat', i.e. copulation can occur.

olfactory organs Organs of smell.

omasum Third chamber of a ruminant's stomach.

ommatidium A single unit in the compound eye of arthropods.

omnivore Plant- and animal-eating animal.

operculum Muscular flap covering the gills in bony fish.

optic chiasma Point at which the optic nerves cross over between the vertebrate eyes and brain. It is important in binocular vision.

optic nerve The nerve connecting the vertebrate eye with the brain.

orbit Socket of the vertebrate skull in which the eye lies.

ossification Process by which bone is formed from cartilaginous or other tissue.

ovary Reproductive organ of female animals, producing ova and female sex hormones.

oviparous Fertilized ova are laid as eggs and the embryo develops within the egg.

ovoviviparous The fertilized ova develop within the female's body but do not make contact with the body and do not receive nourishment from it.

ovulation Release of an ovum from the ovary.

ovum (plural ova) Unfertilized non-motile female gamete.

pacemaker Group of cells that provide a rhythmic series of electrical impulses that drives an organ. Most commonly applied to the cells in the vertebrate heart that are responsible for providing the electrical impulses for the heartbeat.

palate The roof of the mouth in vertebrates.

palp A head or mouth appendage found in many invertebrates.

parasympathetic nervous system Part of the autonomic nervous system in vertebrates.

parturition The passage of the foetus out of the female's body at the end of pregnancy in mammals.

pecking order Social hierarchy found in many animals that live in groups.

pectoral fins Forward pair of lateral fins found in fishes.

pectoral girdle Ring of bones in vertebrates to which the fore limbs articulate.

pelagic Inhabiting the open waters of the sea or a lake.

pelvic fins Rear pair of lateral fins in fishes.

pelvic girdle Ring of bones in vertebrates to which the hind limbs articulate.

pentadactyl limb The characteristic limb of the vertebrates, with five digits or 'fingers'.

peripheral nervous system Those parts of the nervous system not included in the central nervous system.

peristalsis Waves of contraction that pass down

tubular organs, particularly the digestive tract.

phalange One of the types of bones of the pentadactyl limb.

pheromone Chemical produced by one animal, designed to elicit a response in another animal of the same species.

pineal body Downgrowth of the vertebrate brain with endocrine functions. In some lower vertebrates it functions as the median eye.

pinna Outermost part of the outer ear in some mammals.

pituitary gland The major endocrine gland in vertebrates, occurring as downgrowth of the brain. It produces a wide range of hormones, many of them controlling other endocrine glands.

placenta The series of membranes within the uterus of viviparous animals that nourishes the developing foetus. It allows a close association of the foetal and maternal blood systems.

pleural membranes Membranes enclosing the mammalian lungs.

plexus A network of nerve cells.

poikilothermy Inability to regulate the body temperature, which therefore assumes that of the surroundings.

pollex The inner digit on the forelimbs of the higher vertebrates. It is often vestigial, or may be adapted for a variety of purposes.

polyp Non-motile form of those coelenterates that have the medusoid motile form.

premolar Grinding and chewing teeth occurring between the canines and molars in the jaws of mammals.

pupa A non-feeding form in which metamorphosis from a larva to an adult occurs in insects.

pupil Opening in the iris of the eye of vertebrates and some invertebrates, through which light enters the eye.

rachis The shaft of a feather.

radial symmetry Form of symmetry found in sedentary animals, e.g. the coelenterates, in which the body is symmetrical about a number of planes passing through a central axis.

radula A strip on the tongue of molluscs that carries teeth to rasp food off rocks, etc. As the teeth are worn away they are replaced.

reflex Automatic response to a stimulus.

regeneration Regrowth or replacement of tissues and body parts lost due to injury. Extensive regeneration is possible in many invertebrates, but regeneration is much more limited in the vertebrates.

retina Layer of sensory cells in the eyes of vertebrates and some molluscs.

rod Light-sensitive cell in the retina of vertebrate eyes.

rumen The first chamber in the stomach of ruminants.

ruminants Group of higher mammals, including cattle and sheep, in which the digestive system allows food to be swallowed and then digested later.

saliva Secretion of mucus and enzymes which moistens the food and starts off the process of digestion.

scolex The head of a tapeworm, which anchors it to the intestinal wall of the host.

sebum A greasy material produced by the sebaceous glands in the skin of mammals. It greases the hair and protects the skin.

sessile Animals attached to a fixed surface or to another animal.

sibling One of a number of offspring of the same two parents.

sinus A cavity or recess.

smooth muscle Vertebrate muscle tissue, under involuntary control, usually found around hollow organs. It can produce long-term contractions.

sperm Motile male gamete formed in the testes of male animals.

sphincter Ring of muscle around the opening to a hollow organ.

spinal cord That part of the central nervous system in vertebrates enclosed within the spinal column.

spinneret The openings on the abdomen of a spider out of which silk is produced to make webs, tie up prey, spin cocoons, etc.

spiracle Gill slit in fish, or opening of the tracheae in insects.
striated muscle Vertebrate muscle with a striped appearance. It is under voluntary control, important in locomotion. It produces rapid powerful contractions.
stridulation The production of sound by insects, usually by rubbing body parts together.
succus entericus Digestive secretions of the walls of the small intestine in vertebrates.
swim bladder An air bladder found in many fish. It is used in maintaining depth when swimming.
sympathetic nervous system Part of the vertebrate autonomic nervous system.
synapse Point of contact between nerve cells at which the nerve impulse passes from one cell to another.
systole The phase of the heart beat in which the heart muscle is contracted.

tarsals Bones in the rear pentadactyl limbs of vertebrates.
telson The tail appendage found in some arthropods.
tendon Fibrous band connecting a muscle to a bone.
testis Male reproductive organ that produces sperms and male sex hormones.
tetrapod Vertebrate having four limbs.
thorax The middle section of arthropods, particularly of insects. In vertebrates the thorax is the body cavity containing the heart and lungs.
tone State of partial contraction of a muscle which maintains body posture.
trachea In arthropods the tracheae are tubes that take air to the tissues. In vertebrates the trachea is the windpipe, taking air from the larynx to the lungs.

umbilical cord The connection between the embryo and the placenta in pregnant mammals.
ungulate Group of mammals that graze, that have hooves and that walk on the tips of elongated and adapted pentadactyl limbs.
urea Waste product of mammals and many other animals.
uric acid Waste product of birds and some other animals.
urine Liquid produced in the kidney, containing waste products such as urea or uric acid.
uterus The womb in mammals.

vascular system Fluid-filled spaces in the body, e.g. the blood vascular system.
vasoconstriction Constriction of a blood vessel.
vasodilatation Increase in the diameter of a blood vessel.
vein Blood vessel that carries blood from the tissues to the heart.
venation Arrangement of veins in an insect's wing.
ventral Surface of an animal furthest away from the notochord or spinal column.
venule Small blood vessel linking a vein to the capillary network.
vertebra Separate bone of the vertebral column.
vertebral column Bones or cartilage in close apposition, running in a line from the skull to the tail of vertebrates and enclosing the spinal cord.
vertebrate Having a backbone or vertebral column or notochord.
villus A projection from a body surface. It is usually designed to increase the surface area of a tissue.
viviparous Embryos develop within and are nourished by the mother.
vocal cords Elastic fibres in the larynx that produce sounds in vertebrates.

white matter Region of the vertebrate central nervous system consisting of nerve cell fibres.

yolk Nutrient store in eggs.

The Animal Kingdom

The Animal Kingdom Metazoa (greek, *meta* = later in time, *zoon* = an animal) is composed of multicellular animals that may lose their boundaries in the adult state, and with at least two layers of cells. The Kingdom contains 21 Phyla, with over a million species identified and described. Animals inhabit most of the planet's seas and land surfaces. As far as its classification is concerned, an animal's full modern hierarchy can extend to 20 strata:

Kingdom	*Order*
Sub-kingdom	Sub-order
Phylum	Super-family
Sub-phylum	*Family*
Super-class	Sub-family
Class	Tribe
Sub-class	Genus
Infra-class	*Species*
Cohort	Sub-species
Super-order	

Animal dimensions by species

Mollusca – 128 000 species: ranging in size between the minute coin shell *Neolepton sykesi* 1,2 mm *0·047 in* long, and a giant octopus weighing 6–7 tons, which is the heaviest of all invertebrates.
Insecta – 950 000 (1974) described species of a suspected total of perhaps some 3 million: ranging in size between the Battledore wing fairy fly (*Hymenoptera mymaridae*) 0,2 mm *0·008 in* long to the bulky 100 g *3·5 oz* African goliath beetle (*Goliathus goliathus*).
Crustacea – 25 000 species: ranging in size from the water flea *Alonella* species at 0,25 mm *0·01 in* long to the Giant Japanese Spider crab (*Macrocheira kaempferi*) with a spread of 3,66 m *12 ft* between claws.
Pisces – 30 000 species: ranging in size between the 12–16 mm *0·47–0·63 in* long *Schindleria praematurus* at 2 mg or 17·750 to the oz and the 43 tonne 18,5 m *60 ft* long Whale shark (*Rhiniodon typus*).
Amphibia – 3000 species: ranging in size between minute poisonous frogs 12,5 mm *0·05 in* long and the 1,5 m *5 ft* long giant salamander (*Andrias davidianus*) weighing up to 45 kg *100 lb*.
Reptilia – 6000 species: ranging in size between 38 mm *1·5 in* long geckoes and the South American snake anaconda (*Eunectes murinus*), which has been reported to attain 13,7 m *45 ft* in length.
Aves – *c.* 8950 species: ranging in size from the 1,6 g *0·06 oz* Bee humming bird (*Calypte helenae*) up to the 156,5 kg *345 lb*, 2,7 m *9 ft* tall ostrich (*Struthio camelus*).
Mammalia – *c.* 4500 species: ranging in size, on land, between the 2 g *0·07 oz* Kitt's hog-nosed bat (*Craseonycteris thonglongyai*) and the African elephant (*Loxodonta africana africana*) which may very rarely attain 12 tons; and, at sea, between the 35 kg *77 lb* Commerson's dolphin (*Cephalorhynchus commersoni*) and the 190 tonne *187 ton* Blue Whale (*Balaenoptera musculus*).

Animal longevity

Age determination based on ring-producing structures (e.g. teeth) or length of time animal kept in captivity.

Maximum life span (years)		*Species*
152+	(a)	Marion's tortoise (*Testudo sumeirii*)
c. 150		Quahog (*Venus mercenaria*)
120+		Man (*Homo sapiens*) – highest proven age
116+		Spur-thighed tortoise (*Testudo graeca*)
c. 100		Deep sea clam (*Tindaria callistiformis*)
>90		Killer whale (*Orcinus orca*)
80–90		Sea anemone (*Cereus pedunculatus*)
88		European eel (*Anguilla anguilla*)
82	(b)	Lake sturgeon (*Acipenser fulvescens*)
70–80		Freshwater mussel (*Margaritana margaritifera*)
78		Asiatic elephant (*Elephans maximus*)
77		Tuatara (*Sphenodon punctatus*)
72+	(a)	Andean condor (*Vultur gryphus*)
c. 70		African elephant (*Loxodonta africana*)
69¾		Sterlet (*Acipenser ruthenus*)
68+		Great eagle-owl (*Bubo bubo*)
66		American alligator (*Alligator mississipiensis*)
64		Blue macaw (*Ara macao*)
62+		Siberian white crane (*Grus leucogeranus*)
62		Horse (*Equus caballus*)
62		Ostrich (*Struthio camelus*)
60+		European catfish (*Silurus glanis*)
58¾		Alligator snapping turtle (*Macrochelys temminckii*)
58+	(d)	Royal albatross (*Diomedea immutabilis*)
57+		Orang-utan (*Pongo pygmaeus*)
56	(c)	Sulphur-crested cockatoo (*Cacatua galerita*)
55½		Chimpanzee (*Pan troglodytes*)
55		Pike (*Esox lucius*)
54⅓		Hippopotamus (*Hippopotamus amphibius*)
54+		Slow-worm (*Anguis fragilis*)
53½		Gorilla (*Gorilla gorilla*)
53⅓		Stinkpot (*Sternotherus odoratus*)
51+		Japanese giant salamander (*Andrias japonicus*)
51		White pelican (*Pelecanus onocrotalus*)
50+		Green turtle (*Chelonia mydas*)
>50		Koi carp (*Cyprinus carpio*)
c. 50		North American lobster (*Homarus americanus*)
49¾		Domestic goose (*Anser a. domesticus*)
49+		Short-nosed echidna (*Tachyglossus aculeatus*)
49	(e)	Grey parrot (*Psittacus erythacus*)
49		Indian rhinoceros (*Rhinoceros unicornis*)
47		European brown bear (*Ursus a. arctos*)
46+		White-throated capuchin (*Cebus capucinus*)
46+		Grey seal (*Halichoerus gypus*)
c. 46		Mandrill (*Mandrillus sphinx*)
c. 45		Blue whale (*Balaenoptera musculus*)
44		Herring gull (*Larus argentatus*)
42+	(d)	Emu (*Dromaius novaehollandiae*)
42		Metallic wood borer (*Buprestis aurulenta*)
41		Goldfish (*Carassius auratus*)
40¼		Common boa (*Boa constrictor*)
>40		Common toad (*Bufo bufo*)
36¼		Cape giraffe (*Giraffa camelopardalis*)
35+		Bactrian camel (*Camelus ferus*)
34+		Hoffman's two-toed sloth (*Choloepus hoffmanni*)
34		Domestic cat (*Felis catus*)
34		Canary (*Severius canaria*)
33		American bison (*Bison bison*)
32⅓		Bobcat (*Lynx rufus*)
32+		Australian school shark (*Galeorhinus australis*)
31+		Indian flying fox (*Pteropus giganteus*)
30+	(d)	American manatee (*Trichechus manatus*)
c. 30		Red kangaroo (*Macropus rufus*)
29½		African buffalo (*Syncerus caffer*)
29½		Domestic dog (*Canis familiaris*)
29+		Budgerigar (*Melopsittacus undulatus*)
29+		Neptune crab (*Neptunus pelagines*)
c. 29		Lion (*Panthera leo*)
28		African civet (*Viverra civetta*)
c. 28		Theraphosid spider (*Mygalomorphae*)
27¼		Sumatran crested porcupine (*Hystrix brachyura*)
27		Medicinal leech (*Hirudo medicinalis*)
27		Domestic pig (*Sus scrofa*)
26¾		Red deer (*Cervus elephus*)
26¼		Tiger (*Panthera tigris*)
26+	(d)	Giant panda (*Ailuropoda melanoleuca*)
26		Common wombat (*Vombatus ursinus*)
24¾		Vicuna (*Vicugna vicugna*)
23½		Grey squirrel (*Sciurus carolinensis*)
21+		Coyote (*Canis latrans*)
21		Canadian otter (*Lutra canadensis*)
20¾		Domestic goat (*Capra hircus domesticus*)
20¼		Blue sheep (*Pseudois nayaur*)
20+		Feather-star (*Promachocrinus kerguelensis*)
18+		Queen ant (*Myrmecina graminicola*)
18+		Common rabbit (*Oryctolagus cuniculus*)
16+		Hedgehog (*Echinops telfairi*)
15		Land snail (*Helix spiriplana*)
c. 15		Brittlestar (*Amphiura chiajei*)
14⅞		Guinea pig (*Cavia porcellus*)
13½		Indian pangolin (*Manis crassicaudata*)
12		Capybara (*Hydrochoerus hydrochoaeris*)
11½		Philippine tree shrew (*Urogale everetti*)
>10		Giant centipede (*Scolopendra gigantea*)
10		Golden hamster (*Mesocricetus auratus*)
9+		Purse-web spider (*Atypus affinis*)
8⅔		Fat dormouse (*Glis glis*)
8+		Greater Egyptian gerbil (*Gerbillus pyramidum*)
7+		Spiny starfish (*Marthasterias glacialis*)
7		Millipede (*Cylindroiulus londinensis*)
6		House mouse (*Mus musculus*)
5+		Segmented worm (*Allolobophora longa*)
4½		Moonrat (*Echinosorex gymnurus*)
3¾		Siberian flying squirrel (*Pteromys volans*)
2		Pygmy white-toothed shrew (*Suncus etruscus*)
1⅛		Monarch butterfly (*Danaus plexippus*)
0·5		Bedbug (*Cimex lectularius*)
0·27	(f)	Black widow spider (*Latrodectus mactans*)
0·04	(f)	Common housefly (*Musca domestica*)

(a) *Fully mature at time of capture*
(b) *Still actively growing when caught*
(c) *Unconfirmed claims up to 120 years*
(d) *Still alive*
(e) *Another less well substantiated record of 72 years*
(f) *Males*

Velocity of animal movement

The data on this topic are notoriously unreliable because of the many inherent difficulties of timing the movement of most animals – whether running, flying, or swimming – and because of the absence of any standardisation of the method of timing, of the distance over which the performance is measured, or of allowance for wind conditions.

The most that can be said is that a specimen of the species below has been timed to have attained as a maximum the speed given.

mph	*km/h*		*Species*
225	*362*	(a)	Peregrine falcon (*Falco peregrinus*)
150+	*240+*	(b)	Golden eagle (*Aquila chrysaetos*)
106·25	*171*		White-throated spinetail swift (*Hirundapus caudacutus*)
c. 100	*c. 160*		Alpine swift (*Apus melba*)
95·7	*154*		Magnificent frigatebird (*Fregata magnificens*)
88	*142*		Spur-winged goose (*Plectropterus gambensis*)
80	*129*		Red-breasted merganser (*Mergus serrator*)
77	*124*		White-rumped swift (*Apus caffer*)
72	*116*		Canvasback duck (*Aythya valisineria*)
70	*113*		Common eider (*Somateria mollissima*)
60–70	*96,5–113*	(c)	Racing pigeon (*Columba livia*)
68	*109*		Sailfish (*Istiophorus platypterus*)
65	*105*		Mallard (*Anas platyrhynchos*)
60+	*96,5+*		Cheetah (*Acinonyx jubatus*)
60	*96,5*		Golden plover (*Pluvialis apricaria*)
57	*92*		Common quail (*Coturnix coturnix*)
57	*92*		Common swift (*Apus apus*)
56	*90*		Red grouse (*Lagopus lagopus*)
55+	*88,5+*		Pronghorn antelope (*Antilocapra americana*)
55	*88,5*		Green violetear (*Colibri thalassinus*)
55	*88,5*		Whooper swan (*Cygnus cygnus*)
53	*85*		Grey partridge (*Perdix perdix*)
50+	*80+*		Blackbuck (*Antilope cervicapra*)
50+	*80+*		Mongolian gazelle (*Procapra gutturosa*)

mph	km/h		Species
50	80		House martin (*Delichon urbica*)
50	80		Marlin (*Istophoridae*)
50	80		Springbok (*Antidorcas marsupialis*)
49	79		Royal albatross (*Diomedea epomophora*)
48·15	77,48		Wahoo (*Acanthocybium solandri*)
47·2	75,9		Long-tailed sylph (*Aglaiocercus kingi*)
47	75,5		Grant's gazelle (*Gazella granti*)
46·61	75		Yellowfin tuna (*Thunnus albacares*)
45	72		Ostrich (*Struthio camelus*)
45	72		Brown hare (*Lepus europaeus*)
43·4	69,8	(d)	Bluefin tuna (*Thunnus thynnus*)
43·26	69,62	(e)	Race horse (*Equus caballus*) (mounted)
42	67,5		Red deer (*Cervus elephus*)
41·72	67,14	(f)	Greyhound (*Canis familiaris*)
40+	64+		Red fox (*Vulpes vulpes*)
40	64		Bonefish (*Albula vulpes*)
40	64	(g)	Eastern grey kangaroo (*Macropus giganteus*)
40	64		Emu (*Dromaius novahollandiae*)
40	64		Mountain zebra (*Equus zebra*)
c.40	c.64		Swordfish (*Xiphias gladius*)
35–40	56–64		American free-tailed bat (*Tadarida brasiliensis*)
38	61		Barn swallow (*Hirundo rustica*)
37	59,5		Blue wildebeeste (*Connochaetes taurinus*)
36	58		Dragonfly (*Austrophlebia costalis*)
35·5	57		Whippet (*Canis familiaris*)
35	56		Coyote (*Canis latrans*)
30–35	48–56		Deer bot-fly (*Cephenemyia pratti*)
34·5	55,5		Killer whale (*Orcinus orca*)
33·5	53,9		Hawk-moth (*Sphingidae*)
32	51,5		Giraffe (*Giraffa camelopardalis*)
31·25	50,2		Horse-fly (*Tabanus bovinus*)
31	49,8		Mako shark (*Isurus oxyrinchus*)
30+	48+		Butterfly (*Prepona*)
28·75	46		Minke whale (*Balaenoptera acutorostrata*)
28	45		Black rhinoceros (*Diceros bicornis*)
27·89	44,88	(h)	Man (*Homo sapiens*)
27·6	44,4		Common dolphin (*Delphinus delphis*)
25·3	40,7		Short-finned pilot whale (*Globicephala macrorhynchus*)
25	40		Californian sea-lion (*Zalophus californianus*)
24·5	39		African elephant (*Loxodonta africana*)
23	37		Salmon (*Salmo salar*)
22·8	36,5		Blue whale (*Balaenoptera musculus*)
21	34		Mountain goat (*Oremnos americanus*)
20	32		Arabian camel (*Camelus dromedarius*)
c.18	c.29		Pacific leatherback turtle (*Dermochelys coriacea schlegeli*)
18	29		Six-lined race-runner (*Cnemidophorus sexlineatus*)
c.17	c.27		Gentoo penguin (*Pygosterlis papua*)
13·39	21,5		Hornet (*Vespa crabro*)
11·8	18,9		Crabeater seal (*Lobodon carcinophagus*) (land)
10–11	16–17,5		Black mamba (*Dendroaspis polylepsis*)
10	16		N American porcupine (*Erithizon dorsatum*)
7·26	11,5		Honey-bee (*Apis mellifera*)
6	9,5		House rat (*Ratus rattus*)
5·12	8,23		Common house-fly (*Musca domestica*)
4·5	7,24		Common flea (*Pulex irritans*) (jumping)
2·5	4,02		Common shrew (*Sorex araneus*)
2·24	3,6		Yellow-bellied sea snake (*Pelamis platurus*) (swimming)
1·17	1,88		House spider (*Tegenaria atrica*)
1·12	1,80		Centipede (*Scutiger coleoptrata*)
1·07	1,72		Millipede (*Diopsiulus regressus*) (jumping)
0·23	0,37		Giant tortoise (*Geochelone gigantea*)
0·224	0,36		Rosy boa (*Lichanura roseofusca*)
0·068– 0·098	0,109– 0,151	(i)	Three-toed sloth (*Bradypus tridactylus*)
0·031	0,049		Common garden snail (*Helix aspersa*)
0·000 39	0,000 62	(j)	Neptune crab (*Neptunus pelagines*)

(a) *45-deg angle of stoop in courtship display. Cannot exceed 62·5 mph 100,5 km/h in level flight.*
(b) *Vertical dive.*
(c) *Wind-assisted speeds up to 110·07 mph 177,1 km/h recorded.*
(d) *Credited with burst speeds up to 65 mph 104 km/h.*
(e) *Average over 440 yd 402 m.*
(f) *Average over 410 yd 375 m.*
(g) *Young mature females.*
(h) *Over 15 yd 13,7 m (flying start)*
(i) *Can double this speed in an emergency.*
(j) *Travelled 101·5 miles 163,3 km/h in 29 years.*

Animal classification

THE MOLLUSCS
Phylum *Mollusca* is a large group of soft-bodied animals with shells, found on land, in freshwater and the sea. A typical mollusc consists of a head, a muscular foot, and a hump containing the viscera. The skin covering the hump is folded and secretes the shell. It has a heart, with an open blood system, and a simple nervous system.

Class *Amphineura*
A group of seawater molluscs, with elongated bodies and shells consisting of a number of plates. For example, the chitons.

Class *Gastropoda*
The gastropods are a group of land, sea and freshwater molluscs. There is usually a coiled shell and a distinct head with eyes and tentacles. For example: *Patella*, the limpet; *Buccinium*, the whelk; *Helix*, the land snail; *Planorbis*, the freshwater snail; *Limax*, the slug; *Littorina*, the winkle.

Class *Scaphopoda*
Long worm-like seawater molluscs, with tubular shells open at both ends. The head is little developed, with a number of tentacles. For example, the elephant's-tusk shells.

Class *Lamellibranchia*
In the lamellibranchs the body is compressed sideways and completely enclosed in the bivalved shell. They are largely found in seawater, although some inhabit freshwater. For example: *Mytilus*, the mussel; *Ostrea*, the oyster; *Anodonta*, the freshwater mussel; *Pecten*, the scallop; *Teredo*, the shipworm.

Class *Cephalopoda*
The cephalopods are highly-organized seawater molluscs. They have a well-developed head with complex eyes, tentacles, probably formed from the foot, and often a much reduced shell. For example: *Loligo*, the squid; *Sepia*, the cuttle-fish; *Octopus*; *Nautilus*.

THE ARTHROPODS
Phylum *Arthropoda* is a very large and varied group of animals. In general they have hard exoskeletons and a number of body segments. They have a number of segmented limbs, one pair at least serving as jaws. There is a heart and an open blood system, with a more complex nervous system than in the molluscs.

Class *Onychophora*
A terrestrial group, with a thin soft cuticle (skin). The head is divided into three segments, with one pair of jaws. The remaining body segments are all identical. For example, *Peripatus*.

Class *Crustacea*
The crustaceans are a mainly aquatic group, breathing via gills. There is often a thickened exoskeleton. Three pairs of appendages are found on the head, with many other diverse appendages on the rest of the body.

Order *Phyllopoda*
A primitive order, with many similar paired appendages. For example, *Chirocephalus*, the fairy shrimp.

Order *Isopoda*
Flattening from top to bottom; many similar paired appendages. For example, the woodlice.

Order *Amphipoda*
The amphipods show side-to-side flattening. For example, *Gammarus*, the freshwater shrimp.

Order *Decapoda*
Five pairs of legs, plus other jointed appendages. For example: *Cancer*, a crab; *Astacus*, a crayfish.

Class *Arachnida*
The arachnids have bodies divided into two regions. The first region carries, among other jointed appendages, four pairs of legs. The second region consists of 13 segments. For example: *Scorpio*, a scorpion; *Limulus*, a king-crab; *Epeira*, a spider; *Boophilus*, a cow-tick.

Class *Myriapoda*
A terrestrial group of animals, consisting of many similar limb-bearing segments. There is a clearly-observed head with one pair of jaws.

Order *Chilopoda*
Carnivores with one pair of appendages on each segment. The centipedes.

Order *Diplopoda*
Herbivores with two pairs of appendages on each segment. The millipedes.

Class *Insecta*
The insects are a large, mainly terrestrial group. An insect consists of three regions; the head, thorax and abdomen. The head has a pair of antennae, the body three pairs of legs and two pairs of wings, while the abdominal segments carry no appendages. The two dozen or so orders include the following.

Order *Lepidoptera*
The butterflies and moths.

Order *Coleoptera*
The beetles.

Order *Hymenoptera*
The ants, wasps and bees.

Order *Diptera*
The flies.

Order *Orthoptera*
The cockroaches, grasshoppers, locusts and stick insects.

Order *Anisoptera*
The dragonflies.

THE CHORDATES
Phylum *Chordata* contains the most sophisticated animals. All chordates possess a notochord (a sort of skeletal rod) at some stage in their embryological development. There is a tubular central nervous system, and a closed blood system.

SUB-PHYLUM *PROTOCHORDATA*
A group with no true brain, skull, heart or kidneys. For example: *Balanoglossus*, a burrowing marine worm; *Cionia*, a sea-squirt; *Amphioxus*, a lancelet.

SUB-PHYLUM *VERTEBRATA*
In the vertebrates a vertebral column replaces the notochord of the protochordates, along with a true internal skeleton of bone and/or cartilage. There are usually two pairs of limbs. The kidneys are the organs of excretion. There is a central nervous system, with a brain enclosed in a protective skull.

Class *Pisces*
The fish. A large aquatic class, with gills for breathing, pectoral and pelvic fins as limbs, and scales as a pseudo-exoskeleton.

Sub-class *Chondrichthyes*
A cartilaginous endoskeleton.

Order *Selachii*
There is no operculum covering the gills. There are many teeth, which are constantly being replaced. For example: *Scyliorhinus*, the dogfish; *Selache*, the basking shark; *Raia*, the ray; *Torpedo*, the electric ray.

Sub-class *Teleostomi*
The endoskeleton is entirely of bone, with an exoskeleton of bony scales. An air bladder is usually present.

Order *Dipnoi*
The lung-fishes; there are lungs as well as gills. For example: *Ceratodus*, the Burnett salmon; *Protopterus*, the mud-fish.

Order *Teleostei*
The modern bony fish, in which the endoskeleton is reduced and the exoskeleton consists of bony scales. For example: *Salmo*, the salmon; *Gadus*, the cod; *Exocoetus*, the flying fish; *Hippocampus*, the seahorse.

Class *Amphibia*
Suited for life both in the water and on land. Gills are present in the larvae (tadpoles), lungs in the adult. The legs are modelled on the

pentadactyl (five-fingered) limb.

Order *Urodela*
Limbs are short and there is often a tail. The gills often persist into adulthood. For example: *Triton*, the newt; *Salamandra*, the salamander; *Amblystoma*, the axolotl.

Order *Anura*
The frogs and toads. The adults have neither gills nor tails. For example: *Rana*, the frog; *Bufo*, the toad.

Class *Reptilia*
The reptiles have dry skin with scales or bony plates. They breath with lungs. Typically they have two pairs of pentadactyl limbs. They lay yolk-filled eggs with calcareous (calcium-rich) shells.

Order *Chelonia*
The tortoises and turtles.

Order *Lacertilia*
The lizards.

Order *Ophidia*
The snakes.

Order *Crocodilia*
The crocodiles and alligators.

Class *Aves*
The birds are warm-blooded. Of the two pairs of pentadactyl limbs, the front pair is formed into wings. The skin bears feathers, except on the legs, where there are horny scales, linking them with the reptiles. Lungs are the respiratory organs. They lay yolky eggs with calcareous shells, and show parental care of the young.

Order *Ratitae*
Large running birds with rudimentary wings. For example: *Struthio*, the ostrich; *Dromaeus*, the emu; *Casuarius*, the cassowary; *Apteryx*, the kiwi.

Order *Carinatae*
The flying birds, from wrens up to eagles.

Class *Mammalia*
The mammals are warm-blooded, with pentadactyl limbs. The skin has hair. The respiratory organs are lungs, and the thoracic and abdominal cavities are separated by the diaphragm. In most cases they give birth to live young, which they suckle on milk from the mammary glands and to which they show an often well-developed sense of parental care.

Sub-class *Prototheria*
A primitive group of mammals which lay eggs and have no mammary glands. For example: the duck-billed platypus; the spiny anteater.

Sub-class *Metatheria*
The marsupials of Australia and South America. They give birth to only partly-developed young, which are then suckled in the pouch on the body of the mother. For example: the kangeroos; the koala bears; the opossums.

Sub-class *Eutharia*
These are the placental mammals, whose offspring are born at a more developed stage than those of the other two sub-classes.

Order *Insectivora*
The hedgehogs, shrews and moles.

Order *Chiroptera*
The bats.

Order *Rodentia*
The rats, mice, squirrels, lemmings, beavers and porcupines.

Order *Lagomorpha*
The rabbits and hares.

Order *Cetacea*
The whales and dolphins.

Order *Carnivora*
The cats, lions, dogs, weasels, otters, badgers, bears and seals.

Order *Perissodactyla*
The horses, zebras, tapirs and rhinosceroses.

Order *Artiodactyla*
The cows, goats, deer, giraffe and sheep.

Order *Primates*
The lemurs, monkeys, apes and man.

The Human World

Anthropology

Anthropology, the study of the differences and similarities between the various races of mankind, contains two autonomous sciences: physical anthropology (the study of blood groups and genetic differences) and social anthropology or ethnology (the study of custom).

Physical Anthropology
The classification of the races or gene pools of man is complex and is vulnerable to political controversy. Many terms which have been used to describe racial groupings are hypothetical, being based either upon cultural and linguistic considerations which are not genetically linked (*e.g.* the term 'the Semitic race'), or upon physical similarities (*e.g.* the term negroid).

Formerly classifications of mankind were attempted based purely upon outward physical characteristics such as skin colour (black, brown, white, yellow); body proportions (anthropometry), the shape of the head (craniometry), hair form, teeth and eyelids. A widely adopted system was that based on hair form which recognized three main types: the straight haired, woolly haired and curly haired groups. Although this remains of value no modern description of race relies solely on hair form. External bodily differences are not ignored in the definition of races but are of less scientific importance to such simply inherited or single gene traits as can be easily and precisely quantified.

One of the major factors in modern anthropological studies is the blood group. Certain blood groups predominate in some races but are almost absent in others; *e.g.* B group is very rare in Amerinds. As well as blood groups various related factors are of racial consequence: abnormal haemoglobins and pigments and deficiencies in some type of cell are all known to be racially linked.

Many metabolic differences are now used in anthropological classification: abnormalities in the sense of taste (some races cannot taste phenylthiocarbamide), the incidence of colour blindness, differences in the secretion of amino acids and other biochemical traits have all been scientifically investigated and shown to be excellent aids in the definition of gene pools. Certain medical disorders of genetic origin are useful to the science; *e.g.* thalassemia is confined to the Mediterranean type of the Caucasoid race. The Japanese have studied earwax types and found them to be genetically significant. Thus blood and other genetic traits have taken first place over body measurements and hair types in the definition of races.

The study of genetically transmitted traits has allowed anthropologists to divide man into about ten major types – the exact number depends upon individual interpretation of the scientific evidence. These major divisions, often referred to as geographical races, account for over 99% of mankind. Each geographical race contains many local groupings which, although forming breeding units separate from others to a greater or lesser degree, are nevertheless genetically related to the whole. The remaining groups are sometimes (inaccurately) termed microraces and consist of either small local genetically distinct populations, (*e.g.* the Ainu of Hokkaido) or peoples whose place in the anthropological jigsaw is still the subject of much controversy (*e.g.* the Bushmen of Southern Africa).

The Geographical Races

(1) *The ASIATIC or MONGOLOID Race*
Extent: most of Asia north and east of India.
Classic appearance: 'yellow-brown' skin, straight hair, round head, high cheek bones and flat face.

A northern group includes Lapps, Yakuts and Koreans; a southern group – 'Oceanic Mongoloids' or Indonesians – is very mixed with a tendency to broader heads. The central (Pareoean) type with, in general, less prominent cheek bones and broader noses, includes both Chinese and Japanese.

(2) *The AMERINDIAN Race*
Extent: the Americas.
Classic appearance: Similar to Asiatics though the Eskimos tend to have longer skulls, broader faces and narrower noses, and the Fuegans have curly hair.

Although there are undoubted links between the Indians of the New World and the Asiatics there is sufficient genetic reason to recognize them as separate races.

(3) *The AFRICAN or NEGROID Race*
Extent: Africa south of the Sahara.
Classic appearance: tall, woolly hair, black or dark brown skin, broad nose, thickened lips.

Many sub-groups include Nilotics and the much shorter lighter skinned Pygmies (Negrillos). It is debatable whether the Bushmen belong to this geographical race.

(4) *The POLYNESIAN Race*
Extent: Polynesia including New Zealand.
Classic appearance: similar to 'Oceanic Mongoloids' though with longer heads and some Caucasoid traits.

The ancestral home of the Polynesians was probably South-East Asia.

(5) *The MELANESIAN Race*
Extent: Melanesia including New Guinea. Classic appearance: similar to Africans but some Melanesian islanders tend to be lighter skinned.

This group contains isolated pockets in Asia including Semang tribes in Sumatra and Malaysia, possibly the Andaman Island Negritos, and debatably the short Aeta of the Philippines.

(6) *The MICRONESIAN Race*
Extent: Micronesia.
Classic appearance: slight of stature, light brown skins, curly hair.
  Genetically related to 'Oceanic Mongoloids'.

(7) *The AUSTRALOID Race*
Extent: mainland Australia.
Classic appearance: curly hair, dark brown to black skin, massive skull with protruding jaws and retreating forehead, slender limbs.
  The Australian aboriginals are distantly related to the Indic race, in particular to the Veddah of Sri Lanka, but long isolation has resulted in some special features.

(8) *The INDIC Race*
Extent: Indian sub-continent.
Classic appearance: medium height, curly hair, prominent forehead, light brown skin but considerable variation in colour.
  Local races include the north Indian Caucasoid type, the south Indian 'Dravidians', Singhalese Veddah and some isolated peoples in Sumatra and Sulawesi.

(9) *The CAUCASOID Race*
Extent: Europe, Asia west of India and north Africa. Also widely diffused to the Americas and Australasia.
  Classic appearance: considerable variation in height and build, and hair colour and form although there is a tendency to curly hair; 'white' or light skin, prominent forehead.
  Sub-groups include Proto-Nordics (from Turkestan), Somalis, Ethiops and other Caucasoid peoples of the Horn of Africa and the Red Sea, Eurafricans, Arabs (including Bedouins), the Mediterranean or Romance peoples, the Nordic peoples (of Britain, Scandinavia, the Low Countries and Germany), the Pamiri, the Eurasiatics (including the Alpine type) found from central Europe to the Himalayas, and possibly the Ainu of Hokkaido, who are often categorized as a 'microrace'.

Major anthropological discoveries

Year	Scientific Name	Period and Estimated Date BC	Location	Description	Anthropologist
1856[1]	*Homo neanderthalensis*	Late middle Palaeolithic 120 000	Neander Valley, nr Düsseldorf, Germany	skull, bones	Fuhlrott
1868[2]	*Homo sapiens* (Cromagnon man)	Upper Palaeolithic 35 000	Cromagnon, Les Eyzies, France	4 skeletons, 1 foetus	Lartet
1890	*Pithecanthropus erectus*	Upper Pleistocene 400 000	Kedung Brebus, Java	mandible, tooth	Dubois
1907	*Homo heidelbergensis*	Lower Palaeolithic 450 000	Mauer, nr Heidelberg, Germany	lower jaw	Schoetensack
1912[3]	*Eoanthropus dawsonii*	Holocene (Recent) (fraud)	Piltdown, East Sussex	composite skull	Dawson
1921	*Homo rhodesiensis*	Upper Gamblian c. 50 000	Broken Hill, Zambia	skull	Armstrong
1924	*Australopithecus africanus*	Early Pleistocene 1 000 000	Taung, Botswana	skull	Dart (Izod)
1926[4]	*Proconsul nyanzae*	Miocene c. 25 000 000	Koru, Kenya	fragments (non-hominoid)	Hopwood
1927	*Pithecanthropus pekinensis*	Lower Palaeolithic 400 000	Choukoutien, nr Peking, China	tooth	Bohlin
1929–34	*Neanderthaloid man*	Middle Palaeolithic or Mousterian 120 000	Mt Carmel, Israel	part 16 skeletons	Garrod
1932	*Ramapithecus*	Miocene c. 8–13 000 000	Siwalik Hills, N India	jaws, teeth	G. E. Lewis
1935[5]	*Homo sapiens fossilis*	Lower Palaeolithic 250 000	Boyn Hill, Swanscombe, Kent	parts skull	Marston
1935[6]	*Gigantopithecus blacki*	Middle Pleistocene 450 000	from Kwangsi, China (Hong Kong druggist)	teeth only	von Koenigswald
1936	*Pleisianthropus transvaalensis*	Early Pleistocene 1 000 000	Sterkfontein, Transvaal	skull, part femur	Broom (Barlow)
1938	*Paranthropus robustus*	Pleistocene 700 000	Kromdraai, Transvaal	skull part, bones	Broom (Terblanche)
1947	*Homo sapiens fossilis*	Middle Palaeolithic or Mousterian 125 000	Fontéchevade, France	*2 callottes*	Martin
1949	*Australopithecus prometheus*	Pleistocene 900 000	Makapansgat, Transvaal	fragments[7]	Dart
1953	*Telanthropus capensis*	Pleistocene 800 000	Swartkrans, Transvaal	jaw, skull parts	Broom
1954	*Atlanthropus*	Chelleo-Acheulian 500 000	Ternifine, Algeria	parietal, 3 mandibles	Arambourg
1957	*Neanderthaloid man*	Upper Palaeolithic 45 000	Shanidar, Iraq	skeletons	Solecki
1959	*Zinjanthropus boisei*	Pliocene-Pleistocene c. 1 750 000	Olduvai, Tanzania	skull	Mrs Mary Leakey
1960	*Homo habilis*	Pliocene-Pleistocene *ante supra*	Olduvai, Tanzania	fragments	Louis Leakey
1961	*Kenyapithecus wickeri*	Mid Miocene c. 14 000 000	Fort Ternan, Kenya	palate, teeth (non-hominoid)	Leakey (Mukiri)
1963	*Australopithecus robustus*	Middle Pleistocene 450 000	Chenchiawo, Lantien, NW China	jaw	—
1964	*Sinanthropus lantianensis*	Middle Pleistocene c. 500 000	Kungwangling, Lantien, Shensi, China	skull cap and female jaw in 1963	Wu Ju Kang
1969	*Homo erectus*	Middle Pleistocene 500 000–1 000 000	Sangiran, Java	skull	Sartono
1972	*Homo?*	Plio–Pleistocene 2 000 000	East Turkana, Kenya	mandibular, cranial and limb bones	Richard Leakey
1974	*Australopithecus* or *Homo Australopithecus afarensis*	Pliocene 3–4 000 000	Hadar Afar region, Ethiopia	skull parts, jaws, teeth, skeleton known as 'Lucy'	Johanson and Taieb
1975	*Homo erectus*	Early Pleistocene 1 500 000	Turkana, Kenya	skull**	Richard Leakey
1975	*Homo*	Plio-Pleistocene 3 350 000–3 750 000	Laetoli, Tanzania	8 adults, 3 children	Mrs Mary Leakey
1976	*Homo*	Pleistocene 400 000	Halkidiki, Greece	complete skeleton	Greek Anthropological Society
1977	*Ramapithecus*	Mid-Miocene c. 9–11 million	Potwar Plateau, Pakistan	radius	Pilbeam
1978	*Hominid*	Plio-Pleistocene 3 500 000	Laetoli, Tanzania	footprints	Mrs Mary Leakey and Richard Hay
1980	*Homo sapiens*	Middle Pleistocene 120 000	Laetoli, Tanzania	skull	—

[1] Female skull discovered in Gibraltar in 1848 but unrecognised till 1864.
[2] Earliest specimen found at Engis, near Liége, Belgium, in 1832 by Schmerling.
[3] Exposed by X-Ray and radio-activity tests in Nov 1953 as an elaborate fraud.
[4] Non-hominoid. Complete skull discovered 1948 by Mrs Leakey.
[5] Further part discovered 1955.
[6] Since 1957 all the evidence is that these relate to a non-hominoid giant ape.
[7] Complete skull in 1958 (Kitching).
** Of great importance because of its uncanny resemblance to Peking man which Leakey believes is more correctly datable to triple the age advanced by the Chinese.

The 26 civilizations of man

If the duration of the evolution of Homo, now estimated at 3 750 000 years, is likened to a single year, then the earliest of all history's known civilizations began after 5 p.m. on 30 Dec. Put another way, 289/290ths of man's existence has been uncivilized.

Few historians have attempted to classify the world's civilizations because of the natural tendency to specialize. An early attempt was that of the Frenchman, Count de Gobineau, in his four-volume *L'Inégalité des Races Humaines* (Paris, 1853–5). His total was ten. Since that

time western archaeologists have rescued five more ancient civilizations from oblivion – the Babylonic, the Hittite, the Mayan, the Minoan, and the Sumeric. This would have brought his total to 15 compared with a more modern contention of 26.

The most authoritative classification now available is the revised twelve-volume life work of Professor Arnold Joseph Toynbee, *A Study of History*, published between 1921 and 1961. This concludes that there have been 21 civilizations of which eight still survive. Those surviving are the Arabic (Islamic), the Far Eastern (began in AD 589 and now split into two), the Orthodox Christian (now also split into two), the Hindu (begun c. AD 775), the Western civilization and

the Communist civilization. The term 'civilization' in the context of classifications relates purely to entities with separate imperial designs rather than a differing culture or ethos.

Archaeological discoveries in 1960 showed that the Yucatec and Mayan civilizations had the same cradle. The compilation below gives details. The Eskimo, Spartan, Polynesian, and Ottoman civilizations have been listed though Toynbee excludes these from his total on the grounds that they were 'arrested civilizations'. Spontaneous derivations, once favoured by 'isolationists', are under increasing attack by archaeologists of the 'diffusionist' school, who believe there were trans-oceanic contacts at very early dates.

The 26 civilizations of man

No.	Name	Dawn	Final Collapse	Duration in Centuries	Cradle	Dominant States	Religion and Philosophy	Derivation
1	Egyptiac	ante 4000 BC	c. AD 280	c. 43	Lower Nile	Middle Empire c. 2065–1660 BC	Osiris-worship Philosophy of Atonism	Spontaneous
2	Sumeric or Sumerian	ante 3500 BC	c. 1700 BC	c. 18	Euphrates-Tigris Delta	Sumer and Akkad Empire c. 2298–1905 BC	Tammuz-worship	Spontaneous
3	Indic	ante 3000 BC	c. AD 500	35	Mohenjo-Daro, Harappa, Indus and Ganges valleys	Mauryan Empire 322–185 BC Gupta Empire AD 390–475	Hinduism, Jainism, Hinayāna Buddhism	Possibly of Sumeric origin
4	Mayan[1]	c. 2500 BC	AD 1550	c. 45	Guatemalan forests	First Empire AD c. 300–690	Human sacrifice and human penitential self-mortification	Spontaneous
5	Minoan	ante 2000 BC	c. 1400 BC	6	Cnossus, Crete and the Cyclades	Thalassocracy of Minos c. 1750–1400 BC	?Orphism	Spontaneous
6	Hittite	2000 BC	c. 1200 BC	8	Boghazköi, Anatolia, Turkey	—	Pantheonism	Related to Minoan
7	Sinic	c. 1600 BC[3]	AD 220	18	Yellow River Basin	Ts'in and Han Empire 221 BC–AD 172	Mahāyāna Buddhism, Taoism, Confucianism	Believed unrelated
8	Babylonic	c. 1500 BC	538 BC	10	Lower Mesopotamia	Babylonian Empire 610–539 BC	Judaism, Zoroastrianism Astrology	Related to Sumeric
9	Hellenic	c. 1300 BC	AD 558	18½	Greek mainland and Aegean Is	Roman Empire 31 BC–AD 378	Mithraism, Platonism, Stoicism, Epicureanism Pantheonism, Christianity	Related to Minoan
10	Syriac	c. 1200 BC	AD 970	22	Eastern Cilicia	Achaemenian Empire c. 525–332 BC	Islam and Philosophy of Zervanism	Related to Minoan
11	Eskimo	c. 1100 BC	c. AD 1850	c. 30	Umnak, Aleutian Islands	Thule AD c. 1150–1850	Includes Sila, sky god; Sedna, seal goddess	—
12	Spartan	c. 900 BC	AD 396	13	Laconia	620–371 BC	—	Hellenic
13	Polynesian	c. 500 BC	c. AD 1775	22½	Samoa and Tonga	—	Ancestor spirits *Mana* – supernatural power	—
14	Andean	c. 100 BC	AD 1783	19	Chimu, N Peru and Nazca, S Peru	Inca Empire AD 1430–1533	Philosophy of Viracochaism	Spontaneous
15	Khmer[4]	c. AD 100	AD 1432	13	Cambodian coast	Angkor Kingdom AD 802–1432	Hinduism	Possibly related to Indic and Sinic
16	Far Eastern (main)	AD 589	Scarcely survives	14 to date	Si Ngan (Sian-fu) Wei Valley	Mongol Empire AD 1280–1351 Manchu Empire AD 1644–1912	Muhayaniah Buddhism	Related to Sinic
17	Far Eastern (Japan and Korea)	AD 645	Survives	13 to date	Yamato, Japan via Korea	Tokugawa Shogunate AD 1600–1868	Mikado-worship, Shintoism, Buddhism and Zen Philosophy	Related to Sinic
18	Western	c. AD 675	Flourishes	13 to date	Ireland	Habsburg Monarchy AD 1493–1918 and French (Napoleonic) Empire AD 1792–1815 The British Empire 1757–1931	Philosophy of Christianity	Related to Hellenic
19	Orthodox Christian (main)	c. AD 680	Survives	13 to date	Anatolia, Turkey	Byzantine Empire AD 395–1453	Bedreddinism Orthodox Church, Imāmī	Related to Hellenic and Western
20	Hindu	c. AD 775	Survives	11 to date	Kanauj, Jumna-Ganges Duab	Mughul Raj AD c. 1572–1707 British Raj 1818–1947	Hinduism, Sikhism	Related to Indic
21	Orthodox Christian (Russia)	c. AD 950	Survives	10 to date	Upper Dnieper Basin	Muscovite Empire AD 1478–1917	Orthodox Church Sectarianism	Related to Hellenic
22	Arabic	c. AD 975	AD 1525	5½	Arabia, Iraq, Syria	Abbasid Caliphate of Baghdad	Islām (post AD 1516)	Related to Syriac
23	Mexic	c. AD 1075	AD 1821	7½	Mexican Plateau	Aztec Empire AD 1375–1521	Quetzalcoatl	Related to Mayan
24	Ottoman	c. AD 1310	AD 1919	6	Turkey	Ottoman Empire AD 1372–1919	Islām	—

No.	Name	Dawn	Final Collapse	Duration in Centuries	Cradle	Dominant States	Religion and Philosophy	Derivation
25	Iranic (now Islamic)	c. AD 1320	Survives	6½ to date	Oxus-Jaxartes Basin	—	Islām (post AD 1516)	Related to Syriac
26	Communist	1848	Flourishes		Western Europe	USSR and China	Atheism, Marxist-Leninism, Maoism	—

[1] Toynbee regards a Yucatec civilization (c. AD 1075–1680) as a separate entity. Archaeological discoveries in 1960 indicate that Dzibilchaltan, on the Yucatan Peninsula, was in fact the cradle of the whole Mayan civilization.
[2] There is evidence of links with Egyptiac. The early classic period at Tikal dates from c. AD 250–550.
[3] The earliest archaeologically acceptable dynasty was that of Shang, variously dated 1766–1558 BC. The historicity of the First, or Hsia dynasty, allegedly founded by Yü in 2205 BC, is in decided doubt.
[4] Not regarded by Toynbee as a separate civilization but as an offshoot of the Hindu civilization. Modern evidence shows, however, that the Khmer origins antedate those of the Hindu civilization by 7 centuries.

The Human Body

Bones in the human body

Skull	Number
Occipital	1
Parietal – 1 pair	2
Sphenoid	1
Ethmoid	1
Inferior Nasal Conchae – 1 pair	2
Frontal – 1 pair, fused	1
Nasal – 1 pair	2
Lacrimal – 1 pair	2
Temporal – 1 pair	2
Macilla – 1 pair	2
Zygomatic – 1 pair	2
Vomer	1
Palatine – 1 pair	2
Mandible – 1 pair, fused	1
	22

The Ears	
Malleus	2
Incus	2
Stapes	2
	6

Vertebrae	
Cervical	7
Thoracic	12
Lumbar	5
Sacral – 5, fused to form the Sacrum	1
Coccyx – between 3 and 5, fused	1
	26

Vertebral Ribs	
Ribs, 'true' – 7 pairs	14
Ribs, 'false' – 5 pairs of which 2 pairs are floating	10
	24

Sternum	
Manubrium	1
'The Body' (sternebrae)	1
Xiphisternum	1
	3

Hyoid (in the throat)	1

Pectoral Girdle	
Clavicle – 1 pair	2
Scapula – (including Coracoid) – 1 pair	2
	4

Upper Extremity (each arm)	
Humerus	1
Radius	1
Ulna	1
Carpus:	
Scaphoid	1
Lunate	1
Triquetral	1
Pisiform	1
Trapezium	1
Trapezoid	1
Capitate	1
Hamate	1
Metacarpals	5

Phalanges:	
First Digit	2
Second Digit	3
Third Digit	3
Fourth Digit	3
Fifth Digit	3
	30

Pelvic Girdle	
Ilium, Ischium and Pubis (combined) – 1 pair of hip bones, innominate	2

Lower Extremity (each leg)	
Femur	1
Tibia	1
Fibula	1
Tarsus:	
Talus	1
Calcaneus	1
Navicular	1
Cuneiform medial	1
Cuneiform, intermediate	1
Cuneiform, lateral	1
Cuboid	1
Metatarsals	5
Phalanges:	
First Digit	2
Second Digit	3
Third Digit	3
Fourth Digit	3
Fifth Digit	3
	29

Total	
Skull	**22**
The Ears	**6**
Vertebrae	**26**
Vertebral Ribs	**24**
Sternum	**3**
Throat	**1**
Pectoral Girdle	**4**
Upper Extremity (arms) – 2 × 30	**60**
Hip Bones	**2**
Lower Extremity (legs) – 2 × 29	**58**
	206

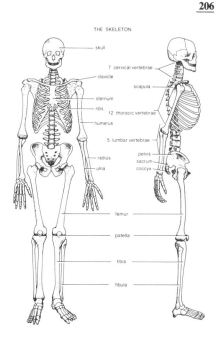

THE SKELETON

skull
clavicle
7 cervical vertebrae
scapula
sternum
ribs
12 thoracic vertebrae
humerus
5 lumbar vertebrae
radius
pelvis
ulna
sacrum
coccyx
femur
patella
tibia
fibula

Organs of the human body

The abdominal organs
These consist of the digestive organs – the oesophagus, stomach, small and large intestines and rectum. In addition there are the liver, spleen, pancreas, kidneys and bladder.

The thoracic organs
The thorax or rib cage contains just three organs – the heart and the two lungs.

Skin
The skin is by far the largest single organ of the human body. It weighs about 16 per cent of the total body weight and in an average adult male has a surface area of $18\,000\,cm^2$ *2800 in²*. The three main groups into which Man is divided by the colour of his skin are *Leukoderms* (white-skinned), *Melanoderms* (black-skinned) and *Xanthroderms* (yellow-skinned). Pigment producing cells in the basal layers of the epidermis are called melanoblasts (Greek *melas* – black; *blastos* – bud).

The number (up to 4000 per sq cm) and the size do not vary significantly in white and negro skin but are more active and productive in the latter so protecting the iris and the retina against the brightness of the sun.

The human brain
It is estimated that a human brain, weighing about $1\cdot36\,kg$ *3 lb* contains 10 000 000 000 nerve cells. Each of these deploys a potential 25 000 interconnections with other cells. Compared with this the most advanced computers are giant electronic morons.

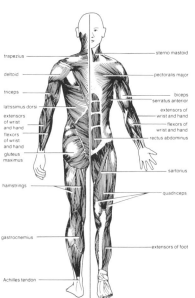

SUPERFICIAL MUSCLES, BACK AND FRONT

trapezius
deltoid
triceps
latissimus dorsi
extensors of wrist and hand
flexors of wrist and hand
gluteus maximus
hamstrings
gastrocnemius
Achilles tendon
sterno mastoid
pectoralis major
biceps
serratus anterior
extensors of wrist and hand
flexors of wrist and hand
rectus abdominus
sartorius
quadriceps
extensors of foot

Human genetics
The normal human has 46 chromosomes. The chromosome is the microscopic thread-like body within cells which carries hereditary factors or genes. These are classified as 22 pairs of non-sex chromosomes (one of each pair derived from the father and one from the mother) and two sex chromosomes making 46. In a female both sex

chromosomes are Xs, one from the father and one from the mother. In a male they are an X from the mother and a Y from the father. The X chromosome is much larger than the Y, thus women possess four per cent more deoxyribonucleic acid than males. This may have a bearing on their greater longevity.

The human sometimes exhibits 47 or more chromosomes. One such instance is the XXX female in which the supernumerary is an extra X. In some cases of hermaphroditism the supernumerary is a Y.

Chimpanzees, gorillas, and orang-utans have 48 chromosomes. It has been suggested that man's emergence from the primitive man-ape population may have occurred by a process known as 'reciprocal translocation'. This is a mechanism whereby two dissimilar chromosomes break and two of the four dissimilar parts join with the possible net loss of one chromosome. It is possible that 47 and 46 chromosome hominoids enjoyed a bipedal advantage on forest edges over brachiating apes and thus the evolution of man began from this point.

Somatotypes

One of the systems used for classifying human physique is somatotyping (from the Greek *soma*, body) first published in 1940 by Sheldon of the USA.

The three components used, some degree of which is present in everyone, are: (1) Endomorphy (a tendency to globularity); (2) Mesomorphy (a tendency to muscularity); and (3) Ectomorphy (a tendency to linearity). The degrees of tendency range from 1 to an extreme of 7.

Extreme endomorphics would be 7—1—1; Hercules would be 1—7—1, and the extreme in ectomorphics would be 1—1—7. In practice such extremes are rarely encountered. The commonest somatotypes are 3—4—4, 4—3—3, and 3—5—2. The components are oblique, not orthogonal, i.e. not independent of each other to the point where it would be impossible to have a 5—5—5 or a 7—7—1.

Research (Tanner, 1964) into a sample of Olympic athletes shows that mean Endomorphy varies between 2·0 (steeplechasers) and 3·8 (shot putters); Mesomorphy between 4·1 (high jumpers) and 6·2 (discus throwers); and Ectomorphy between 4·5 (steeplechasers) and 2·0 (shot and discus throwers). Sprinters averaged 2·5—5·5—2·9 while milers have a mean rating of 2·5—4·3—4·3.

Human dentition

Man normally has two sets of teeth during his life span. The primary (milk or deciduous) set of 20 is usually acquired between the ages of 6 and 24 months. The secondary (or permanent) dentition of 32 teeth grows in usually from about the sixth year.

The four principal types of teeth are: –

Incisors (Lat. *incidere* – to cut into) total eight. Two upper central, flanked by two upper lateral with four lower.

Canine (Lat. *canis* – a dog) total four. These are next to the lateral incisors and are thus the third teeth from the mid-line in each quadrant of the mouth. These are also referred to as *cuspids* (Lat. *cuspis* – a point).

Pre-Molars (Lat. *molare* – to grind) total eight. These are next in line back from the incisors, two in each quadrant. Because these have two cusps these are alternatively known as bicuspids.

Molars (see above) total twelve. These are the furthest back in the mouth – three in each quadrant. The upper molars often have four cusps and the lower five cusps for grinding. The third (hindermost) molars are known also as 'wisdom teeth' and do not usually appear until the age of 18 to 20.

Prediction of Human Stature

The table below shows the average mean percentage of mature height for both boys and girls at each age from birth to 18 years. These percentages, taken from large samples, essentially reflect the proven average expectation of ultimate height.

Age in Years	*Boys, %*	*Girls, %*
Birth	28·6	30·9
¼	33·9	36·0
½	37·7	39·8
¾	40·1	42·2
1	42·2	44·7
1½	45·6	48·8
2	49·5	52·8
2½	51·6	54·8
3	53·8	57·0
4	58·0	61·8
5	61·8	66·2
6	65·2	70·3
7	69·0	74·0
8	72·0	77·5
9	75·0	80·7
10	78·0	84·4
11	81·1	88·4
12	84·7	92·9
13	87·3	96·5
14	91·5	98·3
15	96·1	99·1
16	98·3	99·6
17	99·3	100·0
18	99·8	100·0

Thus a boy measuring 137 cm *54 in* on his ninth birthday could be expected to be

$$137\ (54) \times \frac{100}{75{\cdot}0} = 183\,\text{cm}\ (72\,in)\ \text{as a man.}$$

In practice because of maternal factors, the prediction of adult stature becomes of value only after the age of 2 or 2½ years. After the age of 9½ prediction is more accurately based on skeletal rather than chronological age. The accuracy tends to be greater throughout for girls than for boys, who, at 14 are subject to a standard deviation of error of 4 per cent, *viz.* the 91·5 per cent figure can be 95·8 per cent for a physically advanced boy, and 87·6 per cent for a retarded one.

Human Expenditure of Energy

The 'calorie' used by dieticians is the kilo-calorie based on 15°C, written as $kcal_{15}$, *i.e.* the heat energy necessary to raise 1 kg of water from 14·5°C to 15·5°C and thus equal to 4·1868 kilojoules. The FAO reference man weighs 65 kg *143·3 lb*, is aged 25 years and is 'moderately active', requiring 3200 cal per diem. The reference woman weighs 55 kg *121·2 lb* and requires 2300 cal also living at an annual mean of 10°C or 50°F.

	Rate in calories per hour
Rest in bed (basal metabolic rate)	60
Sitting at ease (man)	108
Sitting and writing	114
Standing at ease	118
Driving a car	168
Washing up (woman)	198
Driving a motor cycle	204
Dressing, washing, shaving	212
Bed making (woman)	420
Walking 6·4 kph 4 mph	492
Climbing 15 cm *6 in* stairs at 2·4 kph *1·5 mph*	620
Tree felling	640
Bicycling at 13 mph	660
Running at 5 mph	850
Running at 7½ mph	975
Rowing at 33 strokes/min	1140
Swimming breaststroke at 56 strokes/min	1212
Nordic skiing (level snow) at 9·15 mph	1572

Note: Women expend less calories in performing the same activity. e.g. a man washing up would expend 275 cals./hour.

Human extremes

tallest recorded man Robert Pershing Wadlow, b. 22 Feb. 1918 in Alton, Illinois, USA, d. 15 July 1940. Height 272 cm *8 ft 11·1 in.*

tallest recorded woman Zeng Jinlian, b. 26 June 1964 in Yujiang village, Hunan Province, China, d. 13 Feb. 1982. Height 247 cm *8 ft 1¾ in.*

shortest recorded man Calvin Phillips, b. 14 Jan. 1791 in Bridgewater, Massachusetts, USA d. April 1812. Height 67 cm *26½ in.*

shortest recorded woman Pauline Musters, b. 26 Feb. 1876 in Ossendrecht, the Netherlands, d. 1 Mar. 1895. Height 59 cm *23·2 in.*

tallest tribe Tutsi tribe in Rwanda and Burundi. Average height for males is over 180 cm *6 ft.*

shortest tribe Mbuti tribe in Zaïre. Average height for males 135 cm *4 ft 6 in.*

heaviest recorded male Jon Bower Minnoch, b. 29 Sept. 1941 in Bainbridge Island, Washington state, USA, d. 10 Sept. 1983. Weight 442 kg *975 lb.*

heaviest recorded female Mrs Percy Pearl Washington, b. 1926, d. 9 Oct. 1972 in Milwaukee, USA. Weight estimated as 399 kg *880 lb.*

oldest recorded male Shigechiyo Izumi, b. 29 June 1865 on Tokunoshima island, Japan, d. 21 Feb. 1986. Age 120 years 237 days.

oldest recorded female Probably Mrs Mamie Eva Keith, b. 22 Mar. 1873 at Anna, Illinois, USA, d. 20 Sept. 1986. Age 113 years 182 days.

most recorded children To the first of two wives of Feodor Vassilyev of Shuya, near Moscow, b. 1707. She had 69 children.

oldest recorded mother Mrs Ruth Alice Kistler, formerly Mrs Shepard, *née* Taylor. She gave birth to a daughter on 18 Oct. 1956 at Glendale, California, USA, when her age was 57 years 129 days.

highest number of recorded multiple births- Nonuplets (9 babies) born to Mrs Geraldine Brodrick in the Royal Hospital, Sydney, Australia, on 13 June 1971. Two males were stillborn and a third only survived 6 days.

highest number of surviving multiple births Six out of six, born to Mrs Susan Jane Rosenkowitz, *née* Scoones, at Mowbray, Cape Town, South Africa, on 11 Jan. 1974.

heaviest recorded baby The heaviest viable babies were born to Sig. Carmelina Fedele of Aversa, Italy in September 1955 and by Caesarian section to Mrs Christina Samane at Sipetu Hospital, Transkei, South Africa, on 24 May 1982. Both babies were boys and both weighed 10·2 kg *22 lb 8 oz.*

lightest recorded baby The lightest viable baby was Marian Chapman, b. 5 June 1938, d. Mrs Marian Taggart, 31 May 1983. Her weight at birth was 283 g *10 oz.*

smallest waist The smallest recorded waist of a woman of normal 20th century stature belonged to Mrs Ethel Grainger, b. 1905, d. 1982, of Peterborough, Cambs. Between 1929 and 1939 she reduced her waist from 56 cm *22 in* to 33 cm *13 in.*

largest chest Robert Earl Hughes (1926–58) of the USA probably had a chest measurement of 265 cm *104 in* at a body weight of 485 kg *1069 lb.* George Macaree of the UK has a chest measurement of 190 cm *75 in* for a body weight of 196·8 kg *434 lb.* Both these gentlemen were endomorphs, i.e. with a tendency towards globularity. Among muscular individuals, Gary Aprahamian (b. 2 Feb. 1962, d. 23 Aug 1984), the US power-lifter, had a normal chest measurement of 155 cm *61 in* at 165 kg *365 lb.*

longest necks The Padaung or Kareni people of Burma successively fit more and more copper coils to their necks, with the result that necks of 40 cm *16 in* are not unknown.

heaviest recorded brain The heaviest non-diseased brain recorded in post mortem was that of the Russian author Ivan Sergeyvich Turgenev (1818–83). It weighed 2012 g *4 lb 6 oz.* (The average male brain weighs about 1420 g *3 lb 2 oz.*)

lightest recorded brain This belonged to a 31-year old woman, examined in post mortem at King's College Hospital, London, in 1977. It weighed 1096 g *2 lb 7 oz.*

longest recorded fingernails On 8 Apr. 1985 Shridhar Chillal (b. 1937) of Poona, India, had a total measurement for the nails on the five digits of his left hand of 363 cm *143 in*, with the thumb nail alone measuring 87·6 cm *34½ in.* He had stopped cutting them in 1952.

longest recorded hair Georgia Sabrantke, b. 10

Jan. 1943, of West Germany, had hair 296 cm *9 ft 8¼ in* long on 6 Mar. 1986.

strongest recorded hair On 9 Sept. 1984 a hair from the head of Miss Pham Thy Lan broke at a strain of 178 g *6¼ oz*, while being tested on BBC TV's *Record Breakers*.

longest beard The beard of Hans N. Langseth, b. 1846 near Eidsroll, Norway, d. 1927 in Iowa, USA, was preserved. It measured 5·33 m *17 ft 6 in* at the time of his death.

longest recorded moustache This belongs to Birger Pellas, b. 21 Sept. 1934, of Mälmo, Sweden. Grown since 1973, his moustache was measured on 8 Jan. 1986 as being 2·64 m *8 ft 8 in*.

fastest intelligible speaking (in English) In March 1983 John Moschitta of the USA spoke at a rate of 552 words per minute for 58 seconds in a test conducted by a radio station.

highest recorded body temperature On 10 July 1980 Willy Jones was admitted to Grady Memorial Hospital, Atlanta, Georgia, USA, with a body temperature of 46·5°C *115·7°F*. He was pronounced well and discharged 24 days later.

lowest recorded body temperature There are two cases of individuals recorded with a body temperature of 16°C *60·8°F* who survived. The first was Dorothy Mae Stevens (1929–74), in Chicago, Illinois, USA, on 1 Feb. 1951; the other was 2-year-old Vickie Mary Davis on 21 Jan. 1956 in Marshalltown, Iowa, USA.

longest recorded heart stoppage Miss Jean Jawbone, aged 20, was revived from a heart stoppage of at least 3 hr 40 m by a team at the Health Sciences Centre, Winnipeg, Canada, on 8 Jan 1977.

longest without food and water Eighteen-year-old Andreas Mihavecz of Bregenz, Austria, was locked in a holding cell in Höchst, Austria, by the police on 1 Apr. 1979. On 18 Apr. 1979, 18 days later, they remembered he was there. Miraculously they found him alive.

(*Top*) The greatest gorge in the world, the Grand Canyon, viewed from Yavapai Point.

(*Left*) Mauna Loa in Hawaii, the world's largest active volcano, erupted as recently as April 1984. (Colorific)

(*Above*) Sir George Everest, a Surveyor-General of India who died in 1866 but whose name lives on with the highest mountain in the world. (Mansell Collection)

(*Opposite*) Angel Falls, Vene-zuela, is the world's highest waterfall with a total drop of 3212 ft *979 m.* (David F. Hoy)

(*Top left*) Gouffre de la Pierre St-Martin in the French Pyrenees is the world's deepest cave at 4370 ft *1332 m.* (Dr A. C. Waltham)

(*Top right*) Crystals of the rare gem Painite discovered in 1951 by A. D. Pain (GB) near Ohn-gaing, Burma. (British Museum, Natural History)

(*Above*) The world's most ex-pensive gem – the 42·92 carat Tereschenko blue diamond auc-tioned for $4 580 000 in 1984.

(*Above right*) The 21 327 carat topaz, 'The Brazilian Princess' is the world's largest cut precious gem.

(*Right*) The largest piece of jade – the 28·25 ton jade boulder discovered in 1977.

(*Above*) Charles Richter, whose scale has been used to measure the severity of earthquakes worldwide since 1935.

(*Right*) The 'Old Faithful' geyser, Yellowstone National Park, California, USA.

(*Right*) Earthquake-struck Valdiva, Chile – 8·9 on the Richter scale.

EDMVND. HALLEIVS LL.D.
GEOM. PROF. SAVIL. & R.S. SECRET.

(*Top left*) The English astronomer Edmond Halley (1656–1742) who predicted exactly the return of the comet named after him (sadly though, he had been dead for 16 years when his prediction came true).

(*Top right*) Sir John Herschel (1792–1871) was the first astronomer to comprehend the universe's massive dimension. (National Gallery London)

(*Far left*) Ole Christensen Rømer (1644–1710), the great Danish astronomer.

(*Left*) A page from Rømer's log.

(*Left*) A total eclipse of the Sun.

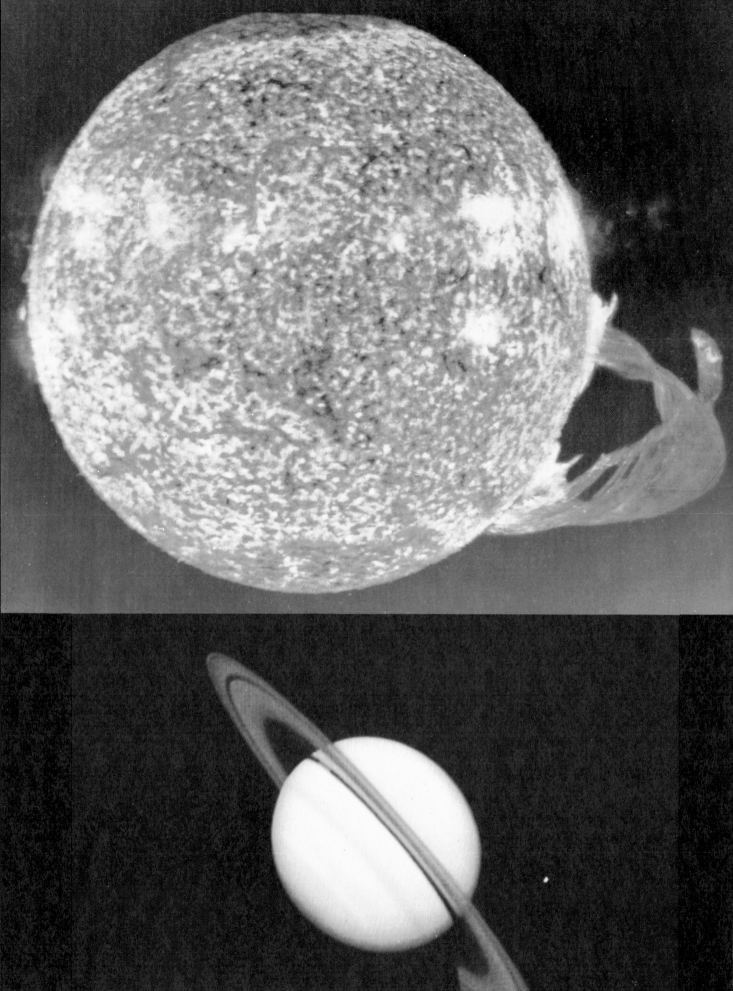

(*Opposite top*) a solar flare.

(*Opposite below*) Saturn, the ringed planet
with at least 21 satellites (NASA).

(*Right*) The brightest type of star – a super
nova.

(*Below*) The 94 ins *239 cm* primary mirror
of NASA's space telescope.

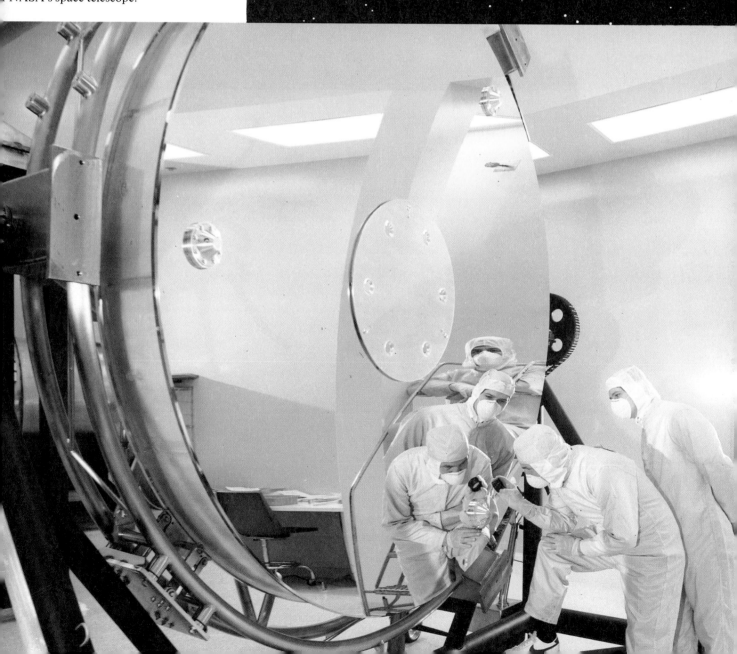

(*Top left*) The largest of all the 8733 species of birds – The North African ostrich.

(*Top right*) The Cuban Bee hummingbird – the smallest bird in the world.

(*Middle left*) The Falabella of Argentina – the smallest breed of horse.

(*Middle right*) The Blue-ringed octopus is the most venomous cephalopod, with enough poison in its bite to kill 7 people.

(*Bottom left*) The Estuarine crocodile is not only the largest of all the crocodilia but also the most predatory on humans.

(*Bottom right*) The *Theraphosa* family of spiders of north-eastern S. America is, along with the *Lasiodora* and *Grammostola* of Brazil, the largest in the world.

Medicine

Medical and surgical specialities

There are in medicine many specialities. It is possible to have Departments of Neurology, Paediatrics and Paediatric-Neurology in the same hospital. This list provides an explanation of medical departments.

Allergy – reaction of a patient to an outside substance, e.g. pollen or Penicillin, producing symptoms which may vary between being inconvenient e.g. hay fever or rashes to fatal, e.g. asthma.
Anaesthetics – the skill of putting a patient to sleep with drugs.
Anatomy – the study of the structure of the body.
Anthropology – the study of man in his environment. Physical anthropology embraces blood grouping and genetic variations.
Apothecary – a pharmacist or, in its old-fashioned sense, a general practitioner was once described as an apothecary.
Audiology – the assessment of hearing.
Aurology – the study of ear disease.
Bacteriology – the study of bacterial infections. This usually includes viruses.
Biochemistry – the study of the variation of salts and chemicals in the body.
Bio-engineering – the study of the mechanical workings of the body, particularly with reference to artificial limbs and powered appliances which the body can use.
Biophysics – the study of electrical impulses from the body. This can be seen with assessment of muscle disease etc.
Cardiology — the study of heart disease.
Community medicine – the prevention of the spread of disease and the increase of physical and mental well being within a community.
Cryo-surgery – the use of freezing techniques in surgery.
Cytogenetics – the understanding of the particles within a cell which help to reproduce the same type of being.
Cytology – the microscopic study of body cells.
Dentistry – the treatment and extraction of teeth.
Dermatology – the treatment of skin diseases.
Diabetics – the treatment of diabetes.
Embryology – the study of the growth of the baby from the moment of conception to about the 20th week.
Endocrinology – the study of the diseases of the glands which produce hormones.
E.N.T. *see* Otorhinolaryngology
Entomology – the study of insects, moths, with particular reference to their transmission of disease.
Epidemiology – the study of epidemics and the way that diseases travel from one person to another.
Forensic medicine – the study of injury and disease caused by criminal activity and the detection of crime by medical knowledge.
Gastro-enterology – the study of stomach and intestinal diseases.
Genetics – the study of inherited characteristics, disease and malformations.
Genito-urinary disease – the study of diseases of the sexual and urine-producing organs.
Geriatrics – the study of diseases and condition of elderly people.
Gerontology – the study of diseases of elderly people and in particular the study of the ageing process.
Gynaecology – the study of diseases of women.
Haematology – the study of blood diseases.
Histochemistry – the study of the chemical environment of the body cells.
Histology – the microscopic study of cells.
Histopathology – the microscopic study of diseased or abnormal cells.
Homeopathy – is a form of treatment by administering minute doses which in larger doses would reproduce the symptoms of the disease that is being treated.
Immunology – the study of the way the body reacts to outside harmful diseases and influences, e.g. the production of body proteins to overcome such diseases as diphtheria or the rejection of foreign substances like transplanted kidneys.
Laryngology – the study of throat diseases.
Metabolic disease – diseases of the interior workings of the body, e.g. disorders of calcium absorption, etc., thyroid disease or adrenal gland disease.
Microbiology – the study of the workings of cells.
Nephrology – the study of kidney disease.
Neurology – the study of a wide range of diseases of the brain or nervous system.
Neurosurgery – operations on the brain or nervous system.
Nuclear medicine – treatment of diseases with radio-active substances.
Obstetrics – the care of the pregnant mother and the delivery of the child.
Oncology – study of cancer.
Ophthalmic Optician (Optometrist) – a practitioner specially trained to assess any visual disorder and examine eyes and provide corrective treatment in the form of visual aids, e.g. spectacles, contact lenses.
Optician, dispensing – a registered dispensing optician is only allowed to dispense spectacles. The prescription is provided either by an Optometrist or an Ophthalmic Medical Practitioner.
Orthodontology – a dental approach to producing teeth that are straight.
Orthopaedics – fractures and bone diseases.
Orthoptics – treatment of squints of the eye (by an orthoptist-medically unqualified but trained practitioner).
Orthotist – an orthopaedic appliance technician.
Otology – the study of diseases of the ear.
Otorhinolaryngology – the study of diseases of the ear, nose and throat often referred to as E.N.T.
Paediatrics – diseases of children.
Parasitology – the study of infections of the body by worms and insects.
Pathology – the study of dead disease by *post mortem* examination either under the microscope or the whole organ.
Pharmacology – the study of the use of drugs in relation to medicine.
Physical medicine – the treatment of damaged parts of the body with exercises, electrical treatments, etc., or the preparation of the body for surgery, e.g. breathing exercises and leg exercises.
Physiology – the study and understanding of the normal workings of the body.
Physiotherapist – a trained person who works in the physical medicine department.
Plastic surgery – the reconstruction and alteration of damaged or normal parts of the body.
Proctology – the study of diseases of the rectum or back passage.
Prosthetics – the making of artificial limbs and appliances.
Psychiatry – the study and treatment of mental disease.
Psycho-analysis – the investigation of the formation of mental illness by long-term repeated discussion.
Psychology – the study of the mind with particular reference to the measurement of intellectual activity.
Psychotherapy – treatment of mental disorder.
Radiobiology – the treatment or investigation of disease using radio-active substances.
Radiography – the taking of X-rays.
Radiology – the study of X-rays.
Radiotherapy – the treatment of disease with X-rays.
Renal diseases – the diseases of the kidney or urinary tract.
Rheumatology – the study of diseases of muscles and joints.
Rhinology – the study of diseases of the nose.
Therapeutics – curative medicine, the healing of physical and/or mental disorder.
Thoracic surgery – surgery on the chest or heart.
Toxicology – the understanding and analysis of poisons.
Urology – the study of diseases of the kidney or urinary tract.
Vascular disease – diseases of the blood vessels.
Venereology – the study of sexually transmitted disease.
Virology – the study of virus diseases.

Glossary

abdomen The space enclosing the digestive tract and organs, in addition to various other organs. The top of the abdomen is limited by the diaphragm, the lower limit being the pelvis.
abortion Ending of a pregnancy before the foetus can survive outside the uterus.
abscess A local infection causing inflammation and the production of pus.
accommodation The action of focusing the eye, caused by altering the thickness of the lens.
acetylsalicylic acid Aspirin. It relieves pain, lowers a raised temperature and reduces inflammation.
Achilles tendon Tendon in the heel, linking the muscles in the calf to the heel-bone.
achondroplasia A form of dwarfism, caused by defective development of the bones of the skull and limbs.
acne An overproduction of grease by the sebaceous glands. The openings of the glands get blocked and act as foci of infection.
acromegaly An excess of growth hormone, resulting in, among other symptoms, enlargement of the hands and feet.
ACTH Adrenocorticotrophic hormone, produced by the pituitary gland and acting on the adrenals.
acute Describing a disease of rapid onset and short duration.
addiction A craving for a drug, resulting in tolerance of the drug and then physical dependence on the drug.
adenoid Lymph tissue at the back of the nose.
ADH Antidiuretic hormone, produced by the pituitary and affecting the kidneys.
adrenaline Produced by the adrenal glands. It stimulates the heart, circulatory system and respiratory system and inhibits digestion.
adrenals The adrenal glands are endocrine glands attached to the upper part of each kidney. They produce adrenaline (prepares body for 'fight and flight') cortisol (affects storage of glucose) and aldosterone (affects kidneys).
afterbirth The placenta.
AIDS Acquired Immune Deficiency Syndrome, disease transmitted sexually, by blood or by other body fluids. As yet (1988) no known cure.
aldosterone A hormone produced by the adrenals, affecting the kidneys. It regulates the excretion of salt.
alimentary canal The mouth, oesophagus, stomach and intestines.
alveolus Air sac in the lungs where oxygen and carbon dioxide are exchanged between the air and the blood.
amenorrhoea Lack of menstrual periods.
amniocentesis Taking a sample of the amniotic fluid from around the foetus in a pregnant woman. Analysis of the sample gives many indications as to the state of the foetus.
amnion Bag of membranes containing the foetus and amniotic fluid during pregnancy.
anaemia Lack of haemoglobin in the blood, due to loss of blood or to defective production of haemoglobin. Haemoglobin carries oxygen in the bloodstream, so anaemia gives rise to symptoms of tiredness and malaise.

anaesthetic A drug that removes sensation in a particular area or throughout the body.

analgesic A drug used to relieve pain.

anastomosis Joining two cut tubes, e.g. two lengths of intestine from which a diseased section has been removed.

aneurysm A bulge in an artery wall, caused by an area of weakness.

angina Pain in the chest caused by insufficient supply of blood (and therefore oxygen) to the heart muscle. It is due to diseased coronary arteries.

ankylosis Loss of movement in a joint, usually caused by arthritis.

anorexia A neurosis involving loss of appetite and rejection of food.

antibiotic Naturally occurring or synthetic drug that kills bacteria. Antibiotics are thus used to treat bacterial infections.

antibody A chemical produced by the body's immune system in order to neutralize a specific harmful chemical or substance, e.g. microorganism.

anticoagulant Drug that prevents blood from clotting.

antigen A chemical against which an antibody is formed and which the antibody 'attacks'.

antiserum Serum extracted from the blood of an animal that is immune to a specific microorganism, e.g. hepatitis.

antitoxin Antibody that neutralizes a specific toxin or antigen.

arrhythmia An alteration in the natural rhythm of the heart.

arteriosclerosis A loss of elasticity in the arteries.

artery Blood vessel carrying blood away from the heart. Apart from the artery carrying blood from the heart in the lungs, all arteries carry oxygenated blood.

arthritis Inflammation of a joint, giving pain and restricted movement.

asthma Contraction of the air tubes in the lungs, caused by infection, allergy or stress. The result is very difficult breathing.

athletes' foot Fungal infection of the skin between the toes.

bacteria Microorganisms, capable of being seen with a light microscope, that live off living, dead or inorganic material.

barbiturates Group of drugs used as sedatives, as anaesthetics and to promote sleep. They are potentially addictive drugs.

bed-sore Pressure of skin and tissue against bone caused by prolonged time spent in bed. The blood supply to the area is reduced and eventually a slow-healing ulcer is formed.

benign Mild, usually self-limiting, form of a disease.

bile A secretion of the liver, formed by the breakdown of haemoglobin. It helps in the digestion of fats in the small intestine.

biopsy Removal of a piece of living tissue for examination.

bladder Muscular bag into which urine drains from the kidneys, before being passed out via the urethra.

blood pressure The pressure in the arteries, caused by the pumping action of the heart. It fluctuates with the heart beat.

breech delivery Delivery of a baby at birth bottom first (instead of head first).

bronchitis Inflammation, often due to infection, of the airways in the lungs, i.e. the bronchi and the bronchioles. Over-production of mucus is a common symptom.

bruise Bump or knock causing bleeding into the skin and surface tissues. As the blood decomposes, it gives the characteristic colours of a bruise.

calcitonin Hormone produced by the thyroid. It lowers the concentration of calcium in the blood.

callus A hard area of skin, formed as a result of pressure or friction.

Calorie The use of the Calorie to indicate energy values of foods is common. A Calorie indicates the amount of energy required to warm 1 kg of water by 1°C; the calorific value of a food indicates the amount of such energy liberated if the food were completely burnt.

cancer An uncontrolled cell growth, in which the body's usual checks and controls are absent for some reason.

capillary Blood vessel of one cell diameter. Capillaries form a network within the tissues and act as a link between the arteries and veins.

carcinogen A substance or drug with the potential of causing cancer.

cardiac Pertaining to the heart.

cataract An opaque area that develops on the lens of the eye.

cautery A small burn, caused electrically or by use of a laser, used to seal small cut blood vessels.

cerebrospinal fluid Fluid, derived from blood, which surrounds, and is found within cavities of, the brain and spinal cord.

cervical Either pertaining to the cervix of the womb or pertaining to the neck of the womb.

chemotherapy Treating a disease with chemicals.

cholesterol A fatty chemical, found throughout the body. However it can be deposited in the blood vessels, causing blockages.

chorea Uncontrolled jerky muscular contractions.

chromosome That part of the cell which contains genetic material.

chronic Describing a disease of slow onset and long duration.

cirrhosis Disease of the liver caused by scarring. The scar tissue is hard and fibrous and eventually is liable to affect the whole liver.

clavicle Collar-bone.

cold An infection, initially viral, of the mucous membranes of the nose and throat.

cold sore An infection with the herpes virus around the mouth, causing raised blisters.

colitis Inflammation of the colon or large intestine, either due to infection or, in the case of ulcerative colitis, due to an unknown cause.

colon The large intestine, from the ileum to the rectum.

congenital An abnormality or disease is congenital if the baby is born with it.

conjunctivitis Inflammation of the conjunctiva of the eye, usually caused by viral or bacterial infection.

consumption Traditionally an alternative name for tuberculosis.

corn A form of callus on the foot.

coronary arteries Arteries providing the blood supply to the heart muscle.

costal Pertaining to the ribs.

cramp A spasm of a muscle or group of muscles.

Crohn's disease Inflammation of the final section of the small intestine (the ileum), due to an unknown cause.

cystitis Inflammation of the bladder, usually due to a bacterial infection.

dandruff Condition in which flakes of skin are shed from the scalp.

diabetes In full, diabetes mellitus. A disease due to a deficiency of, or inability to use properly, insulin formed in the pancreas.

diagnosis The identification of a disease from various signs and symptoms.

dialysis Removal of harmful waste products from the blood by an osmotic process in an artificial kidney.

diaphragm A domed sheet of muscle separating the thoracic cavity from the abdominal cavity.

dilatation A process of widening, either as one of the body's reflexes or by mechanical means.

disc A cartilaginous pad between each vertebra, acting as a shock absorber and imparting flexibility to the spinal column as a whole.

diuretic A drug used to increase the flow of urine.

drug A chemical given to help relieve the symptoms of a disease or to modify any of the body's natural processes.

duodenum The first section of the small intestine, between the stomach and the jejunum.

dysmenorrhoea Painful menstrual periods.

dyspnoea Difficulty in breathing.

ECG Electrocardiogram or measurement of the electrical changes in the heart muscle.

ECT Electroconvulsive therapy. Application of an electric shock to the scalp, used to treat certain mental illnesses, especially depression.

ectopic pregnancy A pregnancy in an abnormal position, e.g. in the Fallopian tube.

eczema An inflammatory condition of the skin, often due to an allergy.

EEG Electroencephalogram or measurement of electrical changes in the brain.

embolism Blockage of an artery by an air bubble or, more commonly, a blood clot.

emetic A drug given to induce vomiting.

emphysema Damage to the lungs whereby the tiny air sacs at the ends of the airways break down, leading to breathlessness.

encephalitis A viral infection of the brain.

endemic A disease that is always present in a given area.

endocrine gland A ductless gland that releases secretions (hormones) into the bloodstream, rather than into a duct for local use.

endoscopy Examination of internal organs using a tube lit from the inside; fibre-optics are invariably used now.

enteritis Inflammation of the intestine, usually due to an infection.

epidemic A disease introduced to a given area. It appears, spreads and then disappears, usually until the next outbreak.

epilepsy Convulsive attacks or fits, of an unknown cause.

erythrocyte A red blood cell.

Eustachian tube A passage leading from the back of the nose to the middle ear.

expectorant A drug that loosens mucus in the respiratory tract, particularly the lungs, and aids coughing.

faeces Waste residue of food, dead and live bacteria, and water, expelled from the rectum.

farmer's lung An allergic response to fungi found in hay, straw, etc.

fibrin A protein produced in the blood during the clotting process. It forms the matrix within which the clot forms.

fibroid A lumpy benign tumour of the uterus.

fistula A passage between two parts of the body, either as a result of a wound, e.g. a stab wound, or as a result of a deliberate operation.

foetus Unborn baby, more advanced than an embryo in that it is recognisably human.

forearm The part of the arm between the elbow and the wrist.

fracture A broken bone, either completely or partially broken.

frostbite Damage to the skin and deeper tissues due to ice crystals forming.

fungi Very simple plant forms with parasitic or saprophytic life style. Some forms cause infections, usually of the skin but sometimes internally.

gall bladder Sac under the lower side of the liver that acts as a storage organ for bile.

gall stone Solid crystalline lump precipitated from the bile in the gall bladder.

gamma globulin Blood proteins responsible for immunity to specific diseases. They can be separated and given to non-immune recipients, thus conferring short-term immunity.

gangrene Death and bacterial decay of tissue.

gastric Pertaining to the stomach.

gastric ulcer A stomach ulcer.

gastritis Inflammation of the stomach lining.

gastro-enteritis Inflammation of the stomach and intestine.

gingivitis Inflammation of the gums, caused by infection.

glaucoma High pressure within the eyeball resulting in defects in vision.

goitre Swelling of the thyroid gland.

gout Formation of uric acid crystals around joints.

gullet The oesophagus.

haemoglobin The complex protein molecule that gives red blood cells their colour. It transports oxygen in the bloodstream.

haemolysis The breakdown of red blood cells.

haemophilia An inherited disease characterized by an inability of the blood to form clots.

haemorrhage Bleeding.

halothane An anaesthetic gas.

hamstring muscles Muscles at the back of the thigh that flex the knee.

hay fever An allergy to pollen, particularly grass pollens. It causes acute irritation to the mucous membranes of the nose and to the conjunctiva of the eye.

hemiplegia Paralysis of one half of the body caused by damage or disease in the opposite half of the brain.

hepatic Pertaining to the liver.

hepatitis Inflammation of the liver, usually viral.

hernia A rupture, or protrusion of an organ from one body compartment into another compartment.

herpes One group of herpes viruses, *Herpes simplex*, causes cold sores and venereal herpes; the other group, *Herpes zoster*, causes shingles.

hiatus hernia Protrusion of a section of the stomach through the oesophageal opening in the diaphragm.

Hodgkin's disease A form of cancer of the lymph tissues, resulting in lowered resistance to infections.

hormone A chemical, released directly into the bloodstream by one organ (an endocrine gland) in order to regulate other organs or body functions.

hyper- Prefix meaning too much.

hypertension Raised blood pressure.

hyperthermia High body temperature.

hypo- Prefix meaning too little.

hypochondria A preoccupation with or anxiety about one's health.

hypoglycaemia Too low a level of glucose in the blood.

hypothermia Lowered body temperature.

iatrogenic Disease or condition produced as a result of treatment given for another disease or condition.

ileum Latter section of the small intestine, leading into the large intestine.

ilium The haunch-bone; part of the pelvis.

immunity The natural or acquired resistance of a body to invading, i.e. 'foreign', chemicals. The immune system can deal with 'invaders' larger than chemicals, e.g. microorganisms, transplants, but this is because it reacts to chemicals on the surface of the microorganism or transplant.

immunization The production of immunity to a specific disease.

incontinence Inability to control the emptying of the bladder or bowels.

incubation period The time it takes between infection with a disease-causing microorganism and the production of disease symptoms.

infarct An area of dead tissue resulting from a blocked blood vessel.

infection The entry of microorganisms into the body, their subsequent multiplication and the production of disease symptoms.

inflammation Heat, redness, pain and swelling produced as defensive reaction by the body to infection or damage.

inoculation Form of immunization in which a live harmless varient of the disease-causing microorganism is used to infect the body, producing immunity to both the harmless and harmful microorganisms.

insulin Hormone produced in the pancreas which regulates the metabolism of sugars by controlling the uptake of glucose from the blood by the body's cells.

intercostal muscles Muscles between the ribs.

ischaemia Lack of blood to part of the body.

islets of Langerhans Groups of cells in the pancreas responsible for the production of insulin.

IUD Intrauterine device. A form of contraception; a coil or loop implanted in the uterus prevents a fertilized ovum from embedding in the uterus wall and developing into an embryo.

jaundice Yellowing of skin. It is caused by a build-up of bile pigments in the blood.

jejunum The middle section of the small intestine, between the duodenum and the ileum.

jugular Pertaining to the neck.

lacrimal Pertaining to tears, e.g. lacrimal gland above the eye.

laparotomy Incision in the abdominal wall, usually for purposes of examination.

large intestine The latter part of the intestine, between the small intestine and the rectum.

larynx The voice box, at the front of the throat.

lesion An injury, wound or harmful disturbance to an organ or tissue.

leucocyte White blood cell.

leukaemia A form of cancer in which there is over-production of under-developed, and therefore useless, white blood cells.

ligament A fibrous band of tissue holding two bones together at a joint.

linctus A syrupy medicine given to soothe coughing.

louse Insects which infest the hair of the body. Their eggs are called nits.

lumbar Pertaining to the lower back.

lymph Fluid from the blood which leaks out of the capillaries, bathes the tissues and returns to the blood system via the lymphatic system.

lymphatic system A network of vessels and glands which collect and filter the lymph before returning it to the blood system.

malignant Severe, often fatal, form of a disease.

malnutrition Deficiency in the quality or quantity of food.

meconium Fluid consisting largely of mucus and bile, passed out of an infant's bowels soon after birth.

menarche The appearance of menstruation at puberty.

meninges Membranes enclosing the brain and spinal cord.

meningitis Inflammation of the meninges due to viral or bacterial infection.

menopause The disappearance of menstruation, usually between the ages of about 40 and 50.

menorrhagia Heavy bleeding during menstruation.

metabolism The sum total of the chemical reactions in the body by which nutrients are converted to energy, tissues are renewed, replaced and regenerated and waste products are broken down.

microorganism Any organism too small to be seen with the naked eye. Usually taken to mean viruses, bacteria and some fungi and protozoans.

migraine Acute form of headache, perhaps allergic in origin, sometimes causing nausea and visual disturbances.

miscarriage Accidental abortion.

multiple sclerosis A chronic disease in which areas of the central nervous system degenerate. A variety of symptoms can be involved, depending on the areas of degeneration, and these symptoms can appear and disappear at random, so it seems.

myasthenia gravis Progressive form of muscle disease in which voluntary muscles become weaker.

myocardial Pertaining to the heart muscle.

narcolepsy Disease characterized by periods of uncontrollable sleepiness.

narcotic Drug producing dulling or loss of consciousness.

nausea Urge to vomit.

neonatal Pertaining to new-born babies.

nephritis Inflammation of the kidney, due to infection, chemical poisoning or other reasons.

neuralgia Acute pain originating in a nerve.

neuritis Inflammation of a nerve.

nit The egg of a louse, found firmly attached to a hair or to fibres of clothing.

nystagmus Reflex rapid movements of the eyes, designed to keep moving objects in view.

obesity An excess of body fat.

oedema An excess of fluid in the tissues, either generally or locally, causing swelling.

oesophagus That section of the digestive tract between the pharynx and the stomach.

organ A distinct structure in the body designed to perform a particular function.

osteoarthritis Destruction of the cartilaginous surfaces that allow bones to move over each other.

osteoporosis Weakening of the bones in old age due to a reduction in the calcium content of the bones.

oxytocin Hormone produced by the pituitary gland that stimulates contractions of the uterus during labour.

palate The roof of the mouth. The hard palate is at the front, the soft palate at the back.

pancreas A gland at the back of the abdomen. It secretes digestive juices into the small intestine, and also acts as an endocrine gland, producing insulin from the islets of Langerhans.

pandemic A widespread epidemic.

paracetamol An analgesic.

paraplegia Paralysis of the lower half of the body.

parathyroids A group of small endocrine glands associated with the thyroid gland. They produce parathormone which controls the level of calcium in the blood.

Parkinson's disease A form of paralysis in which the muscles become stiff, movement awkward, and a rhythmic twitching affects the muscles locally or generally.

patella The kneecap.

pectoral Pertaining to the chest.

pelvis Ring of bone which forms the base of the abdominal cavity and which forms the hip joint on each side.

peptic ulcer Ulcer of the stomach or duodenum.

pericarditis Inflammation of the pericardium or fibrous sheath surrounding the heart.

perinatal Pertaining to the period shortly before, during and shortly after birth.

peristalsis Rhythmic contractions producing flow along the digestive tract.

peritoneum The membrane lining the abdominal cavity.

peritonitis Inflammation of the peritoneum.

pharynx That part of the throat, from the back of the nose to the opening of the oesophagus, concerned with both breathing and swallowing.

phlebitis Inflammation of a vein, usually due to blockage of the vein by a clot.

phlegm Mucus.

phrenic Pertaining to the diaphragm.

piles Haemorrhoids; distended varicose veins just inside the anus.

pituitary An endocrine gland on the underside of the brain. It produces a number of hormones: ACTH, which controls the adrenal glands; thyrotrophic hormone which controls the thyroid gland; gonadotrophic hormones, which control the ovaries and testes; growth hormone, controlling growth; prolactin, controlling milk production in the breasts; oxytocin, controlling contraction of the uterus during labour; and ADH, controlling loss of water from the body in the urine.

plasma The fluid component of blood.

platelet Small particle found in blood. Platelets are involved in the clotting mechanism.

pleura A double membrane surrounding the lungs.

pleurisy Inflammation of the pleura, usually due to infection.

pneumonia Inflammation of the lungs, due to infection. It affects the alveoli or air pockets at the ends of the airways.

pneumothorax Air between the lungs and chest wall, impairing breathing.

polycythaemia The opposite of anaemia; an excess of red blood cells.

polyp Tumour, usually benign, growing out from a mucous membrane and attached to the membrane by a stalk.

poultice A hot dressing applied to inflamed surface areas.

prickly heat Blockage of sweat glands and production of tiny blisters and an irritating rash.

progesterone Hormone produced in the ovaries; it acts on the uterus such that it prepares itself to receive fertilized ovum.

prognosis Forecast of the course a disease will take.

prolactin Hormone produced by the pituitary that stimulates the breasts to secrete milk.

prolapse Displacement of an organ from its normal position, usually due to gravity.

prophylaxis Prevention of disease.

prostate gland Gland found only in males. It secretes part of the seminal fluid into the urethra.

prosthesis Artificial replacement for part of the body.

psoriasis Scaly red blotches formed on the skin. The complaint tends to come and go, for unknown reasons.

puerperal Pertaining to childbirth.

pulmonary Pertaining to the lungs.

pus Dead cells, dead white blood cells, dead bacteria and tissue fluid.

pyloric stenosis A constriction of the outlet from the stomach to the duodenum.

rabies A disease of a variety of animals. Humans can be infected via an animal bite. Symptoms include fever, delirium, muscle spasms and paralysis. Spasm of the throat muscles causes the inability to drink or hydrophobia.

rectum The last section of the digestive tract, between the large intestine and anus.

referred pain Pain which occurs in a different part of the body to the site of injury or trauma.

reflex An automatic response to a stimulus.

remission Temporary subsidence of the symptoms of a disease.

renal Pertaining to the kidneys.

rheumatic fever Acute disease, generally of children and adolescents, involving raised temperature and inflammation of various parts of the body at different times, including the joints and the valves and lining of the heart.

rheumatism Pain or inflammation of the joints or muscles.

rheumatoid arthritis Formation of inflamed knots of fibrous tissue, usually around joints.

rickets Faulty bone growth due to a lack of vitamin D.

rodent ulcer A type of skin cancer in which a hard lump appears on the face. The centre of the lump subsequently breaks down to form an ulcer.

sciatica Pain in the region of the sciatic nerve at the back of the thigh, calf and foot.

sclerosis Thickening or hardening of a particular tissue.

scoliosis Curvature of the spine sideways.

sebum Greasy material formed by the sebaceous glands of the skin.

sedative A drug that calms or renders someone sleepy.

senility Changes in the brain in old age.

sepsis Infection of tissues, causing damage.

septicaemia Spread of an infection into the blood, which thereby carries the infecting agent throughout the body.

serum Straw-coloured fluid that separates from blood as it clots.

shingles Another name for *Herpes zoster*; a viral infection of nerves, causing painful blisters on the skin in the area that the infected nerve serves.

shock Sudden drop in blood pressure causing failure of the blood circulation system.

sign Any indication of a disease observed by the doctor, nurse, etc.

sinew A tendon or ligament.

sinus A hollow cavity opening off a passageway, e.g. the nasal sinuses opening off the nose. It can also mean merely a bulge in a tube.

sinusitis Inflammation of the mucous membrane of the nasal sinuses.

spasm Uncontrolled contraction of a muscle or group of muscles.

spastic paralysis Loss or limitation of controlled movement in various muscles, due to disease of the nervous system.

sphincter Ring of muscle around an opening to a hollow or tubular organ.

spina bifida Congenital disease in which the vertebrae do not close over the spinal column, allowing the meninges to protrude.

spleen An organ at the top of the abdominal cavity, responsible for white blood cell production, breakdown of red blood cells and some control of immunity.

spondylitis Inflammation of the vertebrae, often with loss of mobility.

sputum Mucus.

squint Poor alignment of the eyes; they either turn inwards (convergent squint) or outwards (divergent squint).

stenosis Constriction or narrowing of a tube, e.g. part of the digestive tract.

stroke Interruption of blood supply to part of the brain.

subcutaneous Beneath the skin.

suture The surgical stitching used to close a wound or incision.

symptom Any indication of a disease observed by the patient.

syndrome A group of symptoms that frequently occur together, although they may not always be caused by the same disease.

systemic Pertaining to the body as a whole.

temperature The 'normal' body temperature is between 36°C and 37·5°C (97–9°F) when taken in the mouth. However it will vary between these limits during the day and, for women, during their menstrual cycle.

tendon Fibre joining muscle to bone.

tetanus Infection of a wound with the bacteria *Clostridium tetani*. The bacteria produces a poison which causes the characteristic muscle spasms.

thorax The space enclosing the heart, lungs, and oesophagus. It is bounded by the rib-cage and the diaphragm.

thrombosis Partial or complete blockage of a blood vessel by a blood clot.

thrombus A blood clot formed on the inside surface of a blood vessel.

thrush Infection of a mucous membrane, usually of the mouth, by a fungus.

thyroid Endocrine gland in the neck. It produces thyroxine, which controls energy production in the tissues; and calcitonin, which controls the calcium levels in the blood.

tissue A collection of cells, usually of the same type, specialized to perform a particular function.

tolerance The need to administer larger and larger doses of a drug over time, as the body gets used to it.

tomography An X-ray examination in which a 'slice' of the body is looked at.

tonsil Lymph tissue at the back of the mouth.

topical Pertaining to the surface of the body.

tourniquet A constricting strap or band applied to a limb to stop arterial bleeding.

toxaemia Poisoning of the blood by toxins from infecting bacteria.

toxin Poisonous substance, usually produced by bacteria.

toxoid A toxin that has been chemically modified to render it harmless. It is still able to produce an immune response when used to immunize against the original toxin.

trachea The windpipe. A tube strengthened with cartilage that runs between the larynx and the bronchi that pass into the lungs.

tranquillizer Drug used to calm the mood without inducing sleepiness.

transfusion Transfer of blood from a healthy to an ill person.

transplantation Transfer of a healthy organ to a patient to replace a diseased organ.

trauma Physical damage to tissue, e.g. a wound.

tropical ulcer Ulceration of the skin, usually on the leg, commonly found in the tropics. It is very slow to heal.

tubal pregnancy A form of ectopic pregnancy occurring in the Fallopian tubes.

tumour A group of cells that starts to divide without the usual checks and controls imposed by the body. It may be malignant or benign.

ulcer Breakdown of the skin or mucous membrane that heals very slowly or not at all.

ultrasound Sound waves at a frequency well above the range of human hearing, used to provide an image of internal structures.

ureter Tube leading from the kidney to the bladder.

urethra Tube leading from the bladder to the exterior.

uvula The soft projection hanging down at the back of the mouth.

vaccination Use of dead or a harmless form of microorganism to produce artificial immunity to the harmful form of the microorganism.

vaccine The dead or harmless microorganisms used in a vaccination.

varicose veins Swollen veins, usually in the legs, due to collapse of the valves in the veins allowing backflow of blood.

vascular Pertaining to blood vessels.

vein Blood vessel returning blood from the tissues to the heart. Apart from the vein carrying blood from the lungs to the heart, all veins carry deoxygenated blood.

venereal disease Sexually transmitted disease.

vertigo a form of dizziness in which the subject feels the surroundings are spinning round.

viruses Microorganisms, smaller than bacteria and incapable of being seen with a light microscope. They can only reproduce inside living cells.

vitamins Chemicals found in foodstuffs or synthesized by the body. They are not nutrients, but are essential for the normal functioning of growth, repair and reproduction.

wart A small tumour of the outer layer of the skin caused by a virus.

Vaccines

Anthrax – a killed vaccine which is recommended for workers at particular risk, e.g. farmers, and butchers. Doses should be given yearly.

Bubonic Plague – killed and live vaccines can be used to limit epidemics. They give about six months' protection.

Cholera – two injections of the killed organism should be given 10 days apart and will give 3–6 months' protection. Thereafter injections should be given six-monthly. It only gives moderate protection.

Diphtheria – the toxoid is given in a course of 3 injections to infants and a booster dose at the age of 5 will give long-lasting immunity. Antitoxin is used for those who have caught diphtheria. It gives temporary protection.

German Measles (Rubella) – a modified living vaccine is recommended to be given to all girls between the age of 11 and 13, i.e. before the onset of menstruation, and protects against infection of the foetus and thus congenital malformations.

Influenza – killed vaccines will give about 70 per cent protection for 9 months to a year in epidemics of a similar virus. They are particularly useful in those who tend to have respiratory illness, the infirm or elderly. Modified living virus vaccines are at present under assessment.

Jaundice (Infective Hepatitis) – a vaccine against one of the varieties (hepatitis B) is now being assessed and will soon be available.

Measles – a modified living vaccine is given in the second year of life and will give prolonged protection and, in about 50 per cent, will produce a very mild feverish illness. It does not produce encephalitis.

Meningococcal meningitis – killed vaccines of both types A and C have been produced. They help in the prevention of the spread of epidemics.

Mumps – a modified living vaccine gives long-lasting protection. It is often used for adults who have not had the natural infection.

Pneumonia – (when due to the pneumococcus bacteria). A vaccine is now available for use in the elderly and others vulnerable to this infection. Reimmunization every 2–3 years is recommended.

Poliomyelitis – Sabin modified living oral vaccine gives long-term protection. It is usually given in 3 doses to infants, and a booster dose at the age of 5, and sometimes in the early teens. It rarely causes cases of clinical poliomyelitis. Salk vaccine is the killed virus and gives short-term protection. It is seldom used nowadays.

Rabies – protection is obtained with 3 injections of a vaccine at one and then six months apart. If a person has been bitten injections should be given at once and on the third, seventh and fourteenth days, and then one and three months.

Smallpox – From 1st January 1980 the World

Health Organization has declared the world free from smallpox. Vaccination is only needed for research scientists working with the virus.

Tetanus – the toxoid is usually given in 3 injections combined with diphtheria and sometimes whooping cough. A booster dose at the age of 5 and then boosters every 5 years. Antitoxin (A.T.S.) is given to those in immediate danger of developing tetanus.

Tuberculosis – Bacille Calmette-Guerin (BCG) is a modified living organism which is given to those aged between 10 and 13 in the UK by the school health authorities. It gives lifelong immunity.

Typhoid and Paratyphoid – the vaccine containing the killed organisms of Paratyphoid A & B does not give protection against these infections. A Typhoid vaccine protects about 50% of those immunized with two injections at 4–6 weeks apart. Booster injections are given yearly to those living in areas where the disease is common and every 2–3 years to those less at risk.

Typhus – highly effective killed vaccines will give protection for about a year.

Whooping Cough – this is usually combined in 3 injections with diphtheria and tetanus. There is evidence that it rarely causes brain damage and for this reason some infants should not have the injections. However the risk of damage in healthy infants from the natural disease is greater than that from immunization.

Yellow Fever – a modified living vaccine will give 10 years' protection and this is recognized on an international vaccination certificate.

Principal drugs in order of their discovery

Drugs are listed in order of the date of their introduction to show the development of modern therapeutics.

BC *ante*

c. 2100 *Ethyl alcohol* or *ethanol* (C_2H_5OH). One of the earliest drugs used to stupefy.

AD

c. 1550 *Digitalis*, a mixture of compounds from the leaf of the Foxglove (*Digitalis purpurea* and *D. lanata*), used to treat congestive heart failure. Employed by herbalists since the 16th century and introduced into scientific medicine by William Withering (GB) in 1785. Its components, particularly digoxin, are still in use.

1805 *Morphine*. Addictive narcotic analgesic, an alkaloid of opium which is the dried latex from the unripe capsules of the poppy (*Papaver somniferum*). First recognized by Friedrich Sertürner (Germany) in 1805 but not used in medical practice till 1821. Synthesized in 1952.

1818 *Quinine*. Obtained from Cinchona tree bark. Separated by P J Pelletier and J B Caventou (France) 1818 to 1820. Antimalarial use.

1819 *Atropine*. An anticholinergic agent isolated in 1819 by Rudolph Brandes from belladonna (*Atropa belladonna*). The related drug hyocine is used to prevent motion sickness.

1820 *Colchicine*. Drug derived from meadow saffron (*Colchicum autumnale*), used particularly in the treatment of gout. Isolated in 1820 by P J Pelletier and J B Caventou.

1821 *Codeine*. Occurs naturally in opium and is a derivative of morphine (q.v.). Antitussive, weak analgesic.

1842 *Ether* (diethyl ether). General anaesthetic. First administered by Dr C W Long (1815–78) in Jefferson, Georgia, on 30 Mar. 1842 for a cystectomy.

1844 *Nitrous Oxide* (N_2O) (Laughing Gas). Short-acting general anaesthetic used in dentistry and obstetrics. Discovered in 1776 by Joseph Priestley (GB). First used as anaesthetic in 1844 by an American dentist, Horace Wells.

1846 *Glyceryl Trinitrate* (nitroglycerin). Known mainly as an explosive. Used as a vasodilator in easing cardiac pains in angina pectoris. First prepared in 1846 by Ascanio Sobrero of Italy.

1847 *Chloroform*. Introduced as an anaesthetic by Sir James Simpson (UK) but rarely used today.

1859 *Cocaine* (from the Peruvian coca bean (*Erythroxylon coca* and *E. truxillense*)). First separated by Niemann. Formula established by Wöhler in 1860. Local anaesthetic, which results in dependence.

1867 *Phenol* (Carbolic acid (C_6H_5OH)). Earliest bactericide and disinfectant, discovered by Lister in 1867. Antiseptic and antipruritic.

1891 *Thyroid Extract*. First used as injection in treatment for myxoedema by George Murray in 1891. The active principles are *tri-iodothyronine* and *thyroxine*.

1893 *Aspirin* (acetylsalicylic acid). A nonsteroidal anti-inflammatory and analgesic drug, introduced in 1893 by Hermann Dresser.

1893 *Paracetamol* (Acetaminophen). First used in medicine by Joseph von Mering in 1893, but only gained popularity as an antipyretic analgesic in 1949.

1901 *Adrenaline* (epinephrine). Hormone secreted by medulla of adrenal gland in response to stress. It mimics the effects of stimulation of the sympathetic (adrenergic) autonomic nervous system. First isolated in 1901 by J Takamine (1854–1922) and T B Aldrick and synthesized in 1904 by Friedrich Stolz (1860–1936).

1903 *Barbitone*. Early example of barbituric acid derivatives (barbiturates) with hypnotic, sedative and anti-convulsant properties, e.g. phenobarbitone (long-acting), pentobarbitone (intermediate), thiopentone (short-acting).

1906 *Vitamins*. F G Hopkins (1861–1947) established essentiality of vitamins. Principal vitamins now administered are Vitamin A, B_1, B_2, B_6, B_{12}, C, D, K, M and PP.

1906 *Procaine* (Novocaine). Local anaesthetic, a non-habit forming substitute for cocaine introduced by Alfred Einhorn. Largely superseded by lignocaine.

1907 *Histamine*. Isolated by Adolf Windus (1876–1959) and Karl Vogt (b. 1880). One of a number of substances released by body tissues as part of allergic or inflammatory responses. The earliest anti-histamine was 933 F discovered by G Ungar (France) *et al.* in 1937.

1912 *Acriflavine*. Introduced as an antiseptic by Paul Ehrlich.

1917 *Oxygen*. The most plentiful element in the Earth's crust. Discovered 1771 by the Swede, Carl Wilhelm Scheele and independently in 1774 by Joseph Priestley (GB). First used therapeutically by J S Haldane in 1917.

1921 *Ergometrine*. One of a mixture of ergot alkaloids found in rye grain infected with the fungus *Claviceps purpurea*. Used as a uterine stimulant. First isolated by K Spiro and A Stoll (Germany) in 1921. Another component *Ergotamine* is used to treat migraine.

1921 *Insulin*, the specific antidiabetic hormone from the mammalian pancreas. Isolated by Sir Frederick Banting (1891–1941) and Dr C H Best (1899–1978), Toronto, Canada, in 1921. First synthesized in 1964.

1929 *Progesterone*. Female steroid hormone secreted by ovary following ovulation to prepare uterus for, and to maintain, pregnancy. Isolated by G Corner and W Allen in 1929. Related compounds are used with oestrogen, or alone, in oral contraceptives.

1929 *Testosterone*. Androgenic (masculinising) hormone. First obtained in 1929 by C Moore, T. Gallagher and F. Koch. Related anabolic (muscle-building) steroids abused by participants in sporting activities.

1930 *Mepacrine (quinacrine)*. Antimalarial. Now replaced by Chloroquine.

1933 *Adrenocorticotrophic hormone* (ACTH). First isolated by J B Collip (b. 1892) *et al.* Active against arthritis.

1935 *Thiopentone*. Very short-acting barbiturate intravenous anaesthetic.

1935 *Tubocurarine*. Alkaloid isolated from curare (a S. American Indian arrow-poison) in 1935 by Harold King, used as a skeletal-muscle relaxant.

1936 *Oestradiol*. The principal oestrogenic female hormone, isolated by D MacCorquodale in 1936.

1937 *Dapsone*. Bacteriostatic drug, effects in treatment of leprosy noted in 1937.

1937 *Sulphonamides*. Analogues of p-aminobenzoic acid with antibacterial activity. The most used early 'sulpha' drug was sulphapyridine (May and Baker 693), from 1937 (Dr Arthur Ewins).

1938 *Phenytoin*. Anticonvulsant introduced in 1938 by Merritt and Pulman for most types of epilepsy.

1939 *DDT* (Dichloro-diphenyl-trichloroethane). A powerful insecticide developed by Dr Paul Müller which has vastly lowered the malarial death rate by killing the malaria-carrying mosquitoes.

1939 *Pethidine*. A narcotic analgesic used particularly during childbirth. Introduced 1939 by Hoechst. Synthesized by Eisleb and Schaumann.

1940 *Penicillins*. Group of antibacterial substances (e.g. penicillin G, the benzyl derivative). Discovered in 1928 by Sir Alexander Fleming (1881–1955) by the chance contamination of a petri dish at St Mary's Hospital, London. First concentrated in 1940 by Sir Howard Florey (1898–1968) and E B Chain (1906–79). Not identified as *Penicillium notatum* until 1930. Penicillin G introduced 1946. In 1961 Chain *et al.* isolated *p-aminopenicillanic acid* which is the nucleus for many semi-synthetic derivatives.

1943 *LSD* (Lysergic acid diethylamide). A hallucinogen, discovered by Albert Hofman (Switzerland) in Apr. 1943. Now has no recognized therapeutic use.

1943 *Dimercaprol (BAL)* (formerly British Anti-Lewisite). Developed during the war by L Stocken and R Thompson, to combat lethal war gas, lewisite. Later uses discovered as antidote to poisoning by arsenic, gold or mercury.

1943 *Streptomycin*. An antibiotic discovered by S A Waksman (Russian born, USA) in 1943. Important for its activity against tuberculosis.

1944 *Mepyramine (Pyrilamine)*. First acceptable antihistamine.

1944 *Amphetamine*. A central nervous system stimulant, formerly widely abused.

1944 *Paludrine* (proguanil hydrochloride). An antimalarial drug.

1947 *Chloramphenicol*. An antibiotic from *Streptomyces venezuelae* used for treatment of typhoid. First isolated by Buckholder (USA) in 1947 and first synthesized in 1949.

1948 *Chlortetracycline (Aureomycin)*. An antibiotic first isolated in 1948 at Pearl River, NY, USA, by Dr Benjamin M Duggar.

1948 *Imipramine*. A benzodiazepine derivative, synthesized by Häfliger in 1948. An antidepressant.

1949 *Cortisone*. One of a number of steroid hormones from adrenal cortical extracts so named in 1939. First used in treatment of rheumatoid arthritis in 1949 leading to development of many anti-inflammatory steroids.

1951 *Halothane* ($C_2HBrClF_3$). General anaesthetic first synthesized in 1951 by Suckling.

1952 *Chlorpromazine*. Potent tranquilliser first synthesized by Charpentier in 1952. Acts selectively upon higher centre in brain as a central nervous system depressant.

1952 *Isoniazid* (Isonicotinic Acid Hydrazide, INH). Used in the treatment of tuberculosis, reported on by Edward Robitzek in 1952.

1954 *Methyldopa*. Used in treatment of hypertension. Effects first noted in 1954 by Sourkes.

1954 *Reserpine*. Tranquilliser from Rauwolfia, a genus of plant in the dogbane family, used in treatment of high blood pressure. Effects noted in modern times by Kline in 1954.

1955 *Oral Contraceptives*. The first reported field studies of a pill containing synthetic hormones that prevent ovulation were those by Pincus using Enovid in 1955, in Puerto Rico.

1955 *Metronidazole*. Based on discovery of Azomycin in 1955 by Nakamura. Used in treatment of trichomoniasis, and other protozoal infections.

1956 *Amphotericin*. An antifungal antibiotic used topically. Elucidated in 1956 by Vandeputte *et al*.

1957 *Interferon*. A group of proteins produced by virus-infected cells. They inhibit the multiplication of viruses.

c. 1960 *Tolbutamide*. Reduces blood sugar level in diabetics.

1960 *Chlordiazepoxide* ('Librium'). Tranquillizer for treatment of anxiety and tension states, convulsive states and neuromuscular and cardiovascular disorders. Effects first noted in 1960 by Randall *et al*. Related drug *Diazepam* ('Valium') also used in anxiety states and as premedication for surgery.

c. 1960 *Frusemide*. A diuretic.

1961 *Thiabendazole*. Efficacy in dealing with intestinal tract infestations noted by Brown *et al*. in 1961. Used to treat various worm infections.

1962–3 *Clofibrate*. Lowers the fatty acid and cholesterol levels in the blood. Effects noted in 1962–3 by Thorp and Waring.

1963 *Allopurinol*. Used in treatment of gout, it slows rate at which body forms uric acid. Reported on by Hitchings, Elion *et al*. in 1963.

1963 *Cephalosporins*. Antibiotics discovered in 1945 in Sardinia by Prof Brotzu. First utilized in 1963. Developed by Sir Howard (later Lord) Florey and Glaxo Laboratories.

1964 *Tolnaftate*. An anti-fungal agent announced October 1964. Highly effective against epidermiphytosis (athlete's foot).

1965 *Niridazole*. Discovered in 1961 (announced December 1965) by Dr Paul Schmidt of CIBA, Basle. Treatment of debilitating liver-infestation disease Bilharzia (250 million world incidence).

1966 *Pralidoxime*. Antidote for poisoning by cholinesterase inhibitors, particularly organophosphorus compounds, which are used as insecticides and 'nerve gases'.

1966 *Trometamol* (Tromethamine). A diuretic used to treat acidosis, especially after surgery.

1967 *Nitrazepam* ('Mogadon'). Tranquilliser and hypnotic.

1967 *Laevo-dopa* (L-Dopa). Naturally occurring amino acid reported on by Cotzias and others in 1967. Used in treatment of Parkinson's disease.

1968 *Propranolol*. A β-adrenergic blocking drug used to treat hypertension. More recent related drugs include pindolol, sotalol, timolol.

1969 *Ibuprofen*. First of the proprionic acid derivatives; a non-steroidal anti-rheumatic.

1969 *Salbutamol*. Useful in asthma for its selective bronchodilator effects, whereas earlier unselective drugs were more dangerous in evaluating the heart rate.

1970 *Inosine Pranobex*. Immunomodulator/anti-viral used in the treatment of herpes simplex.

1972 *Prostaglandins*. The name given by von Euler in 1935 to a group of related substances found in the body, based on prostonoic acid. Prostaglandin $F_{2\alpha}$ was the first to be used therapeutically, in 1972, for induction of labour.

1976 *Cimetidine*. Selective antihistamine which prevents excessive acid secretion in the stomach, often the cause of ulcers.

1981 *Captopril*. The first anti-hypertensive drug which acts by inhibiting the formation of the hormone, angiotensin.

1981 *Acyclovir*. The first specific anti-viral: used in the treatment of herpes infections.

Phobias

Acerophobia	Sourness	Kleptophobia	Stealing
Acrophobia	Heights	Koniphobia	Dust
Agoraphobia	Open spaces	Kopophobia	Fatigue
Aichurophobia	Points	Kyphophobia	Stooping
Ailourophobia	Cats	Lalophobia	Speech
Akousticophobia	Sound	Limnophobia	Lakes
Algophobia	Pain	Linonophobia	String
Altophobia	Heights	Logophobia	Words
Amathophobia	Dust	Lyssophobia	Insanity
Ancraophobia	Wind	Maniaphobia	Insanity
Androphobia	Men	Mastigophobia	Flogging
Anginophobia	Narrowness	Mechanophobia	Machinery
Anglophobia	England or things English	Metallophobia	Metals
Anthropophobia	Human beings	Meteorophobia	Meteors
Antlophobia	Flood	Monophobia	One thing
Apeirophobia	Infinity	Musicophobia	Music
Apiphobia	Bees	Musophobia	Mice
Arachnophobia	Spiders	Mysophobia	Dirt
Asthenophobia	Weakness	Myxophobia	Slime
Astraphobia	Lightning	Necrophobia	Corpses
Atelophobia	Imperfection	Negrophobia	Negroes
Atephobia	Ruin	Nelophobia	Glass
Aulophobia	Flute	Neophobia	New
Auroraphobia	Auroral lights	Nephophobia	Clouds
Bacilliphobia	Microbes	Nosophobia	Disease
Barophobia	Gravity	Nyctophobia	Darkness
Bathophobia	Depth	Ochlophobia	Crowds
Batophobia	Walking	Ochophobia	Vehicles
Batrachophobia	Reptiles	Odontophobia	Teeth
Belonephobia	Needles	Oikophobia	Home
Bibliophobia	Books	Olfactophobia	Smell
Blennophobia	Slime	Ommataphobia	Eyes
Brontophobia	Thunder	Oneirophobia	Dreams
Carcinophobia	Cancer	Ophiophobia	Snakes
Cardiophobia	Heart condition	Ornithophobia	Birds
Chaetophobia	Hair	Ouranophobia	Heaven
Cheimatophobia	Cold	Panphobia	
Cherophobia	Cheerfulness	(Pantophobia)	Everything
Chionophobia	Snow	Parthenophobia	Young girls
Chrometophobia	Money	Pathophobia	Disease
Chromophobia	Colour	Patroiophobia	Heredity
Chronophobia	Duration	Peccatophobia	Sinning
Claustrophobia	Enclosed spaces	Pediculophobia	Lice
Clinophobia	Going to bed	Peniaphobia	Poverty
Cnidophobia	Stings	Phagophobia	Swallowing
Coprophobia	Faeces	Phasmophobia	Ghosts
Cryophobia	Ice, frost	Pharmacophobia	Drugs
Crystallophobia	Crystals	Phobophobia	Fears
Cymophobia	Sea swell	Phonophobia	Speaking aloud
Cynophobia	Dogs	Photophobia	Strong light
Demonophobia	Demons	Phronemophobia	Thinking
Demophobia	Crowds	Phyllophobia	Leaves
Dendrophobia	Trees	Pnigerophobia	Smothering
Dermatophobia	Skin	Pogonophobia	Beards
Dikephobia	Justice	Poinephobia	Punishment
Doraphobia	Fur	Polyphobia	Many things
Dromophobia	Crossing streets	Potophobia	Drink
Eisoptrophobia	Mirrors	Pteronophobia	Feathers
Elektrophobia	Electricity	Pyrophobia	Fire
Eleutherophobia	Freedom	Russophobia	Russia or things Russian
Enetephobia	Pins	Rypophobia	Soiling
Entomophobia	Insects	Satanophobia	Satan
Eosophobia	Dawn	Sciophobia	Shadows
Eremitophobia	Solitude	Selaphobia	Flashes
Ergophobia	Work	Siderodromophobia	Travelling by train
Erythrophobia	Blushing	Siderophobia	Stars
Gallophobia	France or things French	Sinophobia	China or things Chinese
Gametophobia	Marriage	Sitophobia	Food
Genophobia	Sex	Spermophobia	
Germanophobia	Germany or things German	(Spermatophobia)	Germs
Geumatophobia	Taste	Stasophobia	Standing
Graphophobia	Writing	Stygiophobia	
Gymnophobia	Nudity	(Hadephobia)	Hell
Gynophobia	Women	Syphilophobia	Syphilis
Haematophobia	Blood	Tachophobia	Speed
Haptophobia	Touch	Taphophobia	Burial alive
Harpaxophobia	Robbers	Teratophobia	Monsters
Hedonophobia	Pleasure	Terdekaphobia	Number thirteen
Hippophobia	Horses	Thaasophobia	Sitting idle
Hodophobia	Travel	Thalassophobia	Sea
Homichlophobia	Fog	Thanatophobia	Death
Hormephobia	Shock	Theophobia	God
Hyalinopygophobia	Glass Bottoms	Thermophobia	Heat
Hydrophobia	Water	Thixophobia	Touching
Hygrophobia	Dampness	Tocophobia	Childbirth
Hypegiaphobia	Responsibility	Toxiphobia	Poison
Hypnophobia	Sleep	Traumatophobia	Wounds, injury
Hypsophobia	High place	Tremophobia	Trembling
Ideophobia	Ideas	Trypanophobia	Inoculations, injections
Kakorraphiaphobia	Failure	Xenophobia	
Katagelophobia	Ridicule	(Zenophobia)	Foreigners
Kenophobia	Void	Zoöphobia	Animals
Keraunothnetophobia	Fall of man-made satellites		
Kinesophobia			
(Kinetophobia)	Motion		

Psychiatric conditions

actual neurosis Term coined by Freud to describe the physiological results of current disturbances.
affective disorder Psychoses in which disturbances of mood occur.
agitated An adjective used to describe depressions when they make the patient anxious, tense and restless.
alienation Being set apart from or removed from either oneself or others.
amnesia Inability to remember.
anhedonia An inability to experience pleasure.
anorexia An absence of appetite.
anxiety An irrational fear, often in response to an unrecognized stimulus.
apathy An absence of emotion.
aphanisis The fear of losing the ability to experience pleasure.
autism A childhood disorder, often persisting into adulthood, in which the patient appears to be cut off from his environment; the senses function normally, but there appears to be little perception.

behaviour disorder A group of conditions in which the behaviour of the patient is frowned on by society.
boredom A condition, distinct from apathy in that the patient is irritable and restless in his search for an activity or interest with which to occupy himself.

catatonia Schizophrenic condition in which the patient suffers periods of excitement and/or stupor, during which he seems out of touch with his environment.
conversion hysteria One of the psychoneuroses in which the patient's symptoms are physical complaints, i.e. the symptoms are physical in their expression but psychoneurotic in their origin.

delusion A fixed idea, held by a patient, that is at variance with beliefs and ideas held by normal people.
dementia A physical deterioration in the brain, resulting in mental deterioration and disorder.
depersonalization A feeling of unreality.
depression A disorder of mood in which the patient suffers from low spirits (the traditional 'melancholy'), an impairment of some mental processes and often a lack of sleep, appetite, etc.
dissassociation Existence of two or more mental processes which lack any connection.

elation A feeling of high spirits accompanying mania.
engulfment An extreme form of anxiety in which all relationships with others are seen as threatening.
exhibitionism Usually taken to mean the sexual perversion, invariably on the part of the male, in which the sex organs are exposed to a female. It can also be taken more widely to mean showing off.
extraversion Outgoing behaviour. This is a component, to a greater or lesser extent, of most people's behaviour; it only becomes a problem when taken to extremes.

fixation Attachment to a concept, object or person, usually appropriate to an earlier stage of development.
frigidity An inability for a woman to be sexually aroused. It may involve an aversion to sexual arousal.
fugue Seemingly automatic behaviour which the subject subsequently cannot remember.

guilt Guilt is attached to an action that has already occurred. It becomes neurotic when the action has not transgressed any value systems of the patient.

hallucination A sensation with no physical origin. Hallucinations can occur as a result of physical illness, or they can be psychotic, usually associated with schizophrenia.

hebephrenia A form of schizophrenia in which the sufferer neglects his person and appears withdrawn, often with unusual mannerisms.
hypochondriasis An imagined belief on the patient's part that he is ill, often with an incurable complaint.
hypomania A mild form of mania.
hysteria A form of neurosis, involving anxiety, physical symptoms, usually attaching to a part of the body about which the patient is concerned, and an absence of any physical foundation for these symptoms.

illusion A misinterpretation of something that has actually occurred.
implosion Fear of being destroyed by reality.
impotence Inability of a man to perform sexual intercourse, either for physical or psychological reasons.
inferiority complex A feeling of inadequacy.
inhibition The suppression of a function by the operation of another function.
introversion Introspective behaviour. This is a component, to a greater or lesser extent, of most people's behaviour; it only becomes a problem when taken to extremes.
involutional melancholia Severe depression occurring at the time of the menopause.

mania A psychosis in which elation, excitement, insomnia and perhaps exhaustion eventually lead to rapid and aimless thought.
manic depressive psychosis A psychosis in which a cycle of depression and elation repeats itself, the patient seemingly unable to control the cycle.
melancholia Another term for depression.

neuralgia Pain originating in a nerve.
neurasthenia An ill-defined form of tiredness that can almost be seen as a neurosis.
neuritis Inflammation of a nerve or nerves.
neurosis Mental disorder of the personality in which there is no organic damage to the nervous system. Someone suffering from a neurosis is aware that something is wrong.

obsessional neurosis Neurosis characterized by obsessions, i.e. ideas that constantly impose themselves on the patient's thinking. The resulting behaviour is repetitive, even ritualistic.
organic mental illness Mental illness resulting from damage to or a disorder of the brain.

paranoia A psychosis in which the patient suffers from delusions of persecution, often organized into a complex and coherent system which controls the patient's life.
phobia An unrealistic and excessive fear of an object or situation. A form of anxiety.
psychomotor acceleration The speeding up of thoughts and actions that occurs in mania.
psychomotor retardation The slowing down of thoughts and actions that occurs in depression.
psychopathy Antisocial irresponsible aggressive behaviour that is often impulsive.
psychosis Mental disorder which leaves the patient out of touch with reality; he is unaware of his disorder. Psychoses can either be organic, in which case disease of the brain can be shown, or functional, in which no damage to the brain can be observed.
psychosomatic illness Physiological symptoms and disturbances of function caused by the patient's personality and psychological disturbances.

regression Behaviour more appropriate to an earlier stage of life, often sparked off by stress.

schizophrenia Functional psychoses characterized by disturbances of thinking, motivation and mood, coupled with hallucinations and delusions.
stupor Complete lack of movement and responsiveness, either due to organic or psychiatric causes.

traumatic neurosis Neurosis which develops shortly after an unexpected and traumatic experience. The neurosis involves the periodic reliving of the traumatic experience.

Schools of Psychology

Adler, Alfred Psychoanalyst who developed individual psychology.
analytical psychology That branch of psychology developed by Jung.

behavioural psychology This school of psychology is largely based on the work of B. F. Skinner. Its central tenet is that human behaviour can be modified by reinforcement, i.e. the provision of a 'reward', either physical or social, or the avoidance of punishment. It assumes that the symptom is the illness and that the patient can be 'cured' by deconditioning and reconditioning.

body-centred psychology This is not so much a school of psychology as a loose grouping of therapies and ideas in which work on the physical body results in an alteration in the personality or the image of self. It includes such diverse philosophies and therapies as yoga, the Alexander technique. Rolfing, bioenergetics, T'ai Chi and Feldenkrais.

clinical psychology An essential practically-based area of psychology in which research findings and methods are applied to human behaviour, both normal and abnormal. It is now a very broadly-based discipline, encompassing experimental psychology, social psychology, environmental psychology and ethology.

developmental psychobiology The study of biological processes and systems that affect the development of behaviour. In particular, interest focuses on the behavioural characteristics which enable species to cope with environmental challenges, and the behaviour and development of the young as they relate to their environment.

ego psychology This is a branch of psychoanalytical theory that has developed from Freud's book *The Ego and the Id*. It is now associated with Freud's daughter, Anna Freud, who developed the thinking in her *The Ego and the Mechanism of Defence*. It concentrates on the manner in which the individual develops and acquires functions which enable him to control his impulses and his environment and to act independently.
existential analysis This area of psychology is heavily influenced by the existential philosophers such as Sartre and Heidegger. Essentially it lays emphasis on the here and now, expecting the patient to take responsibility for his actions, through which his life will take on meaning. There is little emphasis on the unconscious mental processes dwelt on by other schools of psychology.

Freudian psychoanalysis Psychoanalysis was developed in the first place by Sigmund Freud. It has subsequently been adapted by various psychoanalysts so that there are now many branches of psychoanalysis. However classical psychoanalysis can be traced back directly to Freud's teachings and writings, particularly to his *An Outline of Psychoanalysis*.
Fromm, Erich One of the neo-Freudians, he at first subscribed to Freud's ideas but subsequently broke away to develop his own thinking. He was much affected by existential philosophy and came to emphasize the part that society as a whole – its structures, expectations, etc. – has to play in determining the way in which an individual copes with basic human needs.

Horney, Karen Another of the neo-Freudians who at first subscribed to Freud's thinking, then later broke away to develop their own ideas. Horney concentrated on the experience of childhood as the basis for neurosis, postulating that such neuroses can be avoided by good child care.

individual psychology This was the name Alfred Adler gave to his branch of psychoanalysis, formed when he departed from Freud's thinking. Adler saw the individual as responsible for his own actions and able to work towards his own goals.

Jungian theory Carl Jung was at first associated with Sigmund Freud in the development of psychoanalysis, but subsequently developed his own ideas. These cover a very wide spectrum of psychology, but one of his most important contributions was to develop a 16-category typology of character, e.g. intraversion, extraversion, thinking, feeling, etc.

Kleinian theory Melanie Klein's theories lie within the mainstream of Freudian psychoanalysis, but there are important departures. Primarily she lays emphasis on the first year of a child's life as being a time rich in phantasy and a time during which the origins of neurosis occur.

Lacan, Jacques A French psychoanalyst who introduced elements of structuralism and linguistics into psychoanalysis and psychology.
Laing, R. D. Scottish psychiatrist responsible for much pioneering work in the area of radical therapy and for bringing a more humanistic approach to psychology.
learning theory Psychological theories which aim to explain individual behaviour and personality arising as a result of learned reactions and responses to the environment. This is in contrast to psychoanalysis, which sees behaviour and personality arising as a result of developmental processes.

neo-Freudian theory This encompasses a wide variety of psychological thought. The common thread running through the ideas is that those that have formulated the ideas were at first espoused Freud's ideas on psychoanalysis. They have subsequently broken away from or modified or added to Freud's thinking. In general they have put forward ideas that emphasize the social needs of individuals more than Freud did.
neurolinguistics A combination of psychology, linguistics and neurology that looks at the acquisition of language, its production and processing, and its disruption or disturbances, especially those disturbances related to organic brain disease.
neuropsychiatry The study of organic brain disorders and the effects they have on behaviour and personality.

phenomenology Literally, the study of phenomena, i.e. of the experiences that we have and the effect they have on personality and behaviour.
psychiatry The treatment and study of mental, emotional, personality and behavioural disorders.
psychoanalysis A method of treating mental illness, originated by Sigmund Freud. Psychoanalysis aims to bring to the surface those fears and conflicts between instinct and conscience that have been pushed into the unconscious.
psychology The study of the mind, of behaviour and of thinking.
psychopathology The study of the abnormal workings of the mind and of abnormal behaviour.
psychosynthesis Psychological thinking developed by the Italian Roberto Assagioli, who trained under Freud. His ideas diverged widely from Freud's, in that he recognized that mental disturbance can arise when the elements of personality are at odds with each other, and that a release occurs when these elements can be merged. Psychosynthesis aims to bring these elements together in a greater whole.
psychotherapy Treatment of mental disturbance, personality problems, behavioural difficulties, etc., by psychological means. Invariably a strong link is forged between the therapist and the patient, who often meet on a one-to-one basis.

radical therapy A relatively recent move in psychology has been to call into question society's definition of such words as 'sane' and 'insane', undermining the medical model of psychology. This move was catalysed by R. D. Laing, and owes a lot to the existentialists and humanists; insanity, if there is such a thing, is seen as a social problem needing social solutions.

Rogers, Carl Ransom Rogers developed what is known as humanistic psychology, in which the self-image the patient (client) has of himself is paramount. The therapist should therefore be open and honest with the patient, and not seek to change the patient by any approval or disapproval.

social psychiatry The examination of mental disorder as a part of society. Both the social causes of such disorders and the social methods of prevention are looked at.
Sullivan, Harry Stack One of the neo-Freudians who at first subscribed to Freud's thinking, Sullivan subsequently broke away to develop his own ideas of personality. These ideas are based on his observations of the patterns existing in social and inter-personal relations, and development of personality with these patterns.

Nobel prizewinners in physiology and medicine since 1950

1987 Susumu Tonegawa, Japanese.
1986 Rita Levi-Montalcini, Italy.
1985 Michael Brown, Joseph Goldstein, both US.
1984 Cesar Milstein, British/Argentine; Georges J. F. Kohler, W. German; Neils K. Jerne, British/Danish
1983 Barbara McClintock, US
1982 Sune Bergstrom, Bengt Samuelsson, both Swedish; John R. Vane, British
1981 Roger W. Sperry, David H. Hubel, Tosten N. Wiesel, all US
1980 Baruj Benacerraf, George Snell, both US; Jean Dausset, France
1979 Allan M. Cormack, US, Geoffrey N. Hounsfield, British
1978 Daniel Nathans, Hamilton O. Smith, both US; Werner Arber, Swiss
1977 Rosalyn S. Yalow, Roger C. L. Guillemin, Andrew V. Schally, all US
1976 Baruch S. Blumberg, US; Daniel Carleton Gajdusek, US
1975 David Baltimore, Howard Temin, both US; Renato Dulbecco, Ital.-US
1974 Albert Claude, Lux.-US; George Emil Palade, Rom.-US; Christian Rene de Duve, Belg.
1973 Karl von Frisch, Ger.; Konrad Lorenz, Ger.-Austrian; Nikolaas Tinbergen, Brit.
1972 Gerald M. Edelman, US; Rodney R. Porter, British
1971 Earl W. Sutherland Jr., US
1970 Julius Axelrod, US; Sir Bernard Katz, British; Ulf von Euler, Swedish
1969 Max Delbruck, Alfred D. Hershey, Salvador Luria, all US

1968 Robert W. Holley, H. Gobind Khorana, Marshall W. Nirenberg, all US
1967 Ragnar Granit, Swedish; Haldan Keffer Hartline, US; George Wald, US
1966 Charles B. Huggins, Francis Peyton Rous, both US
1965 Francois Jacob, André Lwoff, Jacques Monod, all French
1964 Konrad E. Bloch, US; Feodor Lynen, German
1963 Sir John C. Eccles, Australian; Alan L. Hodgkin, British; Andrew F. Huxley, British
1962 Francis H. C. Crick, British; James D. Watson, US; Maurice H. F. Wilkins, British
1961 Georg von Bekesy, US
1960 Sir F. MacFarlane Burnet, Australian; Peter B. Medawar, British
1959 Arthur Kornberg, US; Severo Ochoa, US
1958 George W. Beadle, US; Edward L. Tatum, US; Joshua Lederberg, US
1957 Daniel Bovet, Italian
1956 André F. Cournand, US; Werner Forssmann, German; Dickinson W. Richards, Jr, US
1955 Alex H. T. Theorell, Swedish
1954 John F. Enders, Frederick C. Robbins, Thomas H. Weller, all US
1953 Hans A. Krebs, British; Fritz A. Lipmann, US
1952 Selman A. Waksman, US
1951 Max Theiler, US
1950 Philip S. Hench, Edward C. Kendall, both US; Tadeus Reischstein, Swiss

Alternative medicine

acupuncture Chinese medicine maintains that the organs are linked to points on the surface of the body – the acupuncture points. Points affecting specific organs lie along lines or meridians. Stimulation of these points, usually with a needle, has an effect on the organ and, if the organ is diseased, specific points can be chosen to remedy the disease.
Alexander technique The Alexander technique, developed by Matthias Alexander and passed on by teachers throughout the world, aims to teach correct posture and balance. As such it is rarely used to remedy specific ailments; more, it is a means of inducing an inner harmony and sense of well-being from which good health will flow.
anthroposophical medicine A system of medicine, in part developed out of our Western system of medicine, that was put forward by Rudolf Steiner. It involves an understanding of all aspects of a 'patient', both physical and spiritual; to this end, modification of diet, exercises known as curative eurythmics, painting therapy, homeopathy and other holistic treatments are all incorporated. The most important feature, though, is that the practitioners of anthroposophical medicine should have a spiritual awareness of the people they treat.
aromatherapy The use of a wide range of oils extracted from plants as part of a programme of massage. Different aromatic oils from different

plants are used to treat a wide range of complaints and symptoms; indeed different concentrations of the same oil can have different results. In addition to massage, administration of the oils can be by mouth, inhalation, baths and even a form of acupuncture.
ayurvedic medicine This is the traditional system of medicine in India, still much used there. It treats the patient as a whole, and therefore looks initially at his whole life, not just his signs and symptoms. Treatment may include fasting, meditation, breathing exercises and drugs taken from an enormous range of pills, ointments, powders, etc., all prepared by the practitioner himself.

biochemics This is a type of homeopathic treatment which aims to remedy imbalances in the inorganic salts and oxides in the body. These remedies are widely sold; for example Combination A is used for neuritis, Combination E for indigestion, Combination Q for sinusitis.
biofeedback This uses an electronic device to convert the electrical activity of the body, e.g. brainwaves, heart beat, or other activity, to an easily observed signal, e.g. a variable sound or a moving needle. The user of the device can then monitor his control of a bodily function, say heart beat, and learn to gain greater control over it.

chiropractic A system of manipulation of the spine, developed by Daniel Palmer. This manipulation relieves pressure on the nerves, thus allowing them to function freely and restoring the body to health.

colour therapy This is a form of therapy in which the whole body, or a particular part of it, is illuminated with a particular colour, depending on the ailment. Practised therapists observe the patient through a screen of glass containing an indigo dye; the image of the patient so observed gives an indication of the colours in which he is deficient.

herbalism The use of plants, in various forms, to treat and remedy diseases. The emphasis is on restoring a balance in the body by the use of these plants or plant extracts; small doses are given that are designed to boost the body's defences, and recommendations are given as to diet, breathing and other aspects of lifestyle.

homeopathy A system of medicine first propounded by Samuel Hahnemann nearly 200 years ago. The basic principle is that a drug that produces symptoms the same as those of the disease is diluted and then administered. The dilution factor is so great that no or only a few molecules of the drug are actually received by the patient. There is at the moment no 'scientific' explanation as to why the system works, but it is certainly a very successful and widely used branch of medicine.

hydrotherapy This is the use of water in a variety of treatments. It might merely involve bathing in spa water, bathing in special baths with sprays or air jets built into them, the use of muds, the use of spa waters as an addition to the diet or as the sole item in the diet during a period of fasting or even for colonic irrigation.

macrobiotics This is not so much a system of medicine as an approach to life. It involves principally keeping yin (the passive female principle of the universe) and yang (the active male principle of the universe) in balance. This is achieved by eating fresh, largely vegetarian, foods, taking great care over their preparation and ensuring that the two principles are balanced in the diet.

megavitamin treatment The premise of this form of treatment is that disease is caused by deficiencies of particular vitamins. Prevention of disease can thus be effected by taking large doses of the appropriate vitamins. This treatment is used significantly in the USA for psychiatric disorders, but it is a controversial system with results that are much argued over.

naturopathy This system of medicine is based on the principle that natural processes will keep the body fit and healthy. Emphasis is therefore placed on a simple diet, regular exercise, the avoidance of drugs and unnatural foods.

negative ion therapy The air in rural and seaside areas contains a predominance of negative ions. Built up areas have much lower levels of negative ions in the air, and air conditioning may remove these ions completely. Negative ion therapy aims to redress this imbalance by supplying air which is rich in negative ions. In addition to promoting good health, negative ions have been shown to alleviate the symptoms of burns, migraine, respiratory disorders and eczema.

osteopathy Osteopathy was developed by Dr Andrew Still and involves manipulation of the bones of the body and the spine. This brings the body back into balance, promotes good posture and takes the pressure off various organs.

radiesthesia The use of pendulums as a diagnostic tool, often in association with homeopathic remedies. The patient provides a sample, e.g. hair, spot of blood, nail clipping. This is then compared to other standard samples by oscillating a pendulum over the samples and noting changes in direction. Once a diagnosis has been arrived at, movement of the pendulum is again used in the selection of the appropriate remedy.

reflexology Just as acupuncture works on points on the surface of the body that are linked to specific organs, so reflexology works on the areas of the feet, particularly the soles of the feet, that are linked to specific areas and organs of the body. If a particular organ or area of the body is troubled, the associated area on the feet will also feel tender. Massage of this area of the feet will in turn alleviate the troubled organ or area of the body.

rolfing This is a kind of deep massage whose aim is to break down layers of connective tissue in the body that have been deposited as a reaction to bad posture. The hypothesis is that by breaking down these layers, better posture and physical well-being will be promoted. The technique was developed by Ida Rolf.

shiatsu Shiatsu is the use of finger massage over the acupuncture points along the body's meridians, both to remedy diseased parts of the body and to promote general health and well-being. Shiatsu is massage of one person by another; often such practitioners will make allied suggestions as to diet, exercise, etc. A self-administered form of shiatsu is called do-in.

yoga Yoga is not so much a system of medicine as a way of life. Yoga is divided into many branches, and it is hatha yoga that most people will recognize; this is the use of various positions and movements to keep the body healthy and supple. However yoga also involves breathing exercises, chanting, meditation – in fact a whole outlook on life. The aim of all aspects of yoga is to promote health, well-being and a spiritual oneness with life.

Philosophy

'Philosophy' is a word derived from the Greek words meaning 'love of wisdom', and philosophy in the Western world began with the ancient Greeks. It is used to cover a wide area: the scientific arrangement of those principles which underlie all knowledge and existence.

The sphere of philosophy can be roughly delineated by stating how it is distinct from other areas of thought. It differs from religion since its quest for the underlying causes and principles of being and thinking does not depend on dogma and faith; and from science, since it does not depend solely on fact, but leans heavily on speculation. Its inter-relation with both science and religion can be seen in the large number of philosophers who were also either theologians or scientists, and the few such as Blaise Pascal and Roger Bacon, who were all three. Philosophy developed from religion, becoming distinct when thinkers sought truth independent of theological considerations. Science in turn developed from philosophy, and eventually, all the branches of science from physics to psychology broke away – psychology being the last to do so in the 20th century.

Philosophy can be split into three particularly important categories: ethics, metaphysics and epistemology. Such a division leaves out some important areas of philosophical speculation, including logic, which is the increasingly formalized technique of exact analysis of reasoning, but it serves to introduce a few of the most important writings.

1. **Ethics** is the study of human conduct and morality. Philosophers have held many points of view about ideal human conduct but their opinions tend to resolve into an opposition between two main schools. One school, the 'Idealist', considers that the goodness or badness of a course of action must be judged by standards dictated from the other world – from God or from some force for good – external to man. The second school, who might be grouped under the term 'Utilitarians', feels that the effect which a course of action produces in this world makes it good or bad.

The Idealist school was represented quite early in the history of Western philosophy by the Greek philospher Plato, who wrote in the 4th century BC. Plato, in a series of dialogues, has his ex-teacher Socrates discuss the problems of philosophy with friends and opponents.

Socrates' procedure is to draw out the wisdom from the gentleman with whom he is discussing the question. Socrates, in fact, rarely makes a statement. He prefers what advertising men call 'the soft sell'. That is to say, he asks questions which compel the others either to make the statement he wants them to make or to appear foolish.

In three of these dialogues, especially – *The Protagoras, The Phaedo*, and *The Gorgias* – Plato develops a system of ethics which is essentially idealistic. Socrates propounds that the good comes from the realm of 'ideas' or 'forms'. This is a sort of perfect other world which projects distorted copies of everything good down to the world we have to contend with. For Plato, individual conduct is good in so far as it is governed by the emanated spirit from above. Plato does not, of course, use the word 'heaven' for the world of ideas, but he was adapted – after being modified by Aristotle, Plotinus, and others – for Christian purposes. One of the ways in which the knowledge from the realm of the 'ideas' was communicated to mortals was by a voice or 'demon'. In the *Apology*, Socrates describes how this individual conscience has prevented him from wrongdoing.

Another important work which has to be classed with the idealists is Aristotle's *Nicomachean Ethics*. Aristotle was a pupil of Plato, and, like Plato, he thinks of the good as a divine emanation, or overflow, but his ethics have a more 'practical' bent. He equates happiness with the good and is responsible for the doctrine of the 'golden mean'. This states that every virtue is a mean, or middle-point, between two vices. Generosity, for instance, is the mean between prodigality and stinginess.

A more cynical approach was introduced by Niccolò Machiavelli, founder of the modern science of politics. In his famous book, *The Prince*, Machiavelli drew his conclusions from the very nature of man.

The same tendency to give idealism a practical bent is found in a more modern philosopher, Immanuel Kant. His idealistic aspect may be compared with Socrates' 'demon'. Kant maintains that there is in each man a voice which guides him as to right or wrong.

But the part of Kant's ethics which is most famous is that connected with the phrase 'categorical imperative'. In Kant's own words: 'Act only according to a maxim by which you can at the same time will that it shall become a general law'. In other words, before acting in a certain way, the individual must ask himself: 'If everybody did the same thing what would be the moral condition of the universe?' This is a practical consideration in the sense that it concerns the *result* of an action, but Kant's concern is for the morality of the universe and not its happiness or earthly welfare. Kant's principal ethical works are *The Critique of Pure Reason, The Critique of Practical Reason, The Metaphysics of Morality*, and *The Metaphysics of Ethics*.

The opposing group of 'utilitarian' ethics is concerned with the matter of earthly welfare. The earliest Western philosopher to represent this tradition is Epicurus, a Greek philosopher of the 4th century BC.

Instead of deriving ideas of right and wrong from above, as did the Socratics for example, Epicurus maintained that 'we call pleasure the beginning and end of the blessed life'. The term 'Epicurean' was used – and often still is used – to describe one who indulges in excessive pleasure, but this usage is neither accurate nor just. Epicurus did not condone excesses. On the contrary, he said that pleasure was only good when moderate or 'passive'. 'Dynamic' pleasure, which caused painful after-effects, was not good.

The utilitarian tradition has on the whole had more adherents than the idealistic tradition in modern philosophy. Jeremy Bentham, for example, writing in the 18th century, acknowledged his debt to Epicurus in his *Principles of Morals and Legislation*. Bentham agreed that pain and pleasure were the 'sovereign masters' governing man's conduct. He added to this a doctrine of *utility* which argued that 'the greatest happiness of the greatest number is the measure of right and wrong'.

John Stuart Mill is perhaps the most famous of the Utilitarians. He extended Bentham's doctrines pointing out that there were different *qualities* of pleasure and pain; and that 'some *kinds* of pleasure are more valuable than others'. These articles were later put out in book form: *Utilitarianism*.

In the USA the Utilitarians made an impact on the Pragmatists, who held that 'the *right* is only the expedient in our way of thinking' – to quote William James, whose *Pragmatism* is the best-known book produced by this school.

2. **Metaphysics.** The term 'metaphysics' originated as the title of one of Aristotle's treatises. It probably meant only that he wrote it after his *Physics*, but it was once thought to signify study beyond the realm of physics. Today it is usually employed to describe the speculation as to the ultimate nature of reality and the structure of the universe.

The sort of questions asked by metaphysicians concern the origin and condition of the universe in which man lives, and, as we might expect, they came up early in the history of philosophy. Before Aristotle had invented the term 'metaphysics' – as early as the 6th Century BC – pre-Socratic Greek philosophers were offering their solutions of the mysteries of the universe.

Much of the speculation of these pre-Socratic philosophers was centred on speculation about the four *elements* which they thought made up the universe. Empedocles, who, according to legend, threw himself into the volcano at Mt Etna to prove his immortality – and failed – first defined earth, air, fire and water as the four basic elements. Others attempted to make one of these the most important, or *primary*, element from which the others were derived. Thales – one of the seven wise men of Greece – thought water was on top. Heraclitus' primary element was fire. Anaximander reasoned that none of the four was primary. They must, he said, exist in perpetual balance.

3. **Epistemology** is the study of the nature, grounds and validity of man's knowing – how we come to know and how far we can rely on what we think we have discovered.

Some epistemologists assert that knowledge is born in the individual and has only to be drawn forth. The other point of view is that at birth the mind is a *tabula rasa* – blank sheet – on which knowledge is imprinted.

The first school is represented classically by Plato. In the *Theaetetus* especially, he discusses various theories of knowledge and discards those built on the shifting sands of sense perception. The senses are, he feels, too fallible. True knowledge comes from those general notions which are derived from the realm of the *ideas* – which the soul possesses prior to birth.

The classic representative of the second school is John Locke – a 17th century English philosopher. In his *Essay Concerning Human Understanding*, Locke defines what is really the opposite point of view to Plato's. He is the pioneer proponent of the *tabula rasa*. Locke regards the mind at birth as comparable to an empty cabinet with two compartments. As we live, one compartment is filled with our *perceptions* and the other with our *sensations*. From these two combined we get our *ideas*.

This theory tends to make knowledge a matter of experience and mental processing rather than one of religious insight. As one might expect, Locke's theories are important influences in those fields which investigate the processes of mental activity – such as psychology and education.

Philosophical Terms

a posteriori Used to describe knowledge that comes from experience

a priori Used to describe knowledge that can be acquired independently of experience through pure reason.

aesthetics The science of feelings and sensations; a branch of philosophy concerned with value – judgments about beauty and taste, especially in art.

analytic A system of logical analysis; that which discovers the function of pure reason; describes a judgment whose truth is found by analyzing the concepts involved.

axiom A necessary and self-evident proposition, requiring no proof.

causality The relationship between a cause and its effect.

deduction The act of reaching a conclusion by arguing from the general to the particular.

dialectic Means of discovering the truth by proceeding from a thesis to a denial of it or antithesis and finally reconciling the two through a synthesis.

epistemology Branch of philosophy that attempts to answer questions about the nature of knowledge and the means by which it is acquired. Study of the origins of human knowledge. (See also above.)

ethics Branch of inquiry that attempts to answer questions about right and wrong, good and evil; pertaining to how human life should be lived. (See also above.)

induction The logic of drawing general conclusions from particular instances.

logic Branch of philosophy (and especially mathematics) that, by abstracting the subject matter of statements and deductive arguments, seeks to investigate their structure and form.

metaphysics Branch of philosophy concerned with systems of ideas that attempt to explain a general theory of the universe and man's place in it, relying on *a priori* arguments rather than empirical proofs. (See also above.)

paradox, logical Any conclusion that at first sounds ridiculous but has an argument to sustain it; e.g. the Cretan philosopher Epimenides said 'All Cretans are liars.' As he was Cretan himself, is his statement true or false?

predestination Postulation that all the events of a human's life are determined beforehand.

sense datum (data) What one actually sees, hears, touches, smells, tastes of an object, from which the receiver of such data projects his understanding of and identification of the whole object.

sophistry Containing a fallacious argument.

synthesis The outcome of the confrontation of two arguments, by which a truth is discovered.

teleology Argument or theory that postulates that things can be explained better in terms of what they will become rather than what they are now or have been.

thesis A proposition or argument.

value-judgment Assessment of a thing's worth in aesthetic terms.

Schools and Theories

Since the days of the early Greeks, philosophers have been divided into different schools and have advanced opposing theories. Among the many basic outlooks and theories not already discussed but which have developed since Thales of Miletus (624–550 BC) first questioned the nature of ultimate reality, the following may be listed:

1. *Absolutism:* the theory that there is an ultimate reality in which all differences are reconciled.

2. *Agnosticism:* the position that the ultimate answer to all fundamental inquiries is that we do not know.

3. *Altruism:* the principle of living and acting in the interest of others rather than oneself.

4. *Asceticism:* the belief that withdrawal from the physical world into the inner world of the spirit is the highest good attainable.

5. *Atheism:* rejection of the concept of God as a workable hypothesis.

6. *Atomism:* the belief that the entire universe is composed of distinct and indivisible units.

7. *Conceptualism:* the doctrine that universal ideas are neither created by finite (human) minds, nor entirely apart from an absolute mind (God).

8. *Critical Idealism:* the concept that man cannot determine whether there is anything beyond his own experience.

9. *Critical Realism:* the theory that reality is tripartite, that in addition to the mental and physical aspects of reality, there is a third aspect called essences.

10. *Criticism:* the theory that the path to knowledge lies midway between dogmatism and scepticism.

11. *Determinism:* the belief that the universe follows a fixed or pre-determined pattern.

12. *Dialectical Materialism:* the theory that reality is strictly material and is based on a struggle between opposing forces, with occasional interludes of harmony.

13. *Dogmatism:* assertion of a belief without authoritative support.

14. *Dualism:* the belief that the world consists of two radically independant and absolute elements, e.g. good and evil, spirit and matter.

15. *Egoism:* in ethics the belief that the serving of one's own interests is the highest end.

16. *Empiricism:* rejection of all *a priori* knowledge in favour of experience and induction.

17. *Evolutionism:* the concept of the universe as a progression of inter-related phenomena.

18. *Existentialism:* denial of objective universal values – man must create values for himself through action; the self is the ultimate reality.

19. *Hedonism:* the doctrine that pleasure is the highest good.

20. *Humanism:* any system that regards human

interest and the human mind as paramount in the universe.

21. *Idealism:* any system that regards thought or the idea as the basis either of knowledge or existence; in ethics, the search for the best or the highest.

22. *Instrumentalism:* the concept of ideas as instruments, rather than as goals of living.

23. *Intuitionism:* the doctrine that the perception of truth is by intuition, not analysis.

24. *Materialism:* the doctrine that denies the independent existence of spirit, and asserts the existence of only one substance – matter; belief that physical well-being is paramount.

25. *Meliorism:* the belief that the world is capable of improvement, and that man has the power of helping in its betterment, a position between optimism and pessimism.

26. *Monism:* belief in only one ultimate reality, whatever its nature.

27. *Mysticism:* belief that the ultimate reality lies in direct contact with the divine.

28. *Naturalism:* a position that seeks to explain all phenomena by means of strictly natural (as opposed to supernatural) categories.

29. *Neutral Monism:* theory that reality is neither physical nor spiritual, but capable of expressing itself as either.

30. *Nominalism:* the doctrine that general terms have no corresponding reality either in or out of the mind, and are, in effect, nothing more than words. (*c.f.* Realism).

31. *Optimism:* any system that holds that the universe is the best of all possible ones, and that all will work out for the best.

32. *Pantheism:* the belief that God is identical with the universe.

33. *Personalism:* theory that ultimate reality consists of a plurality of spiritual beings or independent persons.

34. *Pessimism:* belief that the universe is the worst possible and that all is doomed to evil.

35. *Phenomenalism:* theory that reality is only appearance.

36. *Pluralism:* belief that there are more than two irreducible components of reality.

37. *Positivism:* the doctrine that man can have no knowledge except of phenomena, and that the knowledge of phenomena is relative, not absolute.

38. *Pragmatism:* a method that makes practical consequences the test of truth.

39. *Rationalism:* the theory that reason alone, without the aid of experience, can arrive at the basic reality of the universe.

40. *Realism:* the doctrine that general terms have a real existence. *c.f.* Nominalism.

41. *Relativism:* rejection of the concept of the absolute.

42. *Scepticism:* the doctrine that no facts can be certainly known.

43. *Theism:* acceptance of the concept of God as a workable hypothesis.

44. *Transcendentalism:* belief in an ultimate reality that transcends human experience.

45. *Voluntarism:* the theory that will is the determining factor in the universe.

Chronology of philosophers and their theories

Pre-Socratic Greeks

Thales of Miletas (624–550 BC). Regarded as the starting point of Western philosophy; the first exponent of monism.

Anaximander (611–547 BC). Continued Thales' quest for universal substance, but reasoned that that substance need not resemble known substances.

Anaximenes (588–524 BC). Regarded air as the ultimate reality.

Pythagoras (572–497 BC). Taught a dualism of body and soul.

Heraclitus (533–475 BC). Opposed concept of a single ultimate reality; held that one permanent thing is change.

Parmenides (c. 495 BC). Formulated the basic doctrine of idealism; member of Eleatic school,

so called because based at Elea in southern Italy.

Anaxogorus (500–428 BC). Believed in an indefinite number of basic substances.

Zeno of Elea (c. 495–430 BC). Argued that plurality and change are appearances, not realities.

Empedocles (c. 495–435 BC). Held that there were four irreducible substances (water, fire, earth and air) and two forces (love and hate).

Protagoras (481–411 BC). An early relativist and humanist; doubted human ability to attain absolute truth.

Classic Greek Philosophers

Socrates (c. 470–399 BC). Developed Socratic method of inquiry; teacher of Plato, through whose writings his idealistic philosophy was disseminated.

Democritus (460–370 BC). Began tradition in Western thought of explaining universe in mechanistic terms.

Antisthenes (c. 450–c. 360 BC). Chief of group known as the Cynics; stressed discipline and work as the essential good.

Plato (c. 428–347 BC). Founded the Academy at Athens; developed the idealism of his teacher Socrates; teacher of Aristotle.

Diogenes of Sinope (c. 412–c. 325 BC). Famous Cynic.

Aristotle (384–322 BC). Taught that there are four factors in causation: the interrelated factors of form and matter; motive cause, which produces change; and the end, for which a process of change occurs. Perhaps the greatest influence on western civilization.

Hellenistic Period

Pyrrho of Elis (c. 365–275 BC). Initiated the Sceptic school of philosophy; believed that man could not know anything for certain.

Epicurus (341–270 BC). Taught that the test of truth is in sensation; proponent of atomism and hedonism.

Zeno of Citium [Cyprus] (c. 335–263 BC). Chief of the Stoics, so called because they met in the Stoa Poikile or Painted Porch at Athens; proponent of pantheism, evolutionism; taught that man's role is to accept nature and all it offers, good or bad.

Plotinus (AD 205–270). Chief expounder of Neo-Platonism, a combining of the teachings of Plato with Oriental concepts.

Augustine (AD 354–430). Known to history as St Augustine; expounder of optimism and absolutism; believed that God transcends human comprehension; one of greatest influences on medieval Christian thought.

Boethius (c. AD 480–524). Late Roman statesman and philosopher. A Neo-Platonist, his great work, *The Consolations of Philosophy*, served to transmit Greek philosophy to medieval Europe.

Medieval Period

Avicenna (980–1037). Arabic follower of Aristotle and Neo-Platonism; his works led to a revival of interest in Aristotle in 13th century Europe.

Anselm (1033–1109). Italian Augustinian; known to history as St. Anselm; a realist, he is famous for his examination of the proof of God's existence.

Peter Abelard (1079–1142). Leading theologian and philosopher of medieval France; his nominalism caused him to be declared a heretic by the Church.

Averroes (1126–98). Great philosopher of Mohammedan Spain, and leading commentator on Aristotle; regarded religion as allegory for the common man, philosophy as the path to truth.

Moses Maimonides (1135–1204). Leading Jewish student of Aristotle in medieval Mohammedan world; sought to combine Aristotelian teaching with that of the Bible.

Roger Bacon (c 1214–92). English student of Aristotle, advocated return to Hebrew and Greek versions of Scripture; an empiricist.

St Bonaventure (c. 1217–74). Born John of Fidanza in Italy; friend of Thomas Aquinas; student of Plato and Aristotle; a mystic and ascetic.

St Thomas Aquinas (1225–74). Italian; leading philosopher of the Scholastics or Christian philosophers of the Middle Ages; evolved a compromise between Aristotle and Scripture, based on the belief that faith and reason are in agreement; his philosophical system is known as Thomism.

The Renaissance

Desiderius Erasmus (1466–1536). Greatest of the humanists, he helped spread the ideas of the Renaissance in his native Holland and throughout Northern Europe.

Niccolò Machiavelli (1469–1527). Italian politician and political thinker; a realist, he placed the state as the paramount power in human affairs.

Thomas More (1478–1535). Statesman and later saint; early influence in the English Renaissance. Stressed a return to Greek sources and political and social reform. All these traits appeared in his famous *Utopia* (1516).

Transition to Modern Thought

Francis Bacon (1561–1626). English statesman and philosopher of science; in his major work, *Novum Organum*, he sought to replace the deductive logic of Aristotle with an inductive system in interpreting nature.

Thomas Hobbes (1588–1679). English materialist who believed the natural state of man is war; outlined a theory of human government in his book *Leviathan*, whereby the state and men's subordination to it form the sole solution to human selfishness and aggressiveness.

René Descartes (1596–1650). French; dualist, rationalist, theist. Descartes and his system, Cartesianism, are at the base of all modern knowledge. What he furnished is a theory of knowledge that underlies modern science and philosophy. 'All the sciences are conjoined with one another and interdependent' he wrote.

Blaise Pascal (1623–52). French theist who held that sense and reason are mutually deceptive; truth lies between dogmatism and scepticism.

Benedict de Spinoza (1632–77). Dutch rationalist metaphysician, he developed ideas of Descartes while rejecting his dualism.

John Locke (1632–1704). English dualist, empiricist; in his great *Essay Concerning Human Understanding* he sought to refute the rationalist view that all knowledge derives from first principles. His influence in political, religious, educational and philosophical thought was wide and deep.

18th Century

Gottfried Wilhelm von Leibniz (1646–1716). German idealist, absolutist, optimist (his view that this is the best of all possible worlds was ridiculed by Voltaire in *Candide*); held that reality consisted of units of force called monads.

George Berkeley (1685–1753). Irish idealist and theist of English ancestry who taught that material things exist only in being perceived; his system of subjective idealism is called Berkeleianism.

Emmanuel Swedenborg (1688–1772). Swedish mystic, scientist, theologian; author of *Principia Rerum Naturalium*, 1734.

David Hume (1711–76). Scottish philosopher and historian. An empiricist who carried on ideas of Locke, but developed a system of scepticism (Humism) according to which human knowledge is limited to experience of ideas and sensations, whose truth cannot be verified.

Jean-Jacques Rousseau (1712–78). French political philosopher whose concepts have had a profound influence on modern thought; advocated a 'return to nature' to counteract the inequality among men brought about by civilized society.

Adam Smith (1723–90). Founder of modern political economy and a leader of the 'Scottish Renaissance'. His *Wealth of Nations* (1776), with its emphasis on economic liberalism and natural liberty, has had a more profound influence than almost any other philosophical work.

Immanuel Kant (1724–1804). German founder of critical philosophy. At first influenced by

Leibniz, then by Hume, he sought to find an alternative approach to the rationalism of the former and the scepticism of the latter; in ethics, formulated the Categorical Imperative – which states that what applies to oneself must apply to everyone else unconditionally – a restatement of the Christian precept 'Do unto others as you would have them do unto you'.

Jeremy Bentham (1748–1832). English Utilitarian. Believed, like Kant, that the interests of the individual are one with those of society, but regarded fear of consequences rather than basic principle as the motivation for right action.

Johann Gottlieb Fichte (1762–1814). German; formulated a philosophy of absolute idealism based on Kant's ethical concepts.

19th Century

Georg Wilhelm Friedrich Hegel (1770–1831). German; his metaphysical system, known as Hegelianism, was rationalist and absolutist, based on the belief that thought and being are one, and nature is the manifestation of an Absolute Idea.

Arthur Schopenhauer (1788–1860). German who gave the will a leading place in his metaphysics. The foremost expounder of pessimism, expressed in *The World as Will and Idea*. Rejected absolute idealism as wishful thinking, and taught that the only tenable attitude lay in utter indifference to an irrational world; an idealist who held that the highest ideal was nothingness.

Auguste Comte (1798–1857). French founder of positivism, a system which denied transcendant metaphysics and stated that the Divinity and man were one, that altruism is man's highest duty, and that scientific principles explain all phenomena.

John Stuart Mill (1806–73). English; major exponent of Utilitarianism, who differed from Bentham by recognizing differences in quality as well as quantity in pleasure. Most famous work *On Liberty* (1859).

Søren Kierkegaard (1813–55). Danish religious existentialist, whose thought is the basis of modern (atheistic) existentialism; taught that 'existence precedes essence' that only existence has reality, and the individual has a unique value.

Karl Marx (1818–83). German revolutionist, from whom the movement known as Marxism derives its name and many of its ideas; his works became, in the late 19th century, the basis of European socialism; published *The Communist Manifesto* with Friedrich Engels in 1848.

Herbert Spencer (1820–1903). English evolutionist whose 'synthetic philosophy' interpreted all phenomena according to the principle of evolutionary progress.

Charles S Pierce (1839–1914). American physicist and mathematician who founded philosophical school called pragmatism; regarded logic as the basis of philosophy and taught that the test of an idea is whether it works.

William James (1842–1910). American psychologist and pragmatist who held that reality is always in the making and that each man should choose the philosophy best suited to him.

Friedrich Wilhelm Nietzsche (1844–1900). German philosopher and poet. An evolutionist who held that the 'will to power' is basic in life, that the spontaneous is to be preferred to the orderly; attacked Christianity as a system that fostered the weak, whereas the function of evolution is to evolve 'supermen'.

20th Century

Edmund Husserl (1859–1938). German who developed a system called 'phenomenology', which asserts that realities other than mere appearance exist – called essences.

Henri Bergson (1859–1941). French evolutionist who asserted the existence of a 'vital impulse' that carries the universe forward, with no fixed beginning and no fixed end – the future is determined by the choice of alternatives made in the present.

John Dewey (1859–1952). American; basically a pragmatist, he developed a system known as instrumentalism. Saw man as continuous with but distinct from nature.

Alfred North Whitehead (1861–1947). British evolutionist and mathematician who held that reality must not be interpreted in atomistic terms, but in terms of events; that God is intimately present in the universe, yet distinct from it, a view called panentheism, as opposed to pantheism, which simply equates God and Nature.

George Santayana (1863–1952). American born in Spain; a foremost critical realist who held that the ultimate substance of the world is matter in motion – and the mind itself is a product of matter in motion.

Benedetto Croce (1866–1952). The best-known Italian philosopher of 20th century. Noted for his role in revival of historical realism in Italy 1900–1920.

Bertrand Russell (1872–1970). British agnostic who adhered to many systems of philosophy before becoming chief exponent of scientism, the view that all knowledge is solely attainable by the scientific method.

George Edward Moore (1873–1958). Rigorous British moral scientist. Developed doctrine of Ideal Utilitarianism in *Principia Ethica*, 1903.

Karl Jaspers (1883–1969). German existentialist who approached the subject from man's practical concern with his own existence.

Ludwig Wittgenstein (1889–1951). Austrian; developed the philosophy of language.

Martin Heidegger (1889–1976). German student of Husserl, he furthered development of phenomenology and greatly influenced atheistic existentialists.

Friedrich von Hayek (b. 1899). Austrian economist and philosopher. Argues that social science must not try to ape the method of physics. What can be predicted and used for analysis is an abstract pattern which leaves the details unspecified.

Karl Popper (b. 1902). British of Austrian extraction. Exponent of critical rationalism arguing that scientific laws can never be proved to be true; the most that can be claimed is that they have survived attempts to disprove them. Writer from liberal and individualistic standpoint.

Jean-Paul Sartre (1905–1980). French; developed existentialist thought of Heidegger; atheistic supporter of a subjective, irrational human existence, as opposed to an orderly overall reality.

Alfred J. Ayer (b. 1910). British, principal advocate of logical positivism, a modern extension of the thinking of Hume and Comte.

Religion

Religions of The World

(estimates in millions)

Christian	1063
Roman Catholic	628
Eastern Orthodox	63
Protestant	373
Muslim (Islam)	554
Hindu	461
Buddhist	249
Confucian	158
Shinto	32
Taoist	20
Jewish	17

The main religions of the world below are listed in order of their chronological appearance.

Judaism

The word Jew is derived through the Latin *Judaeus*, from the Hebrew *Yehudhi*, signifying a descendant of Judah, the fourth son of Jacob whose tribe, with that of his half brother, Benjamin, made up the peoples of the kingdom of Judah. This kingdom was separate from the remaining tribes of Israel. The exodus of the Israelites from Egypt is believed to have occurred *c.* 1400 BC.

Judaism is monotheistic and based on the covenant that Israel is the bearer of the belief in the one and only God.

From 311 until 1790 Jews existed under severe disabilities and discrimination in most Christian and Moslem areas. Jewish emancipation began with the enfranchisement of Jews in France in Sept. 1791. This touched off antisemitism which in return fired Zionism. The first Zionist Congress was held in Basle, Switzerland, in Aug. 1897.

The Balfour letter written on 2 Nov. 1917 by Arthur Balfour, British foreign secretary, addressed to Lord Rothschild declared 'His Majesty's Government view with favour the establishment of Palestine as a natural home for the Jewish people. . .'.

On 24 July 1922 the League of Nations approved a British mandate over Palestine. These policies led to bitter Arab resistance with revolts in 1929 and 1936–39 claiming the right of self-determination. The irreconcilable aims of Arab nationalism and Zionism led to partition with the creation of Israel (*q.v.*) on 14 May 1948 and the internationalizing of Jerusalem.

There are over 25 000 Thalessa Jews living in Ethiopia and the Horn of Africa.

Jewish holidays including *Pesach* (Passover), celebrating the Exodus, *Shabuoth* (Pentecost), *Rosh Hashana* (New Year) and *Yom Kippur* (Day of Atonement) devoted to fasting, meditation and prayer.

Yiddish, an Eastern Vernacular form of mediaeval German, is unrelated to Semitic Hebrew.

Hinduism

The precise date of the origin of Hinduism, or Sanatān-Dharma (ancient way of life) or Arya-Dharma (Aryan way of life) is not known, although the early Indus and Gangetic civilisations (approx: 3500 BC) may have made some contributions. There are no beliefs common to all Hindus and Hinduism is indeed very diverse for it covers 'Bhakti' (devotion) as well as 'Gyān' (knowledge). The Hindu caste system originally started as division of labour, but later, especially during non-Hindu domination it became very rigid. The Vedas (divine or sacred knowledge) was passed on by the Rishis and Munis (learned sages) to the people in the form of Mantras (Sanskrit verses). Brahma, Vishnu and Shiva represent Creation, preservation and destruction. To be reunited either with the Nirākār (form-less) or Sākār (with form), depending upon one's choice, one could either follow the path of devotion (Bhakti) or knowledge (Gyān) or a mixture of both.

The living status in the next life, if any, is determined by Karma (actions) in present life. When one's Karma are righteous, then, upon death there is unity with the supreme, and Moksha (freedom) from the birth and death cycle. If the way of life is not righteous, the birth and death cycle continues. Life is divided into (1) Brahmacharya (celibate period) (2) Grahastha (householder) (3) Vānprastha (retired stage) (4) Sanyās (renunciation).

Hinduism is not an organised religion. There is absolute freedom with regard to the choice and mode of one's philosophy. It is understood that while choosing one's own philosophy one has to follow basic human rules which are universal and can be summed up in an ancient Sanskrit phrase 'Vasudhaiv Kutumbakam' which means 'the whole world is one family'.

Hinduism and the problems within the present social system of the Hindus are entirely separate matters. Gandhian 'Ahimsa' (non-violence) was inspired by the Hindu philosophy as well. Generally speaking the Hindu philosophy could be summed up in the following translated verse (original in Sanskrit) from the ancient 'Bhagvad-Gitā' 'One has control over one's actions but not over the results'.

The recent interest in Hindu culture and philosophy in Europe and America, e.g. The International Society for Krishna Consciousness, or various other organisations, is a modern facet of Hinduism, absolutely without any parallel in its entire history.

Buddhism

Buddhism is based on the teaching of the Indian prince, Siddhartha (later called Gautama) (*c.* 563–483 BC) of the Gautama clan of the Sakyas, later named Gautama Buddha (*buddha* meaning 'the enlightened one'). Aśoka, a 3rd Century BC King of Magadha [Gonyes] is regarded as a progenitor of Buddhism. After seeing in *c.* 534 BC for the first time a sick man, an old man, a holy man and a dead man, he wandered fruitlessly for six years, after which he meditated for 49 days under a Bodhi tree at Gaya in Magadha. He achieved enlightenment or *nirvana* and taught salvation in Bihar, west of Bengal, until he died, aged 80. Gautama's teaching was essentially a protesting offshoot of early Hinduism. It contains four Noble Truths: (1) Man suffers from one life to the next; (2) the Origin of suffering is craving; craving for pleasure, possessions and the cessation of pain; (3) the cure for craving is non-attachment to all things including self; (4) the way to non-attachment is the Eight-fold path of right conduct, right effort, right intentions, right livelihood, right meditations, right mindfulness, right speech and right views.

Buddhism makes no provisions for God and hence has no element of divine judgement or messianic expectation. It provides an inexorable law or *dharma* of cause and effect which determines the individual's fate.

The vast body or *sangha* of monks and nuns practise celibacy, non-violence, poverty and vegetarianism. Under the *Hinayana*, or Lesser Vehicle, tradition of India only they have hope of attaining *nirvana*. Under the *Mahayana*, or Greater Vehicle, as practised in Indo-China, China and Japan, laymen as well may attain the highest ideal of *bodhisattva*, the enlightened one who liberates himself by personal sacrifice. Under Zen Buddhism enlightenment or *satori* is achieved only by prolonged meditation and mental and physical shock.

Confucianism

Confucius (551–479 BC) was not the sole founder of Confucianism but was rather a member of the founding group of *Ju* or meek ones. Confucius is the Latinized version of K'ung Fu-tzo or Master K'ung who was a keeper of accounts from the province of Lu. He became the first teacher in Chinese history to instruct the people of all ranks in the six arts: ceremonies, music, archery, charioteering, history and numbers.

Confucius taught that the main ethic is *jen* (benevolence), and that truth involves the knowledge of one's own faults. He believed in altruism and insisted on filial piety. He decided that people could be led by example and aimed at the rulers of his own time imitating those in a former period of history, where he attributed the prosperity of the people to the leadership of the Emperors. Confucianism included the worship of Heaven and revered ancestors and great men, though Confucius himself did not advocate prayer, believing that man should direct his own destiny.

Confucianism can be better described as a religious philosophy or code of social behaviour, rather than a religion in the accepted sense, since it has no church or clergy and is in no way an institution. For many years it had a great hold over education, its object being to emphasize the development of human nature and the person. During the early 19th century attempts were made by followers to promote Confucianism to being a state religion, and though this failed, a good deal of the Confucian teachings still remain despite the onslaught of Communist ideology in the traditional area of its influence.

Christianity

The religion Christianity takes its name from Jesus Christ*, son of the Virgin Mary, whose subsequent husband, Joseph of Nazareth, was 27 generations descended from David. His birth is now regarded as occurring at Bethlehem in the summer of 4 BC or earlier. The discrepancy is due to an error in the 6th century by Dionysius Exiguus in establishing the dating of the Christian era.

The principles of Christianity are proclaimed in the New Testament which was written in Greek and of which the earliest complete surviving manuscript dates from AD *c.* 350.

Christ was crucified in the reign of the Roman emperor Tiberius during the procuratorship in Judaea of Pontius Pilate in AD 29 or according to the Roman Catholic chronology, 7 April, AD 30.

The primary commandment of Jesus was to love God. His second commandment (Mark xii, 31) was to 'love thy neighbour' in a way that outward performance alone did not suffice.

Hate was prohibited and not only adultery but evil lust (Matt. v, 21).

Unselfishness and compassion are central themes in Christianity.

Jesus appointed twelve disciples; the following are common to the lists in the books of Matthew, Mark, Luke and the Acts.

---

* Jesus (the Saviour, from Hebrew root *yasha'*, to save) Christ (the anointed one, from Greek, Χριω, *chrio*, to anoint).

1. Peter, Saint Peter (brother of Andrew).
2. Andrew, Saint Andrew (brother of Peter).
3. James, son of Zebedee (brother of John).
4. John, Saint John (the Apostle) (brother of James).
5. Philip.
6. Bartholomew.
7. Thomas.
8. Matthew, Saint Matthew.
9. James, of Alphaeus.
10. Simon the Canaanean (in Matthew and Mark) or Simon Zelotes (in Luke and the Acts).
11. Judas Iscariot (not an apostle).

Thaddaeus in the book of Matthew and Mark is the twelfth disciple, while in Luke and the Acts the twelfth is Judas of James. The former may have been a nickname or place name to distinguish Judas of James from the Iscariot. Matthias succeeded to the place of the betrayer Judas Iscariot.

Roman Catholicism
Roman Catholic Christianity is that practised by those who acknowledge the supreme jurisdiction of the bishop of Rome (the Pope) and recognize him as the lawful successor of St. Peter who was appointed by Christ Himself to be head of the church. Peter visited Rome c. AD 42 and was martyred there c. AD 67. Pope John Paul II is his 263rd successor.

The Roman Catholic Church claims catholicity inasmuch as she was charged (de jure) by Christ to 'teach all nations' and de facto since her adherents are by far the most numerous among Christians. The Roman Catholic Church is regarded as the infallible interpreter both of the written (5 of the 12 apostles wrote) and the unwritten word of God. The organization of the Church is the Curia, the work of which is done by 11 permanent departments or congregations.

The great majority of Catholics are of the Roman rite and use the Roman liturgy. While acknowledging the hierarchical supremacy of the Holy See other Eastern Churches or Uniate Rites enjoy an autonomy. These include (1) the Byzantine or Greek rite, (2) the Armenian rite, and (3) the Coptic rite.

The doctrine of the Immaculate Conception was proclaimed on 8 Dec. 1854, and that of Papal Infallibility was adopted by the Ecumenical Council by 547 votes to 2 on 18 July 1870. The 21st Council was convened by Pope John XXIII. The election of Popes is by the College of Cardinals.

Eastern Orthodox
The church officially described as 'The Holy Orthodox Catholic Apostolic Eastern Church' consists of those churches which accepted all the decrees of the first seven General Councils and such churches as have since sprung up in that tradition.

The origin arises from the splitting of the old Roman Empire into a Western or Latin half, centred on Rome, and an Eastern or Greek half, centred on Constantinople.

Some features of this branch of Christianity are that bishops must be unmarried; the dogma of the immaculate conception is not admitted; icons are in the churches but the only 'graven image' is the crucifix; and fasts are frequent and rigorous.

Protestant
The term 'protestant' had never been used officially in the style of any church until the Anglican community in North America called themselves the 'Protestant Episcopal Church' during the 17th century. The name has never been officially used by the Church of England.

Islam (Mohammedanism)

Islām is the world's second largest religion with its emphasis on an uncompromising monotheism and a strict adherence to certain religious practices. It belongs to the Semitic family and was founded by Muhammad (Mohammed or Mahomet) (AD 575–632) on 16 July AD 622 at Yathrib, now known as Al Madīnah, (Medina) in Saudi Arabia.

Muhammad, a member of the Koreish tribe, was a caravan conductor and later became a shop-keeper in Mekkah (Mecca). There is some evidence that he was semi-literate, at least in early manhood. He did not become a public preacher until 616. Soon after 622 [AH (anno Hegirae or the year of exile) 1] Muhammad turned the direction of his prayer southward from Jerusalem and an Israeli God towards the temple at Mecca and the God Allah. Muhammad soon became an administrator, general, judge and legislator in addition to being one through whom divine revelation was communicated.

The Arabic term islām literally meaning 'surrender' points to the fundamental religious idea of Islām namely that the believer, called a Muslim, accepts 'surrender to the Will of Allāh', who is viewed as the unique God. The Will of Allah is made known through the Qur'ān (Koran), the Book revealed to his messenger Muhammad. The basic belief of Islām is expressed in the Shahādah, the Muslim confession of faith: 'There is no God but Allah and Muhammad is his Prophet!' From this fundamental belief are derived beliefs in (1) angels, (particularly Gabriel), (2) the revealed Books (of the Jewish and Christian faiths in addition to the Qur'ān), (3) a series of prophets and (4) the Last Day, the Day of Judgement. Acceptance of this essential creed involves further duties that are to be strictly observed: five daily prayer sessions, a welfare tax called the zakāt, fasting during the month of Ramadān and a pilgrimage (hajj) to Mecca, all of which – including the profession of faith – are called the Five Pillars. Ramadān is the ninth month of the Muslim lunar calendar.

Shī'ism and Sunnism are the two main forms of Islām, others being Sufism, Mu'tazilah, Khārijism and other minor forms. Although the majority of Muslims are Sunnis, the Shī'ah (who number only about 40 000 000) are the most important surviving sect (the population of Iran is about 93% Shī'i). Shī'ism has exerted a great influence on Sunni Islām, although their doctrines differ greatly. Besides the main body of Twelver (Ithnā 'Asharīyah) Shī'ah, Shī'ism has produced a variety of extremist sects, the most conspicuous being the Ismā'īlī.

Though the sheer variety of races and cultures embraced by Islām has produced differences, all segments of Muslim society are bound by a common faith and a sense of belonging to a single community. With the loss of political power during the period of Western colonialism in the 19th and early 20th centuries, the concept of the Islāmic community, instead of weakening, became stronger. This, in harness with the discovery of immense oil reserves, helped various Muslim peoples in their struggle to gain political freedom and sovereignty in the mid-20th century.

Shinto

Shintō ('the teaching' or 'the way of the gods') came into practice during the 6th century AD to distinguish the Japanese religion from Buddhism which was reaching the islands by way of the mainland. The early forms of Shintō were a simple nature worship, and a religion for those who were not impelled by any complicated religious lore. The help of the deities was sought for the physical and spiritual needs of the people and there was great stress laid upon purification and truthfulness.

The more important national shrines were dedicated to well-known national figures, but there were also those set up for the worship of deities of mountain and forest.

During the 19th century, thirteen Sect Shintō denominations were formed and these were dependent on private support for their teaching and organization. They had very little in common and varied widely in beliefs and practices. Some adhered to the traditional Shintō deites while others did not. Of the 13 denominations Tenrikyō is the one with the greatest following outside Japan.

Theories of Shintō have been greatly influenced by Confucianism, Taoism and Buddhism. In 1868, however, the Department of Shintō was established and attempts were made to do away with the Shintō and Buddhist coexistence, and in 1871 Shintō was proclaimed the Japanese national religion. Following World War II the status was discontinued.

Taoism

Lao-tzu (Lao-tze or Lao-tse), the Chinese philosopher and founder of Taoism, was, according to tradition, born in the sixth century BC. Lao-tzu taught that Taoism (Tao = the Ultimate and Unconditioned Being) could be attained by virtue if thrift, humility and compassion were practised.

Taoism has the following features – numerous gods (though Lao-tzu did not himself permit this); a still persisting, though now decreasing, body of superstition; and two now declining schools – the 13th-century Northern School with its emphasis on man's life, and the Southern School, probably of 10th century origin, stressing the nature of man. Various Taoist societies have been formed more recently by laymen, who though worshipping deities of many religions, promote charity and a more moral culture. The moral principles of Taoism consist of simplicity, patience, contentment and harmony. Since the decline of its espousal by the T'ang dynasty (AD 618–906), it has proved to be chiefly the religion of the semi-literate.

Philosophical Taoism or Tao-chia advocates naturalism and is thus opposed to regulations and organization of any kind. After the 4th century BC when Buddhism and Taoism began to influence each other there was a weakening of this anti-collectivist strain but the philosophy still has a strong hold over the way of life and culture in parts of China.

The religion imitates Buddhism in the matter of clergy and temple, the chief of which is the White Cloud temple in Peking, China.

The Pope

Otherwise known as the Bishop of Rome, the Pope is the chief bishop of the Roman Catholic Church, considered by Catholics to be the Vicar of Christ on earth and the successor of St Peter, the first Bishop of Rome. He is thus looked upon as the supreme head of the Church on earth and the chief pastor of the whole Church.

The Pope is elected by the College of Cardinals in the Vatican City, meeting in secret conclave. The election is by scrutiny and requires a two-thirds majority.

The Popes over the last 300 years have been as follows.

Benedict XIV	(Lambertini)	elected 1740
Clement XIII	(Rezzonico)	elected 1758
Clement XIV	(Ganganelli)	elected 1769
Pius VI	(Braschi)	elected 1775
Pius VII	(Chiaramonti)	elected 1800
Leo XII	(della Genga)	elected 1823
Pius VIII	(Castiglioni)	elected 1829
Gregory XIV	(Cappellari)	elected 1831
Pius IX	(Mastai-Ferretti)	elected 1846
Leo XIII	(Pecci)	elected 1878
Pius X	(Sarto)	elected 1903
Benedict XV	(della Chiesa)	elected 1914
Pius XI	(Ratti)	elected 1922
Pius XII	(Pacelli)	elected 1939
John XXIII	(Roncalli)	elected 1958
Paul VI	(Montini)	elected 1963
John Paul I	(Luciani)	elected 1978
John Paul II	(Wojtyla)	elected 1978

Versions of the Bible in English

The Bible was first brought in Latin form to England by Aidan in the north and St Augustine in the south. After that various parts were translated or summarized: the poem of *Caedmon* (8th century?); the works of *Bede* and *Alfred* are considered to have advanced the cause, but little, if anything remains of their efforts.

The *Lindisfarne Gospels* of the 10th century represent the first extant translation of the gospels into English. From then on, various parts of the Bible as we know it were translated notably by Aelfric and Richard Rolle (d. 1349).

The first complete version of the bible in English was translated by William Wycliffe, whose translations were completed in 1384. A list of versions to the present day is given below.
Tyndale's version (New Testament only) *c.* 1526.
Coverdale's Bible (Old and New Testaments) 1535.
Matthew's Bible 1537.
Taverner's Bible 1539.
The Great Bible 1539.
The Geneva Bible 1557.
The Bishop's Bible 1568.
The Rheims and Douai Bible 1582.
The Authorized Version (King James' Version) 1611.
Since the Authorized Version, there have been many versions in English translation. A list of some of the more well-known is given below.
The Revised Version 1885.
The American Standard Version 1901.
The Jerusalem Bible 1966.
The New English Bible 1970.
The Jerusalem Bible 1976.
The Good News Bible (Today's English Version).

Greek Gods and Goddesses

Adonis God of vegetation and re-birth.
Aeolus God of the winds.
Alphito Barley goddess of Argos
Aphrodite Goddess of love and beauty.
Apollo God of prophecy, music and medicine.
Ares God of war.
Arethusa Goddess of springs and fountains.
Artemis Goddess of fertility.
Asclepius God of healing.
Athene Goddess of prudence and wise council; and protectress of Athens.
Atlas A Titan who bears up the earth.
Attis God of vegetation.
Boreas God of the Northern wind.
Cronus Father of the God *Zeus*.
Cybele Goddess of the earth.
Demeter Goddess of the harvest.
Dionysus God of wine and the 'good life'.
Eos Goddess of the dawn.
Eros God of love.
Gaia Goddess of the earth.
Ganymede God of rain.
Hebe Goddess of youth.
Hecate Goddess of the moon.
Helios God of the sun.
Hera Goddess of the sky.
Hermes God of trade and travellers.
Hestia Goddess of fire.
Hypnos God of sleep.
Iris Goddess of the rainbow.
Morpheus God of dreams.
Nemesis God of destiny.
Nereus God of the sea.
Nike Goddess of victory.
Oceanus Ruler of the sea.
Pan God of male sexuality and of herds.
Persephone Goddess of the underworld and of corn.
Pluto God of the underworld.
Poseidon God of the sea.
Prometheus God of creation.
Rhea The original Mother Goddess; wife of Cronus.
Selene Goddess of the moon.
Thanatos God of death.
Zeus The overlord of the Olympian gods and goddesses; God of the sky and all its properties.

Roman Gods and Goddesses

Bellona Goddess of war.
Ceres Goddess of corn.
Consus God of seed sowing.
Cupid God of love.
Diana Goddess of fertility and hunting.
Dis Pater God of the underworld.
Egreria Goddess of fountains and childbirth.
Epona Goddess of horses.
Fauna Goddess of fertility and herds.
Faunus God of crops and herds.
Feronia Goddess of spring flowers.
Fides God of honesty.
Flora Goddess of fruitfulness and flowers.
Fortuna Goddess of chance and fate.
Genius Protective god of individuals, groups and the state.
Janus God of entrances, travel, the dawn.
Juno Goddess of marriage, childbirth, light.
Jupiter God of the sky and its attributes (sun, moon, thunder, rain, etc.).
Lar God of the house.
Liber Pater God of agricultural and human fertility.
Libitina Goddess of funeral rites.
Maia Goddess of fertility.
Mars God of war and agriculture.
Mercury The messenger god; also god of merchants.
Minerva Goddess of war, craftsmen, education.
Mithras The sun god; god of regeneration.
Neptune God of the sea.
Ops Goddess of the harvest.
Orcus God of death.
Pales Goddess of flocks.
Penates Gods of food and drink.
Picus God of agriculture.
Pomono Goddess of fruit trees.
Portunus God of husbands.
Rumina Goddess of nursing mothers.
Saturn God of the vine, and of working men.
Silvanus God of trees and forests.
Venus Goddess of spring, gardens (later, goddess of love).
Vertumnus God of fruit trees.
Vesta Goddess of fire.
Victoria Goddess of victory.
Vulcan God of fire and thunderbolts.

Norse Gods and Goddesses

Aegir God of the sea.
Alcis Twin gods of the sky.
Baldur Son of Odin.
Bor Father of Odin.
Bragi God of poetry.
Donar God of thunder.
Fafnir A dragon god.
Fjorgynn Mother of Thor.
Freyja Goddess of libido.
Freyr God of fertility.
Frigg Goddess of fertility; wife of Odin.
Gefion Goddess who received virgins after death.
Heimdall Guardian of the bridge Bifrost.
Hel Goddess of death; Queen of Niflheim, the land of mists.
Hermod Son of Odin.
Hoder Blind god who killed Baldur.
Idunn Guardian goddess of the golden apples of youth; wife of Bragi.
Ing Founder God of the Anglo-Saxons and of the dynasty of Berenicia.
Kvasir God of wise utterances.
Logi The fire-god.
Loki God of mischief.
Mimir God of wisdom.
Nanna Goddess wife of Baldur.
Nehallenia Goddess of plenty.
Nerthus Goddess of earth.
Njord God of ships and the sea.
Odin (*Woden, Wotan*) Chief of the Aesir family of gods, the 'father' god, the god of battle, death, inspiration.
Otr The otter-god.
Ran Goddess of the sea.

Sif Goddess wife of Thor.
Sigyn Goddess wife of Loki.
Thor God of thunder and the sky; god of crops.
Tiwaz God of battle.
Valkyries Female helpers of the gods of war.
Weland (*Volundr, Weiland, Wayland*) The craftsman god.

Religious and other Festivals

Muslim festivals
Weekly (Friday) Day of Assembly
1 Muharram New Year's Day
1–10 Muharram New Year Festival (*Muharram*)
12 Rabi' ul-Awwal Festival of the Prophet's Birthday
26 Rajab Festival of the Prophet's Night Journey and Ascension
15 Sha'ban Night of Forgiveness
1–29/30 Ramadan Annual Fast (*Ramadan*)
1 Shawal Festival of Breaking the Fast (*Eid-ul-Fitr*)
9 Dhul-Hijjah Day of Arafat
10 Dhul-Hijjah Festival of Sacrifice (*Eid-ul-Adha*)
NB The dates vary against the Gregorian calendar, from year to year (see Islamic Calendar, p 6).

Buddhist festivals
Weekly Uposatha Days
Different festivals and, in some cases, different dates for similar festivals, are observed in the different countries where Buddhism is practised.

Burma
16/17 April New Year
May/June The Buddha's Birth, Enlightenment and Death
July The Buddha's First Sermon/Beginning of the Rains Retreat
October End of the Rains Retreat
November Kathina Ceremony

China
June/August Summer Retreat
August Festival of Hungry Ghosts
Gautama Buddha's Birth
Kuan-Yin

Sri Lanka
13 April New Year
May/June The Buddha's Birth, Enlightenment and Death
June/July Establishment of Buddhism in Sri Lanka
July The Buddha's First Sermon
July/August Procession of the Month of Asala
September The Buddha's First Visit to Sri Lanka
December/January Arrival of Sanghamitta

Thailand
13–16 April New Year
May The Buddha's Enlightenment
May/June The Buddha's Cremation
July–October Rains Retreat
October End of the Rains Retreat
November Kathina Ceremony
November Festival of Lights
February All Saints' Day

Tibet
February New Year
May The Buddha's Birth, Enlightenment and Death
June Dzamling Chisang
June/July The Buddha's First Sermon
October The Buddha's Descent from Tushita
November Death of Tsongkhapa
January The Conjunction of Nine Evils and the Conjunction of Ten Virtues

Christian festivals
1 January The Solemnity of Mary Mother of God
6 January Epiphany
25 January Conversion of St Paul
February Shrove Tuesday; Ash Wednesday

2 February Hypapante
　　　　The Presentation of Christ in the Temple
February–March/April Lent (The Great Fast)
19 March St Joseph
25 March The Annunciation of the Lord
March/April Holy Week; Palm Sunday; Maundy Thursday; Good Friday; Holy Saturday; Easter
25 April St Mark
May Ascension
1 May St Philip and St James
14 May St Matthias
31 May The Visitation of the Blessed Virgin Mary
May/June The Fathers of the First Ecumenical Church Pentecost; Trinity Sunday; All Saints; Corpus Christi
11 June St Barnabus
29 June St Peter and St Paul
July The Sacred Heart of Jesus
3 July St Thomas
25 July St James
6 August The Transfiguration
24 August St Bartholomew
1 September New Year (Eastern Orthodox Church)
8 September The Nativity of the Blessed Virgin Mary
14 September The Exaltation of the Holy Cross
21 September St Matthew
29 September St Michael and All Angels (Michaelmas)
18 October St Luke
28 October St Simon and St Jude
1 November All Saints
21 November Presentation of the Blessed Virgin Mary in the Temple
30 November St Andrew
November–December Advent
7 December St John
8 December The Immaculate Conception of the Blessed Virgin Mary
25 December Christmas
26 December St Stephen
27 December St John
28 December Holy Innocents

Jewish festivals
Weekly Sabbath (*Shabat*)
Monthly New Moon (*Rosh Hodesh*)
January/February (15 Shevat) Festival of 15 Shevat/New Year for Trees (*Tu B'Shevat*)
February/March (13 Adar) Fast of Ester (*Taanit Ester*), (14 Adar) Festival of Lots (*Purim*)
March/April (14 Nisan) Fast of the First-born (*Taanit Behorim*), (15/16–21/22 Nisan) Passover (*Pesah*), (27 Nisan) Holocaust Day (*Yom Ha-Shoah*)
April/May (4 Iyyar) Remembrance Day (*Yom Ha'Zikharon*), (5 Iyyar) Independence Day (*Yom Ha'Atzmaut*), (18 Iyyar) 33rd Day of Counting the Omer, (28 Iyyar) Jerusalem Day (*Yom Yer Shalayim*)
May/June (6/7 Sivan) Festival of Weeks (*Shavuot*), (20 Sivan) Fast of 20 Sivan
June/July (17 Tammuz) Fast of 17 Tammuz
July/August (9 Av) Fast of 9 Av (*Tisha B'Av*), (15 Av) Festival of 15 Av (*Tu B'Av*)
August/September (1 Ellul) Festival of 1 Ellul/New Year for Cattle
September/October (1/2 Tishri) New Year (*Rosh Hashanah*), (3 Tishri) Fast of Gedaliah (*Tsom Gedaliah*), (10 Tishri) Day of Atonement (*Yom Kippur*), (15/16–22/23 Tishri) Festival of Tabernacles (*Sukkot*), (22/23 Tishri) Eighth Day of Conclusion (*Shemini Atzeret*), (23 Tishri) Rejoicing in the Torah (*Simhat Torah*)
November/December (25 Kislev–2 Tevet) Festival of the Dedication of the Temple/Festival of Lights (*Hanukah*)
December/January (10 Tevet) Feast of 10 Tevet

Hindu festivals
January Makar Sankranti/Til Sankranti/Lohri, Pongal, Kumbha Mela at Prayag (every twelve years)
January/February Vasanta Panchami/Shri Panchami/Saraswati Puja, Bhogali Bihu, Mahashivratri
20 February Ramakrishna Utsav
February/March Holi
March/April Ugadi, Basora, Rama Navami, Hanuman Jayanti
April Vaisakhi

April/May Akshaya Tritiya, Chittrai
May/June Ganga Dasa-hara, Nirjala Ekadashi, Snan-yatra
June/July Ratha-yatra/Jagannatha, Ashadhi Ekadashi/Toli Ekadashi
July/August Teej, Naga Panchami, Raksha Bandhan/Shravana Purnima/Salono/Rakhi Purnima
August/September Onam, Ganesha Chaturthi, Janamashtami/Krishna Jayanti
September/October Mahalaya/Shraddha/Pitri Paksha/Kanagat, Navaratri/Durga Puja/Dassehra, Lakshmi Puja (West Bengal and Himachal Pradesh)
2 October Gandhi Jayanti
October/November Divali/Deepavali, Chhath, Karttika Ekadashi/Devuthna Ekadashi/Tulsi Ekadashi Karttika Purnima/Tripuri Purnima, Hoi, Skanda Shasti
November/December Vaikuntha Ekadashi, Lakshmi Puja (Orissa)

Chinese festivals
January/February Chinese New Year
February/March Lantern Festival
March/April Festival of Pure Brightness
May/June Dragon Boat Festival
July/August Herd Boy and Weaving Maid
August All Souls' Festival
September Mid-Autumn Festival
September/October Double Ninth Festival
November/December Winter Solstice

Painting and Sculpture

Drawing is the process of artistic depiction on a two-dimensional surface by linear (and sometimes tonal) means, of objects or abstractions.

Painting is the visual and aesthetic expression of ideas and emotions primarily in two dimensions, using colour, line, shapes, texture and tones.

Sculpture describes the processes of carving, or engraving, modelling and casting so as to produce representations or abstraction of an artistic nature in relief, in intaglio, or in the round.

Styles and movements

PALAEOLITHIC ART
from 24 000 BC
Cave painting of the Perigordian (Aurignacian period) and the later Solutrean and Magdalenian

periods (18 000–11 000 BC) first discovered at Chaffaud, Vienne, France in 1834. Lascaux examples discovered 1940. Cave painting also discovered in Czechoslovakia, the Urals, USSR, India, Australia (Mootwingie dates from *c.* 1500 BC) and North Africa (earliest is from the Bubulus period in the Sahara *post* 5400 BC).

MESOPOTAMIAN ART 3600–600 BC
Covering the Sumerian, Assyrian and Babylonian epochs, it is epitomised by many styles which incorporate figures, animals, plants and mythical animals. Is seen now mainly in the sculptural works on palaces (Nineveh) and on tiles.

EGYPTIAN ART (3100–341 BC)
It is essentially a decorative tomb art, based on the notion of immortality, and provided that a deceased was recorded and equipped for the

after-life in writing (heiroglyph), pictures and material wealth and goods.

ANCIENT GREEK 2000–27 BC
Minoan and Mycenaean art (2800–1100 BC) consists mainly of sculptured engravings, decorated pottery and some frescoes. The Archaic period (800–500 BC) saw the development of sculpture, especially human figures. This tendency was developed in the Classical period (500–323 BC) where the body was glorified and drapery carved to imitate movement. The Hellenistic period (323–27 BC) expressed the emotions and was noticeable for its portraits. Throughout the entire period pottery was decorated with figures and scenes from story and legend.

ROMAN ART (100 BC – AD 400)
Based on Greek art, it excelled in copying Greek sculpture and relief carving of a very high quality. Portraiture also was popular. Roman painting was mainly executed in fresco in a naturalistic style (Pompeii). Mosaic floors were also highly decorative.

EARLY CHRISTIAN AD 200
Funerary fresco painting in the Roman catacombs ended with Constantine.

MIGRATION PERIOD 150–1000
A general term covering the art of the Huns with strong Asian influence and the Revised post-Roman Celtic art in Ireland and Britain, the pre-Carolingian Frankish art and the art of the Vikings.

BYZANTINE ART c. 330–c. 1450
At first an admixture of Hellenic, Roman, Middle Eastern and Oriental styles, it dates from and has its first centre in the establishment of Constantinople as capital of the Roman Empire in the East. The First Golden Age was reached in the 6th century, when Hagia Sophia (St Sophia) was built in the city. The Second Golden Age occurred between 1051 and 1185 when Western Europe was influenced by its severe, spiritually uplifted style. These two Ages are chiefly artistically dominated by the use of mosaic work, but by the Third Golden Age (1261–1450) this expensive medium was being replaced by fresco painting.

ISLAMIC ART 7th century–17th century
Originally based on superb Koranic calligraphy, it is a highly decorative art form which reaches its apotheosis in the miniature painting, the ceramic tile, and carpetmaking in which floral and geometric motives reach a high peak of formal perfection.

ROMANESQUE ART 1050–1200
A widespread European style, mainly architectural, distinguished by the use of rounded arches. The sculpture is mainly church work intended to inspire awe of the divine power by depicting scenes of heaven and hell, demons and angels and the omnipotent deity. Illuminated manuscripts of high quality include the Winchester Bible.

GOTHIC ART (1125–1450)
The style of architecture, painting and sculpture which succeeded Romanesque art in Europe. The first Gothic building was St Denis, outside Paris, which differed from the previous style mainly by having ribbed vaulting to its roofs which were held up by pointed arches. The sculpture is narrative and realistic, in painting the style evolved more slowly and is seen in manuscripts, which developed into the most decorative style seen in International Gothic.

INTERNATIONAL GOTHIC c. 1380–c. 1470
A mixture of styles of painting and sculpture in Europe due to the movements of notable peripatetic artists and the increase in trade, travel and court rivalry. The main influences were Northern France, The Netherlands and Italy, and its main features are rich and decorative colouring and detail, and flowing line.

THE RENAISSANCE c. 1435–1545
Meaning 'rebirth', the term describes the revival of classical learning and art. At first centred in Florence, it marked the end of the Middle Ages and was probably the outstanding creative period in the history of the arts. Architecture, painting, sculpture, deriving from Greek and Roman models, moved into an unparalleled vigour and prominence, and the artist gained a role in society hitherto unknown, mainly due to the rival city states that employed them. Artistic invention included perspective and painting with oil. Latterly, the Renaissance style moved towards Mannerism.

MANNERISM c. 1520–1700
A style emerging from the Renaissance, it exaggerated the styles of Michaelangelo and Raphael into contorted and extravagantly gestured figures, to achieve a more intense emotional effect. This style influenced the later Baroque movement.

THE BAROQUE c. 1600–1720
Centred on the new stability of the Roman Catholic faith, its main artistic aim was to unite the main parts of building, sculpture and painting into an overall dramatic effect. It is mainly 'frontal', that is it is best seen from one, rather than many, viewpoints. Its exuberance and monumentality make it one of the most robust movements in art history.

ROCOCO c. 1735–65
A mainly French style, it is characterized by a wealth of elaborate and superficial decoration. Elegance was the keynote and Rococo reflected the extravagance and brilliance of Court Life.

NEO-CLASSICISM (c. 1750–1850)
More of a discipline than a movement, it expresses the qualities of harmony, clarity and order associated with Greek and Roman art. The antithesis of Romanticism, it espouses accepted notions of beauty and rejects individual inspiration.

ROMANTICISM c. 1780–1850
A mainly literary movement, it was a reaction to Classicism and the growing Industrial Revolution. Deriving its inspiration from untamed nature, the Romantic belief centred on the importance of spontaneity of individual feeling towards the natural world.

THE PRE-RAPHAELITE BROTHERHOOD 1848–1856
A brotherhood of seven London artists formed to make a return to the pre-Raphael (hence the name) Italian forms as a protest against the frivolity of the prevailing English School of the day. The founders and most important demonstrators of the style were William Holman Hunt, John Everett Millais and Dante Gabriel Rossetti.

ARTS AND CRAFTS MOVEMENT c. 1870–1900
Based on the revival of interest in the mediaeval craft system led by William Morris, its aims were to fuse the functional and the decorative, and to restore the worth of handmade crafts in the face of the growing mass-produced wares of the late 19th century.

SYMBOLISM c. 1880–1905
Influenced by the Pre-Raphaelites and the Romantics, it was a movement that provided an intellectual alternative to the straight visual work of the Impressionists. Its twin sources were either literary or pictorially formal and the results were intended to engage the emotions. Symbolism influenced the Surrealists and was the forerunner of Expressionist and abstract art.

IMPRESSIONISM 1875–1886
The term was inadvertently introduced by the journalist Leroy in *Charivari* to describe the work of Monet, Sisley, Pissarro and others, taking the name from Monet's *Impression: Soleil levant*. The painters in this manner were concerned with light and its effects, and the use of 'broken' colour.

POINTILLISM c. 1880–1915
Based on the colour theories of Chevreul, its aim was to achieve greater pictorial luminosity by placing small marks of pure primary colour on the surface, allowing them to merge at a viewing distance to create an optical mixture. Sometimes called Divisionism.

POST-IMPRESSIONISM c. 1880–1910
Term used to describe any breakaway tendencies from pure impressionism that took place during the period, and embraces Pointillism and the beginnings of Expressionism, especially the works of Gauguin, Van Gogh and Cézanne.

ART NOUVEAU c. 1890–1915
A decorative style deriving from the Arts and Crafts movement of the UK, it is represented by two streams, one of fluid asymmetry and flowing linear rhythms inspired by nature, the other of a geometrical austerity. Called Jugendstil (Germany) and Sezessionstil (Austria).

20th century forms

FAUVISM c. 1905–7
A short-lived but highly influential French movement of artists surrounding Matisse, it is summarised by the daring and spontaneous handling of paint in bold, brilliant, sometimes non-representational colour, in a subjective, joyous response to the visual world. 'Fauve' means 'wild beast', a critic's response to seeing paintings by Matisse and others at the 1905 Salon d'Automne.

DIE BRUCKE (The Bridge) c. 1905–13
A group of German Expressionist artists, including Kirchner, whose manifesto was to overthrow the concept of art as an end in itself and to integrate art and life by using art as a means of communication. Influenced by tribal art and Van Gogh, the founders lived and worked communally, forcing the intensity of their work by using clashing colours and aggressive distortions.

EXPRESSIONISM c. 1905–25
Used loosely, a term that denotes an emphasis on pictorial distortion or chromatic exaggeration within a work of art of any given period. More specifically it is used to define certain 20th century North European art where the emphasis is on stress or heightened emotion, as portrayed through the artists' subjective vision. Influenced by Gauguin, Van Gogh, Munch and Fauvism, the movement includes the most specific groups of Die Brucke and Der Blaue Reiter.

CUBISM c. 1907–23
The style formulated from investigations by Picasso and Braque into Cezanne's late works and African tribal sculpture. The first painting to combine these influences was Picasso's 'Les Demoiselles d'Avignon'. The term 'Cubist' was coined by a French critic on seeing Braque's work in that style of 1908. 'Analytic' (early) Cubism presents the subject from a variety of viewpoints: 'Synthetic' (late) Cubism introduced decorative elements such as lettering and applied materials such as newspaper (collage) to achieve a balance between the depiction of reality and the picture as an object in its own right. The movement had many followers, but in a few years Picasso and Braque moved away from it to independent paths.

FUTURISM c. 1909–19
Initially a literary movement, its manifesto concerned itself with incorporating the thrust of modern technology with art. Anti art-establishment, it approached abstract art, especially cubism, to express its dynamism. Its founder-member Marinetti described speed as 'a new form of beauty'.

SCHOOL OF PARIS c. 1910–50
Term used to distinguish the large international group of Paris-based artists which made the city the centre of the Art World until the emergence of the New York School.

DER BLAUE REITER (the Blue Rider) c. 1911–14
A loosely-knit group of Expressionist painters including Kandinsky, Klee and Marc, united by a dictum of Kandinsky that stated 'the creative spirit is concealed within matter'.

DADA c. 1915–23
A total rejection of established values; anti-aesthetic and anti-rational, by European and American artists, sculptors and photographers.

BAUHAUS c. 1919–33
A post-First World War resolution to re-integrate the disparate visual arts and crafts within the discipline of architecture, function dictating the form. It exerted, and still exerts a profound influence on 20th century architecture and crafts.

SURREALISM c. 1924–
A French avant-garde movement of literary origin inspired by Dada, and greatly influenced by Freud's theories of psychoanalysis. Irrational association, spontaneous techniques and an elimination of premeditation to free the workings of the unconscious mind, as well as an interest in dreams, were the main motivations of its practitioners.

KINETIC ART c. 1930–
A term which broadly covers art which incorporates movement, in the work in space, generated by air currents, motors, artificial lights, etc.

ABSTRACT IMPRESSIONISM c. 1940–
Placing emphasis on spontaneous personal expression, it rejects contemporary, social and aesthetic values. Recognised as the first movement in the USA to develop independently of and actually influence Europe. Notable practitioners include Jackson Pollock and De Kooning. Includes Action Painting (USA), and Tachisme (Europe).

NEW YORK SCHOOL c. 1945–60
A group of avant-garde artists whose aim was to find a uniquely American mode of expression. The group included such artists as Pollock, De Kooning and Rothko.

OP ART c. 1950–
An abstract art that bases itself on creating optical effects which appear to move on a flat surface.

POP ART c. 1955–
A reaction against Abstract Expressionism, the movement started almost simultaneously in UK and USA and uses the images of mass media, advertising and pop culture, presenting the common, everyday object as art.

MINIMAL ART c. 1960–
A rejection of the aesthetic qualities of art in favour of the physical reality of the art object. The material used is important, as are their strictly geometrical formats and placings within settings. A famous (some might say, notorious) example was Andre's *Equivalent VIII*, 120 firebricks arranged in a solid rectangle on the Tate Gallery floor in 1966.

Media

ACRYLIC RESIN
A quick-drying waterproof emulsion that can be mixed with dry pigments to give paints that can be applied with heavy knife-laid impasto or diluted with water to wash-like consistency.

ETCHING
The process of biting out a design on a metal plate with acid, so that the resultant indentations hold ink, which will subsequently print the image onto paper.

FRESCO
(Ital.: *fresco*, fresh.) Developed by Minoan and other ancient civilisations. *Buon fresco* is executed with pigments ground in water or lime-water on to a freshly prepared lime-plaster wall while the plaster is still damp.

GOUACHE
A water-colour painting carried out with opaque colours as opposed to pure water colour which employs transparent colours.

INKS
Liquids for drawing or painting; generally the colours are in suspension or present as a dye. Sometimes, as with Indian ink or white ink, there may be opaque pigments in suspension. Inks may be applied with different types of pen or soft hair brushes.

INTAGLIO
Any method where a metal plate is bitten into, etched or cut to hold ink for a design to be printed from it. Engraving, Drypoint, Etching, Aquatint and Mezzotint fall into this category.

LITHOGRAPHY
Planar printing method where design is drawn on limestone or metal plate with greasy ink or crayon. The surface is then wetted; the ink applied to it adheres only to the greasy part, the wetted part repelling it. A print is then taken from the surface.

MONOTYPE
Single print taken from a design painted on a flat surface while the paint is still wet.

OIL
Dry pigments ground in an oil; this is generally linseed, but may be poppy, walnut or other similar oils. It is a technique that gradually evolved during the latter part of the Middle Ages. The Van Eyck brothers did much to perfect the medium.

PASTEL
A stick of colour made from powdered pigment bound with gum. Applied dry to paper the colours can be blended and mixed but the result can be fragile and impermanent unless fixed with spray varnish (fixative).

TEMPERA
A loose term in painting in which the dry pigments are mixed with such substances as egg white, egg yolk, glue, gelatine or casein. True tempera is when the colours are ground with egg yolk only.

WATER COLOUR
Pigments are ground with gum arabic and thinned in use with water. The technique as used today started with Albrecht Dürer but did not achieve widespread use until the emergence of the English School of water-colourists in the first half of the 19th century. Applied with squirrel or sable brushes on white or tinted paper.

WOODCUT
Design incised on wood, the grain of which runs lengthwise. The negative areas are cut away, leaving the raised design to take ink, from which is taken the paper print. The Japanese perfected this medium.

WOOD ENGRAVING
As in woodcut, except that the printing surface is on the end grain of the wood block, allowing fine detail to be cut with a graver or burin. Extensively used in book illustration until the invention of photo-mechanical engraving.

Highest Price Paintings   Progressive Records

Price	Equivalent 1987 Value	Painter, title, sold by and sold to	Date
£6500	£276 297	Antonio Correggio's *The Magdalen Reading* (in fact spurious) to Elector Friedrich Augustus II of Saxony	1746
£8500	£331 812	Raphael's *The Sistine Madonna* (1513–14) from Placenza to Elector Friedrich Augustus II of Saxony	1759
£16 000	£376 480	Van Eyck's *Adoration of the Lamb*, 6 outer panels of Ghent altarpiece by Edward Solby to the Government of Prussia	1821
£24 600*	£848 640	Murillo's *The Immaculate Conception* by estate of Marshal Soult to the Louvre (against Czar Nicholas I) in Paris	1852
£70 000	£3 738 800	Raphael's *Ansidei Madonna* (1506) from Perugia by the 8th Duke of Marlborough to the National Gallery	1885
£100 000	£5 416 320	Raphael's *The Colonna Altarpiece* (1503–05) from Perugia by Seldemeyer to J. Pierpont Morgan	1901
£102 880	£4 253 600	Van Dyck's *Elena Grimaldi-Cattaneo* (portrait) by Knoedler to Peter Widener (1834–1915)	1906
£102 880	£4 253 600	Rembrandt's *The Mill* by 6th Marquess of Lansdowne to Peter Widener	1911
£116 500	£4 032 080	Raphael's smaller *Panshanger Madonna* by Joseph (later Baron) Duveen (1869–1939) to Peter Widener	1913
£310 400	£10 677 680	Leonardo da Vinci's *Benois Madonna* (c. 1477) to Czar Nicholas II in Paris	1914
£821 429*	£6 926 400	Rembrandt's *Aristotle Contemplating the Bust of Homer* by estate of Mr and Mrs Alfred W. Erickson to New York Metropolitan Museum of Art	1961
£1 785 714	£11 211 200	Leonardo da Vinci's *Ginerva de' Benci* (c. 1475) by Prince Franz Josef II of Liechtenstein to National Gallery of Art, Washington DC, USA	1967
£2 310 000*	£12 093 120	Velázquez's *Portrait of Juan de Pareja* by the Earl of Radnor to the Wildenstein Gallery, New York	1970
£2 729 000*	£4 352 400	Turner's *Juliet and Her Nurse* by Trustees of Whitney Museum, New York to undisclosed bidder at Sotheby Parke Bernet, New York	1980
£7 470 500*	£8 647 600	Turner's *Seascape: Folkestone* from estate of Lord Clark (1903–83) to Leggatt's of London for an unknown buyer	1984
£8 100 000*	£8 845 200	Mantegna's *The Adoration of the Magi* by the Marquess of Northampton to the J. Paul Getty Museum, Malibu, California	1985
£22 500 000	—	Van Gogh's *Les Tournesols* ('Sunflowers') at Sotheby's, London	1987
£30 187 623	—	Van Gogh's *Irises* from John Whitney Payson to an undisclosed bidder at Sotheby's, New York	1987

* Indicates price at auction, otherwise prices were by private treaty.

Renowned painters by country

Some of the world's most renowned painters with well-known examples of their work.

AUSTRALIA
Nolan, Sidney (b. 1917) *Themes from the Career of Ned Kelly.*

AUSTRIA
Klimt, Gustav (1862–1918) *Mosaic mural for the Palais Stoclet in Brussels.*
Kokoschka, Oskar (b. 1886) *View of the Thames.*
Schiele, Egon (1890–1918) *The Artist's Mother Sleeping.*

BELGIUM
Brueghel, Pieter (The Elder) (c. 1525–69) *The Adoration of the Kings, The Peasant Dance.*
Ensor, James (1860–1949) *Entry of Christ into Brussels.*
Gossaert, Jan (c. 1478–1533) *Adoration.*
Jordaens, Jacob (1593–1678) *The Bean King.*
Magritte, René (1898–1967) *The Key of Dreams.*
Memlinc, Hans (c. 1430–94) *Mystic Marriage of St. Catherine.*
Rubens, Peter Paul (1577–1640) *Adoration of the Magi, Battle of the Amazons.*
Teniers, David (The Younger) (1610–90) *Peasants Playing Bowls.*
Van der Weyden, Rogier (c. 1400–64) *Deposition, The Magdalen Reading.*
Van Dyck, Anthony (1599–1641) *Charles I of England, Elena Grimaldi-Cattaneo.*
Van Eyck, Hubert (c. 1370–c. 1426) Jan (c. 1390–1441) *Ghent Altarpiece, The Three Mary's at the Open Sepulchre.* Jan alone *The Arnolfini Marriage, Adoration of the Lamb.*

CZECHOSLOVAKIA
Kupka, Frank (Frantisek) (1871–1957) *Amorpha, fugue in two colours.*

FRANCE
Arp, Hans (Jean) (1887–1966) *Berger et Nuage.*
Bonnard, Pierre (1867–1947) *The Window.*
Boucher, François (1703–70) *Diana Bathing.*
Braque, Georges (1882–1963) *Vase of Anemones.*
Cézanne, Paul (1839–1906) *Mont Sainte-Victoire, Bathers.*
Chagall, Marc (1887–1985) *I and the Village, Calvary.*
Chardin, Jean-Baptiste Siméon (1699–1779) *The Skate, The Lesson.*
Corot, Jean-Baptiste Camille (1796–1875) *Ponte de Mantes, Sens Cathedral.*
Courbet, Gustave (1819–77) *A Burial at Ornans.*
Daumier, Honoré (1808–79) *The Third-Class Carriage.*
David, Jacques Louis (1748–1825) *The Rape of the Sabines.*
Degas, Hilaire-Germain-Edgar (1834–1917) *La Danseuse au Bouquet.*
Delacroix, Eugène (1798–1863) *The Massacre of Chios.*
Derain, André (1880–1954) *Mountains at Collioure.*
Fouquet, Jean (c. 1420–c. 1480) *Etienne Chevalier with St Stephen.*
Fragonard, Jean-Honoré (1732–1806) *The Love Letter, Baigneuses.*
Gauguin, Paul (1848–1903) *Ta Matete.*
Gellée, Claude (called Claude Lorraine) (1600–82) *Ascanius and the Stag.*
Gericault, Theodore (1791–1824) *The Raft of the Medusa.*
Ingres, Jean-Auguste Dominique (1780–1867) *Odalisque.*
La Tour, George de (1593–1652) *St. Sebastian tended by the Holy Women.*
Leger, Fernand (1881–1955) *Three Women.*
Lorraine, Claude (1600–82) *Embarkation of St Ursula.*
Manet, Edouard (1823–83) *Déjeuner sur l'Herbe.*
Matisse, Henri (1869–1954) *Odalisque.*
Millet, Jean-François (1814–75) *Man with the Hoe, Angelus.*
Monet, Claude (1840–1926) *Rouen Cathedral, Water-lilies.*

Pissarro, Camille (1830–1903) *The Harvest, Montfoucault.*
Poussin, Nicolas (1593/4–1665) *Worship of the Golden Calf.* (Damaged Mar. 1978)
Renoir, Pierre Auguste (1841–1919) *Luncheon of the Boating Party.*
Rouault, Georges (1871–1958) *Christ Mocked.*
Rousseau, Henri Julien ('Le Douanier') (1844–1910) *The Dream.*
Seurat, Georges (1859–91) *Sunday Afternoon on the Grande Jatte.*
Stael, Nicholas de (1914–55) *The Roofs.*
Toulouse-Lautrec, Henri de (1864–1901) *At the Moulin Rouge.*
Utrillo, Maurice (1883–1955) *Port St Martin.*
Vlaminck, Maurice de (1876–1958) *The Bridge at Chatou.*
Watteau, Antoine (1684–1721) *The Embarkation for Cythera.*

GERMANY
Altdorfer, Albrecht (c. 1480–1538) *Battle of Arbela.*
Beckmann, Max (1884–1950) *The Night.*
Beuys, Joseph (b. 1921) *Fond IV/4.*
Cranach, Lucas (The Elder) (1472–1553) *Venus, Rest on Flight into Egypt.*
Dix, Otto (1891–1969) *The War.*
Ernst, Max (1891–1976) *The Elephant Celebes.*
Durer, Albrecht (1471–1528) *The Four Apostles, Apocalypse.*
Friedrich, Caspar David (1774–1840) *The Cross in the Mountains.*
Grosz, George (1893–1959) *Suicide.*
Grunewald, Mathias (c. 1460–1528) *Isenheim Altarpiece.*
Holbein, Hans (The Younger) (c. 1497–1543) *Henry VIII, The Ambassadors.*
Kirchner, Ernst Ludwig (1880–1938) *Self-portrait with Model.*
Marc, Franz (1880–1916) *The Blue Horse.*
Nolde, Emil (Emil Hansen) (1867–1956) *Masks and Dahlias.*

GREAT BRITAIN
Auerbach, Frank (b. 1931) *E.O.W. Nude.*
Bacon, Francis (b. 1909) *Three Studies at the Base of a Crucifixion.*
Blake, William (1757–1827) *The Book of Job: Divine Comedy.*
Bonington, Richard Parkes (1801–28) *A Sea Piece.*
Constable, John (1776–1837) *The Hay Wain.*
Crome, John (1768–1821) *The Slate Quarries.*
Dobson, William (1610–46) *Endymion Porter.*
Freud, Lucian (b. 1922) *Francis Bacon.*
Fuseli, Henry (Johann Heinrich Fussli) (1741–1825) *Nightmare.*
Gainsborough, Thomas (1727–88) *Blue Boy.*
Girtin, Thomas (1775–1802) *Kirkstall Abbey: Evening.*
Hamilton, Richard (b. 1922) *Portrait of Hugh Gaitskell as a Famous Monster of Filmland.*
Hilliard, Nicholas (c. 1537–1619) *Elizabeth I, Sir Walter Raleigh.*
Hockney, David (b. 1937) *Mr. & Mrs. Clark and Percy.*
Hogarth, William (1697–1764) *Rake's Progress, Marriage à la Mode.*
Hunt, William Holman (1827–1910) *The Scapegoat, Light of the World.*
John, Augustus Edwin (1878–1961) *The Smiling Woman.*
John, Gwen (1876–1939) *Self Portrait.*
Landseer, Sir Edwin (1802–73) *The Old Shepherd's Chief Mourner, Shoeing.*
Millais, Sir John Everett (1829–96) *Order of Release.*
Nash, Paul (1889–1946) *British. Dead Sea.*
Nicholson, Ben (b. 1894) *White Relief.*
Raeburn, Sir Henry (1756–1823) *Sir John Sinclair.*
Ramsay, Allan (1713–84) *The Artist's Wife.*
Reynolds, Sir Joshua (1723–92) *Mrs Siddons as the Tragic Muse, The Three Graces.*
Rossetti, Dante Gabriel (1828–82) *Beata Beatrix.*
Sickert, Walter Richard (1860–1942) *Ennui.*
Sisley, Alfred (1839–99) *Flood at Port Marly.*
Smith, Sir Matthew (1879–1959) *Fitzroy Street Nudes.*

Spencer, Sir Stanley (1891–1959) *The Resurrection, Cookham.*
Stubbs, George (1724–1806) *Horse frightened by a Lion.*
Sutherland, Graham (1903–80) *Christ in Glory, Coventry Cathedral.*
Turner, Joseph Mallord William (1775–1851) *The Grand Canal, Venice, Shipwreck, Juliet and Her Nurse.*
Wilson, Richard (1713–82) *Okehampton Castle.*

HUNGARY
Moholy-Nagy, Laszlo (1895–1946) *Light prop.*
Vasarely, Victor (b. 1908) *Timbres II.*

ITALY
Balla, Giacomo (1871–1958) *Dynamism of a Dog on a Leash.*
Bellini, Giovanni (c. 1429–1561) *Pieta, Coronation of the Virgin, Agony in the Garden.*
Botticelli, Sandro (Alessandro di Mariano Filipepi) (1445–1510) *Birth of Venus, Mystic Nativity.*
Canaletto, Giovanni Antonio Canal (1697–1768) *Venice: A Regatta on the Grand Canal.*
Caravaggio, Michelangelo Merisi (1573–1610) *St Matthew, Deposition.*
Carra, Carlo (1881–1966) *Metaphysical Muse.*
Del Castagno, Andrea (Andrea di Bartolo di Bargilla) (1421–57) *The Vision of St. Jerome.*
Chirico, Giorgio de (1888–1978) *Mystery and Melancholy of a Street: Nostalgia of the Infinite.*
Correggio, Antonio Allegri (c. 1489–1534) *Jupiter and Io, Assumption of the Virgin, The Magdalene reading* (attributed but spurious).
Duccio (Di Buoninsegna) (active 1278–1318) *The Rucellai Madonna.*
Da Fabriano Gentile (1370–1427) *The Adoration of the Magi.*
Francesca, Piero della (c. 1415–92) *Nativity.*
Fra Angelico, Giovanni da Fiesole (1387–1455) *Annunciation.*
Fra Filippo Lippi (c. 1406–69) *Tarquinia Madonna.*
Giorgione, Giorgio da Castelfranco (1475–1510) *Sleeping Venus.*
Giotto di Bondone (c. 1267–1337) *Life of St. Francis.*
Leonardo da Vinci (1452–1519) *Mona Lisa (La Gioconda), Last Supper, Cinerva de' Benci, Benois Madonna.*
Lorenzetti, Ambrogio (active c. 1319–48?) *Good and Bad Government, Palazzo Pubblico, Siena.*
Mantegna, Andrea (c. 1430–1506) *The Triumph of Caesar.*
Martini, Simone (c. 1285–1344) *Annunciation.*
Masaccio (1401–28?) *Scenes from the Life of St. Peter, Brancacci Chapel.*
Da Messina, Antonello (1430–79) *Salvador Mundi.*
Michelangelo, Buonarroti (1475–1564) *Creation of Adam.*
Modigliani, Amedeo (1884–1920) *Portrait of Madame Zborowski.*
Morandi, Giorgio (1890–1964) *Still Life.*
Orcagna (Andrea di Cione) (active 1343–68) *The Redeemer with the Madonna and Saints.*
Parmigianino (Girolamo Francesco Maria Mazzola) (1503–40) *The Vision of St. Jerome.*
Raphael (1483–1520) *Sistine Madonna, Panshanger Madonna, The Colonna altarpiece, Ansidei Madonna.*
Romano, Giulio (1499?–1546) *The Hall of the Giants.*
Del Sarto, Andrea (Andrea d'Agnolo) (1486–1530) *The Madonna of the Harpies: A Young Man.*
Signorelli, Luca (active 1470–1523) *The Last Judgment, Orvieto.*
Tiepolo, Giovanni Battista (1696–1770) *The Finding of Moses.*
Tintoretto, Jacopo Robusti (1518–94) *Last Supper, Il Paradiso.*
Titian (c. 1487–1576) *The Tribute Money, Bacchus and Ariadne.*
Uccello, Paolo (1396/7–1475) *The Battle of San Romano: The Night Hunt.*
Veronese, Paolo Caliari (1528–88) *Marriage at Cana.*

JAPAN

Hiroshige, Ando (1797–1858) *A Hundred Famous Views of Edo*.

Hokusai, Katsushika (1760–1849) *Thirty-six Views of Mount Fuji*.

Motonobu, Kano (1476–1559) *Eight Views of Hsiao-hsiang*.

Utamaro, Kitagawa (1753–1806) *Mushierabi (Book of Insects)*.

MEXICO

Orozco, Jose Clemente (1883–1949) *Hidalgo and Castillo*.

Rivera, Diego (1886–1957) *Creation*.

Siqueiros, David Alfaro (1896–1974) *The March of Humanity on Earth: Towards the Cosmos*.

NETHERLANDS

Appel, Karel (b. 1921) *Cry of Liberty*.

Bosch, Hieronymus (c. 1450–1516) *Christ Crowned with Thorns, The Garden of Earthly Delights*.

Hals, Frans (c. 1580–1666) *Laughing Cavalier*.

Hooch, Pieter de (1629–83) *An Interior*.

Leyden, Lucas van (1494–1533) *Last Judgment*.

Mondrian, Piet (1872–1944) *Composition*.

Rembrandt, Harmensz van Rijn (1606–69) *The Night Watch, The Anatomy Lesson, Aristotle contemplating the Bust of Homer, The Mill*.

Ruisdael, Jacob van (c. 1628–82) *View of Haarlem*.

Van Gogh, Vincent (1853–90) *Road with Cypresses, Old Peasant, L'Eglise d'Auvers*.

Vermeer, Jan (1632–75) *Woman with a Water Jug*.

NORWAY

Munch, Edvard (1863–1944) *Dance of Death, Shriek*.

SPAIN

Dali, Salvador (b. 1904) *Crucifixion, The Persistence of Memory*.

El Greco (1541–1614) *The Burial of Count Orgaz, View of Toledo*.

Goya, Francisco de (1746–1828) *The Naked Maja, The Shootings of May 3rd*.

Gris, Juan (Jose Gonsalez) (1887–1927) *Violin and Fruit Dish*.

Murillo, Bartolomé Esteban (1617–82) *Virgin and Child, Immaculate Conception*.

Picasso, Pablo (1881–1973) *Guernica, Les Demoiselles d'Avignon*.

Ribera, José (1591–1652) *The Martyrdom of St. Bartholomew*.

Tapies, Antonio (b. 1923) *Large Painting*.

Velázquez, Diego (1599–1660) *Rokeby Venus, The Water-Carrier, Juan de Pareja*.

SWITZERLAND

Klee, Paul (1879–1940) *Twittering Machine*.

USSR

Kandinsky, Wassily (1866–1944) *Compositions, Improvisations and Impressions*.

Larionov, Mikhail Fedorovich (1881–1964) *Glass*.

Malevich, Kasimir Severinovich (1878–1935) *Black Square*.

Soutine, Chaim (1893–1943) *The Madwoman*.

Tatlin, Vladimir (1885–1953) *Constructivist Sculptures*.

UNITED STATES OF AMERICA

Audubon, John James (1785–1851) *Birds of America*.

Cassatt, Mary (1845–1926) *The Bath*.

Eakins, Thomas (1844–1916) *The Gross Clinic*.

Homer, Winslow (1836–1910) *Northeaster*.

O'Keeffe, Georgia (b. 1887) *Cityscapes of New York*.

De Kooning, Willem (b. 1904) *Woman Series*.

Lichtenstein, Roy (b. 1923) *Wham!*

Moses, Grandma (Anna Mary Robertson) (1860–1961) *The Thanksgiving Turkey*.

Pollock, Jackson (1912–56) *Autumn Rhythm*.

Rauschenberg, Robert (b. 1925) *Monogram*.

Rothko, Mark (1903–70) *Green on Blue*.

Sargent, John Singer (1856–1925) *Carnation, Lily, Lily, Rose*.

Warhol, Andy (1930–87) *Campbell's Soupcans*.

Whistler, James Abbott McNeill (1834–1903) *Arrangement in Grey and Black – The Artist's Mother*.

Renowned sculptors by country

FRANCE

Brancusi, Constantin (1876–1957) Romanian French.

Gaudier-Brzeska, Henri (1891–1915) French.

Pevsner, Antoine (1886–1962) French.

Pigalle, Jean-Baptiste (1714–85) French.

Rodin, Auguste (1840–1917) French.

Roubiliac, Louis-Francois (c. 1705–62) French.

GREAT BRITAIN

Caro, Anthony (b. 1924) British.

Epstein, Sir Jacob (1880–1959) English.

Flaxman, John (1755–1826) English.

Hepworth, Barbara (1903–75) British.

Moore, Henry (1898–1986) British.

Paolozzi, Eduardo (b. 1924) British.

GREECE

Phidias (died c. 432 BC) Greek.

Praxiteles (active mid-4th century BC) Greek.

ITALY

Bernini, Gianlorenzo (1598–1680) Italian.

Cellini, Benvenuto (1500–71) Italian.

Donatello (Donato di Niccolo) (1386–1466) Italian.

Ghiberti, Lorenzo (1378–1455) Italian.

Michelangelo, Buonarroti (1475–1564) Italian.

Pisano, Giovanni (active c. 1265–1314) Italian.

Pisano, Nicola (active c. 1258–84) Italian.

Robbia, Luca della (1400–82) Italian.

SPAIN

Gonzalez, Julio (1876–1942) Spanish.

SWITZERLAND

Giacometti, Alberto (1901–66) Swiss.

USSR

Archipenko, Alexander (1887–1964) Russian.

Gabo, Naum (Naum Neemia Pevsner) (1890–1977) Russian.

Zadkine, Ossip (1890–1967) Russian.

UNITED STATES OF AMERICA

Calder, Alexander (1898–1976) American.

Nevelson, Louise (b. 1900) American.

Smith, David (1906–65) American.

Photography

The camera obscura (Latin, 'darkened room') and its principles were familiar as far back in time as the 4th century BC, when Aristotle observed that if a very small aperture was made in one wall of an otherwise light-free room, the scene outside the wall was cast, but inverted, on the opposite inside wall of the room. Perfected with lenses in the aperture during the 19th century, this device was used as an aid to artists.

In 1725 the German, Johann Heinrich Schultze, discovered that silver salts darken in ratio to the strength of light exposed to them. The first actual use of this phenomenon was made in England by Thomas Wedgwood and Sir Humphrey Davy, who coated silver salts onto paper and produced silhouette images on it from leaves and other natural sources. They published a joint paper on their findings in 1802.

In 1826, a Frenchman, Joseph Nicéphore Niepce, made and fixed permanently the first photographic image, a view from his workroom. His camera obscura lens resolved the image onto a bituminous, light-sensitive coating supported by a plate of pewter. Development of the image was obtained by acid etching the unexposed bitumen, the relief image left on the pewter

giving a printing surface to obtain copies. Niepce then went into partnership with Louis Jacques Mandé Daguerre. Adapting Schultze's discovery, they used copper plates covered with silver iodide. In 1835 Daguerre succeeded in developing his images with mercury vapour; two years later he was able to permanently fix the images by immersing the plates in a solution of common salt (sodium chloride). Announcing his discovery in 1839, he patented it, using the name Daguerrotype, for which the French government awarded him an annual pension on condition that his process be made public.

Numerous experiments using silver salts then took place, the most important being those of William Henry Fox Talbot in England who, by using impregnated paper with silver salts, obtained negative images from which multiple positives could be made. The process was called Calotype, but was not as sharp and brilliant as Daguerrotype, which remained the more popular.

In 1850 an English sculptor, Frederick Scott Archer, invented the wet-plate process. The image was formed on a glass plate coated with light-sensitive collodion, a jelly-like substance that remained wet for some time. While still wet, the plate was exposed in the camera and straightway developed. Such methods were cumbersome and technical and it was not until the introduction of the dry-plate process, invented in 1871 by Englishman, Richard L. Maddox, did amateur photography catch on.

By 1884 George Eastman in the United States was manufacturing silver bromide printing papers; in 1891 the Belgian, Leo Backland, marketed the first commercially successful contact papers, calling them Velox papers.

Dry-plate photography, though a great improvement on previous processes, was still awkward and cumbersome. John Carbutt, an American, coated sheets of celluloid with emulsion. Eastman was quick to realise its commercial aspects and in 1880 introduced the first Kodak, a simple hand camera already loaded at the factory with celluloid film for 100 shots. After the film was exposed the whole equipment was returned to the factory; the film developed and printed, and the camera reloaded. Eastman introduced paper-backed roll film for daylight loading in 1891, and, together with camera improvements, photography became a hobby for the masses.

Colour in photography is based on the principle that an admixture in varying ratios of the three primary colours, red, blue and green, will give any colour in the spectrum. In 1810 a German physicist found that wet silver chloride exposed to a spectrum would reproduce faintly the spectrum colours but would disappear when the image was dried. In 1860 James Clark Maxwell, a British physicist, made three wet-collodion photographs of a tartan ribbon, each one through a red, blue and green filter. He then projected them through similar filters, superimposing the images on a screen. A crude colour reproduction resulted, but lacking in sensitivity to red and green.

After various experiments the three-layer emulsion method, each layer being sensitive to a different primary colour, was perfected in the Kodachrome film, marketed in 1935. The film was developed layer by layer, each being dyed in the appropriate complementary colours yellow, magenta and cyan blue, thus giving a transparency of the true image colours. About the same time Agfacolour was introduced, the difference between it and Kodachrome being that the three layers contained not only the sensitive emulsions but also colour formers, all of which reacted with a special developer to produce an accurate colour image in one step, instead of the separate three-step development of Kodachrome. From these two methods, most modern colour film has been developed.

CAMERAS

From the camera obscura to a light-free box with a lens was an obvious step. Camera development followed that of the development of the image plate, and it was not until dryplate and celluloid roll film was introduced that the camera became truly portable. However, the first single-lens reflex camera had been patented in 1861 by Thomas Sutton, and in 1880 the British firm of R. & J. Beck produced a twin-lens reflex camera. A roll-film camera, the Kodak, was brought out in 1888 by George Eastman, followed in 1895 by the folding 'Brownie' camera.

In 1914 Oscar Bernak of Germany invented the Leica principle, a small precision instrument of considerable sophistication using 35 mm roll film. This was marketed successfully in 1925 and is still the most widely used format, there being a host of refinements from Germany and later Japan up to the present day. Beck's twin-lens reflex camera was marketed in 1928 under the name Rolleiflex.

In 1963 Edwin Land introduced the revolu-tionary Polaroid camera, which was able to produce black-and-white and colour pictures in less than a minute after exposure. After the picture is taken, the negative forms a sandwich with the positive, which is passed through rollers that break open plastic pods containing devel-oper and fixer. After an appropriate time lapse, the camera back is opened and the print is peeled away from the negative, giving a positive image of the picture.

Architecture and Civil Engineering

Architecture

Architecture is a reflection of the life of the people, countries and civilizations who build it. The earliest architecture, built of mud, brick and wood, has long since vanished; only stone-built buildings and those hewn out of rock have left any traces to tell us what the first architecture may have looked like. Egyptian tombs, dating from 2700 BC are the first remnants; the mastabas, a small flat-topped building with sloping sides, and pyramids, the first built at Sakkara about 2700 BC. The rise of the Egyptian civilisation along the Nile saw the building of the great pyramids and, latterly (1600 BC), the great temples. Roughly parallel in time the Babylonians of Mesopotamia were building temples whose decoration reflected their reli-gion. In Crete, the palace of Knossos was built in about 1600 BC and this was the prelude to the magnificent flowering of Greek architecture.

Greek architecture is characterized by three orders which manifest themselves in the design of the columns supporting the roof structures and the entablatures above the columns. The Doric order is simple and sturdy, very often undecorated. The Ionic order, possibly of Asiatic origin, was more slender, and carried scrolls and simple decoration on the capitals. The columns were also fluted. The Corinthian order has an elaborate capital decorated with stylised acan-thus leaves. Temples and public buildings were built in these styles, and their position shows that the Greeks were adept and skilful in town planning.

The spread of the Roman Empire brought Greek influence to Roman architecture but the Romans added one architectural feature of outstanding importance – the arch. Arch con-struction enabled the Romans to supply their cities with water from outside by building aqueducts, which were arched to carry the load. From the arch they developed the cross-vault: the point where two tunnel-shaped roofs meet and cross each other at right angles.

The Middle Ages saw the rise of the Byzantine empire in Eastern Europe and the Middle East (330 AD) and the development of the dome. In the West, architecture scarcely moved forward until the beginning of the 11th century, when the Romanesque style, using cross-vaulting techniques and the plan of the early Christian Roman basilica was adopted.

About the middle of the 12th century the Romanesque style gave way to Gothic. This saw the invention or development of five features: the pointed arch, the rib (which supported the arch), the buttress on the outside of the building, the tracery window, and architectural decoration of a high order. In this style, especially in France and Britain, abbeys and cathedrals sprang up of immense ambition and scale. The style contin-ually developed, mainly in the art of decoration. The Decorated style (14th century) moved to the Flamboyant style in France, where the decora-tive stone was carved in flame-like patterns, and in England to the Perpendicular style, with its huge windows with flattened pointed arches and elaborate fan vaulting of the roofs.

The Renaissance period in Italy (early 15th century) was generated by powerful and rich families in the city-states in and around Flor-ence, notably the Medicis. Drawing upon the styles of the Roman and Byzantine periods the architects of the early Renaissance (the first whose names we actually know with certainty) developed the dome (Brunelleschi, Florence Cathedral) and the design of the multi-storied town house or 'palazzo' (Palazzo Pitti, Florence). For the next 400 years the Renaissance move-ment spread rapidly through Europe, a peak being represented in St Peter's, Rome, which took 150 years to build to designs and alterations by 14 architects, including Bramante, Michel-angelo (The Dome) and Maderna.

In and around Venice in the mid-16th century Palladio was designing elegant churches and exquisite houses, and in France the Loire Chateaux or hunting lodges of the French kings were being built in elaborate and fantastic styles, with turrets, pinnacles and chimneys. Such a flowering of ideas did not produce a coherent style as such until the 17th century, when the Classical style emerged in France with the building of the Louvre and Versailles. In England these influences were late in taking hold, but the first Renaissance building, the Queen's House, Greenwich, was built to designs by Inigo Jones after he had visited Italy in 1613. This was the starting point for such architects as Wren, Vanbrugh and Hawksmoor, whose churches and country houses represent a high point in English Architecture. At the same time in Italy, Spain, Austria and southern Germany, the Baroque style predominated, characterised by its bold, curving lines, large-scale planning and dramatic effects bordering on the theatrical, as exemplified by the piazza in St Peter's, Rome (Bernini) and the Belvedere Palace in Vienna, which is decorated inside in the Rococo style. The style was most restrained in England, and in the 18th century gave way to the Palladian style, derived from Palladio's villas around Venice. Domestic architecture in England be-came classical in the mid-1750s onward in the style popularly known as Georgian.

From then onward, in Europe and to a lesser extent in America, the various Renaissance styles were adapted or modified until the Gothic revival of the 1830s in Britain, where the Gothic and the Classical styles were equally prominent. A new building material was cast iron (the Crystal Palace, London), but which did not change the appearance of architecture.

The Modern Movement came out of the development of the steel frame, from which hung the masonry walls. Its first use in Chicago at the end of the 19th century was the start of a revolutionary change in the look of cities throughout the world. Within a generation reinforced concrete was invented and from then on the skycrapers of America and elsewhere sprang into being. The strength of reinforced concrete allowed cantilevering and the construc-tion of thin skins of vast area, and building styles were freed to take on sweeping and sculptured shapes. After the Second World War the large-scale use of glass for curtain walls gave a transparent and airy quality to skyscrapers, factories and public buildings.

Glossary of Terms

abacus Flat top of the capital of a column.
apse Semicircular termination or recess at the end of a church chancel.
architrave The beam which extends across the top of the columns in classical architecture.
baptistry Building used for baptisms. Sometimes merely a bay or chapel reserved for baptisms.
bay Compartment or unit of division of an interior or of a façade – usually between one window or pillar and the next.
belvedere Open-sided structure designed to offer extensive views, usually in a formal garden.
boss Projection, usually carved, at the intersec-tion of stone ribs of Gothic vaults and ceilings.
buttress Vertical mass of masonry built against a wall to strengthen it and to resist the outward pressure of a vault.
campanile Bell-tower.
capital Top of a column, usually carved.
caryatid Sculptured female figure serving as a supporting column.
cornice Projecting upper part of the entablature in classical architecture.
dado Lower part of an interior wall when panelled or painted separately from the main part.
drum Cylindrical lower part of a dome or cupola.
entablature In classical architecture, the beam-like division above the columns, comprising architrave, freize and cornice.

flying buttress Arch conveying the thrust of a vault towards an isolated buttress.

frieze Decorated central division of an entablature, between the architrave and the cornice.

keystone Central, wedge-shaped stone of an arch, so called because the arch cannot stand up until it is in position.

lancet window Window with a single, sharply pointed arch. The style is associated with the Early English period of Gothic architecture, around the 13th century.

mezzanine Low storey introduced between two loftier ones, usually the ground and first floors.

order Basic elements of classical and Renaissance architecture, comprising the base, column, capital and entablature.

oriel Bay window on an upper floor, supported by projecting stonework.

pediment In classical architecture, the low-pitched gable above the entablature, usually filled with sculpture.

pier Vertical masonry support for a wall arch.

rustication Heavy stonework with the surface left rough, or with deeply channelled joints, used principally on Renaissance buildings.

spandrel Triangular space between the curves of two adjacent arches and the horizontal moulding above them.

tracery Ornamental stonework in the upper part of a Gothic window.

tympanum Triangular surface bounded by the mouldings of a pediment; also, the space, often carved, between the lintel and arch of a Gothic doorway.

vault A roof or ceiling built in stone, brick or concrete, as opposed to wood.

SOME NOTABLE ARCHITECTS

Aalto, Alvar (1898–1976) Finnish.
Adam, Robert (1728–1772) Scottish.
Alberti, Leone Battista (1404–72) Italian.
Barry, Sir Charles (1795–1860) English.
Bernini, Gianlorenzo (1598–1680) Italian.
Borromini, Francesco (1599–1667) Italian.
Brunelleschi, Filippo (1377–1446) Italian.
Burlington, Richard Boyle (Earl of) (1694–1753) English.
Campbell, Colen (1660?–1729) Scottish.
Gibbs, James (1682–1754) Scottish.
Hawksmoor, Nicholas (1661–1736) English.
Jones, Inigo (1573–1652) English.
Kent, William (1685–1748) English.
Le Corbusier (Charles Edouard Jeanmerat) (1887–1965) French.
Le Vau, Louis (1612–70) French.
Maderna, Carlo (1556–1629) Italian.
Mansart, François (1598–1666) French.
Mansart, Jules (1646–1708) French.
Michelangelo, Buonarroti (1475–1564) Italian.
Mies van der Rohe, Ludwig (1886–1969) German.
Nash, John (1752–1835) English.
Neimeyer, Oscar (b. 1907) Brazilian.
Palladio, Andrea (1508–1580) Italian.
Paxton, Sir Joseph (1801–1865) English.
Pugin, Augustus (1812–1852) English.
Saarinen, Eero (1910–1961) Finnish.
Soane, Sir John (1753–1837) English.
Vanbrugh, Sir John (1664–1726) English.
Wren, Sir Christopher (1632–1723) English.
Wright, Frank Lloyd (1869–1959) American.
Wyatt, James (1746–1813) English.

World's tallest inhabited buildings

Height (ft)	Height (m)	No of storeys	Building	Location
1454	443	110	Sears Tower (1974)	Wacker Drive, Chicago, Illinois
1350	412	110	World Trade Centre (1973)[1]	Barclay and Liberty Sts, New York City
1250	381	102	Empire State Building (1930)[2]	5th Av and 34th St, New York City
1136	346	80	Standard Oil Building (1973)	Chicago, Illinois
1127	343	100	John Hancock Center (1968)	Chicago, Illinois
1046	319	77	Chrysler Building (1930)	Lexington Av and 42nd St, New York City
1002	305	75	Texas Commercial Plaza	Houston, Texas
985	300	71	Allied Bank Plaza	1000 Louisiana, Houston, Texas
954	290	76	Columbia Center	Seattle, Washington State
952	290	72	First Bank Tower	First Canadian Place, Toronto, Ontario
939	286	73	Main Center	901 Main St, Dallas, Texas
927	282	71	40 Wall Tower	New York City
914	279	59	Citicorp Center (1977)	New York City
899	274	64	Transco Tower	Houston, Texas
886	270	68	Scotia Squava	Toronto, Ontario
859	262	74	Water Tower Plaza (1975)[3]	Chicago, Illinois
858	261	62	United California Bank (1974)	Los Angeles, California
853	259	48	Transamerica Pyramid	San Francisco, California
851	259	66	United California Bank	New York City
850	259	70	RCA Building	Rockefeller Centre, 5th Av, New York City
844	257	60	First National Bank of Chicago (1969)	Chicago, Illinois
841	256	64	US Steel Building (1971)	Pittsburgh, Pennsylvania
838	255	66	Bank of Nova Scotia	Toronto, Ontario
813	248	60	One Chase Manhattan Plaza	Liberty St and Nassau St, New York City
808	246	59	Pan American Building (1963)	Park Av, and 43rd St, New York City
800	244	68	MLC Office Tower (1977)	Sydney, Australia
794	242	60	Rialto Tower†	Collins St, Melbourne, Australia
792	241	57	Woolworth Building (1911–13)	233 Broadway, New York City
790	241	60	John Hancock Tower	Boston, Mass
790	241	42	Palace of Culture and Science	Warsaw, Poland
787	240	60	Sunshine 60 (1978)	Tokyo, Japan
787	240	28	Mikhail Lomonosov University	Moscow, USSR

[1] Two TV antennae bring the overall height to 1559 ft *475,18 m.*
[2] Between 27 July 1950 and 1 May 1951 a 222 ft TV tower was added.
[3] World's tallest reinforced concrete building.
† Under construction.

World's tallest structures

Height (ft)	Height (m)	Structure	Location
2120	646	Warszawa Radio Mast (May 1974)	Konstantynow, nr Płock, Poland
2063	629	KTHI-TV (December 1963)	Fargo, North Dakota, USA
1815	553	CN Tower, Metro Centre (April 1975)	Toronto, Canada
1762	537	Ostankino TV Tower (1967) (4 m added in 1973)	near Moscow, USSR
1749	533	WRBL-TV & WTVM (May 1962)	Columbus, Georgia, USA
1749	533	WBIR-TV (September 1963)	Knoxville, Tennessee, USA
1732	528	Moscow TV Tower	Moscow, USSR
1673	510	KFVS-TV (June 1960)	Cape Girardeau, Missouri, USA
1638	499	WPSD-TV	Paducah, Kentucky, USA
1619	493	WGAN-TV (September 1959)	Portland, Maine, USA
1610*	490	KSWS-TV (December 1956)	Roswell, New Mexico, USA
1600	487	WKY-TV	Oklahoma City, Okla, USA
1572	479	KW-TV (November 1954)	Oklahoma City, Okla, USA
1527	465	BREN Tower (unshielded atomic reactor) (April 1962)	Nevada, USA

* Fell in a gale, 1960; re-erected.

Below: left to right

Warszawa Radio Mast Poland 2120 ft 646 m

GPO Tower London 619 ft 188 m

Sears Tower Chicago USA 1454 ft 443 m

CN Tower Toronto Canada 1815 ft 553 m

OTHER TALL STRUCTURES

Height (ft)	Height (m)	Structure	Location
1345	410	Danish Govt Navigation Mast	Greenland
1312	399	Peking Radio Mast	Peking, China
1272†	387	Anglia TV Mast (1965–September 1967)	Belmont, Lincolnshire
1271	387	Tower Zero (1967)	North West Cape, W Australia
1253	382	Lopik Radio Mast	Netherlands
1251	381	International Nickel Co Chimney (1970)	Sudbury, Ontario, Canada
1212	369	Thule Radio Mast (1953)	Thule, Greenland
1206	368	American Electric Power Smokestack (1969)	Cresap, West Virginia, USA
1200	366	Kennecott Copper Corp Chimney (1975)	Magna, Utah, USA
1179	359	Television Centre	Moscow
1150	350	TV Tower	Vinnitsa, Ukraine, USSR
1093	333	CHTV Channel II Mast	Hamilton, Ontario, Canada
1092	332	Tokyo Television Mast	Tokyo, Japan
1080	329	IBA Transmitter Tower (September 1971)	Emley Moor, West Yorkshire
1065	325	Leningrad TV Mast	Leningrad, USSR
1052	320	La Tour Eiffel (1887–9)	Paris, France

† Highest structure in Great Britain.

Seven wonders of the world

The seven Wonders of the World were first designated by Antipater of Sidon in the second century BC. They are, or were:

Name	Location	Built (circa)	Fate
1. Three Pyramids of Giza (El Gîzeh)*	near El Gîzeh, Egypt	from 2580 BC	still stand
2. Hanging Gardens of Semiramis, Babylon	Babylon, Iraq	600 BC	no trace
3. Statue of Zeus (Jupiter) by Phidias	Olympia, Greece	post 432 BC	destroyed by fire
4. Temple of Artemis (Diana) of the Ephesians	Ephesus, Turkey	ante 350 BC	destroyed by Goths AD 262
5. Tomb of King Mausolus of Caria	Halicarnassus (now Bodrum), Turkey	post 353 BC	fragments survive
6. Statue of Helios (Apollo) by Charles of Lindus, called the Colossus of Rhodes (117 ft 36 m tall)	Rhodes, Aegean Sea	292–280 BC	destroyed by earthquakes 224 BC
7. Lighthouse (400 ft 122 m) on island of Pharos	off Alexandria, Egypt	270 BC	destroyed by earthquakes AD 400 and 1375

* Built by the Fourth Dynasty Pharaohs, Hwfw (Khufu or Cheops), Kha-f-Ra (Khafre or Khefren) and Menkaure (Mycerinus). The Great pyramid ('Horizon of Khufu') originally had a height of 480 ft 11 in 146·5 m now, since the loss of its topmost stone or pyramidion, reduced to 449 ft 6 in 137 m, Khafre's pyramid was 470 ft 9 in 143 m, and Menkaure's was 218 ft 66 m tall. The estimated weight of the 2 300 000 limestone blocks is 5 840 000 metric tonnes.

Tallest smokestacks and towers in the United Kingdom

Height (ft)	Height (m)	Building	Location
850	259	Drax Power Station	Drax, N. Yorkshire
800	244	Grain Power Station	Isle of Grain, Kent
700	213	Pembroke Power Station	Pembroke, Dyfed
670	204	Littlebrook 'D'	Dartford, Kent
670	204	Ironbridge 'B' Power Station (1 chimney)	Ironbridge, Salop
654	199	Didcot Power Station	Didcot, Oxfordshire
650	198	Eggborough Power Station (1 chimney)	Eggborough, N. Humberside
650	198	Ferrybridge 'C' Power Station (2 chimneys) (1 completed, 1966)	Ferrybridge, W. Yorkshire
650	198	Fiddler's Ferry	Cuerdley, Warrington
650	198	Kingsnorth Power Station (1 chimney)	Kingsnorth, Kent
650	198	Fawley Power Station (1 chimney)	Fawley, Hampshire
650	198	West Fife Power Station (2 chimneys)	West Fife
619	188	GPO Tower (1963)	Cleveland Mews, London, W1
600	182	West Burton Power Station (2 chimneys)	Retford, Nottinghamshire
558	170	Tilbury 'B' Power Station (2 chimneys)	Tilbury, Essex
550	167	Drakelow 'C' Power Station (2 chimneys)	Burton-on-Trent, Derbyshire

Note: The 474 ft 144 m Townsend's stack, Port Dundas, Glasgow (1857–9) was demolished in 1928. The 455 ft 139 m Tennant's Stalk, St Rollox, Glasgow (1841–2) has also been demolished. No power stations of or below 400 ft 122 m are listed. Battersea Power Station, London, is 337 ft 103 m.

OTHER TALL STRUCTURES IN THE UNITED KINGDOM

Height (ft)	Height (m)	Building	Location
820	250	Post Office Radio Masts (1925)	Rugby, Warwickshire
630	192	Transmission line pylons	West Thurrock, Thames Estuary
600·3	183	National Westminster Bank (1971–1979)	Old Broad Street–Bishopsgate, London
533	162	Humber Estuary Bridge Towers	Hessle and Barton
518·7	158,1	Blackpool Tower (1894)	Blackpool, Lancashire
512	156	Forth Road Bridge (1964)	Lothian–Fife, Scotland
488	148	Transmission line pylons	Severn Estuary
450	137	St John's Beacon	Liverpool
404	123	Salisbury Cathedral (ante 1305)	Salisbury, Wiltshire
399	121	Co-operative Insurance Society Building (1962)	Miller Street, Manchester
387	118	Vickers Building (1959–63)	Millbank, London
385	117	Centre Point (1966)	St Giles Circus, London
380	116	Penta Hotel (1971–73)	Kensington, London
370	113	Forth Rail Bridge (1882–90)	Lothian–Fife, Scotland
365	111	St Paul's Cathedral (1675–1710)	London
365	111	Stock Exchange (1972)	London
343	104	Shell Upstream Tower (1957–61)	South Bank, London
340	103	Victoria Tower (1840–67)	Palace of Westminster, London
328	100	Hilton Hotel (1960–63)	Park Lane, London
327	99	Portland House	Victoria, London

Longest bridge spans in the world

STEEL ARCH BRIDGES

Steel was first used in bridge construction in 1828 (Danube Canal Bridge, Vienna) but the first all-steel bridge was the Chicago and Alton Railway Bridge over the Missouri at Glasgow, South Dakota, USA, in 1878. The longest concrete arch bridge is the KRK Island Bridge, Yugoslavia with a span of 390 m 1280 ft.

Length (ft)	Length (m)	Name	Year of completion	Location
1700	518,2	New River Gorge	1977	Fayetteville, West Virginia, USA
1652	503,5	Bayonne (Kill Van Kull)	1931	Bayonne, NJ-Staten I, NY, USA
1650	502,9	Sydney Harbour	1932	Sydney, Australia
1255	382,5	Fremont	1972	Portland, Oregon, USA
1200	365,7	Port Mann	1964	Vancouver, BC, Canada
1128	343,8	Thatcher Ferry	1962	Balboa, Panama
1100	335,2	Laviolette (St Lawrence)	1967	Trois-Rivières, Quebec, Canada
1090	332,2	Zdakov	1967	Vltava River, Czechoslovakia
1082	330,0	Runcorn–Widnes	1961	Runcorn, Cheshire–Widnes, Lancashire, England
1080	329,2	Birchenough	1935	Sabi River, Rhodesia

CANTILEVER BRIDGE

The term cantilever came in only in 1883 (from *cant* and *lever*, an inclined or projecting lever). The earlier bridges of this type were termed Gerber bridges from Heinrich Gerber, engineer, of the 425 ft *129,5 m* Hassfurt am Main, Germany, bridge completed in 1867.

Length (ft)	Length (m)	Name	Year of completion	Location
1800	548,6	Quebec*	1917	St Lawrence, Canada
1710	521,2	Firth of Forth*	1890	Firth of Forth, Scotland
1673	510,0	Minato	1974	Osaka, Japan
1644	501,0	Commodore Barry Delaware River	1970	Chester, Pennsylvania, USA
1575	480,0	Greater New Orleans	1958	Algiers, Mississippi River, Louisiana, USA
1500	457,2	Howrah	1943	Calcutta, India
1400	426,7	Transbay (Oakland)	1936	San Francisco, California, USA
1235	376,4	Baton Rouge	1968	Mississippi River, Louisiana, USA
1235	376,4	Astoria	1966	Oregon, USA
1212	369,4	Nyack-Tarrytown (Tappan Zee)	1955	Hudson River, NY, USA
1200	365,7	Longview	1930	Columbia River, Washington, USA
1200	365,7	Baltimore	1976	Maryland, USA
1182	360,2	Queensboro	1909	East River, NY City, USA
1100	335,2	Carquinez Strait†	1927	nr San Francisco, California, USA
1100	335,2	Second Narrows	1959	Burrard Inlet, Vancouver, BC, Canada

* Rail bridge.   † New parallel bridge completed 1958.

LONGEST BRIDGING

Length (miles)	Length (km)	Name	Date Built	Location
23·87	38,422	Lake Pontchartrain Causeway II	1969	Mandeville–Jefferson, Louisiana, USA
23·83	38,352	Lake Pontchartrain Causeway I	1956	Mandeville–Jefferson, Louisiana, USA
17·99	28,952	Swampland Expressway	1973	Louisiana, USA
17·65	28,400	Chesapeake Bay Bridge-Tunnel	1964	Delmarva Peninsula–Norfolk, Virginia, USA
11·85*	19,070	Great Salt Lake Viaduct (Lucin cut-off)	1904	Great Salt Lake, Utah, USA
7·5	12,102	Ponte President Costa e Silva	1974	Rio de Janeiro–Niteroi, Brazil
6·7	10,78	San Mateo–Hayward	1967	San Francisco, California, USA

Other notable bridging

5·40	8,69	Lake Pontchartrain	1963	Slidell, Louisiana, USA
4·23	6,81	Sunshine Skyway I	1954	Lower Tampa Bay, Florida, USA
4·23	6,81	Sunshine Skyway II	1970	Lower Tampa Bay, Florida, USA
4·2	6,8	Nanking	1968–9	Yangtze Kiang, China
4·03	6,48	Chesapeake Bay I	1952	Maryland, USA

SUSPENSION BRIDGES

The suspension principle was introduced in 1741 with a 70 ft *21 m* span iron bridge over the Tees, England. Ever since 1816 the world's longest span bridges have been of this construction except for the reign of the Forth Bridge (1889–1917) and Quebec Bridge (1917–29).

Length (ft)	Length (m)	Name	Year of completion	Location
5840	1780	Akashi-Kaikyo†	1988	Honshu-Shikoku, Japan
4626	1410	Humber Estuary Bridge	1980	Humber, England
4260	1298	Verrazano–Narrows (6+6 lanes)	1964	Brooklyn–Staten I, USA
4200	1280	Golden Gate	1937	San Francisco Bay, USA
3800	1158	Mackinac Straits	1957	Straits of Mackinac, Mich, USA
3524	1074	Bosphorus Bridge	1973	Bosphorus, Istanbul, Turkey
3500	1067	George Washington (2 decks, lower has 6 lanes, upper has 8 lanes since 1962)	1931	Hudson River, NY City, USA
3323	1013	Ponte 25 Abril (Tagus) (4 lanes)	1966	Lisbon, Portugal
3300	1006	Firth of Forth Road Bridge	1964	Firth of Forth, Scotland
3240	988	Severn–Wye River (4 lanes)	1966	Severn Estuary, England
2874	876	Ohnaruto*	1983	Kobe-Naruto Route, Japan
2800	853	Tacoma Narrows II	1952	Washington, USA
2526	770	Innoshima*	1982	Onomichi-Impari Route, Japan
2336	712	Angostura	1967	Ciudad Bolívar, Venezuela
2336	712	Kammon Straits	1973	Shimonoseki, Japan
2310	704	Transbay (2 spans)	1936	San Francisco–Oakland, Calif, USA
2300	701	Bronx–Whitestone (Belt parkway)	1939	East River, NY City, USA
2190	668	Pierre Laporte Bridge	1970	Quebec City, Canada
2150	655	Delaware Memorial I	1951	Wilmington, Delaware, USA
2150	655	Delaware Memorial II	1968	Wilmington, Delaware, USA
2000	610	Melville Gaspipe	1951	Atchafalaya River, Louisiana, USA
2000	610	Walt Whitman	1957	Philadelphia, Pennsylvania, USA
1995	608	Tancarville	1959	Seine, Le Havre, France
1968	600	Lillebaelt	1970	Lillebaelt, Denmark

† Under design.   * Under construction.

Length (miles)	Length (km)	Name	Date Built	Location
4·0	6,43	Champlain	1962	Montreal, Canada
3·98	6,41	Chesapeake Bay II	1972	Maryland, USA
3·77	6,06	Oeland	1972	Sweden
3·75	6,03	London Bridge–Deptford Creek (878 brick arches)	1836	London
3·5	5,63	North Beveland to Schouwen Duiveland (52 arches)	1966	Netherlands
3·12	5,02	Oosterschelde	1965	Middelburg-Zierikzee, Netherlands
2·38	3,83	Evergreen Point	1963	Seattle, Washington
2·28*	3,67	Lower Zambezi (46 spans)	1935	Dona Ana–Vila de Sena, Mozambique
2·24*	3,60	Lake of Venice (222 arches)	1846	Mestre–Venice, Italy
2·21*	3,55	New Tay Bridge (85 spans)	1887	Wormit, Fife–Dundee, Tayside, Scotland
2·2	3,54	Laveka Bay Causeway	1961	Texas, USA
2·13	3,42	Newport Bridge	1969	Rhode Island, USA
1·99	3,20	Storstrom (3 arches, 51 piers)	1937	Sjaelland–Falster, Denmark
1·9	3,1	Upper Sone	1900	Sone River, India

* Rail viaduct.

Canals

A canal, from the Latin *canalis* – a water channel – is an artificial channel used for purposes of drainage, irrigation, water supply, navigation or a combination of these purposes.

Navigation canals were originally only for specially designed barges, but were later constructed for sea-going vessels. This important latter category consists either of improved barge canals, or, since the pioneering of the Suez in 1859–69, canals specially constructed for ocean-going vessels.

The world's major deep-draught ship canals (of at least 5 m *16·4 ft* depth) in order of length

Length of Waterway (miles)	Length of Waterway (km)	Name	Year Opened	Minimum Depth (ft)	Minimum Depth (m)	No of Locks	Achievement and Notes
141	227	White Sea (Beloye More)–Baltic (formerly Stalin) Canal	1933	16·5	5,0	19	Links with Barents Sea and White Sea to the Baltic with a chain of a lake, canalised river, and 32 miles *51,5 km* of canal.
100·6	162	Suez Canal	1869	39·3	12,9	Nil	Eliminates the necessity for 'rounding the Cape'. Deepening in progress.
62·2	100	V I Lenin Volga–Don Canal	1952	—	—	13	Interconnects Black, Azov and Caspian Seas.
60·9	98	North Sea (or Kiel) Canal	1895	45	13,7	2	Shortens the North Sea–Baltic passage; south of German–Danish border. Major reconstruction 1914.
56·7	91	Houston (Texas) Canal	1940	34	10,4	Nil	Makes Houston, although 50 miles from the coast, the United States' eighth busiest port.
53	85	Alphonse XIII Canal	1926	25	7,6	13	Makes sea access to Seville safe. True canal only 4 miles, *6,4 km* in length.
50·71	82	Panama Canal	1914	41	12,5	6	Eliminates the necessity for 'rounding the Horn'. 49 miles *78,9 km* of the length was excavated.
39·7	64	Manchester Ship Canal	1894	28	8,5	4	Makes Manchester, although 54 miles *86,9 km* from the open sea, Britain's third busiest port.
28·0	45	Welland Canal	1931	29	8,8	7	Circumvents Niagara Falls and Niagara River rapids.
19·8	32	Brussels or Rupel Sea Canal	1922	21	6,4	4	Makes Brussels an inland port.

Notes: (1) The Volga–Baltic canal system runs 1850 miles *2300 km* from Leningrad *via* Lake Ladoga, Gor'kiy, Kuybyshev and the Volga River to Astrakhan. The Grand Canal of China, completed in the 13th century over a length of 1107 miles *1780 km* from Peking to Hangchou had silted up to a maximum depth of 6 ft *1,8 m* by 1950 but is now being reconstructed.
(2) The world's longest inland navigation route is the St Lawrence Seaway of 2342 miles *3769 km* from the North Atlantic up the St Lawrence estuary and across the Great Lakes to Duluth, Minnesota, USA. It was opened on 26 Apr. 1959.

World's highest dams

Name	River	Country	Completion	Height (ft)	Height (m)
Rogunsky	Vakhsh	USSR	Building	1066	325
Nurek	Vakhsh	USSR	Building	1040	317
Grande Dixence	Dixence-Rhône	Switzerland	1962	935	285
Ingurskaya	Inguri	USSR	Building	892	272
Chicoasen	Grijalva	Mexico	1980	869	265
Vajont	Piave	Italy	1961	858	262
Tehri	Upper Ganges	India	Building (1989)	856	261
Mica	Columbia	Canada	1976	794	242
Sayano-Shushenskaya	Yenisey	USSR	1980	794	242
Patia	Patia	Colombia	Building	787	240
Chivor	Bata	Colombia	1975	778	237
Mauvoisin	Rhône	Switzerland	1957	777	237
Oroville	Feather-Sacramento	USA	1968	770	235
Chirkyi	Sulak-Caspian Sea	USSR	1975	764	233

World's most massive earth and rock dams

Name	Volume (millions of cubic yards)	Volume (millions of cubic metres)
New Cornelia Tailings, Arizona (1973)	274·0	209,4
Tarbela, Indus, Pakistan (1975)	159·2	121,7
Fort Peck, Missouri, Montana, USA (1940)	125·6	96,0
Guri, Caroni, Venezuela*	102·0	78,0
Rogunsky, Vakhsh, Tadjikistan, USSR*	98·7	75,5
Oahe, Missouri, S Dakota, USA (1963)	92·0	70,0
Oosterschelde, Netherlands (1980)	91·5	70,0
Mangla, Jhelum, Pakistan (1967)	85·8	65,6
Gardiner, South Saskatchewan, Canada (1968)	85·6	65,4
Afsluitdijk, Netherlands (1932)	82·9	63,3
Yacyreta-Apípe, Paraguay–Argentina*	80·0	61,2
Oroville, Feather, Calif, USA (1968)	78·0	60,0
San Luis, Calif, USA (1967)	77·9	59,5
Nurek, Vakhsh, Tadjikistan, USSR*	75·8	57,9
Garrison, Missouri, N Dakota, USA (1956)	66·5	50,8
Cochiti, USA (1975)	62·1	47,5
Tabka, Syria (1976)	60·1	45,9
W A C Bennett (formerly Portage Mt), Peace River, BC, Canada (1967)	57·2	43,7
Kiev, Dnieper, Ukraine, USSR (1964)	56·0	42,7
Aswan High Dam (Sadd-el-Aali), Nile river, Egypt (1970)	55·7	41,3

* under construction.

World's greatest man-made lakes

Name of Dam	Capacity miles³	Capacity km³
Owen Falls, Uganda (1964)	49·16	204,9
Bratsk, Angara River, USSR (1964)	40·59	169,2
Aswan High Dam (Sadd-el-Aali), Nile, Egypt (1970)	39·36	164
Kariba, Rhodesia-Zambia (1959)	39·38	160
Akosombo, Volta, Ghana (1965)†	35·5	148
Daniel Johnson, Manicouagan, Quebec, Canada (1968)	34·07	142
Guri (Raul Leon), Caroni-Orinoco, Venezuela*	32·66	131,1
Krasnoyarsk, Yenisey, USSR	17·58	73,3
WAC Bennett (Portage Mt) Peace River, BC, Canada (1967)	16·79	70
Zeya, E Siberia, USSR*	16·41	68,4
Wadi Tharthar, Tigris, Iraq (1956)	16	66,7
Ust-Ilim, Angara, USSR*	14·23	59,3

† Lake Volta, Ghana is the largest artificial lake measured by area (3275 miles² 8482 km²).
* under construction.
Note: Owen Falls Dam regulates the natural Victoria Nyanza which is the world's third largest by area.

World's longest vehicular tunnels

Miles	km	Name	Location
33·49	53,9	Seikan (rail) 1972–85*	Tsugaru Channel, Japan
19·07	30,7	Moscow Metro (1979)	Belyaevo to Medvedkovo, Moscow, USSR
17·30	27,84	Northern Line (Tube) 1939	East Finchley-Morden, London
13·78	22,17	Oshimizu 1981	Honshū, Japan
12·31	19,82	Simplon II (rail) 1918–22	Brigue, Switzerland-Iselle, Italy
12·30	19,80	Simplon I (rail) 1898–1906	Brigue, Switzerland-Iselle, Italy
11·61	18,68	Shin-Kanmon (rail) 1975	Kanmon Strait, Japan
11·49	18,49	Great Apennine (rail) 1923–34	Vernio, Italy
10·14	16,32	St Gotthard (road) 1971–80	Göschenen-Airolo, Switzerland
10·00	16,0	Rokko (rail) 1972	Japan
9·94	16,0	Hong Kong Subway (1975–80)	Hong Kong
9·85	15,8	Henderson (rail) 1975	Rocky Mts, Colorado, USA
9·26	14,9	St Gotthard (rail) 1872–82	Göschenen-Airolo, Switzerland
9·03	14,5	Lötschberg (rail) 1906–13	Kandersteg-Goppenstein, Switzerland
8·7	14,0	Arlberg (road) (1978)	Langen-St Anton, Austria
8·61	13,85	Hokkuriku (rail) 1957–62	Tsuruga-Imajo-Japan
8·5	13,6	Mont Cenis (rail extension) (1857–81)	Modane, France-Bardonecchia, Italy
8·3	13,35	Shin-shimizu (rail) (1967)	Japan
8·1	13,03	Aki (rail) (1975)	Japan
7·99	12,87	Fréjus II (road) 1974–80	Lanslebourg, France-Susa, Italy
7·78	12,52	Cascade (rail) 1925–29	Berne-Senic, Washington, USA
7·27	11,69	Mont Blanc (road) 1959–65	Pèlerins, France-Entrèves, Italy

* under construction

World's longest non-vehicular tunnels

Miles	km	Name	Location
105	168,9	Delaware Aqueduct 1937–44	New York State, USA
51·5	82,9	Orange-Fish Irrigation 1974	South Africa
49·7	80	Blomen water tunnel	Blomen, Sweden
44	70,8	West Delaware 1960	New York City, USA
31	50	Central Outfall 1975	Mexico City, Mexico
29·8	48	Arpa-Sevan hydro-electric*	Armenia, USSR
20·2	32.1	Kielder water tunnel	Tyne, Wear, Tees, England
18·8	30,3	Thames-Lea Water Supply 1960	Hampton-Walthamstow, London
18·1	29,1	Shandfaken Aqueduct 1923	Catskill, New York State
18·0	29	San Jacinto Aqueduct 1938	California, USA
17·7	28,5	Rendalen hydro-electric*	Norway
17·5	28,2	Kielder Aqueduct 1980	Tyne-Tees, England
15	24,1	Lochaber-hydro-electric 1930	Ben Nevis, Scotland
14·6	23,4	Encumbene-Snowy hydro-electric	New South Wales, Australia
13·7	22	Third Water Tunnel 1970–7	New York City, USA
13	20,9	Florence lake Tunnel 1925	California, USA
13	20,9	Continental Divide Tunnel 1946	Colorado, USA
12	20	Ely-Ouse 1969	Cambridgeshire, England

* under construction
Note: The Chicago Tunnels and Reservoir Plan (TARP), Illinois, USA involves 120 miles 193 km of sewerage tunnelling. The Majes hydro-electric and water supply in Peru comprises 60·9 miles 98 km of tunnels. The whole Snowy Mountain system New South Wales, Australia comprises 30·9 miles 49,7 km of tunnels. It was completed in 1966.

Music and Dance

Orchestral instruments

(Woodwind 1–9; Brass 10–13; Percussion 14–23; Strings 24–28; Keyboard 29–30.)

1 Piccolo or Octave Flute
Earliest concerto: Vivaldi, *c.* 1735. *Earliest orchestral use:* 1717 Handel's Water Music. *History:* Name 'piccolo' dates from 1856, but the origin goes back to prehistory via flute and sopranino recorder.

2 Flute – transverse or cross-blown
Earliest concerto Vivaldi, *c.* 1729. *Earlist orchestral use:* 1672 Lully. *History:* Prehistoric (*c.* 18,000 BC); the modern Boehm flute dates from 1832.

3 Oboe
Earliest concerto: Marcheselli, 1708. *Earliest orchestral use:* 1657 Lully's *L'amour malade*. *History:* Originated Middle Ages in the schalmey family. The name comes from Fr. *hautbois* (1511) = high wood.

4 Clarinet
Earliest concerto: Vivaldi, *c.* 1740?: 2 clarinets; Molter, *c.* 1747: 1 clarinet. *Earliest orchestral use:* 1726 Faber: Mass. *History:* Developed by J C Denner (1655–1707) from the recorder and schalmey families.

5 Cor anglais
Earliest concerto: J M Haydn, *c.* 1755? *Earliest orchestral use:* 1760 in Vienna. *History:* Purcell wrote for 'tenor oboe' *c.* 1690; this *may* have originated the name English Horn. Alternatively, it may be from 'angled horn', referring to its crooked shape.

6 Bass Clarinet
Earliest orchestral use: 1838 Meyerbeer's *Les Huguenots*. *History:* Prototype made in 1772 by Gilles Lot of Paris. Modern Boehm form from 1838.

7 Bassoon
Earliest concerto: Vivaldi, *c.* 1730? *Earliest orchestral use:* *c.* 1619. *History:* Introduced in Italy *c.* 1540 as the lowest of the double-reed group.

8 Double Bassoon
Earliest orchestral use: *c.* 1730 Handel. *History:* 'Borrowed' from military bands for elemental effects in opera.

9 Saxophone
Earliest concerto: Debussy's *Rhapsody*, 1903. *Earliest orchestral use:* 1844 Kastner's *Last King of Judah. History:* Invented by Adolphe Sax, *c.* 1840.

10 Trumpet
Earliest concerto: Torelli, before 1700, Haydn, 1796: keyed trumpet. *Earliest orchestral use:* *c.* 1800 keyed, 1835 valved, in Halévy's *La Juive. History:* The natural trumpet is of prehistoric origin; it formed the basis of the earliest orchestras.

11 Trombone
Earliest concerto: Wagenseil, *c.* 1760. *Earliest orchestral use:* *c.* 1600, as part of bass-line. *History:* From Roman *buccina* or slide-trumpet, via the mediaeval sackbut to its modern form *c.* 1500.

12 Horn
Earliest concerto: Bach, 1717–21, or Vivaldi, Bach ... Vivaldi: 2 horns; Telemann, before 1721: 1 horn. *Earliest orchestral use:* 1639,

Cavalli. *History:* Prehistoric. The earliest music horns were the German helical horns of the mid-16th century. Rotary valve horn patented in 1832.

13 Tuba
Earliest concerto: Vaughan Williams, 1954. *Earliest orchestral use:* 1830, Berlioz' *Symphonie Fantastique. History:* Patented by W Wieprecht and Moritz, Berlin, 1835.

14 Timpani/Kettle Drum
Earliest concerto: Masek, *c.* 1790: 1 set, Tausch, *c.* 1870: 6 timpani. *Earliest orchestral use:* 1607, Monteverdi's *Orfeo. History:* Originated in the ancient Orient.

15 Bass Drum
Earliest orchestral use: 1748, Rameau's *Zais. History:* As timpani.

16 Side or Snare Drum
Earliest orchestral use: 1749, Handel's *Fireworks Music. History:* Derived from the small drums of prehistory, via the mediaeval tabor. Achieved its modern form in the 18th century.

17 Tenor Drum
Earliest orchestral use: 1842.

18 Tambourine
Earliest orchestral use: 1820. *History:* Dates back to the mediaeval Arabs; prototype used by Assyrians and Egyptians. Earliest use of the word 1579.

19 Cymbals
Earliest orchestral use: 1680, Strungk's *Esther. History:* From Turkish military bands of antiquity.

20 Triangle
Earliest orchestral use: 1774, Glantz: Turkish Symphony. *History:* As cymbals.

21 Xylophone
Earliest orchestral use: 1873, Lumbye's *Traumbilder. History:* Primitive; earliest 'art' mention 1511.

22 Gong or Tam tam
Earliest orchestral use: 1791, Gossec's *Funeral March. History:* Originating in the ancient Far East.

23 Glockenspiel
Earliest orchestral use: 1739, Handel's *Saul. History:* Today strictly a keyboard instrument, in the 19th century the metal plates were struck by hand-held hammers. The original instrument dates from 4th century Rome.

24 Violin
Earliest concerto: Torelli, 1709. *Earliest orchestral use:* *c.* 1600. *History:* Descended from the Lyre via the 6th century crwth, rebec and fiddle. Modern instrument of Lombardic origin *c.* 1545. The words violin and fiddle derive ultimately from Roman *vitulari* ('to skip like a calf').

25 Violoncello
Earliest concerto: Jacchini, 1701. *Earliest orchestral use:* *c.* 1600. *History:* As violin.

26 Viola
Earliest concerto: Telemann *ante* 1722. *Earliest orchestral use:* *c.* 1600. *History:* As violin.

27 Double Bass
Earliest concerto: Vanhal, *c.* 1770. *Earliest orchestral use:* *c.* 1600. *History:* Developed alongside the violin family, but is a closer relative to the bass viol or Violone.

28 Harp
Earliest concerto: Handel, 1738. *Earliest orchestral use:* *c.* 1600. *History:* Possibly prehistoric: attained its modern form by 1792.

29 Vibraphone
Earliest orchestral use: 1934. *History:* First used in dance bands in the 1920s.

30 Celesta
Earliest orchestral use: 1880, Widor's *Der Korrigane. History:* Invented by Mustel in 1880.

Popular and folk instruments

Accordion/concertina
Accordion invented (as Handäoline) in Germany, 1822. Concertina invented in England, 1829. The accordion produces two notes, one drawn, the other pressed, to a key, the concertina only one; further, the accordion sometimes has a keyboard, the concertina never has.

Bagpipes
A prehistoric Middle Eastern or Chinese instrument made by shepherds of a lamb or goat skin with pipes attached. The bag acts as a bellows to actuate chanter and drone pipes. First concerto, 1755. Much used today as a military instrument in Scotland and elsewhere.

Balalaika
East European (predominantly Russian) triangular development of the long-necked lute, reaching its present form about a century ago. Currently made in six sizes, each with three strings.

Guitar
A fretted, six-stringed development of the antique lute (qv), possibly introduced into Europe by the Moors (8th century) and settling as Spain's national instrument, attaining its present basic form *c.* 1750. Earliest printed music, 1546. Earliest concerto, 1808.

Harmonium
Invented (as *orgue expressif*) in France, 1830s. A bellows reed organ, perfected during the 1840s as a modest-sized keyboard instrument for church, cinema and home use (known in England sometimes as 'cottage organ').

Harpsichord
Evolved from the psaltery during the 14th century; earliest surviving example dated 1521. Mainly a domestic instrument, it also supported the bass line in early orchestras. First solo concerto, *c.* 1720. Eclipsed *c.* 1800 by pianoforte (qv), but reintroduced progressively since 1903.

Keyboards
Generic term for keyboard instrument(s) connected to electronic device which produces extensive variations in tone-colour and note duration.

Lute
Extremely ancient (*c.* 3000 BC or before) source of all subsequent bowed and plucked stringed instruments, including violin, guitar, sitar, mandolin, etc. Earliest published music, 1507. Popularity subsided during 18th century, but currently revived for performance of early music.

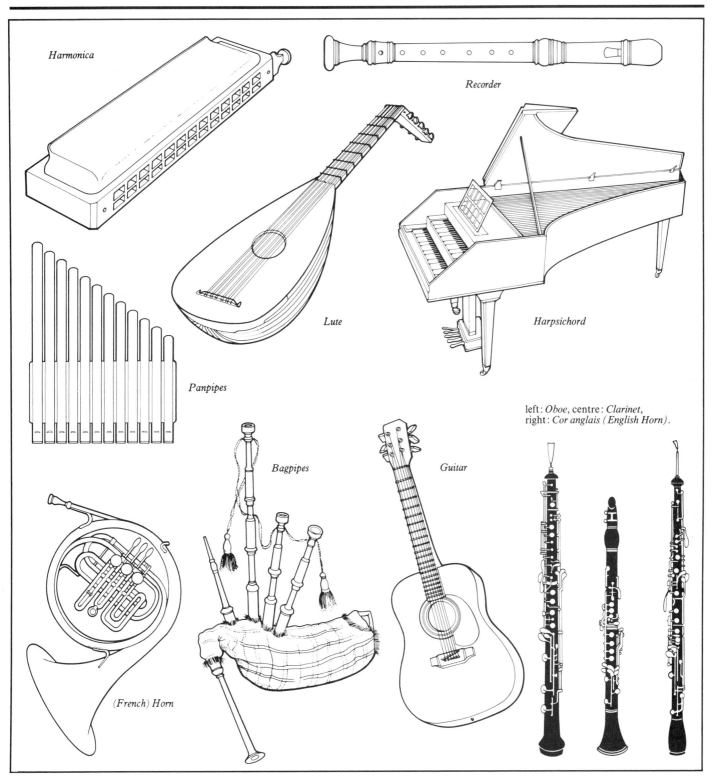

Harmonica

Recorder

Lute

Harpsichord

Panpipes

left: *Oboe*, centre: *Clarinet*,
right: *Cor anglais (English Horn)*.

Bagpipes

Guitar

(French) Horn

Mouth organ/harmonica
The most popular of all instruments. Invented in Germany, 1821. First concerto, 1951.

Organ
Ultimate origin lies in the antique panpipes (qv), but subsequent developments make it the biggest and most powerful of all instruments. First concerto by Handel, *c.* 1730. Saint-Saëns first used it in a symphony, 1886.

Panpipes
The simplest and most primitive organ, each pipe producing only one note. Named after the god Pan. An important instrument in Balkan folk music, it has recently achieved more widespread recognition.

Pianoforte
Descended from the dulcimer. Invented by Cristofori, *c.* 1709. Earliest printed music, 1732; first concert use in London, 1767; first concerto by J C Bach, 1776. Attained its modern basic form, *c.* 1850.

Recorder
End-blown flute, developed from prehistoric pipes. First mentioned, 1388. Popular during 17th and 18th centuries until being succeeded by the transverse flute.

Synthesiser
Electronic device, invented *c.* 1950 to create pitch, tone-colour and duration of any note or notes or sounds. Used especially in popular and jazz music, where it is often attached to a keyboard.

The history and development of music

PREHISTORIC
Improvisatory music-making. Music and magic virtually synonymous.

PRIMITIVE (Ancient Greece and Rome; Byzantium) 8th century BC to 4th century AD
Improvisatory music-making in domestic surroundings. Competitive music-making in the arena.

Viola   Violin

Violoncello

Double Bass

AMBROSIAN (4th to 6th century AD)

The beginnings of plainsong and the establishment of order in liturgical music.

Principal composer
Bishop Ambrose of Milan (*c.* 333–97) established four scales.

GREGORIAN (6th to 10th century)

Church music subjected to strict rules, e.g.: melodies sung only in unison.

Principal composer
Pope Gregory I, 'The Great' (540–604) extended the number of established scales to eight.

MEDIAEVAL (1100–1300)

Guido d'Arezzo (*c.* 980–1050) was called the 'inventor of music': his teaching methods and invention of a method of writing music transformed the art. Beginning of organized instrumental music; start of polyphony in church music.

Principal composers
Minstrels (10th–13th centuries). Goliards (travelling singers of Latin songs: 11th–12th centuries). Troubadours (*c.* 1100–1210). Trouvères (from 1100).
Bernart de Ventadorn (*c.* 1150–95) encouraged singing in the vernacular.

RENAISSANCE (1300–1600)

The great age of polyphonic church music. Gradual emergence of instrumental music. Appearance of Madrigals, chansons, etc. The beginnings of true organization in music and instruments.

Principal composers
Guillaume de Machut (*c.* 1300–77)
John Dunstable (*c.* 1380–1453)
Guillaume Dufay (*c.* 1400–74)
Johannes Ockeghem (1430–95)
Josquin des Prés (*c.* 1450–1521)
John Taverner (*c.* 1495–1545)
Giovanni da Palestrina (*c.* 1525–94)
Orlando di Lasso (*c.* 1530–94)
Thomas Morley (1557–1603)
John Dowland (1563–1626)
Michael Praetorius (1571–1621)

BAROQUE (1600–1750)

Beginnings of opera and oratorio. Rise of instrumental music; the first orchestras, used at first in the opera house but gradually attaining separate existence. Beginnings of sonata, concerto, suite, and symphony. The peak of polyphonic writing.

Principal composers
Giovanni Gabrieli (1557–1612)
Claudio Monteverdi (1567–1643)
Orlando Gibbons (1583–1625)
Pietro Cavalli (1602–76)
Jean-Baptiste Lully (1632–87)
Arcangelo Corelli (1653–1713)
Henry Purcell (*c.* 1659–95)
Alessandro Scarlatti (1660–1725)
François Couperin (1668–1733)
Reinhard Keiser (1674–1739)
Antonio Lucio Vivaldi (1678–1741)
Georg Philipp Telemann (1681–1767)
Jean-Philippe Rameau (1683–1764)
Domenico Scarlatti (1685–1757)
Johann Sebastian Bach (1685–1750)
George Frideric Handel (1685–1759)

CLASSICAL (1750–1800+)

The age of the concert symphony and concerto. Beginning of the string quarter and sinfonia concertante. Decline of church music. Important developments in opera.

Principal composers
Giovanni Battista Sammartini (*c.* 1700–75)
Christoph Willibald von Gluck (1714–87)
Carl Philipp Emanuel Bach (1714–88)
Franz Joseph Haydn (1732–1809)
Wolfgang Amadeus Mozart (1756–91)
Luigi Cherubini (1760–1842)

EARLY ROMANTIC (1800–50)

High maturity of the symphony and concerto, etc. in classical style. Romantic opera. The age of the piano virtuosi. Invention of the Nocturne. Beginnings of the symphonic poem. Lieder. Beginnings of nationalism.

Principal composers
Ludwig van Beethoven (1770–1827)
Nicolo Paganini (1782–1840)
Carl Maria von Weber (1786–1826)
Gioacchino Rossini (1792–1868)
Franz Schubert (1797–1828)
Hector Berlioz (1803–69)
Mikhail Glinka (1804–57)
Jakob Ludwig Felix Mendelssohn Bartholdy (1809–47)
Frédéric François Chopin (1810–49)
Robert Schumann (1810–56)

HIGH ROMANTICISM (1850–1900)

The development of nationalism. Maturity of the symphonic and tone poems. Emergence of music drama.

Principal composers
Franz Liszt (1811–86)
Richard Wagner (1813–83)
Giuseppe Verdi (1813–1901)
César Franck (1822–90)
Bedřich Smetana (1824–84)
Anton Bruckner (1824–96)
Johannes Brahms (1833–97)
Peter Ilyitch Tchaikovsky (1840–93)
Antonin Dvořák (1841–1904)
Edvard Hagerup Grieg (1843–1907)
Gustav Mahler (1860–1911)

MODERN (1900–)

Impressionism and post-romanticism. Gigantism. Neo-classicism and other reactionary movements. Atonalism.

Principal composers
Giacomo Puccini (1858–1924)
Claude Debussy (1862–1918)
Richard Strauss (1864–1949)
Carl Nielsen (1865–1931)
Jean Sibelius (1865–1957)
Alexander Scriabin (1872–1915)
Ralph Vaughan Williams (1872–1958)
Sergei Rachmaninov (1873–1943)
Arnold Schoenberg (1874–1951)
Charles Ives (1874–1954)
Maurice Ravel (1875–1937)
Béla Bartók (1881–1945)
Igor Stravinsky (1882–1971)
Anton Webern (1883–1945)
Alban Berg (1885–1935)
Sergei Prokofiev (1891–1953)
Aaron Copland (b 1890)
Sir William Walton (1902–82)
Sir Michael Tippett (b 1905)
Dmitri Shostakovich (1906–75)
Samuel Barber (b. 1910)
Benjamin Britten (1913–77)

AVANT-GARDE (Today)

Avant-Garde is history in the making and any list of composers would be arbitrary since one cannot tell which of the many directions taken by modern music will prove most influential. There have always been avant-garde composers, without which the art of music would never have developed: we would take many names from the above chart as good examples. Here are some names of avant-gardistes of prominence.

Principal composers
Luigi Dallapiccola (1904–75)
Oliver Messiaen (b. 1908)
John Cage (b. 1912)
Witold Lutostawski (b. 1913)
Iannis Xenakis (b. 1922)
Luigi Nono (b. 1924)
Pierre Boulez (b. 1925)
Hans Werner Henze (b. 1926)
Karlheinz Stockhausen (b. 1928)
Steve Reich (b. 1936)

A chart of the main works of 72 of history's major composers from the 13th to the 20th century was published in the Guinness Book of Answers (2nd Edition) at pages 94–97.

Some musical comedy composers

Kern, Jerome (1885–1945) *Show Boat*; *Swing Time*
Berlin, Irving (b. 1888) *Annie Get Your Gun*; *Call Me Madam*
Porter, Cole (1891–1964) *Kiss Me Kate*; *Can Can*
Novello, Ivor (1893–69) *The Dancing Years*; *King's Rhapsody*
Gershwin, George (1898–1937) *Lady Be Good*; *Porgy and Bess*
Coward, Noel (1899–1973) *Bitter Sweet*; *Sail Away*
Weill, Kurt (1900–50) *Threepenny Opera*; *One Touch of Venus*
Rogers, Richard (b. 1902) *The King and I*; *Oklahoma*
Loesser, Frank (1910–69) *Guys and Dolls*
Bernstein, Leonard (b. 1918) *On the Town*; *West Side Story*
Wilson, Sandy (b. 1924) *The Boy Friend*
Sondheim, Stephen (b. 1930) *Company*; *A Little Night Music*
Lloyd Webber, Andrew (b. 1948) *Jesus Christ Superstar*; *Evita*

Some jazz musicians and composers

Handy, (W)illiam (C)hristopher (1873–1958) Composer
Bolden, Buddy (1878–1931) Cornet
Morton, (Ferdinand la Menthe) 'Jellyroll' (1885–1941) Piano
Oliver, Joe 'King' (1885–1938) Cornet
Ory, Edward 'Kid' (1886–1973) Trombone
Bechet, Sidney (1891–1959) Soprano saxophone
Smith, Bessie (1895–1937) Singer
Ellington, Edward Kennedy (Duke) (1899–1974) Pianist, bandleader
Armstrong, Louis 'Satchmo' (1900–1971) Trumpet, singer
Beiderbecke, Leon 'Bix' (1903–31) Cornet
Basie, William 'Count' (1904–84) Pianist, bandleader
Dorsey, Thomas (Tommy) (1905–56) Trombone, bandleader
Goodman, Benjamin David, 'Benny' (b. 1909) Clarinet, bandleader
Tatum, Arthur 'Art' (1910–56) Piano
Herman, Woodrow Charles, 'Woody' (b. 1913) Clarinet, bandleader
Holiday, Billie (1915–59) Singer
Monk, Theolonius Sphere (1917–82) Piano
Gillespie, John Birks, 'Dizzy' (b. 1917) Trumpet
Fitzgerald, Ella (b. 1918) Singer
Parker, Charles Christopher 'Bird' (1920–55) Saxophone
Peterson, Oscar Emmanuel (b. 1925) Piano
Roach, Maxwell, 'Max' (b. 1925) Drums
Coltrane, John (1926–67) Saxophone
Davis, Miles (b. 1926) Trumpet

Some popular singers and pop groups

Abba (formed 1971)
Baez, Joan (b. 1941)
The Beatles (formed 1960–1970)
Bowie, David (b. 1947)
Cash, Johnny (b. 1932)
Charles, Ray (b. 1930)
Crosby, Bing (1904–1977)
Dylan, Bob (b. 1941)
Haley, Bill (1925–1981)
Hendrix, Jimi (1942–1970)
Jackson, Michael (b. 1958)
John, Elton (b. 1947)
Holly, Buddy (1936–1959)
Marley, Bob (1945–1981)
Mitchell, Joni (b. 1943)
Parton, Dolly, (b. 1946)
Presley, Elvis (1935–1977)
Ross, Diana (b. 1944)
Richard, Cliff (b. 1940)
The Rolling Stones (formed 1962)
Sinatra, Frank (b. 1915)
Wonder, Stevie (b. 1950)

Musical terms

adagio slow and leisurely.
aleatory music Allowing performers freedom of interpretation or which introduces other random elements.
allegro Quick, lively.
andante Gently moving, flowing.
anthem Church choral work.
aria Solo song in opera or oratorio.
arpeggio Notes of a chord played upward or downward in quick succession.
atonal music Use of all twelve semitones; having no key.
cadence Musical punctuation used to end phrases, sections or complete works.
cadenza Solo virtuoso piece before the final cadence in an aria, or at any stated place in a concerto.
canon Repetition of tune or tunes that overlap each other.
chord Notes played together simultaneously.
chromatic relating to notes and chords comprising the twelve-note scale.
coda Theme introduced at the end of a movement to emphasize its finality.
concrete music (Musique concrète). Music constructed from previously recorded natural sounds.
continuo Keyboard augmentation of a 17th or 18th century orchestral work.
counterpoint Two or more independent tunes sung or played at the same time.
diatonic Relating to notes of the major and minor scales.
dominant key Key whose keynote is the fifth note of the tonic key.
electronic music Consisting of electronically produced sounds.

forte (f) Loudly.
fortissimo (ff) Very loudly.
fugue A polyphonic composition. The first tune is in the tonic; the second, introduced later, in the dominant key, and so on.
interval Difference in pitch between two notes.
largo Slow, stately.
libretto Text of oratoria or opera.
lieder German romantic songs of the 19th century.
madrigal Secular composition for voices.
Mass Roman Catholic sung service of Communion.
motet Unaccompanied part song of a religious nature.
movement A division of a long musical work.
obbligato Accompaniment by solo instrument.
opera Drama set to music.
operetta Light opera, often with dialogue.
oratorio Religious equivalent of opera without costume or scenery.
overture Instrumental introduction to opera or oratorio.
pentatonic scale A primitive five-note octave.
pianissimo (pp) Very soft.
piano (p) Soft.
pitch The height or depth of a note, measured according to its vibration (e.g. A above middle C equals 440 vibrations a second).
pizzicato Notes played by plucking strings of normally bowed instruments.
polyphonic 'Many voiced', combining independent melodic lines. As in motets and fugues.
recitative Solo vocal music that follows speech patterns.
Requiem Mass for the dead.
rondo Musical composition where the first and main section returns alternatively after different contrasting sections.
scherzo Lively movement.
serial music Compositions of the twelve-tone scale using all notes with equal importance, and each one once only before all have been used.
sonata form A form of musical composition developed during the 18th century. The first part sets out two main themes, each in a different key. The second part develops these two themes. The third is a recapitulation in which both themes are presented in the key of the first theme.
suite A work made up of several movements.
symphony Major orchestral work, usually made up of four movements.
syncopation Accentuation of a beat in each bar that is normally not accentuated.
tempo Pace at which a work is performed.
tertiary form A simple three-part musical structure in which the central part contrasts with the first and third, which are similar (ABA form).
theme A basic tune.
tutti Passage for whole orchestra.
vibrato Wavering of a note's pitch in singing, string playing and wind playing, to give vibrancy.
vivace Lively.

The Dance

MAIN TRENDS	TYPES OF DANCE POPULAR AT THE TIME (Basic rhythmic pulse in brackets)
Pre-history Unorganized or loosely organized dances for warlike and communal purposes.	
c. 50 BC Mimes: dancing and singing spectacles (Rome).	
14th Century Danse basse: low, slow gliding steps. Hault danse: with high fast steps.	Pavane (4); derived from instrumental music from Padua; possibly the first stylised dance. Galliard (3), also from Italy, where the name implies gaiety.

MAIN TRENDS	TYPES OF DANCE POPULAR AT THE TIME (*Basic rhythmic pulse in brackets*)
15th Century First true ballet, with settings by Leonardo da Vinci, danced at Tortona, 1489. Introduced at the court of Henry VIII of England as Masque.	Court ballet: Branle (2), English clog dance with circular figures. Allemande (2,4,), i.e. 'from Germany'. Courante (3), i.e. 'running', from It. *corrente* (current). Volta (3), very lively (It. *volta*: vault).
16th Century Ballet comique. First complete printed account (15 Oct. 1581) of a ballet to celebrate the marriage of duc de Joyeuse and Marguerite of Lorraine. It was based on the story of Circe and choreographed by Baldassarino de Belgiojoso.	Morris dance, from Morocco.
17th Century Ballet Masquerade, often with hideous and elaborate masks. Playford's *English Dancing Master* published 1651; a collection of tunes and steps. First waltz, developed from minuet and Ländler in 1660; word 'waltz' first used in 1754 in Austria. Ballet systematique: Louis XIV established the Academie Royale de Danse 1661. Five classic positions codified; first history of dancing published in 1682.	Gigue (3,6,12), originally from English jig, the word from German *Geige*: 'fiddle'. Sarabande (3), slow and graceful, introduced to Spain *c.* 1588 from Morocco or West Indies. Bouree (4), lively dance, starting on the upbeat. Chaconne (3), graceful dance introduced from Peru (*guacones, c.* 1580) via Spain. Gavotte (2), medium pace, from Provencale; *gavoto*: a native of the Alps. Minuet (3), 'small steps'; rustic minuets occur in Strasbourg in 1682, but origin in the 15th century Branle. Passacaglia (3), as chaconne above, but in minor key. Rigaudon; Rigaudon: Rigadoon (2,4), lively French dance. Ländler (3), rustic dance, from *Ländl*: 'small country'. Matelot (2), Dutch sailors' clog dance. Contredanse (2,4) from Eng. 'country dance', but mistranslated as 'counter-dance', i.e. for opposing groups, and re-introduced into England in this form. Cotillion (6), from French word for 'petticoat', for 2 groups of 4 pairs each; developed into quadrille at the end of the 19th century.
18th Century Ballet steps on toe-tips (on point) (*c.* 1800).	Reel (4), stylised form of Scottish dance.
19th Century Square dance (*c.* 1815). Can-can (*c.* 1835); high-kicking exhibitionist female dance popular on Parisian stages. Age of the great waltz composers: Josef Lanner; Johann Strauss; Emil Waldteufel, etc.	Quadrille (2,4). Polka (2), introduced to Paris in 1843 from Bohemian courtship dance (1-2-3-hop). Cakewalk (2), graceful walking dance of competitive type with cakes as prizes, popular in Black America in 1872; introduced into ballrooms *c.* 1900.

MAIN TRENDS	TYPES OF DANCE POPULAR AT THE TIME (*Basic rhythmic pulse in brackets*)
20th Century Ballets Russes established in Paris by Diaghilev, 1909. New free dance forms emerging.	 Samba (2), emerged from Brazil, 1885; known *c.* 1920 as Maxixe; resumed name 'samba' *c.* 1940. Quickstep (2), invented in America 1900; reached peak of popularity in 1920s. Tango (2), earliest contest in Nice, France, in 1907. Barn dance (4), associated in America with festivities surrounding the completion of a new barn. Two-step (2). Boston (2), predecessor of the foxtrot. Turkey Trot (2).
Ballroom dance craze, mostly couples dancing to small instrumental groups (*c.* 1920).	Foxtrot (4), slow and quick varieties, introduced in 1912 in America, allegedly named after Harry Fox. The slow foxtrot evolved *c.* 1927 into the 'blues' dance.
Growth of very energetic dancing, often to jazz or pseudo-jazz groups (from 1939). Modern Discotheque style, i.e. recorded music for dancing; originated in Parisian clubs (*c.* 1951).	Charleston (2), side kick from the knee. Named after a Mack and Johnson song (1923) about the town that saw the first ballet in America in 1735. Pasodoble (2), Spanish-style two-step. Rumba (8, i.e. 3 + 3 + 2), authentic Cuban dance popularised in 1923. Black Bottom (4), first mentioned in New York Times (19 Dec. 1926), a type of athletic and jerky foxtrot. Conga (4, i.e. 1–2–3–kick), single-file dance developed in 1935 from Rumba and from aboriginal African dances. Jive (2,4) derived from Jitterbug.
Popularity of dances closely linked to the 'hit-parade' progress of popular music and the consequent invention of many new dance styles.	Mambo (8), an off-beat Rumba (1948) of Cuban origin. Rock 'n' Roll (2), introduced in 1953 by Bill Haley and his Comets in America; heavy beat and simple melody for energetic and free dancing. Cha cha cha (2,4) (1954), a variation of the Mambo, couples dancing with lightly linked hands. Twist (2) (1961), body-torsion and knee-flexing lively dance, with partners rarely in contact. Bossa nova (2), lively Latin American dance. Go-go (2,4) (1965), repetitious dance of verve, often exhibitionist. Reggae (4) (1969), introduced from Jamaica, strong accentuations off-beat. Pogo (2) (1976), introduced by 'Punk Rockers'. Dancers rise vertically from the floor in imitation of a pogo stick. Robotic-dancers imitate clockwork dolls with rigid limb movements. 1980 Break dancing; dancers perform acrobatic feats while dancing.

Ballet terms

á terre Steps which do not entail high jumps. They include the *glissade, pas balloné* and *pas brisé*.

battement Ballet exercises

batterie, battu Jump during which a dancer beats the calves sharply together.

corps de ballet Group of dancers who support the principal dancers.

divertissement Self-contained dance within a ballet, designed purely as entertainment or to show off a dancer's technique.

elevation Any high jump in ballet. Elevations include the *entrechat, rivoltade, pas de chat* and *cabriole*.

enchaînement. Sequence of steps linked to make a harmonious whole.

entrechat Vertical jump during which the dancer changes the position of the legs after beating the calves together.

fouetté Spectacular pirouette in which the dancer throws his raised leg to the front and side in order to achieve momentum for another turn.

jeté Jump from one leg to the other, basic to many ballet steps. These include the *grand jeté en avant*, in which the dancer leaps forward as if clearing an obstacle, and the *jeté foutté* where the dancer performs a complete turn in mid-air.

pas Basic ballet step in which the weight is transferred from one leg to another. The term is also used in combination to indicate the number of performers in a dance; a *pas seul* is a solo and a *pas de deux* a dance for a pair of dancers.

pirouette Complete turn on one leg, performed either on the ball of the foot or on the toes.

plié Bending the legs from a standing position; *demi-plié* involves bending the knees as far as possible while keeping the heels on the ground.

relevé Bending the body from the waist to one side or the other during a turn or a pirouette.

rivoltade, revoltade Step in which a dancer raises

one leg in front, jumps from the other and turns in the air, landing in his original position but facing the other way.

saut A plain jump into the air without embellishment.

soutenu Movement executed at a slower tempo than usual.

sur les pointes On the toes.

variation Solo by a male dancer in a *pas de deux*.

Some well known ballet companies

Royal Danish Ballet
Founded 1748
Bolshoi Ballet
Founded in Moscow in 1776
Kirov Ballet Formerly the Imperial Russian Ballet of St. Petersburg (Leningrad)
Founded 1860
Ballets Russes
Founded by Diaghilev in Paris 1909
Martha Graham Dance Company
Founded by Graham in 1930

Ballet Rambert
Founded by Marie Rambert in 1930
Vic-Wells Ballet (afterwards, Sadlers Wells Ballet)
Founded in 1931 by Ninette de Valois
Ballets Jooss
Founded by Kurt Jooss in 1932
New York City Ballet
Founded in 1934
American Ballet Theatre
Founded in 1940 by Lucia Chase
Merce Cunningham Dance Company
Founded by Cunningham in 1952
Royal Ballet Successor to Sadlers Wells Ballet.
Founded 1956

Film and Television

Cinema

ORIGINS OF THE CINEMA
The creation of the cinema as we know it today was preceded by various developments in photography and the study of movement that go back to the early 19th century. The illusion of movement was first obtained by projecting images mechanically in rapid succession and was used in toys made in the 1830s.

An English photographer, Edward Muybridge, used up to 36 still cameras to capture the movements of animals and humans in a series of experiments; the results he projected in succession. The first motion picture films were taken on a camera patented in Britain by French-born Louis Le Prince, who used sensitized paper rolls to obtain images taken in 1888. A year later Eastman celluloid film was available in Britain and Le Prince used this to develop the commercial aspects of his patent.

The kinetoscope, invented in 1891 at the laboratories of Edison in the USA was the first apparatus for viewing cine film: the intermittent 'gate', which holds each frame of film stationary while it is being exposed was invented in Britain by William Friese-Greene in 1888. Rapidly, all these experiments and inventions were integrated into one apparatus, a combined movie camera and projector, by the French brothers, Auguste and Louis Lumière. They started the first movie shows, the first public performance taking place in Paris on 22 March 1894. Meanwhile in New York, on 14 April 1894, the first commercial showing of motion pictures took place, using kinetoscopes. The cinema, as we know it, was born.

The public's interest in the new medium became unassuageable, and showmen were quick to exploit its commercial potential. Programmes were shown in fairgrounds and hired halls; soon purpose-built cinemas were being built and by 1910 there were over 5,000 in Britain alone.

At first, cinema presentations were confined to the showing of a number of short films, but in 1906 the first feature film was made in Australia. Lasting 60–70 minutes, it was made by Charles Tait and was called *The Story of the Kelly Gang*. Europe and the United States soon followed Tait's lead, and by the outbreak of World War I in 1914, 22 countries were producing feature films.

COLOUR MOVIES
Colour photography experiments were being carried out throughout the latter half of the 19th century, and in July 1906 the first commercially successful colour film was made. Developed by G. A. Smith in Britain, he called his process Kinemacolor, and the first public presentation of a film in his new process was shown in a programme of 21 films on 26 February 1909. Britain led the United States in the production of Kinemacolor films, producing the first full-length feature in colour in 1914. The first (non-subtractive) Technicolor film was made in the United States in 1917, using (like Kinemacolor) colour filters on both camera and projector. Two-colour subtractive Technicolor film was made and used in 1922.

By 1932, three-colour subtractive Technicolor film was available and was first used for a Walt Disney cartoon shown on 17 July 1932. Meanwhile, two-colour processes continued to be developed, the most notable being Cinecolor. Eastman Color was introduced in 1952 and steadily displaced its rivals. It is now almost universally used in Western countries.

THE INTRODUCTION OF SOUND
Although *The Jazz Singer*, starring Al Jolson, made in Hollywood in 1927, is credited with being the first 'talkie', there is a long list of precedents stretching back to 1896. Short sound films were shown in Berlin in September of that year, using synchronised discs for the sound. Sound-on-disc continued to be used in various forms until 1929, and as far back as 1906 the first sound-on-film process was patented by French-born Eugene Lauste of London, but it was not until 1910 that he succeeded in recording and reproducing speech on film. By 1913 he had perfected the apparatus to record and reproduce sound on films, but World War I put an end to his hopes of commercially exploiting his invention. Sound track was added to Technicolor film in 1924. The first presentation of a sound-on-film production before a paying audience was shown in New York on 15 April 1923. *The Jazz Singer* takes its place in the record as being the first talking feature film, and used the sound-on-disc system. The first sound-on-film feature was shown on 1 September 1928, in New York: its title, *The Air Circus*.

Stereophonic sound was patented in France in 1932 and its first use was three years later. Sensurround was first used in 1974 in *Earthquake*, having not only all-round sound, but vibrations set up by low-frequency sound.

OTHER TECHNICAL DEVELOPMENTS
The first wide screen showings date back to the 1890s, when film stock of exceptional width was used. It was first used in a feature film in Italy in 1923. Anamorphic lenses – used to contract a wide image onto standard film (as in Cinemascope) – were first used in France in 1927. 70 mm film for use with a wide screen was used in the United States in 1929. The first system to combine wide-gauge film and anamorphic lenses was called Ultra-Panavision which was first used in 1957. Cinemascope was developed by the Frenchman, Henri Chrétien, from an anamorphic system he invented in 1927. The patent rights were bought by the Hollywood Fox Studios and used in the first Cinemascope feature in 1953, *The Robe*.

Cinerama was shown at the New York World Fair in 1939, but was not launched commercially until 1952.

Three-dimensional films date from 1915, using red and green spectacles worn by the viewers. Intermittent attempts to popularize the development have not been successful. A Russian development in 1947 was the first to dispense successfully with spectacles, and used a specially designed corrugated screen to reflect the two images to the left and right eye.

Holography gives the illusion of three-dimensional substance without resort to spectacles or screens, and uses lasers to create an effect whereby a spectator can move from one position to another and 'see' the object projected from these different vantages or angles. It was first presented in Moscow in 1977.

CINEMAS
(more than 3000)

USSR	142 146	(1981)
USA	14 732	(1981)
Italy	7726	(1981)
India	6991	(1981)
France	4532	(1981)
China	4000	(1979)
Spain	3970	(1981)
W. Germany	3530	(1981)
Bulgaria	3006	(1981)
Japan	2298	(1981)
UK	1541	(1981)
Sweden	1239	(1981)

CINEMAS
(more than 3000)

Argentina	1010	(1981)
South Africa	700	(1979)
Australia	564	(1979)
New Zealand	172	(1979)

ATTENDANCE IN MILLIONS OF SEATS PER YEAR

China	22 500	(1979)
India	3676	(1981)
USA	1067	(1981)
Italy	215	(1981)
France	187	(1981)
Japan	149	(1981)
West Germany	141	(1981)
UK	86	(1981)

FILM PRODUCTION (1984)
(Feature films of 1 hour or more)

India	800
Japan	379
USA	262
France	161
USSR	150
Thailand	141
Hong Kong	125
Italy	103
Brazil	90
Pakistan	82
Indonesia	78
Germany, West	77
Mexico	77
Spain	75
Bangladesh	50
UK	42

SOME NOTABLE CINEMA ACTORS, ACTRESSES AND DIRECTORS

Allen, Woody (b. 1935) American actor, director. *Manhattan*; *Annie Hall*

Antonioni, Michelangelo (b. 1912) Italian director. *La Notte*

Attenborough, Sir Richard (b. 1923) British actor, director. *A Bridge Too Far*; *Ghandi*

Barrymore, John (1882–1942) American actor. *Beau Brummel*

Barrymore, Lionel (1878–1954) American actor. *You Can't Take it with You*

Bergman, Ingmar (b. 1918) Swedish director. *The Seventh Seal*; *Fanny and Alexander*

Bergman, Ingrid (1915–82) Swedish actress. *Anastasia*; *Indiscreet*

Bogart, Humphrey (1899–1957) American actor. *The Big Sleep*; *Casablanca*

Bunuel, Luis (1900–83) Spanish director. *L'Age d'Or*; *Le Chien Andalou*

Burton, Richard (1925–1984) British actor. *Beckett*; *Who's Afraid of Virginia Woolf?*

Carné, Marcel (b. 1909) French director. *Les Enfants du Paradis*

Chaplin, Sir Charles (1889–1977) British actor, director. *The Gold Rush*; *City Lights*; *Modern Times*

Colman, Ronald (1891–1958) British actor. *Lost Horizon*

Cooper, Gary (1901–61) American actor. *High Noon*; *For Whom the Bell Tolls*

Coppola, Francis Ford (b. 1939) American director. *The Godfather*; *Apocalypse Now*

Cukor, George (1899–1983) American director. *My Fair Lady*

Curtiz, Michael (1888–1962) Hungarian born director. *Casablanca*

Davis, Bette (b. 1908) American actress. *All About Eve*

Dean, James (1931–55) American actor. *Rebel Without a Cause*

De Mille, Cecil B. (1881–1959) American director. *The Ten Commandments*

De Sica, Vittorio (1902–72) Italian director. *Bicycle Thieves*

Dietrich, Marlene (b. 1901) German actress. *The Blue Angel*

Disney, Walt (1901–66) American animator and director. *Mickey Mouse*; *Snow White and the Seven Dwarfs*

Dreyer, Carl (1889–1968) Danish director. *The Passion of Joan of Arc*

Eastwood, Clint (b. 1930) American actor, director. *A Fistful of Dollars*

Eisenstein, Sergei (1898–1948) Russian director. *The Battleship Potemkin*; *Alexander Nevsky*

Fairbanks, Douglas (1883–1939) American actor. *The Three Musketeers*

Fassbinder, Rainer Werner (1946–85) German director. *The Marriage of Maria Braun*

Fellini, Frederico (b. 1920) Italian director. *La Dolce Vita*

Fields, W. C. (1879–1946) American actor. *David Copperfield*; *Never give a Sucker an Even Break*

Flaherty, Robert (1884–1951) American director. *Man of Aran*

Fonda, Jane (b. 1937) American actress. *Klute*; *The China Syndrome*

Ford, John (1895–1973) American director. *Stagecoach*; *The Quiet Man*

Gabin, Jean (1904–76) French actor. *Le Jour se Leve*; *Pepe Le Moko*

Gable, Clark (1901–60) American actor. *Gone with the Wind*; *The Misfits*

Gance, Abel (1889–1982) French director. *Napoleon*

Garbo, Greta (b. 1905) Swedish actress. *Ninotchka*; *Camille*

Garland, Judy (1922–69) American actress. *The Wizard of Oz*; *A Star is Born*

Godard, Jean-Luc (b. 1930) French director. *Breathless*; *Une Femme Mariée*

Goldwyn, Samuel (1882–1974) American producer. *The Goldwyn Follies*; *Wuthering Heights*

Griffith, D. W. (1875–1948) American director. *Birth of a Nation*; *Intolerance*

Hepburn, Katherine (b. 1907) American actress. *The Lion in Winter*; *The African Queen*

Herzog, Werner (b. 1942) German director. *Nosferatu*; *Fitzcarraldo*

Hitchcock, Alfred (1899–1980) British director. *Rear Window*; *Psycho*

Huston, John (b. 1906) American director. *Treasure of the Sierra Madre*; *The Asphalt Jungle*

Kazan, Elia (b. 1909) American director. *On The Waterfront*; *East of Eden*

Keaton, Buster (1895–1966) American actor, director. *The Navigator*; *The General*

Kubrick, Stanley (b. 1928) American director. *2001: A Space Odyssey*; *Dr. Strangelove*

Kurosawa, Akira (b. 1910) Japanese director. *The Seven Samurai*; *Rashomon*

Lang, Fritz (1890–1976) Austrian director. *The Cabinet of Dr. Caligari*; *Metropolis*

Lean, David (b. 1908) British director. *Bridge on the River Kwai*; *Lawrence of Arabia*; *A Passage to India*

Leigh, Vivien (1913–67) British actress. *Gone with the Wind*; *Streetcar Named Desire*

Loren, Sophia (b. 1934) Italian actress. *Two Women*

Losey, Joseph (1909–85) American director. *The Concrete Jungle*; *The Servant*

Lubitsch, Ernst (1892–1947) German director. *Ninotchka*; *Heaven Can Wait*

McQueen, Steve (1930–83) American actor. *Bullitt*; *The Magnificent Seven*

Magnani, Anna (b. 1908) Italian actress. *Open City*; *The Rose Tattoo*

Marx Brothers (Chico (1886–1961) Harpo (1888–1964) Groucho (1890–1977) American comedy actors. *Duck Soup*; *A Night at the Opera*

Mason, James (1909–84) British actor. *The Wicked Lady*; *Odd Man Out*

Méliès, Georges (1861–1938) French director. *A Trip to the Moon*

Mifune, Toshiro (b. 1920) Japanese actor. *Rashomon*; *Seven Samurai*

Monroe, Marilyn (1926–62) American actress. *Seven Year Itch*; *Some Like It Hot*

Newman, Paul (b. 1925) American actor. *Butch Cassidy and the Sundance Kid*

Nicholson, Jack (b. 1937) American actor. *Chinatown*; *One Flew over the Cuckoo's Nest*

Olivier, Laurence (Lord Olivier) (b. 1907) British actor, director. *Henry V*; *Hamlet*; *Richard III*; *The Entertainer*

Pickford, Mary (1893–1979) American actress. *America's Sweetheart*; *The Mary Pickford Story*

Television

The invention of television, the instantaneous viewing of distant objects by electrical transmission, was a process of successive discoveries. The first commercial cathode ray tube was introduced in 1897 by Karl Braun but was not linked to electronic vision until 1907 by Boris Rosing. A A Campbell Swinton published the basis of television transmission in a letter to *Nature* in 1908. The earliest public demonstration was given on 27 Jan 1926 by John Logie Baird (1888–1946). The potential of modern technical developments, such as satellite and cable television, video-discs and video-cassettes, is widely recognized.

RECEIVERS (THOUSANDS)*

	1965	1970	1980	1985
World	177 000	273 000	546 000	737 000
W Europe	49 400	81 900	139 400	162 900
USSR & E Europe	24 000	45 300	105 500	130 100
Middle East & N Africa	1 250	2 600	11 800	19 500
South Africa	—	—	2 000	3 000
Other African countries	98	237	2 400	7 900
China	70	300	7 000	56 000
India	2	16	1 000	2 300
Japan	18 000	23 000	60 000	70 000
Other Asian countries	700	2 700	18 900	31 000
Australasia, Pacific & Oceania	3 200	4 000	6 800	8 600
United States	68 000	89 000	140 000	175 000
Canada	5 000	7 200	12 000	14 000
Latin America	7 400	16 100	37 500	54 900
West Indies	101	725	1 500	2 000

Source: BBC.

BROADCASTING RECEIVING LICENCES IN THE UK:

	total	radio only	monochrome	colour
31 Mar 1940	8 951 045	8 897 618	—	—
31 Mar 1950	12 219 448	11 819 190	343 882	—
31 Mar 1968	17 645 821	2 529 750	15 068 079	20 428
31 Mar 1975	17 700 815	—	10 120 493	7 580 322
31 Mar 1981	18 667 211	—	4 887 663	13 779 548
31 Mar 1982	18 554 200	—	4 293 668	14 260 552
31 Mar 1983	18 494 235	—	3 795 587	14 698 648
31 Mar 1984	18 631 753	—	3 261 273	15 370 481
31 Mar 1985	18 715 937	—	2 896 263	15 819 674
31 Mar 1986	18 704 732	—	2 679 396	16 025 336

Polanski, Roman (b. 1933) Polish director. *Chinatown*; *Rosemary's Baby*
Porter, Edwin (1869–1941) American director. *The Great Train Robbery*
Ray, Satyajit (b. 1921) Indian director. *Pathar Panchali*; *The Chess Players*
Redford, Robert (b. 1937) American actor. *The Sting*; *All the President's Men*
Reed, Sir Carol (b. 1906) British director. *The Third Man*; *Our Man in Havana*
Renoir, Jean (1894–1979) French director. *La Grande Illusion*; *Le Regle du Jeu*
Rossellini, Roberto (1906–77) Italian director. *Open City*
Schlesinger, John (b. 1926) British director. *Midnight Cowboy*; *Darling*

Sennett, Mack (1880–1960) American director. *The Keystone Cops series*
Spielberg, Steven (b. 1946) American director. *E.T. The Extra-Terrestrial*; *Jaws*
Sternberg, Josef von (1894–1969) American director. *Shanghai Express*; *The Blue Angel*
Stewart, James (b. 1908) American actor. *Rear Window*; *Destry Rides Again*
Streep, Meryl (b. 1951) American actress. *The French Lieutenant's Woman*; *Kramer vs Kramer*
Stroheim, Erich von (1885–1957) Austrian director. *Sunset Boulevard*
Tati, Jacques (1908–84) French director, actor. *Jour de Fête*; *M. Hulot's Holiday*
Taylor, Elizabeth (b. 1932) British actress. *Cleopatra*; *Who's Afraid of Virginia Woolf?*

Tracy, Spencer (1900–67) American actor. *Adam's Rib*; *Bad Day at Black Rock*
Truffaut, Francois (1932–84) French director. *Day for Night*; *Jules et Jim*
Valentino, Rudolph (1895–1926) American actor. *The Sheik*; *Blood and Sand*
Vidor, King (1894–1982) American director. *Wizard of Oz*; *War and Peace*
Visconti, Luchino (b. 1906) Italian director. *The Leopard*; *The Damned*
Wajda, Andrzej (b. 1926) Polish director. *Kanal*; *Ashes and Diamonds*
Wayne, John (1907–79) American actor. *Stagecoach*; *True Grit*
Welles, Orson (b. 1915) American director, actor. *Citizen Kane*; *The Third Man*

Radio and the Press

Radio

The first advertised broadcast was on 24 December 1906 from Brant Rock, Mass., USA. The first regular broadcast entertainment in the UK started on 14 February 1922.

Radio sets (thousands)*

	1965	1975	1985
World	529 000	1 010 000	1 650 000
W Europe	116 500	186 600	297 800
USSR & E Europe	59 700	92 600	164 300
Middle East & N Africa	12 300	29 300	58 100
South Africa	2 600	4 800	10 000
Other African countries	4 800	18 500	42 600
China	6 000	35 000	120 000
India	4 800	24 000	50 000
Japan	27 000	87 000	100 000
Other Asian countries	13 300	49 700	111 600
Australasia, Pacific & Oceania	7 800	13 000	24 700
United States	230 000	380 000	500 000
Canada	14 000	23 000	32 000
Latin America	29 400	62 800	133 500
West Indies	860	4 000	5 600

* *Source: BBC.*

The amount of listening in the UK (1985–86) averaged 8 hours 45 minutes a week per head of population.

Frequencies

Frequencies are measured in hertz (Hz) (cycles per second). 1000 Hz equals 1 kilohertz (kHz). 1000 kHz equals 1 megahertz (MHz) or 1 million hertz. Low frequencies between 150 kHz (2000 metres) and 285 kHz (1053 metres) comprise the long-wave band. Medium frequencies between 525 kHz (571 metres) and 1605 kHz (187 metres) comprise the medium-wave band. High frequencies between 3 MHz (75 metres) and 30 MHz (10 metres) comprise the short-wave band.

EXTERNAL RADIO BROADCASTING

Estimated total programme hours per week of some external broadcasters

	1950	1955	1960	1965	1970	1975	1980	1985	1986
United States of America	497	1690	1495	1832	1907	2029	1901	2339	2411
USSR	533	656	1015	1417	1908	2001	2094	2211	2229
Chinese People's Republic	66	159	687	1027	1267	1423	1350	1446	1446
German Federal Republic	—	105	315	671	779	767	804	795	821
United Kingdom (BBC)	643	558	589	667	723	719	719	729	733
Albania	26	47	63	154	487	490	560	581	588
Egypt	—	100	301	505	540	635	546	560	560
North Korea	—	53	159	392	330	455	597	535	535
East Germany	—	9	185	308	274	342	375	413	446
India	116	117	157	175	271	326	389	408	408
Cuba	—	—	—	325	320	311	424	379	381
Australia	181	226	257	299	350	379	333	352	359
Iran	12	10	24	118	155	154	175	310	324
Nigeria	—	—	—	63	62	61	170	322	322
Poland	131	359	232	280	334	340	337	320	320
Netherlands	127	120	178	235	335	400	289	336	316
Bulgaria	30	60	117	154	164	197	236	290	315
Turkey	40	100	77	91	88	172	199	307	307
Japan	—	91	203	249	259	259	259	287	282
France	198	191	326	183	200	108	125	272	274
Czechoslovakia	119	147	196	189	202	253	255	268	267
Spain	68	98	202	276	251	312	239	252	267
Israel	—	28	91	92	158	198	210	223	220
Romania	30	109	159	163	185	190	198	212	208
South Africa	—	127	63	84	150	141	183	205	205
Italy	170	185	205	160	165	170	169	173	173
Canada	85	83	80	81	98	159	134	169	171
Portugal	46	102	133	273	295	190	214	140	155
Sweden	28	128	114	142	140	154	155	196	154
Hungary	76	99	120	121	105	127	127	122	122
Yugoslavia	80	46	70	78	76	82	72	86	86

(i) USA includes Voice of America (1226 hours per week), Radio Free Europe (566 hours per week), Radio Liberty (497 hours per week) and Radio Marti (122 hours per week). (1986 figures).
(ii) USSR includes Radio Moscow, Radio Station Peace & Progress and regional stations.
(iii) German Federal Republic includes Deutsche Welle (568 hours per week) and Deutschlandfunk (253 hours per week). (1986 figures).
(iv) The list includes fewer than half the world's external broadcasters. Among those excluded are Taiwan, Vietnam, South Korea, and various international commercial and religious stations, as well as clandestine radio stations. Certain countries transmit part of their domestic output externally on shortwaves; these broadcasts are mainly also excluded.
(v) 1986 figures for June; all other years as at December or nearest available month.
International Broadcasting and Audience Research (August 1986)

BBC Local Radio

(BBC's network of local radio stations)

Bedfordshire	Kent	Northampton
Bristol	Lancashire	Nottingham
Cambridgeshire	Leeds	Oxford
Cleveland	Leicester	Sheffield
Cornwall	Lincolnshire	Shropshire
Cumbria	London	Solent
Derby	Manchester	Stoke-on-Trent
Devon	Merseyside	Sussex
Essex	Newcastle	WM (Birmingham)
Humberside	Norfolk	York

IBA LOCAL RADIO STATIONS

Area	Company	Air date
Aberdeen	Northsound Radio	27.7.81
Ayr (with Girvan)	West Sound	16.10.81
Belfast/Londonderry/ Enniskillen & Omagh	Downtown Radio	Greater Belfast 16.3.76 Londonderry & Limavady 1.10.86 Enniskillen & Omagh late 1987 1987
Birmingham	BRMB Radio	19.2.74
Bournemouth	2CR	15.9.80
Bradford/Huddersfield & Halifax	Pennine Radio	Bradford 16.9.75 Huddersfield & Halifax 14.12.84
Brighton	Southern Sound Radio	29.8.83
Bristol/Swindon/West Wiltshire	GWR Radio	Bristol 27.10.81 Swindon & West Wiltshire 12.10.82
Bury St Edmunds	Saxon Radio	6.11.82
Cardiff/Newport	Red Dragon Radio	Cardiff 11.4.80 Newport 13.6.83
Coventry	Mercia Sound	23.5.80
Dundee/Perth	Radio Tay	Dundee 17.10.80 Perth 14.11.80
Edinburgh	Radio Forth	22.1.75
Exeter/Torbay	DevonAir Radio	Exeter 7.11.80 Torbay 12.12.80
Glasgow	Radio Clyde	31.12.73
Gloucester & Cheltenham	Severn Sound	23.10.80
Great Yarmouth & Norwich	Radio Broadland	1.10.84
Guildford	County Sound	4.4.83
Hereford/Worcester	Radio Wyvern	4.10.82
Hertford & Harlow	to be appointed	
Humberside	Viking Radio	17.4.84
Inverness	Moray Firth Radio	23.2.82

Area	Company	Air date
Ipswich	Radio Orwell	28.10.75
Leeds	Radio Aire	1.9.81
Leicester	Leicester Sound	7.9.84
Liverpool	Radio City	21.10.74
London	Capital Radio	16.10.73
London	LBC	8.10.73
Luton/Bedford	Chiltern Radio	Luton 15.10.81 Bedford 1.3.82
Maidstone & Medway/ East Kent	Invicta Radio	1.10.84
Manchester	Piccadilly Radio	2.4.74
Northampton	Northants 96	30.11.86
Nottingham/Derby	Radio Trent	Nottingham 3.7.75 Derby 3.3.87
Peterborough	Hereward Radio	10.7.80
Plymouth	Plymouth Sound	19.5.75
Portsmouth/ Southampton	Ocean Sound	12.10.86
Preston & Blackpool	Red Rose Radio	5.10.82
Reading/Basingstoke & Andover	Radio 210	Reading 8.3.76 Basingstoke & Andover 1.1.87
Reigate & Crawley	Radio Mercury	20.10.84
Sheffield & Rotherham/ Barnsley/Doncaster	Radio Hallam	Sheffield & Rotherham 1.10.74 Barnsley/ Doncaster 1.10.85
Southend/Chelmsford	Essex Radio	Southend 12.9.81 Chelmsford 10.12.81
Stoke-on-Trent	Signal Radio	5.9.83
Swansea	Swansea Sound	30.9.74
Teesside	Radio Tees	24.6.75
Tyne & Wear	Metro Radio	15.7.74
Wolverhampton & Black Country/ Shrewsbury & Telford	Beacon Radio	Wolverhampton 12.4.76 Shrewsbury 14.7.87
Wrexham & Deeside	Marcher Sound	5.9.83

Telephones

Zone	In service	% of World	Per 100 pop.
1 North America	198 882 227	40·9	74·2
2 Africa	6 135 956	1·3	1·8
3,4 Europe	172 098 479	35·4	38·0
5 South and Central America	23 011 120	4·7	6·7
6 South Pacific	5 407 086	1·1	2·0
7 USSR	18 000 000		
8 Far East	71 296 677	14·7	26·5
9 Middle East and South East Asia	9 818 924	2·0	1·1
10 World Total	486 055 001	100	17·1

	Number of Phones	Per 100 pop.
USA	181 893 000	78·7
Japan	60 349 857	51·0
UK	28 375 982	50·7
W. Germany	30 122 023	48·8
USSR	23 707 000	8·8 (at Jan 81)
France	26 940 296	49·8
Italy	20 444 037	36·3
Canada	15 741 723	64·7

At January 1, 1982. *Source AT & T*

World Press

DAILY NEWSPAPERS

	Total	Estimated Total approx.	per 100 approx.
World	8 107	304 000 000	142
Africa	128	4 501 000	8·6
America, N. & S.	2 441	77 308 000	117
Asia	3 137	16 200 000	24
Europe	1 601	98 000 000	200
Oceania	110	6 300 000	262
USSR	690	102 000 000	369*

By Country (a selection)

	Total	Estimated approx. in 000s	approx. per 000 popula-tion
USA	1 787	62 223	282
India	1 087	13 033	20
Turkey	1 115	3 880	—
W Germany	380	20 410	339
USSR (see above)			
Japan	178	65 881	569

Scale Rates per 1000 inhabitants

Japan	569	Liechtenstein	477
Iceland	557	Norway	456
Sweden	528	Austria	453
E. Germany	517	Netherlands	432
Finland	480		

* at 1979

MAJOR DAILY NEWSPAPERS WITH CIRCULATIONS

		Circulation
Australia	Sun News Herald	646 454
Canada	Toronto Globe & Mail	310 069
China	People's Daily	6 000 000
Egypt	Al Akhbar	751 115
France	Le Figaro	361 363
	Le Monde	405 674
W. Germany	Die Welt	200 636
	Frankfurter Allgemeine Zeitung	345 194
	Bild Zeitung	5 966 369
Italy	Corriere della Sera	533 615
	La Stampa	358 005
Japan	Yomiuri Shimbun[1]	8 704 470
	Asahi Shimbun[1]	7 485 632
Spain	El Pais	296 167
USA	Washington Post	768 286
	Chicago Sun-Times	657 275
	Chicago Tribune	756 857
	New York Daily News	1 554 604
	New York Times	963 443
	Wall Street Journal[2]	1 798 416
	Los Angeles Times	1 024 322
USSR	Pravda	10 700 000

[1] all editions.
[2] national edition.

Christian Science Monitor ⎫
Financial Times ⎬ Available
International Herald Tribune ⎬ worldwide
Wall Street Journal ⎭

UNITED KINGDOM
Principal national newspapers   *Circulation*

Sun	3 993 031
Daily Mirror	3 121 454
Daily Mail	1 759 455
Daily Express	1 697 229
Star, The	1 288 583
Daily Telegraph, The	1 146 917
Guardian	493 582
Times	442 375
Today	307 256
Independent, The	292 703
Financial Times	279 762
Sporting Life, The	90 000
Morning Star	28 544

National Sundays

News of the World	4 941 966
Sunday Mirror	3 018 910
Sunday People	2 932 472
Sunday Express	2 214 612
Mail on Sunday	1 688 015
Sunday Times	1 220 021
Observer, The	773 514
Sunday Telegraph	720 902

Regional morning papers

(Glasgow) Daily Record	767 000
Glasgow Herald	122 238
(Aberdeen) Press and Journal	110 784
(Edinburgh) Scotsman	92 461
(Leeds) Yorkshire Post	92 374
(Norwich) Eastern Daily Press	90 179
(Darlington) Northern Echo	88 468
(Cardiff) Western Mail	81 119
(Liverpool) Daily Post	71 000
(Bristol) Western Daily Press	70 714
(Newcastle Upon Tyne) The Journal	67 637
(Plymouth) Western Morning News	59 000
(Ipswich) East Anglian Daily Times	49 000
(Belfast) Irish News	43 000
Birmingham Post	34 050

Evening papers

London Standard	522 407
Manchester Evening News	300 386
Birmingham Evening Mail (all eds)	275 528
Liverpool Echo	210 889
(Glasgow) Evening Times	192 561
(Newcastle upon Tyne) Evening Chronicle	149 313
(Sheffield) The Star	145 975
Belfast Telegraph	143 396
(Leeds) Evening Post	140 762

MAGAZINES
Largest UK circulation[1]

Radio Times	3 204 087
TV Times	3 109 059
Woman's Weekly	1 386 411
Reader's Digest	1 460 350
Woman's Own	1 284 559
Woman	1 222 659
Family Circle	536 358
Woman & Home	578 038

Largest US circulation

TV Guide	17 670 543
Reader's Digest	17 926 542
National Geographic	10 215 000
Family Circle	7 427 979
McCall's Magazine	6 266 090
National Enquirer	4 602 524
Time	4 337 988
Newsweek	2 960 073
Sports Illustrated	2 286 069

[1] ABC July–Dec 1983

Language

World's principal languages

The world's total of languages and dialects is now estimated to be about 5000. The most widely spoken, together with the countries in which they are used, are as follows.

1. Guoyu (standardized Northern Chinese or Běifānghuà)
Alphabetized into *Zhùyīn fùhào* (37 letters) in 1918 and converted to the *Pinyin* system of phonetic pronunciation in 1958. Spoken in China (Mainland). Language family: Sino-Tibetan. 700 000 000.

2. English
Evolved from an Anglo-Saxon, Norman-French and Latin amalgam *c.* 1350. Spoken in Australia, Bahamas, Canada, Sri Lanka (3rd), Cyprus (3rd), The Gambia, Ghana, Guyana, India (non-constitutional), Ireland, Jamaica, Kenya (official with Swahili), Malaysia, Malta (official with Maltese), New Zealand, Nigeria (official), Pakistan (now only 1 per cent), Sierra Leone (official), Singapore (2nd at 24 per cent), South Africa (38 per cent of white population), Tanzania (official with Swahili), Trinidad and Tobago, Uganda (official), UK, USA, Zimbabwe and also widely as the second language of educated Europeans and of citizens of the USSR. Language family: Indo-European. 395 000 000.

3. Great Russian
The foremost of the official languages used in the USSR and spoken as the first language by 60 per cent of the population. Language family: Indo-European. 250 000 000.

4. Spanish
Dates from the 10th century AD; spoken in Argentina, Bolivia, Canary Islands, Chile, Colombia, Costa Rica, Cuba, Dominican Republic, Ecuador, El Salvador, Guatemala, Honduras, Mexico, Nicaragua, Panama, Paraguay, Peru, The Philippines, Puerto Rico, Spain, Uruguay, Venezuela. Language family: Indo-European. 230 000 000.

5. Hindustani (a combination of Hindi and Urdu) foremost of the 845 languages of India of which 15 are 'constitutional'. Hindi (official) is spoken by more than 25 per cent, Urdu by nearly 4 per cent and Hindustani, as such, by 10 per cent. In Pakistan, Hindustani is the third most prevalent language ($7\frac{1}{2}$ per cent). Language family: Indo-European. 220 000 000.

=6. Bengali
Widely spoken in the Ganges delta area of India and Bangladesh. Language family: Indo-European. 135 000 000.

=6. Arabic
Dates from the early 6th century. Spoken in Algeria, Bahrain, Egypt, Iraq (81 per cent), Israel (16 per cent), Jordan, Kuwait, Lebanon, Libya, Maldives, Morocco (65 per cent), Oman, Qatar, Saudi Arabia, Somalia, Sudan (52 per cent), Syria, Tunisia, United Arab Emirates and both Yemens. Language family: Hamito-Semitic. 135 000 000.

=6. Portuguese
Distinct from Spanish by 14th century and, unlike it, was more influenced by French than by Arabic. Spoken in Angola, Brazil, Goa, Guinea–Bissau, Macao, Mozambique, Portugal, East Timor (Indonesia). Language family: Indo-European. 135 000 000.

9. German
Known in written form since the 8th century AD. Spoken in the Federal Republic of Germany (West) and the German Democratic Republic (East), Austria, Liechtenstein, Luxembourg and Switzerland plus minorities in the USA, USSR, Hungary, Poland, Romania and in formerly colonised German territories in eastern and southern Africa and the Pacific. Language family: Indo-European. 120 000 000.

10. Japanese
Earliest inscription (in Chinese characters) dates from the 5th century. Spoken in Japan, Formosa (Taiwan), Hawaii and some formerly colonised Pacific Islands. Unrelated to any other language. 110 000 000.

11. Malay-Indonesian
Originated in Northern Sumatra, spoken in Indonesia (form called Bahasa is official), Malaysia, Sabah, Sarawak, Thailand (southernmost parts). Language family: Malayo-Polynesian. 100 000 000.

12. French
Developed in 9th century as a result of Frankish influence on Gaulish substratum. Fixed by Académie Française from 17th century. Spoken in France, French Pacific Is., Belgium, Guadeloupe, Haiti, Luxembourg, Martinique, Monaco, Switzerland, the Italian region of Aosta, Canada, USA (Louisiana) and widely in former French colonies in Africa. Language family: Indo-European. 95 000 000.

=13. Italian
Became very distinct from Latin by 10th century. Spoken in Eritrea, Italy, Libya, Switzerland and widely retained in USA among Italian population. Language family: Indo-European. 60 000 000.

=13. Punjabi
One of the 15 constitutional languages of India spoken by the region of that name. Also spoken in parts of Pakistan. 60 000 000.

=13. Urdu
One of the 15 official languages of India. Also spoken in parts of Pakistan and Bangladesh. 60 000 000.

16. Korean
Not known to be related to any other tongue. 55 000 000.

=17. Cantonese
A distinctive dialect of Chinese spoken in the Kwang-tung area. Language family: Sino-Tibetan. 50 000 000.

=17. Telugu
Used in south India. Known in a written, grammatic form from the 11th century. Language family: Dravidian. 50 000 000.

=17. Tamil
The second oldest written Indian language. Cave graffiti date from the 3rd century BC. Spoken in Sri Lanka, southern India, and among Tamils in Malaysia. Language family: Dravidian. 50 000 000.

=17. Marathi.
A language spoken in west and central India, including Goa and part of Hyderabad and Poona with written origins dating from about AD 500. Language family: Indo-European. 50 000 000.

21. Javanese
Closely related to Malay. Serves as the language of 50 per cent of Indonesian population. Language family: Malayo-Polynesian. 45 000 000.

=22. Ukrainian (Little Russian)
Distinction from Great Russian discernible by 11th century, literary zenith late 18th and early 19th century. Banned as written language in Russia 1876–1905. Discouraged since 1931 in USSR. Spoken in Ukrainian SSR, parts of Russian SFSR and Romania. Language family: Indo-European. 40 000 000.

=22. Wu
A dialect in China spoken, but not officially encouraged, in the Yang-tse delta area. Language family: Sino-Tibetan. 40 000 000.

=22. Min (Fukien)
A dialect in China which includes the now discouraged Amoy and Fuchow dialects and Hainanese. Language family: Sino-Tibetan. 40 000 000.

=22. Turkish
Spoken in European and Asian Turkey – a member of the Oghuz division of the Turkic group of languages. 40 000 000.

=26. Vietnamese
Used in the whole of eastern Indo-China. Classified as a Mon-Khmer by some and as a Thai language by other philologists. 35 000 000.

=26. Polish
A western Slavonic language with written records back to the 13th century, 300 years before its emergence as a modern literary language. Spoken in Poland, and western USSR and among émigré populations notably in the USA. Language family: Indo-European. 35 000 000.

Origins of the English language

The three Germanic dialects on which English is based are descended from the Indo-Germanic or Aryan family of languages, spoken since c. 3000 BC by the nomads of the Great Lowland Plain of Europe, which stretches from the Aral Sea in the Soviet Union to the Rhine in West Germany. Now only fragments of Old Lithuanian contain what is left of this ancestral tongue.

Of the three inherited Germanic dialects, the first was Jutish, brought into England in AD 449 from Jutland. This was followed 40 years later by Saxon, brought from Holstein, and Anglian, which came from the still later incursions from the area of Schleswig-Holstein.

These three dialects were superimposed on the 1000-year-old indigenous Celtic tongue, along with what Latin had survived in the towns from nearly 15 generations of Roman occupation (AD 43–410). The next major event in the history of the English language was the first of many Viking invasions, beginning in 793, from Denmark and Norway. Norse and Danish left permanent influences on the Anglo-Frisian Old English, though Norse never survived as a separate tongue in England beyond 1035, the year of the death of King Canute (Cnut), who had then reigned for 19 years over England, 16 years over Denmark and 7 years over Norway.

The Scandinavian influence now receded before Norman French, though Norse still struggled on in remote parts of Scotland until about 1630 and in the Shetland Islands until c. 1750. The Normans were, however, themselves really Vikings, who in five generations had become converts to the Latin culture and language of northern France.

For three centuries after the Norman conquest of 1066 by William I, descendant of Rollo the Viking, England lived under a trilingual system. The mother tongue of all the first 13 Kings and Queens, from William I (1066–1087) until as late as Richard II (1377–99), was Norman. English became the language of court proceedings only during the reign of Edward III, in October 1362, and the language for teaching in the Universities of Oxford and Cambridge in c. 1380.

English did not really crystallize as an amalgam of Anglo-Saxon and Latin root forms until the 14th century, when William Langland (c.1330–c.1400), and Geoffrey Chaucer (c.1340–1400) were the pioneers of a literary tradition, which culminated in William Shakespeare, who died in 1616, just four years before the sailing of the *Mayflower*.

World's longest words

Japanese[1]
Chi-n-chi-ku-ri-n (12 letters)
—very short person (slang)

Spanish
Superextraordinarisimo (22 letters)
—extraordinary

French
Anticonstitutionnellement (25 letters)
—anticonstitutionally.
Anthropoclimatologiquement[2] (26 letters)
—anthropoclimatologically

Croatian
Prijestolonasljednikovica (25 letters)
—wife of an heir apparent.

Italian
Precipitevolissimevolmente (26 letters)
—as fast as possible.

Portuguese
inconstitucionalissimamente (27 letters)
—with the highest degree of unconstitutionality.

Icelandic
Hæstaréttarmálaflutningsmaôur (29 letters)
—supreme court barrister

The Russian alphabet

The Russian alphabet is written in Cyrillic script, so called after St. Cyril, the 9th century monk who is reputed to have devised it. It contains thirty-three characters, including five hard and five soft vowels. Five other Cyrillic letters appear only in Bulgarian (one) and Serbian (four).

Capital	Lower case	Name	English equivalent	Capital	Lower case	Name	English equivalent
А	а	ah	ā	Т	т	teh	t
Б	б	beh	b	У	у	oo	oo
В	в	veh	v	Ф	ф	eff	f
Г	г	gheh	g	Х	х	hah	h
Д	д	deh	d	Ц	ц	tseh	ts
Е	е	yeh	ye	Ч	ч	cheh	ch
Ж	ж	zheh	j	Ш	ш	shah	sh
З	з	zeh	z	Щ	щ	shchah	shch
И	и	ee	ee	Ъ	ъ	(hard sign)	—
К	к	kah	k	Ы	ы	yerih	I
Л	л	ell	l	Ь	ь	(soft sign)	—
М	м	em	m	Э	э	eh	e
Н	н	en	n	Ю	ю	you	yu
О	о	aw	aw	Я	я	ya	yā
П	п	peh	p				
Р	р	err	r	Е	е	yaw	yo
С	с	ess	s	Й	й	short й	elided 'y'

The Greek alphabet

The Greek alphabet consists of twenty-four letters – seven vowels and seventeen consonants. The seven vowels are alpha (short a), epsilon (short e), eta (long e), iota (short i), omicron (short o), upsilon (short u, usually transcribed y), and omega (long o).

Name	Capital	Lower case	English equivalent	Name	Capital	Lower case	English equivalent
Alpha	A	α	a	Nu	N	ν	n
Beta	B	β	b	Xi	Ξ	ξ	x
Gamma	Γ	γ	g	Omicron	O	ο	ō
Delta	Δ	δ	d	Pi	Π	π	p
Epsilon	E	ε	ĕ	Rho	P	ρ	r
Zeta	Z	ζ	z	Sigma	Σ	σ ς	s
Eta	H	η	ē	Tau	T	τ	t
Theta	Θ	θ	th	Upsilon	Y	υ	u or y
Iota	I	ι	i	Phi	Φ	φ	ph
Kappa	K	κ	k	Chi	X	χ	kh
Lambda	Λ	λ	l	Psi	Ψ	ψ	ps
Mu	M	μ	m	Omega	Ω	ω	o

Greek has no direct equivalent to our c, f, h, j, q, u, v, or w.

Longest words (cont.)
English
The longest word in the *Oxford English Dictionary* is:

floccinaucinihilipilification (29 letters)

—the action of estimating as worthless.

The longest regularly formed English word is:

praetertranssubstantiationalistically (37 letters) found in Mark McShane's novel *Untimely Ripped*.

Russian
ryentgyenoelyektrokardiografichyeskogo (33 Cyrillic letters, transliterating as 38)

—of the radioelectrocardiographic.

Hungarian
Megszentségtelenithetetlenségeskedéseitekért (44 letters)

—for your unprofaneable actions.

Turkish
Cekoslovakyalilastiramadik-larimizdanmiymissiniz (47 letters)

—'are you not of that group of persons that we were said to be unable to Czechoslovakian-ise?'

Dutch[5]
Kindercarnavalsoptochtvoor-bereidingswerkzaamheden (49 letters)

—preparation activities for a children's carnival procession

Mohawk[3]
tkanuhstasrihsranuhw-e'tsraaksahsrakaratattsrayeri' (50 letters)

—the praising of the evil of the liking of the finding of the house is right.

German[4, 5]
Donaudampfschiffahrtselec-trizitaetenhauptbetrieb-swerkbauunterbeamtengesellschaft (80 letters)

—The club for subordinate officials of the head office management of the Danube steamboat electrical services (Name of a pre-war club in Vienna).

Swedish[5]
Spårvagnsaktiebolagsskensmutsskjutarefack-föreningspersonalbeklädnadsmagasins-förrådsförvaltaren (94 letters)

—Manager of the depot for the supply of uniforms to the personnel of the track cleaners' union of the tramway company.

[1] Patent applications sometimes harbour long compound 'words'. An extreme example is one of 13 kana which transliterates to the 40 letter Kyūkitsūrohekimenfuchakunen-ryōsekisanryō meaning 'the accumulated amount of fuel condensed on the wall face of the air intake passage'.

[2] Not accepted by *savants* to be an acceptable French word.

[3] Lengthy concatenations are a feature of Mohawk. Below is an example.

[4] The longest dictionary word in every day usage is Kraftsfahr-zeugreparaturwerkstätten (33 letters or 34 if the ä is written as ae) meaning motor vehicle repair shops (or service garages).

[5] Agglutinative words are only limited by imagination and are not found in standard dictionaries. The first 100 letter such word was published in 1975 by the late Eric Rosenthal in Afrikaans.

Literature

Glossary

abridged edition Condensed or shortened version of a work.

acrostic Poem in which the initial letters of the word of each line makes a word or words when read downwards.

act Major division in a dramatic work.

adage Maxim or proverb.

addendum Addition or appendix to a book.

allegory Story or tale with double meaning.

alliteration Figure of speech where consonants at the beginning of words, or stressed syllables, are repeated.

almanac Book or table comprising a calendar of days, weeks and months indicating special occasions or events.

anagram Letters or word or phrase which, when re-arranged, form a new word.

anecdote Brief account or story about an individual.

annotation Textual comment on a book.

anthology Collection of poetry or prose from diverse sources.

aphorism Short statement of a truth or dogma couched in memorable terms.

argot Slang or coarse vernacular language.

assonance Repetition of similar vowel sounds in speech or writing to achieve a particular effect.

autobiography An account of a person's life by himself or herself.

avant-garde Advanced (in style or thought); ahead of its time.

ballad Story that tells a narrative.

belles lettres Essays on literary studies and the aesthetics of literature.

bibliography List of works on a particular subject or author.

biography An account of a person's life.

blank verse Poetry with unrhymed line endings.

blurb Brief description of a book printed on the dust cover or jacket.

bowdlerize To 'cleanse' a work by omitting or cutting out indecent passages, phrases or words.

canon Collection of works established as genuine.

canto Division of an epic or narrative poem.

caption Short description accompanying an illustration.

catalogue List of books or works.

chronicle A compilation of events in sequence, either actual or fictional.

cipher Writing that employs substitution or transposition of letters.

cliché Over-used expression that has become trite.

colloquialism Word, phrase or expression in everyday use.

concordance Alphabetical index of words in a work, or works by a single author.

copyright Protective law to prevent pirating or plagiarism of an author's work.

couplet Two successive rhyming lines in poetry.

cycle Group of works united by an overall theme.

dialect Manner of speaking pertaining to a particular class or geographical region.

dialogue The speech of characters in a story or play; part of a work in which characters speak.

diary Sequential private record of personal and other events kept by an individual.

dictionary Book containing the words of a language, and their definitions, alphabetically; two-language dictionaries contain the corresponding words of both languages and their meanings, also alphabetically; any book that gives words and phrases about a particular subject, arranged alphabetically.

digest Publication where works are abridged.

documentary Form of fiction or drama based on documentary evidence provided by newspapers, recent historical reports or other contemporary or recent factual evidence.

doggerel Rough, ill-constructed verse.

double entendre Ambiguity in a word or expression, one of which meanings is usually bawdy or frivolous.

drama Work to be performed on a stage by actors.

dramatis personae Characters in a play.

duologue Conversation between two characters in a play, story or poem.

edition Total number of copies of a book printed from unchanged set of type.

elegy Serious meditative poem; lament.

encyclopedia Comprehensive work encompassing and describing many aspects of knowledge; specialist work covering comprehensively a subject or discipline.

epic Long narrative poem incorporating myth, legend, folklore and history, about the deeds of heroes, warriors, important people; a grandiose treatment of an individual's or nation's story.

epigram Short witty statement in verse or prose.

epistle Direct address to another person; a 'letter' in the form of verse.

epitaph Valediction to dead person or persons; inscription on a tomb or grave.

eponymous Person whose name becomes the title of the work.

essay Composition, usually in prose, discussing a topic or variety of topics.

euphemism Substitution of a bland expression for a harsh or blunt one.

exposition Summary of plot and events given at the beginning of a play.

fable A short narrative in prose or verse that points a moral.

fiction General term for an imaginative work, usually in prose.

foreword Short introduction to a work.

gazetteer Geographical dictionary or index.

ghost writer Person who undertakes literary work for another who takes the credit.

glossary Alphabetical list of unfamiliar or uncommon words, usually appended to work in which they appear.

hyperbole Figure of speech that contains exaggeration for emphasis.

idiom Form of expression of phrase peculiar to its language and possessing a meaning other than its literal one.
introduction Essay stating author's intention to reader.

jingle Verse or verses with strong rhyme and rhythm.
journal Paper, periodical or magazine.

legend Story about a particular person containing myth and historical fact; explanation of symbols on a map or chart.
lexicon Dictionary, especially for Classical and Middle Eastern languages.
libretto Text of an opera or operetta.
limerick Type of light or amusing verse, of five lines.
linguistics The scientific study of language.
lyric Words to a song.

manuscript Book or work written by hand.
maxim Short statement or even sentence containing a general truth about human conduct and human nature.
melodrama Exaggeratedly and emotionally written story, usually tragic.
metaphor Figure of speech in which one thing is described in terms of another, by implication.
meter Patterns of stressed and unstressed syllables in verse.
monologue Single person addressing an audience alone, in drama, verse or prose. *Interior* monologue; unspoken but thought speech in verse or prose.
myth Non-factual story that embodies explanation of how something comes to exist, usually involving supernatural or superhuman creatures.

narrative Story or tale in prose or verse.
neologism Newly-coined word.
nom de plume Term used to indicate a fictitious name used by a writer to represent his work.
novel Extended piece of prose fiction.
novella Prose fiction, longer than a short story, shorter than a novel, concentrating upon a single event.
ode Lyric poem describing an event or feelings about a person, object or event.

paradox Apparently self-contradicting statement that, on closer examination, is found to contain a truth reconciling the two opposites.
parody Imitation of words, style, sense, subject of a writer to make them appear ridiculous.
patois Local dialect.
periodical Magazine or journal published regularly.
philology Study of literature, language and linguistics.
plagiarism Wrongful appropriation and publication of another's work as one's own.
plot Plan or organization of events and characters in a play, work of fiction or poem as to induce curiosity and suspense in the audience or reader.
poem Literary work which may be in rhyme, blank verse or a combination of the two.
poetry Any kind of metrical composition in a literary work.
pornography Work in which there is a deliberate emphasis on the sexual behaviour of characters, in order to arouse sexual excitement.
potboiler Work written essentially to gain the author a livelihood.
précis Concise statement; short summary of a work.
preface Introduction to a work.
prologue Opening section of the work itself.
propaganda Work devoted to the dissemination of an idea or belief, usually biased.
pseudonym Name other than the true one used by an author to represent his work.
pun Figure of speech that involves a play upon the words used.

refrain Phrase, line or lines repeated at intervals or at the end of a stanza in poetry.
review Notice or critical article on musical, artistic or literary work.

revue Theatrical entertainment made up of sketches, dances, songs, recitals and improvised pieces, usually humorous, satirical or topical.
rhetoric Art of using language, in speaking or writing, to persuade. The persuasive style (rather than the content) of a work.
rhyme Echoing sound or audible similarity in two or more words, especially at endings. Device used to construct much poetry.
riddle Puzzle, question or enigma; conundrum.

saga Lengthy prose work, sometimes in several parts, describing the history and events surrounding medieval kings, warriors and, recently, fictitious families.
satire Any work in which wickedness, folly, vice and corruption in individuals and society is exposed by ridicule and scorn.
semantics Branch of linguistics dealing with meaning, and the change of meaning, in words.
semiology General study or science of signs with which humans communicate with each other (including words and their use in every context).
sermon Verbal instruction of some length, usually religious.
sic Included in brackets after a printed word or quoted passage to indicate that it is quoted accurately, however actually incorrect.
simile Figure of speech where one thing is likened to another explicitly.
slang Colourful and vernacular language of the street, marketplace, barrackroom, workplace, sportsplace and playground.
soliloquy Kind of monologue in which a stage character expresses his thoughts and feelings.
song Poem or verse set to music.
sonnet Formal poem of 14 lines.
style Characteristic manner of expression in prose or verse; the way in which a thing is written by an author.
synonym A word similar in meaning to another.
synopsis Outline of the main points of a work; a summary.

tale Spoken or written narrative.
tautology Overuse of synonyms or repetition of ideas in sentence.
theme Central idea of a work, rather than its subject.
thesis Long essay or treatise on a subject, usually expository; work presented to examiners for academic qualification.
tract Short printed treatise on religious or political subject.
tragedy Serious dramatic composition in prose or verse in which the principal character or characters are victims, often fatally so, of circumstance, or of a fatal flaw of character, of a crime of violence, especially one involving the death of an innocent person.
translation Rendering of a work into another language.
treatise Formal work examining a subject and the principles underlying it.

vade mecum Manual or handbook carried for frequent reference.
vernacular Domestic or native language.

yarn Story or tale, sometimes improbable and far-fetched.

English Literature

Nothing definite has survived of the stories or songs possessed by the ancient Britons who were invaded by Julius Caesar on 26 Aug. 55 BC. Barely anything has survived from the 367-year Roman occupation until AD 410. English literature thus begins at least by being English.

The earliest known British born author was Pelagius (fl. 400–18) from whom survive some remains of theological disputations written in Rome.

The earliest English poem known to us is Widseth, about a wandering minstrel of the 6th century. In the Exeter Book 150 lines of this poem survive.

The oldest surviving record of a named English poet who composed on British soil is from the paraphrase by Bede (673–735) of a hymn attributed to Caedmon of Streanashalch (Whitby, North Yorkshire), who was living in 670. This survives in the Cambridge manuscript of Bede (or Baeda) in a hand possibly of the 8th century.

The first great book in English prose is the Anglo-Saxon Chronicle supervised by King Alfred until 892. Alfred himself translated some of the writings of Bede and of Gregory the Great's *Pastoral Care* into West Saxon.

The Lindisfarne Gospels, a beautiful vellum quarto Latin manuscript now in the British Library, London, was written c. 696–8. In c. 950 Alred, Bishop of Durham, added an interlinear gloss in Northumbrian dialect.

The leading authors of the Old English Period are:

Alfric	c. 955—c. 1020
King Alfred	849—99
Venerable Bede	c. 673—735
Caedmon	fl. 670
Cynewulf	? 9th century
Wulfstan	d. 1023

Bibliography

Below are brief notes and a list of the major works of the 10 British writers who have the longest entries in the *Oxford Dictionary of Quotations*. They are listed in order of length of their entry.

Shakespeare, William (1564–1616)
The greatest contribution to the world's store of poetry and drama has been made by William Shakespeare (1564–1616). Born at Stratford-upon-Avon, this eldest surviving child of an Alderman and trader produced in the space of the seventeen years between 1594 (*Titus Andronicus*) and 1611 (*The Tempest*) thirty-seven plays which total 814 780 words.

Shakespeare's outpouring of sheer genius has excited and amazed critics of every age since. His contemporary Ben Jonson called him 'The applause! delight! the wonder of our stage!' Milton refers to him as 'Sweetest Shakespeare, Fancy's child'. To Thomas Carlyle, looking at his massive brow, he was 'The greatest of intellects'. Matthew Arnold refers to him as 'out-topping knowledge'.

Venus and Adonis (narrative poem)	1593
The Rape of Lucrece (narrative poem)	1594
Titus Andronicus	1594
*Henry VI Part 2**	1594
The Taming of the Shrew (see also 1623, First Folio)	1594
*Henry VI Part 3**	1595
Romeo and Juliet	1597
Richard II	1597
Richard III	1597
Henry IV Part I	1598
Love's Labour's Lost (Revised version, original (?1596) probably lost)	1598
Henry IV Part 2	1600
A Midsummer Night's Dream	1600
The Merchant of Venice	1600
Much Ado About Nothing	1600
Henry V (First 'true' text published 1623 in First Folio)	1600
*Sir John Falstaff and the Merry Wives of Windsor** (First 'true' text published in 1623 in First Folio)	1602
*Hamlet**	1603
Hamlet ('according to the true and perfect copy')	1604
King Lear	1608
Pericles, Prince of Tyre	1609
Troilus and Cressida	1609
Sonnets (1640 in 'Poems')	1609

* Bad quartos or unauthorised editions.

Posthumously Published

Othello	1622
First Folio – 36 plays in all including the first publication of *The Taming of the Shrew* (Shakespeare's revised version of the 1594 version)	1623

Henry VI Part I	*Macbeth*
The Two Gentlemen of Verona	*Timon of Athens*
	Antony and Cleopatra
The Comedy of Errors	*Coriolanus*
King John	*Cymbeline*
As You Like It	*A Winter's Tale*
Julius Caesar	*The Tempest*
Twelfth Night	*Henry VIII*
Measure for Measure	
All's Well That Ends Well	

The Second Folio (1632), the Third Folio (1663 1st issue, 1664 2nd issue) and the Fourth Folio (1685) added nothing of authority to Heming and Condell's monumental First Folio.

Scientific study of Shakespeare began with Edward Capell (1713–81) and his researches published from 1768. The eminently honest and painstaking work of Alexander Dyce's edition of 1857 led to the publication in 1863–66 of what is regarded as the standard text, *The Cambridge Shakespeare*, edited by W C Clark and J Glover.

Tennyson, Alfred, First Baron (1809–92)

Poems [including *The Lotos Eaters* and *The Lady of Shalott* (dated 1833)]	1832
Poems (two volumes) (including *Ulysses*, *Sir Galahad*, *Morte d'Arthur*, *Locksley Hall*)	1842
In Memoriam A.H.H. (Arthur Henry Hallam)	1850
Ode on the Death of the Duke of Wellington	1852
Charge of the Light Brigade	1854
Maud and Other Poems	1859
Idylls of the King	1857–85
	(completed edition 1889)
Enoch Arden (including *Old Style*)	1864
Holy Grail	1869
The Revenge: A Ballad of the Fleet	1878
Becket	1884
Locksley Hall 60 Years After	1886
Demeter and Other Poems (including *Crossing the Bar*)	1889

Milton, John (1608–74)

On the Death of Fair Infant Dying of a Cough	1625
L'Allegro and Il Penseroso	1632
Arcades	1633
Comus (2 Masques)	1634
Lycidas	1638
A Tractate of Education	1644
Doctrine and Discipline of Divorce	1644
Areopagitica (a Tract)	1644
Tenure of Kings and Magistrates (a Pamphlet)	1649
Paradise Lost (written *c.* 1640–57)	1657
Paradise Regained (written 1665–66)	1671
Samson Agonistes	1671

Kipling, Joseph Rudyard (1865–1936)

Departmental Ditties	1886
Plain Tales from The Hills	1888
Soldiers Three	1888
Wee Willie Winkie	1888
The Light That Failed	1891
Barrack Room Ballads	1892
Many Inventions	1893
Jungle Books (Two volumes)	1894–95
The Seven Seas (including *Mandalay*)	1896
Captains Courageous	1897
Recessional	1897
Stalky & Co.	1899
Kim	1901
Just So Stories for Children	1902
Puck of Pook's Hill	1906
Rewards and Fairies	1910
A School History of England	1911

Wordsworth, William (1770–1850)

The Evening Walk (written 1787–92)	1793
Descriptive Sketches (written 1787–92)	1793
Guilt and Sorrow	1794
Lyrical Ballads (with Coleridge)	1798 & 1800
Prelude	1805
Poems in Two Volumes (including *Ode to Duty* and *Ode on Intimations of Immortality*)	1807
Excursion: a portion of the *Recluse*	1814
Poems, including the *Borderers*	1842

Shelley, Percy Bysshe (1792–1822)

Alastor	1816
Ode to The West Wind	1819
The Cenci	1819
Prometheus Unbound	1820
The Witch of Atlas	1820
To a Skylark	1820
The Cloud	1820
Epipsychidion	1821
Adonais	1821
Queen Mab	1821
Hellas	1822
Defence of Poetry (uncompleted)	

Johnson, Dr Samuel (1709–84)

A Voyage to Abyssinia by Father Jerome Lobo (Translation)	1735
London: a Poem, in Imitation of the Third Satire of Juvenal (anon.)	1738
Parliamentary Reports disguised as Debates in the Senate of Magna Lilliputia (Senate of Lilliput)	July 1741–Mar. 1744
Life of Savage	1744
Plan of a Dictionary of the English Language	1747
Irene (Theatrical tragedy produced by Garrick at Drury Lane)	1748
The Vanity of Human Wishes	1749
The Rambler (essays in 208 bi-weekly issues)	Mar. 1750–Mar. 1752
A Dictionary of the English Language (8 years' work, 1747–55)	1755
The Prince of Abyssinia, A Tale	1759
The Idler (essays in the *Universal Chronicle* or the *Weekly Gazette*)	Apr. 1758–Apr. 1760
Rasselas	1759
Shakespeare, a new Edition	1765
A Journey to the Western Highlands	1775
The Lives of the Poets	vols. i–iv 1779, vols. v–x 1781
Dr Johnson's Diary, posthumously published	1816

Browning, Robert (1812–89)

Paracelsus	1835
Sordello	1840
Christmas-Eve and Easter-Day	1850
Men and Women (including *One Word More* and *Bishop Blougram's Apology*)	1855
Dramatis Personae (including *Rabi ben Ezera* and *Caliban upon Setebos*)	1864
The Ring and The Book	1868–69
A Grammarian's Funeral	
Soliloquy of the Spanish Cloister	
The Pied Piper of Hamelin	
Asolando	posthumously 1890
New Poems (with Elizabeth Barrett Browning)	posthumously 1914

Byron, George Gordon, sixth baron (1788–1824)

Fugitive Pieces (privately printed) originally called *Juvenilia*	1806
Hours of Idleness (reprint of the above with amendments)	1807
English Bards and Scotch Reviewers	1809
Childe Harold (began at Janina, 1809), Cantos i and ii	1812
The Giaour	1813
The Corsair	1814
Lora	1814

The Siege of Corinth	1816
The Prisoner of Chillon	1816
Childe Harold (written in Switzerland), Canto iii	1816
Childe Harold (written in Venice), Canto iv	1817
Manfred	1817
Don Juan (first five cantos)	1818–20
Autobiography	(burnt 1824)
Cain	1821
Don Juan (later cantos)	1821–22
Contribution to *The Liberal* newspaper 'Vision of Judgement'	1822
The Island	1823
Heaven and Earth	1824

Dickens, Charles John Huffam (1812–70)

Sketches of Young Gentlemen, Sketches of Young Couples, The Mudfog Papers	unpublished
A Dinner at Poplar Walk (re-entitled *Mr. Minns and his Cousin*)	Dec. 1833
Sketches by Boz. Illustrative of Every Day Life and Every-Day People published in *Monthly Magazine* (1833–35) and *Evening Chronicle*	1835
The Posthumous Papers of the Pickwick Club	from Apr. 1836
Oliver Twist (in Bentley's *Miscellany*)	1837–39
Nicholas Nickleby (in monthly numbers)	1838–39
Master Humphrey's Clock (*Barnaby Rudge* and *The Old Curiosity Shop*)	1840–41
The Old Curiosity Shop (as a book)	1841
Barnaby Rudge (as a book)	1841
American Notes	1842
Martin Chuzzlewit (parts)	1843–44
A Christmas Carol	1843
The Chimes (written in Italy)	1844
The Cricket on the Hearth	1845
Pictures from Italy	1846
Daily News (later the *News Chronicle*) Editor	Jan.–Feb. 1846
The Battle of Life	1846
The Haunted Man	1847
Dombey and Son (parts) (written in Switzerland)	1847–48
Household Word (weekly periodical) Editor (included *Holly-Tree*)	1848–59
David Copperfield	1849–50
Bleak House (in parts)	1852–53
A Child's History of England (in three volumes)	1852-3-4
Hard Times. For These Times (book form)	1854
Little Dorrit	1857–58
All the Year Round (Periodical) Editor	1859–70
Great Expectations	1860–61
The Uncommercial Traveller (collected parts of *A Tale of Two Cities*)	1861
Our Mutual Friend	1864–65
The Mystery of Edwin Drood (unfinished)	1870

Other British writers (14th to 20th centuries)

The writers below are listed in chronological order of year of birth, together with their best known work or works.

14th Century

Langland, William (*c.* 1330–*c.* 1400). *Vision of Piers Plowman*.

Chaucer, Geoffrey (*c.* 1340–1400). *Canterbury Tales*.

15th Century

Malory, Sir Thomas (*c.* 1400–1470). *Morte d'Arthur*.

More, Sir Thomas (1478–1535). *Utopia*.

16th Century

Leland or Leyland (c. 1506–1552) *Itinerary.*

Spenser, Edmund (1552–99). *The Faerie Queene.*

Lyly, John (c. 1554–1606). *Euphues.*

Sidney, Sir Philip (1554–86). *The Countesse of Pembrokes Arcadia; Astrophel and Stella; The Defence of Poesie.*

Bacon, Francis (Baron Verulam, Viscount St Albans) (1561–1626). *The Advancement of Learning.*

Marlowe, Christopher (1564–1593). *Tamburlaine The Great; Dr Faustus.*

Donne, John (1572–1631). *Poems; Songs and sonnets; Satyres; Elegies.*

Jonson, Benjamin (1572–1637). *Every Man in his humour* (produced 1598, published 1601); *Every Man out of his humour* (1600); *Volpone: or the foxe* (1607); *The Alchemist* (1610, published 1612); *Bartholomew Fayre* (1614, published 1631).

Burton, Robert (1577–1640). *Anatomy of Melancholy.*

Beaumont, Francis (1584–1616) and Fletcher, John (1579–1625). *The Scornful Lady; Philaster; The Maid's Tragedy; A King and No King.*

Hobbes, Thomas (1588–1679). *Leviathan; Behemoth.*

Herrick, Robert (1591–1674). *Hesperides.*

Walton, Izaak (1593–1683). *The Complete Angler.*

17th Century

Clarendon, Edward Hyde, Earl of (1608–74). *History of the Rebellion and Civil Wars in England.*

Butler, Samuel (1612–80). *Hudibras.*

Evelyn, John (1620–1706). *Diary.*

Bunyan, John (1628–88). *The Pilgrim's Progress.*

Dryden, John (1631–1700). *All For Love.*

Locke, John (1632–1704). *Essay Concerning Human Understanding.*

Pepys, Samuel (1633–1703). *Diary.*

Newton, Sir Isaac (1643–1727). *Philosophiae Naturalis Principia Mathematica; Opticks.*

Ottway, Thomas (1652–85). *Venice Preserved.*

Defoe, Daniel (1660–1731). *The Life and Adventures of Robinson Crusoe.*

Swift, Jonathan (1667–1745). *Gulliver's Travels.*

Congreve, William (1670–1729). *The Way of the World.*

Addison, Joseph (1672–1719). *The Spectator.*

Pope, Alexander (1688–1744). *An Essay on Criticism; The Rape of the Lock; The Dunciad; An Essay on Man.*

Richardson, Samuel (1689–1761). *Pamela; Clarissa.*

18th Century

Fielding, Henry (1707–54). *Tom Thumb; The History of Tom Jones.*

Sterne, Laurence (1713–68). *Tristram Shandy.*

Gray, Thomas (1716–71). *An Elegy Written in a Country Churchyard.*

Walpole, Horace, 4th Earl of Orford (1717–97). *Letters.*

Smollett, Tobias George (1721–71). *Roderick Random; Peregrine Pickle; Humphrey Clinker.*

Smith, Adam (1723–1790). *Wealth of Nations.*

Goldsmith, Oliver (1728–74). *The Vicar of Wakefield; She Stoops to Conquer; The Deserted Village.*

Burke, Edmund (1729–97). *Reflections on the Revolution in France.*

Cowper, William (1731–1800). *Poems.*

Gibbon, Edward (1737–94). *A History of the Decline and Fall of the Roman Empire.*

Paine, Thomas (1737–1809). *Rights of Man.*

Boswell, James (1740–95). *Life of Johnson.*

Sheridan, Richard Brinsley (1751–1816). *The Rivals; The School For Scandal.*

Burney, Frances 'Fanny' (Madame D'Arblay), (1752–1840). *Evelina.*

Blake, William (1757–1827). *Songs of Innocence; Songs of Experience.*

Burns, Robert (1759–96). *Poems chiefly in the Scottish dialect; Tam O'Shanter; The Cotters Saturday Night; The Jolly Beggars.*

Cobbett, William (1762–1835). *Rural Rides.*

Smith, Rev Sydney (1771–1845). *The Letters of Peter Plymley; Edinburgh Review.*

Scott, Sir Walter (1771–1832). *Waverley; Rob Roy; Ivanhoe; Kenilworth; Quentin Durward; Redgauntlet; Lady of the Lake.*

Coleridge, Samuel Taylor (1772–1834). *Lyrical Ballads (Ancient Mariner); The Kubla Khan.*

Southey, Robert (1774–1843). *Quarterly Review* (contributions); *Life of Nelson.*

Austen, Jane (1775–1817). *Sense and Sensibility; Pride and Prejudice; Mansfield Park; Emma; Northanger Abbey; Persuasion.*

Lamb, Charles (1775–1834). *Tales from Shakespeare* [largely by his sister, Mary Lamb (1764–1847)]; *Essays of Elia.*

Hazlitt, William (1778–1830). *My First Acquaintance with Poets; Table Talk; The Plain Speaker.*

Hunt, James Henry Leigh (1784–1859). *The Story of Rimini; Autobiography.*

De Quincey, Thomas (1785–1859). *Confessions of an English Opium Eater.*

Peacock, Thomas Love (1785–1866). *Headlong Hall; Nightmare Abbey.*

Marryat, Frederick (1792–1848). *Mr Midshipman Easy.*

Clare, John (1793–1864). *Poems Descriptive of Rural Life.*

Keats, John (1795–1821). *Endymion; Ode to a Nightingale: Ode on a Grecian Urn; Ode to Psyche; Ode to Autumn; Ode on Melancholy; La Belle Dame sans Merci; Isabella.*

Carlyle, Thomas (1795–1881). *The French Revolution; Oliver Cromwell's Letters and Speeches.*

Shelley, Mary Wollstonecraft (Godwin) (1797–1851). *Frankenstein.*

Hood, Thomas (1799–1845). *The Song of the Shirt; The Bridge of Sighs; To The Great Unknown.*

Macaulay, Thomas Babington (Lord) (1800–59). *Lays of Ancient Rome; History of England.*

19th Century

Newman, John Henry, Cardinal (1801–90). *The Dream of Gerontius.*

Surtees, Robert Smith (1803–64). *Handley Cross.*

Borrow, George (1803–1881). *Lavengro.*

Disraeli, Benjamin (Earl of Beaconsfield) (1804–81). *Coningsby; Sybil; Tancred.*

Browning, Elizabeth Barrett (1806–61). *Poems; Aurora Leigh.*

Mill, John Stuart (1806–1873). *Liberty.*

Darwin, Charles Robert (1809–82). *On the Origin of Species; The Descent of Man.*

Fitzgerald, Edward (1809–83). *Rubáiyát of Omar Khayyám.*

Gaskell, Mrs (Elizabeth Cleghorn Stevenson) (1810–65). *Mary Barton; Cranford; North and South.*

Thackeray, William Makepeace (1811–63). *Vanity Fair; The History of Henry Esmond Esq.*

Smiles, Samuel (1812–1904). *Self-Help.*

Lear, Edward (1812–88). *A Book of Nonsense; Nonsense Songs.*

Read, Charles (1814–84). *The Cloister and the Hearth.*

Trollope, Anthony (1815–82). *The six Barsetshire novels (The Warden; Barchester Towers; Doctor Thorne; Framley Parsonage; The Small House at Allington; The Last Chronicle of Barset).*

Brontë, (later Nicholls), Charlotte (1816–55). *Jane Eyre; Shirley; Villette.*

Brontë, Emily Jane (1818–48). *Wuthering Heights.*

Ruskin, John (1819–1900). *Modern Painters.*

'Eliot, George' (Mary Ann [or Marian] Evans, later Mrs J W Cross) (1819–80). *Adam Bede; The Mill on the Floss; Silas Marner; Middlemarch.*

Kingsley, Charles (1819–75). *Westward Ho!; The Water Babies.*

Brontë, Anne (1820–49). *Tenant of Wildfell Hall.*

Arnold, Matthew (1822–88). *The Strayed Reveler; Poems.*

Collins, William Wilkie (1824–89). *The Woman in White; The Moonstone.*

Bagehot, Walter (1826–77). *The English Constitution.*

Meredith, George (1828–1909). *Modern Love; Diana of the Crossways.*

Rossetti, Dante Gabriel (1828–82). *Poems; Ballads and Sonnets.*

'Carroll, Lewis' (Rev. Charles Lutwidge Dodgson) (1832–98). *Alice's Adventures in Wonderland; Through The Looking Glass.*

Morris, William (1834–96) *News from Nowhere.*

Gilbert, Sir William Schwenck (1836–1911). *The Mikado; The Gondoliers; HMS Pinafore; The Pirates of Penzance; The Yeomen of the Guard; Patience.*

Swinburne, Algernon Charles (1837–1909). *Poems and Ballads; Rosamund.*

Hardy, Thomas (1840–1928). *Under The Greenwood Tree; Tess of the D'Urbervilles; Far From the Madding Crowd; The Return of the Native; The Mayor of Casterbridge; Jude the Obscure.*

Hudson, W(illiam) H(enry) (1841–1922). *Green Mansions.*

Bridges, Robert Seymour (1844–1930). *The Testament of Beauty.*

Hopkins, Gerard Manley (1844–89). *The Notebooks and Papers of Gerard Manley Hopkins.*

Stoker, Bram (Abraham) (1847–1912). *Dracula.*

Jefferies, Richard (1848–1887). *The Amateur Poacher.*

Stevenson, Robert Louis (1850–94). *Travels with a Donkey in the Cévennes; New Arabian Nights; Treasure Island; Strange Case of Dr Jekyll and Mr Hyde; Kidnapped; Catriona; The Black Arrow; The Master of Ballantrae; Weir of Hermiston* (unfinished).

Moore, George (1852–1933). *Esther Waters.*

Wilde, Oscar Fingal O'Flahertie Wills (1854–1900). *The Picture of Dorian Gray; Lady Windermere's Fan; The Importance of Being Ernest.*

Haggard, Sir Henry Rider (1856–1925). *King Solomon's Mines; She; Alain Quartermain.*

Shaw, George Bernard (1856–1950). *Plays Pleasant and Unpleasant* (including *Mrs Warren's Profession, Arms and the Man; Candida); Three Plays for Puritans (The Devil's Disciple, Caesar and Cleopatra* and *Captain Brassbound's Conversion); Man and Superman; John Bull's Other Island; Major Barbara; Androcles and the Lion; Pygmalion; Saint Joan; Essays in Fabian Socialism.*

Gissing, George (Robert) (1857–1903). *The Private Papers of Henry Ryecroft.*

Conrad, Joseph (né Teodor Józef Konrad Nalecz Korzeniowski) (1857–1924). *Almayer's Folly; An Outcast of the Islands; The Nigger of the 'Narcissus'; Lord Jim; Youth; Typhoon; Nostromo; The Secret Agent; Under Western Eyes.*

Doyle, Sir Arthur Conan (1859–1930). *The White Company; The Adventures of Sherlock Holmes; The Hound of the Baskervilles; The Exploits of Brigadier Gerard; The Lost World.*

Thompson, Francis (1859–1907). *The Hound of Heaven; The Kingdom of God.*

Housman, Alfred Edward (1859–1936). *A Shropshire Lad.*

Grahame, Kenneth (1859–1932). *The Wind in the Willows.*

Barrie, Sir James Matthew (1860–1937). *Quality Street; The Admirable Crichton; Peter Pan.*

Quiller-Couch, Sir Arthur Thomes ('Q') (1863–1944). *On the Art of Writing; Studies in Literature.*

Yeats, William Butler (1865–1939). *Collected Poems; The Tower; Last Poems; The Hour Glass.*

Wells, Herbert George (1866–1946). *The Invisible Man; The History of Mr Polly; Kipps; The Shape of Things to Come; The War of the Worlds.*

Murray, George Gilbert Aimé (1866–1957). *History of Ancient Greek Literature.*

Bennett, Enoch Arnold (1867–1931). *Anna of the Five Towns; The Old Wives' Tale; Clayhanger; The Card; Riceyman Steps.*

Galsworthy, John (1867–1933). *The Forsyte Saga; Modern Comedy; The White Monkey.*

Douglas, Norman (1868–1952). *Old Calabria; South Wind.*

Belloc, Joseph Hilaire Pierre (1870–1953). *The Path to Rome; The Bad Child's Book of Beasts; Cautionary Tales.*

Synge, John Millington (1871–1909). *The Playboy of the Western World.*

Beerbohm, Sir Max (1872–1956). *Zuleika Dobson.*

Powys, John Cowper (1872–1963). *Weymouth Sands.*

Ford, Ford Madox (1873–1939). *The Good Soldier.*

De La Mare, Walter (1873–1956). *Poems; Come Hither; O Lovely England.*

Chesterton, Gilbert Keith (1874–1936). *The Innocence of Father Brown; The Ballad of The White Horse.*

Churchill, Sir Winston Spencer (1874–1965). *Life of Marlborough; The Second World War; A History of The English-Speaking Peoples; The World Crisis.*

Maugham, William Somerset (1874–1965). *Of Human Bondage; The Moon and Sixpence; The Razor's Edge.*

Buchan, John (1st Baron Tweedsmuir) (1875–1940). *Montrose; The Thirty-Nine Steps; Greenmantle; Prester John; Huntingtower.*

Powys, Theodore Francis (1875–1953). *Mr Weston's Good Wine.*

Trevelyan, George Macaulay (1876–1962). *History of England; English Social History.*

Masefield, John (1878–1967). *Salt-Water Ballads; The Everlasting Mercy; So Long to Learn; Jim Davis; Collected Poems.*

Thomas, Edward (1878–1917). *Poems.*

Forster, Edward Morgan (1879–1970). *Where Angels Fear to Tread; A Room with a View; Howard's End; A Passage to India.*

O'Casey, Sean (1880–1964). *Juno and the Paycock; The Plough and the Stars.*

Wodehouse, Sir Pelham Grenville (1881–1975). *Summer Lightning; Much Obliged Jeeves.*

Joyce, James (1882–1941). *Ulysses; Finnegans Wake; Portrait of the Artist as a Young Man.*

Woolf, (née Stephen), Virginia (1882–1941). *The Voyage Out; Night and Day; Jacob's Room; The Years.*

Milne, Alan Alexander (1882–1956). *Winnie the Pooh; The House at Pooh Corner.*

Keynes, John Maynard (Baron) (1883–1946). *The Economic Consequences of the Peace; The General Theory of Employment.*

Mackenzie, Sir Compton (1883–1972). *Whisky Galore; Sinister Street.*

Lewis, (Percy) Wyndham (1884–1957). *The Apes of God.*

Ransome, Arthur Michell (1884–1967). *Swallows and Amazons.*

Walpole, Sir Hugh Seymour (1884–1941). *Herries Chronicle.*

Flecker, James Elroy (1884–1915). *The Golden Journey to Sarmarkand.*

Lawrence, David Herbert (1885–1930). *Sons and Lovers; Love Poems and Others.*

Sassoon, Siegfried (1886–1967). *Memoirs of a Fox-Hunting Man; Memoirs of an Infantry Officer.*

Sitwell, Dame Edith (1887–1964). *Collected Poems; Aspects of Modern Poetry.*

Brooke, Rupert Chawner (1887–1915). *1914 and Other Poems; Letters from America.*

Muir, Edwin (1887–1959). *First Poems.*

Cary, (Arthur) Joyce (Lunel) (1888–1957). *The Horse's Mouth.*

Eliot, Thomas Stearns (1888–1965). *Murder in the Cathedral; The Waste Land.*

Lawrence, Thomas Edward (later Shaw) (1888–1935). *Seven Pillars of Wisdom.*

Mansfield, Katherine (Beauchamp) (1888–1923). *In a German Pension: The Dove's Nest and Other Stories.*

Toynbee, Arnold Joseph (1889–1975). *A Study of History.*

Herbert, Sir Alan Patrick (1890–1971). *Misleading Cases.*

Rosenberg, Isaac (1890–1918). *Poems.*

Christie, Agatha Mary Clarissa (1891–1976). *The Murder of Roger Ackroyd.*

Tolkien, J(ohn) R(onald) R(euel) (1892–1973). *The Hobbit; The Lord of the Rings.*

Owen, Wilfred (1893–1918). *Poems.*

Sayers, Dorothy Leigh (1893–1957). *The Nine Tailors.*

Priestley, John Boynton (1894–1985). *The Good Companions; The Linden Tree; An Inspector Calls.*

Huxley, Aldous Leonard (1894–1963). *Brave New World; Point Counter Point.*

Hartley, Leslie Poles (1895–1972). *The Go-Between.*

Graves, Robert Ranke (b. 1895). *I Claudius; Goodbye to All That.*

Blunden, Edmund (1896–1974). *Poems 1914–1930.*

Sheriff, Robert Cedric (1896–1975). *Journey's End.*

Williamson, Henry (1897–1977). *Tarka the Otter.*

Coward, Sir Noel (1899–1973). *Hay Fever; Private Lives; Blithe Spirit.*

Hughes, Richard (1900–1976). *A High Wind in Jamaica.*

20th Century

Orwell, George (Eric Arthur Blair) (1903–50). *Animal Farm; 1984.*

Waugh, Evelyn (1903–66). *Scoop, Men at Arms; Officers and Gentlemen; Unconditional Surrender; Brideshead Revisited.*

Day-Lewis, Cecil (1904–72). *Collected Poems.*

Isherwood, Christopher (b. 1904). *Goodbye to Berlin.*

Greene, Graham (b. 1904). *Brighton Rock; Our Man in Havana; The Power and the Glory.*

Green, Henry (pseud. of Henry Vincent Yorke) (1905–1973). *Living; Loving; Concluding.*

Snow, Sir Charles Percy (1905–1980). *Strangers and Brothers.*

Bates, Herbert Ernest (1905–74). *'Flying-Officer X' Stories.*

Powell, Anthony (b. 1905). *The Music of Time novel sequence.*

Beckett, Samuel (b. 1906). *Waiting for Godot.*

Betjeman, John (1906–84). *Mount Zion; Collected Poems.*

Fry, Christopher (b. 1907). *The Lady's Not for Burning; Venus Observed.*

MacNeice, Louis (1907–63). *Autumn Journal; Collected Poems.*

Auden, Wystan Hugh (1907–73). *Poems; Look Stranger; The Dance of Death.*

Fleming, Ian (Lancaster) (1908–65). *Dr No; Goldfinger.*

Lowry, (Clarence) Malcolm (1909–57). *Under the Volcano.*

Golding, William (b. 1911). *Lord of the Flies.*

Rattigan, Terence (1911–77). *French Without Tears; The Winslow Boy.*

Durrell, Lawrence (b. 1912). *Selected Poems; The Alexandria Quartet.*

Thomas, Dylan (1914–53). *Portrait of the Artist as a Young Dog; Under Milk Wood.*

Burgess, Anthony (b. 1917). *A Clockwork Orange; Napoleon Symphony.*

Wilson, Angus (b. 1913). *Hemlock and After; The Old Men at the Zoo.*

Lessing, Doris (May) (b. 1919). *Children of Violence; The Golden Notebooks.*

Murdoch, Iris (b. 1919). *An Unofficial Rose; The Italian Girl; An Accidental Man.*

Amis, Kingsley (b. 1922). *Lucky Jim.*

Larkin, Phillip (b. 1922). *High Windows.*

Osborne, John (b. 1929). *Look Back in Anger.*

Arden, John (b. 1930). *Serjeant Musgrave's Dance.*

Hughes, Ted (b. 1930). *The Hawk in the Rain; Lupercal.*

Pinter, Harold (b. 1930). *The Caretaker; The Birthday Party.*

Wesker, Arnold (b. 1932). *Roots; Chips with Everything.*

Stoppard, Tom (b. 1937). *Rosencrantz and Guildenstern are Dead; Dirty Linen.*

Ayckbourn, Alan (b. 1939). *How the Other Half Loves; The Norman Conquests.*

Poets Laureate

The office of poet laureate is one of great honour, conferred on a poet of distinction, In 1616, James I granted a pension to the poet Ben Jonson, but it was not until 1668 that the laureateship was created as a royal office. When the position of poet laureate falls vacant, the prime minister is responsible for putting forth names for a new laureate, to be chosen by the sovereign. The sovereign then commands the Lord Chamberlain to appoint the poet laureate, and he does so by issuing a warrant to the laureate-elect. The Chamberlain also arranges for the appointment – for life – to be announced in the *London Gazette.*

John Dryden (1631–1700; laureate 1668–88)

Thomas Shadwell (1642?–92; laureate 1688–92)

Nahum Tate (1652–1715); laureate 1692–1715)

Nicholas Rowe (1674–1718; laureate 1715–18)

Laurence Eusden (1688–1730; laureate 1718–30)

Colley Cibber (1671–1757; laureate 1730–57)

William Whitehead (1715–85; laureate 1757–85) (Appointed after Thomas Gray declined the offer)

Thomas Warton (1728–90; laureate 1785–90)

Henry James Pye (1745–1813; laureate 1790–1813)

Robert Southey (1774–1843; laureate 1813–43)

William Wordsworth (1770–1850; laureate 1843–50)

Alfred, Lord Tennyson (1809–92); laureate 1850–92) (Appointed after Samuel Rogers declined the offer)

Alfred Austin (1835–1913; laureate 1896–1913)

Robert Bridges (1844–1930; laureate 1913–30)

John Masefield (1878–1967; laureate 1930–67)

Cecil Day-Lewis (1904–72; laureate 1968–72)

Sir John Betjeman (1906–84; laureate 1972–84)

Ted Hughes (b. 1930 laureate 1984–)

Some well-known writers

Listed by country

Argentina
Borges, Jorge Luis (b. 1899). *The Labyrinth; Ficciones.*

Austria
Kafka, Franz (1883–1924). *The Trial; The Castle.*

Belgium
Maeterlinck, Maurice (1862–1949). *The Blue Bird.*

Chile
Neruda, Pablo (pseud. of Neftali Ricardo Reyes) (b. 1904). *Poems.*

Colombia
Marques, Gabriel Garcia (b. 1920). *One Hundred Years of Solitude.*

Denmark
Anderson, Hans Christian (1807–75). *The Emperor's New Clothes.*

France
Rabelais, François (1494?–1553?). *Gargantua; Pantagruel.*

Corneille, Pierre (1606–84). *Le Cid.*

Molière, *nom de théâtre* of Jean-Baptiste Poquelin (1622–73). *Tartuffe; La Malade Imaginaire.*

Racine, Jean (1639–99). *Phèdre.*

Voltaire, pseud. of François-Marie Arouet (1694–1778). *Candide.*

Stendhal, pseud. of Henri Beyle (1783–1842). *The Red and the Black.*

Balzac, Honoré de (1799–1850). *La Comedie Humaine.*

Dumas, Alexandre (père) (1802–70). *The Three Musketeers.*

Hugo, Victor Marie (1802–85). *Les Misérables.*

Baudelaire, Charles-Pierre (1821–67). *Les Fleurs du Mal.*

Flaubert, Gustave (1821–1880). *Madame Bovary.*

Zola, Emile (1840–1902). *Nana; Germinal.*

Maupassant, Guy de (1850–93). *Stories.*

Rimbaud, Arthur (1854–91). *Illuminations.*

Gide, André (1869–1951). *Strait is the Gate.*

Proust, Marcel (1871–1922). *Remembrance of Things Past.*

Colette, Sidonie Gabrielle (1873–1954). *Cheri.*
Sartre, Jean-Paul (1905–80). *The Age of Reason.*
Genet, Jean (b. 1910–). *The Thief's Journal; The Maids.*

Germany
Goethe, Johann Wolfgang von (1749–1832). *Faust.*
Schiller, Friedrich (1759–1805). *Poems; Wallenstein.*
Heine, Heinrich (1797–1856). *Poems.*
Mann, Thomas (1875–1955). *Death in Venice; The Magic Mountain.*
Rilke, Rainer Maria (1875–1926). *Poems.*
Hesse, Hermann (1877–1962). *Steppenwolf.*
Brecht, Bertolt (1898–1956). *Mother Courage.*
Grass, Gunter (b. 1927–). *The Tin Drum.*

India
Tagore, Rabindranath (1861–1941). *Poems.*

Italy
Dante Alighieri (1265–1321). *Divine Comedy.*
Petrarch (Petrarca), Francesco (1304–74). *Sonnets.*
Machiavelli, Niccolo (1469–1527). *The Prince.*
D'Annunzio, Gabriele (1863–1938). *Francesca da Rimini.*
Pirandello, Luigi (1867–1936). *Six Characters in Search of an Author; The Rules of the Game.*
Lampedusa, Giuseppe Tomasi de (1896–1957). *The Leopard.*
Silone, Ignazio, pseud. of Secondo Tranquilli (1900–78). *Bread and Wine.*
Moravia, Alberto, pseud. of Alberto Pincherle (b. 1907–). *The Woman of Rome.*
Calvino, Italo (b. 1923–). *Adam One Afternoon and Other Stories.*

Japan
Murasaki Shikibu (*c.* 980–*c.* 1030). *Tale of Genji.*
Sei Shonagon (fl. 1000). *The Pillow-Book of Sei Shonagon.*

Norway
Ibsen, Henrik (1828–1906). *Ghosts; A Doll's House; Hedda Gabler.*
Hamsun, Knut (1859–1952). *The Growth of the Soil.*

Russia
Pushkin, Aleksandr Sergeyevich (1799–1837). *Eugene Onegin; Stories.*
Turgenev, Ivan (1818–83). *A Month in the Country.*
Dostoyevsky, Fyodor Mikhailovich (1821–1881). *The Idiot; The Brothers Karamazov; Crime and Punishment.*
Tolstoy, Count Leo Nikolayevich (1828–1910). *War and Peace; Anna Karenina.*
Chekhov, Anton Pavlovich (1860–1904). *The Seagull; The Cherry Orchard.*
Pasternak, Boris Leonidovich (1890–1960). *Dr. Zhivago.*
Solzhenitsyn, Aleksandr Isayevich (1918–). *One Day in the Life of Ivan Denisovich.*

Spain
Cervantes Saavedra, Miguel de (1547–1616). *Don Quixote.*
Lorca, Federico Garcia (1898–1936). *Poems; Blood Wedding.*

Sweden
Strindberg, August (1849–1912). *Miss Julie.*

United States
Hawthorne, Nathaniel (1804–64). *The Scarlet Letter.*
Longfellow, Henry Wadsworth (1807–82). *The Wreck of the Hesperus; The Song of Hiawatha.*
Poe, Edgar Allan (1809–49). *The Murders in the Rue Morgue; The Raven.*
Thoreau, Henry David (1817–62). *Walden.*
Melville, Herman (1819–91). *Moby Dick; Billy Budd.*
Whitman, Walt (1819–92). *Leaves of Grass.*
Twain, Mark (Samuel Langhorne Clemens) (1835–1910). *Adventures of Tom Sawyer; Adventures of Huckleberry Finn.*
James, Henry (1843–1916). *The Turn of the Screw; The Golden Bowl; Portrait of a Lady.*
Frost, Robert (1874–1963). *Poems.*
London, Jack (John Griffith London) (1876–1916). *The Call of the Wild; White Fang.*
O'Neill, Eugene (1888–1953). *The Iceman Cometh; Long Day's Journey into Night.*
Fitzgerald, F. Scott (1896–1940). *The Great Gatsby; Tender is the Night; The Last Tycoon.*
Faulkner, William (1897–1962). *The Sound and the Fury.*
Hemingway, Ernest (1898–1961). *A Farewell to Arms; For Whom the Bell Tolls; The Old Man and the Sea.*
Nabokov, Vladimir (b. 1899). *Pale Fire; Lolita.*
Pound, Ezra (1900–). *Pisan Cantos; Hugh Selwyn Mauberley.*
Steinbeck, John (1902–68). *The Grapes of Wrath; Of Mice and Men.*
O'Hara, John (1905–70). *Appointment in Samarra; Pal Joey.*
Williams, Tennessee (1911–83). *A Streetcar Named Desire; The Glass Menagerie.*
Bellow, Saul (b. 1915). *Herzog; The Dean's December.*
Miller, Arthur (b. 1915). *Death of a Salesman; The Crucible.*
Lowell, Robert (1917–80). *Poems.*
Mailer, Norman (b. 1923). *The Naked and the Dead.*
Roth, Philip (b. 1933). *Portnoy's Complaint; Letting Go.*

Nobel prizewinners in literature since 1950

1987 Joseph Brodsky, US
1986 Wole Sayinka, Nigeria
1985 Claude Simon, France
1984 Jaroslav Seifert, Czechoslovakian.
1983 William Golding, British
1982 Gabriel Garcia Marquez, Colombian-Mex.
1981 Elias Canetti, Bulgarian-British
1980 Czeslaw Milosz, Polish-US
1979 Odysseus Elytis, Greek
1978 Isaac Bashevis Singer, US (Yiddish)
1977 Vincente Aleixandre, Spanish
1976 Saul Bellow, US
1975 Eugenio Montale, Ital.
1974 Eyvind Johnson, Harry Edmund Martinson, both Swedish
1973 Patrick White, Australian
1972 Heinrich Boll, W. German
1971 Pablo Naruda, Chilean
1970 Aleksandr I. Solzhenitsyn, Russ.
1969 Samuel Beckett, Irish
1968 Yasunari Kawabata, Japanese
1967 Miguel Angel Asturias, Guate.
1966 Samuel Joseph Agnon, Israeli
      Nelly Sachs, Swedish
1965 Mikhail Sholokhov, Russian
1964 Jean-Paul Sartre, French (Prize declined)
1963 Giorgos Seferis, Greek
1962 John Steinbeck, US
1961 Ivo Andric, Yugoslavian
1960 Saint-Jean Perse, French
1959 Salvatore Quasimodo, Italian
1958 Boris L. Pasternak, Russian (Prize declined)
1957 Albert Camus, French
1956 Juan Ramon Jimenez, Puerto Rican-Span.
1955 Halldor K. Laxness, Icelandic
1954 Ernest Hemingway, US
1953 Sir Winston Churchill, British
1952 François Mauriac, French
1951 Pär F. Lagerkvist, Swedish
1950 Bertrand Russell, British

Booker prizewinners

1969 P. H. Newby, *Something to Answer For*
1970 Bernice Rubens, *The Elected Member*
1971 V. S. Naipaul, *In a Free State*
1972 John Berger, *G*
1973 J. G. Farrell, *The Siege of Krishnapur*
1974 (joint prizewinners)
      Nadine Gordimer, *The Conservationist*
      Stanley Middleton, *Holiday*
1975 Ruth Prawer Jhabvala, *Heat and Dust*
1976 David Storey, *Saville*
1977 Paul Scott, *Staying On*
1978 Iris Murdoch, *The Sea, The Sea*
1979 Penelope Fitzgerald, *Offshore*
1980 William Golding, *Rites of Passage*
1981 Salman Rushdie, *Midnight's Children*
1982 Thomas Keneally, *Schindler's Ark*
1983 J. M. Coetzee, *The Life and Times of Michael K.*
1984 Anita Brookner, *Hotel du Lac*
1985 Keri Hulme, *The Bone People*
1986 Kingsley Amis, *The Old Devils*
1987 Penelope Lively, *Moon Tiger*

Whitbread Literary Award-winners

1971 Novel: Gerda Charles, *The Destiny Waltz*
      Biography: Michael Meyer, *Henrik Ibsen*
      Poetry: Geoffrey Hill, *Mercian Hymns*
1972 Novel: Susan Hill, *The Bird of Night*
      Biography: James Pope-Hennessey, *Trollope*
      Children's Book: Rumer Godden, *The Diddakoi*
1973 Novel: Shiva Naipaul, *The Chip Chip Gatherers*
      Biography: John Wilson, *CB: A Life of Sir Henry Campbell-Bannerman*
      Children's Book: Alan Aldridge and William Plomer, *The Butterfly Ball and the Grasshopper's Feast*
1974 Novel: Iris Murdoch, *The Sacred and Profane Love Machine*
      Biography: Andrew Boyle, *Poor Dear Brendan*
      Joint Children's Books: Russell Hoban and Quentin Blake, *How Tom Beat Captain Najork and His Hired Sportsmen*
      Jill Paton Walsh, *The Emperor's Winding Sheet*
      First Book: Clare Tomalin, *The Life and Death of Mary Wollstonecraft*
1975 Novel: William McIlvanney, *Docherty*
      Autobiography: Helen Corke, *In Our Infancy*
      First Book: Ruth Spalding, *The Improbable Puritan: A Life of Bulstrode Whitelock*
1976 Novel: William Trevor, *The Children of Dynmouth*
      Biography: Winifred Gerin, *Elizabeth Gaskell*
      Children's Book: Penelope Lively, *A Stitch in Time*
1977 Novel: Beryl Bainbridge, *Injury Time*
      Biography: Nigel Nicolson, *Mary Curzon*
      Children's Book: Shelagh Macdonald, *No End to Yesterday*
1978 Novel: Paul Theroux, *Picture Palace*
      Biography: John Grigg, *Lloyd George: The People's Champion*
      Children's Book: Philippa Pearce, *The Battle of Bubble and Squeak*
1979 Novel: Jennifer Johnston, *The Old Jest*
      Autobiography: Penelope Mortimer, *About Time*
      Children's Novel: Peter Dickinson, *Tulku*
1980 Novel: David Lodge, *How Far Can You Go?*
      Biography: David Newsome, *On the Edge of Paradise: A. C. Benson the Diarist*
      Children's Novel: Leon Garfield, *John Diamond*
      Book of the Year: David Lodge, *How Far Can You Go?*
1981 Novel: Maurice Leitch, *Silver's City*
      Biography: Nigel Hamilton, *Monty: The Making of a General*
      Children's Novel: Jane Gardam, *The Hollow Land*
      First Novel: William Boyd, *A Good Man in Africa*
1982 Novel: John Wain, *Young Shoulders*
      Biography: Edward Crankshaw, *Bismarck*
      Children's Novel: W. J. Corbett, *The Song of Pentecost*
      First Novel: Bruce Chatwin, *On the Black Hill*

1983 Novel: William Trevor, *Fools of Fortune*
Joint Biography: Victoria Glendinning, *Vita*
Kenneth Rose, *King George V*
Children's Novel: Roald Dahl, *The Witches*
First Novel: John Fuller, *Flying to Nowhere*
1984 Novel: Christopher Hope, *Kruger's Alp*
First Novel: James Buchan, *A Parish of Rich Women*
Biography: Peter Ackroyd, *T. S. Eliot*
Children's Novel: Barbara Willard, *Queen of the Pharisees Children*
Short Story: Diana Rowe, *Tomorrow is Our Permanent Address*
1985 Novel: Peter Ackroyd, *Hawksmoor*
First Novel: Jeanette Winterson, *Oranges Are Not the Only Fruit*
Children's Novel: Janni Howker, *The Nature of the Beast*
Biography: Ben Pimlott, *Hugh Dalton*
Poetry: Douglas Dunn, *Elegies*
Book of the Year: Douglas Dunn, *Elegies*
1986 Novel: Kazuo Ishiguro, *An Artist of the Floating World*
First Novel: Jim Crace, *Continent*
Children's Novel: Andrew Taylor, *The Coal House*
Poetry: Peter Reading, *Stet*
Biography: Richard Mabey, *Gilbert White*
Book of the Year: Kazuo Ishiguro, *An Artist of the Floating World*
1987 Novel: Ian McEwan, *The Child in Time*
First Novel: Francis Wyndham, *The Other Garden*
Children's Novel: Geraldine McCaughrean, *A Little Later than the Angels*
Poetry: Seamus Heaney, *The Haw Lantern*
Biography: Christopher Nolan, *Under the Eye of the Clock*
Book of the Year: Christopher Nolan, *Under the Eye of the Clock*

Pulitzer Fiction Award-winners

1917 No award
1918 Ernest Poole, *His Family*
1919 Booth Tarkington, *The Magnificent Ambersons*
1920 No award
1921 Edith Wharton, *The Age of Innocence*
1922 Booth Tarkington, *Alice Adams*
1923 Willa Cather, *One of Ours*
1924 Margaret Wilson, *The Able McLaughlins*
1925 Edna Ferber, *So Big*
1926 Sinclair Lewis, *Arrowsmith*
1927 Louis Bromfield, *Early Autumn*
1928 Thornton Wilder, *The Bridge at San Luis Rey*
1929 Julia Peterkin, *Scarlet Sister Mary*
1930 Oliver La Farge, *Laughing Boy*
1931 Margaret Ayer Barnes, *Years of Grace*
1932 Pearl S. Buck, *The Good Earth*
1933 T. S. Stribling, *The Store*
1934 Caroline Miller, *Lamb in His Bosom*
1935 Josephine Winslow Johnson, *Now in November*
1936 Harold L. Davis, *Honey in the Horn*
1937 Margaret Mitchell, *Gone With the Wind*
1938 John Phillips Marquand, *The Late George Apley*
1939 Marjorie Kinnan Rawlings, *The Yearling*
1940 John Steinbeck, *The Grapes of Wrath*
1941 No award
1942 Ellen Glasgow, *In This Our Life*
1943 Upton Sinclair, *Dragon's Teeth*
1944 Martin Flavin, *Journey in the Dark*
1945 John Hersey, *A Bell For Adano*
1946 No award
1947 Robert Penn Warren, *All the King's Men*
1948 James A. Michener, *Tales of the South Pacific*
1949 James Gould Cozzens, *Guard of Honor*
1950 A. B. Guthrie, Jr, *The Way West*
1951 Conrad Richter, *The Town*
1952 Herman Wouk, *The Caine Mutiny*
1953 Ernest Hemingway, *The Old Man and the Sea*
1954 No award
1955 William Faulkner, *A Fable*
1956 Mackinley Kantor, *Andersonville*
1957 No award
1958 James Agee, *A Death in the Family*
1959 Robert Lewis Taylor, *The Travels of Jamie McPheeters*
1960 Allen Drury, *Advise and Consent*
1961 Harper Lee, *To Kill a Mockingbird*
1962 Edwin O'Connor, *The Edge of Sadness*
1963 William Faulkner, *The Reivers*
1964 No award
1965 Shirley Ann Grau, *The Keepers of the House*
1966 Katherine Anne Porter, *The Collected Stories of Katherine Anne Porter*
1967 Bernard Malamud, *The Fixer*
1968 William Styron, *The Confession of Nat Turner*
1969 N. Scott Momaday, *House Made of Dawn*
1970 Jean Stafford, *Collected Stories*
1971 No award
1972 Wallace Stegner, *Angle of Repose*
1973 Eudora Welty, *The Optimist's Daughter*
1974 No award
1975 Michael Shaara, *The Killer Angels*
1976 Saul Bellow, *Humboldt's Gift*
1977 No award
1978 James Alan McPherson, *Elbow Room*
1979 John Cheever, *The Stories of John Cheever*
1980 Norman Mailer, *Executioner's Song*
1981 John Kennedy Toole, *Confederacy of Dunces*
1982 John Updike, *Rabbit is Rich*
1983 Alice Walker, *The Color Purple*
1984 William Kennedy, *Ironweed*
1985 Alison Lurie, *Foreign Affairs*
1986 Larry McMurtry, *Lonesome Dove*

US National Book Award-winners, 1950–79

1950 Nelson Algren, *The Man with the Golden Arm*
1951 William Faulkner, *The Collected Stories of William Faulkner*
Brendan Gill, *The Trouble of One House* (special citation)
1952 James Jones, *From Here to Eternity*
1953 Ralph Ellison, *Invisible Man*
1954 Saul Bellow, *The Adventures of Augie March*
1955 William Faulkner, *A Fable*
1956 John O'Hara, *Ten North Frederick*
1957 Wright Morris, *The Field of Vision*
1958 John Cheever, *The Wapshot Chronicle*
1959 Bernard Malamud, *The Magic Barrel*
1960 Philip Roth, *Goodbye, Columbus*
1961 Conrad Richter, *The Water of Kronos*
1962 Walker Percy, *The Moviegoer*
1963 J. F. Powers, *Morte D'Urban*
1964 John Updike, *The Centaur*
1965 Saul Bellow, *Herzog*
1966 Katherine Anne Porter, *The Collected Stories of Katherine Anne Porter*
1967 Bernard Malamud, *The Fixer*
1968 Thornton Wilder, *The Eighth Day*
1969 Jerzy Kosinski, *Steps*
1970 Joyce Carol Oates, *Them*
1971 Saul Bellow, *Mr Sammler's Planet*
1972 Flannery O'Connor, *Flannery O'Connor: The Complete Stories*
1973 John Barth, *Chimera*
John Williams, *Augustus*
1974 Isaac Bashevis Singer, *A Crown of Feathers and Other Stories*
Thomas Pynchon, *Gravity's Rainbow*
1975 Robert Stone, *Dog Soldiers*
Thomas Williams, *The Hair of Harold Roux*
1976 William Gaddis, *J R*
1977 Wallace Stegner, *The Spectator Bird*
1978 Mary Lee Settle, *Blood Tie*
1979 Tim O'Brien, *Going after Cacciato*

After 1979 the awards were discontinued.

Sport

Origins and Antiquity of Sports

Date	Sport	Location and Notes
BC		
c. 3000	Coursing	Egypt. Saluki dogs. Greyhounds used in England AD 1067. Waterloo Cup 1836.
c. 2700	Wrestling	Nintu Temple, Khafaje, Iraq; ancient Olympic games c. 708 BC, Greco-Roman style, France c. AD 1860; Internationalised 1912.
c. 2050	Hockey	Beni Hasan tomb, Egypt. Lincolnshire AD 1277. Modern forms c. 1875. Some claims to be of Persian origin in 2nd millennium BC.
c. 1600	Falconry	China-Shang dynasty. Earliest manuscript evidence points to Persian origin.
c. 1520	Boxing	Thera fresco, Greece. First ring rules 1743 England. Queensberry Rules 1867.
c. 1360	Fencing	Egyptians used masks and blunted swords. Established as a sport in Germany c. AD 1450. Hand guard invented c. 1510. Foil 17th century, épée mid-19th century, and sabre in Italy, late 19th century.
c. 1300	Athletics	Ancient Olympic Games. Modern revival c. 1810, Sandhurst, England.
c. 800	Ice Skating	Bone skates superseded by metal blades c. AD 1600.
c. 776	Gymnastics	Ancient Olympic Games. Modern Sport developed c. AD 1776 in Germany.
c. 648	Horse Racing	Thirty-third ancient Olympic Games. Roman diversion c. AD 210 Netherby, Cumbria. Chester course 1540.
c. 600	Equestrianism	Riding of horses dates from c. 3000 BC Persia. Show jumping London AD 1869.
c. 525	Polo	As *Pulu*, Persia. Possibly of Tibetan origin.
c. 10	Fly Fishing	Earliest reference by the Roman Martial.
ante 1	Ju Jitsu	Pre-Christian Chinese origin, developed as a martial art by Japan.
AD		
c. 300	Archery	Known as a Mesolithic skill (as opposed to a sport), Natal, South Africa *ante* 46 000 BC. Practised by the Genoese. Internationalised 1931.
c. 1050	Tennis (Royal or Real)	Earliest surviving court, Paris, France, 1496. First 'world' champion c. 1740.
1278	Fox Hunting	Earliest reference in England. Popularised at end 18th century. Previously deer, boar or hare hunted.
ante 1300	Bowls	On grass in Britain, descended from the Roman game of boccie.
c. 1410	Football (Association)	*Calcio* in Italy. First modern rules, Cambridge University, 1846. Eleven-a-side standardised 1870. Chinese ball-kicking game *Tsu-chin* known c. 350 BC.
1429	Billiards	First treatise by Marot (France) c. 1550. Rubber cushions 1835, slate beds 1836.
c. 1450	Golf	Earliest reference: parliamentary prohibition in March 1457, Scotland. Rubber core balls 1902, steel shafts 1929.
1472	Shooting	Target shooting recorded in Zurich, Switzerland.
ante 1492	Lacrosse	Originally American Indian *baggataway*. First non-Indian club, Montreal, 1856.
c. 1550	Cricket	Earliest recorded match, Guildford, Surrey, England. Earliest depictment c. 1250. Eleven-a-side Sussex 1697. Earliest recorded women's match, Surrey, 1745.
c. 1560	Curling	Netherlands. Kilsyth, Scotland 1716.
1600	Ice Yachting	Earliest patent in Low Countries. Sand yacht reported Belgian beach 1595.
c. 1600	Ice Hockey	Netherlands. Kingston, Ontario, Canada 1855. Rules devised in Montreal 1879.
1603	Swimming	Inter-school contests in Japan by Imperial edict. Sea-bathing at Scarborough by 1660. Earliest bath, Liverpool in 1828.
1661	Yachting	First contest Thames (1 Sept.). Earliest club in Cork, Ireland, 1720.
c. 1676	Caving	Pioneer explorer, John Beaumont, Somerset, England.
1698	Mountaineering	Rock climbing in St Kilda. First major alpine ascent (Mont Blanc) 1786. Continuous history since only 1854. Fujiyama climbed *ante* AD 806.
c. 1700	Bull Fighting	Francisco Romero of Ronda, Andalusia, Spain. Referred to by Romans c. 300 BC.
c. 1700	Baseball	English provenance. Cartwright Rules codified 1845.
1716	Rowing	Earliest contest, sculling race on Thames (1 Aug.). First English regatta, 1775, Henley Regatta 1839.
c. 1750	Trotting	Harness racing sulky introduced 1829.
1760	Roller Skating	Developed by Joseph Merlin (Belgium). Modern type devised by J L Plimpton (USA) in 1863.
1765	Fives (Eton Type)	Buttress hand-ball, Babcary, Somerset. New Courts at Eton, 1840. Rules codified 1877.
c. 1770	Shinty	Inter-village or clan game, West and Central Highlands of Scotland as gaelic *lomain* (driving forward). Rules suggested 1879.
1771	Surfing	Canoe surfing first recorded by Capt. James Cook in the Hawaiian Islands. Board surfing reported by Lt. James King, 1779. Sport revived by 1900 at Waikiki, Honolulu.
1787	Beagling	Newcastle Harriers, England.
1793	Lawn Tennis	Field tennis, as opposed to Court tennis, first recorded in England (29 Sept.). Leamington Club founded 1872. Patent as *sphairistike* by Major W C Wingfield Feb. 1874.
1798	Rackets	Earliest covered court, recorded, Exter. Of 17th century origin.
1823	Rugby	Traditional inventor Rev William Webb Ellis (c. 1807–72) at Rugby School (Nov.). Game formulated at Cambridge, 1839. The Rugby Union founded in 1871.
c. 1835	Croquet	Ireland as 'Crokey'. Country house lawn game in England, c. 1856. First rules 1857. The word dated back to 1478.
1843	Skiing (Alpine)	Tromsö, Norway. Kiandra Club, New South Wales 1855. California 1860. Alps 1883.
1845	Bowling (Ten-Pin)	Connecticut State, USA, to evade ban on nine-pin bowling. *Kegel* – a German cloister sport known since 12th century.
1847	Rodeo	Sante Fe, New Mexico, USA. Steer wrestling, 1900.
c. 1850	Fives (Rugby Type)	Earliest inter-school matches c. 1872.
c. 1850	Squash Rackets	Evolved at Harrow School, England. First US championship 1906.
1853	Gliding	Earliest flight by coachman to Sir George Cayley (possibly John Appleby) Brompton Hall, Yorkshire. World championships 1948.
1853	Australian Rules Football	Ballarat goldfields, Australia.
1865	Canoeing	Pioneered by John Macgregor (Scotland).
1868	Cycling	First International Race 31 May, Parc de St Cloud, Paris.
1869	Water Polo	Developed in England from 'Water Soccer'. An Olympic event since 1900.
1869	Equestrianism (Show Jumping)	London. Pignatelli's academy, Naples c. 1580.
c. 1870	Badminton	Made famous at Badminton Hall, Avon, England. First rules codified India 1876.
1875	Snooker	Devised by Col Sir Neville Chamberlain, Ootacamund Club, India as a variant of 'black pool'.
1876	Greyhound Racing	Railed 'hare' and windlass, Hendon, North London (Sept.). Race with mechanical hare, Emeryville, California, USA, 1919. First race in UK, Manchester 24 July 1926.
1878	Motor Racing	Earliest competitive race Green Bay – Madison, Wisconsin, USA. First real race, Paris to Bordeaux and back 1895 (11–13 June).
1879	Tug of War	First rules framed by New York AC. 'Rope pulling' known in neolithic times.
1879	Ski Jumping	Huseby, near Oslo, Norway.

Origins and Antiquity of Sports continued

Date	Sport	Location and Notes
1881	Lugeing	First competition, Klosters, Switzerland.
1882	Judo	Devised (February) by Dr Jigoro Kano (Japan) from Ju Jitsu (see above).
1884	Tobogganing	First toboggan contests, St Moritz, Switzerland. Referred to in 16th century.
1887	Softball	Invented by George Hancock, Chicago, USA.
1889	Bobsledding	First known bobsleigh race, Davos, Switzerland.
1889	Table Tennis	Devised by James Bigg as 'Gossima' from a game known in 1881. Ping Pong Association formed in London, 1902. Sport resuscitated, 1921.
1891	Weightlifting	First international contest, Cafe Monico, London (28 Mar.).
1891	Netball	Invented in USA. Introduced to England 1895.
1891	Basketball	Invented by Dr James A Naismith. First played 20 Jan. 1892, Springfield, Mass, USA. Mayan Indian game *Pok-ta-Pok* dated *c.* 1000 BC.
1895	Rugby League	Professional breakaway, 1895 (29 Aug.). Team reduced from 15 to 13 in 1906 (12 June).
1895	Volleyball	Invented by William G Morgan at Holyoke, Mass, USA as *Minnonette*. Internationalised 1947.
1896	Marathon Running	Marathon to Athens, 1896 Olympics. Standardised at 26 miles 385 yds, *42,195 km* in 1924. Named after the run from the Marathon battlefield, Greece by Pheidippides in 490 BC.
1897	Motorcycle Racing	Earliest race over a mile, Sheen House, Richmond, Surrey (29 Nov.).
c. 1900	Water Skiing	Aquaplaning, US Pacific coast; plank-riding behind motor boat, Scarborough, England 1914; shaped skis by Ralph Samuelson, Lake Pepin, Minnesota, USA, 1922; devised ramp jump at Miami, Florida, 1928.
1901	Small Bore Shooting	·22 calibre introduced as a Civilian Army training device.
1912	Modern Pentathlon	First formal contest, Stockholm Olympic Games.
1918	Orienteering	Invented by Major Ernst Killander, Sweden (based on military exercises of the 1890s).
1922	Skiing (Slalom)	Devised by Sir Arnold Lunne, Mürren, Switzerland (21 Jan.).
1923	Speedway	West Maitland, NSW, Australia (Nov.); first World Championships Sept. 1936.
1936	Trampoline	Developed by George Nissen (US). First championships 1948. Used in show-business since 1910.
1951	Sky Diving (Parachuting)	First world championships in Yugoslavia.
1952	Synchronised Swimming	Given international status by FINA: US championships 1945.
1958	Hang Gliding	Modern revival by Prof. Rogallo; origins attributable to Otto Lilienthal (Germany) 1893.
1960	Aerobatics	First world championships instituted. First aerobatic manoeuvre 1913.
1964	Board Sailing	First appearance in California, USA.
1966	Skate Boarding	First championship in USA; upsurge from 1975; motorized boards from 1977.

Human Limitations in Sport

The basic physiological limitations to human performance in physical achievement embrace the following:

1) No human can survive more than 18 days without food and water.
2) Speed limit for transmission of messages through the nervous system is 180 mph *228 km/h.*
3) No human can survive prolonged blood temperatures above 105·8°F *41°C* or below 60·8°F *16°C* unharmed.
4) No human (except perhaps some asthmatic children) can detect sounds of a frequency above 20 000 Hz.
5) No human can detect sounds below 2×10 pascal and the most sensitive a frequency below 2750 Hz.
6) The human eye cannot resolve an object smaller than 100 microns at 25,4 cm *10 in.*
7) Visual stimuli rapidly repeated appear fused or continuous at frequencies between 4 and 60 per second according to the level of luminance.
8) No human can detect a vibration with an amplitude of less than 0·02 micron.
9) The human lung volume or vital capacity at maturity tends to a limit of 5,5 litres with up to 300 million alveoli.
10) The heart, as a pump, has a limited capacity above the normal circulatory volume of 5 to 6 litres per minute of which 60 per cent is liquid plasma.

The Olympic Games

The ancient Olympic Games were staged every four years at Olympia, 120 miles west of Athens. The earliest celebration of which there is a certain record is that of July 776 BC, from which all subsequent Games are dated. However, earlier Games were certainly held, perhaps dating back to 1370 BC. These early Games had considerable religious significance.

The Games grew in size and importance to the height of their fame in the 5th and 4th centuries BC. Events included running, jumping, wrestling, throwing the discus, boxing and chariot racing. They were much more than sporting contests, great artistic festivals upholding the Greek ideal of perfection of mind and body. Winners were awarded a branch of wild olive, the Greeks' sacred tree.

The final Olympic Games of the ancient era were held in 393 AD before the Emperor of Rome, Theodosius I, decreed the prohibition of the Games, which were not favoured by the early Christians and which were then long past their great days.

The first modern Games, in Athens in 1896, were at the instigation of Pierre de Fredi, Baron de Coubertin (1863–1937). A far cry from today's huge organisation, just 311 competitors (from 13 countries) took part, of whom 230 were from Greece and others were foreign tourists. By contrast, the 1984 Los Angeles Games, despite the absence of most of the eastern bloc, had record participants of 140 countries comprising 7 400 athletes, and record attendances totalling 5 767 923.

CELEBRATIONS OF THE MODERN OLYMPIC GAMES

	Year	Venue	Date	Countries	Male	Female
I	1896	Athens, Greece	6–15 Apr.	13	311	—
II	1900	Paris, France	20 May–28 Oct.	22	1319	11
III	1904	St Louis, USA	1 July–23 Nov.	13[1]	617	8
*	1906	Athens, Greece	22 Apr.–2 May	20	877	7
IV	1908	London, England	27 Apr.–31 Oct.	22	2013	43
V	1912	Stockholm, Sweden	5 May–22 July	28	2491	55
VI	1916	Berlin, Germany	Not held due to war	—	—	—
VII	1920	Antwerp, Belgium	20 Apr.–12 Sept.	29	2618	74
VIII	1924	Paris, France	4 May–27 July	44	2956	136
IX	1928	Amsterdam, Netherlands	17 May–12 Aug.	46	2724	290
X	1932	Los Angeles, USA	30 July–14 Aug.	37	1281	127
XI	1936	Berlin, Germany	1–16 Aug.	49	3738	328
XII	1940	Tokyo, then Helsinki	Not held due to war	—	—	—
XIII	1944	London, England	Not held due to war	—	—	—
XIV	1948	London, England	29 July–14 Aug.	59	3714	385
XV	1952	Helsinki, Finland	19 July–3 Aug.	69	4407	518
XVI	1956[2]	Melbourne, Australia	22 Nov.–8 Dec.	67	2958	384
XVII	1960	Rome, Italy	25 Aug.–11 Sept.	83	4738	610
XVIII	1964	Tokyo, Japan	10–24 Oct.	93	4457	683
XIX	1968	Mexico City, Mexico	12–27 Oct.	112	4749	781
XX	1972	Munich, FRG	26 Aug.–10 Sept.	122	6086	1070
XXI	1976	Montreal, Canada	17 July–1 Aug.	92	4834	1251
XXII	1980	Moscow, USSR	19 July–3 Aug.	81	4238	1088
XXIII	1984	Los Angeles, USA	28 July–12 Aug.	140		
XXIV	1988	Seoul, South Korea	20 Sept.–5 Oct.	—		

* This celebration to mark the tenth anniversary of the Modern Games was officially intercalated but is not numbered.
[1] Including newly discovered French national.
[2] The equestrian events were held in Stockholm, Sweden, 10–17 June with 158 competitors from 29 countries.

CELEBRATIONS OF THE WINTER GAMES

	Year	Venue	Date	Countries	Male	Female
I*	1924	Chamonix, France	25 Jan.–4 Feb.	16	281	13
II	1928	St Moritz, Switzerland	11–19 Feb.	25	468	27
III	1932	Lake Placid, USA	4–15 Feb.	17	274	32
IV	1936	Garmisch-Partenkirchen, Germany	6–16 Feb.	28	675	80
V	1948	St Moritz, Switzerland	30 Jan.–8 Feb.	28	636	77
VI	1952	Oslo, Norway	14–25 Feb.	22	623	109
VII	1956	Cortina d'Ampezzo, Italy	26 Jan.–5 Feb.	32	687	132

	Year	Venue	Date	Countries	Male	Female
VIII	1960	Squaw Valley, USA	18–28 Feb.	30	521	144
IX	1964	Innsbruck, Austria	29 Jan.–9 Feb.	36	893	200
X	1968	Grenoble, France	6–18 Feb.	37	1065	228
XI	1972	Sapporo, Japan	3–13 Feb.	35	1015	217
XII	1976	Innsbruck, Austria	4–15 Feb.	37	900	228
XIII	1980	Lake Placid, USA	13–24 Feb.	37	833	234
XIV	1984	Sarajevo, Yugoslavia	7–19 Feb.	49	1287	223
XV	1988	Calgary, Canada	23 Feb.–6 Mar.	57	1226	336

* There were Winter Games events included in the Summer Games of 1908 (London) and 1920 (Antwerp) which attracted six countries, 14 males and seven females for the first, and 10 countries, 73 males and 12 females for the latter.

TABLE OF OLYMPIC MEDAL WINNERS – SUMMER GAMES, 1896–1984

		Gold	Silver	Bronze	TOTAL
1.	USA	710	529	448	1687
2.	USSR	340	292	253	885
3.	Great Britain	168	212	197	577
4.	Germany[1]	146	193	192	531
5.	France	147	163	171	481
6.	Sweden	131	135	162	428
7.	Italy	141	117	120	378
8.	Hungary	113	106	130	349
9.	GDR[2]	116	94	97	307
10.	Finland	96	74	108	278
11.	Japan	83	72	75	230
12.	Australia	68	61	82	211
13.	Romania	48	53	76	177
14.	Poland	38	51	86	175
15.	Canada	36	60	68	164
16.	Switzerland	40	64	55	159
17.	Netherlands	41	45	58	144
18.	Denmark	31	57	52	140
19.	Czechoslovakia	42	45	47	134
20.	Belgium	35	48	40	123
21.	Bulgaria	27	50	39	116
22.	Norway	40	30	33	103
23.	Greece	22	39	38	99
24.	Austria	18	26	34	78
25.	Yugoslavia	23	25	23	71
26.	Cuba	23	21	15	59
27.	South Africa[3]	16	15	21	52
28.	Turkey	23	12	10	45
29.	Argentina	13	18	13	44
30.	New Zealand	23	4	15	42
31.	Mexico	9	12	16	37
32.	South Korea	7	12	18	37
33.	China	15	8	9	32
34.	Brazil	6	7	17	30
35.	Iran	4	10	15	29
36.	Kenya	6	7	9	22
37.	Estonia[4]	6	6	9	21
38.	Jamaica	4	8	8	20
39.	Spain	3	11	6	20
40.	Egypt	6	6	6	18
41.	India	8	3	3	14
42.	Ireland	4	4	5	13
43.	Portugal	1	4	7	12
44.	North Korea[5]	2	5	5	12
45.	Ethiopia	5	1	4	10

		Gold	Silver	Bronze	TOTAL
46.	Mongolia	0	5	5	10
47.	Uruguay	2	1	6	9
48.	Pakistan	3	3	2	8
49.	Venezuela	1	2	5	8
50.	Trinidad	1	2	4	7
51.	Chile	0	5	2	7
52.	Philippines	0	1	5	6
53.	Uganda	1	3	1	5
54.	Tunisia	1	2	2	5
=55.	Lebanon	0	2	2	4
=55.	Colombia	0	2	2	4
=57.	Puerto Rico	0	1	3	4
=57.	Nigeria	0	1	3	4
59.	Morocco	2	1	0	3
60.	Latvia[4]	0	2	1	3
=61.	Taipei	0	1	2	3
=61.	Ghana	0	1	2	3
=63.	Luxembourg	1	1	0	2
=63.	Peru	1	1	0	2
65.	Bahamas	1	0	1	2
66.	Tanzania	0	2	0	2
=67.	Cameroun	0	1	1	2
=67.	Haiti	0	1	1	2
=67.	Iceland	0	1	1	2
=67.	Thailand	0	1	1	2
=71.	Algeria	0	0	2	2
=71.	Panama	0	0	2	2
73.	Zimbabwe	1	0	0	1
=74.	Ivory Coast	0	1	0	1
=74.	Singapore	0	1	0	1
=74.	Sri Lanka	0	1	0	1
=74.	Syria	0	1	0	1
=78.	Bermuda	0	0	1	1
=78.	Dominican Repub.	0	0	1	1
=78.	Guyana	0	0	1	1
=78.	Iraq	0	0	1	1
=78.	Niger	0	0	1	1
=78.	Zambia	0	0	1	1

[1]Germany 1896–1964, West Germany from 1968.
[2]GDR, East Germany, from 1968.
[3]South Africa, up to 1960.
[4]Estonia and Latvia, up to 1936.
[5]North Korea, from 1964.

TABLE OF OLYMPIC MEDAL WINNERS – WINTER GAMES, 1924–88

		Gold	Silver	Bronze	TOTAL
1.	USSR	79	57	59	195
2.	Norway	54	60	54	168
3.	USA	42	47	34	123
4.	GDR[1]	39	36	35	110
5.	Finland	33	43	34	110
6.	Austria	28	38	32	98
7.	Sweden	36	25	31	92
8.	Germany[2]	26	26	23	75
9.	Switzerland	23	25	25	73
10.	Canada	14	13	17	44
11.	Netherlands	13	17	12	42
12.	France	13	10	16	39
13.	Italy	14	10	9	33
14.	Czechoslovakia	2	8	13	23
15.	Great Britain	7	4	10	21
16.	Liechtenstein	2	2	5	9
17.	Japan	1	4	2	7
18.	Hungary	—	2	4	6
=19.	Belgium	1	1	2	4
=19.	Poland	1	1	2	4
21.	Yugoslavia	0	3	1	4
22.	Spain	1	0	0	1
23.	North Korea[3]	0	1	0	1
=24.	Bulgaria	0	0	1	1
=24.	Romania	0	0	1	1

Totals include all first, second and third places, including those events not on the current schedule.
[1] GDR, East Germany, from 1968.
[2] Germany, 1924–64, West Germany, from 1968.
[3] From 1964.

Speed in Sport

mph	km/h	Record	Name	Place	Date
739·666	1190,377	Highest land speed – unofficial	Stan Barrett (USA) in *Budweiser Rocket*	Edwards Air Force Base, California, USA	17 Dec. 1979
633·468	1019,467	Highest land speed (official one mile record, jet powered)	Richard Noble (UK) in *Thrust II*	Black Rock Desert, Nevada, USA	4 Oct. 1983
625·2	1006	Parachuting freefall in mesosphere (military research)	Capt J W Kittinger (USA)	Tularosa, New Mexico, USA	16 Aug. 1960
429·311	690,909	Highest land speed (wheel driven)	Donald Campbell (UK) in *Bluebird*	Lake Eyre, South Australia	17 July 1964
418·504	673,516	Highest land speed (4-wheel direct drive)	Robert Summers (USA) in *Golden-rod*	Bonneville Salt Flats, Utah, USA	12 Nov. 1965
345	556	Highest water borne speed – estimated	Ken Warby (Aus) in *The Spirit of Australia*	Blowering Dam, NSW, Australia	20 Nov. 1977
319·627	514,39	Official water speed record	Ken Warby (Aus) in *The Spirit of Australia*	Blowering Dam, NSW, Australia	8 Oct. 1978
318·866	513,165	Highest speed motor cycle	Don Vesco (USA)	Bonneville Salt Flats, Utah	28 Aug. 1978
250·958	403,878	Motor Racing – closed circuit	Dr Hans Liebold (FRG)	Nardo, Italy	5 May 1979
215·33	346,54	Hydroplane record (propeller driven)	Eddie Hill (USA)	Lake Irvine, California	5 June 1983
214·158	344,654	Motor Racing – race lap record	Mario Andretti (USA)	Texas World Speedway	6 Oct. 1973
188	302,5	Pelota (Fastest ball game)	Jose Areitio	Newport, Rhode Island	3 Aug. 1979
170	273	Golf ball (Electrically timed)		USA	1960
163·6	263	Lawn tennis – serve	Bill Tilden	USA	1931
156·62	252,05	Lap record (practice) 24 Hr Endurance Motor Racing	Hans Stuck (W. Germany)	Le Mans, France	14 June 1985
152·284	245,077	Cycling, motor paced	John Howard (USA)	Bonneville Salt Flats, Utah	20 July 1985
143·08	230,26	Water skiing	Christopher Massey (Aus)	Hawkesbury River, NSW, Australia	6 Mar. 1983
143	230	Ice yacht	John D Buckstaff (USA)	Lake Winnebago, Wisconsin, USA	1938
138	222	Lawn tennis – serve (modern equipment)	Steve Denton (USA)	Colorado, USA	29 July 1984
129·827	208,936	Alpine skiing – Downhill Schuss	Franz Weber (Austria)	Les Arcs, France	19 Apr. 1984
121·28	195,18	Gliding (*100 km* triangular course)	Ingo Renner (Aus) in a Nimbus 3	Tocumwal, NSW, Australia	14 Dec. 1982
118·3	190,3	Ice Hockey – puck slap shot	Bobby Hull (Canada)	Chicago, Illinois, USA	1965
113·67	182,93	Water skiing, Barefoot	Lee Kirk (USA)	Firebird Lake, Phoenix, USA	11 June 1977
100·9	162,3	Baseball (pitch)	Lynn Nolan Ryan (USA)	Anaheim, California, USA	20 Aug. 1974
88·4	142,26	Sand Yacht	Nord Embroden (USA) in *Midnight at the Oasis*	Superior Dry Lake, California, USA	15 Apr. 1976

mph	km/h	Record	Name	Place	Date
66·48	107	Sand Yacht – official record	Christian-Yves Nau (Fra) in *Mobil*	Le Touquet, France	22 Mar. 1981
64·95	104,53	Alpine Skiing – Olympic Downhill course (average)	William Johnson (USA)	Sarajevo, Yugoslavia	16 Feb. 1984
52·57	84,60	Speedway (4 laps of 430 yds *393 m*)	Scott Autrey	Exeter, England	19 June 1978
52·40	84,33	Tobogganing – Cresta Run (3977 ft *1212,25 m* course in 51·75 secs)	Franco Gansser (Sui)	St. Moritz, Switzerland	19 Feb. 1984
44·645	71,849	Track Cycling (200 m unpaced in 10·021 secs)	Lutz Hesslich (GDR)	Moscow, USSR	22 Aug. 1984
43·26	69,62	Horse racing (440 yds *402 m* in 20·8 secs)	Big Racket	Mexico City, Mexico	5 Feb. 1945
41·72	67,14	Greyhound racing (410 yds *374 m* straight in 26·13 secs)	The Shoe (Aus)	Richmond, NSW, Australia	25 Apr. 1968
41·50	66,78	Sailing (36·04 knots)	Tim Coleman (UK) in *Crossbow II*	Portland, Dorset, England	17 Nov. 1980
37·22	59,91	Boardsailing (in Force 9 wind)	Michael Pucher (Austria)	Marseille, France	17 Apr. 1985
35·06	56,42	Horse Racing – The Derby (1 mile 885 yds, *2,41 km*)	Mahmoud	Epsom, Surrey, England	27 May 1936
35	56	Boxing – speed of punch	Sugar Ray Robinson (USA)	USA	Jan. 1957
31·784	51,151	Cycling – 1 hour, unpaced	Francesco Moser (Italy)	Mexico City, Mexico	23 Jan. 1984
30·58	49,21	Speed skating on ice (500 m *546 yds* in 36·57 secs on 400 m *437 yds* rink)	Pavel Pegov (USSR)	Medeo, USSR	26 Mar. 1983
29·80	47,96	Steeplechasing – The Grand National (4 miles 856 yds, *7,280 km* in 9 min 1·9 sec)	Red Rum ridden by Brian Fletcher	Aintree, Liverpool, England	31 Mar. 1973
25·78	41,48	Roller skating (440 yds *402 m* in 34·9 secs)	Giuseppe Cantarella (Italy)	Catania, Sicily	28 Sept. 1963
25·13	40,45	Sprinting (during 100 m of 4 × 100 m relay)	Carl Lewis (USA)	Helsinki, Finland	14 Aug. 1983
13·676	22,009	Rowing (2000 m)	USA Eight	Lucerne, Switzerland	17 June 1984
12·36	19,90	Marathon run (average over 26 miles 385 yds *42,195 km*)	Carlos Lopes (Portugal)	R. Herdan, Netherlands	20 Apr. 1985
12·24	19,70	Canoeing (1000 m in 3 min 02·70 sec)	USSR Olympic K4	Moscow, USSR	31 July 1980
9·478	15,253	Walking, 1 hour	Ernesto Canto (Mexico)	Fana, Norway	5 May 1984
5·28	8,50	Swimming (50 yds) – short course in 19·36 secs	Robin Leamy (USA)	Austin, Texas, USA	27 Mar. 1981
4·56	7,35	Swimming (100 m) – long course in 48·95 secs	Matthew Biondi (USA)	Mission Viejo, Cal., USA	7 Aug. 1985
2·74	4,40	Channel swimming (effective speed)	Penny Dean (USA)	England to France	29 July 1978
0·00084	0,00135	Tug 'o War (2 hr 41 min pull – 12 ft *3,6 m*)	2nd Derbyshire Regt (UK)	Jubbulpore, India	12 Aug. 1889

AMERICAN FOOTBALL
Evolved at American universities in the second half of the 19th century as a descendant from soccer and rugby in Britain. The first professional game was played in 1895 at Latrobe, Pennsylvania; organization into National Football League (NFL) took place in 1922 and was divided into two divisions. The American Football League (AFL) was formed in 1960. The two leagues merged in 1970, and under the NFL was reorganised into the National Football Conference (NFC) and the American Football Conference (AFC).

The major trophy is the Super Bowl, held annually since 1967 as a competition between firstly champions of the NFL and AFL, and since 1970 between the champions of the NFC and AFC.

The game is 11-a-side (12-a-side in Canada) with substitutes freely used. Pitch dimensions: 360 ft (*109·7 m*) × 160 ft (*48·8 m*). Ball length 280–286 mm (*11–11¼ ins*), weighing 397–425 g (*14–15 oz*).

ARCHERY
Although developed as an organized sport from the 3rd century AD, archery is portrayed, much earlier, as a skill in Mesolithic cave paintings. Internationalized as a sport in 1931 with the founding of the governing body, *Fédération Internationale de Tir à l'Arc* (FITA); FITA now has more than 45 affiliated countries, and is widespread in USA, UK and Japan. The most popular form of archery is termed Target Archery. Other forms are Field Archery, shooting at animal figures, and Flight Shooting, which has the sole object of achieving distance.

World Target Championships were first held in Poland in 1931, and biennially since 1957. Competitors shoot Double FITA rounds, 144 arrows from four different distances. An Olympic event in 1900, it disappeared between 1920 and 1972. The 1984 champions were: (men) Darrell Pace (USA), and (women) Seo Hyang-Soon (S. Korea).

ATHLETICS (TRACK AND FIELD)
There is evidence that running was involved in early Egyptian rituals at Memphis *c.* 3800 BC, but organised athletics is usually dated to the ancient Olympic Games *c.* 1370 BC. The earliest accurately known Olympiad was in July 776 BC, where Coroibos of Elis is recorded as winning the foot race, about 180–185 m (164–169 yds).

The modern Olympics were revived in 1896 (see Olympic section). The inaugural World Championships were held at Helsinki, Finland in August 1983 and attracted entries from 157 countries, making it the greatest number of nations represented at any sports meeting in history. The Championships are to be quadrennial, the next in Rome in 1987.

Marathon events, held since 1896, commemorate the legendary run of an unknown Greek courier, possibly Pheidippides, who in 490 BC ran some 24 miles (*38·6 km*) from the Plain of Marathon to Athens with news of a Greek victory over the numerically superior Persian army. Delivering his message – 'Rejoice! We have won' – he collapsed and died. Since 1908 the distance has been standardized as 26 miles 385 yds (*42,195 m*).

Dimensions in field events: Shot (men) – weight 7,26 kg (*16 lb*), diameter 110–130 mm (*4·33–5·12 ins*); Shot (women) – weight 4 kg (*8 lb 13 oz*), diameter 95–110 mm (*3·74–4·33 ins*); Discus (men) – weight 2 kg (*4·409 lb*), diameter 219–221 mm (*8·622–8·701 ins*); Discus (women) – weight 1 kg (*2·204 lb*), diameter 180–182 mm (*7·086–7·165 ins*); Hammer – weight 7,26 kg (*16 lb*), length 117,5–121,5 cm (*46·259–47·835 ins*), diameter of head 110–130 mm (*4·33–5·12 ins*); Javelin (men) – weight 800 g (*28·219 oz*), length 260–270 cm (*102·362–106·299 ins*); Javelin (women) – weight 600 g (*21·164 oz*) length 220–230 cm (*86·61–90·55 ins*).

AUSTRALIAN RULES FOOTBALL
Originally a hybrid of soccer, Gaelic football and rugby, laws were codified in 1866 in Melbourne, with the oval (rather than round) ball in use by 1867. The first football body in Australia, the Victoria Football Association, was formed in 1877 and the Australian Football Council (AFC) in 1906.

Teams are 18-a-side. Pitch dimensions are: width 110–155 m (*120–170 yds*), length 135–185 m (*150–200 yds*), encompassing an oval boundary line. The oval ball measures 736 mm (*29¼ ins*) in length, 572 mm (*22½ in*) in diameter and weighs 452–482 g (*16–17 oz*).

BADMINTON
The modern game is believed to have evolved from Badminton Hall, Avon, England, *c.* 1870, or from a game played in India at about the same time. Modern rules were first codified in Poona, India in 1876. A similar game was played in China 2000 years earlier.

The International Badminton Federation was founded in 1934, with affiliations in over 70 countries. Main countries today: Canada, China, Denmark, India, Indonesia, Japan, Malaysia, New Zealand, S. Africa, USA, and the UK.

World Championships were instituted in 1977 and are held triennially. Previously, the All England Championships (instituted 1899) was considered premier. International men's teams compete for the Thomas Cup (first held 1949); and women's for the Uber Cup (first held 1957). Both are held triennially; the 1984 winners were Indonesia and China respectively. Court dimensions: 13·41 m (*44 ft*) × 6·1 m (*20 ft*) (singles game 3 ft narrower). The net is 5 ft high at the centre; two or four players.

BASEBALL
The modern rules, or Cartwright rules, were introduced in New Jersey on 19 June 1846, although a game of the same name had been played in England prior to 1700. Baseball is mainly played in America, where there are two leagues, the National (NL) and the American (AL), founded in 1876 and 1901 respectively. It is also very popular in Japan. The winners of each US league meet annually in a best of seven series of games, the World Series, established permanently in 1905.

The game is 9-a-side. A standard ball weighs 5–5¼ oz (*148 g*) and is 9–9½ ins (*23 cm*) in circumference. Bats are up to 2¾ ins (*7 cm*) in diameter and up to 42 in (*1·07 m*) in length.

BASKETBALL
A game not dissimilar to Basketball was played in Mexico in the 10th century BC, but the modern game was devised by (Canadian born) Dr James Naismith in Massachusetts, December 1891.

The governing body is the Fédération Internationale de Basketball Amateur (FIBA), formed in 1932, and the game is played worldwide. By 1973, 133 national federations were members of FIBA. An Olympic sport since 1936 for men, for women since 1976. America won both 1984 titles. World titles for men (instituted 1950) and for women (instituted 1953) are held every four years. Russia won both golds in the last respective championships.

Teams are 5-a-side, with seven substitutes allowed. The rectangular court is 26·0 m (*85 ft*) in length, and 14·0 m (*46 ft*) wide, and the ball is 75–78 cms (*30 ins*) in circumference and weighs 600–650 grams.

BILLIARDS
Probably deriving from the old French word *billiard* (a stick with a curved end), an early

reference exists, dated 1429, to the game played on grass. Louis XVI of France (1461–83) is believed to be the first to have played on a table. Rubber cushions were introduced in 1835, and slate beds in 1836.

World Professional and Amateur Championships have been held since 1870 and 1926 respectively.

Dimensions of table: 3·66 × 1·87 m (*12 ft × 6 ft*).

BOARDSAILING (WINDSURFING)
Following a High Court decision, Peter Chilvers has been credited with devising the prototype boardsail in 1958. As a sport, it was pioneered by Henry Hoyle Schweitzer and Jim Drake in California in 1968. World Championships were first held in 1973 and boardsailing was added to the Olympic Games in 1984.

BOBSLEIGH AND TOBOGGANING
Although the first sledge dates back to *c.* 6500 BC in Heinola, Finland, organized bobsleighing began in Davos, Switzerland in 1889.

The International Federation of Bobsleigh & Tobogganing was formed in 1923, followed by the International Bobsleigh Federation in 1957. There are less than a dozen major courses in the world.

World and Olympic Championships began in 1924, and competition is for crews of two or four. The driver steers whilst the rear man operates brakes and corrects skidding. With the four-man, the middle two riders alter weight transference for cornering.

The oldest tobogganing club is the St Moritz in Switzerland, founded in 1887, and home of the Cresta Run which dates to 1884. The course is 1212·25 m (*3977 ft*) long with a drop of 157 m (*514 ft*). A solo activity, speeds reach 145 km/h (*90 mph*). In Lugeing, the rider sits or lies back, as opposed to lying prone face down in tobogganing.

BOWLING (TEN-PIN)
Evolved from the ancient German game of ninepins, which having been exported to America was banned in Connecticut in 1847 and then in other States. Ten pins were introduced to beat the ban. Rules were first standardized by the American Bowling Congress (ABC), formed in September 1895.

Concentrated in the USA, the game is also very popular in Japan and Europe. World Championships were introduced for men in 1954 and women in 1963, under the Fédération Internationale des Quilleurs (FIQ), which governs a number of bowling games.

The ten pins are placed in a triangle at the end of a lane of total length 19·16 m (*62 ft 10¾ in*), and width 1·06 m (*42 in*).

BOWLS
Outdoor bowls goes back as far as 13th century England, but was forbidden by Edward III since its popularity threatened the practice of archery. The modern rules were not framed until 1848–9, in Scotland by William Mitchell. There are two types of greens, the crown and the level, the former being played almost exclusively in Northern England and the Midland counties.

Lawn bowls is played mostly in the UK and Commonwealth countries. The International Bowling Board was formed in July 1905. Men and Women's World Championships are held every four years, with singles, pairs, triples and fours events. World Championships for Indoor Bowls were introduced in 1979.

BOXING
Competitively, boxing began in Ancient Greece as one of the first Olympic sports. Boxing with gloves was first depicted on a fresco, however, from the Isle of Thera, *c.* 1520 BC. Prize-fighting rules were formed in England in 1743 by Jack Broughton, but modern day fights evolved from 1867 when the 8th Marquess of Queensberry gave his name to rules. Boxing only became a legal sport in 1901.

Professional boxing has two world governing bodies, the World Boxing Council and the World

Boxing Association, based in Mexico City and Manila respectively. Each body has a world champion at each of 15 recognised weights: Light-flyweight (limit 108 lbs); Flyweight (limit 112 lbs); Super-flyweight (limit 115 lbs); Bantamweight (118 lbs); Featherweight (126 lbs); Junior Lightweight (130 lbs); Lightweight (135 lbs); Light Welterweight (140 lbs); Welterweight (147 lbs); Light middleweight (153½ lbs); Middleweight (160 lbs); Light Heavyweight (175 lbs); Cruiserweight (190 lbs) and Heavyweight.

CANOEING
Modern canoes and kayaks originated among the Indians and Eskimos of North America, but canoeing as a sport is attributed to an English barrister, James MacGregor, who founded the Royal Canoe Club in 1866.

With a kayak, the paddler sits in a forward-facing position and uses a double-bladed paddle, whereas in a canoe the paddler kneels in a forward-facing position and propels with a single-bladed paddle. An Olympic sport since 1936, Olympic titles are now held in nine events for men – New Zealand took four golds at Los Angeles, Canada two – and three for women of which Sweden won two.

CHESS
Derived from the Persian word *Shah*, meaning a king or ruler, the game itself originated in India under the name Chaturanga, a military game (literally 'four corps'). The first chessmen, of ivory, found in Russia, are dated *c.* 200 AD. By the 10th century, chess was played in most European countries. There are today some 40 million enthusiasts in the USSR alone. The governing body, founded in 1922, is the *Fédération Internationale des Echecs* (FIDE), which has been responsible for the World Chess Championship competitions since 1946, although official champions date from 1886 and unofficial before then.

Players are graded according to competitive results on the official ELO scoring system. Bobby Fischer (USA), world champion 1972–5, achieved the highest-ever rating of 2785.

CRICKET
A drawing dated *c.* 1250 shows a bat and ball game resembling cricket, although the formal origins are early 18th century. The formation of the MCC (Marylebone Cricket Club) in 1787 resulted in codified laws by 1835.

The International Cricket Conference (ICC), so called since 1965, having allowed membership from non-Commonwealth countries, now numbers seven. There are additionally 18 associate members. Recognized Test matches are played between England, Australia, West Indies, India, Pakistan, New Zealand and Sri Lanka.

There are four domestic competitions. The UK County Championship, a league of the 17 first class counties with matches over three days; the one-day knockouts of the Nat. West (previously Gillette) Trophy of 60-over matches and the Benson & Hedges of 55, and the one-day John Player League (40-over matches). The domestic competitions of Australia, New Zealand, India and the West Indies are the Sheffield Shield, the Shell Trophy, the Ranji Trophy and the Shell Shield respectively.

The World Cup, the international one day tournament, is held every four years, with the seven Test-playing countries plus the winner of the ICC Trophy which is competed for by non-Test playing countries. Australia won the 1987 tournament, India in 1983, the West Indies the first two.

Dimensions: Ball circumference 20·79–22·8 cms (*8 $\frac{3}{16}$ – 9 in*), weight 155–163 g (*5½–5¾ oz*); pitch 20·11 m (*22 yds*) from stump to stump.

CURLING
Similar to bowls on ice, curling dates from the 15th century although organized administration only began in 1838 with the Grand (later Royal) Caledonian Curling Club in Edinburgh. The sport is traditionally popular in Scotland and Canada. The International Curling Federation

was formed in 1966, and curling is to be added to the 1988 Olympic Games as a demonstration sport.

CYCLING
The first known race was held over 2 km (*1·2 miles*) in Paris on 31 May 1868. The Road Record Association in Britain was formed in 1888, whilst F. T. Bidlake devised the time trial (by 1890) as a means of avoiding traffic congestion caused by ordinary mass road racing.

Competitive racing, popular worldwide, is now conducted both on road and track. The Tour de France (founded in 1903) is the longest lasting non-motorised sporting event in the world, taking 23 days to stage annually. The yellow jersey, to distinguish the leading rider, was introduced in 1919.

Included since the first of the modern Olympic Games in 1896, there were seven men's events in 1984 and one women's, the Individual Road Race.

DARTS
Brian Gamlin of Bury, Lancashire, is credited with devising the present numbering system on the board, although in non-sporting form darts began with the heavily weighted throwing arrows used in Roman and Greek warfare.

Immensely popular in the UK – there are today some 6 000 000 players – the sport is rapidly spreading in America and parts of Europe.

EQUESTRIANISM
Horse riding is some 5000 years old, but schools of horsemanship, or equitation, were not established until the 16th century, primarily in Italy and then in France. The earliest jumping competition was in Islington, London in 1869.

An Olympic event since 1912, events are held in dressage, showjumping and Three Day Event, with team and individual titles for each. Dressage (the French term for the training of horses) is a test of riders' ability to control horses through various manoeuvres within an area of 60 × 20 m (*66 × 22 yds*). In showjumping riders jump a set course of fences, incurring four faults for knocking a fence down or landing (one or more feet) in the water, three faults for a first refusal, six faults then elimination for 2nd and 3rd, and eight for a fall. The Three Day event encompasses dressage, cross country and jumping.

The governing body is the Fédération Equestre Internationale, founded in May 1921.

FENCING
Fencing (fighting with single sticks) was practiced as a sport, or as part of a religious ceremony, in Egypt as early as 1360 BC. The modern sport developed directly from the duelling of the Middle Ages.

There are three types of sword used today. With the foil (introduced 17th century), only the trunk of the body is acceptable as a target. The épée (mid-19th century) is marginally heavier and more rigid and the whole body is a valid target. The sabre (late 19th century) has cutting edges on both sides of the blade and scores on the whole body from the waist upwards. Only with the sabre can points be scored with the edge of the blade rather than the tip.

For men, there are individual and team events for each type of sword in the Olympics. Women compete in foil only. Governed by the Fédération Internationale d'Escrine (f. 1913), the sport has taken off in the eastern bloc having once been dominated by France and Italy.

FIVES
Eton Fives originates from a handball game first recorded as being played against the buttress of Eton College Chapel in 1825. Rules were codified in 1877, and last amended in 1981.

Rugby Fives, a variation, dates from *c.* 1850. Both are more or less confined to the UK.

FOOTBALL (Association)
Tsu-Chu – Tsu meaning 'to kick the ball with feet' (*chu* means 'leather'), was played in China around 400 BC. Calcio, closer to the modern

game, existed in Italy in 1410. Official references date to Edward II's reign in Britain – he banned the game in London in 1314. Later monarchs issued similar edicts. The first soccer rules were formulated at Cambridge University in 1846; previously football was brutal and lawless. The Football Association (FA) was founded in England on 26 October 1863. Eleven per side became standard in 1870.

The governing body, the Fédération Internationale de Football Association (FIFA) was founded in Paris on 21 May 1904; football is played throughout the world.

Professionally, domestic competitions in England are the League Championship (the Football League was formed in 1888 with 12 teams), now with 4 divisions totalling 92 teams; the FA Challenge Cup, inst. 1871; and the Littlewoods (previously League and Milk) Cup, inst. 1960. 'Non-League' or semi-professional football is also widespread. Internationally, the World Cup has been held every four years since 1930 (not 1942 or 1946); the European Championship, instituted in 1958 as the Nations Cup, held every four years; the European Champions Club Cup, instituted in 1955 as the European Cup, contested annually by the League Champions of the member countries of the Union of European Football Associations (UEFA); the European Cup Winners Cup, instituted in 1960 for National Cup winners (or runners-up if the winners are in the European Cup); the UEFA Cup instituted in 1955 as the Inter-City Fairs Cup, held annually since 1960; the European Super Cup (inst. 1972) played between the winners of the European Champions Club Cup and the Cup Winners Cup; and the World Club Championship (inst. 1960) a contest between the winners of the European Cup and the Copa Libertadores (the S. American championship).

Football is an 11-a-side game; the ball's circumference is 68–71 cm (27–28 ins) and weight 396–453 g (14–16 oz). Pitch length 91–120 m (100–130 yds), width 45–91 m (50–100 yds).

The World Cup

Year	Winner	Venue
1930	Uruguay	Uruguay
1934	Italy	Italy
1938	Italy	France
1950	Uruguay	Brazil
1954	W. Germany	Switzerland
1958	Brazil	Sweden
1962	Brazil	Chile
1966	England	England
1970	Brazil	Mexico
1974	W. Germany	W. Germany
1978	Argentina	Argentina
1982	Italy	Spain
1986	Argentina	Mexico

The FA Cup (UK)

The FA Cup, or Football Association Challenge Cup, was instituted in 1871, 17 years before the birth of the Football League. The first final was played at Kennington Oval, London in 1872, when the Wanderers defeated Royal Engineers 1–0. Southern amateur clubs dominated the early years and the Cup did not 'go north' until Blackburn Olympic won in 1883. The final has been played at Wembley Stadium since 1923, when Bolton Wanderers defeated West Ham.

1872	Wanderers
1873	Wanderers
1874	Oxford University
1875	Royal Engineers
1876	Wanderers
1877	Wanderers
1878	Wanderers
1879	Old Etonians
1880	Clapham Rovers
1881	Old Carthusians
1882	Old Etonians
1883	Blackburn Olympic
1884	Blackburn Rovers
1885	Blackburn Rovers
1886	Blackburn Rovers
1887	Aston Villa
1888	West Bromwich Albion
1889	Preston North End
1890	Blackburn Rovers
1891	Blackburn Rovers
1892	West Bromwich Albion
1893	Wolverhampton Wanderers
1894	Notts County
1895	Aston Villa
1896	Sheffield Wednesday
1897	Aston Villa
1898	Nottingham Forest
1899	Sheffield United
1900	Bury
1901	Tottenham Hotspur
1902	Sheffield United
1903	Bury
1904	Manchester City
1905	Aston Villa
1906	Everton
1907	Sheffield Wednesday
1908	Wolverhampton Wanderers
1909	Manchester United
1910	Newcastle United
1911	Bradford City
1912	Barnsley
1913	Aston Villa
1914	Burnley
1915	Sheffield United
1920	Aston Villa
1921	Tottenham Hotspur
1922	Huddersfield Town
1923	Bolton Wanderers
1924	Newcastle United
1925	Sheffield United
1926	Bolton Wanderers
1927	Cardiff City
1928	Blackburn Rovers
1929	Bolton Wanderers
1930	Arsenal
1931	West Bromwich Albion
1932	Newcastle United
1933	Everton
1934	Manchester City
1935	Sheffield Wednesday
1936	Arsenal
1937	Sunderland
1938	Preston North End
1939	Portsmouth
1946	Derby County
1947	Charlton Athletic
1948	Manchester United
1949	Wolverhampton Wanderers
1950	Arsenal
1951	Newcastle United
1952	Newcastle United
1953	Blackpool
1954	West Bromwich Albion
1955	Newcastle United
1956	Manchester City
1957	Aston Villa
1958	Bolton Wanderers
1959	Nottingham Forest
1960	Wolverhampton Wanderers
1961	Tottenham Hotspur
1962	Tottenham Hotspur
1963	Manchester United
1964	West Ham United
1965	Liverpool
1966	Everton
1967	Tottenham Hotspur
1968	West Bromwich Albion
1969	Manchester City
1970	Chelsea
1971	Arsenal
1972	Leeds United
1973	Sunderland
1974	Liverpool
1975	West Ham United
1976	Southampton
1977	Manchester United
1978	Ipswich Town
1979	Arsenal
1980	West Ham United
1981	Tottenham Hotspur
1982	Tottenham Hotspur
1983	Manchester United
1984	Everton
1985	Manchester United
1986	Liverpool
1987	Coventry City

GAELIC FOOTBALL

The game developed from inter-parish 'free for all' with no time limit, no defined playing area nor specific rules. The Gaelic Athletic Association established the game in its present form in 1884. Teams are 15-a-side. Played throughout Ireland.

GOLF

A prohibiting law passed by the Scottish Parliament in 1457, which declared 'goff be utterly cryit doune and not usit', is the earliest mention of golf, although games of similar principle date as far back as AD 400. Golf is today played worldwide.

Competition is either 'match play', contested by individuals or pairs and decided by the number of holes won, or 'stroke play' decided by the total number of strokes for a round. The modern golf course measures total distance 5500–6400 metres, divided into 18 holes of varying lengths. Clubs are currently limited to a maximum of 14, comprising 'irons' Nos. 1–10 (with the face of the club at increasingly acute angles), and 'woods' for driving. Golf balls in the UK have minimum diameter 41·55 mm (1·62 ins) and maximum weight 45·93 grams (1·62 oz). In America, the minimum diameter is 42·62 mm (1·68 ins).

Professionally, the four major tournaments are the British Open, the US Open, the US Masters and the US Professional Golfers' Association (USPGA).

The British Open Golf Championship

The oldest open championship in the world, 'The Open', was first held on 17 October 1860 at the Prestwick Club, Ayrshire. It was then over 36 holes; since 1892 it has been over 72 holes of stroke play. Since 1920, the Royal and Ancient Golf Club have managed the event.

		Score
1860	Willie Park, Sr	174
1861	Tom Morris, Sr	163
1862	Tom Morris, Sr	163
1863	Willie Park, Sr	168
1864	Tom Morris, Sr	167
1865	Andrew Strath	162
1866	Willie Park, Sr	169
1867	Tom Morris, Sr	170
1868	Tom Morris, Jr	170
1869	Tom Morris, Jr	154
1870	Tom Morris, Jr	149
1871	Not held	
1872	Tom Morris, Jr	166
1873	Tom Kidd	179
1874	Mungo Park	159
1875	Willie Park, Sr	166
1876	Robert Martin	176
1877	Jamie Anderson	160
1878	Jamie Anderson	157
1879	Jamie Anderson	170
1880	Robert Ferguson	162
1881	Robert Ferguson	170
1882	Robert Ferguson	171
1883	Willie Fernie	159
1884	Jack Simpson	160
1885	Bob Martin	171
1886	David Brown	157
1887	Willie Park, Jr	161
1888	Jack Burns	171
1889	Willie Park, Jr	155
1890	John Ball	164
1891	Hugh Kirkcaldy	169
1892	Harold Hilton	305
1893	William Auchterlonie	322
1894	John Taylor	326
1895	John Taylor	322
1896	Harry Vardon	316
1897	Harry Hilton	314
1898	Harry Vardon	307
1899	Harry Vardon	310
1900	John Taylor	309
1901	James Braid	309
1902	Alexander Herd	307
1903	Harry Vardon	300
1904	Jack White	296
1905	James Braid	318
1906	James Braid	300
1907	Arnaud Massy (Fra)	312

Year	Player	Score
1908	James Braid	291
1909	John Taylor	295
1910	James Braid	299
1911	Harry Vardon	303
1912	Edward (Ted) Ray	295
1913	John Taylor	304
1914	Harry Vardon	306
1920	George Duncan	303
1921	Jock Hutchinson (USA)	296
1922	Walter Hagen (USA)	300
1923	Arthur Havers	295
1924	Walter Hagen (USA)	301
1925	James Barnes (USA)	300
1926	Robert T. Jones, Jr (USA)	291
1927	Robert T. Jones, Jr (USA)	285
1928	Walter Hagen (USA)	292
1929	Walter Hagen (USA)	292
1930	Robert T. Jones, Jr (USA)	291
1931	Tommy Armour (USA)	296
1932	Gene Sarazen (USA)	283
1933	Denny Shute (USA)	292
1934	Henry Cotton	283
1935	Alfred Perry	283
1936	Alfred Padgham	287
1937	Henry Cotton	283
1938	Reg Whitcombe	295
1939	Richard Burton	290
1946	Sam Snead (USA)	290
1947	Fred Daly	293
1948	Henry Cotton	284
1949	Bobby Locke (Saf)	283
1950	Bobby Locke (Saf)	279
1951	Max Faulkner	285
1952	Bobby Locke (Saf)	287
1953	Ben Hogan (USA)	282
1954	Peter Thomson (Aus)	283
1955	Peter Thomson (Aus)	281
1956	Peter Thomson (Aus)	286
1957	Bobby Locke (Saf)	279
1958	Peter Thomson (Aus)	278
1959	Gary Player (Saf)	284
1960	Kel Nagle (Aus)	278
1961	Arnold Palmer (USA)	284
1962	Arnold Palmer (USA)	276
1963	Bob Charles (NZ)	277
1964	Tony Lema (USA)	279
1965	Peter Thomson (Aus)	285
1966	Jack Nicklaus (USA)	282
1967	Roberto de Vicenzo (Arg)	278
1968	Gary Player (Saf)	299
1969	Tony Jacklin	280
1970	Jack Nicklaus (USA)	283
1971	Lee Trevino (USA)	278
1972	Lee Trevino (USA)	278
1973	Tom Weiskopf (USA)	276
1974	Gary Player (Saf)	282
1975	Tom Watson (USA)	279
1976	Johnny Miller (USA)	279
1977	Tom Watson (USA)	268
1978	Jack Nicklaus (USA)	281
1979	Severiano Ballesteros (Spa)	283
1980	Tom Watson (USA)	271
1981	Bill Rogers (USA)	276
1982	Tom Watson (USA)	284
1983	Tom Watson (USA)	275
1984	Severiano Ballesteros (Spa)	276
1985	Sandy Lyle	282
1986	Greg Norman (Aus)	280
1987	Nick Faldo	279

GLIDING

Leonardo da Vinci around AD 1500 defined the difference between gliding and powered flight in some drawings. However, the first authenticated man-carrying glider was designed by Sir George Cayley in 1853.

In competitive terms, gliders contest various events – pure distance, distance to a declared goal, to a declared goal and back, height gain and absolute altitude. World Championships were first held in 1937 and biennially from 1948.

Hang gliding has flourished in recent years, boosted by the invention of the flexible 'wing' by Professor Francis Rogallo in the early 1960s. The first official World Championships were held in 1976.

GREYHOUND RACING

Greyhounds were first used in sport at coursing – chasing of hares by pairs of dogs – brought to England by the Normans in 1067. Use of mechanical devices was first practised in England, but the sport was popularized in the USA. The first regular track was opened at Emeryville, California in 1919.

Races are usually conducted over distances of between 210 m (230 yds) for the sprint and 1097 m (1200 yds) for the marathon. The Derby, the major race in Britain, was instituted in 1927.

GYMNASTICS

Tumbling and similar exercises were performed c. 2600 BC as religious rituals in China, but it was the ancient Greeks who coined the word gymnastics, which encompassed various athletic contests including boxing, weightlifting and wrestling. A primitive form was practised in the ancient Olympic Games, but the foundations of the modern sport were laid by German Johann Friedrich Simon in 1776, and the first national federation was formed in Germany in 1860.

The International Gymnastics Federation was founded in Belgium in 1881, and gymnastics was included in the first modern Olympic Games in 1896. Current events for men are: floor exercises, horse vaults, rings, pommel horse, parallel bars and horizontal bar, while for women are: floor exercises, horse vault, asymmetrical bars and balance beam. Rhythmic Gymnastics for women was introduced for the first time at the 1984 Los Angeles games. The USSR, USA, Romania, China, and Japan are now the strongest nations.

HANDBALL

Handball, similar to soccer only using hands not feet, was first played at the end of the 19th century. A growing sport, by 1982 there were 80 countries affiliated to the International Handball Federation (founded 1946) and an estimated 10 million participants.

Handball was introduced into the Olympic Games in 1936 as an 11-a-side outdoor game but on its reintroduction in 1972, it became indoor 7-a-side, the standard size of team since 1952. (In Britain it is often 5-a-side.) Yugoslavia won both men and women's events at the Los Angeles Olympics.

HARNESS RACING

Trotting races were held in Valkenburg, Netherlands in 1554 but harness racing developed and is most popular in North America. The sulky, the lightweight vehicle, first appeared in 1829. Horses may trot, moving their legs in diagonal pairs, or pace, moving fore and hind legs on one side simultaneously.

HOCKEY

Early Greek wall carvings c. 500 BC show hockey-like games, whilst curved-stick games appear on Egyptian tomb paintings c. 2050 BC. Hockey in its modern form, however, developed in England in the second half of the 19th century, with Teddington HC (formed 1871) standardizing the rules. The English Hockey Association was founded in 1886; hockey was included in the 1908 and 1920 Olympic Games, and re-introduced on a permanent basis in 1928. Pakistan, Germany, and the Netherlands have joined India as the strong nations. The 1984 Olympic titles were taken by Pakistan (men) and Netherlands (women).

Dimensions: ball circumference 223–234 cm ($8\frac{3}{16}$–$9\frac{1}{4}$ ins) and weight 155–163 g ($5\frac{1}{2}$–$5\frac{3}{4}$ oz); pitch length 91·44 m (100 yds); width 50–55 m (55–60 yds).

HORSE RACING

Early organized racing appears to have been confined to chariots – Roman riders had a foot on each of two horses. The first horse-back racing was by the Greeks in the 33rd Ancient Olympiad in 648 BC. The first recognizable race meeting was held at Smithfield, London in 1174, whilst the first known prize money was a purse of gold presented by Richard I in 1195.

The Jockey Club is now the governing body of flat racing, steeplechasing and hurdle racing, having merged with the National Hunt Committee in 1968. The flat racing season in England takes place between late March and early November. Thoroughbreds may not run until they are two year olds. The five classic races are the Two Thousand Guineas and the One Thousand Guineas (Newmarket, 1600 m one mile), the Derby and the Oaks (Epsom, 2400 m $1\frac{1}{2}$ miles) and the St. Leger (Doncaster, 2800 m $1\frac{3}{4}$ miles).

Steeplechase and hurdle races are run over distances of 2 or more miles, with at least one ditch and six birch fences for every mile. The National Hunt season can last from early August to 1st June, and the two most important steeplechases are the Grand National, first run in 1839, at Aintree over a course of 7220 m (4 miles 856 yds) with 30 jumps, and the Gold Cup at Cheltenham.

HURLING

An ancient game that has been played in Ireland since pre-Christian times, but standardized only since the founding of the Gaelic Athletic Association in 1884. The hurl, or stick, is similar to a hockey stick only flat on both sides. All-Ireland Championships have been held since 1887.

ICE HOCKEY

A game similar to hockey on ice was played in Holland in the early 16th century, but the birth of modern ice hockey took place in Canada, probably at Kingston, Ontario in 1855. Rules were first formulated by students of McGill University in Montreal who first formed a club, in 1880.

The International Ice Hockey Federation was formed in 1908, and World and Olympic Championships inaugurated in 1920. The USSR have won six of the last seven Olympic titles. The major professional competition is the National Hockey League (NHL) in North America, founded in 1917, whose teams contest the Stanley Cup.

Teams are 6-a-side; the ideal rink size is 61 m (200 ft) long and 26 m (85 ft) wide.

ICE AND SAND YACHTING

Ice, sand and land yachting require, in basic form, a wheeled chassis beneath a sailing dinghy. Dutch ice yachts date to 1768, but ice yachting today is mainly in North America. Land and sand yachts of Dutch construction go back even further to 1595. The sports are governed by the International Federation of Sand and Land Yacht Clubs who recognize speed records. International championships were first staged in 1914.

ICE SKATING

Second century Scandinavian literature refers to ice skating, although archaeological evidence points to origins ten centuries earlier. The first English account is dated 1180, while the first club, the Edinburgh Skating Club, was formed around 1742. Steel blades, allowing precision skating, were invented in America in 1850. The International Skating Union was founded in the Netherlands in 1892.

Competitively, ice skating is divided into figure skating, speed skating and ice dancing. Figure skating has been an Olympic event since the Winter Games were first organized in 1924, but there were also events at the 1908 and 1920 Games. Ice dancing was not included until 1976.

The first international speed skating competition was in Hamburg, Germany, in 1885, with World Championships officially dated from 1893. Included for men in the 1924 Olympics, women's events were included in 1960.

JUDO

Developed from a mixture of pre-Christian Japanese fighting arts, the most popular of which was ju-jitsu which is thought to be of ancient Chinese origin. 'Ju' means 'soft', i.e. the reliance on speed and skill as opposed to 'hard' brute force. Judo is a modern combat sport first devized in 1882 by Dr Jigoro Kano. Today, students are graded by belt colours from white to black, the 'master' belts. Grades of black belts are 'Dans', the highest attainable being Tenth Dan.

The Wimbledon Championships

Wimbledon, 'The All England Championships', dates back to 1877 when it comprised just one event, the men's singles. Women's singles and men's doubles were introduced in 1884, with women's doubles and mixed doubles becoming full Championship events in 1913.

Champions since 1947

	Men's Singles	Women's Singles
1947	Jack Kramer (USA)	Margaret Osborne (USA)
1948	Bob Falkenburg (USA)	Louise Brough (USA)
1949	Ted Schroeder (USA)	Louise Brough (USA)
1950	Budge Patty (USA)	Louise Brough (USA)
1951	Dick Savitt (USA)	Doris Hart (USA)
1952	Frank Sedgman (Aus)	Maureen Connolly (USA)
1953	Vic Seixas (USA)	Maureen Connolly (USA)
1954	Jaroslav Drobny (Cz)	Maureen Connolly (USA)
1955	Tony Trabert (USA)	Louise Brough (USA)
1956	Lew Hoad (Aus)	Shirley Fry (USA)
1957	Lew Hoad (Aus)	Althea Gibson (USA)
1958	Ashley Cooper (Aus)	Althea Gibson (USA)
1959	Alex Olmedo (USA)	Maria Bueno (Bra)
1960	Neale Fraser (Aus)	Maria Bueno (Bra)
1961	Rod Laver (Aus)	Angela Mortimer (GB)
1962	Rod Laver (Aus)	Karen Susman (USA)
1963	Chuck McKinley (USA)	Margaret Smith (Aus)
1964	Roy Emerson (Aus)	Maria Bueno (Bra)
1965	Roy Emerson (Aus)	Margaret Smith (Aus)
1966	Manuel Santana (Spa)	Billie Jean King (USA)
1967	John Newcombe (Aus)	Billie Jean King (USA)
1968	Rod Laver (Aus)	Billie Jean King (USA)
1969	Rod Laver (Aus)	Ann Jones (GB)
1970	John Newcombe (Aus)	Margaret Smith-Court (Aus)
1971	John Newcombe (Aus)	Evonne Goolagong (Aus)
1972	Stan Smith (USA)	Billie Jean King (USA)
1973	Jan Kodes (Cz)	Billie Jean King (USA)
1974	Jimmy Connors (USA)	Chris Evert (USA)
1975	Arthur Ashe (USA)	Billie Jean King (USA)
1976	Bjorn Borg (Swe)	Chris Evert (USA)
1977	Bjorn Borg (Swe)	Virginia Wade (GB)
1978	Bjorn Borg (Swe)	Martina Navratilova (Cz)
1979	Bjorn Borg (Swe)	Martina Navratilova (Cz)
1980	Bjorn Borg (Swe)	Evonne Goolagong-Cawley (Aus)
1981	John McEnroe (USA)	Chris Evert-Lloyd (USA)
1982	Jimmy Connors (USA)	Martina Navratilova (USA)
1983	John McEnroe (USA)	Martina Navratilova (USA)
1984	John McEnroe (USA)	Martina Navratilova (USA)
1985	Boris Becker (W. Germany)	Martina Navratilova (USA)
1986	Boris Becker (W. Germany)	Martina Navratilova (USA)
1987	Pat Cash (Aus)	Martina Navratilova (USA)

Women's Doubles

1947 Pat Todd & Doris Hart (USA)
1948 Louise Brough & Margaret Osborne-du Pont (USA)
1949 Louise Brough & Margaret Osborne-du Pont (USA)
1950 Louise Brough & Margaret Osborne-du Pont (USA)
1951 Doris Hart & Shirley Fry (USA)
1952 Doris Hart & Shirley Fry (USA)
1953 Doris Hart & Shirley Fry (USA)
1954 Louise Brough & Margaret Osborne-du Pont (USA)
1955 Angela Mortimer & Anne Shilcock (GB)
1956 Angela Buxton (GB) & Althea Gibson (USA)
1957 Althea Gibson & Darlene Hard (USA)
1958 Maria Bueno (Bra) & Althea Gibson (USA)
1959 Jean Arth & Darlene Hard (USA)
1960 Maria Bueno (Bra) & Darlene Hard (USA)
1961 Karen Hantze & Billie Jean Moffitt (USA)
1962 Karen Hantze-Susman & Billie Jean Moffitt (USA)
1963 Maria Bueno (Bra) & Darlene Hard (USA)
1964 Margaret Smith & Lesley Turner (Aus)
1965 Maria Bueno (Bra) & Billie Jean Moffitt (USA)
1966 Maria Bueno (Bra) & Nancy Richey (USA)
1967 Rosemary Casals & Billie Jean Moffitt-King (USA)
1968 Billie Jean King & Rosemary Casals (USA)
1969 Margaret Smith-Court & Judy Tegart (Aus)
1970 Billie Jean King & Rosemary Casals (USA)
1971 Billie Jean King & Rosemary Casals (USA)
1972 Billie Jean King (USA) & Betty Stove (Hol)
1973 Billie Jean King & Rosemary Casals (USA)
1974 Evonne Goolagong (Aus) & Peggy Michel (USA)
1975 Ann Kiyomura (USA) & Kazuko Sawamatsu (Jap)
1976 Chris Evert (USA) & Martina Navratilova (Cz)
1977 Helen Cawley (Aus) & Joanne Russell (USA)
1978 Kerry Reid & Wendy Turnbull (Aus)
1979 Billie Jean King (USA) & Martina Navratilova (Cz)
1980 Kathy Jordan & Anne Smith (USA)
1981 Martina Navratilova (Cz) & Pam Shriver (USA)
1982 Martina Navratilova & Pam Shriver (USA)
1983 Martina Navratilova & Pam Shriver (USA)
1984 Martina Navratilova & Pam Shriver (USA)
1985 Kathy Jordan (USA) & Liz Smylie (Aus)
1986 Martina Navratilova & Pam Shriver (USA)
1987 C. Kohde-Kilsch (W. Germ) & H. Sukova (Czech)

Men's Doubles

1947 Bob Falkenburg & Jack Kramer (USA)
1948 John Bromwich & Frank Sedgman (USA)
1949 Ricardo Gonzales & Frank Parker (USA)
1950 John Bromwich & Adrian Quist (Aus)
1951 Ken McGregor & Frank Sedgman (Aus)
1952 Ken McGregor & Frank Sedgman (Aus)
1953 Lew Hoad & Ken Rosewall (Aus)
1954 Rex Hartwig & Mervyn Rose (Aus)
1955 Rex Hartwig & Lew Hoad (Aus)
1956 Lew Hoad & Ken Rosewall (Aus)
1957 Budge Patty & Gardnar Mulloy (USA)
1958 Sven Davidson & Ulf Schmidt (Swe)
1959 Roy Emerson & Neale Fraser (Aus)
1960 Rafael Osuna (Mex) & Dennis Ralston (USA)
1961 Roy Emerson & Neale Fraser (Aus)
1962 Bob Hewitt & Fred Stolle (Aus)
1963 Rafael Osuna & Antonio Palafox (Mex)
1964 Bob Hewitt & Fred Stolle (Aus)
1965 John Newcombe & Tony Roche (Aus)
1966 Ken Fletcher & John Newcombe (Aus)
1967 Bob Hewitt & Frew McMillan (Saf)
1968 John Newcombe & Tony Roche (Aus)
1969 John Newcombe & Tony Roche (Aus)
1970 John Newcombe & Tony Roche (Aus)
1971 Roy Emerson & Rod Laver (Aus)
1972 Bob Hewitt & Frew McMillan (Saf)
1973 Jimmy Connors (USA) & Ilie Nastase (Rom)
1974 John Newcombe & Tony Roche (Aus)
1975 Vitas Gerulaitis & Sandy Mayer (USA)
1976 Brian Gottfried (USA) & Raul Ramirez (Mex)
1977 Ross Case & Geoff Masters (Aus)
1978 Bob Hewitt & Frew McMillan (Saf)
1979 John McEnroe & Peter Fleming (USA)
1980 Peter McNamara & Paul McNamee (Aus)
1981 John McEnroe & Peter Fleming (USA)
1982 Peter McNamara & Paul McNamee (Aus)
1983 John McEnroe & Peter Fleming (USA)
1984 John McEnroe & Peter Fleming (USA)
1985 Balazs Taroczy (Hun) & Heinz Gunthardt (Switz)
1986 J. Nystrom & M. Wilander (Sweden)
1987 K. Flach & R. Seguso (USA)

Mixed Doubles

1947 Louise Brough (USA) & John Bromwich (Aus)
1948 Louise Brough (USA) & John Bromwich (Aus)
1949 Sheila Summers & Eric Sturgess (Saf)
1950 Louise Brough (USA) & Eric Sturgess (Saf)
1951 Doris Hart (USA) & Frank Sedgman (Aus)
1952 Doris Hart (USA) & Frank Sedgman (Aus)
1953 Doris Hart & Vic Seixas (USA)
1954 Doris Hart & Vic Seixas (USA)
1955 Doris Hart & Vic Seixas (USA)
1956 Shirley Fry & Vic Seixas (USA)
1957 Darlene Hard (USA) & Mervyn Rose (Aus)
1958 Loraine Coghlan & Bob Howe (Aus)
1959 Darlene Hard (USA) & Rod Laver (Aus)
1960 Darlene Hard (USA) & Rod Laver (Aus)
1961 Lesley Turner & Fred Stolle (Aus)
1962 Margaret Osborne-du Pont (USA) & Neale Fraser (Aus)
1963 Margaret Smith & Ken Fletcher (Aus)
1964 Lesley Turner & Fred Stolle (Aus)
1965 Margaret Smith & Ken Fletcher (Aus)
1966 Margaret Smith & Ken Fletcher (Aus)
1967 Billie Jean Moffitt-King (USA) & Owen Davidson (Aus)
1968 Margaret Smith-Court & Ken Fletcher (Aus)
1969 Ann Jones (GB) & Fred Stolle (Aus)
1970 Rosemary Casals (USA) & Ilie Nastase (Rom)
1971 Billie Jean King (USA) & Owen Davidson (Aus)
1972 Rosemary Casals (USA) & Ilie Nastaste (Rom)
1973 Billie Jean King (USA) & Owen Davidson (Aus)
1974 Billie Jean King (USA) & Owen Davidson (Aus)
1975 Margaret Smith-Court (Aus) & Marty Reissen (USA)
1976 Françoise Durr (Fra) & Tony Roche (Aus)
1977 Greer Stevens & Bob Hewitt (Saf)
1978 Betty Stove (Hol) & Frew McMillan (Saf)
1979 Greer Stevens & Bob Hewitt (Saf)
1980 Tracy Austin & John Austin (USA)
1981 Betty Stove (Hol) & Frew McMillan (Saf)
1982 Anne Smith (USA) & Kevin Curren (Saf)
1983 Wendy Turnbull (Aus) & John Lloyd (GB)
1984 Wendy Turnbull (Aus) & John Lloyd (GB)
1985 Martina Navratilova (USA) & Paul McNamee (Aus)
1986 K. Flach & Kathy Jordan (USA)
1987 M. J. Bates & J. M. Durie (GB)

The International Judo Federation was founded in 1951; World Championships were first held in Tokyo in 1956, with women competing from 1980. Included in the Olympics since 1964 (except 1968), there are currently eight weight divisions. Points are scored by throws, locks on joints, certain pressures on the neck, and immobilizations.

KARATE
Literally meaning 'empty hand' fighting, karate is based on techniques devised from the 6th century Chinese art of Shaolin boxing (Kempo), and was developed by an unarmed populace in Okinawa as a weapon against Japanese oppressors *c*.1500. Transmitted to Japan in the 1920s by Funakoshi Gichin, the sport was refined and organized with competitive rules.

There are five major styles in Japan: Shotokan, Wado-ryu, Goju-ryu, Shito-ryu and Kyokushinkai, each placing different emphases on speed and power. The military form of Tae Kwon-do is a Korean equivalent of Karate. Wu shu is a comprehensive term embracing all Chinese martial arts. Kung fu is one aspect of these arts popularized by the cinema. Many forms of the martial arts have gained devotees in Europe and the Americas.

LACROSSE
North American Indians played *baggataway*, and a French clergyman likening the curved stick to a bishop's crozier called it *la crosse*. The French may also have named it after their game *Chouler a la crosse*, known in 1381. Certainly in its recognizable form the game had reached Europe by the 1830s, and was introduced into Britain in 1867.

The International Federation of Amateur Lacrosse (AFAL) was founded in 1928, but the game was not standardized sufficiently to hold World Championships until 1967 for men and 1969 for women. Now every four years, America won both titles in 1982. It was played in the Olympic Games of 1904 and 1908, and was a demonstration sport in 1928, 1932 and 1948.

The game is 10-a-side (12-a-side for women at international level); pitch dimensions 100×64 m (110×70 yds). Ball weight in England 142 g (5 oz), circumference 184–203·2 mm ($7\frac{1}{4}$–8 ins), colour yellow; in USA weight 142–149 g (5–$5\frac{1}{4}$ oz), circumference 196·9–203·2 mm ($7\frac{3}{4}$–8 ins), colour orange or white.

LAWN TENNIS
Lawn tennis evolved from the indoor game of real tennis; 'field tennis' is mentioned in a 1793 magazine; Major Harry Gem founded the first club in Leamington Spa in 1872. The All England Croquet Club added Lawn Tennis to their title in 1877 and held their first Championships. The United States Lawn Tennis Association (now USLTA) was founded in 1881, the English in 1888. The International Lawn Tennis Federation was formed in Paris in March 1913.

The Wimbledon or All England, Championships (see p. 147) have since 1877 been regarded as the most important in the world, alongside the US Open, French and Australian Opens. Together these four make up the 'Grand Slam', the elusive distinction of holding all four titles at once. The US Open (instituted 1881) is now held at Flushing Meadows, New York, and the French at Roland Garros, Paris. The Australian Championships were first held in 1905.

Men and women today compete in various 'circuits' in the second richest sport in the world to golf. 'Grand Prix' tournaments are scaled according to a standard, with points awarded for results, totted to decide world rankings. The international team competition for men is the Davis Cup, won most times by the USA. The Federation Cup (first held 1963) is the women's equivalent and has again been dominated by USA, and Australia. The Wightman Cup is an annual USA-GB match begun in 1923 when only these two showed interest in a multi-nation tournament.

Tennis was part of the Olympic programme until 1924, and was a demonstration sport at Mexico 1968 and Los Angeles 1984. It is to be re-instituted to the Games proper in 1988.

MODERN PENTATHLON AND BIATHLON
In the ancient Olympic Games, the Pentathlon was the most prestigious event. It then consisted of discus, javelin, running, jumping and wrestling. The modern pentathlon, introduced into the Olympics in 1912, consists of riding (an 800 m course with 15 fences, riders do not choose their mounts); fencing (épée), shooting, swimming (300 m freestyle) and finally a cross-country run of 4000 m. Each event is held on a different day, with scaled points awarded for each activity.

L'Union Internationale de Pentathlon Moderne et Biathlon (UIPMB) was founded in 1948. Originally the UIPM, the administration of Biathlon (cross-country skiing and shooting) was added in 1957. Biathlon has been an Olympic event since 1960.

MOTORCYCLE RACING
The earliest motorcycle race was held at Sheen House, Richmond, Surrey in 1897 over a one mile (1·6 km) oval course. The first international motorcycle-only race (early races had included motorcars) was held in 1905, the International Cup Race, after the same race had been declared void in 1904 following bad organisation and underhand intrigues. The new Fédération Internationale des Clubs Motocyclistes (FICM) had organized the 1905 event, but has since been succeeded by the Fédération Internationale Motocycliste (FIM).

World Championships were started in 1949 by the FIM, in which competitors gain points from a series of Grand Prix races. Races are currently held for the following classes of bike: 50 cc, 125 cc, 250 cc, 350 cc, 500 cc and sidecars.

In road racing, the TT races (Auto-Cycle Union Tourist Trophy), first held in 1907, are the most important series. The 60·72 km (37·73 miles) 'Mountain' course, with 264 corners and curves, has been in use since 1911.

In Moto-Cross, or Scrambling, competitors race over rough country including steep climbs and drops, sharp turns, sand, mud and water. Originated at Camberley, Surrey in 1924; the Belgians have dominated in recent years.

MOTOR RACING
The first known race between automobiles was over 323 km (201 miles) in Wisconsin in 1878, but it is generally accepted that the first 'real' race was the Paris-Bordeaux-Paris run of 1178 km (732 miles) in 1895. Emile Levassor (Fra), the winner, averaged 24·15 km/h (15·01 mph). The first closed circuit race was at Rhode Island, 1896; the oldest Grand Prix is the French, inaugurated in 1906.

Competition in the highest bracket, the Formula One, is over the series of Grand Prix races (each usually about 200 miles in length) held worldwide, scoring points according to placing. The first World Championships were held in 1950, with the Manufacturers' Championships starting in 1958. Formula Two and Three Championships are held for cars with lesser cubic capacities.

Other forms of competition include the Le Mans circuit, a 24-hour race for touring cars; 'rallying' over public roads through several thousand miles, and drag racing, a test of sheer acceleration, most firmly established in USA.

NETBALL
Modern netball grew out of basketball, and reached England in 1895 having been invented in America in 1891. Rings instead of baskets date to 1897, and the term netball was coined in 1901 in England. National Associations date to 1924 and 1926 in New Zealand and England; the International Federation was formed in 1960. World Championships are held every four years, since 1963, with Australia winning in 1983 and maintaining their dominance.

Netball is no-contact, 7-a-side and played almost exclusively by females. The court measures 30·48 × 15·24 m (100 × 50 ft); ball circumference 68–71 cms (27–28 ins), weight 397–454 g (14–16 oz).

ORIENTEERING
'Orienteering' was first used to describe an event held in Oslo in 1900, based on military exercises, but the founding of the modern sport is credited to Major Ernst Killander (Swe) in 1918.

Basically a combination of cross-country running and map-reading, the sport is very popular in Scandinavia and has a keen band of followers in Britain. The International Orienteering Federation was founded in 1961, with World Championships from 1966, largely dominated by Sweden.

PELOTA VASCA (Jaï Alaï)
The sport, which originated in Italy as *longue paume* and was introduced into France in the 13th century, is said to be the fastest of all ball games. Various forms of pelota are played according to national character or local custom throughout the world. 'Gloves' and 'chisteras' (curved frames attached to a glove) are of varying sizes, and courts can be open or enclosed with wide differences in dimensions and detail. The Federacion Internacional de Pelota Vasca has staged World Championships every four years since 1952.

PÉTANQUE
Pétanque, or *boules*, originated in France from its parent game Jeu Provencal, where it is still immensely popular. Origins go back over 2000 years, but it was not until 1945 that the Fédération Français de Pétanque et Jeu Provencal was formed, and subsequently the Fédération Internationale (FIPJP).

POLO
Thought to be of Persian origin, having been played as *Pulu c*. 525. Brought to England from India in 1869. Teams are 4-a-side, mounted on horses of any type.

POWERBOAT RACING
Steamboat races date from 1827, petrol engines from 1865, but actual powerboat racing started in about 1900. International racing was largely established by the presentation of a Challenge Trophy by Sir Alfred Harmsworth in 1903, heralding thereafter 'circuit' or shorter course competition (America has been the most prominent winner of the trophy). Offshore events for (planing) cruises began in 1958, and speed records are recognised in various categories by the various governing bodies.

REAL TENNIS
Evolved from the game *jeu de paume* ('game of the palm') played in French monasteries in the 11th century, using the hands. The long-handled racket was not invented until about 1500. The world championship at real tennis is the oldest world championship of any sport, dating to approximately 1740. Today, real tennis is only played in five countries – England, Scotland, USA, France and Australia and the total number of courts in use throughout the world has dwindled to approximately 30.

ROLLER SKATING
The first roller skate was devised by Jean-Joseph Merlin of Belgium in 1760, but proved disastrous in demonstration. The present four-wheeled type was patented by New Yorker James L. Plimpton in 1863. Competition is along similar lines to ice skating – speed, figure and dance.

ROWING
A literary reference to rowing is made by the Roman poet Virgil in the *Aeneid*, published after his death in 19 BC; regattas were held in Venice *c*. 300 AD. The earliest established sculling race is the Doggett's Coat and Badge, first rowed in August 1716 from London Bridge to Chelsea, and still contested annually.

The governing body, the Fédération Internationale de Sociétés d'Aviron was founded in 1892, with the first major international meeting, the European Championships, held a year later.

Olympic Championships were first held in 1900 for men and 1976 for women. Current events are held for: (men) single, double and coxless quadruple sculls, coxless and coxed pairs, coxless and coxed fours and eights; (women) single and double skulls, coxless pairs, coxless quadruple sculls, coxed fours and eights. With sculling, the sculler has a smaller oar in each hand rather than pulling one oar with both hands.

The Oxford-Cambridge Boat Race was first held in 1829, from Hambledon Lock to Henley Bridge, and won by Oxford. The current course, used continuously since 1864, is from Putney to Mortlake and measures 6·779 km (*4 miles 374 yds*). To 1988, there has been only one dead heat, in 1877.

RUGBY LEAGUE

The game originated as a breakaway from Rugby Union on 29 August 1895, on account of the governing body forbidding northern clubs paying players, who thus lost Saturday wages. Three years later full professionalism came into being. In 1906 the major change from 15-a-side to 13 was made, and the title 'Rugby League' was created in 1922.

Rugby League is played principally in Great Britain, Australia, New Zealand and France. Major trophies in England are the Challenge Cup (inst. 1897), the League Championship (inst. 1907), the Premiership Trophy (inst. 1975) and the John Player Trophy (inst. 1972).

Dimensions: Pitch length maximum 100·58 m (*110 yds*), width maximum 68·58 m (*75 yds*). Ball length 27·3–29·2 cms (*10¾–11½ ins*), circumference at widest point 584–610 mm (*23–24 ins*).

RUGBY UNION

Developed at Rugby School, England. A traditional yarn tells of William Webb Ellis illegally picking up the ball and running with it during a football game, although this may be apocryphal. Certainly the game was known to have been played at Cambridge University by 1839. The Rugby Football Union was formed on 26 January 1871.

The International Rugby Football Board was formed in 1890. Teams representing the British Isles have toured Australia, New Zealand and South Africa since 1888, although they were not composed of players from all the Home Countries until 1924, when the term 'British Lions' was first coined.

The International Championship – between England, Ireland, Scotland, and Wales – was first held in 1884, with France included from 1910. Now also known as the Five Nations tournament, the 'Grand Slam' is prized for winning all four matches. The 'Triple Crown' is achieved for a Home Countries side defeating the other three.

The game is 15-a-side. Dimensions: pitch of maximum 68·58 m (*75 yds*) width, and 91·44 m (*100 yds*) between goal lines. Ball length 27·9–28·5 cms (*10¾–11½ in*) and weight 382–439 g (*13½–15½ oz*).

SHINTY

Shinty (from the Gaelic *sinteag*, a bound) goes back some 2000 years to Celtic history and legend, to the ancient game of *camanachd*, the sport of the curved stick. Having been introduced by the invading Irish Gaels it kept close associations with hurling but is essentially native to Scotland. The governing body, the Camanachd Association, was set up in 1893.

SHOOTING

The first recorded club for gun enthusiasts was the Lucerne Shooting Guild in Switzerland, dating from *c.* 1466, and the first known shooting match took place in Zurich in 1472. The National Rifle Association in Britain was founded in 1860; the Clay Pigeon Shooting Association developed from trap shooting in the USA and descended from the Inanimate Bird S.A. Skeet shooting is a form of clay pigeon designed to simulate a range of bird game-shot and was invented in the USA in 1915. Pistol events, like air rifle, are judged by accuracy in scoring on a fixed target, from various distances and positions.

Shooting events for men were held in the first modern Olympic Games in 1896, but the 1984 Games included two mixed events for the first time. Only two other Olympic sports have mixed competition, equestrianism and yachting.

SKIING

A well preserved ski found in Sweden is thought to be 4500 years old, and various other evidence from Russia and Scandinavia chronicles primitive skiing, but the modern sport did not develop until 1843 with a competition in Tromsö, Norway. The first modern slalom was held at Murren, Switzerland in 1922. The International Ski Federation (FIS) was founded in 1924.

Alpine skiing is racing on prepared slopes, against the clock, whereas Nordic skiing is either cross-country or ski jumping. Alpine world championships date to 1931, and have been included in the Olympics since 1936, as a combination event, but events are now split into Slalom, Giant Slalom and Downhill. Nordic events date to the 1924 Olympics, and include a combination event of cross-country and jump.

SNOOKER

Colonel Sir Neville Chamberlain concocted the game of snooker as a cross between 'Black Pool', 'Pyramids' and billiards, in 1875 at Madras, India. The term 'Snooker' came from the nickname given to first-year cadets at the Royal Military Academy, Woolwich. The game reached England in 1885 via world billiards champion, John Roberts who had been introduced to snooker in India.

Rules were codified in 1919, and the World Professional Championship instituted in 1927. Since 1970 the professional game has been controlled by the World Professional Billiards and Snooker Association.

A full size table measures 3·66 × 1·87 m (*12 × 6 ft*); ball values are: red (1), yellow (2), green (3), brown (4), blue (5), pink (6) and black (7).

SOFTBALL

Softball, the indoor derivative of baseball, was invented by George Hancock in Chicago, USA in 1887, and rules were first codified in Minnesota in 1895. The name softball was not adopted until 1930. A 9-a-side game (except in the USA) softball is played in Canada, Japan, the Philippines, most of Latin America, New Zealand and Australia. The ball is as hard as a baseball, but as distinct from baseball must be pitched underarm and released below hip level. The pitching distance is 14 m (*45 ft 11 ins*) for men, 11·11 m (*36 ft 5½ ins*) for women and 18·3 m (*60 ft ½ in*) between bases for both. 'Slow pitch' softball is a modern variation.

SPEEDWAY

Motorcycle racing on dust track surfaces has been traced back to 1902 in the USA, but the first 'short track' races were in Australia in 1923. Evolving in Britain in the 1920s, the National League was instituted in 1932. The first World Championships were held in September 1936 at Wembley under the auspices of the Fédération Internationale Motocycliste (FIM). A team competition was inaugurated only as late as 1960. Each race is contested by four riders (six in Australia) over four laps; the bikes have no brakes, one gear and are limited to 500 cc.

SQUASH

Squash developed at Harrow School, England in 1817 from a game used for practising rackets but substituted a softer, 'squashy' ball. There was no recognised champion of any country however until 1907 in America. A rapidly growing game in modern times, World Open Championships have been held since 1976, and since 1979 the ISRF (International Squash Rackets Federation), previously for amateurs only, has been open to all players and includes a team event won always by either Australia, Great Britain or Pakistan. The British Open has been held since 1922 for women and 1930 for men.

Court dimensions: 9·75 m (*31 ft 11¾ ins*) long and 6·40 m (*21 ft*) wide, with front wall height 4·75 m (*15 ft 7 ins*) up to the boundary line. The 'tin' runs along the bottom of the front wall, above which the ball must be hit.

SURFING

Originating in Polynesia, the first reference to surfing on a board dates to 1779 by a Naval Officer in Hawaii. Revived in the early 20th century in Australia; hollow boards were introduced in 1929. World Amateur Championships began in 1964.

SWIMMING

Competitive swimming dates to 36 BC in Japan, the first country to seriously adopt the sport, Emperor G-Yozei decreeing its introduction in schools. In Britain, organized competitive swimming was only introduced in 1837 when the National Swimming Society was formed. Australia led modern developments with an unofficial world 100 yd championship in 1858 at Melbourne.

The first widely-used technique (possibly excepting the 'doggy paddle') was the breaststroke. From this developed the side-stroke, a similar action performed sideways, last used by an Olympic Champion, Emil Rausch (Ger) to win the 1904 one mile event. A style resembling the front crawl had been seen in various parts of the world by travellers in the mid-19th century. Backstroke developed as inverted breaststroke, which modified towards inverted crawl. Butterfly began as an exploitation of a loophole in the rules for breaststroke allowing the recovery of arms from the water, and was recognized as a separate stroke in 1952. The medley event, using all four strokes in turn, came from America in the 1930s.

The world governing body for swimming, diving, water polo and synchronized swimming is the Fédération Internationale de Natation Amateur (FINA), founded in 1908. World Championships in swimming were first held in 1973, and are now held quadrennially. Last held in 1982, East Germany dominated the women's events, America and the USSR the men's.

Swimming has been an integral part of the Olympics since 1896, the first modern Olympic Games, with 100 m, 400 m, 1500 m and 100 m (sailors) freestyle events for men. Women first competed in 1912. Diving was introduced in 1904 (1912 for women), and water polo in 1900. Current events are: (Men) 100 m, 200 m, 400 m and 1500 m freestyle; 100 m, 200 m backstroke, breaststroke and butterfly; 200 m and 400 m medley; 4 × 100 m medley relay; 4 × 100 m and 4 × 200 m freestyle relay; springboard diving; high diving and water polo. (Women) 100 m, 200 m, 400 m and 800 m freestyle; 100 m and 200 m backstroke, breaststroke and butterfly; 200 m and 400 m medley; 4 × 100 m medley relay; 4 × 100 m freestyle medley; springboard diving, high diving, and solo and duet synchronized swimming.

Synchronized swimming, a form of water ballet, was first recognized internationally in 1952 and was included in the first World Championships in 1973. It appeared in the Olympics for the first time in 1984.

TABLE TENNIS

Earliest evidence of a game resembling table tennis goes back to London sports goods manufacturers in the 1880s. Known as *gossima*, it was the introduction of the celluloid ball and the noise it made when hit that brought the name 'ping pong' and the Ping Pong Association in 1902. Interest declined until the use of attached rubber mats to the wooden bats (allowing spin) in the early 1920s. The International Table Tennis Association was founded in 1926, with World Championships held since 1927. The Swaythling and Corbillon Cups are held as world team championships, instituted in 1927 and 1934 for men and women respectively. China has been particularly dominant in recent years. Dimensions: ball diameter 37·2–38·2 mm (*1·46–1·5 in*), weight 2·4–2·53 g, table length 2·74 m (*9 ft*); 1·525 m (*5 ft*) wide.

TRAMPOLINING

Equipment similar to today's trampoline was used by a show business group, 'The Walloons', just prior to World War I. The word originates from the Spanish *trampolin*, a springboard, and indeed springboards date to circus acrobats of the Middle Ages. The birth of the sport follows the invention of the prototype 'T' type by the American, George Nissen in 1936. World Championships, administered by the International Trampolining Association, were instituted in 1964 and held biennially since 1968.

VOLLEYBALL

Although an Italian game *pallone* was played in the 16th century, the modern game was invented as *Minnonette* in 1895 by William Morgan at Massachusetts, USA, as a game for those who found basketball too strenuous. The name volleyball came a year later. The game spread rapidly worldwide and reached Britain in 1914. The first international tournament was the inaugural European Championship in 1948, the year after the founding of the International Volleyball Federation.

Although proposed for the 1924 Games by the USA, volleyball was not included in the Olympics until 1964. America won the 1984 men's title, although the USSR has dominated the World (instituted 1949) and European Championships in recent years. China won the women's Olympic event and also the 1982 World Championship (instituted 1959). The two are equated in Olympic year.

Court dimensions are 18 × 9 m (*89 ft 0¾ ins* × *29 ft 6⅜ ins*); ball circumference 65–67 cm (25 19/32–26⅜ ins), 250–260 g (*8·85–9·9 oz*) in weight. Net height is 2·43 m (*7 ft 11¾ ins*) for men and 2·24 m (*7 ft 4¼ ins*) for women.

WALKING

Walking races have been included in the Olympic events since 1906 but walking matches have been known since 1859. Walking as a sport is defined as 'progression by steps so that unbroken contact with the ground is maintained'. Road walking has become more prevalent than track walking, and the Olympic distances are currently 20 km and 50 km.

WATER SKIING

Water skiing as we now know it was pioneered by Ralph Samuelson (USA) on Lake Pepin, Minnesota in 1922. Having tried and failed with snow skis, he gave exhibitions with pine board skis culminating in the first jump, off a greased ramp, in 1925. The Union Internationale de Ski Nautique was set up in July 1946 and the British Water Ski Federation was formed in 1954.

Competitively, the sport is divided into trick skiing, slalom and skijumping. (Trick skiing, performed at lower speeds, involves gymnastic feats rewarded according to difficulty.) The World Championships, begun in 1947 and held biennially, include an overall title, in which the USA have figured prominently in recent years, both for men and women.

Skiing barefoot brought a new element to the sport and competitions are held for straight speed records.

WEIGHTLIFTING

In China during the Chou Dynasty, which ended in 249 BC, weightlifting became a necessary military test, and as an exercise could date as far back as 3500 BC. Competitions for lifting weights of stone were held in the ancient Olympic Games. The amateur sport, however, is of modern vintage with competitions dating to *c.* 1850 and the first championship termed 'world' to 1891. The International Weightlifting Federation was established in 1920, and its first official championships held in 1922 in Estonia.

Weightlifting was included in the first modern Olympics in 1896, and then from 1920. In 1984 there were ten weight divisions, from up to 52 kg to over 110. Competition is decided by aggregate of two forms of lifting, the snatch and the clean and jerk. A third form, the press, was dropped in 1976 because of the difficulty in judging it. The Eastern bloc, especially the USSR, has dominated the sport in which world records are broken more frequently than in any other.

Powerlifting involves different techniques which perhaps have greater emphasis on sheer strength rather than technique. The three basic lifts are the squat (or deep knee bend), bench press and dead lift. The International Powerlifting Federation was founded in 1972, with the USA recently dominant as world record holders in the 11 weight divisions stretching to 125+ kg.

WRESTLING

One of the oldest sports in the world, organized wrestling may date to *c.* 2750–2600 BC; certainly it was the most popular sport in the ancient Olympic Games, and victors were recorded from 708 BC. Wrestling developed in varying forms in varying countries, with the classical Greco-Roman style popular in Europe, and free style more to the liking of countries in the East and the Americas. The main distinction is that in Greco-Roman the wrestler cannot seize his opponent below the hips nor grip with the legs. The International Amateur Wrestling Federation (FILA) also recognizes Sambo wrestling, akin to judo and popular in the USSR. FILA was founded in 1912, although the sport was in the first modern Olympics in 1896. There are currently ten weight divisions in both free-style and Greco-Roman events at the Games.

Sumo wrestling is a traditional form in Japan dating to 23 BC. Conducted with ceremony and mysticism, weight and bulk are vital since the object is to force the opponent out of the circular ring, using any hold.

YACHTING

Yachting dates to the race for a £100 wager between Charles II and his brother James, Duke of York, on the Thames in 1661 from Greenwich to Gravesend and back. The first recorded regatta was held in 1720 by the Cork Harbour Water Club (later Royal Cork Yacht Club), the oldest club, but did not prosper until the seas became safe after the Napoleonic Wars in 1815. That year the Yacht Club (later the Royal Yacht Squadron) was formed and organized races at Cowes, Isle of Wight, the beginning of modern yacht racing. The International Yacht Racing Union (IYRU) was established in 1907.

Yachting forms an Olympic event for six classes of boat; other competitions include the Admiral's Cup, a biennial inter-nation, 200 mile Channel and inshore race from Cowes to Fastnet Rock, Ireland and back to Plymouth, and the Whitbread Round the World Race, instituted in 1973 and quadrennial. The America's Cup was originally won as an outright prize by the schooner *America* on 22 August 1851 at Cowes and later offered by the New York Yacht Club as a challenge trophy. Since 1870 the Cup has been challenged by Great Britain in 16 contests, by Canada in two and seven times by Australia, but the USA were undefeated until 1983 when *Australia II* defeated the American boat *Liberty*.

Inventions

The invention and discovery of drugs, and musical instruments are treated separately (see Index)

Object	*Year*	*Inventor*	*Notes*
Adding Machine	1623	Wilhelm Schickard (Ger)	Earliest commercial machine devised by William Burroughs (US) in St Louis, Missouri, in 1885
Aeroplane	1903	Orville (1871–1948) and Wilbur Wright (1867–1912) (US)	Kitty Hawk, North Carolina (17 Dec). First sustained controlled flight
Airship (non-rigid)	1852	Henri Giffard (Fr) (1825–82)	Steam-powered propeller, near Paris (24 Sept.)
(rigid)	1900	Graf Ferdinand von Zeppelin (Ger) (1838–1917)	Bodensee (2 July) Getafe, Spain (9 Jan.)
Bakelite	1907	Leo H Baekeland (Belg/US) (1863–1944)	First use, electrical insulation by Loando & Co, Boonton, New Jersey
Balloon	1783	Jacques (1745–99) and Joseph Montgolfier (1740–1810) (Fr)	Tethered flight, Paris (15 Oct.) manned free flight, Paris, (21 Nov.) by François de Rozier and Marquis d'Arlandes. Father Bartolomeu de Gusmão (*né* Lourenço) (b. Brazil, 1685) demonstrated hot air balloon in Portugal on 8 Aug. 1709
Ball-Point Pen	1888	John J Loud (US)	First practical and low cost models by Lazlo and Georg Biro (Hungary) in 1938
Barbed Wire	1867	Lucien B Smith (patentee) (25 June)	Introduced to Britain in 1880 by 5th Earl Spencer in Leicestershire
Barometer	1644	Evangelista Torricelli (It) (1608–47)	Referred to in a letter of 11 June
Battery (Electric)	1800	Alessandro Volta (1745–1827)	Demonstrated to Napoleon in 1801

Object	Year	Inventor	Notes
Bicycle	1839–40	Kirkpatrick Macmillan (Scot) (1810–78)	Pedal-driven cranks. First direct drive in March 1861 by Ernest Michaux (Fr)
Bicycle Tyres (pneumatic)	1888	John Boyd Dunlop (GB) (1840–1921)	Principle patented but undeveloped by Robert William Thomson (GB), 10 June 1845. First motor car pneumatic tyres adapted by André and Edouard Michelin (Fr) 1895 (see Rubber tyres)
Bifocal Lens	1780	Benjamin Franklin (1706–90) (US)	His earliest experiments began c. 1760
Bronze (copper with tin) Working	c.2800 BC	SW Asia and Mediterranean	Copper smelting with arsenical ores was practised earlier
Bunsen Burner	1855	Robert Willhelm von Bunsen (1811–99) (Ger) at Heidelberg	Michael Faraday (1791–1867) (UK) had previously designed an adjustable burner
Burglar Alarm	1858	Edwin T Holmes (US)	Electric installed, Boston, Mass (21 Feb.)
Car (steam)	1769	Nicolas Cugnot (Fr) (1725–1804)	Three-wheeled miliary tractor. Oldest surviving automobile is the Italian Bordino (1854) in Turin
(petrol)	1888	Karl Benz (Ger) (1844–1929)	First run Mannheim Nov. or Dec. Patented 29 Jan. 1886. First powered hand cart with internal combustion engine was by Siegfried Marcus (Austria), c. 1864
Carburettor	1876	Gottlieb Daimler (Ger) (1834–1900)	Carburettor spray: Charles E Duryea (US) (1892)
Carpet Sweeper	1876	Melville R Bissell (US)	Grand Rapids, Mich (Patent, 19 Sept.)
Cash Register	1879	James Ritty (US) (Patent 4 Nov.)	Built in Dayton, Ohio. Taken over by National Cash Register Co 1884
Cellophane	1908	Dr Jacques Brandenberger (Switz), Zurich	Machine production not before 1911
Celluloid	1861	Alexander Parkes (GB) (1813–90)	Invented in Birmingham, England; developed and trade marked by J W Hyatt (US) in 1870
Cement (Portland)	1824	Joseph Aspdin (GB) (1779–1885)	Wakefield, Yorkshire (21 Oct.)
Chronometer	1735	John Harrison (GB) (1693–1776)	Received in 1772 Government's £20 000 prize on offer since 1714
Cinema (see also Film)	1895	Auguste Marie Louis Nicolas Lumière (1862–1954) and Louis Jean Lumière (1864–1948) (Fr)	Development pioneers were Etienne Jules Marey (Fr) (1830–1903) and Thomas A Edison (US) (1847–1931). First public showing, Blvd. des Capucines, Paris (28 Dec.)
Clock (mechanical)	725	I-Hsing and Liang-Tsan (China)	Earliest escapement, 600 years before Europe
(pendulum)	1656	Christiaan Huygens (Neth) (1629–95)	
Copper working	c.4500 BC	Earliest smelting sites	Rudna Glava, Yugoslavia (Vinça culture)
Dental Plate	1817	Anthony A Plantson (US) (1774–1837)	
Dental Plate (rubber)	1855	Charles Goodyear (US) (1800–60)	
Diesel Engine	1895	Rudolf Diesel (Ger) (1858–1913)	Lower pressure oil engine patent by Stuart Akroyd, 1890. Diesel's first commercial success, Augsburg, 1897
Disc Brake	1902	Dr F Lanchester (GB) (1868–1946)	First used on aircraft 1953 (Dunlop Rubber Co)
Dynamo	1832	Hypolite Pixii (Fr), demonstrated, Paris 3 Sept.	Rotative dynamo, demonstrated by Joseph Saxton, Cambridge, England June 1833
Electric Blanket	1883	Exhibited Vienna, Austria Exhibition	
Electric Flat Iron	1882	H W Seeley (US)	New York City, USA (Patent 6 June)
Electric Lamp	1879	Thomas Alva Edison (US) (1847–1931)	First practical demonstration at Menlo Park, New Jersey, USA, 20 Dec. Pioneer work on carbon filaments, Sir Joseph Swan (1828–1914), 1860
Electric motor (DC)	1873	Zénobe Gramme (Belg) (1826–1901)	Exhibited in Vienna. First demonstrated by Michael Faraday (1791–1867) in 1821. Patent by Thomas Davenport (US) of Vermont, 25 Feb. 1837
Electric motor (AC)	1888	Nikola Tesla (b. Yugoslavia) (US) (1856–1943)	
Electromagnet	1824	William Sturgeon (GB) (1783–1850)	Improved by Joseph Henry (US) (1797–1878)
Electronic Computer (see also Micro-processor)	1943	Dr Alan M Turing (GB) (1912–54)	Designed 'Colossus' for decyphering German codes, Bletchley Park, Herts, England: Alterable stored programme Manchester University Mark I by Sir Frederick Williams and Prof T Kilburn 1948: Point-contact transistor announced by John Bardeen and Walter Brattain, July 1948. Junction transistor announced by R L Wallace, Morgan Sparks and Dr William Shockley in early 1951
Film (moving outlines)	1885	Louis le Prince	Institute for the Deaf, Washington Hts, NY, USA
(talking)	1922	Josef Engl, Josef Mussolle and Hans Vogt (Germany)	Der Brandstifter, Alhambra, Berlin (17 Sept.)
(musical sound)	1923	Dr Lee de Forest (US) (1873–1961)	New York demonstration (13 Mar.)
Fountain Pen	1884	Lewis E Waterman (US) (1837–1901)	Patented by D Hyde (US), 1830, undeveloped
Galvanometer	1834	André-Marie Ampère (1755–1836)	First measurement of flow of electricity with a free-moving needle
Gas Lighting	1792	William Murdock (GB) (1754–1839)	Private house in Cornwall, 1792; Factory Birmingham, 1798; London Streets, 1807
Glass (stained)	c.1080	Augsburg, Germany	Earliest English, c. 1150, York Minster
Glassware	c.1500 BC	Egypt and Mesopotamia	Glass blowing Syria, c. 50 BC
Glider	1853	Sir George Cayley (GB) (1773–1857)	Near Brompton Hall, Yorkshire. Passenger possibly John Appleby. Emmanuel Swedenborg (1688–1772) sketches dated c. 1714
Gramophone	1878	Thomas Alva Edison (US) (1847–1931)	Hand-cranked cylinder at Menlo Park, NJ. Patent, 19 Feb. First described on 30 Apr 1877 by Charles Cros (1842–88) (Fr)
Gyro-compass	1911	Elmer A Sperry (US) (1860–1930)	Tested on USS Delaware, (28 Aug.). Gyroscope devised 1852 by Jean Foucault (Fr) (1819–68)
Helicopter	1924	Etienne Oehmichen (Fr)	First FAI world record set on 14 Apr. 1924. Earliest drawing of principle Le Mans Museum, France c. 1460. First serviceable machine by Igor Sikorsky (US), 1939
Hovercraft	1955	Sir Christopher Cockerell (GB) (b. 1910)	Patented 12 Dec. Earliest air-cushion vehicle patent was in 1877 by J I Thornycroft (1843–1928) (GB). First 'flight' Saunders Roe SRN-1 at Cowes, England, 30 May 1959
Iron Working (Carburized iron)	c.1200 BC	Cyprus and Northern Palestine	Introduced into Britain, c. 550 BC

Object	Year	Inventor	Notes
Jet Engine	1937	Sir Frank Whittle (GB) (b. 1907)	First test bed run (12 Apr.). Principles announced by Merconnet (Fr) 1909 and Maxime Guillaume (Fr) 1921. First flight 27 Aug. 1939 by Heinkel He-178
Laser	1960	Dr Charles H Townes (US) (b. 1915). First demonstration by Theodore Maiman (US) (b. 1927)	Demonstrated at Hughes Research, Malibu, California in July. Abbreviation for Light amplification by stimulated emission of radiation
Launderette	1934	J F Cantrell (US)	Fort Worth, Texas (18 Apr.)
Lift (Mechanical)	1857	Elisha G Otis (US) (1811–61)	Earliest elevator at Yonkers, NY
Lightning Conductor	1752	Benjamin Franklin (US) (1706–90)	Philadelphia, Pennsylvania, USA in Sept.
Linoleum	1860	Frederick Walton (GB)	
Locomotive	1804	Richard Trevithick (GB) (1771–1833)	Penydarren, Wales, 9 miles *14,4 km* (21 Feb.)
Loom, power	1785	Edmund Cartwright (GB) (1743–1823)	
Loudspeaker	1900	Horace Short (GB) Patentee in 1898	A compressed air Auxetophone. First used atop the Eiffel Tower, Summer 1900. Earliest open-air electric public address system used by Bell Telephone on Staten Island, NY on 30 June 1916
Machine Gun	1718	James Puckle (GB) patentee, 15 May 1718. White Cron Alley factory in use 1721	Richard Gatling (US) (1818–1903) model dates from 1861
Maps	c.3800 BC	Sumerian (clay tablets of river Euphrates)	Earliest measurement by Eratosthenes c. 220 BC. Earliest printed map printed in Bologna, Italy, 1477
Margarine	1869	Hippolyte Mège-Mouriès (Fr)	Patented 15 July
Match, safety	1826	John Walker (GB), Stockton, Teeside	
Microphone	1876	Alexander Graham Bell (1847–1922) (US)	Name coined 1878 by Prof David Hughes, who gave demonstration in London in January 1878
Micro-processor	1971	Drs Robert Noyce and Gordon Moore (USA)	Launched by US company Intel
Microscope	1590	Zacharias Janssen (Neth)	Compound convex-concave lens
Motor Cycle	1885	Gottlieb Daimler (1834–1900) of Cannstatt, Germany, patent 29 Aug.	First rider Paul Daimler (10 Nov. 1885); first woman rider Mrs Edward Butler near Erith, Kent, 1888
Neon Lamp	1910	Georges Claude (Fr) (1871–1960)	First installation at Paris Motor Show (3 Dec.)
Night Club	1843	Paris, France	First was Le Bal des Anglais, Paris 5me. (Closed c. 1960)
Nylon	1937	Dr Wallace H Carothers (US) (1896–1937) at Du Pont Labs, Seaford, Delaware, USA (Patent, 16 Feb.)	First stockings made about 1937. Bristle production 24 Feb. 1938. Yarn production December 1939
Paper	AD 105	Mulberry based fibre, China	Introduced to West *via* Samarkand, 14th century
Parachute	1785	Jean-Pierre F Blanchard (Fr) (1753–1809)	Dropped small mammal over London. Earliest jump from aircraft 1 Mar. 1912 by Albert Berry (US) over St Louis, Missouri, USA
Parchment	c.1300 BC	Egypt	Modern name from Pergamum (now Bergama), Asia Minor, c. 250 BC
Parking Meter	1935	Carlton C Magee (US)	Oklahoma City (16 July)
Pasteurization	1867	Louis Pasteur (1822–1895)	Destruction of pathogenic micro-organisms by heat. Effective against tuberculous milk
Photography (on metal)	1826	J Nicéphore Niépce (Fr) (1765–1833)	Sensitised pewter plate, 8 hr exposure at Chalon-sur-Saône, France
(on paper)	1835	W H Fox Talbot (GB) (1807–1877)	Lacock Abbey, Wiltshire (August)
(on film)	1888	John Carbutt (US)	Kodak by George Eastman (US) (1854–1932), August 1888
Plastics	c.1852	Alexander Parks (1813–90)	Discovered pyroxylin, the first plastic
Porcelain	851	Earliest report from China	Reached Baghdad in ninth century
Potter's Wheel	c.6500 BC	Asia Minor	Used in Mesopotamia c. 3000 BC
Printing Press	c.1455	Johann Gutenberg (Ger) (c. 1400–68)	Hand printing known in Korea by 704
Printing (rotary)	1846	Richard Hoe (US) (1812–86)	Philadelphia Public Ledger rotary printed, 1847
Propeller (ship)	1837	Francis Smith (GB) (1808–74)	Hand propeller screw used in 1776 submarine (q.v.)
Pyramid	2650 BC	Imhotep	Earliest was Zoser step pyramid, Saqqâra
Radar	1922	Dr Albert H Taylor and Leo C Young	Radio reflection effect first noted. First harnessed by Dr Rudolph Kühnold, Kiel, Germany 20 Mar. 1934. Word coined in 1940 by Cdr S M Tucker USN
Radio Telegraphy	1864	Dr Mahlon Loomis (US) demonstrated over 14 miles *22 km* Bear's Den, Loudoun County, Virginia (October)	First advertised radio broadcast by Prof R A Fessenden (b. Canada, 1868–1932) at Brant Rock, Massachusetts on 24 Dec. 1906
Radio Telegraphy (Transatlantic)	1901	Guglielmo Marconi (It) (1874–1937)	Morse signals from Poldhu, Cornwall, to St John's, Newfoundland (12 Dec.)
Rayon	1883	Sir Joseph Swan (1828–1914) (GB)	Production at Courtauld's Ltd, Coventry, England November 1905. Name 'Rayon' adopted in 1924
Razor (electric)	1931	Col Jacob Schick (US)	First manufactured Stamford, Conn (18 Mar.)
(safety)	1895	King C Gillette (US) Patented 2 Dec. 1901	First throw-away blades. Earliest fixed safety razor by Kampfe
Record (long-playing)	1948	Dr Peter Goldmark (US)	Micro-groove developed in the CBS Research Labs and launched 21 June by Columbia, so ending 78 rpm market supremacy
Refrigerator	1850	James Harrison (GB) and Alexander Catlin Twining (US)	Simultaneous development at Rodey Point, Victoria, Australia and in Cleveland, Ohio. Earliest domestic refrigerator 1913 in Chicago, Illinois
Rubber (latex foam)	1928	Dunlop Rubber Co (GB)	Team led by E A Murphy at Fort Dunlop, Birmingham
(tyres)	1846	Thomas Hancock (GB) (1786–1865)	Introduced solid rubber tyres for vehicles (1847) (*see also* Bicycle)
(vulcanised)	1841	Charles Goodyear (US) (1800–60)	
(waterproof)	1823	Charles Macintosh (GB) (1766–1843) Patent	First experiments in Glasgow with James Syme. G Fox in 1821 had marketed a Gambroon cloth, but no detail has survived
Rubik Cube	1975	Prof. Ernö Rubik (Hungary)	Patented device with $4 \cdot 3 \times 10^{22}$ combinations
Safety Pin	1849	Walter Hunt (US)	First manufactured New York City, NY (10 Apr.)
Scotch Tape	1930	Richard Drew (US) (1899–1980)	Developed from opaque masking tape
Self-Starter	1911	Charles F Kettering (US) (1876–1958)	Developed at Dayton, Ohio, sold to Cadillac

Object	Year	Inventor	Notes
Sewing Machine	1829	Barthélemy Thimmonnier (Fr) (1793–1854)	A patent by Thomas Saint (GB) dated 17 July 1790 for an apparently undeveloped machine was found in 1874. Earliest practical domestic machine by Isaac M Singer (1811–75) of Pittstown, NY, USA, in 1851. AB Wilson machine of 1850, Farrington Museum, Conn., USA.
Ship (sea-going)	*c.*40 000 BC	Possibly double dug-out canoes	Traversed Indonesia to Australia
(steam)	1775	J C Périer (Fr) (1742–1818)	On the Seine, near Paris. Propulsion achieved on river Saône, France by Marquis d'Abbans, 1783. First sea-going Phoenix by John Stevens (1749–1838) built 1808. Clement Fulton first commercially successful
(turbine)	1894	Hon Sir Charles Parsons (GB) (1854–1931)	*SS Turbinia* attained 34·5 knots on first trial. Built at Heaton, Tyne and Wear
Silk Manufacture	*c.* 50 BC	Reeling machines devised, China	Silk mills in Italy *c.* 1250, world's earliest factories
Skyscraper	1882	William Le Baron Jenny (US)	Home Insurance Co Building, Chicago, Ill, 10 storey (top 4 steel beams)
Slide Rule	1621	William Oughtred (1575–1660) (Eng)	Earliest slide between fixed stock by Robert Bissaker, 1654
Spectacles	1289	Venice, Italy (convex)	Concave lens for myopia not developed till *c.* 1450
Spinning Frame	1769	Sir Richard Arkwright (GB) (1732–92)	
Spinning Jenny	1764	James Hargreaves (GB) (1745–78)	
Spinning Mule	1779	Samuel Crompton (GB) (1753–1827)	
Steam Engine	1698	Thomas Savery (GB) (*c.* 1650–1715)	Recorded on 25 July. Denis Papin (Fr) (1647–1712) invented the pressure cooker 1679
Steam Engine (piston)	1712	Thomas Newcomen (GB) (1663–1729)	
Steam Engine (condenser)	1765	James Watt (Scot) (1736–1819)	
Steel Production	1855	Henry Bessemer (GB) (1813–1898)	At St Pancras, London. Cementation of wrought iron bars by charcoal contact known to Chalybes people of Asia Minor *c.* 1400 BC
Steel (stainless)	1913	Harry Brearley (GB)	First cast at Sheffield (Eng) (20 Aug.). Krupp patent, Oct. 1912 for chromium carbon steel; failed to recognise corrosion resistance
Submarine	1776	David Bushnell (US), Saybrook, Conn	Hand propelled screw, one man crew, used off New York. A twelve man wooden and leather submersible devised by Cornelius Drebbel (Neth) demonstrated in Thames in 1624
Tank	1914	Sir Ernest Swinton (GB) (1868–1951)	Built at Lincoln, designed by William Tritton. Tested 8 Sept. 1915
Telegraph	1787	M Lammond (Fr) demonstrated a working model, Paris	
Telegraph Code	1837	Samuel F B Morse (US) (1791–1872)	The real credit belonged largely to his assistant Alfred Vail (US) who first transmitted at Morristown, NJ on 8 Jan. 1838
Telephone	1849	Antonio Meucci (It) in Havana, Cuba	Caveat not filed until 1871. Instrument worked imperfectly by electrical impulses
	1876	Alexander Graham Bell (US) (1847–1922) Patented 7 Mar. 1876	First exchange at Boston, Mass, 1878
Telescope (refractor)	1608	Hans Lippershey (Neth)	(2 Oct.)
Television (mechanical)	1926	John Logie Baird (GB) (1888–1946)	First successful experiment 30 Oct. 1925. First public demonstration 27 Jan. 1926, London, of moving image with gradations of light and shade at 22 Frith Street, London. First transmission in colour on 3 July 1928 at 133 Long Acre, London
Television (electronic)	1927	Philo Taylor Farnsworth (US) (1906–71)	First images (Nov.) 202 Green St, Los Angeles. Patent granted 26 Aug. 1930
Terylene	1941	J R Whinfield (1901–66), J T Dickson (GB) at Accrington, Lancashire	First available 1950, marketed in USA as 'Dacron'
Thermometer	1593	Galileo Galilei (It) (1564–1642)	Gas thermoscope built at Royal Institution, London (29 Aug.)
Transformer	1831	Michael Faraday (GB) (1791–1867)	
Transistor	1948	John Bardeen, William Shockley and Walter Brattain (US)	Researched at Bell Telephone Laboratories. First application for a patent was by Dr Julius E Lilienfeld in Canada on October 1925 (*see* Electronic Computer)
Typewriter	1808	Pellegrine Tarri (It)	First practical 27 character keyed machine with carbon paper built in Reggio Emilia, Italy
Washing Machine (electric)	1907	Hurley Machine Co (US)	Marketed under the name of 'Thor' in Chicago, Illinois, USA
Watch	1462	Bartholomew Manfredi (It)	Earliest mention of a named watchmaker (November) but in reference to an earlier watchmaker
Water Closet	1589	Designed by Sir John Harington (GB)	Installed at Kelston, near Bath. Built by 'T C' (full name unknown)
Welder (electric)	1877	Elisha Thomson (US) (1853–1937)	
Wheel	*c.*3300 BC	Sumerian civilization	Spoked as opposed to solid wheels *c.* 1900 BC
Windmill	*c.* 600	Persian corn grinding	Oldest known English post mill, 1191, Bury St Edmunds
Writing	*c.*3500 BC	Sumerian civilisation	Earliest evidence found in SE Iran, 1970
X-Ray	1895	Wilhelm Konrad Röntgen (Ger) (1845–1923)	University of Wurzburg (8 Nov.)
Zip Fastener	1891	Whitcomb L Judson (US) Exhibition 1893 at Chicago Exposition	First practical fastener invented in USA by Gideon Sundback (Sweden) in 1913

Transport

Shipping

WORLD'S LARGEST SHIPS
The largest liner of all-time was *Queen Elizabeth* (UK) of 82 998 gross tons and 1031 ft *314 m* completed in 1940 and destroyed by fire in Hong Kong as *Seawise University* on 9 Jan. 1972. The largest and active liner is the *Norway* of 70 202·19 grt and 315,66 m *1035 ft 7½ in* in length. She was built as the *France* in 1961 and put out of service in 1975. In June 1979 she was bought by the Norwegian Knut Kloster, renamed *Norway*, and recommissioned as a cruise ship in August 1979.

SHIPPING TONNAGES
There are four tonnage systems in use, viz. gross tonnage (GRT), net tonnage (NRT), deadweight tonnage (DWT) and displacement tonnage.

(1) *Gross Registered Tonnage*, used for merchantmen, is the sum in cubic ft of all the enclosed spaces divided by 100, such that 1 grt = 100 ft^3 of enclosed space.

(2) *Net Registered Tonnage*, also used for merchantmen, is the gross tonnage (above) less deductions for crew spaces, engine rooms and ballast which cannot be utilised for paying passengers or cargo.

(3) *Deadweight Tonnage*, mainly used for tramp ships and oil tankers, is the number of UK long tons (of 2240 lb) of cargo, stores, bunkers and, where necessary, passengers which is required to bring down a ship from her height line to her load-water line, i.e. the carrying capacity of a ship.

(4) *Displacement Tonnage*, used for warships and US merchantmen, is the number of tons (each 35 ft^3) of sea water displaced by a vessel charged to its load-water line, i.e. the weight of the vessel and its contents in tons.

Oil tankers (over 450 000 tons dwt)

Name	Flag	High DWT	GRT	Length ft	Length m	Breadth ft	Breadth m
Seawise Giant	Liberia	564 763	238 558	1504	*458*	209	*63*
Pierre Guillaumat	France	555 051	274 838	1359	*414*	206	*62*
Prairial	France	554 974	274 838	1359	*414*	206	*62*
Bellamya	France	553 662	275 276	1359	*414*	206	*62*
Batillus	France	553 662	273 550	1358	*413*	206	*62*
Esso Atlantic	Liberia	516 893	234 638	1333	*406*	233	*71*
Esso Pacific	Liberia	516 423	234 626	1333	*406*	233	*71*
King Alexander	Sweden	491 120	245 140	1194	*363*	259	*78*
Nissei Maru	Japan	484 337	238 517	1243	*378*	203	*61*
Globtik London	Liberia	483 933	213 894	1243	*378*	203	*61*
Globtik Tokyo	Liberia	483 662	213 886	1243	*378*	203	*61*
Burmah Enterprise	UK	457 927	231 629	1241	*378*	224	*68*
Burmah Endeavour	UK	457 841	231 629	1241	*378*	223	*67*

Bulk Ore, Bulk Oil and Oil Carriers (over 250 000 tons DWT)

Name	Flag	High DWT*	GRT*	Length ft	Length m	Breadth ft	Breadth m
World Gala	Liberia	282 462	133 748	1109	*338*	179	*55*
Dode Canyon	Liberia	275 588	131 473	1114	*340*	180	*54*
Mary R Koch	Liberia	270 656	136 991	1099	*335*	171	*51*
Weser Ore	Liberia	270 000	139 401	1099	*335*	171	*51*
Rhine Ore	Panama	270 000	139 406	1099	*335*	171	*51*
Jose Bonifacio	Brazil	266 088	126 760	1106	*337*	179	*55*
Castor	Liberia	264 484	132 305	1101	*335*	176	*53*
Licorne Atlantique	France	260 429	131 619	1101	*335*	176	*53*
Alkisima Alarabia	Saudi Arabia	260 412	143 959	1101	*335*	176	*53*

*NB Seagoing carriers are subject to modification and change, which is why high DWT and GRT's differ from previous information.

MAIN COMMERCIAL AIRCRAFT IN AIRLINE SERVICE 1985*

Name of Aircraft**	Nationality	No. in service	Wingspan	Length	Max. cruising speed	Range with max. payload	Max. takeoff weight	Max. seating capacity
Yakolev YAK-40	USSR	2641	82 ft 0 in *(25·00 m)*	66 ft 9½ in *(20·36 m)*	297 knots *(550 km/h)*	782 naut miles *(1450 km)*	35 275 lb *(16 000 kg)*	32
Boeing 727 (−200)	USA	1769	108 ft 0 in *(32·92 m)*	153 ft 2 in *(46·69 m)*	520 knots *(964 km/h)*	2140 naut miles *(3966 km)*	209 500 lb *(95 025 kg)*	189
McDonnell Douglas DC9 (Super 81)	USA	1091	107 ft 10 in *(32·87 m)*	*147 ft 10 m* in *(45·06 m)*	487 knots *(902 km/h)*	2657 naut miles[1] *(4925 km)*	140 000 lb *(63 500 kg)*	172
Boeing 737 (−200)	USA	1011	93 ft 0 in *(28·35 m)*	100 ft 2 in *(30·53 m)*	500 knots *(927 km/h)*	2300 naut miles *(4262 km)*	124 500 lb *(56 472 kg)*	130
Boeing 747 (−200)	USA	597	195 ft 6 in *(70·66 m)*	231 ft 10 in *(70 66)*	520 knots *(964 km/h)*	5700 naut miles[3] *(10 562 km)*	833 000 lb *(377 840 kg)*	516
Fokker F27 (Mk 500)	Netherlands	495	95 ft 2 in *(29·00 m)*	82 ft 2½ in *(25·06 m)*	259 knots *(480 km/h)*	935 naut miles *(1741 km)*	45 000 lb *(20 410 kg)*	60
McDonnell Douglas DC8 (Srs 63)	USA	402	148 ft 5 in *(45·23 m)*	187 ft 5 in *(57·12 m)*	521 knots *(965 km/h)*	3907 naut miles *(7240 km)*	350 000 lb *(158 000 kg)*	259
McDonnell Douglas DC10 (Srs 40)	USA	357	165 ft 5 in *(50·41 m)*	182 ft 1 in *(55·50 m)*	498 knots *(922 km/h)*	4050 naut miles *(7505 km)*	572 000 lb) *(259 450 kg)*	380
Boeing 707/720 (707–320)	USA	310	145 ft 9 in *(44·42 m)*	152 ft 11 in *(46·61 m)*	525 knots *(973 km/h)*	5000 naut miles[2] *(9265 km)*	333 600 lb *(151 315 kg)*	219
Lockheed L-1011 Tristar (−500)	USA	242	155 ft 4 in *(47·34 m)*	164 ft 2½ in *(50·05 m)*	525 knots *(973 km/h)*	5209 naut miles[5] *(9653 km)*	496 000 lb *(224 980 kg)*	400

Name of Aircraft**	Nationality	No. in service	Wingspan	Length	Max. cruising speed	Range with max. payload	Max. takeoff weight	Max. seating capacity
Airbus A300B (A300B4-200)	International	238	147 ft 1 in (44·84 m)	175 ft 11 in (53·62 m)	492 knots (911 km/h)	2750 naut miles[6] (5095 km)	363 760 lb (165 000 kg)	336
BAC One-eleven (Srs 500)	UK	210	93 ft 6 in (28·50 m)	107 ft 0 in (32·61 m)	470 knots (871 km/h)	1480 naut miles (2744 km)	104 500 lb (47 400 kg)	119
Antonov AN 24/-26 (An 26)	USSR	107	95 ft 10 in (29·20 m)	78 ft 1 in (23·80 m)	237 knots (440 km/h)	594 naut miles (1100 km)	52 911 lb (24 000 kg)	40
Tupolev Tu-154(−154B)	USSR	49	123 ft 3 in (37·55 m)	157 ft 1¾ in (47·90 m)	513 knots (950 km/h)	1485 naut miles[5] (2750 km)	211 650 lb) (96 000 kg)	169
Ilyushin IL-18 (11-18D)	USSR	47	122 ft 9 in (37·40 m)	117 ft 9½ in (35·90 m)	364 knots (675 km/h)	1997 naut miles (3700 km)	141 095 lb (64 000 kg)	110[4]
BAC/Aérospatiale Concorde	International	14	83 ft 10 in (25·56 m)	203 ft 9 in (62·10 m)	1176 knots (2179 km/h)	3360 naut miles (6230 km)	408 000 lb (185 065 kg)	128

* No details available for Fokker F28.
**Scheduled and non-circulated services including all-freight. Specifications apply to version in brackets.
[1] Range quoted with max. fuel.
[2] With 147 passengers.
[3] With 442 passegers.
[4] 122 seats in summer with wardrobes deleted.
[5] With 52 passegers.
[6] With 269 passengers.

MAJOR WORLD AIRLINES (ICAO STATISTICS 1983)

Airline	Passenger km (000)	Aircraft km (100)	Passengerrs carried (000)	Aircraft departures
Aeroflot, USSR	176 799 900	122 390 (est.)	109 483 781	52 592 (est.)
United Airlines, USA	70 478 226	610 589	38 267 068	458 075
American Airlines USA	50 397 984	443 030	28 842 686	326 031
Pan American World Airways, USA	48 464 348	282 166	15 199 679	144 255
Eastern Airlines USA	45 587 420	487 098	37 431 110	514 922
Transworld Airlines (TWA), USA	43 873 548	305 547	18 640 216	195 233
Delta Airlines USA	43 078 743	450 048	36 947 666	509 722
British Airways, UK	34 812 358	214 819	14 259 539	167 131
Japan Airlines (JAL), Japan	32 695 163	178 003	13 717 592	76 111
Northwest Airlines, USA	29 036 295	216 994	12 904 157	168 336
Air France, France	27 710 514	182 584	11 715 494	133 312
Lufthansa, Germany	22 852 517	208 901	13 134 493	195 707
Air Canada, Canada	20 480 551	201 978	10 502 637	164 268
Singapore Int. Airlines, Singapore	18 544 115	70 864	4 545 292	34 686
All Nippon Airways, (ANA) Japan	17 190 937	117 400	22 136 357	168 901
KLM-Royal Dutch Airlines, Netherlands	16 647 273	108 507	4 582 464	65 605
Iberia, Lineas Areas de Espana, Spain	15 806 614	146 268	12 866 458	160 257
Republic Airlines, USA	15 574 399	269 916	17 898 725	452 246
Western Airlines, USA	15 094 739	159 145	13 388 906	162 970
Saudia Airlines, Saudi Arabia	14 981 824	115 282	10 936 631	108 849
Continental Airlines, USA	14 957 635	178 296	10 353 533	168 800
Quantas Airways, Australia	14 362 062	64 184	2 094 961	16 972
Alitalia, Italy	12 752 121	95 462	7 410 096	85 104
Swissair, Switzerland	12 252 727	98 434	6 105 491	89 842
US Airlines, USA	11 871 507	181 599	16 630 155	316 153
CP Air, Canada	10 871 207	72 957	3 694 179	47 682
Frontier Airlines, USA	10 557 252	94 558	6 457 565	138 884
Air New Zealand, New Zealand	10 035 575	44 361	3 102 125	68 241
Cathay Pacific Airlines, Hong Kong	9 655 507	40 963	3 238 690	19 734
Korean Airlines, Korea	9 275 395	58 074	3 612 549	31 340
South African Airways (SAA), South Africa	8 663 323	66 837	3 851 879	56 424
Air India, India	8 484 549	46 114	1 818 051	18 217
Thai International Airlines, Thailand	7 794 669	42 616	2 208 541	17 157
Pakistan International Airlines, Pakistan	7 656 537	34 235	2 571 704	32 986
Malaysian Air Services, Malaysia	7 616 981	41 719	4 904 620	87 777
Varig International, Brazil	7 322 761	71 478	3 751 557	61 904

WORLD'S MAJOR AIRPORTS 1984

Airport name and location	Terminal passengers (000)	International passengers (000)	Air transport movements (000)	Cargo (000 tonnes)
O'Hare International, Chicago, Ill., USA	44 028	3177	732	614
Hartfield Int., Atlanta, Ga., USA	38 989	na	na	na
Los Angeles Int., Calif, USA	34 394	5397	548	722
Dallas/Fort Worth Regional, Texas, USA	32 267	487	526	269
John F. Kennedy Int., New York, USA	29 935	16 334	318	1121
Heathrow Airport, London, UK	29 164	24 105	297	541
Stapleton Int. Denver, Colorado, USA	28 806	na	na	na
Tokyo Int. (Hameda), Tokyo, Japan	26 377	471	158	279
San Francisco Int., Calif., USA	24 193	2474	362	388
Newark International, NY, USA	23 654	1001	355	206
La Guardia Airport, NY, USA	20 303	na	356	43

Airport name and location	Terminal passengers (000)	International passengers (000)	Air transport movements (000)	Cargo (000 tonnes)
Logan Int., Boston, Mass., USA	19 418	2134	343	252
Miami Int. Airport, Florida, USA	19 328	6986	353	470
Flughafen Frankfurt Main, Frankfurt, Germany	18 297	13 348	212	686
Osaka Int. Airport, Osaka, Japan	17 670	3355	127	128
Aeroport de Paris, Orly, Paris, France	17 174	7311	158	205
Lambert Airport, St Louis, Missouri, USA	16 629	na	na	na
Honolulu Int. Airport, Oahu, USA	16 551	2371	344	199
Toronto Int. (Pearson), Toronto, Canada	14 752	na	na	na
Washington National, Washington DC, USA	14 574	na	na	na

International information: distance in kilometres between airports

	Athens	Bahrain	Bangkok	Bombay	Buenos Aires	Cairo	Chicago	Copenhagen	Frankfurt	Hong Kong	Johannesburg	Karachi	Lagos	Lima	London	Madrid	Manila	Mexico City	Montreal	Moscow	Nairobi	New York	Paris	Peking (Beijing)	Rio de Janeiro	Rome	San Francisco	Singapore	Sydney	Tehran	Tokyo	Vancouver
Athens		2829	7916	5164	11699	1117	8758	2136	1807	8541	7131	4320	4043	11762	2414	2359	9637	11274	7616	2251	4564	7914	2093	7617	9704	1047	10918	9053	15315	2458	9543	9792
Bahrain	2829		5358	2411	13293	1929		4461	4437	6389	6297	1661	5457	14333	5090	5185	7364	13963		3467	3399	10614	4822	6182	11460	3862		6326	12504	1048	8314	
Bangkok	7916	5358		3008	16877	7249		8601	8963	1719	8989	3701	10604	19676	9540	10157	2199	15717	13378	7069	7207	13912	9433	3296	16073	8814	12730	1443	7538	5457	4642	11782
Bombay	5164	2411	3008		14935	4339	12934		6564	4298		876	7617		7207	7512	5132		12069	5047	4529	12523	6999	4763		6160		3917	10152	2803	6782	
Buenos Aires	11699	13293	16877	14935		11844	9043	12086	11494	18443	8109	14716	7932	3151	11129	10079	11745	7391	9051	13488	10411	8528	11062	19277	1996	11170	10395	15867	11760	13781	18285	11297
Cairo	1117	1929	7249	4339	11844		9866	3197	2922	8123	6258	3556	3927	12435	3531	3349	9162	12363	8722	2913	3540	9009	3204	7530	9893	2125	11994	8255	14395	1955	9588	10835
Chicago	8758			12934	9043	9866		6849	6966		14009				6343		13062	2718	1198	7968		1187	6665	10554		7734		15039	14857		10067	2828
Copenhagen	2136	4461	8601		12086	3197	6849		678	8662	9204	5537	5511	11086	982	2058	9780	9507	5799	1539	6699	6184	1035	7191	10178	1535	8801	9959	16031	3657	8706	7657
Frankfurt	1807	4437	8963	6564	11494	2922	6966	678		9165	8684	5690	4853	10717	654	1420	10290	9545	5851	2021	6312	6185	471	7783	9560	966	9142	10270	16484	3765	9360	8057
Hong Kong	8541	6389	1719	4298	18443	8123		8662	9165		10694	4775	11835	18344	9640	10519	1125	14122	12425	7149	8750	12956	9627	1985	17687	9271	11097	2576	7374	6186	2936	10245
Johannesburg	7131	6297	8989		8109	6258	14009	9204	8684	10694		7041	4522	10901	9068	8097	10975	14588	12962	9164	2910	12822	8707	11699	7146	7718	16966	8649	11019	7283	13513	
Karachi	4320	1661	3701	876	14716	3556		5537	5690	4775	7041				6334	6658	5716		11241	4202	4367	11675	6128	4862	13004	5303	12983		11003	1930	6969	11706
Lagos	4043	5457	10604	7617	7932	3927		5511	4853	11835	4522				5000	3827			8498	6251	3828	8440	4685	11455	6022	4018		11160		5850	13506	11938
Lima	11762	14333	19676		3151	12435		11086	10717	18344	10901				10143	9520		4241	6419	12620		5861	10248	16605	3776	10834	7255	18812			15413	8154
London	2414	5090	9540	7207	11129	3531	6343	982	654	9640	9068	6334	5000	10143		1244	10759	8901	5213	2506	6830	5536	365	8148	9245	1460	8610	10873	17008	4411	9585	7574
Madrid	2359	5185	10157	7512	10079	3349		2058	1420	10519	8097	6658	3827	9520	1244		11644	9063	5550	3418	6189	5758	1031	9199	8140	1360		11373	17661	4753	10764	8422
Manila	9637	7364	2199	5132	11745	9162	13062	9780	10290	1125	10975	5716			10759	11644		14218		8273	9401	13686	10752	2873	18107	10390	11221	2373	6258	7247	2993	
Mexico City	11274	13963	15717		7391	12363	2718	9507	9545	14122	14588			4241	8901	9063	14218		3712	10683		3366	9195	12427	7661		3027	16587	12978		11247	3940
Montreal	7616		13378	12069	9051	8722	1198	5799	5851	12425	12962	11241	8498	6419	5213	5550		3712		7036	11701	536	5523	10440	8189	6605	4072	14794	16011	9433	10384	3679
Moscow	2251	3467	7069	5047	13488	2913	7968	1539	2021	7149	9164	4202	6251	12620	2506	3418	8273	10683	7036		6366	7477	2479	5802	11526	2397		8443		2486	7502	8180
Nairobi	4564	3399	7207	4529	10411	3540		6699	6312	8750	2910	4367	3828		6830	6189	9401		11701	6366		11828	6475	9219	8937	5380	15446	7456	12128	4374	11296	
New York	7914	10614	13912	12523	8528	9009	1187	6184	6185	12956	12822	11675	8440	5861	5536	5758	13686	3366	536	7477	11828		5829	10971	7723	6886	4149	15329	16002	9839	10824	3926
Paris	2093	4822	9433	6999	11062	3204	6665	1035	471	9627	8707	6128	4685	10248	365	1031	10752	9195	5523	2479	6475	5829		8214	9144	1100	8971	10728	16954	4198	9736	7938
Peking (Beijing)	7617	6182	3296	4763	19277	7530	10554	7191	7783	1985	11699	4862	11455	16605	8148	9199	2873	12427	10440	5802	9219	10971	8214		17302	8120		4486		5617	2132	8487
Rio de Janeiro	9704	11460	16073		1996	9893		10178	9560	17687	7146	13004	6022	3776	9245	8140	18107	7661	8189	11526	8937	7723	9144	17302		9186	10633	15738	13516		18519	11206
Rome	1047	3862	8814	6160	11170	2125	7734	1535	966	9271	7718	5303	4018	10834	1460	1360	10390		6605	2397	5380	6886	1100	8120	9186		10052	10010	16302	3396	9880	9007
San Francisco	10918		12730		10395	11994		8801	9142	11097	16966	12983		7255	8610		11221	3027	4072		15446	4149	8971		10633	10052		13579	11941	11829	8222	1286
Singapore	9053	6326	1443	3917	15867	8255	15039	9959	10270	2576	8649		11160	18812	10873	11373	2373	16587	14794	8443	7456	15329	10728	4486	15738	10010	13579		6296	6615	5361	12811
Sydney	15315	12504	7538	10152	11760	14395	14857	16031	16484	7374	11019	11003			17008	17661	6258	12978	16011		12128	16002	16954		13516	16302	11941	6296		12909	7826	12492
Tehran	2458	1048	5457	2803	13781	1955		3657	3765	6186	7283	1930	5850		4411	4753	7247		9433	2486	4374	9839	4198	5617		3396	11829	6615	12909		7713	10556
Tokyo	9543	8314	4642	6782	18285	9588	10067	8706	9360	2936	13513	6969	13506	15413	9585	10764	2993	11247	10384	7502	11296	10824	9736	2132	18519	9880	8222	5361	7826	7713		7500
Vancouver	9792		11782		11297	10835	2828	7657	8057	10245		11706	11938	8154	7574	8422		3940	3679	8180		3926	7938	8487	11206	9007	1286	12811	12492	10556	7500	

To convert kilometres to miles multiply by 0.62137

MILESTONES IN AVIATION

1717 Earliest 'rational' design published by Emmanuel Swedenborg (1688–1772) in Sweden.

1785 7 Jan. First crossing of English Channel by balloon Jean Pierre Blanchard (FRA) and Dr John J Jeffries (USA).

1852 24 Sept. First flight by navigable airship, in France.

1900 2 July. First flight by German Zeppelin airship.

1903 17 Dec. First sustained flight in an aeroplane, by Wright Brothers, near Kitty Hawk, N. Carolina, United States.

1906 12 Nov. First public aeroplane flight in Europe. Alberto Santos-Dumont covers a distance of 220 m *722 ft* near Paris, France.

1909 25 July. Louis Blériot (FRA) completes first aeroplane crossing of the English Channel in 36½ min.

1910 27–8 Aug. Louis Paulhan completes first flight from London to Manchester, in 4 hr 12 min with an overnight stop.

1919 14–15 June. Capt John William Alcock and Lieut Arthur Whitten Brown complete first non-stop crossing of the Atlantic in 16 hr 27 min.

1919 12 Nov.–10 Dec. Capt Ross Smith and Lieut Keith Smith complete first flight from United Kingdom (Hounslow) to Australia (Darwin).

1924 1 Apr. Imperial Airways formed in Great Britain.

1927 20–21 May. First solo non-stop trans-atlantic flight (eastbound) by Charles A Lindbergh (US) in Ryan monoplane in 33 hr 29½ min.

1928 15 May. Inauguration of Australia's Flying Doctor Service.

1928 31 May–9 June. First trans-Pacific flight from San Francisco to Brisbane, by Capt Charles Kingsford Smith and C T P Ulm.

1929 30 March. First commercial air route between London and Karachi inaugurated by Imperial Airways.

1929 8–29 Aug. The first airship flight around the world was made by the German *Graf Zeppelin*, commanded by Dr Hugo Eckener.

1934 8 Dec. The first weekly air mail service between England and Australia was started.

1935 13 April. The first through passenger service by air from England to Australia was initiated.

1935 22 Nov. The first scheduled air mail flight across the Pacific was flown, from San Francisco to Manila, Philippines.

1937 12 Apr. First test-bed run of a jet engine by Fl Off Frank Whittle (GB).

1939 28 June. Inauguration of Pan American's transatlantic New York–Southampton flying-boat service.

1939 27 Aug. First turbo-jet test flight by Fl Kapt Erich Warsitz in He 178 at Marienche, Germany.

1947 14 Oct. First supersonic flight by Capt Charles E Yeager USAF in Bell XS-1 over Maroc, California, USA.

1949 21 June. First flight of a turbojet-powered airliner, the de Havilland Comet 1. (Entered service 2 May 1952.)

1950 29 July. A Vickers Viscount made the world's first scheduled passenger service by a turbine-powered airliner.

1957 19 Dec. The first transatlantic passenger service to be flown by turbine-powered airliners was inaugurated by BOAC with Bristol Britannia aircraft.

1958 4 Oct. The first transatlantic service to be flown by a turbojet-powered airliner was inaugurated by a de Havilland Comet 4 of BOAC.

1968 31 Dec. First flight of the Russian supersonic airliner, the Tupolev TU-144.

1969 9 Feb. First flight of the Boeing 747 'Jumbo-jet'. (Entered service 21 Jan. 1970.)

1969 2 March. First flight of BAC/Aérospatiale Concorde. (Entered scheduled service with Air France and British Airways 21 Jan. 1976.)

1974 1 Sept. Lockheed SR-71A flew the North Atlantic in 1 hr 54 min 56·4 sec.

1977 26 Sept. Laker Airways inaugurated transatlantic cheap fare Skytrain.

1978 12–17 Aug. First crossing of the North Atlantic by a balloon, the American Yost HB-72 *Double Eagle II*, crewed by Ben L Abruzzo, Maxie L Anderson and Larry M Newman.

1979 12 June. First crossing of the English Channel by a man-powered aircraft, Dr Paul MacCready's *Gossamer Albatross*, powered/piloted by Bryan Allen.

1980 5 Dec. Dr Paul MacCready's solar-powered aircraft, *Solar Challenger*, recorded a first significant solar-powered flight of 1 hr 32 min.

1981 14 Apr. The NASA space shuttle *Columbia* made an unpowered, but otherwise conventional landing by a heavier-than-air craft, on the dry bed of Rogers Lake at Edwards Air Force Base, California, after a space mission involving 54 hr 20 min in Earth orbit.

1981 7 July. Piloted by Steve Ptacek, Dr Paul MacCready's *Solar Challenger* became the first solar-powered aircraft to make a crossing of the English Channel, flying from Cormeille-en-Vexin, France, to Manston, Kent.

1986 9 Dec. The strange-looking 2000-lb *900-kg Voyager*, piloted by Dick Rutan and Jeana Yaeger, become the first plane to fly around the Earth without stopping and without refuelling. It took off from the Mojave Desert and landed back there 9 days 3 minutes and 44 seconds later, on the day before Christmas Eve.

Rail

A railway may be defined as a track which guides vehicles travelling along it. Such tracks, formed of parallel lines of stone blocks with grooves in the centres, date back to Babylonian times, about 2245 BC, and can still be found in south-eastern Europe. The word 'railway' was first recorded in 1681 at Pensnett near Stourbridge, West Midlands. 'Railroad' was first used at Rowton near Coalport, Shropshire, in 1702. Both words were used in Britain until about 1850 after which 'railway' was adopted. In the USA 'railroad' became widely, though not universally, used. The first positive record of the use of steam power on a railway was in 1804 when a locomotive built by Richard Trevithick hauled a train at Penydarren Ironworks in South Wales. The first railway to be operated entirely by steam engines from its opening was the Liverpool & Manchester, on 15 September 1830.

The 'standard guage' of 1435 mm (4 ft 8½ in) was first established on the Willington Colliery wagonway near Newcastle upon Tyne in 1764–5. Today this guage is standard in Great Britain, Canada, the USA, Mexico, Europe (except Ireland, Spain, Portugal, Finland and the USSR), North Africa, the Near East countries, Australian National Railways and New South Wales, China, Korea and the Japanese Shinkansen lines. In South America it is found in Paraguay, Uraguay, the Argentine Urquiza system, Central and Southern Railways of Peru, Venezuela and short lines in Brazil.

PRINCIPAL RAILWAY SYSTEMS OF THE WORLD

Railway system	Year of first railway	Gauge mm	ft	in	Route length km	miles
Argentina	1857	1676	5	6	22 101	13 733
		1435	4	8½	3 088	1 919
		1000	3	3⅜	11 844	7 359
		750	2	5½	285	177
					37 318	23 188
Australia	1854	1600	5	3	8 396	5 217
		1435	4	8½	14 243	8 850
		1067	3	6	16 749	10 407
					39 388	24 474
Brazil	1854	1600	5	3	3 385	2 104
		1000	3	3⅜	25 330	15 739
		762	2	6	202	126
					28 917	17 969
Canada	1836	1435	4	8½	68 023	42 267
		1067	3	6	1 146	712
		915	3	0	178	111
					69 347	43 090
Chile	1851	1676	5	6	4 282	2 661
		1435	4	8½	370	230
		1000	3	3⅜	3 300	2 050
					7 952	4 941
China	1880	1435	4	8½	c. 50 000	c. 31 000
Czechoslovakia	1839	1435	4	8½	13 029	8 095
France	1832	1435	4	8½	34 362	21 351
Germany	1835					
Federal (West)		1435	4	8½	28 450	17 678
State (East)		1435	4	8½	14 215	8 833
					42 665	26 511
Great Britain	1830	1435	4	8½	17 229	10 706
		600	1	11½	19	12
India	1853	1676	5	6	31 789	19 753
		1000	3	3⅜	25 209	15 664
		762	2	6	3 521	2 188
		610	2	0	390	242
					60 909	37 847
Italy	1839	1435	4	8½	16 133	10 024
Japan	1872	1435	4	8½	1 177	731
		1067	3	6	20 145	12 517
					21 322	13 248
Mexico	1850	1435	4	8½	14 223	8 838
		913	3	0	451	280
					14 674	9 118
Pakistan	1861	1676	5	6	7 754	4 818
		1000	3	3⅜	444	276
		762	2	6	610	379
					8 808	5 473
Poland	1842	1435	4	8½	23 855	14 822
Romania	1869	1435	4	8½	10 515	6 534
		762	2	6	568	353
		610	2	0		
					11 083	6 887
South Africa	1860	1065	3	6	22 891	14 223
		610	2	0	705	438
					23 596	14 661

Railway system	Year of first railway	Gauge mm	ft	in	Route length km	miles
Spain	1848	1668	5	6	13 531	8 407
Sweden	1856	1435	4	8½	11 158	6933
		891	2	11	182	113
					11 340	7046
Turkey	1896	1435	4	8½	8 140	5 857
USA	1830	1435	4	8½	294 625	183 077

Railway system	Year of first railway	Gauge mm	ft	in	Route length km	miles
USSR	1837	1520	4	11	c. 140 000	c. 87 000
Yugoslavia	1846	1435	4	8½	9 762	6066

The modern standard system of railway electrification at 25 kV 50 Hz was first used in France in 1950 and in England, on the Colchester – Clacton – Walton lines, in 1959.

Road Transport

Average Mileage
The average estimated mileage for a car in the UK rose from 8700 miles *14 000 km* per year in 1970 to 9500 miles *15 300 km* per year in 1978.

Car ownership
Car ownership per 1000 inhabitants in the UK in 1984 was 284·22, or a total of 16 055 000 cars.

Petrol prices
Petrol prices for four-star petrol rose from 32½ p in 1970 to 76½ p per gallon in 1978. The price reached its peak in the 1985 Budget when it reached £2 a gallon, then dropped sharply in 1986 as crude oil prices plummetted as a result of a world recession and overproduction. Since then the price has fluctuated according to market trends, in March 1987 standing at 175 p per gallon.

Accidents
The cumulative total of fatalities since the first in the UK on 17 Aug. 1896 surpassed 250 000 in 1959 and by the end of 1984 it had reached about 399 000. There are only estimated figures for Northern Ireland in the period 1923 and 1930. The peak year for fatalities was 1941 when there were wartime restrictions on the use of headlamps; in that year 9444 people were killed or 26 per day in Great Britain alone. L plates were introduced in May 1935.

Traffic signals: dates of introduction
1868   Parliament Square, Westminster, London, semaphore-arms with red and green gas lamps for night use.
1925   Piccadilly Circus, London, police-operated.
1926   Wolverhampton, Staffordshire, modern type electric.
1932   First vehicle actuation sets introduced.

Right and Left Hand Driving
Of the 221 separately administered countries and territories in the world 58 drive on the left and 163 on the right. In Britain it is believed that left hand driving is a legacy from the preference of passing an approaching horseman or carriage right side to right side to facilitate right armed defence against sudden attack. On the Continent postillions were mounted on the rearmost left horse in a team and thus preferred to pass left side to left side. While some countries have transferred from left to right the only case recorded of a transfer from right to left is in Okinawa on 30 July 1978.

Purchase and Value Added Tax on cars

Oct.	1940	33⅓*	Nov.	1962	25
June	1947	33⅓*	July	1966	27½
Apr.	1950	33⅓	Apr.	1973	
Apr.	1951	66⅔	*Purchase tax*		
Apr.	1953	50	*replaced by VAT*		
Oct.	1955	60	Apr.	1973	10
Apr.	1959	50	Apr.	1974	10
July	1961	55	July	1974	8
Apr.	1962	45	June	1979	15

* 66⅔% if retail value exceeded £1280.

UNITED KINGDOM MOTOR VEHICLES AND ROADS

Year	No. of Vehicles	Roads Miles	km	Motorways miles	km	Road per vehicle yds	m	Fatalities
1904	c. 18 000	c. 176 000	283 200	—	—	—	—	—
1914	388 860	c. 176 000	283 200	—	—	796	727·8	—
1920	c. 652 000	c. 176·000	283 200	—	—	475	434·3	—
1925	1 538 235	c. 178 000	286 400	—	—	203	185·6	—
1930	2 309 515	179 286	288 532	—	—	136·7	124·9	c. 7400
1939	3 208 410	180 527	290 530	—	—	99·0	90·5	8419
1945	1 654 364	c. 183 000	294 500	—	—	194·7	178	5380
1950	4 511 626	197 076	317 163	—	—	77·1	70·5	5156
1960	9 610 432	207 939	334 645	95	152·8	38·1	34·8	7142
1980	18 644 210	210 937	339 471	1589	2557	19·9	18·2	5953
1981	18 663 565	212 341	341 730	1630	2623	20·0	18·3	5844
1982	18 683 335	213 333	343 327	1653	2661	20·1	18·4	5934
1983	18 703 551	214 393	345 032	1683	2709	20·2	18·4	5445
1984	18 724 324	215 536	346 872	1736	2794	20·3	18·5	5599

Notes: Vehicles surpassed 1 million early in 1923. Cars surpassed 1 million early in 1930, 5 million early in 1949. Motor cycles (including mopeds, scooters and three-wheelers) surpassed 1 million in 1953. Trams reached their peak in 1927 with 14413 and sank by 1965 to 110. Diesel vehicles surpassed 25% of all goods vehicles in 1961 (2·1% in 1935) and 35% in 1965. The road mileage includes Trunk roads, Class I, Class II and Unclassified. Statistics prior to 1925 apply to Great Britain only. The earliest dual carriageway was the Southend arterial in 1937 though parts of both the Great West Road and the Kingston by-pass were converted to separate carriageways in 1936.

International vehicle registration letters

A	Austria
ADN	Yemen, People's Democratic Republic
AFG	Afghanistan
AL	Albania
AND	Andorra
AUS	Australia
B	Belgium
BD	Bangladesh
BDS	Barbadas
BG	Bulgaria
BH	Belize
BR	Brazil
BRN	Bahrain
BRU	Brunei
BS	Bahamas
BUR	Burma
C	Cuba
CDN	Canada
CH	Switzerland
CI	Ivory Coast
CL	Sri Lanka
CO	Colombia
CR	Costa Rica
CS	Czechoslovakia
CY	Cyprus
D	Germany, Federal Republic
DDR	German Democratic Republic
DK	Denmark
DOM	Dominican Republic
DY	Benin
DZ	Algeria
E	Spain, Balearic Islands, Canary Islands, Spanish Guinea, Spanish Sahara
EAK	Kenya
EAT	Tanganyika (Tanzania)
EAU	Uganda
EAZ	Zanzibar (Tanzania)
EC	Ecuador
ES	El Salvador
ET	United Arab Republic (Egypt)
ETH	Ethiopia
F	France and territories
FJI	Fiji
FL	Liechtenstein
FR	Faroe Islands
GB	Great Britain and Northern Ireland
GBA	Alderney
GBG	Guernsey
GBJ	Jersey
GBM	Isle of Man
GBZ	Gibraltar
GCA	Guatemala
GH	Ghana
GR	Greece
GUY	Guyana
H	Hungary
HK	Hong Kong
HKJ	Jordan
I	Italy
IL	Israel
IND	India
IR	Iran
IRL	Republic of Ireland
IRQ	Iraq
IS	Iceland
J	Japan
JA	Jamaica
K	Kampuchea
KWT	Kuwait
L	Luxemburg
LAO	Lao, People's Democratic Republic
LAR	Libya
LB	Liberia
LS	Lesotho
M	Malta
MA	Morocco
MAL	Malaysia
MC	Monaco

MEX	Mexico	**RH**	Haiti	**TG**	Togo
MS	Mauritius	**RI**	Indonesia	**TN**	Tunisia
MW	Malawi (Nyasaland)	**RIM**	Mauritania	**TR**	Turkey
		RL	Lebanon	**TT**	Trinidad and Tobago
N	Norway	**RM**	Madagascar		
NA	Netherlands Antilles	**RMM**	Mali	**USA**	United States of America
NIC	Nicaragua	**RN**	Niger		
NL	Netherlands	**RO**	Romania	**V**	Vatican City
NZ	New Zealand	**ROK**	Republic of Korea	**VN**	Viet-Nam
		ROU	Uruguay		
P	Portugal, Cape Verde Islands, Moz-	**RP**	Philippines	**WAG**	Gambia
	ambique, Portuguese Guinea, Por-	**RSM**	San Marino	**WAL**	Sierra Leone
	tugese Timor, Angola, Sao Tome, and	**RU**	Burundi	**WAN**	Nigeria
	Principe Islands	**RWA**	Republic of Rwanda	**WD**	Dominica (Leeward Islands)
PA	Panama			**WG**	Grenada (Windward Islands)
PAK	Pakistan	**S**	Sweden	**WL**	St Lucia (Windward Islands)
PE	Peru	**SD**	Swaziland	**WS**	Western Samoa
PL	Poland	**SF**	Finland	**WV**	St Vincent and the Grenadines (Wind-
PNG	Papua New Guinea	**SGP**	Singapore		ward Islands)
PY	Paraguay	**SME**	Suriname		
		SN	Senegal	**YU**	Yugoslavia
RA	Argentina	**SU**	Union of Soviet Socialist Republics	**YV**	Venezuela
RB	Botswana (Bechuanaland)	**SWAZA**	Namibia		
RC	Taiwan	**SY**	Seychelles	**Z**	Zambia
RCA	Central African Republic	**SYR**	Syria	**ZA**	South Africa
RCB	Congo (Brazzaville)			**ZRE**	Zaire
RCH	Chile	**T**	Thailand	**ZW**	Zimbabwe

Spaceflight

Manned spaceflights

1 USSR 1
12 April 1961
Vostok 1
Yuri Gagarin
1 hr 48 min
Landed separately from craft.

2 USA 1
5 May 1961
Freedom 7
Alan Shepard
15 min 28 sec
Suborbital; splashdown.

3 USA 2
21 July 1961
Liberty Bell 7
Gus Grissom
15 min 37 sec
Spacecraft sank,

4 USSR 2
6 August 1961
Vostok 2
Gherman Titov
1 day 1 hr 18 min
At 25, youngest person in space.

5 USA 3
20 February 1962
Friendship 7
John Glenn
4 hr 55 min 23 sec
First American to orbit.

6 USA 4
24 May 1962
Aurora 7
Scott Carpenter
4 hr 56 min 5 sec
Landing overshoot of 250 miles.

7 USSR 3
11 August 1962
Vostok 3
Andrian Nikolyev
3 day 22 hr 22 min
Bachelor in space.

8 USSR 4
12 August 1962
Vostok 4
Pavel Popovich
2 day 22 hr 57 sec
Came to within four miles of Vostok 3.

9 USA 5
3 October 1962
Sigma 7
Wally Schirra
9 hr 13 min 11 sec
Pacific splashdown.

10 USA 6
15 May 1963
Faith 7
Gordon Cooper
1 day 10 hr 19 min 49 sec
Final US one-man flight.

11 USSR 5
14 June 1963
Vostok 5
Valeri Bykovsky
4 day 23 hr 6 min
Solo flight record-holder.

12 USSR 6
16 June 1963
Vostok 6
Valentina Tereshkova
2 day 22 hr 50 min
First woman in space.

13 USSR 7
12 October 1964
Voskhod 1
Vladimir Komarov, Konstantin Feoktistov, Boris Yegerov
1 day 0 hr 17 min 3 sec
Riskiest flight, no spacesuits, no ejection seats, inside a 'Vostok'.

14 USSR 8
18 March 1965
Voskhod 2
Pavel Belayev, Alexei Leonov

1 day 2 hr 2 min 17 sec
Leonov makes first walk in space.

15 USA 7
25 March 1965
Gemini 3
Gus Grissom, John Young
4 hr 52 min 51 sec
Grissom first man in space twice.

16 USA 8
3 June 1965
Gemini 4
James McDevitt, Edward White
4 day 1 hr 56 min 12 sec
White walks in space.

17 USA 9
21 August 1965
Gemini 5
Gordon Cooper, Charles Conrad
7 day 22 hr 55 min 14 sec
Breaks endurance record.

18 USA 10
4 December 1965
Gemini 7
Frank Borman, James Lovell
13 day 18 hr 35 min 1 sec
Acted as rendezvous target; breaks endurance record.

19 USA 11
15 December 1965
Gemini 6
Wally Schirra, Tom Stafford
1 day 1 hr 51 min 54 sec
First rendezvous in space.

20 USA 12
16 March 1966
Gemini 8
Neil Armstrong, David Scott
10 hr 41 min 26 sec
Emergency landing after first space docking.

21 USA 13
3 June 1966
Gemini 9
Tom Stafford, Eugene Cernan
3 day 0 hr 20 min 50 sec
Rendezvous; spacewalk; bullseye splashdown.

22 USA 14
18 July 1966
Gemini 10
John Young, Michael Collins
2 day 22 hr 46 min 39 sec
Docking; spacewalk; record altitude of 474 miles *763 km.*

23 USA 15
12 September 1966
Gemini 11
Charles Conrad, Richard Gordon
2 day 23 hr 17 min 8 sec
Docking; spacewalk; altitude of 850 miles *1368 km*; automatic landing.

24 USA 16
11 November 1966
Gemini 12
James Lovell, Edwin Aldrin
3 day 22 hr 34 min 31 sec
Docking; record spacewalk of over 2 hr.

USA
27 January 1967
Apollo 1
Gus Grissom, Edward White, Roger Chaffee
Killed in spacecraft fire.

25 USSR 9
23 April 1967
Soyuz 1
Vladimir Komarov
1 day 2 hr 47 min 52 sec
Komarov killed when parachute fails; intended to dock with Soyuz 2.

USSR
24 April 1967
Soyuz 2
Valeri Bykovsky, Alexei Yeliseyev and Yevgeny Khrunov
Flight cancelled; was to have docked with Soyuz 1 but this craft had problems.

26 USA 17
11 October 1968
Apollo 7
Wally Schirra, Donn Eisele, Walt Cunningham
10 day 20 hr 9 min 3 sec
Earth orbit shakedown of Command and Service Module.

27 USSR 10
26 October 1968
Soyuz 3
Georgi Beregovoi
3 day 22 hr 50 min 45 sec
Failed to dock with unmanned Soyuz 2.

USSR
December 1968
Zond
Pavel Belayev
Circumlunar flight cancelled.

28 USA 18
21 December 1968
Apollo 8
Frank Borman, James Lovell, William Anders
6 day 3 hr 0 min 42 sec
Ten lunar orbits over Christmas.

29 USSR 11
14 January 1969
Soyuz 4
Vladimir Shatalov
2 day 23 hr 20 min 47 sec
Launched with one man, returned with three.

30 USSR 12
15 January 1969
Soyuz 5

Boris Volynov, Alexei Yeleseyev, Yevgeny Khrunov
3 day 0 hr 54 min 15 sec
Yeliseyev and Khrunov spacewalk to Soyuz 4 after docking.

31 USA 19
3 March 1969
Apollo 9
James McDivitt, David Scott, Russell Schweickart
10 day 1 hr 0 min 54 sec
Test of Lunar Module in Earth orbit; spacewalk.

32 USA 20
18 May 1969
Apollo 10
Tom Stafford, John Young, Eugene Cernan
8 day 0 hr 3 min 23 sec
Lunar Module tested in lunar orbit; came to 9 miles *14·5 km* of surface of Moon.

33 USA 21
16 July 1969
Apollo 11
Neil Armstrong, Michael Collins, Edwin Aldrin
8 day 3 hr 18 min 35 sec
Armstrong and Aldrin walk on Moon for over 2 hours.

34 USSR 13
11 October 1969
Soyuz 6
Georgi Shonin, Valeri Kubasov
4 day 22 hr 42 min 47 sec
Welding tests.

35 USSR 14
12 October 1969
Soyuz 7
Anatoli Filipchenko, Vladislav Volkov, Viktor Gorbatko
4 day 22 hr 40 min 23 sec
Rendezvous to within 1600 feet *488 m* of Soyuz 8.

36 USSR 15
13 October 1969
Soyuz 8
Vladimir Shatalov, Alexei Yeliseyev
4 day 22 hr 50 min 49 sec
Third flight in strange troika mission by Soviets.

37 USA 22
14 November 1969
Apollo 12
Charles Conrad, Richard Gordon, Alan Bean
10 day 4 hr 36 min 25 sec
Pinpoint landing near Surveyor.

38 USA 23
11 April 1970
Apollo 13
James Lovell, Jack Swigert, Fred Haise
5 day 22 hr 54 min 41 sec
Service module exploded 55 hours into mission; crew limped home using Lunar Module as lifeboat.

39 USSR 16
1 June 1970
Soyuz 9.
Andiran Nikolyev, Vitali Sevastyanov
17 day 16 hr 58 min 50 sec
Crew carried from craft on stretchers suffering acute stress of readapting to gravity after longest flight.

40 USA 24
31 January 1971
Apollo 14
Alan Shepard, Stuart Roosa, Edgar Mitchell
9 day 0 hr 1 min 57 sec
Shepard only Mercury Astronaut to walk on Moon.

41 USSR 17
23 April 1971
Soyuz 10
Vladimir Shatalov, Alexei Yeliseyev, Nikolai Ruckavishnikov

1 day 23 hr 45 min 54 sec
Failed to enter Salyut 1 space station after soft docking.

42 USSR 18
6 June 1971
Soyuz 11
Georgi Dobrovolsky, Vladislav Volkov, Viktor Patsayev
23 day 18 hr 21 min 43 sec
Crew died as craft depressurized before re-entry; not wearing spacesuits.

43 USA 25
26 July 1971
Apollo 15
David Scott, Alfred Worden, James Irwin
12 day 7 hr 11 min 53 sec
First lunar rover.

44 USA 26
16 April 1972
Apollo 16
John Young, Ken Mattingly, Charles Duke
11 day 1 hr 51 min 5 sec
Space Shuttle approved during mission; Mattingley in lunar orbit makes longest solo US flight.

45 USA 27
7 December 1972
Apollo 17
Eugene Cernan, Ron Evans, Jack Schmitt
12 day 13 hr 51 min 59 sec
Last manned expedition to Moon this century?

46 USA 28
25 May 1973
Skylab 2
Charles Conrad, Joe Kerwin, Paul Weitz
28 day 0 hr 49 min 49 sec
Spacewalk to repair severely disabled Skylab 1 space station.

47 USA 29
28 July 1973
Skylab 3
Alan Bean, Owen Garriott, Jack Lousma
59 day 11 hr 9 min 4 sec
Stranded in space temporarily as Command Module malfunctions.

48 USSR 19
27 September 1973
Soyuz 12
Vasili Lazarev, Oleg Makarov
1 day 23 hr 15 min 32 sec
Test of space-station ferry.

49 USA 30
16 November 1973
Skylab 4
Gerry Carr, Edward Gibson, Bill Pogue
84 day 1 hr 15 min 31 sec
Longest US manned spaceflight.

50 USSR 20
18 December 1973
Soyuz 13
Pyotr Klimuk, Valetin Lebedev
7 day 20 hr 55 min 35 sec
Russians and Americans in space together for first time, although they don't meet.

51 USSR 21
3 July 1974
Soyuz 14
Pavel Popvich, Yuri Artyukhin
15 day 17 hr 30 min 28 sec
First space spies, on Salyut 3.

52 USSR 22
26 August 1974
Soyuz 15
Gennadi Serfanov, Lev Demin
2 day 0 hr 12 min 11 sec
Failed to dock with Salyut 3.

53 USSR 23
2 December 1974
Soyuz 16
Anatoli Filipchenko, Nikolai Ruckavishnikov

5 day 22 hr 23 min 35 sec
Rehearsal for US–USSR joint flight, ASTP.

54 USSR 24
11 January 1975
Soyuz 17
Alexei Gubarev, Georgi Grechko
29 day 13 hr 19 min 45 sec
Aboard Salyut 4.

55 USSR 25
5 April 1975
Soyuz 18-1
Vasili Lazarev, Oleg Makarov
21 min 27 sec
Second stage failed; flight aborted.

56 USSR 26
24 May 1975
Soyuz 18
Pyotr Klimuk, Vitali Sevastyanov
62 day 23 hr 20 min 8 sec
Aboard Salyut 4.

57 USSR 27
15 July 1975
Soyuz 19
Alexei Leonov, Valeri Kubasov
5 day 22 hr 30 min 51 sec
Docked with Apollo 18 in joint ASTP mission.

58 USA 31
15 July 1975
Apollo 18
Tom Stafford, Vance Brand, Deke Slayton
9 day 1 hr 28 min 24 sec
Docked with Soyuz 19; flight for Mercury astronaut Slayton at 51; crew gassed during landing, recovered.

59 USSR 28
6 July 1976
Soyuz 21
Boris Volynov, Vitali Zholobov
49 day 6 hr 23 min 32 sec
Evacuated Salyut 5. (Soyuz 20 was Progress tanker test, unmanned.)

60 USSR 29
22 September 1976
Soyuz 22
Valeri Bykovsky, Vladimir Aksyonov
7 day 21 hr 52 min 17 sec
Independent Earth survey flight.

61 USSR 30
14 October 1976
Soyuz 23
Vyacheslav Zudov, Valeri Rozhdestvensky
2 day 0 hr 6 min 35 sec
Failed to dock with Salyut 5; splashed down in lake.

62 USSR 31
7 February 1977
Soyuz 24
Viktor Gorbatko, Yuri Glazkov
17 day 17 hr 25 min 50 sec
Aboard Salyut 5.

63 USSR 32
9 October 1977
Soyuz 25
Vladimir Kovalyonok, Valeri Ryumin
2 day 0 hr 44 min 45 sec
Failed to dock with Salyut 6.

64 USSR 33
10 December 1977
Soyuz 26
Yuri Romanenko, Georgi Grechko
96 day 10 hr 0 min 7 sec
Aboard Salyut 6; broke endurance record.

65 USSR 34
10 January 1978
Soyuz 27
Vladimir Dzhanibekov, Oleg Makarov
5 day 22 hr 58 min 58 sec
Visitors to Salyut 6.

66 USSR 35
2 March 1978
Soyuz 28
Alexei Gubarev, Vladimir Remek
7 day 22 hr 16 min
Remek was from Czechoslovakia, first non-American, non-Russian in space; visit to Salyut 6.

67 USSR 36
15 June 1978
Soyuz 29
Vladimir Kovalyonok, Alexander Ivanchenkov
139 day 14 hr 47 min 32 sec
Aboard Salyut 6; landed in Soyuz 31.

68 USSR 37
27 June 1978
Soyuz 30
Pyotr Klimuk, Miroslaw Hermaszewski
7 day 22 hr 2 min 59 sec
Visit to Salyut 6; Hermaszewski from Poland.

69 USSR 38
26 August 1978
Soyuz 31
Valeri Bykovsky, Sigmund Jahn
7 day 29 hr 49 min 4 sec
Visit to Salyut 6; Jahn from East Germany; landed in Soyuz 29.

70 USSR 39
25 February 1979
Soyuz 32
Vladimir Lyakhov, Valeri Ryumin
175 day 0 hr 35 min 37 sec
Visit to Salyut 6; landed in Soyuz 34 which was launched unmanned.

71 USSR 40
10 April 1979
Soyuz 33
Nikolai Ruckavishnikov, Georgi Ivanov
1 day 23 hr 1 min 6 sec
Failed to dock with Salyut 6; Bulgarian Ivanov only Intercosmos visitor not to reach space station.

72 USSR 41
9 April 1980
Soyuz 35
Leonid Popov, Valeri Ryumin
184 day 20 hr 11 min 35 sec
Salyut 6 mission takes Ryumin to 361 days space experience.

73 USSR 42
26 May 1980
Soyuz 36
Valeri Kubasov, Bertalan Farkas
7 day 20 hr 45 min 44 sec
Visit to Salyut 6; Farkas from Hungary; landed in Soyuz 35.

74 USSR 43
5 June 1980
Soyuz T2
Yuri Malyshev, Vladimir Aksyonov
3 day 22 hr 19 min 30 sec
Test of new Soyuz model to Salyut 6. (Soyuz T1 was unmanned.)

75 USSR 44
23 July 1980
Soyuz 37
Viktor Gorbatko, Pham Tuan
7 day 20 hr 42 min
Visit to Salyut 6; Tuan from Vietnam; landed in Soyuz 36.

76 USSR 45
18 September 1980
Soyuz 38
Yuri Romanenko, Arnaldo Mendez
7 day 20 hr 43 min 24 sec
Visit to Salyut 6; Mendez from Cuba.

77 USSR 46
27 November 1980
Soyuz T3

Leonid Kizim, Oleg Makarov, Gennadi Strekalov
12 day 19 hr 7 min 42 sec
Maintenance crew to Salyut 5; first three-man Soyuz since Soyuz 11 accident.

78 USSR 47
12 March 1981
Soyuz T4
Vladimir Kovalyonok, Viktor Savinykh
74 day 17 hr 37 min 23 sec
Final Salyut 6 long-stay crew; Savinykh 100th person in space.

79 USSR 48
22 March 1981
Soyuz 39
Vladimir Dzhanibvekov, Jugderdemidyin Gurragcha
7 day 20 hr 42 min 3 sec
Salyut 6 visit; Gurragcha from Mongolia.

80 USA 32
12 April 1981
Columbia STS 1
John Young, Bob Crippen
2 day 6 hr 20 min 52 sec
Maiden flight of Space Shuttle.

81 USSR 49
15 May 1981
Soyuz 40
Leonid Popov, Dumitru Prunariu
7 day 20 hr 41 min 52 sec
Final visiting crew to Salyut 6; Prunariu from Romania.

82 USA 33
12 November 1981
Columbia STS 2
Joe Engle, Dick Truly
2 day 6 hr 13 min 11 sec
First flight of used vehicle.

83 USA 34
22 March 1982
Columbia STS 3
Jack Lousma, Gordon Fullerton
8 day 0 hr 4 min 46 sec
Third test flight.

84 USSR 50
13 May 1982
Soyuz T5
Anatoli Berezevoi, Valentin Lebedev
211 day 9 hr 4 min 32 sec
First, record-breaking, visit to Salyut 7.

85 USSR 51
24 June 1982
Soyuz T6
Vladimir Dzhanibekov, Alexander Ivanchenkov, Jean-Loup Chretien
7 day 21 hr 50 min 52 sec
Visit to Salyut 7; Chretien from France, first Western European in space.

86 USA 35
27 June 1982
Columbia STS 4
Ken Mattingly, Hank Hartsfield
7 day 1 hr 9 min 31 sec
Military flight; final test flight.

87 USSR 52
Soyuz T7
Leonid Popov, Alexander Serebrov, Svetlana Savitskaya
7 day 21 hr 52 min 24 sec
Savitskaya second woman in space after 20 years.

88 USA 36
11 November 1982
Columbia STS 5
Vance Brand, Robert Overmyer, Joe Allen, William Lenoir
5 day 2 hr 14 min 26 sec
First commercial mission of Shuttle; deployed two communications satellites; first four-person flight.

89 USA 37
4 April 1983
Challenger STS 6
Paul Weitz, Karol Bobko, Don Peterson, Story Musgrave
5 day 0 hr 23 min 42 sec
Deployed TDRS 1; limped into orbit after upper stage failure; performed spacewalk.

90 USSR 53
20 April 1983
Soyuz T8
Vladimir Titov, Gennadi Strekalov, Alexander Serebrov
2 day 0 hr 17 min 48 sec
Failed to dock with Salyut 7; Titov first spaceman with same name as previous one; Serebrov first person to fly consecutive missions.

91 USA 38
18 June 1983
Challenger STS 7
Bob Crippen, Rick Hauck, John Fabian, Sally Ride, Norman Thagard
6 day 2 hr 24 min 10 sec
Satellite deployment mission is first by five people; includes first US woman in space.

92 USSR 54
27 June 1983
Soyuz T9
Valdimir Lyakhov, Alexander Alexandrov
149 day 10 hr 46 min
Trouble with space station, Salyut 7, halts flight.

93 USA 39
30 August 1983
Challenger STS 8
Richard Truly, Dan Brandenstein, Guion Bluford, Dale Gardner, William Thornton
6 day 1 hr 8 min 40 sec
Night launch and landing.

USSR
27 September 1983
Soyuz T10-1
Vladimir Titov, Gennadi Strekalov
Launcher explodes on pad; crew saved by launch escape system.

94 USA 40
28 November 1983
Columbia STS 9
John Young, Brewster Shaw, Owen Garriott, Robert Parker, Byron Lichtenberg, Ulf Merbold
10 day 7 hr 47 min 23 sec
Flight of European Spacelab 1; Merbold from West Germany; first six-up flight.

95 USA 41
3 February 1984
Challenger STS 41B
Vance Brand, Robert Gibson, Bruce McCandless, Robert Stewart, Ronald McNair
7 day 23 hr 15 min 54 sec
First independent spacewalk using MMU by McCandless; first space mission to end at launch site (Kennedy/Canaveral).

96 USSR 55
8 February 1984
Soyuz T10
Leonid Kizim, Vladimir Solovyov, Oleg Atkov
236 day 22 hr 49 min
Longest manned space mission; Kizim and Solovyov made record six spacewalks.

97 USSR 56
3 April 1984
Soyuz T11
Yuri Malyshev, Gennadi Strekalov, Rakesh Sharma
7 day 21 hr 40 min
Visit to Salyut 7; Sharma from India.

98 USA 42
6 April 1984
Challenger STS 41C
Bob Crippen, Dick Scobee, George Nelson, Terry Hart, James van Hoften
6 day 23 hr 40 min 5 sec

Repaired Solar Max; with Soyuz T10 and T11 crews in space, 11 people are up at once.

99 USSR 57
17 July 1984
Soyuz T12
Vladimir Dhzanibekov, Svetlana Savitskaya, Oleg Volk
11 day 19 hr 14 min 36 sec
Savitskaya becomes first woman spacewalker, outside Salyut 7.

100 USA 43
30 August 1984
Discovery STS 41D
Hank Hartsfield, Michael Coats, Judy Resnik, Steven Hawley, Michael Mullane, Charlie Walker
6 day 0 hr 56 min 4 sec
Launch pad abort in June; three satellites deployed; Walker first industry-engineer astronaut.

101 USA 44
5 October 1984
Challenger STS 41G
Bob Crippen, Jon McBride, Sally Ride, Kathy Sullivan, David Leestma, Marc Garneau, Paul Scully Power
8 day 5 hr 23 min 33 sec
First seven-up flight; first carrying two women; Ride first US woman in space twice; Sullivan first US woman to spacewalk; Garneau from Canada.

102 USA 45
8 November 1984
Discovery STS 51A
Rick Hauck, Dave Walker, Joe Allen, Dale Gardner, Anna Fisher
7 day 23 hr 45 min 54 sec
Two spacewalks to retrieve lost communications satellites and return them to Earth.

103 USA 46
24 January 1985
Discovery STS 51C
Ken Mattingly, Loren Shriver, Ellison Onizuka, James Buchli, Gary Payton
3 day 1 hr 33 min 13 sec
Military mission; Payton first USAF Manned Space Flight Engineer.

104 USA 47
12 April 1985
Discovery STS 51D
Karol Bobko, Don Williams, Rhea Seddon, Jeff Hoffman, David Griggs, Charlie Walker, Jake Garn
6 day 23 hr 55 min 23 sec
Deployed three communications satellites; unscheduled EVA to attempt repair of one; Senator Jake Garn first passenger observer in space.

105 USA 48
29 April 1985
Challenger STS 51B
Bob Overmyer, Fred Gregory, Don Lind, William Thornton, Norman Thagard, Lodewijk van den Berg, Taylor Wang
7 day 0 hr 8 min 50 sec
Spacelab 3 research mission; Lind in space after 19-year wait.

106 USSR 58
6 June 1985
Soyuz T13
Vladimir Dzhanibekov, Viktor Savinykh
112 day 3 hr 12 min
Complete overhaul of Salyut 7 after systems failures; Savinykh came home in Soyuz T14 and Georgi Grechko in Soyuz T13.

107 USA 49
17 June 1985
Discovery STS 51G
Dan Brandenstein, John Creighton, Shannon Lucid, Steve Nagel, John Fabian, Patrick Baudry, Abdul Aziz Al-Saud
7 day 1 hr 38 min 58 sec
Satellite deployment and research mission; first

with three nations represented, Baudry from France (first non-US, non-USSR nation to make two flights), Al Saud a Sultan Prince from Saudi Arabia.

108 USA 50
29 July 1985
Challenger STS 51F
Gordon Fullerton, Roy Bridges, Karl Henize, Anthony England, Story Musgrave, John-David Bartoe, Loren Acton
7 day 22 hr 45 min 27 sec
Launch pad abort on July 12; one engine shutdown during launch, causing abort-to-orbit; Henize oldest man in space at 58; Spacelab 2 research mission.

109 USA 51
27 August 1985
Discovery STS 51I
Joe Engle, Dick Covey, William Fisher, James van Hoften, Mike Lounge
7 day 2 hr 14 min 42 sec
Three satellites deployed; Leasat 3 captured, repaired and redeployed.

110 USSR 59
17 September 1985
Soyuz T14
Vladimir Vasyutin, Georgi Grechko, Alexander Volkov
64 day 21 hr 52 min
Mission cut short after Vasyutin becomes mentally disturbed; Grechko returned in Soyuz T13; Savinykh stayed with Soyuz T14 and clocked up mission time of 168 days.

111 USA 52
3 October 1985
Atlantis STS 51J
Karol Bobko, Ron Grabe, Dale Hilmers, Bob Stewart, William Pailes
4 day 1 hr 45 min 30 sec
Military mission.

112 USA 53
30 October 1985
Challenger STS 61A
Hank Hartsfield, Steve Nagel, Bonnie Dunbar, Guion Gluford, James Buchli, Ernst Messerschmitt, Reinhard Furrer, Wubbo Ockels
7 day 0 hr 44 min 51 sec
West German-funded Spacelab D1 mission; Messerschmitt and Furrer from West Germany; Ockels from Holland; first eight-up mission.

113 USA 54
27 November 1985
Atlantis STS 61B
Brewster Shaw, Bryan O'Connor, Mary Cleave, Jerry Ross, Sherwood Spring, Rudolpho Neri Vela, Charlie Walker
6 day 21 hr 4 min 50 sec
Neri Vela from Mexico; Walker's third flight as Shuttle payload specialist; Ross and Spring assemble structures during EVAs.

114 USA 55
12 January 1986
Columbia STS 61C
Robert Gibson, Charles Bolden, Franklin Chang-Diaz, George Nelson, Steve Hawley, Robert Cenker, Bill Nelson
6 day 2 hr 4 min 9 sec
Much-delayed flight; first with crew members of same name; Bill Nelson, a Congressman, second political passenger.

USA
28 January 1986
Challenger STS 51L
Dick Scobee, Mike Smith, Judith Resnik, Ronald McNair, Ellison Onizuka, Christa McAuliffe, Gregory Jarvis
73 sec
Exploded at 47 000 ft *14 330 m*; crew killed; first flight to take off but not to reach space; first American in-flight fatalities.

115 USSR 60
13 March 1986

Soyuz T15
Leonid Kizim, Vladimir Solovyov
125 day 0 hr 1 min
First mission to new space station Mir 1; also docked with Salyut 7; Kizim clocks up over a year in space experience.

Most experienced spacemen

Name	Experience (days)	Country	No. of flights
Kizim	374	USSR	3
Solovyov	361	USSR	2
Ryumin	361	USSR	2
Lyakhov	324	USSR	2
Savinykh	242	USSR	2
Atkov	236	USSR	1
Lebedev	219	USSR	2
Kovalyonok	216	USSR	3
Berezovoi	211	USSR	1
Popov	200	USSR	3
Alexandrov	149	USSR	1
Ivanchencko	147	USSR	2
Dzhanibekov	145	USSR	5
Grechko	132	USSR	3
Romanenko	102	USSR	2
Carr	84	USA	1
Gibson	84	USA	1
Pogue	84	USA	1

SPACEWOMEN

Savitskaya	19	USSR	2
Ride	14	USA	2

National manned spaceflight totals

Country	Day (to nearest days)	No. of flights
USSR	1964	60
USA	479	55
France	15	2 (1 USSR, 1 USA)
West Germany	10	2 (USA)
Canada	8	1 (USA)
Czechoslovakia	8	1 (USSR)
Poland	8	1 (USSR)
India	8	1 (USSR)
East Germany	8	1 (USSR)
Hungary	8	1 (USSR)
Romania	8	1 (USSR)
Cuba	8	1 (USSR)
Mongolia	8	1 (USSR)
Vietnam	8	1 (USSR)
Saudi Arabia	7	1 (USA)
Holland	7	1 (USA)
Mexico	7	1 (USA)
Bulgaria	2	1 (USSR)

TOTALS: 18 countries 2571 days

National man-days in space

Country	Days (to nearest day)
USSR	4239
USA	1767
West Germany	24

Rest: see National Manned Spaceflight Totals

PEOPLE WHO HAVE FLOWN IN SPACE

199 in total
120 USA (9 women)
60 USSR (2 women)
3 West Germany
2 France
1 each from Canada, Poland, India, East Germany, Hungary, Cuba, Mongolia, Vietnam, Romania, Czechoslovakia, Bulgaria, Saudi Arabia, Mexico, Holland

People who have flown two missions:
83 (includes two women, Svetlana Savistskaya, USSR, and Sally Ride, USA)
People who have flown three missions:
28
People who have flown four missions:
6
People who have flown five missions:
2 (John Young, USA; Vladimir Dzhanibekov, USSR)
People who have flown six missions:
1 (John Young, USA)

Youngest and oldest in space

Oldest: Karl Henize, 58, USA.
Oldest Russian: Georgi Grechko, 53.
Oldest other country: Reinhard Furrer, 44, West Germany.
Oldest woman: Shannon Lucid, 42, USA.
Oldest Russian woman: Svetlana Savitskaya, 35.
Youngest: Gherman Titov, 25, USSR.
Youngest American: Sally Ride, 32.
Youngest American male: Eugene Cernan, 32.
Youngest Russian woman: Valentina Tereshkova, 26.
Youngest other country: Dumitru Prunariu, 28, Romania.

IN-FLIGHT FATALITIES

Vladimir Komarov	USSR	Soyuz 1	24 April 1967
Georgi Dobrovolsky	USSR	Soyuz 11	6 June 1971
Vladislav Volkov	USSR		
Viktor Patsayev	USSR		
Dick Scobee	USA	Space Shuttle*	28 January 1986
Mike Smith	USA	Challenger	
Judith Resnik	USA	STS 51L	
Ellison Onizuka	USA		
Ronald McNair	USA		
Gregory Jarvis	USA		
Christa McAulliffe	USA		

* did not reach space

DECEASED SPACEPERSONS

Gus Grissom	USA	27 January 1967	Spacecraft fire on launch pad
Edward White	USA	27 January 1967	Spacecraft fire on launch pad
Vladimir Komarov	USSR	24 April 1967	Soyuz 1
Yuri Gagarin	USSR	27 March 1968	Air crash
Pavel Belyayev	USSR	20 January 1970	Peritonitis
Georgi Dobrovolsky	USSR	26 June 1971	Soyuz 11
Vladislav Volkov	USSR	26 June 1971	Soyuz 11
Viktor Patsayev	USSR	26 June 1971	Soyuz 11
Jack Swigert	USA	27 December 1982	Cancer
Dick Scobee	USA	28 January 1986	Challenger
Judith Resnik	USA	28 January 1986	Challenger
Ellison Onizuka	USA	28 January 1986	Challenger
Ronald McNair	USA	28 January 1986	Challenger

SPACEWALKING RECORDS

34 flights have involved EVAs: **11** USSR; **23** USA.
58 people have walked in space once: **41** USA; **17** USSR.
30 people have walked in space twice: **25** USA; **5** USSR.
14 people have walked in space three times: **11** USA; **3** USSR.
5 people have walked in space four times: **3** USA; **2** USSR.
2 people have walked in space five, six, seven and eight times: **2** USSR.

Longest spacewalk: Cernan and Schmitt on Moon, Apollo 17, 7 hr 37 min.
Longest spacewalk in Earth orbit: Nelson and van Hoften, STS 41C, 7 hr 18 min.
Most experienced spacewalkers: Kizim and Solovyov, eight EVAs, 31 hr 40 min.
Untethered spacewalker (with manned manoeuvring units): McCandless, Stewart, Nelson, van Hoften, Allen and Gardner (all USA).

MOON TRAVELLERS

24 Americans have travelled to the moon.
22 Americans have orbited the Moon.
12 Americans have walked on the Moon: Armstrong, Aldrin, Conrad, Bean, Shepard, Mitchell, Scott, Irwin, Young, Duke, Cernan, Schmitt.
3 Americans have travelled to the Moon twice: Lovell, Young, Cernan.
2 Americans have orbited the Moon twice: Young, Cernan.
Moonwalk totals: 3 days 8 hrs 22 min.
Lunar stay time total: 12 days 11 hrs 40 min.
Weight of Moon returned to Earth: 850·2 lb *386·0 kg*.

Energy

World Crude Oil Production, 1985

Region/country	thousand barrels per day
North America	
Canada	1465
Mexico	2735
United States	8971
TOTAL	13 171
Central and South America	
Argentina	449
Brazil	554
Colombia	176
Ecuador	278
Peru	190
Trinidad and Tobago	175
Venezuela	1674
Other	73
TOTAL	3569
Western Europe	
Denmark	58
Germany, West	81
Italy	36
Netherlands	76
Norway	788
Spain	44
United Kingdom	2530
Yugoslavia	84
Other	137
TOTAL	3834
Eastern Europe and USSR	
Albania	80
Romania	242
USSR	11 250
Other	53
TOTAL	11 625
Middle East	
Iran	2201
Iraq	1433
Kuwait	1016
Oman	486
Qatar	301
Saudi Arabia	3388
Syria	178
United Arab Emirates	1193
Other	43
TOTAL	10 239
Africa	
Algeria	643
Angola	231
Cameroon	134
Congo	117
Egypt	887
Gabon	153
Libya	1059
Nigeria	1471
Tunisia	118
Other	66
TOTAL	4879
Far East and Oceania	
Australia	564
Brunei	153
China	2480
India	603
Indonesia	1258
Malaysia	439
Other	140
TOTAL	5637
WORLD TOTAL	52 954

World Coal Production, 1985

Region/country	million short tons
North America	
Canada	67
Mexico	10
United States	886
TOTAL	963
Central and South America	
Brazil	8
Chile	1
Colombia	8
Other	1
TOTAL	18
Western Europe	
Austria	3
Belgium	7
France	19
Germany, West	231
Greece	38
Italy	1
Norway	1
Spain	44
Turkey	35
United Kingdom	100
Yugoslavia	72
TOTAL	552
Eastern Europe and USSR	
Albania	2
Bulgaria	36
Czechoslovakia	142
Germany, East	343
Hungary	27
Poland	275
Romania	49
USSR	798
TOTAL	1671
Middle East	
Iran	1
TOTAL	1
Africa	
Morocco	1
South Africa	180
Zambia	1
Zimbabwe	3
Other	1
TOTAL	185
Far East and Oceania	
Australia	170
China	937
India	171
Indonesia	1
Japan	18
Korea, North	51
Korea, South	25
Mongolia	6
New Zealand	3
Pakistan	2
Philippines	1
Thailand	5
Vietnam	6
Other	3
TOTAL	1400
WORLD TOTAL	4790

World Dry Natural Gas Production, 1985

Region/country	trillion ft³
North America	
Canada	2·83
Mexico	1·05
United States	16·43
TOTAL	20·31
Central and South America	
Argentina	0·50
Bolivia	0·09
Brazil	0·07
Chile	0·05
Colombia	0·15
Trinidad and Tobago	0·20
Venezuela	0·61
Other	0·05
TOTAL	1·74
Western Europe	
France	0·19
Germany, West	0·61
Italy	0·48
Netherlands	2·84
Norway	0·94
United Kingdom	1·49
Yugoslavia	0·07
Other	0·15
TOTAL	6·78
Eastern Europe and USSR	
Germany, East	0·44
Hungary	0·26
Poland	0·22
Romania	1·36
USSR	22·71
Other	0·04
TOTAL	25·04
Middle East	
Bahrain	0·14
Iran	0·50
Kuwait	0·15
Oman	0·05
Qatar	0·21
Saudi Arabia	0·27
United Arab Emirates	0·40
Other	0·03
TOTAL	1·75
Africa	
Algeria	1·40
Egypt	0·14
Libya	0·15
Nigeria	0·10
Other	0·05
TOTAL	1·85
Far East and Oceania	
Australia	0·41
Bangladesh	0·07
Brunei	0·30
China	0·47
India	0·11
Indonesia	1·20
Japan	0·09
Malaysia	0·35
New Zealand	0·12
Pakistan	0·35
Thailand	0·07
Other	0·16
TOTAL	3·71
WORLD TOTAL	61·17

World Natural Gas Plant Liquids Production, 1985

Region/country	thousand barrels per day
North America	
Canada	337
Mexico	271
United States	1609
TOTAL	2217
Central and South America	
Argentina	20
Bolivia	1
Brazil	17
Chile	11
Colombia	4
Cuba	2
Peru	3
Trinidad and Tobago	3
Venezuela	61
Other	2
TOTAL	124
Western Europe	
Austria	1
France	17
Greece	2
Italy	1
Netherlands	11
Norway	98
United Kingdom	145
Yugoslavia	4
TOTAL	279
Eastern Europe and USSR	
Hungary	25
Poland	1
Romania	15
USSR	635
TOTAL	676
Middle East	
Bahrain	8
Iran	10
Iraq	8
Kuwait	54
Qatar	30
Saudi Arabia	338
United Arab Emirates	156
TOTAL	604
Africa	
Algeria	335
Egypt	27
Libya	26
TOTAL	388
Far East and Oceania	
Australia	65
Brunei	28
Indonesia	44
Malaysia	10
Pakistan	2
New Zealand	3
Other	2
TOTAL	154
WORLD TOTAL	4443

World Net Hydroelectric Power Production, 1985

Region/country	billion kilowatt hours
North America	
Canada	300·7
Mexico	25·0
United States	284·3
TOTAL	610·0
Central and South America	
Argentina	20·4
Brazil	170·0
Chile	9·3
Colombia	20·0
Costa Rica	3·0
Peru	8·7
Uruguay	3·5
Venezuela	20·0
Other	10·0
TOTAL	264·8
Western Europe	
Austria	31·8
Finland	12·0
France	63·7
Germany, West	17·4
Iceland	3·7
Italy	44·0
Norway	101·8
Portugal	10·6
Spain	33·2
Sweden	70·3
Switzerland	32·7
Turkey	11·9
United Kingdom	6·8
Yugoslavia	26·0
Other	5·9
TOTAL	471·8
Eastern Europe and USSR	
Bulgaria	3·0
Czechoslovakia	3·3
Poland	3·4
Romania	11·0
USSR	250·0
Other	4·4
TOTAL	275·2
Middle East	
Iran	6·3
Other	4·1
TOTAL	10·4
Africa	
Egypt	10·5
Zaire	4·3
Zambia	10·0
Zimbabwe	3·4
Other	17·4
TOTAL	45·6
Far East and Oceania	
Australia	14·9
China	86·0
India	55·0
Japan	81·1
Korea, North	27·0
Korea, South	3·6
New Zealand	18·7
Pakistan	13·0
Philippines	7·5
Thailand	5·0
Other	13·2
TOTAL	325·1
WORLD TOTAL	2002·9

World Net Nuclear Electric Power Production, 1985

Region/country	billion kilowatt hour
North America	
Canada	59·7
United States	383·7
TOTAL	443·4
Central and South America	
Argentina	5·5
Brazil	3·2
TOTAL	8·7
Western Europe	
Belgium	32·8
Finland	17·8
France	212·8
Germany, West	119·4
Italy	6·7
Netherlands	3·7
Spain	26·6
Sweden	55·7
Switzerland	21·3
United Kingdom	56·7
Yugoslavia	3·8
TOTAL	557·3
Eastern Europe and USSR	
Bulgaria	11·3
Czechoslovakia	7·0
Germany, East	12·3
Hungary	6·2
USSR	140·0
TOTAL	176·8
Africa	
South Africa	5·5
TOTAL	5·5
Far East and Oceania	
India	4·3
Japan	144·4
Korea, South	15·7
Pakistan	0·2
Taiwan	27·3
TOTAL	191·9
WORLD TOTAL	1383·6

World Uranium Production (Uranium Content)

Region/country	tonnes
Africa	14 175
Gabon	980
Niger	3426
S. Africa	9769
North America	15 275
Canada	7140
United States	8135
South America	368
Argentina	179
Brazil	189
Asia	4
Japan	4
Europe	3637
Belgium	45
France, incl. Monaco	3271
Germany, West	47
Portugal	104
Spain	170
Oceania	3211
Australia	3211
WORLD	36 670

SOLAR ENERGY

Solar technology has an inexhaustible free fuel – the sun. Financial outlay to produce energy is concerned with initial investment to acquire equipment, but from then on, unlike coal, gas, oil, etc., the fuel is free. This makes economic comparisons of solar against other sources of energy difficult because one-time investment has to be weighed against frequent fuel purchases.

At present solar energy is unable to compete with cheap fossil fuels. However solar energy could provide a substantial percentage of world energy needs. To do so it will need to overcome economic and institutional barriers and prejudices.

The solar industry appears to lack cohesion and that, combined with the apathy greeted by those outside it, is making the solar contribution to world energy needs slow to expand. This is further illustrated in the lack of any recognized national or international source of data.

TIDAL ENERGY

Estimates vary, but it is generally agreed that tidal energy could never provide more than 1–2% of the world's electricity. For the time being, the problems of producing tidal energy appear to outweigh the benefits, particularly considering cost-effectiveness. Tidal energy is too expensive, is difficult to 'control' and 'store', and would be problematic to integrate successfully into a grid system.

NB The following tidal energy figures provided do not include any indication of year.

Tidal Power Sites

Location	Average tidal range (m)	Hydraulic energy ($10^9 kWh/yr$)
North America		
Bay of Fundy		
Passamaquoddy	5·5	15·8
Cobscook	5·5	6·3
Annapolis	6·4	6·7
Minas-Cobequid	10·7	175·0
Amherst Point	10·7	2·25
Shepody	9·8	22·1
Cumberland	10·1	14·7
Petitcodiac	10·7	7·0
Memramcook	10·7	5·2
Cook Inlet, Alaska		

Tidal Power Sites

Location	Average tidal range (m)	Hydraulic energy ($10^9 kWh/yr$)
Knik Arm	7·5	6·0
Turnagin Arm	7·5	12·5
South America		
Argentina		
San José	5·9	51·5
Europe		
England		
Severn	9·8	14·7
France		
Aber-Benoit	5·2	0·16

Tidal Power Sites

Location	Average tidal range (m)	Hydraulic energy ($10^9 kWh/yr$)
Aber-Wrach	5·0	0·05
Arguenon/Lancieux	8·4	3·9
Frenaye	7·4	1·3
La Rance	8·4	3·1
Rotheneuf	8·0	0·14
Mont St Michel	8·4	85·1
Somme	6·5	4·1
USSR		
Kislaya Inlet	2·4	0·02
Lumbovskii Bay	4·2	2·4
White Sea	5·7	126·0
Mezen Estuary	6·6	12·0

Defence

APPROXIMATE COST OF THE TWO WORLD WARS TO THE MAIN CONTESTANTS IN PEOPLE AND MONEY

	Mobilized (000)	Military Killed (000)	Civilians Killed (000)	Cost in $ million (000)		Mobilized (000)	Military Killed (000)	Civilians Killed (000)	Cost in $ million (000)
World War I					**World War II**				
The Central Powers					*The Axis Powers*				
Germany	11 000	1808	760	58	Germany	11 000	3 250	3 810	300
Austria Hungary	7 800	1200	300	24	Italy	4 500	330	500	50
Turkey	2 850	325	2150	3·5	Japan	6 095	1 700	360	100
Bulgaria	1 200	87	275	1					
					The Allied Powers				
The Allied Powers					British Empire	8 720	452	80	150
British Empire	8 904	908	30	52	France	6 000	250	360	100
France	8 410	1357	40	50	Poland	1 000	120	5 300	na
Russia (USSR post-1917)	12 000	1700	2000	25·6	USSR	12 500	7 500	17 500	200
Serbia	707	45	650	2·5	USA	14 900	407	Small	350
Italy	5 615	650	Small	18	China[1]	8 000	1 500	7 800	na
USA	4 355	126	Small	33					
Other Allied Powers	2 200	365	—	—					
Total all countries involved	65 000	8500	6642	282	Total from above countries	72 700	15 600	35 800[2]	1600

[1] 1937–45. Figures highly speculative.   [2] Does not include full total of victims of wartime genocides.   na – not available.

THE TWO GREAT WARS

History's two greatest wars have both been fought in the 20th century. World War I (1914–18) resulted in 9 700 000 fatalities including 765 399 from the United Kingdom. World War II (1939–45) resulted in 54·8 million battle and civilian deaths including 25 million in the USSR, and 6 028 000 or 22·2% of her population in Poland. The UK losses were 265 000.

NAVAL FORCES

Apart from contributing to the nuclear deterrent, navies continue to pursue their time honoured role of maintaining an armed presence at sea while contributing to the protection of trade and of anti-submarine warfare.

LAND AND AIR FORCES

The many confrontations since World War II have been combined action by land and air forces with a minor naval role. The arbiters of decision since the 1930s have been close support aircraft and armoured fighting vehicles, of which the predominant weapon has been the tank.

PRINCIPAL WARS SINCE 1945

1945– China and Taiwan: Nationalist Chinese (with US assistance) *versus* Communist Chinese. Intensive phase lapsed in 1949 with establishment of Communist state.
1946–79 Indo-China/Vietnam: French/South Vietnamese and then USA and South Vietnamese *versus* Communists and North Vietnamese.

China *versus* Vietnam 1979; Cambodian (Kampuchean) genocide under Pol Pot regime 1976–79.
1947–71 Indian sub-continent: India *versus* Pakistan, intermittently in Kashmir, plus short intensive confrontations in 1947, 1965 and 3–16 Dec. 1971.
1948–73 Middle East: Israel *versus* Arab States (with interventions by Britain and France). Continuous state of war with intensive confrontations in 1948, 1956, 5–10 June 1967 (6-day war) and 6–24 Oct. 1973.
1950–1953 Korea: North Korea and China *versus* United Nations forces. 25 June 1950 invasion of South Korea. Armistice signed 27 July 1953.

1979 Afghanistan: USSR military incursion 24 Dec. 1979. Occupation continues.

Strategic nuclear delivery vehicles

For over three decades a factor in the deterrence from world war has been the threat of nuclear attack by one or other of the major powers linked to the achievement of a measure approaching parity in the means of delivery. It is now possible for five nations to use tactical nuclear weapons on the battlefield by means of aircraft, rockets, artillery or from mines. For strategic delivery six major systems are available:

Inter-continental ballistic missiles with ranges in excess of 4000 miles *6400 km* ICBM
Intermediate-range ballistic missiles with ranges between 1500 and 4000 miles *2400–6400 km* IRBM
Medium-range ballistic missiles with ranges between 500 and 1500 miles *800–2400 km* MRBM
Short-range ballistic missiles with ranges less than 500 miles *800 km* SRBM
Long-range bombers with ranges over 6000 miles *9650 km*
Medium-range bombers with ranges between 3500 and 6000 miles *5600–9650 km*
Ballistic missiles can be launched from ground sites or submarines.

The warheads may be productive of explosions ranging between 25 Megaton (MT) in the largest SS 9 Scarp (USSR) ICBM, with its range of 7500 miles *12 000 km* to 50 kiloton (kT) in the SRBMs. One kT is equivalent to 1000 tons of TNT and one MT or megaton to one million tons of TNT. The USSR SS-18 has 10 'Mirved' warheads (multiple independently targetable re-entry vehicles) each of 1 MT.

Air-launched medium-range nuclear weapons (1984–85)*

USA	USSR
1008	0

Ground-launched medium-range nuclear weapons (1984–85)*

USA/NATO	USSR
48	0

Land-based medium-range nuclear weapons (1984–85)*

USA/NATO	USSR
48	620

Force comparisons of major nuclear systems

Land-based long-range (strategic) nuclear weapons*

	Total no of launchers	Yield of warhead	Number of warheads per launcher	Accuracy, m (circle of error probable)	Range, km
USA					
Titan II	37	9MT	1	1500	15 000
Minuteman II	450	1.2MT	1	370	11 300
Minuteman III (1970)	250	170kT	3	280	14 800
Minuteman III (1980)	300	335kT	3	220	12 900
TOTAL	1037		2137		
USSR					
SS11	520	1MT/300kT	3 or 1†	1200	8–10 000
SS13	60	750kT	1	2000	10 000
SS17	150	20kT/1MT	4 or 1	450	10 000
SS18	308	900kT/20MT	8 or 1	300–450	10 000
SS19	360	550kT/5MT	6 or 1	300	10 000
TOTAL	1398		approx. 6000		

* Source *The Military Balance 1984–85* (published annually by The International Institute for Strategic Studies, London)
† Many Soviet missiles are produced in a range of modes, each with differing configurations of numbers and yields of warheads

Long-range (strategic) nuclear-capable aircraft (1984–85)*

	No. deployed	Range, km
USA		
B-52G	151	12 000
B-52H	90	16 000
TOTAL	241	
USSR		
TU-95	100	12 800
MYA-4	43	11 200
TOTAL	143	

* Source *The Military Balance 1984–85*, International Institute for Strategic Studies, London

Conventional armed force comparisons (1984–85)*

	NATO	Warsaw Pact
Total uniformed manpower	5 024 000	6 169 000
Total reserves	5 424 000	7 119 000
Total manpower deployed in Europe	1 767 000	1 960 000
Main battle tanks	20 742	50 500
Submarines	188	193
Surface ships	1 110	1 132
Naval aircraft	1 458	786
Land-based aircraft	4 382	11 325

* Source *The Military Balance 1984–85*, International Institute for Strategic Studies

Sea-based long-range (strategic) nuclear weapons (1984–85)*

	Total missiles	Total warheads
USA	592	5344
UK	64	384†
France	80	80
TOTAL	736	5808
USSR TOTAL	980*	2–3000

* Source *The Military Balance 1984–85*, International Institute of Strategic Studies, London
† assumes completion of the Chevaline improvements to Polaris in which three warheads per launcher have been replaced by six per launcher

Abbreviations

AAM	air-to-air missile
AB	airburst
ABM	anti-ballistic missile
ACDA	Arms Control and Disarmament Agency
ACHDF	Air Command Home Defence Forces
ACM	Advanced Cruise missile
ADM	atomic demolition munition
AEA	Atomic Energy Authority
AEC	Atomic Energy Commission
AERE	Atomic Energy Research Establishment
AEW	airborne early warning
AFAP	artillery-fired atomic projectile
AfP	Atoms for Peace
AGM	air-to-ground missile
AGR	advanced gas-cooled reactor
ALBM	air-launched ballistic missile
ALCM	air-launched cruise missile
ASALM	advanced strategic air-launched missile
ASAT	anti-satellite
ASBM	air-to-surface ballistic missile
ASC	American Security Council
ASM	air-to-surface missile
ASROC	anti-submarine rocket
ASW	anti-submarine warfare
ATB	advanced technology bomber (Stealth)
AUR	all-up round
AWACS	airborne warning and control system
AWDREY	atomic weapons detection, recognition, and estimation of yield
AWRE	Atomic Weapons Research Establishment
BIT	built-in test
BMD	ballistic missile defence
BMEWS	ballistic missile early warning system
BWR	boiling water reactor
C³I	command, control, communication and intelligence
CCD	Conference of the Committee on Disarmament
CD	Committee on Disarmament
CDS	command disable system
CEP	circular error probable
CINCUSEUR	Commander in Chief, US Forces, Europe
CM	Cruise missile
CMP	counter military potential
CND	Campaign for Nuclear Disarmament
CPS	Coalition for Peace through Strength
CSCE	Conference on Security and Cooperation in Europe
CTB	comprehensive test ban
DDRE	Directorate of Defense Research and Engineering (US)
DGZ	desired ground zero
DMA	Defense Mapping Agency (US)
DP	deep basing
DSMAC	digital scene matching area correlation
ECM	electronic counter-measures
ELINT	electronic intelligence
EMt	equivalent megatonnage
EMP	electromagnetic pulse
END	European Nuclear Disarmament
ENDC	Eighteen Nation Disarmament Committee
ER-RB	enhanced radiation-reduced blast
ERW	enhanced radiation weapon
FBR	fast-breeder reactor
FBS	forward based systems
FOBS	fractional orbital bombardment system
FOST	Force Océanique Stratégique
FROD	functionally related observable differences
GAMA	GLCM alert and maintenance area

GAO	General Accounting Office (US Congress)
GB	ground burst
GCI	ground-controlled intercept
GLCM	ground-launched cruise missile
GZ	ground zero
HLG	High Level Group (NATO)
IAEA	International Atomic Energy Agency
ICBM	intercontinental ballistic missile
IISS	International Institute of Strategic Studies
INF	intermediate-range nuclear force
IOC	initial operational capability
IRBM	intermediate-range ballistic missile
ISMA	International Satellite Monitoring Agency
JANE	Journalists Against Nuclear Extermination
JCMPO	Joint Cruise Missile Project Office
kT	kiloton
LCC	launch control centre
LNO	limited nuclear options
LNW	limited nuclear war
LORAN	long-range navigation
LOW	launch-on warning
LRTNF	long-range theatre nuclear force
LRTNW	long-range theatre nuclear weapons
LTA	launch-through attack
LWR	light water reactor
MAD	mutual assured destruction
MAPW	Medical Association for Prevention of War
MARV	manoeuvring re-entry vehicle
MBFR	mutual and balanced force reductions
MCANW	Medical Campaign Against Nuclear War
MIRV	multiple independently retargetable re-entry vehicle
MLF	multi-lateral force
MRASM	Medium-range air-to-surface missile
MRBM	medium-range ballistic missile
MRL	multiple rocket launchers
MRTNF	medium-range theatre nuclear force
MRV	multiple re-entry vehicle
MT	megaton
M-X	missile experimental
NATO	North Atlantic Treaty Organization
NFZ	nuclear free zone
NND	non-nuclear defence
NOP	nuclear operations plans
NORAD	North American Aerospace Defense Command
NPG	Nuclear Planning Group (NATO)
NPT	Non-Proliferation Treaty
NVDA	non-violent direct action
OPANAL	Agency for the Prohibition of Nuclear Weapons in Latin America
PAL	permissive action link
PBV	post-boost vehicle
PGW	precision guided weapon
PLS	pre-launch survivability
PNET	Peaceful Nuclear Explosions Treaty
PTBT	Partial Test Ban Treaty
PTP	probability to penetrate
QRA	quick reaction alert
RW	radiological weapon
RV	re-entry vehicle
SAC	Strategic Air Command (USAF)
SACEUR	Supreme Allied Command, Europe (NATO)
SALT	Strategic Arms Limitation Talks
SAM	surface-to-air missile
SANA	Scientists against Nuclear Arms

SCC	Standing Consultative Commission
SCG	Special Consultative Group (NATO)
SEO	selective employment options
SHAPE	Supreme Headquarters Allied Powers, Europe (NATO)
SICBM	small intercontinental ballistic missile
SIOP	single integrated operational plan
SIPRI	Stockholm International Peace Research Institute
SLBM	submarine-launched ballistic missile
SLCM	sea-launched cruise missile
SOSUS	sound surveillance system
SRAM	short-range attack missile
SRBM	short-range ballistic missile
SRDB	Scientific Research and Development Branch (of UK Home Office)

SSBN	nuclear-powered ballistic missile submarine
SSPK	single shot probability of kill
SSM	surface-to-surface missile
SSN	nuclear-powered attack submarine
START	Strategic Arms Reductions Talks
SUBROC	submarine rocket
TAC	Tactical Air Command
TEL	transporter-erector-launcher
TERCOM	terrain contour matching
TNF	theatre nuclear forces
TNW	theatre nuclear war
TTBT	Threshold Test Ban Treaty
UNA	United Nations Association
UNSSD	United Nations Special Session on Disarmament
USAF	United States Air Force
VLS	vertical launch system
WDC	World Disarmament Campaign
WTO	Warsaw Treaty Organization

The trusteeship council

This council administers territories under UN trusteeship. Twelve territories have been under UN trusteeship:

Original Trust Territory	Subsequent Status
Tanganyika (UK)	Independent, 9 Dec. 1961; merged with Zanzibar, 26 Apr. 1964, as Tanzania
Ruanda–Urundi (Belgium)	Two independent states, 1 July 1962
Somaliland (Italy)	Independent, 1 July 1960
Cameroons (UK)	Northern part joined Nigeria, 1 June 1961; southern part joined Cameroon, 1 Oct. 1961.
Cameroons (France)	Independent republic of Cameroon, 1 Jan. 1960
Togoland (UK)	United with Gold Coast, to form Ghana, 6 Mar. 1957
Togoland (France)	Independent republic of Togo, 27 Apr. 1960
Western Samoa (NZ)	Independent, 1 Jan. 1962
Nauru (Australia, NZ and UK)	Independent, 31 Jan. 1968
New Guinea (Australia)	Merged with Papua to form Papua New Guinea, independent 16 Sept. 1975
Pacific Islands (USA) comprising the Carolines, Marshalls and Marianas (excepting Guam)	The Northern Mariana Islands became a Commonwealth territory of the USA on 9 Jan. 1978 but remain legally part of the Trust Territory until the termination of the trusteeship. The other islands are grouped in three territories which are to enter into 'free association' with the USA.

The United Nations

'A general international organization . . . for the maintenance of international peace and security' was recognized as desirable in Clause 4 of the proposals of the Four-Nation Conference of Foreign Ministers signed in Moscow on 30 Oct. 1943 by R Anthony Eden, later the Earl of Avon (1897–1977) (UK), Cordell Hull (1871–1955) (USA), Vyacheslav M Skryabin, *alias* Molotov (b. 1890) (USSR), and Ambassador Foo Ping-sheung (China).

Ways and means were resolved at the mansion of Dumbarton Oaks, Washington, DC, USA, between 21 Aug. and 7 Oct. 1944. A final step was taken at San Francisco, California, USA, between 25 Apr. and 26 June 1945 when delegates of 50 participating states signed the Charter (Poland signed on 15 Oct. 1945). This came into force on 24 Oct. 1945, when the four above-mentioned states, plus France and a majority of the other 46 states, had ratified the Charter. The first regular session was held in London on 10 Jan.–14 Feb. 1946.

Of the 168 *de facto* sovereign states of the world, 158 are now in membership including the two USSR republics of Byelorussia and the Ukraine which have separate membership.
The non-members are:
Andorra
China (Taiwan)
Kiribati
Korea, Democratic People's Republic of
Korea, Republic of
Liechtenstein
Monaco
Nauru
San Marino
Switzerland
Tonga
Tuvalu
Vatican City (Holy See)

UN member states, with year of joining

Afghanistan	1946
Albania	1955
Algeria	1962
Angola	1976
Antigua and Barbuda	1981
Argentina*	1945
Australia*	1945
Austria	1955
Bahamas	1973
Bahrain	1971
Bangladesh	1974
Barbados	1966
Belgium*	1945
Belize	1981
Benin	1960
Bhutan	1971
Bolivia*	1945
Botswana	1966
Brazil*	1945
Brunei Darussalam	1984
Bulgaria	1955

Burkina Faso	1960	Poland*	1945
Burma	1948	Portugal	1955
Burundi	1962	Qatar	1971
Byelorussia*	1945	Romania	1955
Cambodia	1955	Rwanda	1962
Cameroon	1960	St Christopher and Nevis	1983
Canada*	1945	St Lucia	1979
Cape Verde	1975	St Vincent and the Grenadines	1980
Central African Rep.	1960	Samoa, Western	1976
Chad	1960	São Tomé and Príncipe	1975
Chile*	1945	Saudi Arabia*	1945
China*	1945	Senegal	1960
Colombia*	1945	Seychelles	1976
Comoros	1975	Sierra Leone	1961
Congo	1960	Singapore	1965
Costa Rica*	1945	Solomon Islands	1978
Cuba*	1945	Somalia	1960
Cyprus	1960	South Africa*	1945
Czechoslovakia*	1945	Spain	1955
Denmark*	1945	Sri Lanka	1955
Djibouti	1977	Sudan	1956
Dominica	1978	Suriname	1975
Dominican Republic*	1945	Swaziland	1968
Ecuador*	1945	Sweden	1946
Egypt*	1945	Syrian Arab Rep.*	1945
El Salvador*	1945	Tanzania	1961
Equatorial Guinea	1968	Thailand	1946
Ethiopia*	1945	Togo	1960
Fiji	1970	Trinidad and Tobago	1962
Finland	1955	Tunisia	1956
France*	1945	Turkey*	1945
Gabon	1960	Uganda	1962
Gambia	1965	Ukrainian Soviet	
German Democratic Rep.	1973	Socialist Rep.*	1945
Germany, Federal Rep. of	1973	USSR*	1945
Ghana	1957	United Arab Emirates	1971
Greece*	1945	UK*	1945
Grenada	1974	USA*	1945
Guatemala*	1945	Uruguay*	1945
Guinea	1958	Vanuatu	1981
Guinea-Bissau	1974	Venezuela*	1945
Guyana	1966	Vietnam	1977
Haiti*	1945	Yemen Arab Republic	1947
Honduras*	1945	Yemen, P.D.R.	1967
Hungary	1955	Yugoslavia*	1945
Iceland	1946	Zaïre	1960
India*	1945	Zambia	1964
Indonesia	1950	Zimbabwe	1980
Iran*	1945		
Iraq*	1945		
Ireland	1955		
Israel	1949		
Italy	1955		
Ivory Coast	1960		
Jamaica	1962		
Japan	1956		
Jordan	1955		
Kenya	1963		
Kuwait	1963		
Laos People's Dem. Rep.	1955		
Lebanon*	1945		
Lesotho	1966		
Liberia*	1945		
Libyan Arab Jamahiriya	1955		
Luxemburg*	1945		
Madagascar	1960		
Malawi	1964		
Malaysia	1957		
Maldives	1965		
Mali	1960		
Malta	1964		
Mauritania	1961		
Mauritius	1968		
Mexico*	1945		
Mongolia	1961		
Morocco	1956		
Mozambique	1975		
Nepál	1955		
Netherlands*	1945		
New Zealand*	1945		
Nicaragua*	1945		
Niger	1960		
Nigeria	1960		
Norway*	1945		
Oman	1971		
Pakistan	1947		
Panama*	1945		
Papua New Guinea	1975		
Paraguay*	1945		
Peru*	1945		
Philippines*	1945		

* Original member.

The United Nations' principal organs are:

The General Assembly consisting of all member nations, each with up to five delegates but one vote, and meeting annually in regular sessions with provision for special sessions. The Assembly has seven main committees, on which there is the right of representation by all member nations. These are (1) Political and Security, (2) Economic and Financial, (3) Social, Humanitarian and Cultural, (4) Decolonization, (5) Administration and Budgetary, (6) Legal, and the Special Political.

The Security Council, consisting of 15 members, each with one representative, of whom there are five permanent members (China, France, the USSR, the United Kingdom and the USA) and 10 elected members serving a two-year term. Apart from procedural questions, an affirmative majority vote of at least nine must include that of all five permanent members. It is from this stipulation that the so-called veto arises.

The Economic and Social Council, consisting of 54 members elected for three-year terms, is responsible for carrying out the functions of the General Assembly's second and third Committees, viz. economic, social, educational, health and cultural matters. It had the following Functional Commissions in 1983: (1) Statistical, (2) Population, (3) Social Development, (4) Narcotic Drugs, (5) Human Rights, (6) Status of Women. The Council has also established Economic Commissions, as follows: (1) for Europe (ECE), (2) for Asia and the Pacific (ESCAP), (3) for Latin America (ECLA), (4) for Africa (ECA) and (5) for Western Asia (ECWA).

The International Court of Justice or World Court, comprising 15 Judges (quorum of nine) of different nations, each serving a nine-year term and meeting at 's-Gravenhage (The Hague), Netherlands. All members of the UN plus Liechtenstein, San Marino and Switzerland are parties to the Statute of the Court. Only States may be parties in contentious cases. In the event of a party's failing to adhere to a judgment, the other party may have recourse to the Security Council. Judgments are final and without appeal but can be reopened on grounds of a new decisive factor within ten years.

The Secretariat. The principal administrative officer is the Secretary General who is appointed by the General Assembly for a five-year term. This office has been held thus:
Trygve Halvdan Lie (1896–1968) (Norway) 1 Feb. 1946–10 Nov. 1952.
Dag Hjalmar Agne Carl Hammarskjöld (1905–61) (Sweden) 10 Apr. 1953–18 Sept. 1961.
U Maung Thant (1909–74) (Burma) (acting) 3 Nov. 1961–30 Nov. 1962, (permanent) 30 Nov. 1962–31 Dec. 1971.
Kurt Waldheim (b. 21 Dec. 1918) (Austria) 1 Jan. 1972–31 Dec. 1981.
Javier Pérez de Cuéllar (b. 19 Jan. 1920) (Peru) 1 Jan. 1982 (in office).

Specialized Agencies of the United Nations
There are 15 specialized agencies, which in order of absorption or creation are as follows:

ILO
International Labour Organization (Headquarters – Geneva). Founded 11 Apr. 1919 in connection with the League of Nations. Re-established as the senior UN specialized agency, 14 Dec. 1946. Especially concerned with social justice, hours of work, unemployment, wages, industrial sickness, and protection of foreign workers.

FAO
Food and Agriculture Organization of the United Nations (Headquarters – Rome). Established, 16 Oct. 1945. Became UN agency, 14 Dec. 1946. Objects: to raise levels of nutrition and standards of living; to improve the production and distribution of agricultural products. FAO provides an Intelligence Service on Agriculture, Forestry and Fisheries.

UNESCO
United Nations Educational, Scientific and Cultural Organization (Headquarters – Paris). Established, 4 Nov. 1946. Objects: to stimulate popular education and the spread of culture, and to diffuse knowledge through all means of mass communication; to further universal respect for justice, the rule of law, human rights and fundamental freedoms. Became a UN agency, 14 Dec. 1946.

ICAO
International Civil Aviation Organization (Headquarters – Montreal). Established, 4 Apr. 1947. Objects: to study the problems of international civil aviation; to encourage safety measures and co-ordinate facilities required for safe international flight. A UN agency from 13 May 1947.

IBRD
International Bank for Reconstruction and Development (The World Bank) (Headquarters – Washington). Established, 27 Dec. 1945. Objects: to assist in the reconstruction and development of territories of members by aiding capital investment. Became a UN agency, 15 Nov. 1947.

IMF
International Monetary Fund (Headquarters – Washington). Established, 27 Dec. 1945. Objects: to promote international monetary co-operation, the expansion of international trade and stability of exchange rates. A UN agency from 15 Nov. 1947.

UPU
Universal Postal Union (Headquarters – Berne, Switzerland). Established 1 July 1875; became a UN specialized agency, 1 July 1948. Objects: to unite members in a single postal territory.

WHO
World Health Organization (Headquarters – Geneva). Established, 7 Apr. 1948. Objects: to promote the attainment by all peoples of the highest possible standard of health. Its services are both advisory and technical. A UN agency from 10 July 1948.

ITU
International Telecommunication Union (Headquarters – Geneva). Founded 17 May 1865; incorporated in the United Nations, 10 Jan. 1949. Objects: to seek the standardization of procedures concerning greater efficacy of telecommunications and to allocate frequencies.

WMO
World Meteorological Organization (Headquarters – Geneva). Established 11 Oct. 1947. Objects: to standardize meteorological observations; to secure their publication, and apply the information for the greater safety of aviation and shipping and benefit of agriculture, etc. A UN agency from 20 Dec. 1951.

IFC
International Finance Corporation (Headquarters – Washington). Established, 24 July 1956. Objects: to promote the flow of private capital internationally and to stimulate the capital markets. Membership is open only to those countries that are members of the World Bank. A UN agency from 20 Feb. 1957.

IMCO
Inter-Governmental Maritime Consultative Organization (Headquarters – London). Established 17 Mar. 1958. Objects: to co-ordinate safety at sea and to secure the freedom of passage. A UN agency from 13 Jan. 1959.

IDA
International Development Association (Headquarters – Washington). Established, 24 Sept 1960. Object: to assist less developed countries by providing credits on special terms. Membership limited as in IFC. A UN agency from 27 Mar. 1961.

WIPO
World Intellectual Property Organization (Headquarters – Geneva). Established, 26 Apr. 1970; became a UN specialized agency, 17 Dec. 1974. Objects: to promote the protection of intellectual property (inventions, designs, copyright, etc.) and to centralize administration of its legal and technical aspects.

IFAD
International Fund for Agricultural Development (Headquarters – Rome). Established, 30 Nov. 1977; became a UN specialized agency, 15 Dec. 1977. Objects: to mobilise substantial additional resources (grants or loans) on concessional terms to increase food production in developing countries.

NATO

North Atlantic Treaty Organization
NATO, an idea first broached by the Secretary of State for External Affairs for Canada on 28 Apr. 1948, came into existence on 4 Apr. 1949 and into force on 24 Aug. 1949, with Belgium, Canada, Denmark, France, Iceland, Italy, Luxemburg, the Netherlands, Norway, Portugal, the United Kingdom and the USA. Greece and Turkey were admitted on 18 Feb. 1952, the Federal Republic of Germany on 5 May 1955, and Spain on 30 May 1982 bringing the total of countries to 16. France withdrew from NATO's military affairs on 1 July 1966 and the HQ was moved from Paris to Brussels. Greece left the military command structure on 14 Aug. 1974 but its re-integration was approved by NATO's Defence Planning Committee on 20 Oct. 1980.

OECD

Organization for Economic Co-operation and Development
Founded as a European body (OEEC) on 20 Sept. 1961, the Organization after 14 years was reconstituted to embrace other Western countries. It now comprises 24 countries: Australia, Austria, Belgium, Canada, Denmark, Finland, France, Federal Republic of Germany, Greece, Iceland, Ireland, Italy, Japan, Luxembourg, Netherlands, New Zealand, Norway, Portugal, Spain, Sweden, Switzerland, Turkey, United Kingdom and USA, with Yugoslavia (special status).

Headquarters are in Paris. The aims are to achieve the highest sustainable economic growth and level of employment with a rising standard of living compatible with financial stability.

EFTA

European Free Trade Association
Established 3 May 1960.
With the departure of the United Kingdom and Denmark, EFTA comprised six countries, viz. Austria, Iceland, Norway, Portugal, Sweden and Switzerland, with Finland as an associate member. EFTA was established on 27 Mar. 1961.

The EFTA countries (except Norway) signed a free trade agreement with the EEC on 22 July 1972 and Norway did so on 14 May 1973.

OAU

Organization of African Unity
In Addis Ababa, Ethiopia, on 25 May 1963, 32 African countries established the organization for common defence of independence, the elimination of colonialism and co-ordination of economic policies. By 1980 the OAU had 50 members. English and French are recognized as official languages in addition to African languages.

OPEC

Organization of the Petroleum Exporting Countries
Established 21 Jan. 1961. Founded by a group of 13 major oil exporting countries to represent their interests in dealings with the major oil companies, it sets price levels per barrel of crude oil for their markets that effectively control the world market price. Members include Algeria, Ecuador, Gabon, Indonesia, Iran, Iraq, Kuwait, Libya, Nigeria, Qatar, Saudi Arabia, United Arab Emirates, Venezuela.

The European Communities

ECSC
European Coal and Steel Community

EEC
European Economic Community

EURATOM
European Atomic Energy Community
The ECSC was established by a treaty signed on 18 April 1951, effective from 25 July 1952. The founding members were Belgium, France, the Federal Republic of Germany, Italy, Luxembourg and the Netherlands. These six countries were also the original members of the EEC (or Common Market) and EURATOM, established by two treaties signed in Rome on 25 March 1957, both effective from 1 Jan. 1958. Common institutions for the three Communities were established by a treaty signed on 8 April 1965, effective from 1 July 1967. The six original members established a complete customs union, and introduced a common external tariff, on 1 July 1968.

Denmark, Ireland and the United Kingdom joined the three Communities on 1 Jan. 1973, having signed a treaty of accession on 22 Jan. 1972. The first direct elections to the European Parliament were held on 7–10 June 1979, when 410 members were elected.

Greece signed a treaty of accession on 28 May 1979 and joined the Communities on 1 Jan. 1981, increasing the membership to 10. The European Parliament was increased to 434 members with 24 elected from Greece on 18 Oct. 1981.

Spain and Portugal signed Treaties of Accession in June 1985, and became full members on 1 Jan. 1986. They have nominated 60 and 24 representatives respectively to sit in the European Parliament until the next elections.

The Council of Europe

The Council of Europe, with headquarters in Strasbourg (France), was established in May 1949. It was founded in the wake of the trauma of World War II caused by extremist political régimes in Germany and Italy. Its object was to achieve greater unity between its member nations to safeguard their European heritage and to facilitate both economic and social progress.

The principal organ of the Council is its Committee of Ministers, consisting of the Foreign Ministers of the 21 member countries.

The Council's principal achievement has been the signing of the European convention for the Protection of Human Rights and Fundamental Freedoms in 1950, under which was established the European Commission and the European Court of Human Rights. All the member states' inhabitants (about 390 million at mid-1980) are thus protected against their own Governments on matters of basic human rights such as the right to life; freedom from torture; right to liberty and security of person; right to respect for private and family life; freedom of thought, conscience and religion; freedom of expression; freedom of association and the right to marry.

The 21 member nations and their dates of adherence are:

Austria	1957
Belgium	1950
Cyprus	1961
Denmark	1950
France	1950
Germany (Fed. Rep.)	1950
Greece	1950
Iceland	1950
Ireland	1950
Italy	1950
Liechtenstein	1978
Luxemburg	1950
Malta	1966
Netherlands	1950
Norway	1950
Portugal	1978
Spain	1978
Sweden	1950
Switzerland	1972
Turkey	1950
United Kingdom	1950

Warsaw Pact

The Warsaw Pact refers to a treaty of friendship and non-aggression signed between the USSR and its satellite countries in May 1955. The aim was to set up a joint military command structure and to ensure that all countries of the Pact would come to the defence of any one member who suffered aggression.

The member countries were Albania, Bulgaria, Czechoslovakia, East Germany, Hungary, Poland, Romania and the USSR. Since 1962 Albania has no longer been invited to Warsaw Pact meetings, but it has never formally been expelled from the Pact.

Council for Mutual and Economic Assistance (Comecon)

The aim of the CMEA is to foster the economies and development within, and trade between, the member countries. It can therefore be seen as a form of 'economic community' of socialist countries. Founder members were: Bulgaria, Czechoslovakia, Hungary, Poland, Romania and the USSR. Albania joined in 1949, but left in 1961. East Germany joined in 1950, Mongolia in 1962, Cuba in 1972, Vietnam in 1978. Yugoslavia has participated in the working of some of the CMEA's bodies since 1964. Afghanistan, Angola, Ethiopia, Laos, Mexico, Mozambique, Nicaragua and the People's Democratic Republic of Yemen attend CMEA meetings as observers.

Economics

Among the history of sciences, economics has a relatively modern development.

The word *economics* was earlier (since 1393) used for the art of housekeeping. Its modern sense of the practical and theoretical science of the production and distribution of wealth first came in the context of rural economics in 1792. The earliest attempt at a rigorous treatment however dates from Galiani's *Della Moneta* published in 1751.

The first major landmark in the history of economic thought was in 1776 with the publication of *An Enquiry into the Nature and Causes of the Wealth of Nations* by Adam Smith (1723–90), the Scottish professor of Logic and Moral Philosophy. He propounded the theory that a whole community achieves the benefit of the largest possible total wealth through the delicate market balance of free competition and man's conflicting self-interests. The main stages in the development of economics are:

1776 Smith, Adam (1723–90) *An Enquiry into the Nature and Causes of the Wealth of Nations.* Argued that wealth arose out of labour (especially the division of labour). The handbook of the industrial revolution.
1798 Malthus, Thomas (1766–1834) *An Essay on the Principle of Population.* Over-population was the death knell of economic growth and prosperity.
1848 Mill, John Stuart (1806–73) *Principles of Political Economy.* Value of any commodity depended upon the amount of all factors going into its production.
1848 Marx, Karl (1818–83). *The Communist Manifesto.* Written with Friedrich Engels.
1867 Marx (see above). *Das Kapital* (Vol 2, 1885, Vol 3, 1894). Theory of 'surplus value' accruing to the insatiable capitalist. Free enterprise system is self-destructive and a 'dictatorship of the proletariat' would follow.
1890 Marshall, Alfred (1842–1924). *Principles of Economics.* Utility and costs are the joint determinants of value.
1936 Keynes, John Maynard (1883–1946). *The General Theory of Employment, Interest and Money.* Duty of state to dispel depressions by higher public expenditure even at the price of persistent inflation.
1962 Friedman, Milton (b. 1912). *Capitalism and Freedom.* Duty of states with large inflationary public sector economies to restore prosperity by cutting public spending and borrowing.

Glossary

arbitrage Process of making a buying or selling margin out of differences in commodity prices or currency values in different markets.
assets Resources employed within an enterprise to conduct its business.
asset stripping Purchasing a business with the motive of selling off its assets at a profit above the purchase price instead of perpetuating it.

Austrian School A group of University of Vienna deductive economists led by Carl Menger (1840–1921), von Wieser (1851–1926) and von Böhm-Bawerk (1851–1914). Followed in the 20th century by Ludwig von Mises (1881–1973) and Friedrich Hayek (b. 1899) who oppose the Keynesian ascendancy of macro-economics.

backwardation A percentage charge paid by the seller of stock for the right to delay delivery.
balance of payments Balance of international transactions and transfers for goods (imports and exports) and services (invisibles).
balance of trade The solely *current* account sector of the balance of payments. This latter embraces also the capital account.
bank rate The rate at which a central bank will lend to its national banking system. In Britain this rate was pivotal to interest levels until replaced by Minimum Lending Rate or MLR.
banks, joint stock Banks whose principal function is to receive deposits and make short term loans, mainly for working capital. Also described as commercial banks.
bear A speculator who sells on a falling market in the hope that he may buy back at a lower level.
bill of exchange A transferable and unconditional order drawn by a creditor on a debtor for discharge on an agreed fixed date – hence a 90 day bill.
bridging loan Often applied to bank or other loans where the borrower is prepared to bear interest for a fixed period, to avoid losing an intended new investment, while anticipating the sale of another.
bull A speculator who buys stock in the belief that he will be able to sell it at a profit (see bear).

capitalism A social system in which work is undertaken for individual reward, under a system of free contract, and capital is ownable by private persons.
cartels Associations which limit competition by price-fixing and/or market-sharing.
CIF Cost, insurance, freight. The inclusion of these on-costs in the quoted price.
communism The official doctrine, originating from Lenin's interpretation of the writings of Marx, which controls the USSR, China, Eastern European and other countries. A system of society with vesting of property in the community, each member working for the common benefit according to his capacity and receiving according to his needs.

demurrage Payment by a shipper to a shipowner for discharging or loading delays beyond the stipulated time contracted.
depreciation The decrease in the value of an asset due to wear and tear, age, obsolescence or fall in market price.
devaluation Reducing the value of the nation's currencies thereby cheapening exports and raising the price of imports.
discounted cash flow The discounting of cash flows to present value to determine or compare the viability of a project.
disinflation Measures to relieve inflationary stress such as running a budget surplus, credit squeezes or hire purchase controls.
dividend Money yield per share from the profits or reserves of a company.

elasticity of demand Responsiveness or sensitivity of demand to a change in price. Inelastic demand is insensitive.
entrepreneur One who risks his own capital in an enterprise.
equity Ordinary (as opposed to preference) shares holding in a limited company.
exports Sales overseas or abroad of a country's goods (visible exports) or services (invisible exports).

fiduciary issues Issue of notes 'in faith' unbacked by gold or tangible assets.
floating exchange rate Exchange rates which are not fixed and which fluctuate according to foreign exchange market supply or demand.
foreign exchange market Financial centres in which foreign currency is bought and sold by dealers. In Britain these include banks, finance houses and exchange brokers.
free trade Trade which flows freely and without tariffs or other distortions so that the benefit of international specialisation is globally maximised.
funded debt Perpetual loans or debts with no fixed repayment date.

general agreement on tariffs and trade (GATT) Established in Geneva in 1947 it aims to eliminate all barriers to trade through non-discrimination and a negotiated reduction in tariffs.
gilt-edged securities Those considered absolutely safe for purposes of interest and redemption at par when they mature.
gold standard A monetary system in which the gold value of the currency is fixed by law.
Gresham's Law Tendency for money of lower intrinsic value to circulate more freely than money of higher intrinsic and equal nominal value.

hard currency Currency is 'hard' if it has an underlying strength based on internal stability and external surplus on balance of trade.
hyper-inflation Inflation so rapid that contracts can be shortened no further and flight from the currency is total, thus leading to a total economic breakdown, e.g. Germany (1922–23), Hungary (1946), China (1948–49).

indexed pension Pension rates annually or periodically adjusted to preserve value by allowing for rises (and falls) in the Retail Price Index.
indirect taxes Taxes on goods and services collected indirectly through traders or manufacturers (as opposed to direct collection as in case of income tax).

inflation A fall in the value of money caused by expansion of money supply, high public spending, credit creation, high wage settlements etc.
interest The price payable for the use of loanable funds or credit.

Keynesianism The doctrine of the macro-economist Lord Keynes (1883–1946), adopted by the British Government in 1944, that generation of demand by public spending (or budget deficit) will promote faster expansion, more private investment and higher employment levels.

liquidity The ease and speed with which an asset can be exchanged. Cash has 'perfect' liquidity whereas a deposit account requiring notice of withdrawal has not.

M1 Total money supply in its most liquid form (coin, banknotes, and immediately encashable assets).
M2 (Not used since 1972) M1 plus clearing bank and discount house deposits.
M3 M1 plus assets liquefiable in the short term, *viz* Building Society deposits and shares encashable within the account period.
market economy Conditions of competitive, non-centralized supply and demand that operates like a continuous referendum, between consumers and manufacturers, buyers and sellers, and lenders and borrowers.
Marxism The doctrine of the co-author of the *Communist Manifesto* (1848), Karl Marx (1818–1883). He advocated the abolition of private property, and State provision of work and subsistence for all.
monetarism The doctrine that the avoidance of inflation and deflation is better achieved by monetary rather than fiscal methods, i.e. by control over money supply (*via* interest rates, hire purchase and other credit creations, and levels of public spending and borrowing).

national income The total of incomes of all residents, companies and government bodies derived from goods and services produced through economic activity.
negative income tax A device for alleviating poverty by 'topping up' the lowest band of incomes by fiscal rebate rather than by conventional social benefits.

overmanning The employment of more labour than required to achieve efficient production due to unfulfilled expectations of rising demand, anxiety to deny skilled workers to a competitor, or trade union pressure to prevent job losses.

PAYE Pay As You Earn system of collection of income tax from current earnings. Developed from a German model by Sir Paul Chambers. Introduced into Britain in 1944.
public sector borrowing requirement (PSBR) The amount by which the revenue of public sector organizations falls short of expenditure. This deficit, by central and local authorities and nationalized industries, is financed by sales of securities, increases in currency, borrowing from overseas and bank lending to the public sector.

reflation The initial and temporary phase in the upturn from a slump in which extra spending is matched by increased supply. Reflation ends and inflation starts if demand continues or grows to the point of raising prices.
reverse income tax *See* Negative Income Tax.

stagflation A simultaneous presence of rises in prices and rises in unemployment levels once thought by economists to be mutually exclusive.
syndicalism A doctrine whereunder industry is controlled by workers.

treasury bills Bills issued by the Treasury (originating in 1873) in multiples of £5000 for short term (3 months) funding of Government debt.

value added tax A tax levied on the basis of the cost of 'inputs' of materials and labour as opposed to a turnover or sales tax.

zero price Economists jargon for a state service supplied at no cost to the eligible recipient at the time. The tax-price, paid by most people, is paid only later and indirectly.

Gross national product

The economic power of a nation is reflected in its gross national product (GNP) and its national income.

Gross national product is derived from gross domestic product at factor cost plus net property income from overseas. National income is GNP less capital consumption.

Gross domestic product at factor cost can be determined in two ways, (A) by the expenditure generating it, or (B) the incomes, rent and profits which enable the expenditure. The components in any year are thus:

A	B
Consumers' expenditure	Income from employment
Public authority current spending	Income from self-employment
Gross fixed capital formation	Gross trading profits of companies
Value of work in progress	Gross profits and surpluses of public corporations
Value of physical increase in stocks	Rent *less* stock appreciation
Exports *less* imports	
Income from abroad *less* payments abroad	
Subsidies *less* taxes on expenditure	
= Gross Domestic Product	= Gross Domestic Product

GNP of countries of the world, 1983

Country/territory	Gross national product ($ million)
Afghanistan	2290
Albania	1930
Algeria	49 450
American Samoa	140
Andorra	na
Angola	3320
Antigua and Barbuda	140
Argentina	58 560
Aruba	na
Australia	166 230
Austria	69 830
Bahamas	900
Bahrain	4120
Bangladesh	12 530
Barbados	1020
Belgium	90 540
Belize	170
Benin	1110
Bermuda	840
Bhutan	110
Bolivia	3070
Botswana	920
Brazil	245 590
Brunei	4420
Bulgaria	37 390
Burkina Faso	1210
Burma	6500
Burundi	1050
Cameroon	7640
Canada	300 400
Cape Verde	110
Central African Republic	690
Chad	360
Channel Islands	1380
Chile	21 890
China, People's Republic	301 840
China (Taiwan)	38 200

Country/territory	Gross national product ($ million)
Colombia	38 830
Comoros	120
Congo, People's Republic	2180
Costa Rica	2420
Cuba	12 330
Cyprus	2430
Czechoslovakia	89 260
Denmark	58 850
Djibouti	180
Dominica	80
Dominican Republic	8170
East Timor	100
Ecuador	11 690
Egypt	31 880
El Salvador	3690
Equatorial Guinea	62
Ethiopia	4860
Faeroe Islands	440
Fiji	1190
Finland	50 730
France	568 690
French Guiana	210
French Polynesia	1260
Gabon	2950
Gambia	200
German Democratic Republic	120 940
Germany, Federal Republic	702 440
Ghana	3980
Gibraltar	130
Greece	39 210
Greenland	550
Grenada	110
Guadeloupe	1370
Guam	690
Guatemala	8890
Guinea	1740
Guinea-Bissau	150
Guyana	410
Haiti	1700
Honduras	2740
Hong Kong	31 900
Hungary	23 050
Iceland	2430
India	190 710
Indonesia	87 120
Iran	69 170
Iraq	39 500
Ireland	16 960
Isle of Man	340
Israel	21 990
Italy	357 570
Ivory Coast	6730
Jamaica	2940
Japan	1 204 270
Jordan	4400
Kampuchea	570
Kenya	6450
Kiribati	30
Korea, Democratic People's Republic	17 040
Korea, Republic	80 310
Kuwait	30 290
Laos	290
Lebanon	3290
Lesotho	670
Liberia	990
Libya	25 100
Liechtenstein	na
Luxembourg	4470
Macao	780
Madagascar	2730
Malawi	1390
Malaysia	27 760
Maldives	40
Mali	1110
Malta	1310
Martinique	1330
Mauritania	720
Mauritius	1250
Mexico	168 070
Monaco	na
Mongolia	1100
Morocco	15 620
Mozambique	2810
Namibia	1920

Country/territory	Gross national product ($ million)
Nauru	na
Nepal	2660
Netherlands	142 420
Netherlands Antilles	1370
New Caledonia	1140
New Zealand	24 000
Nicaragua	2690
Niger	1460
Nigeria	71 030
Norway	57 090
Oman	7070
Pacific Islands (Trust Territory)	140
Pakistan	35 000
Panama	4070
Papua New Guinea	2510
Paraguay	4540
Peru	18 650
Philippines	39 420
Poland	139 780
Portugal	22 490
Puerto Rico	12 830
Qatar	5960
Réunion	2060
Romania	57 030
Rwanda	1540
St Christopher and Nevis	40
St Lucia	130
St Vincent and the Grenadines	90
San Marino	na
São Tomé and Príncipe	30
Saudi Arabia	127 080
Senegal	2730
Seychelles	160
Sierra Leone	1230
Singapore	16 560
Solomon Islands	160
Somalia	1140
South Africa	76 890
Spain	182 760
Spanish North Africa	90
Sri Lanka	5140
Sudan	8420
Suriname	1280
Swaziland	610
Sweden	103 240
Switzerland	105 060
Syria	16 510
Tanzania	4880
Thailand	40 380
Togo	790
Tonga	80
Trinidad and Tobago	7870
Tunisia	8860
Turkey	58 260
Tuvalu	5
Uganda	3090
USSR	1 212 030
United Arab Emirates	25 770
United Kingdom	505 610
USA	3 292 340
US Virgin Islands	890
Uruguay	7390
Vanuatu	40
Venezuela	70 820
Viet-Nam	7750
Western Sahara	na
Western Samoa	50
Yemen Arab Republic	3930
Yemen, People's Democratic Republic	1020
Yugoslavia	58 520
Zaïre	5050
Zambia	3630
Zimbabwe	5820

World statistics

Population and Gross National Product per Capita

Country or territory	Population 1984 (thousands)	GNP per capita 1983 (US$)
Afghanistan	17 150	160
Albania	2900	740
Algeria	21 265	2320
American Samoa	35	4500
Angola	8420	470
Antigua and Barbuda	79	1690
Argentina	30 104	2510
Australia	15 562	11 460
Austria	7527	9230
Bahamas	226	4050
Bahrain	407	10 480
Bangladesh	98 012	130
Barbados	255	3990
Belgium	9856	9130
Belize	156	1130
Benin	3921	290
Bermuda	58	13 540
Bhutan	1213	80
Bolivia	6198	480
Botswana	1031	880
Brazil	132 582	1870
Brunei	216	20 520
Bulgaria	8960	4150
Burkina Faso	6559	180
Burma	36 212	180
Burundi	4587	240
Cameroon	9868	820
Canada	25 183	12 280
Cape Verde	321	320
Central African Rep.	2534	280
Chad	4900	80
Channel Islands	130	11 070
Chile	11 880	1890
China	1 030 150	300
Colombia	28 076	1410
Comoros	381	340
Congo, People's Rep.	1838	1220
Costa Rica	2435	1070
Cuba	9782	2696
Cyprus	665	3670
Czechoslovakia	15 464	5820
Denmark	5110	11 540
Djibouti	358	480
Dominica	72	970
Dominican Rep.	6102	1160
Ecuador	8451	1420
Egypt	46 172	690
El Salvador	5386	680
Equatorial Guinea	366	180
Ethiopia	42 019	120
Faeroe Islands	45	11 220
Fiji	677	1780
Finland	4902	10 710
France	55 089	10 480
French Guiana	80	3230
French Polynesia	159	8210
Gabon	812	3430
Gambia	712	290
German Dem. Rep.	16 701	7180
German Fed. Rep.	61 205	11 400
Ghana	13 372	320
Gibraltar	30	4630
Greece	9888	3910
Greenland	53	7640
Grenada	92	830
Guadeloupe	318	4330
Guam	115	6490
Guatemala	8167	1110
Guinea	5948	300
Guinea-Bissau	877	190
Guyana	806	560
Haiti	5401	290
Honduras	4234	670
Hong Kong	5394	6070
Hungary	10 692	2150
Iceland	240	10 240
India	749 880	260
Indonesia	158 907	560
Iran	43 815	2060
Iraq	15 164	3020

Country or territory	Population 1984 (thousands)	GNP per capita 1983 (US$)
Ireland	3533	4990
Isle of Man	69	5980
Israel	4172	5270
Italy	57 033	6390
Ivory Coast	9876	710
Jamaica	2289	1270
Japan	120 075	10 100
Jordan	3372	1720
Kampuchea	6888	70
Kenya	19 723	340
Kiribati	61	460
Korea, Dem. People's Rep.	19 633	1000
Korea, Rep. of	40 576	2010
Kuwait	1790	16 200
Laos	3738	80
Lebanon	2635	1070
Lesotho	1490	560
Liberia	2122	480
Libya	3620	8460
Luxembourg	365	14 620
Macao	310	2560
Madagascar	9712	310
Malawi	6831	210
Malaysia	15 206	1870
Maldives	173	260
Mali	7341	150
Malta	360	3480
Martinique	311	4260
Mauritania	1664	480
Mauritius	1003	1160
Mexico	76 949	2180
Mongolia	1852	700
Montserrat	14	2420
Morocco	21 347	760
Mozambique	13 427	270
Namibia	1128	1670
Nepal	16 054	160
Netherlands	14 411	9870
Netherlands Antilles	259	5430
New Caledonia	147	6600
New Zealand	3249	7710
Nicaragua	3116	880
Niger	6252	240
Nigeria	96 816	770
Norway	4151	13 990
Oman	1186	6230
Pacific Islands (Trust Territory)	143	1080
Pakistan	92 411	390
Panama	2009	2110
Papua New Guinea	3253	760
Paraguay	3291	1320
Peru	18 297	1040
Philippines	53 404	750
Poland	36 918	3900
Portugal	10 202	2230
Puerto Rico	3331	3800
Qatar	292	21 160
Réunion	529	3920
Romania	22 628	2540
Rwanda	5864	270
St Christopher and Nevis	46	1320
St Lucia	134	1050
St Vincent	109	840
São Tomé and Príncipe	106	340
Saudi Arabia	10 833	12 220
Senegal	6393	440
Seychelles	64	2430
Sierra Leone	3668	330
Singapore	2533	6660
Solomon Islands	263	640
Somalia	5231	250
South Africa	32 722	2240
Spain	38 523	4770
Sri Lanka	15 646	330
Sudan	21 467	400
Suriname	384	3390
Swaziland	730	870
Sweden	8337	12 440
Switzerland	6572	16 250
Syria	9927	1790
Tanzania	21 489	240
Thailand	50 109	820
Togo	2928	280

Country or territory	Population 1984 (thousands)	GNP per capita 1983 (US$)
Tonga	106	780
Trinidad and Tobago	1170	6830
Tunisia	7068	1290
Turkey	48 266	1250
Uganda	14 325	220
USSR	275 029	4550
United Arab Emirates	1277	23 770
United Kingdom	56 327	9180
US	236 961	14 080
Uruguay	2990	2470
Vanuatu	131	350
Venezuela	17 829	3830
Viet-Nam	60 069	160
Virgin Islands (US)	102	8460
Western Samoa	163	350
Yemen Arab Rep.	7790	550
Yemen, PDR	2021	520
Yugoslavia	22 955	2490
Zaïre	30 583	170
Zambia	6477	580
Zimbabwe	8173	740

The World's Capital Cities

Country	Capital city	Population (1983)
AFRICA		
Algeria	Algiers	1 523 000
Angola	Luanda	475 328
Benin	Porto Novo	144 000
Botswana	Gaborone	59 657
Burkina Faso	Ouagadougou	77 500
Burundi	Bujumbura	78 810
Cameroon	Yaounde	291 071
Cape Verde	Praia	3628
Central African Republic	Bangui	300 723
Chad	N'djaména	179 000
Comoros	Moroni	17 267
Congo	Brazzaville	136 200
Djibouti	Djibouti	6200
Egypt	Cairo	5 074 016
Equatorial Guinea	Malabo	37 237
Ethiopia	Addis Ababa	1 412 575
Gabon	Libreville	57 000
Gambia	Banjul	49 181
Ghana	Accra	564 194
Guinea	Conakry	197 267
Guinea-Bissau	Bissau	109 214
Ivory Coast	Abidjan	282 000
Kenya	Nairobi	1 103 554
Lesotho	Maseru	13 312
Liberia	Monrovia	166 507
Libya	Bengazi	137 295
	Tripoli	213 506
Madagascar	Antananarivo	347 466
Malawi	Lilongwe	219 011
Mali	Bamako	399 869
Mauritania	Nouakchott	134 986
Mauritius	Port Louis	148 040
Morocco	Rabat-Salé	435 510
Mozambique	Maputo	383 795
Namibia	Windhoek	36 051
Niger	Niamey	130 299
Nigeria	Lagos	1 060 848
Réunion	St Denis	115 687
Rwanda	Kigali	116 227
St Helena	Jamestown	1475
São Tomé and Príncipe	São Tomé	5114
Senegal	Dakar	798 792
Seychelles	Port Victoria	23 012
Somalia	Mogadishu	230 000
South Africa	Capetown	697 513
	Pretoria	545 450
Sudan	Khartoum	561 000
Tunisia	Tunis	468 997
Tanzania	Dar Es Salaam	880 000
Uganda	Kampala	330 700
Western Sahara	El Aaiun	20 010
Zaïre	Kinshasa	2 242 297
Zambia	Lusaka	538 469
Zimbabwe	Harare	681 000
NORTH AMERICA		
Antigua	St John City	21 814
Bahamas	Nassau	135 437
Barbados	Bridgetown	8789
Belize	Belmopan	2932
Bermuda	Hamilton	1669
Br. Virgin Islands	Road Town	891
Canada	Ottawa	295 160
Cayman Islands	Georgetown	7617
Costa Rica	San José	274 832
Cuba	Havana	1 972 363
Dominica	Roseau	10 417
Dominican Republic	Santo Domingo	673 460
El Salvador	San Salvador	335 930
Greenland	Godthab	8425
Grenada	St George's	7303
Guadaloupe	Pointe-à-Pitre	29 522
Guatemala	Ciudad de Guatemala	793 336
Haiti	Port au Prince	461 464
Honduras	Tegucigalpa	444 230
Jamaica	Kingston	696 300
Martinique	Fort-de-France	97 814
Mexico	Mexico City	9 191 295
Montserrat	Plymouth	1267
Netherlands Antilles (Curaçao)	Willemstad	43 546
Nicaragua	Managua	608 020
Panama	Panama	389 172
Puerto Rico	San Juan	424 600
St Christopher-Nevis	Basse-Terre	14 161
St Lucia	Castries	40 451
St Pierre and Miquelon	St John's	5416
St Vincent and the Grenadines	Kingstown	4308
Trinidad and Tobago	Port-of-Spain	59 649
Turks and Caicos Islands	Grand Turk	3098
United States	Washington DC	623 100
SOUTH AMERICA		
Argentina	Buenos Aires	2 922 829
Bolivia	La Paz	881 404
Brazil	Brazilia	410 999
Chile	Santiago	4 132 293
Colombia	Bogotá	2 836 361
Ecuador	Quito	820 971
Falkland Islands	Port Stanley	1079
French Guiana	Cayenne	38 093
Guyana	Georgetown	72 049
Paraguay	Asunción	457 210
Peru	Lima	4 164 597
Surinam	Paramaribo	110 867
Uruguay	Montevideo	1 173 254
Venezuela	Caracas	1 816 901
ASIA		
Afghanistan	Kabul	1 127 417
Bahrain	Manama	108 684
Bangladesh	Dacca	3 458 602
Bhutan	Thimphu	8922
Brunei	Banda Seribegawan	49 902
Burma	Rangoon	2 276 000
China	Beijing (Peking)	5 531 460
Cyprus	Nicosia	180 000
East Timor	Diw	52 158
Hong Kong	Victoria	633 138
India	New Delhi	6 273 036
Indonesia	Jakarta	6 503 449
Iran	Teheran	5 734 000
Iraq	Baghdad	1 490 759
Israel	Jerusalem	428 668
Japan	Tokyo	8 361 054
Jordan	Amman	744 000
Kampuchea	Phnom Penh	393 995
Korea	Seoul	8 364 379
Kuwait	Kuwait City	78 116
Laos	Vientaine	132 253
Lebanon	Beirut	474 870
Macau	Macau	241 413
Malaysia	Kuala Lumpur	451 997
Maldives	Male	29 522
Mongolia	Ulan Bator	435 400
Nepal	Kathmandu	235 160
Oman	Muscat	5080
Pakistan	Islamabad	204 364
Philippines	Quezon City	1 165 865
Qatar	Doha	45 000
Sabah	Kuta Kinabalu	40 939
Sarawak	Kuching	63 535
Saudi Arabia	Riyadh	666 840
Singapore	Singapore	2 529 100
Sri Lanka	Colombo	123 000
Syria	Damascus	1 112 214
Thailand	Bangkok	4 697 071
Turkey	Ankara	1 981 300
United Arab Emirates	Abu Dhabi	242 975
Viet-Nam	Hanoi	414 620
Yemen Arab Rep.	Sana	140 339
People's Rep. of Yemen	Aden	271 590
EUROPE		
Albania	Tirana	206 118
Austria	Vienna	1 562 000
Belgium	Brussels	139 678
Bulgaria	Sofia	1 076 737
Channel Islands	St Helier	25 698
Czechoslovakia	Prague	1 184 862
Denmark	Copenhagen	486 593
Faroe Islands	Thorshaven	10 726
Finland	Helsinki	484 365
France	Paris	2 188 960
German-Democratic Republic	Berlin	1 189 353
Germany, Federal Republic	Bonn	291 509
Gibraltar	Gibraltar	26 479
Greece	Athens	885 737
Hungary	Budapest	2 064 341
Iceland	Reykjavik	87 309
Ireland	Dublin	525 360
Isle of Man	Douglas	19 821
Italy	Rome	2 836 123
Leichtenstein	Vaduz	4904
Luxembourg	Luxembourg	78 912
Malta	Valetta	14 040
Monaco	Monaco	27 063
Netherlands	Amsterdam	681 918
Norway	Oslo	448 016
Poland	Warsaw	1 634 789
Portugal	Lisbon	807 167
Romania	Bucharest	1 979 076
San Marino	San Marino	6567
Spain	Madrid	3 188 297
Sweden	Stockholm	650 952
United Kingdom England and Wales	London	6 696 008
N. Ireland	Belfast	322 600
Scotland	Edinburgh	440 902
USSR	Moscow	8 396 000
Yugoslavia	Belgrade	1 087 915
OCEANIA		
American Samoa	Pago Pago	3075
Australia	Canberra	255 900
Fiji	Suva	63 628
French Polynesia	Papeete	25 342
Guam	Agana	896
Kiribati	Tarawa	17 921
New Caledonia	Noumea	56 078
New Zealand	Wellington	133 700
Papua New Guinea	Port Moresby	116 952

Country	Capital city	Population (1983)
Pitcairn	Adamstown	55
Samoa	Apia	32 099
Solomon Islands	Honiara	14 942
Tonga	Nuku' Alofa	18 312
Vanuatu	Vila	3072

Car ownership (1980)

Country	Cars per 1000 inhabitants	Total
United States	529·92	121 723 650
Monaco	518·11	13 471
Luxembourg	480·72	173 061
Australia	470·46	6 977 000
Canada	426·95	10 255 511
New Zealand	421·98	1 346·124
West Germany	384·30	23 680 911
Switzerland	378·86	2 394 455
Iceland	373·58	85 924
France	367·85	19 750 000
Falkland Islands	360·00	720
Sweden	347·32	2 893 242
Netherlands	325·77	4 600 000
Belgium	320·35	3 158·737
Italy	313·81	17 900·000
Norway	311·14	1 278 817
Kuwait	308·71	435 291
Austria	307·98	2 312 932
United Kingdom	272·57	15 267 000
Martinique	269·34	91 578
Finland	267·05	1 279 192
Gibraltar	266·66	8000
Denmark	266·44	1 366 867
Guadeloupe	265·78	87 709
Puerto Rico	262·59	929 583
French Guiana	243·31	16 789
Ireland	226·48	774 594
New Caledonia	219·20	30 250
Spain	212·38	7 943 325
Japan	208·64	24 612 277
Bahamas	206·68	49 605
Bermuda	200·27	14 420
Réunion	199·70	99 850
Malta	194·61	66 170
Czechoslovakia	156·79	2 475 774
Cyprus	152·53	96 097
Trinidad and Tobago	146·10	170 948
Israel	115·95	459 178
Venezuela	104·99	1 501 382
Hungary	103·11	1 105 446
Yugoslavia	101·94	2 284 693
Portugal	99·83	995 387
Barbados	97·61	24 600
Lebanon	95·67	310 000
Greece	94·50	912 016
Argentina	92·67	2 576 300
Saudi Arabia	87·76	757 395
South Africa	81·20	2 446 000
Brazil	75·20	9 565 914
Poland	73·99	2 634 338
Netherlands Antilles	73·64	20 620
Singapore	68·26	165 198
Suriname	67·94	26 500
Cook Island	65·82	1119
Mexico	61·75	4 808 014
Uruguay	58·73	172 099
Gabon	58·68	32 274
Seychelles	56·06	3700
Bulgaria	54·00	480 000
Malaysia	53·41	729 089
Panama	47·28	90 310
St Christopher-Nevis	44·78	2329
Chile	44·72	505 000
St Lucia	44·55	5302
Grenada	43·88	4783
Hong Kong	43·61	227 658
Taiwan	40·77	717 595
Fiji	39·80	25 475
Guyana	36·54	32 521
Djibouti	32·14	8035

Country	Cars per 1000 inhabitants	Total
Algeria	30·34	573 573
Zimbabwe	29·14	221 536
USSR	29·00	7 500 000
Iran	28·00	1 020 000*
Dominica	27·97	2238
Jordan	27·40	90 439
Jamaica	27·27	60 000
Ecuador	26·91	232 564
Mauritius	24·96	25 215
Swaziland	24·19	13 308
Colombia	24·13	672 385
Ivory Coast	23·92	193 564
Costa Rica	20·86	48 188
Tunisia	20·34	132 439
Morocco	20·20	425 000
Zambia	19·00	105 000*
Dominican Republic	18·23	102 127
Turkey	18 06	812 122
Peru	15·58	284 518
Iraq	15·56	210 000
El Salvador	14·39	72 547
Honduras	14·18	54 200
Togo	12·00	29 000
Yemen Arab Republic	11·97	72 698
Gambia	11·65	7400
Romania	10·50	230 000
Botswana	10·27	8836
Egypt	9·54	410 558
Senegal	8·75	50 875
Paraguay	8·73	27 530
Thailand	8·56	413 249
Nicaragua	8·52	24 887
Sri Lanka	8·36	126 256
Bolivia	8·35	48 274
Central African Republic	7·40	14 200*
Madagascar	7·22	64 806
Mauritania	6·70	11 262
South Korea	6·55	267 605
Kenya	6·49	113 629
Philippines	6·32	318 085
Papua New Guinea	5·68	17 730
Indonesia	4·91	579 995
Niger	4·73	25 844
Somalia	4·58	17 200
Sierra Leone	4·48	16 009
Haiti	3·40	17 377
Lesotho	3·13	4301
Zaïre	3·11	89 471
Nigeria	2·97	262 550
Ghana	2·81	33 000
Malawi	2·30	14 102
Tanzania	2·28	43 248
Upper Volta	2·18	15 537
Afghanistan	2·12	34 506
Pakistan	1·92	164 099
Ethiopia	1·29	41 227
Burundi	1·28	5984
Rwanda	1·27	6465
Cameroon	1·22	10 692
India	1·10	757 247
Liberia	0·84	1632
Uganda	0·78	11 020

* 1978

Home ownership (1980)

Country	Householders owning their dwellings (%)
Mongolia	100·0
Tokelau	97·7
Pacific Islands	94·3
Samoa	93·4
Niue Island	90·8
Indonesia	87 0
Cyprus	86·3
Thailand	85·9
India	84·6
Philippines	83·3
Iraq	83·0

Country	Householders owning their dwellings (%)
Haiti	82·9
Cayman Islands	82·0
Paraguay	81·8
Syria	81·6
St Pierre and Miquelon	81·4
Pakistan	80·3
San Marino	78·2
Faeroe Islands	77·8
Nepal	75·8
Cuba	74·7
St Vincent and the Grenadines	74·7
Bolivia	74·2
Barbados	73·5
Montserrat	72·7
Honduras	71·8
Iran	71·6
Puerto Rico	71·5
Bulgaria	71·0
Venezuela	70·9
American Samoa	70·7
Tunisia	70·7
Yugoslavia	70·7
Greece	70·6
Dominican Republic	70·5
Iceland	70·3
Turks and Caicos	70·3
Peru	69·5
Ireland	68·8
Vietnam	68·4
Australia	67·3
Israel	67·2
Nicaragua	66·1
Mexico	66·0
Norfolk Island	66·0
Guadeloupe	65·9
St Lucia	63·8
Sri Lanka	63·3
Hungary	62·9
Panama	62·9
United States	62·9
Réunion	62·8
Martinique	61·2
Ecuador	60·8
Bahrain	60·6
Brazil	60·4
Canada	60·0
Trinidad and Tobago	59·3
Sudan	59·2
Argentina	58·9
Japan	58·8
Netherlands Antilles	58·6
Finland	58·5
Belize	57·9
Spain	57·2
St Christopher-Nevis	57·2
Guyana	56·8
Guatemala	56·7
Costa Rica	56·3
Antigua	55·9
Luxembourg	55·9
Bahamas	55·1
British Virgin Islands	54·5
Congo	54·5
Belgium	53·6
Colombia	53·5
Norway	52·6
Chile	52·3
Jamaica	52·1
Italy	50·9
New Caledonia	50·8
Czechoslovakia	50·4
Malaysia: Sarawak	49·8
Austria	49·4
Turkey	49·3
Malaysia: Sabah	48·8
Jordan	48·5
Mauritius	48·5
Zimbabwe	48·0
El Salvador	47·9
Zaïre	47·4
St Helena	46·6
Greenland	46·2
Guam	46·0

Country	Householders owning their dwellings (%)
Denmark	45·7
United Kingdom: Northern Ireland	45·6
France	45·5
Portugal	44·5
Suriname	44·0
French Guiana	43·5
Egypt	43·0
United Kingdom: England and Wales	43·0
Malawi	39·6
Uruguay	39·4
Bermuda	39·1
Seychelles	37·2
Morocco	37·0
Sweden	35·2
West Germany	33·5
Malta	32·4
Virgin Islands	30·5
Kuwait	29·9
United Kingdom: Scotland	29·3
Switzerland	28·5
Ethiopia	28·1
New Zealand	26·5
Monaco	26·3
Netherlands	25·7
Tanzania	25·7
East Germany	23·0
Singapore	22·0
Brunei	20·6
Hong Kong	18·1
Papua New Guinea	16·3
Nauru	11·0
Nigeria	8·0
Gibraltar	4·4
Cocos (Keeling) Islands	0·7
Christmas Island	0·6
USSR	n.a.

Life expectancy, years at birth, 1981

Males Country	Life expectancy	Females Country	Life expectancy
Iceland	73·00	Iceland	79·20
Norway	72·31	Norway	78·65
Sweden	72·23	Netherlands	78·40
Japan	72·15	Sweden	78·14
Netherlands	72·00	France	77·85
Denmark	71·50	Denmark	77·50
Israel	71·50	Japan	77·35
Switzerland	70·29	Finland	77·12
Puerto Rico	70·21	Puerto Rico	77·11
Greece	70·13	United States	76·50
Cyprus	70·00	Canada	76·36
France	69·73	Switzerland	76·22
Spain	69·69	United Kingdom: England and Wales	75·82
United Kingdom: England and Wales	69·62	West Germany	75·64
Canada	69·30	Austria	75·60
West Germany	68·99	Ireland	75·32
Italy	68·97	Hong Kong	75·01
East Germany	68·82	Israel	75·00
Ireland	68·77	Poland	75·00
United States	68·70	Spain	74·96
Bulgaria	68·68	Italy	74·88
New Zealand	68·55	New Zealand	74·60
Austria	68·54	East Germany	74·42
Cuba	68·50	Belgium	74·21
Fiji	68·50	Luxembourg	73·90
Finland	68·49	United Kingdom: Northern Ireland	73·84
Malta	68·27	Greece	73·64
Belgium	67·79	United Kingdom: Scotland	73·61
Australia	67·63	Hungary	73·26
United Kingdom: Northern Ireland	67·54	Malta	73·10
Romania	67·42	Cyprus	72·90
Hong Kong	67·36	Bermuda	72·35
Poland	67·30	Romania	72·06
United Kingdom: Scotland	67·23	Portugal	72·03
Luxembourg	67·00	Cuba	71·80
Czechoslovakia	66·99	Fiji	71·70
Hungary	66·72	Uruguay	71·56
Kuwait	66·40	Kuwait	71·50
Costa Rica	66·26	Argentina	71·38
Bermuda	65·60	Costa Rica	70·49
Uruguay	65·51	Yugoslavia	70·22
Yugoslavia	65·42	Singapore	70·00
Portugal	65·29	Malaysia	69·95
Argentina	65·16	Seychelles	69·90
Singapore	65·10	Venezuela	69·70
American Samoa	65·00	American Samoa	69·10
Venezuela	65·00	Trinidad and Tobago	68·11
Malaysia	64·92	Panama	67·50
Albania	64·90	Barbados	67·43
Sri Lanka	64·80	Martinique	67·40
Samoa	64·30	Bahamas	67·30
Panama	64·26	Guadeloupe	67·30
Trinidad and Tobago	64·08	Albania	67·00
Bahamas	64·00	South Korea	67·00
Soviet Union	64·00	Sri Lanka	66·90
Martinique	63·30	Suriname	66·76
South Korea	63·00	Jamaica	66·63
Mexico	62·76	Mexico	66·57
Barbados	62·70	Greenland	66·20
Jamaica	62·65	Chile	66·01
Seychelles	62·50	Netherlands-Antilles	65·70
Suriname	62·50	Grenada	65·60
Brunei	61·90	Mauritius	65·31
Lebanon	61·40	Lebanon	65·10
China	60·70	China	64·40
Greenland	60·70	Antigua	64·32
Mauritius	60·60	Samoa	64·30
Chile	60·48	Paraguay	63·60
Antigua	60·40	Guyana	63·01
Paraguay	60·30	North Korea	62·50
Grenada	60·14	Réunion	62·40
Mongolia	59·10	Mongolia	62·30
Guyana	59·03	Brunei	62·10
Netherlands-Antilles	58·90	Turkey	62·00
North Korea	58·80	St Christopher-Nevis	61·90
Colombia	58·50	Colombia	61·20
St Vincent and the Grenadines	58·46	Brazil	61·10
St Christopher-Nevis	57·97	El Salvador	60·42
Iran	57·63	Cape Verde	60·00
Brazil	57·61	Philippines	60·00
Dominican Republic	57·15	St Vincent and the Grenadines	59·67
Dominica	56·97	South Africa	59·40

Country (Males)	Life expectancy	Country (Females)	Life expectancy
		Dominica	59·18
Kiribati	56·90	Kiribati	59·00
Philippines	56·90	Thailand	58·70
South Africa	56·60	Syria	58·63
El Salvador	56·56	Dominican Republic	58·59
Cape Verde	56·30	St Lucia	58·47
Solomon Islands	56·00	Ecuador	58·07
Réunion	55·80	Solomon Islands	58·00
St Lucia	55·13	Iran	57·44
Ecuador	54·89	Tunisia	56·00
Syria	54·49	Honduras	55·90
Tunisia	54·00	Peru	55·48
Pakistan	53·72	Algeria	55·00
Turkey	53·70	British Virgin Isles	54·76
Thailand	53·60	Montserrat	54·76
Algeria	52·90	Nicaragua	54·60
Jordan	52·60	Libya	54·50
Peru	52·59	Morocco	54·50
Guadeloupe	52·50	Iraq	54·30
Honduras	52·40	Egypt	53·80
Egypt	51·60	Zimbabwe	53·30
Libya	51·40	Jordan	52·00
Morocco	51·40	Uganda	51·70
Iraq	51·20	Burma	51·50
Nicaragua	51·20	Kenya	51·20
Zimbabwe	49·80	Bolivia	51·10
Montserrat	49·53	Haiti	50·00
British Virgin Isles	49·50	Mozambique	50·00
Burma	48·60	Guatemala	49·74
Uganda	48·30	Tanzania	49·70
Guatemala	48·29	Belize	48·97
Indonesia	47·50	Lesotho	48·90
Namibia	47·50	Pakistan	48·80
Papua New Guinea	47·50	Botswana	47·50
Haiti	47·10	Indonesia	47·50
Kenya	46·90	Zambia	47·50
Lesotho	46·70	Papua New Guinea	47·00
Bolivia	46·50	Kampuchea	46·90
India	46·40	Bangladesh	46·60
Tanzania	46·40	Comoros	46·60
Bangladesh	45·80	Saudi Arabia	46·50
Liberia	45·80	Vietnam	46·00
Belize	44·90	Cameroon	45·10
Benin	44·80	Congo	45·10
Botswana	44·30	Equatorial Guinea	45·10
Zambia	44·30	Ghana	45·10
Saudi Arabia	44·20	Ivory Coast	45·10
Kampuchea	44·00	Namibia	45·10
Comoros	43·40	Zaïre	45·10
Vietnam	43·20	Benin	45·00
Sudan	43·00	Gabon	45·00
Nepal	42·20	Nepal	45·00
Bhutan	42·00	Rwanda	45·00
Cameroon	41·90	Sierra Leone	45·00
Congo	41·90	Sudan	45·00
Equatorial Guinea	41·90	Swaziland	45·00
Ghana	41·90	India	44·70
Ivory Coast	41·90	Malawi	44·20
Mozambique	41·90	Liberia	44·00
Zaïre	41·90	Burundi	43·00
Rwanda	41·80	Guinea	42·60
Sierra Leone	41·80	Somalia	42·60
Swaziland	41·80	Gambia	42·50
Malawi	40·90	Mali	42·50
South Yemen	40·60	Mauritania	42·50
Burundi	40·00	Niger	42·50
Afghanistan	39·90	Senegal	42·50
Gambia	39·40	South Yemen	42·40
Guinea	39·40	Laos	41·80
Mali	39·40	Afghanistan	40·70
Mauritania	39·40	Bhutan	40·50
Niger	39·40	Angola	40·10
Senegal	39·40	Ethiopia	40·10
Somalia	39·40	Guinea-Bissau	40·10
Laos	39·10	Yemen Arab Republic	38·70
Madagascar	37·50	Togo	38·50
Yemen Arab Republics	37·30	Madagascar	38·30
Nigeria	37·20	Nigeria	36·70
Angola	37·00	Central African Republic	36·00
Ethiopia	37·00	Chad	35·00
Guinea-Bissau	37·00	Upper Volta	31·10
Central African Republic	37·00		
Upper Volta	32·10		
Togo	32·10		
Chad	29·00		
Gabon	25·00		

Alcoholic liquor consumption per year

Country	Per capita consumption of alcoholic liquors (litres)
Japan	26·9
Canada	11·0
United States	9·0
Brazil	6·8
Hong Kong	6·3
Luxembourg	5·8
Poland	5·5
Singapore	5·5
Venezuela	5·3
Hungary	4·5
East Germany	4·3
New Zealand	4·0
Argentina	3·8
Czechoslovakia	3·5
Netherlands	3·4
West Germany	3·4
Soviet Union	3·3
Spain	3·0
Sweden	3·0
Finland	2·9
Malta	2·6
Yugoslavia	2·6
France	2·5
Belgium	2·4
Iceland	2·4
Philippines	2·3
Romania	2·3
Ireland	2·2
Thailand	2·2
Bulgaria	2·0
Italy	2·0
Switzerland	2·0
Cyprus	1·9
United Kingdom	1·9
Norway	1·8
Austria	1·6
South Africa	1·6
Denmark	1·4
Greece	1·4
Australia	1·0
Israel	0·9
Mexico	0·9
Portugal	0·9
Turkey	0·5
Malaysia	0·3
Egypt	0·2
India	0·2
Indonesia	0·1

Broadcasting: Numbers of radios and televisions, 1983

Country	No. of radio receivers in use or licences issued (thousands)	No. of television receivers in use or licences issued (thousands)
AFRICA		
Algeria	4400	1325
Angola	162	33
Benin	290	13
Botswana	120	na
Burkina Faso	122	35
Burundi	178	na
Cameroon	820	na
Cape Verde	47	na
Central African Republic	140	1·4
Chad	1050	na
Comoros	54	na
Congo	100	4·5
Djibouti	23	11
Egypt	8000	2000
Equatorial Guinea	115	2
Ethiopia	3300	40
Gabon	102	20
Gambia	90	na
Ghana	2200	76
Guinea	160	8
Guinea-Bissau	28	na
Ivory Coast	1200	370

Country	No. of radio receivers in use or licences issued (thousands)	No. of television receivers in use or licences issued (thousands)
Kenya	640	75
Lesotho	40	na
Liberia	380	24
Libya	750	220
Madagascar	2000	71
Malawi	310	na
Mali	121	na
Mauritania	180	na
Mauritius	210	85
Morocco	3600	860
Mozambique	275	2·1
Niger	280	11
Nigeria	7000	457
Réunion	120	90
Rwanda	300	na
St Helena	1·8	na
São Tomé and Príncipe	25	na
Senegal	440	6
Seychelles	23	0·5
Sierra Leone	700	22
Somalia	134	na
South Africa	8700	2300
Sudan	5000	1000
Swaziland	93	2·5
Togo	590	13
Tunisia	1124	370
Uganda	320	81
Tanzania	591	9
Western Sahara	32	2·7
Zaïre	3000	12
Zambia	170	76
Zimbabwe	350	97

NORTH AMERICA

Country	No. of radio	No. of television
Antigua and Barbuda	20	19
Bahamas	118	36
Barbados	191	55
Belize	79	na
Bermuda	65	39
British Virgin Isles	6	2·5
Canada	18 950	11 530
Cayman Islands	18	3·5
Costa Rica	205	181
Cuba	3121	1658
Dominica	39	na
Dominican Republic	1200	550
El Salvador	1900	330
Greenland	19	4·4
Grenada	38	na
Guadeloupe	39	38
Guatemala	340	202
Haiti	120	19
Honduras	200	52
Jamaica	890	200
Martinique	55	42
Mexico	21 800	8300
Montserrat	6	na
Netherlands Antilles	175	57
Nicaragua	850	200
Panama	335	255
Former Canal Zone	46	20
Puerto Rico	2450	980
St Christopher and Nevis and Anguilla	21	4·5
St Lucia	96	2
St Pierre and Miquelon	4	3·4
Trinidad and Tobago	355	300
Turks and Caicos Islands	4	na
United States	479 000	185 300
US Virgin Islands	90	56

Country	No. of radio receivers in use or licences issued (thousands)	No. of television receivers in use or licences issued (thousands)
SOUTH AMERICA		
Argentina	16 000	5910
Bolivia	3500	386
Brazil	50 000	16 500
Chile	3550	1350
Colombia	3650	2700
Ecuador	2950	570
Falkland Islands	1·5	na
French Guiana	60	12
Guyana	350	na
Paraguay	260	81
Peru	3000	920
Suriname	220	43
Uruguay	1700	376
Venezuela	6650	2050
ASIA		
Afghanistan	1350	51
Bahrain	160	121
Bangladesh	770	84
Bhutan	12	na
Brunei	49	29
Burma	864	6
China	70 000	7000
Cyprus	400	91
Hong Kong	2710	1195
India	45 000	2096
Indonesia	22 000	3500
Iran	7500	2300
Iraq	2750	800
Israel	1107	1050
Japan	85 000	66 342
Jordan	620	220
Kampuchea	900	60
Korea	18 000	7000
Kuwait	477	431
Laos	400	na
Lebanon	2100	780
Macau	100	na
Malaysia	6500	1425
Maldives	15	na
Mongolia	182	11
Nepal	390	na
Oman	700	45
Pakistan	7000	1100
Philippines	2342	1350
Qatar	129	130
Saudi Arabia	3075	2650
Singapore	681	472
Sri Lanka	1800	50
Syria	1970	423
Thailand	7200	840
Turkey	5800	5600
United Arab Emirates	280	110
Yemen Arab Republic	125	17
People's Republic of Yemen	132	39
EUROPE		
Albania	476	196

Country	No. of radio receivers in use or licences issued (thousands)	No. of television receivers in use or licences issued (thousands)
Andorra	7	5
Austria	4000	2348
Belgium	4617	2981
Bulgaria	2055	1691
Czechoslovakia	4165	4323
Denmark	2005	1889
Faeroe Islands	17	na
Finland	4800	2100
France	47 000	20 500
German Democratic Republic	6415	5970
Germany, Federal Republic of	24 604	22 132
Gibraltar	34	7
Greece	4000	1700
Hungary	5770	3970
Iceland	139	70
Ireland	1600	838
Italy	14 213	13 831
Liechtenstein	17	8
Luxembourg	196	93
Malta	150	100
Netherlands	11 385	6460
Norway	1700	1316
Poland	9050	8542
Portugal	1700	1500
Romania	3223	3912
San Marino	11	7
Spain	10 900	9850
Sweden	7150	3245
Switzerland	2358	2450
United Kingdom	56 000	27 000
Yugoslavia	5419	4618
OCEANIA		
American Samoa	45	6
Australia	20 000	6500
Cook Islands	10	na
Fiji	400	na
French Polynesia	84	26
Guam	140	78
Kiribati	13	na
Nauru	6	na
New Caledonia	82	30
New Zealand	2850	922
Niue Island	1	na
Norfolk Island	2	na
Pacific Islands	na	7
Papua New Guinea	215	na
Samoa	70	3·5
Solomon Islands	24	na
Tonga	75	na
Vanuatu	30	na
USSR		
USSR	140 000	84 000
Byelorussian SSR	2300	2250
Ukrainian SSR	33 594	14 761

Percentage of labour force engaged in agriculture, 1984

Country	%	Country	%
Afghanistan	76·1	Brazil	35·1
Albania	57·8	Bulgaria	28·4
Algeria	45·4	Burkina Faso	78·7
Angola	55·2	Burma	49·0
Argentina	11·8	Burundi	81·1
Australia	5·0	Cambodia	71·9
Austria	7·5	Cameroon	78·9
Bahamas	7·8	Canada	4·1
Bangladesh	82·4	Cape Verde	53·7
Barbados	15·2	Central African Republic	85·3
Belgium-Luxembourg	2·5	Chad	80·1
Benin	44·4	Chile	16·6
Bhután	93·0	China, People's Republic of China	56·4
Bolivia	47·8	Colombia	24·1
Botswana	76·9	Comoros	62·2

Country	%	Country	%	Country	%
Congo	31·3	Ivory Coast	76·9	Portugal	23·6
Costa Rica	32·4	Jamaica	17·8	Romania	43·7
Cuba	20·7	Japan	8·6	Rwanda	87·6
Cyprus	32·5	Jordan	22·9	Saudi Arabia	57·7
Czechoslovakia	8·3	Kenya	75·5	Senegal	72·0
Denmark	5·8	Korea	33·9	Sierra Leone	62·3
Dominican Republic	54·0	North Korea	42·3	Singapore	1·8
Ecuador	41·9	Kuwait	1·7	Somalia	77·9
Egypt	48·8	Laos	71·5	South Africa, Republic of	27·2
El Salvador	48·1	Lebanon	7·3	Spain	14·4
Equatorial Guinea	72·4	Lesotho	80·6	Sri Lanka	52·1
Ethiopia	76·8	Liberia	67·1	Sudan	74·5
Fiji	37·3	Libya	11·3	Suriname	16·0
Finland	10·5	Madagascar	80·1	Swaziland	68·5
France	7·1	Malawi	81·0	Sweden	4·1
Gabon	74·0	Malaysia	44·7	Switzerland	4·4
Gambia	76·2	Malta	4·3	Syria	46·0
German Democratic Republic	8·4	Mauritania	80·5	Tanzania	78·7
Germany, Federal Republic of	3·1	Mauritius	26·0	Thailand	73·4
Ghana	47·7	Mexico	32·7	Togo	65·5
Greece	34·2	Mongolia	43·7	Trinidad and Tobago	15·0
Guatemala	52·4	Morocco	48·8	Tunisia	37·0
Guinea	78·0	Mozambique	60·4	Turkey	48·8
Guinea-Bissau	79·8	Nepál	92·0	Uganda	78·5
Guyana	19·5	Netherlands	4·5	UK	1·8
Haiti	63·3	New Zealand	8·4	USSR	14·0
Honduras	61·0	Nicaragua	39·4	USA	1·8
Hong Kong	2·0	Niger	85·2	Uruguay	10·7
Hungary	12·8	Nigeria	49·6	Venezuela	15·5
Iceland	9·8	Norway	6·4	Vietnam	68·0
India	60·2	Pakistan	51·3	Yemen Arab Republic	73·1
Indonesia	55·7	Panama	31·8	Yemen, People's Democratic	
Iran	35·6	Papua New Guinea	80·6	Republic of	56·1
Iraq	37·8	Paraguay	47·4	Yugoslavia	32·7
Ireland	18·8	Peru	34·5	Zaïre	72·0
Israel	6·0	Philippines	43·2	Zambia	63·9
Italy	8·9	Poland	27·2	Zimbabwe	56·5

United Kingdom

Physical and Political Geography

The various names used for the islands and parts of islands off the north-west coast of Europe geographically known as the British Isles are confusing. Geographical, political, legal and popular usages unfortunately differ, thus making definition necessary.

The British Isles is a convenient but purely *geographical* term to describe that group of islands lying off the north-west coast of Europe, comprising principally the island of Great Britain and the island of Ireland. There are four political units: the United Kingdom of Great Britain and Northern Ireland; the Republic of Ireland; the Crown dependencies of the Isle of Man and, for convenience, also the Channel Islands.
Area: 121 689 miles² *315 173 km².*
Population: 60 039 800 (1984/5 estimate).

The United Kingdom (UK) (of Great Britain and Northern Ireland)
The political style of the island of Great Britain, with its offshore islands and, since the partition of Ireland (see below), the six counties of Northern Ireland. The term United Kingdom, referring to Great Britain and (the whole island of) Ireland, first came into use officially on 1 Jan. 1801 on the Union of the two islands. With the coming into force of the Constitution of the Irish

Free State as a Dominion on 6 Dec. 1922, the term 'United Kingdom of Great Britain and Ireland' had obviously become inappropriate. It was dropped by Statute from the Royal style on 13 May 1927 in favour of 'King of Great Britain, Ireland and of, etc.'. On the same date Parliament at Westminster adopted as its style 'Parliament of the United Kingdom of Great Britain and Northern Ireland'. On 29 May 1953 by Proclamation the Royal style conformed to the Parliamentary style – Ireland having ceased to be a Dominion within the Commonwealth on 18 Apr. 1949.
Area: 94 220 miles² *244 030 km².*
Population: 56 487 800 (1984 estimate).

Great Britain (GB) is the geographical and political name of the main or principal island of the solely geographically named British Isles group. In a strict geographical sense, off-shore islands, for example the Isle of Wight, Anglesey, or Shetland, are not part of Great Britain. In the political sense Great Britain was the political name used unofficially from 24 Mar. 1603, when James VI of Scotland succeeded his third cousin twice removed upwards, Queen Elizabeth of England, so bringing about a Union of the Crowns, until on 1 May 1707 the style was formally adopted with the Union of the Parliaments of England and Scotland and was used until 1 Jan. 1801. The government of Great Britain is unitary.
Area: 88 799 miles² *229 988 km².*
Population (mid-1985): 55 060 000.

England is geographically the southern and greater part of the island of Great Britain. The islands off the English coast, such as the Isle of Wight and the Isles of Scilly, are administratively part of England. Politically and geographically England (historically a separate Kingdom until 1707) is that part of Great Britain governed by English law which also pertains in Wales and, since 1746, in Berwick-upon-Tweed.
The term 'England' is widely (but wrongly) used abroad to mean the United Kingdom or Great Britain.
Area: 50 366 miles² *130 477 km².*
Population: 47 111 700 (mid-1985 estimate).

Isles of Scilly
Area: 4041 acres *1 635 ha* (6·31 miles² *16,35 km²*).
Population: 2006 (1981 estimate). There are five populated islands (1981 estimates) – Bryher (pop. 155), St Agnes (pop. 60), St Martin's (pop. 80), St Mary's (pop. 1650) and Tresco (pop. 155). There are 19 other islands and numerous rocks and islets.
The islands are administered by 25 councillors, which is a unique type of local government unit set up by an Order made under the Local Government Act, 1974. For some purposes the Isles are administered in company with the Cornwall County Council. The islands form part of the St Ives electoral division.

Wales (The principality of) now comprises eight instead of twelve counties. The area was incorporated into England by Act of Parliament in

1536. The former county of Monmouthshire, though for all administrative intents and purposes part of Wales, only became an integral part of Wales on 1 Apr. 1974. The other boundaries between England and Wales expressly could not be altered by the ordinary processes of local government reorganisation.

Wales may not, by Statute, be represented by fewer than 35 MPs at Westminster.
Area: 8018 miles² *20 766 km²*.
Population: 2 811 800 (mid-1985 estimate).

Scotland consists of the northern and smaller part of the island of Great Britain. The separate Kingdom of Scotland ceased on 24 March 1603 when King James VI of Scotland (ascended 1567) became also King James I of England. Both countries continued, however, to have their separate Parliaments until the Union of the Parliaments at Westminster, London, on 1 May 1707. Scotland continues to have its own distinctive legal system. By Statute Scotland may not be represented by less than 71 MPs at Westminster. On 16 May 1975 the 33 traditional counties were reduced to 9 geographical regions and 3 island authorities.
Area: 30 415 miles² *78 774 km²*.
Population: 5 137 000 (1985 estimate).

Ireland is the name of the second largest island in the geographical British Isles. Henry VIII assumed the style 'King of Ireland' in 1542, although Governors of Ireland (the exact title varied) ruled on behalf of the Kings of England from 1172. The viceroyalty did not disappear until 1937. The Union of the Parliaments of Great Britain and Ireland occurred on 1 Jan. 1801.

Northern Ireland consists of six counties in the north-eastern corner of the island. County government has been replaced by 26 districts. They are all within the larger ancient province of Ulster which originally consisted of nine counties. The government's relationship to the Imperial Parliament in England was federal in nature. Certain major powers were reserved by the Imperial Parliament, the sovereignty of which was unimpaired. There is a provision in the Ireland Act of 1949 that Northern Ireland cannot cease to be part of the United Kingdom, or part of the Queen's Dominions without the express consent of her Parliament. This Parliament, known as Stormont and established in 1921, was however abolished by the Northern Ireland Constitution Act, 1973. Devolved government came into effect on 1 Jan. 1974, but the Northern Ireland Assembly was prorogued on 29 May 1974 after the Executive collapsed. Arrangements for a Constitutional Convention, under the Northern Ireland Constitution Act 1974, which came into force in July 1974, collapsed in February 1976. Northern Ireland is represented by the fixed number of twelve Members of the Imperial Parliament at Westminster.
Area: 5450 miles² *14 120 km²*.
Population: 1 557 800 (mid-1985 estimate).

The Republic of Ireland
Te Irish Free State came into being on 15 Jan. 1922 and consists of 26 of the pre-partition total of 32 Irish counties. The original name was 'The Irish Free State' (or in Irish Gaelic 'Saorstát Eireànn') and the country had Dominion status within the British Commonwealth. A revised Constitution, which became operative on 29 Dec. 1937, abolished the former name and substituted the title 'Eire', which is the Gaelic word for 'Ireland'. On 18 Apr. 1949 the official description of the State became 'The Republic of Ireland' (Poblacht na h-Eireann), but the name of the State remains 'Ireland' in the English and 'Eire' in the Irish Gaelic language. On the same date the Republic of Ireland ceased to be a member of the British Commonwealth.
Area: 27 136 miles² *70 282 km²*.
Population (mid-1986 estimate): 3 537 195.

UNITED KINGDOM MOUNTAIN AND HILL RANGES

Scotland

Range	Length (miles)	Length (km)	Culminating peak	Height (ft)	Height (m)
Grampian Mountains	155	250	Ben Macdhui, Grampian	4300	1310
North West Highlands	140	225	Càrn Eige, Highland	3877	1181
*Southern Uplands (Scottish Lowlands)	125	200	Merrick, Dumfries & Galloway	2764	842
Liath Mountains	35	55	Càrn Dearg, Highland	3093	942

England

Range	Length (miles)	Length (km)	Culminating peak	Height (ft)	Height (m)
Pennines	120	195	Cross Fell, Cumbria	2930	893
North Downs	85	135	Leith Hill, Surrey	965	294
Cotswold Hills	60	95	Cleeve Hill, Gloucestershire	1083	330
South Downs	55	85	Butser Hill, Hampshire	888	271
Cheviot Hills	45	70	The Cheviot, Northumberland	2676	815
Chiltern Hills	45	70	Coombe Hill, Buckinghamshire	852	259
Berkshire Downs (White Horse Hills)	35	55	Walbury Hill, Berkshire	974	296
Cumbrian Mountains	30	50	Scafell Pike, Cumbria	3210	978
Exmoor	30	50	Dunkery Beacon, Somerset	1706	519
North Yorkshire Moors (Cleveland and Hambleton Hills)	30	50	Urra Moor, Bottom Head North Yorkshire	1491	454
Hampshire Downs	25	40	Pilot Hill, Hampshire	938	285
Yorkshire Wolds	22	35	Garrowby Hill, Humberside	808	246

Wales

Range	Length (miles)	Length (km)	Culminating peak	Height (ft)	Height (m)
Cambrian Mountains	110	175	Snowdon (Yr Wyddfa), Gwynedd	3560	1085
Berwyn Mountains	40	65	Aran Fawddwy, Gwynedd	2972	905

Northern Ireland

Range	Length (miles)	Length (km)	Culminating peak	Height (ft)	Height (m)
Sperrin Mountains	40	65	Sawel Mt, Londonderry-Tyrone	2240	682
Mountains of Mourne	30	50	Slieve Donard, County Down	2796	852
Antrim Hills	25	40	Trostan, Antrim	1817	553

* Includes: Lammermuir Hills (Lammer Law, Lothian 1733 ft *528 m*); Lowther Hills (Green Lowther, Strathclyde, 2403 ft *732 m*); Pentland Hills (Scald Law, Lothian, 1898 ft *578 m*) and the Tweedsmuir Hills (Broad Law, Borders, 2754 ft *839 m*).

BRITISH ISLES EXTREMITIES

Island of Great Britain
Great Britain, the eighth largest island in the world, has extreme (mainland) dimensions thus:

Most Northerly Point	Easter Head, Dunnet Head, Highland	Lat	58° 40′ 24″ N
Most Westerly Point	Corrachadh Mor, Ardnamurchan, Highland	Long	6° 14′ 12″ W
Most Southerly Point	Lizard Point, Cornwall	Lat	49° 57′ 33″ N
Most Easterly Point	Lowestoft Ness, Lowestoft, Suffolk	Long	1° 46′ 20″ E

Other extreme points (mainland) in its 3 constituent countries are:

Most Southerly Point in Scotland	Gallie Craig, Mull of Galloway, Dumfries & Galloway	Lat	54° 38′ 27″ N
Most Easterly Point in Scotland	Keith Inch, Peterhead, Grampian	Long	1° 45′ 49″ W
Most Northerly Point in England	Meg's Dub, Northumberland	Lat	55° 48′ 37″ N
Most Westerly Point in England	Dr Syntax's Head, Land's End, Cornwall	Long	5° 42′ 15″ W
Most Northerly Point in Wales	Point of Air, Clwyd	Lat	53° 21′ 08″ N
Most Westerly Point in Wales	Porthtaflod, Dyfed	Long	5° 19′ 43″ W
Most Southerly Point in Wales	Rhoose Point, South Glamorgan	Lat	51° 22′ 40″ N
Most Easterly Point in Wales	Lady Park Wood, Gwent	Long	2° 38′ 49″ W

Island of Ireland (20th largest island in the world)

Most Northerly Point in Ireland	Malin Head, Donegal	Lat	55° 22′ 30″ N
Most Northerly Point in Northern Ireland	Benbane Head, Moyle, Antrim	Lat	55° 15′ 0″ N
Most Westerly Point in Ireland	Dunmore Head, Kerry	Long	10° 28′ 55″ W
Most Westerly Point in Northern Ireland	Cornaglah, Fermanagh	Long	8° 10′ 30″ W
Most Southerly Point in Ireland	Brow Head, Cork	Lat	51° 26′ 30″ N
Most Southerly Point in Northern Ireland	Cranfield Point, Newry and Mourne, Down	Lat	54° 01′ 20″ N
Most Easterly Point in Ireland (Northern)	Townhead, Ards Peninsula, Down	Long	5° 26′ 52″ W
Most Easterly Point in Republic of Ireland	Wicklow Head, Wicklow	Long	5° 59′ 40″ W

The Crown Dependencies

The Isle of Man
The Isle of Man (Manx-Gaelic, *Ellan Vannin*) is a Crown dependency.
Area: 141 440 acres *57 200 ha* (221 miles² *572 km²*).
Population: 64 282 (1986 census).
Administrative headquarters: Douglas 20 368.

The ancient capital was Castletown (3019).
History: Habitation of the island has been traced to the Mesolithic period. The island was converted to Christianity in the 5th or 6th century probably by monks from Ireland. At this time the island's people spoke Gaelic. Norsemen from Scandinavia plundered the island towards the end of the 8th century but became settled around the middle of the 9th century. During the ensuing period of Norse rule, Tynwald was established as the national Parliament. In 1266 the island was sold by Norway to Scotland, but

the island alternated between English and Scottish rule until 1333 when it came under England. The island was held by a succession of English noblemen until 1405, when Henry IV granted it to the Stanley family who ruled until 1736 apart from the period 1651 to 1660 when it was under the rule of the English Commonwealth. The Stanleys became the Earls of Derby in 1485 and adopted the title Lord of Mann and the Isles. The Stanleys were succeeded by the Dukes of Atholl who sold the Lordship of Mann to the British Crown in 1765, when the island became a Crown dependency, although it has never been part of the United Kingdom. A period of rule under English officialdom followed. In 1866 the House of Keys became a popularly elected legislature for the first time since the rule of the Norse and women in the Isle of Man got the right to vote in 1881. More recent times have seen the Isle of Man gaining increasing independence from the United Kingdom. Tynwald is the oldest continuous national Parliament in the world and celebrated its millenium in 1979.

Legislature: Her Majesty the Queen as Lord of Mann appoints the Lieutenant Governor who is the nominal head of the Isle of Man Government. The island's legislative assembly is the Court of Tynwald which comprises the Legislative Council and the House of Keys. The upper house, the Legislative Council, consists of 8 members elected by the House of Keys and 2 ex-officio members, the Lord Bishop of Sodor and Man and the Attorney-General. The House of Keys is made up of 24 members who are elected from the island's 13 constituencies.

Highest point above sea-level: Snaefell (2034 ft *619 m*).
Leading Industries: Finance, agriculture, manufacturing, tourism.
Events and Attractions: Tynwald Hill, St John's; Peel Castle; Castle Rushen; Castletown; Laxey waterwheel; steam railway; electric railway; TT motor-cycle races.

THE CHANNEL ISLANDS
The Channel Islands (French: *Iles Anglo-Normandes*) are a Crown dependency. There is a Channel Isle department in the Home Office, Whitehall, London.
Area: 48 083 acres *19 458 ha* (75·13 miles² *194,6 km²*).
Guernsey (French: *Guernesey*) – 15 654 acres *6334 ha* (24·46 miles² *63,3 km²*).
Jersey – 28 717 acres *11 621 ha* (44·87 miles² *116,2 km²*).
Dependencies of Guernsey:
Alderney (French: *Aurigny*) – 1962 acres *794 ha* (3·07 miles² *7,9 km²*).
Sark (Sercq) – 1274 acres *515 ha* (1·99 miles² *5,1 km²*). (Greak Sark, 1035 acres *419 ha 4,2 km²*; Little Sark 239 acres *96 ha 0,9 km²*).
Herm – 320 acres *129 ha 1,29 km²*.
Brechou (Brecqham) – 74 acres *30 ha 0,3 km²*.
Jethou – 44 acres *18 ha*.
Lihou (Libon) – 38 acres *15 ha*.
Other islands include Ortach, Burhou, the Casquets, Les Minquiers (including Maîtresse Ile) and the Ecrehou Islands (including Marmaoutier, Blanche Ile, and Maître Ile).
Population: 137 200 (1986 estimate).

Jersey – 80 212   Alderney – 2000.
Guernsey – 54 380   Sark – 604.
Administrative headquarters: Jersey – St Helier, Guernsey and dependencies – St Peter Port.
History: The islands are known to have been inhabited by Acheulian man (before the last Ice Age) and by Neanderthal man. Continuously inhabited since Iberian settlers, who used flint implements, arrived in the 2nd millennium BC. The islands were later settled by the Gauls, and after them the Romans; Christian missionaries came from Cornwall and Brittany in the 6th century AD. The Vikings began raiding the islands in the 9th century. Rollo, the Viking nobleman, established the duchy of Normandy in AD 911. His son, the second duke, William I 'Longsword' annexed the Channel Islands in 933. Jethou was ceded to England in 1091. The other islands were annexed by the crown in 1106. Normandy was conquered by France, and the King (John) was declared to have forfeited all his titles to the duchy. The islanders, however, remained loyal to John. Administration has since been under the control of his successors, while maintaining a considerable degree of home rule and, until 1689, neutrality. Before the Reformation the islands formed part of the diocese of Coutances, but were later placed under the bishops of Winchester. From the 9th century everyone in the islands spoke Norman French, but English became dominant by the mid-19th century. The islands were occupied by Nazi Germany on 30 June–1 July 1940, and fortified for defence. They were relieved by British forces on 9 May 1945.

WATERFALLS
The principal waterfalls of the British Isles are:

Height (ft)	Height (m)	Name
658	*200*	Eas-Coul-Aulin, Highland
370	*112*	Falls of Glomach, Highland
350	*106*	Powerscourt Falls, County Wicklow
>300	*>90*	Pistyll-y-Llyn, Powys-Dyfed
240	*73*	Pistyll Rhaiadr, Clwyd
205	*62*	Foyers, Highland
204 (total)	*62*	Falls of Clyde, Strathclyde (comprises Bonnington Linn (30 ft *9m*), Corra Linn (84 ft *25 m*), Dundaff Linn (10 ft *3 m*) and Stonebyres Linn (80 ft *24 m*) cataracts)
200	*60*	Falls of Bruar, Tayside (upper fall)
200	*60*	Cauldron (or Caldron) Snout, Cumbria
200	*60*	Grey Mare's Tail, Dumfries & Galloway

DEPRESSIONS
A very small area of Great Britain is below sea-level. The largest such area is in the Fenland of East Anglia, and even here a level of 9 ft *2,7 m* below sea-level is not exceeded in the Holme Fen near Ely, Cambridgeshire. The beds of three Lake District lakes are below sea-level with the deepest being part of the bed of Windermere, Cumbria at −90 ft *−27 m*. The bed of Loch Morar, Highland, Scotland reaches 987 ft *301 m* below sea-level.

CAVES
Large or deep caves are few in Great Britain. Great Britain's deepest cave is Ogof Ffynnon Ddu (1010 ft *308 m*) in Powys, Wales. The largest system is the Easegill system with 46,3 km *28·8 miles* of surveyed passages. England's deepest cave is Giant's Hole, Oxlow Caverns, Derbyshire which descends 702 ft *214 m*. Scotland's largest cave is Great Smoo, Highland. The Republic of Ireland's deepest is Carrowmore Cavern, County Sligo being 459 ft *140 m* deep. Northern Ireland's deepest is Reyfad Pot, Fermanagh being 587 ft *179 m* deep.

UK LOCHS AND LAKES

Area (miles²)	Area (km²)	Name and Country	Max. Length (miles)	Max. Length (km)	Max. Breadth (miles)	Max. Breadth (km)	Max. Depth (ft)	Max. Depth (m)
Northern Ireland								
147·39	*381,7*	Lough Neagh, Antrim, Down, Armagh, Tyrone, Londonderry	18	*28*	11	*17*	102	*31*
40·57	*105,0*	Lower Lough Erne, Fermanagh	18	*28*	5·5	*8,8*	226	*68*
12·25	*31,7*	Upper Lough Erne, Fermanagh – Cavan	10	*16*	3·5	*5,6*	89	*27*
Scotland (Fresh-water (inland) lochs, in order of size of surface area)								
27·5	*71,2*	Loch Lomond, Strathclyde-Central	22·64	*36,4*	5	*8*	623	*189*
21·87	*56,6*	Loch Ness, Highland	22·75	*36,6*	2	*3,2*	751	*228*
14·95	*38,7*	Loch Awe, Strathclyde	25·5	*41,0*	2	*3,2*	307	*93*
11·0	*28,4*	Loch Maree, Highland	13·5	*21,7*	2	*3,2*	367	*111*
10·3	*26,6*	Loch Morar, Highland	11·5	*18,5*	1·5	*2,4*	1017	*309*
10·19	*26,3*	Loch Tay, Tayside	14·55	*23,4*	1·07	*1,7*	508	*154*
8·70	*22,5*	Loch Shin, Highland	17·35	*27,7*	1	*1,6*	162	*49*
7·56	*19,5*	Loch Shiel, Highland	17·5	*28,1*	0·9	*1,4*	420	*128*
7·34	*19,0*	Loch Rannoch, Tayside	9·75	*15,6*	1·1	*1,7*	440	*134*
7·18	*18,5*	Loch Ericht, Highland–Tayside	14·6	*23,4*	1·1	*1,7*	512	*156*
6·25	*16,1*	Loch Arkaig, Highland	12·0	*19,3*	0·9	*1,4*	359	*109*
5·9	*15,2*	Loch Lochy, Highland	9·9	*15,9*	1·25	*2,0*	531	*161*

England (Lake District lakes in order of size of surface area)
(all in Cumbria)

Area (miles²)	Area (km²)	Name	Max. Length (miles)	Max. Length (km)	Max. Breadth (yd)		Max. Depth (ft)	Max. Depth (m)
5·69	*14,7*	Windermere	10·50	*16,8*	1610	*1,47*	219	*66*
3·44	*8,9*	Ullswater	7·35	*11,8*	1100	*1,0*	205	*62*
2·06	*5,3*	Bassenthwaite Water	3·83	*6,1*	1300	*1,18*	70	*21*
2·06	*5,3*	Derwentwater	2·87	*4,6*	2130	*1,94*	72	*21*
1·89	*4,8*	Coniston Water	5·41	*8,7*	870	*0,79*	184	*56*
1·12	*2,9*	Ennerdale Water	2·40	*3,8*	1000	*0,9*	148	*45*
1·12	*2,9*	Wastwater	3·00	*4,8*	880	*0,8*	258	*78*
0·97	*2,5*	Crummock Water	2·50	*4,0*	1000	*0,9*	144	*43*
0·54	*1,3*	Haweswater	2·33	*3,7*	600	*0,54*	103	*31*
0·36	*0,9*	Buttermere	1·26	*2,0*	670	*0,61*	94	*28*
Wales								
3·18	*8,2*	Lake Vyrnwy (dammed), Powys	4·7	*7,5*	1000	*0,06*	120	*36*
1·69	*4,3*	Bala Lake (Llyn Tegid), Gwynedd	3·8	*6,1*	850	*0,53*	125	*38*

Administration: The islands are divided into two Bailiwicks, the States of Jersey and the States of Guernsey. The two Bailiwicks each have a Lieutenant-Governor and Commander-in-Chief, who is the personal representative of the Monarch and the channel of communication between HM Government and the Insular Governments. The Crown appoints Bailiffs, who are both Presidents of the Assembly of the States (the Legislature) and of the Royal Court. In Jersey the States consists of elected senators, *connétables* (constables) and deputies; in Guernsey, *conseillers* (councillors), elected by an intermediate body called the States of election, people's deputies, representatives of the *douzaines* (parish councils) and representatives of Alderney.

Highest points above sea-level:
Jersey – 453 ft *138 m*
Guernsey – 349 ft *106 m*
Alderney – 281 ft *85,5 m*
Sark – 375 ft *114 m*
Herm – 235 ft *71,5 m*
Jethou – 267 ft *81 m*
Lihou – 68 ft *21 m*
Leading Industries: Agriculture, chiefly cattle, potatoes, tomatoes, grapes, and flowers; tourism; finance and industry.
Places of Interest: The Museum of the Société Jersiaise; the church of St Peter Port.

New Towns

There are 28 New Towns built by government-appointed Development Corporations in England (21), Wales (2) and Scotland (5). When development of a New Town in England and Wales is substantially completed it is transferred to the *Commission for the New Towns.* **Between 1862 and April 1986 this stage was reached in 13 towns (*below).**

Population (1984).
*Stevenage, Herts. (1946) – 75 700
*Crawley, Sussex. (Jan. 1947) – 72 900
*Hemel Hempstead, Herts. (Feb. 1947) – 77 100
*Harlow, Essex. (May 1947) – 78 000
Aycliffe, Durham. (July 1947) – 25 500
East Kilbride, Strathclyde. (Aug. 1947) – 70 500
Peterlee, Durham. (Mar. 1948) – 23 400
*Welwyn Garden City, Herts. (June 1948) – 40 500
*Hatfield, Herts. (June 1948) – 25 200
Glenrothes, Fife. (Oct. 1948) – 37 500
*Basildon, Essex. (Feb. 1949) – 101 800
*Bracknell, Berks. (Oct. 1949) – 50 800
Cwmbran. Gwent. (Nov. 1949) – 45 600
*Corby, Northants. (1950) – 48 500
Cumbernauld, Strathclyde. (1956) – 49 500
*Skelmersdale, Lancashire. (1962) – 41 800
Livingston, Lothian. (1962) – 39 300
Telford, Shropshire. (1963) – 107 400
Runcorn, Cheshire. (1964) – 66 000
*Redditch, Hereford & Worcester. (1964) – 70 000
Washington, Tyne & Wear. (1964) – 55 000
Irvine, Strathclyde. (1966) – 57 150
Milton Keynes, Buckinghamshire. (1967) – 115 000
Newtown, Powys. (1967) – 10 000
*Northampton. (1968) – 160 000
Peterborough. (1968) – 125 400
Warrington, Cheshire. (1968) – 140 000
*Central Lancashire New Town. (1970)
Stonehouse, Strathclyde was scheduled in 1973 but development plans were abandoned in 1976.

HIGHEST PEAKS IN THE BRITISH ISLES

Though the eighth largest island in the world, Great Britain does not possess any mountains of great height.

In only two Scottish regions, those of Grampian and Highland, does the terrain surpass a height of 4000 ft *1219 m.* In Great Britain there are seven mountains and five subsidiary points (tops) above 4000 ft *1219 m* all in Scotland, and a further 283 mountains and 271 tops between 3000 ft and 4000 ft *914–1219 m* of which only 21 (see below) are in England or Wales. South of the border, 3000 ft *914 m* is only surpassed in Gwynedd and Cumbria, Scotland possesses 54 mountains higher than Snowdon and 165 higher than the Scafell Pike. Ben Nevis was probably first climbed about 1720 and Ben Macdhui was thought to be Great Britain's highest mountain until as late as 1847.

Scotland's ten highest peaks

	ft	*m*
1. Ben Nevis, Highland	4406	*1392*
2. Ben Macdhui, Grampian	4300	*1310*
3. Braeriach, Grampian-Highland border	4248	*1294*
North top (Ben Macdhui)	*4244*	*1293*
4. Cairn Toul, Grampian	4241	*1292*
South Plateau (Braeriach) (also *c. 4160 ft* 1268 m)	*4149*	*1264*
Sgor an Lochan Uaine (Cairn Toul)	*4116*	*1254*
Coire Sputan Dearg (Ben Macdhui)	*4095*	*1248*
5. Cairngorm, Grampian-Highland border	4084	*1244*
6. Aonach Beag, Highland	4060	*1237*
Coire an Lochain (Braeriach)	*4036*	*1230*
7. Càrn Mor Dearg, Highland	4012	*1222*
8. Aonach Mor, Highland	3999	*1218*
Carn Dearg (Ben Nevis)	*3990*	*1216*
Coire an t-Saighdeir (Cairn Toul)	*3989*	*1215*
9. Ben Lawers, Tayside	3984	*1214*
Cairn Lochan (Cairngorm)	*3983*	*1214*
10. Beinn a'Bhùird (North Top), Grampian	3924	*1196*

Wales' ten highest peaks
(all in Gwynedd)

	ft	*m*
1. Snowdon (Yr Wyddfa)	3560	*1085*
Garnedd Ugain or Crib Y Ddisg (Yr Wyddfa)	*3493*	*1065*
2. Carnedd Llewelyn	3484	*1062*
3. Carnedd Dafydd	3426	*1044*
4. Glyder Fawr	3279	*999*
5. Glyder Fâch	3262	*994*
Pen Yr Oleu-wen (Carnedd Dafydd)	*3210*	*978*
Foel Grach (Carnedd Llewelyn)	*3195*	*974*
Yr Elen (Carnedd Llewelyn)	*3151*	*960*
6. Y Garn	3104	*946*
7. Foel Fras	3091	*942*
8. Elidir Fawr	3029	*923*
Crib Goch (Yr Wyddfa)	*3023*	*921*
9. Tryfan	3010	*917*
10. Aran Fawddwy	2970	*905*

Ireland's ten highest peaks

	ft	*m*
1. Carrauntual (or Carrauntoohil), Kerry	3414	*1041*
2. Beenkeragh, Kerry	3314	*1010*
3. Caher, Kerry	3200	*975*
4. Ridge of the Reeks (*two* other tops of the same height, a *third* of 3141 ft *957 m,* and a *fourth* of *c.* 3050 ft *930 m*), Kerry	3200	*c. 975*
5. Brandon, Kerry	3127	*953*
Knocknapeasta (Ridge of the Reeks)	*3062*	*933*
6. Lugnaquillia, Wicklow	3039	*926*
7. Galtymore, Tipperary	3018	*920*
8. Slieve Donard, County Down	*2796	*852*
9. Baurtregaum, Kerry	2796	*852*
10. Mullaghcleevaun, Wicklow	2788	*849*

* Highest peak in Northern Ireland.

England's ten highest peaks
(all in Cumbria)

	ft	*m*
1. Scafell Pike	3210	*978*
2. Sca Fell	3162	*963*
3. Helvellyn	3116	*950*
Broad Crag (Scafell Pikes)	*3054*	*930*
4. Skiddaw	3053	*930*
Lower Man (Helvellyn)	*3033*	*922*
Ill Crags (Scafell Pikes)	*c. 3025*	*c. 922*
Great End (Scafell Pikes)	*2984*	*909*
5. Bow Fell	2960	*902*
6. Great Gable	2949	*898*
7. Cross Fell	2930	*893*
8. Pillar Fell	2927	*892*
Catstye Cam (Helvellyn)	*2917*	*889*
9. Esk Pike	2903	*884*
Raise (Helvellyn)	*2889*	*880*
10. Fairfield	2863	*872*

UNITED KINGDOM'S LARGEST ISLANDS

England (12 largest)

	mile²	km²
Isle of Wight	147·09	380,99
*Sheppey	36·31	94,04
*Hayling	10·36	26,84
*Foulness	10·09	26,14
*Portsea	9·36	24,25
*Canvey	7·12	18,45
*Mersea	6·96	18,04
*Walney	5·01	12,99
*Isle of Grain	4·96	12,85
*Wallasea	4·11	10,65
St Mary's, Isles of Scilly	2·43	6,29
*Thorney	1·91	4,96

Scotland (12 largest)

	mile²	km²
Lewis with Harris	859·19	2225,30
Skye	643·28	1666,08
Mainland, Shetland	373·36	967,00
Mull	347·21	899,25
Islay	246·64	614,52
Mainland, Orkney	206·99	536,10
Arran	168·08	435,32
Jura	142·99	370,35
North Uist	135·71	351,49
South Uist	128·36	332,45
Yell, Shetland	82·69	214,16
Hoy, Orkney	52·84	136,85

Wales (12 largest)

	mile²	km²
*Anglesey (Ynys Mon)	275·60	713,80
Holy I	15·22	39,44
Skomer	1·12	2,90
Ramsey	0·99	2,58
Caldey	0·84	2,79
Bardsey	0·76	1,99
Skokholm	0·41	1,06
Flat Holm	0·13	0,33
*Llanddwyn I	0·12	0·31
Puffin Island	0·11	0,28
The Skerries	0·06	0,15
Cardigan Island	0·06	0,15

Crown Dependencies:

	mile²	km²
Isle of Man	220·72	571,66
Calf of Man	0·96	2,49

The principal Channel Isles comprise

	mile²	km²
Jersey	44·87	116,21
Guernsey	24·46	63,34
Alderney	3·07	7,94
Sark	1·99	5,15
Herm	0·50	1,29

Northern Ireland's principal offshore island is Rathlin Island (5·56 mile² *14,41 km²*)

* Bridged or causewayed to the mainland

LONGEST RIVERS IN THE UNITED KINGDOM
Specially compiled maps issued by the Ordnance Survey in the second half of the last century are still the authority for the length of the rivers of the United Kingdom. It should, however, be noted that these measurements are strictly for the course of a river bearing the one name; thus for example where the principal head stream has a different name its additional length is ignored – unless otherwise indicated.

Length (miles)	Length (km)	Names	Remotest source	Mouth	Area of basin (miles²)*	Area of basin (km²)	Extreme Discharge (cusecs)†
220	354	Severn (for 158 miles)	Lake on E side of Plinlimmon, Powys	Bristol Channel	4409·7	11421	23 100 (1937)
215	346	Thames (for 111 miles) – Isis (43 miles) – Churn	Severn Springs, Gloucestershire	North Sea (The Nore)	3841·6	9948	27 900 (1894)
185	300	Trent (147) – Humber (38)	Biddulph Moor, Staffs	North Sea (as Humber)	4029·2	10436	5 510
161	260	Aire (78) – (Yorkshire) Ouse (45) and Humber (38)	NW of North Yorks	North Sea (as Humber)	4388·4	11366	4 580 (Aire only)
143	230	Ouse (Great or Bedford)	nr Brackley, Northamptonshire	The Wash	3313·6	8 582	11 000
135	215	Wye (or Gwy)	Plinlimmon, Powys	Into Severn 2½ miles S of Chepstow, Gwent	1615·3	4 184	32 000
117	188	Tay (93·2) – Tummel	(Tay) Beinn Oss' Tayside	North Sea	1961·6	5 080	49 000
100	161	Nene (formerly Nen)	nr Naseby, Northants	The Wash	914·5	2 369	13 500
98·5	158	Clyde (inc. Daer Water)	nr Earncraig Hill, Extreme S Strathclyde	Atlantic Ocean (measured to Port Glasgow)	1173·8	3 040	20 200
98·0	157,5	Spey	Loch Spey, Highland	North Sea	1153·5	2 988	34 200
96·5	155,3	Tweed	Tweed's Well, Borders	North Sea	1992·3	5 160	21 400
85·2	137,1	Dee (Aberdeenshire)	W of Cairn Toul, Grampian	North Sea	817·2	2 116	40 000
85	136,7	Avon (Warwickshire or Upper)	nr Naseby, Northants	Into Severn at Tewkesbury	(part of Severn Basin)		8 560
80·5	129,5	Don (Aberdeenshire)	Carn Cuilchathaidh, Grampian	North Sea	515·7	1 336	Not available
79	127	Tees	Cross Fell, Cumbria	North Sea	863·6	2 237	13 600
76	122	Bann (Upper Bann – Lough Neagh – Lower Bann)	Mountains of Mourne, SW Down	Atlantic Ocean	—	—	—
73	117,5	Tyne (34) – North Tyne (39)	Cheviots between Peel Fell and Carter Fell	North Sea	1126·4	2 917	42 000
70	112,5	Dee (Cheshire)	Bala Lake, Gwynedd	Irish Sea	818·1	2 119	16 000
69	111	Eden (Cumberland)	Pennines, SE of Kirby Stephen	Solway Firth, Irish Sea	926·7	2 400	—
65	104,5	Usk	Talsarn Mt, Powys	Bristol Channel	672·0	1 740	23 700
65	104,5	Wear	W of Wearhead, Northumberland	North Sea	462·6	1 198	6 130
65	104,5	Wharfe	7½ miles S of Hawes, North Yorks	Into York Ouse, nr Cawood	(part of Yorks Ouse Basin)		15 300
64·5	103,5	Forth	Duchray Water (13½ miles), Ben Lomond	Firth of Forth, North Sea	627·9	1 626	—

* This column gives the hydrometric area of the whole river system as per *The Surface Water Survey*.
† This column gives the highest recorded discharge in cubic feet per second (*note*: 1 cusec = 0·0283168 m³/sec 538 170 gallons per day) taken at the lowest sited gauging on the name river.

The 58 cities of the United Kingdom

The term City as used in the United Kingdom is a title of dignity applied to 58 towns of varying local Government status by virtue of their importance as either archiepiscopal or episcopal sees or former sees, or as commercial or industrial centres. The right has been acquired in the past by (1) traditional usage – for example, the Domesday Book describes Coventry, Exeter and Norwich as *civitas*; by (2) statute; or by (3) royal prerogative, and in more recent times solely by royal charter and letters patent – the most recent examples are Lancaster (1937), Cambridge (1951). Southampton (1964), Swansea (1969), the extension of the City of Westminster to include the former Metropolitan Boroughs of Paddington and St Marylebone in 1965 and Derby (1977). St David's (Dyfed) is a city only by repute; the title is used ecclesiastically because it has a cathedral.

Name of City with Geographical County or Region	First Recorded Charter	Title of Civic Head
Aberdeen, Grampian, Scotland	1179	Lord Provost
Bangor, Gwynedd, Wales	1883	Mayor
Bath, Avon	1590	Mayor
Belfast, Antrim, Northern Ireland	1613	Lord Mayor*
Birmingham, West Midlands	1838	Lord Mayor
Bradford, West Yorkshire	1847	Lord Mayor
Bristol, Avon	1188	Lord Mayor
Cambridge, Cambridgeshire	1207	Mayor
Canterbury, Kent	1448	Mayor
Cardiff, South Glamorgan, Wales	1608	Lord Mayor
Carlisle, Cumbria	1158	Mayor
Chester, Cheshire	1506	Mayor
Chichester, West Sussex	1135–54	Mayor
Coventry, West Midlands	1345	Lord Mayor
Derby, Derbyshire	1154 (present charter 1977)	Mayor
Dundee, Tayside, Scotland	c.1179	Lord Provost
Durham, Durham	1602	Mayor
Edinburgh, Lothian, Scotland	c.1124	Lord Provost
Elgin, Grampian, Scotland	1234	Lord Provost
Ely, Cambridgeshire	no charter	Chairman
Exeter, Devon	1156	Mayor
Glasgow, Strathclyde, Scotland	1690	Lord Provost*
Gloucester, Gloucestershire	1483	Mayor
Hereford, Hereford and Worcester	1189	Mayor
Kingston upon Hull, Humberside	1440	Lord Mayor

Name of City with Geographical County or Region	First Recorded Charter	Title of Civic Head
Lancaster, Lancashire	1193	Mayor
Leeds, West Yorkshire	1626	Lord Mayor
Leicester, Leicestershire	1589	Lord Mayor
Lichfield, Staffordshire	1549	Mayor
Lincoln, Lincolnshire	1154	Mayor
Liverpool, Merseyside	1207	Lord Mayor
London, Greater London	1066–87	Lord Mayor*
Londonderry, Londonderry, Northern Ireland	1604	Mayor
Manchester, Greater Manchester	1838	Lord Mayor
Newcastle upon Tyne, Tyne and Wear	1157	Lord Mayor
Norwich, Norfolk	1194	Lord Mayor
Nottingham, Nottinghamshire	1155	Lord Mayor
Oxford, Oxfordshire	1154–87	Lord Mayor
Perth, Tayside, Scotland	1210	Lord Provost
Peterborough, Cambridgeshire	1874	Mayor
Plymouth, Devon	1439	Lord Mayor
Portsmouth, Hampshire	1194	Lord Mayor
Ripon, North Yorkshire	886	Mayor
Rochester, Kent	1189	Mayor
St Albans, Hertfordshire	1553	Mayor
Salford, Greater Manchester	1835	Mayor
Salisbury, Wiltshire	1227	Mayor
Sheffield, South Yorkshire	1843	Lord Mayor
Southampton, Hampshire	1447	Mayor
Stoke-on-Trent, Staffordshire	1874 (present charter 1910)	Lord Mayor
Swansea, West Glamorgan, Wales	1169 (present charter 1969)	Mayor
Truro, Cornwall	1589	Mayor
Wakefield, West Yorkshire	1848	Mayor
Wells, Somerset	1201	Mayor
Westminster, Greater London	1256 (present charter 1965)	Lord Mayor
Winchester, Hampshire	1155	Mayor
Worcester, Hereford & Worcester	1189	Mayor
York, North Yorkshire	1396	Lord Mayor*

* Is styled 'Rt Hon'.

Cities, towns and districts in the United Kingdom with a population of over a quarter of a million

Since the recent reform of local government the definition of many towns has been difficult: a few new districts show an improved delineation of towns, but many new districts have Borough status, although the towns from which they take their nomenclature may represent but a fraction of their population. Also, some urban districts, usually with Borough status, do not bear the name of the principal town; e.g. the Borough in which West Bromwich is the main town is called Sandwell.

Estimated mid 1985:

1.	London	Greater London	6 767 500
2.	Birmingham	West Midlands	1 007 500
3.	Glasgow City	Strathclyde	733 794
4.	Leeds	West Yorkshire	710 500
5.	Sheffield	South Yorkshire	538 700
6.	Liverpool	Merseyside	491 500
7.	Bradford	West Yorkshire	463 500
8.	Manchester	Greater Manchester	451 100
9.	Edinburgh City	Lothian	439 672
10.	Bristol	Avon	393 800
11.	Kirklees	West Yorkshire	376 900
12.	Wirral	Merseyside	336 500
13.	Coventry	West Midlands	312 200
14.	Wakefield	West Yorkshire	310 200
15.	Wigan	Greater Manchester	306 700
16.	Sandwell	West Midlands	303 300
17.	Belfast City	N. Ireland	301 600
18.	Dudley	West Midlands	300 800
19.	Sunderland	Tyne and Wear	298 900
20.	Sefton	Merseyside	298 400
21.	Stockport	Greater Manchester	291 200
22.	Doncaster	South Yorkshire	288 500
23.	Leicester	Leicestershire	282 900
24.	Newcastle-upon-Tyne	Tyne and Wear	282 200
25.	Nottingham	Nottinghamshire	279 400
26.	Cardiff	South Glamorgan	278 900
27.	Walsall	West Midlands	262 900
28.	Kingston-upon-Hull	Humberside	262 000
29.	Bolton	Greater Manchester	261 200
30.	Plymouth	Devon	253 400
31.	Wolverhampton	West Midlands	253 200
32.	Rotherham	South Yorkshire	252 700
33.	Stoke-on-Trent	Staffordshire	248 700

The United Kingdom counties

The United Kingdom of Great Britain and Northern Ireland's traditional 91 counties were in 1974 and 1975 reduced to 66 in Great Britain and six in Northern Ireland.

England has 46 *geographical* counties (formerly 40)
Scotland has 9 *geographical* regions and 3 island authorities (formerly 33 counties)
Wales has 8 *geographical* counties (formerly 12)

Northern Ireland has 6 *geographical counties* (*divided into 26 districts*)

Names of the counties: For some counties there are alternatives such as Devon and Devonshire. We however have generally only added the suffix 'shire' where there is a town of the same name as its county. This occurs in 17 cases but to these must be added four others which traditionally (but not statutorily) use 'shire': Berkshire,

Cheshire, Lancashire, and Wiltshire. 'Hampshire' was adopted in 1959 in place of the County of Southampton.

Population: A mid-1985 estimate is given.

County worthies by birth: The term 'worthy' is used in its sense of famous man or woman and in some cases fame includes notoriety.

* Metropolitan Counties that were abolished on 31 March 1986.

Avon

First recorded name and derivation: 1973. From the river of that name. (Afon is Welsh for river.)
Area: 516 miles² *1338 km²*.
Population: 942 000.
Density: 1821 per mile² *702 per km²*.
Administrative HQ: Avon House, The Haymarket, Bristol.
Highest point above sea-level: Nett Wood, East Harptree – 825 ft *251 m*.

Road lengths:	miles	km
motorway and trunk	76·44	*122,31*
principal	248·3	*399,6*
other	2567·5	*4132,0*

Schools and colleges: Nursery 17; Primary 392; Secondary 62; Special 31; Colleges of further education 8; College of education 1; Polytechnic 1.
Places of interest: Bath (Roman remains); Bath Abbey; Clevedon Court; Bristol Cathedral; Stanton Drew (standing stones); Clifton Suspension Bridge.
County worthies by birth: John Locke (1632–1704); Thomas Chatterton (1752–70); Robert Southey (1774–1843); Samuel Plimsoll (1824–98); W G Grace (1848–1915).

Bedfordshire

First recorded use of name and derivation: 1011 (Bedanfordscir), Beda's ford, or river crossing.
Area: 477 miles² *1235 km²*.
Population: 516 700.
Density: 1081 per mile² *418 per km²*.
Administrative HQ: County Hall, Cauldwell St, Bedford.
Highest point above sea-level: Dunstable Downs 798 ft *243 m*.

Road lengths:	miles	km
motorway	16·0	*25,7*
trunk	70·0	*112,6*
principal	133·0	*214,0*
others	1150·0	*1850,7*

Schools and colleges: Nursery 12; Lower/primary 217; Middle 43; Upper/secondary 33; Sixth form college 1; Special 15; Colleges of higher education 2; Colleges of further education 2.
Places of interest: Woburn Abbey; Whipsnade Park (Zoo); Luton Hoo; Elstow Moot Hall; Dunstable Priory Church; Wrest Park; Old Warden Shuttleworth Collection.
County worthies by birth: John Bunyan (1628–88); John Howard (1726–90); Sir Joseph Paxton (1801–65); Thomas Tompion (1638–1713).

Berkshire

First recorded use of name and derivation: AD 860, wooded hill district named after Bearruc hill.
Area: 485 miles² *1256 per km²*.
Population: 724 000.
Density: 1475 per mile² *570 per km²*.
Administrative HQ: Shire Hall, Shinfield Park, Reading.
Highest point above sea-level: Walbury Hill, 974 ft *296 m*.

Road lengths:	miles	km
motorway	69·1	*111,3*
trunk	22·9	*37,0*
principal	205·6	*331,0*
others	1639·7	*2639,0*

Schools and colleges: Nursery 18; Primary (various) 293; Secondary 65; Special 17; Establishments of further education 19.
Places of interest: Windsor Castle (St George's Chapel); Reading Abbey (ruin); Sandhurst; Eton College.
County worthies by birth: Edward III (1312–77); Henry VI (1421–71); Archbishop William Laud (1628–88); Sir John Herschel (1792–1871).

Borders

First recorded use of name and derivation: 1975, from the district bordering on the boundary between England and Scotland from the Middle English word *bordure*; Term 'border' used in Act of the English Parliament, 1580.
Area: 1800 miles² *4662 km²*.
Population: 101 705.
Density: 56 per mile² *22 per km²*.
Administrative HQ: Regional Headquarters, Newtown St Boswells.
Highest point above sea-level: Broad Law (Southern summit) 2756 ft *840 m*.
Districts: Berwickshire 18 370; Ettrick and Lauderdale 33 249; Roxburgh 35 210; Tweeddale 14 373.

Road lengths:	miles	km
trunk	113·6	*182,8*
principal	270·7	*385,1*
classified	836·5	*1346,2*
unclassified	640·3	*1030,4*

Schools and colleges: Primary 84; Secondary 9; Colleges of further education 2.
Places of interest: Dryburgh Abbey; Jedburgh Abbey; Kelso Abbey; Condingham Priory; Jedburgh Castle; Cessford Tower; Drochill Castle.
County worthies by birth: Johannes Duns Scotus (*c.* 1266–1308); James Thomson (1700–48); James Hogg (1770–1835); Mungo Park (1711–1806); Dr John Leyden (1775–1811); Sir David Brewster (1781–1868); Henry Lyte (1793–1847); James Parish Lee (1831–1904); Sir James Murray (1837–1915).

Buckinghamshire

First recorded use of name and derivation: 1016 (Buccingahamscir) the hamm (watermeadow) of Bucca's people.
Area: 727 miles² *1883 per km²*.
Population: 601 600.
Density: 818 per mile² *316 per km²*.
Administrative HQ: County Hall, Aylesbury.
Highest point above sea-level: Nr. Aston Hill 876 ft *267 m*.

Road lengths:	miles	km
motorway	35·0	*56,3*
trunk	38·0	*61,1*
principal	251·0	*403,9*
classified	690·0	*1110,4*
unclassified	1262·0	*2030,9*

Schools and colleges: Nursery 5; First 134; Middle 72; Combined 96; Secondary 52; Special 20; Colleges of further education 4.
Places of interest: Claydon House; Cliveden House; Hughenden Manor; Stowe House; Chequers; Hellfire Caves (West Wycombe); Chiltern Open Air Museum; Milton's Cottage; Waddesdon Manor; Ascott House.
County worthies by birth: Edmund Waller (1605–87); Sir William Herschel (1792–1871); James Brudenell, 7th Earl of Cardigan (1797–1868); Sir (George) Gilbert Scott (1811–78); William Grenfell, Baron Desborough (1855–1945); William Malcolm, Baron Hailey (1872–1969).

Cambridgeshire

First recorded use of name and derivation: 1010 (Grantabricscir), a Norman corruption of Grantabrice (bridge over River Granta).
Area: 1316 miles² *3409 km²*.
Population: 621 400.
Density: 463 per mile² *179 per km²*.
Administrative HQ: Shire Hall, Castle Hill, Cambridge.
Highest point above sea-level: 300 yd *275 m* south of the Hall, Great Chishill, 478 ft *145 m*.

Road lengths:	miles	km
motorway	44	*70,8*
trunk	181	*291,2*
principal	280	*450,6*
others	2417	*3889,7*

Schools and colleges: Nursery and Primary 28; Secondary 49; Special 18; Colleges of further education 6.
Places of interest: Burghley House; Cambridge University; The Backs, Cambridge; Ely Cathedral; Peterborough Cathedral; Sawston Hall, near Cambridge; Peckover House and The Brinks, Wisbech; Kimbolton Castle, near Huntingdon; Imperial War Museum, Duxford; Cromwell Museum, Huntingdon; Wimpole Hall, near Cambridge; Fitzwilliam Museum, Cambridge.
County worthies by birth: Orlando Gibbons (1583–1625); Oliver Cromwell (1599–1658); Jeremy Taylor (1613–67); Octavia Hill (1838–1912); Lord Keynes (1883–1946).

Central Scotland

First recorded use of name and derivation: self-explanatory, pertaining to the centre, the word *central*, first recorded in this sense, 1647.
Area: 1000 miles² *2590 km²*.
Population: 272 792.
Density: 273 per mile² *105 per km²*.
Administrative HQ: Central Region Offices, Viewforth, Stirling.
Highest point above sea-level: Ben More, 3852 ft *1174 m*.
Districts (with population): Clackmannan 47 875; Falkirk 143 921; Stirling 80 866.

Road lengths:	miles	km
motorway	42·9	*68,9*
trunk	70·1	*112,9*
principal	207·8	*334,5*
classified	379·9	*611,5*
unclassified	564·7	*908,8*

Schools and colleges: Nursery 11; Primary 121; Secondary (various) 22; Colleges of further education 2.
Places of interest: Stirling Castle; Old Stirling Bridge; Cambuskenneth Abbey; Field of Bannockburn; Loch Lomond (east side); Doune Castle; Castle Campbell; Dunblane Cathedral; Wallace Monument.
County worthies by birth: George Buchanan (1506–82); Rob Roy McGregor (1671–1734); Sir George Harvey (1806–76); Marshal of the RAF Lord Tedder (1890–1967).

Cheshire

First recorded use of name and derivation: AD 980 (Legeceastersir), corrupted from the camp (*castra*) of the legions (*legiones*).
Area: 896 miles² *2322 km²*.
Population: 942 400.
Density: 1046 per mile² *404 km²*.
Administrative HQ: County Hall, Chester.
Highest point above sea-level: Shining Tor 1834 ft *559 m*.

Road lengths:	miles	km
motorway	120·5	*194,0*
trunk	127·3	*205,0*
principal	427·5	*688,4*
classified	860·7	*1386,0*
unclassified	1851·4	*2981,4*

Schools and colleges: Nursery 8; Primary 482; Secondary 79; Special 26; Colleges of further education 8.
Places of interest: Roman remains within walled city of Chester; Chester Cathedral; Gawsworth Hall; Jodrell Bank; Tatton Hall.
County worthies by birth: John Bradshaw (1602–59); Emma, Lady Hamilton (*c.* 1765–1815); Rev Charles Dodgson (Lewis Carroll) (1832–98).

Cleveland

First recorded use of name and derivation: 1110, *Clivelanda*, 'the hilly district'.
Area: 225 miles² *583 km²*.
Population: 559 900.
Density: 2501 per mile² *965 per km²*.
Administrative HQ: Municipal Buildings, Middlesbrough.
Highest point above sea-level: Hob on the Hill 1078 ft *328 m*.

Road lengths:	miles	km
trunk	34	*55,5*
principal	167	*268,57*
others	1183	*1905,50*

Schools and colleges: Nursery 4; Primary 218; Secondary 57; Special 22; Colleges of further

education 6; Polytechnic 1.
Places of interest: Church of St Hilda (Hartlepool); Capt James Cooke Museum (Marton); Guisborough Priory; Preston Hall; Ormesby Hall.
County worthies by birth: Capt James Cook (1728–79); Thomas Sheraton (1751–1806); John Walker (1781–1859); Sir Compton Mackenzie (1823–1972).

Clwyd

First recorded use of name and derivation: 1973 from the river of that name.
Area: 936 miles² *2425 km²*.
Population: 397 900.
Density: 423 per mile² *163 per km²*.
Administrative HQ: Shire Hall, Mold.
Highest point above sea-level: Moel Sych 2713 ft *826 m*.
Road lengths:

	miles	km
trunk	119·0	*191,5*
principal	263·0	*423,2*
classified	1190·0	*1915,1*
unclassified	1255·0	*2019,7*

Schools and colleges: Nursery 5; Primary 257; Secondary 33; Special 14; Colleges of further education 6; College of education 1.
Places of interest: Denbigh Castle; Valle Crucis (Cistercian Abbey); Rhuddlan Castle (ruins); Bodrhyddan Hall; Wrexham Church; Erddig Hall; Brenig Reservoir.
County worthies by birth: William Salisbury (*c.* 1520–84); Sir Hugh Myddleton (1560–1631); Judge George Jeffreys (1648–1689); Sir Henry M Stanley (1841–1904).

Cornwall (and Isles of Scilly)

First recorded use of name and derivation: 884 (Cornubia) and 981 (Cornwalum), possibly the territory of the Welsh tribe Cornovii.
Area: 1369 miles² *3546 km²*.
Population: 443 800.
Density: 321 per mile² *124 per km²*.
Administrative HQ: County Hall, Truro.
Highest point above sea-level: Brown Willy 1375 ft *419 m*.
Road lengths:

	miles	km
trunk	147	*236,5*
principal	293	*471,4*
classified	1894	*3047,4*
unclassified	2212	*3559,1*

Schools and colleges: Nursery 2; Primary 257; Secondary 33; Special 4; Colleges of further education 4.
Places of interest: Chun Castle (ring-fort); Chysauster (Iron Age village); Cotehele House (Tudor house); Land's End; Lanhydrock House (17th century house); Lanyon Quoit; The Lizard; Rame Head; Restormel (moated castle); St Buryan (Bronze Age stone and 15th century church); St Michael's Mount; St Neot church (stained glass); Tintagel (ruins); Kynance Cove; Truro Cathedral.
County worthies by birth: Samuel Foote (1720–77); John Opie (1761–1807); Richard Trevithick (1771–1833); Sir Humphrey Davy (1778–1829); Richard (1804–34) and John (1807–39) Lander; Sir Arthur Quiller-Couch (1863–1944); Robert Fitzsimons (1862–1917).

Cumbria

First recorded use of name and derivation: AD 935 Cumbra land, land of the Cumbrians from the Welsh *Cymry*.
Area: 2628 miles² *6809 km²*.
Population: 484 400.
Density: 184 per mile² *71 per km²*.
Administrative HQ: The Courts, Carlisle.
Highest point above sea-level: Scafell Pike 3 210 ft *978 m*.
Road lengths:

	miles	km
motorway	60·2	*97,0*
trunk	217·4	*349,0*

principal 399·4 *643,0*
others 3895·2 *6268,0*
Schools and colleges: Nursery 8; Primary 329; Secondary 44; Special 12; Colleges of further education 4; Other colleges 2; College of education 1.
Places of interest: Hadrian's Wall; Lake District; Grasmere (Wordsworth monuments – museum, cottage, grave); Levens Hall; Carlisle Cathedral.
County worthies by birth: John Dalton (1766–1844); William Wordsworth (1770–1850); John Peel (1776–1854); Sir William H Bragg (1862–1942); George Romney (1734–1802); Queen Catherine Parr (*c.* 1512–48).

Derbyshire

First recorded use of name and derivation: 1049 (Deorbyscir), village with a deer park.
Area: 1016 miles² *2631 km²*.
Population: 912 400.
Density: 897 per mile² *346 per km²*.
Administrative HQ: County Offices, Matlock.
Highest point above sea-level: Kinder Scout 2088 ft *636 m*.
Road lengths:

	miles	km
motorway	21·3	*34,3*
trunk	159·7	*257,0*
principal	331·7	*533,9*
classified	1129·2	*1817,2*
unclassified	1873·0	*3014,2*

Schools and colleges: Nursery 14; Primary 460; Middle 2; Secondary 79; Special 28; Colleges of further education 6; College of higher education 1.
Places of interest: Peak District; Chatsworth House; Repton School; Haddon Hall; Hardwick Hall; Melbourne Hall; Dove Dale.
County worthies by birth: Samuel Richardson (1689–1761); Marquess Curzon of Kedleston (1859–1925); James Brindley (1716–72); Thomas Cook (1808–92).

Devon

First recorded use of name and derivation: AD 851 (Defenascir), territory of the Dumonii (an aboriginal Celtic tribal name adopted by the Saxons).
Area: 2592 miles² *6715 km²*.
Population: 988 000.
Density: 377 per mile² *146 per km²*.
Administrative HQ: County Hall, Exeter.
Highest point above sea-level: High Willhays 2038 ft *621 m*.
Road lengths:

	miles	km
motorway	23·3	*37,5*
trunk	187·0	*301,0*
principal	562·0	*905,0*
classified	3188·0	*5131,0*
unclassified	4191·0	*6744,0*

Schools and colleges: Nursery 2; Primary 447; Secondary 85; Special 23; Establishments of further education 9; Polytechnic 1.
Places of interest: Exeter Castle (ruins); Exeter Cathedral; Devonport dockyard; Dartmoor; Buckfast Abbey; Clovelly; Powderham Castle; Dartmouth (port, castle and Royal Naval College).
County worthies by birth: St Boniface (*c.* 680–755); Sir John Hawkins (1532–95); Sir Francis Drake (*c.* 1540–96); Sir Walter Raleigh (?1552–1618); 1st Duke of Albermarle (George Monk) (1608–70); 1st Duke of Marlborough (1650–1722); Thomas Newcomen (1663–1729); Sir Joshua Reynolds (1723–92); Samuel Taylor Coleridge (1772–1834); Sir Charles Kingsley (1819–75); William Temple (1881–1944); Dame Agatha Christie (1891–1976).

Dorset

First recorded use of name and derivation: AD 940 (Dorseteschire), (suggested meaning) dwellers (*saete*) of the place of fist-play (*Dorn-gweir*).
Area: 1024 mile² *2654 km²*.
Population: 627 700.

Density: 603 per mile² *233 per km²*.
Administrative HQ: County Hall, Dorchester.
Highest point above sea-level: Pilsdon Pen 909 ft *277 m*.
Road lengths:

	miles	km
trunk	59·0	*94,9*
principal	286·0	*460,7*
classified	979·0	*1575,5*
unclassified	1563·0	*2514,9*

Schools and colleges: Primary/First 193; Middle 26; Secondary/Upper 45; Special 14; Colleges of further/higher education 5.
Places of interest: Corfe Castle; Sherborne Abbey; Wimborne Minster; Maiden Castle; Clouds Hill (Nat. Trust); Cerne Giant; Forde Abbey; Milton Abbey; Poole Harbour; Christchurch Priory; Compton Acres Gardens.
County worthies by birth: John, Cardinal Morton (*c.* 1420–1500); 1st Earl of Shaftesbury (1621–83); Sir James Thornhill (1676–1734); Thomas Love Peacock (1785–1866); William Barnes (?1800–86); Thomas Hardy (1840–1928); Sir Frederick Treves (1853–1923).

Dumfries and Galloway

First recorded use of name and derivation: Dumfries *c.* 1183, Fort *Dum*, of the Welsh *prys* (copse). Galloway: *c.* 990, Gall-Gaidheal, the foreign Gael.
Area: 2499 miles² *6475 km²*.
Population: 146 562.
Density: 58 per mile² *23 per km²*.
Administrative HQ: Regional Headquarters, Dumfries.
Highest point above sea-level: Merrick, 2770 ft *844 m*.
Districts (with population): Annandale and Eskdale 35 338; Nithsdale 56 493; Stewartry 23 138; Wigtown 30 109.
Road lengths:

	miles	km
trunk	216	*347,5*
principal	309	*497,2*
classified	1121	*1803,7*
unclassified	1004	*1615,4*

Schools and colleges: Nursery 2; Primary 119; Secondary 17; Special 18; Establishments of further education 5.
Places of Interest: Stranraer Castle; Dunskey Castle; St Ninian's Cave; Glenluce Abbey; Threave Castle (ruins); Glentrool National Park; The Ruthwell Cross; Caerlaverock Castle; Drumlanrig Castle; Burns' House and Muasoleum (Dumries); Gretna Green; Dundrennan Abbey; Costume Museum, New Abbey.
County worthies by birth: John Dalrymple, 1st Earl of Stair (1646–95); William Paterson (1660–1719); Thomas Telford (1757–1834); Sir John Ross (1777–1856); Thomas Carlyle (1795–1881); John Paul Jones (1747–1792); Hugh MacDiarmid (1892–1978).

Durham

First recorded use of name and derivation: *c.* 1000 (Dunholme), the hill (old English, *dun*) crowning a holm or island.
Area: 940 miles² *2436 km²*.
Population: 600 900.
Density: 642 per mile² *248 per km²*.
Administrative HQ: County Hall, Durham.
Highest point above sea-level: Mickle Fell 2591 ft *798 m*.
Road lengths:

	miles	km
motorway	26·5	*42,76*
trunk	51·4	*82,87*
principal	236·1	*380,01*
classified	727·2	*1170,40*
unclassified	1330·6	*2141,50*

Schools and colleges: Nursery 25; Primary 347; Secondary 50; Special 21; Colleges of further education 4; College of education 1.
Places of interest: Durham Cathedral, Bowes Museum, Raby Castle.
County worthies by birth: Earl of Avon (Anthony Eden) (1897–1977); Elizabeth Barrett Browning (1806–61).

Dyfed

First recorded use of name and derivation: The name of an ancient 5th century province.
Area: 2225 miles² *5765 km²*.
Population: 335 900.
Density: 151 per mile² *58 per km²*.
Administrative HQ: County Hall, Carmarthen.
Highest point above sea-level: Carmarthen Fan Foel 2500+ ft *762+ m*.

Road lengths:	miles	km
trunk	237	381,6
principal	260	418,3
classified	2410	3877,7
unclassified	1979	3184,2

Schools and colleges: Nursery 4; Primary 356; Secondary 36; Special 6; Colleges of further education 3; other colleges 3.
Places of interest: Cardigan Castle (ruins); Aberystwyth Castle (ruins); Strata Florida Abbey; Nanteos Mansion; Kidwelly Castle; Carreg-Cennen Castle, Talley Abbey; Pendine Sands, Laugharne; St David's Cathedral and Bishop's Palace; Pentre Ifan (burial chamber), near Newport; Pembroke Castle; Carew Castle; Bishop's Palace, Lamphey; Manorbier Castle; Cilgerran Castle; Pembrokeshire Coast National Park.
County worthies by birth: Griffith Jones of Llanddowror (1683–1761); Henry VII (1457–1509); Giraldus Cambrensis (*c.* 1147–*c.* 1223); John Dyer (1701–1757); Sir Lewis Morris (1833–1907); Dafydd ap Gwilym (*c.* 1340–1370); Sir John Rhys (1840–1915); St David (d. 601 ?); Bishop Asser (d. 909 or 910); Augustus John (1878–1961); Robert Recorde (1510?–58).

East Sussex

First recorded use of name and derivation: AD 722 (Suth Seaxe), the territory of the southern Saxons or suthseaxa.
Area: 693 miles² *1795 km²*.
Population: 682 400.
Density: 980 per mile² *378 per km²*.
Administrative HQ: Pelham House, St Andrew's Lane, Lewes.
Highest point above sea-level: Ditchling Beacon 813 ft *248 m*.

Road lengths:	miles	km
trunk	62·2	100,08
principal	245·6	394,92
classified	635·44	1022,78
unclassified	1254·4	2018,5

Schools and colleges: Nursery 3; Primary 222; Secondary 37; Sixth form colleges 3; Special 20; Colleges of further education 5; Polytechnic 1.
Places of interest: Pevensey Castle; Bodiam Castle; Brighton Pavilion; Lewes Castle; Herstmonceux (Royal Observatory); Bentley Wildfowl; Battle Abbey.
County worthies by birth: John Fletcher (1579–1625); Aubrey Beardsley (1872–98).

Essex

First recorded use of name and derivation: AD 604 (East Seaxe), territory of the eastern Saxons.
Area: 1418 miles² *3674 km²*.
Population: 1 504 700.
Density: 1056 per mile² *407 per km²*.
Administrative HQ: County Hall, Chelmsford.
Highest point above sea-level: In High Wood, Langley 480 ft *146 m*.

Road lengths:	miles	km
motorway	58·0	94,0
trunk	88·0	141,0
principal	401·0	645,8
classified	1465·0	2357,5
unclassified	2600·0	4183,4

Schools and colleges: Nursery 2; Primary 601; Secondary 116; Sixth form colleges 2; Special 40; Colleges of further education 10; College of education 1.
Places of interest: Waltham Abbey; Colchester Castle; Epping Forest (part of); Thaxted Church and Guildhall; Hadleigh Castle; Castle Hedingham Keep; St Osyth Priory.

County worthies by birth: Dick Turpin (1705–39); Field Marshal Lord Wavell (1883–1950).

Fife

First recorded use of name and derivation: AD *c.* 590, from Fibh (disputed), possibly one of the seven sons of Cruithne, British patriot.
Area: 505 miles² *1308 km²*.
Population: 344 019.
Density: 602 per mile² *263 per km²*.
Administrative HQ: The Regional Council meets at: Fife House, North Street, Glenrothes.
Highest point above sea-level: West Lomond 1713 ft *522 m*.
Districts (with population): Dunfermline 127 484, Kirkcaldy 149 491, North East Fife 65 851.

Road lengths:	miles	km
motorway }	86·9	139,9
trunk		
principal	204·3	328,8
classified	339·8	546,9
unclassified	727·0	1170,0

Schools and colleges: Nursery 69; Primary 149; Secondary 20; Special 6; Establishments of further education 4.
Places of interest: St Andrew's; Dunfermline; Falkland Palace; Isle of May; Culross; Inchcolm; Dysart; East Neuk Villages; Aberdour Castle.
County worthies by birth: Sir David Lyndsay (*c.* 1486–1555); David, Cardinal Beaton (1494–1546); Charles I (1600–49); Alexander Selkirk (1676–1721); Adam Smith (1723–90); Robert (1728–92) and James (1730–94) Adams; Dr Thomas Chalmers (1780–1847); Sir David Wilkie (1785–1841); Sir Joseph Noel Paton (1821–1901); Andrew Carnegie (1835–1919).

Gloucestershire

First recorded use of name and derivation: AD 1016 (Gleawcestrescir), the shire around the fort (*ceaster*) at the splendid place (Old Welsh, *gloiu*).
Area: 1018 miles² *2638 km²*.
Population: 511 400.
Density: 500 per mile² *193 per km²*.
Administrative HQ: Shire Hall, Gloucester.
Highest point above sea-level: Cleeve Cloud 1083 ft *330 m*.

Road lengths:	miles	km
motorway	30·4	49,0
trunk	121·7	196,0
principal	286·2	459,0
classified	1118·5	1800,0
unclassified	1505·6	2423,0

Schools and colleges: Primary 273; Secondary 51; Special 17; Colleges of further education 4.
Places of interest: Tewkesbury Abbey; Gloucester Cathedral; Roman remains at Chedworth and Cirencester; Berkeley Castle; Sudeley Castle; Forest of Dean; The Cotswolds; Prinknash Abbey.
County worthies by birth: Edward Jenner (1749–1823); Rev. John Keble (1792–1866); Ralph Vaughan Williams (1872–1958); Gustav Theodore Holst (1874–1934).

Grampian Region

First recorded use of name and derivation: 1526 derivation uncertain, perhaps from Gaelic *greannich* 'gloomy or rugged', or from the Celtic root *grug* 'curved, rounded' and related to the old Welsh *crwb* 'a haunch or hump'.
Area: 3300 miles² *8550 km²*.
Population: 500 566.
Density: 151 per mile² *58 per km²*.
Administrative HQ: Woodhill House, Ashgrove Road West, Aberdeen AB9 2LU.
Highest point above sea-level: Ben Macdhui 4300 ft *1310 m*.
Districts (with population): Aberdeen (city) 214 100; Banff and Buchan 83 086; Gordon 67 344; Kincardine and Deeside 44 314; Moray 85 647.

Road lengths:	miles	km
trunk	213·0	342,7
principal	525·0	844,7
classified	1931·0	3107,0
unclassified	2062·0	3317,8

Schools and colleges: Nursery 19; Primary 278; Secondary 39; Special 20; Colleges of further education 5.
Places of interest: Balmoral Castle (near Crathie); Kildrummy Castle (ruins); Aberdeen University; Braemar (annual Highland games); Findlater Castle; Duff House (Banff); Maiden Stone; Haddo House; Leith Hall; Huntly Castle; Elgin Cathedral (ruins); Cairngorms (National Nature Reserve).
County worthies by birth: John Barbour (*c.* 1316–95); James Sharp (1618–79); Alexander Cruden (1701–1770); James Ferguson (1710–76); Sir James Clark (1788–1870); James Gordon Bennett (1795–1872); William Dyce (1806–64); Mary Slessor (1848–1915); James Ramsay Macdonald (1866–1937); John Charles Walsham Reith, 1st Baron (1889–1971).

Greater London*

First recorded use of name and derivation: AD 115 (*Londinium*), possibly from the Old Irish *Londo*, a wild or bold man.
Area: 610 miles² *1580 km²*.
Population: 6 767 500.
Density: 11 075 per mile² *4276 per km²*.
Administrative HQ: County Hall, London SE1.
Highest point above sea-level: 809 ft *246 m* 33 yd *30 m* South-east of Westerham Heights (a house) on the Kent-GLC boundary.

Population of London boroughs (1984 estimate)

Barking and Dagenham	149 400	Islington	165 200
Barnet	298 200	Kensington and Chelsea	136 000
Bexley	218 400	Kingston upon Thames	134 100
Brent	254 900		
Bromley	298 400	Lambeth	244 100
Camden	177 300	Lewisham	232 100
Croydon	318 900	Merton	164 000
Ealing	288 700	Newham	209 400
Enfield	263 300	Redbridge	226 500
Greenwich	216 600	Richmond-on-Thames	160 600
Hackney	187 900		
Hammersmith and Fulham	150 700	Southwark	215 600
		Sutton	169 600
Haringey	200 100	Tower Hamlets	144 600
Harrow	201 400	Waltham Forest	215 100
Havering	239 700	Wandsworth	258 300
Hillingdon	232 200	Westminster, City of	182 000
Hounslow	197 800		

The City of London, population 5400 (1984 estimate) is not a London borough.

Road Lengths:	miles	km
motorway	44	70,81
trunk	129·2	208,0
principal	879·6	1415,6
classified	909·1	1463,1
unclassified	6046·7	9731,2

Schools and colleges: (including ILEA). Nursery 89; Primary and Middle 2177; Secondary and Middle 535; Sixth form Colleges 6; Special 231; Establishments of further education 78.
Places of interest: Buckingham Palace; Houses of Parliament; St Paul's Cathedral; Tower of London; Westminster Abbey; British Museum; National Gallery; Trafalgar Square; Port of London; Hampton Court Palace; Syon House, Isleworth; Chiswick House, W4; Osterley Park, Osterley; Harrow School; London Airport (Heathrow); Kew Gardens; Tower Bridge; Greenwich (Cutty Sark, Maritime Museum and Royal Observatory); South Kensington Museums; Westminster Cathedral; Post Office Tower.
County worthies by birth:
The following 18 Kings and Queens (see separate section for details): Mathilda, Edward I, Edward V, Henry VIII, Edward VI, Mary I, Elizabeth I, Charles II, James II, Mary II, Anne, George III, George IV, William IV, Victoria, Edward VII, George V, Elizabeth II.
The following 15 Prime Ministers (see separate section for details): Earl of Chatham, Duke of Grafton, Lord North, William Pitt, Henry Addington, Spencer Perceval, George Canning, Viscount Goderich, Viscount Melbourne, Lord

John Russell, Benjamin Disraeli, Earl of Rosebery, Earl Attlee, Harold Macmillan, Lord Home of the Hirsel.

Thomas à Becket (1118–70); Geoffrey Chaucer (c. 1340–1400); Sir Thomas More (1478–1535); Thomas Cromwell, Earl of Essex (c. 1485–1540); Edmund Spenser (1552–99); Sir Francis Walsingham (c. 1530–90); Francis Bacon (1561–1626); Ben Jonson (1572–1637); Inigo Jones (1573–1652); Earl of Stafford, Thomas Wentworth (1593–1641); John Hampden (c. 1595–1643).

Sir Thomas Browne (1605–82); John Milton (1608–74); Samuel Pepys (1633–1703); William Penn (1644–1718); Edmond Halley (1656–1742); Henry Purcell (c. 1658–95); Daniel Defoe (1660–1731); Viscount Bolingbroke (1678–1751); Alexander Pope (1688–1744); Earl of Chesterfield (1694–1773).

Thomas Gray (1716–71); Horace Walpole (1717–97); Richard Howe (1726–99); Edward Gibbon (1737–94); Charles James Fox (1749–1806); John Nash (1752–1835); Joseph Turner (1775–1851); Sir Charles Napier (1782–1853); Viscount Palmerston (1784–1865); Viscount Stratford de Redcliffe (1786–1880); George Gordon, Lord Byron (1788–1824); Michael Faraday (1791–1867); John Keats (1795–1821); Thomas Hood (1799–1855).

John Stuart Mill (1806–73); Robert Browning (1812–89); Anthony Trollope (1815–82); George F. Watts (1817–1904); John Ruskin (1819–1900); Lord Lister (1827–1912); Dante Gabriel Rossetti (1828–82); William Morris (1834–96); Sir William Gilbert (1836–1911); Algernon Charles Swinburne (1837–1909); Sir Arthur Sullivan (1842–1900); Lord Baden-Powell (1857–1941); Marquess of Reading (1860–1935); Gerard Manley Hopkins (1844–89); H G Wells (1866–1946); John Galsworthy (1867–1933); Sir Max Beerbohm (1873–1956); G K Chesterton (1874–1936); Virginia Woolf (1882–1941); Sir Charles Chaplin (1889–1978); Evelyn Waugh (1903–66).

Greater Manchester*

First recorded use of name and derivation: AD 923 *Mameceaster*, first element reduced from the Old British *Mamucion* to which was added the Old English *ceaster*, a camp.
Area: 496 miles² *1286 km²*.
Population: 2 582 600.
Density: 5218 per mile² *2013 per km²*.
Administrative HQ: County Hall, Piccadilly Gardens, Manchester.
Highest point above sea-level: Featherbed Moss 1774 ft *540 m*.

Road lengths:	miles	km
motorway	105·0	169,0
trunk	26·7	43,0
principal	506·4	815,0
classified	502·6	809,0
unclassified	3733·1	6008,0

Schools and colleges: Nursery 59; Primary 1203; Middle 16; Secondary 238; Sixth form Colleges 9; Special 99; Establishments of further education 35; Polytechnic 1.
Places of interest: Castlefield (Britain's first urban heritage park); Foxdenton Hall; Haigh Hall; Peel Tower; Salford Art Gallery and Museum; Manchester: Chethams School and Library, Cathedral, Ship Canal, Bramhall Hall; Dunham Massey Hall; Heaton Hall; Lyme Hall and Park.
County worthies by birth: Samuel Crompton (1753–1827); Sir Robert Peel (1788–1850); William Harrison Ainsworth (1805–82); John Bright (1811–89); James Prescott Joule (1818–89); Emmeline Pankhurst (1858–1928); 1st Earl Lloyd-George of Dwyfor (1863–1945); L S Lowry (1887–1976); John William Alcock (1892–1919); Gracie Fields (1898–1979); Sir William Walton (b. 1902).

Gwent

First recorded use of name and derivation: The

name of an ancient province dating from 5th century.
Area: 531 miles² *1376 km²*.
Population: 440 200.
Density: 828 per mile² *320 per km²*.
Administrative HQ: County Hall, Cwmbran.
Highest point above sea-level: Chwarel-y-Fan. 2228 ft *679 m*.

Road lengths:		miles	km
motorway		31·16	50,1
trunk		96·72	155,6
principal		131·42	211,5
classified unclassified	} 1831·60		2947,0

Schools and colleges: Nursery 17; Primary 254; Secondary 35; Special 7; Colleges of further education 7.
Places of interest: Tintern Abbey; Caldicot Castle; Caerleon (Roman remains); Chepstow Castle; Wye Valley; Raglan Castle; Bit Pit; Blaenavon, Sirhowy Ironworks; Penhow Castle; Tredegar House.
County worthies by birth: Henry V (1387–1422); Bertrand Russell (1872–1970); Charles S Rolls (1877–1910); W H Davies (1877–1940); Aneurin Bevan (1897–1960); Neil Kinnock (b. 1942).

Gwynedd

First recorded use of name and derivation: The name of an ancient kingdom or principality dating from the 5th century.
Area: 1493 miles² *3868 km²*.
Population: 233 600.
Density: 156 per mile² *60 per km²*.
Administrative HQ: County Offices, Caernarfon (formerly Caernarvon).
Highest point above sea-level: Snowdon. 3560 ft *1085 m*.

Road lengths:	miles	km
trunk	208·0	334,7
principal	258·0	415,2
classified	1192·0	1918,3
unclassified	1292·0	2079,3

Schools and colleges: Primary 198; Secondary 24; Special 7; Establishments of further education 4.
Places of interest: Castles: Harlech, Beaumaris, Caernafon, Conwy (Conway), Criccieth, Dolbadarn (Llanberis), Dolwyddelan, Penrhyn, Gwydyr; Snowdonia National Park (840 sq miles); Bryn Celli Ddu; Portmeirion; Lloyd George Memorial and Museum, Llanystumdwy; Snowdon Mountain Railway; Ffestiniog Narrow Gauge Railway.
County worthies by birth: Edward II (1284–1327); Lewis Morris (1700–65); Goronwy Owen (1723–69); Sir Hugh Owen (1804–81); T E Lawrence (1888–1935).

Hampshire

First recorded use of name and derivation: AD 755 (Hamtunscir), the shire dependent on Hamtun (*hamm*, a meadow; *tun*, a homestead).
Area: 1456 miles² *3772 km²*.
Population: 1 523 900.
Density: 1037 per mile² *400 per km²*.
Administrative HQ: The Castle, Winchester.
Highest point above sea-level: Pilot Hill 937 ft *285 m*.

Road lengths:	miles	km
motorway	71·0	114,0
trunk	119·0	191,5
other	5450·0	8760,0

Schools and colleges: Primary 603; Secondary 100; Sixth form colleges 10; Special 49; Colleges of Further education 14; Polytechnic 1.
Places of interest: Winchester Cathedral; Beaulieu Palace House and Motor Museum; New Forest; Art Gallery, Southampton; Portsmouth dockyard (with HMS Victory).
County worthies by birth: Henry III (1207–72); William of Wykeham (1324–1404); Gilbert White (1720–93); Jane Austen (1775–1817); Isambard Kingdom Brunel (1806–59); Charles Dickens (1829–70); Sir John Everett Millais (1829–96); Admiral Lord Jellicoe (1859–1935);

Lord Denning (b. 1899); James Callaghan MP (b. 1912).

Hereford and Worcester

First recorded use of name and derivation: AD c. 1038 Hereford, *herepaeth*, military road, meaning ford, a river crossing and AD 889 *Ueogorna ceastre*, the fort (Latin *caester*) of the Weogoran tribe, probably named from the Wyre Forest.
Area: 1516 miles² *3927 km²*.
Population: 650 800.
Density: 426 per mile² *164 per km²*.
Administrative HQ: County Hall, Worcester.
Highest point above sea-level: In Black Mountains 2306 ft *702 m*.

Road lengths:	miles	km
motorway	56·4	90,8
trunk	110·8	178,4
principal	474·4	763,8
other	3888·9	6260,9

Schools and colleges: Primary 279; Middle 54; Secondary 45; Special 27; Sixth form colleges 2; Colleges of further education 10; College of education 1.
Places of interest: Offa's Dyke; Hereford Cathedral; Worcester Cathedral; Malvern Priory; Pershore Abbey; Dinmore Manor; Symond's Yat and Wye Valley; Brockhampton Court; Goodrich Castle; Bulmer Railway Centre; Hereford Museum of Cider; Hergest Croft Gardens; Eastnor Castle; Croft Castle; Severn Valley Railway; West Midlands Safari Park; Avoncroft Museum of Buildings; Hagley Hall; Hanbury Hall; Harvington Hall; Hartlebury Castle; County Museum; Elgar's Birthplace; National Needle Museum.
County worthies by birth: Richard Hakluyt (1553–1616); Robert Devereux, Earl of Essex (1567–1601); Samuel Butler (1612–80); David Garrick (1717–79); Sir Rowland Hill (1795–1879); Sir Edward Elgar (1857–1934); A E Housman (1859–1936); Stanley Baldwin (1867–1947).

Hertfordshire

First recorded use of name and derivation: AD 866 (Heortfordscir), the river crossing (ford) of the stags (harts).
Area: 631 miles² *1634 km²*.
Population: 986 100.
Density: 1554 per mile² *600 per mile²*.
Administrative HQ: County Hall, Hertford.
Highest point above sea-level: Hastoe 802 ft *244 m*.

Road lengths:	miles	km
motorway	64·0	102,0
trunk	81·0	129,0
principal	227·0	363,0
other	2314·0	3703,0

Schools and colleges: Primary and Nursery 474; Secondary and Middle 102; Special 35; Further education establishments 13; Polytechnic 1.
Places of interest: St Albans Cathedral, Roman remains of Verulamium (now at St Albans); Hatfield House; Knebworth House; Salisbury Hall.
County worthies by birth: Nicholas Breakspear (Pope Adrian IV) (1100–59); Sir Henry Bessemer (1813–98); Henry Manning (1808–92); Queen Elizabeth, the Queen Mother (b. 1900); Third Marquess of Salisbury (1830–1903); William Cowper (1731–1800); Cecil Rhodes (1853–1902); Sir Richard Fanshawe (1608–66).

Highland Region

First recorded use of name and derivation: c. 1425 (implied in *hielandman*) from adjective *high*, noun *land*.
Area: 10 088 miles² *26 136 km²*.
Population: 198 617.
Density: 20 per mile² *8 per km²*.
Administrative HQ: Regional Buildings, Glenurquhart Road, Inverness. Regional Council meets at County Buildings, Dingwall.

Highest point above sea-level: Ben Nevis 4406 ft *1342 m*.
Districts (with population): Badenoch and Strathspey 10 003; Caithness 27 494; Inverness 57 526; Lochaber 19 561; Nairn 10 039; Ross and Cromarty 47 351; Skye and Lochalsh 10 963; Sutherland 13 142.

Road lengths:	miles	km
trunk	484	*778,9*
principal	1006	*1619*
classified	1522	*2450*
other	1637	*2535*

Schools and colleges: Primary 219; Secondary 29; Special 7; Establishments of further education 3.
Places of interest: St Mary's Chapel (Forse Thurso); Site of John O'Groat's House (Pentland Firth); Girnigoe Castle; Dunrobin Castle; Culloden Battlefield; Glenfinnan Monument (raising of Prince Charles Stewart's standard); Loch Ness; Eilean Donan Castle; Dunvegan Castle (Skye); Cawdor Castle (Nairn); Castle Tioram; Beauly Priory (Inverness); Clava Cairns (Inverness); Fortrose Cathedral; Glenelg Brochs; Highland Folk Museum; Strathnaver Museum.
County worthies by birth: Hugh Mackay (?1640–92); Simon Fraser, Lord Lovat (?1667–1749); Duncan Forbes (1685–1746); Flora MacDonald (1722–90); Gen Arthur St Clair (1734–1818); Sir John Sinclair (1754–1835); Sir Alexander Mackenzie (1755–1820); Hugh Miller (1802–56); Alexander Bain (1810–77); Sir Hector MacDonald (1853–1903); William Smith (1854–1914).

Humberside

First recorded use of name and derivation: AD c. 730 *humbri*, the British river name, side.
Area: 1356 miles[2] *3512 km[2]*.
Population: 850 000.
Density: 628 per mile[2] *242 per km[2]*.
Administrative HQ: County Hall, Beverley, N. Humberside.
Highest point above sea-level: Cot Nab 808 ft *246 m*.

Road lengths:	miles	km
motorway	70·8	*114,0*
trunk	80·2	*129,0*
principal	343·6	*553,0*
other	3031·8	*4879,0*

Schools and colleges: Nursery 9; Primary 350; Junior high 74; Comprehensive 64; Special 18; Colleges of further and higher education 8.
Places of interest: Kingston upon Hull: Trinity House, Wilberforce House, Town Docks Museum; Beverley Minster; Thornton Abbey; St Mary's Church; Museum of Army Transport; Burton Agnes Hall; Burton Constable Hall; Elsham Hall; Old Rectory, Epworth; Danes Dyke, Flamborough; Humber Bridge; Sandtoft Transport Centre; Normanby Hall, Scunthorpe; Spurn Point.
County worthies by birth: John Fisher (c. 1469–1535); Andrew Marvell (1621–78); John (1703–91) and Charles (1707–88) Wesley; William Wilberforce (1759–1833); Amy Johnson (1903–41); Sir Mark Sykes (1879–1919); Henry Frederick Lindley, 1st Earl of Halifax (1881–1959).

Isle of Wight

First recorded use of name and derivation: The Celtic name Ynys-yr-Wyth, from which the Romans derived Vectis predates the Roman conquest.
Area: 147 miles[2] *381 km[2]*.
Population: 122 900.
Density: 822 per mile[2] *317 per km[2]*.
Administrative HQ: County Hall, Newport.
Highest point above sea-level: St Boniface Down 787 ft *240 m*.

Road lengths:	miles	km
trunk	nil	*nil*
principal	76	*122,3*
classified	167	*268,7*
unclassified	218	*350,8*

Schools and colleges: Primary 47; Middle 16; Secondary 5; Special 2; College of further education 1.
Places of interest: Osborne House; Carisbrooke Castle; Brading and Newport (Roman Villas); Blackgang Chine Fantasy Theme Park.
County worthies by birth: Sir Thomas Fleming (1544–1613); Dr Thomas James (1580–1629); Robert Hooke (1635–1703); Dr Thomas Arnold (1795–1842).

Kent

First recorded use of name and derivation: c. 308 BC Celtic *canto*, a rim or coastal area.
Area: 1441 miles[2] *3732 km[2]*.
Population: 1 495 200.
Density: 1035 per mile[2] *400 per km[2]*.
Administrative HQ: County Hall, Maidstone.
Highest point above sea-level: Betsom's Hill, Westerham 824 ft *251 m*.

Road lengths:	miles	km
motorway	86·9	*139,9*
trunk	123	*198,0*
principal	483·4	*777,8*
non-principal	4538	*7303,0*

Schools and colleges: Nursery and primary 602; Middle 10; Secondary 143; Special 39; Colleges of further and higher education 12.
Places of interest: Canterbury Cathedral; Dover Cliffs; Pilgrim's Way; North Downs; Knowle; Penshurst Place; Deal Castle; Chartwell; Rochester Castle and Cathedral; Leeds Castle.
County worthies by birth: Christopher Marlow (1564–93); Sir William Jenner (1815–98); Sir William Harvey (1578–1657); Robert Bridges (1844–1930); General James Wolfe (1727–59); William Caxton (c. 1422–91); Edward Richard George Heath (b. 1916); William Hazlitt (1778–1830).

Lancashire

First recorded use of name and derivation: the shire around *Lancastre* AD 1087; camp, (*castrum*) on the River Lune.
Area: 1175 miles[2] *3043 km[2]*.
Population: 1 380 300.
Density: 1174 per mile[2] *453 per km[2]*.
Administrative HQ: County Hall, Preston.
Highest point above sea-level: Greygarth Hill 2058 ft *627 m*.

Road lengths:	miles	km
motorway	82·0	*132,0*
trunk	118·8	*180,0*
principal	369·0	*594,0*
classified	1109·1	*1785,0*
unclassified	2818·5	*4536,0*

Schools and colleges: Nursery 38; Primary 675; Secondary 125; Special 49; Establishments of further education 12; Polytechnic 1.
Places of interest: Blackpool Tower; Gawthorpe Hall; Lancaster Castle; Browsholme Hall.
County worthies by birth: Sir Richard Arkwright (1732–92); James Hargreaves (?1745–78); Sir Ambrose Fleming (1849–1945).

Leicestershire

First recorded use of name and derivation: 1086 (Domesday Book) Ledecestrescire. From the camp (*castra*) of the *Ligore*, dwellers on the River Legra (now the R Soar).
Area: 985 miles[2] *2553 km[2]*.
Population: 872 200.
Density: 879 per mile[2] *339 per km[2]*.
Administrative HQ: County Hall, Glenfield, Leicester.
Highest point above sea-level: Bardon Hill 912 ft *277 m*.

Road lengths:	miles	km
motorway	51·6	*83,0*
trunk	109·4	*176,0*
principal	257·2	*414,0*
classified	1023·5	*1647,0*
unclassified	1674·8	*2695,0*

Schools and colleges: Nursery 1; Primary 347; Secondary 79; Sixth form colleges 4; Special 21;

Colleges of further education 7; other colleges 5; Polytechnic 1.
Places of interest: Belvoir Castle; Ashby-de-la-Zouche Castle; Kirby Muxloe Castle; Stanford Hall; Battlefield of Bosworth; Oakham Castle; Rutland Water; Stapleford Park.
County worthies by birth: Queen Jane (1537–54); George Fox (1624–91); Thomas Babington Macaulay (1800–59); George Villiers, Duke of Buckingham (1592–1628); Hugh Latimer (?c. 1485–1555); Titus Oates (1649–1705); Francis Beaumont (1584?–1616); Robert Burton (1577–1640); Robert Hall (1764–1831); C. P. Snow (1905–1980).

Lincolnshire

First recorded use of name and derivation: 1016 (Lincolnescire), a colony (*colonia*) by the *lindum* (a widening in the river, i.e. River Witham).
Area: 2272 miles[2] *5885 km[2]*.
Population: 560 300.
Density: 245 per mile[2] *95 per km[2]*.
Administrative HQ: County Offices, Lincoln.
Highest point above sea-level: Normanby-le-Wold 548 ft *167 m*.

Road lengths:	miles	km
motorway	nil	*nil*
trunk	221·4	*355,10*
principal	475·2	*765,29*
classified	2204	*3549,05*
unclassified	2410·0	*3877,69*

Schools and colleges: Nursery 5; Primary 326; Secondary 70; Special 21; Establishments of further education 7.
Places of interest: Lincoln: Cathedral, Castle, Art Gallery; Tattershall Castle; Boston Stump.
County worthies by birth: Henry IV (1367–1413); John Foxe (1516–87); William Cecil, Lord Burghley (1520–98); Sir Isaac Newton (1642–1727); Sir John Franklin (1786–1847); Alfred, Lord Tennyson (1809–92); Sir Malcolm Sargent (1895–1967); Margaret Thatcher (b. 1925).

Lothian

First recorded use of name and derivation: c. AD 970 from personal name, possibly a Welsh derivative of Laudinus.
Area: 678 miles[2] *1756 km[2]*.
Population: 745 229.
Density: 1098 per mile[2] *424 per km[2]*.
Administrative HQ: Regional Headquarters, George IV Bridge, Edinburgh.
Highest point above sea-level: Blackhope Scar 2137 ft *651 m*.
Length of coastline: 63 miles *101 km*.
Districts (with population): East Lothian 80 838; Edinburgh (city) 440 902; Midlothian 82 362; West Lothian 140 700.

Road lengths:	miles	km
motorway	30	*48,3*
trunk	64	*103,0*
principal	272	*438,0*
classified	573	*922,0*
unclassified	1184	*1905,0*

Schools and colleges: Primary 244; Secondary 51; Special 26; Establishments of further education 5.
Places of interest: Dunbar Castle; Tantallon Castle (ruins); Muirfield Golf Centre (Gullane); Aberlady (bird sanctuary); Rosslyn chapel; Borthwick Castle; Newbattle Abbey; Dalkeith Palace; Edinburgh Castle; St Giles Cathedral; Crichton Castle; Palace of Holyrood House; Craigmillar Castle; Linlithgow Palace; Dundas Castle; The Binns (near Queensferry); Torphichen Church; Hopetoun House; The Forth Bridges.
County worthies by birth: John Knox (c. 1505–72); Mary, Queen of Scots (1542–87); John Napier (1550–1617); James VI of Scotland and I of England (1566–1625); David Hume (1711–76); James Boswell (1740–95); Sir Walter Scott (1771–1832); George Gordon, 4th Earl of Aberdeen (1784–1860); James Nasmyth (1808–90); Alexander Melville Bell (1819–1905); Sir Herbert Maxwell (1845–1937); Alexander Graham

Bell (1847–1922); Arthur James Balfour (1848–1930); Robert Louis Stevenson (1850–94); Sir Arthur Conan Doyle (1859–1930); Field Marshal Douglas Haig (1861–1928).

Merseyside*

First recorded use of name and derivation: AD 1002 *Maerse* from Old English *Maeres-ea* boundary river (between Mercia and Northumbria).
Area: 252 miles² *652 km²*.
Population: 1 481 000.
Density: 5915 per mile² *2286 per km²*.
Administrative HQ: Metropolitan House, Old Hall St, Liverpool.
Highest point above sea-level: Billinge Hill 588 ft *179 m*.
Length of coastline: 56 miles *93 km*.

Road lengths:	miles	km
motorway	30·26	48,71
trunk	41·44	66,70
principal	225·13	362,3
classified	301·19	484,7
unclassified	2220·44	3573,4

Schools and colleges: Nursery 9; Primary 693; Combined 10; Middle 56; Secondary 171; Special 76; Establishments of further and higher education 24; Polytechnic 1.
Places of interest: Liverpool: Roman Catholic Cathedral and Anglican Cathedral, Speke Hall, Croxteth Hall; Walker Art Gallery; Sudley Art Gallery; Merseyside: County Museum, Maritime Museum; Pilkington Glass Museum; Knowsley Safari Park; Ainsdale Nature Reserve; Albert Dock Village; Festival Gardens; Beatle City Museum.
County worthies by birth: George Stubbs (1724–1806); William Ewart Gladstone (1809–98); 1st Earl of Birkenhead (1872–1930); Edward Stanley, 14th Earl of Derby (1799–1869); Sir Thomas Beecham (1879–1961).

Mid-Glamorgan

First recorded use of name and derivation: 1242 (Gwlad Morgan) the terrain of Morgan, a 10th century Welsh Prince.
Area: 393 miles² *1019 km²*.
Population: 533 900.
Density: 1359 per mile² *524 per km²*.
Administrative HQ: County Hall, Cathays Park, Cardiff, South Glamorgan (i.e. outside the county).
Highest point above sea-level: Near Craig-y-Llyn 1919 ft *585 m*.

Road lengths:	miles	km
motorway and trunk	104·4	167,9
principal	299·1	481,5
classified	470·5	797,5
unclassified	1782·5	2869,8

Schools and colleges: Nursery 23; Primary 314; Secondary 42; Special 10; Colleges of higher and further education 7; Polytechnic 1.
Places of interest: Ewenny Priory; Caerphilly Castle; Brecon Mountain Railway; Dare Valley Country Park; Stuart Crystal Glassworks, Aberdare; Llanharan House; Ogmore Castle; Kenfig Nature Reserve; Glyncornel Environmental Centre.
County worthies by birth: Richard Price (1723–91); Dr William Price (1800–93); Joseph Parry (1841–1903); Sir Geraint Evans (b. 1922); Stuart Burrows (b. 1933).

Norfolk

First recorded use of name and derivation: AD 1043 (Norfolk), the territory of the *nor* (northern) *folk* (people) of East Anglia.
Area: 2067 miles² *5355 km²*.
Population: 719 100.
Density: 346 per mile² *133 per km²*.
Administrative HQ: County Hall, Martineau Lane, Norwich NR1 2DH.
Highest point above sea-level: Sandy Lane, east of Sheringham 335 ft *102 m*.

Road lengths:	miles	km
trunk	241·0	388,01
principal	660·0	1062,0
classified	3853·0	6203,0
unclassified	4528·0	7290,0

Schools and colleges: Nursery 4; Primary and middle 272; Secondary 64; Special 19; Colleges of further education 2.
Places of interest: The Broads; Sandringham House; Blickling Hall; Holkham Hall; Breckland; Scolt Head; Norwich Cathedral; The Castle, Norwich; Maddermarket Theatre, Norwich; Castle Acre; Grimes Graves; Walsingham.
County worthies by birth: Sir Edward Coke (1552–1634); 2nd Viscount Townshend (1674–1738); Sir Robert Walpole (1676–1745); Thomas Paine (1737–1809); Fanny Burney (1752–1840); 1st Viscount Nelson (1758–1805); Elizabeth Fry (1780–1845); George Borrow (1803–81); 1st Earl of Cromer (1841–1917); H Rider Haggard (1856–1925); Edith Cavell (1865–1915); George VI (1895–1952).

Northamptonshire

First recorded use of name and derivation: *c.* AD 1011 (Hamtunscir) [see Hampshire], the northern homestead.
Area: 914 miles² *2367 km²*.
Population: 546 100.
Density: 591 per mile² *228 per km²*.
Administrative HQ: County Hall, Northampton.
Highest point above sea-level: Arbury Hill, 734 ft *223 m*.

Road lengths:	miles	km
motorway	28·0	45,1
trunk	129·3	208,1
principal	246·6	397,0
classified	719·4	1157,8
unclassified	1197·0	1926,5

Schools and colleges: Nursery 34; Primary 271; Middle and secondary 67; Special 21; Establishments of further education 5.
Places of interest: Earls Barton Church; Sulgrave Manor; Fotheringhay; Brixworth Church.
County worthies by birth: Richard III (1452–85); John Dryden (1631–1700); Christopher Hatton (1540–91).

Northumberland

First recorded use of name and derivation: AD 895 (Norohymbraland), the land to the north of the Humber.
Area: 1943 miles² *5033 km²*.
Population: 300 600.
Density: 155 per mile² *60 per km²*.
Administrative HQ: County Hall, Morpeth.
Highest point above sea-level: The Cheviot 2676 ft *815 m*.

Road lengths:	miles	km
trunk	140	224,0
primary	181·2	290,0
secondary	351·9	563,0
local district	225·6	361,0
access	2176·9	3483,0

Schools and colleges: First 146; Middle 46; Secondary 16; Special 13; Establishments of further education 2.
Places of interest: Hadrian's Wall; Lindisfarne Priory; Alnwick Castle; Warkworth Castle; Hexham Abbey; Bamburgh Castle; Norham Castle; Chillingham Castle (wild cattle); Blanchland.
County worthies by birth: William Turner (1508–68); Lancelot ('Capability') Brown (1716–83); Thomas Bewick (1753–1828); 2nd Earl Grey (1764–1845); George Stephenson (1781–1848); Grace Darling (1815–42); Robert ('Bobby') Charlton (b. 1937).

North Yorkshire

First recorded use of name and derivation: *c.* AD 150 Ebórakon (Ptolemy); AD 1050 *Eoferwicscir*, land possessed by Eburos.

Area: 3210 miles² *8317 km²*.
Population: 696 600.
Density: 215 per mile² *83 per km²*.
Administrative HQ: County Hall, Northallerton.
Highest point above sea-level: Whernside 2419 ft *737 m*.

Road lengths:	miles	km
motorway	6·5	10,4
trunk	254·0	408,7
principal	446·7	718,7
other	5015·1	8069,3

Schools and colleges: Nursery 5; Primary 416; Secondary (various) 68; Special 18; Establishments of further and higher education 11.
Places of interest: Richmond Castle; Scarborough Castle; City of York (the Minster and the Five Sisters Windows); Byland Abbey; Castle Howard; Rievaulx Abbey; Fountains Abbey; Bolton Priory (ruins); Ripon Cathedral; The Yorkshire Dales; The North York Moors; Selby Abbey.
County worthies by birth: Alcuin (735–804); Henry I (1068–1135); Miles Coverdale (1488–1568); Roger Ascham (1515–68); Guy Fawkes (1570–1606); Thomas Fairfax (1612–71); Sir George Cayley (1773–1857); John Flaxman (1755–1826); William Etty (1787–1849); William Powell Frith (1819–1909); William Stubbs (1825–1901); Sir William Harcourt (1827–1904); Frederick, Lord Leighton (1830–78); Edith Sitwell (1887–1964); Sir Herbert Read (1893–1968); Wystan Hugh Auden (1907–73).

Nottinghamshire

First recorded use of name and derivation: 1016 (Snotingahamscir), the shire around the dwelling (ham) of the followers of Snot, a Norseman.
Area: 835 miles² *2164 km²*.
Population: 1 005 900.
Density: 1198 per mile² *462 per km²*.
Administrative HQ: County Hall, West Bridgford, Nottingham.
Highest point above sea-level: Herrod's Hill, 652 ft *198 m*.

Road lengths:	miles	km
motorway	9·32	15,0
trunk	134·2	216,0
principal	304·4	490,0
classified	683·5	1100,0
unclassified	1710·6	2753,0

Schools and colleges: Nursery 7; Primary 428; Secondary 92; Special 29; Further education establishments 10; Polytechnic 1.
Places of interest: Southwell Cathedral; Sherwood Forest; The Dukeries; Wollaton Hall; Newstead Abbey.
County worthies by birth: Thomas Cranmer (1489–1556); Edmund Cartwright (1743–1823); Richard Bonington (1801–28); Gen William Booth (1829–1912); Samuel Butler (1835–1902); D H Lawrence (1885–1930).

Orkney

First recorded use of name and derivation: *c.* 308 BC as Orcas (Pytheas) from Celtic Innse Orc, islands of the Boars, the Boars being a Pictish tribe; later altered to the Norse Orkneyjar, islands of the Young Seals.
Area: 376 miles² *974 km²*. Consists of 54 islands.
Population: 19 351.
Density: 51 per mile² *20 per km²*.
Administrative HQ: Council Offices, Kirkwall.
Highest point above sea level: Ward Hill, Hoy 1570 ft *478 m*.

Road lengths:	miles	km
principal	100	160,9
classified	225	362,0
unclassified	252	405,5

Schools and colleges: Primary 20; Secondary 6; Special 1; College of further education 1.
Places of interest: Noltland Castle (ruins); the prehistoric village of Skara Brae; the stone circle at Brogar; Old Man of Hoy; Kirkwall Cathedral; Scapa Flow.
County worthies by birth: John Rae (1813–93); Sir Robert Strange (1721–92).

Oxfordshire

First recorded use of name and derivation: AD 1010 (Oxnfordscir), the shire around Oxford (a river ford for oxen). The town (city) was first recorded (as Osnaforda) in AD 912.
Area: 1008 miles² *2611 km²*.
Population: 565 400.
Density: 551 per mile² *213 per km²*.
Administrative HQ: County Hall, New Road, Oxford.
Highest point above sea-level: White Horse Hill, 856 ft *260 m*.

Road lengths:	miles	km
motorway	8·5	*13,6*
trunk	169·0	*272,0*
principal	242·9	*391,0*
classified	950·0	*1529,0*
unclassified	1060·0	*1706,0*

Schools and colleges: Nursery 7; First/primary 246; Middle and secondary 49; Special 16; Establishments of further education 6; Polytechnic 1.
Places of interest: Oxford University; Blenheim Palace, nr Woodstock; Rollright Stones; Broughton Castle; Radcliffe Camera; Bodleian Library, Oxford; Christ Church Cathedral, Oxford; Iffley Road running track; White Horse of Uffington.
County worthies by birth: Alfred (849–99); St Edward the Confessor (c. 1004–66); Richard I (1157–99); John (1167–1216); Sir William D'Avenant (1606–68); Warren Hastings (1732–1818); Lord Randolph Churchill (1849–95); Sir Winston Churchill (1874–1965); William Morris, 1st Viscount Nuffield (1877–1963).

Powys

First recorded use of name and derivation: The name of an ancient province probably dating from c. 5th century AD.
Area: 1960 miles² *5077 km²*.
Population: 111 400.
Density: 56 per mile² *22 per km²*.
Administrative HQ: County Hall, Llandrindod Wells.
Highest point above sea-level: Pen-y-Fan (Cadet Arthur) 2907 ft *885 m*.

Road lengths:	miles	km
trunk	262	*421,6*
principal	155	*249,4*
classified	1607	*2585,7*
unclassified	1464	*2355,6*

Schools and colleges: Primary 119; Secondary 13; Special 3; Colleges of further education 3.
Places of interest: Brecon Beacons; Elan Valley Reservoirs; Brecon Cathedral; Powis Castle and gardens; Lake Vyrnwy; Montgomery Castle; Gregynog Hall; Dan-y-Ogof Caves.
County worthies by birth: Owain Glyndwr (c. 1354–fl 1416); George Herbert (1593–1633); Robert Owen (1771–1858).

Shetland

First recorded use of name and derivation: 1289, land of Hjalto (Old Norse personal name c.f. Scots, Sholto) or hilt-shaped land.
Area: 551 miles² *1427 km²*. Consists of 117 islands.
Population: 23 440.
Density: 42 per mile² *16 per km²*.
Administrative HQ: Town Hall, Lerwick.
Highest point above sea-level: Ronas Hill, Mainland, 1475 ft *449 m*.

Road lengths:	miles	km
principal	140·0	*225,3*
classified	210·0	*337,9*
unclassified	200·0	*321,9*

Schools and colleges: Primary 37; Secondary 9; Further Education Centre 1.
Places of interest: Scalloway Castle; Jarlshof; Broch of Mousa; Broch of Clickimin; St Ninian's Isle; Lerwick Museum; Muckle Flugga lighthouse. Sullem Voe Terminal; Lerwick Town Hall.
County worthies by birth: Arthur Anderson (1792–1868); Sir Robert Stout (1844–1930).

Shropshire

First recorded use of name and derivation: AD 1006 *Scrobbesbyrigscir* from Scrobbesbyrig or Shrewsbury.
Area: 1347 miles² *3490 km²*.
Population: 390 300.
Density: 287 per mile² *111 per km²*.
Administrative HQ: Shirehall, Abbey Foregate, Shrewsbury.
Highest point above sea-level: Brown Clee Hill 1790 ft *545 m*.

Road lengths:	miles	km
motorway	5·0	*11,6*
trunk	154·0	*247,8*
principal	262·0	*421,6*
classified	1513·0	*2434,4*
unclassified	1467·0	*2360,4*

Schools and colleges: Nursery 2; Primary 223; Secondary (various) 44; Special 10; Colleges of further and higher education 5.
Places of interest: Offa's Dyke; Ludlow Castle; Stokesay Castle; Coalbrookdale and Ironbridge; The Wrekin; Hodnet Hall Gardens; Severn Valley Railway; Bridgnorth; Acton Scott Working Farm Museum; Buildwas Abbey; Wenlock Priory; Wroxeter.
County worthies by birth: Lord Clive of Plassey (1725–74); Thomas Minton (1766–1836); Charles Darwin (1809–82); Capt Matthew Webb (1848–83); Mary Webb (1881–1927).

Somerset

First recorded use of name and derivation: AD 878 *Sumorsaete*, the people who looked to Somerton (Sumortun) as the tribal capital of the 'land of summer' (Welsh *gwlad yr haf*).
Area: 1335 miles² *3458 km²*.
Population: 447 000.
Density: 330 per mile² *128 per km²*.
Administrative HQ: County Hall, Taunton.
Highest point above sea-level: Dunkery Beacon 1705 ft *519 m*.

Road lengths:	miles	km
motorway	33·0	*53,1*
trunk	60·0	*96,6*
principal	393·0	*632,5*
classified	1575·0	*2534,7*
unclassified	1861·0	*2995,0*

Schools and colleges: Nursery 1; Primary 239; Middle 9; Secondary 29; Special 8; Colleges of further and higher education 6.
Places of interest: Cheddar Gorge; Wookey Hole; Wells Cathedral; Exmoor National Park; Glastonbury Abbey (ruins).
County worthies by birth: St Dunstan (c. 925–88); Roger Bacon (1214–94); John Pym (1584–1643); Robert Blake (1599–1657); Henry Fielding (1707–54); Sir Henry Irving (1838–1905); John Hanning Speke (1827–64); Ernest Bevin (1881–1951).

South Glamorgan

First recorded use of name and derivation: 1242 (Gwlad Morgan) the terrain of Morgan, a 10th century Welsh Prince.
Area: 161 miles² *416 km²*.
Population: 394 800.
Density: 2450 per mile² *948 per km²*.
Administrative HQ: County offices, Newport Road, Cardiff.
Highest point above sea-level: Near Lisvane 866 ft *264 m*.

Road lengths:	miles	km
motorway and trunk	38·3	*61,70*
principal	61·2	*98,60*
other	968·9	*1559,44*

Schools and colleges: Nursery 12; Primary 162; Secondary 29; Special 17; Establishments of further and higher education 4.
Places of interest: Cardiff: Castle, National Museum of Wales, The Welsh Industrial and Maritime Museum; Llandaff Cathedral; St Fagan's Castle (Welsh Folk Museum); St Donat's Castle; Fonmon Castle; Llantwit Major.

South Yorkshire*

First recorded use of name and derivation: c. AD 150 Ebórakon (Ptolemy). 1050 (Eoferwicscir), land possessed by Eburos.
Area: 602 miles² *1560 km²*.
Population: 1 303 200.
Density: 2168 per mile² *837per km²*.
Administrative HQ: County Hall, Barnsley.
High point above sea-level: Margery Hill, 1793 ft *546 m*.

Road lengths:	miles	km
motorway	73·3	*118,0*
trunk	82·6	*133,0*
classified	832·0	*1339,0*
unclassified	2120·7	*3413,0*

Schools and colleges: Nursery 10; Primary 571; Secondary 116; Special 43; Establishments of further education 31; Polytechnic 1.
Places of interest: Sheffield: Cathedral Church of ss Peter and Paul, Cutler's Hall, Abbeydale Industrial Hamlet, Bishops House, Kelham Island Industrial Museum, Cusworth Hall; Conisbrough Castle, Doncaster; Roche Abbey, Rotherham (ruins); Barnsley: Cannon Hall, Cawthorne Victoria Jubilee, Monk Bretton Priory, Worsborough Mill.
County worthies by birth: Thomas Osborne, Earl of Danby (1631–1712); Gordon Banks (b. 1938).

Staffordshire

First recorded use of name and derivation: 1016 (Staeffordscir), the shire around a ford by a *staeth* or landing place.
Area: 1048 miles² *2716 km²*.
Population: 1 020 400.
Density: 973 per mile² *375 per km²*.
Administrative HQ: County Buildings, Stafford.
Highest point above sea-level: Oliver Hill, near Flash, 1684 ft *513 m*.

Road lengths:	miles	km
motorway	43·04	*69,30*
trunk	178·04	*286,70*
principal 'A'	343·39	*552,96*
class II	209·02	*336,59*
class III	850·37	*1369,35*
unclassified	2 147·78	*3458,59*

Schools and colleges: Nursery 27; Primary/Infants 430; Middle 36; Secondary 83; Special 32; Sixth form college 1; Establishments of further and higher education 14; Polytechnic 1.
Places of interest: Lichfield Cathedral; Croxden Abbey; Cannock Chase; Alton Towers; Blithfield Hall; Tamworth Castle; Shugborough Hall and County Museum; Stafford Castle; Gladstone Pottery Museum.
County worthies by birth: Isaak Walton (1593–1683); Dr Samuel Johnson (1709–84); Josiah Wedgwood (1730–95); Admiral Earl of St Vincent (1735–1823); Arnold Bennett (1867–1931); Havergal Brian (1876–1972).

Strathclyde

First recorded use of name and derivation: c. AD 85 Clota, the river (per Tacitus) AD 875 Straecled Wenla cyning.
Area: 5348 miles² *13 856 km²*.
Population: 2 358 727.
Density: 444 per mile² *171 per km²*.
Administrative HQ: Strathclyde House, 20 India St, Glasgow G2 4PF.
Highest point above sea-level: Bidean nam Bian 3766 ft *1147 m*.
Districts (with population): Argyll and Bute 64 290; Bearsden and Milngavie 39 180; Clydebank 51 870; Clydesdale 56 730; Cumbernauld and Kilsyth 64 620; Cumnock and Doon Valley 45 820; Cunninghame 135 980; Dumbarton 79 570; East Kilbride 82 760; Eastwood 51 940; Glasgow (city) 781 700; Hamilton 107 520; In-

verclyde 100 860; Kilmarnock and Loudoun 81 560; Kyle and Carrick 112 360; Monklands 109 360; Motherwell 150 760; Renfrew 214 570; Strathkelvin 87 360.

Road lengths:	miles	km
regional motorway	28·5	46,0
trunk motorway	60·8	98,0
trunk	447·3	727,0
principal	1042·6	1678,0
non principal	2269·2	3652,0
unclassified	4180·5	6728,0

Schools and colleges: Nursery 207; Primary 924; Secondary 191; Special 57; Establishments of further education 21.

Places of interest: Fingal's Cave (Isle of Staffa); Iona; Loch Lomond: Rossdhu House; Cameron House; Dumbarton Rock and Castle; Newark Castle; Glasgow Cathedral; Bothwell Castle (ruins); Culzean Castle (National Trust for Scotland); Burns' Cottage and Museum (Alloway); Inveraray Castle; Brodick Castle; Rothesay Castle (Isle of Bute); Paisley Abbey; Kelvingrove Art Galleries and Museum, Burrell Collection, Glasgow; Livingstone Memorial, Blantyre.

County worthies by birth: Sir William Wallace (1274–1305); James Watt (1736–1819); William Murdoch (1754–1839); Robert Burns (1759–96); David Livingstone (1813–73); John Boyd Dunlop (1840–1921); James Chalmers (1841–1901); Sir Alexander Fleming (1881–1955); John Logie Baird (1888–1946).

Suffolk

First recorded use of name and derivation: AD 895 (Suthfolchi), the territory of the southern folk (of East Anglia).
Area: 1467 miles² 3800 km².
Population: 624 200.
Density: 420 per mile² 162 per km².
Administrative HQ: County Hall, Ipswich.
Highest point above sea-level: Rede, 420 ft 128 m.

Road lengths:	miles	km
trunk	157·4	253,3
principal	293·0	471,6
classified	1539·7	2478,0
unclassified	1879·9	3025,4

Schools and colleges: Nursery 2; Primary 283; Middle 41; High 39; Special 10; Colleges of further and higher education 5.

Places of interest: Flatford Mill and Willy Lott's Cottage; Framlingham Castle; Kyson Hill; Saxtead Green Windmill; Gainsborough's House; Lavenham (Guild Hall, Wool Hall); Long Melford Church; Newmarket; Bury St Edmunds (Abbey ruins) and Cathedral (nave); Ickworth Mansion; The Maltings, Snape.

County worthies by birth: Sir Joseph Hooker (1817–1911); John Constable (1776–1837); Cardinal Thomas Wolsey (c. 1475–1530); Edward Fitzgerald (1809–83); Thomas Gainsborough (1727–88); Robert Bloomfield (1766–1823); Benjamin Britten (1913–76).

Surrey

First recorded use of name and derivation: AD 722 (Suthrige), from the Old English, suthergé or southern district.
Area: 639 miles² 1655 km².
Population: 1 013 700.
Density: 1587 per mile² 613 per km².
Administrative HQ: County Hall, Kingston upon Thames (i.e. outside the county). The traditional county town is Guildford.
Highest point above sea-level: Lieth Hill 965 ft 294 m.

Road lengths:	miles	km
motorway	47·0	75,6
trunk	38·0	61,1
principal	354·0	569,7
classified	604·0	972,0
unclassified	1607·0	2586,2

Schools and colleges: Nursery 6; Primary and middle 400; Secondary 70; Special 35; Establishments of further and higher education 11.

Places of interest: Guildford Cathedral; Waverley Abbey; Royal Horticultural Soc Gardens,

Wisley; Box Hill, Polesden Lacey; Loseley House.
County worthies by birth: William of Ockham (d. 1349?); Thomas Malthus (1766–1834); Aldous Huxley (1894–1936); Sir Lawrence Olivier (b. 1907); John Evelyn (1620–1706); William Cobbett (1762–1835); Matthew Arnold (1822–88).

Tayside

First recorded use of name and derivation: c. AD 85 Taus or Tanaus (Tacitus).
Area: 2960 miles² 7668 km².
Population: 394 322.
Density: 133 per mile² 51 per km².
Administrative HQ: Tayside House, Dundee.
Highest point above sea-level: Ben Lawers 3984 ft 1214 m.
Length of coastline: 76 miles 122 km.
Districts (with population): Angus 93 163, Dundee 180 748; Perth and Kinross 120 984.

Road lengths:	miles	km
motorway	28·5	46,0
trunk	137·3	221,0
principal	433·7	698,0
classified	1163·8	1873,0
unclassified	1199·2	1930,0

Schools and colleges: Nursery 16; Primary 200; Secondary 32; Special 16; Establishments of further education 4.

Places of interest: Glamis Castle; Arbroath Abbey (ruins); Brechin Cathedral and Round Tower; Scone Palace; Bridge of Dun (near Montrose); Guthrie Castle; Blair Castle; Edzell Castle; Loch Leven Castle; Queen's View, Loch Tummel; Pitlochry Ladder and Fish Dam.

County worthies by birth: Pontius Pilate fl AD 36; James Chalmers (1822–53); Sir James Barrie (1860–1937); John Buchan 1st Baron Tweedsmuir (1875–1940); HRH The Princess Margaret, Countess of Snowdon (b. 1930).

Tyne and Wear*

First recorded use of name and derivation: c. AD 150 Tina (river) (Ptolemy) and c. AD 720 Wirus (river) (Bede).
Area: 208 miles² 540 km².
Population: 1 139 900.
Density: 5492 per mile² 2116 per km².
Administrative HQ: Sandyford House, Newcastle-upon-Tyne.
Highest point above sea-level: Leadgate near Chopwell 851 ft 259 m.

Road lengths:	miles	km
motorway	5·5	9,0
trunk	39·1	63,0
principal	198·8	320,0
classified	283·3	456,0
unclassified	1982·1	3190,0

Schools and colleges: (administered at District Council level) Nursery 35; Primary 516; Middle 33; Secondary 88; Special 65; Colleges of further education 7; Polytechnics 2.

Places of interest: Church of St Andrew's Byker; Monkwearmouth (ruins); Tynemouth Castle and Priory; Washington Old Hall Plummer Tower; South Shields Roman Fort.

County worthies by birth: The Venerable Bede (673–735); Admiral (1st) Lord Collingwood (1750–1810); Sir Joseph Swann (1828–1914); Owen Brannigan (1908–73); Cardinal Basil Hume, Archbishop of Westminster (b. 1923).

Warwickshire

First recorded use of name and derivation: the name was recorded in 1001 and means dwellings by the weir.
Area: 765 miles² 1981 km².
Population: 479 700.
Density: 624 per mile² 241 per km².
Administrative HQ: Shire Hall, Warwick.
Highest point above sea-level: Ilmington Downs 854 ft 260 m.

Road lengths:	miles	km
motorway	29·1	46,91
trunk	145·7	234,5
principal	186·9	300,8
classified	730·7	1175,8
unclassified	1105·0	1778,1

Schools and colleges: Nursery 9; Primary 252; Secondary 41; Special 17; Establishments of further and higher education 5.

Places of interest: Warwick Castle; Kenilworth Castle; Stratford-upon-Avon (Shakespeare's birthplace); Compton Wynyates; Charlecote; Coughton Court; Ragley Hall; Arbury Hall.

County worthies by birth: William Shakespeare (1564–1616); Joseph Arch (1826–1919); Walter Savage Landor (1775–1864); Marion Evans (George Eliot) (1819–80); Rupert Brooke (1887–1915); Michael Drayton (1563–1631); Sir William Dugdale (1605–1686); Sir Fulke Greville, 1st Baron Brooke (1554–1628); Francis Willughby (1635–1672).

West Glamorgan

First recorded use of name and derivation: 1242 (Gwlad Morgan) the terrain of Morgan, a 10th century Welsh Prince.
Area: 315 miles² 815 km².
Population: 364 100.
Density: 1157 per mile² 447 per km².
Administrative HQ: County Hall, Swansea.
Highest point above sea-level: Cefnffordd 1969 ft 600 m.

Road lengths:	miles	km
motorway	23·0	37,0
trunk	29·0	46,7
principal	126·0	202,8
classified	199·0	320,2
unclassified	676·0	1088,0

Schools and colleges: Nursery 2; Primary 176; Secondary 26; Special 7; Colleges of further education 3; Other college 1; Institute of higher education.

Places of interest: Neath Abbey (ruins); Penrice Castle; Gower Peninsula; Margam Park; Aberdulais Falls and Basin; Afan Argoed Forest Park; Cefn Coed Coal and Steam Museum.

County worthies by birth: Dylan Thomas (1914–53); Wynford Vaughan Thomas (b. 1908); Daniel Jones (b. 1912); Harry Secombe CBE (b. 1921); Richard Burton (1925–1984).

West Midlands*

First recorded use of name and derivation: 1555 mydlande, mid lands (applied to the middle counties of England).
Area: 347 miles² 899 km².
Population: 2 641 800.
Density: 7628 per mile² 2944 per km².
Administrative HQ: County Hall, Lancaster Circus, Birmingham.
Highest point above sea-level: Turner's Hill 876 ft 267 m.

Road lengths:	miles	km
motorway	43·5	70,0
trunk	42·6	68,5
principal	370·9	596,9
classified	455·5	732,8
unclassified	3135·4	5045,6

Schools and colleges: Nursery 53; Primary 962; Middle 34; Secondary 236; Special 97; Establishments of further and higher education 28; Polytechnics 3.

Places of interest: Dudley Castle; Birmingham: Aston Hall, City Museum and Art Gallery, Museum of Science and Industry; Coventry Cathedral.

County worthies by birth: Sir Edward Burne-Jones (1833–98); George Cadbury (1839–1922); Sir Henry Newbolt (1862–1938); Neville Chamberlain (1869–1940); Sir Frank Whittle (b. 1907).

West Sussex

First recorded use of name and derivation: AD 722 (Suth Seaxe), the territory of the southern Saxons

or *suthseaxa*.
Area: 778 miles² *2016 km²*.
Population: 687 700.
Density: 876 per mile² *339 per km²*.
Administrative HQ: County Hall, West St, Chichester.
Highest point above sea-level: Blackdown Hill 919 ft *280 m*.

Road lengths:	miles	km
motorway	4·3	*6,9*
trunk	54·6	*87,9*
principal	299·3	*481,7*
classified	697·4	*1122,3*
unclassified	1164·3	*1873,7*

Schools and colleges: Nursery 4; Primary 237; Middle 17; Secondary 44; Sixth form colleges 3; Special 14; Colleges of further and higher education 6.
Places of interest: Chichester Cathedral; Arundel Castle; Goodwood House; Petworth House; Uppark; Fishbourne Roman Palace.
County worthies by birth: John Selden (1584–1654); William Collins (1721–59); Percy Bysshe Shelley (1792–1822); Richard Cobden (1804–65).

West Yorkshire*

First recorded use of name and derivation: *c*. AD 150 Ebórakon (Ptolemy), 1050 (Eoferwicscir), land possessed by Eburos.
Area: 787 miles² *2039 km²*.
Population: 2 052 800.
Density: 2613 per mile² *1008 per km²*.
Administrative HQ: County Hall, Wakefield.
Highest point above sea-level: Black Hill 1908 ft *581 m*.
Districts (with population): Bradford 464 700; Calderdale 191 800; Kirklees 377 100; Leeds 716 100; Wakefield 313 400.

Road lengths:	miles	km
motorway	39·1	*63,0*
trunk	62·1	*100,0*
principal	310·0	*499,0*
classified	377·7	*608,0*
unclassified	2206·4	*3551,0*

Schools and colleges: Nursery 79; Primary and middle 940; Secondary (various) 160; Sixth form colleges 3; Special 80; Establishments of further and higher education 33; Polytechnics 2.
Places of interest: Bronte Museum (Haworth); Kirkstall Abbey; Ilkley Moor; Temple Newsam House; Harewood House; Wakefield Cathedral.
County worthies by birth: Sir Martin Frobisher (*c*. 1535–94); Thomas Fairfax (1612–71); Thomas Chippendale (1718–79); Joseph Priestley (1733–1804); Charlotte Bronte (1816–55); Anne Bronte (1820–49); Emily Bronte (1818–48); Henry Herbert, Lord Asquith (1852–1928); Frederick Delius (1862–1934); Barbara Hepworth (1903–75); John Boynton Priestley (1894–1984); Wilfred Rhodes (1877–1973); James Harold Wilson (b. 1916).

Western Isles

First recorded use of name and derivation: Possibly 14th century (during the reign of David II the style 'Lord of the Isles' appears, whereas in the Treaty of Perth, 1266, the Norse name *sudreys* is used).
Area: 1120 miles² *2901 km²*.
Population: 31 545.
Density: 28 per mile² *11 per km²*.
Administrative HQ: Council Offices, Stornoway, Isle of Lewis.
Highest point above sea-level: Clisham, Harris 2622 ft *799 m*.
Main Islands: The largest islands in the Long Island archipelago.

	miles²	km²
Lewis with Harris	859·19	*2225*
North Uist	135·71	*351*
South Uist	128·36	*332*

Road lengths:	miles	km
principal	197	*316,9*
classified	229	*368,5*
unclassified	271	*436*

Schools and colleges: Nursery 3; Primary 45; Secondary 16; College of further education 1.
Places of interest: Kisimul Castle (Isle of Barra); Kilpheder (South Uist); Callanish – stone circle and cairn (Isle of Lewis); St Kilda, Rockall; St Clement's Church, Rodel (Isle of Harris).
Islands worthies by birth: Flora Macdonald (1722–90).

Wiltshire

First recorded use of name and derivation: AD 878 (Wiltunscire), the shire around *Wiltun* (tun, town) on the River Wylye.
Area: 1344 miles² *3481 km²*.
Population: 540 800.
Density: 399 per mile² *154 per km²*.
Administrative HQ: County Hall, Trowbridge.
Highest point above sea-level: Milk Hill and Tan Hill (or St Anne's Hill) 964 ft *293 m*.

Road lengths:	miles	km
motorway	33·0	*53,1*
trunk	84·0	*135,2*
principal	402·0	*647,0*
classified	1218·0	*1960,2*
unclassified	1187·0	*1910,3*

Schools and colleges: Primary 302; Middle and Secondary 51; Special 13; Establishments of further education 7.
Places of interest: Salisbury Cathedral; Longleat; Stonehenge; Avebury Stone Circle; Wilton House; Stourhead; Windmill Hill.

Northern Ireland

Area: 5450 miles² *14 120 km²*.
Population: 1 557 800 (mid-1985 estimate).
Density: 290 per mile² *112 per km²*.
Administrative HQ: Belfast.
Districts: The province is now divided into 26 districts, whose councils have similar functions to English district councils. The six geographical counties no longer exist as administrative units. Northern Ireland is divided into nine areas: five education and library areas plus four health and social services areas (other functions such as police, planning, roads, water, housing, fire services, etc., are run centrally from Stormont). The area boards are not directly elected: about a third of their members are district councillors while the rest are persons appointed by the appropriate United Kingdom minister. The six traditional geographic counties of Northern Ireland in order of size are:

COUNTY TYRONE
First recorded use of name and derivation: From Tir Eoghan, land of Eoghan (Owen, son of Niall).
Area: 126 miles² *327 km²*.
Former capital: Omagh on the river Strule.
Highest point: Sawel (in Sperrin Mts) 2240 ft *683 m*.
Coastline length: nil.

COUNTY ANTRIM
First recorded use of name and derivation: From the 5th century monastery of Aentrebh.
Area: 112 miles² *291 km²*.
Former capital: City of Belfast on the river Lagan.
Highest point: Trostan 1817 ft *544 m*.
Coastline length: 90 miles *145 km*.

County worthies by birth: 1st Duke of Somerset (*c*. 1500–52); Edward (Hyde) 1st Earl of Clarendon (1609–74); Sir Christopher Wren (1632–1723); Joseph Addison (1672–1719); William H F Talbot (1800–77); Sir Isaac Pitman (1813–97); Thomas Hobbes (1588–1679).

England's Regises

The use of the suffix 'Regis' – meaning 'of the King' – is used in the names of 12 places in England. In most cases the term has arisen from local usage to distinguish a Royal Manor, rather than from any exercise of prerogative by the sovereign.

	Earliest Mention
Bere Regis, Dorset	1244
Bognor Regis, West Sussex (1929)†	680
Grafton Regis, Northamptonshire	1204
Houghton Regis, Bedfordshire	1353
Kingsbury Regis, Somerset	1200
Letcombe Regis, Berkshire	1136
Lyme Regis, Dorset	1285
Lynn Regis, Norfolk (1537)†	1085
Melcombe Regis, Dorset	1280
Milton Regis, Kent	
Rowley Regis, West Midlands (1933)†	1173
Wyke Regis, Dorset	998

† By royal prerogative.

COUNTY DOWN
First recorded use of name and derivation: From Dun, Irish gaelic for fort (i.e. St Patrick's fort).
Area: 95 miles² *247 km²*.
Former capital: Downpatrick on the river Quoile.
Highest point: Slieve Donard 2796 ft *852 m*.
Coastline length: 125 miles *201 km*.

COUNTY LONDONDERRY
First recorded use of name and derivation: From the charter granted by James I in 1613 to the City of London (England) livery companies. 'Derry' is a corruption of the celtic *doire*, an oak grove *c*. AD 500.
Area: 80 miles² *208 km²*.
Former capital: City of Londonderry on the river Foyle.
Highest point: Sawel 2240 ft *683 m*.
Coastline length: 18 miles *29 km*.

COUNTY FERMANAGH
First recorded use of name and derivation: From Fir Mhanach, territory of the men of Managh.
Area: 71 miles² *185 km²*.
Former capital: Enniskillen.
Highest point: Cuilcagh 2188 ft *667 m*.
Coastline length: nil.

COUNTY ARMAGH
First recorded use of name and derivation: From Queen Macha *c*. 3rd century BC.
Area: 49 miles² *127 km²*.
Former capital: Armagh on the Blackwater tributary Callan.
Highest point: Slieve Gullion 1894 ft *577 m*.
Coastline length: 2 miles *3,2 km*.

NORTHERN IRELAND: THE 26 DISTRICTS

District	HQ	Pop. (mid-1985)	Area acres	Area hectares
Antrim	Antrim	45 900	100 142	40 527
Ards	Newtownards	62 200	90 881	36 779
Armagh	Armagh	50 400	164 897	66 733
Ballymena	Ballymena	55 800	156 622	63 384
Ballymoney	Ballymoney	23 800	103 009	41 687
Banbridge	Banbridge	31 600	109 048	44 131
Belfast	Belfast	301 600	32 165	13 017
Carrickfergus	Carrickfergus	28 400	20 964	8484
Castlereagh	in Belfast, i.e. out of the district	58 400	20 858	8441
Coleraine	Coleraine	47 300	118 022	47 763
Cookstown	Cookstown	27 900	126 533	51 207
Craigavon	Lurgan and Portadown	75 300	69 161	27 989
Down	Downpatrick	55 400	157 736	63 835
Dungannon	Dungannon	43 900	188 453	76 266
Fermanagh	Enniskillen	51 400	419 951	169 952
Larne	Larne	28 600	83 381	33 744
Limavady	Limavady	28 900	144 610	58 523
Lisburn	Lisburn	90 900	107 723	43 595
Londonderry	Londonderry	95 300	92 065	37 258
Magherafelt	Magherafelt	33 000	138 836	56 186
Moyle	Balleycastle	15 000	122 013	49 378
Newry and Mourne	Newry	84 700	218 903	88 589
Newtownabbey	Newtownabbey	72 100	37 332	15 108
North Down	Bangor	69 300	17 893	7241
Omagh	Omagh	44 900	277 627	112 354
Strabane	Strabane	35 800	212 728	86 090
Total		1 557 800	3 331 553	1 348 261

Note: The name Ulster is sometimes (but mistakenly) used as an alternative for the Province of Northern Ireland. Ulster is in fact one of the four ancient provinces of the island of Ireland [viz Connaught (5 counties), Leinster (12 counties), Munster (6 counties) and Ulster (9 counties)] and comprised the six counties of Northern Ireland and the three of the 26 counties (viz Cavan, Donegal and Monaghan) in the Republic of Ireland.

Education and library areas: BELFAST AREA (HQ Belfast): Nursery 27; Primary 108; Secondary Intermediate 33; Grammar 18; Special 10; Colleges of further education 3. NORTH-EASTERN AREA (HQ Ballymena): Nursery 17; Primary 248; Secondary Intermediate 42; Grammar 18; Special 5; Colleges of further education 8. SOUTH-EASTERN AREA (HQ Belfast): Nursery 16; Primary 168; Secondary Intermediate 33; Grammar 11; Special 5; Colleges of further education 5. SOUTHERN AREA (HQ Armagh): Nursery 14; Primary 284; Secondary Intermediate 39; Grammar 18; Special 1; Colleges of further education 6. WESTERN AREA (HQ Omagh): Nursery 10; Primary 209; Secondary Intermediate 36; Grammar 13; Special 4; Colleges of further education 4.

Health and social services: EASTERN AREA (HQ Belfast); NORTHERN AREA (HQ Ballymena); WESTERN AREA (HQ Londonderry); SOUTHERN AREA (HQ Craigavon).

Highest point above sea-level: Slieve Donard (in Newry and Mourne District) 2796 ft *852 m*.

Places of interest: Lakes of Fermanagh; Mourne Mountains; Armagh Cathedrals; Florence Court; Antrim Coast Road; Giant's Causeway; Mount Stewart; Carrickfergus Castle; Sperrin Mountains; Downpatrick Cathedral.

Worthies by birth: St Malachy (c. 1095–1148); Sir Hans Sloane (1660–1753); Robert Stewart, Lord Castlereagh (1769–1822); Thomas Andrews (1813–85); Thomas Mayne Reid (1818–83); John Nicholson (1822–57); Lord Kelvin (1824–1907); Lord Alexander of Tunis (1891–1969).

Britain's pre-history

British history starts with the earliest written references dating from c. 525 BC by Himilco of the Tunisian city of Carthage. Events prior to that belong to pre-history – a term invented by Daniel Wilson in 1851.

Pre-historic events are subject to continuous reassessment as new dating methods are advanced. Most notable among these has been radiocarbon dating invented by Dr Willard F Libby (US) in 1949. This is based upon the decay rate of the radioactive carbon isotope C14, whose half-life is 5730 years (formerly thought to be 5568 years). Other modern methods include dendrochronology (calibration by study of tree-rings), developed by Professor C W Ferguson since 1969 and thermoluminescence, pollen analysis and amino-acid testing.

BC
c. 400 000
Disputed evidence for *Homo erectus*, predecessor of *H. sapiens* in paleolithic hand-axes found 1975 near Westbury-sub-Mendip, Somerset.

? 285 000–240 000
Anglian glaciation possibly contemporary with the alpine Mindel glaciation with ice sheets reaching the Thames valley. Human occupation (known as pre-Hoxnian) may have occurred during a warmer interstadial phase of this glaciation, e.g. course hand-axe culture at Fordwich, Kent (published 1968) and Kents Cavern, near Torquay, Devon (reassessed 1971).

? 240 000–130 000
Hoxnian interglacial (so named after Hoxne site, Suffolk, disc. 1797). Clactonian flake assemblages followed by Acheulian hand-axe industry, which latter yielded earliest British human remains at Swanscombe, Kent found by Marston in 1935–6. Sea level 30–35 m *98–114 ft* above present datum.

130 000–105 000
Wolstonian glaciation, probably contemporary with the alpine Riss glaciation.

105 000–75 000
Ipswichian interglacial – sea level 8 m *26 ft* above present datum.

75 000–19 000
Last or Devensian glaciation, contemporary with the alpine Würm glaciation, reaching to the latitude of York. Britain probably discontinuously unpopulated but populated during the warmer Chelford interstadial of 59 000 BC and during a further interstadial of 40 000 to 36 000 BC.

26 700 ± 450
Earliest upper palaeolithic radiocarbon dating from Kents Cavern.

18 000–14 000
Maximum extension of ice-sheets. Sea-level fall of 100–150 m *328–492 ft*.

10 500–8000
Mesolithic Creswellian period and the close of the late Upper Palaeolithic era.

c. 9050
Irish Sea land-bridge breached.

8400
Start of the present Flandrian post-glacial period. Earliest (Maglemosian) to latest (Lussa, Jura) datings of Mesolithic finds. Mesolithic man may have had herds by 4300 BC.

c. 6850
The North Sea land bridge between East Yorkshire and Holland breached by rising sea-level.

c. 6450
The English Channel attained its current width under the impact of the Flandrian transgression.

6100
Earliest dated habitation in Scotland, microlithic industry at Morton in Fife.

4580
Earliest dated habitation in Ireland – neolithic site at Ballynagilly, Tyrone two centuries earlier than England's earliest neolithic sites at Broome Heath, Norfolk; Findon, West Sussex and Lambourne, Berkshire.

4210–3990
Earliest dated British farming site at Hembury, Devon (first excavated 1934–5).

3795
Earliest dated pottery at Ballynagilly (see above).

3650–3400
Avebury Stone Circle building, Wiltshire.

2930–2560
Giant Silbury Hill round barrow, Wiltshire.

2760
Earliest Bronze Age dating with Beaker pottery from Ballynagilly (see above), four centuries before earliest English datings at Chippenham, Cambridge and Mildenhall, Suffolk.

2285–2075
Phase I at Stonehenge (ditch construction).

1260
Earliest dated hill-fort, Ivinghoe, Buckinghamshire.

c. 750
Introduction of iron into Britain from Hallstatt by the Celts. Hill-forts proliferate.

c. 308
First circumnavigation of Great Britain by Pytheas the Greek sea-captain from Massilia (Marseille).

c. 125
Introduction of Gallo-Belgic gold coinage via Kent from the Beauvais region of France.

c. 90
Earliest British coinage – Westerham gold staters so named after the hoard find in Kent in 1927.

55 (26 Aug.)
Julius Caesar's exploratory expedition with 7th and 10th legions and 98 ships from Boulogne and Ambleteuse.

54 (18 or 21 July)
Second Julian invasion with five legions and 2000 cavalry.

**AD
43**
Claudian invasion and the start of the Roman Occupation.

Roman Era, 55 BC–AD 410

Caesar arrived off Dover from Boulogne with 98 transports and two legions in the early hours of 26 Aug. 55 BC. He landed against beach opposition between Deal and Walmer. Repeated skirmishing prevented the reconnaisance being a success and Caesar withdrew. He returned in 54 BC (variously on 18 or 21 July) with five legions and 800 vessels, and encamped on the Kentish shore and crossed the Thames near Brentford. He was much harried by the British leader, Cassivellaunus, based on the old Belgic capital of St Albans (*Verulamium*). The occupation was not sustained.

It was nearly a century later in AD 43 when the third Roman landing was made with some 20 000 men in three waves under the command of Plautius. This invasion is referred to as the Claudian Invasion, after the Roman emperor of that time. The British leader, Cunobelinus, was aged but resistance remained bitter. Roman cruelties against the king of the Iceni tribe and his family in East Anglia fired a native 'death or liberty' revolt under his widow, Queen Bodicca (Boadicea) in AD 61. Colchester (*Camulodunum*), London (*Londinium*) and St Albans were in turn sacked. The total death roll was put at 70 000 by Tacitus. Boadicea's horde of some 80 000 was met by Suetonius' 14th and 20th Legions of 10 000 men on a battlefield perhaps near Hampstead Heath, North London. For the loss of only about 400 of the fully-armed Romans, 70 000 Britons were claimed to have been killed. Subjugation, however, was not achieved until AD 83, when Agricola, the Roman Governor, won the Battle of Mons Graupius, suggested by some to be the Pass of Killiecrankie, Tayside.

For nearly 300 years the Roman régime brought law, order, peace, food, and even unknown warmth and cleanliness for the few who aspired to villas. The legions recruited locally to maintain 40 000 troops, garrisoned at Chester, Caerleon-on-Usk, York, and Hadrian's Wall. Hadrian arrived in Britain in 122 after the annihilation of the 9th Legion by the Picts. The 74½-mile-long *120 km* wall across the Tyne-Solway isthmus was built between AD 122 and 129. The 37-mile-long *59,5 km* Forth-Clyde or Antonine Wall was built c. 150, but was abandoned within 40 years. Emperor Severus reestablished military order in the period 208–11, but by the time of Carausius, who ruled in 287–93, raids by the Saxons (*Seax*, short, one-handed sword) from the Schleswig-Holstein area were becoming increasingly troublesome. Demands were made by the Saxons, Scots and Picts that Emperor Valentinian send his general, Theodosius, in 367 to restore order in the Province. In 400 Theodosius in turn sent his general, Stilicho, to deliver the Province from the ever-increasing pressure of the barbarians, but by 402 he was forced to recall the Roman garrison to help resist the incursions in Northern Italy of the Visigoths under Alaric. In 405 there was mutiny in the remaining garrison in Britain, who elected Gratianus, a Briton, as rival emperor. In 410 Emperor Honorius told the Britons from Rome that they must 'defend themselves' against the Saxons, Picts, and Scots.

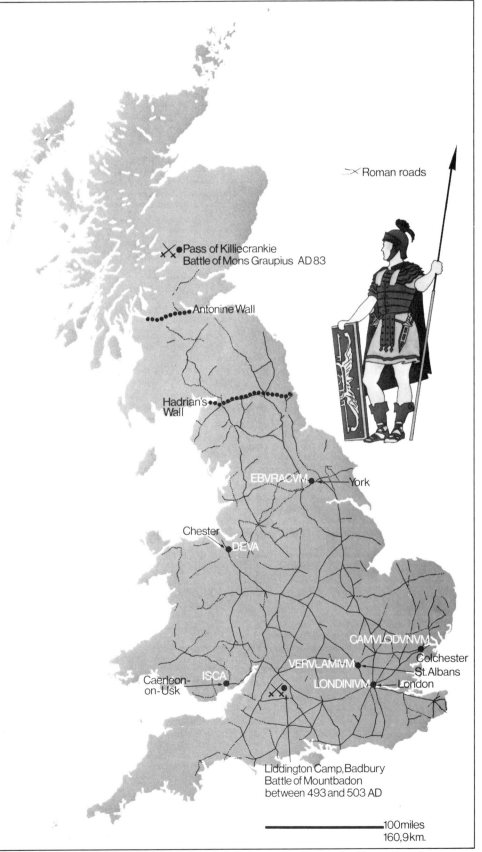

Roman roads

Pass of Killiecrankie
Battle of Mons Graupius AD 83

Antonine Wall

Hadrian's Wall

EBVRACVM — York

Chester
DEVA

CAMVLODVNVM
VERVLAMIVM
Colchester
St. Albans
LONDINIVM — London

Caerleon-on-Usk
ISCA

Liddington Camp, Badbury
Battle of Mountbadon
between 493 and 503 AD

100 miles
160,9 km.

AD 410–1066

British rulers between the end of the Roman occupation (AD 410) and the Norman conquest (1066)

By 449 a Jutish Kingdom had been set up in Kent by Hengist and Horsa. The 5th and 6th centuries were a period of utter confusion and misery with conflict between English and the remaining Britons, whose last champion was reputedly King Arthur. Some time between 493 and 503 Arthur fought the Battle of Mountbadon against the cruel Saxon invaders on an uncertain site, now ascribed to Liddington Camp, Badbury, near Swindon, Wiltshire.

England (excluding Cumbria) did not again become a unified state before AD 954. Some earlier kings exercised direct rule over all England for intermittent periods during their reigns. Edward the Elder (899–924 or 925), son of Alfred (871–99) the most famous of the Kings of the West Saxons, had suzerainty over the whole of England though he did not directly rule the Danish kingdom of York, which was not finally extinguished until 954.

The following nine kingdoms existed in England before it became a unified kingdom. All existed contemporaneously during the first half of the 7th century (c. AD 604 to 654), but became absorbed in each other until the Kings of Wessex established overall authority.

1.	Kings of Kent	c. 455 to 825, conquered by West Saxons.
2.	Kings of the South Saxons	477–c. 786, absorbed by Wessex.
3.	Kings of West Saxons	519–954, established authority over all England.
4.	Kings of Bernicia	547–670, annexed by Northumbria.
5.	Kings of Northumbria	c. 588–?878, reduced by the Danish Kingdom of York.
6.	Kings of Mercia	c. 595–ante 883, first acknowledged overlordship of West Saxons 829.
7.	Kings of Deira	599 or 560 to 654, annexed by Bernicia.
8.	Kings of the East Angles	c. 600–870, conquest by Danes.
9.	Kings of the East Saxons	ante 604–825, submitted to West Saxons.
	Danish Kingdom of York	875 or 876–954, expulsion by Edred, the King of West Saxons.

The West Saxon King Egbert (802–39), grandfather of King Alfred, is often quoted as the first King of All England from AD 829, but in fact he never reduced the Kingdom of Northumbria ruled by Eanred (808 or 810 to 840 or 841).

Kings of All England

Athelstan, eldest son of the eldest son of King Alfred of the West Saxons, acceded 924 or 925. The first to establish rule over all England (excluding Cumbria) in 927. d. 27 Oct. 939 aged over 40 years.

Edmund, younger half-brother of Athelstan; acceded 939 but did not regain control of all England until 944–45. Murdered, 26 May 946 by Leofa at Pucklechurch, near Bristol, Avon.

Edred, younger brother of Edmund; acceded May 946. Effectively King of All England 946–48, and from 954 to his death, on 23 Nov. 955. Also intermittently during the intervening period.

Edwy, son of Edmund, b. c. 941; acceded November 955 (crowned at Kingston, Greater London); lost control of Mercians and Northumbrians in 957. d. 1 Oct. 959 aged about 18.

Edgar, son of Edmund, b. 943; acceded October 959, as King of All England (crowned at Bath, 11 May 973). d. 8 July 975, aged c. 32.

Edward the Martyr, son of Edgar by Aethelflaed, b. c. 962; acceded 975. d. 18 Mar. 978 or 979, aged 16 or 17.

Ethelred (*Unraed*, i.e. ill-counselled), second son of Edgar by Aelfthryth, b. ?968–69; acceded 978 or 979 (crowned at Kingston, 14 Apr. 978 or 4 May 979); dispossessed by the Danish king, Swegn Forkbeard, 1013–14. d. 23 Apr. 1016, aged c. 47 or 48.

Swegn Forkbeard, King of Denmark 987–1014, acknowledged King of All England from about September 1013 to his death, 3 Feb. 1014.

Edmund Ironside, prob. 3rd son of Ethelred, b. c. 992; chosen King in London, April 1016. In summer of 1016 made agreement with Cnut whereby he retained dominion only over Wessex. d. 30 Nov. 1016.

Cnut, younger son of King Swegn Forkbeard of Denmark, b. c. 995. Secured Mercia and Danelaw, summer 1016; assumed dominion over all England December 1016; King of Denmark 1019–35. King of Norway 1028–1035; overlord of the King of the Scots and probably ruler of the Norse-Irish kingdom of Dublin. d. 12 Nov. 1035, aged c. 40 years.

Harold Harefoot, natural son of Cnut by Aelfgifu of Northampton, b. ?c. 1016–17; chosen regent for half-brother, Harthacnut, late 1035 or early 1036; sole King 1037, d. 17 Mar. 1040, aged c. 23 or 24 years.

Harthacnut, son of Cnut by Emma, widow of King Ethelred (d. 1016) b. ?c. 1018; titular King of Denmark from 1028; effectively King of England from June 1040. d. 8 June 1042, aged c. 24 years.

Edward the Confessor, senior half-brother of Harthacnut and son of King Ethelred and Emma, b. 1002–05; resided with Harthacnut from 1041, acceded 1042, crowned 3 Apr. 1043. d. 5 Jan. 1066, aged between 60 and 64. Sanctified.

Harold Godwinson, brother-in-law of Edward the Confessor and brother of his Queen Edith, son of Godwin, Earl of Wessex, b. ?c. 1020; acceded 6 Jan. 1066, d. or k. 14 Oct. 1066.

Edgar Etheling, chosen by Londoners as king after the Battle of Hastings. Oct. 1066; not apparently crowned, submitted to William I before 25 Dec. 1066; believed still living c. 1125.

Rulers in Wales (844–1289)

Province of Gwynedd (North Wales) (844–1283) last prince executed for treason by Edward I.

Province of Deheubarth (Dyfed) (South Central and South West Wales) (844–1231), last of line imprisoned in Norwich.

Province of Powys (North Central Wales) (1063–1160), split into Southern and Northern Powys. Southern Powys (1160–1277), dispossessed, Northern Powys (1160–ante 1289) became marcher lordship.

Kings of Scotland (1005–1603)

The chronology of the early kings of Alba (north of the Clyde and the Forth) before the 10th century is highly obscure.

Malcolm II (1005–34), b. c. 954. d. 25 Nov. 1034, aged c. 80 years. Formed the Kingdom of Scotland by annexing Strathclyde, c. 1016.

Duncan I (1034–40), son of Malcolm II's daughter, Bethoc.

Macbeth (1040–57), ?son of Malcolm II's daughter, Donada. d. aged c. 52 years.

Lulach (1057–8), stepson of Macbeth and son of his wife Gruoch. d. aged c. 26.

Malcolm III (Canmore) (1058–93), son of Duncan I. d. aged c. 62.

Donald Bane (1093–94 and 1094–97), son of Duncan I, twice deposed.

Duncan II (May to October 1094), son of Malcolm III. d. aged c. 34.

Edgar (1097–1107), son of Malcolm III, half-brother of Duncan II. d. aged c. 33.

Alexander I (1107–24), son of Malcolm III, brother of Edgar. d. aged c. 47.

David I (1124–53), son of Malcolm III and brother of Edgar. d. aged c. 68.

Malcolm IV (1153–65), son of Henry, Earl of Northumberland. d. aged c. 24.

William I (*The Lion*) (1165–1214), brother of Malcolm IV. d. aged c. 72 (from 1174 to 1189 King of England, acknowledged as overlord of Scotland).

Alexander II (1214–49), son of William I. d. aged 48.

Alexander III (1249–1286), son of Alexander II. d. aged 44.

Margaret (*Maid of Norway*) (1286–90), daughter of Margaret, daughter of Alexander III by King Eric II of Norway. Never visited her realm. d. aged 7.

First Interregnum 1290–92.

John (*Balliol*) (1292–96), son of Dervorguilla, a great-great-granddaughter of David I, awarded throne from 13 contestants by adjudication of Edward I who declared after four years that John would have to forfeit his throne for contumacy.

Second Interregnum 1296–1306.

Robert I (1306–29), son of Robert Bruce and grandson of a 1291 competitor. d. aged c. 55.

David II (1329–71), son of Robert I. d. aged 46. *Note:* Edward Balliol, son of John, was crowned King in 1332, acknowledged Edward III of England as overlord in 1333 and surrendered all claims to Scottish crown to him in 1356.

Robert II (1371–90), founder of the Stewart dynasty, son of Walter the Steward and Marjorie Bruce. d. aged 74.

Robert III (1390–1406), legitimated natural son of Robert II. d. aged c. 69.

James I (1406–37), son of Robert III, captured by English 13 days before accession and kept prisoner in England till March 1424. d. aged 42.

James II (1437–60), son of James 1. d. aged 29.

James III (1460–88), son of James II. d. aged 36.

James IV (1488–1513), son of James III and Margaret of Denmark, married Margaret Tudor. d. aged 40.

James V (1513–42), son of James IV and Margaret Tudor. d. aged 30.

Mary (*Queen of Scots*) (1542–67), daughter of James V and Mary of Lorraine, acceded aged 6 or 7 days, abdicated 24 July 1567 and was succeeded by her son (James VI) by her second husband, Henry Stuart, Lord Darnley. She was executed, 8 Feb. 1587, aged 44.

James VI (1567–1625), son of Mary and Lord Darnley (see above), succeeded to the English throne as James I on 24 Mar. 1603, so effecting a personal union of the two realms. d. aged 58.

The eleven royal houses of England since 1066

A royal dynasty normally takes its house name from the family's patronymic. It does not change by reason of a Queen Regnant's marriage – for example, Queen Victoria, a member of the

House of Hanover and Brunswick, did not become a member of the House of Saxe-Coburg and Gotha (her husband's family) but her son, Edward VII, and her grandson, George V (until renamed in 1917), were members of the house of their respective fathers.

The House of Normandy (by right of conquest) (69 years)
The house name derives from the fact that William I was the 7th Duke of Normandy with the style William II. This was despite the fact that he was illegitimate because his father, Duke Robert II, had him formally instituted as his legal heir.

William I (1066–87); William II (1087–1100); Henry I (1100–35) and Matilda.

The House of Blois (19 years)
The house name derives from the fact that the father of King Stephen was Stephen (sometimes called Henry), Count of Blois.

Stephen (1135–54).

The House of Anjou (331 years)
The house name derives from the fact that the father of King Henry II was Geoffrey V, 10th Count of Anjoy and Maine. This family was alternatively referred to as the Angevins, the name deriving from Angers, the town and diocese within the boundaries of Anjou.

Henry II (1154–89) and the next thirteen kings down to and including Richard III (1483–5).

Note: (1) This house, but only since the mid-15th century, and in fact less than 50 years before its male line became extinct, has been referred to as The House of Plantagenet. This name originates from Count Geoffrey's nickname 'Plantagenet', which in turn derived, it is said, from his habit of wearing a sprig of broom (*Planta genista*) in his cap during a crusade.

(2) The House of Anjou (or Plantagenet) may be sub-divided after the deposing of Richard II in 1399 into The House of Lancaster with Henry IV (1399–1413); Henry V (1413–22); Henry VI (1422–61 and 1470–1), and The House of York with Edward IV (1461–83 – except 1470–1); Edward V (1483); Richard III (1483–5).

(3) The names Lancaster and York derived respectively from the titles of the 4th and 5th sons of Edward III; John of Gaunt (1340–99) was 1st Duke of Lancaster (of the second creation), and the father of Henry IV, and Edmund of Langley (1341–1402) was 1st Duke of York and a great-grandfather of Edward IV.

The House of Tudor (118 years)
This house name derives from the surname of Henry VII's father, Edmund Tudor, Earl of Richmond, and son of Sir Owen Tudor, by Catherine, widow of King Henry V.

Henry VII (1485–1509); Henry VIII (1509–47); Edward VI (1547–53); after the reign of Queen Jane, Mary I (1553–8); Elizabeth I (1558–1603).

The House of Grey (14 days)
This house name derives from the family and surname of the 3rd Marquess of Dorset, the father of Lady Guil(d)ford Dudley, who reigned as Queen Jane from 6 July, 1553 for 14 days until 19 July when the House of Tudor regained the throne.

The House of Stuart and the House of Stuart and Orange (98 years and 5 years)
This house name is derived from the family and surname of Henry Stuart, Lord Darnley and Duke of Albany, the eldest son of Matthew, 4th Earl of Lennox. Lord Darnley was the second of three husbands and cousin of Mary Queen of Scots and the father of James VI of Scotland and I of England.

James I (1603–25); Charles I (1625–49); Charles II (*de jure* 1649 but *de facto* 1660–85); James II (1685–8).

The house name became The House of Stuart and Orange when in 1689 William III, son of William II, Prince of Orange, became the sovereign conjointly with his wife, Mary II, the

5th Stuart monarch.

The House of Stuart resumed from 1702 to 1714 during the reign of Queen Anne.

The House of Orange
William III reigned alone during his widowerhood from 1694 to 1702. William in fact possessed the sole regal power during his entire reign from 1689.

The House of Hanover and Brunswick-Lüneburg (187 years)
This house name derives from the fact that George I's father, Ernest Augustus, was the Elector of Hanover and a duke of the House of Brunswick-Lüneburg.

George I (1714–27); George II (1727–60); George III (1760–1820); George IV (1820–30); William IV (1830–7); Queen Victoria (1837–1901).

The House of Saxe-Coburg and Gotha (16 years)
This house name derives from the princely title of Queen Victoria's husband, Prince Albert, later Prince Consort.

Edward VII (1901–10); George V (1910–1917); on 17 July 1917 King George V declared by Royal Proclamation that he had changed the name of the royal house to the House of Windsor.

The House of Windsor
George V (1917–36); Edward VIII (1936); George VI (1936–52); Elizabeth II (from 1952).

In the normal course of events Prince Charles, Prince of Wales, on inheriting the throne would become the first monarch of the House of Mountbatten but by further Proclamations the Queen first declared in 1952 that her children and descendants will belong to the House of Windsor, and later in 1960 that this Declaration would only affect her descendants in the male line who will bear a royal style and title. Descendants outside this class will bear the surname 'Mountbatten-Windsor'.

Titles of the Royal House

Husbands of Queens Regnant
The husband of a queen regnant derives no title from his marriage. Philip II of Spain, husband of Queen Mary I, was termed 'King Consort'. Prince George of Denmark, husband of Queen Anne, was created Duke of Cumberland. Prince Albert of Saxe-Coburg-Gotha was created 'Royal Highness' and seventeen years after his marriage 'Prince Consort'. The Duke of Edinburgh, husband of Queen Elizabeth II, is HRH and a prince of the United Kingdom of Great Britain and Northern Ireland.

Queens Consort
A queen consort ranks with and shares the king's titles. In the event of her being widowed she cannot continue to use the title 'The Queen'. She must add to it her christian name or use the style additionally, or by itself, of 'Queen Mother' (if she has children), or, as in the case of the widow of King William IV, 'Queen Dowager'.

In the event of her re-marriage, which can only be with the consent of the Sovereign, she does not forfeit her royal status. The last such example was when Queen Catherine (Parr) married, as her fourth husband, Lord Seymour of Sudeley, KG, in 1547.

The Heir to the Throne
The Heir Apparent to the throne can only be the son or grandson (as in the case of the Prince of Wales from 1751 to 1760) of the reigning Sovereign. Should the first person in the order of succession bear any relationship other than in the direct male line, they are the Heir (or Heiress) Presumptive. The last Heiress Presumptive to the Throne was HRH the Princess Elizabeth (1936–52). A female could be an Heiress Apparent if she were the only or eldest daughter of a deceased Heir Apparent who had no male issue.

The eldest surviving son of a reigning Sovereign is born The Duke of Cornwall, The Duke

of Rothesay, the Earl of Carrick and The Baron Renfrew, together with the styles of Lord of the Isles, Prince and Great Steward (or Seneschel) of Scotland. The titles Prince of Wales and Earl of Chester are a matter of creation and not of birthright. The Prince of Wales is part of the establishment of The Order of the Garter. If, however, a Prince of Wales died, as in 1751, his eldest son would automatically succeed to that title and the Earldom of Chester but not to the Dukedom of Cornwall and the other honours because they are expressly reserved for the son (and not the grandson) of a Sovereign.

Princes, Princesses and Royal Highnesses
Since 1917 the style HRH Prince or Princess has been limited to the children of the Monarch and the children of the sons of the Monarch and their wives. Grand-children of a Prince of Wales also would enjoy this style. In practice the sons of a Sovereign have a dukedom bestowed upon them after they become of age. Such 'Royal Dukedoms' only enjoy their special precedence (i.e. senior to the two Archbishops and other dukes) for the next generation. A third duke would take his seniority among the non-royal dukes according to the date of the original creation.

The title 'Princess Royal' is conferred (if vacant) for life on the eldest daughter of the Sovereign.

The order of Succession to the Crown

The order of succession is determined according to ancient Common Law rules but these may be upset by an enactment of the Crown in Parliament under powers taken in the Succession to the Crown Act of 1707, provided always (since 1931) that the parliaments of all the Members of the Commonwealth assent. At Common Law the Crown descends lineally to the legitimate issue of the sovereign, males being preferred to females, in their respective orders of age. In the event of failure of such issue (e.g. King Edward VIII in 1936) the Crown passes to the nearest collateral being an heir at law. The common law of descent of the Crown specifically departs from the normal feudal rules of land descent at two points. First, in the event of two or more sisters being next in succession the eldest alone (e.g. The Princess Elizabeth from 1936 to 1952) shall be the heiress and shall not be merely a coparcener with her sister or sisters. Secondly, male issue by a second or subsequent marriage takes precedence over half sisters (e.g. King Edward VI, son of King Henry VIII's third wife, took precedence over Queen Mary I, daughter of his first marriage, and Queen Elizabeth I, daughter of his second marriage).

Below is set out the Order of Succession to the Crown.

1 The heir apparent is HRH The Prince CHARLES Philip Arthur George, KG, KT, The Prince of Wales, The Duke of Cornwall, The Duke of Rothesay, The Earl of Carrick, and the Baron Renfrew, Lord of the Isles and Great Steward of Scotland, born 14 Nov. 1948, then follows his son:

2 HRH The Prince WILLIAM Arthur Philip Louis, born 21 June 1982, then his brother:

3 HRH The Prince HENRY Charles Albert David, born 15 Sept. 1984, then his uncle:

4 HRH The Prince ANDREW Albert Christian Edward, born 19 Feb. 1960, then his brother:

5 HRH The Prince EDWARD Antony Richard Louis, born 10 Mar. 1964, then his sister:

6 HRH The Princess ANNE Elizabeth Alice Louise, Mrs Mark Phillips, born 15 Aug. 1950, then her son:

7 PETER Mark Andrew Phillips, born 15 Nov. 1977, then his sister:

8 Miss ZARA Anne Elizabeth Phillips, born 15 May 1981, then her great aunt:

9 HRH The Princess MARGARET Rose, CI, GCVO, The Countess of Snowdon, born 21 Aug. 1930, then her son:

10 DAVID Albert Charles Armstrong-Jones, commonly called Viscount Linley, born 3 Nov. 1961, then his sister:

11 The Lady SARAH Frances Elizabeth Armstrong-Jones, born 1 May 1964, then her cousin, once removed:

12 HRH Prince RICHARD Alexander Walter George, Duke of Gloucester, born 26 Aug. 1944, then his son:

13 Lord ALEXANDER Patrick George Richard, Earl of Ulster, born 24 Oct. 1974, then his sister:

14 The Lady DAVINA Elizabeth Alice Benedikte Windsor, born 19 Nov. 1977, then her sister:

15 The Lady ROSE Victoria Birgitte Louise WINDSOR, born 1 Mar. 1980, then her cousin once removed:

16 HRH Prince EDWARD George Nicholas Paul Patrick, GCVO, the (2nd) Duke of Kent, the Earl of St Andrews and the Baron Downpatrick, born 9 Oct. 1935, then his son:

17 Lord GEORGE Philip Nicholas WINDSOR, commonly called Earl of St Andrews, born 26 June 1962, then his brother:

18 Lord NICHOLAS Charles Edward Jonathan WINDSOR, born 25 July 1970, then his sister:

19 The Lady HELEN Marian Lucy WINDSOR, born 28 Apr. 1964, then her cousin:

20 Lord FREDERICK Michael George David Louis WINDSOR, born 6 Apr. 1979, (his father, HRH Prince MICHAEL George Charles Franklin of Kent, born 4 July 1942, having forfeited his claim to the Throne by his marriage (30 June 1978) to a Roman Catholic, Baroness Marie-Christine von Reibnitz), then his sister:

21 The Lady GABRIELA Marina Alexandra Ophelia WINDSOR, born 23 Apr. 1981, then her aunt:

22 HRH Princess ALEXANDRA Helen Elizabeth Olga Christabel of Kent, GCVO, the Hon Mrs Angus J B Ogilvy, born 25 Dec. 1936, then her son:

23 JAMES Robert Bruce Ogilvy, Esq, born 29 Feb. 1964, then his sister:

24 Miss MARINA Victoria Alexandra Ogilvy, born 31 July 1966, then her second cousin, once removed upwards.

Factors affecting the order
Two further factors should be borne in mind in determining the order of succession. First, no person may unilaterally renounce their right to succeed. Only an Act of Parliament can undo what another Act of Parliament (the Act of Settlement, 1701) has done. Secondly, some marriages among the descendants of George II are null and void and hence the descendants are not heirs at law, by failure to obtain the consent to marry as required by the Royal Marriage Act of 1772. In some cases this failure, prior to 1956, may have been inadvertent because it was only then confirmed by the House of Lords that every such descendant, born before 1948, is by a statute of 1705 deemed a British subject. So the escape from the requirements of the Royal Marriage Act accorded to all female descendants of George II who apparently married into *foreign* families is not so readily available as was once thought.

The Act of Settlement
On 6 Feb. 1701 the Act of Settlement came into force. It laid down that failing issue from HRH The Princess (later Queen Anne) George (of Denmark) and/or secondly from any subsequent marriage by her first cousin and brother-in-law, the widower King William III, the crown would vest in Princess Sophia, Dowager Electress of Hanover (1630–1714), the granddaughter of King James I, and the heirs of her body, with the proviso that all Roman Catholics, or persons marrying Roman Catholics, were for ever to be excluded, as if they 'were naturally dead'.

The Duke of Windsor
The only subsequent change in statute law was on 11 Dec. 1936 by His Majesty's Declaration of Abdication Act, 1936, by which the late HRH The Prince Edward, MC (later HRH The Duke of Windsor), and any issue he might subsequently have had were expressly excluded from the succession.

Conditions of tenure
On succeeding to the Crown the Sovereign must (1) join in Communion with the established Church of England; (2) declare that he or she is a Protestant; (3) swear the oaths for the preservation of both the Established Church of England and the Presbyterian Church of Scotland, and (4), and most importantly, take the coronation oath, which may be said to form the basis of the contract between Sovereign and subject, last considered to have been broken, on the Royal side, by King James II in 1688.

'The King never dies'
The Sovereign can never be legally a minor, but in fact a regency is provided until he or she attains the age of 18.

There is never an interregnum on the death of a Sovereign. In pursuance of the common law maxim 'the King never dies' the new Sovereign succeeds to full prerogative rights instantly on the death of his or her predecessor.

Notes on the British peerage

There are five ranks in the British temporal peerage – in ascending order they are: 1. Barons or Baronesses; 2. Viscounts or Viscountesses; 3. Earls or Countesses; 4. Marquesses (less favoured, Marquises) or Marchionesses; 5. Dukes or Duchesses.

The British spiritual peerage is of two ranks, Archbishops (of Canterbury and of York) who rank between Royal Dukes and dukes, and twenty-four of the bishops (but always including the Bishops of London, Durham, and Winchester with the Bishop of Sodor and Man always excluded), based on their seniority, who rank between Viscounts and Barons.

A few women hold peerages in their own right and since The Peerage Act, 1963, have become peers of Parliament. The remaining category of membership of the House of Lords is life peers. These are of two sorts: (a) The Lords of Appeal in Ordinary, who are appointed by virtue of the Appellate Jurisdiction Act, 1876. Their number has been increased from the original four to six in 1913, to seven in 1929, and to nine since 1947; (b) by virtue of The Life Peerages Act, 1958, both men and women may be appointed for life membership of The House of Lords. Such creations so far have been confined to the fifth and junior temporal rank of baron or baroness.

1. Peerages of England, i.e. those created prior to the union with Scotland on 1 May 1707.
2. Peerages of Scotland, i.e. those created before the union with England.
3. Peerages of Ireland (the last creation was in 1898 and no further ones are at present likely).
4. Peerages of Great Britain, i.e. those created between the union with Scotland (1707) and the union with Ireland (2 July 1800).
5. Peerages of the United Kingdom of Great Britain and (Northern) Ireland, i.e. those created since 2 July 1800.

All holders of peerages of England, Great Britain and the United Kingdom and (only since The Peerage Act, 1963) also of Scotland, are also peers of Parliament provided they are over 21 and are not unpardoned major felons, bankrupts, lunatics or of alien nationality. Peers who are civil servants may sit but neither speak nor vote.

The single exception to the rule concerning minors is that the Duke of Cornwall (HRH The Prince of Wales) has been technically entitled to a seat from the moment of his mother's accession, when he was only three years of age.

The peers (and peeresses in their own right) of Ireland are not peers of Parliament but they are entitled to stand for election to the House of Commons for any seat in the United Kingdom. The previous system by which this category of peer could elect 28 of its number to sit in the House of Lords has now fallen into disuse because since the Partition of Ireland in 1922 there has been no machinery available to carry out that election and all the representative peers elected prior to that date have since died.

Only the holder of a substantive peerage can be described as noble. In the eyes of the law the holder of a courtesy title is a commoner. For example, the Duke of Marlborough's son is known by courtesy as Marquess of Blandford. Note the omission of the definite article 'the'. The reason is that the Duke of Marlborough is also *the* Marquess of Blandford and his secondary peerage style is merely lent to this son.

Life Peers
The Crown in the past used on occasions to grant life peerages, both to men and women. The Wensleydale peerage case of 1856 acknowledged the Crown's right to do this but denied the consequent right of a seat in the House of Lords to such a peer. The two current categories of life peers are treated above. It should be noted that there is no provision for these non-hereditary peers or peeresses to disclaim their peerages.

Widows of Peers
The only correct style for the widow of a peer is 'The Dowager' prefixed to her peerage title of duchess, marchioness, countess, viscountess, or lady (*note:* 'baroness' is only normally used by a peeress in her own right). But in fact most widowed peeresses dislike this title because of its association with advanced age, so they prefix their Christian name to their title. In the event of a widow remarrying, she should forfeit her previous title but some, quite unjustifiably, retain it.

The Effect of Divorce
Some peeresses who divorce their husbands or have been divorced by them continue to bear their former husband's style though in strict English law they are probably no longer peeresses. If a new wife appears they adopt the practice of most widows and prefix their christian name to their title. With Scottish peerages, however, the position of a divorced peeress is exactly the same as if her husband were dead and hence she takes her legal rights as a widow.

Courtesy Titles
According to the preamble of The Peerage Act, 1963, 'Courtesy titles are, by definition, not matters of law'. They are governed by custom and fall into two categories – those borne by all the children of a peer and those reserved for the heir. The children (except the eldest son) of a duke or marquess take the title 'Lord' or 'Lady' before their christian name and the family name (e.g. Lord Charles Cavendish). The same applies to the daughters of an earl but not, oddly enough, to the younger sons who take the style 'Honourable' which is borne by *all* the children of a viscount, a baron and a temporal life peer. When male holders of this title marry, their wives also become 'The Honourable'. The heir to a dukedom is given the courtesy style 'Marquess', provided, of course, his father has a marquessate, which failing he takes the title 'Earl' but enjoys the precedence of a duke's eldest son. Likewise, the heir to a marquessate takes the courtesy style of 'Earl' (if available) and similarly the heir of an earldom takes the title of his father's viscountcy (if any) or barony.

In the Scottish peerage the term 'Master of' is

used by the male heir to many peerages as of right. If he is married, his wife is styled 'The Hon Mrs'.

Courtesy titles in the second generation extend only to the grandchildren who are the children of an elder son.

The Signature of Peers
A peer's signature, whether on a formal or informal document, is simply his title without any qualification of rank or the use of a christian name. This also applies to peeresses in their own right. Members of the Royal Family who hold peerages, however, sign with their principal Christian name.

The Prefix 'Lady'
This title causes more confusion than any other, simply because of the wide range of its use. It can be used as a less formal alternative by marchionesses, countesses, viscountesses and the wives of barons. It is never used by duchesses. It is used, but only with the addition of their christian names, by the daughters of dukes, marquesses and earls. It is also used by the wives of the younger sons of dukes and marquesses, e.g. Lady Charles Cavendish. It is used, but never with the definite article, by the wives of baronets and knights. There is one baroness.

Special Remainders
The Crown has power to create what are termed 'special remainders' so that a peerage can, for example, pass to an elder brother or some other relative. An example is that the earldom of Mountbatten of Burma passed to the first earl's elder daughter and her male issue.

Dormant Peerages
A peerage is deemed dormant when there is no discoverable heir but there is a reasonable presumption that there may be an heir if he or she could be found. The Crown will not permit the use of a name of a peerage for a subsequent creation unless there is absolute certainty that the former creation is truly extinguished.

The Descent of Peerages
Usually a peerage descends in the male line. Illegitimate offspring are, of course, excluded. If the direct male line fails, then the succession may go back to the male line in an earlier cadet branch of the family. The ancient category of English baronies by writ provides its own rules of descent. These peerages date back to the time when the original holder was deemed to be a peer solely by virtue of receiving a Writ of Summons to attend Parliament. The invariable practice since those days has been to grant a peerage specifically by Letters Patent.

Kings and Queens of England and Great Britain

The precise dates of all the main events in the lives of the earlier monarchs are not known, and probably now never will be. Where recognised authorities are in dispute, as quite frequently occurs in the first twenty or so reigns, we have adhered to the dates given by the Royal Historical Society's *Handbook of British Chronology* (second edition, 1961). This work includes the fruits of recent researches based on only acceptable evidence.

King or Queen Regnant Date of Accession and Final Year of Reign; Style	Date and Place of Birth and Parentage	Marriages and No. of Children	Date, Cause and Place of Death, and Place of Burial	Notes and Succession
1. **WILLIAM I** 25 Dec. 1066–87 'The Bastard' 'The Conqueror' *Style:* 'Willielmus Rex Anglorum'	1027 or 1028 at Falaise, north France; illegitimate son of Robert I, 6th Duke of Normandy, and Herleva, dau. of Fulbert the Tanner	m. at Eu in 1050 or 1051 MATILDA (d. 1083), d of Baldwin V, Count of Flanders. 4s 5d	d., aged 59 or 60, 9 Sept. 1087 of an abdominal injury from his saddle pommel at the Priory of St Gervais, nr. Rouen. The Abbey of St Stephen at Caen (remains lost during French Revolution).	William I succeeded by right of conquest by winning the 'Battle of Hastings', 14 Oct. 1066, from Harold II, the nominated heir of Edward III ('The Confessor'). Succeeded as King of England by his third, but second surviving, son, William
2. **WILLIAM II** 26 Sept. 1087–1100 'Rufus' *Style:* 'Dei Gratia Rex Anglorum'	between 1056 and 1060 in Normandy; third son of William I and Matilda	unmarried. Had illegitimate issue	d., aged between 40 and 44, 2 Aug. 1100 (according to tradition) of impalement by a stray arrow while hunting in the New Forest nr. Brockenhurst, Hants. Winchester Cathedral	Succeeded by his younger brother, Henry
3. **HENRY I** 5 Aug. 1100–35 'Beauclerc' *Style:* As No. 2 but also Duke of Normandy from 1106	in the latter half of 1068 at Selby, Yorks; fourth son of William I and Matilda	m. (1) at Westminster Abbey, 11 Nov. 1100 EADGYTH (Edith), known as MATILDA (d. 1118), d of Malcolm III, King of the Scots, and Margaret (grand-d of Edmund 'Ironside') 1s, 1d and a child who died young. m. (2) 29 Jan 1121 ADELA (d. 1151), d of Godfrey VII, Count of Louvain. No issue	d., aged 67, 1 Dec. 1135, from a feverish illness at St Denis-le-Ferment, nr. Grisors. Reading Abbey	Succeeded by his nephew, Stephen (the third, but second surviving, son of Adela, the fifth d of William I) who usurped the throne from Henry's only surviving legitimate child and d, Matilda (1102–67)
4. **STEPHEN** 22 Dec. 1135–54 *Style:* As No. 2.	between 1096 and 1100 at Blois, France; third son of Stephen (sometimes called Henry), Count of Blois, and Adela	m. 1125, MATILDA (d. 1151), d of Eustace II, Count of Boulogne, and Mary, sister of Queen Matilda, wife of Henry I. 3s 2d	d., aged between 54 and 58, 25 Oct. 1154, from a heart attack at St Martin's Priory, Dover. Faversham Abbey	Succeeded by his first cousin once removed downwards, Henry. Between April and November 1141 he was not *de facto* King and was imprisoned in Bristol Castle
5. **MATILDA** April–Nov. 1141 'Empress Maud' *Style:* 'Imperatrix Henrici Regis filia et Anglorum domina'	Feb. 1102 in London, only legitimate d of Henry I	m. (1) 1114 Henry V, Emperor of Germany (d. 1125). No issue. m. (2) 1130 GEOFFREY V, Count of Anjou (d. 1151). 3s	d., aged 65, 10 Sept. 1167 of uncertain cause, nr. Rouen in Normandy. Fontevraud(?), France	Succeeded by her cousin, Stephen, whom she had deposed

King or Queen Regnant Date of Accession and Final Year of Reign; Style	Date and Place of Birth and Parentage	Marriages and No. of Children	Date, Cause and Place of Death, and Place of Burial	Notes and Succession
6. **HENRY II** 19 Dec. 1154–1189 Style: 'Rex Angliae, Dux Normaniae et Aquitaniae et Comes Andigaviae'	5 Mar. 1133 at Le Mans, France; eldest son of Geoffrey V, Count of Anjou (surnamed Plantagenet), and Matilda (only d of Henry I)	m. at Bordeaux, 18 May, 1152, ELEANOR (c. 1122–1204), d of William X, Duke of Aquitaine, and divorced wife of Louis, later Louis VII, King of France, 5s 3d	d., aged 56, 6 July 1189, of a fever at the Castle of Chinon, nr. Tours, France. Fontevraud abbey church in Anjou Reburied Westminster Abbey	Succeeded by his third and elder surviving son, Richard. On 14 June 1170, Henry II's second and eldest surviving son Henry was crowned with his wife at Winchester as King of England. Contemporaneously he was called King Henry III. He predeceased his father, 11 June 1183
7. **RICHARD I** 3 Sept. 1189–99 'Coeur de Lion' Style: As No. 6	8 Sept. 1157 at Oxford; third son of Henry II and Eleanor	m. at Limassol, Cyprus, 12 May 1191, BERENGARIA (d. soon after 1230), d of Sancho VI of Navarre. No issue	d., aged 41, 6 Apr. 1199 from a mortal arrow wound while besieging the Castle of Châlus in Limousin, France. Fontevraud abbey church in Anjou. Reburied Westminster Abbey	Succeeded by his younger brother, John, who usurped the throne from his nephew Arthur, the only son of Geoffrey, Duke of Brittany (1158–86); and from his niece, Eleanor (1184–1241). Arthur (b, post-humously 1187) was murdered (unmarried) 3 Apr. 1203 in his 17th year
8. **JOHN** 27 May 1199–1216 'Lackland' Style: 'Joannes Rex Angliae et Dominus Hiberniae' etc.	24 Dec. 1167 at Beaumont Palace, Oxford; fifth son of Henry II and Eleanor	m. (1) at Marlborough, Wilts, 29 Aug. 1189, ISABEL (d. 1217). No issue. m. (2) at Angoulême, 24 Aug. 1200, ISABELLA (d. 1246), d of Aimir, Count of Angoulême. 2s 3d	d., aged 48, 18–19 Oct. 1216, of dysentery at Newark Castle, Notts. Worcester Cathedral	In late 1215 the Crown was offered to Louis, son of Philip II of France but despite a visit in 1216 the claim was abandoned in Sept. 1217. Succeeded by his elder son, Henry
9. **HENRY III** 28 Oct. 1216–72 Style: 'Rex Angliae, Dominus Hiberniae et Dux Aquitaniae'	1 Oct. 1207 at Winchester; elder son of John and Isabella	m. at Canterbury, 20 Jan 1236, ELEANOR (d. 1291), d of Raymond Berengar IV, Count of Provence. 2s 3d at least 4 other children who died in infancy	d., aged 65, 16 Nov. 1272, at Westminster. Westminster Abbey church	The style 'Dux Normaniae' and Count of Anjou was omitted from 1259. Succeeded by Edward, his first son to survive infancy (probably his third son)
10. **EDWARD I** 20 Nov. 1272–1307 'Longshanks' Style: As the final style of No. 8	17/18 June 1239 at Westminster; eldest son to survive infancy (probably third son) of Henry III and Eleanor	m. (1) at the monastery of Las Huelgas, Spain, 13–31 Oct. 1254, ELEANOR (d. 1290), d of Ferdinand III, King of Castille. 4s 7d m. (2) at Canterbury, 10 Sept. 1299, MARGARET (1282–1317), d of Philip III, King of France. 2s 1d	d., aged 68, 7 July 1307, at Burgh-upon-the-Sands, nr. Carlisle. Westminster Abbey	Succeeded by the fourth, and only surviving, son of his first marriage, Edward (created Prince of Wales, 7 Feb. 1301)
11. **EDWARD II** 8 July 1307 (deposed 20 Jan. 1327) 'of Caernarfon' Style: As the final style of No. 8	25 Apr. 1284 at Caernarfon Castle; fourth and only surviving son of Edward I and Eleanor	m. at Boulogne, c. 25 Jan. 1308, ISABELLA (1292–1358), d of Philip IV, King of France, 2s 2d	murdered, aged 43, 21 Sept. 1327 (traditionally by disembowelling with red-hot iron) at Berkeley Castle. The abbey of St Peter (now the cathedral), Gloucester	Succeeded by his elder son, Edward of Windsor. Edward II was deposed by Parliament on 20 Jan. 1327, having been imprisoned on 16 Nov. 1326
12. **EDWARD III** 25 Jan. 1327–1377 Style: As No. 10, until 13th year when 'Dei Gratiâ, Rex Angliae, et Franciae et Dominus Hiberniae'	13 Nov. 1312 at Windsor Castle; elder son of Edward II and Isabella	m. at York, 24 June 1328, PHILIPPA (c. 1314–69), d of William I, Count of Holland and Hainault. 7s 5d	d. peacefully, aged 64, 21 June 1377 at Sheen (now in Greater London). Westminster Abbey	Succeeded by his grandson Richard, the second and only surviving son of his eldest son Edward, the Black Prince
13. **RICHARD II** 22 June 1377–99 Style: As final style of No. 12	6 Jan. 1367 at Bordeaux; second, but only surviving, son of Edward, the Black Prince, and Joane, commonly called The Fair Maid of Kent (grand-d of Edward I)	m. (1) at St Stephen's Chapel, Westminster, 20 Jan. 1382, ANNE of Bohemia (1366–94), d of Emperor Charles IV. No issue. m. (2) at St Nicholas' Church, Calais, probably 4 Nov. 1396, ISABELLE (1389–1409), d of Charles VI of France. No issue	d., aged 33, probably 14 Feb. 1400, a sufferer from neurasthenia at Pontefract Castle, Yorks. Westminster Abbey	He was a prisoner of Henry, Duke of Lancaster, later Henry IV, from 19 Aug. 1399 until death. He was deposed 30 Sept. 1399. Henry usurped the throne from the prior claims of the issue of his father John of Gaunt's deceased elder brother, Lionel of Antwerp

King or Queen Regnant Date of Accession and Final Year of Reign; Style	Date and Place of Birth and Parentage	Marriages and No. of Children	Date, Cause and Place of Death, and Place of Burial	Notes and Succession
14. **HENRY IV** 30 Sept. 1399–1413 *Style:* As No. 12	probably Apr. 1366 at Bolingbroke Castle, nr. Spilsby, Lincs.; eldest son of John of Gaunt, 4th son of Edward III, and Blanche, great-great-grand-d of Henry III	m. (1) at Rochford, Essex, between July 1380 and Mar. 1381, Lady MARY de Bohun (?1368/70–94), younger d of Humphrey, Earl of Hereford. 5s 2d. m. (2) at Winchester, 7 Feb. 1403, JOAN (c. 1370–1437), second d of Charles II, King of Navarre. No issue	d., aged probably 46, 20 Mar. 1413, of pustulated eczema and gout in the Jerusalem Chamber, Westminster. Canterbury Cathedral	Succeeded by his second, but eldest surviving, son, Henry of Monmouth
15. **HENRY V** 21 Mar. 1413–1422 *Style:* As No. 13, until 8th year when 'Rex Angliae, Haeres, et Regens Franciae, et Dominus Hiberniae'	probably 16 Sept. 1387 at Monmouth; second and eldest surviving son of Henry IV and the Lady Mary de Bohun	m. at the church of St John, Troyes, 2 June 1420, CATHERINE of Valois (1401–37), youngest d of Charles VI of France. 1s	d., aged probably 34, 31 Aug./Sept. 1422, of dysentery at Bois de Vincennes, France. Chapel of the Confessor, Westminster Abbey	Succeeded by his only child Henry
16. **HENRY VI** 1 Sept. 1422–1461 and 6 Oct. 1470–1471 *Style:* 'Dei Gratiâ Rex Angliae et Franciae et Dominus Hiberniae'	6 Dec. 1421 at Windsor; only son of Henry V and Catherine	m. at Tichfield Abbey, 23 Apr. 1445, MARGARET (1430–82), d of René, Duke of Anjou. 1s	murdered by stabbing, aged 49, 21 May 1471 at Tower of London. Windsor	Succeeded by the usurpation of his third cousin, Edward IV
17. **EDWARD IV** 4 Mar. 1461–1470 and 11 April 1471–1483 *Style:* As No. 16	28 Apr. 1442 at Rouen; eldest son of Richard, 3rd Duke of York ('The Protector') and the Lady Cecily Nevill	m. at Grafton, Northants, 1 May 1464, ELIZABETH (c. 1437–92), eldest d of Sir Richard Woodville. 3s 7d	d., aged 40, 9 Apr. 1483, of pneumonia at Westminster. Windsor	Edward IV was a prisoner of the Earl of Warwick in Aug. and Sept. of 1469; he fled to the Netherlands 3 Oct. 1470; returned to England 14 Mar. 1471, and was restored to kingship 11 Apr. 1471. Succeeded by his eldest son, Edward
18. **EDWARD V** 9 Apr.–25 June 1483 *Style:* As No. 16	2 Nov. 1470 in the Sanctuary at Westminster; eldest son of Edward IV and Elizabeth Woodville	unmarried	d. (traditionally murdered), possibly in 1483 or in 1486, at the Tower of London. A body of the stature and dentition of a 12 year old male discovered at the Tower on 6 July 1933	Edward V was deposed 25 June 1483, when the throne was usurped by his uncle, Richard III (the only surviving brother of his father)
19. **RICHARD III** 26 June 1483–5 *Style:* As No. 16	2 Oct. 1452 at Fotheringay Castle, Northants; fourth and only surviving, son of Richard, 3rd Duke of York ('The Protector'), and the Lady Cecily Nevill	m. 12 July 1472, the Lady ANNE (1456–85), younger d of Richard Nevill, Earl of Warwick ('The King Maker') and widow of Edward, Prince of Wales, only child of Henry VI. 1s	killed aged 32, 22 Aug. 1485, at the battle of Bosworth Field. The Abbey of the Grey Friars, Leicester	Richard III was succeeded by his third cousin once removed downwards, Henry Tudor, 2nd Earl of Richmond
20. **HENRY VII** 22 Aug. 1485–1509 *Style:* As No. 16	27 Jan. 1457 at Pembroke Castle; only child of Edmund Tudor, 1st Earl of Richmond, and Margaret Beaufort, great-great-grand-d of Edward III	m. at Westminster, 18 Jan. 1486, ELIZABETH (1466–1503) d of Edward IV. 3s and 4d, of whom 2 died in infancy	d., aged 52, 21 Apr. 1509, had rheumatoid arthritis and gout at Richmond. In his own chapel at Westminster	Succeeded by his second and only surviving son, Henry
21. **HENRY VIII** 22 Apr. 1509–47 *Style:* (from 35th year) 'Henry the eighth, by the Grace of God, King of England, France, and Ireland, Defender of the Faith and of the Church of England, and also of Ireland, on earth the Supreme Head'	28 June 1491 at Greenwich; second and only surviving son of Henry VII and Elizabeth	m. (1) secretly at the chapel of the Observant Friars, 11 June 1509, CATHERINE of Aragon (1485–1536), d of Ferdinand II, King of Spain and widow of Arthur, Prince of Wales. 2s 2d (one of whom died young)	d., aged 55, 28 Jan. 1547, had chronic sinusitis and periostitis of the leg at the Palace of Westminster. Windsor	Henry was the first King to be formally styled with a post nominal number, i.e. VIII. Succeeded by his only surviving son, Edward
		Subsequent marriages of HENRY VIII:	m. (2) secretly 25 Jan. 1533, ANNE Marchioness of Pembroke (b. 1507, beheaded 1536), d of Sir Thomas Boleyn, the Viscount Rochford. A daughter and possibly another child	m. (3) in the Queen's Closet, York Place, London, 30 May 1536, JANE (d. 1537), eldest d of Sir John Seymour. 1s

King or Queen Regnant Date of Accession and Final Year of Reign; Style	Date and Place of Birth and Parentage	Marriages and No. of Children	Date, Cause and Place of Death, and Place of Burial	Notes and Succession
HENRY VIII		m. (4) at Greenwich, 6 Jan. 1540, ANNE (1515–57), second d of John, Duke of Cleves. No issue.	m. (5) at Oatlands, 28 July 1540, CATHERINE (beheaded 1542), d of Lord Edmund Howard. No issue	m. (6) at Hampton Court, 12 July 1543, CATHERINE (c. 1512–48), d of Sir Thomas Parr and widow of 1. Sir Edward Borough and 2. John Neville, 3rd Lord Latimer. No issue
22. **EDWARD VI** 28 Jan. 1547–53 Style: As No. 21	12 Oct. 1537 at Hampton Court; only surviving son of Henry VIII, by Jane Seymour	unmarried	d., aged 15, 6 July 1553, of pulmonary tuberculosis at Greenwich. Henry VII's Chapel, Westminster Abbey	Succeeded briefly by Lady Guil(d)ford Dudley (Lady Jane Grey), his first cousin once removed
23. **JANE** 6 July (proclaimed 10 July) 1553 (deposed 19 July)	Oct. 1537 at Bradgate Park, Leics.; eldest d of Henry Grey, 3rd Marquess of Dorset, and Frances (d of Mary Tudor, sister of Henry VIII)	m. at Durham House, London, 21 May 1553, Lord GUIL(D)FORD DUDLEY (beheaded 1554), 4th son of John Dudley, Duke of Northumberland. No issue	beheaded, aged 16, 12 Feb. 1554, in the Tower of London. St Peter ad Vincula, within the Tower	Succeeded by her second cousin once removed upwards, Mary
24. **MARY I** 19 July 1553–8 Style: As No. 21 (but supremacy title was dropped) until marriage	18 Feb. 1516 at Greenwich Palace; only surviving child of Henry VIII and Catherine of Aragon	m. at Winchester Cathedral, 25 July 1554, PHILIP (1527–98), King of Naples and Jerusalem, son of Emperor Charles V and widower of Maria, d of John III of Portugal. No issue	d., aged 42, 17 Nov. 1558 of endemic influenza at London. Westminster Abbey	Philip was styled, but not crowned, king. Mary was succeeded by her half sister, Elizabeth, the only surviving child of Henry VIII
25. **ELIZABETH I** 17 Nov. 1558–1603 Style: 'Queen of England, France and Ireland, Defender of the Faith' etc.	7 Sept. 1533 at Greenwich; d of Henry VIII and Anne Boleyn	unmarried	d., aged 69, 24 Mar. 1603, of sepsis from tonsillar abscess at Richmond. Westminster Abbey	Succeeded by her first cousin twice removed, James
26. **JAMES I** 26 Mar. 1603–25 and VI of Scotland from 24 July 1567 Style: 'King of England, Scotland, France and Ireland, Defender of the Faith' etc.	19 June 1566 at Edinburgh Castle; only son of Henry Stuart, Lord Darnley, and Mary, Queen of Scots (d of James V of Scotland, son of Margaret Tudor, sister of Henry VIII)	m. 20 Aug. 1589 (by proxy) ANNE (1574–1619), d of Frederick II, King of Denmark and Norway. 3s 4d	d., aged 58, 27 Mar. 1625, of Bright's disease at Theobalds Park, Herts. Westminster Abbey	Succeeded by his second and only surviving son, Charles
27. **CHARLES I** 27 Mar. 1625–49 Style: As No. 26	19 Nov. 1600 at Dunfermline Palace, second and only surviving son of James I and Anne	m. in Paris, 1 May 1625 (by proxy) HENRIETTA MARIA (1609–69) d of Henry IV of France. 4s 5d	beheaded, aged 48, 30 Jan. 1649, in Whitehall. Windsor	The Kingship was de facto declared abolished 17 Mar. 1649
28. **CHARLES II** 29 May 1660 (but de jure 30 Jan. 1649) to 1685 Style: As No. 26	29 May 1630 at St James's Palace, London; eldest surviving son of Charles I and Henrietta Maria	m. at Portsmouth, 21 May 1662, CATHERINE (1638–1705), d of John, Duke of Braganza. No legitimate issue	d., aged 54, 6 Feb. 1685, of uraemia and mercurial poisoning at Whitehall. Henry VII's Chapel, Westminster Abbey	Succeeded by his younger and only surviving brother, James
29. **JAMES II** 6 Feb. 1685–8 Style: As No. 26	14 Oct. 1633 at St James's Palace, London; only surviving son of Charles I and Henrietta Maria	m. (1) at Worcester House, The Strand, London, 3 Sept. 1660, ANNE (1637–71), eldest d of Edward Hyde. 4s 4d. m. (2) At Modena (by proxy), 30 Sept. 1673, MARY D'ESTE (1658–1718), only d of Alfonso IV, Duke of Modena. 2s 5d	d., aged 67, 6 Sept. 1701, of a cerebral haemorrhage at St Germains, France. His remains were divided and interred at five different venues in France. All are now lost except for those at the parish church of St Germains	James II was deemed by legal fiction to have ended his reign 11 Dec. 1688 by flight. A Convention Parliament offered the Crown of England and Ireland 13 Feb. 1689 to Mary, his eldest surviving d, and her husband, his nephew, William Henry of Orange
30. **WILLIAM III** 13 Feb. 1689–1702	4 Nov. 1650 at The Hague; only son of William II, Prince of Orange, and Mary (Stuart), d of Charles I	They were married at St James's Palace, London, 4 Nov. 1677. No issue	d., aged 51, 8 Mar. 1702, of pleuro-pneumonia following fracture of right collarbone, in Kensington	The widower, King William III, was succeeded by his sister-in-law, Anne, who was also his first cousin

King or Queen Regnant Date of Accession and Final Year of Reign; Style	Date and Place of Birth and Parentage	Marriages and No. of Children	Date, Cause and Place of Death, and Place of Burial	Notes and Succession
MARY II 13 Feb. 1689–94 Style: 'King and Queen of England, Scotland, France and Ireland, Defenders of the Faith etc.'	30 Apr. 1662 at St James's Palace, London; elder surviving d of James II and Anne Hyde		d., aged 32, 28 Dec. 1694, of confluent haemorrhagic smallpox with pneumonia, at Kensington. They were buried in Henry VII's Chapel, Westminster Abbey	
31. **ANNE** 8 Mar. 1702–14 Style: Firstly as No. 25; secondly (after Union with Scotland 6 Mar. 1707) 'Queen of Great Britain, France and Ireland, Defender of the Faith' etc.	6 Feb. 1665 at St James's Palace, London; only surviving d of James II and Anne Hyde	m. at the Chapel Royal, St James's Palace, 28 July 1683, GEORGE (1653–1708), second son of Frederick III, King of Denmark. 2s 3d from 17 confinements	d., aged 49, 1 Aug. 1714, of a cerebral haemorrhage and possibly chronic Bright's disease at Kensington. Henry VII's Chapel, Westminster Abbey	Succeeded in the terms of the Act of Settlement (which excluded all Roman Catholics and their spouses) by her second cousin, George Lewis, Elector of Hanover
32. **GEORGE I** 1 Aug. 1714–27 Style: 'King of Great Britain, France and Ireland, Duke of Brunswick-Lüneburg, etc., Defender of the Faith'	28 May 1660 at Osnabrück; eldest son of Ernest Augustus, Duke of Brunswick-Lüneburg and Elector of Hanover, and Princess Sophia, 5th and youngest d and 10th child of Elizabeth, Queen of Bohemia, the eldest d of James I	m. 21 Nov. 1682 (div. 1694), SOPHIA Dorothea (1666–1726), only d of George William, Duke of Lüneburg-Celle. 1s 1d	d., aged 67, 11 June 1727, of coronary thrombosis, at Ibbenbüren or Osnabrück. Hanover	The Kings of England were Electors of Hanover from 1714 to 1814. Succeeded by his only son, George Augustus
33. **GEORGE II** 11 June 1727–60 Style: As No. 32	30 Oct. 1683 at Hanover; only son of George I and Sophia Dorothea	m. 22 Aug. (O.S.), 2 Sept. (N.S.), 1705, Wilhelmina Charlotte CAROLINE (1683–1737), d of John Frederick, Margrave of Brandenburg-Ansbach. 3s 5d	d., aged 76, 25 Oct. 1760, of coronary thrombosis at the Palace of Westminster. Henry VII's Chapel, Westminster Abbey	Succeeded by his elder son's eldest son, George William Frederick
34. **GEORGE III** 25 Oct. 1760–1820 Style: As No. 31 (until Union of Great Britain and Ireland, 1 Jan. 1801), whereafter 'By the Grace of God, of the United Kingdom of Great Britain and Ireland, King, Defender of the Faith'	24 May (O.S.) 1738 at Norfolk House, St James's Square, London; eldest son of Frederick Lewis, Prince of Wales (d. 20 Mar. 1751) and Princess Augusta of Saxe-Gotha	m. at St James's Palace, London, 8 Sept. 1761, CHARLOTTE Sophia (1744–1818), youngest d of Charles Louis Frederick, Duke of Mecklenburg-Strelitz. 9s 6d	d., aged 81 years 239 days, 29 Jan. 1820, of senility at Windsor. St George's Chapel, Windsor	His eldest son became Regent owing to his insanity 5 Feb. 1811. Hanover was made a kingdom in 1814. Succeeded by his eldest son, George Augustus Frederick
35. **GEORGE IV** 29 Jan. 1820–30 Style: As later style of No. 34	12 Aug. 1762 at St James's Palace, London; eldest son of George III and Charlotte	m. (2)* at the Chapel Royal, St James's Palace, 8 Apr. 1795, CAROLINE Amelia Elizabeth (1768–1821), his first cousin, second d of Charles, Duke of Brunswick-Wolfenbüttel. 1d. *First married Maria FitzHerbert	d., aged 67, 26 June 1830, of rupture of the stomach blood vessels; alcoholic cirrhosis; and dropsy at Windsor. St George's Chapel, Windsor	Succeeded by his eldest surviving brother, William Henry (George's only child, Princess Charlotte, having died in child-birth 6 Nov. 1817)
36. **WILLIAM IV** 26 June 1830–7 Style: As No. 34	21 Aug. 1765 at Buckingham Palace; third and oldest surviving son of George III and Charlotte	m. at Kew, 11 July 1818, ADELAIDE Louisa Theresa Caroline Amelia (1792–1849), eldest d of George, Duke of Saxe-Meiningen. 2d	d., aged 71, 20 June 1837, of pleuro-pneumonia and alcoholic cirrhosis at Windsor. St George's Chapel, Windsor	On William's death the crown of Hanover passed by Salic law to his brother, Ernest, Duke of Cumberland. Succeeded by his niece, Alexandrina Victoria
37. **VICTORIA** 20 June 1837–1901 Style: As (except for 'Queen') No. 34 until 1 May 1876, whereafter 'Empress of India' was added	24 May 1819 at Kensington Palace, London; only child of Edward, Duke of Kent and Strathearn, 4th son of George III, and Victoria, widow of Emich Charles, Prince of Leiningen and d of Francis, Duke of Saxe-Coburg-Saafeld	m. at St James's Palace, London, 10 Feb. 1840, her first cousin Francis ALBERT Augustus Charles Emmanuel (1819–61), second son of Ernest I, Duke of Saxe-Coburg-Gotha. 4s 5d	d., aged 81 years 243 days, 22 Jan. 1901 of senility at Osbourne, I.o.W. Frogmore	Assumed title Empress of India 1 May 1876. Succeeded by her elder surviving son, Albert Edward

King or Queen Regnant Date of Accession and Final Year of Reign; Style	Date and Place of Birth and Parentage	Marriages and No. of Children	Date, Cause and Place of Death, and Place of Burial	Notes and Succession
38. **EDWARD VII** 22 Jan. 1901–10 *Style:* 'By the Grace of God, of the United Kingdom of Great Britain and Ireland and of the British Dominions beyond the Seas, King, Defender of the Faith, Emperor of India'	9 Nov. 1841 at Buckingham Palace, London; elder surviving son of Victoria and Albert	m. at St George's Chapel, Windsor, 10 Mar. 1863, ALEXANDRA Caroline Maria Charlotte Louisa Julia (1844–1925), d of Christian IX of Denmark. 3s 3d	d., aged 68, 6 May, 1910, of bronchitis at Buckingham Palace. St George's Chapel, Windsor	Succeeded by his only surviving son, George Frederick Ernest Albert
39. **GEORGE V** 6 May 1910–36 *Style:* As for No. 37 until 12 May 1927, whereafter 'By the Grace of God, of Great Britain, Ireland, and of the British Dominions beyond the Seas, King, Defender of the Faith, Emperor of India'	3 June 1865 at Marlborough House, London; second and only surviving son of Edward VII and Alexandra	m. at St James's Palace, London, 6 July 1893, Victoria MARY Augusta Louise Olga Pauline Claudine Agnes (1867–1953), eldest child and only d of Francis, Duke of Teck. 5s 1d	d., aged 70, 20 Jan. 1936, of bronchitis at Sandringham House, Norfolk. St George's Chapel, Windsor	Succeeded by his eldest son, Edward Albert Christian George Andrew Patrick David
40. **EDWARD VIII** 20 Jan. 1936–11 Dec. 1936 *Style:* As for No. 39	23 June 1894 at the White Lodge, Richmond Park; eldest son of George V and Mary	m. at the Château de Candé, Monts, France, 3 June 1937, Bessie Wallis Warfield (b. 1896), previous wife of Lt. Earl Winfield Spencer, USN (div. 1927) and Ernest Simpson (div. 1936). No issue	d., aged 77, 28 May, 1972, of cancer of the throat at 4, Route du Champ, D'Entrainement, Paris XVIᵉ, France	Edward VIII abdicated for himself and his heirs and was succeeded by his eldest brother, Albert Frederick Arthur George
41. **GEORGE VI** 11 Dec. 1936–52 *Style:* As for No. 39 until the Indian title was dropped 22 June 1947	14 Dec. 1895 at York Cottage, Sandringham; second son of George V and Mary	m. at Westminster Abbey, 26 Apr. 1923, Lady ELIZABETH Angela Marguerite Bowes-Lyon (b. 1900), youngest d of 14th Earl of Strathmore and Kinghorne. 2d	d., aged 56, 6 Feb. 1952, of lung cancer at Sandringham House, Norfolk. St George's Chapel, Windsor	Succeeded by his elder d, Elizabeth Alexandra Mary
42. **ELIZABETH II** Since 6 Feb. 1952 *Style:* (from 29 May 1953) 'By the Grace of God, of the United Kingdom of Great Britain and Northern Ireland and of Her other Realms and Territories, Queen, Head of the Commonwealth, Defender of the Faith'	21 Apr. 1926 at 17 Bruton Street, London, W1; elder d of George VI and Elizabeth	m. at Westminster Abbey, 20 Nov. 1947, her third cousin PHILIP (b. Corfu, Greece, 10 June 1921), only son of Prince Andrea (Andrew) of Greece and Princess Alice (great-grand-d of Queen Victoria). 3s 1d	—	The Heir Apparent is Charles Philip Arthur George, Prince of Wales, b. 14 Nov. 1948

UK Legislature

THE COMPOSITION OF THE TWO HOUSES OF PARLIAMENT

House of Lords

Peers of the Blood Royal	3
Archbishops of Canterbury and York	2
Dukes	27
Marquesses	36
Earls	171
Countesses in their own right	5
Viscounts	110
Anglican Bishops (by seniority)	23
Barons and Scots Lords (hereditary)	428
Baronesses in their own right (hereditary)	13
Life Peers (Barons)	312
Life Peeresses (Baronesses)	46
	1176

House of Commons

The size of the House of Commons has frequently been altered:

1885 By a Representation of the People Act (RPA) membership was increased by 12 to total 670.

1918 By an RPA, membership was increased by 37 to an all-time high point of 707.

1922 By two Acts of Parliament (the Partition of Ireland) membership was reduced by 92 to 615. (*Note:* Irish representation was reduced from 105 to 13 members representing Northern Ireland.)

1945 By an RPA, membership was increased by 25 to 640.

1948 By an RPA, membership was decreased by 15 to 625. (*Note:* This took effect in 1950 and involved the abolition of the 12 university seats and 12 double-member constituencies.)

1955 By an Order in Council under the House of Commons (Redistribution of Seats) Act, membership was increased by five to a total of 630.

1974 By an Order in Council membership was increased by 5 to a total of 635.

1983 By an Order in Council membership was increased by 15 to the present total of 650.

The results of the 24 general elections 1900–1987

No.	Election and Date	Total Seats	Result (and % share of Total Poll)					% Turn-out of Electorate
			Conservatives	Liberals	Labour	Others		
1	1900 (28 Sept.–24 Oct.)	670	**402**(51·1)	184(44·6)	2 (1·8)	82 (2·5)		74·6 of 6 730 935
2	1906 (12 Jan.–7 Feb.)	670	157(43·6)	**400**(49·0)	30 (5·9)	83 (1·5)		82·6 of 7 264 608
3	1910 (14 Jan.–9 Feb.)	670	273(46·9)	**275**(43·2)	40 (7·7)	82 (2·2)		86·6 of 7 694 741
4	1910 (2–19 Dec.)	670	272(46·3)	272(43·8)	42 (7·2)	84 (2·7)		81·1 of 7 709 981
5	1918 (14 Dec.)	707	**383**(38·7)	161(25·6)	73(23·7)	90(12·0)		58·9 of 21 392 322
6	1922 (15 Nov.)	615	**345**(38·2)	116(29·1)	142(29·5)	12 (3·2)		71·3 of 21 127 663
7	1923 (6 Dec.)	615	**258**(38·1)	159(29·6)	191(30·5)	7 (1·8)		70·8 of 21 281 232
8	1924 (29 Oct.)	615	**419**(48·3)	40(17·6)	151(33·0)	5 (1·1)		76·6 of 21 731 320
9	1929 (30 May)	615	260(38·2)	59(23·4)	**288**(37·1)	8 (1·3)		76·1 of 28 850 870
10	1931 (27 Oct.)	615	**521**(60·5)	37 (7·0)	52(30·6)	5 (1·7)		76·3 of 29 960 071
11	1935 (14 Nov.)	615	**432**(53·7)	20 (6·4)	154(37·9)	9 (2·0)		71·2 of 31 379 050
12	1945 (5 July)	640	213(39·8)	12 (9·0)	**393**(47·8)	22 (2·4)		72·7 of 33 240 391
13	1950(23 Feb.)	625	298(43·5)	9 (9·1)	**315**(46·4)	3 (1·3)		84·0 of 33 269 770
14	1951 (25 Oct.)	625	**321**(48·0)	6 (2·5)	295(48·7)	3 (0·7)		82·5 of 34 465 573
15	1955 (25 May)	630	**344**(49·8)	6 (2·7)	277(46·3)	3 (1·2)		76·7 of 34 858 263
16	1959 (8 Oct.)	630	**365**(49·4)	6 (5·9)	258(43·8)	1 (0·9)		78·8 of 35 397 080
17	1964 (15 Oct.)	630	303(43·4)	9(11·1)	**317**(44·2)	1 (1·3)		77·1 of 35 894 307
18	1966 (31 Mar.)	630	253(41·9)	12 (8·5)	**363**(47·9)	2 (1·7)		75·9 of 35 965 127
19	1970 (18 June)	630	**330**(46·4)	6 (7·5)	288(43·0)	6 (3·1)		72·0 of 39 247 683
20	1974 (28 Feb.)	635	297(38·2)	14(19·3)	**301**(37·2)	23 (5·3)		78·8 of 39 752 317
21	1974 (10 Oct.)	635	277(35·8)	13(18·3)	**319**(39·3)	26 (6·6)		72·8 of 40 083 286
22	1979 (3 May)	635	**339**(43·9)	11(13·8)	268(36·9)	17 (5·4)		75·9 of 41 093 262
23	1983 (9 June)	650	**397**(42·4)	17(25·4) (Alliance)	209(27·6)	21 (4·6)		72·7 of 42 197 344
24	1987 (11 June)	650	375(42·3)	17(12·8)	229(30·8)	24(3·4)		75·4 of 43 181 321

The 24 General Elections of 1900 to 1987

1900 Lord Salisbury's Conservative Government exercised its undoubted constitutional right to cash in on the apparently victorious (Mafeking and Pretoria) outcome of the Boer War two years before its 7 years of life was expired. The Liberal opposition called these tactics immoral and dubbed the election the 'Khaki Election'. The Government were given the most triumphant encore seen since the Reform Act of 1832 with an overall majority of 134 compared with the Dissolution figure of 128. The Liberal opposition was divided into the 'pro-Boers', comprising Gladstonians with the young Lloyd George, and the followers of Asquith, Haldane and Grey, who were Empire men.

1906 By December 1905 A J Balfour, who had succeeded his uncle as Prime Minister in 1902, had his majority reduced to 68 because of losses in by-elections. Feeling out of tune with the objects of the Tariff Reform League, he resigned. The King asked Campbell-Bannerman to form a government which he did and then immediately went to the country. The result was a landslide victory for the Liberals, who won an overall majority of 130. The Conservatives lost support mainly because of alarm over Chamberlain's Tariff Reform campaign and State support for Church of England schools, which offended nonconformist opinion. Liberal policy was the trinity of Free Trade, Home Rule for Ireland, and Humanitarianism.

1910 (Jan./Feb.) Asquith took over the premiership in 1908 shortly before the death of Campbell-Bannerman. The stock of the Tories rose because of Liberal pacifism in the face of the 'German Menace' and the Government lost 10 by-elections. The Liberal hopes of securing a second term rested on their taking advantage of the Conservative peers' inevitable rejection of Lloyd George's deliberately provocative budget. The government were thus handed on a plate the priceless slogan 'Lords versus the People'. The Liberals, however, only ended up with 125 seats fewer than their 1906 highwater mark. More seriously, they were now at the mercy of the jubilant 82 Irish Nationalists and 40 Labourites.

1910 (Dec.) The Government's House of Lords policy was: (1) abolition of Lords' power to veto

over certified Money Bills; (2) a delaying power only of three sessions for other Bills, and (3) the life of a Parliament to be reduced from seven to five years. The ostensible reason for another General Election was that the country should vote on these policies. But the real reason was that secretly King George V, who had succeeded his father that May, had insisted on a second appeal to the nation before giving his promise to create if necessary the required number of Liberal peers to vote the Parliament Bill through. The result of the election was almost a carbon copy of that eleven months previously.

1918 The victorious wartime premier, Lloyd George, at the head of the Coalition which had superseded Asquith's Liberal administration in 1916, went to the country in December 1918. The election was called by the opposition the 'coupon election'. This was because Lloyd George (Lib.) and Bonar Law (Con.) jointly signed letters (nicknamed 'coupons') giving support to those they regarded as loyal supporters of the Coalition. The Government's election policy in terms of slogans was 'Hang the Kaiser'; make the Germans pay for the war 'until the lemon pips squeak'; and make the country 'fit for heroes to live in'. Women over 30 were first given the vote. The Coalition won a crushing victory on a very low (58·9 per cent) poll.

1922 The Coalition Government under Lloyd George progressively lost the confidence of its predominant Conservative wing. The Conservatives disliked the Liberal Prime Minister's vacillating and extravagant domestic policies, especially in regard to agriculture and what they regarded as naïve foreign policies. Left-wing opinion was displeased with the rate of social progress on the home front. Many major strikes were organised. In Oct. 1922 the Conservatives resolved to fight the next election as an independent party. Lloyd George promptly resigned. Bonar Law formed a Government and went to the country. The Conservatives, with Bonar Law's policy of 'Tranquillity', won a majority of 75 over all other parties. The Labour Party overtook the divided Liberals by nearly doubling their representation to 142 and became the official Opposition.

1923 Bonar Law, who had started his premiership a sick man, retired in May 1923, and died

shortly afterwards. His successor, in preference to Lord Curzon, was Stanley Baldwin. The main domestic problem was unemployment. Baldwin took the view that protective tariffs would alleviate it: but he was bound by Bonar Law's promise not to introduce such a measure. The only way out was to appeal to the country. The election saw a tiny change from the 1922 percentages but a dramatic loss of 87 seats by the Conservatives. Baldwin, although now in a minority of 99, waited to face the new Parliament and was inevitably defeated by a Labour-Liberal alliance and then resigned in favour of Ramsay MacDonald (Labour).

1924 MacDonald found himself embarrassingly short of talented Ministers and under intense pressure and scrutiny from the National Executive of the Labour Party. His greatest success was to sort out the Franco-German squabble over war reparation payments. The Government were brought down when their often unwilling allies, the Liberals, voted with the Tories for a motion for enquiry into the circumstances under which a journalist, J R Campbell, was to have his prosecution by the Attorney General for sedition (he advocated British soldiers disobeying orders if confronted with strikers) withdrawn. The Labour Party lost 40 seats and the Conservatives, profiting from there being fewer Liberal candidates, won an overall majority of 225 seats under Baldwin.

1929 Despite Baldwin's Government's surviving overall majority of 185 seats, Labour won this election with 288 seats, but could not command an absolute majority (Conservatives 260, Liberals 59, Others 8 = 327). Over 5 million women between the ages of 21 and 30 were eligible to vote for the first time. The Conservatives had adopted the uninspiring slogan 'Safety First'. The Labour Party, with the slogan 'Socialism In Our Time', had a three-pronged policy of world peace, disarmament, and a desire to deal more energetically with unemployment. The Liberals also based their appeal on unemployment remedies. The Liberal leader, Mr Lloyd George, decided to support Labour in office.

1931 The Labour Government committed themselves to increased expenditure and the unemployment figures rose alarmingly. A loss of confidence in sterling caused a summer crisis and Ramsay MacDonald suggested to his Cabinet an economy scheme which included the reduction of unemployment insurance benefits. The National Executive of the Labour Party and the TUC characteristically flatly refused to support any such measure. On 24 Aug. the Labour Government resigned and MacDonald formed a National Government which went to the polls on 27 Oct. The extent of their victory amazed contemporary opinion as the National Government won 554 seats, including 13 by National Labour candidates, while the opposition was reduced to 52 Labour and 4 Liberal Members.

1935 Ramsay MacDonald (National Labour) resigned his premiership in June 1935 and was logically succeeded by Stanley Baldwin (Conservative), who held a snap November General Election by dissolving Parliament two days short of the fourth anniversary of the 1931 election. The main issue was simply, did the nation approve of the work of the National Government in restoring the economy after the slump and want it to continue, or did the Nation want to revert to a Labour Government? The result was a massive vote of confidence in the National (predominantly Conservative) Government which won an overall majority of 249 seats. The Labour Party's main attack was over the 'Means Test' for unemployment assistance ('the dole'), although their own 1929 Government had accepted the principle of it, and the National Government had quickly withdrawn the new unsatisfactory regulations introduced earlier that year. Broadcasting for the first time played a significant rôle in the campaign with the public listening to a series of speeches made by the various Party Leaders every night during the first part of the election campaign.

1945 During the ten years since the previous election the country underwent the traumatic total war of 1939–45. Baldwin resigned in 1937 and was succeeded by Neville Chamberlain who resigned in 1940 at the nadir of our wartime fortunes. For the remaining five years Winston Churchill gave dynamic leadership which secured victory over Nazi Germany in May 1945. In that month the wartime Coalition broke up and was replaced by a predetermined Conservative administration. This Government, despite Churchill's premiership, was defeated by a Labour landslide. The new Government had Labour's first overall majority – 146 seats.

1950 Mr Attlee's administration launched the 'Welfare State' along the lines set out by various wartime White Papers, but his nationalisation measures, especially as regards steel, met fierce resistance. A balance of payments crisis in the autumn of 1949 compelled the Government to devalue the pound against the dollar and make drastic economies. The result of the February election was a narrow Labour victory with an overall majority of only 5.

1951 After 20 months of precarious administration, during which time the Conservatives ceaselessly harried the Government ranks, especially over the nationalisation of steel, Mr Attlee resigned. The last straw was another balance of payments crisis in September following the earlier resignation of Aneurin Bevan (Minister of Labour) and Harold Wilson (Pres., Board of Trade). The nation's reply to Mr Attlee's appeal over the radio for a larger majority was to elect the Conservatives with an overall majority of 17. Winston Churchill returned as Prime Minister.

1955 In April 1955, after 4½ years of government with a small majority, Sir Winston Churchill resigned as Prime Minister in favour of Sir Anthony Eden, who seven weeks later went to the country for a vote of confidence. The Conservatives had succeeded in restoring the nation's finances, had denationalised steel and road haulage, and twice reduced the standard rate of income tax by 6d. The Government's

majority rose to 58 and the five years of near deadlock in the House was broken.

1959 In Jan. 1957, following the strain of the Suez crisis, Eden resigned and Harold Macmillan became Prime Minister. The Government had been losing support, largely owing to some unpopularity over the Rent Act. The new Prime Minister, despite a number of difficulties, managed to repair Conservative fortunes. His 1959 visit to the USSR and the further reduction of income tax in April added to general contentment. The election was fought on the Conservative theme 'life is better with us' while Labour got into difficulties with Mr Gaitskell's promises of no higher taxes, yet very expensive projects. The result was that the Government again increased their overall majority to 100 seats.

1964 The Conservative Government, after 13 consecutive years of rule, went to the country in October, as required every five years by the Parliament Act of 1911. After the post-war high water mark of 1959 (majority 100) Conservative fortunes declined owing notably to the Profumo scandal and a public wrangle over the successorship to Mr Macmillan who resigned in Oct. 1963 owing to ill health. The nation wanted a change: the Conservatives were however defeated by a rise in the Liberal vote from 5·9 per cent to 11·2 per cent rather than the Labour vote which was less than their 1959 total. Labour won by an overall majority of only 4.

1966 After 20 months in power, Mr Wilson became convinced (on the death of the Member for Falmouth in February) of the danger of continuing with his hairline majority. Labour fought the campaign on the slogan 'You Know Labour Government Works'. The Conservatives fought on a policy of entering the Common Market, reforming the 'over-mighty' Trade Unions and making the Welfare State less indiscriminate. Mr Wilson increased his overall majority from 3 to 97 and declared his intention to govern for five years to achieve 'a juster society'.

1970 Having completed four of the five years of his second term in power, Mr Wilson called the Labour Party to action in a bid for his hat-trick in May 1970. Remembered as the General Election most dominated by the pollsters, their findings consistently showed strong leads for Labour. Wages rates had risen in an unrestrained way in the five month run-up but prices levels were also just beginning to erode the reality of these monetary gains. Within six days of polling NOP showed a massive Labour lead of 12·4 per cent. In reality, however, the voters gave the Conservatives a 3·4 per cent lead, thus an overall majority of 30 seats.

1974 (Feb.) This was the first 'crisis' election since 1931. It was called to settle 'Who governs Britain?' under the duress of the National Union of Mineworkers' coal strike against the restraints of Stage III of the Incomes Policy. The situation was exacerbated by the Arab decision the previous November to raise the price of oil fourfold. A three-day week for most industries was decreed under Emergency Powers to start on 1 Jan. A ballot inviting the miners to give the NUM authority to call a strike was announced on 4 Feb., an election was called on 7 Feb., and a strike began on 10 Feb. after 81 per cent of the miners had voted in favour of giving the NUM Executive the authority they sought. Mr Wilson spoke of conciliation in place of confrontation and the alternative possibilities under a 'Social Contract' agreed between the Labour Party and the TUC on 18 Feb. 1973. The electorate, largely due to the impact of a successful Liberal campaign, spoke equivocally, giving Labour a majority of four over the Conservatives but 10 less than the combined Conservatives and Liberals. The Liberals rejected a coalition and appealed for a government of National Unity. Two hours after Mr Heath's resignation on 4 Mar., the Queen sent for Mr Wilson for a third time.

1974 (Oct.) For the first time since 1910 there were two elections within the same year. On 11 Mar. the miners returned to full working accepting a National Coal Board offer to raise their wage bill by 29 per cent. In June and July HM Opposition, with Liberal support, defeated Mr Wilson's precarious lobby strength 29 times, notably on the Trade Union and Labour Relation Bill. An election was called by Mr Wilson on 18 Sept. The campaign was fought mainly on the issue of inflation statistics, unemployment prospects and the promise by Labour to hold an EEC ballot. Though less than 29 out of each 100 persons eligible to vote cast votes for Labour candidates, only 27 such voters supported Conservative candidates. Thus Mr Wilson won his fourth General Election, with an overall majority of three seats, but with a secure working majority of 42 over the Conservatives, who were by far the largest party in a fragmented Opposition. Mr Wilson resigned and was replaced by Mr Callaghan, who had been elected leader of the Labour Party on 5 Apr. 1976.

1979 (May) During the 1974–79 Parliament all three parties had changed their leaders: Callaghan for Wilson; Steel for Thorpe; and Mrs Thatcher for Heath. The period was one of falling living standards due in part to oil prices and inflation. The Conservatives fought the ensuing general election on trade union reform, cutting public expenditure, reducing taxation and Whitehall intervention. Mrs Thatcher gained 51 seats from Labour in a 5·2% swing mainly in the Midlands and South East to win a 44 overall majority. She became Britain's first and the world's 4th woman Prime Minister and had the largest margin of the popular vote since 1935.

1983 (June) Mrs Thatcher's success was only the second time a Conservative Prime Minister has ever been re-elected after a full term (Lord Salisbury in 1900 was the other). The Conservatives' increase of 58 seats over the 1979 result was also the largest ever by an incumbent government although allowance should be made for an estimated 21 seats gained through boundary changes. By contrast, Labour lost more than a quarter of its previous vote – the lowest ever share won by the principal party of opposition.

1987 (June) Mrs Thatcher's historic third successive electoral victory not only put her into the history books as the longest serving Prime Minister of the twentieth century, but also returned her with an unexpectedly healthy 105 overall majority. Despite attacks by Labour and the Alliance on the Conservative's social policies, particularly education and the National Health Service, Mrs Thatcher won through primarily on economic performance and pronuclear defence. However, the voting pattern showed a nation divided North and South.

Prime Ministers of Great Britain and the United Kingdom

Below is a complete compilation of the 51 Prime Ministers of Great Britain and the United Kingdom. The data run in the following order: final style as Prime Minister (with earlier or later styles); date or dates as Prime Minister with party affiliation; date and place of birth and death and place of burial; marriage or marriages with number of children; education and membership of Parliament with constituency and dates.

1. The Rt Hon, Sir Robert **WALPOLE**, KG (1726) KB (1725, resigned 1726), (PC 1714), cr. 1st Earl of Orford (of the 2nd creation) in the week of his retirement; ministry, 3 April 1721 to 8 Feb. 1742, (i) reappointed on the accession of George II on 11 June 1727, (ii) Walpole's absolute control of the Cabinet can only be said to have dated from 15 May 1730; Whig; b. 26 Aug. 1676 at Houghton, Norfolk; d. 18 Mar. 1745 at No. 5 Arlington St, Piccadilly, London; bur. Houghton, Norfolk m. 1 (1700) Catherine Shorter (d. 1717), m. 2ndly (1738) Maria Skerrett

(d. 1738); children, 1st, 3s and 2d; 2nd, 2d (born prior to the marriage); ed. Eton and King's, Camb. (scholar); MP (Whig) for Castle Rising (1701–2); King's Lynn (1702–42) (expelled from the House for a short period 1712–13).

2. The Rt Hon, the Hon Sir Spencer Compton, 1st and last Earl of **WILMINGTON**, KG (1733), KB (1725, resigned 1733), (PC 1716), cr. Baron Wilmington 1728; cr. Earl 1730; ministry, 16 Feb. 1742 to 2 July 1743; Whig; b. 1673 or 1674; d. 2 July 1743; bur. Compton Wynyates, Warwickshire; unmarried; no legitimate issue; ed. St Paul's School, London, and Trinity, Oxford (originally Tory until about 1704) for Eye (1698–1710); East Grinstead (1713–15); Sussex (Whig) (1715–28); Speaker 1715–27.

3. The Rt Hon, the Hon Henry **PELHAM** (PC 1725); prior to 1706 was Henry Pelham, Esq.; ministry 27 Aug. 1743 to 6 Mar. 1754 (with an interregnum 10–12 Feb. 1746); Whig; b. c. 1695; d. 6 Mar. 1754 at Arlington St, Piccadilly, London; bur. Laughton Church, nr. Lewes, E. Sussex; m. (1726) Lady Catherine Manners; children, 2s and 6d; ed. Westminster School and Hart Hall, Oxford; MP Seaford (1717–22); Sussex (1722–54).

4. The Rt Hon Sir William Pulteney, 1st and last Earl of **BATH** (cr. 1742) PC (1716) (struck off 1731); kissed hands 10 Feb. 1746 but unable to form a ministry; Whig; b. 22 Mar. 1684 in London; d. 7 July 1764; bur. Westminster Abbey; m. Anna Maria Gumley; ed. Westminster School and Christ Church, Oxford; MP Hedon (or Heydon) 1705–34; Middlesex 1734–42.

5. His Grace the 1st Duke of **NEWCASTLE** upon Tyne and 1st Duke of Newcastle under Lyme (The Rt Hon, the Hon Sir Thomas Pelham-Holles), Bt, KG (1718). (PC 1717); added the surname Holles in July 1711; known as Lord Pelham of Laughton (1711–14); Earl of Claire (1714–15); cr. Duke of Newcastle upon Tyne 1715 and cr. Duke of Newcastle under Lyme 1756; ministry, (a) 16 Mar. 1754 to 26 Oct. 1756, (b) 2 July 1757 to 25 Oct. 1760, (c) 25 Oct. 1760 to 25 May 1762; Whig; b. 21 July 1693; d. 17 Nov. 1768 at Lincoln's Inn Field, London; bur. Laughton Church, nr. Lewes, E. Sussex; m. (1717) Lady Henrietta Godolphin (d. 1776); no issue; ed. Westminster School and Claire Hall, Camb.

6. His Grace the 4th Duke of **DEVONSHIRE** (Sir William Cavendish, KG (1756), (PC 1751, but struck off roll 1762)); known as Lord Cavendish of Hardwick until 1729 and Marquess of Hartington until 1755; ministry, 16 Nov. 1756 to May 1757; Whig; b. 1720; d. 2 Oct. 1764 at Spa, Belgium; bur. Derby Cathedral; m. (1748) Charlotte Elizabeth, Baroness Clifford (d. 1754); children, 3s and 1d; ed. privately; MP (Whig) for Co. Derby (1741–51). Summoned to Lords (1751) in father's Barony Cavendish of Hardwick.

7. The Rt Hon James **WALDEGRAVE**, 2nd Earl of Waldegrave (pronounced Wallgrave) from 1741, PC (1752), KG (1757); kissed hands 8 June 1757 but returned seals 12 June being unable to form Ministry; b. 14 Mar. 1715; d. 28 Apr. 1763; m. Marion Walpole (niece of No. 1); children 3d; ed. Eton; took seat in House of Lords, 1741.

8. The 3rd Earl of **BUTE** (The Rt Hon, the Hon Sir John Stuart, KG (1762), KT (1738, resigned 1762), (PC 1760)); until 1723 was The Hon John Stuart; ministry, 26 May 1762 to 8 April 1763; Tory; b. 25 May 1713 at Parliament Square, Edinburgh; d. 10 Mar. 1792 at South Audley St, Grosvenor Square, London; bur. Rothesay, Bute; m. (1736) Mary Wortley-Montagu later (1761) Baroness Mount Stuart (d. 1794); children, 4s and 4d (with other issue); ed. Eton.

9. The Rt Hon, the Hon George **GRENVILLE** (PC 1754); prior to 1749 was G. Grenville Esq;

ministry, 16 Apr. 1763 to 10 July 1765; Whig; b. 14 Oct. 1712 at? Wotton, Bucks; d. 13 Nov. 1770 at Bolton St, Piccadilly, London; bur. Wotton, Bucks; m. (1749) Elizabeth Wyndham (d. 1769); children, 4s and 5d; ed. Eton and Christ Church, Oxford; MP for Buckingham (1741–70).

10. The Most Hon The 2nd Marquess of **ROCKINGHAM** (The Rt Hon Lord Charles Watson-Wentworth), KG (1760), (PC 1765); known as Hon Charles Watson-Wentworth until 1739; Viscount Higham (1739–46); Earl of Malton (1746–50); succeeded to Marquessate 14 Dec. 1750; ministry, (a) 13 July 1765 to July 1766, (b) 27 March 1782 to his death on 1 July 1782; Whig; b. 13 May 1730; d. 1 July 1782; bur. York Minster; m. (1752) Mary Bright (her father was formerly called Liddell) (d. 1804); no issue; ed. Westminster School (and possibly St John's Camb.). Took his seat in House of Lords 21 May 1751.

11. The 1st Earl of **CHATHAM** (The Rt Hon William Pitt (PC 1746)); cr. Earl 4 Aug. 1766; ministry, 30 July 1766 to 14 Oct. 1768; Whig; his health in 1767 prevented his being PM in other than name; b. 15 Nov. 1708 at St James's, Westminster, London; d. 11 May 1788 at Hayes, Kent; bur. Westminster Abbey; m. (1754) Hon. Hester Grenville*, later (1761) cr. Baroness Chatham in her own right (d. 1803); children, 3s and 2d; ed. Eton, Trinity, Oxford (took no degree owing to gout), and Utrecht; MP (Whig) Old Sarum (1735–47); Seaford (1747–54); Aldborough (1754–6); Okehampton (1756–7) (also Buckingham (1756), Bath (1757–66)).

12. His Grace the 3rd Duke of **GRAFTON** (The Rt Hon Sir Augustus Henry FitzRoy) KG (1769), (PC 1765); prior to 1747 known as the Hon. Augustus H. FitzRoy; 1747–57 as Earl of Euston; succeeded to dukedom in 1757; ministry, 14 Oct. 1768 to 28 Jan. 1770; Whig; he was virtually PM in 1767 when Lord Chatham's ministry broke down; b. 28 Sept. 1735 at St Marylebone, London; d. 14 Mar. 1811 at Euston Hall, Suffolk; bur. Euston, Suffolk; m. 1st (1765) Hon. Anne Liddell (sep. 1765, mar. dis. by Act of Parl. 1769) (d. 1804), m. 2ndly (1769) Elizabeth Wrottesley (d. 1822); children, 1st, 2s and 1d; 2nd, 6s and 6d (possibly also another d. who died young); ed, private school at Hackney, Westminster School, and Peterhouse, Camb; MP (Whig) Bury St Edmunds (1756–7).

13. Lord **NORTH** (The Rt Hon, the Hon Sir Frederick North), KG (1772), (PC 1766); succ. (Aug. 1790) as 2nd Earl of Guildford; ministry 28 Jan. 1770 to 20 Mar. 1782; Tory; b. 13 Apr. 1732 at Albemarle St, Piccadilly, London; d. 5 Aug. 1792 at Lower Grosvenor Street, London; bur. All Saints' Church, Wroxton, Oxfordshire; m. (1756) Anne Speke (d. 1797); children, 4s and 3d; ed. Eton, Trinity, Oxford, and Leipzig; MP (Tory) for Banbury (1754–90) (can be regarded as a Whig from 1783). Took his seat in the House of Lords 25 Nov. 1790.

14. The 2nd Earl of **SHELBURNE** (Rt Hon, the Hon Sir William Petty, KG (1782) (PC 1763); formerly, until 1751, William Fitz-Maurice; Viscount Fitz-Maurice (1753–61); succeeded to Earldom 10 May 1761; cr. The 1st Marquess of Lansdowne (6 Dec. 1784); Col. 1760; Maj. Gen. 1765; Lt. Gen. 1772, and Gen. 1783; ministry, 4 July 1782 to 24 Feb. 1783; Whig, b. 20 May 1737 at Dublin, Ireland, d. 7 May 1805 at Berkeley Square, London; bur. High Wycombe, Bucks; m. 1st (1765) Lady Sophia Carerett (d. 1771), 2ndly (1779) Lady Louisa FitzPatrick (d. 1789); children, 1st, 2s, 2nd, 1s and 1d; ed. local school in S. Ireland, private tutor, and Christ Church, Oxford; MP Chipping Wycombe (1760–1). Took seat in House of Lords (as Baron Wycombe) 3 Nov. 1761.

---

* This lady had the extraordinary distinction of being the wife, the mother, the sister and the aunt of four British Prime Ministers. They were Nos. 11, 16, 9, and 18 respectively.

---

15. His Grace the 3rd Duke of **PORTLAND** (The Most Noble Sir William Henry Cavendish Bentinck, KG (1794) (PC 1765)); assumed additional name of Bentinck in 1775; assumed by Royal Licence surname of Cavendish-Bentinck in 1801; Marquess of Titchfield from birth until he succeeded to the dukedom on 1 May 1762; ministry (a) 2 April 1783 to Dec. 1783, (b) 31 Mar. 1807 to Oct. 1809; (a) coalition and (b) Tory; b. 14th Apr. 1738; d. 30 Oct. 1809 at Bulstrode, Bucks; bur. St Marylebone, London; m. (1766) Lady Dorothy Cavendish (d. 1794); children, 4s and 1d; ed. Westminster or Eton and Christ Church, Oxford, MP (Whig) Weobley, Herefordshire (1761–2).

16. The Rt Hon, the Hon William **PITT** (PC 1782) prior Aug. 1766 was William Pitt, Esq.; ministry (a) 19 Dec. 1783 to 14 Mar. 1801, (b) 10 May 1804 to his death on 23 Jan. 1806; Tory; b. 28 May 1759 at Hayes, nr. Bromley, Kent; d. 23 Jan. 1806 at Bowling Green House, Putney, Surrey; bur. Westminster Abbey; unmarried, ed. privately and Pembroke Hall, Cambridge, MP (Tory) Appleby.

17. The Rt Hon Henry **ADDINGTON** (PC 1789); cr. 1st Viscount Sidmouth 1805; ministry, 17 Mar. 1801 to 30 April 1804; Tory; b. 30 May 1757 at Bedford Row, London; d. 15 Feb. 1844 at White Lodge, Richmond Park, Surrey; bur. Mortlake; m. 1st (1781) Ursula Mary Hammond (d. 1811), 2ndly (1823) Hon Mrs Marianne Townshend (née Scott) (d. 1842); children, 1st, 3s and 4d, 2nd, no issue; ed. Cheam, Winchester Col., Lincoln's Inn, and Brasenose, Oxford (Chancellor's Medal for English Essay); MP (Tory) Devizes (1783–1805). Speaker 1789–1801. As a peer he supported the Whigs in 1807 and 1812 administration.

18. The Rt Hon the 1st Baron **GRENVILLE** of Wotton-under-Bernewood (William Wyndham Grenville (PC(I) 1782; PC 1783)); cr. Baron 25 Nov. 1790; ministry, 10 Feb. 1806 to Mar. 1807; b. (the son of No. 9) 25 Oct. 1759; d. 12 Jan. 1834 at Dropmore Lodge, Bucks; bur. Burnham, Bucks; m. (1792) Hon Anne Pitt (d. 1864 aged 91); no issue; ed. Eton, Christ Church, Oxford (Chancellor's prize for Latin Verse), and Lincoln's Inn; MP Buckingham (1782–4), Buckinghamshire (1784–90). Speaker Jan.–June 1789.

19. The Rt Hon, the Hon Spencer **PERCEVAL** (PC 1807), KC (1796); ministry, 4 Oct. 1809 to 11 May 1812; b. 1 Nov. 1762 at Audley Sq., London; murdered 11 May 1812 in lobby of the House; bur. at Charlton; m. (1790) Jane Spencer-Wilson (later Lady Carr) (d. 1844); children, 6s and 6d; ed. Harrow, Trinity, Camb., and Lincoln's Inn; MP (Tory) Northampton (1796– and 1797).

20. The Rt Hon the 2nd Earl of **LIVERPOOL** (Sir Robert Banks Jenkinson, KG (1814) (PC 1799)); from birth to 1786 R B Jenkinson, Esq.; from 1786–96 The Hon R B Jenkinson; from 1796–1808 (when he succeeded to the earldom) Lord Hawkesbury; ministry, (a) 8 June 1812 to 29 Jan. 1820, (b) 29 Jan. 1820 to 17 Feb. 1827; Tory; b. 7 June 1770; d. 4 Dec. 1828 at Coombe Wood, near Kingston-on-Thames; bur. at Hawkesbury; m. 1st (1795) Lady Louisa Theodosia Hervey (d. 1821), 2ndly (1822) Mary Chester (d. 1846); no issue; ed. Charterhouse and Christ Church, Oxford; summoned to House of Lords in his father's barony of Hawkesbury 15 Nov. 1803 (elected MP (Tory) for Appleby (1790) but did not sit as he was under age); Rye (1796–1803).

21. The Rt Hon George **CANNING** (PC 1800); ministry, 10 Apr. 1827 to his death; Tory; b. 11 Apr. 1770 in London; d. 8 Aug. 1827 at Chiswick Villa, London; m. (1800) Joan Scott (later, 1828, cr. Viscountess) (d. 1837); children, 3s and 1d; ed. in London; Hyde Abbey (nr. Winchester); Eton; Christ Church, Oxford (Chancellor's prize, Latin Verse), and Lincoln's Inn; MP (Tory) Newton, I.o.W. (1793–6); Wendover

(1796–1802); Tralee (1802–6); Newton (1806–7); Hastings (1807–12); Liverpool (1812–23); Harwich (1823–6); Newport (1826–7), and Seaford (1827).

22. The Viscount **GODERICH** (Rt Hon, the Hon Frederick John Robinson (PC 1812, PC (I) *c*. 1833); cr. Earl of Ripon 1833; ministry 31 Aug. 1827 to 8 Jan. 1828; Tory; b. 1 Nov. 1782 in London; d. 28 Jan. 1859 at Putney Heath, London; bur. Nocton, Lincs; m. (1814) Lady Sarah Albinia Louisa Hobart (d. 1867); children, 2s and 1d; ed. Harrow; St John's Col., Camb., and Lincoln's Inn; MP Carlow (1806–7); Ripon (1807–27).

23. His Grace The 1st Duke of **WELLINGTON** (The Most Noble, The Hon Sir Arthur Wellesley, KG (1813), GCB (1815), GCH (1816), (PC 1807, PC (I) (1807); known as The Hon Arthur Wesley until 1804; then as The Hon Sir Arthur Wellesley, KB, until 1809 when cr. The Viscount Wellington; cr. Earl of Wellington Feb. 1812; Marquess of Wellington Oct. 1812 and Duke May 1814. Ensign (1787); Lieut. (1787); Capt. (1791); Major (1793); Lt-Col (1793); Col (1796); Maj. Gen. (1802); Lt. Gen. (1808); Gen. (1811); Field Marshal (1813); ministry, (a) 22 Jan. 1828 to 26 June 1830, (b) 26 June 1830 to 21 Nov. 1830, (c) 17 Nov. to 9 Dec. 1834; Tory; b. 1 May 1769 at Mornington House, Upper Merrion St., Dublin; d. 14 Sept. 1852 at Walmer Castle, Kent; bur. St Paul's Cathedral; m. (1806) the Hon Catherine Sarah Dorothea Pakenham (d. 1831); children, 2s; ed. Browns Seminary, King's Rd., Chelsea, London; Eton; Brussels, and The Academy at Angiers; MP Rye (1806); St Michael (1807); Newport, Isle of Wight (1807–9). Took seat in House of Lords as Viscount, Earl, Marquess, and Duke 28 June 1814. Physical height: 5 ft 9½ in *1,76 m.*

24. The 2nd Earl **GREY** (The Rt Hon, the Hon Sir Charles Grey, Bt (1808), KG (1831), (PC 1806)); styled Viscount Howick 1806–7 and previously The Hon Charles Grey; ministry, 22 Nov. 1830 to July 1834; Whig; b. 13 Mar. 1764 at Fallodon, Northumberland; d. 17 July 1845 and bur. at Howick House, Northumberland; m. (1794) Hon Mary Elizabeth Ponsonby (d. 1861); children, 8s and 5d; ed. at a private school in Marylebone, London; Eton; Trinity, Camb., and Middle Temple; MP (Whig) Northumberland (1786–1807); Appleby (1807); Tavistock (1807).

25. The 3rd Viscount **MELBOURNE** (The Rt Hon, The Hon Sir William Lamb, Bt (PC (UK & I) 1827)); ministry, (a) 16 July 1834 to Nov. 1834, (b) 18 April 1835 to 20 June 1837, (c) 20 June 1837 to Aug. 1841; Whig; b. (of disputed paternity) 15 March 1779 Melbourne House, Piccadilly, London; d. 24 Nov. 1848 at Brocket; bur. at Hatfield; m. (1805) Lady Caroline Ponsonby, separated 1824 (d. 1828); only 1s survived infancy; ed. Eton; Trinity, Cambridge, Glasgow University, and Lincoln's Inn; MP (Whig) Leominster (1806); Haddington Borough (1806–7); Portarlington (1807–12); Peterborough (1816–19); Herts (1819–26); Newport, Isle of Wight (1827); Bletchingley (1827–8). Took his seat in House of Lords 1 Feb. 1829.

26. The Rt Hon Sir Robert **PEEL**, Bt (PC 1812); prior to May 1830 he was Robert Peel, Esq., MP, when he succeeded as 2nd Baronet; ministry, (a) 10 Dec. 1834 to 8 Apr. 1835, (b) 30 Aug. 1841 to 29 June 1846; Conservative; b. 5 Feb. 1788 prob. at Chamber Hall, nr. Bury, Lancashire; d. 2 July 1850 after fall from horse; bur. at Drayton Bassett; m. (1820) Julia Floyd (d. 1859); children, 5s and 2d; ed. Harrow; Christ Church, Oxford (Double First in Classics and Mathematics), and Lincoln's Inn; MP (Tory) Cashel (Tipperary) (1809–12); Chippenham (1812–17); Univ. of Oxford (1817–29); Westbury (1829–30); Tamworth (1830–50).

27. The Rt Hon Lord John **RUSSELL** (PC 1830), and after 30 July 1861 1st Earl **RUSSELL**, KG (1862), GCMG (1869); ministry, (a) 30 June

1846 to Feb. 1852, (b) 29 Oct. 1865 to June 1866; (a) Whig and (b) Liberal; b. 18 Aug. 1792 in Hertford St, Mayfair; d. 28 May 1878 at Pembroke Lodge, Richmond Park, Surrey; bur. Chenies, Bucks; m. 1st (1835) Adelaide (*née* Lister), Dowager Baroness Ribblesdale (d. 1838), 2ndly (1841) Lady Frances Anna Maria Elliot-Murray-Kynynmound (d. 1898); children, 1st, 2d and 3s and 3d; ed. Westminster School and Edinburgh University; MP (Whig) Tavistock (1813–17, 1818–20 & 1830–1); Hunts (1820–6); Bandon (1826–30); Devon (1831–2); S. Devon (1832–5); Stroud (1835–41); City of London (1841–61). Took seat in the House of Lords on 30 July 1861.

28. The 14th Earl of **DERBY**, Rt Hon Sir Edward Geoffrey Smith-Stanley, Bt, KG (1859), GCMG (1869), PC 1830, PC (I) (1831); prior to 1834 known as the Hon E G Stanley, MP; then known as Lord Stanley MP until 1844; ministry, (a) 23 Feb. 1852 to 18 Dec. 1852, (b) 20 Feb. 1858 to 11 June 1859, (c) 28 June 1866 to 26 Feb. 1868; Tory and Conservative; b. 19 March 1799 at Knowsley, Lancs; d. 23 Oct. 1869; and bur. at Knowsley, Lancs; m. (1825) Hon Emma Caroline Wilbraham-Bootle (d. 1876); 2s, 1d; ed. Eton; Christ Church Oxford (Chancellor's prize for Latin Verse); MP (Whig) Stockbridge (1822–6); Preston (1826–30); Windsor (1831–2); North Lancs (1832–44). Summoned 1844 to House of Lords as Lord Stanley (of Bickerstaffe); succeeded to Earldom 1851; became a Tory in 1835.

29. The Rt Hon Sir George Hamilton Gordon, Bt, 4th Earl of **ABERDEEN**, KG (1855), KT (1808), (PC 1814); prior to Oct. 1791 known as the Hon G Gordon; from 1791 to Aug. 1801 known as Lord Haddo; assumed additional name of Hamilton Nov. 1818; ministry, 19 Dec. 1852 to 5 Feb. 1855; Peelite; b. 28 Jan. 1784 in Edinburgh; d. 14 Dec. 1860 at Argyll House, St James's, London; bur. at Stanmore, G. London; m. 1st (1805) Lady Catherine Elizabeth Hamilton (d. 1812), 2ndly (1815) to her sister-in-law Harriet (*née* Douglas), Dowager Viscountess Hamilton (d. 1833); children, 1st, 1s and 3d, 2nd 4s and 1d; ed. Harrow and St John's, Camb.; House of Lords 1814.

30. The Rt Hon Sir Henry John Temple, 3rd and last Viscount **PALMERSTON** (a non-representative peer of Ireland), KG (1856), CGB (1832), (PC 1809); known (1784–1802) as the Hon H J Temple; ministry, (a) 6 Feb. 1855 to 19 Feb. 1858, (b) 12 June 1859 to 18 Oct. 1865; Liberal; b. 20 Oct. 1784 at Broadlands, nr. Romsey, Hants (or possibly in Park St, London); d. 18 Oct. 1865 at Brocket Hall, Herts; bur. Westminster Abbey; m. (1839) Hon. Emily Mary (*née* Lamb), the Dowager Countess Cowper (d. 1869); no issue; ed. Harrow; Univ. of Edinburgh, and St John's Camb., MP (Tory) Newport, Isle of Wight (1807–11); Camb. Univ. (1811–31); Bletchingley (1831–2); S. Hants. (1832–4); Tiverton (1835–65); from 1829 a Whig and latterly a Liberal.

31. The Rt Hon Benjamin **DISRAELI**, 1st and last Earl of **BEACONSFIELD**, KG (1878), (PC 1852); prior to 12 Aug. 1876 Benjamin Disraeli (except that until 1838 he was known as Benjamin D'Israeli); ministry, (a) 27 Feb. 1868 to November 1868, (b) 20 Feb. 1874 to Apr. 1880; Conservative; b. 21 Dec. 1804 at either the Adelphi, Westminster, or at 22 Theobald's Rd, or St Mary Axe; d. 19 Apr. 1881 at 19 Curzon St, Mayfair, London; bur. Hughenden Manor, Bucks (monument in Westminster Abbey); m. (1839) Mrs Mary Anne Lewis (*née* Evans) later (1868) Viscountess (in her own right) Beaconsfield; no issue; ed. Lincoln's Inn; MP (Con.) Maidstone (1837–41); Shrewsbury (1841–7); Buckinghamshire (1847–76), when he became a peer.

32. The Rt Hon William Ewart **GLADSTONE** (PC 1841); ministry, (a) 3 Dec. 1868 to February 1874, (b) 23 April 1880 to 12 June 1885, (c) 1 Feb. 1886 to 20 July 1886, (d) 15 Aug. 1892 to 3

March 1894; Liberal; b. 29 Dec. 1809 at 62 Rodney St, Liverpool; d. 19 May 1898 (aged 88 yr 142 days) at Hawarden Castle, Clwyd; bur. Westminster Abbey; m. (1839) Catherine Glynne (d. 1900); children, 4s and 4d; ed. Seaforth Vicarage; Eton and Christ Church, Oxford (Double First in Classics and Mathematics); MP Tory, Newark (1832–45); Univ. of Oxford (1847–65) (Peelite to 1859, thereafter a Liberal); S. Lancs. (1865–8); Greenwich (1868–80); Midlothian (1880–95).

33. The Rt Hon Robert Arthur Talbot Gascoyne-Cecil, the 3rd Marquess of **SALISBURY**, KG (1878), GCVO (1902), (PC 1866); known as Lord Robert Cecil till 1865; and as Viscount Cranbourne, MP, from 1865 to 1868; ministry, (a) 23 June 1885 to 28 Jan. 1886, (b) 25 July 1886 to Aug. 1892, (c) 25 June 1895 to 22 Jan. 1901, (d) 23 Jan. 1901 to 11 July 1902; Conservative; b. 3 Feb. 1830 at Hatfield House, Herts; d. 22 Aug. 1903 at Hatfield House; bur. at Hatfield; m. (1857) Georgiana Charlotte (*née* Alderson), Lady of the Royal Order of Victoria and Albert and C.I. (1899) (d. 1899); Children, 4s and 3d; ed. Eton and Christ Church, Oxford (Hon. 4th Cl. Maths.); MP (Con.) for Stamford (1853–68).

34. The Rt Hon Sir Archibald Philip Primrose, Bt, 5th Earl of **ROSEBERY**, KG (1892), KT (1895), VD (PC 1881); b. the Hon A P Primrose; known as Lord Dalmeny (1851–68); Earl of Midlothian from 1911 but style not adopted by him; ministry, 5 Mar. 1894 to 21 June 1895; Liberal; b. 7 May 1847 at Charles St, Berkeley Square, London; d. 21 May 1929 at 'The Durdans', Epsom, Surrey; bur. at Dalmeny; m. (1878) Hannah de Rothschild (d. 1890); children, 2s and 2d; ed. Eton and Christ Church, Oxford.

35. The Rt Hon Arthur James **BALFOUR** (PC 1885, PC (I) 1887); KG (1922), later (1922) the 1st Earl of Balfour, OM (1916); ministry, 12 July 1902 to 4 Dec. 1905; Conservative; b. 25 July 1848 at Whittingehame, E. Lothian, Scotland; d. 19 Mar. 1930 at Fisher's Hill, Woking, Surrey; bur. at Whittingehame; unmarried; ed. Eton and Trinity, Camb; MP (Con.) Hertford (1874–85); E. Manchester (1885–1906); City of London (1906–22).

36. The Rt Hon Sir Henry **CAMPBELL-BANNERMAN**, GCB (1895), (PC 1884); known as Henry Campbell until 1872; ministry, 5 Dec. 1905 to 5 Apr. 1908; Liberal; b. 7 Sept. 1836 at Kelvinside House, Glasgow; d. 22 Apr. 1908 at 10 Downing Street, London; bur. Meigle, Scotland; m. (1860) Sarah Charlotte Bruce (d. 1906); no issue; ed. Glasgow High School; Glasgow Univ. (Gold Medal for Greek); Trinity, Camb. (22nd Sen. Optime in Maths Tripos; 3rd Cl. in Classical Tripos); MP (Lib.) Stirling District (1868–1908).

37. The Rt Hon Herbert Henry **ASQUITH** (PC 1892, PC (I) 1916); later (1925) 1st Earl of **OXFORD AND ASQUITH**, KG (1925); ministry, (a) 7 Apr. 1908 to 7 May 1910, (b) 8 May 1910 to 5 Dec. 1916 (coalition from 25 May 1915); Liberal; b. 12 Sept. 1852 at Morley, W. Yorks; d. 15 Feb. 1928 at 'The Wharf', Sutton Courtney, Berks; bur. Sutton Courtney Church; m. 1st (1877) Helen Kelsall Melland (d. 1891), 2ndly (1894) Emma Alice Margaret Tennant; children, 1st, 4s and 1d, 2nd 1s and 1d; ed. City of London School; Balliol, Oxford (Scholar, 1st Class Lit. Hum.); MP (Lib.) East Fife (1886–1918); Paisley (1920–4).

38. The Rt Hon (David) Lloyd **GEORGE**, OM (1919), (PC 1905); later (1945) 1st Earl **LLOYD-GEORGE** of Dwyfor; ministry, 7 Dec. 1916 to 19 Oct. 1922; Coalition; b. 17 Jan. 1863 in Manchester; d. 26 Mar. 1945 at Ty Newydd, nr. Llanystumdwy; bur. on the bank of the river Dwyfor; m. 1st (1888) Margaret Owen, GBE (1920) (d. 1941), 2ndly (1943) Frances Louise Stevenson, CBE; children, 1st 2s and 3d, 2nd no issue; ed. Llanystumdwy Church School and privately; MP Caernarvon Boroughs (1890–

1945) (Lib. 1890–1931 and 1935–45; Ind. Lib. 1931–5). Physical height: 5 ft 6 in *1,67 m.*

39. The Rt Hon (Andrew) Bonar **LAW** (PC 1911); ministry, 23 Oct. 1922 to 20 May 1923; Conservative; b. 16 Sept. 1858 at Kingston, nr. Richibucto, New Brunswick, Canada; d. 30 Oct. 1923 at 24 Onslow Grdns., London; bur. Westminster Abbey; m. (1891) Annie Pitcairn (d. 1909); children, 4s and 2d; ed. Gilbertfield School, Hamilton; Glasgow High School; MP (Con.) Blackfriars Div. of Glasgow (1900–6); Dulwich Div. of Camberwell (1906–10); MP Bootle Div. of Lancs (1911–18); Central Div. of Glasgow (1918–23). Physical height: 6 ft 0 in *1,83 m.*

40. The Rt Hon Stanley **BALDWIN** (PC 1920, PC (Can.) 1927); later (1937) 1st Earl Baldwin of Bewdley, KG (1937); ministry, (a) 22 May 1923 to 22 Jan. 1924 (Con.), (b) 4 Nov. 1924 to 4 June 1929 (Con.), (c) 7 June 1935 to 20 Jan. 1936 (Nat.), (d) 21 Jan. 1936 to 11 Dec. 1936 (Nat.), (e) 12 Dec. 1936 to 28 May 1937 (Nat.); b. 3 Aug. 1867 at Bewdley; d. Astley, 14 Dec. 1947; bur. Worcester Cathedral; m. (1892) Lucy Ridsdale, GBE (1937) (d. 1945); children, 2s and 4d; ed. Harrow and Trinity, Camb.; MP (Con.) Bewdley Div. of Worcestershire (1908–37). Physical height: 5 ft 8½ in *1,74 m.*

41. The Rt Hon (James) Ramsay **MACDON-ALD** (PC 1924, PC (Canada) 1929); ministry, (a) 22 Jan. 1924 to 4 Nov. 1924 (Labour), (b) 5 June 1929 to 7 June 1935 (Labour and from 1931 National Coalition); b. 12 Oct. 1866 at Lossie-mouth, Grampian; d. 9 Nov. 1937 at sea, mid-Atlantic; bur. Spynie Churchyard, nr. Lossie-mouth, Scotland; m. (1896) Margaret Ethel Gladstone (d. 1911); children, 3s and 3d; ed. Drainie Parish Board School; MP (Lab.) Leices-ter (1906–18); (Lab.) Aberavon (1922–9); (Lab.) Seaham Div. Co. Durham (1929–31); (Nat. Lab.) (1931–5); MP for Scottish Univs. (1936–7). Physical height: 5 ft 10½ in *1,79 m.*

42. The Rt Hon (Arthur) Neville **CHAMBER-LAIN** (PC 1922); ministry, 28 May 1937 to 10 May 1940; National; b. 18 Mar. 1869 at Edgbaston, Birmingham; d. 9 Nov. 1940 at High Field Park, Hickfield, nr. Reading; ashes interred Westminster Abbey; m. (1911) Annie Vere Cole (d. 12 Feb. 1967); children, 1s and 1d; ed. Rugby School; Mason College (later Birmingham Univ.) (Metallurgy & Engineering Design); MP (Con.) Ladywood Div. of Birming-ham (1918–29); Edgbaston Div. of Birmingham (1929–40). Physical height: 5 ft 10 in *1,77 m.*

43. The Rt Hon Sir Winston (Leonard **SPEN-CER-)CHURCHILL**; KG (1953) OM (1946), CH (1922), TD (PC 1907); ministry, (a) 10 May 1940 to 26 July 1945 (Coalition but from 23 May 1945 Conservative), (b) 26 Oct. 1951 to 6 Feb. 1952 (Conservative), (c) 7 Feb. 1952 to 5 Apr. 1955 (Conservative); b. 30 Nov. 1874 at Blenheim Palace, Woodstock, Oxon; d. 24 Jan. 1965 Hyde Park Gate, London; bur. Bladon, Oxfordshire; m. (1908) Clementine Ogilvy Hozier, GBE (1946), cr. 1965 (Life) Baroness Spencer-Churchill (d. 13 Dec. 1977); children, 1s and 4d; ed. Harrow School and Royal Military College; MP (Con. until 1904, then Lib.) Oldham (1900–6); (Lib.) N.-W. Manchester (1906–8); (Lib.) Dundee (1908–18 and (Coalition Lib.) until 1922); Epping Div. of Essex (1924–45); Woodford Div. of Essex (1945–64); Physical height: 5 ft 8½ in *1,74 m.*

44. The Rt Hon Clement (Richard) **ATTLEE** CH (1945), (PC 1935); created 1955 1st Earl Attlee, KG (1956), OM (1951); ministry, 26 July 1945 to 26 Oct. 1951; Labour; b. 3 Jan. 1883 at Putney, London; d. Westminster Hospital, 8 Oct. 1967; m. (1922) Violet Helen Millar, children, 1s and 3d; ed. Haileybury College and Univ. College, Oxford (2nd Cl. Hons. (Mod. Hist)); MP Limehouse Div. of Stepney (1922–50); West Walthamstow (1950–5). Physical height: 5 ft 8 in *1,73 m.*

45. The Rt. Hon Sir (Robert) Anthony **EDEN**, KG (1954), MC (1917), (PC 1934); cr. 1961 1st Earl of Avon; ministry, 6 Apr. 1955 to 9 Jan. 1957; Conservative; b. 12 June 1897 Windle-stone, Durham; d. Alvediston, Wilts. 14 Jan. 1977; m. 1st (1923) Beatrice Helen Beckett (m. dis. 1950) (d. 1957), 2ndly (1952) Anne Clarissa Spencer-Churchill, children, 1st, 2s 2nd, no issue; ed. Eton and Christ Church, Oxford (1st Cl. Hons (Oriental Langs)); MP Warwick and Leamington (1923–57). Physical height: 6 ft 0 in *1,83 m.*

46. The Rt Hon (Maurice) Harold **MACMIL-LAN** OM (1976) (PC 1942); ministry, 10 Jan. 1957 to 18 Oct. 1963; Conservative; b. 10 Feb. 1894, 52 Cadogan Place, London; d. 29 Dec. 1986; m. (1920) Lady Dorothy Evelyn Caven-dish, GBE; children, 1s and 3d; ed. Eton (Scholar); Balliol, Oxford ((Exhibitioner) 1st Class Hon Mods.); MP Stockton-on-Tees (1924–9 and 1931–45); Bromley (1945–64). Physical height: 6 ft 0 in *1,83 m.*

47. The Rt Hon Sir Alexander (Frederick) **DOUGLAS-HOME**, KT (1962) (PC 1951); known until 30 April 1918 as the Hon A F Douglas-Home; thence until 11 July 1951 as Lord Dunglass; thence until his disclaimer of 23 Oct. 1963 as the (14th) Earl of Home, Lord Home of the Hirsel; ministry, 19 Oct. 1963 to 16 Oct. 1964; Conservative; b. 2 July 1903, 28 South St, London; m. (1936) Elizabeth Hester Alington; children, 1s and 3d; ed. Eton; Christ Church, Oxford; MP South Lanark (1931–45); Lanark (1950–1); Kinross and West Perthshire (1963–74). Physical height: 5 ft 11 in *1,80 m.*

48. The Rt Hon Sir (James) Harold **WILSON**; KG (1976) OBE (civ.) (1945) (PC 1947); ministry, (a) 16 Oct. 1964 to 30 Mar. 1966 (b) 31 Mar. 1966 to 17 June 1970, (c) 4 Mar. 1974 to 10 Oct. 1974, (d) 10 Oct. 1974 to 5 Apr. 1976; Labour; b. Linthwaite, W. Yorks, 11 Mar. 1916; m. (1940) Gladys Mary Baldwin; children, 2s; ed. Milnsbridge C.S.; Royds Hall S.; Wirral G.S.; Jesus College, Oxford (1st Cl. Philosophy, Politics and Economics); MP Ormskirk (1945–50); Huyton (1950 to date). Physical height: 5 ft 8½ in *1,74 m.*

49. The Rt Hon Edward Richard George **HEATH**, MBE (mil.) (1946), (PC 1955); ministry, 18 June 1970 to 3 Mar. 1974; Conservative; b. 9 July 1916 at Broadstairs, Kent; unmarried; ed. Chatham House School, Ramsgate and Balliol College, Oxford; MP Bexley (1950–74); Bexley-Sidcup from 1974. Physical height: 5 ft 11 in *1,80 m.*

50. The Rt Hon (Leonard) James **CAL-LAGHAN** (PC 1964); ministry 5 Apr. 1976 to 4 May 1979; Labour; b. 27 Mar. 1912 at 38 Funtingdon Rd, Portsmouth, Hampshire; m. (1938) Audrey Elizabeth Moulton, children 1s and 2d; ed. Portsmouth Northern Secondary Sch.; MP South Cardiff (1945–50); Southeast Cardiff (1950 to date). Physical height: 6 ft 1½ in *1,87 m.*

51. The Rt Hon Mrs Margaret (Hilda) **THATCHER** *née* Roberts (PC 1970); ministry (a) 4 May 1979 to 9 June 1983 (b) 10 June 1983 to 4 May 1987 (c) 12 June 1987 to date; Conservative; b. 13 Oct. 1925, Grantham, Lincolnshire; m. (13 Dec. 1951) Denis Thatcher MBE (b. 10 May 1915, he prev. m. Margaret D. Kempson, who in 1948 m. Sir Howard Hickman 3rd Bt.); 1s 1d (twins); ed. Kesteven & Gran-tham Girls' Sch.; Somerville Coll., Oxford (MA, BSc); MP Finchley (1959–74); Barnet, Finchley (1974 to date). Physical height: 5 ft 5 in *1,65 m.*

Authorized Post nominal letters in their correct order

There are 72 Orders, Decorations, and Medals which have been bestowed by the Sovereign that carry the entitlement to a group of letters after the name. Of these, 54 are currently awardable. The order (*vide London Gazette*, supplement 27 Oct. 1964) is as follows:

1	VC	Victoria Cross.
2	GC	George Cross.
3	KG	(but *not* for Ladies of the Order), Knight of the Most Noble Order of the Garter.
4	KT	(but *not* for Ladies of the Order), Knight of the Most Ancient and Most Noble Order of the Thistle.
5	GCB	Knight Grand Cross of the Most Honourable Order of the Bath.
6	OM	Member of the Order of Merit.
7*	GCSI	Knight Grand Commander of the Most Excellent Order of the Star of India.
8	GCMG	Knight (or Dame) Grand Cross of the Most Distinguished Order of St Michael and St George.
9*	GCIE	Knight Grand Commander of the Most Eminent Order of the Indian Empire.
10*	CI	Lady of The Imperial Order of the Crown of India.
11	GCVO	Knight (or Dame) Grand Cross of the Royal Victorian Order.
12	GBE	Knight (or Dame) Grand Cross of the Most Excellent Order of the British Empire.
13	CH	Member of the Order of Compan-ions of Honour.
14	KCB	(but *not* if also a GCB) Knight Commander of the Most Honour-able Order of the Bath.
15	DCB	(but *not* if also a GCB) Dame Commander of the Most Honour-able Order of the Bath.
16*	KCSI	(but *not* if also a GCSI), Knight Commander of the Most Excellent Order of the Star of India.
17	KCMG	(but *not* if also a GCMG), Knight Commander of the Most Distin-guished Order of St Michael and St George.
18	DCMG	(but *not* if also a GCMG) Dame Commander of the Most Distin-guished Order of St Michael and St George.
19*	KCIE	(but *not* if also a GCIE), Knight Commander of the Most Eminent Order of the Indian Empire.
20	KCVO	(but *not* if also a GCVO), Knight Commander of the Royal Victo-rian Order.
21	DCVO	(but *not* if also a GCVO), Dame Commander of the Royal Victo-rian Order.
22	KBE	(but *not* if also a GBE), Knight Commander of the Most Excellent Order of the British Empire.
23	DBE	(but *not* if also a GBE), Dame Commander of the Most Excellent Order of the British Empire.
24	CB	(but *not* if also a GCB and/or a KCB), Companion of the Most Honoura-ble Order of the Bath.
25*	CSI	(but *not* if also a GCSI and/or a KCSI), Companion of the Most Excellent Order of the Star of India.
26	CMG	(but *not* if also a GCMG and/or a KCMG or DCMG), Companion of the Most Distinguished Order of St Michael and St George.
27*	CIE	(but *not* if also a GCIE and/or a KCIE), Companion of the Most Eminent Order of the Indian Em-pire.
28	CVO	(but *not* if also a GCVO and/or a KCVO or DCVO), Commander of the Royal Victorian Order.
29	CBE	(but *not* if also a GBE and/or a KBE or DBE), Commander of the Most Excellent Order of the British Empire.
30	DSO	Companion of the Distinguished Service Order.
31	MVO	(but *not* if also either a GCVO and/ or a KCVO or a DCVO, and/or a CVO),

32	OBE	Lieutenant of the Royal Victorian Order. (but *not* if also either a GBE and/or a KBE or DBE and/or a CBE), Officer of the Most Excellent Order of the British Empire.
33	QSO	Queen's Service Order (NZ only).
34	ISO	Companion of the Imperial Service Order.
	MVO	(but *not* if also either a GCVO and/or a KCVO or a DCVO, and/or a CVO and/or an LVO), Member of the Royal Victorian Order.
35	MBE	(but *not* if also either a GBE and/or a KBE or DBE and/or a CBE and/or an OBE), Member of the Most Excellent Order of the British Empire.
36*	IOM	(if in Military Division), Indian Order of Merit.
37*	OB	Order of Burma (when for gallantry).
38	RRC	Member of the Royal Red Cross.
39	DSC	Distinguished Service Cross.
40	MC	Military Cross.
41	DFC	Distinguished Flying Cross.
42	AFC	Air Force Cross.
43	ARRC	(but *not* if also an RRC), Associate of the Royal Red Cross.
44*	OBI	Order of British India.
*	OB	Order of Burma (when for distinguished service).
45	DCM	Distinguished Conduct Medal.
46	CGM	(both the Naval and the Flying decorations), Conspicuous Gallantry Medal.
47	GM	George Medal.
48*	KPM	King's or Queen's Police Medal.
49*	KPFSM	or Police & Fire Services Medal for Gallantry.
50	QPM	
51	QFSM	
*	DCM	(if for Royal West African Frontier Force), Distinguished Conduct Medal.

*	DCM	(if for the King's African Rifles), Distinguished Conduct Medal.
52*	IDSM	Indian Distinguished Service Medal.
53*	BGM	Burma Gallantry Medal.
54	DSM	Distinguished Service Medal.
55	MM	Military Medal.
56	DFM	Distinguished Flying Medal.
57	AFM	Air Force Medal.
58	SGM	Medal for Saving Life at Sea (Sea Gallantry Medal).
*	IOM	(if in Civil Division), Indian Order of Merit.
59*	EGM	Empire Gallantry Medal (usable only in reference to pre-1940 honorary awards unexchangeable for the GC)
60	CPM	Colonial Police Medal for Gallantry.
61	QGM	Queen's Gallantry Medal.
62	QSM	Queen's Service Medal (NZ only).
63	BEM	British Empire Medal, for Gallantry, or the British Empire Medal.
64*	CM	(or for French speakers M du C, Medaille du Canada), Canada Medal.
*	KPM	See 48–51 above, but for distinguished or good service.
*	KPFSM	
	QPM	
	QFSM	
65*	MSM	(but only if awarded for Naval service prior to 20 July 1928), Medal for Meritorious Service.
66	ERD	Emergency Reserve Decoration (Army).
67	*VD	Volunteer Officers' Decoration (1892–1908); for India and the Colonies (1894–1930) and the Colonial Auxiliary Forces Officers' Decoration (1899–1930).
68	TD	(for either the obsolescent Territorial Decoration (1908–30) or for the current Efficiency Decoration

(inst. 1930) when awarded to an officer of the (*Home*) Auxiliary Military Forces and the TAVR (inst. 1969)).

69	ED	(if for the current Efficiency Decoration (inst. 1930) when awarded to an officer of *Commonwealth* or Colonial Auxiliary Military Forces).
70	RD	Decoration for Officers of the Royal Naval Reserve.
71*	VRD	Decoration for Officers of the Royal Naval Volunteer Reserve.
72	CD	Canadian Forces Decoration.

* This distinction is no longer awarded, but there are surviving recipients.

Any of the above post nominal letters precede any others which may relate to academic honours or professional qualifications. The unique exception is that the abbreviation 'Bt.' (or less favoured 'Bart.'), indicating a Baronetcy, should be put before *all* other letters, e.g. The Rt Hon Sir John Smyth, Bt., VC, MC.

The abbreviation PC (indicating membership of the Privy Council), which used to be placed after KG, is now not to be used, except possibly with peers, because in their case the style 'Rt Hon' cannot be used to indicate membership of the Privy Council, since Barons, Viscounts and Earls already enjoy this style *ipso facto* and Marquesses and Dukes have the superior styles 'Most Hon' and 'Most Noble' respectively.

Obsolete post nominal letters include: KP Knight of St Patrick; KB Knight of the Bath (prior to its division into 3 classes in 1815); GCH, KCH and KH Knights Grand Cross, Knight Commanders or Knights of the Order of the Guelphs (1815–1837); KSI Knights of the Star of India (1861–1866); CSC Conspicuous Service Cross (1901–1914); AM Albert Medal; EM Edward Medal; VD Volunteer Decoration.

UK Economics

British Isles – Progressive populations for Great Britain and Ireland combined

Date	Estimate
c. 400 000 BC	200
c. 250 000 BC	1000
12 000 BC	3000
2000 BC	50 000
1000 BC	100 000
200 BC	500 000
AD 43	800 000
600	900 000
1068[1]	2 250 000
1348[2]	5 000 000
1355	3 500 000
1500	5 500 000
1600[3]	6 250 000
1650	7 500 000
1700	9 250 000
1750	10 000 000
1800	16 000 000

[1] Partly on the evidence of the Domesday Book.
[2] Prior to onset of the Black Death.
[3] Of which 4 811 000 in English parishes.

Expectation of life

(Average expectation at birth)

	Male	Female
1900	46	50
1910	52	55
1920	56	60
1930	59	63
1938	61	66
1950	66	72
1958	68	74
1961	67·9	73·8
1971	68·8	75·0
1981	70·8	76·8
1984	71·5	77·4

Decennial Censuses*

Date	Total
1801	11 944 000
1811	13 368 000
1821	15 472 000
1831	17 835 000
1841	20 183 000
1851	22 259 000
1861	24 525 000
1871	27 431 000
1881	31 015 000
1891	34 264 000
1901	38 237 000
1911	42 082 000
1921	44 027 000
1931	46 038 000
1951	50 225 000
1961	52 676 000
1971	55 515 000
1981	55 633 683

* These figures are in respect of the United Kingdom (i.e. the figures for the present area of the Republic of Ireland are excluded). The 1921 and 1931 figures for Northern Ireland are estimates only but were based on censuses subsequently held in 1926 and 1937 respectively.

Birth and Death Rates – Rates for 1000 of population

	1871	1901	1911	1921	1931	1951	1961	1971	1981	1985	1986
Birth Rate	35·0	28·6	24·6	23·1	16·3	15·7	17·9	16·1	13·0	13·3	13·3
Death Rate	22·1	17·3	14·1	12·7	12·2	12·6	12·0	11·5	11·7	11·8	11·6
Rate of Natural Increase	12·9	11·3	10·5	10·4	4·1	3·1	5·9	4·6	1·3	1·5	1·7
Illegitimacy	60	43	45	48	48	48	57	82	125	189	210

National Employment and Unemployment

	Working Population (Thousands)	Unemployment Excluding School Leavers and Students	Percentage Rate		Working Population (Thousands)	Unemployment Excluding School Leavers and Students	Percentage Rate
1965	25 504	338 200	1·4%	1978	26 433	1 375 700	5·2%
1970	25 293	602 000	2·6%	1979	26 443	1 307 300	4·9%
1971	25 124	775 800	3·4%	1980	26 324	1 667 600	6·3%
1972	25 234	855 000	3·7%	1981	26 079	2 464 300	9·4%
1973	25 578	611 000	2·6%	1982	23 373	2 687 900	11·5%
1974	25 515	600 100	2·6%	1983	24 013	3 025 700	12·6%
1975	25 665	929 000	3·6%	1984	24 108	3 013 600	12·5%
1976	25 886	1 273 500	4·9%	1985 (Mar)	24 204	3 146 600	13·0%
1977	26 310	1 378 200	5·2%				

Strikes

	Working Days Lost	Workers Involved
1960	3 024 000	814 000
1965	2 933 000	867 800
1970	10 980 000	1 793 000
1973	7 197 000	1 513 000
1974	14 750 000	1 622 000
1975	6 012 000	789 000
1976	3 284 000	666 000
1977	10 142 000	1 155 000
1978	9 405 000	1 001 000
1979	29 116 000	4 432 000
1980	11 910 000	789 400
1981	4 266 000	1 513 000
1982	5 313 000	2 103 000
1983	3 754 000	574 000
1984	27 135 000	1 391 000
1985	6 402 000	791 000
1986	1 920 000	720 000

Standard of living – in 21·31 mil. households

	1983
TV (Colour 81%)	98%
Refrigerator	94%
Washing machine	80%
Telephone	77%
Central heating	64%
Car	43% with one, 16% with two or more, 59% with one or more

Average from Weekly Earnings mid-1984 — £159·3 (£8,183 p.a.)

[1] There were 16 401 000 cars in Britain by Dec. 1984 of which 47% were foreign made

Distribution of work force of the UK as at June 1983

Agriculture, forestry and fishing	349 000
Energy and water supply industries	662 000
Extractive industries, metal and mineral products and chemicals	821 000
Metal goods, engineering and vehicles	2 651 000
Other manufacturing industries	2 170 000
Construction	1 016 000
Distribution, hotels, catering and repairs	4 209 000
Transport and communication	1 332 000
Banking, finance, insurance, business services and leasing	1 837 000
Other services	6 164 000
All industries and Services	**21 210 000**
Self-employed	2 199 000
Public corporations	1 700 000
Central and local government	5 200 000
Total employed labour force	**23 700 000**

The United Kingdom's National Debt

The National Debt is the nominal amount of outstanding debt chargeable on the Consolidated Fund of the United Kingdom Exchequer only, i.e. the debt created by the separate Northern Ireland Exchequer is excluded.

The National Debt became a permanent feature of the country's economy as early as 1692. The table below shows how the net total Debt has increased over the years (data being for 31 March of year shown):

Year	National Debt (£ million)	Year	National Debt (£ million)
1697	14	1910	713·2
1727	52	1914	649·8
1756	75	1915	1 105·0
1763	133	1916	2 133·1
1775	127	1917	4 011·4
1781	187	1918	5 871·9
1784	243	1919	7 434·9
1793	245	1920[1]	7 828·8
1802	523	1921	7 574·4
1815	834	1923	7 742·2
1828	800	1931	7 413·3
1836	832	1934	7 822·3
1840	827	1935[2]	6 763·9
1854	802	1936	6 759·3
1855	789	1937	6 764·7
1857	837	1938	6 993·7
1860	799	1939	7 130·8
1899	635	1940	7 899·2
1900	628·9	1941	10 366·4
1903	770·8	1942	13 041·1
1909	702·7	1943	15 822·6

Year	National Debt (£ million)	Year	National Debt (£ million)
1944	18 562·2	1965	30 440
1945	21 365·9	1966	31 340
1946	23 636·5	1967	31 985
1947	25 630·6	1968	34 193
1948	25 620·8	1969	33 984
1949	25 167·6	1970	33 079
1950	25 802·3	1971	33 441
1951	25 921·6	1972	35 839
1952	25 890·5	1973	36 884
1953	26 051·2	1974	40 124
1954	26 538	1975	45 886
1955	26 933	1976	56 577
1956	27 038	1977	54 041
1957	27 007	1978	79 000
1958	27 232	1979	82 597
1959	27 376	1980	91 245
1960	27 732	1981	112 780
1961	28 251	1982	117 959
1962	28 674	1983	127 072
1963	29 847	1984	142 545
1964	30 226	1985	158 101

[1] Beginning 1920, total excludes bonds tendered for death duties and held by the National Debt Commissioner.
[2] Beginning 1935, total excludes external debt, then £1036·5 million, arising out of the 1914–18 war.

Balance of Payments

(Expressed in £, million)

	Visible Exports	Visible Imports	Visible Balance	Invisible Balance	Current Balance (− Deficit + surplus)
1965	4848	5071	−223	+198	−27
1970	8121	8163	−42	+818	+776
1971	9060	8799	+261	+889	+1150
1972	9450	10 172	−722	+930	+208
1973	12 115	14 498	−2383	+1508	−875
1974	16 538	21 773	−5235	+1928	−3307
1975	19 463	22 699	−3236	+1615	−1621
1976	25 441	29 012	−3601	+2759	−842

(Expressed in £, million)

	Visible Exports	Visible Imports	Visible Balance	Invisible Balance	Current Balance (− Deficit + surplus)
1977	32 148	33 892	−1744	+2037	+293
1978	35 432	36 607	−1175	+2207	+1032
1979	40 678	44 136	−3458	+2595	−863
1980	47 389	46 211	+1178	+2028	+3206
1981	50 977	47 325	+3652	+3620	+7272
1982	55 565	53 181	+2384	+3167	+5551
1983	60 658	61 158	−500	+2549	+2049
1984	[1]70 377	74 632	−4255	+4879	+624

[1] Provisional.

Internal purchasing power of the £

The worth of the £ at various periods compared with its worth in mid 1985 may be regarded thus:

1870	£1	worth	£26·76
1886	£1	worth	£36·51
1896	£1	worth	£35·30
1909	£1	worth	£31·66
1925	£1	worth	£17·17
1931	£1	worth	£23·65
1949	£1	worth	£12·30
1957	£1	worth	£8·00
1967	£1	worth	£6·99
1970	£1	worth	£5·35
1976	£1	worth	£2·76
1977	£1	worth	£2·31
1978	£1	worth	£1·92
1979	£1	worth	£1·68
1980	£1	worth	£1·40
1985 (mid)	£1	worth	£1·00

Sterling – US Dollar Exchange Rates

$4·50–$5·00	Post War of Independence	1776
$12·00	All-time Peak (Civil War)	1864
$4·86 21/32	Fixed parity	1880–1914
$4·76 7/16	Pegged rate World War I	Dec. 1916
$3·40	Low point after £ floated, 19 May 1919	Feb. 1920
$4·86 21/32	Britain's return to gold standard	28 Apr. 1925
$3·14½	Low point after Britain forced off Gold Standard (20 Sept. 1931 [$3·43])	Nov. 1932
$5·20	High point during floating period	Mar. 1934
$4·03	Fixed rate World War II	4 Sept. 1939
$2·80	First post-war devaluation	18 Sept. 1949
$2·40	Second post-war devaluation	20 Nov. 1967
$2·42	Convertibility of US dollar into gold was suspended on	15 Aug. 1971
$2·58	£ Refloated	22 June 1972
$1·99	£ broke $2 barrier	5 Mar. 1976
$1·56	£ at new all-time low	28 Oct. 1976
$1·76	Bank of England buying pounds	10 Oct. 1977
$2·00	£ breaks back to $2 level (1978 av. $1·91)	15 Aug. 1978
$2·26	Dollar weakens	June 1979
$2·19	Iranian crisis unresolved	8 Dec. 1979
$1·99	£ again falls below $2	3 June 1981
$1·90	One year of 'Reaganomics'	20 Jan. 1982
$1·04	Strength of dollar against all currencies	6 Mar. 1985
$1·21	Recovery after Ohio Bank anxiety	11 Apr. 1985

Imports

Principal Imports into the UK (1984)	£ millions c.i.f.*
Petroleum, petroleum products and related materials	8078·4
Road vehicles (including air cushion vehicles)	5958·3
Office machines and automatic data processing equipment	4112·3
Electrical machinery, apparatus and appliances and electrical parts thereof	3848·1
Miscellaneous manufactured articles	3235·1
Textile yarn, fabrics, made-up articles and related products	2706·2
Paper, paperboard and articles of paper pulp, of paper or of paperboard	2281·5
Non-metallic mineral manufactures	2269·2
General industrial machinery and equipment and machine parts	2249·7
Coal, coke, gas and electric current	2114·2
Machinery specialised for particular industries	2072·0
Articles of apparel and clothing accessories	2013·1
Non-ferrous metals	1996·6
Vegetables and fruit	1931·1
Organic chemicals	1874·4
Telecommunications and sound recording and reproducing apparatus and equipment	1848·6
Power generating machinery and equipment	1782·6
Artificial resins and plastic materials, and cellulose ester and ethers	1609·6
Professional scientific and controlling instruments and apparatus	1592·8
Iron and steel	1487·2
Manufactures of metal	1385·2
Other transport equipment	1362·7
Metalliferous ores and metal scrap	1344·2
Meat and meat preparations	1342·4

Exports

Principal Exports from the UK (1984)	f.o.b.*
Petroleum, petroleum products and related materials	14 909·8
Road vehicles (including air cushion vehicles)	3311·9
Office machines and automatic data processing equipment	3046·2
Miscellaneous manufactured articles	2921·4
Electrical machinery, apparatus and appliances and electrical parts thereof	2804·9
Other transport equipment	2763·9
Power generating machinery and equipment	2686·4
Machinery specialised for particular industries	2678·6
General industrial machinery and equipment and machine parts	2572·1
Organic chemicals	2381·7
Non-metallic mineral manufactures	2298·7
Commodities and transactions not specified elsewhere	1795·3
Professional, scientific and controlling instruments and apparatus	1778·7
Non-ferrous metals	1656·6
Iron and steel	1529·1
Textile yarn, fabrics, made up articles and related products	1484·8
Manufactures of metal	1464·6
Medicinal and pharmaceutical products	1222·4
Chemical materials and products, not elsewhere specified	1183·7
Artificial resins and plastic materials and cellulose esters and ethers	1179·9
Beverages	1157·0
Telecommunications and sound recording and reproducing apparatus and equipment	1117·1
Articles of apparel and clothing accessories	996·4

* c.i.f., cost, insurance and freight. f.o.b., free on board.

25 Top Nations – Imports into UK: (1984)

	£ million	% of total UK imports
West Germany	1 090·2	14·1
United States	9489·8	12·1
Netherlands	6147·3	7·8
France	5885·7	7·5
Norway	3852·7	4·9
Italy	3814·2	4·8
Japan	3768·0	4·8
Belgium & Luxemburg	3691·8	4·7
Irish Republic	2635·0	3·3
Switzerland	2490·6	3·2
Sweden	2416·4	3·1
Spain	1667·4	2·1
Denmark	1660·4	2·1
Canada	1617·5	2·1
Hong Kong	1267·0	1·6
Finland	1248·6	1·6
Soviet Union	854·3	1·1
South Africa	725·6	0·9
Portugal	644·5	0·8
Brazil	637·7	0·8
Australia	612·1	0·8
Taiwan	585·2	0·7
India	571·5	0·7
Saudi Arabia	545·1	0·7
Austria	529·6	0·7

25 Top Nations – Exports from UK: (1984)

	£ million	% of total exports
United States	10 225·8	14·5
West Germany	7458·0	10·6
France	7082·4	10·0
Netherlands	6128·0	8·7
Irish Republic	3393·5	4·8
Belgium & Luxemburg	3051·7	4·3
Italy	2902·7	4·1
Sweden	2888·6	4·1
Switzerland	1549·5	2·2
Saudi Arabia	1387·2	2·0
Spain	1322·4	1·9
South Africa	1205·1	1·7
Denmark	1197·4	1·7
Australia	1186·5	1·7
Canada	1183·2	1·7
Norway	968·4	1·4
Japan	925·3	1·3
Hong Kong	897·4	1·3
India	781·0	1·1
Nigeria	768·5	1·1
Soviet Union	735·2	1·0
Iran	703·1	1·0
Finland	684·5	1·0
Singapore	556·4	0·8
Egypt	427·7	0·6

GROSS NATIONAL PRODUCT

The economic power of a nation is reflected in its Gross National Product (GNP) and its National Income.

Gross National Product is derived from Gross Domestic Product at factor cost plus net property income from overseas. National Income is GNP less capital consumption.

Gross Domestic Product at factor cost can be determined in two ways, (A) by the expenditure generating it, or (B) the incomes, rent and profits which enable the expenditure. The components in any year are thus:

A	B
Consumers' expenditure	Income from employment
Public authority current spending	Income from self-employment
Gross fixed capital formation	Gross trading profits of companies
Value of work in progress	Gross profits and surpluses of public corporations
Value of physical increase in stocks	Rent *less* stock appreciation
Exports *less* imports	
Income from abroad *less* payments abroad	
Subsidies *less* taxes on expenditure	
= Gross Domestic Product	= Gross Domestic Product

MINIMUM LENDING RATE

The Bank Rate was maintained at its record low level of 2 per cent for 12 years 13 days from 26 Oct. 1939 to 7 Nov. 1951, throughout World War II and the post-war period of the Cheap Money Policy under the Attlee government. The only previous occasion that such a low rate had been available was in 1852.

On 13 Oct. 1972 the Bank Rate was more descriptively named Bank of England Minimum Lending Rate when standing at 7¼ per cent. On 13 Nov. 1973 the MLR attained its then all-time peak of 13 per cent with the Arab Oil Price crisis. The devaluation crisis of October 1976 produced a new record rate of 15 per cent. By 14 Oct. 1977 this had subsided to 5 per cent. On 25 May 1978 MLR was fixed by administrative decision. By 8 Feb. 1979 it was back up to 14%. An all-time record of 17% was announced on 15 Nov. 1979. On 20 Aug. 1981 MLR was discontinued and was for practical purposes replaced by the London Clearing Banks base rate.

AVERAGE WEEKLY HOUSEHOLD EXPENDITURE

The average household weekly income in 1983 was £142·59. The breakdown of the average expenditure was as follows:

Food	29·56
Housing	23·99
Transport and vehicles	20·96
Services	16·09
Other Goods	10·81
Durable household goods	10·26
Clothing and footwear	10·00
Fuel, light and power	9·22
Alcoholic drink	6·91
Tobacco	4·21
Miscellaneous	0·58

The Judicial System

The supreme judicial court for the United Kingdom is the House of Lords as an ultimate court of appeal from all courts, except the Scottish criminal courts. Leave to appeal to it is not as of right and is usually reserved for important points of law. The work is executed by the Lord High Chancellor and nine Lords of Appeal in Ordinary. Only one case in 40,000 ever reaches them.

The Supreme Court of Judicature consists of the Court of Appeal under the Master of the Rolls and 21 Lord Justices of Appeal and The High Court of Justice with (a) the Chancery Division with 13 judges (b) the Queen's Bench Division under the Lord Chief Justice of England and 49 judges (c) the Court of Appeal (Criminal Division) with all the foregoing judges excepting the Chancery Division judges (d) the Family Division with a President and currently 13 male and 3 female judges.

On 1 January 1972 the Crown Court replaced Assizes and Quarter Sessions. Under the Courts Service, First tier centres deal with both civil and criminal cases and Second tier centres with only criminal cases. Both are served by High Court (see above) and Circuit Judges. Third tier centres deal with criminal cases only but are served by Circuit Judges only. There are six circuits in England and Wales viz.

Northern Circuit	(46 Judges)
North Eastern Circuit	(40 Judges)
Midland and Oxford	(52 Judges)
Wales and Chester	(22 Judges)
South Eastern Circuit	(181 Judges)
Western Circuit	(31 Judges)

There are in addition 422 Recorders.

Major urban areas have courts presided over by whole-time salaried magistrates known as Stipendiaries thus –
London
Bow Street (Chief Metropolitan Stipendiary and

Public expenditure
£s million cash

Programme	1978–79	1979–80	1980–81	1981–82	1982–83	1983–84	1984–85
Social security	16 934	20 006	24 145	29 435	33 440	36 431	38 391
Health and personal social services	9 227	11 057	14 084	15 817	17 179	18 283	19 217
Education and science, arts and libraries	9 856	11 372	13 837	15 100	16 181	17 009	16 600
Housing	4 503	5 665	5 687	4 193	3 762	3 912	3 604
Environmental services	2 818	3 362	3 875	3 957	4 469	4 812	4 452
Transport	3 263	3 962	4 773	5 146	5 309	5 547	5 324
Employment services	981	1 159	1 842	2 152	2 252	2 762	3 009
Law, order, and protective services	2 438	3 076	3 780	4 434	4 937	5 519	5 806
Defence, overseas aid, and other overseas services	9 342	11 304	12 793	14 289	16 571	18 010	19 314
Other expenditure on programmes	6 391	6 958	8 210	10 075	9 767	9 443	9 784
Total public expenditure on programmes	65 752	77 921	93 028	104 597	113 865	121 728	125 503
Of which, expenditure by local authorities	17 995	21 613	25 103	26 690	29 232	32 780	32 127

Income, Expenditure and Savings

	Population Mid-Year Thousands	Gross National Product GNP (at factor cost) £ millions	Total Personal Income Pre-tax £ millions	Real Personal Disposable Income at 1980 prices £ millions	Consumer Expenditure at prices current £ millions	Personal Saving as % of Disposable Income
1955	51 199	£17 240	£15 609	£79 708	£13 177	3·9
1960	52 508	£23 097	£21 324	£94 453	£17 124	7·3
1965	54 218	£31 934	£30 581	£110 942	£23 110	9·8
1970	55 421	£44 528	£43 853	£122 845	£31 935	9·8
1975	55 900	£96 575	£97 239	£143 924	£65 216	13·3
1976	55 886	£115 154	£112 401	£143 146	£75 712	12·6
1977	55 852	£129 226	£125 573	£140 943	£86 537	11·6
1978	55 836	£149 291	£144 138	£151 197	£99 486	13·1
1979	55 883	£171 999	£170 605	£159 821	£117 912	14·1
1980	55 901	£199 156	£201 118	£161 364	£136 789	15·2
1981	55 671	£219 076	£220 912	£158 106	£152 125	13·5
1982	56 258	£236 924	£240 868	£158 554	£166 477	12·9
1983	56 376	£259 437	£258 360	£161 578	£182 427	10·9

4 Stipendiaries); Camberwell Green (4); Clerkenwell (3); Greenwich and Woolwich (3); Highbury Corner (4); Horseferry Road (3); Marlborough Street (2); Marylebone (4); Old Street (2); South Western (3); Thames (2); Tower Bridge (3); Wells Street (4); West London (2).

Other Stipendiaries operate in Kingston-upon-Hull, Leeds, Greater Manchester, Merseyside, Merthyr Tydfil, Mid Glamorgan, South Glamorgan, South Yorkshire and West Midlands.

In Scotland the Court of Session (established 1532) has an Inner House of 8 Judges (in which the Lord President presides over the First Division and the Lord Justice Clerk over the Second Division) and an Outer House of 12 Judges. The country is divided into 6 Sheriffdoms, each with a Sheriff Principal, Sheriffs and Procurators Fiscal: these are Grampian, Highland and Islands; Tayside, Central and Fife; Lothian and Borders; Glasgow and Strathkelvin; North Strathclyde; and South Strathclyde and Dumfries and Galloway.

Criminal Statistics

ENGLAND AND WALES

Offences recorded by the Police – 1984

Offences	Number of Offences 1984
VIOLENCE AGAINST THE PERSON:	
Murder ⎫	
Manslaughter ⎬ Homicide	620
Infanticide ⎭	
Attempted murder	156
Threat or conspiracy to murder	836
Child destruction	Nil
Causing death by dangerous driving	222
Wounding or other act endangering life	5 276
Endangering railway passenger	40
Endangering life at sea	Nil
Other wounding, etc.	106 352
Assault	587
Abandoning child under two years	15
Child stealing	56

Procuring illegal abortion	1
Concealment of birth	24
SEXUAL OFFENCES:	
Homosexual offences	4 003
Rape	1 433
Indecent assault on a female	10 837
Incest	290
Procuration	102
Abduction	99
Bigamy	94
BURGLARY:	
Burglary in a dwelling	475 787
Burglary in a building other than a dwelling	415 078
ROBBERY:	
Robbery	24 890
THEFT AND HANDLING STOLEN GOODS:	
Theft from the person of another	30 107
Theft or unauthorised taking from mail	2 134
Theft from vehicle	454 943
Theft from shops	248 792
Theft or unauthorised taking of motor vehicle	344 806
Handling stolen goods	45 046
FRAUD AND FORGERY:	
Fraud and forgery	126 093
CRIMINAL DAMAGE:	
Arson	18 889
Criminal damage	478 264
OTHER OFFENCES:	
Blackmail	653
Kidnapping	131
High treason	Nil
Treason felony	Nil
Riot	5
Unlawful assembly	31
Other offence against the State or public order	778
Perjury	304
Criminal libel	3
Aiding suicide	11
Perverting the course of justice	331
Absconding from lawful custody	1 434

SCOTLAND

Crimes and Offences recorded by the Police – 1983

TOTAL CRIMES	448 260
NON-SEXUAL CRIMES OF VIOLENCE	13 025
Serious assault etc.	4 985
Handling offensive weapons	3 097
Robbery	4 170
Other	771
CRIMES OF INDECENCY	5 474
Sexual assault	1 262
Lewd and libidinous practices	2 450
Other	1 762
CRIMES OF DISHONESTY	342 452
Housebreaking	108 520
Theft by opening lockfast places	50 693
Theft of a motor vehicle	29 888
Shoplifting	24 041
Other theft	101 533
Fraud	17 317
Other	10 460
FIRE-RAISING, VANDALISM ETC.	73 060
Fire-raising	3 683
Vandalism etc.	69 377
OTHER CRIMES	14 251
Crimes against public justice	10 856
Drugs	3 227
Other	168
TOTAL OFFENCES	351 308
MISCELLANEOUS OFFENCES	114 807
Petty assault	30 329
Breach of the peace	51 305
Drunkenness	15 046
Other	18 127
MOTOR VEHICLE OFFENCES	236 501
Reckless and careless driving	25 352
Drunk driving	15 373
Speeding	37 674
Unlawful use of vehicle	90 710
Vehicle defect offences	29 412
Other	37 980

The 46 United Kingdom universities

There are 46 institutions of university or degree-giving status in the UK.
The list below is given in order of seniority of date of foundation, and the data run as follows: name, year of foundation, location, and population full-time as at 1 January 1984.

1. **The University of Oxford** 1249*
Oxford OX1 2JD
11 708
Colleges, Halls and Societies: University (1249), Balliol (1263), Merton (1264), Exeter (1314), Oriel (1326), Queen's (1340), New College (1379), Lincoln (1427), All Souls (1438), Magdalen (1458), Brasenose (1509), Corpus Christi (1517), Christ Church (1546), Trinity (1554), St John's (1555), Jesus (1571), Wadham (1612), Pembroke (1624), Worcester (1714), Hertford (1874), St Edmund Hall (1270), Keble (1868), St Catherine's (1962), Campion Hall (1962), St Benet's Hall (1947), St Peter's (1929), St Antony's (1950), Nuffield (1937), Linacre House (1962), Mansfield (1886), Regent's Park (1810), Greyfriars Hall (1910), St Cross (1965), and Wolfson (1965). Lady Margaret Hall (1878), Somerville (1879), St Hugh's (1886), St Hilda's (1893), St Anne's (1952) [originally 1893].

2. **The University of Cambridge** 1284*
Cambridge
11 598

Peterhouse (1284), Clare (1326), Pembroke (1347), Gonville and Caius (1348), Trinity Hall (1350), Corpus Christi (1352), King's (1441), Queen's (1448), St Catherine's (1473), Jesus (1496), Christ's (1505), St John's (1511), Magdalene (1542), Trinity (1546), Emmanuel (1584), Sidney Sussex (1596), Downing (1800), Selwyn (1882), Churchill (1960), Fitzwilliam House (1896), Girton (1869), Newnham (1871), Hughes Hall (1885), New Hall (1954).

3. **The University of St Andrews** 1411
St Andrews KY16 9AJ
3 454
Colleges: United College of St Salvator and St Leonard; College of St Mary; Queen's College, Dundee.

4. **The University of Glasgow** 1451
Gilmorehill, Glasgow G12 8QQ
10 043

5. **The University of Aberdeen** 1495
Aberdeen AB9 1FX
5 470

6. **The University of Edinburgh** 1583
South Bridge, Edinburgh EH8 9YL
9 866

7. **The University of Durham** 1832
Old Shire Hall, Durham DH1 3HP
4 704
Colleges: University, Hatfield, Grey, St Chad's, St John's, St Mary's, St Aidan's, Bede, St Hild's, Neville's Cross, St Cuthbert's Society, Van Mildert, Trevelyan, Collingwood, Ushaw, Graduate Society.

8. **The University of London** 1836
Greater London
40 764
Schools: Bedford College, Birkbeck College, Chelsea College, Imperial College of Science and Technology, King's College, London School of Economics, Queen Elizabeth College, Queen Mary College, Royal Holloway College, Royal Veterinary College, School of Oriental and African Studies, School of Pharmacy, University College, Westfield College, Wye College.
Medical Schools: Charing Cross Hospital, Guy's Hospital, King's College Hospital, The London Hospital, The Middlesex Hospital, Royal Dental Hospital of London, Royal Free Hospital, St Bartholomew's Hospital, St George's Hospital, St Mary's Hospital, St Thomas's Hospital, University College Hospital, Westminster Hospital, British post-graduate Medical Federation, London School of Hygiene and Tropical Medicine, Royal post-graduate Medical School, and

numerous post-graduate teaching hospitals; and various training colleges.

Institutes: Courtauld Institute of Art, Institute of Advanced Legal Studies, Institute of Archaeology, Institute of Classical Studies, Institute of Commonwealth Studies, Inter-collegiate Computer Science, Institute of Education, Institute of Germanic Studies, Institute of Historical Research, Institute of Latin American Studies, Institute of United States Studies, School of Slavonic and East European Studies, Warburg Institute, British Institute, Paris.

9. The University of Manchester[1] 1851
Oxford Road, Manchester M13 9PL
15 438

10. The University of Newcastle upon Tyne 1852
Newcastle upon Tyne NE1 7RU
7 538

11. The University of Wales 1893
see colleges
18 735
Colleges: Aberystwyth, Bangor, Cardiff, Swansea, National School of Medicine (Cardiff), Institute of Science and Technology (Cardiff), St David's College, Lampeter.

12. The University of Birmingham 1900
P.O. Box 363, Birmingham B15 2TT
8 736

13. The University of Liverpool 1903
P.O. Box 147, Liverpool L69 3BX
7 519

14. The University of Leeds 1904
Leeds LS2 9JT
10 569

15. The University of Sheffield 1905
Sheffield S10 2TN
7 648

16. The Queen's University of Belfast 1908
Belfast BT7 1NN
6 645
College: Magee University College (1865), Londonderry.

17. The University of Bristol 1909
Bristol BS8 1TH
6 907

18. The University of Reading 1926
London Road, Reading RG6 2AH
5 576

19. The University of Nottingham 1948
University Park, Nottingham NG7 2RD
6 829

20. The University of Southampton 1952
Southampton SO9 5NH
6 416

21. The University of Hull 1954
Kingston upon Hull HU6 7RX
5 025

22. The University of Exeter 1955
Exeter EX4 4QJ
4 758

23. The University of Leicester 1957
Leicester LE1 7RH
4 668

24. The University of Sussex 1961
Brighton BN1 9RH
4 360

25. The University of Keele 1962
Keele, Staffordshire ST5 5BG
2 729

26. The University of Strathclyde† 1964
George Street, Glasgow G1 1XQ
7 163

27. The University of East Anglia 1963
Norwich NR4 7TJ
4 031

28. The University of York 1963
Heslington, York YO1 5DD
3 338

29. The University of Lancaster 1964
Bailrigg, Lancaster LA1 4YW
4 438

30. The University of Essex 1964
Wivenhoe Park, Colchester CO4 3SQ
3 188

31. The University of Warwick 1965
Coventry CV4 7AL
5 377

32. The University of Kent 1965
Canterbury CT2 7NZ
4 159

33. New University of Ulster 1965
Coleraine, Co. Londonderry BT52 1SA, Northern Ireland
2 226

34. Heriot-Watt University 1966
Edinburgh EH14 4AS
3 185

35. Loughborough University of Technology 1966
Loughborough, Leicestershire LE11 3TU
5 232

36. The University of Aston in Birmingham 1966
Gosta Green, Birmingham B4 7ET
4 054

37. The City University 1966
London, EC1V 0NB
2 798

38. Brunel University 1966
Uxbridge UB8 3PH
2 654

39. University of Bath 1966
Claverton Down, Bath BA2 7AY
3 730

40. University of Bradford 1966
Bradford BD7 1DP
4 574

41. University of Surrey 1966
Guildford GU2 5XH
3 240

42. University of Salford 1967
Salford M5 4WT
3 835

43. University of Dundee 1967
Dundee DD1 4HN
3 198

44. University of Stirling 1967
Stirling FK9 4LA
2 470

45. The Open University 1969
Walton Hall, Milton Keynes MK7 6AA
76 140

46. University of Buckingham§ 1976
Buckingham MK18 1EG
518

* Year of foundation of oldest constituent college
† Formerly the Royal College of Science and Technology, founded 1796
‡ Tuition mainly by correspondence
§ Financed independently from the University Grants Committee and HM Treasury
[1] Includes Manchester Business School and Manchester Institute of Science and Technology
[2] Excludes short courses

Note: The Royal College of Art (1837) Kensington Gore, London (568 post graduates) and The Cranfield Institute of Technology (1969), Cranfield, Bedford (575 post graduates, 2500 short course students) grant degrees.

Basic educational statistics

ENGLAND AND WALES 1982/83

	Number of Schools	Number of Pupils	Number of Teachers	Pupil Teacher Ratio
PUBLIC SECTOR SCHOOLS				
Nursery	1 259	56 300	2 600	21·8
Primary	25 755	4 659 000	211 100	22·1
Secondary	5 437	4 493 600	277 000	16·2
NON-MAINTAINED SCHOOLS	2 637	583 400	47 800	12·2
SPECIAL SCHOOLS	1 989	142 200	19 400	7·3
ALL SCHOOLS	37 077	9 934 200	558 000	17·8

FURTHER EDUCATION (1982/3) (Excluding Universities)

	No. of Establishments	Course Enrolments[1]	Full-time Teachers[2]
Polytechnics	30	204 803	16 699
Other Major Establishments	563	1 685 637	75 301
Adult Education Centres	4 542	1 847 464	1 654

[1] All Modes of attendance
[2] Full-time only

SCOTLAND 1982/83

SCHOOLS	Number of Schools	Number of Pupils	Number of Teachers
Education Authority Nursery	537	34 700	700
Education Authority Primary	2 489	468 000	23 000
Education Authority Secondary	442	399 100	27 900
Education Authority Special	320	10 300	1 500
Grant Aided	55	17 900	1 200
All Schools	3 843	930 000	53 600

POST-SCHOOL	Number of Colleges	Number of Students	Number of Teachers
Colleges of Vocational Further Education	175		
Education Authority Colleges/Centres	161	206 800	7 100
Central Institutions	14		
Voluntary Bodies	—		
Colleges of Education	7	7 200	900

The 30 Polytechnics of England and Wales

City of Birmingham Polytechnic   1971
Perry Bar, Birmingham B42 2SU

Brighton Polytechnic   1970
Moulsecoomb, Brighton BN2 4AT

Bristol Polytechnic   1969
Coldharbour Lane, Frenchay, Bristol BS16 1QY

Polytechnic of Central London   1970
309 Regent Street, London W1R 8AL

City of London Polytechnic   1970
Admissions Office, 31 Jewry Street, London EC3N 2EY

Coventry Lanchester Polytechnic   1970
Priory Street, Coventry CV11 5FB

Hatfield Polytechnic   1970
P.O. Box 109, Hatfield, Herts AL10 9AB

Huddersfield Polytechnic   1970
Queensgate, Huddersfield HD1 3DH

Kingston Polytechnic   1970
Penrhyn Road, Kingston upon Thames, Surrey KT1 2EE

Leeds Polytechnic   1970
Calverley Street, Leeds LS1 3HE

Leicester Polytechnic   1969
P.O. Box 143, Leicester LE1 9BH

Liverpool Polytechnic   1970
Rodney House, 70 Mount Pleasant, Liverpool L3 5UX

Manchester Polytechnic   1970
All Saints, Manchester M15 6BH

Middlesex Polytechnic   1973
114 Chase Side, London N14 5PN

Newcastle upon Tyne Polytechnic   1969
Ellison Building, Ellison Place, Newcastle upon Tyne NE1 8ST

North East London Polytechnic   1970
Romford Road, London E15 4LZ

Polytechnic of North London   1971
Holloway Road, London N7 8DB

Oxford Polytechnic   1970
Gypsy Lane, Headington, Oxford OX3 0BP

Plymouth Polytechnic   1970
Drake Circus, Plymouth PL4 8AA

Portsmouth Polytechnic   1969
Museum Road, Portsmouth PO1 2QQ

Lancashire Polytechnic   1972
Corporation Street, Preston PR1 2TQ

Sheffield City Polytechnic   1969
Pond Street, Sheffield S1 1WB

South Bank Polytechnic   1970
Borough Road, London SE1 0AA

Sunderland Polytechnic   1969
Langham Tower, Ryhope Road, Sunderland SR2 7EE

North Staffordshire Polytechnic   1970
College Road, Stoke on Trent, Staffordshire ST4 2DE

Teesside Polytechnic   1970
Borough Road, Middlesbrough, Cleveland TS1 3BA

Thames Polytechnic   1970
Wellington Street, Woolwich, London SE18 6PF

Trent Polytechnic   1971
Burton Street, Nottingham NG1 4BU

The Polytechnic – Wolverhampton   1969
The Molineux, Molineux Street, Wolverhampton WV1 1SB

WALES
Polytechnic of Wales   1970
Llantwit Road, Treforest, Pontypridd, Mid-Glamorgan CF37 1DL

Countries of the World

NON-SOVEREIGN COUNTRIES
The trend towards full national sovereign status has substantially reduced the total number of non-sovereign territories. With a few obvious exceptions, these territories now tend to have too small a population and/or resources to sustain statehood.

The non-sovereign territories are divided below into four parts:
(*a*) Territories administered by the United Kingdom.
(*b*) Territories administered by Australia or New Zealand.
(*c*) Territories administered by the United States of America.
(*d*) Other non-sovereign territories.

TERRITORIES ADMINISTERED BY THE UNITED KINGDOM

(excluding the Channel Islands and the Isle of Man)

Anguilla

Location: Anguilla (with Scrub I. and other off-shore islands) lies about 5 miles *8 km* north of St Martin, in the Leeward Islands, West Indies. Sombrero I. lies about 30 miles *48 km* north of Anguilla.
Area: 37 miles² *96 km²* (Anguilla 35 miles² *91 km²*, Sombrero 2 miles² *5 km²*).

Population: 7000 (1984 estimate).
Capital: The Valley.

Bermuda

Location: The Bermudas (or Somers Islands) are a group of islands in the western North Atlantic Ocean, about 570 miles *917 km* east of Cape Hatteras in North Carolina, USA.
Area: 20·59 miles² *53,3 km²*.
Population: 54 893 (census of 12 May 1980); 57 145 (1985 estimate). 20 islands are inhabited.
Capital: Hamilton (population about 3000 in 1985), on Bermuda I.

British Antarctic Territory

Location: Comprises all the land south of latitude 60°S, situated between longitude 20°W and 80°W. This includes the South Shetland Islands, the South Orkney Islands, Graham Land and a part of the mainland of Antarctica.
Area: The total area within the sector is about 2 095 000 miles² *5 425 000 km²*, of which land (excluding ice-shelves) occupies about 150 000 miles² *388 498 km²*. The South Shetland Is. are about 130 miles² *336 km²* and the South Orkney Is. 240 miles² *621 km²*.
Population: There are no permanent inhabitants. The only occupants are scientific workers, of whom UK personnel number about 300.
Capital: There being no settlements, the Territory is administered from Stanley, Falkland Is. (*q.v.*).

British Indian Ocean Territory

Location: The territory is now confined to the Chagos Archipelago (or Oil Islands) which is 1180 miles *1899 km* north-east of (and formerly administered by) Mauritius. The islands of Aldabra, Farquhar and Desroches (originally parts of the territory) were restored to Seychelles when the latter became independent on 29 June 1976.
Area: about 20 miles² *52 km²*.
Population: The territory has a 'floating' population of contract labourers, but no permanent population.

British Virgin Islands

Location and Composition: Comprises the eastern part of the Virgin Islands group (the western part is a US colony), and lies to the east of Puerto Rico, in the West Indies.
Area: About 59 miles² *153 km²* (Tortola 21 miles² *54 km²*, Virgin Gorda 8¼ miles² *21 km²*, Anegada 16 miles² *39 km²*, Jost van Dyke 3¼ miles² *8 km²*).
Population: 12 034 in 1980 (Tortola 9322; Virgin Gorda 1443; Anegada 169; Jost van Dyke 136; other islands 82; marine population 220; institutional population 662).
Capital: Road Town (population 3976 in 1980); on Tortola.

Cayman Islands

Location: A group of three islands, in the Caribbean Sea, south of Cuba. The principal island, Grand Cayman, is 178 miles *286 km* west of Jamaica.
Area: approximately 100 miles² *259 km²* (Grand Cayman 76 miles² *197 km²*, Cayman Brac 14 miles² *36 km²*, Little Cayman 10 miles² *26 km²*).
Population: 16 677 (Grand Cayman 15 000, Cayman Brac 1607, Little Cayman 70) at census of 1 July 1979 20 300 (1985 estimate).
Capital: George Town (population 8900 in 1985).

Falkland Islands and Dependencies

Location: A group of islands in the south-western Atlantic Ocean, about 480 miles *772 km* north-east of Cape Horn, South America. The Dependencies are South Georgia, an island 800 miles *1287 km* to the east, and the South Sandwich Islands, 470 miles *756 km* south-east of South Georgia.
Area: approximately 6280 miles² *16 265 km²*, of which the Falklands are approximately 4700

miles² *12 173 km²* (East Falkland and adjacent islands 2610 miles² *6760 km²*, West Falkland, etc., 2090 miles² *5413 km²*). South Georgia is 1450 miles² *3755 km²* and the Sandwich Is. 130 miles² *336 km²*.
Population: Falkland Islands 1919 (census of 1986). South Goergia has a small population (22 residents in 1980) which is highest during the summer whaling season.
Capital: Port Stanley (population 1100 in 1984), on East Falkland.

City of Gibraltar

Location: A narrow peninsula on the south coast of Spain, commanding the north side of the Atlantic entrance to the Mediterranean Sea.
Area: 2·1 miles² *5,5 km²* (2¾ miles *4,4 km* long, greatest breadth nearly 1 mile *1,6 km*).
Population: 28 843 (1985 estimate).
Chief (and only) Town: Gibraltar, at north-western corner of the Rock.

Hong Kong

Location: A peninsula in the central south coast of the Guangdong (Kwangtung) province of southern China, the island of Hong Kong and some 235 other islands, the largest of which is Lantao (58 miles² *150 km²*).
Area: 409·2 miles² *1059,8 km²* (Hong Kong Island 30·1 miles² *78,0 km²*, Kowloon peninsula 4·1 miles² *10,5 km²*, Stonecutters Island ¼ mile² *0,6 km²*, New Territories (leased) 374·8 miles² *970,7 km²*). Including the ocean area within administrative boundaries, the total is 1126 miles² *2916 km²*.
Population: 5 431 200 (1986 estimate). About 98% are Chinese, many being British subjects by virtue of birth in the Colony.
Languages: Mainly Chinese (Cantonese); English 8·5%.
Religion: Predominantly Buddhist.
Capital City and Other Principal Towns (population at Census, 1976): Victoria (501 680), on Hong Kong Island; Kowloon; New Kowloon; North Point; Tsuen Wan; Cheung Chau (an island).
Status and Government: A Crown Colony with the Governor assisted by an Executive Council (16 in 1980) and a Legislative Council (47, including 26 elected, in 1980).
Recent History: British colony, 1841. New Territories leased in 1898 for 99 years. Attacked by Japan, 8 Dec. 1941. Surrendered, 25 Dec. 1941. Recaptured by UK forces, 30 Aug. 1945. UK military administration, 3 Sept. 1945 to May 1946. Formal Japanese surrender, 16 Sept. 1945. Many refugees during Chinese civil war 1948–50, and subsequently, notably on 1–25 May 1962.
Economic Situation: The principal occupations are manufacturing (notably cotton piece goods, shirts, electric products, cameras, toys and games, footwear); services and commerce. Agriculture (poultry and pigs), fishing and mining (notably iron) are carried on.
Currency: 100 cents = 1 Hong Kong dollar (£1 sterling = HK $ 9·431 at 26 April 1985).
Climate: The sub-tropical summer (28°C *82°F* July) is hot and humid with the winter cool and dry (15°C *59°F* February). The average annual rainfall is 2160 mm *85 in*, three-quarters of which falls from June to August in the south-west monsoon season.

Montserrat

Location: An island about 35 miles *56 km* north of Basse Terre, Guadeloupe, in the Leeward Islands, West Indies.
Area: 38 miles² *98 km²*.
Population: 11 698 (census of 7 Apr. 1970); 12 073 (census of 12 May 1980).
Capital: Plymouth (population 3200 in 1980), on south-west coast.

Pitcairn Islands Group

Location: Four islands in the south Pacific Ocean, about 3000 miles *4828 km* east of New Zealand and 3500 miles *5632 km* south-west of Panama: Pitcairn, Henderson, Ducie, Oeno.
Area: 18·5 miles² *48 km²*, including Pitcairn 1·75 miles² *4,5 km²*.
Population: Pitcairn 64 (1986 count).
Principal settlement: Adamstown.

St Christopher (St Kitts) and Nevis

Location: In the northern part of the Leeward Islands, in the West Indies. The main island is St Christopher (or St Kitts), with Nevis 3 miles *5 km* to the south-east.
Area: 101 miles² *262 km²* (St Christopher 65 miles² *168 km²*, Nevis 36 miles² *93 km²*).
Population: 44 404 in 1980.
Capital: Basse-terre (population 14 725 in 1980), on south coast of St Christopher.

St Helena and Dependencies

Location and Composition: An island in the South Atlantic Ocean, 1200 miles *1931 km* west of Africa. The dependencies are: (*a*) Ascension, an island 700 miles *1126 km* to the north-west; (*b*) the Tristan da Cunha group, comprising: Tristan da Cunha, 1320 miles *2124 km* south-west of St Helena; Inaccessible Island, 20 miles *32 km* west of Tristan; the three Nightingale Islands (Nightingale, Middle Island and Stoltenhoff Island), 20 miles *32 km* south of Tristan; Gough Island (Diego Alvarez), 220 miles *354 km* south of Tristan.
Area: 162 miles² *419 km²* (St Helena 47·3 miles² *122 km²*. Ascension 34 miles² *88 km²*, Tristan da Cunha 38 miles² *98 km²*. Gough 35 miles² *90 km²*, Inaccessible 4 miles² *10 km²*, Nightingale ¾ mile² *2 km²*).
Population: St Helena 5499 (1982); Ascension 1625; Tristan da Cunha 325.
Capital: Jamestown (population 1862 at 31 Dec. 1978).
Principal Settlements: Ascension – Georgetown (or Garrison); Tristan da Cunha – Edinburgh.

Turks and Caicos Islands

Location: Two groups of islands at the south-eastern end of the Bahamas, 120 miles *193 km* north of Hispaniola (Haiti and Dominican Republic), in the West Indies. There are over 30 islands, including eight Turks Islands.
Area: 166 miles² *430 km²*.
Population: 7436 (1980 census). There are six inhabited islands (two in the Turks Islands, four in the Caicos Islands).
Capital: Cockburn Town, on Grand Turk Island (population 2897 in 1978).

TERRITORIES ADMINISTERED BY AUSTRALIA OR NEW ZEALAND
Australian Dependencies

The Australian Antarctic Territory

Location: Comprises all land south of latitude 60°S, between 45°E and 160°E, except for French territory of Terre Adélie, whose boundaries were fixed on 1 Apr. 1938 as between 136°E and 142°E.
Area: 2 333 624 miles² *6 044 068 km²* of land and 29 251 miles² *75 759 km²* of ice shelf.

Location of Commonwealth and other non-sovereign Countries of the World

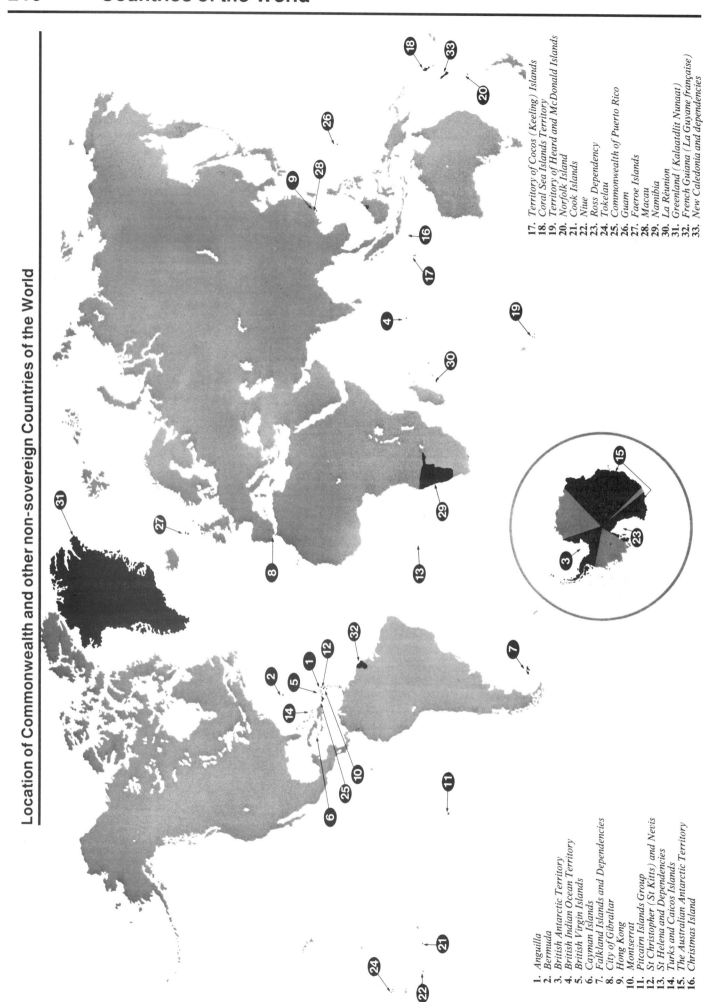

1. Anguilla
2. Bermuda
3. British Antarctic Territory
4. British Indian Ocean Territory
5. British Virgin Islands
6. Cayman Islands
7. Falkland Islands and Dependencies
8. City of Gibraltar
9. Hong Kong
10. Montserrat
11. Pitcairn Islands Group
12. St Christopher (St Kitts) and Nevis
13. St Helena and Dependencies
14. Turks and Caicos Islands
15. The Australian Antarctic Territory
16. Christmas Island

17. Territory of Cocos (Keeling) Islands
18. Coral Sea Islands Territory
19. Territory of Heard and McDonald Islands
20. Norfolk Island
21. Cook Islands
22. Niue
23. Ross Dependency
24. Tokelau
25. Commonwealth of Puerto Rico
26. Guam
27. Faeroe Islands
28. Macau
29. Namibia
30. La Réunion
31. Greenland (Kalaatdlit Nunaat)
32. French Guiana (La Guyane française)
33. New Caledonia and dependencies

Christmas Island

Location: In the Indian Ocean, 223 miles *360 km* south of Java Head.
Area: Approximately 52 miles² *135 km²*.
Population: 3214 (1983 estimate) (1967 Chinese, 800 Malays, 341 Europeans, 106 others).
Principal settlement: Flying Fish Cove.

Territory of Cocos (Keeling) Islands

Location: In the Indian Ocean, about 1720 miles *2768 km* north-west of Perth. The territory contains 27 islands. North Keeling Island lies about 15 miles *24 km* north of the main group.
Area: Approximately 5½ miles² *14 km²*.
Population: 579 (Home Island 363, West Island 216) at 30 June 1983.
Principal settlement: Bantam Village (on Home Island).

Coral Sea Islands Territory

Location: East of Queensland, between the Great Barrier Reef and 157° 10′ E longitude.
Population: 3 meteorologists on an island in the Willis Group.

Territory of Heard and MacDonald Islands

Location: In the southern Indian Ocean, south-east of the Kerguelen Islands, and about 2500 miles *4023 km* south-west of Fremantle.
Area: 113 miles² *292 km²*. No permanent inhabitants.

Norfolk Island

Location: In south-west Pacific Ocean 1042 miles *1676 km* from Sydney and about 400 miles *643 km* from New Zealand. Philip Island is about 4 miles *6 km* south of Norfolk Island.
Area: 13·34 miles² *34,55 km²*.
Population: 2175 (census of 30 June 1981). Figures include visitors. Philip Island and Nepean Island are uninhabited.
Seat of Government: Kingston.

New Zealand Dependencies

Cook Islands

Location: In the southern Pacific Ocean, between about 1750 miles *2816 km* and 2350 miles *3782 km* north-east of New Zealand, between 8°S and 23°S, and 156°W and 167°W. Comprises 15 atolls or islands (Northern group 7, Lower group 8).
Area: 90·3 miles² *234 km²*. Main islands are Rarotonga (16602 acres *6718 ha*), Mangaia (12800 acres *5180 ha*), Atiu (6654 acres *2693 ha*), Mitiaro (5500 acres *2226 ha*), Mauke (Parry Is.) (4552 acres *1842 ha*), Aitutaki (4461 acres *1805 ha*) and Penrhyn (Tongareva) (2432 acres *985 ha*).
Population: 17754 (1981); approx. 24500 Cook Islanders in New Zealand (1982).
Chief Town: Avarua, on Rarotonga Island.

Niue

Location: Niue Island is in the southern Pacific Ocean, 1343 miles *2161 km* north of Auckland, New Zealand, between Tonga and the Cook Islands.
Area: 64028 acres (100·04 miles² *259 km²*).
Population: 3298 (1981); approx. 10000 Niueans in New Zealand (1982).
Capital: Alofi.

Ross Dependency

Location: All the land between 160°E and 150°W longitude (moving eastward) and south of 60°S latitude, comprising a sector of the mainland of Antarctica, including the Ross Ice Shelf, and some off-shore islands.
Area: The mainland area is estimated at 160000 miles² *414400 km²* and the permanent ice shelf at 130000 miles² *336700 km²*.
Population: No permanent inhabitants, but some bases are permanently occupied by scientific personnel.

Tokelau

Location: Tokelau (formerly known as Tokelau Islands) consist of three atolls in the central Pacific Ocean, about 300 miles *483 km* north of Western Samoa.
Area: Approximately 2500 acres *1010 ha* (Nukunonu 1350 acres *545 ha*, Fakaofo 650 acres *260 ha*, Atafu 500 acres *200 ha*), or about 4 miles² *10 km²*.
Population: 1572 in 1981 (Nukunonu 368, Fakaofo 650, Atafu 554).

SOVEREIGN COUNTRIES
By 1985 there were 169 sovereign countries in the world. In this book the United Kingdom has been treated separately, and in the pages which follow, the salient details of the 168 other sovereign countries are given.

Afghanistan

Official name: De Afghanistan Democrateek

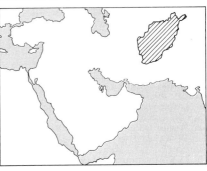

AFGHANISTAN

Jamhuriat (Pushtu) or Jamhuriat Democrateek ye Afghanistan (Dari): The Democratic Republic of Afghanistan.
Population: 15551358 (census of 23 June 1979); 17672000 (1984 estimate, including an estimated 2750000 nomads and about 5000000 Afghan refugees living in other countries).
Area: 250000 miles² *647497 km²*.
Languages: Dari (a Persian dialect), Pushtu (Pushtu or Pakhto).
Religion: Muslim.
Capital city: Kabul, population 1036407 (including suburbs) at 1982 estimate.
Other principal towns (1982): Qandahar (Kandahar) 191345; Herat 150497; Mazar-i-Sharif 110367; Jalalabad 57824; Kunduz 57824.
Highest point: Noshaq, 24581 ft *7492 m* (first climbed 17 Aug. 1960).
Principal mountain ranges: Hindu Kush, Koh-i-Baba, Band-i-Baian, Band-i-Baba, Paropamisus, Paghman.

Territories administered by the United States of America

Territory	Area (miles²)	Area (km²)	Population		Capital
North America					
Commonwealth of Puerto Rico	3435	*8897*	3187570	(1/4/80)	San Juan
Virgin Islands of the United States	133	*344*	95214	(1/4/80)	Charlotte Amalie
Oceania					
American Samoa	76	*197*	32395	(1/4/80)	Pago Pago
Guam	212	*549*	115756	(1984 estimate)	Agaña
Johnston and Sand Islands	<½	*1*	327	(1/4/80)	—
Midway Islands	2	*5*	453	(1/4/80)	—
Wake Island	3	*8*	300	(1/4/80)	—
Trust Territory of the Pacific Islands	687*	*1779**	116974	(1/4/80)	Saipan

* Inhabited dry land only.

Other non-sovereign territories

Territory	Administering Country	Area (miles²)	Area (km²)	Population		Capital
Europe						
Faeroe Islands	Denmark	540	*1399*	13951	(31/12/81)	Thorshavn
Svalbard and Jan Mayen Islands	Norway	24101	*62422*	4012	(31/12/82)*	Ny Ålesund
Asia						
Macao (or Macau)	Portugal	6	*16*	261680	(1981 census)	Macau
Africa						
French Southern and Antarctic Territories	France	2918	*7557*	168	(1983 estimate)	—
Mayotte†	France	144	*374*	47246	(1982 estimate)	Dzaoudzi
Namibia (South West Africa)‡	South Africa§	318261	*824292*	1039800	(1982 estimate)	Windhoek
La Réunion	France	969	*2510*	515814	(1982 census)	Saint-Denis
North America						
Greenland	Denmark	840000	*2175600*	51903	(1/1/83)	Godthåb (Nuuk)
St Pierre and Miquelon	France	93	*242*	6041	(1982 census)	St Pierre
Central America						
Guadeloupe and dependencies	France	687	*1779*	328400	(1982 census)	Pointe-à-Pitre
Martinique	France	425	*1102*	328566	(1982 census)	Fort-de-France
Netherlands Antilles	Netherlands	371	*961*	260000	(1981)	Willemstad
South America						
French Guiana	France	35000	*91000*	73022	(1982 census)	Cayenne
Oceania						
French Polynesia	France	c.1500	*c.4000*	148000	(1983 estimate)	Papeete
New Caledonia and dependencies	France	7358	*19058*	146600	(1983 estimate)	Nouméa
Wallis and Futuna Islands	France	77	*200*	11943	(1982 census)	Mata-Utu

* Inhabited only during winter season.
† Mayotte is part of the Comoros archipelago and is regarded by the Comoros government as part of its territory. However, since the Comoros declared independence in July 1975 the island of Mayotte has remained under French administration.
‡ Including data for Walvis Bay (area 434 miles² *1124 km²*, population 23461 in 1970), an integral part of South Africa.
§ South Africa's jurisdiction is disputed by the UN, which claims a protectorate over the territory.

Principal rivers: Helmand, Bandihala-Khoulm, Kabul, Murghab, Kunduz, Hari Rud, Farah Rud, Ab-i-Panja.
Head of State: Babrak Karmal (b. 1929), President of the Revolutionary Council and General Secretary of the Central Committee of the People's Democratic Party.
Prime Minister: Soltan Ali Keshtmand (b. 1935).
Climate: Wide variations between highlands and lowlands. Average annual rainfall 300 mm *12 in*. In Kabul, July (16°C *61°F* to 33°C *92°F*) and August (15°C *59°F* to 33°C *91°F*) hottest; Jan. (−8°C *18°F* to 2°C *36°F*) coldest; March rainiest (7 days). Maximum temperature up to 49°C *120°F*; minimum below −23°C *−10°F*.
Labour force: 3 868 081 (settled population only) aged 8 and over (1979 census): Agriculture, forestry and fishing 61·3%; Industry (mining, manufacturing, utilities) 12·8% (manufacturing 10·9%); Services 24·6%. Figures exclude persons seeking work for the first time.
Net material product: 94 billion afghanis in 1982–3 (1978 prices): Agriculture, Forestry and Fishing 68·8%; Mining and Manufacturing 13·8%; Trade 9·1%.
Exports: US$694·3 million in 1981: Natural gas 39·3%; Dried fruit and nuts 25·2%; Fresh fruit 7·3%; Raw cotton 3·3%.
Monetary unit: Afghani. 1 afghani = 100 puls (puli).
Denominations:
    Coins 25, 50 puls; 1, 2, 5 afghanis.
    Notes 10, 20, 50, 100, 500, 1000 afghanis.
Exchange rate to £ sterling: 99·2 (26 Jan. 1987).
Political history and government: Formerly an hereditary kingdom, under British influence until 1919. Afghanistan became a limited constitutional monarchy, without political parties, on 1 Oct. 1964. A bicameral parliament was inaugurated on 16 Oct. 1965. The last king was deposed by a military *coup* on 17 July 1973, when the Republic of Afghanistan was proclaimed, the constitution abrogated and parliament dissolved. The king abdicated on 24 Aug. 1973. Government was assumed by a 13-man Central Council of the Republic, led by Lt-Gen. Muhammad Da'ud, a former Prime Minister, who, became President. Da'ud was deposed and killed in another *coup* (known, from the month, as the 'Saur Revolution') on 27 Apr. 1978, when power was assumed by an Armed Forces Revolutionary Council (AFRC). On 30 Apr. 1978 the Democratic Republic of Afghanistan (DRA) was proclaimed and the AFRC incorporated into a new Revolutionary Council. Nur Muhammad Taraki, imprisoned leader of the formerly banned People's Democratic Party of Afghanistan (PDPA), was released and installed as President of the Revolutionary Council. The 1977 republican constitution was abolished. On 16 Sept. 1979 Taraki was overthrown and succeeded as President by the Prime Minister, Hafizullah Amin. On 27 Dec. 1979 Amin was deposed and killed in a Soviet-backed *coup*, supported by the entry into Afghanistan of thousands of USSR troops, which brought Babrak Karmal into office as Head of State. Since then opponents of the government have waged an inconclusive guerrilla war.

ALBANIA

A provisional constitution, 'Basic Principles of the DRA', was ratified by the PDPA on 13 April 1980 and by the Revolutionary Council on the following day. This provided for the establishment of a *Loya Jirgah* (National Assembly), to be directly elected by adult suffrage. Pending elections to the Assembly, supreme power was vested in the 57-member Revolutionaty Council. This body rules by decree and appoints the Council of Ministers. Political power is held by the Central Committee of the pro-Communist PDPA.
Afghanistan has 26 provinces, each administered by an appointed governor.
Length of roadways: 11 652 miles *18 752 km* (31 Dec. 1978).
Universities: 2.
Adult illiteracy: 80% (1982 estimate).
Expectation of life: Males 39·9 years; females 40·7 years (UN estimates for 1970–75).
Defence: Military service two years; total armed forces 47 000 (1985 estimate); defence expenditure: 28·4% of total government expenditure in 1979–80.
Foreign tourists: 9200 in 1981.

Albania

Official name: Republika Popullore Socialiste e Shqipërisë (Socialist People's Republic of Albania).
Population: 2 591 000 (census of Jan. 1979); 2 899 000 (estimate for 1984).
Area: 11 100 miles² *28 748 km²*.
Language: Albanian.
Religions: Muslim; eastern Orthodox; Roman Catholic (religious activity is officially forbidden).
Capital city: Tiranë (Tirana), population 206 100 (estimate for 1983).
Other principal towns (1983): Shkodër (Scutari) 71 200; Durrës (Durazzo) 72 400; Vlorë (Valona) 61 100; Elbasan 69 900; Korçë (Koritsa) 57 100; Berat 36 600; Fier 37 000.
Highest point: Mount Korabi, 9028 ft *2751 m*.
Principal mountain ranges: Albanian Alps, section of the Dinaric Alps.
Principal rivers: Semani (157 miles *253 km*), Drini (174 miles *280 km*), Vjosa (147 miles *236 km*), Mati (65 miles *105 km*), Shkumbini (91 miles *146 km*).
Head of State: Ramiz Alia, President of the Presidium of the People's Assembly.
Head of Government: Adil Çarçani, Chairman of the Council of Ministers.
Climate: Mild, wet winters and dry, hot summers along coast; rainier and colder inland. Maximum temperature 45·3°C *113·5°F*, Lezhe, 23 Aug. 1939; minimum −25,0°C *−13·0°F*, Voskopje, 29 Jan. 1942.
Labour force: 1 286 000 (1984 estimate): Agriculture, forestry and fishing 57·8%.
Gross national product: $1930 million in 1978 (World Bank estimate).
Exports: 2996 million old leks (299·6 million new leks) in 1964: Foodstuff 23·1%; Fuels, minerals and metals 54·2%.
Monetary unit: Lek. 1 lek = 100 qindarka (qintars).
Denominations:
    Coins 5, 10, 20, 50 qintars; 1 lek.
    Notes 1, 3, 5, 10, 25, 50 and 100 leks.
Exchange rate to £ sterling: 10·19 (26 Jan. 1987).
Political history and government: Formerly part of Turkey's Ottoman Empire. On 28 Nov. 1912 a group of Albanians established a provisional government and declared the country's independence. Albania was occupied by Italy in 1914 but its independence was re-established in 1920. A republic was proclaimed on 22 Jan. 1925 and Ahmet Beg Zogu was elected President. He was proclaimed King Zog on 1 Sept. 1928 and reigned until invading Italian forces occupied Albania on 7 April 1939. Italian rule ended in 1943 but German forces then occupied Albania. After they withdrew a provisional government was established in October 1944. The Communist-led National Liberation Front, a wartime resistance group, took power on 29 Nov. 1944. A Communist-dominated assembly

was elected on 2 Dec. 1945. This body proclaimed the People's Republic of Albania on 12 Jan. 1946. The new régime's first constitution was adopted in March 1946. The Communist Party was renamed the Albanian Party of Labour (APL) in 1948. A new constitution, introducing the country's present name, was adopted by the People's Assembly on 27 Dec. 1976. In April 1985 Enver Hoxha, who had led Albania since the Second World War, died. At the time of his death he was the world's longest serving head of state.
The supreme organ of state power is the unicameral People's Assembly, with 250 members elected for four years by universal adult suffrage. The assembly elects a Presidium (13 members) to be its permanent organ. Executive and administrative authority is held by the Council of Ministers, elected by the Assembly.
Political power is held by the APL (or Worker's Party), the only permitted political party, which dominates the Democratic Front. The Front presents a single list of approved candidates for elections to all representative bodies. The APL's highest authority is the Party Congress, convened every five years. The Congress elects a Central Committee (88 full members and 40 candidate members were elected on 7 Nov. 1981) to supervize Party work. To direct its policy the Committee elects a Political Bureau (Politburo), with 13 full and five candidate members.
For local government Albania is divided into 26 districts, each with a People's Council elected for three years.
Length of roadways: 1926 miles *3100 km*.
Length of railways: 253·6 miles *408 km*.
Universities: 1.
Adult illiteracy: 28·5% (males 20·1%; females 36·9%) in 1955 (population aged 9 and over).
Expectation of life: Males 67·0 years; females 69·9 years (UN estimates for 1970–75).
Defence: Military service: Army two years, Air Force, Navy and special units three years; total armed forces 40 400 (20 000 conscripts) in 1985; defence expenditure: 18·5% of total government expenditure in 1985.
Foreign tourists: about 6000 each year.

Algeria

Offical name: El Djemhouria El Djazaïria Demokratia Echaabia, or la République algérienne démocratique et populaire (the Democratic and Popular Republic of Algeria).
Population: 20 499 277 (1983 estimate) plus about 800 000 nationals living abroad.
Area: 919 595 miles² *2 381 741 km²*.
Languages: Arabic; Berber; French.
Religion: Muslim.
Capital city: El Djazaïr or Alger (Algiers), population 1 721 607 (1983 estimate).
Other principal towns (1983): Ouahran (Oran) 663 504; Qacentina (Constantine) 448 578; Annaba (Bône) 348 322; El Boulaïda (Blida) 191 314; Sétif 186 978; Sidi-Bel-Abbès 146 653.
Highest point: Mt Atakor 9573 ft *2918 m*.
Principal mountain ranges: Atlas Saharien, Ahaggar (Hoggar), Hamada de Tinrhert.
Principal river: Chéliff (430 miles *692 km*).
Head of State: Col Bendjedid Chadli (b. 14 Apr. 1929), President.
Prime Minister: Abdelhamid Brahimi (b. 2 Apr. 1936).
Climate: Temperate (hot summers, fairly mild winters, adequate rainfall) along the coast, more extreme inland, hot and arid in the Sahara. In Algiers, August hottest (22°C *71°F* to 29°C *85°F*), January coldest (9°C *49°F* to 15°C *59°F*), December rainiest (12 days). Maximum temperature 53·0°C *127·4°F*, Ouargla, 27 Aug. 1884.
Labour force: 3 567 000 in 1983: Agriculture, Forestry and Fishing 26·9%; Mining and Manufacturing 13·3%; Construction 17·1%; Trade and transport 4·4%; services 38·3%.
Gross domestic product: 68 692 million dinars in 1976: Mining and quarrying 26·4% (crude petroleum and natural gas 25·9%); Manufacturing 14·0%; Construction 14·3%; Trade, restaurants and hotels 12·2% (trade 11·3%);

Government services 11·9%.
Exports: 60 722 million dinar in 1983: Energy and lubricants 98·5%; Primary products and raw materials 1·2%; Food and tobacco 0·3%.
Monetary unit: Algerian dinar. 1 dinar = 100 centimes.
Denominations:
Coins 1, 2, 5, 10, 20, 50 centimes; 1, 5, 10 dinars.
Notes 5, 10, 100, 200 dinars.
Exchange rate to £ sterling: 7·077 (26 Jan. 1987).
Political history and government: A former French possession, 'attached' to metropolitan France. A nationalist revolt, led by the *Front de libération nationale* (FLN) or National Liberation Front, broke out on 1 Nov. 1954. This ended with a cease-fire and independence agreement on 18 March 1962. A provisional government was formed on 28 March 1962. Following a referendum on 1 July 1962, Algeria became independent on 3 July 1962. The provisional government transferred its functions to the Political Bureau of the FLN on 7 Aug. 1962. A National Constituent Assembly was elected, from a single list of candidates adopted by the Bureau, on 20 Sept. 1962. The Republic was proclaimed on 25 Sept. 1962 and a new government was formed with Ahmed Ben Bella as Prime Minister. The government's draft constitution, providing for a presidential régime with the FLN as sole party, was adopted by the Assembly on 28 Aug. 1963 and approved by popular referendum on 8 Sept. 1963. Ben Bella was elected President on 15 Sept. 1963 and a new National Assembly elected on 20 Sept. 1964. The President was deposed by a military *coup* on 19 June 1965, when the Assembly was dissolved and power was assumed by a Revolutionary Council, led by Col. Houari Boumédienne, Minister of Defence.

The régime's National Charter, proclaiming Algeria's adherence to socialism, was approved by referendum on 27 June 1976. A new constitution, embodying the principles of the Charter, was similarly approved on 19 Nov. 1976 and promulgated on 22 Nov. 1976. It continues the one-party system, with the FLN as sole party. Executive power is vested in the President, who is Head of State and Head of Government. He is nominated by the FLN and elected by universal adult suffrage. The President appoints the Council of Ministers. Legislative power is held by the National People's Assembly, with 261 members elected by popular vote for five years (subject to dissolution by the Head of State). Boumédienne was elected President (unopposed) on 10 Dec. 1976 and members of the Assembly elected (from 783 candidates – three per constituency – nominated by the FLN) on 25 Feb. 1977. President Boumédienne died on 27 Dec. 1978. His successor was elected on 7 Feb. 1979, and sworn in two days later. A Prime Minister was appointed on 8 Mar. 1979. Legislation approved on 30 June 1979 shortened the President's term of office from 6 to 5 years.

Algeria comprises 48 *wilayaat* (regions), each *wilaya* having an appointed governor (*wali*).
Length of roadways: 48 720 miles *78 408 km* (31 Dec. 1974).
Length of railways: 2431 miles *3912 km*.
Universities: 12.
Adult illiteracy: 73·6% (males 58·2%; females 87·4%) in 1971.
Expectation of life: Males 57·04 years; females 59·77 years.
Defence: Military service 24 months; total armed forces 170 000 (1985); defence expenditure: 5% of total government expenditure in 1981.
Foreign tourists: 321 478 (1981).

Andorra

Official name: Les Valls d'Andorrà (Catalan); also Los Valles de Andorra (Spanish), or Les Vallées d'Andorre (French).
Population: 42 712 (1984).
Area: 180 miles² *465 km²*.
Languages: Catalan (official), French, Spanish.
Religion: Roman Catholic.

Capital city: Andorra la Vella, population 12 800 in 1979.
Other principal towns: Les Escaldes; Sant Julià de Lòria.
Highest point: Pla del'Estany, 9678 ft *3011 m*.
Principal mountain range: Pyrenees.
Principal river: Valira.
Head of State: Co-Princes (the Bishop of Urgel and the President of France), each represented by a Permanent Delegate and, in Andorra, by the Viguier Episcopal and the Viguier Français.
First Syndic: Francesc Cerqueda-Pascuet.
Head of Government: Josef Pintat Solans.
Climate: Mild (cool summers, cold winters) and dry. May–October are rainiest months.
Monetary unit: French and Spanish currencies (*q.v.*).
Political history and government: In 1278 Andorra was placed under the joint suzerainty of the Bishop of Urgel, in Spain, and the Comte de Foix, in France. The rights of the Comte passed to France in 1589. Andorra is an autonomous principality (*seigneurie*) in which legislative power is held by the unicameral General Council of the Valleys, with 28 members (four from each of the seven parishes) elected by adult Andorran citizens for four years, half the seats being renewable every two years. Female suffrage was introduced by decree on 23 April 1970. The Council elects the First Syndic to act as chief executive for a three-year term. Political parties are technically illegal but one sought recognition in 1979.

In January 1982 an Executive Council was appointed, following elections held in 1981. Legislative and executive powers were thus separated.
Foreign tourists: 6 000 000 in 1982.

Angola

Official name: A República Popular de Angola (the People's Republic of Angola).
Population: 5 646 166 (census of 15 Dec. 1970); 8 960 000 (1986 estimate).
Area: 481 354 miles² *1 246 700 km²*.
Languages: Portuguese (official), Ovimbundu, Kimbundu, Bakongo, Chokwe.
Religions: Catholic 38%; Protestant 12%; traditional beliefs 50%.
Capital city: São Paulo de Luanda, population 480 613 (1970 census); 1 200 000 (1982 estimate).
Other principal towns (1970): Huambo (Nova Lisboa) 61 885; Lobito 59 258; Benguela 40 996; Lubango (Sá de Bandeira) 31 674; Malanje 31 559.
Highest point: Serra Môco, 8563 ft *2610 m*.
Principal mountain ranges: Rand Plateau, Benguela Plateau, Bié Plateau, Humpata Highlands, Chela mountains.
Principal rivers: Cunene (Kunene), Cuanza (Kwanza), Congo (Zaire), Cuando (Kwando), Cubango (Okavango), Zambezi, Cassai (Kasai).
Head of State: José Eduardo dos Santos (b. 28 Aug. 1942), President.
Climate: Tropical, tempered locally by altitude. Two distinct seasons (wet and dry) but with little variation in temperature. Very hot and rainy in lowlands, with lower temperatures inland. Rainy season October to May; average annual rainfall 1780 mm *70 in* Cabina, 280 mm *11 in* at Lobito. Average annual temperature 26°C *79°F* at Santo António do Zaire, 19°C *67°F* at Huambo.
Labour force: 2 206 000 (1984 estimate): Agriculture, forestry and fishing 55·2%.
Gross domestic product: $2701 million in 1975 (estimate).
Exports: 39 531 million kwanza in 1979: Crude petroleum 74%; Petroleum products 10%; Coffee 5%; Diamonds 10%.
Monetary unit: Kwanza. 1 kwanza = 100 lwei.
Denominations:
Coins 50 lwei; 1, 2, 5, 10 kwanza.
Notes 20, 50, 100, 500, 1000 kwanza.
Exchange rate to £ sterling: 45·163 (26 Jan. 1987).
Political history and government: A former Portuguese territory, independent since 11 Nov. 1975. Before and after independence, rival nationalist groups fought for control of the

country. By February 1976 the dominant group was the *Movimento Popular de Libertação de Angola* (MPLA), the Popular Movement for the Liberation of Angola, supported by troops from Cuba. The MPLA's first Congress, on 4–11 Dec. 1977, restructured the Movement into a Marxist-Leninist political party called MPLA-*Partido de Trabalho* (MPLA-PT) or MPLA-Party of Labour. No other parties are permitted. The supreme organ of state is the National People's Assembly, with 206 members serving a three-year term. Members are chosen by electoral colleges composed of representatives elected by 'loyal citizens'. The first Assembly was installed

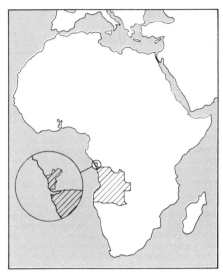

ANGOLA

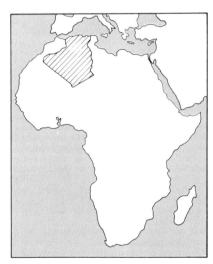

ALGERIA

ANDORRA

on 11 Nov. 1980. Executive power is vested in the President, who is also Chairman of the Council of Ministers and Chairman of the MPLA-PT. Angola has 18 provinces, each with a legislature elected by 'loyal citizens'.
Length of roadways: 44 939 miles *72 323 km* (31 Dec. 1974).
Length of railways: 1739 miles *2798 km*.
Universities: 1.
Adult illiteracy: 75% in 1982.
Expectation of life: Males 37·0 years; females 40·1 years (UN estimates for 1970–75).
Defence: Military service two years; total armed forces 49 500 (1985); also about 20 000 Cuban troops; defence expenditure: 35·8% of total government expenditure in 1984.

Antigua and Barbuda

Population: 65 525 (census of 7 April 1970); 81 500 (1986 estimate).
Area: 170½ miles² *442 km²*.
Language: English.
Religion: Christian (mainly Anglican).
Capital city: St John's (St John City), population 36 000.
Highest point: Boggy Peak, 1319 ft *402 m*.
Head of State: HM Queen Elizabeth II, represented by Sir Wilfred Ebenezer Jacobs, KCVO, OBE (b. 19 Oct. 1919), Governor-General.
Prime Minister: Vere Cornwall Bird (b. 7 Dec. 1910).
Climate: Generally warm and pleasant. Temperatures range from 15°C *60°F* to 34°C *93°F*, with an average of 27°C *81·5°F*. Average annual rainfall 1090 to 1140 mm *43 to 45 in*.
Labour force: 23 067 (1970 census): Agriculture, forestry and fishing 11·8%; Construction 13·9%; Trade, restaurants and hotels 16·5%; Community, social and personal services 31·9%.
Gross domestic product: EC$399·2 million in 1983.
Exports: EC$39·1 million in 1983.
Monetary unit: East Caribbean dollar (EC$). 1 dollar = 100 cents.
Denominations:
  Coins 1, 2, 5, 10, 25, 50 cents.
  Notes 1, 5, 20, 100 dollars.
Exchange rate to £ sterling: 4·13 (26 Jan. 1987).
Political history and government: A former British dependency, comprising Antigua, Barbuda (formerly Dulcina) and Redonda. The islands (collectively known as Antigua) were administered as part of the Leeward Islands, under a federal arrangement. Antigua became a separate Crown Colony on 30 June 1956, although under the Governor of the Leeward Islands until 31 Dec. 1959. From 1 Jan. 1960 the colony had a new constitution, with its own Administrator. On 27 Feb. 1967 Antigua became one of the West Indies Associated States, with full internal self-government. The Administrator was replaced by a Governor and the Chief Minister was restyled Premier.
  Following a constitutional conference on 4–16 Dec. 1980, the islands became fully independent, within the Commonwealth, on 1 Nov. 1981, when the Governor became Governor-General and the Premier took office as Prime Minister. Executive power is vested in the British monarch and is exercisable by the Governor-General, who is appointed on the advice of the Prime Minister and acts in almost all matters on the advice of the Cabinet. Legislative power is vested in the bicameral Parliament, comprising a Senate (17 members appointed by the Governor-General) and a House of Representatives (17 members elected by universal adult suffrage for 5 years, subject to dissolution). The Governor-General appoints the Prime Minister and, on the latter's recommendation, other Ministers. The Cabinet is responsible to the House.
Length of roadways: 600 miles *960 km*.
Adult illiteracy: 11·3% (males 10·4%; females 12·0%) in 1960.
Expectation of life: Males 60·48 years; females 64·32 years (1959–61).
Defence: Total armed forces: about 700; there are also two US bases on Antigua.
Foreign tourists: 129 047 in 1984.

Argentina

Official name: República Argentina (the Argentine Republic).
Population: 27 862 771 (census of 22 Sept. 1980); 30 097 000 (1984 estimate).
Area: 1 072 163 miles² *2 776 889 km²*.
Language: Spanish.
Religion: Roman Catholic.
Capital city: Buenos Aires, population 2 908 000 (1980 census).
Other principal towns (1980): Córdoba 969 000; Rosario 750 455; La Plata 455 000; San Miguel de Tucumán 497 000; Mar de Plata 302 282; Santa Fé 287 000.
Highest point: Cerro Aconcagua, 22 834 ft *6960 m* (first climbed 14 Jan. 1897).
Principal mountain range: Cordillera de los Andes.
Principal rivers: Paraná (2485 miles *4000 km*), Negro, Salado.
Head of State: Dr Raul Alfonsín, President.
Climate: Sub-tropical in Chaco region (north), sunny and mild in pampas, cold and windy in southern Patagonia. In Buenos Aires, January hottest (17°C *63°F* to 29°C *85°F*), June coldest (5°C *41°F* to 14°C *57°F*), August, October and November rainiest (each 9 days). Absolute maximum temperature 48,8°C *119·8°F*, Rivadavia, 27 Nov. 1916; minimum −33,0°C *−27·4°F*, Sarmiento.
Labour force: 10 815 220 (1983 estimate): Agriculture, forestry and fishing 12·0%; Manufacturing 19·9%; Trade, restaurants and hotels 17·0%; Community, social and personal services (incl. business services) 28·0%.
Gross domestic product: 92 360 million pesos in 1984: Agriculture, forestry and fishing 15%; Manufacturing 25%; Trade, restaurants and hotels 13%; Transport and communications 12%; Community, social and personal services 24%.
Exports: $7625 million in 1982: Vegetable products 34%; Prepared foodstuffs 12%; Live animals and animal products 12%.
Monetary unit: Austral (=1000 pesos): 1 austral = 100 centavos.
Denominations:
  Coins 1, 5, 10, 50, 100 centavos.
  Notes 1, 5, 10, 100, 1000 australes.
Exchange rate to £ sterling: 1·99 (26 Jan. 1987).
Political history and government: A federal republic of 22 states and two centrally administered territories. Lt-Gen. Juan Perón was elected President on 23 Sept. 1973 and took office on 12 Oct. 1973. Gen. Perón died on 1 July 1974 and was succeeded by his wife, the former Vice-President. She was deposed by an armed forces *coup* on 24 March 1976, when a three-man military junta took power. The bicameral Congress (a Senate and a Chamber of Deputies) and provincial legislatures were dissolved and political activities suspended. In 1982 Argentina invaded the British-ruled Falkland Islands (Islas Malvinas). After early success they were defeated and the Argentine troops forced to surrender. This brought about the collapse of the military junta, and elections in 1983 ushered in a civilian government. Each province is administered by an elected Governor.
Length of roadways: 129 015 miles *207 630 km* (31 Dec. 1978).
Length of railways: 21 176 miles *34 079 km*.
Universities: 40.
Adult illiteracy: 5·5% in 1980.
Expectation of life: Males 68·6 years; females 73·3 years (1981).
Defence: Military service: Army and Air Force one year, Navy 14 months; total armed forces 105 500 (47 000 conscripts) in 1986; defence expenditure: 11% of total government expenditure in 1982.
Foreign tourists: 950 000 (1983).

Australia

Official name: The Commonwealth of Australia.
Population: 13 915 000 (census of 30 June 1976); 15 276 100 (1982 estimate).

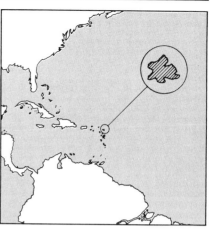

ANTIGUA AND BARBUDA

ARGENTINA

Area: 2 966 150 miles² *7 682 300 km²*.
Language: English.
Religions: Church of England; Roman Catholic; Methodist; Presbyterian.
Capital city: Canberra, population 264 300 (1984 estimate).
Other principal towns (1984): Sydney 3 355 300; Melbourne 2 888 400; Brisbane 1 145 400; Adelaide 978 900; Perth 982 700; Newcastle 418 500; Wollongong 235 800; Hobart 175 700; Geelong 145 200.
Highest point: Mt Kosciusko, 7316 ft *2230 m*.
Principal mountain ranges: Great Dividing Range, Macdonnell Ranges, Flinders Ranges, Australian Alps.
Principal rivers: Murray (with Darling), Flinders, Ashburton, Fitzroy.
Head of State: HM Queen Elizabeth II, represented by the Rt Hon. Sir Ninian Stephen, AK, GCMG, GCVO, KBE, Governor-General.
Prime Minister: The Rt. Hon. Robert Hawke.
Climate: Hot and dry, with average temperatures of about 27°C *80°F*. Very low rainfall in interior. In Sydney, January and February warmest (each average 18°C *65°F* to 25°C *78°F*), July coldest (8°C *46°F* to 15°C *60°F*), each month has an average of between 11 and 14 rainy days. In Perth, average daily maximum of 17°C *63°F* (July) to 29°C *85°F* (January, February), minimum 9°C *48°F* (July, August) to 17°C *63°F* (January, February), July and August rainiest (each 19 days), January and February driest (each 3 days). In Darwin, average maximum 30°C *87°F* (July) to 34°C *94°F* (November),

minimum 19°C *67°F* (July) to 25°C *78°F* (November, December), January rainiest (20 days), no rainy days in July or August. Absolute maximum temperature 53,1°C *127·5°F*, Cloncurry, 13 Jan. 1889; absolute minimum −22,2°C *−8·0°F*, Charlotte Pass, 14 July 1945 and 22 Aug. 1947.

Labour force: 7 127 500 in 1984: Agriculture, forestry and fishing 5·6%; Mining 1·4%; Manufacturing 16·1%; Construction 6·1%; Trade 18%; Services 34·7%; Unemployed 8·9%.

Gross domestic product: A$164 287 million in 1983–4.

Exports: A$24 766·6 million in 1983–4: Meat 5·6%; Cereals 10·9%; Wool 7·7%: Metal ores and scrap 16·6%; Mineral fuels and lubricants 21%; Basic manufactures 10·4%; Machinery and transport equipment 5·4%.

Monetary unit: Australian dollar (A$). 1 dollar = 100 cents.

Denominations:
 Coins 1, 2, 5, 10, 20, 50 cents.
 Notes 1, 2, 5, 10, 20, 50 dollars.

Exchange rate to £ sterling: 2·3473 (26 Jan. 1987).

Political history and government: Britain's six Australian colonies merged to form a federation of states as the Commonwealth of Australia, a dominion under the British Crown, on 1 Jan. 1901. The Northern Territory was separated from South Australia, and the Australian Capital Territory was acquired from New South Wales, on 1 Jan. 1911. The capital was transferred from Melbourne to Canberra in May 1927. Australia became fully independent, within the Commonwealth, under the Statute of Westminster, a law promulgated in Britain on 11 Dec. 1931 and adopted by Australia on 9 Oct. 1942 (with effect from 3 Sept. 1939).

Executive power is vested in the Queen and exercised by her representative, the Governor-General, advised by the Federal Executive Council (the Cabinet), led by the Prime Minister. The Governor-General appoints the Prime Minister and, on the latter's recommendation, other Ministers. Legislative power is vested in the Federal Parliament. This consists of the Queen, represented by the Governor-General, and two chambers elected by universal adult suffrage (voting is compulsory). The Senate has 64 members (10 from each state and two from each of the federal territories) elected by proportional representation for six years (half the seats renewable every three years). The House of Representatives has 125 members elected for three years (subject to dissolution) from single-member constituencies. The Cabinet is responsible to Parliament. Australia comprises six states (each with its own Government and judicial system) and two federally-administered territories.

Length of roadways: 495 314 miles *796 960 km* (1982).

Length of railways: 25 362 miles *40 807 km* (1982).

Universities: 19.

Expectation of life: Males 67·63 years; females 74·15 years (1965–67), excluding full-blooded aborigines.

Defence: Military service voluntary; total armed forces 70 731 (1985); defence expenditure, 1984–5: A$ 6252 million.

Foreign tourists: 943 900 in 1983.

NEW SOUTH WALES

Population: 4 914 300 (1976 census); 5 406 900 (1984 estimate).

Area: 309 500 miles² *801 600 km²*.

Capital city: Sydney, population 3 355 300 (1984 estimate).

Other principal towns (1984): Newcastle 418 500; Wollongong 235 900; Lake Macquarie 161 000; Wagga Wagga 49 650; Shoalhaven 56 600; Shellharbour 46 000; Albury 39 150.

Highest point: Mt Kosciusko, 7316 ft *2230 m*.

Principal mountain ranges: Great Dividing Range, Australian Alps, New England Range, Snowy Mountains, Blue Mountains, Liverpool Range.

Principal rivers: Darling, Murray.

Governor: Air Marshal Sir James Anthony Rowland, KBE, DFC, AFC (b. 1 Nov. 1922).

Premier: Neville Kenneth Wran.

Climate: Most of the state has hot summers and mild winters, with rainfall well distributed, but in the east drought and storms sometimes occur.

Length of roadways: 121 534 miles *195 548 km* (1983).

Length of railways: 6218 miles *10 005 km* (1984).

Universities: 6.

QUEENSLAND

Population: 2 295 123 (1981 census); 2 505 300 (1984 estimate).

Area: 666 875 miles² *1 727 200 km²*.

Capital city: Brisbane, population 1 145 400 (1984 estimate).

Other principal towns (1984): Gold Coast 174 530; Townsville 100 530; Sunshine Coast 81 300; Cairns 64 840; Rockhampton 56 520.

Highest point: Mt Bartle Frere, 5287 ft *1611 m*.

Principal mountain ranges: Great Dividing Range, Selwyn, Kirby.

Principal rivers: Brisbane, Mitchell, Fitzroy, Barcoo, Flinders.

Governor: Sir Walter Benjamin Campbell, QC

Premier: Sir Johannes Bjelke-Petersen (b. 13 Jan. 1911).

Length of roadways: 101 563 miles *163 415 km* (1983).

Length of railways: 6359 miles *10 231 km* (1983).

Universities: 3.

SOUTH AUSTRALIA

Population: 1 294 509 (1981 census); 1 352 900 (1984 estimate).

Area: 379 925 miles² *984 000 km²*.

Capital city: Adelaide, population 978 900 (1984 estimate).

Other principal towns (1984): Whyalla 31 820; Mount Gambier 18 880; Port Pirie 15 970.

Principal mountain ranges: Middleback, Mt Lofty Range, Flinders Range, Musgrave Range.

Principal river: Murray.

Governor: Lt-Gen. Sir Donald Dunstan, KBE, CB.

Premier: John Charles Bannon.

Climate: Mediterranean type.

Length of roadways: 63 931 miles *102 866 km* (1984).

Length of railways: 3793 miles *6105 km*.

Universities: 2.

TASMANIA

Population: 427 300 (1981 census); 437 300 (1984 estimate).

Area: 26 175 miles² *67 800 km²*.

Capital city: Hobart, population 175 700 (1984 estimate).

Other principal towns (1981): Launceston 64 555; Devonport 21 424; Burnie-Somerset 20 368.

Highest point: Cradle Mountain, 5069 ft *1545 m*.

Principal mountain range: Highlands.

Principal rivers: Derwent, Gordon, Tamar.

Governor: Sir James Plimsoll, AC, CBE.

Premier: R. Gray.

Length of roadways: 13 804 miles *22 210 km* (1983).

Length of railways: 612 miles *985 km* (1983).

Universities: 1.

VICTORIA

Population: 4 075 500 (1984 estimate).

Area: 87 875 miles² *227 600 km²*.

Capital city: Melbourne, population 2 888 400 (1984 estimate).

Other principal towns (1981): Geelong 125 279; Ballarat 62 641; Bendigo 52 741; Shepparton-Mooroopna 28 373.

Principal mountain ranges: Australian Alps, Great Dividing Range.

Principal rivers: Murray, Yarra-Yarra.

Governor: Rev. Dr. Davis McCaughey.

Premier: John Cain.

Length of roadways: 97 701 miles *157 201 km* (1982).

Length of railways: 3592 miles *5780 km* (1984).

Universities: 4.

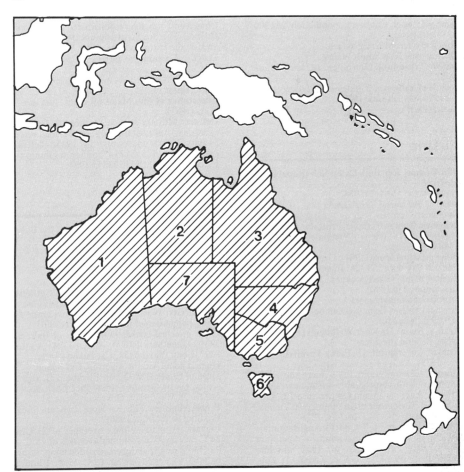

AUSTRALIA—1. **Western Australia** 2. **Northern Territory** 3. **Queensland** 4. **New South Wales** 5. **Victoria** 6. **Tasmania** 7. **South Australia.**

WESTERN AUSTRALIA

Population: 1 299 100 (1981 census); 1 382 500 (1984 estimate).
Area: 975 100 miles² *2 525 500 km²*.
Capital city: Perth, population 982 700 (1984 estimate).
Other principal towns (1984): Fremantle 23 480; Bunbury 23 940; Geraldton 19 840; Kalgoorlie-Boulder 22 200; Albany 13 990.
Highest point: Mt Meharry, 4082 ft *1244 m*.
Principal mountain ranges: Darling, Hamersley.
Principal rivers: Fitzroy, Ashburton, Fortescue, Swan, Murchison.
Governor: Prof. Gordon Stanley Reid (b. 26 Sept. 1923).
Premier: Hon. Brian Thomas Burke.
Length of roadways: 73 994 miles *119 057 km* (1984).
Length of railways: 4672 miles *7518 km* (1984).
Universities: 2.

THE NORTHERN TERRITORY OF AUSTRALIA

Population: 138 800 (1984 estimate).
Area: 519 750 miles² *1 346 200 km²*.
Capital: Darwin, population 66 100 (1984 estimate).
Other principal town: Alice Springs, population 22 000 (1984 estimate).
Highest point: Mount Ziel, 4955 ft *1510 m*.
Principal mountain range: MacDonnell Ranges.
Principal rivers: Victoria, Roper.
Administrator: Commodore E E Johnston, OBE.
Chief Minister: Ian Lindsay Tuxworth.
Climate: Tropical, but with considerable variations. Dry in the south, with very hot summers. On the coast, the rainy season is from November to April and the dry season from May to October.
Length of roadways: 12 479 miles *20 080 km* (1985).
Length of railways: 516 miles *831 km*.

THE AUSTRALIAN CAPITAL TERRITORY

Population: 244 500 (1984 estimate).
Area: 925 miles² *2400 km²*.
Principal town: Canberra, population 264 300 (1984 estimate).
Principal river: Murrumbidgee.
Climate: (see New South Wales).
Length of roadways: 1356 miles *2182 km* (30 June 1978).
Length of railways: 5 miles *8 km* (government railways only, 30 June 1978).
Universities: 1.

Austria

Offical name: Republik Österreich (Republic of Austria).
Population: 7 552 551 (1984).
Area: 32 367 miles² *83 855 km²*.
Language: German.
Religions: Roman Catholic, Protestant minority.
Capital city: Wien (Vienna), population 1 489 153 (1985).
Other principal towns (1981): Graz 243 166; Linz 199 910; Salzburg 139 426; Innsbruck 117 287.
Highest point: Grossglockner, 12 462 ft *3798 m* (first climbed in 1800).
Principal mountain range: Alps.
Principal rivers: Donau (Danube) (1770 miles *2850 km*), Inn, Mur.
Head of State: Dr Kurt Waldheim (b. 21 Dec. 1918), Federal President.
Head of Government: Dr Franz Vranitzky (b. 4 Oct. 1937), Acting Federal Chancellor.
Climate: Generally cold, dry winters and warm summers, with considerable variations due to altitude. Average annual temperature 7°C *45°F* to 9°C *48°F*. Most of rain in summer. In Vienna, July hottest (15°C *59°F* to 24°C *75°F*), January coldest (−3°C *26°F* to 1°C *34°F*), August rainiest (10 days). Absolute maximum temperature 39,4°C *102·9°F*, Horn, 5 July 1957; absolute minimum −36,6°C *−33·9°F*, Zwettl, 11 Feb. 1929.
Labour force: 2 759 700 in 1985 (excludes 139 000 unemployed): Agriculture and forestry 6·7%;

Industry and manufacturing 20%; Services 36·4%.
Gross domestic product: 1371 billion Schilling in 1985: Agriculture and forestry 3·2%; Mining and metal goods production 28·3%; Construction 6·9%; Commerce, hotels and restaurants 15·9%; Transport and communications 5·7%.
Exports: 353 962 million Schilling in 1985: Machinery and vehicles 31·3%; Processed goods 33·8%; Other finished goods 13·7%; Raw materials (excluding fuels) 5·4%; Food 3·8%.
Monetary unit: Schilling. 1 Schilling = 100 Groschen.
Denominations:
　Coins 1, 2, 5, 10, 50 Groschen; 1, 5, 10, 20, 25, 50, 100, 500, 1000 Schilling.
　Notes 20, 50, 100, 500, 1000 Schilling.
Exchange rate to £ sterling: 19·635 (26 Jan. 1987).
Political history and government: Formerly the centre of the Austro-Hungarian Empire. In 1918 the Empire was dissolved and Austria proper became a republic. Troops from Nazi Germany entered Austria on 11 March 1938. It was annexed on 12 March 1938 and incorporated in the German Reich. After liberation by Allied forces, a provisional government was established on 27 April 1945. Austria was divided into four occupation zones, controlled by France, the USSR, the United Kingdom and the USA. It regained independence by the Austrian State Treaty, signed on 15 May 1955 and effective from 27 July 1955. Occupation forces were withdrawn on 25 Oct. 1955.
Austria is a federal state, divided into nine provinces. Legislative power is vested in the bicameral Federal Assembly, comprising the *Nationalrat* (National Council) of 183 members, directly elected by universal adult suffrage for four years (subject to dissolution), and the *Bundesrat* (Federal Council) of 63 members elected for varying terms by the provincial assemblies. The Federal President is a constitutional Head of State, elected by direct popular vote for six years. He normally acts on the advice of the Council of Ministers, led by the Federal Chancellor, which is responsible to the National Council. The President appoints the Chancellor and, on the latter's advice, other Ministers.
Length of roadways: 66 633 miles *107 212 km* (1983).
Length of railways: 3584 miles *5766 km* (1985).
Universities: 18.
Expectation of life: Males 69 years; females 76 years (1983).
Defence: Military service six months, followed by 60 days' reservist training; total armed forces 54 700 (27 000 conscripts) in 1985; defence expenditure, 1985: $17 147 million schilling.
Foreign tourists: 15 110 233 in 1984.

The Bahamas

Official name: The Commonwealth of the Bahamas.
Population: 223 455 (census of 12 May 1980); 226 000 (1984 estimate).
Area: 5382 miles² *13 939 km²*.
Languages: English.
Religions: Anglican, Baptist, Roman Catholic, Methodist, Saints of God and Church of God.
Capital city: Nassau (on New Providence Island), population of island 135 537 (1980).
Other principal islands (1980): Grand Bahama 33 102; Eleuthera 10 600; Abaco 7324; Andros 8397; Long Island 3358; Cat Island 2143.
Highest point: Mount Alvernia, Cat Island.
Head of State: HM Queen Elizabeth II, represented by Sir Gerald Christopher Cash, KCVO, OBE (b. 28 May 1917), Governor-General.
Prime Minister: The Rt Hon. Lynden Oscar Pindling (b. 22 Mar. 1930).
Climate: Equable. Winter averages of 21°C to 24°C *70°F to 75°F*. Summer averages of 26°C to 32°C *80°F to 90°F*. Highest recorded temperature is 34°C *94°F* and lowest 10°C *51°F*. Rainfall mainly between May and September.
Labour force: 69 791 (including unemployed) aged 14 and over (1970 census): Construction

13·6%; Trade, restaurants and hotels 25·9%; Community, social and personal services 27·1%; 84 288 (household survey, Oct. 1975).
Gross domestic product: B$1448·8 million in 1982.
Exports: B$2383 million in 1984.
Monetary unit: Bahamian dollar (B$). 1 dollar = 100 cents.
Denominations:
　Coins 1, 5, 10, 15, 25, 50 cents; B$ 1, 2, 5.
　Notes 50 cents; B$ 1, 3, 5, 10, 20, 50, 100.
Exchange rate to £ sterling: 1·5280 (26 Jan. 1987).
Political history and government: A former British colony, with internal self-government from 7 Jan. 1964. Following a constitutional conference on 12–20 Dec. 1972, the Bahamas became independent, within the Commonwealth, on 10 July 1973. Executive power is vested in the Queen and exercisable by her appointed representative, the Governor-General, advised by the Cabinet. The Governor-General appoints the Prime Minister and, on the latter's advice, other members of the Cabinet. Legislative power is vested in the bicameral Parliament, comprising the Senate (16 appointed members) and the House of Assembly, with 38 members elected for five years by universal adult suffrage. The Cabinet is responsible to Parliament.
Length of roadways: 1450 miles *2334 km*.
Adult illiteracy: 10·2% (males 9·8%; females 10·5%) in 1963.
Expectation of life: Males 64·0 years; females 67·3 years (1969–71).
Defence: A force was established in 1977.
Foreign tourists: 2 500 000 in 1986.

Bahrain

Official name: Daulat al-Bahrain (State of Bahrain).
Population: 350 798 (1981 census); 435 065 (1986 estimate).
Area: 240 miles² *622 km²*.
Language: Arabic.
Religions: Muslim, Christian minority.
Capital city: Manama, population 121 986 (1981 census).
Other principal towns (1981): Muharraq 61 853; Rifa'a 28 150; Isa Town 21 275; Hidd 7111.
Highest point: Jabal ad-Dukhan, 440 ft *134 m*.
Head of State: H H Shaikh Isa bin Sulman al-Khalifa, Hon GCMG (b. 3 July 1933), Amir.
Prime Minister: Shaikh Khalifa bin Sulman al-Khalifa (b. 1935).
Climate: Very hot and humid. Average maximum 20°C *68°F* (January) to 38°C *100°F* (August), minimum 14°C *57°F* (January) to 29°C *85°F* (July, August), December and February rainiest (each two days).
Labour force: 81 503 (1984): Agriculture 1·8%; Manufacturing 12·5%; Construction 33·8%; Trade 13·8%.
Gross domestic product: 1740·1 million Bahrain dinars in 1982.
Exports: 1180·1 million Bahrain dinars in 1984: Refined petroleum 86·4%; Aluminium 7·1%.
Monetary unit: Bahrain dinar. 1 dinar = 1000 fils.
Denominations:
　Coins 1, 5, 10, 25, 50, 100, 250, 500 fils.
　Notes 500 fils; 1, 5, 10, 20 dinars.
Exchange rate to £ sterling: 0·5795 (26 Jan. 1987).
Political history and government: A shaikhdom under British protection from 1882 until full independence on 15 Aug. 1971. Now an amirate, with a Cabinet appointed by the Ruler. A new constitution came into force on 6 Dec. 1973. This provided for a National Assembly, containing Cabinet ministers and 30 elected members serving a four-year term. Elections were held on 7 Dec. 1973 but the Assembly was dissolved by Amiri decree on 26 Aug. 1975.
Expectation of life: Males 54·8 years; females 58·2 years (UN estimates, average for Bahrain, Qatar and the United Arab Emirates, 1970–75).
Adult illiteracy: 36·6% (males 25·2%; females 48·1%) in 1981.

(*Above*) Yale University anthropologists Pilbeam and Simons examine fragments (foreground) of Ramapithecus which date from 14 million BC – the oldest of homonid remains.

(*Above right*) The Walton sextuplets (born 1983) are one of four all-surviving sextuplets in the world.

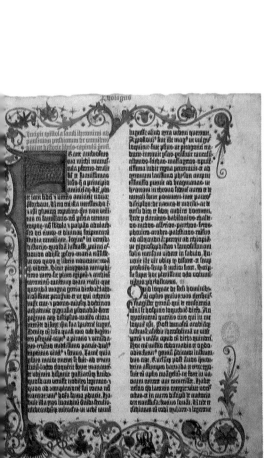

(*Above*) The largest Old Master painting is 'Il Paradiso' by Tintoretto for the Doge's Palace, Venice (painted 1587–90).

(*Left*) A page from one of the only 21 extant copies of the world's most expensive printed book, the Gutenberg Bible.

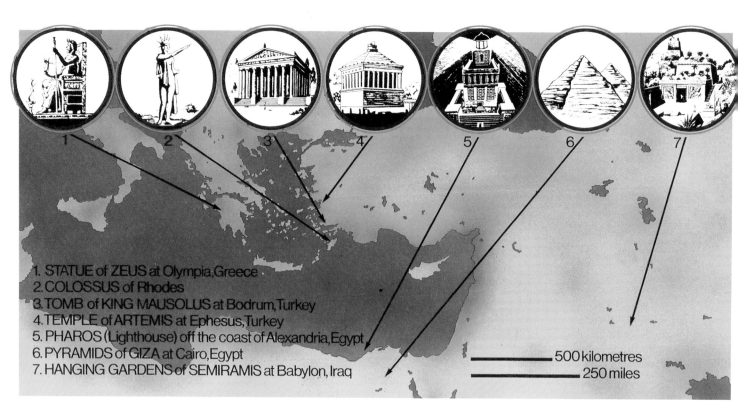

1. STATUE of ZEUS at Olympia, Greece
2. COLOSSUS of Rhodes
3. TOMB of KING MAUSOLUS at Bodrum, Turkey
4. TEMPLE of ARTEMIS at Ephesus, Turkey
5. PHAROS (Lighthouse) off the coast of Alexandria, Egypt
6. PYRAMIDS of GIZA at Cairo, Egypt
7. HANGING GARDENS of SEMIRAMIS at Babylon, Iraq

500 kilometres
250 miles

(*Top*) The Seven Wonders of the Ancient World.

(*Above*) A satellite view of the Gulf of Suez, the Gulf of Aqbar and Red Sea. Africa is on the right-hand side.

(*Right*) Sears Tower, Chicago, Illinois is 1454 ft *443 m* high – the tallest office block in the world.

(*Left*) The Baird Televisor was the first commercially available TV set. It was launched in May 1930.

(*Below left*) *Ben Hur* (1959) holds the record for the most Oscars ever awarded to a single film – 11.

(*Below right*) Steven Spielberg's *E.T.* has grossed $700 million – the highest grossing movie.

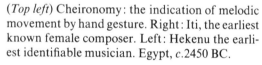

(*Top left*) Cheironomy: the indication of melodic movement by hand gesture. Right: Iti, the earliest known female composer. Left: Hekenu the earliest identifiable musician. Egypt, *c*.2450 BC.

(*Top right*) The oldest extant harpsichord, built by Hieronymous of Bologna in 1521 and preserved at the Victoria and Albert Museum, London.

(*Above*) Peter Goldmark and William S. Bachman, developers of the first successful long-playing disc.

(*Right*) Michael Jackson's album *Thriller* is the best-selling of all time with global sales of 38·5 million copies by August 1, 1987.

(*Left*) US *Nimitz*-class aircraft carriers at 91 487 tonnes, 1092 ft *322·9 m* long and 4½ acres *1·82 ha* of flight deck are the largest warships in the world.

(*Below*) The *Seawise Giant* is the largest ship of any kind at 564 739 tonnes deadweight. Completed in 1979, she is 1504 ft *458·4 m* long.

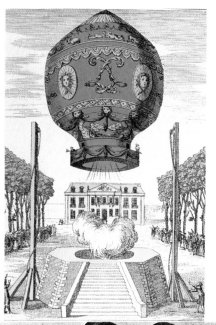

(*Left*) The first free-flight hot-air balloon ascent took place in November 1783 and lasted 22 minutes.

(*Below left*) Wilbur and Orville Wright were the first to fly a controlled and sustained-power aircraft on December 17, 1903.

(*Below right*) The Wright brothers flew *Flyer I* 120 ft *36·5 m* at 30 mph *48 kmh* to become the first true airmen.

(*Bottom*) Four Concordes. At Mach 2·2 (1450 mph *2333 kmh*) the fastest airliners in service.

(*Opposite right*) *Solar Challenger*, powered entirely by solar energy, was the first of its type to cross the English Channel. It flew 163 miles *262·3 km* on July 7, 1981.

(*Opposite*) Space shuttle orbiter *Columbia* was the first re-usable space craft. It made its maiden flight on April 12, 1981.

(*Opposite left*) The interior of NASA's Vehicle Assembly Building, Cape Canaveral, Florida – the most capacious scientific building in the world.

(*Opposite right*) Apollo 11 and Edwin 'Buzz' Aldrin during the first moon landing, July 16, 1969.

(*Above*) The last steam locomotive built by British Railways, No. 92220 *Evening Star*, March 1960.

(*Left*) Gottlieb Daimler (1834–1900) who, with the help of Wilhelm Maybach, designed the first practicable four-stroke internal combustion engine. In 1883 they produced the first 'high speed' (800 rpm) petrol engine with enclosed crank and hot tube ignition.

(*Below*) The *official* one mile land speed record is 633·468 mph *1019·467 kmh* set by Richard Noble OBE (born 1946) on October 4, 1983 over the Black Rock Desert, Nevada, USA in his 17 000 lbs thrust Rolls-Royce Avon 302 jet-powered *Thrust 2* designed by John Ackroyd.

Defence: Military service voluntary; total armed forces 2800 (1985); defence expenditure: 7·9% of total government expenditure in 1983.
Foreign tourists: 154 000 (largely from other Gulf states) in 1984.

Bangladesh

Official name: Gana Praja Tantri Bangla Desh (People's republic of Bangladesh).
Population: 99 235 000 (1985 estimate).
Area: 55 598 miles² *143 998 km²*.
Language: Bengali.
Religions: Muslim, with Hindu, Christian and Buddhist minorities.
Capital city: Dhaka (Dacca), population 3 458 602 (census 1981).
Other principal towns (1981): Chittagong 1 388 475; Khulna 623 184; Narayanganj 298 400; Rajshahi 171 600; Barisal 166 680.
Principal rivers: Ganga (Ganges), Jumna, Meghna.
Head of State: Lt-Gen. Hossain Mohammad Ershad, President.
Prime Minister: Mizanur Rahman Chowdhury.
Climate: Tropical and monsoon. Summer temperature about 30°C *86°F*; winter 20°C *68°F*. Rainfall is heavy, varying from 1270 to 3430 mm *50 in to 135 in* per year in different areas, and most falling from June to September (the monsoon season).
Labour force: 27 972 000 employed in 1983–4: Agriculture, forestry and fishing 58·6%; Trade, hotels and restaurants 11·7%; Manufacturing 7·5%.
Gross domestic product: 397 746 million taka in 1984–5: Agriculture, forestry and fishing 48% (agriculture 41%); Trade 9%.
Exports: 20 250 million taka in 1983: Jute and jute products 57%.
Monetary unit: Taka. 1 taka = 100 paisa.
Denominations:
    Coins 1, 2, 5, 10, 25, 50 paisa.
    Notes 1, 5, 10, 50, 100 taka.
Exchange rate to £ sterling: 46·30 (26 Jan. 1987).
Political history and government: Formerly the eastern wing of Pakistan, formed by the partition of British India on 15 Aug. 1947. In elections for a Pakistan National Assembly on 7 Dec. 1970 the Awami League, led by Sheikh Mujibur Rahman, won all but two seats in East Pakistan and an overall majority in the Assembly. The League advocated autonomy for East Pakistan within a loose federation but this was unacceptable to the main party in West Pakistan. When constitutional talks failed, the League declared East Pakistan's independence as Bangladesh on 26 Mar. 1971. Civil war broke out and the League was outlawed. Mujib was arrested but the League announced on 11 Apr. 1971 that he was President of Bangladesh. After Indian intervention, Pakistani forces surrendered and Bangladesh's secession became effective on 16 Dec. 1971. Mujib was released and became Prime Minister on 12 Jan. 1972. Bangladesh joined the Commonwealth on 18 Apr. 1972. Mujib was deposed by a *coup* and killed on 15 Aug. 1975, when martial law was imposed. Political parties were banned on 30 Aug. 1975. After an army mutiny on 3 Nov. 1975, the new President resigned on 6 Nov. 1975, when the Chief Justice of the Supreme Court became President and Chief Martial Law Administrator. He immediately dissolved Parliament and on the next day the mutiny was crushed. Political parties were again legalized by a regulation of 28 July 1976. The President's deputy, Maj-Gen. Ziaur Rahman, took over martial law powers on 29 Nov. 1976 and became President on 21 Apr. 1977. A Presidential proclamation of 22 Apr. 1977 amended the constitution to change Bangladesh from a secular to an Islamic state. Zia was elected President by a large majority of the popular vote on 3 June 1978 and sworn in for a 5-year term on 12 June. On 29 June 1978 he formed a Cabinet in place of his Council of Advisers. Elections were held on 18 Feb. 1979 for 300 members to serve a 5-year term in a new *Jatiya Sangsad* (Parliament). In a further 30 seats, reserved for women, candidates were

unopposed. The state of emergency was revoked on 27 Nov. 1979. President Zia was killed on 30 May 1981, during an attempted insurrection, and the Vice-President became acting Head of State. He was elected President on 15 Nov. 1981. The elected President was deposed and the Jatiya Sangsad (Parliament) dissolved following promulgation of martial law and the take-over of power by Lt-Gen. H M Ershad on 24 March 1982. Gen. Ershad appointed a retired judge to be President on 27 March 1982, but assumed the Presidency himself on 11 December 1983. A parliamentary election was held on 7 May 1986 and a presidential election held on 15 October 1986, in which Ershad was voted to the presidency.
Length of roadways: 3900 miles *6276 km*.
Length of railways: 2828 miles *4551 km* (1984).
Universities: 6.
Adult illiteracy: 80·3% in 1981.
Expectation of life: 53·9 (1983).
Defence: Military service voluntary; total armed forces 92 300 (1986); estimated defence expenditure, 1984–5; 12·6% of total government expenditure.
Foreign tourists: 103 130 in 1984.

Barbados

Population: 246 082 (census of 12 May 1980); 253 055 (estimate 1985).
Area: 166 miles² *430 km²*.
Language: English.
Religions: Anglican, with Methodist, Roman Catholic and Moravian minorities.
Capital city: Bridgetown, population 7517 (parish of Bridgetown and St Michael 97 872) at 1980 census.
Other principal towns: Speightstown.
Highest point: Mount Hillaby, 1115 ft *340 m*.
Head of State: HM Queen Elizabeth II, represented by Sir Hugh Springer, GCMG, KA, CBE (b. 22 June 1913), Governor-General.
Prime Minister: H. Bernard St John.
Climate: Pleasant, with temperatures rarely rising above 30°C *86°F* or falling below 18°C *67°F*. Average annual rainfall, which varies from district to district, 1270 mm to 1778 mm *50 in to 75 in*. Subject to hurricanes.
Labour force: 112 600 in 1983: Agriculture, forestry and fishing 6·8%; Manufacturing and mining 11·3% Trade 19·1% Community, social and personal services 31·3%; Unemployed 15%.
Gross domestic product: B$1 798 040 in 1982: Sugar 3·1%; Other agriculture 3·7%; Manufacturing 12·2%; Wholesale and retail trade 22·1%; Tourism 10·1%; Financial, insurance and business services 13·9%.
Exports: B$717·4 million in 1983: Electrical components 30·8%; Clothing 11·9%; Sugar 6·6%.
Monetary unit: Barbados dollar (B$). 1 dollar = 100 cents.
Denominations:
    Coins 1, 5, 10, 25 cents; B$1.
    Notes B$ 1, 2, 5, 10, 20, 100.
Exchange rate to £ sterling: 3·0733 (26 Jan. 1987).
Political history and government: A former British colony, with internal self-government from 16 Oct. 1961. A member of the West Indies Federation from 3 Jan. 1958 to 31 May 1962. Following a constitutional conference on 20 June–4 July 1966, Barbados became independent, within the Commonwealth, on 30 Nov. 1966. Executive power is vested in the Queen and exercisable by her appointed representative, the Governor-General, advised by the Cabinet. The Governor-General appoints the Prime Minister and, on the latter's advice, other members of the Cabinet. Legislative power is vested in the bicameral Parliament, comprising the Senate (21 appointed members) and the House of Assembly, with 27 members elected by universal adult suffrage for five years (subject to dissolution) from 27 constituencies. The Cabinet is responsible to Parliament.
Length of roadways: 1020 miles *1642 km*.
Universities: 1.
Adult illiteracy: About 98% in 1988.
Expectation of life: Males 67 years; females 72·5

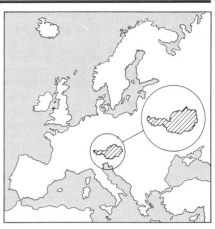

AUSTRIA

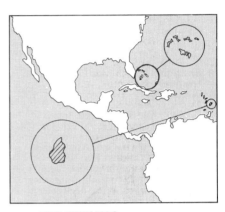

centre: **THE BAHAMAS**

right **BARBADOS**

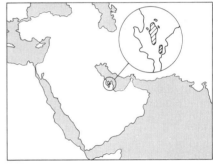

BAHRAIN

years (1982).
Defence: The Barbados Defence Force was established in April 1978 with 154 regular personnel; defence expenditure: 2% of total government expenditure in 1982.
Foreign tourists: 367 652 in 1984.

Belgium

Official name: Royaume de Belgique (in French), Koninkrijk België (in Dutch) or Königreich Belgien (in German): Kingdom of Belgium.
Population: 9 650 944 (census of 31 Dec. 1970); 9 857 721 (1984 estimate).
Area: 11 783 miles² *30 519 km²*.
Languages: Dutch (Flemish), French, German.
Religion: Roman Catholic.
Capital city: Bruxelles (Brussel, Brussels), population 980 196 (1985 estimate).
Other principal towns (1985): Antwerpen (Anvers, Antwerp) 486 576; Gent (Gand, Ghent) 234 563; Charleroi 211 943; Liège (Luik) 202 314; Brugge (Bruges) 117 747; Namur (Namen) 102 022,
Highest point: Botrange, 2277 ft *694 m*.

Principal mountain range: Ardennes.
Principal rivers: Schelde, Meuse (575 miles *925 km*).
Head of State: HM Baudouin Albert Charles Léopold Axel Marie Gustave, KG (b. 7 Sept. 1930), King of the Belgians. The King's name is also written Boudewijn (in Dutch) or Balduin (in German).
Prime Minister: Wilfried Martens.
Climate: Mild and humid on coast. Hotter summers, colder winters inland. In Brussels, January coldest (−0,5°C *31°F* to 5°C *42°F*), July hottest (12°C *54°F* to 23°C *73°F*), December rainiest (13 days). Absolute maximum temperature 40,0°C *104°F* on the coast, 27 June 1947; absolute minimum −29,8°C *−21·6°F*, Vieslam, 10 Dec. 1879.
Labour force: 4 180 000 in 1982: Agriculture 2·6%; Manufacturing 21·1%; Trade 16·6%; Services 34·2% Unemployed 11·2%.
Gross domestic product: 4486 billion Belgian francs in 1984: Agriculture 2·3%; Manufacturing 24·1%; Trade 5·4%; Services 32%.
Exports: 2987·5 billion Belgian francs (including Luxembourg) in 1984: Food and live animals 9·3%; Chemicals 12·6%; Basic manufactures 31·2%; Machinery and transport equipment 21%.
Monetary unit: Belgian franc (frank). 1 franc = 100 centimes (centiemen).
Denominations:
  Coins 50 centimes; 1, 5, 20, francs.
  Notes 50, 100, 500, 1000, 5000 francs.
Exchange rate to £ sterling: 57·75 (26 Jan. 1987).
Political history and government: A constitutional and hereditary monarchy, comprising nine provinces. Legislative power is vested in the King and the bicameral Parliament. comprising the Senate (181 members, including 106 directly elected by universal adult suffrage, 50 elected by provincial councils and 25 co-opted by the elected members) and the Chamber of Representatives (212 members directly elected, using proportional representation). Members of both Houses serve for up to four years. Executive

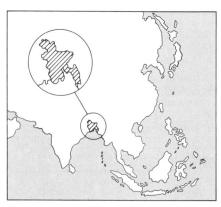

BANGLADESH

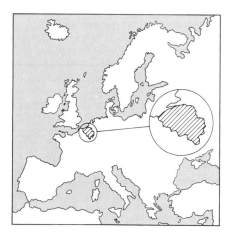

BELGIUM

power, nominally vested in the King, is exercised by the Cabinet. The King appoints the Prime Minister and, on the latter's advice, other Ministers. The Cabinet is responsible to Parliament.
Length of roadways: 80 989 miles *130 311 km* (1984).
Length of railways: 2325 miles *3741 km* (1984).
Universities: 7.
Expectation of life: Males 67·79 years; females 74·21 years (1968–72).
Defence: Military service 10 months (in Germany) or 12 months (in Belgium); total armed forces 91 428 in 1986; defence expenditure, 1985: 5·6% of total government expenditure.

Belize

Population: 144 857 (census of 12 May 1980); 162 100 (1984 estimate).
Area: 8867 miles² *22 965 km²*.
Languages: English (official), Spanish.
Religion: Christian (Roman Catholic 55%, Protestant 43%).
Capital city: Belmopan, population 3000 (1984 estimate).
Other principal towns (1980): Belize City 39 771; Dangriga 6061; Orange Walk Town 8439; Corozal Town 6899; San Ignacio 5616.
Highest point: Victoria Peak, 3681 ft *1122 m*.
Principal mountain range: Maya Mountains.
Principal rivers: Hondo (on Mexican border), Belize, New River.
Head of State: HM Queen Elizabeth II, represented by Dame Elmira Minita Gordon, GCMG, Governor-General.
Prime Minister: Manuel Esquivel.
Climate: Sub-tropical. At Belize City, on the coast, temperatures range from 10°C *50°F* to 36°C *96°F*, with an annual average of 31°C *78·5°F*. There are greater variations inland. Rainfall increases from north (annual average 1295 mm *51 in* at Corozal) to south (4445 mm *175 in* at Toledo).
Labour force: 33 121 (census of 7 April 1970).
Gross domestic product: BZ$314·7 million in 1984.
Exports: BZ$142·3 million in 1984: Sugar 45·7%; Bananas 4·3%; Citrus products 13·7%; Fish products 8·3%; Garments 20·8%.
Monetary unit: Belizean dollar (BZ$). 1 dollar = 100 cents.
Denominations:
  Coins 1, 5, 10, 25, 50 cents.
  Notes 1, 2, 5, 10, 20, 100 dollars.
Exchange rate to £ sterling: 3·056 (26 Jan. 1987).
Political history and government: Formerly British Honduras, a dependency of the United Kingdom. The colony was granted internal self-government on 1 Jan. 1964, when the First Minister became Premier. Renamed Belize on 1 June 1973. There has been a continuing territorial dispute with Guatemala.
  Following a constitutional conference on 6–14 Apr. 1981, Belize became independent within the Commonwealth, on 21 Sept. 1981, when the Premier was restyled Prime Minister. Executive power is vested in the British monarch and is exercisable by the Governor-General, who is appointed on the advice of the Prime Minister and acts in almost all matters on the advice of the Cabinet. Legislative power is vested in the bicameral National Assembly, comprising a Senate (8 members appointed by the Governor-General) and a House of Representatives (28 members elected by universal adult suffrage for 5 years, subject to dissolution). The Governor-General appoints the Prime Minister and, on the latter's recommendation, other Ministers. The Cabinet is responsible to the House.
Length of roadways: 2600 miles *4180 km*.
Adult illiteracy: 8% (estimate).
Defence: The Belize Defence Force was formed on 1 Jan. 1978; there are currently about 1800 British forces in Belize—defence expenditure: about 2% of government expenditure in 1984.
Foreign tourists: 62 735 in 1981.

Benin

Official name: La République populaire du Bénin (the People's Republic of Benin).
Population: 3 825 000 (1984 estimate).
Area: 43 484 miles² *112 622 km²*.
Languages: French (official), Fon, Adja, Bariba, Yoruba.
Religions: Animist, with Christian and Muslim minorities.
Capital city: Porto-Novo, population 208 258 (1982 estimate).
Other Principal towns (1979): Cotonou 487 020 (1982 estimate); Natitingou 50,800; Abomey 41 000; Kandi 31 000; Ouidah 30 000.
Highest point: 2083 ft *635 m*.
Principal mountain range: Châine de l'Atakora.
Principal rivers: Ouémé, Niger (2600 miles *4184 km*) on frontier.
Head of State: Brig.-Gen. Mathieu Kerekou (b. 2 Sept. 1933), President and Head of the Government.
Climate: Tropical (hot and humid). Average temperatures 20°C *68°F* to 34°C *93°F*. Heavy rainfall near the coast, hotter and drier inland. In Cotonou the warmest month is April (daily average high 28°C *83°F*), coldest is August (23°C *73°F*).
Labour force: 1 704 405 (1979).
Gross domestic product: 152 669 CFA francs in 1978: Agriculture, forestry and fishing 48%; Manufacturing 5·8% trade 22·7%; transport and communications 8·1%; Public administration and defence 8·3%.
Exports: 13 270 million CFA francs in 1980: Cocoa beans 22·2%; Cotton 18·5%; Palm products 27·8%.
Monetary unit: Franc de la Communauté financière africaine.
Denominations:
  Coins 1, 2, 5, 10, 25 CFA francs.
  Notes 50, 100, 500, 1000, 5000 CFA francs.
Exchange rate to £ sterling: 464·75 (26 Jan. 1987).
Political history and government: Formerly part of French West Africa, became independent as the Republic of Dahomey on 1 Aug. 1960. The latest in a series of *coups* took place on 26 Oct. 1972, when power was assumed by army officers, led by Maj. Mathieu Kerekou. On 1 Sept. 1973 President Kerekou announced the creation of a National Council of the Revolution (CNR), with 69 members (including 30 civilians), under his leadership, to develop state policy. The military régime proclaimed its adherence to Marxist-Leninist principles and on 1 Dec. 1975 it introduced the country's present name, with a single ruling political party. In August 1977 the CNR adopted a *Loi fondamentale* (Fundamental Law) providing for the establishment of a National Revolutionary Assembly comprising 336 People's Commissioners representing socio-professional classes. The first Assembly was elected by universal adult suffrage on 20 Nov. 1979, from a single list of candidates, and the CNR was disbanded. The Assembly elects the President, who appoints the National Executive Council (Cabinet).
Length of roadways: 5221 miles *8400 km*.
Length of railways: 360 miles *580 km*.
Universities: 1.
Adult illiteracy: 72·1% (males 60·2%; females 83·4%) in 1980.
Expectation of life: Males 41·8 years; females 45·0 years (UN estimates for 1970–75).
Defence: Total armed forces 5460 (1985); defence expenditure: 16·3% of total government expenditure in 1982.
Foreign tourists: 48 000 in 1982.

Bhutan

Official name: Druk-yul or, in Tibetan, Druk Gyalkhap (Realm of the Dragon). The name Bhutan is Tibetan for 'the End of the Land'.
Population: 1 286 275 (1985 estimate).
Area: 18 000 miles² *47 000 km²*.
Languages: Dzongkha, Bumthangka, Sarchapkkha.

Religions: Buddhist, with Hindu minority.
Capital city: Thimphu, population 20 000 (1985 estimate).
Other principal towns: Paro Dzong; Punakha; Tongsa Dzong.
Highest point: Khula Kangri 1, 24 784 ft *7554 m.*
Principal mountain range: Himalaya.
Principal rivers: Amo-Chu, Wang-chu, Machu, Manas.
Head of State: Jigme Singye Wangchuk (b. 11 Nov. 1955), Druk Gyalpo ('Dragon King').
Climate: Steamy hot in lowland foothills. Cold most of the year in higher areas.
Labour force: 650 000 in 1981–2: Agriculture, forestry and fishing 94·3%; Public services 3·4%.
Gross domestic product: $104 million in 1975 (UN estimate).
Monetary unit: Ngultrum. 1 ngultrum = 100 chetrums (Indian currency is also legal tender).
Denominations:
  Coins 5, 10, 25, 50 chetrums; 1 ngultrum.
  Notes 1, 5, 10 and 100 ngultrums.
Exchange rate to £ sterling: 19·82 (26 Jan. 1987).
Political history and government: A hereditary monarchy, under the Wangchuk dynasty since 1907. The Treaty of Punakha in 1910 provided that Bhutan's external relations were to be guided by British India. After the independence of India in 1947, an Indo-Bhutan Treaty of 8 Aug. 1949 transferred this protection to India.
The King is Head of State and Head of Government but a Royal Advisory Council (nine members), established in 1965, is the principal policy-making body. Bhutan's first Cabinet was formed in May 1968. The government is assisted by the unicameral National Assembly (*Tsogdu*), established in 1953. The Assembly has 150 members, of whom 110 are indirectly elected by village headmen, 10 represent ecclesiastical bodies and 30 are appointed officials. Members of the Assembly serve a three-year term. The Royal Advisory Council and the Council of Ministers are responsible to the Assembly.
Length of roadways: 1271 miles *2050 km* (1982).
Expectation of life: Males 47 years; females 50 years.
Defence: Army: 4000 men, Indian trained.
Foreign tourists: 2000 in 1984.

Bolivia

Official name: República de Bolivia.
Population: 6 081 722 (1983 estimate).
Area: 424 164 miles² *1 098 581 km².*
Languages: Spanish, Amyará, Quéchua.
Religion: Roman Catholic.
Capital city: La Paz de Ayacucho, population 835 283 (1983 estimate).
Other principal towns (1982): Santa Cruz de la Sierra 376 912; Cochabamba 281 962; Oruro 132 213; Potosí 103 183; Sucre (constitutional capital) 79 941.
Highest point: Nevado Sajama, 21 391 ft *6520 m* (first climbed in 1937).
Principal mountain ranges: Cordillera de los Andes, Cordillera Real, Cordillera Oriental, Cordillera Central.
Principal rivers: Beni, Mamoré, Pilcomayo, Paraguai (Paraguay) (1500 miles *2410 km*) on frontier.
Head of State: Dr Víctor Paz Estenssoro, President.
Climate: Dry, with cold winds on Altiplano, hot and humid in eastern lowlands. In La Paz, average maximum 17°C *62°F* (June, July) to 19°C *67°F* (November), minimum 0,5°C *33°F* (July) to 6°C *43°F* (January, February), January rainiest (21 days).
Labour force: 1 501 391 (1976 census): Agriculture, forestry and fishing 48·1%; Manufacturing 10·1%; Community, social and personal services 19·6%.
Gross domestic product: 16 049 million pesos in 1983 (at 1970 prices): Agriculture 16·6%; Mining (including petroleum exploration) 7·8%; Industry 14·7%; Transport and fuel 12·4%; Commerce and finance 12·9%; Public administration 11·9%.
Exports: US$817·5 million in 1983: Minerals 42·5%; Natural gas 46·3%; Coffee 1·6%.

Monetary unit: Bolivian peso. 1 peso = 100 centavos.
Denominations:
  Coins 20, 25, 50 centavos; 1 peso.
  Notes 5, 10, 20, 50, 100 pesos.
Exchange rate to £ sterling: 2 922 492 (26 Jan. 1987).
Political history and government: A republic, divided into nine departments. A series of military régimes held power from 1969 to 1979. Elections were held on 1 July 1979 for a President and for a bicameral Congress. No candidate gained a majority in the presidential election. Congress was convened on 1 Aug. 1979 but it also failed to give a majority to any presidential candidate. On 8 Aug. 1979 the President of the Senate was sworn in to serve as interim President. He was deposed by a military *coup* on 1 Nov. 1979. The *coup* leader resigned on 16 Nov. Congress elected the President of the Chamber of Deputies to be interim Head of State until fresh elections for a President and Congress, to hold office for four years. These were held on 29 June 1980 but the presidential election again proved inconclusive. Congress, comprising a Senate (27 members) and a Chamber of Deputies (130 members), was due to meet on 4 Aug. 1980 to elect a President but an armed forces junta again seized power on 17 July 1980. The *coup* leader, Gen Luis García Meza, was sworn in as President on the next day and Congress was suspended. On 4 Aug. 1981 President García resigned and ceded power to the junta. In 1982 the junta handed back power to the Congress elected in 1980, and Dr Siles Suazo was elected President for a four-year term. Elections were eventually held in 1985 after labour unrest.
Length of roadways: 25 473 miles *40 987 km.*
Length of railways: 2320 miles *3733 km.*
Universities: 9.
Adult illiteracy: 37·3% in 1976.
Expectation of life: Males 46·5 years; females 51·1 years (UN estimates for 1970–75).
Defence: Military service 12 months, selective; total armed forces 27 600 in 1985; defence expenditure: 7·4% of total government expenditure in 1982.
Foreign tourists: 163 000 in 1984.

Botswana

Official name: The Republic of Botswana.
Population: 941 027 (1981 census); 1 047 000 (1984 estimate).
Area: 224 711 miles² *582 000 km².*
Languages: Setswana, English.
Religions: Christian, ancestral beliefs.
Capital city: Gaborone, population 59 657 (1981 census).
Other principal towns (1981): Francistown 31 065; Selebi-Pikwe 29 469; Kanye 20 215; Lobatse 19 034; Mochudi 18 386; Molepole 20 565; Mahalapye 20 712; Maun 14 925.
Principal rivers: Chobe, Shashi.
Head of State: Dr Quett Ketumile Joni Masire (b. 23 July 1925), President.
Climate: Sub-tropical but variable. Hot summers. In winter, warm days and cold nights in higher parts. Average annual rainfall 457 mm *18 in*, varying from 635 mm *25 in* in north to 228 mm *9 in* or less in western Kalahari. Sand and dust blown by westerly wind in August.
Labour force: 128 894 in 1984: Agriculture 4·2%; Mining 5·8%; Manufacturing 7·4%; Trade 14%; Transport and communications 4·3%; Financial services 4·8%; Community, social and personal services 34·7%; South African mines 14·7%.
Gross domestic product: 1021·7 million pula in 1982–3: Agriculture 7·3%; Mining 27·9%; Manufacturing 7·7%; Trade 22·1%; Financial services 9·6%; Government services 16·6%.
Exports: 860 million pula in 1984: Meat and meat products 7·2%; Diamonds 71·9% Copper-nickel matte 7·9%; Textiles 4·7%.
Monetary unit: Pula. 1 pula = 100 thebe.
Denominations:
  Coins 1, 5, 10, 25 and 50 thebe.
  Notes 1, 2, 5 and 10 pula.

Exchange rate to £ sterling: 2·615 (26 Jan. 1987).
Political history and government: Formerly the Bechuanaland Protectorate, under British rule. In February 1965 the seat of government was moved from Mafeking (now Mafikeng), in South Africa, to Gaberones (now Gaborone). The first elections were held on 1 Mar. 1965, when internal self-government was achieved, and the first Prime Minister was appointed two days later. Bechuanaland became the independent Republic of Botswana, within the Commonwealth, on 30 Sept. 1966, when the Prime Minister became President.
Legislative power is vested in the unicameral National Assembly, with 38 members, including 32 directly elected by universal adult suffrage from single-member constituencies. Members of the Assembly serve for up to five years. Executive power is vested in the President, who

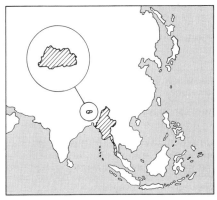

left: **BHUTAN**   *right:* **BURMA**

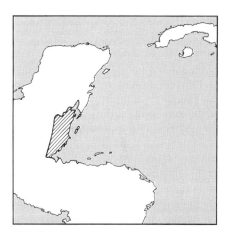

BELIZE

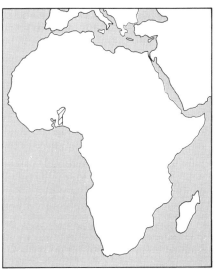

BENIN

is leader of the majority party in the Assembly. He governs with the assistance of an appointed Cabinet, responsible to the Assembly. The government is also advised by the House of Chiefs, with 15 members, including the chiefs of the eight principal tribes, four sub-chiefs and three others.
Length of roadways: 9300 miles *15 000 km* (1983).
Length of railways: 441 miles *710 km*.
Universities: 1.
Adult illiteracy: 59% (males 63%; females 56%) in 1971.
Expectation of life: Males 44·3 years; females 47·5 years (UN estimates for 1970–75).
Defence: Total armed forces 3000 (1984); defence expenditure, 1982: US$26·7 million.
Foreign tourists: 82 193 in 1983.

Brazil

Official name: A República Federativa do Brasil (the Federative Republic of Brazil).
Population: 132 580 000 (1984 estimate).
Area: 3 286 488 miles² *8 511 965 km²*.
Language: Portuguese.
Religion: Roman Catholic.
Capital city: Brasília, population 1 434 000 (1983 estimate).
Other principal towns (1980): Sao Paulo 7 032 547; Rio de Janeiro 5 090 700; Salvador 1 491 642; Belo Horizonte 1 441 567; Recife 1 183 391; Porto Alegre 1 114 867; Curitiba 842 818; Belem 755 984; Goiãna 702 858; Fortaleza 647 917.
Highest point: Pico da Bandeira, 9482 ft *2890 m*.
Principal mountain ranges: Serra do Mar, Serra Geral, Serra de Mantiqueira.
Principal rivers: Amazonas (Amazon) (4007 miles *6448 km*) and tributaries, Paraná, São Francisco.
Head of State: José Sarney, President.
Climate: Hot and wet in tropical Amazon basin; sub-tropical in highlands; temperate (warm summers and mild winters) in southern uplands. In Rio de Janeiro, average maximum 24°C *75°F* (July, September) to 29°C *85°F* (February), minimum 17°C *63°F* (July) to 23°C *73°F* (January, February), December rainiest (14 days). In São Paulo, maximum 22°C *71°F* (June, July) to 28°C *82°F* (February), minimum 9°C *49°F* (July) to 18°C *64°F* (February), January rainiest (19 days). Absolute maximum temperature 43·9°C *111·0°F*, Ibipetuba, 16 Sept. 1927: absolute minimum −11°C *+12·2°F*, Xanxerê, 14 July 1933.
Labour force: 43 235 712 in 1980: Agriculture, forestry and fishing 29·3%; Manufacturing 16·1%; Construction 7·3% Trade 9·3%; Services (inc. hotels and restaurants) 16·3% Social services 6·9%; Persons seeking work 2·2%.
Gross domestic product: 50 815·3 billion cruzeiros in 1982.
Exports: US$27 005·3 million in 1984: Coffee 10·6%; Food, beverages, vinegar and tobacco 21·2%; Mineral products 13·8%; Products of chemical and allied industries 4·2%; Textiles 4·5%; Machinery and transport equipment 12·4%.
Monetary unit: The cruzado was introduced in 1986: 1 cruzado = 1000 cruzeiros.
Exchange rate to £ sterling: 24·45 (26 Jan. 1987).
Political history and government: Under a military-backed government since the army revolution of 31 Mar.–1 Apr. 1964. Existing political parties were banned on 27 Oct. 1965. Two new parties (one pro-government, one against) were formed in Dec. 1965. New constitutions were introduced on 15 Mar. 1967 and 20 Oct. 1969. Brazil is a federal republic comprising 23 States, four Territories and a Federal District (Brasília). Legislative power is exercised by the National Congress, comprising the Chamber of Deputies (420 members, elected for four years) and the Federal Senate (66 members, elected in rotation for eight years). One-third of the Senate is elected indirectly. All literate adults may vote. Executive power is exercised by the President, elected for six years by an electoral college composed of members of Congress and representatives of State legislatures. He is assisted by a

Vice-President and an appointed Cabinet. The President has far-reaching powers. On 22 Nov. 1979 Congress approved legislation to end the two-party system. Several opposition parties were later formed.
Length of roadways: 860 241 miles *1 384 423 km* (31 Dec. 1979).
Length of railways: 18 584 miles *29 901 km*.
Universities: 67.
Adult illiteracy: 21·8% in 1984.
Expectation of life: 61·8 (1975–80).
Defence: Military service one year; total armed forces 276 000 in 1984; defence expenditure: 8·2% of total government expenditure in 1984.
Foreign tourists: 1 146 881 in 1982.

Brunei

Population: 192 832 (1981 census); 215 943 (1984 estimate).
Area: 2226 miles² *5765 km²*.
Language: Malay, English.
Religion: Islam.
Capital city: Bandar Seri Begawan, population 54 000 (1984 estimate).
Principal river: Brunei River.
Head of State: HH Muda Sir Hassanal Bolkiah Mu'izzaddin Waddaulah, Sultan of Brunei (b. 15 July 1946).
Climate: Hot and wet, tropical marine, rainfall ranging from 2500 mm *100 inches* on the coast to 5000 mm *200 inches* inland. Bandar Seri Begawan, Jan. 27°C *80°F*, July 28°C *82°F*.
Labour force: 70 690 in 1981: Construction 17·9%; Trade 10·4%; Transport, storage and communications 6·4%; Community, social and personal services 41·4%; Unemployed 3·6%.
Gross domestic product: B$8051·5 million in 1984.
Exports: B$6813·9 million in 1984: Crude petroleum 56·4%; Natural gas 41·9%.
Currency: Brunei dollar = 100 cents.
Exchange rate to £ sterling: 3·2823 (24 Jan. 1987).
Political history and government: The Sultanate of Brunei once controlled all of the island of Borneo, as well as parts of the Sulu Islands and the Philippines. After the 16th century its power declined until, by the middle of the 19th century, it had been reduced to its present boundaries, under the protection of Great Britain.
The present Sultan formed a constitution in 1959, whereby there would be a Privy Council, an Executive and a Legislative Council. On 6 Jan. 1965 amendments were made to the constitution so that elections could be made to the Legislative Council. The Executive Council was renamed the Council of Ministers. The Council of Ministers is presided over by the Sultan and consists of six ex-officio members and four other members, all of whom, except one, are members of the Legislative Council. The Mentri Besar, or Acting Chief Minister (one of the ex-officio members of the Legislative Council and the Council of Ministers) is responsible to the Sultan for the exercise of executive authority in the State.
On 7 Jan. 1979 the Sultan and the British government signed a treaty by which Brunei became an independent state on 31 December 1983.
Length of roadways: 916 miles *1474 km*.
Defence: Total armed forces, 4050 (1985); defence expenditure: 12·8% of total government expenditure in 1984.
Foreign tourists: 7513 in 1984.

Bulgaria

Official name: Narodna Republika Bulgariya (People's Republic of Bulgaria).
Population: 8 972 000 (1984 estimate).
Area: 42 823 miles² *110 912 km²*.
Languages: Bulgarian 88%; Turkish and Macedonian minorities.
Religions: Eastern Orthodox, with Muslim, Roman Catholic and Protestant minorities.
Capital city: Sofiya (Sofia), population 1 093 752 (1983 estimate).

Other principal towns (1983): Plovdiv 373 235; Varna 295 218; Ruse 181 185; Burgas 183 477; Stara Zagora 144 904; Pleven 140 440; Shumen 104 089.
Highest point: Musala, 9596 ft *2925 m*.
Principal mountain range: Stara Planina (Balkan Mountains).
Principal rivers: Dunav (Danube) (1770 miles *2850 km*), Iskŭr (Iskar) (229 miles *368 km*), Maritsa (326 miles *524 km*), Tundzha.
Head of State: Todor Zhivkov (b. 7 Sept. 1911), Chairman of the State Council and General Secretary of the Central Committee of the Bulgarian Communist Party.
Head of Government: Grisha Filipov (b. 13 July 1919), Chairman of the Council of Ministers.
Climate: Mild in the south, more extreme in the north. In Sofia, July (14°C *57°F* to 28°C *82°F*), August (13°C *56°F* to 28°C *82°F*) hottest, January (−5°C *22°F* to 1°C *34°F*) coldest, May rainiest (11 days).
Labour force: 4 113 546 in 1983: Agriculture 22·4%; Industry 34·3%; Construction 8·6%; Commerce 8·7%; Education and culture 7·4%; Public health, welfare and sports 4·8%.
Net material product: 23 479 million leva in 1983: Agriculture and livestock 16·5%; Industry 56·5%; Construction 9·7%; Trade 6·5%; Transport and storage 6·8%.

left: **BOLIVIA**   *right:* **BRAZIL**

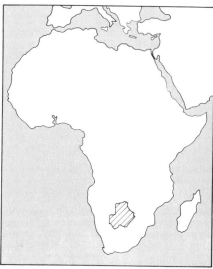

BOTSWANA

Exports: 12987·3 million leva in 1984: Machinery and equipment 47·7%; Fuels, mineral raw materials and metals 10·8%; Foodstuffs, beverages and tobacco products 17·5%.
Monetary unit: Lev. 1 lev = 100 stotinki (singular: stotinka).
Denominations:
Coins 1, 2, 5, 10, 20, 50 stotinki; 1, 2, 5 leva.
Notes 1, 2, 5, 10, 20 leva.
Exchange rate to £ sterling: 1·2967 (26 Jan. 1987).
Political history and government: Formerly part of Turkey's Ottoman Empire, becoming an autonomous principality in 1878. Bulgaria became a fully independent kingdom on 22 Sept. 1908. The government allied with Nazi Germany in the Second World War. On 9 Sept. 1944 the Fatherland Front, a Communist-dominated coalition, seized power in a *coup*. The monarchy was abolished by a popular referendum on 8 Sept. 1946 and a republic proclaimed on 15 Sept. 1946. A constitution for a People's Republic was adopted on 4 Dec. 1947. A new constitution was promulgated, after approval by referendum, on 18 May 1971.

The supreme organ of state power is the unicameral National Assembly, with 400 members elected for five years (unopposed) by universal adult suffrage in single-member constituencies. The Assembly elects the State Council (28 members were elected on 17 June 1981) to be its permanent organ. The Council of Ministers, the highest organ of state administration, is elected by (and responsible to) the Assembly.

Political power is held by the Bulgarian Communist Party (BCP), which dominates the Fatherland Front. The Front presents an approved list of candidates for elections to all representative bodies. The BCP's highest authority is the Party Congress, convened every five years. The Congress elects a Central Committee (197 members were elected in April 1981) to supervise Party work. To direct its policy, the Committee elects a Political Bureau (Politburo), with 12 full members and three candidate members in 1981.

Bulgaria comprises 27 provinces and three cities, each with a People's Council elected for 2½ years.
Length of roadways: 22583 miles *36336 km* (1984).
Length of railways: 3996 miles *6430 km* (1984).
Universities: 3.
Adult illiteracy: 9·8% (males 4·8%; females 14·7%) in 1965.
Expectation of life: Males 68·68 years; females 73·91 years (1974–76).
Defence: Military service: Army and Air Force two years, Navy three years; total armed forces 148500 (94000 conscripts) in 1985; defence expenditure: 5·5% of total government in 1985.
Foreign tourists: 6100000 (including about 3000000 in transit) in 1984.

Burkino Faso

Official name: Burkina Faso (previously Upper Volta).
Population: 7919895 (1985 census).
Area: 105869 miles² *274200 km²*.
Languages: French (official), Mossi, other African languages.
Religions: Animist; Muslim and Christian minorities.
Capital city: Ouagadougou, population 375000 (1985 estimate).
Other principal towns (1985): Bobo-Dioulasso 211538; Koudougou 52431; Ouahigouya 36564.
Highest point: Mt Tema, 2457 ft *749 m.*
Principal rivers: Volta Noire (Black Volta), Volta Rouge (Red Volta), Volta Blanche (White Volta).
Head of State: Capt. Thomas Sankara, President.
Climate: Hot (average temperature 28°C *83°F*). Dry from November to March. Very dry in north and north-east. Rainy season June to October in south. In Ouagadougou, average maximum temperature 30°C *87°F* (August) to

40°C *104°F* (March), minimum 15°C *60°F* to 26°C *79°F*.
Labour force: 3537000 in 1984: Agriculture, forestry and fishing 79%.
Gross domestic product: 252340 million CFA francs in 1979. Agriculture, forestry and fishing 37·9% Manufacturing 11·5%; Trade 15·8% Transport, storage and communications 6·4%; Financial services 5·3%.
Exports: 18109 million francs CFA in 1982: Cotton 41·9%; Almonds 16%; Livestock 14·1%.
Monetary unit: Franc de la Communauté financière africaine.
Denominations:
Coins 1, 2, 5, 10, 25, 50, 100 CFA francs.
Notes 50, 100, 500, 1000, 5000 CFA francs.
Exchange rate to £ sterling: 464·75 (26 Jan. 1987).
Political history and government: Formerly a part of French West Africa, independent since 5 Aug. 1960. The civilian President was deposed on 3 Jan. 1966 in a military *coup* led by Lt-Col (later Maj-Gen) Sangoulé Lamizana, the army Chief of Staff. He took office as President and Prime Minister, the constitution was suspended, the National Assembly dissolved and a Supreme Council of the Armed Forces established. Political activities were suspended on 21 Sept. 1966 but the restriction was lifted in Nov. 1969. A new constitution was approved by popular referendum on 14 June 1970 and introduced on 21 June. This provided for a four-year transitional régime, under joint military and civilian control, leading to the return of civilian rule. Elections for a unicameral National Assembly of 57 members were held on 20 Dec. 1970. The leader of the majority party was appointed Prime Minister by the President, took office on 13 Feb. 1971 and formed a mixed civilian and military Council of Ministers. On 8 Feb. 1974, after a dispute between the Premier and the Assembly, the President dismissed the former and dissolved the latter. The army again assumed power, with the constitution and political activity suspended. The Head of State also became President of the Council of Ministers on 11 Feb. 1974. Political parties were banned on 30 May. The Assembly was replaced by a National Consultative Council for Renewal, formed on 2 July 1974, with 65 members nominated by the President.

Political parties were allowed to resume activities from 1 Oct. 1977. A referendum on 27 Nov. 1977 approved a draft constitution providing for a return to civilian democratic rule, with legislative elections on a multi-party basis, a President directly elected for a 5-year term and a separate Prime Minister nominated by the President. Elections were held on 30 Apr. 1978 for a new National Assembly (57 members serving a 5-year term). Under the constitution, only the three parties which obtained most votes were allowed to continue their activities (other parties being obliged to merge with them). A presidential election was held on 14 May 1978 but no candidate gained an overall majority. A 'run-off' election between the two leading candidates on 28 May was won by Lamizana. On 7 July 1978 the Assembly elected the President's nominee for Prime Minister. The President appointed other Ministers on the Prime Minister's recommendation. On 29 May 1979 the Assembly passed a law limiting the number of authorised political parties to the three strongest in the 1978 elections.

On 25 Nov. 1980 the government was overthrown in a military *coup*, led by Col Saye Zerbo, military commander of the capital region. He was overthrown in Nov. 1982, Maj. Jean-Baptiste Oedraogo assuming power, who was himself overthrown by Capt. Thomas Sankara in Aug. 1983. Sankara has subsequently survived a number of attempts to overthrow him. Supreme political power resides with a council of Ministers.

The country is divided into 30 provinces.
Length of roadways: 10299 miles *16574 km.*
Length of railways: 321 miles *517 km.*
Universities: 1.
Adult illiteracy: 91·2% (males 85·7%; females 96·7%) in 1975.

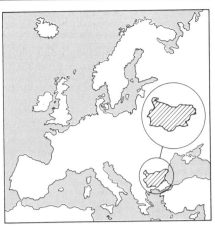

BULGARIA

Expectation of life: Males 39·4 years; females 42·5 years (UN estimates for 1970–75).
Defence: Total armed forces 3900 (1985); defence expenditure, 1984: $28·6 million.
Foreign tourists: 44000 in 1982.

Burma

Official name: Pyidaungsu Socialist Thammada Myanma Nainggnan (The Socialist Republic of the Union of Burma).
Population: 35313905 (1983 census); 36392000 (1984 estimate).
Area: 261218 miles² *676552 km².*
Languages: Burmese, English.
Religions: Buddhist, with Muslim, Hindu and Animist minorities.
Capital city: Yangon (Rangoon), population 2458712 (1983 census).
Other principal towns (1983): Mandalay 532895; Moulmein 219991; Bassein 335000; Akyab 143000.
Highest Point: Hkakado Razi, 19296 ft *5881 m.*
Principal mountain ranges: Arakan Yoma, Pegu Yoma.
Principal rivers: Irrawaddy (including Chindwin), Salween, Sittang, Mekong (2600 miles *4180 km*) on frontier.
Head of State: Brig-Gen. U. San Yu (b. 1919), President.
Prime Minister: U Maung Maung Kha (b. 2 Nov. 1917).
Climate: Hot March–April, monsoon May–October, cool November–February. In Rangoon, average maximum 29°C *85°F* (July, August) to 36°C *97°F* (April), minimum 18°C *65°F* (January) to 25°C *77°F* (May), July (26 days) and August (25 days) rainiest. Absolute maximum temperature 45,56°C *114°F*, Mandalay, 29 Apr. 1906, Monywa, 15 May 1934; absolute minimum −0,56°C *31°F*, Maymyo, 29 Dec. 1913.
Labour force: 14792000 in 1985: Agriculture, forestry and fishing 66·1%; Manufacturing 8·3%; Trade 9·8%; Administration 3·9%.
Gross domestic product: 54042 million kyats in 1984–5: Agriculture, forestry and fishing 48% Manufacturing 9·4%; Transport 3·4%; Financial institutions 2·3%; Social and administrative services 4·7%.
Exports: 3419·5 million kyats in 1983–4: Rice and rice products 40·8%; Teak 24·6%; Base metals and ores 8·8%.
Monetary unit: Kyat. 1 kyat = 100 pyas.
Denominations:
Coins 1, 5, 10, 25, 50 pyas; 1 kyat.
Notes 1, 5, 10, 20, 25, 50, 100 kyats.
Exchange rate to £ sterling: 10·1192 (26 Jan. 1987).
Political history and government: Formerly part of British India. Burma became a separate British dependency, with limited self-government, in 1937. It was invaded and occupied by Japanese forces in February 1942 but reoccupied by British forces in May 1945. Burma became independent, outside the Common-

wealth, on 4 Jan. 1948. The government was deposed by a military *coup* on 2 Mar. 1962 and Parliament was dissolved the next day. Power was assumed by a Revolutionary Council, led by Gen Ne Win. The military régime established the Burmese Socialist Programme Party (BSPP), the only permitted party since 28 Mar. 1964.

A new one-party constitution, approved by popular referendum on 15–31 Dec. 1973, was introduced on 4 Jan. 1974, when the country's present name was adopted. Legislative power is vested in the People's Assembly, with 475 members elected for four years by universal adult suffrage. The first Assembly was elected on 27 Jan.–10 Feb. 1974 and inaugurated on 2 Mar. 1974, when the Revolutionary Council was dissolved. The Assembly elects a Council of State (29 members) to be the country's main policy-making body. The Chairman of the Council of State is President of the Republic. The Council of Ministers, elected by the Assembly, has executive responsibility. Burma comprises 7 states and 7 administrative regions.
Length of roadways: 14 333 miles *23 067 km* (1985).
Length of railways: 1961 miles *3156 km* (1985).
Universities: 2.
Adult illiteracy: 34% (males 24%, females 44%) in 1980.
Expectation of life: Males 48·6 years; females 51·5 years (UN estimates for 1970–75).
Defence: Military service voluntary; total armed forces 186 000 (1985); defence expenditure: 19% of total government expenditure in 1982–3.
Foreign tourists: 28 575 in 1984.

Burundi

Official name: La République du Burundi or Republika y'Uburundi (the Republic of Burundi).
Population: 4 537 000 (1984 estimate).
Area: 10 747 miles² *27 834 km²*.
Languages: French, Kirundi, Kiswahili.
Religions: Roman Catholic, with Animist and Protestant minorities.
Capital city: Bujumbura (formerly Usumbura), population 172 201 (1979).
Other principal town: Gitega (Kitega), population 35 000 (1982).
Highest point: 8809 ft *2685 m*.
Principal rivers: Kagera, Ruzizi.
Head of State: Col Jean-Baptiste Bagaza (b. 29 Aug. 1946), President.
Climate: Hot and humid in lowlands, cool in highlands.
Labour force: 2 480 841 in 1983: Agriculture and fishing 93·7% Traditional trades 0·9%; Private sector 1·5%; Public sector 3·8%.
Gross domestic product: 105 503 million Burundi francs in 1984: Agriculture, forestry and fishing 52·2%; Manufacturing 5·4%; Construction 6·1%; Trade 8·5%; Government services 8·3%.
Exports: 11 828·1 million Burundi francs in 1984: Coffee 84%; Tea 7·3%; Cotton 0·7%; Hides and skins 0·7%.
Monetary unit: Burundi franc. 1 franc = 100 centimes.
Denominations:
Coins 1, 5, 10 francs.
Notes 10, 20, 50, 100, 500, 1000 francs.
Exchange rate to £ sterling: 183·31 (26 Jan. 1987).
Political history and government: Formerly a monarchy, ruled by a *Mwami* (King). Part of German East Africa from 1899. Occupied in 1916 by Belgian forces from the Congo (now Zaire). From 1920 Burundi was part of Ruanda–Urundi, administered by Belgium under a League of Nations mandate and later as a UN Trust Territory. Became independent on 1 July 1962. A one-party state since 24 Nov. 1966. The monarchy was overthrown, and a republic established, by a military *coup* on 28 Nov. 1966, when the Prime Minister, Col (later Lt-Gen) Michel Micombero, took power and became President. Another military *coup* deposed Micombero on 1 Nov. 1976. A Supreme Revolutionary Council (SRC) with 30 members, all military officers, was established on 2 Nov. 1976

and its leader became President of the Second Republic. The office of Prime Minister was abolished on 13 Oct. 1978. The ruling party's National Congress, opening on 26 Dec. 1979, elected a Central Committee to take over the SRC's functions.
Length of roadways: 3196 miles *5144 km.*
Universities: 1.
Adult illiteracy: 73·2% (males 61·1%, females 84·6%) in 1980.
Expectation of life: Males 40 years; females 43 years (sample survey, 1970–71).
Defence: Total armed forces 5200 (1985); defence expenditure: 24·6% of total government expenditure in 1984.
Foreign tourists: 38 000 in 1982.

Cameroon

Official name: La République unie du Cameroun (the United Republic of Cameroon).
Population: 9 165 000 (1984 estimate).
Area: 183 569 miles² *475 442 km².*
Languages: French, English (both official).
Religions: Animist, with Christian and Muslim minorities.
Capital city: Yaoundé, population 650 000 (1984 estimate).
Other principal towns (1981): Douala 636 980; Nkongsamba 86 870; Garoua 77 856; Maroua 81 861; Bamenda 58 697; Bafoussam 75 832; Foumban 41 538.
Highest point: Cameroon Mt, 13 350 ft *4069 m.*
Principal mountain range: Massif de Ladamaoua.
Principal rivers: Sanaga, Nyong.
Head of State: Paul Biya (b. 13 Feb. 1933), President.
Climate: Hot and rainy on the coast; cooler and drier inland. Average temperature 27°C *80°F.* In Yaoundé average maximum 27°C *80°F* to 29°C *85°F,* minimum around 19°C *66°F.*
Labour force: 3 543 000 in 1982.
Gross domestic product: 3195 billion CFA francs in 1983–4: Agriculture, forestry and fishing 22%; Mining 16·3%; Manufacturing 11·2%; Construction 6%; Trade 13%; Financial services 12·4%.
Exports: 440 470 million CFA francs in 1984: Cocoa 22·8%; Coffee 21·3%; Cotton fibre 2·3%; Cotton fabric 2·1%; Timber 4·2%; Aluminium 6·8%; Petroleum 21·6%.
Monetary unit: Franc de la Communauté financière africain (CFA).
Denominations:
Coins 1, 2, 5, 10, 25, 50, 100, 500 CFA francs.
Notes 100, 500, 1000, 5000, 10 000 CFA francs.
Exchange rate to £ sterling: 464·75 (26 Jan. 1987).
Political history and government: The former German colony of Cameroon was divided into British and French zones, both parts becoming UN Trust Territories. The French zone became independent as the Republic of Cameroon on 1 Jan. 1960. The northern part of the British zone joined Nigeria on 1 June 1961 and the southern part became West Cameroon when it joined the former French zone (renamed East Cameroon) to form a federal republic on 1 Oct. 1961. A one-party state since 8 Sept. 1966. After approval by a referendum on 21 May 1972, the federal arrangement ended and Cameroon became a unitary state on 2 June 1972. The legislature is a unicameral National Assembly of 120 members elected for five years by universal suffrage. The President, elected by the people every five years, appoints the Prime Minister, other Ministers and a governor for each of the seven provinces.
Length of roadways: 16 730 miles *26 920 km* (1977).
Length of railways: 729 miles *1173 km.*
Universities: 1.
Adult illiteracy: 59·5% (males 45·4%, females 75·5%) in 1976.
Expectation of life: Males 41·9 years; females 45·1 years (UN estimates for 1970–75).
Defence: Total armed forces 6600 (1985); defence expenditure: 9·1% of total government expenditure in 1984–5.
Foreign tourists: 116 152 in 1983.

Canada

Official name: Canada.
Population: 24 343 181 (1981 census); 25 591 100 (1986 estimate).
Area: 3 851 809 miles² *9 976 139 km².*
Languages: English 60·1%; French 26·9%; German 2·6%; Italian 2·5%; Ukrainian 1·4% (1971).
Religions: Roman Catholic, United Church of Canada, Anglican.
Capital city: Ottawa, population 756 600 (1984 estimate).
Other principal towns (1984): Toronto 3 140 500; Montreal 2 865 900; Vancouver 1 331 000; Edmonton 687 500; Winnipeg 603 500; Quebec 589 100; Hamilton 554 400; Calgary 619 760.
Highest point: Mt Logan, 19 850 ft *6050 m* (first climbed 23 June 1925).
Principal mountain ranges: Rocky Mts, Coast Mts, Mackenzie Mts.
Principal rivers: Mackenzie (2635 miles *4240 km,* including Peace 1195 miles *1923 km*), Yukon (1979 miles *3185 km*), St Lawrence (1945 miles *3130 km*), Nelson (1600 miles *2575 km,* including Saskatchewan 1205 miles *1940 km*), Columbia (1150 miles *1850 km*), Churchill (1000 miles *1609 km*).
Head of State: HM Queen Elizabeth II, represented by Mme Jeanne Sauvé (b. 1922), Governor-General.
Prime Minister: The Rt Hon Brian Mulroney (b. 1939).
Climate: Great extremes, especially inland. Average summer temperature 65°F, very cold winters. Light to moderate rainfall, heavy snowfalls. Below are listed a selection of towns showing the extreme monthly variations in average maximum and minimum daily temperatures and the month with the maximum number of rainy days.

Calgary: Average maximum −4°C *24°F* (January) to 24°C *76°F* (July). Average minimum −17°C *2°F* (January) to 8°C *47°F* (July). Rainiest month (rainy days) June (12).
Halifax: Average maximum −0,5°C *31°F* (February) to 23°C *74°F* (July, August). Average minimum −9°C *15°F* (January, February) to 13°C *56°F* (August). Rainiest month (rainy days) January (17).
Ottawa: Average maximum −6°C *21°F* (January) to 27°C *81°F* (July). Average minimum −16°C *3°F* (January, February) to 14°C *58°F* (July). Rainiest month (rainy days) December (14).
St John's: Average maximum −2°C *28°F* (February) to 20°C *69°F* (August). Average minimum −9°C *16°F* (February) to 12°C *53°F* (August). Rainiest months (rainy days) November, December (17).
Vancouver: Average maximum 5°C *41°F* (January) to 23°C *74°F* (July). Average minimum 0°C *32°F* (January) to 12°C *54°F* (July, August). Rainiest month (rainy days) December (22).
Winnipeg: Average maximum −14°C *7°F* (January) to 26°C *79°F* (July). Average minimum −25°C *−13°F* (January) to 13°C *55°F* (July). Rainiest months (rainy days) January, June (12).
Yellowknife: Average maximum −23°C *−10°F* (January) to 20°C *69°F* (July). Average minimum −33°C *−26°F* (January) to 11°C *52°F* (July). Rainiest month (rainy days) December (13).

Absolute maximum temperature 46,1°C *115°F,* Gleichen, Alberta, 28 July 1903; absolute minimum −62,8°C *−81°F,* Snag, Yukon, 3 Feb. 1947.
Labour force: 12 399 000 in 1984: Agriculture 4·7%; Manufacturing 15·9%; Trade 15·6%; Services 39·6%; unemployed 11·3%.
Gross domestic product: C$234 215 million in 1978: Manufacturing (excl. government) 20·7%; Trade (excl. government) 11·3%; Community, social and personal services (incl. restaurants, hotels and business services) 26·2% (government services 16·8%).
Exports: C$109·5 billion in 1984 (estimate): Raw materials 15·8%; Agricultural products 9·4%; Manufactured goods 73·8%.

Monetary unit: Canadian dollar (C$). One dollar = 100 cents.

Denominations:

Coins 1, 5, 10, 25, 50 cents; $1.

Notes $1, 2, 5, 10, 20, 50, 100, 500, 1000.

Exchange rate to £ sterling: 2·07 (26 Jan. 1987).

Political history and government: The Dominion of Canada, under the British Crown, was established on 1 July 1867 by the British North America Act. It was originally a federation of four provinces (Quebec, Ontario, Nova Scotia and New Brunswick). These were later joined by Manitoba (15 July 1870), British Columbia (20 July 1871), Prince Edward Island (1 July 1873), Alberta and Saskatchewan (1 Sept. 1905). Canada acquired its Arctic islands from the United Kingdom on 1 Sept. 1880. The country achieved full independence, within the Commonwealth, by the Statute of Westminster on 11 Dec. 1931. Newfoundland, previously a separate British dependency, became the tenth province on 1 Apr. 1949.

In November 1981 the Canadian government agreed on the provisions of an amended constitution, to the end that it should replace the British North America Act and that its future amendment should be the prerogative of Canada. These proposals were adopted by the Parliament of Canada and were enacted by the UK Parliament as the Canada Act of 1982.

The Act gave to Canada the power to amend the Constitution according to procedures determined by the Constitutional Act 1982, which was proclaimed in force by the Queen on 17 April 1982. The Constitution Act 1982 added to the Canadian Constitution a charter of Rights and Freedoms, and provisions which recognize the nation's multi-cultural heritage, affirm the existing rights of native peoples, confirm the principle of equalization of benefits among the provinces, and strengthen provincial ownership of natural resources.

Canada is a federal parliamentary state. Executive power is vested in the Queen and exercisable by her representative, the Governor-General, whom she appoints on the advice of the Canadian Prime Minister. The Federal Parliament comprises the Queen, a nominated Senate (104 members, appointed on a regional basis) and a House of Commons (282 members elected by universal adult suffrage). A Parliament may last no longer than 5 years. The Governor-General appoints the Prime Minister and, on the latter's recommendation, other Ministers to form the Cabinet. The Prime Minister must have majority support in Parliament, to which the Cabinet is responsible. Canada contains 10 provinces (each with a Lieutenant-Governor and a legislature from which a Premier is chosen) and two centrally-administered territories.

Length of roadways: 575 520 miles *928 258 km* (1981).

Length of railways: 41 150 miles *66 370 km*.

Universities: 47.

Expectation of life: Males 69·34 years; females 76·36 years (1970–72).

Defence: Military service voluntary; total armed forces 82 000 (1983); defence expenditure, 1985–6: 8·9% of total government expenditure.

Foreign tourists: 34 864 981 in 1984.

ALBERTA

Population: 2 237 724 (1981 census); 2 344 600 (1985 estimate).

Area: 255 285 miles² *661 199 km²*.

Languages: English, German, Ukrainian, French.

Religions: United Church of Canada, Roman Catholic, Anglican, Lutheran.

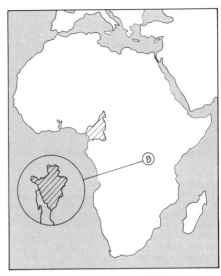

above: **CAMEROON**   *encircled:* **BURUNDI**

Capital city: Edmonton, population 560 085 (1985).

Other principal towns (1985): Calgary 625 143; Lethbridge 59 901; Red Deer 52 620; Medicine Hat 41 717.

Principal mountain range: Rocky Mountains.

Principal rivers: Peace, Athabasca.

Lieutenant-Governor: Helen Hunley.

Premier: Hon. Donald Getty.

Length of roadways: 94 335 miles *151 785 km*.

Length of railways: 5613 miles *9031 km*.

Universities: 4.

BRITISH COLUMBIA

Population: 2 744 467 (1981 census); 2 892 000 (1985 estimate).

Area: 366 255 miles² *948 596 km²*.

Languages: English, German.

Religions: United Church of Canada, Anglican, Roman Catholic, Lutheran.

Capital city: Victoria, population 242 000 (1984 estimate).

Other principal towns (1984): Vancouver 1 331 000; Prince George 69 293; Kamloops 64 661; Kelowna 61 847; Nanaimo 50 317.

Principal mountain range: Rocky Mountains.

Principal rivers: Fraser, Thompson, Kootenay, Columbia.

Lieutenant-Governor: Robert Gordon Rogers.

Premier: William Vander Zalm.

Length of roadways: 27 308 miles *43 939 km*.

Length of railways: 4826 miles *7766 km*.

Universities: 3.

MANITOBA

Population: 1 026 241 (1981 census); 1 070 300 (1985 estimate).

Area: 251 000 miles² *650 087 km²*.

Languages: English, Ukrainian, German, French.

Religions: United Church of Canada, Roman Catholic, Anglican, Lutheran.

Capital city: Winnipeg, population 603 500 (1984 estimate).

Other principal towns (1981): Brandon 36 247; Thompson 14 288; Portage la Prairie 13 086.

Highest point: Duck Mountain, 2727 ft *831 m*.

Lieutenant-Governor: Pearl McGonigal.

Premier: Howard Pawley.

Length of roadways: 11 813 miles *19 007 km*.

Length of railways: 4900 miles *7886 km*.

Universities: 3.

NEW BRUNSWICK

Population: 696 403 (1981 census); 714 200 (1984 estimate).

Area: 28 354 miles² *73 437 km²*.

Languages: English, French.

Religions: Roman Catholic, Baptist, United Church of Canada, Anglican.

Capital city: Fredericton, population 45 248 (1976 census).

**CANADA—1. Yukon Territory   2. Northwest Territories   3. British Columbia
4. Alberta   5. Saskatchewan   6. Manitoba   7. Ontario   8. Quebec   9. Newfoundland
10. New Brunswick   11. Nova Scotia   12. Prince Edward Island**

Other principal towns (1976): Saint John 85 956;
Moncton 55 934; Bathurst 16 301; Edmundston
12 710.
Highest point: Mt Carleton, 2690 ft *820 m.*
Principal river: St John.
Lieutenant-Governor: George F. S. Stanley.
Premier: Richard Bennett Hatfield (b. 9 Apr.
1931).
Length of roadways: 12 854 miles *20 686 km.*
Universities: 4.

NEWFOUNDLAND (Terre-Neuve) AND LABRADOR
Population: 567 681 (1981 census); 579 000 (1984
estimate).
Area: 156 185 miles² *404 517 km².*
Language: English.
Religions: Roman Catholic, Anglican, United
Church of Canada, Salvation Army.
Capital city: St John's, population 154 820 (1981
census).
Other principal towns (1981): Corner Brook
24 339; Labrador City 11 538; Gander 10 404;
Stephenville 8876.
Highest point: Mt Gras Morne, 2666 ft *812 m.*
Principal mountain range: Long Range Mountain.
Principal rivers: Humber, Exploits, Gander.
Lieutenant-Governor: James McGrath.
Premier: (Alfred) Brian Peckford (b. 27 Aug.
1942).
Length of roadways: 5415 miles *8713 km* (1984).
Length of railways: 906 miles *1458 km* (1984).
Universities: 1.

NOVA SCOTIA
Population: 847 442 (1981 census); 881 300 (1985
estimate).
Area: 21 425 miles² *55 490 km².*
Language: English.
Religions: Roman Catholic, United Church of
Canada, Anglican, Baptist.
Capital city: Halifax, population 114 594 (1981
census).
Other principal towns (1981): Dartmouth 62 277;
Sydney 29 444; Glace Bay 21 466; Truro 12 552.
Lieutenant-Governor: Alan R. Abraham.
Premier: John MacLennan Buchanan (b. 22
April 1931).
Length of roadways: 15 899 miles *25 582 km*
(1984).
Length of railways: 890 miles *1432 km* (1984).
Universities: 8.

ONTARIO
Population: 8 625 107 (1981 census); 8 946 900
(1985 estimate).
Area: 412 582 miles² *1 068 582 km².*
Languages: English, French, Italian, German.
Religions: Roman Catholic, United Church of
Canada, Anglican, Presbyterian.
Capital city: Toronto, population 2 998 947 (1981
census).
Other principal towns (1981): Hamilton 542 095;
Ottawa 717 978; London 254 280; Windsor
192 083.
Principal rivers: St Lawrence, Ottawa.
Lieutenant-Governor: Rt. Hon. Lincoln M. Alexander.
Premier: David Peterson.
Length of roadways: 95 471 miles *153 613 km*
(1984).
Length of railways: 10 375 miles *16 693 km*
(1984).
Universities: 15.

PRINCE EDWARD ISLAND
Population: 124 200 (1981 census); 127 000 (1985
estimate).
Area: 2184 miles² *5657 km².*
Languages: English, French.
Religions: Roman Catholic, United Church of
Canada, Presbyterian.
Capital city: Charlottetown, population 15 282
(1981).
Other principal town: Summerside 7828 (1981).
Lieutenant-Governor: Lloyd G. MacPhail.
Premier: Joseph Ghiz.
Length of roadways: 3280 miles *5278 km* (1984).
Length of railways: 274 miles *441 km* (1984).
Universities: 1.

QUEBEC
Population: 6 438 403 (1981 census); 6 553 492
(1984 estimate).
Area: 594 860 miles² *1 540 680 km².*
Languages: French, English.
Religion: Roman Catholic.
Capital city: Quebec, population 164 000 (1984
estimate).
Other principal towns (1984): Montreal 1 001 300;
Laval 278 280; Sherbrooke 72 000; Verdun
58 400; Hull 55 000; Trois-Rivières 50 000.
Highest point: Mt Jacques Cartier, 4160 ft
1268 m.
Principal mountain ranges: Notre Dame, Appalachian.
Principal river: St Lawrence.
Lieutenant-Governor: Hon. Gilles Lamontagne.
Premier: Robert Bourassa.
Length of roadways: 35 800 miles *57 602 km*
(1984).
Length of railways: 2801 miles *4507 km* (1984).
Universities: 7.

SASKATCHEWAN
Population: 968 313 (1981 census); 1 019 500
(1985 estimate).
Area: 251 700 miles² *651 900 km².*
Languages: English, German, Ukrainian.
Religions: United Church of Canada, Roman
Catholic, Lutheran, Anglican.
Capital city: Regina, population 175 159 (1985
estimate).
Other principal towns (1985): Saskatoon 175 859;
Moose Jaw 35 525; Prince Albert 33 540; Yorkton 16 055; Swift Current 16 049.
Highest point: 4546 ft *1385 m.*
Principal rivers: N. Saskatchewan, Cree, Geokie.
Lieutenant-Governor: Frederick W. Johnson.
Premier: Grant Devine.
Length of roadways: 128 962 miles *207 500 km*
(1985).
Length of railways: 7330 miles *11 800 km* (1984).
Universities: 2.

NORTHWEST TERRITORIES
Population: 50 454 (1984).
Area: 1 304 903 miles² *3 379 683 km².*
Languages: Eskimo and Indian languages, English, French.
Religions: Roman Catholic, Anglican, United
Church of Canada.
Capital city: Yellowknife, population 10 884
(1984).
Other principal towns (1984): Hay River 3112;
Inuvik 3421; Frobisher Bay 2904; Fort Smith
2408.
Principal mountain range: Mackenzie.
Principal river: Mackenzie.
Commissioner: John Havelock Parker (b. 2 Feb.
1929).

YUKON TERRITORY
Population: 23 153 (1981 census).
Area: 186 299 miles² *482 515 km².*
Languages: English, Indian languages.
Religions: Anglican, Roman Catholic, United
Church of Canada.
Capital city: Whitehorse, population 17 742
(1981).
Other principal towns (1981): Watson Lake 1559;
Dawson City 1530.
Highest point: Mt Logan, 19 850 ft *6050 m.*
Principal mountain range: St Elias.
Principal river: Yukon.
Commissioner: Douglas Bell.
Length of roadways: 2918 miles *4695 km* (1984).

Cape Verde

Official name: A República de Cabo Verde (the
Republic of Cape Verde).
Population: 296 093 (1980 census); 308 000 (1985
estimate).
Area: 1557 miles² *4033 km².*
Languages: Portuguese, Crioulo (a patois).
Religion: Roman Catholic 98·7% (1965).
Capital city: Praia, population 37 676 (1980
census).

encircled: **CAPE VERDE** *top:* **CHAD**
immediately below: **THE CENTRAL AFRICAN
REPUBLIC**

Other principal towns: Mindelo 36 746 (1980);
São Filipe.
Highest point: 9285 ft *2829 m.*
Head of State: Aristides Maria Pereira (b. 17
Nov. 1924) President.
Prime Minister: Maj. Pedro Verona Rodrigues
Pires (b. 29 Apr. 1934).
Climate: Hot and semi-arid, tempered by oceanic
situation. Average temperature in Praia varies
from 22°C *72°F* to 27°C *80°F.* Prevailing northeasterly wind. Rainfall is scarce (falling almost
entirely between August and October) and
drought sometimes chronic.
Labour force: 84 869 (census of 15 Dec. 1970).
Gross domestic product: 2251 million escudos
Caboverdianos in 1979: Agriculture and forestry
23·6%; Fishing 5·5%; Construction 17·3% Trade
and transport 31·5%; Services 16·5%.
Exports: 147 million escudos Caboverdianos in
1981: Vegetables and vegetable products 58·9%;
Animals and animal products 11·4%; Foodstuffs
and beverages 9·5%.
Monetary unit: Escudo Capoverdianos. 1 escudo = 100 centavos.
Denominations:
Coins 20, 50 centavos; 1, 2½, 10, 20, 50 escudos.
Notes 100, 500, 1000 escudos.
Exchange rate to £ sterling: 136·40 (26 Jan.
1987).
Political history and government: A former
Portuguese territory, the Cape Verde Islands
were part of Portuguese Guinea (now GuineaBissau) until 1879 and formed a separate
territory from then until independence on 5 July
1975. The independence movement was dominated by the *Partido Africano da Independência
da Guiné e Cabo Verde* (PAIGC), the African
Party for the Independence of Guinea and Cape
Verde. At independence Portugal transferred
power to a PAIGC régime. The country's first
constitution was approved on 7 Sept. 1980.
Legislative power is vested in the National
People's Assembly, with 56 members elected by
universal adult suffrage for five years. Executive
power is held by the President, elected for five
years by the Assembly. He appoints and leads a
Council of Ministers. Following the *coup* in
Guinea-Bissau on 14 Nov. 1980, the Cape Verde
branch of the PAIGC was renamed the African
Party for the Independence of Cape Verde on
20 Jan. 1981. Constitutional articles relating to
the proposed union with Guinea-Bassau were
revoked on 12 Feb. 1981.
Length of roadways: 1398 miles *2250 km* (1981).
Adult illiteracy: 63·1% (population aged 14 and
over) in 1970.
Expectation of life: Males 56·3 years; females
60·0 years (UN estimates for 1970–75).
Defence: Total armed forces 1145 in 1986.

The Central African Republic

Official name: La République centrafricaine.
Population: 2 700 000 (1986 estimate).
Area: 240 535 miles² *622 984 km²*.
Languages: Sangho, French (official).
Religions: Protestant, Roman Catholic, Animist.
Capital city: Bangui, population 473 800 (1984).
Other principal towns (1981): Berberati 95 000; Bouar 51 000.
Highest point: Mt Gaou, 4659 ft *1420 m*.
Principal mountain range: Chaîne des Mongos.
Principal river: Oubangui.
Head of State: Gen. André Kolingba, Chairman of the Military Committee for National Recovery.
Climate: Tropical (hot and humid). Heavy rains June to October, especially in south-western forest areas. Average temperature 26°C *79°F*. Daily average high temperature 29°C *85°F* to 34°C *93°F*, low 19°C *66°F* to 22°C *71°F*.
Labour force: 900 000 (1970): Agriculture, forestry and fishing 91·3% (ILO estimates).
Gross domestic product: 49 175 million CFA francs in 1977 at 1967 prices: Agriculture 32%; Forestry 8·3%; Manufacturing 10·7%; Trade 27·3%.
Exports: 35 454 million CFA francs in 1982: Diamonds 24·4%; Cotton 6·4%; Coffee 33·2%; Wood 20·1%.
Monetary unit: Franc de la Communauté financière africaine.
Denominations:
    Coins 1, 2, 5, 10, 25, 50, 100 CFA francs.
    Notes 100, 500, 1000, 5000, 10 000 CFA francs.
Exchange rate to £ sterling: 464·75 (26 Jan. 1987).
Political history and government: Formerly Ubangi-Shari (Obangui-Chari), part of French Equatorial Africa. Became the Central African Republic (CAR) on achieving self-government, 1 Dec. 1958. Independent since 13 Aug. 1960. The first President, David Dacko, was deposed on 31 Dec. 1965 by a military *coup*, led by his uncle, Col (later Marshal) Jean-Bédel Bokassa. The National Assembly was dissolved on 1 Jan. 1966 and the constitution revoked on 4 Jan. Bokassa assumed full powers and became 'President for life' in Feb. 1972. On 4 Dec. 1976 he proclaimed the Central African Empire with himself as Emperor. He crowned himself on 4 Dec. 1977. Bokassa was deposed on 20–21 Sept. 1979, when ex-President Dacko and the CAR were restored. The imperial constitution was abrogated. A new constitution, providing for a multi-party system, was approved by referendum on 1 Feb. 1981 and promulgated on 6 Feb. Dacko was elected President on 15 March and sworn in for a six year term on 3 April. On 21 July he declared a 'state of siege', to be administered by Gen André Kolingba, the Army Chief of Staff. On 1 Sept. 1981 President Dacko was deposed in a military *coup* by Gen Kolingba as leader of a 23-man *Comité militaire pour le redressement national* (CMRN). The constitution and political parties were suspended, and all legislative and executive powers assumed by the CMRN. An all-military Council of Ministers was formed.
Length of roadways: 13 670 miles *22 000 km* (31 Dec. 1978).
Universities: 1.
Adult illiteracy: 67% (males 52%; females 81%) in 1980.
Expectation of life: Males 41·9 years; females 45·1 years (UN estimates for 1970–75).
Defence: Total armed forces 2300 (1985); defence expenditure: 13·1% of total government expenditure in 1982.
Foreign tourists: 7000 in 1982.

Chad

Official name: La République du Tchad (the Republic of Chad).
Population: 5 061 000 (1985 estimate).
Area: 495 750 miles² *1 284 000 km²*.
Languages: French (official), Arabic, African languages.
Religions: Muslim, Animist, Christian.
Capital city: N'Djaména (formerly Fort-Lamy), population 225 000 (1983 estimate).
Other principal towns (1979): Moundou 87 000; Sarh (Fort-Archambault) 124 000; Bongor 69 000; Doba 64 000.
Highest point: Emi Koussi, 11 204 ft *3415 m*.
Principal mountain ranges: Tibesti, Ennedi.
Principal rivers: Chari, Bahr Kéita.
Head of State: Hissène Habré, President.
Climate: Hot and dry in the Sahara desert (in the north) but milder and very wet (annual rainfall 4980 mm *196 in*) in the south. In N'Djaména, average maximum 30°C *87°F* (August) to 42°C *107°F* (April), minimum 14°C *57°F* (December, January) to 25°C *77°F* (May), August rainiest (22 days).
Labour force: 1 738 000 in 1981: Agriculture, forestry and fishing 83%.
Gross domestic product: 148 570 million CFA francs in 1975: Agriculture, forestry and fishing 41·4% (agriculture 34·4%); Manufacturing 11·2%; Trade, restaurants and hotels 28·7% (trade 27·9%).
Exports: 4120 million CFA francs in 1983: Raw cotton 91·1%; Live cattle 1·2%.
Monetary unit: Franc de la Communauté financière africaine.
Denominations:
    Coins 1, 2, 5, 10, 25, 50, 100 CFA francs.
    Notes 100, 500, 1000, 5000, 10 000 CFA francs.
Exchange rate to £ sterling: 464·75 (26 Jan. 1987).
Political history and government: Former province of French Equatorial Africa, independent since 11 Aug. 1960. From the time of independence the central government was opposed by Muslim rebels, who formed the *Front de libération nationale du Tchad* (FROLINAT), or Chad National Liberation Front, in 1966. The Front later split into several factions but most insurgent groups remained linked to it. On 13 April 1975 the central government was overthrown by a military *coup*. The new régime formed a Supreme Military Council (SMC), led by Gen Félix Malloum. On 25 Aug. 1978 the SMC signed a 'fundamental charter' with a section of one of Chad's rebel groups, the Northern Armed Forces Command Council (CCFAN). The charter was to serve as the country's interim constitution. On 29 Aug. 1978 the SMC was dissolved. Gen Malloum was confirmed as President and a CCFAN leader became Prime Minister. Following a peace conference between the various factions, the President and Prime Minister resigned on 23 Mar. 1979 and a Provisional State Council was formed. Fighting continued, however, and this body was replaced by a transitional Council of Ministers on 29 April 1979. After a further reconciliation conference, this Government resigned on 29 Aug. 1979 to make way for a new régime dominated by FROLINAT, whose Chairman Goukouni Oueddei, became Head of State. A Provisional Administrative Committee (including only northern guerrilla representatives) was set up on 3 Sept. 1979 but this was replaced on 10 Nov. by a Transitional Government of National Unity, including most faction leaders.
    In 1980 a treaty of friendship was signed with Libya, who supported the northern rebels, and in 1981 there was even talk of a merger between the two countries. Since then the country has been effectively divided between government forces in the south and rebel forces in the north.
Length of roadways: 19 092 miles *30 725 km* (31 Dec. 1974).
Universities: 1.
Adult illiteracy: 86% in 1977.
Expectation of life: Males 40·0 years; females 42·6 years (UN estimates for 1970–75).
Defence: Total armed forces 12 200 (1985); defence expenditure: 46·5% of total government expenditure in 1984.
Cinemas: 13 (seating capacity 12 400) and 3 mobile units (1977).

Chile

Official name: República de Chile.
Population: 11 275 440 (1982 census); 11 700 000 (1986 estimate).
Area: 292 258 miles² *756 945 km²*.
Language: Spanish.
Religions: Roman Catholic, Protestant minority.
Capital city: Santiago, population 4 630 000 (1986 estimate).
Other principal towns (1986 estimates): Viña del Mar 286 000; Valparaíso 280 000; Concepción 240 000; Talcahuano 210 000; Antofagasta 170 000; Temuco 180 000.
Highest point: Ojos del Salado, 22 588 ft *6885 m* (first climbed 1937).
Principal mountain range: Cordillera de los Andes.
Principal rivers: Loa (273 miles *439 km*), Maule, Bio-Bio, Valdiva.
Head of State: Gen Augusto Pinochet Ugarte (b. 25 Nov. 1915), President.
Climate: Considerable variation north (annual rainfall 1 mm *0·04 in*) to south (2665 mm *105 in*). Average temperatures 12°C *53°F* winter, 17°C *63°F* summer. In Santiago, December (10°C *51°F* to 28°C *83°F*), January (12°C *53°F* to 29°C *85°F*), and February (11°C *52°F* to 29°C *84°F*) hottest, June (3°C *37°F* to 14°C *58°F*) and July (3°C *37°F* to 15°C *59°F*) coldest and rainiest (6 days each). Absolute maximum temperature 41,6°C *106·9°F*, Los Angeles, February 1944; absolute minimum −21,2°C *−6·16°F*, Longuimay, July 1933.
Labour force: 3 216 100 in 1983: Agriculture, forestry and fishing 15·8%; Manufacturing 12·6%; Commerce 17·1%; Services 42·9%.
Gross domestic product: 1557·7 billion pesos in 1983: Mining and quarrying 10·1%; Manufacturing 20·6%; Trade 15·0%; Services 36·0%.
Exports: US$332·8 million in 1984: Copper 44·3%; Fruit and vegetables 9·1%; wood pulp 3·2%.
Monetary unit: Chilean peso. 1 peso = 100 centavos.
Denominations:
    Coins 1 peso.
    Notes 5, 10, 50, 100, 500, 1000 pesos.
Exchange rate to £ sterling: 309·51 (26 Jan. 1987).
Political history and government: A republic, divided into 12 regions and one metropolitan region (Santiago). The last civilian President was deposed by a military *coup* on 11 Sept. 1973. A 'state of siege' was proclaimed; the bicameral National Congress (a Senate and a Chamber of Deputies) was dissolved on 13 Sept. 1973, and

CHILE

the activities of political parties were suspended on 27 Sept. 1973. Power is held by the *Junta Militar de Gobierno*, whose leader was proclaimed President of the Republic on 17 Dec. 1974. All political parties were banned on 12 Mar. 1977. The state of siege was lifted on 11 Mar. 1978 but a state of emergency remained in force. A new constitution was approved in a plebiscite on 11 Sept. 1980, signed by the President on 21 Oct. 1980 and entered into force on 11 Mar. 1981. It provided for the separation of the junta and presidency, with the military régime retaining power for a 'transitional' period of eight years. Legislative elections are scheduled for 1990, when the junta is to submit a single presidential candidate to referendum.

Length of roadways: 48 493 miles *78 025 km* (1981).

Length of railways: 4625 miles *7441 km* (1984).

Universities: 8.

Adult illiteracy: 5·8% (1985).

Expectation of life: 67·01 years (1980).

Defence: Military service one year (Army and Navy only); total armed forces 101 000 (30 000 conscripts) in 1986; defence expenditure: 22·7% of total government expenditure in 1984.

Foreign tourists: 295 406 in 1983.

China (mainland)

Official name: Zhonghua Renmin Gongheguo (People's Republic of China).

Population: 1 008 200 000 (1982 census); 1 036 040 000 (1984 estimate).

Area: 3 691 500 miles² *9 561 000 km²*.

Language: Chinese (predominantly Mandarin dialect).

Religions: Confucianism, Buddhism, Daoism (Taoism); Roman Catholic and Muslim minorities.

Capital city: Beijing, population 5 760 000 (1983 estimate).

Other principal towns (1983): Shanghai 6 390 000; Tianjin 5 220 000; Chengdu 2 510 000; Jinan 1 360 000; Zhengzhou 1 517 000; Nanjing 2 170 000; Shijiazhuang 1 098 000; Guangzhou 3 170 000; Changsha 1 098 000; Hefei 830 000; Wuhan 3 280 000; Hangzhou 1 201 000; Shenyang 4 080 000; Kunming 1 450 000; Nanchang 1 061 000; Xian 2 220 000; Harbin 2 560 000; Taiyuan 1 790 000; Guiyang 1 330 000; Fuzhou 1 142 000; Changchun 1 770 000; Lanzhou 1 430 000; Xining 364 000; Nanning 876 000; Hohhot 754 000; Urumqi 944 000; Yinchuan 576 000; Lhasa 105 000.

Highest point: Mt Everest (on Tibet-Nepal border), 29 028 ft *8848 m* (first climbed 29 May 1953).

Principal mountain ranges: Himalaya, Kunlun Shan, Tien Shan, Nan Shan, Astin Tagh.

Principal rivers: Changjiang (Yangtze Kiang) (3436 miles *5530 km*), Huanghe (Yellow), Mekong.

Head of State: Li Xiannian, State President.

Political Leader: Hu Yaobang (b. 1915), General Secretary of the Politburo.

Head of Government: Zhao Ziyang (b. 1919), Premier of the State Council.

Climate: Extreme variations. Warm, humid summers and long cold winters in north (annual average below 10°C *50°F*); sub-tropical in extreme south; monsoons in the east; arid in the north-west. In Beijing, July hottest (22°C *71°F* to 32°C *89°F*) and rainiest (13 days), January coldest (−9°C *15°F* to 2°C *35°F*).

Labour force: 460 040 000 in 1983: Industry 13·1%; Construction 3·2%; Agriculture 70·7%; Trade 4·4%.

Net material product: 467 300 million yuan in 1983: agriculture 44·9%; Industry 41·9%; construction 5%; Transport 3·5%; Commerce 4·6%.

Exports: 43 833 million yuan in 1983: Food and live animals 12·8%; Crude materials 8·5%; Mineral fuels 21%; Chemicals 5·6%; Basic manufactures 19·6%; Machinery and transport equipment 5·5%; Miscellaneous manufactures 17·1%.

Monetary unit: Yuan. 1 yuan = 10 jiao (chiao) = 100 fen.

Denominations:
   Coins 1, 2, 5 fen.
   Notes 1, 2, 5, jiao; 1, 2, 5, 10 yuan.

Exchange rate to £ sterling: 5·6558 (26 Jan. 1987).

Political history and government: Under Communist rule since September 1949. The People's Republic was inaugurated on 1 Oct. 1949. The present constitution was adopted on 5 Mar. 1978. China is a unitary state comprising 21 provinces, 5 'autonomous' regions (including Tibet) and 3 municipalities. The Communist Part is 'the core of leadership' and the Chairman of the Party's Central Committee commands the People's Liberation Army (PLA), which includes naval and air forces. The highest organ of state power is the National People's Congress, with (in 1980) 3478 deputies indirectly elected for 5 years by provinces, regions, municipalities and the PLA. The Congress, under the leadership of the Party, elects a Standing Committee (196 members in March 1978) to be its permanent organ. The executive and administrative arm of government is the State Council (a Premier, Vice-Premiers and other Ministers), appointed by and accountable to the Congress.

Political power is held by the Communist Party of China (CPC). The CPC's highest authority is the Party Congress, convened normally every five years. The 11th Congress, meeting on 12–18 Aug. 1977, elected a Central Committee (201 full and 132 alternate members) to supervise Party work. To direct its policy, the Committee elects a Political Bureau (Politburo), with 24 full and two alternate members in 1980. The Politburo has a seven-member Standing Committee (the Chairman and six Vice-Chairmen).

A new constitution was introduced in 1982 which, among other things, restored the post of State President.

Length of roadways: 568 750 miles *915 100 km* (1978).

Length of railways: 32 300 miles *52 000 km* (1984).

Universities: 37.

Adult illiteracy: 23% in 1983.

Expectation of life: Males 66·43 years; females 69·35 years (1981).

Defence: Military service selective (Army three years, Air and Army technicians four years, Navy five years); total regular forces 3 900 000 (1985); defence expenditure: 11·9% of total government expenditure in 1985.

Foreign tourists: 12 400 000 in 1984.

China (Taiwan)

Official name: Chung-hua Min Kuo (Republic of China).

Population: 19 012 512 (1984 estimate).

Area: 13 892·5 miles² *35 981,4 km²*.

Language: Northern Chinese (Amoy dialect).

Religions: Buddhist, with Muslim and Christian minorities.

Capital city: Taipei, population 2 449 702 (1984 estimate).

Other principal towns (1984): Kaohsiung 1 285 132; Taichung 655 196; Tainan 631 614; Panchiau 467 754; Keelung 352 666; Shanchung 349 927.

Highest point: Yü Shan (Mt Morrison), 13 113 ft *3997 m*.

Principal mountain range: Chunyang Shanmo.

Principal rivers: Hsia-tan-shui Chi (99 miles *159 km*), Choshui Chi (106 miles *170 km*), Tan-shui Ho (89 miles *144 km*), Wu Chi (70 miles *113 km*).

Head of State: Gen Chiang Ching-kuo (b. 18 Mar. 1910) President.

Prime Minister: Yu Kuo-hwa.

Climate: Rainy summers and mild winters, average temperature 23°C *73°F*, average annual rainfall 2565 mm *101 in*. In Taipei, July (24°C *76°F* to 34°C *93°F*) and August (24°C *75°F* to 33°C *91°F*) warmest, January (12°C *54°F* to 19°C *66°F*) and February (12°C *53°F* to 18°C *65°F*) coolest, April rainiest (14 days).

Labour force: 7 491 000 in 1984: Agriculture, forestry and fishing 17·2%; Manufacturing 33·3%; Commerce 17·1%; Construction 7%; Transport, storage and communications 5%; Other services 14·6%.

Gross domestic product: NT$2 275 679 million in 1984: Agriculture, forestry and fishing 6·5%; Manufacturing 41·7%; Construction 4·4%; Transport, storage and communications 6%; Trade 13·6%; Government services 9·9%.

Exports: NT$1 204 696·7 million in 1984: Synthetic yarn 1%; Synthetic fabrics 1·7%; Clothing 11·4%; Electronic components 3%; Calculators 3·4%; TVs 2%; Radios 1·4% Plastic articles 7·9%; Dolls and toys 2·4%.

Monetary unit: New Taiwan dollar (NT $). 1 dollar = 100 cents.

Denominations:
   Coins 10, 20, 50 cents; 1, 5, dollars.
   Notes 1, 5, 10, 50, 100, 500, 1000 dollars.

Exchange rate to £ sterling: 53·55 (26 Jan. 1987).

Political history and government: After the Republic of China was overthrown by Communist forces on the mainland, the government withdrew to Taiwan on 8 Dec. 1949. As it claims to be the legitimate administration for all China, the régime continues to be dominated by mainlanders who came to the island in 1947–49. The first elections since the Communist victory were held in Taiwan on 23 Dec. 1972. There are five governing bodies (*yuans*). The highest legislative organ is the Legislative Yuan, comprising (in 1980) 320 life members and 48 elected for 3 years. This body submits proposals to the National Assembly (1128 life members and 62 elected for 6 years), which elects the President and Vice-President for 6 years. The Executive Yuan (Council of Ministers) is the highest administrative organ and is responsible to the Legislative Yuan.

Length of roadways: 12 326 miles *19 833 km*.

Length of railways: 1887 miles *3036 km*.

Universities: 11.

Adult illiteracy: 27·6% (males 15·2%; females 42·0%) in 1966.

Expectation of life: Males 66·82 years; females 74·13 years (1977).

Defence: Military service two years; total armed forces 444 000 (1985); defence expenditure: 39% of total government expenditure in 1985–6.

Foreign tourists: 1 516 138 in 1984.

Colombia

Official name: La República de Colombia.

Population: 22 551 811 (census of 24 Oct. 1973); 25 900 000 (1986 estimate).

Area: 439 737 miles² *1 138 914 km²*.

Language: Spanish.

Religion: Roman Catholic.

Capital city: Bogotá, population 4 208 000 (1985).

Other principal towns (1985): Medellín 2 690 000; Cali 1 654 000; Barranquilla 1 120 000; Cartagena de Indias 530 000; Bucaramanga 545 000; San José de Cúcuta 411 000.

Highest point: Pico Cristóbal Colón, 18 947 ft *5775 m* (first climbed 1939).

Principal mountain range: Cordillera de los Andes.

Principal rivers: Magdalena, Cauca, Amazonas (Amazon, 4007 miles *6448 km*) on frontier.

Head of State: Dr Virgilio Barco, President.

Climate: Hot and humid on the coasts and in the jungle lowlands, temperate in the Andean highlands, with rainy seasons March–May and September–November. In Bogotá, daily average low temperature 9°C *48°F* to 10°C *51°F*, high 18°C *64°F* to 20°C *68°F*, April and October rainiest (20 days).

Labour force: 8 467 000 in 1980: Agriculture, forestry and fishing 28·5%; Manufacturing 13·4%; Trade 14·9%; Community, social and personal services 23·6%.

Gross domestic product: 3 828 582 million pesos in 1984: Agriculture 22·4%; Industry 21·4%; Mining 1·8%; Construction 4%; Transport and communication 9·6%.

Exports: US$3·8 billion in 1985: Coffee 49·1%; Bananas 4·4%; Flowers 3·7%; Fuel oil 12·6%; Coal 3·5%; Textiles 3·2%.

Monetary unit: Colombian peso. 1 peso = 100 centavos.

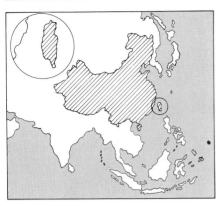

CHINA (MAINLAND)

encircled: **CHINA (TAIWAN)**

COLOMBIA

Denominations:
  Coins 1, 2, 5, 10, 20 pesos.
  Notes 10, 20, 50, 100, 200, 500, 1000 and 2000 pesos.
Exchange rate to £ sterling: 342·74 (26 Jan. 1987).
Political history and government: A republic. Legislative power is vested in Congress, which is composed of the Senate (112 members) and the House of Representatives (199 members). Members of both Houses are elected for 4 years. Executive power is exercised by the President (elected for 4 years by universal adult suffrage), assisted by a Cabinet. The country is divided into 22 departments, 5 intendancies and 4 commissaries.
Length of roadways: 47 000 miles *75 000 km* (1986).
Length of railways: 2115 miles *3403 km*.
Universities: 37 (21 state, 16 private).
Adult illiteracy: 14·8% (males 13·6%; females 16·1%) in 1981.
Expectation of life: Males 58·5 years; females 61·2 years (UN estimates for 1970–75).
Defence: Military service two years; total armed forces 66 200 in 1985; defence expenditure: 8·5% of total government expenditure in 1985.
Foreign tourists: 715 277 in 1984.

The Comoros

Official name: La République fédérale islamique des Comores (the Federal Islamic Republic of the Comoros).
Population: 421 000 (1983 estimate).
Area: 838 miles² *2171 km²* (including Mayotte, 144 miles² *373 km²*).
Languages: French (official), Comoran (a blend of Swahili and Arabic).
Religions: Muslim, with a Christian minority.
Capital city: Moroni, population 16 000 (1978 estimate).
Other principal towns: Dzaoudzi (on Mayotte), Mutsamudu.
Highest point: Mt Kartala, 7746 ft *2361 m*.
Head of State: Ahmed Abdallah Abderemane (b. 1918), President.
Climate: Tropical climate with two distinct seasons. Dry between May and October, hot and humid from November to April. Most rain in January (up to 380 mm *15 in*). Cyclones, waterspouts and tidal waves occur in the summer. The November monsoon brings the maximum temperature of 28°C *82°F*, while the minimum temperature (July) falls to 20°C *68°F*.
Labour force: 104 000 (mid-1970): Agriculture, forestry and fishing 67·1%; Industry 20·8%; Services 12·1% (ILO estimates).
Gross domestic product: $70 million (estimate) in 1975.
Exports: 54·2 million CFA francs in 1980: Vanilla 7·2%; Ylang-ylang 14·9%; Cloves 45·9%; Copra 3·1%.
Monetary unit: Franc de la Communauté financière africaine (French currency is used on Mayotte).
Denominations:
  Coins 1, 2, 5, 10, 20 CFA francs.
  Notes 50, 100, 500, 1000, 5000 CFA francs.
Exchange rate to £ sterling: 464·75 (26 Jan. 1987).
Political history and government: A former French dependency. Attached to Madagascar in 1912, the Comoro Islands became a separate French Overseas Territory in 1947. The Territory achieved internal self-government by a law of 29 Dec. 1961, with a Chamber of Deputies (in place of the Territorial Assembly) and a Government Council to control local administration. Ahmed Abdallah, President of the Council from 26 Dec. 1972, was restyled President of the Government on 15 June 1973. In a referendum on 22 Dec. 1974 the Comorans voted 95·6% in favour of independence, though on the island of Mayotte the vote was 65% against. The French Government wanted each island to ratify a new constitution separately by referendum. To avoid the expected separation of Mayotte, the Chamber of Deputies voted for immediate independence on 6 July 1975. A unilateral declaration of independence, as the *Etat Comorien* (Comoran State), was made on the same day. On 7 July the Chamber elected Abdallah as President of the Comoros and constituted itself as the National Assembly. France kept its hold on Mayotte but the three other main islands achieved *de facto* independence. On 3 Aug. 1975 Abdallah was deposed in a *coup*. France recognized the independence of the three islands on 31 Dec. 1975. The new régime was overthrown by a *coup* on 12–13 May 1978. A Political-Military Directory was formed and on 23 May ex-President Abdallah and his former deputy were appointed its co-presidents. On 24 May 1978 the country's present name was announced. A new constitution was approved by referendum on 1 Oct. 1978 and Abdallah was elected President (unopposed) for a 6-year term on 22 Oct. 1978. A 39-member Federal Assembly was elected for a 5-year term on 8 and 15 Dec. 1978, and in 1979 the assembly approved the formation of a one-party state.
  A referendum on Mayotte on 8 Feb. 1976 resulted in a 99·4% vote for retaining links with France. In a second referendum, on 11 Apr. 1976, Mayotte voted against remaining a French Overseas Territory. In Dec. 1976 France enacted legislation to give the island a special status as a *collectivité particulière*. It is thus an integral part of the French Republic and administered by a Government Commissioner.
Length of roadways: 466 miles *750 km* (1973).
Adult illiteracy: 41·6% in 1966.
Expectation of life: Males 43·3 years; females 46·6 years (UN estimates for 1970–75).
Defence: About 800 personnel; defence expenditure: 15% of total government expenditure in 1982.
Foreign tourists: About 2000 per year.

The Congo

Official name: La République populaire du Congo (the People's Republic of the Congo).
Population: 1 764 000 (1985 estimate).
Area: 132 047 miles² *342 000 km²*.
Languages: French (official), Bantu languages.
Religions: Animist, Christian minority.
Capital city: Brazzaville, population 456 383 (1983 estimate).
Other principal towns (1983): Pool 219 329; Pointe-Noire 214 466; Bouenza 135 999; Cuvette 127 558; Niari 114 229; Plateaux 110 379.
Highest point: 3412 ft *1040 m*.
Principal mountain range: Serro do Crystal.
Principal rivers: Zaïre (Congo) (2920 miles *4700 km*), Oubangui.
Head of State: Col Denis Sassou-Nguesso (b. 1943), President.
Prime Minister: Ange-Edouard Poungi.
Climate: Tropical (hot and humid). Equatorial rains for seven to eight months per year. In Brazzaville, daily average low temperature 17°C *63°F* to 21°C *70°F*, high 28°C *82°F* to 33°C *91°F*.
Labour force: 428 000 (1970): Agriculture, forestry and fishing 41·8%; Industry 21·5%; Services 36·7% (ILO estimates); 487 267 (1974 census).
Gross domestic product: 541 706 million CFA francs in 1981: Agriculture, forestry and fishing 7·9%; Mining 39·3%; Manufacturing 6·3%; Trade 11·1%; Transport, storage and communications 8·1% Government services 10%.
Exports: 326 150 million CFA francs in 1982: Petroleum and petroleum products 90·4%; Wood 4·7%.
Monetary unit: Franc de la Communauté financière africaine.
Denominations:
  Coins 1, 2, 5, 10, 25, 50, 100 CFA francs.
  Notes 100, 500, 1000, 5000, 10000 CFA francs.
Exchange rate to £ sterling: 464·75 (26 Jan. 1987).
Political history and government: Formerly, as Middle Congo, a part of French Equatorial Africa. Became independent as the Republic of the Congo on 15 Aug. 1960. A one-party state since 2 July 1964. Present name adopted on 3 Jan. 1970. On 18 Mar. 1977 the President was assassinated and the Central Committee of the ruling party transferred its powers to an 11-member Military Committee. The new régime suspended the 1973 constitution on 5 Apr. 1977 and dissolved the National Assembly the next day. On 5 Feb. 1979 the Military Committee resigned and handed over powers to the party's

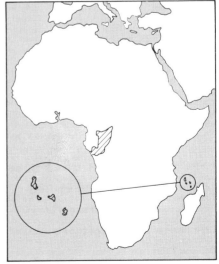

left: **THE CONGO**   *right:* **THE COMOROS**

Central Committee. On 8 July 1979 a new constitution was approved by referendum and a National People's Assembly of 89 members elected (unopposed). The Congress of the ruling party elects a Central Committee (60 members) whose Chairman is also the country's President (serving a five-year term). The President leads the Council of Ministers, including a Prime Minister who is responsible to the party. The Assembly is responsible to the Prime Minister.
Length of roadways: 5124 miles *8246 km* (31 Dec. 1977).
Length of railways: 494 miles *795 km*.
Universities: 1.
Adult illiteracy: 83·5% (males 76·2%; females 92·7%) in 1960–61.
Expectation of life: Males 41·9 years; females 45·1 years (UN estimates for 1970–75).
Defence: Military service voluntary; total armed forces 8700 (1985), plus 500 Cuban troops; defence expenditure: 6·8% of total government expenditure in 1984.
Foreign tourists: 62 000 in 1981.

Costa Rica

Official name: República de Costa Rica (the 'rich coast').
Population: 2 416 809 (1984 census).
Area: 19 730 miles² *51 100 km²*.
Language: Spanish.
Religion: Roman Catholic.
Capital city: San José, population 245 370 (1984 census).
Other principal towns (1984): Limón (43 158; Puntarenas 47 851; Alajuela 33 929; Heredia 20 867; Cartago 23 884.
Highest point: Chirripó, 12 533 ft *3820 m*.
Principal mountain ranges: Cordillera del Guanacaste, Cordillera de Talamanca.
Principal river: Río Grande.
Head of State: Dr Oscar Arias Sánchez, President.
Climate: Hot and wet on Caribbean coast, hot but drier on Pacific coast, cooler on central plateau. In San José, May hottest (17°C *62°F* to 27°C *80°F*), December and January coolest (14°C *58°F* to 24°C *75°F*), rainy season May–November, October rainiest (25 days). Absolute maximum temperature 42°C *107·6°F*, Las Cañas de Guanacaste, 26 Apr. 1952; absolute minimum −1·1°C *30°F*, Cerro Buena Vista, 11 Jan. 1949.
Labour force: 827 176 in 1983: Agriculture, forestry and fishing 28·3%; Mining and manufacturing 16·7% Commerce 17·9%; Community, social and personal services 25·3%.
Gross domestic product: 29 764·2 million colones in 1978: Agriculture, forestry and fishing 20·0% (agriculture 19·3%); Mining and manufacturing 18·2%; Trade, restaurants and hotels 20·2% (trade 18·7%); Government services 14·2%.
Exports: US$837·5 million in 1984: Coffee 25·9%; Bananas 27%; Sugar 2·1%; Cattle and meat 4·1%.
Monetary unit: Costa Rican colón. 1 colón = 100 céntimos.
Denominations:
Coins 5, 10, 25, 50 céntimos; 1, 2 colones.
Notes 5, 10, 20, 50, 100, 500, 1000 colones.
Exchange rate to £ sterling: 89·9981 (26 Jan. 1987).
Political history and government: A republic. Legislative power is vested in the unicameral Legislative Assembly (57 deputies elected for four years by compulsory adult suffrage). Executive power is vested in the President, similarly elected for four years. He is assisted by two Vice-Presidents and a Cabinet. There are 7 provinces, each administered by an appointed governor.
Length of roadways: 18 081 miles *29 093 km* (1984).
Length of railways: 549 miles *883 km* (1984).
Universities: 3.
Adult illiteracy: 6%. Highest rate of literacy in Central America.
Expectation of life: Males 66·26 years; females 70·49 years (1972–74).
Defence: There have been no armed forces since 1948. Paramilitary forces number about 5000.
Foreign tourists: 273 901 in 1984.

Cuba

Official name: La República de Cuba.
Population: 9 706 369 (1981 census); 10 042 800 (1984 estimate).
Area: 42 803 miles² *110 860 km²*.
Languages: Spanish, English.
Religions: Roman Catholic, Protestant minority.
Capital city: Ciudad de la Habana (Havana), population 1 924 886 (1981 census); 1 972 400 (1984 estimate).
Other principal towns (1984): Santiago de Cuba 353 373; Santa Clara 175 525; Camaguey 253 836; Holguín 192 182; Guantánamo 171 065; Cienfuegos 106 478; Matanzas 103 605; Bayamo 103 366.
Highest point: Pico Turquino, 6467 ft *1971 m*.
Principal mountain range: Sierra Maestra.
Principal river: Cauto (155 miles *249 km*).
Head of State: Dr Fidel Castro Ruz (b. 13 Aug. 1927), President of the State Council and Chairman of the Council of Ministers; also First Secretary of the Communist Party of Cuba.
Climate: Semi-tropical. Rainy season May–October. High winds, hurricanes frequent. In Havana, July and August warmest (24°C *75°F* to 32°C *89°F*), January and February coolest (18°C *65°F* to 26°C *79°F*), September and October rainiest (11 days each).
Labour force: 2 999 700 in state sector in 1983: Industry 21%; Agriculture 19·8%; Trade 11·6%; Services 23·2%.
Net material product: 12 905·5 million pesos in 1983: Agriculture, forestry and fishing 10·4%; Industry 32·2%; Construction 8·4%; Trade 41%.
Exports: 5430 million pesos in 1984: Sugar 75% approx.
Monetary unit: Cuban peso. 1 peso = 100 centavos.
Denominations:
Coins 1, 5, 20, 40 centavos; 1 peso.
Notes 1, 3, 5, 10, 20, 50, 100 pesos.
Exchange rate to £ sterling: 1·2177 (26 Jan. 1987).
Political history and government: On 1 Jan. 1959 the dictatorship of Gen Fulgencio Batista was overthrown by revolutionary forces, led by Dr Fidel Castro. The constitution was suspended and a Fundamental Law of the Republic was instituted from 7 Feb. 1959. Executive and legislative authority was vested in the Council of Ministers, led by a Prime Minister, which appointed the Head of State. A 'Marxist-Leninist programme' was proclaimed on 2 Dec. 1961 and revolutionary groups merged into a single political movement, called the Communist Party of Cuba (CPC) since 2 Oct. 1965. On 24 Nov. 1972 the government established an Executive Committee (including the President and Prime Minister) to supervise State administration. The first elections since the revolution were held for municipal offices in one province on 30 June 1974.

A new constitution, approved by referendum on 15 Feb. 1976 and in force from 24 Feb. 1976, provides for assemblies at municipal, provincial and national levels. On 10 Oct. 1976 elections were held for 169 municipal assemblies, with 'run-off' elections a week later. Members are elected by universal adult suffrage for 2½ years. On 31 Oct. 1976 the municipal assemblies elected delegates to 14 provincial assemblies. On 2 Nov. 1976 the municipal assemblies elected 481 deputies to the National Assembly of People's Power, inaugurated on 2 Dec. 1976. The National Assembly, whose members hold office for five years, is the supreme organ of state. The Assembly elects 31 of its members to form a Council of State, its permanent organ. The Council's President is Head of State and Head of Government. Executive power is vested in the Council of Ministers, appointed by the National Assembly on the proposal of the Head of State, who presides over it. The CPC, the only permitted political party, is 'the leading force of society and the state'. To direct its policy, the Central Committee of the CPC appoints a Political Bureau (Politburo).
Length of roadways: 7300 miles *11 746 km* (1982).
Length of railways: 9041 miles *14 547 km* (1984).

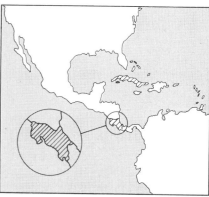

above: **CUBA**　*below:* **COSTA RICA**

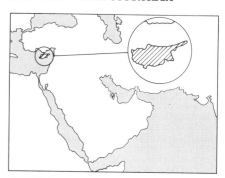

CYPRUS

Universities: 4.
Adult illiteracy: estimated 4%.
Expectation of life: Males 68·5 years; females 71·8 years (1970).
Defence: Military service three years; total armed forces 158 000 (1986); defence expenditure, 1981: 13·3% of total government expenditure in 1985.
Cinemas: 439 (seating capacity 294 300) and one drive-in (capacity 2000) in 1972; 458 and 637 mobile units (1976).
Foreign tourists: 201 000 in 1984.

Cyprus

Official name: Kypriaki Dimokratia (in Greek), or Kibris Cumhuriyeti (in Turkish), meaning Republic of Cyprus.
Population: 657 300 including 157 894 in Turkish Republic of Northern Cyprus (1984 estimate).
Area: 3572 miles² *9251 km²*. including Turkish area of 1295 miles² *3355 km²*.
Languages: Greek 77%; Turkish 18%; English 3% (1960).
Religions: Greek Orthodox 77·0%; Moslem 18·3%.
Capital city: Nicosia, population: Government-controlled, 164 400 (1985 estimate); Turkish 68 286 (1978).
Other principal towns (1982): Limassol (107 200); Famagusta (39 500); Larnaca (48 400).
Principal mountain ranges: Troödos, Kyrenian Mts.
Principal rivers: Seranhis, Pedieas.
Head of State: Spyros Kyprianou (b. 28 Oct. 1932), President; Head of State of Turkish Republic of Northern Cyprus: Rauf Denktash, President.
Climate: Generally equable. Average rainfall is about 380 mm *15 in* but the summers are often rainless. The average daily high temperature in Nicosia reaches 36°C *97°F* (July) and the average daily low 5°C *42°F* (January).
Labour force: 220 089 (in 1983, for whole island): Agriculture, forestry, fishing 19·7%; Manufacturing 18·9%; Trade, restaurants and hotels 17·4%; Transport, storage and communication 4·8%; Services 18·1%.
Gross domestic product: C£1091·8 million in 1983, for Government-controlled area: Agriculture 9·3%; Mining, manufacturing, electricity

and gas 19·9%; Services 15·2%; Construction 12·0%; Transport 8·7%; Trade 14·8%; Banking 7·7%; Public administration 8·1%.
Exports: C£234·96 million in 1983, for Government-controlled area: Potatoes 12·8%; Citrus fruit 6·1%; Beverages 5·2%; Basic manufactures 9·3%; Clothing 26·3%; Footwear 7·5%.
Monetary unit: Cyprus pound. C£1 = 100 cents; Turkish lira (q.v.) in Turkish area.
Denominations:
Coins ½, 1, 2, 5, 10, 20 cent.
Notes 50 cent, £1, £5, £10.
Exchange rate to £ sterling: 0·742 (26 Jan 1987).
Political history and government: A former British dependency, independent since 16 August 1960 and a member of the Commonwealth since 13 March 1961. Under the 1960 constitution, Cyprus is a unitary republic with executive authority vested in one President (who must be a Greek Cypriot) and the Vice-President (who must be a Turkish Cypriot). They are elected for 5 years by universal suffrage (among the Greek and Turkish communities respectively) and jointly appoint a Council of Ministers (seven Greeks, three Turks). The national legislature is the unicameral House of Representatives, comprising 50 members (35 Greek and 15 Turkish, separately elected for 5 years). Each community was also to have a communal chamber.

The first President of Cyprus was Archbishop Makarios III, who proposed amendments to the constitution on 30 November 1963. These were unacceptable to the Turks, who have ceased to participate in the central government since December 1963. After the Turkish withdrawal, the all-Greek House of Representatives abolished the Greek Communal Chamber and the separate electoral rolls. The Turkish community continued to elect a Vice-President for Cyprus (not recognised by the Greeks) and established separate administrative, legal and judicial organs.

After the temporary overthrow of President Makarios in a coup in July 1974, the armed forces of Turkey intervened and occupied northern Cyprus. On 17 February 1975 the Turkish Cypriots unilaterally proclaimed this area the Turkish Federated State of Cyprus, for which a constitution was approved by referendum on 8 June 1975. Makarios died on 3 August 1977, when Spyros Kyprianou, President of the House of Representatives, became acting Head of State. On 31 August 1977 he was elected unopposed to complete Makarios's term of office. He was returned unopposed as President on 26 January 1978 and inaugurated on 1 March. He was again re-elected for a further five year term on 13 February 1983.

In November 1983 the Turkish Cypriot leadership declared the Turkish-held area of Cyprus to be the Turkish Republic of Northern Cyprus. To date this action remains unrecognised by the world community. UN sponsored talks between the Greek and the Turkish Cypriot sides have made no progress in resolving the Cyprus problem.
Length of roadways: 6978 miles *11 227 km* (1983).
Adult illiteracy: 9·5% (1976).
Expectation of life: Males 72·3 years; females 76·0 years (1978–81).
Defence: *Greek Cypriots:* military service 26 months; total armed forces 10 000 (1985); defence expenditure, 1981: $27·0 million. *Turkish Cypriots:* 36 500 (1985).
Foreign tourists: 736 972 to Government-controlled area in 1984; 113 318 to Turkish-controlled area in 1984.

Czechoslovakia

Official name: Československá Socialistická Republika (Czechoslovak Socialist Republic).
Population: 15 479 642 (1985 estimate).
Area: 49 375 miles[2] *127 881 km[2]*.
Languages: Czech 64%; Slovak 30%; Hungarian 4%.
Religions: Roman Catholic 70%; Protestant 15%.
Capital city: Praha (Prague), population 1 186 253 at 1 Jan. 1984.

Other principal towns (1 Jan. 1984): Bratislava 401 383; Brno 380 871; Ostrava 323 732; Košice 214 270; Plzeň 174 094.
Principal mountain ranges: Bohemian–Moravian Highlands, Krkonoše (Giant Mountains), High Tatras, Low Tatras.
Principal rivers: Labe (Elbe, 525 miles *845 km*), Vltava (Moldau), Dunaj (Danube, 1770 miles *2850 km*), Morava, Váh, Nitra, Hron.
Head of State: Dr Gustáv Husák (b. 10 Jan. 1913), President; also General Secretary of the Central Committee of the Communist Party of Czechoslovakia.
Prime Minister: Dr L'ubomír Štrougal (b. 19 Oct. 1924).
Climate: Cold winters and warm, rainy summers. Average temperature 9°C *49°F*. In Prague, July warmest (14°C *58°F* to 23°C *74°F*), January coldest (−4°C *25°F* to 1°C *34°F*), June and July rainiest (14 days each). Absolute maximum temperature 39,0°C *102·2°F*, Hurbanovo, 5 Aug. 1905; absolute minimum −41,0°C *−41·8°F*, Vigľaš-Pstruša, 11 Feb. 1929.
Labour force: 7 808 000 in 1983: Agriculture and forestry 13·1%; Mining and manufacturing 36·1%; Construction 9·2%; Trade 8·5%; Education and culture 6·9%.
Net material product: 507·3 billion Kčs in 1983: Agriculture, forestry and fishing 8·9%; Industry 61%; Construction 10·4%; Trade 14·3%; Transport and storage 4·2%.
Exports: 103 877·9 million Kčs in 1983: Mineral fuels and lubricants 4·8%; Chemicals 6·0%; Basic manufactures 17·3%; Machinery and transport equipment 52%; Miscellaneous manufactures 12%.
Monetary unit: Koruna (Kčs) or Czechoslovak crown. 1 koruna = 100 haléřu (singular: halér).
Denominations:
Coins 5, 10, 20, 50 haléřů; 1, 2, 5 korunas.
Notes 10, 20, 50, 100, 500 korunas.
Exchange rate to £ sterling: 14·28 (26 Jan. 1987).
Political history and government: Formerly part of Austria-Hungary, independent since 28 Oct. 1918. Under the Munich agreement, made on 29 Sept. 1938 by France, German, Italy and the United Kingdom, Czechoslovakia ceded the Sudetenland to Germany and other areas to Hungary and Poland. German forces entered Czechoslovakia on 1 Oct. 1938. In 16 Mar. 1939 Germany invaded and occupied the rest of the country. At the end of the Second World War in May 1945 the pre-1938 frontiers were restored but Czechoslovakia ceded Ruthenia to the U.S.S.R. in June 1945. The Communist Party won 38% of the vote at the 1946 election and dominated the government. After Ministers of other parties resigned, Communist control became complete on 25 Feb. 1948. A People's Republic was established on 9 June 1948. A new constitution, introducing the country's present name, was proclaimed on 11 July 1960. Czechoslovakia has been a federal republic since 1 Jan. 1969.

The country comprises two nations, the Czechs and the Slovaks, each forming a republic with its own elected National Council and government. Czechoslovakia comprises 10 administrative regions and two cities.

The supreme organ of state power is the bicameral Federal Assembly, elected for 5 years by universal adult suffrage. Its permanent organ is the elected Presidium. The Assembly comprises the Chamber of the People, with 200 members (136 Czechs and 64 Slovaks), and the Chamber of Nations, with 150 members (75 from each republic). The Assembly elects the President of the Republic for a 5-year term and he appoints the Federal Government, led by the Chairman of the Government (Prime Minister), to hold executive authority. Ministers are responsible to the Assembly.

Political power is held by the Communist Party of Czechoslovakia, which dominates the National Front (including four other minor parties). All candidates for representative bodies are sponsored by the Front. The Communist Party's highest authority is the Party Congress, which elects the Central Committee to supervise Party work. The Committee elects a Presidium (12 full members and one alternate member

were elected in April 1981) to direct policy.
Length of roadways: 46 031 miles *74 064 km* (excluding local roads).
Length of railways: 8167 miles *13 141 km* (1983).
Universities: 5 (plus 7 technical universities).
Adult illiteracy: under 1%.
Expectation of life: Males 66·7 years; females 73·6 years (1977).
Defence: Military service: Army 2 years, Air Force 3 years; total regular forces 214 000 in 1985; defence expenditure: 7·8% of total government expenditure in 1983.
Foreign tourists: 14 301 839 in 1983.

Denmark

Official name: Kongeriget Danmark (Kingdom of Denmark).
Population: 5 116 273 (1 Jan. 1986).
Area: Denmark and the Faroes 17 180 miles[2] *44 500 km[2]*; Greenland 131 930 miles[2] *341 700 km[2]*.
Language: Danish.
Religions: Evangelical Lutheran 94%, other Christian minorities.
Capital city: København (Copenhagen), population 626 899 (1 Jan. 1986); including suburbs 1 351 999.
Other principal towns (1 Jan. 1986): Aarhus 253 650; Odense 172 751; Aalborg 154 905; Esbjerg 80 639.
Highest point: Yding Skovhøj, 568 ft *173 m*.
Principal river: Gudenå.
Head of State: HM Queen Margrethe II (b. 16 Apr. 1940).
Prime Minister: Poul Schlüter (b. 3 Apr. 1929).
Climate: Temperate: Mild summers (seldom above 21°C *70°F*) and cold winters (although seldom below freezing). The days are often foggy and damp. In Copenhagen, July warmest (13°C *55°F* to 22°C *72°F*), February coldest (−2°C *28°F* to 2°C *36°F*), August rainiest (12 days). Absolute maximum temperature 35,8°C *96·4°F*, Antvorskov, 13 Aug. 1911; absolute minimum −31,0°C *−23·8°F*, Løndal, 26 Jan. 1942.
Labour force: 2 753 000 aged 15 to 74 in 1985: Agriculture and fishing 6·3%; Construction 6·8%; Manufacturing 20·8%; Trade 16·2%; Hotels and restaurants 7·5%; Services 33·2%.
Gross domestic product: 482 658 billion kroner in 1984: Agriculture, forestry and fishing 6·2%; Manufacturing 20·5%; Construction 6·3%; Trade 13·3%; Transport, storage and communications 8·2%; Government services 22·6%.
Exports: 157·75 billion kroner in 1984: Industrial products 65·7%; Agricultural exports 24·4%; Fish and fur 5·7%.
Monetary unit: Danish krone. 1 krone = 100 øre.
Denominations:
Coins 5, 10, 25 øre; 1, 5, 10 kroner.
Notes 2, 10, 50, 100, 500, 1000 kroner.
Exchange rate to £ sterling: 10·55, (26 Jan. 1987).
Political history and government: A constitutional monarchy since 1849. Under the constitutional charter (*Grundlov*) of 5 June 1953, legislative power is held jointly by the hereditary

above: **DENMARK**
below: **CZECHOSLOVAKIA**

monarch (who has no personal political power) and the unicameral Parliament (*Folketing*), with 179 members (175 from metropolitan Denmark and two each from the Faeroe Islands and Greenland). Members are elected by universal adult suffrage for 4 years (subject to dissolution), using proportional representation. Executive power is exercised by the monarch through a Cabinet, led by the Prime Minister, which is responsible to Parliament. Denmark comprises 14 counties, one city and one borough.
Length of roadways: 43 611 miles *70 170 km* (1984).
Length of railways: 1586 miles *2552 km*.
Universities: 5 (plus 3 technical universities).
Adult illiteracy: under 1%.
Expectation of life: Males 71·5 years; females 77·5 years (1983–4).
Defence: Military service nine months; total armed forces 29 600 in 1985; defence expenditure: 6·2% of total government expenditure in 1985.
Foreign tourists: 3 690 000 in 1982.

Djibouti

Official name: Jumhuriya Jibuti (Arabic) or République de Djibouti (French): Republic of Djibouti.
Population: 297 000 (1985 estimate).
Area: 8880 miles² *23 000 km²*.
Languages: Somali, Afar, Arabic, French (official).
Religions: Muslim; Christian minority.
Capital city: Djibouti (Jibuti), population 200 000 (1985 estimate).
Other principal towns: Tadjoura, Obock, Dikhil, Ali-Sabieh.
Head of State: Gouled Aptidon Hassan (b. 1916), President.
Prime Minister: Gourad Hamadou Barkat.
Climate: Very hot and dry.
Gross domestic product: 60 234 million Djibouti francs in 1984.
Exports: 2220 million Djibouti francs in 1980: skins and leather 6·1%; Cereals 3·7%.
Monetary unit: Djibouti franc. 1 franc = 100 centimes.
Denominations:
   Coins 1, 2, 5, 10, 20, 50, 100 francs.
   Notes 500, 1000, 5000, 10 000 francs.
Exchange rate to £ sterling: 266 (26 Jan. 1987).
Political history and government: Formerly a dependency of France. Known as French Somaliland until 5 July 1967 and from then until independence as the French Territory of the Afars and the Issas. Also in 1967 the Territorial Assembly became the Chamber of Deputies. A provisional independence agreement was signed on 8 June 1976. A popular referendum approved independence on 8 May 1977, when an enlarged Chamber of Deputies (65 members) was also elected. The Chamber elected a Prime Minister on 16 May 1977. The Territory became independent on 27 June 1977, when the Prime Minister became President and the Chamber became a Constituent Assembly. Executive power is held by the President, directly elected for a six-year term as Head of State and Head of Government. The President appoints the Prime Minister and, on the latter's recommendation, other members of the Council of Ministers. The Assembly is to draw up a new constitution.
Length of roadways: 1806 miles *2906 km*.
Length of railways: 62 miles *100 km*.
Defence: Total armed forces 3000 (1986); Defence expenditure: 22·4% of total government expenditure in 1984.
Foreign tourists: 10 000 in 1980.

Dominica

Official name: The Commonwealth of Dominica.
Population: 74 069 (census of 1981).
Area: 289·8 miles² *751 km²*.
Language: English.
Religion: Roman Catholic 80%.

Capital city: Roseau, population 28 346 (1981).
Other principal towns: Portsmouth, Marigot.
Highest point: Imray's View, 4747 ft *1447 m*.
Principal river: Layou.
Head of State: Sir Clarence A. Seignoret, President.
Prime Minister: Mary Eugenia Charles (b. 1919).
Climate: Warm and pleasant. Cool from December to May. Rainy season generally June to October, dry February to May. Sometimes in the path of severe hurricanes.
Labour force: 27 380 (1980 estimate).
Gross domestic product: EC$194·4 million in 1982.
Exports: EC$61 516 000 in 1982: Bananas 43·7%; Soap 38·1%; Copra 4·9%.
Monetary unit: East Caribbean dollar (EC$). 1 dollar = 100 cents.
Denominations.
   Coins 1, 2, 5, 10, 25, 50 cents.
   Notes 1, 5, 20, 100 dollars.
Exchange rate to £ sterling: 4·13 (26 Jan. 1987).
Political history and government: A former British dependency, Dominica was part of the Leeward Islands until 31 Dec. 1939, when it was transferred to the Windward Islands. The federal arrangement in the British-ruled Windward Islands ended on 31 Dec. 1959. Under a new constitution, effective from 1 Jan. 1960, Dominica achieved a separate status, with its own Administrator. On 1 Mar. 1967 Dominica became one of the West Indies Associated States, gaining full autonomy in internal affairs. The Administrator became Governor and the Chief Minister was restyled Premier.
   Dominica became an independent republic on 3 Nov. 1978, with the Premier as Prime Minister. Legislative power is vested in the unicameral House of Assembly, with 31 members (21 elected by universal adult suffrage, 9 appointed by the President and 1 *ex officio*) serving a term of five years (subject to dissolution). Executive authority is vested in the President, elected by the House, but he generally acts on the advice of the Cabinet. The President appoints the Prime Minister, who must be supported by a majority in the House, and (on the Prime Minister's recommendation) other Ministers. The Cabinet effectively controls government and is responsible to the House.
Length of roadways: 467 miles *752 km* (31 Dec. 1976).
Adult illiteracy: 5·9% in 1970.
Expectation of life: Males 56·97 years; females 59·18 years (1958–62).
Foreign tourists: 27 315 (1984).

The Dominican Republic

Official name: La República Dominicana.
Population: 6 102 000 (1984 estimate).
Area: 18 703 miles² *48 442 km²*.
Language: Spanish.
Religion: Roman Catholic.
Capital city: Santo Domingo de Guzmán, population 1 313 172 (1981 census).
Other principal towns (1981): Santiago de los Caballeros 278 638; La Romana 91 571; San Pedro de Macoris 78 562; San Francisco de Macoris 64 906; La Vega 52 432.
Highest point: Pico Duarte (formerly Pico Trujillo), 10 417 ft *3175 m*.
Principal mountain range: Cordillera Central.
Principal river: Yaque del Norte.
Head of State: Dr Joaquín Balaguer, President.
Climate: Sub-tropical. Average temperature 27°C *80°F*. The west and south-west are arid. In the path of tropical cyclones. In Santo Domingo, August is hottest (23°C *73°F* to 31°C *88°F*), January coolest (19°C *66°F* to 29°C *84°F*), June rainiest (12 days). Absolute maximum temperature 43°C *109·4°F*, Valverde, 31 Aug. 1954; absolute minimum −3,5°C *+25·7°F*, Valle Nuevo, 2 Mar. 1959.
Labour force: 1 107 468 (1970 census): Agriculture, forestry and fishing 54·9%; Manufacturing 10·7%; Community, social and personal services 16·1%; 1 592 072 (estimate for 1 July 1979).

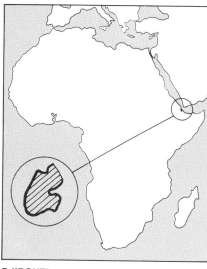

DJIBOUTI

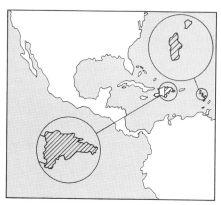

left: **THE DOMINICAN REPUBLIC**
right: **DOMINICA**

Gross domestic product: RD$7917·5 million in 1982: Agriculture, forestry and fishing 17·9%; Mining 2·4%; Manufacturing 18·4%; Construction 7%; Trade 16·7%; Transport 4·5%; Finance 3·9%; Government services 8·4%.
Exports: US$868 076 000 in 1984: Raw sugar 31·3%; Molasses 1·6%; Cocoa beans 8·1%; Coffee 11%; Tobacco 2·8%; Ferro-nickel 12·5%; Alloy of gold and silver 15·2%.
Monetary unit: Dominican Republic peso. 1 peso = 100 centavos.
Denominations:
   Coins 1, 5, 10, 25, 50 centavos; 1 peso.
   Notes 1, 5, 10, 20, 50, 100, 500, 1000 pesos.
Exchange rate to £ sterling: 4·6619 (26 Jan. 1987).
Political history and government: A republic comprising 27 provinces (each administered by an appointed governor) and a *Distrito Nacional* (DN) containing the capital. Legislative power is exercised by the bicameral National Congress, with a Senate of 28 members (one for each province and one for the DN) and a Chamber of Deputies (91 members). Members of both houses are elected for four years by universal adult suffrage. Executive power lies with the President, elected by direct popular vote for four years. He is assisted by a Vice-President and an appointed Cabinet containing Secretaries of State.
Length of roadways: 7643 miles *12 297 km*.
Length of railways: 365 miles *588 km*.
Universities: 4 (plus 1 technical university).
Adult illiteracy: 23% in 1983.
Expectation of life: 62 years for both males and females.
Defence: military service is voluntary; 4 years; total armed forces 22 200 (1985); defence expenditure: 12·8% of total government expenditure in 1984.
Foreign tourists: 341 000 in 1982.

Ecuador

Official name: La República del Ecuador ('the equator').
Population: 9 052 331 (1985 estimate).
Area: 109 484 miles² *283 561 km²*.
Language: Spanish.
Religion: Roman Catholic.
Capital city: Quito, population 1 110 248 at 1982 census.
Other principal towns (1982): Guayaquil 1 300 868; Cuenca 272 397; Ambato 221 392; Machala 117 243; Esmeraldas 141 030; Portoviejo 167 070; Riobamba 149 757.
Highest point: Chimborazo, 20 561 ft *6267 m* (first climbed 1879).
Principal mountain range: Cordillera de los Andes.
Principal rivers: Napo, Pastaza, Curaray, Daule.
Head of State: Leòn Febres Cordero, President.
Climate: Tropical (hot and humid) in coastal lowlands. Temperate (mild days, cool nights) in highlands, average temperature 13°C *55°F*, rainy season November–May. In Quito, average maximum 21°C *70°F* (April, May) to 23°C *73°F* (August, September), minimum 7°C *44°F* (July) to 8°C *47°F* (February–May), April rainiest (22 days). Absolute maximum temperature 38°C *100·4°F*, Babahoyo, 4 Jan. 1954; absolute minimum −3,6°C *25·5°F*, Cotopaxi, 9 Sept. 1962.
Labour force: 3 017 650 in 1984: Agriculture, forestry and fishing 46·4%; Manufacturing 10·9%; Trade, 11·7%; Community, social and personal services 16·2%.
Gross domestic product: 565 802 million sucres in 1983; Agriculture, hunting and fishing 13·3%; Mining and quarrying 12·8%; Manufacturing 20·3%; Trade 14·4%.
Exports: US$2622 million in 1984: Petroleum 68·4%; Bananas 4·7%; Cocoa 1·9%; Coffee 6·5%; Fish and fish products 8·8%.
Monetary unit: Sucre. 1 sucre = 100 centavos.
Denominations:
   Coins 5, 10, 20, 50 centavos; 1 sucre.
   Notes 5, 10, 20, 50, 100, 500, 1000 sucres.
Exchange rate to £ sterling: 222·95 (26 Jan. 1987).
Political history and government: A republic comprising 19 provinces (each administered by an appointed governor) and a National Territory, the Archipiélago de Colón (the Galapagos Islands). On 22 June 1970 the President dismissed the National Congress (a Senate of 54 members and a 72-member Chamber of Deputies) and assumed dictatorial powers. He was deposed by the armed forces on 15 Feb. 1972 and a National Military Government was formed. All political activity was suspended on 11 July 1974. A three-man military junta took power on 11 Jan. 1976 as the Supreme Council of Government. On 2 June 1976 the régime announced plans for a return to civilian rule. A referendum on 15 Jan. 1978 approved a new constitution providing for an executive President and a unicameral Congress with legislative power, both to be directly elected by universal adult suffrage. A presidential election was held on 16 July 1978 but no candidate obtained a majority of the votes. A 'run-off' election between the two leading candidates was held on 29 Apr. 1979, when the new Congress (69 members) was also elected. Jaime Roldós Aguilera was elected President and took office for a 4-year term on 10 Aug. 1979, when the Congress was inaugurated and the new constitution came into force. President Roldós was killed in an air crash on 24 May 1981 and his Vice-President succeeded him for the remainder of his term. Elections in 1984 were won by León Cordero. The President appoints and leads the Council of Ministers.
Length of roadways: 22 400 miles *35 900 km* (1980).
Length of railways: 606 miles *971 km* (1984).
Universities: 8 (plus 8 technical universities).
Adult illiteracy: 25·8% (males 21·8%; females 29·6%) in 1974.
Expectation of life: Males 54·89 years; females 58·07 years (1962–74, excluding nomadic Indian tribes).

Egypt

Official name: Jumhuriyat Misr al-'Arabiya (Arab Republic of Egypt).
Population: 51 000 000 (1987 estimate).
Area: 386 662 miles² *1 001 449 km²*.
Language: Arabic.
Religions: Muslim 92·6% Christian 7·3% (1960).
Capital city: El Qahira (Cairo), population 8 540 000 (1979 estimate).
Other principal towns (1976): El Iskandariyah (Alexandria) 2 318 655; El Giza 1 246 713; Subra-El Khema 393 700; El Mahalla el Kubra 292 853; Tanta 284 636; Bur Sa'id (Port Said) 262 620; El Mansura 257 866.
Highest point: Jebel Katherina, 8651 ft *2609 m*.
Principal mountain ranges: Sinai, Eastern Coastal Range.
Principal river: Nile (4145 miles *6670 km*).
Head of State: Lt-Gen. (Muhammad) Husni Mubarak (b. 1928), President.
Prime Minister: Dr. Atef Sedki.
Climate: Hot and dry. Over 90% is arid desert. Annual rainfall generally less than 50 mm *2 in*, except on Mediterranean coast (maximum of 200 mm *8 in* around Alexandria). Mild winters. In Cairo, average maximum 18°C *65°F* (January) to 35°C *96°F* (July), minimum 8°C *47°F* (January) to 22°C *71°F* (August). In Luxor, average maximum 23°C *74°F* (January) to 42°C *107°F* (July), minimum 5°C *42°F* (January) to 23°C *73°F* (July, August), rain negligible.
Labour force: 10 517 900 in 1981: Agriculture, forestry and fishing 38·1%; Manufacturing 15%; Construction 5%; Trade 8·1%; Transport, storage and communications 5·3%; Social and personal services 19·5%; Unemployed 5·4%.
Gross domestic product: £E7341·0 million in 1977: Agriculture, forestry and fishing 27·6%; Manufacturing, mining and quarrying 24·4%; Trade, restaurants and hotels (incl. finance and insurance services) 12·3%; Community, social and personal services 20·5%.
Exports: £E2250·3 million in 1983: Raw cotton and cotton products 22·7%; Edible Fruits 2·7%; Crude petroleum 47·6%; Fuel oils 9·2%.
Monetary unit: Egyptian pound (£E). £E1 = 100 piastres = 1000 millièmes.
Denominations:
   Coins 1, 5 millièmes; 1, 2, 5, 10, 20 piastres.
   Notes 5, 10, 25, 50 piastres; 1, 5, 10, 20, 100 pounds.
Exchange rate to £ sterling: 2·08 (26 Jan. 1987).
Political history and government: A former British protectorate, Egypt became independent, with the Sultan as King, on 28 Feb. 1922. Army officers staged a *coup* on 23 July 1952 and the King abdicated, in favour of his son, on 26 July 1952. Political parties were dissolved on 16 Jan. 1953. The young King was deposed, and a republic proclaimed, on 18 June 1953. Egypt merged with Syria to form the United Arab Republic on 1 Feb. 1958. Syria broke away and resumed independence on 29 Sept. 1961 but Egypt retained the union's title until the present name was adopted on 2 Sept. 1971. A new constitution, proclaiming socialist principles, was approved by referendum on 11 Sept. 1971. Legislative authority rests with the unicameral People's Assembly of 458 members (10 appointed and 400 elected according to the list system and 48 individual system for 5 years). Half the elected members must be workers or peasants. The Assembly nominates the President, who is elected by popular referendum for six years. He has executive authority and appoints one or more Vice-Presidents, a Prime Minister and a Council of Ministers to perform administrative functions. The Arab Socialist Union (ASU), created on 7 Dec. 1962, was the only recognised political organisation of the state until the formation of political parties was again legalised on 29 June 1977. The three parties initially permitted were based on the

ECUADOR

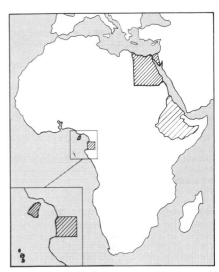

left : **EQUATORIAL GUINEA**
top right : **EGYPT**   *lower right :* **ETHIOPIA**

three 'platforms' of the ASU which presented separate candidates at the Assembly elections of 28 Oct. and 4 Nov. 1976. Elections were again held in 1984 to the People's Assembly, but the electoral requirements for the opposition parties were very tightly drawn. The country is composed of 25 governorates (5 cities, 16 provinces, 4 frontier districts).
Length of roadways: 17 964 miles *28 910 km* (main and secondary roads only) at 31 Dec. 1979.
Length of railways: 3018 miles *4857 km*.
Universities: 18.
Adult illiteracy: 61·8% (males 46·4%; females 77·6%) in 1976.
Expectation of life: Males 51·6 years; females 53·8 years (1960).
Defence: Military service; 3 years (selective); total armed forces 445 000 (1985); defence expenditure: £E2900 million in 1985–6.
Foreign tourists: 1 500 000 in 1983.

El Salvador

Offical name: La República de El Salvador ('The Saviour').
Population: 4 672 900 (1981 census); 5 480 000 (1985 estimate).
Area: 8124 miles² *21 041 km²*.

Defence: Military service: two years, selective; total armed forces 43 600 (1986); defence expenditure: 9·4% of total government expenditure in 1982.
Foreign tourists: 219 357 (1984).

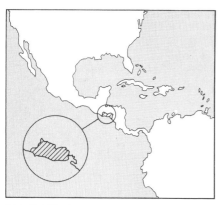

EL SALVADOR

Language: Spanish.
Religion: Roman Catholic.
Capital city: San Salvador, population 444 052 (1982).
Other principal towns (1981): Santa Ana 208 322; San Miguel 161 156; Zacatecoluca 78 751; Ahuachapán 69 852; Usulutain 65 462.
Highest point: 9200 ft *2804 m*.
Principal rivers: Lempa (250 miles *402 km*), San Miguel.
Head of State: José Napoleón Duarte, President.
Climate: Tropical (hot and humid) in coastal lowlands, temperate in uplands. In San Salvador, maximum temperature is 32°C *90°F* (April and May), minimum around 15°C *60°F* (December, January, February).
Labour force: 2 490 000 in 1984: Agriculture 50%; Industry 22%; Services 27%.
Gross domestic product: 9754 million colones in 1983: Agriculture, forestry and fishing 21·6%; Manufacturing 15·6%; Commerce 23·9%; Public administration 11·1%; Personal services 8·1%.
Exports: 1814 million colones in 1984: Coffee 62%.
Monetary unit: Salvadorian colón. 1 colón = 100 centavos.
Denominations:
  Coins 1, 5, 10, 25, 50 centavos.
  Notes 1, 2, 5, 10, 25, 100 colones.
Exchange rate to £ sterling: 7·625 (26 Jan. 1987).
Political history and government: A republic composed of 14 departments. From 1932 a series of military officers held power, either as elected Presidents (often after disputed polls) or by means of a *coup*. On 20 Feb. 1977 Gen Carlos Humberto Romero Mena was elected President (despite allegations of fraud) and on 1 July 1977 he was sworn in. On 15 Oct. 1979 President Romero was deposed in a military *coup*. The unicameral Legislative Assembly was dissolved. The new régime formed a 5-member junta (including 3 civilians). On 15 Oct. 1980 the junta announced that elections to a constituent assembly would be held in 1982 and general elections in 1983. On 22 Dec. 1980 two members of the junta were sworn in as President and Vice-President. Presidential elections were held in 1984.
Length of roadways: 7643 miles *12 297 km* (1982).
Length of railways: 374 miles *602 km* (1985).
Universities: 12.
Adult illiteracy: 31·5% (1979).
Expectation of life: Males 62·9 years; females 66·4 years (1980–5).
Defence: Total armed forces 52 130 (1986); defence expenditure, 23% of total expenditure in 1984.
Foreign tourists: 106 100 (1983).

Equatorial Guinea

Official name: La República de Guinea Ecuatorial.
Population: 375 000 (1986 estimate).
Area: 10 831 miles² *28 051 km²*.
Languages: Spanish (official), Fang, Bubi.
Religions: Roman Catholic, Protestant minority.

Capital city: Malabo (formerly Santa Isabel), population 37 237 at 1960 census.
Other principal town: Bata, population 27 024 (1960).
Highest point: Pico de Moca (Moka), 9350 ft *2850 km*.
Principal rivers: Campo, Benito, Muni.
Head of State: Lt-Col Teodoro Obiang Nguema Mbasogo (b. 1946), President.
Prime Minister: Cristino Seriche Bioke Malabo.
Climate: Tropical (hot and humid), with average temperatures of over 26°C *80°F* and heavy rainfall (about 2000 mm *80 in* per year).
Labour force: 111 000 in 1984: Agriculture, forestry and fishing 73%.
Gross domestic product: 3311 million ekuele (at 1962 prices) in 1967; $112 million (estimate) in 1975.
Exports: 2502 million bipkwele in 1981: Cocoa 71·5%; Timber 24·4%; Coffee 2·8%.
Monetary unit: Franc de la Commonauté financière africaine. (Until 1985 it was the epkwele, plural bipkwele, linked to the Spanish peseta at 1 peseta = 2 epkwele since 1980.) céntimos.
Denominations:
  Coins 1, 2, 5, 10, 25, 50, 100 aand 500 CFA francs.
  Notes 100, 500, 1000, 5000, 10000 CFA francs.
Exchange rate to £ sterling: 279·54 (14 Jan. 1985).
Political history and government: Formed on 20 Dec. 1963 by a merger of two Spanish territories, Río Muni on the African mainland and the adjacent islands of Fernando Póo (later renamed Macías Nguema Biyogo, then Bioko) and Annobón (now Pagalu). Became an independent republic, as a federation of two provinces, on 12 Oct. 1968. All political parties were merged into one on 2 Feb. 1970. The first President, Francisco Macías Nguema, was proclaimed 'President for Life' on 14 July 1972. A revized constitution, approved by referendum on 29 July 1973 and effective from 4 Aug. 1973, gave absolute power to the President and established a unitary state, abolishing the provincial autonomy of the islands. President Macías was deposed by a *coup* on 3 Aug. 1979, when a Supreme Military Council assumed power.
Length of roadways: 730 miles *1175 km*.
Expectation of life: Males 41·9 years; females 45·1 years (UN estimates for 1970–75).
Defence: Total armed forces: 2200 (1985); defence expenditure US$6 million in 1982.

Ethiopia

Official name: Socialist Ethiopia.
Population: 42 169 203 (1984 census).
Area: 471 800 miles² *1 221 900 km²*.
Languages: Amharic, Galla, Somali.
Religions: Muslim 50%, Christian (mainly Coptic).
Capital city: Addis Ababa ('New Flower'), population 1 277 159 (1980 estimate).
Other principal towns (1980): Asmara 424 532; Dire Dawa 82 024; Gondar 76 932; Dessie 75 616; Nazret 69 865; Jimma 63 837; Harar 62 921; Bahr Dar 52 188.
Highest point: Ras Dashen, 15 158 ft *4620 m*.
Principal mountain ranges: Eritrean highlands, Tigre Plateau, Eastern Highlands, Semien mountains.
Principal rivers: Abbay, Tekeze, Awash, Omo, Sagan, Webi, Shebele.
Head of State: Lt-Col Mengistu Haile Mariam (b. 1937), President of the Derg (Provisional Military Administrative Council).
Climate: Mainly temperate and cool on the high plateau, with average annual temperature of 13°C *55°F*, abundant rainfall (June to August) and low humidity. Very hot and dry in desert lowlands and valley gorges. In Addis Ababa, average maximum 21°C *69°F* (July, August) to 25°C *77°F* (March–May), minimum 5°C *41°F* (December) to 10°C *50°F* (April–August). Absolute maximum 47,5°C *117·5°F*, Kelaffo, May 1959; absolute minimum −5,6°C *−22·0°F*, Maichew, November 1956.

Labour force: 14 264 000 in 1984: Agriculture, forestry and fishing 76·8%.
Gross domestic product: 9118·6 million birr in 1981–2: Agriculture, forestry and fishing 44·2%; Manufacturing 6·6%; Handicrafts and small industry 3·5%; Construction 3·6%; Trade 9·8%; Transport and communications 4·8%; Financial services 3·3%.
Exports: 833·3 million birr in 1983: Coffee 62·6%; Hides and skins 10·1%.
Monetary unit: Birr (formerly Ethiopian dollar). 1 birr = 100 cents.
Denominations:
  Coins 1, 5, 10, 25, 50 cents.
  Notes 1, 2, 10, 50, 100 birr.
Exchange rate to £ sterling: 3·18 (26 Jan. 1987).
Political history and government: Formerly a monarchy, ruled by an Emperor with near-autocratic powers. Political parties were not permitted. The former Italian colony of Eritrea was merged with Ethiopia, under a federal arrangement, on 15 Sept. 1952. Its federal status was ended on 14 Nov. 1962.
The last Emperor was deposed by the armed forces on 12 Sept. 1974. The constitution and the bicameral Parliament (a Senate and a Chamber of Deputies) were suspended. The *coup* was engineered by the Armed Forces Coordinating Committee (the Derg). The Committee established a Provisional Military Government and on 28 Nov. 1974 created the Provisional Military Administrative Council (PMAC) as its executive arm. Ethiopia was declared a socialist state on 20 Dec. 1974 and the monarchy was abolished on 21 Mar. 1975. Under a government re-organization, announced on 29 Dec. 1976 and modified by proclamation on 11 Feb. 1977, the PMAC was renamed the Derg and was re-constituted. In 1979 all political groupings were replaced by a Commission for Organizing the Party of the Working People in Ethiopia. In 1984 this was in turn replaced by the Workers' Party of Ethiopia, modelled on the Communist Party in the USSR. Ethiopia has 14 provinces.
Length of roadways: 23 172 miles *37 291 km* (31 Dec. 1979).
Length of railways: 614 miles *988 km*.
Universities: 2.
Adult illiteracy: 54% (1983).
Expectation of life: Males 37·0 years; females 40·1 years (UN estimates for 1970–75).
Defence: Military service: conscription; total armed forces 210 000 (1985), plus an estimated 5000 Cubans; defence expenditure: 25·1% of total government expenditure in 1983–4.
Foreign tourists: 69 000 in 1983–4.

Fiji

Population: 588 068 (census of 13 Sept. 1976); 690 684 (1984 estimate).
Area: 7056 miles² *18 274 km²*.
Languages: English, Fijian, Hindi.
Religions: Christian 50·8% (mainly Methodist), Hindu 40·3%, Muslim 7·8% (1966).
Capital city: Suva, population 71 000 (1982 estimate).
Other principal towns (1982): Lautoka 26 000; Vatukoula 7000; Ba 7000; Nausori 6000; Labasa 5000.
Highest point: Mt Victoria (Tomaniivi) on Viti Levu, 4341 ft *1323 m*.
Principal rivers: Rewa, Sigatoka, Navua, Nadi, Ba.
Head of State: HM Queen Elizabeth II, represented by Ratu Sir Penaia Ganilau, GCMG, KCVO, KBE, CMG, CVO, Governor General.
Prime Minister: Ratu the Rt Hon Sir Kamisese Kapaiwai Tuimacilai Mara, GCMG, KBE (b. 13 May 1920).
Climate: Temperate, with temperatures rarely falling below 15,5°C *60°F* or rising above 32,2°C *90°F*. Copious rainfall on windward side; dry on leeward side. Rainy season Nov.–March, driest month July.
Labour force: 240 000 in 1985: Unemployed 10·2%.
Gross domestic product: $F1157·9 million in 1984: Agriculture, forestry and fishing 24·3%;

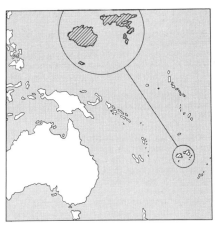

FIJI

Manufacturing 12·2%; Distribution (inc. tourism) 16·8%; Government services 17·8%.

Exports: $F279 418 000 in 1984: Sugar 39·4%; Gold 7·3%; coconut oil 6·6%; Prepared fish 5·1%.

Monetary unit: Fiji dollar (F$). 1 dollar = 100 cents.

Denominations:
Coins 1, 2, 5, 10, 20, 50 cents.
Notes 1, 2, 5, 10, 20 dollars.

Exchange rate to £ sterling: 1·7144 (26 Jan. 1987).

Political history and government: A former British colony, an independent member of the Commonwealth since 10 Oct. 1970. Executive power is vested in the Queen and exercisable by her personal representative, the Governor-General, appointed on the recommendation of the Cabinet. The Governor-General normally acts in accordance with the Cabinet's advice. The bicameral legislature comprises a Senate (22 members nominated for staggered six-year terms) and a House of Representatives (52 members elected for five years, subject to dissolution). Elections to the House are on three rolls: Fijian (22), Indian (22) and general (8). The Cabinet, which effectively directs the government, is responsible to the legislature. The Prime Minister is chosen by the House and other Ministers are appointed on his recommendation. There are 14 provinces, each headed by a chairman.

Length of roadways: 2675 miles *4300 km*.

Length of railways: 450 miles *725 km*.

Universities: 1.

Expectation of life: Males 68·5 years; females 71·7 years (UN estimates for 1970–75).

Defence: Military service voluntary; total armed forces 2670 (1985); defence expenditure, 1985: $F15·9 million.

Foreign tourists: 235 227 in 1984.

Finland

Official name: Suomen Tasavalta (Republic of Finland).

Population: 4 893 748 (1984 estimate).

Area: 130 557 miles² *338 145 km²*.

Languages: Finnish 93·6%; Swedish 6·2%.

Religions: Lutheran 90·1%; Orthodox 1·1%.

Capital city: Helsinki (Helsingfors), population 484 263 (31 Dec. 1984).

Other principal towns (1983): Tampere (Tammerfors) 168 150; Turku (Åbo) 162 282; Espoo (Esbo) 152 929; Vantaa (Vandu) 141 991; Lahti 97 347; Oulu (Uleåborg) 96 525.

Highest point: Haltiatunturi, 4344 ft *1324 m*.

Principal mountain ranges: Suomenselkä, Maanselkä.

Principal rivers: Paatsjoki, Torniojoki, Kemijoki, Kokemäenjoki.

Head of State: Dr Mauno Henrik Koivisto (b. 25 Nov. 1923), President.

Climate: Warm summers, very cold winters. Average annual temperature 17°C *62°F*. Winters are long and extreme in the north. In Helsinki, July warmest (14°C *57°F* to 22°C *71°F*), Feb-

ruary coldest (−9°C *15°F* to −3°C *26°F*), August and October rainiest (12 days each). Absolute maximum temperature 35,9°C *96·6°F*, Turku, 9 July 1914; absolute minimum −48,8°C −55·8°F, Sodankylä, January 1868.

Labour force: 2 572 000 in 1984: Agriculture, forestry and fishing 11·4%; Manufacturing 21·9%; Trade 13·3%; Community, personal and social services 25·8%; Unemployed 6·1%.

Gross domestic product: 307 876 million markkaa in 1984; Agriculture, forestry and fishing 7·4%; Manufacturing 23·6%; Trade 9·9%; Financial services 8·2%; Other community, personal and social services 14·7%.

Exports: $80 904·1 million markka in 1984: Paper and paperboard 23·5%; Machinery and transport equipment 24·9%; Wood and wood pulp 11·1%.

Monetary unit: Markka (Finnmark). 1 markka = 100 penniä (singular: penni).

Denominations:
Coins 5, 10, 20, 50 penniä; 1, 5, 10 markkaa.
Notes 5, 10, 50, 100, 500, 1000 markkaa.

Exchange rate to £ sterling: 6·96 (26 Jan 1987).

Political history and government: Formerly a Grand Duchy within the Russian Empire. After the Bolshevik revolution in Russia, Finland's independence was declared on 6 Dec. 1917. A republic was established by the constitution of 17 July 1919. This combines a parliamentary system with a strong presidency. The unicameral Parliament (*Eduskunta*) has 200 members elected by universal adult suffrage for 4 years (subject to dissolution by the President), using proportional representation. The President, entrusted with supreme executive power, is elected for 6 years by a college of 301 electors, chosen by popular vote in the same manner as members of Parliament. Legislative power is exercised by Parliament in conjunction with the President. For a general administration the President appoints a Council of State (Cabinet), headed by a Prime Minister, which is responsible to Parliament. Finland has 12 provinces, each administered by an appointed Governor.

Length of roadways: 47 140 miles *75 848 km* (1985).

Length of railways: 3728 miles *9035 km* (1985).

Universities: 17 universities of science, 3 universities of art and 1 educational institution for social work at third level.

Adult illiteracy: Under 1%.

Expectation of life: Males 70·08 years; females 78·13 years (1982).

Defence: Military service: 8 to 11 months; total armed forces 36 300 (1986); defence expenditure: 5·7% of total government expenditure in 1984.

Tourism: Foreign exchange receipts on travel and ticket balances totalled $3039 million markkaa (1984).

France

Official name: La République française (the French Republic).

Population: 55 282 000 (1986 estimate).

Area: 211 208 miles² *547 026 km²*.

Language: French; Breton and Basque minorities.

Religions: Roman Catholic, Protestant, Jewish, Moslem.

Capital city: Paris, population 8 706 973 (1982 census).

Other principal towns (1982): Lyon 1 220 844; Marseille 1 110 511; Lille 936 295; Bordeaux 640 012; Toulouse 541 271; Nantes 464 857; Nice 449 496; Grenoble 392 021; Rouen 379 879; Toulon 410 393; Strasbourg 373 470; Valenciennes 349 505; St-Étienne 317 228; Lens 327 383; Nancy 306 982; Cannes 295 525; Tours 262 786; Béthune 258 383; Clermont-Ferrand 256 189; Le Havre 254 595; Rennes 234 418; Montpellier 221 307; Mulhouse 220 613; Orléans 220 478; Dijon 215 865; Douai 202 366; Brest 201 145.

Highest point: Mont Blanc, 15 771 ft *4807 m* (first climbed on 8 Aug. 1786).

Principal mountain ranges: Alps, Massif Central, Pyrenees, Jura Mts, Vosges, Cévennes.

Principal rivers: Rhône, Seine, Loire (625 miles *1006 km*), Garonne, Rhin (Rhine).

Head of State: François Mitterand (b. 26 Oct. 1916), President.

Prime Minister: Jacques Chirac.

Climate: Generally temperate, with cool summers in the west and warm summers elsewhere. Mediterranean climate (warm summers, mild winters) in the south. In Paris, average maximum 5°C *42°F* (January) to 24°C *76°F* (July), minimum 0°C *32°F* (January) to 13°C *55°F* (July, August), December rainiest (17 days). Absolute maximum temperature 44,0°C *111·2°F*, Toulouse, 8 Aug. 1923; absolute minimum −33°C −27·4°F, Langres, 9 Dec. 1879.

Labour force: 23 045 000 in 1983: Agriculture, forestry and fishing 7·3%; Manufacturing 22%; Construction 7·3%; Trade 15%; Community, social and personal services 26·2%; Unemployed 8·1%.

Gross domestic product: 3 094 419 million francs in 1981: Agriculture 3·4%; Manufacturing 25·1%; Construction 6·6%; Trade 10% Financial services 17·7%; Community, social and personal services 8·1%.

Exports: 850·9 billion francs in 1984: Agriculture 16·6%; Semi-manufactured goods 26·7%; Capital goods 26·7%; Consumer goods 14·3%; Surface transport equipment 11%.

Monetary unit: French franc. 1 franc = 100 centimes.

Denominations:
Coins 5, 10, 20, 50 centimes; 1, 2, 5, 10 francs.
Notes 10, 50, 100, 500 francs.

Exchange rate to £ sterling: 9·295 (26 Jan. 1987).

Political history and government: A republic whose present constitution (establishing the Fifth Republic and the French Community) was approved by referendum on 28 Sept. 1958 and promulgated on 6 Oct. 1958. Legislative power is held by a bicameral Parliament. The Senate has 319 members (296 for metropolitan France, 13 for the overseas departments and territories and 10 for French nationals abroad) indirectly elected for 9 years (one third renewable every three years). The National Assembly has 577 members directly elected by universal adult suffrage (using two ballots if necessary) for 5 years, subject to dissolution. In 1986 the elections were held under the departmental list system of proportional representation according to the principle of the highest average. The system has now been changed back to direct election by universal adult suffrage, using two ballots if necessary. Executive power is held by the President. Since 1962 the President has been directly elected by universal adult suffrage (using two ballots if necessary) for 7 years. The President appoints a Council of Ministers, headed by the Prime Minister, which governs the country and is responsible to Parliament. Metropolitan France comprises 22 administrative regions containing 96 departments. There are also five overseas departments (French Guiana, Guadeloupe, Martinique, La Réunion) which are integral parts of the French Republic. Each department is administered by an elected President of the Regional Council.

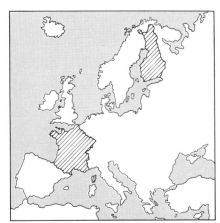

left: **FRANCE**   *right:* **FINLAND**

Length of roadways: 945 526 miles *1 521 351 km* (1984).
Length of railways: 21 559 miles *34 688 km* (1984).
Universities: 69.
Expectation of life: Males 70·4 years; females 78·5 years (1981).
Defence: Military service; 12 months (18 months for overseas); total armed forces 519 924; (1985) defence expenditure, 1985: 15·7% of total government expenditure in 1983.
Foreign tourists: 34 018 000 in 1983.

Gabon

Official name: La République gabonaise (the Gabonese Republic).
Population: 1 336 000 in 1986.
Area: 103 347 miles² *267 667 km²*.
Languages: French (official), Fang, Eshira, Mbété.
Religions: Christian 60%, Animist minority.
Capital city: Libreville, population 350 000 (1983).
Other principal towns (1978): Port-Gentil 123 300; Lambaréné 26 257.
Highest point: Mont Iboundji, 5185 ft *1580 m.*
Principal river: Ogooué (Ogowe).
Head of State: *El Hadj* Omar Bongo (b. Albert-Bernard Bongo, 30 Dec. 1935), President and Head of Government.
Prime Minister: Léon Mébiame (b. 1 Sept. 1934).
Climate: Tropical (hot and humid). Average temperature 26°C 79°F. Heavy rainfall (annual average 2490 mm *98 in*). In Libreville, average maximum 30°C 86°F to 34°C 94°F, minimum 18°C 65°F to 22°C 71°F.
Labour force: 381 400 in 1972: Agriculture 70%; Forestry, mining and construction 15·7%; Commerce and industry 2·1%; Civil service 2·1%.
Gross domestic product: 600 203 million CFA francs in 1978: Mining and quarrying (excluding government) 36·3% (crude petroleum and natural gas 30·2%); Construction 14·1%.
Exports: 669 300 million CFA francs in 1982: Crude petroleum 81·3%; Timber 7·8%; Manganese ores and concentrates 4·9%; Agricultural products 3%.
Monetary unit: Franc de la Communauté financière africaine.
Denominations:
  Coins 1, 2, 5, 10, 25, 50, 100 CFA francs.
  Notes 100, 500, 1000, 5000, 10 000 CFA francs.
Exchange rate to £ sterling: 464·75 (26 Jan. 1987).
Political history and government: Formerly part of French Equatorial Africa, independent since 17 Aug. 1960. A one-party state since March 1968. The legislature is a unicameral National Assembly of 93 members, of whom nine are nominated by the President and 84 directly elected by universal adult suffrage for five years. Executive power is held by the President,

GABON

directly elected for seven years. He appoints, and presides over, a Council of Ministers, including a Prime Minister. Gabon comprises nine regions, each administered by an appointed Prefect.
Length of roadways: 4511 miles *7276 km* (1981).
Length of railways: 200 miles *325 km.*
Universities: 1.
Adult illiteracy: 87·6% in 1960.
Expectation of life: Males 39·4 years; females 42·6 years (UN estimates for 1970–75).
Defence: Military service voluntary; total armed forces 2400 (1985); defence expenditure: 4·7% of total government expenditure in 1984.
Foreign tourists: 16 000 in 1982.

The Gambia

Official name: The Republic of the Gambia.
Population: 695 886 (1983 census, excluding seasonal farming immigrants).
Area: 4361 miles² *11 295 km².*
Languages: English (official), Mandinka, Fula, Wollof.
Religions: Muslim, Christian minority.
Capital city: Banjul (formerly Bathurst), population 65 000 (1983 census).
Other principal towns: Brikama; Salikeni; Bakau; Gunjur.
Principal river: Gambia.
Head of State: *Alhaji* Sir Dawda Kairaba Jawara (b. 11 May 1924), President.
Climate: Long dry season, normally November to May, with pleasant weather on coast (best in West Africa) due to effect of the *harmattan*, a northerly wind. Hotter up-river, especially February to May. Average annual rainfall 1000 mm *40 in* on coast, less inland. Rainy season June to October. Average annual temperature in Banjul 27°C 80°F.
Labour force: 300 000 in 1984: Agriculture, Forestry and Fishing 76·3%.
Gross domestic product: 451·2 million dalasi in 1981: Agriculture, foresty and fishing 35%; Manufacturing 5·5%; Construction 5·5%; Trade 21%; Transport and storage 7·6%; Financial services 12·7%.
Exports: 64·82 million dalasi in 1979–80: Groundnuts 52·2%; Groundnut meal and cake 7·9%; Groundnut oil 22·7%; Fish 10·2%.
Monetary unit: Dalasi. 1 dalasi = 100 butut.
Denominations:
  Coins 1, 5, 10, 25, 50 butut; 1 dalasi.
  Notes 1, 5, 10, 25 dalasi.
Exchange rate to £ sterling: 11·00 (26 Jan. 1987).
Political history and government: A former British dependency, an independent member of the Commonwealth since 18 Feb. 1965. A republic since 24 April 1970. Legislative power is held by a unicameral House of Representatives containing 43 members (35 directly elected for 5 years by universal adult suffrage, 4 Chiefs' Representative Members elected by the Chiefs in Assembly, 3 non-voting nominated members and the Attorney-General). Executive power is held by the President, the leader of the majority party in the House. He appoints a Vice-President (who is leader of government business in the House) and a Cabinet from elected members of the House. The country has four political parties. On 1 Feb. 1982 the Gambia and Senegal formed a confederation named Senegambia.
Length of roadways: 1916 miles *3083 km* (1983).
Adult illiteracy: 79·9% (males 70·9%, females 88·4%) in 1980.
Expectation of life: Males 39·4 years; females 42·5 years (UN estimates for 1970–75).
Defence: Military service voluntary; total armed forces 475 in 1985.
Foreign tourists: 41 950 in 1983–84.

Germany (East)

Official name: Deutsche Demokratische Republik (German Democratic Republic).
Population: 16 705 635 (census of 31 Dec. 1981); 16 660 000 (1984 estimate).
Area: 41 828 miles² *108 333 km².*

Language: German.
Religions: Protestant 50%, Roman Catholic 8%.
Capital city: (East) Berlin, population 1 185 500 (1983 estimate).
Other principal towns (1983): Leipzig 559 000; Dresden 522 500; Karl-Marx-Stadt (Chemnitz) 318 900; Magdeburg 289 100; Rostock 241 100; Halle 236 100.
Highest point: Fichtelberg, 3983 ft *1214 m.*
Principal mountain ranges: Thüringer Wald, Erz Gebirge.
Principal rivers: Elbe (525 miles *845 km*) (with Havel and Saale), Oder (with Neisse).
Head of State: Erich Honecker (b. 25 Aug. 1912), Chairman of the Council of State; also General Secretary of the Central Committee of the Socialist Unity Party.
Head of Government: Willi Stoph (b. 9 July 1914), Chairman of the Council of Ministers.
Climate: Temperate (warm summers, cool winters), greater range inland. In Berlin, July warmest (13°C 55°F to 23°C 74°F), January coldest (−3°C 26°F to 2°C 35°F), December rainiest (11 days). Absolute maximum temperature 38,3°C 102·7°F, Blankenberg, 7 July 1957; absolute minimum −33,8°C −28·8°F, Zittau-Hirschfelde, 11 Feb. 1939.
Labour force: 8 499 000 (1984, excluding apprentices): Agriculture and forestry 10·8%; Mining, manufacturing, power and building 47·8%; Trade 10·1%; Transport and communications 7·4%.
Net material product: 210 080 million DDR-marks (1983); Agriculture and forestry 8·2%; Industry and productive crafts 74·6%; Trade 9·7%.
Exports: 84 227 million Valuta marks (1983): Machinery 47·8%; Fuels, mineral raw materials, metals 17·7%; Other raw materials and semi-manufactured goods 7·9%; Industrial consumer goods 14·1%; Chemical products, building materials and other goods 12·5%.
Monetary unit: Mark der Deutschen Demokratischen Republik (DDR-Mark). 1 Mark = 100 Pfennige.
Denominations:
  Coins 1, 5, 10, 20, 50 Pfennige; 1, 2, 5, 10, 20 DDR-Marks.
  Notes 5, 10, 20, 50, 100 DDR-Marks.
Exchange rate to £ sterling: 2·785 (26 Jan. 1987).
Political history and government: The territory was the USSR's Zone of Occupation in Germany from May 1945. The republic, a 'people's democracy' on the Soviet pattern, was proclaimed on 7 Oct. 1949. The USSR granted full sovereignty on 25 Mar. 1954. The present constitution was promulgated on 9 Apr. 1968. The supreme organ of state power is the *Volkskammer* (People's Chamber), with 500 members elected for 5 years by universal adult suffrage (from a single list of candidates). The Chamber elects a 24-member *Staatsrat* (Council of State) to be its permanent organ. The executive branch of government is the *Minister-rat* (Council of Ministers), under a Chairman (Minister-President) appointed by the Chamber, which also approves his appointed Ministers. The Council's work is directed by a Presidium of 16 members. Political power is held by the (Communist) Socialist Unity Party of Germany (SED), formed in 1946 by a merger of the Communist Party and the Social Democratic Party in the Soviet Zone. The SED dominates the National Front of Democratic Germany, which also includes four minor parties and four mass organisations. The SED's highest authority is the Party Congress. The Congress elects the Central Committee to supervise Party work (on 15 Apr. 1981 the Congress elected a Committee of 156 full members and 57 candidate members). The Central Committee elects a Political Committee (Politburo), with 17 full members and eight candidate members in 1981, to direct its policy. The country is divided into 14 districts (*Bezirke*) and the city of East Berlin.
Length of roadways (classified): 74 891 miles *120 500 km* (1984).
Length of railways: 8820 miles *14 226 km* (1983).
Universities: 7.
Expectation of life: Males 68·82 years; females 74·42 years (1976).

Defence: Military service 18–24 months; total regular forces 174 000 in 1985; defence expenditure: 7·8% of total government expenditure in 1985.
Foreign tourists: 933 889 in 1983.

Germany (West)

Official name: Bundesrepublik Deutschland (Federal Republic of Germany).
Population: 61 020 000 (estimate for 31 Dec. 1985).
Area: 96 025 miles² *248 706 km²*.
Language: German.
Religions: Protestant 49%, Roman Catholic 44·6%.
Capital city: Bonn, population 291 700 (estimate 1984).
Other principal towns (1984): Berlin (West) 1 851 800; Hamburg 1 600 300; München (Munich) 1 277 000; Köln (Cologne) 932 400; Frankfurt 604 600; Dortmund 584 800; Düsseldorf 570 700; Stuttgart 563 200; Bremen 535 800; Duisberg 528 000; Hannover (Hanover) 517 900; Nürnberg (Nuremberg) 471 700; Bochum 387 100; Wuppertal 381 900; Bielefeld 303 900; Mannheim 297 200; Gelsenkirchen 290 700; Münster 273 500; Wiesbaden 268 900; Karlsruhe 268 700; Mönchengladbach 256 300; Braunschweig (Brunswick) 255 400.
Highest point: Zugspitze, 9721 ft *2963 m* (first climbed 1820).
Principal mountain ranges: Alps, Schwarzwald (Black Forest).
Principal rivers: Rhein (Rhine) (820 miles *1320 km*), Ems, Weser, Elbe, Donau (Danube) (1770 miles *2850 km*).
Head of State: Dr Richard von Weizsäcker (b. 15 Mar. 1920), Federal President.
Head of Government: Dr Helmut Kohl (b. 3 April 1930), Federal Chancellor.
Climate: Generally temperate (average annual temperature 9°C *48°F*) with considerable variations from northern coastal plain (mild) to Bavarian Alps (cool summers, cold winters). In Hamburg, July warmest (13°C *56°F* to 20°C *69°F*), January coolest (−2°C *28°F* to 2°C *35°F*), January, July and December rainiest (each 12 days). Absolute maximum temperature 39,8°C *103·6°F*, Amberg, 18 Aug. 1892; absolute minimum −35,4°C −*31·7°F*, 12 Feb. 1929.
Labour force: 27 835 000 in 1985: Agriculture, forestry and fishing 5·4%; Production 41%; Trade, transport and communications 18·3%; Others 35·3%; Unemployed 8·3%.
Gross domestic product: 1830·4 billion DM in 1985: Agriculture and forestry 1·7%; Producing industries 41·5%; Trade, transport and communications 15%; Services 25·8%.
Exports: 537 164 million DM in 1985: Road vehicles 17·1%; Products of mechanical engineering 14·7%; Chemical products 13·9%.
Monetary unit: Deutsche Mark (DM). 1 Deutsche Mark = 100 Pfennige.
Denominations:
 Coins 1, 2, 5, 10, 50 Pfennige; 1, 2, 5, 10 DM.
 Notes 5, 10, 20, 50, 100, 500, 1000 DM.
Exchange rate to £ sterling: 2·785 (26 Jan. 1987).
Political history and government: The territory was the British, French and US Zones of Occupation in Germany from May 1945. A provisional constitution, the *Grundgesetz* (Basic Law), came into force in the three Zones (excluding Saarland) on 23 May 1949 and the Federal Republic of Germany (FRG) was established on 21 Sept. 1949. Sovereignty was limited by the continuing military occupation, and subsequent defence agreements, until 5 May 1955, when the FRG became fully independent. Saarland (under French occupation) was rejoined with the FRG administratively on 1 Jan. 1957 and economically incorporated on 6 July 1959. The FRG is composed of 10 states (*Länder*) – each *Land* having its own constitution, parliament and government – plus the city of West Berlin which retains a separate status. The country has a parliamentary regime, with a bicameral legislature. The Upper House is the *Bundesrat* (Federal Council) with 45 seats, including 41 members of *Land* governments

(which appoint and recall them) and 4 non-voting representatives appointed by the West Berlin Senate. The term of office varies with *Land* election dates. The Lower House, and the FRG's main legislative organ, is the *Bundestag* (Federal Assembly), with 519 deputies, including 497 elected for four years by universal adult suffrage (using a mixed system of proportional representation and direct voting) and 22 members (with limited voting rights) elected by the West Berlin House of Representatives. Executive authority rests with the *Bundesregierung* (Federal Government), led by the *Bundeskanzler* (Federal Chancellor) who is elected by an absolute majority of the *Bundestag* and appoints the other Ministers. The Head of State, who normally acts on the Chancellor's advice, is elected for a five-year term by a Federal Convention, consisting of the *Bundestag* and an equal number of members elected by the *Land* parliaments.
Length of roadways: 107 548 miles *173 045 km* (1984).
Length of railways: 19 008 miles *30 584 km* (1984).
Universities: 48 (and 10 technical universities).
Expectation of life: Males 70·8 years; females 77·5 years (1985).
Defence: Military service 15 months; total armed forces 495 000 (236 000 conscripts) in 1985; defence expenditure: 8·7% of total government expenditure in 1984.
Foreign tourists: 10 000 000 arrivals and 22 000 000 overnight stays in 1984–5.

Ghana

Official name: The Republic of Ghana ('land of gold').
Population: 12 205 574 (1984 census).
Area: 92 100 miles² *238 537 km²*.
Languages: English (official), Asante, Ewe, Fante, Ga, and Dagbani.
Religions: Christian, Muslim, Animist.
Capital city: Accra, population 953 500 (1984 census).
Other principal towns (1984): Kumasi 399 300; Tamale 136 800; Tema 99 600; Takoradi 61 500; Cape Coast 57 700; Sekondi 32 400.
Highest point: Afadjato 2860 ft *872 m*.
Principal rivers: Volta (formed by the confluence of the Black Volta and the White Volta) and its tributaries (principally the Oti, Tano, Ofin).
Head of State: Flight-Lieutenant Jerry John Rawlings (b. 1947), Chairman Provisional National Defence Council.
Climate: Tropical. In north hot and dry. Forest areas hot and humid. Eastern coastal belt warm and fairly dry. In Accra average maximum 27°C *80°F* (August) to 31°C *88°F* (February to April and December), average minimum 22°C *71°F* (August) to 24°C *76°F* (March, April), June rainiest (10 days).
Labour force: 3 331 618 (including 198 571 unemployed) aged 15 and over (1970 census); 3 351 000 (mid-1970): Agriculture forestry and fishing 58·4%; Industry 16·7%; Services 24·9% (ILO estimates).
Gross domestic product: 6526·2 million cedis in 1976: Agriculture, forestry and fishing (excluding government) 50·3% (agriculture 43·3%); Industry 19·1% (manufacturing 13·1%); Trade, restaurants and hotels 13·1% (trade 12·3%).
Exports: 6999 million cedis in 1983: Cocoa 75%.
Monetary unit: New cedi. 1 cedi = 100 pesewas.
Denominations:
 Coins ½, 1, 2½, 5, 10, 20 pesewas.
 Notes 1, 2, 5, 10, 50 cedis.
Exchange rate to £ sterling: 233·861 (26 Jan. 1987).
Political history and government: On 6 Mar. 1957 the British dependency of the Gold Coast merged with British Togoland to become independent, and a member of the Commonwealth, as Ghana. Became a republic on 1 July 1960. The President, Dr Kwame Nkrumah, was deposed by a military *coup* on 24 Feb. 1966. Civilian rule was restored on 30 Sept. 1969 but again overthrown by the armed forces on 13 Jan. 1972. The 1969 constitution was abolished, the National Assembly dissolved and political

encircled left: **THE GAMBIA**
GHANA

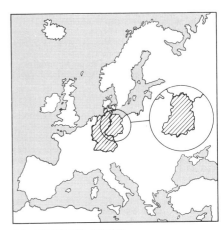

left: **GERMANY (WEST)**
encircled right: **GERMANY (EAST)**

parties banned. Power was assumed by the National Redemption Council (NRC), comprising military commanders and Commissioners of State with ministerial responsibilities. The first Chairman of the NRC was Lt-Col (later Gen) Ignatius Acheampong. On 14 Oct. 1975 a 7-man Supreme Military Council (led by Acheampong) was established, with full legislative and administrative authority, to direct the NRC. Acheampong was removed from office by the SMC on 5 July 1978. A constitutional drafting commission, appointed by the military government, reported on 17 Nov. 1978. Its recommendations were debated by a Constitutional Assembly of 120 members (64 elected by local councils, the remainder nominated by the SMC and other national bodies), which was inaugurated on 21 Dec. 1978 and presented its final report on 15 May 1979. The ban on political parties had been lifted on 1 Jan. 1979 and the return to civilian rule planned for 1 July. The régime was overthrown by another military *coup* on 4 June 1979, when an Armed Forces Revolutionary council (AFRC) took power. The AFRC postponed the return to civilian rule but on 14 June it promulgated the new constitution, providing for an executive President (serving a four-year term) and a unicameral parliament (with a five-year term) both to be elected by universal adult suffrage. Elections were held on 18 June 1979 for a President and the 140 members of Parliament. No presidential candidate received a majority of votes and a 'run-off' election between the two leading candidates was held on 9 July. Civilian rule was restored, and the President took office, on 24 Sept. 1979, but was subsequently overthrown in a bloodless coup by

Flt-Lt Rawlings on 31 Dec. 1981. Ghana comprises ten regions, each the responsibility of a Minister.

Length of roadways: 33 000 miles *53 100 km* (1980).
Length of railways: 592 miles *953 km* (1985).
Universities: 3.
Adult illiteracy: 69·8% in 1970.
Expectation of life: Males 41·9 years; females 45·1 years (UN estimates for 1970–75).
Defence: Military service voluntary; total armed forces 15 000 (1986); defence expenditure: 4·7% of total government expenditure in 1982.
Foreign tourists: 42 000 in 1981.

Greece

Official name: Elleniki Dimokratia (Hellenic Republic).
Population: 9 740 417 (1981 census); 9 896 000 (1984 estimate).
Areas: 50 944 miles² *131 944 km²*.
Language: Greek.
Religions: Eastern Orthodox Church 97%; Roman Catholic and other minorities.
Capital city: Athínai (Athens), population 3 027 331 (1981).
Other principal towns (1981): Thessaloniki (Salonika) 406 413; Piraeus 196 389; Patras 142 163; Heraklion 102 398; Larisa 102 426; Volos 71 378; Kavála 56 705.
Highest point: Óros Ólimbos (Olympus), 9550 ft *2911 m*.
Principal mountain range: Pindus Mountains.
Principal rivers: Aliákmon (195 miles *314 km*), Piniós, Akhelóös.
Head of State: Christos Sartzetakis (b. 1929), President.
Prime Minister: Andreas Georgios Papandreou (b. 5 Feb. 1919).
Climate: Mediterranean (hot, dry summers and mild, wet winters). Colder in the north and on higher ground. In Athens, July and August hottest (22°C *72°F* to 32°C *90°F*), January coolest (5°C *42°F* to 12°C *54°F*), December and January rainiest (seven days each). Absolute maximum temperature 45,7°C *114·3°F*, Heraklion, Crete, 16 June 1914; absolute minimum −25°C −13°F, Kavála, 27 Jan. 1954.
Labour force: 3 543 797 in 1981: Agriculture, forestry and fishing 27·4%; Manufacturing 18·7%; Construction 9·2%; Trade 12·2%; Transport, storage and communications 7·5%; Financial services 3·6%; Community, social and personal services 15%; Unemployed 4·4%.
Gross domestic product: 1 157 670 million drachmae in 1978: Agriculture, forestry and fishing 17·2% (agriculture 16·5%); Manufacturing 18·9%; Trade 12·9%; Community, social and personal services (including restaurants, hotels and business services) 21·7%.
Exports: 542 676 million drachmae in 1984: Fruit and vegetables 14%; Beverages and tobacco 4·6%; Crude materials 7·2%; Mineral fuels, lubricants, etc. 10·1% Basic manufactures 29·8%; Clothing 12·6%.
Monetary unit: Drachma. 1 drachma = 100 leptae (singular: lepta).
Denominations:
 Coins 10, 20, 50 leptae; 1, 2, 5, 10, 20 drachmae.
 Notes 50, 100, 500, 1000 drachmae.
Exchange rate to £ sterling: 203·82 (26 Jan. 1987).
Political history and government: While Greece was a monarchy a *coup* by army officers, led by Col Georgios Papadopoulos, deposed the constitutional government on 21 Apr. 1967. Parliament was suspended and political parties banned. Papadopoulos became Prime Minister on 13 Dec. 1967, a Regent was appointed and the King left the country the next day. A Republic was proclaimed on 1 June 1973 and Papadopoulos became President. He was deposed by another military *coup* on 25 Nov. 1973. Civilian rule was re-established on 24 July 1974, when a Government of National Salvation took office. The ban on political parties was lifted and free elections for a Parliament were held on 17 Nov. 1974. A referendum on 8 Dec. 1974

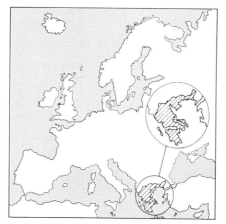

GREECE

rejected the return of the monarchy. A new republican constitution, providing for a parliamentary democracy, came into force on 11 June 1975. Greece became a full member of the EEC in 1981. Executive power rests with the President, elected for 5 years by the legislature, a unicameral parliament (*Vouli*) of 300 members directly elected by universal adult suffrage for 4 years. The President appoints a Prime Minister and, on his recommendation, the other Ministers to form a Cabinet to govern the country. The Cabinet is accountable to Parliament. The country is divided into 51 prefectures (*Nomoi*). The district of Mount Athos, with its autonomous monastic community, has a privileged status as a self-governing part of the Greek state.
Length of roadways: 22 999 miles *37 013 km* (main and secondary roads only) at 30 Apr. 1979.
Length of railways: 1602 miles *2577 km*.
Universities: 6.
Adult illiteracy: 10% in 1981.
Expectation of life: males 70·13 years; females 73·64 years (1970).
Defence: Military service 22–26 months; total armed forces 201 500 (1985); defence expenditure: 13·7% of total government expenditure in 1984.
Foreign tourists: 6 000 000 in 1984.

Grenada

Official name: State of Grenada.
Population: 88 000 (1985 estimate).
Area: 133 miles² *344 km²*.
Language: English.
Religion: Christian.
Capital city: St. George's, population 30 813 (1978 estimate).
Other principal towns: Grenville, Victoria, Sauteurs, Gouyave (Charlotte Town), Hillsborough.
Highest point: Mount St Catherine's, 2756 ft *840 m*.
Head of State: HM Queen Elizabeth II, represented by Sir Paul Scoon, GCMG, GCVO, OBE (b. 4 July 1935), Governor-General.
Prime Minister: Rt Hon. H. A. Blaize.
Climate: Tropical maritime, with equable temperature averaging 28°C *82°F* in the lowlands. Annual rainfall averages 1524 mm *60 in* in coastal area and 3810–5080 mm *150–200 in* in mountain areas. Rainy season June to December (November wettest), dry season January to May.
Labour force: 45 000 (1986).
Gross domestic product: EC$235·6 million (at factor cost) in 1985.
Exports: EC$51·09 in 1983: Cocoa 31·7%; Bananas 16·6%; Nutmeg 15·2%; Mace 4%.
Monetary unit: East Caribbean dollar (EC$). 1 dollar = 100 cents.
Denominations:
 Coins 1, 2, 5, 10, 25, 50 cents.
 Notes 1, 5, 20, 100 dollars.
Exchange rate to £ sterling: 4·13 (26 Jan. 1987).
Political history and government: A former British dependency. An Associated State, with

internal self-government, from 3 Mar. 1967 until becoming fully independent, within the Commonwealth, on 7 Feb. 1974. Executive power is vested in the Queen and exercised by the Governor-General, who acts on the advice of the Cabinet, led by the Prime Minister. At independence the Grenada United Labour Party (GULP) was in power. The GULP government was overthrown on 13 Mar. 1979 in a *coup* by supporters of the main opposition party, the New Jewel Movement. A 'People's Revolutionary Government' took power, dissolved Parliament, suspended the constitution and announced plans to create a People's Consultative Assembly to draft a new one. Maurice Bishop, the Prime Minister was subsequently killed in a power struggle, whereupon the army took control (19 Oct. 1983). At the request of other Caribbean countries, the US then led an invasion of the island, and a state of emergency was declared. An interim government took over, to be succeeded by an elected government in December 1984.
Length of roadways: 577 miles *928 km*.
Adult illiteracy: 2·2% in 1986.
Expectation of life: Males 60·14 years; females 65·60 years (1959–61).
Defence: A Special Security Unit.
Foreign tourists: 82 600 in 1983.

Guatemala

Official name: República de Guatemala.
Population: 6 043 559 (1981 census); 8 403 025 (1985 estimate).
Area: 42 042 miles² *108 889 km²*.
Languages: Spanish, with some twenty Indian dialects (most important is Quiché).
Religion: Roman Catholic 90%.
Capital city: Ciudad de Guatemala (Guatemala City), population 1 300 000 (1983 estimate).
Other principal towns (1983): Quezaltanango 65 733; Puerto Barrios 38 956; Mazatenango 38 319; Antigua 26 631; Zacapa 35 769; Coban 43 538.
Highest point: Volcán Tajumulco, 13 881 ft *4220 m*.
Principal mountain ranges: Sierra Madre, Sierra de las Minas, Sierra de los Cuchumatanes, Sierra de Chuacús.
Principal rivers: Motagua (249 miles *400 km*), Usumacinta (688 miles *1107 km*).
Head of State: Vinicio Cerezo Arevalo, President.
Climate: Tropical (hot and humid) on coastal lowlands, with average temperature of 28°C *83°F*. More temperate in central highlands, with average of 21°C *68°F*. Mountains cool. In Guatemala City, average maximum 22°C *72°F* (December) to 29°C *84°F* (May), minimum 12°C *53°F* (January) to 16°C *61°F* (June), June rainiest (23 days). Absolute maximum temperature 45°C *113°F*, Guatemala City, 17 Dec. 1957; absolute minimum −7,1°C *19·2°F*, Quezaltenango, 15 Jan. 1956.
Labour force: 2 382 908 in 1984: Agriculture, forestry and fishing 58·1%; Manufacturing 13·6%; Trade 7·3%; Services 12%.
Gross domestic product: 2874·6 million quetzales (at 1958 prices) in 1978: Agriculture, forestry and fishing 25·9%; Manufacturing 16·2%; Trade 28·2%; Community, social and personal services (including restaurants and hotels) 10·6%.
Exports: 1150 million quetzals in 1984: Coffee 31·3%; Cardamom 8·9%; Cotton 6·1%; Sugar 6·5%; Bananas 5·1%.
Monetary unit: Quetzal. 1 quetzal = 100 centavos.
Denominations:
 Coins 1, 5, 10, 25 centavos.
 Notes 50 centavos; 1, 5, 10, 20, 50, 100 quetzales.
Exchange rate to £ sterling: 1·528 (26 Jan. 1987).
Political history and government: A republic comprising 22 departments. Under the constitution, promulgated on 15 Sept. 1965 and effective from 1 July 1966, legislative power is vested in the unicameral National Congress, with 61 members elected for 4 years by universal

adult suffrage. Executive power is held by the President, also directly elected for 4 years. If no candidate obtains an absolute majority of votes, the President is chosen by Congress. He is assisted by a Vice-President and an appointed Cabinet.
Length of roadways: 11 200 miles *18 000 km* (1985).
Length of railways: 510 miles *820 km* (1985).
Universities: 5.
Adult illiteracy: 53·9% (males 46·1%; females 61·5%) in 1973.
Expectation of life: Males 48·29 years; females 49·74 years (1963–65).
Defence: Military service: 2 years; total armed forces 31 550 (1986); defence expenditure 16% of total government expenditure in 1984.
Foreign tourists: 235 166 in 1983.

Guinea

Official name: La République populaire et révolutionnaire de Guinée (the People's Revolutionary Republic of Guinea).
Population: 5 177 000 (1983 estimate).
Area: 94 926 miles² *245 857 km²*.
Languages: French (official), Fulani (Poular), Susu, Malinké.
Religions: Muslim, Animist minority.
Capital city: Conakry, population 763 000 (1980 estimate).
Other principal towns (1972); Kankan 85 310; Kindia 79 861; Labé 79 670; N'Zérékoré 23 000.
Highest point: Mt Nimba, 5748 ft *1752 m*.
Principal mountain range: Fouta Djalon.
Principal rivers: Niger (2600 miles *4184 km*), Bafing, Konkouré, Kogon.
Head of State: Brig.-Gen. Lansana Conté.
Climate: Hot and moist, with heavy rainfall in coastal areas. Cooler in higher interior. In Conakry, average maximum 28°C *82°F* to 32°C *90°F*, minimum around 23°C *74°F*, annual rainfall 4300 mm *169 in*.
Labour force: 1 870 000 (mid-1970): Agriculture, forestry and fishing 84·7% (ILO estimates).
Gross domestic product: $723 million in 1975 (UN estimate).
Exports: 8852 million sylis in 1980: Bauxite and alumina 96·8%; Pulses and oilseeds 2·9%.
Monetary unit: Syli. 1 syli = 100 cauris (corilles). In 1986 the syli was replaced by the Guinea Franc and the currency devalued by about 90%.
Denominations:
    Coins 50 cauris; 1, 2, 5 sylis.
    Notes 10, 25, 50, 100 sylis.
Exchange rate to £ sterling: 519·69 (26 Jan. 1987).
Political history and government: Formerly French Guinea, part of French West Africa. Became independent as the Republic of Guinea, outside the French Community, on 2 Oct. 1958. A provisional constitution was adopted on 12 Nov. 1958. Legislative power is vested in the unicameral National Assembly, with 210 members elected by universal adult suffrage for 7 years. The Assembly elects a Commission to be its permanent organ. Full executive authority is vested in the President, also directly elected for 7 years. He appoints and leads a Cabinet, including a Prime Minister. Guinea has a single political party, the *Parti démocratique de Guinée* (PDG), which exercises 'sovereign and exclusive control of all sections of national life'. The party's directing organ is the Central Committee, 25 members elected for 5 years at Congress. The PDG Congress of 17–22 Nov. 1978 decided to alter the country's name from 1 Jan. 1979. It was also decided to increase the PDG Central Committee to 75.
    Elections were held in 1980, and in 1984 the government was overthrown by the military on the death of President Sekou Touré. The military have held on to power since then.
Length of roadways: 17 650 miles *28 400 km*.
Length of railways: 584 miles *940 km*.
Adult illiteracy: 91·4% (estimate) in 1965.
Expectation of life: Males 39·4 years; females 42·6 years (UN estimates for 1970–75).
Defence: Military service voluntary; total armed forces 8500 (1985); defence expenditure 1850

million sylis in 1982.

Guinea-Bissau

Official name: República da Guiné-Bissau (the Republic of Guinea-Bissau).
Population: 858 000 (1985 estimate).
Area: 13 948 miles² *36 125 km²*.
Languages: Portuguese (official), Creole, Balante, Fulani, Malinké.
Religions: Animist; Muslim minority.
Capital city: Bissau, population 109 486 (1979 census).
Other principal towns (1979): Oio 135 114; Cacheu 130 227; Bafatá 116 032; Gabú 104 227.
Principal rivers: Cacheu, Mansôa, Gêba, Corubel.
Head of State: Maj. João Bernardo Vieira (b. 1939), President of the Council of the Revolution.
Climate: Tropical, with an average annual temperature of 25°C *77°F*. Rainy season June to November. In dry season (December to May) the northerly *harmattan*, a dust-laden wind, blows from the Sahara.
Labour force: 158 000 (1970): Agriculture, forestry and fishing 87·0% (ILO estimates).
Gross domestic product: $177 million in 1975 (UN estimate).
Exports: 382 million pesos in 1980: Fish 33%; Groundnuts 24%; Coconuts 17%.
Monetary unit: Guinea peso. 1 peso = 100 centavos.
Denominations:
    Coins 5, 10, 20, 50 centavos; 1, 2½, 5, 10, 20 pesos.
    Notes 50, 100, 500 pesos.
Exchange rate to £ sterling: 260·58 (26 Jan. 1987).
Political history and government: Formerly Portuguese Guinea. Independence declared on 24 Sept. 1973, recognized by Portugal on 10 Sept. 1974. The independence movement was dominated by the *Partido Africano da Independência da Guiné e Cabo Verde* (PAIGC), the African Party for the Independence of Guinea and Cape Verde. In 1973 the PAIGC established a National People's Assembly as the supreme organ of the state and formulated the independence constitution, which provided for the eventual union of Guinea-Bissau with Cape Verde (*q.v.*). In elections held between 19 Dec. 1976 and January 1977 voters chose regional councils from which a new National Assembly of 150 members was subsequently selected. The Assembly, to hold office for up to four years, was convened on 13 Mar. 1977. The Head of State was elected for a four-year term by the Assembly. The constitution proclaimed the PAIGC, the only permitted party, to be 'the supreme expression of the sovereign will of the people'. Executive power was vested in the State Council, with 15 members elected for three years from deputies to the Assembly. Administrative authority lay with the Council of State Commissioners, appointed by the Head of State. On 10 Nov. 1980 the Assembly approved a new constitution, increasing the powers of the Head of State, but on 14 Nov. he was overthrown in a *coup*. A nine-member Revolutionary council, led by the former Chief State Commissioner, took power. The Assembly and State Council were dissolved on 19 Nov. 1980 and a Provisional Government announced on the next day.
Length of roadways: 3144 miles *5058 km* (1982).
Adult illiteracy: 95·1% in 1962.
Expectation of life: Males 37·0 years; females 40·1 years (UN estimates for 1970–75).
Defence: Total armed forces 6500 (1986).

Guyana

Official name: The Co-operative Republic of Guyana.
Population: 758 619 (1980 census); 900 000 (1983 estimate).
Area: 83 000 miles² *214 969 km²*.
Languages: English (official), Hindu, Urdu.

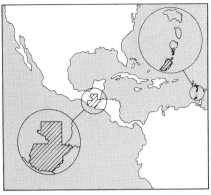

left: **GUATEMALA**
right: **GRENADA**

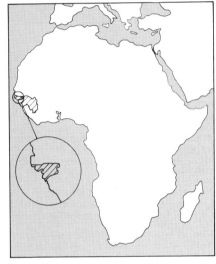

encircled left : **GUINEA-BISSAU**
right : **GUINEA**

Religions: Christian 56·7%; Hindu 33·4%; Muslim 8·8% (1960).
Capital city: Georgetown, population 188 000 (1983 estimate).
Other principal towns (1970): Linden 29 000; New Amsterdam 23 000; Mackenzie 20 000; Corriverton 17 000.
Highest point: Mt Roraima (9094 ft *2772 m*), on the Brazil-Venezuela frontier.
Principal mountain ranges: Pakaraima, Serra Acarai, Kanuku, Kamoa.
Principal rivers: Essequibo, Courantyne (on the frontier with Suriname), Mazaruni, Berbice, Demarara.
Head of State: Hugh Desmond Hoyte, President.
Prime Minister: Hamilton Green.
Climate: Generally warm and pleasant. Average temperature 27°C *80°F*, with daily range of about 10°C *18°F* on coast, increasing inland. Average annual rainfall 2360 mm *93 in*, 2030-2540 mm *80 to 100 in* on coast (mainly April to August and November to January), 1520 mm *60 in* inland (May to August).
Labour force: 239 331 in 1980: Agriculture, forestry and fishing 20·3%; Mining 3·9%; Manufacturing 11·7%; Trade 6·1%; Transport, storage and communications 3·8% Community, social and personal services 24%; Unemployed 18·7%.
Gross domestic product: $G 1455 million in 1983.
Exports: $G697·7 million in 1982: Bauxite 40·5%; Sugar 37·8%; Rice 8·7%.
Monetary unit: Guyana dollar ($G). 1 dollar = 100 cents.
Denominations:
    Coins 1, 5, 10, 25, 50 cents.
    Notes 1, 5, 10, 20 dollars.
Exchange rate to £ sterling: 6·226 (26 Jan. 1987).
Political history and government: Formerly the colony of British Guiana. Became independent, within the Commonwealth, on 26 May 1966,

taking the name Guyana. A republic since 23 Feb. 1970. Legislative power is held by the unicameral National Assembly. Following a referendum on 10 July 1978, which gave the Assembly power to amend the constitution, elections to the Assembly were postponed for 15 months. It assumed the role of a Constituent Assembly, established on 6 Nov. 1978, to draft a new constitution. A new constitution was promulgated on 6 Oct. 1980. Elections took place in 1980 and 1985, in which the ruling Peoples' National Congress party were accused of malpractice on both occasions.

The National Assembly has 65 members, including 12 regional representatives and 53 members elected for five years by universal adult suffrage, using proportional representation. Executive power is vested in the President, who is leader of the majority party in the Assembly and holds office for its duration. The President appoints and leads a Cabinet, responsible to the Assembly.

Length of roadways: 3000 miles *4830 km*.
Length of railways: 116 miles *187 km*.
Universities: 1.
Adult illiteracy: 8·7% in 1970.
Expectation of life: males 59·03 years; females 63·01 years (1959–61), excluding Amerindians.
Defence: Total armed forces 6600 (1985); defence expenditure US$43 million (1985).

Haiti

Official name: République d'Haïti.
Population: 5 053 792 (1982 census); 5 185 000 (1984 estimate).
Area: 10 714 miles[2] *27 750 km*[2].
Languages: French (official), Créole 90%.
Religions: Roman Catholic, Vodum (Voodoo).
Capital city: Port-au-Prince, population 719 617 (1982 census).
Other principal towns (1982): Cap Haïtien 64 406; Gonaïves 34 209; Les Cayes 34 090; Port de Paix 21 733 (1975).
Highest point: Pic La Selle, 8793 ft *2680 m*.
Principal mountain range: Massif de la Hotte.
Principal river: Artibonite (147 miles *237 km*).
Head of State: There is a five-man Council of Government consisting of: Gen. Henry Namphy, Col. Max Valles, Col. William Regala, Alix Cinéas, Gerard Gourgue.
Climate: Tropical but cooled by sea winds. Rainy season May to September. North warmer than south. In Port-au-Prince, average maximum 31°C *87°F* (December, January) to 34°C *94°F* (July), minimum 20°C *68°F* (January, February) to 23°C *74°F* (July), May rainiest (13 days).
Labour force: 2 016 200 in 1982–3: Agriculture, forestry and fishing 65·9%; Manufacturing 6·8%; Trade 10·3%; Community, social and personal services 7·1%.
Gross domestic product: 2303·6 million gourdes (at 1955 prices) in year ending 30 Sep. 1978: Agriculture, forestry and fishing 40·6% (agriculture, excluding, livestock, 36·1%); Manufacturing 11·7%; Trade 10·3%; Community, social and personal services (incl. restaurants and hotels) 17·3%.
Exports: 951·8 million gourdes in 1982–3: Coffee 26·9%; Cocoa 2·1%; Essential oils 3·7%; Light industrial products 21·4%; Manufactured articles 28·9%; Rope and cord 2·6%.
Monetary unit: Gourde. 1 gourde = 100 centimes.
Denominations:
Coins 5, 10, 20, 50 centimes.
Notes 1, 2, 5, 10, 50, 100, 250, 500 gourdes.
Exchange rate to £ sterling: 7·64 (26 Jan. 1987).
Political history and government: A republic comprising 9 departments. Dr François Duvalier was elected President on 22 Sept. 1957 and took office on 22 Oct. 1957. Under the constitution of June 1964, the unicameral Legislative Chamber has 58 members elected for 6 years by universal adult suffrage. The constitution granted absolute power to the President, who took office for life on 22 June 1964. On 14 Jan. 1971 the constitution was amended to allow the President to nominate his own successor. The

President named his son, Jean-Claude, to succeed him as President for life. Dr Duvalier died on 21 Apr. 1971 and his son was sworn in on the following day.

However popular feeling against Jean-Claude Duvalier increased and in Feb. 1986 he was forced to flee the country. Government was subsequently assumed by a ruling council in which the military figured strongly.
Length of roadways: 2500 miles *400 km*.
Universities: 1.
Adult illiteracy: 76·7% (males 71·3%; females 81·6%) in 1971.
Expectation of life: Males 47·1 years; females 50·0 years (UN estimates for 1970–75).
Defence: Total armed forces 6900 (1985); defence expenditure: US$30 million in 1984.
Foreign tourists: 221 094 in 1982–3.

Honduras

Official name: Republica de Honduras.
Population: 3 717 000 (1984 estimate).
Area: 43 277 miles *112 088 km*.
Language: Spanish, some Indian dialects.
Religion: Roman Catholic.
Capital city: Tegucigalpa, population 510 000 (1984).
Other principal towns (1983): San Pedro Sula 325 000; La Ceiba 60 000; El Progreso 52 000; Puerto Cortes 38 000; Choluteca 52 000.
Highest point: Cerro las Minas 9400 ft *2865 m*.
Principal rivers: Patuca, Ulúa.
Head of State: José Azcona Hoyo.
Climate: Tropical (hot and humid) and wet on coastal plains. Rainy season May to November. More moderate in central highlands. In Tegucigalpa, average maximum 25°C *77°F* (December, January) to 30°C *86°F* (June), September and October rainiest (each 14 days). Absolute maximum temperature 43,3°C *110°F*, Neuva Octepeque, 13 Mar. 1958; absolute minimum −0·6°C *31°F*, La Esperanza, 17 Feb. 1956.
Labour force: 1 074 000 in 1984: Agriculture, forestry and fishing 53·3%; Manufacturing 13·3%; Construction 4·3%; Transport, storage and communications 4%; Trade 9·7%; Services 13·8%.
Gross domestic product: 6297 million lempiras in 1984: Agriculture, forestry and fishing 24·2%; Manufacturing 13·2%; Construction 5·4%; Trade 11·6%; Transport, storage and communications 6·7%; Services 8·1%.
Exports: 1471·6 million lempiras in 1984: Bananas 30%; Coffee 23%; Wood 4·6%; Lead and zinc 5·8%; Shellfish 5·3%.
Monetary unit: Lempira. 1 lempira = 100 centavos.
Coins 1, 2, 5, 10, 20, 50 centavos.
Notes 1, 2, 5, 10, 20, 50, 100 lempiras.
Exchange rate to £ sterling: 3·05 (26 Jan. 1987).
Political history and government: A republic comprising 18 departments. The last elected President was deposed on 4 Dec. 1972 by a military *coup*, led by a former President, Brig-Gen Oswaldo López Arellano. The military regime suspended the legislature, a unicameral Congress of Deputies, and introduced government by decree. On 22 Apr. 1975 Gen López was overthrown by army officers and replaced by Col (later Gen) Juan Melgar Castro. On 7 Aug. 1978 Gen Melgar was deposed by another *coup* and a 3-man military junta took power. Its leader became President and rules with the assistance of an appointed Cabinet. On 20 Apr. 1980 a 71-member Constituent Assembly was elected by universal adult suffrage. On 20 July 1980 the junta transferred power to the Assembly and on 25 July the Assembly elected the President to continue in office as interim Head of State. A presidential election on 29 Nov. 1981 was won by Dr Roberto Suazo Córdova, who took office on 27 Jan. 1982. His government was still dominated by the military, however, a situation that continued to a varying degree until the next elections in 1985.
Length of roadways: 7494 miles *12 058 km* (1984).
Length of railways: 1106 miles *1780 km*.
Universities: 1.
Adult illiteracy: 43·1% (males 41·1%; females

GUYANA

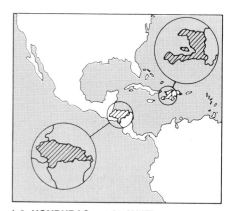

left: **HONDURAS**   *right:* **HAITI**

44·9%) in 1974.
Expectation of life: Males 52·4 years; females 55·9 years (UN estimates for 1970–75).
Defence: Military service: 14 months; total armed forces 16 600 (1985); defence expenditure: 6·6% of total government expenditure in 1984.
Foreign tourists: 144 232 in 1984.

Hungary

Official name: Magyar Népkőztársaság (Hungarian People's Republic).
Population: 10 640 000 (1 Jan. 1986).
Area: 35 921 miles[2] *93 036 km*[2].
Language: Magyar.
Religions: Roman Catholic; Protestant, Orthodox and Jewish minorities.
Capital city: Budapest, population 2 080 000 (1 Jan. 1986).
Other principal towns (1 Jan. 1986): Miskolc 212 000; Debrecen 212 000; Szeged 183 000; Pécs 177 000; Győr 129 000; Nyíregyháza 118 000; Székesfehérvár 112 000; Kecskemét 103 000.
Highest point: Kékes, 3330 ft *1015 m*.
Principal mountain ranges: Cserhát, Mátra, Bükk, Bakony.
Principal rivers: Duna (Danube) (1770 miles *2850 km*, 273 miles *439 km* in Hungary), with its tributaries (Drava, Tisza, Rba).
Head of State: Pál Losonczi (b. 18 Sept. 1919), President of the Presidential Council.
Political Leader: János Kádár (b. 22 May 1912), General Secretary of the Hungarian Socialist

Workers' Party.

Head of Government: György Lázár (b. 15 Sept. 1924), Chairman of the Council of Ministers.

Climate: Continental (long, dry, hot summers, cold winters). In Budapest, July warmest (16°C *61°F* to 28°C *82°F*), January coldest (−3°C *26°F* to 2°C *35°F*), May and December rainiest (each nine days). Absolute maximum temperature 41,3°C *106·3°F*, Pécs, 5 July 1950; absolute minimum −34,9°C − *30·8°F*, Asófügöd, 16 Feb. 1940.

Labour force: 4 912 900 in 1985: Industry 31·3%; Agriculture and forestry 22·2%; Trade 10·4%; Sanitary, social and cultural services 11·4%.

Net material product: 914 300 million forints in 1985: Agriculture, forestry and fishing 18·8%; Industry 46·4%; Construction 11%; Trade 13·3%.

Exports: 424 600 million forints in 1985: Machinery, transport equipment and other capital goods 29·6%; Industrial consumer goods 15·2%; Food products 13·2%; Semi-finished products 18·2%.

Monetary unit: Forint. 1 forint = 100 fillér.
Coins 10, 20, 50 fillér; 1, 2, 5, 10, 20 forints.
Notes 20, 50, 100, 500, 1000 forints.

Exchange rate to £ sterling: 67·29 (26 Jan. 1987).

Political history and government: After occupation by Nazi Germany, a Hungarian provisional government signed an armistice on 20 Jan. 1945. Following elections in October 1945, a republic was proclaimed on 1 Feb. 1946. The Communist Party took power in May–June 1947. A new constitution was introduced on 18 Aug. 1949 and a People's Republic established two days later.

The highest organ of state is the unicameral National Assembly which currently has 387 members elected for 5 years by universal adult suffrage; 352 of these members represent territorial constituencies, all of which must be contested in a general election under the amended electoral law of 1983. In addition there are 35 members who are presented on a national list. The Assembly elects from its members a Presidential Council (21 members) to be its permanent organ and the state's executive authority, responsible to the Assembly. The Council of Ministers, the highest organ of state administration, is elected by the Assembly on the recommendation of the Presidential Council.

Political power is held by the (Communist) Hungarian Socialist Workers' party (HSWP), the only legal party, which dominates the Patriotic People's Front. The Front presents a list of candidates for elections for representative bodies, nominations being made in public nomination meetings in the various constituencies and local council wards. The HSWP's highest authority is the Party Congress, which elects a Central Committee to supervise Party work (the 13th Congress, held on 25–28 March 1985, elected a Central Committee of 105). The Central Committee elects a Political Committee (Politburo) of 13 members to direct policy.

Hungary comprises 19 counties and the capital city.

Length of roadways: 18 449 miles *29 684 km* (1983).

Length of railways: 4825 miles *7766 km*.

Universities: 10 (plus 9 technical universities).

Adult illiteracy: 2·0% (males 1·6%; females 2·4%) in 1970.

Expectation of life: Males 65·6 years; females 73·7 years (1984).

Defence: Military service: 18 months; total regular forces 105 500 (50 000 conscripts) in 1986; defence expenditure: 4% of total government expenditure in 1984.

Foreign tourists: 9 724 000 in 1985.

Iceland

Official name: Lýđveldiđ Island (Republic of Iceland).

Population: 241 750 (1 Dec. 1984).

Area: 39 784 miles² *103 000 km²*.

Language: Icelandic.

Religion: Lutheran.

Capital city: Reykyavik ('Bay of Smokes'),

---

population 88 745 (1 Dec. 1983).

Other principal towns (1983): Kópavogur 14 546; Akureyri 13 711; Hafnarfjordur 12 979; Keflavik 6907; Akranes 5285; Gardbaer 5896; Vestmannaeyjar 4809.

Highest point: Hvannadalshnúkur, 6952 ft *2119 m*.

Principal rivers: Thjórsá (120 miles *193 km*), Skjálfandafljót, Jökulsa á Fjöllum.

Head of State: Mme Vigdís Finnbogadóttir (b. 15 Apr. 1930), President.

Prime Minister: Steingrímur Hermannsson (b. 22 June 1928).

Climate: Cold. Long winters with average temperature of 1°C *34°F*. Short, cool summers with average of 10°C *50°F*. Storms are frequent. In Reykjavík, average maximum 2°C *36°F* (January) to 14°C *58°F* (July), minimum −2°C *28°F* (January, February) to 9°C *48°F*, (July), December rainiest (21 days). Absolute maximum temperature 32,8°C *91·0°F* Mödrudalur, 26 July 1901; absolute minimum −44,6°C − *48·2°F*, Grímsstaoir, 22 Mar. 1918.

Labour force: 116 105 in 1983: Agriculture 6·8%; Fishing 5·1%; Fish processing 8·9%; Other manufacturing 16·3%; Construction 10·2%; Trade, finance and services 15·5%; Other services 30·2%.

Gross domestic product: 81 532 million krónur in 1984.

Exports: 34 792 million kronur in 1983: Fish products 67·2%; Aluminium 14·5%; Other manufacturing products 13·4%.

Monetary unit: New Icelandic króna. 1 króna = 100 aurar (singular: eyrir).

Denominations:
Coins 5, 10, 50 aurar; 1, 5 krónur.
Notes 10, 50, 100, 500 krónur.

Exchange rate to £ sterling: 60·83 (26 Jan. 1987).

Political history and government: Formerly ruled by Denmark. Iceland became a sovereign state, under the Danish Crown, on 1 Dec. 1918. An independent republic was declared on 17 June 1944. Legislative power is held jointly by the President (elected for 4 years by universal adult suffrage) and the Althing (Parliament), with 60 members elected by universal suffrage for 4 years (subject to dissolution by the President), using a mixed system of proportional representation. The Althing chooses 20 of its members to form the Upper House, the other 40 forming the Lower House. For some purposes, the two Houses sit jointly as the United Althing. Executive power is held jointly by the President and the Cabinet, although the President's functions are mainly titular. The President appoints the Prime Minister and, on the latter's recommendation, other Ministers. The Cabinet is responsible to the Althing. Iceland has seven administrative districts.

Length of roadways: 7238 miles *11 649 km* (31 Dec. 1979).

Universities: 1.

Expectation of life: males 74·0 years; females 80·2 years (1983–4).

Defence: Iceland has no forces but is a member of NATO.

Foreign tourists: 85 190 in 1984.

India

Official name: Bharatiya Ganrajya or Bharat ka Ganatantra (the Republic of India). India is called Bharat in the Hindi language.

Population: 685 184 692 (census of 1 Mar. 1981); 732 256 000 (1983 estimate).

Area: 1 269 213 miles² *3 287 263 km²* (provisional, 31 March 1982).

Languages: Assamese; Bengali 7%; Gujarati; Hindi (official) 24%; Kannada; Kashmiri; Malayalam; Marathi 6%; Oriya; Punjabi; Sanskrit; Sindhi; Tamil; Telugu 7%; Urdu.

Religions: Hinduism 82·7%; Islam 11·2%; Christianity 2·6%; Sikhism 1·9%; Buddhism 0·7%; Jainism 0·5%; plus others (1971).

Capital city: New Delhi, population 6 220 406 (1981 census).

Other principal towns (1981): Mumbai (Bombay) 8 243 405; Calcutta 3 305 006; Madras 3 276 622; Bangalore 2 921 751; Ahmedabad 2 548 057; Hy-

---

HUNGARY

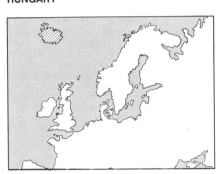

ICELAND

derabad 2 545 836; Pune (Poona) 1 686 109; Kanpur 1 639 064; Nagpur 1 302 066; Jaipur 1 015 160; Lucknow 1 007 604; Indore 970 410; Patna 918 903; Surat 913 806; Madurai 907 732; Varanasi (Benares) 797 162; Jabalpur 757 303; Agra 747 318; Vadodara 744 881; Howrah 744 429; Cochin 685 836; Allahabad 650 070.

Highest point: Nanda Devi, 25 645 ft *7816 m* (first climbed 29 Aug. 1936), excluding Kashmir.

Principal mountain ranges: Himalaya, Gravalti, Sappura, Vindhya, Western Ghats, Chota Nagpur.

Principal rivers: Ganga (Ganges) (1560 miles *2510 km*) and tributaries, Brahmaputra (1800 miles *2900 km*), Sutlej, Narmeda, Tapti, Godavari, Krishna, Cauvery.

Head of State: Giani Zail Singh (b. 5 May 1916), President.

Prime Minister: Rajiv Gandhi (b. 20 August 1944).

Climate: Ranges from temperate in the north (very cold in the Himalayas) to tropical in the south. The average summer temperature in the plains is about 29°C *85°F*. The full weight of the monsoon season is felt in June and July but the rainfall figures vary widely according to locality. Average daily high temperature in Bombay 28°C *83°F* (January, February) to 33°C *91°F* (May); average daily low temperature 19°C *67°F* (January, February) to 27°C *80°F* (May); rainiest, month July (21 days). Average daily high temperature in Calcutta 26°C *79°F* (December) to 36°C *97°F* (April); average daily low 13°C *55°F* (December, January) to 26°C *79°F* (June, July); rainiest months July, August (each 18 days).

Labour force: 220 100 000 (excluding unemployed) at 1981 census: Agriculture 66%; Manufacturing 3%.

Gross domestic product: 1734·2 billion rupees in 1983–4: Agriculture, forestry and fishing 36·1%; Manufacturing 14·9%; Trade 14·3%; Transport, storage and communications 6·1%.

Exports: 98 653 million rupees in 1984–5: Fish 3·3%; Coffee 5·1%; Ready-made garments 6·2%; Pearls, precious and semi-precious stones 12·3%; Iron ore 3·9%; Machinery and transport equipment 5%.

Monetary unit: Indian rupee. 1 rupee = 100 paisa (singular: paise).

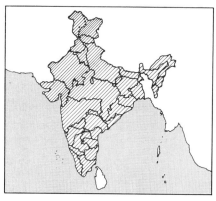

INDIA

Denominations:

Coins 5, 10, 20, 25, 50 paisa; 1 rupee.

Notes 1, 2, 5, 10, 20, 50, 100 rupees.

Exchange rate to £ sterling: 19·82 (26 Jan. 1987).
Political history and government: On 15 Aug. 1947 former British India was divided on broadly religious lines into two independent countries, India and Pakistan, within the Commonwealth.

India was formed as a Union of States, with a federal structure. A republican constitution was passed by the Constituent Assembly on 26 Nov. 1949 and India became a republic, under its present name, on 26 Jan. 1950. France transferred sovereignty of its five Indian settlements on 2 May 1950 (Chandernagore) and 1 Nov. 1954 (Pondicherry, Karikal, Yanam and Mahé). The Portuguese territories of Goa, Daman and Diu were invaded by Indian forces on 19 Dec. 1961 and incorporated in India. Sikkim, formerly an Associated State, became a State of India on 26 Apr. 1975.

Legislative power is vested in a Parliament, consisting of the President and two Houses. The Council of States (*Rajya Sabha*) has 244 members, including 236 indirectly elected by the State Assemblies for 6 years (one-third retiring every two years) and 8 nominated by the President. The House of the People (*Lok Sabha*) has 544 members, including 542 elected by universal adult suffrage for 5 years (subject to dissolution) and two nominated. The President is a constitutional Head of State elected for 5 years by an electoral college comprising elected members of both Houses of Parliament and the State legislatures. He exercises executive power on the advice of the Council of Ministers, which is responsible to Parliament. The President appoints the Prime Minister and, on the latter's recommendation, other Ministers.

India comprises 22 self-governing States (including the disputed territory of Jammu-Kashmir) and 9 Union Territories. Each State has a Governor (appointed by the President for 5 years), a legislature elected for 6 years (to be reduced to 5 years under legislation of 30 Apr. 1979) and a Council of Ministers. The Union

INDONESIA

Territories are administered by officials appointed by the President.
Length of roadways: 1 041 000 miles *1 675 000 km* (1983).
Length of railways: 38 198 miles *61 460 km* (1983).
Universities: 120.
Adult literacy: 36·23% (1981): Males 46·89%; Females 24·82%.
Expectation of life: Males 50·8 years; Females 50 years (1981).
Defence: Military service voluntary; total armed forces: 1 260 000 in 1985; defence expenditure: 15·4% of total government expenditure in 1985–6.
Foreign tourists: 1 210 752 in 1984.

Indonesia

Official name: Republik Indonesia.
Population: 147 490 298 (1980 census); 163 000 000 (1985 estimate).
*Area: 785 766 miles² *2 034 255 km²*.
Languages: Bahasa Indonesia (official), Javanese, Madurese, Sundanese, Bugis, Makassar, Batak.
Religions: Muslim 85%; Christian, Buddhist and Hindu minorities.
Capital city: Jakarta, population 6 503 449 (1980).
Other principal towns (1980): Surabaya 2 027 913; Bandung 1 462 637; Semarang 1 026 671; Medan 1 378 955; Palembang 787 187; Ujungpadang (Makasar) 709 038; Malang 511 780; Surakarta 469 888; Yogyakarta (Jogjakarta) 398 727.
Highest point: Puncak Jaya (formerly Ngga Pulu and Mt Sukarno), 16 020 ft *4883 m* (first climbed on 13 Feb. 1962).
Principal mountain ranges: Bukit, Barisan, Pegunungan Jayawijaya.
Principal rivers: Kapuas (715 miles *1150 km*), Digul (557 miles *896 km*), Barito (560 miles *900 km*), Mahakam, Kajan, Hari.
Head of State: Gen Suharto (b. 8 June 1921), President and Prime Minister.
Climate: Tropical (hot and rainy). Average temperature 27°C *80°F*. Mountain areas cooler. In Jakarta, average maximum 29°C *84°F* (January, February) to 31°C *88°F* (September), minimum 23°C *73°F* (July, August) to 24°C *75°F* (April, May) January rainiest (18 days).
Labour force: 57 802 801 in 1982: Agriculture, forestry and fishing 54·7%; Manufacturing 10·4%; Trade 14·8%; Community, social and personal services 12·3%.
Gross domestic product: 85 914 billion rupiahs in 1984: Agriculture, forestry and fishing 24·9%; Mining and quarrying 17·7%; Manufacturing 12%; Trade 15·6%; Services 17·5%.
Exports: US$21 151·7 million in 1983: Oil and gas 86·8%; Coffee 1·6%; Rubber 2·8%; Wood 4·6%.
Monetary unit: Rupiah. 1 rupiah = 100 sen.
Denominations:

Coins 1, 5, 10, 25, 50 sen.

Notes 1, 2½, 5, 10, 25, 50, 100, 500, 1000, 5000, 10 000 rupiahs.

Exchange rate to £ sterling: 2488·62 (26 Jan. 1987).
Political history and government: Excluding East Timor (see below), Indonesia was formerly the Netherlands East Indies. The islands were occupied by Japanese forces in March 1942. On 17 Aug. 1945, three days after the Japanese surrender, a group of nationalists proclaimed the independence of the Republic of Indonesia. The Netherlands transferred sovereignty (except for West New Guinea) on 27 Dec. 1949. West New Guinea remained under Dutch control until 1 Oct. 1962, when a UN Temporary Executive Authority took over administration of the territory until it was transferred to Indonesia on 1 May 1963.

Military commanders, led by Gen Suharto, assumed emergency executive powers on 11–12 Mar. 1966. The President handed all power to Suharto on 22 Feb. 1967. On 12 Mar. 1967 the People's Consultative Assembly removed the President from office and named Gen Suharto as acting President. He became Prime Minister on 11 Oct. 1967 and, after being elected by the

Assembly, was inaugurated as President on 27 Mar. 1968.

The highest authority of the state is the People's Consultative Assembly, with 920 members who serve for 5 years. The Assembly, which elects the President and Vice-President for 5 years, includes 460 members of the People's Representation Council (House of Representatives), which is the legislative organ. The council has 100 appointed members, 351 directly elected and 9 representatives from West Irian (West New Guinea) chosen in indirect elections. The remaining 460 members of the Assembly include 207 appointed by the government, 130 elected by regional assemblies, 121 allocated to parties and groups in proportion to their elected seats in the Council and 2 allocated to minor parties. The President is assisted by an appointed Cabinet.

Indonesia comprises 27 provinces, including East (formerly Portuguese) Timor, unilaterally annexed on 17 July 1976.
Length of roadways: 52 749 miles *84 891 km* (31 Dec. 1972).
Length of railways: 4273 miles *6877 km*.
Universities: 51 (28 state, 23 private).
Adult illiteracy: 43·4% (males 30·5%; females 55·4%) in 1971.
Expectation of life: males 46·4 years; females 48·7 years (UN estimates for 1970–75).
Defence: Military service selective; total armed forces 276 900 (1986); defence expenditure: 6·7% of total government expenditure in 1985–6.
Foreign tourists: 700 000 in 1985.

Iran

Official name: Jomhori-e-Islami-e-Irân (Islamic Republic of Iran).
Population: 43 414 000 (1984 estimate).
Area: 636 296 miles² *1 648 000 km²*.
Languages: Farsi (Persian), Azerbaizhani, Kurdish, Arabic.
Religions: Muslim 98%; Christian, Jewish, Zoroastrian minorities.
Capital city: Tehrān (Teheran), population 5 734 199 (1982 estimate).
Other principal towns (1982): Mashad 1 119 748; Eşfāhan (Isfahan) 926 601; Tabriz 852 296; Shirāz 800 416; Ahvez (Ahwaz) 470 927; Kermanshah 531 350; Qom (Ghom) 424 048; Karaj 526 272.
Highest point: Qolleh-ye Damāvand (Mt Demavend), 18 386 ft *5604 m*.
Principal mountain ranges: Reshteh-ye Alborz (Elburz Mts), Kūhhā-ye-Zāgros (Zagros Mts).
Principal rivers: Kārūn, Safid (Sefid Rud), Atrak, Karkheh, Zāyandeh.
National Leader: Ayatollah Ruhollah Khomeini (b. 17 May 1900), *Wali Faqih*.
President: Hojatoleslam Ali Khamenei (b. 1939).
Prime Minister: Hossein Mousavi Khameini (b. 1941).
Climate: Extremely hot on Persian Gulf, cooler and dry on central plateau, subtropical on shore of Caspian Sea. In Teheran, July hottest (25°C *77°F* to 37°C *99°F*), January coldest (−3°C *27°F* to 7°C *45°F*), March rainiest (5 days). Absolute maximum temperature 52°C *126°F*, Abādān, 6 July 1951.
Labour force: 8 788 894 (excluding 943 614 unemployed) at 1976 census (5% sample): Agriculture, forestry and fishing 34·3%; Manufacturing 19·1%; Construction 13·6%; Community, social and personal services 17·8%.
Gross domestic product: 4 689 200 million rials in year ending 20 Mar. 1977: Petroleum production 38·0%; Other mining and manufacturing 10·7%; Community, social and personal services (incl. restaurants, hotels and business services) 12·9%.
Exports: 1189·9 billion rials in 1984: Crude petroleum 89·6%.
Monetary unit: Iranian rial. 1 rial = 100 dinars.
Denominations:

Coins 50 dinars; 1, 2, 5, 10, 20 rials.

Notes 5, 10, 20, 50, 100, 200, 500, 1000, 5000, 10 000 rials.

Exchange rate to £ sterling: 111 (26 Jan. 1987).
Political history and government: Formerly the Empire of Persia, renamed Iran on 21 Mar. 1935. The country was an absolute monarchy

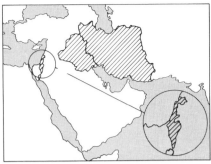

encircled: **ISRAEL** *centre:* **IRAQ** *right:* **IRAN**

until the adoption of the first constitution, approved by the Shah (Emperor) on 30 Dec. 1906. On 31 Oct. 1925 the National Assembly deposed the Shah and handed power to the Prime Minister, Reza Khan. He was elected Shah on 13 Dec. 1925 and took the title Reza Shah Pahlavi. During the Second World War Reza Shah favoured Nazi Germany. British and Soviet forces entered Iran on 25 Aug. 1941, forcing the Shah to abdicate in favour of his son, Mohammad Reza Pahlavi, on 16 Sept. 1941.

Under the Pahlavi dynasty, Iran was a limited constitutional monarchy and executive power remained with the Shah. On 2 Mar. 1975 Shah Mohammad dissolved existing political parties and announced the formation of a single party. Opposition to the Shah's rule later grew and, in response to increasing political violence and demonstrations, other parties were granted the freedom to resume their activities on 29 Aug. 1978. Protests against the Shah intensified and a mainly military government was appointed on 6 Nov. 1978. After further unrest, another civilian Prime Minister was appointed on 4 Jan. 1979. The new Cabinet was approved by the legislature on 16 Jan., when the Shah left the country. Popular opposition to the Shah grouped behind the Islamic traditionalist movement, dominated by the Ayatollah Ruhollah Khomenei, a spiritual leader of the Shi'a Muslims, who had been exiled by the Shah since 1963. Khomeini established a Revolutionary Islamic Council on 13 Jan. 1979, returned to Iran on 1 Feb. and appointed a provisional government on 5 Feb. After heavy fighting, the Shah's government fell, and power was surrendered to Khomeini's movement, on 11 Feb. 1979. Both houses of Parliament requested their own dissolution.

Following a referendum on 30–31 Mar., a republic was proclaimed on 1 Apr. 1979. A draft constitution officially published on 18 June, was submitted to a Constituent Council of Experts, with 73 members elected by popular vote on 3 Aug. 1979. The council, inaugurated on 19 Aug., completed its work on 14 Nov. 1979. The constitution, including the Council's far-reaching amendments, was approved by a referendum on 2–3 Dec. 1979. In accordance with Ayotollah Khomeini's principle of *Wilayat e Faqih* ('Rule of the Theologian'), supreme authority is vested in the *Wali Faqih*, a religious leader (initially Khomeini) agreed by the Muslim clergy, with no fixed term of office. The President is chief executive, elected by universal adult suffrage for a four-year term. Legislative power is vested in the unicameral Islamic Consultative Assembly (*Majlis*), with 270 members, also elected directly for four years. A 12-member Council of Guardians ensures that legislation conforms with Islamic precepts. Abolhasan Bani-Sadr was elected first President on 25 Jan. 1980 and assumed office on 4 Feb. The *Majlis* was elected on 14 Mar. and 9 May 1980.

The Prime Minister appointed by Khomeini had resigned on 5 Nov. 1979. On the next day power was assumed by the 14-man Revolutionary Council. After the transfer of legislative power from this Council to the *Majlis*, the President was formally sworn in on 22 July 1980. The *Majlis* approved a new Prime Minister, Muhammad Ali Rajai, on 11 Aug. 1980 and he was appointed on 20 Aug. A list of Ministers was approved on 10 Sept. 1980 and the Revolutionary Council dissolved itself. After a dispute between the *Majlis* and President Bani-Sadr, the *Wali Faqih* dismissed the President on 22 June 1981. Rajai was elected President on 24 July and sworn in by the *Majlis* on 3 Aug. President Rajai and his Prime Minister were assassinated on 30 Aug. Another presidential election was held on 2 Oct. and the winning candidate sworn in on 13 Oct. A new Prime Minister was approved by the *Majlis* on 29 Oct. 1981. Ali Khameini was re-elected as president in 1985.

Iran and Iraq have been at war since 1980, originally over a border dispute.
Length of roadways: 49 700 miles *80 000 km.*
Length of railways: 2838 miles *4567 km.*
Universities: 22.
Adult illiteracy: 63·8% (males 52·4%; females 75·7%) in 1976.
Expectation of life: Males 57·63 years; females 57·44 years (1973–76).
Defence: Military service 24 months; total regular armed forces 555 000 (1985); defence expenditure: 31% of total government expenditure in 1984–5.
Foreign tourists: 157 000 in 1984.

Iraq

Official name: Al-Jumhuriya al-'Iraqiya (the Republic of Iraq).
Population: 14 110 425 (1984 estimate).
Area: 167 925 miles² *434 924 km².*
Languages (1965): Arabic 81·1%: Kurdish 15·5%; Turkoman 1·7%.
Religions: Muslim, Christian minority.
Capital city: Baghdad, population 3 236 000 (1977 census).
Other principal towns (1977): Al-Basrah 1 540 000; Mosul 1 220 000; Kirkuk 535 000.
Highest point: 12 000 ft *3658 km.*
Principal mountain ranges: Kurdistan Mts.
Principal rivers: Tigris, Euphrates (1700 miles *2740 km*).
Head of State: Saddam Husain (b. 1937), President and Prime Minister.
Climate: Extremely hot, dry summers, humid near coast. Cold, damp winters with severe frosts in highlands. In Baghdad, average maximum 15°C *60°F* (January) to 43°C *110°F* (July, August), minimum −1°C *39°F* (January) to 24°C *76°F* (July, August), December rainiest (5 days). Absolute maximum temperature 52°C *125°F*, Shaiba, 8 Aug. 1937; minimum −14°C *6°F*, Ar Rutbah, 6 Jan. 1942.
Labour force: 3 059 214 (excl. 74 725 unemployed) at 1977 census: Agriculture, forestry and fishing 31·5% Construction 10·7%; Community, social and personal services 31·9%.
Gross domestic product: 4022·4 million dinars in 1975: Mining and quarrying 57·6%; Community, social and personal services (incl. business services) 13·8%.
Exports: 3041·8 million Iraqi dinars in 1983: Crude petroleum 98·6%.
Monetary unit: Iraqi dinar. 1 dinar = 5 riyals = 20 dirhams = 1000 fils.
Denominations:
  Coins 1, 5, 10, 25, 50, 100 fils.
  Notes 250, 5000 fils; 1, 5, 10 dinars.
Exchange rate to £ sterling: 0·4747 (26 Jan. 1987).
Political history and government: Formerly part of Turkey's Ottoman Empire, captured by British forces during the 1914–18 war. After the war Iraq became a Kingdom under a League of Nations mandate, administered by Britain. The mandate was ended on 3 Oct. 1932, when Iraq became independent. In an army-led revolution on 14 July 1958 the King was murdered, the bicameral parliament dissolved and a republic established. A succession of military régimes then held power. The latest of these was established on 17 July 1968. A provisional constitution, proclaiming socialist principles, was introduced on 16 July 1970. A National Charter, to be the basis of a permanent constitution, was issued on 15 Nov. 1971.

An elected National Assembly was envisaged but, before it was formed, the highest authority in the state was the Revolutionary Command Council (RCC). Legislation published on 5 Dec. 1979, and ratified by the RCC on 16 Mar. 1980, provided for a National Assembly, with a four-year term, to perform legislative duties alongside the RCC. The 250 members of the Assembly were elected on 20 June 1980. Executive power remains with the RCC, whose President is Head of State and Supreme Commander of the Armed Forces. The RCC, whose membership was increased to 22 on 4 Sept. 1977, elects the President and the Vice-President. The President appoints and leads a Council of Ministers to control administration. The dominant political organization is the Arab Socialist Renaissance (Ba'ath) Party.

Iraq comprises 18 governorates, each administered by an appointed governor. Three of the governorates form the (Kurdish) Autonomous Region, which has an elected Legislative Council.

Iraq and Iran have been at war since 1980, originally over a border dispute.
Length of roadways: 15 775 miles *25 385 km* (1984).
Length of railways: 1571 miles *2528 km* (1971).
Universities: 6.
Adult illiteracy: 75·7% (males 64·4%; females 87·1%) in 1965.
Expectation of life: Males 51·2 years; females 54·3 years (UN estimates for 1970–75).
Defence: Military service 21–24 months; total armed forces 520 000 (1985); defence expenditure: 4300 million Iraqi dinars in 1984.
Foreign tourists: 2 020 000 in 1982.

Ireland

Official name: Poblacht na h'Éireann (Republic of Ireland), abbreviated to Éire (Ireland).
Population: 3 443 045 (1981 census); 3 537 195 (1986 estimate).
Area: 27 136·3 miles² *70 282·6 km².*
Languages: English, Irish Gaelic.
Religions: Roman Catholic 94·9% (1961); Church of Ireland, Presbyterian, Methodist, Jewish minorities.
Capital city: Dublin (Baile Átha Cliath), population 915 115 (1981 census).
Other principal towns (1981): Cork (Corcaigh) 149 792; Limerick (Luimneach) 75 520; Galway (Gaillimh) 41 861; Waterford (Port Lairge) 39 636.
Highest point: Carrantuohill, 3414 ft *1041 m*, in Co. Kerry.
Principal mountain ranges: Macgillycuddy's Reeks, Wicklow Mts.
Principal rivers: Shannon (224 miles *360 km*), Suir (85 miles *136 km*), Boyne (70 miles *112 km*), Barrow (119 miles *191 km*), Erne (72 miles *115 km*).
Head of State: Dr Patrick John Hillery (Pádraig Ó hIrighile) (b. 2 May 1923), *An Uachtaran* (President).
Head of Government: Charles Haughey, *Taoiseach* (Prime Minister).

IRELAND

Climate: Mild (generally between 0°C *32°F* and 21°C *70°F*). In Dublin, average maximum 8°C *47°F* (December, January, February) to 19°C *67°F* (July, August), minimum 2°C *35°F* (January, February) to 10°C *51°F* (July, August); December rainiest (14 days). Absolute maximum temperature 33°C *92°F*, Dublin (Phoenix Park), 16 July 1876; absolute minimum −19°C *−2°F*, Markee Castle, Co. Sligo, 16 Jan. 1881.
Labour force: 1 110 000 in 1984: Agriculture, forestry and fishing 16·4%; Manufacturing 19·1%; Construction 7·5%; Commerce, insurance and finance 19·1%; Transport and communications 6·2%; Public administration and defence 6·6%.
Gross domestic product: I£14 394 million in 1984: Agriculture, forestry and fishing 12·3%; Mining, manufacturing and construction 35·6%; Public administration and defence 7%; Transport, communication and trade 17·1%; Other services 32·8%.
Exports: I£8897·6 million in 1984: Food and live animals 23·2%; Chemicals 13·9%; Machinery and transport equipment 28·7%; Miscellaneous manufactures 11·1%.
Monetary unit: Irish pound (punt or IR£). 1 pound = 100 pence.
Denominations:
Coins ½, 1, 2, 5, 10, 50 pence.
Notes 1, 5, 10, 20, 50, 100 pounds.
Exchange rate to £ sterling: 1·047 (26 Jan. 1987).
Political history and government: The whole of Ireland was formerly part of the United Kingdom. During an insurrection against British rule in April 1916 a republic was proclaimed but the movement was suppressed. After an armed struggle, beginning in 1919, a peace agreement was signed on 6 Dec. 1921 and became operative on 15 Jan. 1922. It provided that the six Ulster counties of Northern Ireland should remain part of the UK while the remaining 26 counties should become a dominion under the British Crown. Southern Ireland duly achieved this status as the Irish Free State on 6 Dec. 1922. A new constitution, giving full sovereignty within the Commonwealth, became effective on 29 Dec. 1937. Formal ties with the Commonwealth were ended on 18 Apr. 1949, when the 26 counties became a republic.
Legislative power is vested in the bicameral National Parliament (*Oireachtas*): a Senate (*Seanad Éireann*) of 60 members (11 nominated by the Prime Minister, 49 indirectly elected for 5 years) with restricted powers; and a House of Representatives (*Dáil Éireann*) with 166 members elected by universal adult suffrage for 5 years (subject to dissolution), using proportional representation. The President is a constitutional Head of State elected by universal adult suffrage for 7 years. Executive power is held by the Cabinet, led by a Prime Minister, appointed by the President on the nomination of the *Dáil*. The President appoints other Ministers on the nomination of the Prime Minister with the previous approval of the *Dáil*. The Cabinet is responsible to the *Dáil*.
In 1985 the Anglo-Irish Agreement was signed, providing for participation of Eire in political, legal, security and cross-border matters in N. Ireland, via an Intergovernmental Conference.
Length of roadways: 57 349 miles *92 294 km* (31 Dec. 1977).
Length of railways: 1236 miles *1989 km*.
Universities: 4.
Expectation of life: Males 68·77 years; females 73·52 years (1970–72).
Defence: Military service voluntary; total armed forces 13 742 (1985); defence expenditure: 3·6% of total government expenditure in 1985.
Foreign tourists: 2 428 000 in 1984 (excluding excursionists).

Israel

Official name: Medinat Israel (State of Israel).
Population: 4 233 000 (1985 estimate; includes East Jerusalem and Israeli residents in other occupied territories).
Area: 8572 miles² *21 942 km²* (includes Golan

Heights but not the other occupied territories).
Languages (1983): Hebrew (official) 68·8%; Arabic 18·3%; Yiddish 2·6%.
Religions (1984): Jewish 82·7%; Muslim 13·3%.
Capital city: Yerushalayim (Jerusalem), population 457 700 (1985 estimate), including East Jerusalem (Jordanian territory under Israeli occupation since 1967).
Other principal towns (1985): Tel Aviv/Jaffa 322 800; Haifa 224 600; Ramat Gan 116 000; Bat-Yam 131 200; Holon 138 800; Petah Tikva 129 300; Beersheba 115 000.
Highest point: Mt Atzmon (Har Meron), 3963 ft *1208 m*.
Lowest point: The Dead Sea, 1296 ft *395 m* below sea level.
Principal mountain range: Mts of Judea.
Principal rivers: Jordan (200 miles *321 km*), Qishon.
Head of State: Chaim Herzog, President.
Prime Minister: Yitzhak Shamir.
Climate: Mediterranean (hot, dry summers and mild, rainy winters). More extreme in the south. Sub-tropical on coast. In Jerusalem, average maximum 12°C *55°F* (January) to 30°C *87°F* (July, August), minimum 5°C *41°F* (January) to 17°C *64°F* (August), February rainiest (11 days). Absolute maximum temperature 54°C *129°F*, Tirat Zevi, 22 June 1942; absolute minimum −16°C *2°F*, Tel ha Tanim, 8 Nov. 1950.
Labour force: 1 402 600 in 1983: Agriculture, forestry and fishing 5·3%; Manufacturing 21·3%; Trade 12·1%; Financial services 9%; Public and community services 28%; Unemployed 4·5%.
Gross domestic product: 25 966 million new shekels in 1985: Mining and manufacturing 23·4%; Trade 14·5%; Financial services 16·1%; Community services 21·8%.
Exports: US$6256·4 million in 1985: Diamonds 23%; Chemicals 13%; Food, beverages and tobacco 6%; Citrus fruit 2·7%.
Monetary unit: New Israel shekel (= 1000 old shekels). 1 shekel = 100 agorot (singular: agora).
Denominations:
Coins 1, 5, 10, 50 agorot; 1 shekel.
Notes 1, 5, 10, 50, 100 shekels.
Exchange rate to £ sterling; 2·4750 (26 Jan. 1987).
Political history and government: Palestine (of which Israel forms part) was formerly part of Turkey's Ottoman Empire. During the First World War (1914–18) Palestine was occupied by British forces. After the war it was administered by Britain as part of a League of Nations mandate, established in 1922. The British Government terminated its Palestine mandate on 14 May 1948, when Jewish leaders proclaimed the State of Israel. After armed conflict with neighbouring Arab states, Israel's borders were fixed by armistice agreements in 1949. During the war of 5–10 June 1967 Israeli forces occupied parts of Egypt, Syria and Jordan, including East Jerusalem (which Israel unilaterally incorporated into its territory by legislation passed on 27 June 1967).
Israel is a republic. Supreme authority rests with the unicameral *Knesset* (Assembly), with 120 members elected by universal suffrage for 4 years, using proportional representation. The *Knesset* elects the President, a constitutional Head of State, for 5 years. Executive power rests with the Cabinet, led by the Prime Minister. The Cabinet takes office after receiving a vote of confidence in the *Knesset*, to which it is responsible. Israel comprises 6 administrative districts.
Length of roadways: 7758 miles *12 482 km* (1984).
Length of railways: 358 miles *573 km*.
Universities: 6 (plus 2 specialized).
Adult illiteracy: 9·9% (males 5·7%; females 10·5%) in 1985.
Expectation of life: Males 73·1 years; females 76·6 years (1984).
Defence: Military service: men 36 months, women 24 months (Jews and Druses only), Christians and Arabs may volunteer; annual training for reservists thereafter up to age 54 for men, 38 (or marriage) for women; total armed forces 142 000 (193 300 conscripts) in 1985; defence expenditure: 26·8% of total government expenditure in 1982–3.

Foreign tourists: 1 264 400 in 1985.

Italy

Official name: Repubblica Italiana (Italian Republic), abbreviated to Italia.
Population: 56 556 911 (1981 census); 57 202 345 (1985 estimate).
Area: 116 318 miles² *301 263 km²*.
Languages: Italian; small German and other minorities.
Religions; Roman Catholic; Protestant and Jewish minorities.
Capital city: Roma (Rome), population 2 830 650 (estimate Dec. 1983).
Other principal towns (31 Dec. 1983): Milano (Milan) 1 561 438; Napoli (Naples) 1 208 545; Torino (Turin) 1 069 013; Genova (Genoa) 746 785; Palermo 712 342; Bologna 447 971; Firenze (Florence) 440 910; Catania 380 370; Bari 369 576; Venezia (Venice) 340 873; Messina 263 924; Verona 261 947; Trieste 246 315.
Highest point: On Monte Bianco (Mont Blanc), 15 616 ft *4760 m*.
Principal mountain ranges: Appennini (Appenines), Alps.
Principal rivers: Po (418 miles *672 km*), Tevere (Tiber), Arno, Volturno, Garigliano.
Head of State; Francesco Cossiga, President.
Head of Government: Bettino Craxi (b. 24 Feb. 1934), President of the Council of Ministers (Prime Minister).
Climate; Generally Mediterranean, with warm, dry summers (average maximum 26°C *80°F*) and mild winters. Cooler and rainier in the Po Valley and the Alps. In Rome, average maximum 12°C *54°F* (January) to 31°C *88°F* (July, August), minimum 4°C *39°F* (January, February) to 17°C *64°F* (July, August), February rainiest (11 days). Absolute maximum temperature 46°C *114°F*, Foggia, 6 Sept. 1946; absolute minimum −34°C *−29°F*, Pian Rosa, 14 Feb. 1956.
Labour force: 22 982 000 in 1983: Agriculture, forestry and fishing 11·1%; Manufacturing 22·3%; Construction 9·1%; Commerce 18%; Transport, storage and communications 4·9%; Other services 23·9%; Unemployed 9·9%.
Gross domestic product: 489 253 billion lire in 1983: Agriculture, forestry and fishing 6·7%; Industry 38·4%; Public administration 15·4%; Other activities 44·5%.
Exports: 110 537·2 billion lire in 1983: Food and live animals 5·2%; Mineral fuels and lubricants 5·5%; Chemicals 7·1%; Basic manufactures 23·2%; Machinery and transport equipment 32·4%; Miscellaneous manufactures 22·1%.
Monetary unit; Italian lira. 1 lira = 100 centesimi.
Denominations:
Coins 1, 2, 5, 10, 20, 50, 100, 500, 1000 lire.
Notes 500, 1000, 2000, 5000, 10 000, 20 000, 50 000, 100 000 lire.
Exchange rate to £ sterling: 1980·25 (26 Jan. 1987).
Political history and government: Formerly several independent states. The Kingdom of Italy, under the House of Savoy, was proclaimed in 1861 and the country unified in 1870. Italy was under Fascist rule from 28 Oct. 1922 to 25 July 1943. A referendum on 2 June 1946 voted to abolish the monarchy and Italy became a republic on 10 June 1946. A new constitution took effect on 1 Jan. 1948.
Legislative power is held by the bicameral Parliament (*Parlamento*), elected by universal suffrage for 5 years (subject to dissolution), using proportional representation. The Senate has 315 elected members (seats allocated on a regional basis) and 7 life Senators. The Chamber of Deputies has 630 members. The minimum voting age is 25 years for the Senate and 18 for the Chamber. The two houses have equal power. The President of the Republic is a constitutional Head of State elected for 7 years by an electoral college comprising both Houses of Parliament and 58 regional representatives. Executive power is exercised by the Council of Ministers. The Head of State appoints the President of the Council (Prime Minister) and, on the latter's

recommendation, other Ministers. The Council is responsible to Parliament.

Italy has 20 administrative regions, each with an elected legislature and a regional executive.
Length of roadways: 185 021 miles *297 698 km*.
Length of railways: 10 045 miles *16 163 km*.
Universities: 59.
Adult illiteracy: 3%, and only among over-60s.
Expectation of life: Males 70·61 years; females 77·19 years (1977–9).
Defence: Military service: Army and Air Force 12 months, Navy 18 months; total armed forces 385 100 (1985); defence expenditure: 4·9% of total government expenditure in 1983.
Foreign tourists: 46 600 000 in 1983 (including excursionists).

The Ivory Coast

Official name: La République de la Côte d'Ivoire (the Republic of the Ivory Coast).
Population: 6 702 866 (census of 30 Apr. 1975); 10 056 000 (estimate 1985).
Area: 124 504 miles² *322 463 km²*.
Languages: French (official), many African languages.
Religions: Animist, Muslim, Christian.
Capital city: Yamoussoukro, population 70 000 in 1983.
Other principal towns (1983): Abidjan 1 850 000; Bouaké 200 000; Daloa 70 000; Man 50 000; Gagnoa 45 000.
Highest point: Mont Toukui, *c.* 6900 ft *2100 m*.
Principal mountain ranges: Man Mountains, Guinea Highlands.
Principal rivers: Bandama, Sassandra, Komoé.
Head of State: Félix Houphouët-Boigny (b. 18 Oct. 1905), President.
Climate: Generally hot, wet and humid. Temperatures from 14°C *57°F* to 39°C *103°F*. Rainy seasons May to July, October to November. In Abidjan, average maximum 28°C *82°F* to 32°C *90°F*, minimum around 23°C *74°F*.
Labour force: 2 301 000 (1970): Agriculture, forestry and fishing 84·5%; Services 12·9% (ILO estimates); 2 831 705 (excl. unpaid family workers) at 1975 census.
Gross domestic product: 1 539 265 million CFA francs in 1977: Agriculture, forestry and fishing 26·2% (agriculture 22·2%); Manufacturing 11·4%; Trade, restaurants and hotels 30·9% (trade 30·5%).
Exports: 796 774 million CFA francs in 1983: Coffee 20%; Cocoa 20%; Timber 14%; Petroleum products 9%.
Monetary unit: Franc de la Communauté financière africaine.
Denominations:
    Coins 1, 2, 5, 10, 25, 50, 100 CFA francs.
    Notes 100, 500, 1000, 5000, 10 000 CFA francs.
Exchange rate to £ sterling: 464·75 (26 Jan. 1987).
Political history and government: Formerly part of French West Africa, independent since 7 Aug. 1960. The ruling *Parti démocratique de la Côte d'Ivoire* has been the only organized political party since its establishment in 1946.

Under the constitution, promulgated on 31 Oct. 1960, legislative power is vested in the unicameral National Assembly, elected for five years by universal adult suffrage. The first multi-candidate elections were held in two rounds on 9 and 23 Nov. 1980, the Assembly being increased from 120 to 147 members. Executive power is held by the President, also directly elected for five years. On 25 Nov. 1980 the Assembly adopted a constitutional amendment creating the post of Vice-President. The President rules with the assistance of an appointed council of Ministers, responsible to him. The country comprises 34 departments.
Length of roadways: 28 950 miles *46 580 km* (1982).
Length of railways: 407 miles *655 km*.
Universities: 1.
Adult illiteracy: 95% (males 92%; females 98%) in 1962 (UNESCO estimates).
Expectation of life: males 41·9 years; females 45·1 years (UN estimates for 1970–75).

Defence: Military service voluntary; total armed forces 7730 (1986); defence expenditure, 1984: $71·6 million.
Foreign tourists: 194 869 in 1984.

Jamaica

Population: 2 095 878 (1982 census).
Area: 4244 miles² *10 991 km²*.
Language: English.
Religion: Christian (Anglican and Baptist in majority).
Capital city: Kingston, population 750 000 (1982 estimate).
Other principal towns (1982): Montego Bay 60 000; Spanish Town 41 600.
Highest point: Blue Mountain Peak (7402 ft *2256 m*).
Principal mountain range: Blue Mountains.
Principal river: Black River.
Head of State: HM Queen Elizabeth II, represented by Sir Florizel Augustus Glasspole, GCMG (b. 25 Sept. 1909), Governor-General.
Prime Minister: Edward Philip George Seaga (b. 28 May 1930).
Climate: The average rainfall is 1956 mm *77 in*, and the rainfall is far greater in the mountains than on the coast. In Kingston, average maximum 30°C *86°F* (January to March) to 32°C *90°F* (July, August), minimum 19°C *67°F* (January, February) to 23°C *74°F* (June), wettest month is October (nine days). In the uplands the climate is pleasantly equable.
Labour force: 1 022 900 in 1981: Agriculture, forestry and fishing 27·9%; Manufacturing 10·4%; Construction 4·1%; Transport, communications and public utilities 3·9%; Commerce 11·6%; Public administration 13·6%; Other services 16·6%; Unemployed 25·6%.
Gross domestic product: J$2965·5 million in 1977: Mining and quarrying 10·2%; Manufacturing 18·5%; Trade, restaurants and hotels 15·8% (trade 13·9%); Community, social and personal services 18·0% (public administration and defence 14·3%).
Exports: J$ 1392 million in 1983: Food and live animals (including sugar) 16·8%; Crude materials (including bauxite) 60·2%.
Monetary unit: Jamaican dollar (J$). 1 dollar = 100 cents.
Denominations:
    Coins 1, 5, 10, 20, 25, 50 cents.
    Notes 50 cents; 1, 2, 5, 10, 20 dollars.
Exchange rate to £ sterling: 8·766 (26 Jan. 1987).
Political history and government: A former British colony. Became independent, within the Commonwealth, on 6 Aug. 1962. Executive power is vested in the British monarch and exercised by the Governor-General, who is appointed on the recommendation of the Prime Minister and acts in almost all matters on the advice of the Cabinet. Legislative power is held by the bicameral Parliament: the Senate has 21 members, appointed by the Governor-General (13 on the advice of the Prime Minister and 8 on that of the Leader of the Opposition), and the House of Representatives has 60 members elected by universal adult suffrage for 5 years (subject to dissolution) in single-member constituencies. The Governor-General appoints the Prime Minister and, on the latter's recommendation, other Ministers. The Cabinet is responsible to the House.
Length of roadways: 10 206 miles *16 425 km*.
Length of railways: 205 miles *330 km*.
Universities: 1.
Adult illiteracy: 4·6% (1970).
Expectation of life: Males 62·65 years; females 66·63 years (1959–61).
Defence: Total armed forces 3400 (1985); defence expenditure: US$25·4 million (1984–5).
Foreign tourists: 843 775 in 1984.

Japan

Official name: Nippon or Nihon (land of the Rising Sun).
Population: 120 720 542 (1986).
Area: 145 817 miles² *377 765 km²*.
Language: Japanese.

ITALY

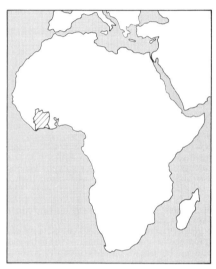

THE IVORY COAST

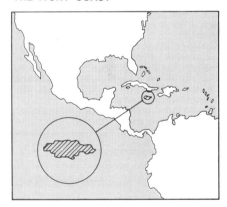

JAMAICA

Religions: Shintō, Buddhist.
Capital city: Tōkyō, population 8 216 000 (1986).
Other principal towns (1986): Yokohama 3 013 000; Osaka 2 541 000; Nagoya 2 077 000; Kyoto 1 469 000; Sapporo 1 529 000; Kobe 1 404 000; Fukuoka 1 127 000; Kitakyushu 1 047 000; Kawasaki 1 079 000.
Highest point: Fuji, 12 388 ft *3776 m* (first climbed before AD 806).
Principal mountain range: Hida.
Principal rivers: Tone (200 miles *321 km*), Ishikari (227 miles *365 km*), Shinano (229 miles *368 km*), Kitakami (156 miles *251 km*).
Head of State: HIM Hirohito (b. 29 Apr. 1901), *Nihon-koku Tennō* (Emperor of Japan).
Prime Minister: Yasuhiro Nakasone.
Climate: Great variation, from north (warm summers with long, cold winters) to south (hot, rainy summers with mild winters). In Tokyo, August warmest (22°C *72°F* to 30°C *86°F*),

January coldest (−6°C *20°F* to 8°C *47°F*), June and September rainiest (each 12 days). Absolute maximum temperature 41°C *105°F*, Yamagata, 25 July 1933; absolute minimum −41°C *−42°F*, Asahikawa, 25 Jan. 1902.
Labour force: 58 070 000 in 1985: Agriculture and forestry 8%; Fishing 0·8%; Construction 9%; Manufacturing 25%; Commerce and finance 37%; Transport and other public utilities 6·9%; Services 20%; Government work 3%; Unemployed 2·6%.
Gross domestic product: 317 305 billion yen in 1985: Manufacturing 33·3%; Trade 14·3%; Construction 7·5%; Transport and communications 6·3%; Agriculture 3·2%; Others, including services 35·3%.
Exports: US$170 113·9 million in 1984: Chemicals 4·5%; Basic manufactures 17·7%; Machinery and transport equipment 60·4%; Misc. manufactures 14·5%.
Monetary unit: Yen. 1 yen = 100 sen.
Denominations:
 Coins 1, 5, 10, 50, 100, 500 yen.
 Notes 1000, 5000, 10 000 yen.
Exchange rate to £ sterling: 233·25 (26 Jan. 1987).
Political history and government: An hereditary monarchy, with an Emperor as Head of State. After being defeated in the Second World War, Japanese forces surrendered on 14 Aug. 1945. Japan signed an armistice on 2 Sept. 1945, agreeing to give up many outer islands, and the country was placed under US military occupation. A new constitution was promulgated on 3 Nov. 1946 and took effect from 3 May 1947. Following the peace treaty of 8 Sept. 1951, Japan regained its sovereignty on 28 Apr. 1952. The Tokara Archipelago and the Amami Islands (parts of the Ryukyu group) were restored on 5 Dec. 1951 and 25 Dec. 1953 respectively. The Bonin Islands were restored on 26 June 1968 and the rest of the Ryukyu Islands (including Okinawa) on 15 May 1972.

Japan is a constitutional monarchy, with the Emperor as a symbol of the state. He has formal prerogatives but no power relating to government. Legislative power is vested in the bicameral Diet (*Kokkai*), elected by universal adult suffrage. The House of Councillors (*Sangiin*), with limited delaying powers, has 252 members elected for 6 years (half retiring every three years) and the House of Representatives (*Shugiin*) has 511 members elected for 4 years (subject to dissolution). Executive power is vested in the Cabinet. The Prime Minister is appointed by the Emperor (on designation by the Diet) and himself appoints the other Ministers. The Cabinet is responsible to the Diet.

Japan has 47 prefectures, each administered by an elected Governor.
Length of roadways: 725 916 miles *1 168 000 km* (1983).
Length of railways: 16 788 miles *27 012 km* (1983).
Universities: 122 (59 national, 12 municipal, 51 private).
Adult illiteracy; 2·2% (males 1·0%; females 3·3%) in 1960.
Expectation of life: Males 74·84 years; females 80·46 (1986).
Defence: Military service voluntary; total armed forces 245 000 (1986); defence expenditure: 6% of total government expenditure in 1985–6.
Foreign tourists: 2 300 000 in 1985.

Jordan

Official name: Al-Mamlaka al-Urduniya al-Hashimiyah (the Hashemite Kingdom of Jordan).
Population: 3 253 408 (1984 estimate).
Area: 37 738 miles² *97 740 km²*.
Language: Arabic.
Religions: Muslim, Christian minority.
Capital city: 'Ammãn, population 956 720 (1984 estimate).
Other principal towns: Az Zarqa (Zarka) 255 500 (1983); Irbid 131 200 (1983); Bait Lahm (Bethlehem) 68 009 (1961); Ariha (Jericho) 66 839 (1961); Al Quds ash Sharif (Jerusalem) 60 337 (Jordanian sector, 1961).
Highest point: Jabal Ramm, 5755 ft *1754 m*.

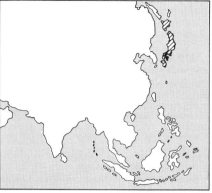
JAPAN

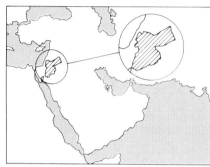
JORDAN

Principal river: Jordan (200 miles *321 km*).
Head of State: HM King Husain ibn Talal, GCVO (b. 14 Nov. 1935).
Prime Minister: Zaid Rifai.
Climate: Hot and dry, average temperature 15°C *60°F* with wide diurnal variations. Cool winters, rainy season December to March. In Ammãn, August hottest (average maximum 32°C *90°F*), January coolest (average minimum −1°C *39°F*). Absolute maximum temperature 51°C *124°F*, Dead Sea North, 22 June 1942; absolute minimum −7°C *18°F*, Ammãn, 28 Feb. 1959.
Labour force: 565 000 (1970): Agriculture, forestry and fishing 33·9%; Industry 32·8%; Services 33·4% (ILO estimates).
Gross domestic product: 1487·4 million Jordanian dinar in 1983.
Exports: 160·1 million Jordanian dinar in 1983: Phosphates 32·2%; Tomatoes 3·7%; Other vegetables and fruit 11%.
Monetary unit: Jordanian dinar. 1 dinar = 1000 fils.
Denominations:
 Coins 1, 5, 10, 20, 25, 50, 100, 250 fils.
 Notes 500 fils; 1, 5, 10 dinars.
Exchange rate to £ sterling: 0·5135 (26 Jan. 1987).
Political history and government: Formerly part of Turkey's Ottoman Empire, Turkish forces were expelled in 1918. Palestine and Transjordan were administered by Britain under League of Nations mandate, established in 1922. Transjordan became an independent monarchy, under an Amir, on 22 Mar. 1946. The Amir became King, and the country's present name was adopted, on 25 May 1946. In the Arab-Israeli war of 1948 Jordanian forces occupied part of Palestine, annexed in December 1949 and fully incorporated on 24 Apr. 1950. This territory was captured by Israel in the war of 5–10 June 1967.

Under the constitution, adopted on 7 Nov. 1951, legislative power is vested in a bicameral National Assembly comprising a Chamber of Notables (30 members appointed by the King for 8 years, half retiring every 4 years) and a Chamber of Deputies with 60 members (50 Muslims and 10 Christians) elected by universal adult suffrage for 4 years (subject to dissolution). In each Chamber there is equal representation for the East Bank and the (occupied) West Bank. Executive power is vested in the King, who rules with the assistance of an appointed Council of Ministers, responsible to the Assembly. On 9

Nov. 1974 both Chambers of the Assembly approved constitutional amendments which empowered the King to dissolve the Assembly and to postpone elections for up to 12 months. The Assembly was dissolved on 22 Nov. 1974 and reconvened on 5–7 Feb. 1976, when it approved a constitutional amendment giving the King power to postpone elections indefinitely and to convene the Assembly as required. A royal decree of 19 Apr. 1978 provided for the creation of a National Consultative Council, with 60 members appointed by the King, on the Prime Minister's recommendation, to debate proposed legislation. The Council, whose members serve for two years (subject to dissolution by the King), first met on 24 Apr. 1978 and was renewed on 20 Apr. 1980. The Council was subsequently dissolved by the King and replaced by the bicameral National Assembly in 1984 (again, appointed by the King).

Jordan comprises 8 administrative districts, including 3 on the West Bank (under Israeli occupation since June 1967).
Length of roadways: 2545 miles *4095 km*.
Length of railways: 384 miles *618 km*.
Universities: 3.
Adult illiteracy: 67·6% (males 49·9%; females 84·8%) in 1961.
Expectation of life: Males 52·6 years; females 52·0 years (1969–63).
Defence: Military service: selective conscription; total armed forces 70 300 (1985); defence expenditure: 25·4% of total government expenditure in 1985.
Foreign tourists: 1 312 000 in 1983.

Kampuchea

Official name: Sathearanakrath Pracheachon Kampuchea (People's Republic of Kampuchea).
Population: 7 200 000 (1984 estimate).
Area: 69 898 miles² *181 035 km²*.
Languages: Khmer (official), French.
Religion: Buddhist.
Capital city: Phnom-Penh, population 600 000 (1983 estimate).
Other principal towns: Battambang, Kompong Chhnang, Kompong Cham, Kompong Som (Sihanoukville).
Highest point: Mt Ka-Kup, 5722 ft *1774 m*.
Principal mountain range: Chaîne des Cardamomes.
Principal river: Mekong (2600 miles *4184 km*).
Head of State: Heng Samrin (b. 1934), Chairman of the People's Revolutionary Council; also Secretary-General of the Kampuchean People's Revolutionary Party.
Prime Minister: Hun Sen.
Climate: Tropical and humid. Rainy season June–November. In Phnom-Penh, average maximum 30°C *86°F* (November, December) to 34°C *94°F* (April), minimum 21°C *70°F* (January) to 24°C *76°F* (April–October), September rainiest (19 days).
Labour force: 2 849 000 in 1970: Agriculture, Forestry and fishing 78·2%; Industry 5·3%; Services 17·6%.
Gross domestic product: 32 000 million riels in 1966 (when $1 = 35 riels); $1192 million (estimate) in 1975.
Exports: 2732·5 million old riels in 1973: Rubber 93·1%; Haricot beans 4·4%.
Monetary unit: New riel. 1 riel = 100 sen.
Denominations:
 Coins 5 sen.
 Notes 10, 20, 50 sen; 1, 5, 10, 20, 50 riels.
Exchange rate to £ sterling: Not available on 26 Jan. 1987; approx. 5·8 on 31 Dec. 1985.
Political history and government: As Cambodia, formerly a monarchy and part of French Indo-China. Norodom Sihanouk became King on 26 Apr. 1941. On 6 May 1947 he promulgated a constitution providing for a bicameral Parliament, including an elected National Assembly. Cambodia became an Associate State of the French Union on 8 Nov. 1949 and a fully independent kingdom on 9 Nov. 1953. Sihanouk abdicated on 2 Mar. 1955 in favour of his father, Norodom Suramarit. King Suramarit died on 3 Apr. 1960 and Parliament elected Prince Sihan-

ouk to become Head of State (without taking the title of King) on 20 June 1960.

On 18 Mar. 1970 Prince Sihanouk was deposed by his Prime Minister, Lt-Gen (later Marshal) Lon Nol, who proclaimed the Khmer Republic on 8 Oct. 1970. Sihanouk went into exile and formed a Royal Government of National Union, supported by the pro-Communist *Khmers Rouges* ('Red Cambodians'). Sihanoukists and the *Khmers Rouges* formed the National United Front of Cambodia (NUFC). Their combined forces defeated the republicans and Phnom-Penh surrendered on 17 April 1975, when the Royal Government took power. On 14 Dec. 1975 a congress of the NUFC approved a new republican constitution, promulgated on 5 Jan. 1976, when the name of the country was changed to Democratic Kampuchea. Elections were held on 20 March 1976 for the People's Representative Assembly (250 members). Prince Sihanouk resigned as Head of State on 4 April 1976. In his place the Assembly chose a three-man State Presidium on 11 April 1976. Pol Pot was appointed Prime Minister two days later. On 27 Sep. 1977 it was officially revealed that the ruling organization was the Communist Party of Kampuchea, with Pol Pot as its Secretary. Rival Communists, opponents of Pol Pot, established the Kampuchean National United Front for National Salvation (KNUFNS), announced on 3 Dec. 1978. After a year of border fighting, Vietnamese forces, supporting the KNUFNS, invaded Cambodia on 25 Dec. 1978, capturing the capital on 7 Jan. 1979. The next day the KNUFNS established the People's Revolutionary Council (8 members) and on 10 Jan. 1979 the country's present name was adopted. The second Congress of the KNUFNS, held on 29–30 Sept. 1979, elected a Central Committee of 35 members.

Elections were held on 1 May 1981 for 117 members of a new National Assembly. The Assembly began its first session on 24 June 1981 and ratified a new constitution on 27 June. The supreme organ of state power is the unicameral Assembly, elected by universal adult suffrage for a five-year term. The Assembly chooses seven of its members to form the Council of State, its permanent organ, which appoints the Council of Ministers. The new régime is based on the Kampuchean People's Revolutionary Party.

Length of roadways: c. 6835 miles *c. 11 000 km.*
Length of railways: 160 miles *260 km.*
Adult illiteracy: 63·9% (males 37·7%; females 89·6%) in 1962.
Expectation of life: Males 44·0 years; females 46·9 years (UN estimates for 1970–75).
Defence: Military service: conscription; total armed forces about 35 000 (1985), also about 180 000 Vietnamese troops.

Kenya

Official name: Jamhuri ya Kenya (Republic of Kenya).
Population: 15 327 061 (1979 census); 19 536 000 (1984 estimate).
Area: 224 081 miles² *580 367 km².*
Languages: Swahili (official), English, Kikuyu, Luo.
Religions; Christian 58% (1962), Muslim.
Capital city: Nairobi, population 1 100 000 (1985 estimate).
Other principal towns (1985 estimates): Mombasa 478 000; Nakuru 130 000; Kisumu 215 000; Machakos 117 000; Meru 98 000; Eldoret 71 000; Thika 57 000.
Highest point: Mount Kenya (17 058 ft *5199 m*).
Principal mountain range: Aberdare Mountains.
Principal rivers: Tana, Umba, Athi, Mathioya.
Head of State: Daniel Toroitich arap Moi (b. Sept. 1924), President.
Climate: Varies with altitude. Hot and humid on coast, with average temperatures of 20°C *69°F* to 32°C *90°F*, falling to 7°C *45°F* to 27°C *80°F* on land over 5000 ft *1524 m.* Ample rainfall in the west and on highlands, but very dry in the north. In Nairobi, average maximum 20°C *69°F* (July) to 26°C *79°F* (February), minimum 10°C *51°F* (July) to 14°C *58°F* (April), May rainiest (17 days).

Labour force: 1 093 300 in 1983: Agriculture, forestry and fishing 21·1%; Manufacturing 13·6%; Construction 5·5%; Trade 7·3%; Community, social and personal services 41·3%.
Gross domestic product: K£3701·1 million in 1984: Traditional economy 6·1%; Monetary economy: Agriculture, forestry and fishing 30%; Manufacturing 12·5%; Trade 13%; Financial services 7·7%; Government services 14·3%.
Exports: 10 926·3 million Kenyan shillings in 1982: Coffee 26·5%; Tea 14·3%; Petroleum products 27·3% Fruit and vegetables 7%; Cement 3·5%.
Monetary unit; Kenya shilling. 1 shilling = 100 cents; 20 shillings = K£1.
Denominations:
  Coins 5, 10, 50 cents; 1 shilling.
  Notes 5, 10, 20, 100 shillings.
Exchange rate to £ sterling: 24·20 (26 Jan. 1987).
Political history and government: Formerly a British colony and protectorate. Became independent, within the Commonwealth, on 12 Dec. 1963 and a republic on 12 Dec. 1964. A one-party state since 30 Oct. 1969. Legislative power is held by the unicameral National Assembly, with 172 members (158 elected by universal adult suffrage, the Attorney-General, the Speaker and 12 members nominated by the President) serving a term of five years (subject to dissolution). Executive power is held by the President, also directly elected for five years. He is assisted by an appointed Vice-President and Cabinet. Kenya has 40 districts, each with a District Development Committee responsible for all development projects.
Length of roadways: 33 298 miles *53 577 km.*
Length of railways: 1658 miles *2668 km.*
Universities: 2.
Adult illiteracy: 50% (males 39%; females 62%) in 1982.
Expectation of life: Males 46·9 years; females 51·2 years (1969).
Defence: Military service voluntary; total armed forces 13 650 (1985); defence expenditure: 9·1% of total government expenditure in 1984–5.
Foreign tourists: 360 000 in 1984.

Kiribati

Population: 63 848 (1985 census).
Area: 277 miles² *717 km².*
Languages: Kiribati (Gilbertese), English.
Religion: Christian (Anglican, Methodist, Roman Catholic, Mormons, Seventh Day Adventists).
Capital city: Tarawa atoll, population 21 393 (1985 census).
Highest point: 265 ft *81 m,* on Banaba (Ocean Island).
Head of State: Ieremia T Tabai, GCMG (b. 16 Dec. 1950), Beretitenti (President).
Climate: Warm and pleasant, with day temperatures between 27°C *80°F* and 32°C *90°F* and a minimum of about 23°C *77°F* at night. Average annual rainfall varies widely between atolls, ranging from 30 in *762 mm* to 150 in *3810 mm.* Rainy season December to February, dry from August to October.
Labour force: 7869 in 1985: Government service and private enterprise 86%; Seamen 8·3%; Phosphate mining in Nauru 5·7%.
Gross domestic product: A$24 million (1982 estimate).
Exports: A$13 006 000 in 1984: Copra 53·7%; Fish 17·6%.
Monetary unit: Australian currency (*q.v.*).
Political history and government: In 1892 a United Kingdom protectorate was established over the 16 atolls of the Gilbert Islands and the 9 Ellice Islands (now Tuvalu) the two groups being administered together. Ocean Island (now Banaba) was annexed on 28 Nov. 1900. The Gilbert and Ellice Islands were annexed on 10 Nov. 1915, effective from 12 Jan. 1916, when the protectorate became a colony. Later in 1916 the new Gilbert and Ellice Islands Colony (GEIC) was extended to include Ocean Island and two of the Line Islands. Christmas Island (now Kiritimati), in the Line Islands, was annexed in 1919 and the 8 Phoenix Islands on

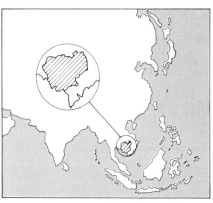

KAMPUCHEA

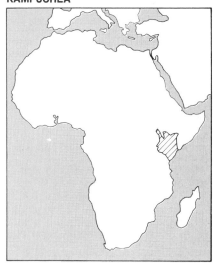

KENYA

18 Mar. 1937. Two of the Phoenix Islands, Canton (now Kanton) and Enderbury, were also claimed by the USA and a joint British-US administration was agreed on 6 Apr. 1939. The 5 uninhabited Central and Southern Line islands became part of the GEIC on 1 Jan. 1972. The Ellice Islands were allowed to form a separate territory, named Tuvalu, on 1 Oct. 1975. The remainder of the GEIC was renamed the Gilbert Islands and obtained self-government on 1 Jan. 1977. Following a constitutional conference on 21 Nov.–7 Dec. 1978, this territory became an independent republic, within the Commonwealth, on 12 July 1979, taking the name Kiribati (pronounced 'Kiribass'). The USA has agreed to renounce its claim to Kanton and Enderbury Islands under a 1982 Treaty of Friendship.

Legislative power is vested in the Maneaba ni Maungatabu, a unicameral body. It has 35 members elected by universal adult suffrage for 4 years (subject to dissolution), one nominated representative of the Banaban community and, if he is not an elected member, the Attorney-General as an *ex officio* member. The 35 elected members of the pre-independence House of Assembly took office as members of the first Maneaba. Executive power is vested in the Beretitenti (President), who is Head of State and Head of Government. The pre-independence Chief Minister became the first Beretitenti but in future the Beretitenti is to be elected. After each general election for the Maneaba, it will nominate, from among its members, three or four candidates from whom the Beretitenti will be elected by universal adult suffrage. The Maneaba is empowered to remove the Beretitenti from office.

The Beretitenti governs with the assistance of a Kauoman-ni-Beretitenti (Vice-President) and Cabinet, whom he appoints from among members of the Maneaba. The Cabinet is responsible to the Maneaba.
Length of roadways: 400 miles *640 km.*
Expectation of life: Males 56·9 years; females 59·0 years (1958–62, including Tuvalu).

Korea (North)

Official name: Chosun Minchu-chui Inmin Konghwa-guk (Democratic People's Republic of Korea).
Population: 19 630 000 (1984 estimate).
Area: 46 540 miles² *120 538 km²* (excluding demilitarized zone).
Language: Korean.
Religions: Buddhist, Confucian, Taoist.
Capital city: Pyongyang, population 1 280 000 (1981 estimate).
Other principal towns (1976): Ch'ongjin 300 000; Hungnam 260 000; Kaesong 240 000.
Highest point: Pektu San (Pait'ou Shan), 9003 ft *2744 m* (first climbed 1886).
Principal mountain range: Nangnim Sanmaek.
Principal rivers: Imjin, Ch'ongch'ŏn, Yalu (300 miles *482 km*) on frontier.
Head of State: Marshall Kim Il Sung (*né* Kim Sung Chu, b. 15 Apr. 1912), President; also General Secretary of the Central Committee of the Korean Workers' Party.
Head of Government: Kang Song San, Premier of the Administration Council.
Climate; Continental; hot, humid, rainy summers (average temperature 25°C *77°F*) and cold, dry winters (average −6°C *21°F*).
Labour force: 8 939 000 in 1984: Agriculture, forestry and fishing 42·3.
Gross national product: $17 040 million in 1978 (World Bank estimate).
Exports: US$1610 million in 1981: Manufactured goods 59%.
Monetary unit: Won. 1 won = 100 chon (jun).
Denominations:
  Coins 1, 5, 10 chon.
  Notes 50 chon; 1, 5, 10, 50, 100 won.
Exchange rate to £ sterling: 1·4363 (26 Jan. 1987).
Political history and government: Korea was formerly a kingdom, for long under Chinese suzerainty. Independence was established on 17 Apr. 1895. Korea was occupied by Japanese forces in Nov. 1905 and formally annexed by Japan on 22 Aug. 1910, when the monarch was

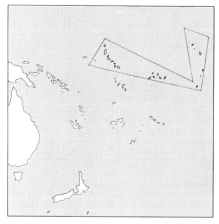

KIRIBATI

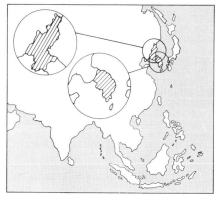

above: **KOREA (NORTH**
below: **KOREA (SOUTH)**

deposed. After Japan's defeat in the Second World War, Korea was divided at the 38th parallel into military occupation zones, with Soviet forces in the North and US forces in the South. After the failure of negotiations in 1946 and 1947, the country remained divided. With Soviet backing, a Communist-dominated administration was established in the North. Elections were held on 25 Aug. 1948 and the Democratic People's Republic of Korea was proclaimed on 9 Sept. 1948. After the Korean War of 1950–53 a cease-fire line replaced the 38th parallel as the border between North and South.

In North Korea a new constitution was adopted on 27 Dec. 1972. The highest organ of state power is the unicameral Supreme People's Assembly, with 579 members elected (unopposed) for four years by universal adult suffrage. The Assembly elects for its duration the President of the Republic and, on the latter's recommendation, other members of the Central People's Committee to direct the government. The Assembly appoints the Premier and the Committee appoints other Ministers to form the Administration Council, led by the President.

Political power is held by the (Communist) Korean Workers' Party (KWP), which dominates the Democratic Front for the Reunification of the Fatherland (including two other minor parties). The Front presents an approved list of candidates for elections to representative bodies. The KWP's highest authority is the Party Congress. The sixth Congress met on 10–14 Oct. 1980 and elected a new Central Committee to supervise Party work. To direct its policy, the Committee elects a Political Bureau (19 full and 15 alternate members were elected on 14 Oct. 1980). The five-member Presidium of the Political Bureau is the Party's most powerful policy-making body.

North Korea comprises nine provinces and two cities, each with an elected People's Assembly.
Length of railways: 2722 miles *4380 km* (1974).
Universities: 3.
Adult illiteracy: 10% (est.).
Expectation of life: 74 years (1982).
Defence: Military service: Army, Navy 5 years, Air Force 3–4 years; total armed forces 838 000 (1985); defence expenditure: 14% of total government expenditure in 1985.

Korea (South)

Official name: Daehan-Minkuk (Republic of Korea).
Population: 40 466 577 (1985 census).
Area: 38 232 miles² *99 022 km²*.
Language: Korean.
Religions: Buddhist, Christian, Confucian, Chundo Kyo.
Capital city: Sŏul (Seoul), population 9 645 824 (1985 census).
Other principal towns (1985): Pusan (Busan) 3 516 768; Taegu (Daegu) 2 030 649; Inchŏn (Incheon) 1 387 475.
Highest point: Halla-san, 6398 ft *1950 m*.
Principal rivers: Han, Naktong (with Nam), Kum, Somjin, Yongsan.
Head of State: Gen Chun Doo Hwan (b. 23 Jan. 1931), President.
Prime Minister: Lho Shin Yong.
Climate: Hot, humid summers (average temperature 25°C *77°F*) and cold, dry winters (average −6°C *21°F*). In Seoul, August hottest (22°C *71°F* to 30°C *87°F*), January coldest (−9°C *15°F* to 0°C *32°F*), July rainiest (16 days). Absolute maximum temperature 40°C *104°F*, Taegu, 1 Aug. 1942; absolute minimum −43,6°C *−46·5°F*, Chungkangjin, 12 Jan. 1933.
Labour force: 14 984 000 in 1984: Agriculture, forestry and fishing 27·1%; Mining, manufacturing 24·2%; Services 48·7%; Unemployed 3·8%.
Gross domestic product: 58 279·7 billion won in 1983: Agriculture, forestry and fishing 14%; Mining and manufacturing 29·5%; Others 56·5%.
Exports: US$26 billion in 1984: Food and live

animals 4%; Manufactured goods 28·3%; Machinery and transport equipment 32%; Miscellaneous manufactured articles 28%.
Monetary unit: Won. 1 won = 100 chun (jeon).
Denominations:
  Coins 1, 5, 10, 50, 100, 500 won.
  Notes 500, 1000, 5000, 10 000 won.
Exchange rate to £ sterling: 1309·6 (26 Jan. 1987).
Political history and government: (For events before partition, *see* North Korea, above). After UN-supervised elections for a National Assembly on 10 May 1948, South Korea adopted a constitution and became the independent Republic of Korea on 15 Aug. 1948. North Korean forces invaded the South on 25 June 1950, and war ensued until 27 July 1953, when an armistice established a cease-fire line (roughly along the 38th parallel) between North and South. This has become effectively an international frontier.

On 16 May 1961 South Korea's government was overthrown by a military *coup*, led by Maj-Gen Pak Chung Hi, who assumed power, dissolved the National Assembly, suspended the constitution and disbanded political parties. A new constitution was approved by referendum on 17 Dec. 1962. Gen Pak was elected President on 15 Oct. 1963 and inaugurated on 17 Dec. 1963, when a newly-elected National Assembly was convened. Martial law was imposed on 17 Oct. 1972 and another constitution approved by referendum on 21 Nov. 1972. This *Yushin* ('Revitalising') Constitution provided for the President to be elected indirectly by a 'National Conference for Unification' (NCU), comprising delegates elected by popular vote. The National Assembly had two-thirds of its members directly elected and one-third nominated by the NCU. Emergency Decree No. 9, issued on 13 May 1975, banned virtually all opposition activities.

President Pak was assassinated on 26 Oct. 1979. On the next day, martial law was introduced (with the Army Chief of Staff as martial law administrator), except on the island of Cheju, and the Prime Minister, Choi Kyu Ha, became Acting President. On 6 Dec. 1979 he was elected President by the NCU and on the next day he rescinded Emergency Decree No. 9. In a virtual *coup* on 12–13 Dec. 1979 the martial law administrator and other officers were arrested by troops under Lt-Gen (later Gen) Chun Doo Hwan, head of the Army Security Command. President Choi was inaugurated on 21 Dec. 1979 to complete his predecessor's last term (1978–84). Following a wave of strikes and demonstrations, martial law was extended throughout the country on 17 May 1980. All political activities were banned and the national Assembly was closed on 19 May. The Cabinet resigned on 20 May and a new Prime Minister was appointed the next day. On 31 May 1980 the government established a Special Committee for National Security Measures, an advisory body controlled by the armed forces, which assumed political power. Following a 'purification' campaign, involving mass arrests and purges, President Choi resigned on 16 Aug. 1980. To succeed him, Gen Chun was endorsed by the armed services and (after retiring from the Army) was elected unopposed on 27 Aug. He was sworn in on 1 Sept. and a new Cabinet was formed.

A new constitution was approved by referendum on 22 Oct. 1980 and came into effect on 27 Oct., when the 'Fifth Republic' was inaugurated. The National Assembly and existing political parties were dissolved. Martial law was lifted on 24 Jan. 1981.

Executive power is held by the President, indirectly elected for a single seven-year term by a presidential electoral college whose members are elected by universal adult suffrage. The first college (5278 members) was elected on 11 Feb. 1981. The college elected President Chun on 25 Feb. and he was sworn in on 3 March, when the college was dissolved. The President rules with the assistance of an appointed State Council (Cabinet), led by a Prime Minister. Legislative power is vested in the unicameral National Assembly, popularly elected for a four-year term. On 25 Mar. 1981 voting took place for an

Assembly of 276 members: 184 directly elected (two each from 92 districts, though no party could have more than one candidate per district) and 92 additional members (61 for the party gaining the most seats by direct election, the remaining 31 for other parties in proportion to seats won directly).

Length of roadways: 33 521 miles *53 936 km* (1983).
Length of railways: 1940 miles *3121 km* (1983).
Universities: 41.
Adult illiteracy: 8% (1983).
Expectation of life: Males 64·2 years; females 70·6 years (1983).
Defence: Military service: Army and Marines 2½ years, Navy and Air Force 3 years; total armed forces 607 000 (1986); defence expenditure: 27·7% of total government expenditure in 1985.
Foreign tourists: 1 426 000 in 1985.

Kuwait

Official name: Daulat al-Kuwait (State of Kuwait). Kuwait means 'little fort'.
Population: 1 695 128 (1985 census).
Area: 6880 miles² *17 818 km²*.
Language: Arabic.
Religions: Muslim; Christian minority.
Capital city: Kuwait City, population 60 525 (1980 census).
Other principal towns (1980): Hawalli 152 402; Salmiya 145 991; Abraq Kheetan 48 104; Farawaniya 57 841.
Highest point: 951 ft *289 m*.
Head of State: HH Shaikh Jabir al-Ahmad al-Jabir as-Sabah (b. 1928), Amir.
Prime Minister: HH Shaikh Saad al-Abdullah as-Salim as-Sabah.
Climate: Humid, average temperature 24°C *75°F*. In Kuwait City, maximum recorded temperature 51°C *124°F*, July 1954; minimum −2·6°C *+27·3°F*, January 1964.
Labour force: 484 033 (including non-Kuwaitis) in 1980: Agriculture, forestry and fishing 1·9%; Manufacturing 8·5%; Construction 20·1%; Trade 12·1%; Transport, storage and communications 6·2%; Services 45·5%.
Gross domestic product: 6218·7 million Kuwaiti dinar in 1983: Mining 49·8%; Manufacturing 6·4%; Construction 4·6%; Trade 8·6%; Financial services 10·1%; Public administration 6·5%; Other services 8·7%.
Exports: 3128·4 million Kuwaiti dinars in 1982: Crude petroleum and petroleum products 81·2%; Gas 2·2%; Basic manufactures 5·7%; Machinery and transport equipment 6·5%.
Monetary unit: Kuwaiti dinar. 1 dinar = 1000 fils.
Denominations:
 Coins 1, 5, 10, 20, 50, 100 fils.
 Notes 250, 500 fils; 1, 5, 10 dinars.
Exchange rate to £ sterling: 0·42655 (26 Jan. 1987).
Political history and government: A monarchy formerly ruled by a Shaikh. Under British protection from 23 Jan. 1899 until achieving full independence, with the ruling Shaikh as Amir, on 19 June 1961. Present constitution adopted on 16 Dec. 1962. Executive power is vested in the Amir (chosen by and from members of the ruling family) and is exercised through a Council of Ministers. The Amir appoints the Prime Minister and, on the latter's recommendation, other Ministers. Legislative power is vested in the unicameral National Assembly, whose members serve for four years (subject to dissolution) and are elected by literate civilian adult male Kuwaiti citizens. On 29 Aug. 1976 the Amir dissolved the Assembly and suspended parts of the constitution, including provisions for fresh elections. In accordance with an Amiri decree of 24 Aug. 1980, a new 50-seat National Assembly (two deputies from each of 25 constituencies) was elected on 23 Feb. 1981. The Assembly's first session opened on 9 Mar. 1981. Political parties are not legally permitted. Kuwait comprises three governorates.
Length of roadways: 1208 miles *1944 km*.
Universities: 1.

Adult illiteracy: 40·4% (males 32·0%; females 52·0%) in 1975.
Expectation of life: 70·4 years (1980–4).
Defence: Military service 18 months; total armed forces 13 100 (1985); defence expenditure: 11·1% of total government expenditure in 1983–4.

Laos

Official name: Saathiaranagrŏat Prachhathippatay Prachhachhon Lao (Lao People's Democratic Republic).
Population: 3 584 803 (1985 census).
Area: 91 400 miles² *236 800 km²*.
Languages: Lao (official), French.
Religions: Buddhist, tribal.
Capital city: Viengchane (Vientiane), population 210 000 (1981 estimate).
Other principal towns (1973): Savannakhet 50 690; Pakse 44 860; Luang Prabang 44 244.
Highest point: Phou Bia, 9252 ft *2820 m*.
Principal mountain range: Annamitic Range.
Principal river: Mekong (2600 miles *4184 km*).
Head of State: Souphanouvong (b. 1902), President.
Prime Minister: Kaysone Phomvihane (b. 13 Dec. 1920), also General Secretary of the Lao People's Revolutionary Party.
Climate: Tropical (warm and humid). Rainy monsoon season May–October. In Vientiane, average maximum 28°C *83°F* (December, January) to 34°C *93°F* (April), minimum 14°C *57°F* (January) to 24°C *75°F* (June to September), July and August rainiest (each 18 days). Maximum recorded temperature 44,8°C *112·6°F*, Luang Prabang, April 1960; minimum 0,8°C *33·4°F*, Luang Prabang, January 1924.
Labour force: 2 002 000 in 1984: Agriculture, forestry and fishing 71·5%.
Gross domestic product: $300 million in 1975 (UN estimate).
Exports: US$48 million in 1981.
Monetary unit: New kip. 1 kip = 100 at.
Denominations:
 Notes 1, 5, 10, 20 kips.
Exchange rate to £ sterling: 53·69 (26 Jan. 1987).
Political history and government: Formerly the three principalities of Luang Prabang, Vientiane and Champassac. Became a French protectorate in 1893. The three principalities were merged in 1946 and an hereditary constitutional monarchy, under the Luang Prabang dynasty, was established on 11 May 1947. The Kingdom of Laos became independent, within the French Union, on 19 July 1949. Full sovereignty was recognized by France on 23 Oct. 1953. After nearly 20 years of almost continuous civil war between the Royal Government and the *Neo Lao Hak Sat* (Lao Patriotic Front or LPF), a Communist-led insurgent movement whose armed forces were known as the *Pathet Lao*, a peace agreement was signed on 21 Feb. 1973. A joint administration was established on 5 Apr. 1974 but the LPF became increasingly dominant. The National Assembly was dissolved on 13 Apr. 1975. The King abdicated on 29 Nov. 1975 and on 1 Dec. 1975 a National Congress of People's Representatives (264 delegates elected by local authorities) proclaimed the Lao People's Democratic Republic, with Prince Souphanouvong, Chairman of the LPF, as President. The Congress installed a Council of Ministers, led by a Prime Minister, and appointed a Supreme People's Council (SPC) of 45 members, chaired by the President, to draft a new constitution. The SPC held its first plenary session on 12–17 June 1976.

Political power is held by the Lao People's Revolutionary Party (LPRP), formerly called the People's Party of Laos. The Communist LPRP has a Central Committee with 14 full and 6 alternate members, headed by a seven-member Political Bureau.
Length of roadways: 8069 miles *12 983 km*.
Universities: 1.
Adult illiteracy: 15% (1981).
Expectation of life: Males 39·1 years; females 41·8 years (UN estimates for 1970–75).
Defence: Military service: 18 months; total armed forces 53 700 (1985), plus about 50 000 Vietnamese troops; defence expenditure: 12% of total government expenditure in 1981.

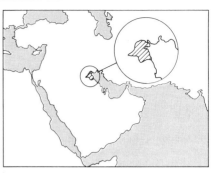

KUWAIT

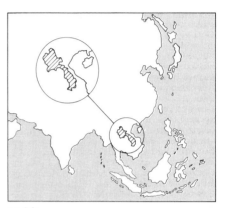

LAOS

Lebanon

Official name: Al-Jumhuriya al-Lubnaniya (the Lebanese Republic), abbreviated to al-Lubnan.
Population: 2 644 000 (1984 estimate).
Area: 3950 miles² *10 400 km²*.
Languages: Arabic (official), French, Armenian, English.
Religions: Christian (Roman Catholic, Orthodox), Muslim.
Capital city: Beirut, population 702 000 (1980 estimate).
Other principal towns (1980): Tripoli 175 000; Zahlé 46 800; Saida (Sidon) 24 740; Tyre 14 000.
Highest point: Qurnat as-Sawdā, 10 131 ft *3088 m*.
Principal mountain ranges: Lebanon, Jabal ash-Sharqī (Anti-Lebanon).
Principal river: Nahr al-Litāni (Leontes).
Head of State: Shaikh Amin Gemayel, President.
Prime Minister: Rashid Karami.
Climate: Coastal lowlands are hot and humid in summer, mild (cool and damp) in winter. Mountains cool in summer, heavy snowfall in winter. In Beirut, average maximum 16°C *62°F* (January) to 32°C *89°F* (August), minimum 10°C *51°F* (January, February) to 23°C *74°F* (August), January rainiest (15 days).
Labour force: 815 000 in 1983.
Gross domestic product: £L6365 million in 1972: Mining, quarrying and manufacturing 13·9%; Trade, restaurants and hotels 31·5%; Community, social and personal services 18·1%.
Exports: L£2694·2 in 1983: Vegetable products 27·3%; Precious metals and jewellery 11%; Machinery and electrical apparatus 8%; Non-precious metals and products 8·4%; Textiles and products 7·1%.
Monetary unit: Lebanese pound (£L). 1 pound = 100 piastres.
Denominations:
 Coins 1, 2½, 5, 10, 25, 50 piastres; 1 pound.
 Notes 1, 5, 10, 25, 50, 100, 250 pounds.
Exchange rate to £ sterling: 129·964 (26 Jan. 1987).
Political history and government: Formerly part of Turkey's Ottoman Empire. Turkish forces were expelled in 1918 by British and French troops, with Arab help. Administered by France under League of Nations mandate from 1 Sept. 1920. Independence declared on 26 Nov. 1941.

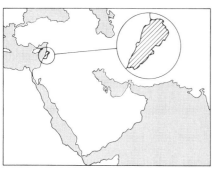

LEBANON

A republic was established in 1943 and French powers transferred on 1 Jan. 1944. All foreign troops left by December 1946.

Legislative power was vested in the unicameral Chamber of Deputies, with 99 members elected by universal adult suffrage for 4 years (subject to dissolution), using proportional representation. Seats are allocated on a religious basis (53 Christian, 45 Muslim). Elections to the Chamber due in April 1976 were postponed because of civil disorder. On 15 Mar. 1979 the Chamber renamed itself the National Assembly. On 15 Mar. 1980 the term of the Assembly was extended, for a third time, until the end of 1981. Executive power is vested in the President, elected for 6 years by the Assembly. He appoints a Prime Minister and other Ministers to form a Cabinet, responsible to the Assembly. By convention, the President is a Maronite Christian, the Prime Minister a Sunni Muslim, and the Speaker of Parliament a Shiite Muslim.

In the late 1970s and 1980s Lebanon has been torn apart by constant feuding between various militias, with the government holding little if any control over the country. The Israelis effectively control south Lebanon and the Syrians east Lebanon; the Palestinians also constitute an important influence on events.

Length of roadways: 4598 miles *7400 km* (1971).
Length of railways: 138 miles *222 km*.
Universities: 5.
Adult illiteracy: Males 21·5%; females 42·1% in 1970.
Defence: Armed forces: 17 400 (1985), plus private militias, 30 000 Syrian troops, the Israeli-backed south Lebanese Army, Palestinian guerillas and UN forces (5660 in 1985).

Lesotho

Official name: The Kingdom of Lesotho.
Population: 1 700 000 (1983 estimate).
Area: 11 720 miles² *30 355 km²*.
Languages: Sesotho, English.
Religion: Christian 73·4% (1966).
Capital city: Maseru, population 45 000 (1976 census).
Other principal towns: Mafeteng, Leribe, Mohale's Hoek.
Highest point: Thabana Ntlenyana (Thadentsonyane), 11 425 ft *3482 m*.
Principal mountain range: Drakensberg.
Principal rivers: Orange, Caledon (on northern frontier).
Head of State: King Motlotlehi Moshoeshoe II (b. 2 May 1938).
Head of government: Maj.-Gen. Justin Lekhanya, Chairman of the Military Council.
Climate: In lowlands, maximum temperature in summer 32°C *90°F*, winter minimum −6°C *20°F*. Range wider in highlands. Average annual rainfall 29 in *736 mm*. Rainy season October–April.
Labour force: 757 000 in 1984: Agriculture, forestry and fishing 80·6%. In 1981 23% of the total labour force worked in South Africa.
Gross domestic product: 95·0 million maloti in year ending 31 Mar. 1975: Agriculture, forestry and fishing 47·5%; Trade, restaurants and hotels 17·4% (trade 14·3%); Owner-occupied dwellings 11·3%.

Exports: 37·9 million maloti in 1979: Wool 8·9%; Mohair 11·4%; Diamonds 56%.
Monetary unit: Loti (plural: maloti). 1 loti = 100 lisente.
Denominations:
Coins 1, 2, 5, 10, 25, 50 lisente; 1 loti.
Notes 2, 5, 10 maloti.
Exchange rate to £ sterling: 3·159 (26 Jan. 1987).
Political history and government: An hereditary monarchy, formerly the British colony of Basutoland. Granted internal self-government, with the Paramount Chief as King, on 30 April 1965. Became independent (under present name), within the Commonwealth, on 4 Oct. 1966. Under the constitution, legislative power was vested in a bicameral Parliament, comprising a Senate of 33 members (22 Chiefs and 11 Senators nominated by the King for 5-year terms) and a National Assembly of 60 members elected by universal adult suffrage for 5 years (subject to dissolution). Executive power is exercised by the Cabinet, led by the Prime Minister, which is responsible to Parliament. The Assembly elections of 27 Jan. 1970 were annulled three days later by the Prime Minister, who declared a state of emergency and suspended the constitution. The Cabinet assumed full power. No more elections have been held but an interim National Assembly of 93 members (the former Senate and 60 nominated members) was inaugurated on 27 Apr. 1973. Elections were to have been held in 1985, but no opposition candidates offered themselves. In January 1986 the government was overthrown by the military. Lesotho comprises 9 administrative districts, each under an appointed District Administrator.
Length of roadways: 1742 miles *2803 km*.
Length of railways: 1 mile *1½ km*.
Universities: 1.
Adult illiteracy: 50% in 1979.
Expectation of life: Males 45·7 years; females 49 years (1975–80).
Defence: There is a paramilitary force, numbering 1500 in 1982; defence expenditure: 29·8 million maloti in 1985–6.
Foreign tourists: 35 000 in 1982.

Liberia

Official name: The Republic of Liberia.
Population: 2 109 000 (1984 estimate).
Area: 43 000 miles² *111 369 km²*.
Languages: English (official), tribal languages.
Religions: Christian; Muslim and Animist minorities.
Capital city: Monrovia, population 425 000 (1984 estimate).
Other principal towns: Harbel, Buchanan, Greenville (Sinoe), Harper (Cape Palmas).
Highest point: On Mt Nimba, 4500 ft *1372 m*.
Principal mountain range: Guinea Highlands.
Principal rivers: St Paul, St John, Cess.

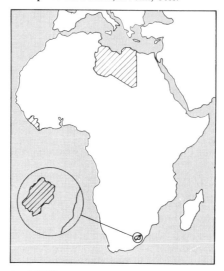

top: **LIBYA**
left: **LIBERIA**
encircled: **LESOTHO**

Head of State: Master Sgt Samuel Kanyon Doe (b. 6 May 1952), Chairman of the People's Redemption Council.
Climate: Tropical (hot and humid), with temperatures from 13°C *55°F* to 49°C *120°F*. Rainy season April to October. In Monrovia, average maximum 27°C *80°F* (July, August) to 30°C *87°F* (March, April), minimum 22°C *72°F* to 23°C *74°F* all year round, June and September rainiest (each 26 days).
Labour force: 548 615 in 1980: Agriculture, forestry and fishing 71·6%; Mining 5·1%; Trade 3·8%; Services 10%.
Gross domestic product: L$699·7 million in 1977: Agriculture, forestry and fishing 16·0%; Mining and quarrying 22·6%; Trade, restaurants and hotels 10·9%; Community, social and personal services (incl. all government services) 16·6%.
Exports: US$427·6 million in 1983: Iron ore and concentrates 62·5%; Rubber 17·1%; Timber 5·5%; Coffee 4·3%.
Monetary unit: Liberian dollar (L$). 1 dollar = 100 cents.
Denominations:
Coins 1, 2, 5, 10, 25, 50 cents; 1, 5 Liberian dollar.
Notes 1, 5, 10, 20 US dollars (There are no Liberian banknotes).
Exchange rate to £ sterling: 1·528 (26 Jan. 1987).
Political history and government: Settled in 1822 by freed slaves from the USA. Became independent on 26 July 1847. The constitution was modelled on that of the USA. Legislative power was vested in a bicameral Congress, comprising a Senate and a House of Representatives, both chambers elected by universal adult suffrage. Executive power was vested in the President, also directly elected. On 26 Apr. 1979, following anti-government riots, legislature granted the President emergency powers for one year. Leaders of an opposition party were arrested on 9 Mar. 1980 and charged with attempting to overthrow the government. They were due to face trial on 14 Apr. but on 12 Apr. the President was deposed and killed in a military *coup*. Power was assumed by a People's Redemption Council (PRC), which released the former President's opponents. On 25 Apr. 1980 the PRC suspended the constitution and imposed martial law. Following the adoption of a new constitution, elections were held in 1985.
Length of roadways: 6268 miles *10 085 km* (1981).
Length of railways: 304 miles *490 km*.
Universities: 2.
Adult illiteracy: 91·1% (males 86·1%; females 95·8%) illiterate in English in 1962.
Expectation of life: Males 45·8 years; females 44·0 years (1971).
Defence: Total armed forces 6995 (1986); defence expenditure: 9·9% of total government expenditure in 1981.
Foreign tourists: 6000 in 1976.

Libya

Official name: Daulat Libiya al-'Arabiya al-Ishtrakiya al-Jumhuriya (Socialist People's Libyan Arab Jamahiriya – 'state of the masses').
Population: 3 637 488 (1984 census).
Area: 679 363 miles² *1 759 540 km²*.
Language: Arabic.
Religion: Muslim.
Capital city: Tripoli (Tarābulus), population 980 000.
Other principal towns (1973): Benghazi 219 317; Misrātah (Misurata) 42 815; Az Zawiyah (Zawia) 39 382; Al Baida 31 796; Ajdabiyah (Agedabia) 31 047; Derna 30 241; Sabhah (Sebha) 28 714; Tubruq (Tobruk) 28 061.
Highest point: Pico Bette, 7500 ft *2286 m*.
Principal mountain ranges: Jabal as-Sawdā, Al Kufrah, Al Harūj al-Aswad, Jabal Nafūsah, Hamada de Tinrhert.
Principal river: Wādi al-Fārigh.
Head of State: Col Mu'ammar Muhammad Abdulsalam Abu Miniar al-Qadhafi (b. Sept. 1942), Revolutionary Leader.
Head of Government: Muhammad az-Zarruq Rajab, Secretary-General of the General People's Congress.

Climate: Very hot and dry, with average temperatures between 13°C *55°F* and 38°C *100°F*. Coast cooler than inland. In Tripoli, August hottest (22°C *72°F* to 30°C *86°F*), January coolest (8°C *47°F* to 16°C *61°F*). Absolute maximum temperature 57,3°C *135·1°F*, Al 'Aziziyah (El Azizia), 24 Aug. 1923; absolute minimum −9°C *+15·8°F*, Hon, 10 Jan. 1938.

Labour force: 773 200 (excl. armed forces and unemployed) in 1978: Agriculture, forestry and fishing 20·8%; Construction 23·1%; Community, social and personal services 26·9%.

Gross domestic product: 5911·5 million dinars in 1978: Mining and quarrying 56·1%; Construction 11·3%; Government services 11·1%.

Exports: 4611·2 million Libyan dinar in 1981: Crude petroleum 99·6%.

Monetary unit: Libyan dinar. 1 dinar = 1000 dirhams.

Denominations:
Coins 1, 5, 10, 20, 50, 100 dirhams.
Notes 250, 500 dirhams; 1, 5, 10 dinars.

Exchange rate to £ sterling: 0·4683 (26 Jan. 1987).

Political history and Government: Formerly part of Turkey's Ottoman Empire. Became an Italian colony in September 1911. Italian forces were expelled in 1942–43 and the country was under British and French administration from 1943 until becoming an independent kingdom, under the Amir of Cyrenaica, on 24 Dec. 1951. The monarchy was overthrown by an army *coup* on 1 Sept. 1969, when a Revolutionary Command Council (RCC) took power and proclaimed the Libyan Arab Republic. The bicameral Parliament was abolished and political activity suspended. On 8 Sept. 1969 the RCC elected Col Mu'ammar al-Qadhafi as its Chairman. A provisional constitution, proclaimed in December 1969, vested supreme authority in the RCC, which appointed a Council of Ministers. On 11 June 1971 the Arab Socialist Union (ASU) was established as the sole political party. Under a decree of 13 Nov. 1975 provision was made for the creation of a 618-member General National Congress of the ASU. This later became the General People's Congress (GPC), comprising members of the RCC, leaders of existing 'people's congresses' and 'popular committees', and trade unions and professional organizations. The Congress held its first session on 5–18 Jan. 1976. On 2 Mar. 1977 the GPC approved a new constitution, which adopted the country's present name. Under the constitution, the RCC and Council of Ministers were abolished and power passed to the GPC, assisted by a General Secretariat. The Council of Ministers was replaced by a General People's Committee. The first Secretary-General of the GPC was Col Qadhafi. At a GPC meeting on 1–2 Mar. 1979 he relinquished this post, although remaining Supreme Commander of the Armed Forces. Libya is divided into 10 governorates.

Length of roadways: *c.* 3232 miles *c. 5200 km.*

Universities: 2.

Adult illiteracy: 49·9% (males 33·1%; females 69·9%) in 1973 (population aged 10 and over).

Expectation of life: Males 51·4 years; females 54·5 years (UN estimates for 1970–75).

Defence: Military service: conscription; total armed forces 73 000 (1985); defence expenditure: 210 million Libyan dinar in 1982.

Foreign tourists: 126 000 in 1980.

Liechtenstein

Official name: Fürstentum Liechtenstein (Principality of Liechtenstein).

Population: 25 215 (census of 1980); 27 076 (1985 estimate).

Area: 61·8 miles² *160·0 km².*

Language: German.

Religions: Roman Catholic; Protestant minority.

Capital city: Vaduz, population 4927 in 1985 (estimate).

Other principal towns (1985): Schaan 4697; Balzers 3460; Triesen 3043; Eschen 2785; Mauren 2703; Triesenberg 2241.

Highest point: Grauspitze, 8526 ft *2599 m.*

Principal mountain range: Alps.

Principal rivers: Rhein (Rhine) (820 miles *1319 km*, 17 miles *27 km* in Liechtenstein), Samina.

Head of State: Prince Franz Josef II (b. 16 Aug. 1906).

Head of Government: Hans Brunhart (b. 28 Mar. 1945).

Climate: Alpine, with mild winters. Temperature extremes for Sargans, in Switzerland, a few miles from the Liechtenstein border: absolute maximum 38,0°C *100·4°F*, 29 July 1947; absolute minimum −25,6°C *−14·1°F*, 12 Feb. 1929.

Labour force: 12 851 (excl. unemployed) in 1985: Industry, commerce and construction 44·1%; Other services 53·1%.

Exports: 1188 million Swiss francs in 1985.

Monetary unit: Swiss currency (*q.v.*).

Political history and government: An hereditary principality, independent since 1866. Present constitution adopted on 5 Oct. 1921. Legislative power is exercised jointly by the Sovereign and the unicameral Diet (*Landtag*), with 15 members elected (by men only) for 4 years, using proportional representation. A 5-man Government (*Regierung*) is elected by the Diet for its duration and confirmed by the Sovereign.

Length of railways: 11·5 miles *18·5 km.*

Foreign tourists: 85 851 in 1985.

Luxemburg

Official name: Grand-Duché de Luxembourg (French), Grouscherzogdem Lezebuurg (Luxembourgois) or Grossherzogtum Luxemburg (German): Grand Duchy of Luxemburg.

Population: 364 600 (1981 census); 365 900 (1984 estimate).

Area: 999 miles² *2586 km².*

Languages: Letzeburgesch (Luxembourgois), French, German.

Religion: Roman Catholic.

Capital city: Luxemburg-Ville, population 78 900 (1981 census).

Other principal towns (1981): Esch-sur-Alzette 25 500; Differdange 17 100; Dudelange 14 100; Petange 12 300.

Highest point: Bourgplatz, 1833 ft *559 m.*

Principal mountain range: Ardennes.

Principal rivers: Mosel (Moselle), Sûre (107 miles *172 km*, 99 miles *159 km* in Luxembourg), Our, Alzette.

Head of State: HRH Prince Jean Benoît Guillaume Marie Robert Louis Antoine Adolphe Marc d'Aviano (b. 5 Jan. 1921), Grand Duke.

Head of Government: Jacques Santer (b. 18 May 1937), President of the Government (Prime Minister).

Climate: Temperate (cool summers and mild winters). Absolute maximum temperature 37,0°C *98·6°F*, Luxembourg-Ville, 28 July 1895, and Grevenmacher, 6 July 1957; absolute minimum −24,3°C *−11·7°F*, Wiltz, 5 Feb. 1917.

Labour force: 158 100 in 1984: Agriculture, forestry and fishing 4·8%; Mining and manufacturing 25·7%; Construction 9·9%; Trade 33·3%; Community, social and personal services 12·8%.

Gross domestic product: 181 400 million francs in 1982: Mining and manufacturing 26·5% (manufacturing 26·4%); Trade, services, hotels and restaurants 29·8% (distributive trades, hotels and catering 16%, services, construction and transport 13·8%); Banking, finance and insurance 12%; Government services 12·3%; Other services 16%; Agriculture and forestry 3·4%.

Exports: 111 421 million Luxemburg francs in 1983: Iron and steel 43·9%; Plastic and rubber manufactures 14·2%; Textile products 6·4%; Animals and animal products 2·8%.

Monetary unit: Luxembourg franc. 1 franc = 100 centimes.

Denominations:
Coins 25 centimes; 1, 5, 10, 20 Luxembourg francs.
Notes 50, 100 Luxembourg francs; 50, 100, 500, 1000, 5000 Belgian francs.

Exchange rate to £ sterling: 57·75 (26 Jan. 1987).

Political history and government: An hereditary grand duchy, independent since 1867. Luxemburg is a constitutional monarchy. Legislative

LIECHTENSTEIN

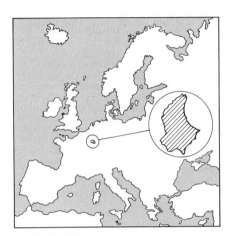

LUXEMBURG

power is exercised by the unicameral Chamber of Deputies, with 64 members elected by universal adult suffrage for 5 years (subject to dissolution) on the basis of proportional representation. Some legislative functions are also entrusted to the advisory Council of State, with 21 members appointed for life by the Grand Duke, but the Council can be overriden by the Chamber. Executive power is vested in the Grand Duke but is normally exercised by the Council of Ministers, led by the President of the Government. The Grand Duke appoints Ministers but they are responsible to the Chamber. Luxemburg is divided into 12 cantons.

Length of roadways: 3205 miles *5157 km.*

Length of railways: 170 miles *274 km.*

Universities: 1.

Expectation of life: Males 66·9 years; females 73·4 years (1982).

Defence: Military service voluntary; total armed forces 720 (1985); defence expenditure: 2·8% of total government expenditure in 1984.

Foreign tourists: 420 674 in 1984.

Madagascar

Official name: Repoblika Demokratika n'i Madagaskar (in Malagasy) or République démocratique de Madagascar (in French): Democratic Republic of Madagascar.

Population: 10 294 000 (1986 estimate).

Area: 226 658 miles² *587 041 km².*

Languages: Malagasy, French (both official).

Religions: Animist, Christian, Muslim.

Capital city: Antananarivo (Tananarive), population 662 585 (1985 estimate).

Other principal towns (1982): Toamasina 82 907; Mahajanga 80 881; Fianarantsoa 72 901; Antseranana 49 000; Toliary 48 929.

Highest point: Maromokotro, 9436 ft *2876 m.*

Principal mountain ranges: Massif du Tsaratanan, Ankaratra.

Principal rivers: Ikopa, Mania, Mangoky.

Head of State: Lt-Cdr Didier Ratsiraka (b. 4 Nov. 1936), President.

Prime Minister: Lt-Col Désiré Rakotoarijaona (b. 19 June 1934).

Climate: Hot on coast (average daily maximum 32°C *90°F*), but cooler inland. Fairly dry in south, but monsoon rains (December to April) in north. In Antananarivo, average maximum 20°C *68°F* (July) to 27°C *81°F* (November), minimum 8°C *48°F* (July, August) to 16°C *61°F* (January, February), January rainiest (21 days). Absolute maximum temperature 44·4°C *111·9°F*, Behara, 20 Nov. 1940; absolute minimum −6·3°C *+20·7°F*, Antsirabé, 18 June 1945.

Labour force: 4629000 in 1984: Agriculture, forestry and fishing 80·1%.

Gross domestic product: 372853 million Malagasy francs in 1974: Agriculture, forestry and fishing 42·8%; Manufacturing 12·2%; Trade 11·2%; Government services 11·6%.

Exports: 192267 million Malagasy francs in 1984: Coffee 40·6%; Vanilla 15·8%; Sugar 2·9%; Cloves and clove oil 12·5%.

Monetary unit: Franc malgache (Malagasy franc). 1 franc = 100 centimes.

Denominations:
Coins 1, 2, 5, 10, 50, 100 francs.
Notes 50, 100, 500, 1000, 5000 francs.

Exchange rate to £ sterling: 1024 (26 Jan. 1987).

Political history and government: Formerly a French colony, Madagascar became the Malagasy Republic on achieving self-government, within the French community, on 14 Oct. 1958. It became fully independent, on 26 June 1960. Following disturbances, the President handed over full powers to the army commander on 18 May 1972, when Parliament was dissolved. A National Military Directorate was formed on 12 Feb. 1975 and suspended all political parties. On 15 June 1975 the Directorate elected Lt-Cdr Didier Ratsiraka to be Head of State, as President of the Supreme Revolutionary Council (SRC). A referendum on 21 Dec. 1975 approved a draft constitution and the appointment of Ratsiraka as Head of State for 7 years. The Democratic Republic of Madagascar was proclaimed on 30 Dec. 1975 and Ratsiraka took office as President of the Republic on 4 Jan. 1976.

Executive power is vested in the President, who rules with the assistance of the SRC and an appointed Council of Ministers. Legislative power is vested in the National People's Assembly, with 137 members elected by universal adult suffrage for 5 years. The Assembly was first elected on 30 June 1977, with a single list of candidates presented by the *Front national pour la défense de la révolution malgache*, a pro-government alliance of political parties. The country is divided into 6 provinces.

Length of roadways: 10752 miles *17300 km*.
Length of railways: 549 miles *884 km*.
Universities: 1.
Adult illiteracy: 66·5% (males 59·2%; females 73·0%) illiterate in Malagasy in 1953 (indigenous population aged 14 and over).
Expectation of life: Males 41·9 years; females 45·1 years (UN estimates for 1970–75).
Defence: Military service 18 months; total armed forces 21100 (1985); defence expenditure: US$52·6 million in 1985.
Foreign tourists: 12000 in 1982.

Malawi

Official name: The Republic of Malaŵi.
Population: 5547460 (census of 20 Sept. 1977); 6839000 (1984 estimate).
Area: 45747 miles² *118484 km²*.
Languages: English (official), Chichewa.
Religions: Mainly traditional beliefs; Christians form 33% of population; Moslem minority.
Capital city: Lilongwe, population 158500 (1983 estimate).
Other principal towns (1983 estimate): Blantyre 313600; Zomba 46000; Mzuzu 59500.
Highest point: Mount Sapitwa, 9843 ft *3000 m*.
Principal river: Shire.
Head of State: Dr Hastings Kamuzu Banda (b.

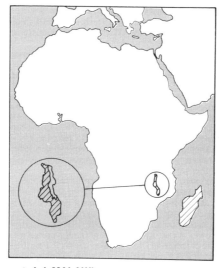

encircled: **MALAWI**
right: **MADAGASCAR**

14 May 1906), President.

Climate: In the low-lying Shire valley temperatures can rise to 46°C *115°F* in October and November, but above 3000 ft *910 m* the climate is much more temperate and at the greatest heights the nights can be frosty. Dry season May to September, very wet season late December to March. Annual rainfall in the highlands is about 1270 mm *50 in* and in the lowlands 900 mm *35 in*.

Labour force: 2967000 in 1984: Agriculture, forestry and fishing 81%.

Gross domestic product: 827·6 million kwacha in 1984 at 1978 prices: Agriculture, forestry and fishing 37·3%; Manufacturing 12·3%; Construction 3·9%; Trade 13·4%; Transport and communications 6%; Financial services 6·4%; Government services 12·8%.

Exports: 430·2 million kwacha in 1984: Tobacco 52·2%; Tea 26·4%; Sugar 6·7%; Beans and peas 1·4%.

Monetary unit: Malawi kwacha. 1 kwacha = 100 tambala.

Denominations:
Coins 1, 2, 5, 10, 20 tambala.
Notes 50 tambala; 1, 5, 10 kwacha.

Exchange rate to £ sterling: 2·828 (26 Jan. 1987).

Political history and government: Formerly the British protectorate of Nyasaland. Granted internal self-government on 1 Feb. 1963 and became independent, within the Commonwealth, on 6 July 1964, taking the name Malawi. Became a republic, and a one-party state, on 6 July 1966, when Dr Hastings Banda (Prime Minister since 1963) became President. Under a constitutional amendment of Nov. 1970, he became President for life on 6 July 1971. Legislative power is held by the unicameral National Assembly, with 87 members elected by universal adult suffrage for 5 years (subject to dissolution) and up to 15 additional members nominated by the President. All members must belong to the ruling Malawi Congress Party. All candidates were returned unopposed in 1964, 1971 and 1976 but on 29 June 1978 voting took place (for 47 seats) for the first time since 1961. There was a similar election in 1983.

Executive power is vested in the President, who rules with the assistance of an appointed Cabinet. Malawi has three administrative regions, each the responsibility of a Cabinet Minister.

Length of roadways: 7173 miles *11542 km*.
Length of railways: 500 miles *800 km*.
Universities: 1 (with five constituent colleges).
Adult illiteracy: 75% (males 60%; females 80%) in 1982.
Expectation of Life: Males 46 years; females 50 years (Africans only, 1982).
Defence: Total armed forces 5250 (1985); defence expenditure: 6·7% of total government expenditure in 1984–5.
Foreign tourists: 37856 in 1983.

Malaysia

Official name: Persekutuan Tanah Melaysiu (Federation of Malaysia).
Population: 15677000 (1985 estimate).
Area: 127581 miles² *330433 km²*.
Languages: Malay (official), Chinese, Tamil, Iban, English.
Religions (1970): Muslim 50·0%; Buddhist 25·7%; Hindu; Christian.
Capital city: Kuala Lumpur, population 937875 (1980 census).
Other principal towns (1980): Ipoh 300727; Georgetown 250578; Johore Bharu 249880; Kuala Trengganu 186608; Kota Bharu 170559; Kuantan 136625; Seremban 136252; Kuching 120000.
Highest point: Mount Kinabalu, 13455 ft *4101 m*, in Sabah.
Principal mountain range: Trengganu Highlands.
Principal rivers: Pahang, Kelantan.
Head of State: HM Sultan Mahmood Iskandar ibni Al-Marhum Sultan Ismail DK, SPMJ, SPDK, DK (Brunei) SSIJ, PIS, BSI, *Yang di-Pertuan Agong* (Supreme Head of State).
Prime Minister: Dato Seri Dr Mahathir bin Mohamad (b. 20 Dec. 1925).
Climate: Peninsular Malaysia is hot and humid, with daytime temperatures around 29°C *85°F* and little variation throughout the year. The average daily range on the coast is 22°C *72°F* to 33°C *92°F*. Rainfall is regular and often heavy. Maximum recorded temperature 39,4°C *103·0°F*, Pulau Langkawi, 27 Mar. 1931; minimum 2,2°C *36·0°F*, Cameron Highlands, 6 Jan. 1937.

Sabah is generally fairly humid but relatively cool. In Kota Kinabalu, average temperatures are 23°C *74°F* to 31°C *87°F*, average annual rainfall 2640 mm *104 in*. The north-east monsoon is from mid-October to March or April, the south-west monsoon from May to August.

Sarawak is humid, with temperatures generally 22°C *72°F* to 31°C *88°F*, sometimes reaching 36°C *96°F*. It has heavy rainfall (annual average 3050 mm *120 in* to 4060 mm *160 in*), especially in the north-east monsoon season (October to March).

Labour force: 5503700 in 1985: Agriculture, forestry and fishing 35·2%; Manufacturing 15·7%; Construction 6·6%; Transport, storage and communications 4·9%; Government services 14·9%.

Gross domestic product: 60729 million ringgit in 1985 at constant 1978 prices: Agriculture, forestry and fishing 19·5%; Mining 9·8%; Manufacturing 20·5%; Construction 5·2%; Transport, storage and communications 6·3%; Trade 12·6%; Financial services 8·6%; Government services 12%.

Exports: 36653·8 million ringgit in 1984: Food and live animals 4·1%; Timber 10·8%; Rubber 10%; Petroleum 23·8%; Palm oil 12·4%; Tin 3·2%; Machinery and transport equipment 20%; Miscellaneous manufactures 3·2%.

Monetary unit: Ringgit (Malaysian dollar). 1 ringgit = 100 sen.

Denominations:
Coins 1, 5, 10, 20, 50 sen; 1, 5, 10, 15, 25, 100, 200, 250, 500 ringgit.
Notes 1, 5, 10, 50, 100, 1000 ringgit.

Exchange rate to £ sterling: 3·9225 (26 Jan. 1987).

Political history and government: Peninsular (West) Malaysia comprises 11 states (nine with hereditary rulers, two with Governors) formerly under British protection. They were united as the Malayan Union on 1 Apr. 1946 and became the Federation of Malaya on 1 Feb. 1948. The Federation became independent, within the Commonwealth, on 31 Aug. 1957. On 16 Sept. 1963 the Federation (renamed the States of Malaya) was merged with Singapore (*q.v.*), Sarawak (a British colony) and Sabah (formerly the colony of British North Borneo) to form the independent Federation of Malaysia, still in the Commonwealth. On 9 Aug. 1965 Singapore seceded from the Federation. On 5 Aug. 1966 the States of Malaya were renamed West Malaysis, now known as Peninsular Malaysia.

Malaysia is an elective monarchy. The nine state rulers of Peninsula Malaysia choose from their number a Supreme Head of State and a Deputy, to hold office for 5 years. Executive power is vested in the Head of State but is normally exercised on the advice of the Cabinet. Legislative power is held by the bicameral Parliament. The Senate (*Dewan Negara*), with limited powers, has 58 members, including 32 appointed by the Head of State and 26 (two from each state) elected by State Legislative Assemblies for 6 years. The House of Representatives (*Dewan Rakyat*) has 154 members (114 from Peninsular Malaysia, 16 from Sabah and 24 from Sarawak) elected by universal adult suffrage for 5 years (subject to dissolution). The Head of State appoints the Prime Minister and, on the latter's recommendation, other Ministers. The cabinet is responsible to Parliament.

Malaysia comprises 13 states and, since 1 Feb. 1974, the Federal Territory of Kuala Lumpur. Each state has a unicameral Legislative Assembly, elected by universal adult suffrage.
Length of roadways: 17 979 miles *28 928 km* (Peninsular Malaysia).
Length of railways: 1377 miles *2215 km* (Peninsular Malaysia).
Universities: 7.
Adult illiteracy: 42·0% (males 30·9%; females 53·2%) in 1970 (population aged 10 and over): Peninsular Malaysia 39·2%; Sabah 55·7%; Sarawak 61·7%.
Expectation of life: Males 68·2 years; females 72·9 years (1983).
Defence: Military service voluntary; total armed forces 110 000 (1985); defence expenditure: 10·9% of total government expenditure in 1986.
Foreign tourists: 2 900 000 in 1984.

Maldives

Official name: Dhivehi Jumhuriya (Republic of Maldives).
Population: 180 453 (1985 census).
Area: 115 miles² *298 km²*.
Language: Dhivehi (Maldivian).
Religion: Muslim.
Capital city: Malé, population 36 593 (1983 estimate).
Head of State: Maumoon Abdul Gayoom (b. 29 Dec. 1937), President.
Climate: Very warm and humid. Average temperature 27°C *80°F*, with little daily variation. Annual rainfall 2540–3800 mm *100–150 in*.
Labour force: 67 384 (Dec. 1977).
Gross domestic product: $10 million in 1975 (UN estimate).
Exports: US$ 8 649 000 in 1981: Fish and fish products 81·6%; Fabricated mica 2·4%.
Monetary unit: Rufiyaa (Maldivian rupee). 1 rufiyaa = 100 laaris (larees).
Denominations:
Notes 1, 2, 5, 10, 50, 100 rufiyaa.
Exchange rate to £ sterling: 10·696 (26 Jan. 1987).
Political history and government: Formerly an elective sultanate, called the Maldive Islands. Under British protection, with internal self-government, from December 1887 until achieving full independence, outside the Commonwealth, on 26 July 1965. Following a referendum in March 1968, the islands became a republic on 11 Nov. 1968, with Ibrahim Nasir (Prime Minister since 1954) as President. Name changed to Maldives in April 1969. Legislative power is held by the unicameral Citizens' Council (*Majilis*), with 48 members, including eight appointed by the President and 40 (two from each of 20 districts) elected for five years by universal adult suffrage. Executive power is vested in the President, also directly elected for five years. He rules with the assistance of an appointed Cabinet, responsible to the *Majilis*. Near the end of his second term, President Nasir announced his wish to retire. The *Majilis* chose a single candidate who was approved by referendum on 28 July 1978 and sworn in on 11 Nov. 1978. There are no political parties. The country has 20 administrative districts: the capital is centrally administered while each of the 19 atoll

groups is governed by an appointed atoll chief (*verin*) who is appointed by the President and advised by an elected committee.
Foreign tourists: 83 814 in 1984.

Mali

Official name: La République du Mali (the Republic of Mali).
Population: 7 719 000 (1984 estimate).
Area: 478 767 miles² *1 240 000 km²*.
Languages: French (official language); Bambara 60%; Fulani.
Religions: Sunni Muslim 65%; traditional beliefs 30%.
Capital city: Bamako, population 404 022 (including suburbs) at 1976 census.
Other principal towns (1976): Ségou 65 000; Mopti 54 000; Sikasso 47 000; Kayes 45 000.
Highest point: Hombori Tondo, 3789 ft *1155 m*.
Principal mountain ranges: Mandingué Plateau, Adrar des Iforas.
Principal rivers: Sénégal, Niger, Falémé.
Head of State: Gen. Moussa Traoré (b. 25 Sept. 1936), President; also President of the Government (Prime Minister).
Climate: Hot. Very dry in the north, wetter in the south (rainy season June to Oct.). Average temperatures in the south 24°C *75°F* to 32°C *90°F*, higher in the Sahara. In Bamako, average maximum 30°C *87°F* (August) to 39°C *103°F* (April), minimum 16°C *61°F* to 24°C *76°F*. In Timbuktu, average maximum 30°C *87°F* (August) to 43°C *110°F* (May), minimum 13°C *55°F* (Jan.) to 26°C *80°F* (June), July and August rainiest (each 9 days).
Labour force: 4 127 000 in 1984: Agriculture, forestry and fishing 84·9%.
Gross domestic product: 127 100 million Mali francs in 1983: Cotton 40·8%; Groundnuts 1%.
Exports: 83 830 million Mali francs in 1981.
Monetary unit: Franc de la Communauté financière africaine (CFA) (= 2 Mali francs).
Denominations:
Coins 1, 2, 5, 10, 25, 50, 100 francs CFA.
Notes 100, 500, 1000, 5000, 10 000 francs CFA.
Exchange rate to £ sterling: 464·75 (26 Jan. 1987).
Political history and government: Formerly French Sudan, part of French West Africa. Joined Senegal to form the Federation of Mali on 4 Apr. 1959. By agreement with France, signed on 4 Apr. 1960, the Federation became independent on 20 June 1960. Senegal seceded on 20 Aug. 1960 and the remnant of the Federation was proclaimed the Republic of Mali on 22 Sept. 1960. The elected National Assembly was dissolved on 17 Jan. 1968. The government was overthrown by an army *coup* on 19 Nov. 1968, when a Military Committee for National Liberation (CMLN), led by Lt (later Brig-Gen) Moussa Traoré, was established. The constitution was abrogated and political parties banned. The CMLN ruled by decree with the assistance of an appointed Council of Ministers. The President of the CMLN assumed the functions of Head of State on 6 Dec. 1968 and became also Prime Minister on 19 Sept. 1969. The CMLN published a new constitution on 26 Apr. 1974 and it was approved by referendum on 2 June 1974. This provides for a one-party state with an elected President and National Assembly, with the CMLN remaining in power for a transitional period of five years. The formation of the ruling party, the *Union démocratique du peuple malien* (UDPM), was announced on 22 Sept. 1976. The UDPM was formally constituted on 30 Mar. 1979 and nominated Traoré as presidential candidate on 18 May. Elections were held on 19 June 1979 for a National Assembly (82 members serving a four-year term) and for a President (with a five-year term). Mali has eight administrative regions.
Length of roadways: 11 200 miles *18 000 km*.
Length of railways: 398 miles *640 km*.
Adult illiteracy: 90·6% (males 86·5%, females 94·3%) in 1976.
Expectation of life: Males 39·4 years; females 42·5 years (UN estimates for 1970–75).

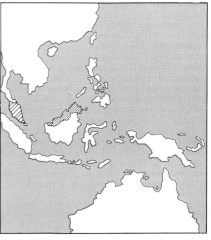

MALAYSIA

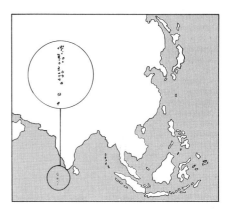

MALDIVES

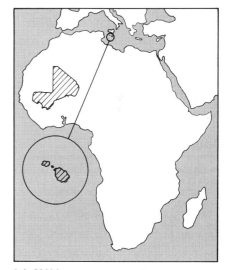

left: **MALI**
encircled: **MALTA**

Defence: Military service voluntary; total armed forces 4950 (1985); defence expenditure: 21·2% of total government expenditure in 1982.
Foreign tourists: 22 000 in 1979.

Malta

Official name: Repubblika ta Malta (Republic of Malta).
Population: 331 997 (1984 estimate).
Area: 122 miles² *316 km²*, including Gozo (25·9 miles² *67 km²*) and Comino (1·07 miles² *2,77 km²*).
Languages: Maltese, English, Italian.
Religion: Roman Catholic.

Capital city: Valletta, population 14 013 (1984 estimate).
Other principal towns (1984): Sliema 20 071; Birkirkara 18 041; Qormi 17 130.
Highest point: 816 ft *249 m*.
Head of State: Miss Agatha Barbara, President.
Prime Minister: Dr Carmelo Mifsud Bonnici.
Climate: Basically healthy without extremes. The temperature rarely drops below 4°C *40°F* and in most years does not rise above 38°C *100°F*. The average annual rainfall in Valletta is 576 mm *22·7 in*. In the summer the nights are cool except when the *Sirocco* desert wind blows from the south-east.
Labour force: 111 314 in 1984: Agriculture and fishing 4·9%; Manufacturing 30·7%; Construction and quarrying 5·2%; Trade 10·3%; Transport and storage 5·5%; Private services 24·3%; Government services 24·3%.
Gross domestic product: 461·1 million Maltese lira in 1984.
Exports: 181 364 000 Maltese lira in 1984: Food and live animals 2·9%; Beverages and tobacco 3·4%; Mineral fuels and lubricants 3·5%; Basic manufactures 10·5%; Machinery and transport equipment 22·2%; Clothing 33·9%.
Monetary unit: Maltese lira (LM). 1 lira = 100 cents = 1000 mils.
Denominations:
Coins 2, 3, 5 mils; 1, 2, 5, 10, 25, 50 cents.
Notes 1, 5, 10 pounds.
Exchange rate to £ sterling: 0·534 (26 Jan. 1987).
Political history and government: A former British colony. Became independent, within the Commonwealth, on 21 Sept. 1964. A republic since 13 Dec. 1974, when the Governor-General became President. Legislative power is held by the unicameral House of Representatives, with 65 members elected for 5 years (subject to dissolution) by universal adult suffrage, using proportional representation. The President is a constitutional Head of State, elected for 5 years by the House, and executive power is exercised by the Cabinet. The President appoints the Prime Minister and, on the latter's recommendation, other Ministers. The Cabinet is responsible to the House.
Length of roadways: 801 miles *1289 km* (1983).
Universities: 1.
Adult illiteracy: 33·5% (males 31%; females 36%) in 1963 (UNESCO estimates).
Expectation of life: Males 68·27 years; females 73·10 years (1976).
Defence: Military service voluntary; total armed forces 775 (1985); defence expenditure 3·2% of total government expenditure in 1984.
Foreign tourists: 479 747 in 1984.

Mauritania

Official name: République Islamique de Mauritanie (French) or Jumhuriyat Muritaniya al-Islamiya (Arabic): Islamic Republic of Mauritania.
Population: 1 874 000 (1985 estimate).
Area: 397 955 miles² *1 030 700 km²*.
Languages: Arabic, Hassaniya, French.
Religion: Muslim.
Capital city: Nouakchott, population 134 986 (including suburbs) at 1976 census.
Other principal towns (1976): Nouadhibou (Port-Etienne) 21 961; Kaédi 20 848; Zouérate 17 474; Rosso 16 466; Atar 16 326.
Highest point: Kediet Ijill, 3002 ft *915 m*.
Principal river: Sénégal.
Head of State: Lt-Col Maouya Ould Sidi Ahmed Taya (b. 1943) Chairman of the Military Committee for National Salvation and Prime Minister.
Climate: Hot and dry, with breezes on coast. In Nouakchott, average maximum 28°C *83°F* to 34°C *93°F*. In interior, F'Derik has average July maximum of 43°C *109°F*.
Labour force: 552 000 in 1984: Agriculture, forestry and fishing 80·4%.
Gross domestic product: 31 728 million ouguiya in 1980.
Exports: 18 497 million ouguiya in 1984: Iron ore 49·7%; Fish 50·3%.
Monetary unit: Ouguiya. 1 ouguiya = 5 khoums.

Denominations:
Coins 1 khoum; 1, 5, 10, 20 ouguiya.
Notes 100, 200, 1000 ouguiya.
Exchange rate to £ sterling: 114·33 (27 Jan. 1987).
Political history and government: Formerly part of French West Africa, Mauritania became a self-governing member of the French Community on 28 Nov. 1958. Moktar Ould Daddah became Prime Minister on 23 June 1959. The country became fully independent on 28 Nov. 1960, with Daddah as Head of State. Under the constitution of 20 May 1961, Daddah became President on 20 Aug. 1961. A one-party state, under the Mauritanian People's Party (PPM), was introduced in 1964. On 28 Feb. 1976 Spain ceded Spanish Sahara to Mauritania and Morocco, to be apportioned between them. Mauritania occupied the southern part of this territory, which it named Tiris el-Gharbia.
President Daddah was deposed by the armed forces on 10 July 1978, when power was assumed by a Military Committee for National Recovery (CMRN), led by Lt-Col Moustapha Ould Mohamed Salek. The constitution was suspended and the National Assembly and ruling party dissolved. On 20 July 1978 the new regime published a Constitutional Charter, under which the Chairman of the CMRN would exercise executive authority. On 6 Apr. 1979 the CMRN was replaced by a Military Committee for National Salvation (CMSN), also led by Salek, but he relinquished the post of Prime Minister to Lt-Col Ahmed Ould Bouceif (Bousseif). On 11 Apr. 1979 the CMSN adopted a new Constitution Charter, assuming legislative power for itself and separating the roles of Head of State and Head of Government. Bouceif was killed in an air crash on 27 May and the CMSN appointed a new Prime Minister, Lt-Col Mohamed Khouna Ould Haidalla, on 31 May. Salek, then only titular Head of State, resigned on 3 June 1979, being replaced by Lt-Col Mohamed Mahmoud Ould Ahmed Louly.
Following negotiations with the *Frente Popular para la Liberación de Sakiet el Hamra y Rio de Oro* (the Polisario Front), a Saharan nationalist group, Mauritania signed an agreement on 5 Aug. 1979 providing for its withdrawal from its portion of Western (formerly Spanish) Sahara. It formally withdrew on 15 Aug. 1979, although Morocco had previously announced its annexation of the area (in addition to the northern part which it already held).
On 4 Jan. 1980 Louly was deposed by Haidalla, who (despite the previous separation of powers) became Head of State while remaining Prime Minister. He relinquished the premiership on 15 Dec. 1980, when an almost entirely civilian Cabinet was formed. This was replaced on 25 Apr. 1982, when the Army Chief of Staff became Prime Minister.

left: **MAURITANIA**
encircled: **MAURITIUS**

On 19 Dec. 1980 the CMSN published a draft constitution, to be submitted to a referendum. The constitution envisages a National Assembly, elected for four years, and a President serving a single six-year term. Executive power would be held by the Prime Minister, to be designated by the President (from among the majority in the Assembly) and approved by the Assembly. Political parties would be permitted but the PPM would remain banned.
Length of roadways: 5550 miles *8900 km*.
Length of railways: 404 miles *650 km*.
Adult illiteracy: 82·6% (population aged 6 and over) in 1977.
Expectation of life: Males 39·4 years; females 42·5 years (UN estimates for 1970–75).
Defence: Total armed forces 8470 (1985); defence expenditure: 29·1% of total government expenditure in 1979.
Foreign tourists: 20 700 in 1975.

Mauritius

Population: 1 002 178 (1983 census).
Area: 789·5 miles² *2045 km²*.
Languages (1984): Arabic 7%; Bhojpuri 19%; Chinese 2%; Creole 29%; French 3%; Hindi 22%; Marathi 2%; Tamil 7%; Telegu 3%; Urdu 6%. The official language is English.
Religions (1962): Hindu 52%; Christian 30%; Muslim 16%.
Capital city: Port Louis, population 135 200 (1984 estimate).
Other principal towns (1984): Beau Bassin-Rose Hill 91 258; Curepipe 62 751; Quatre Bornes 64 203; Vacoas-Phoenix 53 818.
Highest point: Piton de la Rivière Noire (Black River Mountain), 2711 ft *826 m*.
Head of State: HM Queen Elizabeth II, represented by Sir Veerasamy Ringadoo, Governor-General.
Prime Minister: Aneerood Jugnauth.
Climate: Generally humid, with south-east trade winds. Average temperatures between 19°C *66°F* at 2000 ft *610 m* and 23°C *75°F* at sea-level. At Vacoas, 1394 ft *425 m*, maximum 37°C *98·6°F*, minimum 8°C *46·4°F*. Average annual rainfall between 890 mm *35 in* and 5080 mm *200 in* on highest parts. Wettest months are January to March. Tropical cyclones between September and May.
Labour force: 294 739 at 1983 census (island of Mauritius only): Agriculture, forestry and fishing 25·3%; Manufacturing 20·8%; Construction 7·5%; Trade 12%; Transport, storage and communications 6%; Community, social and personal services 24·4%. The island of Rodrigues had a labour force of 8206 in 1972.
Gross domestic product: 11 985 million rupees in 1984: Agriculture, forestry and fishing 14·7%; Manufacturing 17·8%; Trade 13·7%; Transport, storage and communications 11·1%; Financial services 17·1%; Government services 11·6%.
Exports: 2914 million rupees in 1984: Sugar and molasses 88·7%; Tea 8·5%.
Monetary unit: Mauritian rupee. 1 rupee = 100 cents.
Denominations:
Coins 1, 2, 5, 10, 25, 50 cents; 1 rupee.
Notes 5, 10, 25, 50 rupees.
Exchange rate to £ sterling: 19·12 (26 Jan. 1987).
Political history and government: A former British colony. On 12 Mar. 1964 the Chief Minister became Premier. On 8 Nov. 1965 the United Kingdom transferred the Chagos Archipelago, a Mauritian dependency, to the newly-created British Indian Ocean Territory. A new constitution was adopted, and Mauritius achieved self-government, on 12 Aug. 1967, when the Premier became Prime Minister. Following communal riots, a state of emergency was declared on 21–22 Jan. 1968. Mauritius became independent, within the Commonwealth, on 12 Mar. 1968.
Executive power is vested in the British monarch and exercisable by the Governor-General, who is appointed on the recommendation of the Prime Minister and acts in almost all matters on the advice of the Council of Ministers. Legislative power is held by the unicameral

Legislative Assembly, with 71 members: the Speaker, 62 members elected by universal adult suffrage for 5 years and 8 'additional' members (the most successful losing candidates of each community). The Governor-General appoints the Prime Minister and, on the latter's recommendation, other Ministers. The Council of Ministers is responsible to the Assembly.

By a constitutional amendment of 18 Nov. 1969, the term of the Assembly (elected on 7 Aug. 1967) was extended by four years and the election due in 1972 was not held until 20 Dec. 1976. The state of emergency was lifted on 31 Dec. 1970 but, after industrial unrest, it was reimposed on 16 Dec. 1971.
Length of roadways: 1100 miles *1800 km.*
Universities: 1.
Adult illiteracy: 39·2% (males 28·5%; females 49·9%) in 1962 (population aged 13 and over).
Expectation of life: Males 60·68 years; females 65·31 years (island of Mauritius only) in 1971–73.
Defence: No standing force.
Cinemas: 46 (seating capacity 45 000) in 1981.
Foreign tourists: 139 670 in 1984.

Mexico

Official name: Estados Unidos Mexicanos (United Mexican States).
Population: 66 846 833 (1980 census); 78 807 000 (1985 estimate).
Area: 756 062 miles² *1 958 201 km².*
Languages: Spanish 90%, indigenous.
Religion: Roman Catholic 96%.
Capital city: Ciudad de México (Mexico City), population 12 932 116 (1980 census).
Other principal towns (1980): Guadalajara 2 244 715; Monterrey 1 916 472; Heróica Puebla de Zaragoza (Puebla) 835 759; Léon 655 809; Ciudad Juárez 567 365; Rosales 560 011; Mexicali 510 554; Tijuana 461 257; Mérida 424 529; Acapulco 409 335; Chihuahua 406 830; San Luis Potosí 406 630.
Highest point: Pico de Orizaba (Volcán Citlaltepetl), 18 405 ft *5610 m.*
Principal mountain ranges: Sierra Madre Occidental, Sierra Madre Oriental, Sierra Madre del Sur, Sistema Volcánico Transversal.
Principal rivers: Río Bravo del Norte (Río Grande) (1885 miles *3033 km*), Balsas, Grijalva, Pánuco.
Head of State; Miguel de la Madrid Hurtado (b. 12 December 1934), President.
Climate: Tropical (hot and wet) on coastal lowlands and in south, with average temperature of 18°C *64°F.* Temperate on highlands of central plateau. Arid in north and west. In Mexico City, average maximum 19°C *66°F* (December, January) to 25°C *78°F* (May), minimum 5°C *42°F* (January) to 13°C *55°F* (June), July and August rainiest (27 days each). Absolute maximum temperature 58°C *136°F,* San Luis Potosí, 11 Aug. 1933; absolute minimum −28°C *−19°F,* Balerio, 30 Jan. 1949.
Labour force: 22 066 084 (June 1980): Agriculture, forestry and fishing 25%; Mining 2%; Manufacturing 11·7%; Building industry 5·9%; Commerce, restaurants and hotels 7·8%; Transport and communications 3%; Personal, social and communal services 10·9%.
Gross domestic product: 9 417 089 million pesos in 1982: Agriculture, forestry and fishing 7·3%; Mining 9·9%; Manufacturing 21·2%; Building industry 6·3%; Commerce, restaurants and hotels 22·8%; Transport and communications 6·4%; Finance, insurance and real estate 7·5%; Personal, social and communal services 18·8%.
Exports: US$24 054 million in 1984: Crude oil and natural gas 62%; Vehicles 6%; Petroleum products 5%.
Monetary unit: Mexican peso. 1 peso = 100 centavos.
Denominations:
Coins 20 and 50 centavos; 1, 5, 10, 20, 50 and 100 pesos.
Notes 100, 500, 1000, 5000 and 10 000 pesos.
Exchange rate to £ sterling: 1463·23 (26 Jan. 1987).
Political history and government: A federal republic of 31 states and Federal District (around the capital). Present constitution was proclaimed on 5 Feb. 1917. Legislative power is vested in the bicameral National Congress. The Senate has 64 members – two from each state and the Federal District – elected by universal adult suffrage for 6 years. The Chamber of Deputies, directly elected for 3 years, has 400 seats, of which 300 are filled from single-member constituencies. The remaining 100 seats, allocated by proportional representation, are filled from minority parties' lists. Executive power is held by the President, elected for 6 years by universal adult suffrage at the same time as the Senate. He appoints and leads a Cabinet to assist him. Each state is administered by a Governor (elected for 6 years) and an elected Chamber of Deputies.
Length of roadways: 134 043 miles *214 470 km* (1983).
Length of railways: 16 034 miles *25 799 km.*
Universities: 47 plus 2 technical universities.
Adult illiteracy: 17% (males 13·8%, females 20·2%) in 1980.
Expectation of life: 65 years (1980).
Defence: Military service: voluntary, with part-time conscript militia; total regular armed forces 132 940 (1986); defence expenditure: 7·9% of total government expenditure in 1983.
Foreign tourists: 4 749 000 in 1983.

Monaco

Official name: Principauté de Monaco (Principality of Monaco).
Population: 27 063 (1982 census).
Area: 0·70 mile² *1,81 km².*
Language: French.
Religion: Mainly Roman Catholic.
Capital city: Monaco-Ville, population 2422.
Other principal towns: Monte Carlo, population 9948 (1968).
Highest point: On Chemin de Révoirés, 533 ft *162 m.*
Principal river: Vésubie.
Head of State: HSH Prince Rainier III (b. 31 May 1923).
Minister of State: Jean Ausseil.
Climate: Mediterranean, with warm summers (average July maximum 28°C *83°F*) and very mild winters (average January minimum 3°C *37°F*), 62 rainy days a year (monthly average maximum seven days in winter). Absolute maximum temperature 34°C *93°F,* 29 June 1945 and 3 Aug. 1949; absolute minimum −2,3°C *27·8°F.*
Labour force: 10 093 (excluding 232 unemployed) aged 15 and over (census of 1 Mar. 1968): Industry 21·9% (manufacturing 14·8%); Services 77·9% (commerce 18·7%).
Monetary unit: French currency (*q.v.*).
Political history and government: An hereditary principality, in close association with France since 2 Feb. 1861. Monaco became a constitutional monarchy on 5 Jan. 1911. The present constitution was promulgated on 17 Dec. 1962. Legislative power is held jointly by the Sovereign and the unicameral National Council, with 18 members elected by universal adult suffrage for 5 years. The electorate comprises only true-born Monégasque citizens aged 25 years or over. Executive power is vested in the Sovereign and exercised jointly with a 4-man Council of Government, headed by a Minister of State (a French civil servant chosen by the Sovereign). Monaco comprises 3 *quartiers.*
Length of roadways: 29 miles *46 km.*
Length of railways: 1·1 miles *1,7 km.*
Foreign tourists: 227 844 hotel arrivals in 1984.

Mongolia

Official name: Bügd Nairamdakh Mongol Ard Uls (Mongolian People's Republic).
Population: 1 866 300 (1985 estimate).
Area: 604 250 miles² *1 565 000 km².*
Language: Khalkh Mongolian.
Religion: Buddhist.
Capital city: Ulan Bator (Ulaan Baatar), population 470 500 (1984 estimate).

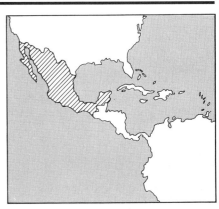

MEXICO

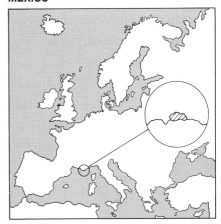

MONACO

Other principal towns (1984): Darhan 63 600; Erdenet 40 500.
Highest point: Mönh Hayrhan Uul, 14 311 ft *4362 m.*
Principal mountain ranges: Altai Mts, Hangayn Nuruu.
Principal rivers: Selenge (Selenga) with Orhon, Hereleng (Kerulen).
Head of State: Jambyn Batmunkh (b. 10 Mar. 1926), Chairman of the Praesidium of the Peoples' Great Hural.
Head of Government: Dumaagyn Sodnom (b. 14 July 1933), Chairman of the Council of Ministers.
Climate: Dry. Summers generally mild, winters very cold. In Ulan Bator, July warmest (10°C *51°F* to 22°C *71°F*) and rainiest (10 days), January coldest (−32°C *−26°F* to −18°C *−2°F*).
Labour force: 365 000 (estimate for 1983): Agriculture and forestry 36·3%; Industry 17·8%; Construction 7·2%; Non-productive sector 25·2%.
Gross national product: $1100 million in 1978 (World Bank estimate).
Exports: 1816 tugriks in 1983: Fuel, mineral raw materials and metals 39·2%; Raw materials and products of its processing 25·6%; Foodstuffs 12·1%; Industrial consumer goods 13·5%.
Monetary unit: Tugrik. 1 tugrik = 100 möngö.
Denominations:
Coins 1, 2, 5, 10, 15, 20, 50 möngö; 1 tugrik.
Notes 1, 2, 5, 10, 25, 50, 100 tugrik.
Exchange rate to £ sterling: 5·1272 (26 Jan. 1987).
Political history and government: Formerly Outer Mongolia, a province of China. With backing from the USSR, the Mongolian People's (Communist) Party – called the Mongolian People's Revolutionary Party (MPRP) since 1921 – established a Provisional People's Government on 31 Mar. 1921. After nationalist forces, with Soviet help, overthrew Chinese rule in the capital, independence was proclaimed on 11 July 1921. The USSR recognized the People's Government on 5 Nov. 1921. The Mongolian People's Republic was proclaimed on 26 Nov.

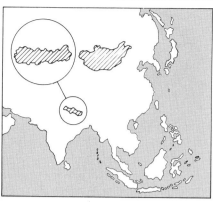

top: **MONGOLIA**   *below:* **NEPAL**

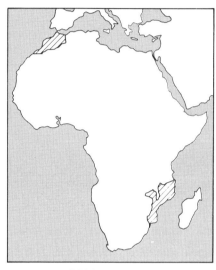

top left: **MOROCCO**
bottom right: **MOZAMBIQUE**

1924 but was not recognized by China. A plebiscite on 20 Oct. 1945 voted 100% for independence, recognized by China on 5 Jan. 1946. A new constitution was adopted on 6 July 1960.

The supreme organ of state power is the People's Great Hural (Assembly), with 370 members elected (unopposed) by universal adult suffrage for five years. The Assembly usually meets only twice a year but elects a Presidium (9 members) to be its permanent organ. The Chairman of the Presidium is Head of State. The highest executive body is the Council of Ministers, appointed by (and responsible to) the Assembly.

Political power is held by the MPRP, the only legal party. The MPRP presents a single list of approved candidates for elections to all representative bodies. The MPRP's highest authority is the Party Congress, which elects the Central Committee (91 full members and 71 candidate members were elected in May 1981) to supervise Party work. The Committee elects a Political Bureau (8 full members and 2 candidate members) to direct its policy.

For local administration, Mongolia is divided into 18 provinces and 3 municipalities.
Length of roadways: *c.* 46 600 miles *c. 75 000 km.*
Length of railways: 1056 miles *1700 km.*
Universities: 1.
Adult illiteracy: 4·6% (population aged 9 to 50) in 1956.
Expectation of life: Males 59·1 years; females 62·3 years (UN estimates for 1970–75).
Defence: Military service: 2 years; total armed forces 33 000 (1985); defence expenditure: 14% of total government expenditure in 1984.
Foreign tourists: 10 000 in 1984.

Morocco

Official name: Al-Mamlaka al-Maghribiya (the Kingdom of Morocco).
*Population: 20 255 687 (Sept. 1982 census).
*Area: 177 115 miles² *458 730 km².*
Languages: Arabic, Berber, French, Spanish.
Religions: Muslim; Christian minority.
Capital city: Rabat, population 1 020 001 (1982 census).
Other principal towns (1982): Casablanca 2 436 664; Marrakech 1 266 695; Fes 805 464; Meknes 626 868; Tanger 436 227; Oujda 780 762; Tetouan 704 205; Kenitra 715 967; Safi 706 618.
Highest point: Jebel Toubkal, 13 665 ft *4165 m* (first climbed in 1923).
Principal mountain ranges: Haut (Grand) Atlas, Moyen (Middle) Atlas, Anti Atlas.
Principal rivers: Oued Dra (335 miles *539 km*), Oued Oum-er-Rbia, Oued Moulouya (320 miles *515 km*), Sebou (280 miles *450 km*).
Head of State: HM King Hassan II (b. 9 July 1929).
Prime Minister: Mohamed Karim Lamrani.
Climate: Semi-tropical. Warm and sunny on coast, very hot inland. Rainy season November to March. Absolute maximum temperature 51,7°C *125·0°F*, Agadir, 17 Aug. 1940; absolute minimum −24°C *−11·2°F*, Ifrane, 11 Feb. 1935.
Labour force: 5 999 260 in 1982: Unemployed 10·7%.
Gross domestic product: 34 637 million dirhams in 1983 at 1969 prices: Agriculture, forestry and fishing 11%; Manufacturing 16·6%; Construction 4·5%; Transport and communications 5·2%; Trade 17·4%; Public administration 19·1%; Other services 15·9%.
Exports: 19 110 million dirhams in 1984: Citrus fruit 5·5%; Phosphates 24·2%; Phosphoric acid 18·4%; Fertilizers 4%; Clothing 5·4%.
Monetary unit: Dirham. 1 dirham = 100 francs (centimes).
Denominations:
  Coins 1, 2, 5, 10, 20, 50 francs; 1, 5 dirhams.
  Notes 5, 10, 50, 100 dirhams.
Exchange rate to £ sterling: 12·70 (26 Jan. 1987).
Political history and government: An hereditary monarchy, formerly ruled by a Sultan. Most of Morocco (excluding the former Spanish Sahara) became a French protectorate on 30 Mar. 1912. A smaller part in the north became a Spanish protectorate on 27 Nov. 1912. Tangier became an international zone on 18 Dec. 1923. The French protectorate became independent on 2 Mar. 1956 and was joined by the Spanish protectorate on 7 Apr. 1956. The Tangier zone was abolished on 29 Oct. 1956. The Sultan became King on 18 Aug. 1957. The northern strip of Spanish Sahara was ceded to Morocco on 10 Apr. 1958 and the Spanish enclave of Ifni was ceded on 30 June 1969. On 28 Feb. 1976 the rest of Spanish Sahara was ceded to Morocco and Mauritania, to be apportioned between them. After Mauritania announced its intention to withdraw from Tiris el-Gharbia, its section of Western (formerly Spanish) Sahara, Morocco annexed that portion also (and renamed it Oued Eddahab) on 14 Aug. 1979.

A new constitution, approved by referendum on 1 Mar. 1972 and promulgated on 10 Mar. 1972, provides for a modified constitutional monarchy. Legislative power is vested in a unicameral Chamber of Representatives, which, after the elections of 14 September 1984, had 306 members, of which 204 are elected directly and 102 chosen by an electoral college.

Executive power is vested in the King, who appoints (and may dismiss) the Prime Minister and other members of the Cabinet. The King can also dissolve the Chamber.
Length of roadways: 35 918 miles *57 792 km.*
Length of railways: 1100 miles *1800 km.*
Universities: 6.
Adult illiteracy: 65% (males 51%, females 78%) in 1982.
Expectation of life: Males 51·4 years; females 54·5 years (UN estimates for 1970–75).
Defence: Military service: 18 months; total

armed forces 149 000 (1985); defence expenditure: 11% of total government expenditure in 1983.
Foreign tourists: 1 877 372 in 1983.

* Figures exclude Western (formerly Spanish) Sahara, with an area of 97 343 miles² *252 120 km²* and a 1982 population of 163 868.

Mozambique

Official name: A República Popular de Moçambique (the People's Republic of Mozambique).
Population: 13 530 000 (1985 estimate).
Area: 308 774 miles² *799 380 km².*
Languages: Portuguese (official), many African languages.
Religions: Animist; Christian and Muslim minorities.
Capital city: Maputo (formerly Lourenço Marques), population 903 621 (1984 estimate).
Other principal towns (1970): Nampula 126 126; Beira 113 770.
Highest point: Monte Binga, 7992 ft *2436 m.*
Principal mountain range: Lebombo Range.
Principal rivers: Limpopo, Zambezi, Rovuma, Shire.
Head of State: Joaquím Alberto Chissano, President.
Climate: Varies from tropical to sub-tropical except in a few upland areas. Rainfall is irregular but the rainy season is usually from November to March, with an average temperature of 28°C *83°F* in Maputo. In the dry season, average temperatures 18°C *65°F* to 20°C *68°F*.
Labour force: 5 671 290 in 1980: Agriculture, forestry and fishing 83·9%; Mining and manufacturing 6·1%; Track 2%; Services 4·3%; Unemployed 1·7%.
Gross domestic product: $83·6 billion meticais in 1984.
Exports: 4060·5 million meticais in 1984: Fish 29·5%; Cashew nuts 16%; Tea 11·3%; Cotton 8·4%.
Monetary unit: Metical (plural: meticais). 1 metical = 100 centavos.
Denominations:
  Coins 10, 20, 50 centavos; 1, 2½, 5, 10, 20 meticais.
  Notes 50, 100, 500, 1000 meticais.
Exchange rate to £ sterling: 59·39 (26 Jan. 1987).
Political history and government: Formerly a Portuguese colony, independent since 25 June 1975. The independence movement was dominated by the *Frente de Libertação de Moçambique* (Frelimo), the Mozambique Liberation Front. Before independence Frelimo was recognized by Portugal and its leader became the first President. The independence constitution proclaims that Frelimo is the directing power of the state and of society. At its third Congress, in February 1977, Frelimo was reconstituted as the Frelimo Party, a 'Marxist-Leninist vanguard party'. Legislative power is vested in the People's Assembly, with 210 members, mainly Frelimo Party officials, indirectly elected on 1–4 Dec. 1977. Executive power is held by the President, who appoints and leads a Council of Ministers. Mozambique has 11 provinces.
Length of roadways: 16 800 miles *27 000 km* (1982).
Length of railways: 2495 miles *4014 km.*
Universities: 1.
Adult illiteracy: 88·6% (males 85%; females 92%) in 1962 (UNESCO estimates).
Expectation of life: Males 41·9 years; females 45·1 years (UN estimates for 1970–75).
Defence: Military service: two years (including women); total armed forces 24 200 (1986); defence expenditure, 1985: $10·3 billion meticais.
Foreign tourists: 68 826 in 1974.

Nauru

Official name: The Republic of Nauru (Naoero).
Population: 8042 (1983 census).
Area: 8·2 miles² *21 km².*
Languages: English, Nauruan.
Religions: Protestant, Roman Catholic.

Highest point: 225 ft *68 m*.
Head of State: Hammer DeRoburt, OBE (b. 25 Sept. 1922), President.
Climate: Tropical; day temperature 30°C *85°F*; rainfall variable, averaging 2000 mm *80 inches*; wettest periods Nov. to Feb.
Labour force: 2473 in 1966: Phosphate mining 56·9%.
Monetary unit: Australian currency (*q.v.*).
Political history and government: Annexed by Germany in October 1888. Captured by Australian forces in November 1914. Administered by Australia under League of Nations mandate (17 Dec. 1920) and later as UN Trust Territory. A new constitution was adopted on 29 Jan. 1968 and Nauru became independent on 31 Jan. 1968. Hammer DeRoburt, Head Chief of Nauru since 1956, was elected the country's first President on 19 May 1968. Under an agreement announced on 29 Nov. 1968, Nauru became a 'special member' of the Commonwealth. Legislative power is held by a unicameral Parliament, with 18 members elected by universal adult suffrage for three years (subject to dissolution). Executive power is held by the President, who is elected by Parliament for its duration and rules with the assistance of an appointed Cabinet, responsible to Parliament. Nauru's first political party was formed in 1976.
Length of roadways: 12 miles *19 km*.
Length of railways: 3·2 miles *5,2 km*.

Nepal

Official name: Sri Nepāla Sarkār (Kingdom of Nepal).
Population: 16 600 000 (1984 estimate).
Area: 54 362 miles² *140 797 km²*.
Languages (1971): Nepali (official) 52·4%; Maithir 11·5%; Bhojpuri 7·0%; Tamang 4·8%; Tharu 4·3%; Newari 3·9%; Abadhi 2·7%; Magar 2·5%; Raikirati 2·0%.
Religions (1971): Hindu 89·4%; Buddhist 7·5%; Muslim 3·0%.
Capital city: Kathmandu, population 393 494 (1981 census).
Other principal towns (1981): Morang 93 544; Lalitpur 79 875; Bhaktapur 48 472.
Highest point: Mount Everest, 29 028 ft *8848 m* (on Chinese border). First climbed 29 May 1953.
Principal mountain range: Nepal Himalaya (Mahabharat Range).
Principal rivers: Karnali, Naryani, Kosi.
Head of State: HM King Birenda Bir Bikram Shah Dev (b. 28 Dec. 1945).
Prime Minister: Lokendra Bahadur Chand.
Climate: Varies sharply with altitude, from Arctic in Himalaya to humid sub-tropical in the central Vale of Kathmandu (annual average 11°C *52°F*), which is warm and sunny in summer. Rainy season June to October. In Kathmandu, average maximum 18°C *65°F* (January) to 30°C *86°F* (May), minimum 2°C *35°F* (January) to 20°C *68°F* (July, August), July (21 days) and August (20 days) rainiest. Maximum temperature recorded in Kathmandu is 37°C *99°F* (2 May 1960) and minimum is −3°C *26°F* (20 Jan. 1964).
Labour force: 6 850 886 in 1981: Agriculture, forestry and fishing 91·1%; Trade 1·6%; Community, social and personal services 4·6%.
Gross domestic product: 30 265 million Nepal rupees in 1981–2: Agriculture, forestry and fishing 55·5%; Manufacturing (including cottage industries) 3·9%; Construction 8·4%; Transport, storage and communications 6·6%; Financial services 7·8%; Community, social and personal services 7·2%.
Exports: 1703·9 million Nepal rupees in 1983–4: Food and live animals 34·3%; Crude materials (except fuels) 21·8%; Basic manufactures 32·6%.
Monetary unit: Nepalese rupee. 1 rupee = 100 paisa.
Denominations:
Coins 1, 5, 10, 25, 50 paisa; 1 rupee.
Notes 1, 5, 10, 100, 500, 1000 rupees.
Exchange rate to £ sterling: 32·71 (26 Jan. 1987).
Political history and government: An hereditary kingdom. A limited constitutional monarchy was proclaimed on 18 Feb. 1951. In a royal *coup*

on 15 Dec. 1960 the King dismissed the Cabinet and dissolved Parliament. A royal proclamation of 5 Jan. 1961 banned political parties. A new constitution, adopted on 16 Dec. 1962, vested executive power in the King and established a National Assembly (*Rashtriya Panchayat*) whose members (most of them indirectly elected, the remainder nominated by the King) had only consultative functions. A referendum held on 2 May 1980 approved the retention of the non-party system. Under a decree of 15 Dec. 1980, the constitution was amended to provide for a National Assembly of 140 members (112 directly elected by universal adult suffrage for five years, 28 nominated by the King). Voting for the elective seats took place on 9 May 1981. The Prime Minister is elected by the Assembly, with other members of the Council of Ministers appointed by the King on the Prime Minister's recommendation. The Council is responsible to the Assembly.

Nepal comprises 14 zones, each administered by an appointed Commissioner.
Length of roadways: 2858 miles *4600 km* (31 Dec. 1978).
Length of railways: 63 miles *101 km*.
Universities: 1.
Adult illiteracy: 80·8% (males 66·6%; females 95·0%) in 1975.
Expectation of life: Males 42·2 years; females 45·0 years (UN estimates for 1970–75).
Defence: Military service voluntary; total armed forces 25 000 (1985); defence expenditure: 17·2% of total government expenditure in 1984–5.
Foreign tourists: 176 634 in 1984.

The Netherlands

Official name: Koninkrijk der Nederlanden (Kingdom of the Netherlands).
Population: 14 529 000 (1986 estimate).
Area: 16 140 miles² *41 785 km²*.
Language: Dutch.
Religions: Roman Catholic 38%; Protestant 33%.
Capital city: Amsterdam, population 1 006 906 in 1986. The seat of government is 's Gravenhage (Den Haag or The Hague), population 674 548 (1986).
Other principal towns (1986): Rotterdam 1 025 585; Utrecht 511 195; Eindhoven 376 185; Arnhem 294 085; Heerlen-Kerkrade 266 617; Enschede-Hengelo 248 052; Nijmegen 238 187; Tilburg 223 043; Haarlem 214 680; Groningen 207 060.
Highest point: Vaalserberg, 1053 ft *321 m*.
Principal rivers: Maas (Meuse), Waal, Rhine, Ijssel.
Head of State: HM Queen Beatrix Wilhelmina Armgard (b. 31 Jan. 1938).
Prime Minister: Ruud F. M. Lubbers.
Climate: Temperate, generally between −17°C *0°F* and 21°C *70°F*. Often foggy and windy. In Amsterdam, average maximum 4°C *40°F* (January) to 20°C *69°F* (July), minimum 1°C *34°F* (January, February) to 15°C *59°F* (July, August). November, December, January rainiest (each 19 days). Absolute maximum temperature 38,6°C *101·5°F*, Warnsveld, 23 Aug. 1944; absolute minimum −27,4°C *−17·3°F*, Winterswijk, 27 Jan. 1942.
Labour force: 4 561 000 in 1986; registered unemployed 691 900.
Gross domestic product: 415·1 billion guilders in 1986: Agriculture and fisheries 4%; Industry 35%; Services 45%.
Exports: 210 691 million guilders in 1984: Food, drink and live animals 18·7%; Fuel and gas 23%; Chemicals 16·7%; Basic manufactures 12·1%; Machinery and transport equipment 16·5%.
Monetary unit: Netherlands gulden (guilder) or florin. 1 guilder = 100 cents.
Denominations:
Coins 1, 5, 10, 25 cents; 1, 2½, 5 guilders.
Notes 1, 2½, 5, 10, 25, 50, 100, 250, 1000 guilders.
Exchange rate to £ sterling: 3·14 (26 Jan. 1987).
Political history and government: A constitutional and hereditary monarchy. Legislative

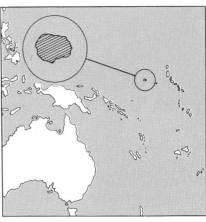

NAURU

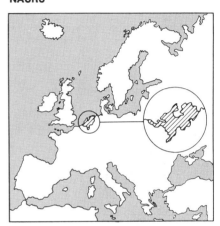

THE NETHERLANDS

power is held by the bicameral States-General. The First Chamber has 75 members indirectly elected for 4 years by the 11 Provincial Councils. The Second Chamber has 150 members directly elected by universal suffrage for 4 years (subject to dissolution), using proportional representation. The Head of State has mainly formal prerogatives and executive power is exercised by the Council of Ministers, which is responsible to the States-General. The monarch appoints the Prime Minister and, on the latter's recommendation, other Ministers. Each of the 12 provinces is administered by an appointed Governor and an elected Council.
Length of roadways: 33 467 miles *53 848 km* (1984).
Length of railways: 1773 miles *2852 km* (1984).
Universities: 9 (plus 3 technical universities and 4 colleges of university standing).
Expectation of life: Males 69·7 years; females 74·9 years (1983).
Defence: Military service: Army 14 months, Navy and Air Force 14–17 months; total armed forces 107 280 (1986); defence expenditure, 7·9% of total government expenditure in 1985.
Foreign tourists: 3 339 300 (hotel arrivals only) in 1984.

New Zealand

Official name: Dominion of New Zealand.
Population: 3 291 300 (1985 estimate).
Area: 103 736 miles² *268 676 km²*.
Languages: English, Maori.
Religions: Church of England, Presbyterian, Roman Catholic.
Capital city: Wellington, population 342 500 (1985 estimate).
Other principal towns (1985): Auckland 894 000; Christchurch 323 500; Hamilton 170 100; Dunedin 110 900; Napier-Hastings 116 900; Palmerston North 95 500.
Highest point: Mt Cook, 12 349 ft *3764 m*.
Principal mountain range: Southern Alps.

NEW ZEALAND

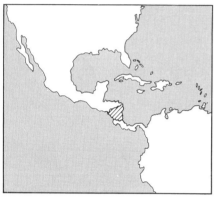

NICARAGUA

Principal rivers: Waikato, Clutha (210 miles *338 km*), Waihou, Rangitaiki, Mokau, Wanganui, Rangitikei, Manawatu.
Head of State: HM Queen Elizabeth II, represented by the Most Rev. Sir Paul Reeves, Governor-General.
Prime Minister: The Rt Hon. David Russell Lange (b. 1942).
Climate: Temperate and moist. Moderate temperatures (annual average 11°C *52°F*) except in the hotter far north. Small seasonal variations. In Wellington, January and February warmest (13°C *56°F* to 20°C *69°F*), July coolest (5°C *42°F* to 12°C *53°F*) and rainiest (18 days), February driest (nine days). In Auckland, average maximum 13°C *56°F* (July) to 23°C *73°F* (January, February), minimum 8°C *46°F* (July, August) to 15°C *60°F* (January, February), July rainiest (21 days).
Labour force: 1 371 000 in 1984: Agriculture, forestry and fishing 10·4%; Manufacturing 22%; Construction 6·4%, Trade 16·1%; Transport, storage and communications 7·5%; Financial services 7·2%; Community, social and personal services 22%; Unemployed 5·7%.
Gross domestic product: NZ$34935 million in 1983–4: Agriculture, forestry and fishing 9·1%; Manufacturing 22·6%; Electricity, gas and water 2·9%; Construction 5·2%; Trade 20·9%; Transport, storage and communications 8·6%; Financial services 14·9%; Community, social and personal services 16·2%.
Exports: NZ$10975·9 million in 1984–5: Meat and meat products 20·3%; Dairy products 8·1%; Fruit and vegetables 4·5%; Wool 13·5%; Forest products 5·7%.
Monetary unit: New Zealand dollar ($NZ). 1 dollar = 100 cents.
Denominations:
  Coins 1, 2, 5, 10, 20, 50 cents.
  Notes 1, 2, 5, 10, 20, 50, 100 dollars.
Exchange rate to £ sterling: 2·806 (26 Jan. 1987).
Political history and government: A former British colony. Became a dominion, under the British crown, on 26 Sept. 1907. Fully independent, within the Commonwealth, under the

Statute of Westminster, promulgated in the United Kingdom on 11 Dec. 1931 and accepted by New Zealand on 25 Nov. 1947. Executive power is vested in the British monarch and exercisable by the Governor-General, who is appointed on the recommendation of the Prime Minister and acts in almost all matters on the advice of the Executive Council (Cabinet), led by the Prime Minister. Legislative power is held by the unicameral House of Representatives, with 95 members (including four Maoris) elected by universal adult suffrage for three years (subject to dissolution). The Governor-General appoints the Prime Minister and, on the latter's recommendation, other Ministers. The Cabinet is responsible to the House.
Length of roadways: 57 581 miles *92 648 kms*.
Length of railways: 2692 miles *4332 kms*.
Universities: 6.
Expectation of life: European males 70·34 years; European females 76·42 years; Maori males 65·44 years; Maori females 69·84 years (1980–2).
Defence: Military service: voluntary, supplemented by Territorial Army service of 12 weeks basic, 20 days per year; total armed forces 12 443 (1985); defence expenditure: 4·7% of total government expenditure in 1985.
Foreign tourists: 597 000 in 1984–5.

Nicaragua

Official name: República de Nicaragua.
Population: 2 908 000 (1984 estimate).
Area: 57 150 miles² *148 000 km²*.
Language: Spanish; English/Miskito on the Atlantic Coast.
Religion: Roman Catholic; Protestant minority.
Capital city: Managua, population 615 000 (1981 estimate).
Other principal towns (1981): León 158 577; Granada 72 640; Masaya 78 308; Chinandega 144 291.
Highest point: Pico Mogotón, 6913 ft *2107 m*.
Principal mountain ranges: Cordillera Isabelia, Cordillera de Darién.
Principal rivers: Coco (Segovia) (300 miles *482 km*), Rio Grande, Escondido, San Juan.
Head of State: Daniel Ortega Saavedra, President.
Climate: Tropical (hot and humid) with average annual temperature of 26°C *78°F*. Rainy season May–December. Annual rainfall 2540 mm *100 in* on east coast. In Managua, annual average over 27°C *80°F* all year round.
Labour force: 813 000 (excluding unemployed) in 1980: Agriculture, forestry and fishing 42%; Manufacturing 16%; Trade, restaurants and hotels 13%; Community, social and personal services 18%.
Gross domestic product: 45 824 million cordobas in 1984: Agriculture, forestry and fishing 23·5%; Manufacturing 24·9%; Trade 19·2%; Services 26·6%.
Exports: 3945·4 million cordobas in 1984: Cotton 42·8%; Coffee 38·1%.
Monetary unit: Córdoba. 1 córdoba = 100 centavos.
Denominations:
  Coins 5, 10, 25, 50 centavos; 1 córdoba.
  Notes 1, 2, 5, 10, 20, 50, 100, 500, 1000, 5000 córdobas.
Exchange rate to £ sterling: 106·75 (26 Jan. 1987).
Political history and government: A republic comprising 16 departments and one territory. At the government's request, US forces intervened in Nicaragua in 1912 and established bases. They left in 1925 but returned in 1927, when a guerrilla group, led by Augusto César Sandino, was organised to oppose the US occupation. The US forces finally left in 1933, when their role was assumed by a newly-created National Guard, commanded by Gen. Anastasio Somoza García. Sandino was assassinated in 1934, apparently on Somoza's orders, but his followers ('Sandinistas') remained active in opposing the new régime. Somoza became President in 1936 and, either in person or through nominees, held power until his assassi-

nation by a 'Sandinista' in 1956. Political power, exercised within a constitutional framework, was retained by a member of the Somoza family, either directly as President or as Commander of the National Guard. From 1960 the régime was opposed by a guerrilla group which in 1962 formed the *Frente Sandinista de Liberación Nacional* (FSLN), the Sandinist National Liberation Front. General Anastasio Somoza Debayle, son of the former dictator, was President from 1967 to 1972 and again from 1 Dec. 1974. The FSLN allied with other opponents of the régime in 1977. Armed clashes with the National Guard developed into civil war. After 6 months of heavy fighting, President Somoza resigned and left the country on 17 July 1979. The President of the National Congress was nominated as interim President but he left after two days, when the capital fell to the Sandinistas.
The guerrilla groups had formed a provisional Junta of National Reconstruction (initially five members) on 16 June 1979. The Junta named a Provisional Governing Council on 16 July and this Council took office as the Government of National Reconstruction on 20 July 1979. The 1974 constitution was abrogated and the bicameral National Congress (a Senate and a Chamber of Deputies) dissolved. The National Guard was also dissolved, being replaced by the 'Sandinista People's Army', officially established on 22 Aug. 1979.
On taking office, the junta published a Basic Statute, providing for the creation of an appointed 33-member Council of State to act as an interim legislature and to draft a new constitution. On 21 Aug. 1979 the junta issued a 'Statute on Rights and Guarantees for the Citizens of Nicaragua', promising a wide range of democratic reforms. The initial membership of the Council of State, announced on 21 Apr. 1980, was increased to 47. The Council first convened on 4 May 1980 and was increased to 51 members on 4 May 1981. Elections took place in March 1985, and a new constitution was approved in Nov. 1986, to be enacted from Jan. 1987.
Length of roadways: 15 500 miles *25 000 km* (1984).
Length of railways: 232 miles *373 km* (1977).
Universities: 3.
Adult illiteracy: Approx. 12·5% after the 1980 literacy campaign.
Expectation of life: 59 years (1985).
Defence: Total armed forces 31 000 (1986); defence expenditure, 1983: $348·3 million.

Niger

Official name: République du Niger.
Population: 6 040 000 (1983 estimate).
Area: 489 191 miles² *1 267 000 km²*.
Languages: French (official), Hausa, Tuareg, Djerma, Fulani.
Religions: Muslim 85%; Animist, Christian.
Capital city: Niamey, population 360 000 (1981 estimate).
Other principal towns (1977): Zinder 58 436; Maradi 45 852; Tahoua 31 265; Agadez 20 475.
Highest point: Mont Gréboun, 6562 ft *2000 m*.
Principal mountain ranges: Aïr (Azbine), Plateau du Djado.
Principal rivers: Niger (370 miles *595 km* in Niger), Dillia.
Head of State: Col Seyni Kountché (b. 1930), President of the Supreme Military Council and Chairman of the Council of Ministers.
Prime minister: Hamid Algabid.
Climate: Hot and dry. Average temperature 29°C *84°F*. In Niamey, average maximum 34°C *93°F* (January) to 42°C *108°F* (April).
Labour force: 1 827 000 in 1984: Agriculture, forestry and fishing 85·2%.
Gross domestic product: 453 800 million CFA francs in 1979: Agriculture, forestry and fishing 44%; Mining 13·4%; Manufacturing, construction and public works 12·5%; Trade, transport and services 23%; Public administration 7·1%.
Exports: US$ 454·8 million in 1981: Food and live animals 13%; Crude materials (largely uranium) 80·5%.

Monetary unit: Franc de la Communauté financière africaine.
Denominations:
  Coins 1, 2, 5, 10, 25, 50, 100 CFA francs.
  Notes 50, 100, 500, 1000, 5000 CFA francs.
Exchange rate to £ sterling: 464·75 (26 Jan. 1987).
Political history and government: Formerly part of French West Africa, independent since 3 Aug. 1960. Under military rule since 15 Apr. 1974, when the constitution was suspended and the National Assembly dissolved. Niger is ruled by a Supreme Military Council, composed of army officers, which has appointed a provisional government. The country has 16 administrative districts.
Length of roadways: 5989 miles *9637 km.*
Universities: 1.
Adult illiteracy: 90·2% (males 86%; females 94·2%) in 1980.
Expectation of life: Males 39·4 years; females 42·5 years (UN estimates for 1970–75).
Defence: Total armed forces 2150 (1985); defence expenditure: US$10·3 million in 1984.
Foreign tourists: 50 453 in 1984.

Nigeria

Official name: The Federal Republic of Nigeria.
Population: 92 037 000 (1984 estimate).
Area: 356 669 miles² *923 768 km².*
Languages: English (official), Hausa, Ibo, Yoruba and other linguistic groups.
Religions: Muslim, Christian.
Capital city: Lagos, population 1 060 848 at 1 July 1975 (estimate).
Other principal towns (1975): Ibadan 847 000; Ogbomosho 432 000; Kano 399 000; Oshogbo 282 000; Ilorin 282 000; Abeokuta 253 000; Port Harcourt 242 000; Zaria 224 000; Ilesha 224 000; Onitsha 220 000; Iwo 214 000; Ado-Ekiti 213 000; Kaduna 202 000; Mushin 197 000.
Highest point: Dimlang, 6700 ft *2042 m.*
Principal mountain range: Jos Plateau.
Principal rivers: Niger (2600 miles *4184 km* in total length), Benue, Cross.
Head of State: Maj.-Gen. Ibrahim Babangida, President.
Climate: On the coast it is hot (average daily maximum temperature at Lagos 32°C *89°F*) and unpleasantly humid. In the north it is drier and semi-tropical. Annual rainfall ranges from 625 to 3800 mm *25 to 150 in.*
Labour force: 33 708 000 (1984 estimate): Agriculture, forestry and fishing 50%.
Gross domestic product: 48 651 million naira in 1983–4: Agriculture, forestry and fishing 25%; Mining and quarrying 20·4%; Manufacturing 4·9%; Trade 21·6%.
Exports: 8704·7 million naira in 1982: Petroleum 98·8%; Cocoa 0·6%.
Monetary unit: Naira. 1 naira = 100 kobo.
Denominations:
  Coins ½, 1, 5, 10, 25 kobo.
  Notes 50 kobo; 1, 5, 10, 20 naira.
Exchange rate to £ sterling: 5·6354 (26 Jan. 1987).
Political history and government: In 1914 the British dependencies of Northern and Southern Nigeria were unified. In 1947 the United Kingdom introduced a new Nigerian constitution, establishing a federal system of government based on three regions. The Federation of Nigeria became independent, within the Commonwealth, on 1 Oct. 1960. The northern part of the British-administered Trust Territory of Cameroon was incorporated into the Northern Region of Nigeria on 1 June 1961. A fourth region was created by dividing the Western Region under legislation approved on 8 Aug. 1963. The country became a republic, under its present name, on 1 Oct. 1963. The government was overthrown by a military *coup* on 15 Jan. 1966 and power was assumed by a Supreme Military Council (SMC), ruling by decree. Political parties were banned on 24 May 1966. The four regions were replaced by 12 States on 1 April 1968. These were reorganised into 19 States on 17 Mar. 1976.

The SMC published a draft constitution on 7

Oct. 1976. Local government councils were elected (directly in some States, indirectly in others) in Nov.–Dec. 1976. A constituent assembly of 233 members (203 selected by the local councils on 31 Aug. 1977, 22 nominated by the SMC and 8 from the constitutional drafting committee) was inaugurated on 6 Oct. 1977 to finalise the constitution in preparation for a return to civilian rule. The assembly closed on 5 June 1978. A new constitution was issued on 21 Sept. 1978, when the régime ended the ban on political parties and the state of emergency in force since 1966.

The constitution came into force on 1 Oct. 1979, when military rule was ended and the civilian President sworn in. The National Assembly opened on 9 Oct. 1979. Elections were held in August 1983, but in December 1983 the military took over control again, and in January 1984 an 18-member Supreme Military Council was sworn in. This was subsequently superseded by a 28-man Armed Forces Ruling Council, which includes the president. The AFRC appoints a National Council of Ministers, as well as the military governors for the 19 states; these latter appoint state executive councils.
Length of roadways: 67 116 miles *107 990 km* (1980).
Length of railways: 2178 miles *3505 km.*
Universities: 23.
Adult illiteracy: 88·5% in 1952–53 (population aged 7 and over); 84·6% (males 75%; females 94%) in 1962 (UNESCO estimates).
Expectation of life: Males 43·4 years; females 46·6 years (UN estimates for 1970–75).
Defence: Military service voluntary; total armed forces 94 000 (1985); defence expenditure, 1980: $1702 million.
Foreign tourists: 113 827 in 1976.

Norway

Official name: Kongeriket Norge (Kingdom of Norway).
Population: 4 145 845 (1 Jan. 1985).
Area: 149 469 miles² *386 958 km²* (including Svalbard and Jan Mayen).
Languages: Norwegian; small Lapp minority.
Religion: Lutheran.
Capital city: Oslo, population 447 351 at 1 Jan. 1985.
Other principal towns (1 Jan. 1985): Bergen 207 416; Trondheim 134 075; Stavanger 94 193; Kristiansand 62 197; Drammen 50 749.
Highest point: Galdhøpiggen 8098 ft *2469 m.*
Principal mountain range: Langfjellene.
Principal rivers: Glomma (Glama) (372 miles *598 km*), Lågen (209 miles *337 km*), Tanaelv (224 miles *360 km*).
Head of State: HM King Olav V, KG, KT, GCB, GCVO (b. 2 July 1903).
Prime Minister: Geo Harlem Brundtland (b. 20 Apr. 1939).
Climate: Temperate on coast, but cooler inland. In Oslo, average maximum −1°C *30°F* (January) to 23°C *73°F* (July), minimum −7°C *20°F* (January, February) to 13°C *56°F* (July), August rainiest (11 days). Absolute maximum temperature 35°C *95°F*, Oslo, 21 July 1901, and Trondheim, 22 July 1901; absolute minimum −51,4°C −60·5°F, Karasjok, 1 Jan. 1886.
Labour force: 2 031 000 in 1984: Agriculture, forestry and fishing 6·8%; Mining and manufacturing 19·0%; Construction, electricity and water 8·5%; Commerce and finance 16·6%; Government and personal services 35%; Unemployed 3%.
Gross domestic product: 466 407 million kroner in 1985: Agriculture, forestry and fishing 3·7%; Crude petroleum and natural gas 18·6%; Manufacturing 13·4%; Construction 4·9%; Wholesale and retail trade 11·7%; Services 30·2%.
Exports: 154 035 million kroner in 1984: Petroleum and petroleum products 36·6%; Natural gas 17·4%; Manufactured goods 16·7%; Machinery and transport equipment 11%.
Monetary unit: Norwegian krone (plural: kroner). 1 krone = 100 øre.

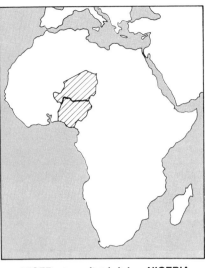

top: **NIGER** *immediately below:* **NIGERIA**

NORWAY

Denominations:
  Coins 50 øre; 1, 5 kroner.
  Notes 10, 50, 100, 500, 1000 kroner.
Exchange rate to £ sterling: 10·775 (26 Jan. 1987).
Political history and government: Formerly linked with Sweden. Independence declared on 7 June 1905; union with Sweden ended on 26 Oct. 1905. Norway is a constitutional monarchy, headed by an hereditary King. Legislative power is held by the unicameral Parliament (*Storting*), with 155 members elected for 4 years by universal adult suffrage, using proportional representation. For the consideration of legislative proposals, the *Storting* divides itself into two chambers by choosing one quarter of its members to form the *Lagting* (upper house), the remainder forming the *Odelsting* (lower house). Executive power is nominally held by the King but is exercised by the Council of Ministers (*Statsråd*), led by the Prime Minister, who are appointed by the King in accordance with the will of the *Storting*, to which the Council is responsible. Norway comprises 19 counties.
Length of roadways: 52 556 miles *84 563 km* (1985).
Length of railways: 2636 miles *4242 km* (1985).
Universities: 4.
Expectation of life: Males 72·64 years; females 79·41 years (1981–2).
Defence: Military service: Army 12 months; Navy and Air Force 12/15 months; total armed forces 40 000 in 1986; defence expenditure: 6·7% of total government expenditure in 1985.

Oman

Official name: Sultanat 'Uman (Sultanate of Oman).

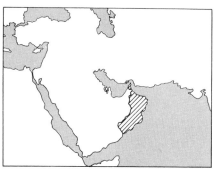

OMAN

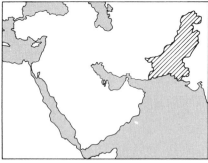

PAKISTAN

Pakistan

Official name: Islami Jamhuria-e-Pakistan (Islamic Republic of Pakistan). 'Pakistan' means 'land of the pure' in the Urdu language.

Population: 84 250 000 (1981 census); 97 670 000 (1986 estimate).
*Area: 307 293 miles² *795 545 km²*.
Languages: Urdu (national), Punjabi, Pashto, Baluchi, Sindhi, English (official).
Religions: Muslim 97·1%; Hindu 1·6%; Christian 1·3% (1961).
Capital city: Islamabad, population 201 000 (1981 census).
Other principal towns (1981): Karachi 5 103 000; Lahore 2 922 000; Faisalabad 1 092 000; Rawalpindi 806 000; Hyderabad 795 000; Multan 730 000; Gujranwala 597 000; Peshawar 555 000.
Highest point: K2 (Mt Godwin Austen), 28 250 ft *8611 m* (first climbed 31 July 1954).
Principal mountain ranges: Hindu Kush, Pamirs, Karakoram.
Principal rivers: Indus and tributaries (Sutlej, Chenab, Ravi, Jhelum).
Head of State: Gen Mohammad Zia ul-Haq (b. 1924), President.
Climate: Dry, and generally hot, with average temperature of 27°C *80°F* except in the mountains, which have very cold winters. Temperatures range from −1°C *30°F* in winter to 49°C *120°F* in summer. In Karachi, June warmest (average 28°C to 34°C *82°F to 93°F*), January coolest (13°C to 25°C *55°F to 77°F*), rainfall negligible throughout the year. In Lahore, average maximum 21°C *69°F* (January) to 41°C *106°F* (June), minimum 5°C *40°F* (December, January) to 27°C *80°F* (July), July and August rainiest (each six days). Absolute maximum temperature 53°C *127°F*, Jacobabad, 12 June 1919.
Labour force: 27 740 000 in 1984: Agriculture, forestry and fishing 50·7%; Manufacturing 12·9%; Trade 11·5%; Community, personal and social services 9·8%; Unemployed 3·9%.
Gross domestic product: 428 178 million rupees in 1984–5: Agriculture and livestock 23·8%; Manufacturing 19·7%; Trade 16·7%; Transport, storage and communications 7·8%; Public administration and defence 8·4%.
Exports: 37 339 million rupees in 1983–4: Raw cotton 4·7%; Rice 15·2%; Cotton fabrics 13%; Cotton yarn and thread 7·8%; Carpets and rugs 6·2%.
Monetary unit: Pakistani rupee. 1 rupee = 100 paisa.
Denominations:
  Coins 1, 5, 10, 25, 50 paisa; 1 rupee.
  Notes 1, 5, 10, 50, 100 rupees.
Exchange rate to £ sterling: 26·2 (26 Jan. 1987).
Political history and government: Pakistan was created as an independent dominion within the Commonwealth on 15 Aug. 1947, when former British India was partitioned. Originally in two parts, East and West Pakistan, the country became a republic on 23 Mar. 1956. The port and peninsula of Gwadur were ceded to Pakistan by Muscat and Oman (now Oman) on 8 Sept. 1958. Military rule was imposed on 27 Oct. 1958. Elections for a Constituent Assembly were held on 7 Dec. 1970, giving a majority to the Awami League, which sought autonomy for East Pakistan. After negotiations on a coalition government failed, East Pakistan declared independence as Bangladesh on 26 Mar. 1971. Following Indian intervention on behalf of the Bengalis, Pakistan's forces surrendered on 16 Dec. 1971, when Bangladesh's independence became a reality. Pakistan was confined to the former western wing. Military rule ended on 20 Dec. 1971. Zulfiqar Ali Bhutto became President and Prime Minister. Pakistan left the Commonwealth on 30 Jan. 1972. A new constitution came into force on 14 Aug. 1973. Under this constitution, Pakistan became a federal republic comprising four provinces (each under a Governor) plus the Federal Capital Territory and 'tribal areas' under federal administration. President Bhutto took office as executive Prime Minister, whose advice was binding on the constitutional President. On 5 July 1977 the government was deposed by a military *coup*. A martial law régime was established, with Gen Mohammad Zia ul-Haq, the Army Chief of Staff, as Chief Martial Law Administrator. The constitution was suspended, although the President remained in office, and a 4-man Military Council was formed to direct the government. The Federal Legislature (a Senate and a National Assembly) and provincial Assemblies were dissolved. Gen Zia appointed a mainly civilian Cabinet on 5 July 1978. The President resigned on 16 Sept. 1978, when Gen Zia assumed his office. He announced on 23 Mar. 1979 that general elections would be held on 17 Nov. Bhutto, the former Prime Minister, was executed (following conviction on a murder charge) on 4 Apr. 1979. Local elections, on a non-party basis, were held on 20–27 Sept. 1979. The President announced on 16 Oct. 1979 that general elections were postponed indefinitely, political parties dissolved and political activity banned. On 24 Mar. 1981 he promulgated an interim constitution. This provided for an advisory Federal Council, to be nominated by the President. On 24 Oct. 1981 President Zia announced that the Council would draft a new constitution. Martial law was lifted at the end of 1985.
Length of roadways: 62 968 miles *101 315 km* (1984).
Length of railways: 5454 miles *8775 km* (1985).
Universities: 20.
Adult illiteracy: 73·8% (1985).
Expectation of life: 55 years (1985).
Defence: Military service voluntary; total armed forces 483 800 (1986); defence expenditure: 40% of total government expenditure in 1985–60.
Foreign tourists: 440 000 in 1984–5.

Panama

Official name: La República de Panamá.
Population: 1 830 175 (census of 11 May 1980); 2 179 000 (1985 estimate).
Area: 30 134 miles² *78 046 km²*.
Language: Spanish.
Religions: Roman Catholic, Protestant minority.
Capital city: Panamá (City), population 542 754 at 1980 census; 660 000 (1982 estimate).
Other principal town: Colón, population 68 000 (1982 estimate).
Highest point: Volcán de Chiriquí, 11 467 ft *3475 m*.
Principal mountain ranges: Serrania de Tabasará, Cordillera de San Blas.
Principal rivers: Tuira (with Chucunaque), Bayano, Santa María.
Head of State: Eric Arturo Del Valle, President.
Climate: Warm, humid days with cool nights. Little seasonal temperature change. Absolute maximum temperature 36,7°C *98°F* at Madden Dam, in the former Canal Zone, 13 Apr. 1920, and Panamá (City), 16 Apr. 1958; absolute minimum 15°C *59°F* at Madden Dam, 4 Feb. 1924.
Labour force: 613 600 in 1984: Agriculture, forestry and fishing 28·6%; Manufacturing 9·7%; Trade 14·6%; Community, social and personal services 28·3%.
Gross domestic product: 4540·5 million balboas in 1984: Agriculture, forestry and fishing 9%; Manufacturing 9%; Trade 14·3%; Transport, storage and communications 20·1%; Financial services 17·4%; Government services 14·5%.
Exports: 256·3 million balboas in 1984; Bananas 29·1%; Shrimps 19·2%; Sugar 13%; Coffee 5·1%.
Monetary unit: Balboa. 1 balboa = 100 centésimos.
Denominations:
  Coins 1, 5, 10, 25, 50 centésimos; 1 and 100 balboas.
  Notes US$1, 2, 5, 10, 20, 50, 100 (there are no Panamanian bank notes).
Exchange rate to £ sterling: 1·528 (26 Jan. 1987).
Political history and government: Formerly part of Colombia, independence declared on 3 Nov. 1903. The elected President was deposed by a *coup* on 11–12 Oct. 1968, when power was seized by the National Guard, led by Col (later Brig-Gen) Omar Torrijos Herrera. A Provisional Junta was established, the National Assembly dissolved and political activity suspended. Political parties were abolished in February 1969. On 6 Aug. 1972 elections were held for a National Assembly of Community Representatives (505 members to hold office for six years)

Oman

Population: 1 810 000 (1984 estimate).
Area: 82 030 miles² *212 457 km²*.
Language: Arabic.
Religion: Muslim.
Capital city: Masqat (Muscat), population 50 000 (1981 estimate).
Other principal towns: Matrah; Salalah.
Highest point: Jabal ash Sham, 10 400 ft *3170 m*.
Principal mountain range: Jabal Akhdas ('Green Mountains').
Head of State: Sultan Qabus ibn Sa'id (b. 18 Nov. 1940).
Climate: Extremely hot summers (temperatures rising to 55°C *130°F*) and mild winters, Cooler in the mountains. Average annual rainfall 75 to 150 mm *3 to 6 in*.
Gross domestic product: 3044·9 million Omani rials in 1984: Crude petroleum 47·6%; Construction 7·4%; Trade 12·1%; Financial services 9·1%; Government services 10·9%.
Exports: 1527·5 million Omani rials in 1984: Petroleum 91·7%.
Monetary unit: Rial Omani. 1 rial = 1000 baiza.
Denominations:
  Coins 2, 5, 10, 25, 50, 100 baiza.
  Notes 100, 250, 500 baiza; 1, 5, 10 rials.
Exchange rate to £ sterling: 0·59 (26 Jan. 1987).
Political history and government: A sultanate, formerly called Muscat and Oman, under British influence since the 19th century. Full independence was recognised by the treaty of friendship with the UK on 20 Dec. 1951. The port and peninsula of Gwadur were ceded to Pakistan on 8 Sept. 1958. Sultan Sa'id ibn Taimur was deposed by his son, Qabus, on 23 July 1970 and the country adopted its present name on 9 Aug. 1970. The Sultan is an absolute ruler and legislates by decree. He is advised by an appointed Cabinet. On 20 Oct. 1981 Sultan Qabus issued decrees creating a State Advisory Council, with 45 members nominated for 2 years. There are no political parties.
Length of roadways: 7425 miles *11 950 km*.
Universities: 1.
Expectation of life: Males 43·7 years; females 45·9 years (UN estimates for 1970–75).
Defence: Military service voluntary; total armed forces 21 500 (1985); defence expenditure: 37·4% of total government expenditure in 1985.

to approve a new constitution. On 13 Sept. 1972 the Assembly approved measures to legalise, for a transitional period of six years from 11 Oct. 1972, the assumption of full executive authority by Gen Torrijos as Chief of Government and Supreme Leader of the Panamanian Revolution. A new Assembly was elected on 6 Aug. 1978, although political parties were still banned. On 11 Oct. 1978 Torrijos resigned as Chief of Government (although remaining Commander of the National Guard until his death in an air crash on 31 July 1981) and the Assembly elected a new President, with full governing powers, for six years. Three political parties were legally registered in Mar.–June 1979. The National Legislative Council, which performs the National Assembly's functions when the Assembly is not in session, was increased from 38 members (all appointed from the Assembly) when elections were held on 28 Sept. 1980 for 19 additional seats, with political parties contesting for the first time since 1968. Full legislative elections and a direct presidential election took place in 1984.

Territorial jurisdiction over the Canal Zone was granted to the USA 'in perpetuity' by treaty of 18 Nov. 1903. Treaties to restore Panamanian rule were signed on 7 Sept. 1977 and approved by a referendum in Panama on 23 Oct. 1977. Under these treaties, ratified on 16 June 1978, the Zone reverted to Panama on 1 Oct. 1979. The Panama Canal itself is to be administered by a joint US-Panamanian commission until 31 Dec. 1999.
Length of roadways: 5349 miles *8606 km* (1984).
Length of railways: 359 miles *578 km* (1984).
Universities: 3.
Adult illiteracy: 21·7% (males 21·1%; females 22·3%) in 1970.
Expectation of life: Males 64·26 years; females 67·50 years (1970, excluding former Canal Zone and tribal Indians).
Defence: Total armed forces (including a paramilitary National Guard) 12 000 (1986); defence expenditure: 6·2% of total government expenditure in 1985.
Foreign tourists: 347 826 in 1984.

Papua New Guinea

Official name: The Independent State of Papua New Guinea.
Population: 3 328 700 (1985 estimate).
Area: 178 704 miles² *462 840 km²*.
Languages: English (official), Pidgin, Moru.
Religion: Christian 92·8% (1966).
Capital city: Port Moresby, population 150 000 (1985 estimate).
Other principal towns (1980): Lae 61 617; Rabaul 14 954; Madang 21 335; Mt Hagen 13 441.
Highest point: Mt Wilhelm, 15 400 ft *4694 m*.
Principal mountain range: Bismarck Range.
Principal rivers: Fly (with Strickland), Sepik (690 miles *1110 km*).
Head of State: HM Queen Elizabeth II, represented by Sir Kingsford Dibela, KGM, Governor-General.
Prime Minister: Paias Wingti.
Climate: Generally hot and humid, cooler in highlands. Average annual rainfall between 1000 and 6350 mm *40 and 250 in.* In Port Moresby, average maximum temperature 28°C *82°F* (August) to 32°C 90°F (December), minimum 23°C *73°F* (July, August) to 25°C *76°F* (November to March), rainiest month is March (9 days).
Labour force: 732 800 in 1980: Agriculture, forestry and fishing 77%; Construction 2·9%; Trade 3·4%; Community, social and personal services 10·5%.
Gross domestic product: 1009·1 million kina (provisional) in year ending 30 June 1975: Agriculture, forestry and fishing 30·5%; Mining and quarrying 13·8%; Community, social and personal services (including restaurants and hotels) 18·9%. Revised total is 1004·0 million kina.
Exports: 805·5 million kina in 1984: Copra 6·1%; Cocoa beans 8·3%; Coffee 14·1%; Timber 7·7%; Copra oil 5%; Palm oil 7·8%; Copper ore and

concentrates 37%.
Monetary unit: Kina. 1 kina = 100 toea.
Denominations:
  Coins 1, 2, 5, 10, 20 toea; 1 kina.
  Notes 2, 5, 10, 20 kina.
Exchange rate to £ sterling: 1·4394 (26 Jan. 1987).
Political history and government: Formed by a merger of the Territory of Papua (under Australian rule from 1906) and the Trust Territory of New Guinea, administered by Australia from 1914, later under a trusteeship agreement with the United Nations. A joint administration for the two territories was established by Australia on 1 July 1949. The combined territory achieved self-government on 1 Dec. 1973 and became independent, within the Commonwealth, on 16 Sept. 1975. Executive authority is vested in the British monarch and exercisable by the Governor-General, who is appointed on the recommendation of the Prime Minister and acts in almost all matters on the advice of the National Executive Council (the Cabinet). Legislative power is vested in the unicameral National Parliament (109 members directly elected for four years by universal adult suffrage). The pre-independence House of Assembly became the first Parliament. The Cabinet is responsible to Parliament, where the Prime Minister, appointed by the Governor-General on Parliament's proposal, must command majority support. Other Ministers are appointed on the Prime Minister's proposal. The country comprises 19 provinces.
Length of roadways: 11 500 miles *18 500 km*.
Universities: 2.
Adult illiteracy: 67·9% (males 60·7%; females 75·6%) in 1971.
Expectation of life: Males 47·5 years; females 47·0 years (UN estimates for 1970–75).
Defence: Military service voluntary; total armed forces 3232 (1985); defence expenditure: 3·9% of total government expenditure in 1984.
Foreign tourists: 33 642 in 1984.

Paraguay

Official name: La República del Paraguay.
Population: 3 035 360 (1982 census); 3 278 000 (1984 estimate).
Area: 157 048 miles² *406 752 km²*.
Languages: Spanish (official), Guaraní.
Religion: Roman Catholic.
Capital city: Asunción, population 455 517 (1982 census).
Other principal towns (1982): San Lorenzo 74 632; Fernando de la Mora 66 810; Lambaré 61 722; Presidente Stroessner 39 676; Pedro Juan Caballero 37 331; Encarnación 27 632.
Highest point: Cerro Tatug, 2297 ft *700 m*.
Principal mountain ranges: Cordillera Amambay, Sierra de Maracaju.
Principal rivers: Paraguay (1500 miles *2414 km*), Paraná (2500 miles *4023 km*), Pilcomayo (1000 miles *1609 km*).
Head of State: Gen Alfredo Stroessner Mattiauda (b. 3 Nov. 1912), President.
Climate: Sub-tropical and humid, average temperatures 18°C to 29°C *65°F to 85°F*. Hot December–March. Cool season May–September. Wet season March–May. In Asunción, average maximum 22°C *72°F* (June) to 35°C *95°F* (January), minimum 12°C *53°F* (June, July) to 22°C *72°F* (January, February), October, November and January rainiest (each 8 days).
Labour force: 1 055 650 in 1982: Agriculture, forestry and fishing 40·9%; Manufacturing 11·8%; Construction 6·4%; Trade 8·1%; Community, personal and social services 16%; Unemployed 4·3%.
Gross domestic product: 818 114 million guaranies in 1983: Agriculture, forestry, fishing and mining 25·9%; Manufacturing 16·4%; Trade, finance and insurance 26·6%; Other services 17·3%.
Exports: US$334·5 million in 1984: Cattle products 3·5%; Timber 6·7%; Tobacco 4·6%; Raw cotton 39·2%; Vegetable oils 5·7%; Seeds for industrial use 30·4%.

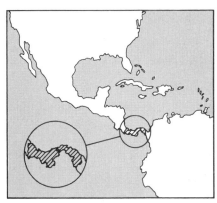

PANAMA

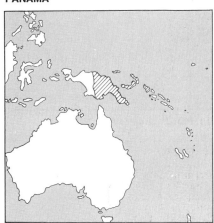

PAPUA NEW GUINEA

Monetary unit: Guaraní. 1 guaraní = 100 céntimos.
Denominations:
  Coins (issued only for commemorative purposes).
  Notes 1, 5, 10, 50, 100, 500, 1000, 5000, 10 000 guaraníes.
Exchange rate to £ sterling: 1025·56 (26 Jan. 1987).
Political history and government: A republic comprising 16 departments. Gen Alfredo Stroessner Mattiauda assumed power by a military *coup* on 5 May 1954. He was elected President on 11 July 1954 to complete his predecessor's term. President Stroessner was re-elected in 1958, 1963, 1968, 1973 and 1978. A new constitution was promulgated on 25 Aug. 1967 and took effect in 1968. Legislative power is held by a bicameral National Congress, whose members serve for 5 years. The Senate has 30 members and the Chamber of Deputies 60 members. The party receiving the largest number of votes (since 1947 the National Republican Association, known as the Colorado Party) is allotted two-thirds of the seats in each chamber, the remaining seats being divided proportionately among the other contending parties. Executive power is held by the President, directly elected for 5 years at the same time as the Congress. He rules with the assistance of an appointed Council of State.
Length of roadways: 7035 miles *11 320 km* (1983).
Length of railways: 274 miles *441 km*.
Universities: 2.
Adult illiteracy: 15·7% in 1983.
Expectation of life: Males 60·3 years; females 63·6 years (UN estimates for 1970–75).
Defence: Military service: 18 months (Navy 2 years); total armed forces 14 370 (1985); defence expenditure: 4·1% of total government expenditure in 1986.
Foreign tourists: 291 956 in 1984.

Peru

Official name: República del Perú.

left: **PERU**   *centre:* **PARAGUAY**

THE PHILIPPINES

Population: 17 005 210 (1981 census); 19 700 000 (1985 estimate).
Area: 496 225 miles² *1 285 216 km²*.
Languages: Spanish, Quéchua, Aymará.
Religion: Roman Catholic.
Capital city: Lima, population 4 164 597 (1981 census); 5 258 600 (1983 estimate).
Other principal towns (1981): Callao 478 500; Arequipa 447 431; Trujillo 354 557; Chiclayo 280 244; Chimbote 216 406; Piura 186 354; Cuzco 181 604; Huancayo 115 693 (1972); Iquitos 173 629.
Highest point: Huascarán, 22 205 ft *6768 m*.
Principal mountain ranges: Cordillera de los Andes (C. Oriental, C. Occidental, C. Blanca).
Principal rivers: Amazonas (Amazon), with Ucayali.
Head of State: Alan García Perez (b. 23 May 1949), President.
Prime Minister: Luis Alva Castro.
Climate: Varies with altitude. Daily fluctuations greater than seasonal. Rainy season October–April. Heavy rains in tropical forests. In Lima, average maximum 19°C *66°F* (August) to 28°C *83°F* (February, March), minimum 13°C *56°F* (August) to 19°C *67°F* (February), August rainiest (two days). Absolute maximum temperature 38,5°C *101·3°F*, Iquitos, 19 June 1948; absolute minimum −20,2°C *−4·4F*, Imata, 1 Aug. 1947.
Labour force: 5 313 891 in 1981: Agriculture, forestry and fishing 36·4%; Manufacturing 10·6%; Trade 12%; Community, social and personal services 20·5%; Unemployed 3·1%.
Gross domestic product: 323·5 million inti in

1984: Agriculture and fishing 15·1%; Mining and petroleum 9·8%; Manufacturing 21·1%; Government 8·4%.
Exports: US$3147 million in 1984: Petroleum and derivatives 19·6%; Copper 14%; Zinc 10·8%; Lead 7·4%; Silver 7·2%.
Monetary unit: Inti. 1 inti = 100 céntimos.
Denominations:
   Coins 50 céntimos; 1, 5, 10 inti.
   Notes 10, 50, 100, 200, 500 inti.
Exchange rate to £ sterling: 30·57 (26 Jan. 1987).
Political history and government: A republic comprising 23 departments and one province. Following disputed presidential elections on 10 June 1962, a military junta took power in a *coup* on 18 July 1962 and annulled the election results. Congressional and presidential elections were held again on 9 June 1963. Fernando Belaúnde Terry, runner-up in 1956 and 1962, was elected President and took office for a six-year term on 28 July 1963, when military rule ended. On 3 Oct. 1968 President Belaúnde was deposed by another military *coup*, led by the army commander, Gen Juan Velasco Alvarado. The bicameral National Congress was abolished, political activity suspended and a revolutionary government of military officers took power, with Gen Velasco as President. Executive and legislative powers were exercised by the armed forces through the President, ruling by decree with the assistance of an appointed Council of Ministers. On 29 Aug. 1975 President Velasco was deposed by the Prime Minister, Gen Francisco Morales Bermúdez.
   On 28 July 1977 President Morales announced plans for the restoration of civilian rule. On 18 June 1978 a Constituent Assembly of 100 members was elected by literate adults, using proportional representation. The Assembly was convened on 28 July 1978. It adopted a new constitution on 12 July 1979 and dissolved itself two days later. The constitution vests executive power in a President, elected for a five-year term by universal adult suffrage (including illiterates for the first time). Legislative power is vested in a bicameral National Congress, also directly elected for five years. The Congress comprises the Senate (60 members chosen on a regional basis plus ex-Presidents of constitutional governments) and the Chamber of Deputies (180 members chosen on the basis of proportional representation). Congressional and presidential elections were held on 18 May 1980, when ex-President Belaúnde was re-elected Head of State. Power was transferred to the new civilian authorities on 28 July 1980, when the new constitution came into force. Each department is administered by an appointed official.
Length of roadways: 40 400 miles *65 000 km* (1984).
Length of railways: 1012 miles *1628 km*.
Universities: 32.
Adult illiteracy: 27·5% (males 16·7%; females 38·2%) in 1972.
Expectation of life: Males 52·59 years; females 55·48 years (1960–65).
Defence: Military service: two years, selective; total armed forces 122 100 (27 000 conscripts) in 1986; defence expenditure: 19·8% of total government expenditure in 1984.
Foreign tourists: 278 782 in 1984.

The Philippines

Official name: República de Filipinas (in Spanish) or Repúblika ñg Pilipinas (in Tagalog): Republic of the Philippines.
Population: 54 668 332 (1985).
Area: 115 831 miles² *300 000 km²*.
Languages: Cebuano; Tagalog; Ilocano; Panay-Hiligaynon; Bikol and about 70 other dialects belonging to the Malayo-Polynesian family of tongues. The national language, Pilipino, is based on Tagalog. English is widely understood and spoken.
Religions (1960): Roman Catholic 84%; Aglipayan 5%; Muslim 5%; Protestant 3%.
Capital city: Manila, population 5 925 884 (1980 census).

Other principal towns (1980): Quezon City 1 165 865; Davao 610 375; Cebu 490 281; Zamboanga 343 722; Pasay 287 770; Bacolod 262 415; Iloilo 244 827; San Carlos (on Pangasinan) 101 243; San Carlos (on Negros Occidental) 91 627.
Highest point: Mt Apo (on Mindanao), 9690 ft *2953 m*.
Principal mountain ranges: Cordillera Central (on Luzon), Diuata Range (on Mindanao).
Principal rivers: Cagayan (180 miles *290 km*) Pampanga, Abra, Agusan, Magat, Laoang, Agno.
Head of State: Corazon Cojuangco Aquino (b. 25 January 1933), President.
Prime Minister: Salvador H. Laurel (b. 18 November 1928).
Climate: Tropical. Hot and humid, except in mountains. Heavy rainfall, frequent typhoons. In Manila, average maximum 30°C *86°F* (December January) to 34°C *93°F* (April, May), minimum 21°C *69°F* (January, February) to 24°C *75°F* (May–August), July rainiest (24 days). Absolute maximum temperature 42,2°C *108·0°F*, Tuguegarao, 29 Apr. 1912; absolute minimum 7,3°C *45·1°F*, Baguio City, 1 Feb. 1930 and 11 Jan. 1932.
Labour force: 20 923 000 in 1984: Agriculture, forestry and fishing 46·5%; Manufacturing 9·3%; Trade 11·8%; Community, social and personal services 15·8%; Unemployed 6%.
Gross domestic product: 548 327 million pesos in 1984: Agriculture, forestry and fishing 25·3%; Manufacturing 25%; Trade 18·2%; Financial services 7·7%.
Exports: US$5265·1 million in 1984: Coconut oil 11%; Electrical machinery 7%; Clothing 4·7%; Sugar 4·5%; Wood and wood products 5·4%.
Monetary unit: Philippine peso. 1 peso = 100 centavos.
Denominations:
   Coins 1, 5, 10, 25, 50 centavos; 1, 5 pesos.
   Notes 2, 5, 10, 20, 50, 100 pesos.
Exchange rate to £ sterling: 20·38 (18 Jan. 1985).
Political history and government: Formerly a Spanish colony. After the Spanish-American War, Spain ceded the Philippines to the USA (10 Dec. 1898). A constitution, ratified by plebiscite on 14 May 1935, gave the Philippines self-government and provided for independence after 10 years. The islands were occupied by Japanese forces in 1942–45. After the restoration of US rule, the Philippines became an independent republic on 4 July 1946.
   The 1935 Constitution provided for a presidential system of government with an independent judiciary and legislature. The Philippines had a succession of six presidents until Ferdinand Edralin Marcos (1966–86) proclaimed martial law on 21 September 1972 and suspended the bicameral Congress. Opposition to his one-man rule and excesses in government power grew over the years. It culminated with the assassination of a prominent opposition figure, former Senator Benigno Aquino, on 21 August 1983. In November 1985 Marcos announced an early presidential election. Mrs Coraon C. Aquino ran against Marcos in the 1986 elections where observers attributed large-scale fraud and intimidation to the ruling party. On 15 February 1986 the national assembly proclaimed Marcos as the winner of the election. The following day, Mrs Aquino announced her party's campaign for civil disobedience which eventually ended Marcos' rule and led to his exile in Hawaii. Mrs Aquino was inaugurated as the seventh President of the Philippine Republic on 25 February 1986. She proclaimed a revolutionary government and appointed a Constitutional Commission to draft a new Constitution. The new constitution would restore the Philippine government to the presidential system with an independent judiciary, a bicameral congress, and a presidential tenure limited to six years without re-election.
   The country is divided into 12 regions and 72 provinces.
Length of roadways: 96 623 miles *155 467 km* (1983).
Length of railways: 711 miles *1144 km*.

Universities: 66.
Adult illiteracy: 17·4% (males 15·7%; females 19·1%) in 1970.
Expectation of life: Males 61·3 years; Females 64·9 years (1985).
Defence: Military service: selective; total armed forces 122 100 (1986); defence expenditure: 8·7% of total government expenditure in 1980.
Foreign tourists: 816 714 in 1984.

Poland

Official name: Polska Rzeczpospolita Ludowa (Polish People's Republic).
Population: 37 063 300 (1984 estimate).
Area: 120 727 miles² *312 683 km²*.
Language: Polish.
Religion: Roman Catholic (over 70%).
Capital city: Warszawa (Warsaw), population 1 649 050 (1984 estimate).
Other principal towns (31 Dec. 1984): Łódź 849 440; Kraków (Cracow) 740 260; Wrocław (Breslau) 635 950; Poznań (Posen) 574 070; Gdańsk (Danzig) 467 110; Szczecin (Stettin) 370 780; Katowice 363 270; Bydgoszcz (Bromberg) 361 390; Lublin 324 150.
Highest point: Rysy, 8199 ft *2499 m*.
Principal mountain ranges: Carpathian Mountains (Tatra range), Beskids.
Principal rivers: Wisła (Vistula) with Narew, Odra (Oder).
Head of State: Gen. Wojciech Jaruzelski (b. 6 July 1923), Chairman of the Council of State.
Head of Government: Zbigniew Messner, Chairman of the Council of Ministers.
Climate: Temperate in west, continental in east. Short, rainy summers, but occasional dry spells; cold, snowy winters. In Warsaw, average maximum −0,4°C *31°F* (January) to 24°C *75°F* (July), minimum −6°C *21°F* (January) to 15°C *59°F* (July), June, July and August rainiest (each 6 days). Absolute maximum temperature 40·2°C *104·4°F*, Prószków, 29 July 1921; absolute minimum −40·6°C *−41·1°F*, Zywiec, 10 Feb. 1929.
Labour force: 17 163 800 aged 15 and over (31 Dec. 1984): Agriculture and forestry 30·8%; Industry (mining, quarrying, manufacturing, electricity, gas and water) 29·1%; Services 7·7%.
Net material product: 7181·8 billion złotys in 1984: Agriculture, forestry and fishing 17·5%; Industry 49·6%; Construction 11·6%; Trade 13·7%; Transport and storage 5%.
Exports: 1336·1 billion złotys in 1984: Hard coal 14·3%; Products of basic metal industries 9·1%; Products of electro-engineering industries 39·3%; Products of chemical industry 9·8%; Products of food industry 6·3%.
Monetary unit: Złoty. 1 złoty = 100 groszy.
Denominations:
  Coins 1, 2, 5, 10, 20, 50 groszy; 1, 2, 5, 10, 20, 50 złotys.
  Notes 50, 100, 200, 500, 1000, 2000, 5000 złotys.
Exchange rate to £ sterling: 291·17 (26 Jan. 1987).
Political history and government: Formerly partitioned between Austria, Prussia and Russia. After the First World War an independent republic was declared on 11 Nov. 1918. Parliamentary government was overthrown in May 1926 by military leaders who ruled until 1939, when invasions by Nazi Germany (1 Sept.) and the USSR (17 Sept.) led to another partition (29 Sept.). After Germany declared war on the USSR (June 1941) its forces occupied the whole of Poland but they were driven out by Soviet forces in March 1945. With the end of the Second World War (May 1945) Poland's frontiers were redrawn. A provisional government was formed on 28 June 1945. A Communist régime took power after the elections of 19 Jan. 1947 and a People's Republic was established on 19 Feb. 1947. At a congress on 15–21 Dec. 1948 the Polish Workers' (Communist) Party merged with the Polish Socialist Party to form the Polish United Workers' Party (PUWP). A new constitution was adopted on 22 July 1952.

The supreme organ of state power is the unicameral Parliament (*Sejm*), with 460 members elected by universal adult suffrage for four years (in the elections of 23 Mar. 1980 there were 646 candidates). The *Sejm* elects a Council of State (17 members) to be its permanent organ. The highest executive and administrative body is the Council of Ministers, appointed by (and responsible to) the *Sejm*.

Political power is held by the Communist PUWP, which dominates the Front of National Unity (including two other smaller parties). The Front presents an approved list of candidates for elections to representative bodies. The PUWP's highest authority is the Party Congress, normally convened every four years. The Congress elects a Central Committee (200 members were elected on 17 July 1981) to supervize Party work. To direct its policy the Committee elects a Political Bureau (Politburo), with 15 full members (including the Committee's First Secretary) and two alternate members in 1981.

On 13 Dec. 1981 the régime declared martial law and established a 20-member military council for national salvation led by the Chairman of the Council of Ministers. Martial law was suspended in Dec. 1982.
Length of roadways: 80 000 miles *128 000 km*.
Length of railways: 16 824 miles *27 070 km*.
Universities: 10 (plus 18 technical universities).
Adult illiteracy: 1·2% (males 0·7%; females 1·7%) in 1978.
Expectation of life: Males 67·0 years; females 75·2 years (1983).
Defence: Military service: Army, internal security forces and Air Force 2 years, Navy and special services 3 years; total regular forces 319 000 (1985); defence expenditure: 7·4% of total government expenditure in 1984.
Foreign tourists: 3 000 000 in 1985.

Portugal

Official name: A República Portuguesa (the Portuguese Republic).
*Population: 9 806 333 (1981 census); 10 089 300 (1984 estimate).
*Area: 35 553 miles² *92 082 km²*.
Language: Portuguese.
Religion: Roman Catholic.
Capital city: Lisboa (Lisbon), population 807 937 (1981 census).
Other principal towns (1981): Oporto 327 368; Amadora 95 518; Coimbra 74 616; Setubal 77 885; Braga 63 033.
*Highest point: 7713 ft *2351 m*.
Principal mountain range: Serra da Estréla.
Principal river: Rio Tejo (Tagus).
Head of State: Dr Mário Alberto Nobre Lopes Soares (b. December 1924), President.
Prime Minister: Professor Aníbal Cavaco Silva.
Climate: Mild and temperate. Average annual temperature 16°C *61°F*, drier and hotter inland. Hot summers, rainy winters in central areas, warm and very dry in south. In Lisbon, average maximum 13°C *56°F* (January) to 27°C *80°F* (August), minimum 8°C *46°F* (January) to 18°C *64°F* (August); March, November and December rainiest (each 10 days). Absolute maximum temperature 45,8°C *114·4°F*, Coimbra, 31 July 1944; absolute minimum −11,0°C *12·2°F*, Penhas Douradas, 25 Jan. 1947.
Labour force: 4 064 000 in 1984: Agriculture, forestry and fishing 24·6%; Manufacturing 25%; Trade 12·9%; Construction 8·6%; Community, social and personal services 9·9%.
Gross domestic product: 2289·6 billion escudos in 1983: Agriculture, forestry and fishing 8·4%; Mining and manufacturing industries 30·2%; Construction 7·4%; Services 55·7%.
Exports: 760 576·6 million escudos in 1984: Food and live animals 5·3%; Alcoholic beverages 3·4%; Crude materials (except fuels) 9%; Chemicals 7·7%; Textile manufactures 12·3%; Machinery and transport equipment 17·3%; Clothing 15·5%.
Monetary unit: Portuguese escudo. 1 escudo = 100 centavos.
Denominations:
  Coins 10, 20, 50 centavos; 1, 2½, 5, 10, 20, 25 escudos.
  Notes 20, 50, 100, 500, 1000, 5000 escudos.

left: **PORTUGAL**   *right:* **POLAND**

Exchange rate to £ sterling: 216·45 (26 Jan. 1987).
Political history and government: Formerly a kingdom. An anti-monarchist uprising deposed the King on 5 Oct. 1910, when a republic was proclaimed. The parliamentary regime was overthrown by a military *coup* on 28 May 1926. Dr António Salazar became Prime Minister, with dictatorial powers, on 5 July 1932. A new constitution, establishing a corporate state, was adopted on 19 Mar. 1933. Dr Salazar retained power until illness forced his retirement on 26 Sept. 1968. His successor, Dr Marcello Caetano, was deposed on 25 Apr. 1974 by a military *coup*, initiated by the Armed Forces Movement. Military leaders formed a Junta of National Salvation and appointed one of its members as President. He appointed a Prime Minister and, on the latter's recommendation, other Ministers to form a provisional government. The 1933 constitution was suspended and the bicameral Parliament dissolved.

On 14 Mar. 1975 the Junta was dissolved and three days later a Supreme Revolutionary Council (SRC) was established to exercise authority until a new constitution took effect. A Constitutional Assembly was elected on 25 Apr. 1975 to formulate a new constitution. After approval by the SRC, the constitution, committing Portugal to make a transition to socialism, was promulgated on 2 Apr. 1976. It provides for a unicameral legislature, the Assembly of the Republic, elected by universal adult suffrage for 4 years (subject to dissolution). The first Assembly, with 263 members, was elected on 25 Apr. 1976, when the constitution entered into force. The SRC was renamed the Council of the Revolution, becoming a consultative body, headed by the President, with powers to delay legislation and the right of veto in military matters. Executive power is vested in the President, directly elected for 5 years. A new President was elected on 27 June and inaugurated on 14 July 1976. The President appoints a Prime Minister to lead a Council of Ministers, responsible to the Assembly. Legislation approved on 2 Oct. 1978 reduced the Assembly to 250 members (including four representing Portuguese abroad) at the next elections. The Assembly was dissolved by the President on 11 Sept. 1979 and new elections held on 2 Dec. 1979 to complete the Assembly's term, ending in Oct. 1980. A new Assembly, also with 250 members, was elected on 5 Oct. 1980.
Length of roadways: 32 274 miles *51 929 km* (1981).
Length of railways: 2229 miles *3588 km*.
Universities: 11.
Adult illiteracy: 29·0% (males 22·4%; females 34·7%) in 1970.
Expectation of life: Males 68·9 years; females 76·5 years (1981).
Defence: Military service: Army 16 months, Navy and Air Force 24 months; total armed forces 73 040 (48 900 conscripts) in 1985; defence

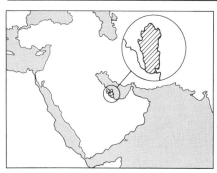

QATAR

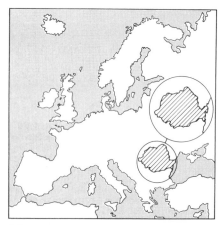

ROMANIA

expenditure: 7% of total government expenditure in 1984.
Foreign tourists: 9 811 000 in 1984.

* Metropolitan Portugal, including the Azores and Maideira Islands.

Qatar

Official name: Dawlat Qatar (State of Qatar).
Population: 287 000 (1985 estimate).
Area: 4416 miles² *11 437 km²*.
Language: Arabic.
Religion: Muslim.
Capital city: Ad Dauhah (Doha), population 190 000 (estimate 1982).
Other principal towns: Dukhan, Umm Said.
Highest point: 240 ft *73 m*.
Head of State: Shaikh Khalifa ibn Hamad al-Thani (b. 1932), Amir and Prime Minister.
Climate: Very hot, with high humidity on the coast. Temperatures reach 49°C *120°F* in summer.
Labour force: 112 785 in 1981: Unemployed 1·3%.
Gross domestic product: 23 365 million Qatar riyals in 1983: Mining and quarrying 45·8%; Manufacturing 5·9%; Building and construction 7·1%; Trade, restaurants and hotels 6·8%; Finance, insurance, real estate and business services 9%.
Exports: 12 002 million Qatar riyals in 1983: Crude petroleum oil 90·8%; Liquefied gas 5·5%.
Monetary unit: Qatar riyal. 1 riyal = 100 dirhams.
Denominations:
Coins 1, 5, 10, 25, 50 dirhams.
Notes 1, 5, 10, 50, 100, 500 riyals.
Exchange rate to £ sterling: 5·5865 (26 Jan. 1987).
Political history and government: Became part of Turkey's Ottoman Empire in 1872. Turkish forces evacuated Qatar at the beginning of the First World War. The UK entered into treaty relations with the ruling Shaikh on 3 Nov. 1916. A provisional constitution was adopted on 2 Apr. 1970. Qatar remained under British protection until achieving full independence on 1 Sept. 1971. On 22 Feb. 1972 the ruler was deposed by his deputy, the Prime Minister.

Qatar is an absolute monarchy, with full powers vested in the ruler (called Amir since independence). It has no parliament or political parties. The ruler appoints and leads a Council of Ministers to exercise executive power. The Ministers are assisted by a nominated Consultative Council with 20 members (increased to 30 in Dec. 1975), whose term was extended for 3 years in May 1975, for a further 4 years in 1978 and for a further 4 years in 1982.
Universities: 1.
Expectation of life: Males 54·8 years; females 58·2 years (UN estimates, average for Bahrain, Qatar and the United Arab Emirates, 1970–75).
Defence: Total armed forces 6000 (1985); defence expenditure: 7·6% of total government expenditure in 1984–5.

Romania

Official name: Republica Socialistă România (Socialist Republic of Romania).
Population: 22 800 000 (1985 estimate).
Area: 91 699 miles² *237 500 km²*.
Languages (1966): Romanian 89·1%; Hungarian 7·7%; German 1·5%.
Religions: Romanian Orthodox (85% of believers), Roman Catholic, Reformed (Calvinist).
Capital city: Bucureşti (Bucharest), population 2 227 568 (1983).
Other principal towns (1983): Brasov 290 722; Constanţa 284 801; Cluj-Napoca 270 820; Iasi 265 176; Timisoara 261 950; Galaţi 254 636; Craiova 243 117; Ploeşti 215 500; Brăila 214 561.
Highest point: Moldoveanu, 8346 ft *2544 m*.
Principal mountain ranges: Carpathian Mountains.
Principal rivers: Dunărea (Danube) (1777 miles *2860 km*, 668 miles *1075 km* in Romania), Mureş (458 miles *768 km*), Prut (445 miles *716 km*).
Head of State: Nicolae Ceauşescu (b. 26 Jan. 1918), President; also General Secretary of the Central Committee of the Romanian Communist Party.
Head of Government: Constantin Dăscălescu, Chairman of the Council of Ministers.
Climate: Hot and humid summers (average temperature 21°C *70°F*); cold, windy, snowy winters (average −2°C *28°F*). Moderate rainfall. Absolute maximum temperature 44,5°C *112·1°F*, Ion Sion, 10 Aug. 1951; minimum −38,5°C *−37·3°F*, Bod, near Braşov, 25 Jan. 1942.
Labour force: 10 457 800 in 1983: Agriculture and forestry 29·2%; Industry 36·7%; Services 12·3%.
Net material product: 750·8 billion lei in 1985.
Exports: 173 324 million lei in 1983: Furniture 3·6%; Tractors and agricultural equipment 3·5%; Oilfield machinery and equipment 2·7%; Textile manufactures 3·4%.
Monetary unit: Leu (plural: lei). 1 leu = 100 bani.
Denominations:
Coins 25 bani; 1, 3, 5 lei.
Notes 10, 25, 50, 100 lei.
Exchange rate to £ sterling: 15·32 (26 Jan. 1986).
Political history and government: Formerly a monarchy. Under the Fascist 'Iron Guard' movement, Romania entered the Second World War as an ally of Nazi Germany. Soviet forces entered Romania in 1944. The Iron Guard régime was overthrown on 23 Aug. 1944 and a predominantly Communist government took power on 6 Mar. 1945. The Romanian Communist Party (RCP) merged with the Social Democratic Party, to form the Romanian Workers' Party (RWP), on 1 Oct. 1947. The King was forced to abdicate on 30 Dec. 1947, when the Romanian People's Republic was proclaimed. The RWP became the RCP again on 2 June 1965. A new constitution, introducing the country's present name, was adopted on 21 Aug. 1965.

The supreme organ of state power is the unicameral Grand National Assembly, with 369 members elected by universal adult suffrage for five years. The Assembly elects from its number the State Council (21 members) to be its permanent organ. The President of the Repub-

lic, elected by the Assembly for its duration, is also President of the State Council. The Council of Ministers, the highest organ of state administration, is elected by (and responsible to) the Assembly.

Political power is held by the RCP, the only legal party, which dominates the Socialist Democracy and Unity Front. The Front presents an approved list of candidates for elections to representative bodies. The Head of State is General Secretary of the RCP and Chairman of the Front. The RCP's highest authority is the Party Congress, convened every five years. The Congress elects a Central Committee (265 full members and 181 alternate members) to supervise Party work. The Central Committee elects from its members an Executive Political Committee (23 full members and 26 alternate members) to direct policy. The Executive Committee has a 11-member Permanent Bureau (including the President), which is the Party's most powerful policy-making body.

Romania comprises 40 administrative districts and the Municipality of Bucharest, each with a People's Council elected for five years.
Length of roadways: 9124 miles *14 681 km* (1983).
Length of railways: 6874 miles *11 061 km* (1983).
Universities: 6 (plus 44 institutes of higher education).
Adult illiteracy: Officially abolished.
Expectation of life: Males 67·4 years; females 72·4 years (1982).
Defence: Military service: Army and Air Force 16 months, Navy 18 months; total armed forces 219 700 in 1986; defence expenditure: 3·4% of total government expenditure in 1985.
Foreign tourists: 6 600 000 in 1984.

Rwanda

Official name: La République rwandaise (in French) or Republika y'u Rwanda (in Kinyarwanda).
Population: 5 757 000 (1983 estimate).
Area: 10 169 miles² *26 338 km²*.
Languages: French, Kinyarwanda (both official), Kiswahili.
Religions: Roman Catholic, Animist; Protestant and Muslim minorities.
Capital city: Kigali, population 117 749 at 1978 census.
Other principal towns (1978): Butare 21 691; Ruhengeri 16 025; Gisenyi 12 436.
Highest point: Mt Karisimbi, 14 787 ft *4507 m*.
Principal mountain range: Chaîne des Mitumba.
Principal river: Luvironza (headwaters of the Nile).
Head of State: Maj-Gen Juvénal Habyarimana (b. 8 Mar. 1937), President.
Climate: Tropical, tempered by altitude. Average temperature at 4800 ft *1463 m* is 23°C *73°F*. Hot and humid in lowlands, cool in highlands. Average annual rainfall 785 mm *31 in*. Main rainy season from February to May, dry season May to September.
Labour force: 2 661 359 in 1978: Agriculture, forestry and fishing 92·9%; Manufacturing 1·3%; Trade 1%; Community, social and personal services 2·8%.
Gross domestic product: 104 497 million Rwanda francs in 1981: Agriculture, forestry and fishing 29·7%; Manufacturing 18·2%; Construction and public works 5·2%; Trade 18·8%; Services 5·1%; Public administration 15·7%.
Exports: 13 476 million Rwanda francs in 1984: Coffee 65·4%; Tea 17·6%; Tin ores and concentrates 9·5%.
Monetary unit: Franc rwandais (Rwanda franc). 1 franc = 100 centimes.
Denominations:
Coins 50 centimes; 1, 2, 5, 10, 20, 50 francs.
Notes 20, 50, 100, 500, 1000 francs.
Exchange rate to £ sterling: 123·22 (26 Jan. 1987).
Political history and government: Formerly a monarchy, ruled by a *Mwami* (King). Part of German East Africa from 1899. Occupied in 1916 by Belgian forces from the Congo (now Zaire). From 1920 Rwanda was part of Ruanda-Urundi, administered by Belgium under League

of Nations mandate and later as a UN Trust Territory. Following a referendum on 25 Sept. 1961, the monarchy was abolished and the republic which had been proclaimed on 28 Jan. 1961 was recognized by Belgium on 2 Oct. 1961. Rwanda became independent on 1 July 1962. On 5 July 1973 the government was overthrown by a military *coup*, led by Maj-Gen Juvénal Habyarimana, who became President. The National Assembly was dissolved and political activity suspended. On 5 July 1975 President Habyarimana established a new ruling party, the *Mouvement révolutionnaire national pour le développement* (MRND), the National Revolutionary Movement for Development. A referendum on 17 Dec. 1978 approved a new constitution legalizing Habyarimana's régime. Executive power is vested in the President, elected by universal adult suffrage for a five-year term. The constitution provides for a 50-member National Development Council (NDC), also to be directly elected for five years. The NDC is granted limited legislative powers but is unable to change government policy. The MRND became the sole political organization. Habyarimana was elected (unopposed) on 24 Dec. 1978 to continue as President. The President appoints and leads a Council of Ministers. Rwanda comprises 10 prefectures, each administered by an appointed official.

Length of roadways: 4239 miles *6820 km*.
Universities: 1.
Adult illiteracy: 83·6% (males 76%; females 91%) in 1962 (UNESCO estimates).
Expectation of life: Males 41·8 years; females 45·0 years (UN estimates for 1970–75).
Defence: Total armed forces 5150 (1985); defence expenditure: 16·5% of total government expenditure in 1983.
Foreign tourists: 19 700 in 1984.

Saint Lucia

Population: 134 000 (1984 estimate).
Area: 238 miles² *616 km²*.
Language: English.
Religion: Christian (mainly Roman Catholic, also Anglican and Methodist).
Capital city: Castries, population 50 700 (1984 estimate).
Other principal town: Vieux Fort, Sarfriere.
Highest point: Morne (Mt.) Gimie, 3145 ft *959 m*.
Head of State: HM Queen Elizabeth II, represented by Sir Allen Lewis GCMG.
Prime Minister: The Rt Hon. John Compton.
Climate: Warm and moist. Dry season Jan.–Apr., rainy May–Aug. In Castries, average annual temperature 28°C *82°F*, rainfall 2235 mm *88 in*, rising to 3480 mm *137 in* inland.
Labour force: 48 012 (1981).
Gross domestic product: EC$294·2 million in 1981: Agriculture, forestry and fishing 13·6%; Manufacturing 9·3%; Construction 15·1%; Trade 19·7%; Transport, storage and communications 10·4%; Financial services 13·2%; Government services 16·3%.
Exports: EC$101·8 million in 1982: Food and live animals 47·5%; Beverages and tobacco 9·5%; Animal and vegetable oils and fats 10·6%; Basic manufactures 14·8%; Miscellaneous manufactures 11·1%.
Monetary unit: East Caribbean dollars (EC$). 1 dollar = 100 cents.
Denominations:
Coins 1, 2, 5, 10, 25, 50 cents.
Notes 1, 5, 20, 100 dollars.
Exchange rate to £ sterling: 4·13 (26 Jan. 1987).
Political history and government: A former British dependency, St. Lucia was administered by the Governor of the Windward Islands until 31 Dec. 1959. From 1 Jan. 1960 it had a new constitution, with its own Administrator. On 1 Mar. 1967 St. Lucia became one of the West Indies Associated States, with full internal self-government. The Administrator became Governor and the Chief Minister was restyled Premier. After a constitutional conference on 24–27 July 1978, Saint Lucia (as it was restyled) became fully independent, within the Commonwealth, on 22 Feb. 1979. The Governor became

Governor-General and the Premier took office as Prime Minister.
Saint Lucia is a constitutional monarchy. Executive power is vested in the British monarch and is exercisable by the Governor-General, who is appointed on the advice of the Prime Minister and acts in almost all matters on the advice of the Cabinet. Legislative power is vested in a bicameral Parliament, comprising a Senate (11 members appointed by the Governor-General) and a House of Assembly (initially 17 members) elected from single-member constituencies by universal adult suffrage for 5 years (subject to dissolution). The Governor-General appoints the Prime Minister and, on the latter's recommendation, other Ministers from among members of the Senate and the House. The Cabinet is responsible to the House.
Length of roadways: 500 miles *800 km*.
Adult illiteracy: 14·8% (population aged 10 and over) in 1970.
Expectation of life: Males 65 years; females 71 years (1983).
Foreign tourists: 87 610 in 1984.

Saint Vincent and the Grenadines

Population: 123 000 (1984 estimate).
Area: 150·3 miles² *389 km²*.
Language: English.
Religion: Christian (mainly Anglican).
Capital: Kingstown, population 24 764 (1982 estimate).
Other principal towns: Georgetown, Barrouallie, Chateaubelair, Layou.
Highest point: Soufrière, 4048 ft *1234 m*.
Head of State: HM Queen Elizabeth II, represented by Joseph Lambert Eustace, Governor-General.
Prime Minister: The Rt Hon. James Mitchell.
Climate: Warm and moist, with average temperatures between 19°C *67°F* and 32°C *89°F*.
Labour force: 40 000 (1983).
Gross domestic product: EC$223·8 million in 1982: Agriculture, forestry and fishing 13%; Manufacturing 9·2%; Construction 10%; Trade 10·1%; Transport, storage and communications 13·3%; Financial services 11·9%; Government services 15·2%.
Exports: EC$84 826 000 in 1982: Bananas 28·6%; Flour 17·8%; Tubers 8·8%; Basic manufactures 9·6%; Machinery and transport equipment 5·8%; Miscellaneous manufactures 8·3%.
Monetary unit: East Caribbean dollar (EC$). 1 dollar = 100 cents.
Denominations:
Coins 1, 2, 5, 10, 25, 50 cents.
Notes 1, 5, 20, 100 dollars.
Exchange rate to £ sterling: 4·13 (26 Jan. 1987).
Political history and government: A former British dependency. The islands, collectively known as St Vincent, were administered by the Governor of the Windward Islands until 31 Dec. 1959. From 1 Jan. 1960 St Vincent had a new constitution, with its own Administrator. On 27 Oct. 1969 it became one of the West Indies Associated States, with full internal self-government. The Administrator became Governor and the Chief Minister was restyled Premier. After a constitutional conference on 18–21 Sept. 1978, the islands, under their present name, became fully independent, as a 'special member' of the Commonwealth, on 27 Oct. 1979. The Governor became Governor-General and the Premier took office as Prime Minister.
The country is a constitutional monarchy. Executive power is vested in the British monarch and is exercisable by the Governor-General, who is appointed on the advice of the Prime Minister and acts in almost all matters on the advice of the Cabinet. Legislative power is vested in the unicameral House of Assembly, with 19 members serving for 5 years (subject to dissolution). The House has 6 Senators (nominated by the Governor-General) and 13 members elected by universal adult suffrage from single-member constituencies. The 13 members of the pre-independence House took office as the

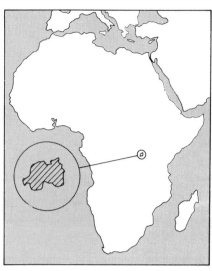

RWANDA

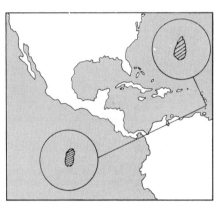

top: **SAINT LUCIA**
below: **SAINT VINCENT AND THE GRENADINES**

elective members of the new House. The Governor-General appoints the Prime Minister and, on the latter's recommendation, other Ministers from among members of the House. The Cabinet is responsible to the House.
Length of roadways: 633 miles *1019 km*.
Adult illiteracy: 15% in 1983.
Expectation of life: Males 58·46 years; females 59·67 years (1959–61).
Foreign tourists: 86 350 in 1983.

San Marino

Official name: Serenissima Repubblica di San Marino (Most Serene Republic of San Marino).
Population: 19 149 (census of 30 Nov. 1976); 22 206 (estimate for 1984).
Area: 23·4 miles² *60,5 km²*.
Language: Italian.
Religion: Roman Catholic.
Capital city: San Marino, population 4620 at 31 Dec. 1984.
Highest point: Mt Titano, 2424 ft *739 m*.
Head of State: There are two Captains-Regent (*Capitani reggenti*) appointed every six months.
Climate: Warm summers, average maximum 29°C *85°F*; dry, cold winters.
Labour force: 8674 in 1976.
Monetary unit: Italian currency (*q.v.*) and San Marino currency.
Political history and government: Founded as a city-state in AD 301. In customs union with Italy since 1862. Legislative power is vested in the unicameral Great and General Council, with 60 members elected by universal adult suffrage for 5 years (subject to dissolution). Women have had the right to vote since 1960 and to stand for

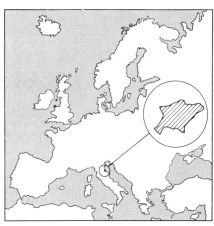

SAN MARINO

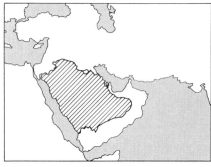

SAUDI ARABIA

election since 1973. The Council elects two of its members (one representing the capital, one the rest of the country) to act jointly as Captains-Regent, with the functions of Head of State and Government, for 6 months at a time. The first female Captain-Regent took office on 1 Apr. 1981. Executive power is held by the Congress of State, with 10 members elected by the Council for the duration of its term. San Marino comprises nine administrative areas, called 'castles', each with an elected committee led by the 'Captain of the Castle', chosen for a 6-month term.
Length of roadways: 137 miles *220 km*.
Foreign tourists: 2 561 221 in 1984.

São Tomé and Príncipe

Official name: A República Democrática de São Tomé e Príncipe (the Democratic Republic of São Tomé and Príncipe).
Population: 102 000 (1984 estimate).
Area: 372 miles² *964 km²*.
Language: Portuguese (official).
Religion: Roman Catholic.
Capital city: São Tomé, population 25 000 (1984 estimate).
Other principal town: Santo António.
Highest point: Pico Gago Coutinho (Pico de São Tomé), 6640 ft *2024 m*.
Head of State: Dr Manuel Pinto da Costa (b. 1910), President.
Climate: Warm and humid, with an average temperature of 27°C *80°F*.
Labour force: 30 607 in 1981: Agriculture, forestry and fishing 53·9%; Mining and manufacturing 5·3%; Trade 6·5%; Community, social and personal services 19%; Unemployed 4·6%.
Gross domestic product: 724·6 million dobra in 1974: Agriculture, forestry and fishing (excluding government) 56·0% (agriculture 49·1%); Trade, restaurants and hotels 14·2% (trade 13·3%); Community, social and personal services 14·3%.
Exports: US$8 million in 1981: Cocoa 90%: Copra 7%.
Monetary unit: Dobra. 1 dobra = 100 centavos.

Denominations:
Coins 10, 20, 50 centavos; 1, 2½, 5, 10, 20, 50 dobra.
Notes 20, 50, 100, 500, 1000 dobra.
Exchange rate to £ sterling: 52·045 (26 Jan. 1987).
Political history and government: A former Portuguese territory, independent since 12 July 1975. Before independence, Portugal recognized the islands' Liberation Movement (MLSTP), whose leader became first President. A Constitutional Assembly, elected on 6 July 1975, approved a new constitution on 12 Dec. 1975. Under the constitution, the MLSTP is 'the leading political force of the nation'. The supreme organ of state is the People's Assembly, with 33 members (mostly MLSTP officials) serving a 4-year term. Executive power is vested in the President, elected for 4 years by the Assembly on the proposal of the MLSTP. He directs the government and appoints Ministers. The government is responsible to the Assembly. The post of Prime Minister was abolished in April 1979.
Length of roadways: 178 miles *287 km* (1973).
Defence: Total armed forces 160 in 1976.

Saudi Arabia

Official name: Al-Mamlaka al-'Arabiya as-Sa'udiya (the Kingdom of Saudi Arabia).
Population: 10 421 000 (1983 estimate).
Area: 830 000 miles² *2 149 690 km²*.
Language: Arabic.
Religion: Muslim.
Capital city: Ar Riyād (Riyadh), population 666 840 at 1974 census.
Other principal towns (1974): Jidda (Jeddah) 561 104; Makkah (Mecca) 366 801; At Ta'if 204 857; Al Madinah (Medina) 198 186; Ad Dammam 127 844; Al Hufuf 101 271.
Highest point: Jebel Razikh, 12 002 ft *3658 m*.
Principal mountain range: Tihā matash Shām.
Principal rivers: The flows are seasonal only.
Head of State and Prime Minister: HM King Fahd bin Abdulaziz.
Climate: Very hot and dry. Mostly desert; frequent sandstorms. Average summer temperature 38°C *100°F* to 49°C *120°F* on coast, up to 54°C *130°F* inland. High humidity. Some places have droughts for years. In Riyadh, average maximum is 42°C *107°F* June–August; January coldest (4°C *40°F* to 21°C *70°F*). In Jeddah, average maximum 29°C *84°F* (January, February) to 37°C *99°F* (July, August), minimum 18°C *65°F* (February) to 27°C *80°F* (August), rainiest month is November (two days).
Labour force: 2 121 000 (mid-1970): Agriculture, forestry and fishing 66·0%; Industry 11·7%; Services 22·3% (ILO estimates).
Gross domestic product: 381 592 million riyals in 1983–4: Mining 39·5%; Manufacturing 7·2%; Construction 13·2%; Trade 7·7%; Transport, storage and communications 6%; Financial services 9·1%.
Exports: 132 250 million riyals in 1984: Crude petroleum 86·6%; Refined petroleum 4·7%.
Monetary unit: Saudi riyal. 1 riyal = 20 qursh = 100 halalah.
Denominations:
Coins 1, 5, 10, 25, 50 halalah; 1, 2, 4 qursh.
Notes 1, 5, 10, 50, 100 riyals.
Exchange rate to £ sterling: 5·7168 (26 Jan. 1987).
Political history and government: Formerly part of Turkey's Ottoman Empire. In 1913 the Sultan of Nejd overthrew Turkish rule in central Arabia. Between 1919 and 1925 he gained control of the Hijaz and was proclaimed King there on 8 Jan. 1926. On 23 Sept. 1932 the Hijaz and Nejd were combined and named Saudi Arabia. The country is an absolute monarchy, with no parliament or political parties. The King rules in accordance with the *Sharia*, the sacred law of Islam. He appoints and leads a Council of Ministers, which serves as the instrument of royal authority in both legislative and executive matters. The King is also assisted by advisory councils, nominated or approved by him.

Length of roadways: 43 144 miles *69 434 km*.
Length of railways: 355 miles *571 km*.
Universities: 7.
Adult illiteracy: 75·4% (males 65·5%; females 87·8%) in 1980.
Expectation of life: Males 44·2 years; females 46·5 years (UN estimates for 1970–75).
Defence: Military service voluntary; total armed forces 62 500 (1985); defence expenditure: 30·7% of total government expenditure in 1984–5.
Foreign tourists: about 1 600 000 in 1985.

Senegal

Official name: La République du Sénégal.
Population: 6 316 000 (1983 estimate).
Area: 75 954 miles² *196 722 km²*.
Languages: French (official), Wolof, Fulani (Peulh), Serer, Toucouleur.
Religions: Muslim 90%; Christian (mainly Roman Catholic) 5%.
Capital city: Dakar, population 978 553 (1979 estimate).
Other principal towns (1979): Thiès 126 886; Kaolack 115 679; Saint-Louis 96 594; Ziguinchor 79 464; Diourbel 55 307.
Highest point: Gounou Mt, 4970 ft *1515 m*.
Principal mountain range: Fouta Djalon.
Principal rivers: Gambie (Gambia), Casamance, Sénégal.
Head of State: Abdou Diouf (b. 7 Sept. 1935), President.
Climate: Tropical. Hot, with long dry season and short wet season. Average annual temperature about 29°C *84°F*. Heavy rainfall on coast. Average maximum 32°C *90°F* to 42°C *108°F* in interior; average minimum about 15°C *60°F*. In Dakar, on coast, average maximum 26°C *79°F* (January) to 32°C *89°F* (September, October); minimum 17°C *63°F* (February) to 24°C *76°F* (July to Oct.); rainiest month is Aug. (13 days).
Labour force: 2 558 000 (1982): Agriculture, forestry and fishing 79·7%; Services 13·8% (ILO estimates).
Gross domestic product: 977·7 billion CFA francs in 1983: Agriculture, forestry and fishing 20·9%; Industry (manufacturing, mining, utilities) 25·5%; Trade, transport and communications 53·6%.
Exports: 100 767 million CFA francs in 1980: Fisheries 24%; Petroleum products 18%; Phosphates 16%; Peanut oil 12%.
Monetary unit: Franc de la Communauté financière africaine.
Denominations:
Coins 1, 2, 5, 10, 25, 50, 100 CFA francs.
Notes 50, 100, 500, 1000, 5000 CFA francs.
Exchange rate to £ sterling: 464·75 (26 Jan. 1987).
Political history and government: Formerly part of French West Africa, Senegal joined French Sudan (now the Republic of Mali) to form the Federation of Mali on 4 Apr. 1959. By agreement with France, signed on 4 Apr. 1960, the Federation became independent on 20 June 1960. Senegal seceded, and became a separate independent state, on 20 Aug. 1960. The Republic of Senegal was proclaimed on 5 Sept. 1960, with Léopold-Sédar Senghor as first President. A new constitution was promulgated on 7 Mar. 1963. Senegal became a one-party state in 1966 but two legal opposition parties were subsequently formed (in July 1974 and Feb. 1976). A constitutional amendment, approved by the government on 10 Mar. 1976, fixed the maximum number of permitted parties at three. On 3 Apr. 1978 the President announced that a fourth party would be permitted. Legislative power rests with the unicameral National Assembly, with 100 members elected for 5 years by universal adult suffrage (the elections of 26 Feb. 1978 were contested by three parties). Executive power is held by the President, also directly elected for 5 years at the same time as the Assembly. He appoints and leads a Cabinet, including a Prime Minister. President Senghor retired on 31 Dec. 1980 and was succeeded by the Prime Minister, Abdou Diouf. On 24 Apr. 1981 the National Assembly adopted a constitutional amendment, effective from 6 May,

lifting restrictions on political parties. By July a further 7 parties had registered. On 1 Feb. 1982 Senegal and The Gambia formed a confederation named Senegambia, led by President Diouf.
Length of roadways: 8681 miles *13 968 km.*
Length of railways: 642 miles *1034 km.*
Universities: 2.
Adult illiteracy: 94·4% (males 89·6%; females 98·9%) illiterate in French (Africans, 1961).
Expectation of life: Males 39·4 years; females 42·5 years (UN estimates for 1970–75).
Defence: Military service: two years, selective; total armed forces 8500 (1985); defence expenditure: US$59·9 million in 1985–6.
Foreign tourists: 240 000 in 1984.

Seychelles

Official name: The Republic of Seychelles.
Population: 65 092 (1985 estimate).
Area: 174·9 miles² *453 km².*
Languages: Creole 94·4%; English 3·0%; French 1·9% (census of 5 May 1971).
Religions: Christian (mainly Roman Catholic) 98·2% (1971).
Capital city: Victoria (formerly Port Victoria), population 23 334 (including suburbs) at 1977 census.
Other principal town: Takamaka.
Highest point: Morne Seychellois, 2992 ft *912 m.*
Head of State: France Albert René (b. 16 Nov. 1935), President.
Climate: Warm and pleasant, with temperatures generally between 24°C *75°F* and 30°C *85°F,* cooler on high ground. Hottest during northwest monsoon, December to May. South-east monsoon is from June to November. Average annual rainfall on Mahé between 1780 mm *70 in* and 3430 mm *135 in.* In Victoria, average annual temperature 29°C *84°F,* rainfall 2300 mm *91 in.*
Labour force: 28 362 in 1982: Unemployed 33·6%.
Gross domestic product: 993·4 million Seychelles rupees in 1983: Agriculture, forestry and fishing 8·4%; Mining, manufacturing and handicrafts 10·4%; Transport, distribution and communications 27·8%; Financial services 11·4%; Government services 17·2%.
Exports: 21 398 000 million Seychelles rupees in 1984: Fish 47·5%; Copra 38·4%; Cinnamon bark 5·3%.
Monetary unit: Seychelles rupee. 1 rupee = 100 cents.
Denominations:
  Coins 1, 5, 25, 50 cents; 1, 5, 10 rupees.
  Notes 5, 10, 20, 50, 100 rupees.
Exchange rate to £ sterling: 8·49 (26 Jan. 1987).
Political history and government: Formerly a British colony, with internal self-government from 1 Oct. 1975. Following a constitutional conference on 19–22 Jan. 1976, Seychelles became an independent republic, within the Commonwealth, on 29 June 1976. At the same time three islands which formed part of the British Indian Ocean territory (established on 8 Nov. 1965) were returned to Seychelles. The pre-independence Prime Minister, James Mancham, became the first President, leading a coalition government comprising members of his own Seychelles Democratic Party and of the Seychelles People's United Party (SPUP), formerly in opposition. The SPUP leader, Albert René, became Prime Minister. President Mancham was deposed on 5 June 1977 in a *coup* by armed opponents of his rule. At the request of the *coup* leaders, René became President. The constitution was suspended and the elected National Assembly dissolved. President René assumed power to rule by decree. In May 1978 the SPUP was renamed the Seychelles People's Progressive Front (SPPF). A new constitution was proclaimed on 26 Mar. 1979 and took effect from 5 June. It provides for a one-party state, with a unicameral People's Assembly of 25 members (two nominated to represent uninhabited islands and 23 elected by universal adult suffrage), serving a four-year term. Executive power is vested in the President, directly elected for five years. Elections for the President (with René as sole candidate) and the Assembly (all

candidates being from the SPPF) were held in June 1979. Similar elections were held for the Assembly in 1983 and the President in 1984. There have been a number of coup attempts.
  The President appoints and leads the Cabinet, his nominations being subject to ratification by the Assembly.
Length of roadways: 160 miles *257 km.*
Adult illiteracy: 42·3% (males 44·4%; females 40·2%) in 1971.
Expectation of life: Males 61·9 years; females 68·0 years (1970–72).
Defence: Total armed forces: 1200 in 1985; total defence expenditure: US$8·6 million in 1983.
Foreign tourists: 72 500 in 1985.

Sierra Leone

Official name: The Republic of Sierra Leone.
Population: 3 517 530 (1985 census).
Area: 27 699 miles² *71 740 km².*
Languages: English (official), Krio, Mende, Temne.
Religions: Animist; Muslim and Christian minorities.
Capital city: Freetown, population 469 776 (1985 census).
Other principal towns (1985): Makeni 20 000; Kenema 13 000; Bo 26 000; Koidu 80 000.
Highest point: Bintimani and Kundukonko peaks, 6390 ft *1948 m.*
Principal mountain range: Loma.
Principal rivers: Siwa, Jong, Rokel.
Head of State: Maj.-Gen. Joseph Saidu Momoh, President.
Climate: Generally hot with two main seasons: wet (May–October), when humidity is tryingly high, and dry (November–April). The average annual rainfall at Freetown is 3505 mm *138 in* and the average daily high temperature nearly 29°C *85°F.*
Labour force: 1 287 000 in 1984: Agriculture, forestry and fishing 66·4%.
Gross domestic product: 1292·2 million leones in 1980–1: Agriculture, forestry and fishing 30·9%; Mining 9·4%; Manufacturing 7·3%; Construction 4·3%; Trade 12·6%; Transport, storage and communications 15·3%; Financial services 7·5%; Government services 2·5%.
Exports: 370·9 million leone in 1984: Coffee 9·2%; Cocoa beans 15·7%; Palm kernels 3·5%; Bauxite 12·8%; Diamonds 34·5%; Rutile 16·1%; Iron ore 2·9%.
Monetary unit: Leone. 1 leone = 100 cents.
Denominations:
  Coins 1, 5, 10, 20, 50 cents.
  Notes 50 cents, 1, 2, 5, 10, 20 leones.
Exchange rate to £ sterling: 43·65 (26 Jan. 1987).
Political history and government: A former British dependency which became independent, within the Commonwealth, on 27 Apr. 1961. At independence the Sierra Leone People's Party was in power, with the All-People's Congress (APC) in opposition. Following disputed elections, the army assumed power on 21 Mar. 1967. Two days later, in a counter-*coup*, another group of officers established a National Reformation Council (NRC), which suspended the constitution. The NRC was overthrown on 17–18 Apr. 1968 by junior officers who restored constitutional government and civilian rule on 26 Apr. 1968, when Dr Siaka Stevens of the APC, appointed Prime Minister in 1967, was sworn in. A republic was established on 19 April 1971 and two days later Dr Stevens was elected President and took office. Legislative power is held by the unicameral House of Representatives, with 104 members: 85 elected by universal adult suffrage for 5 years (subject to dissolution), 12 Paramount Chiefs (one from each District) and 7 members appointed by the President. A constitutional amendment bill, published on 13 May 1978, provided for the repeal of the 1971 constitution and for the introduction of one-party government under the APC; for an extension of the President's term of office from 5 to 7 years; and for the abolition of the office of Prime Minister. After approving the bill, the House was prorogued on 26 May 1978. A referendum on 5–12 June 1978 supported the

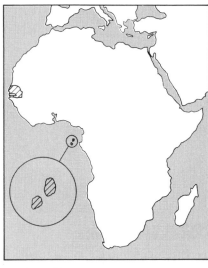

left: **SENEGAL**
encircled: **SÃO TOMÉ AND PRÍNCIPE**

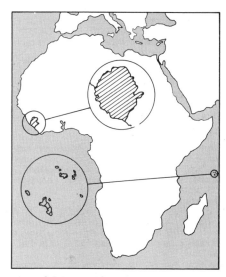

above: **SIERRA LEONE**
below: **SEYCHELLES**

proposed changes and President Stevens was sworn in on 14 June for a 7-year term. Under the new constitution, the President, formerly elected by the House, is elected by the National Delegates' Conference of the APC. He holds executive power and he appoints and leads the Cabinet.
Length of roadways: 4595 miles *7395 km* (31 Dec. 1979).
Length of railways: 52 miles *84 km.*
Universities: 1.
Adult illiteracy: 70·7% (males 62·2%; females 78·7%) in 1985.
Expectation of life: 34 years.
Defence: Total armed forces 3180 (1985); defence expenditure: 6·2% of total government expenditure in 1984–5.
Foreign tourists: 53 000 in 1981.

Singapore

Official name: Hsing-chia p'o Kung-ho Kuo (Chinese) or Republik Singapura (Malay): Republic of Singapore.
Population: 2 558 000 (1985).
Area: 384·2 miles² *620·5 km².*
Languages: Malay, Mandarin Chinese, Tamil, English.
Religions: Muslim, Buddhist, Hindu, Christian.
Capital city: Singapore City, population 1 327 500 at 30 June 1974 (estimate).
Highest point: Bukit Timah (Hill of Tin), 581 ft *177 m.*

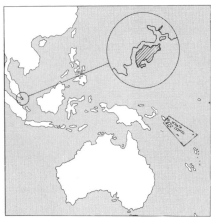

top encircled: **SINGAPORE**
below: **SOLOMON ISLANDS**

Principal river: Sungei Seletar (9 miles *14 km*).
Head of State: Wee Kim Wee, President.
Prime Minister: Lee Kuan Yew (b. 16 Sept. 1923).
Climate: Hot and humid throughout the year, with average maximum of 30°C *86°F* to 32°C *89°F*, minimum 23°C *73°F* to 24°C *75°F*. Frequent rainfall (between 11 and 19 days each month).
Labour force: 1 154 260 aged 15–64 years (1985): Manufacturing 25·4%; Commerce 23·5%; Transport, storage and communication 10·1%; Community, social and personal services 21·5%.
Gross domestic product: S$35 462·7 million in 1984: Manufacturing 25%; Construction 12·2%; Trade 19·9%; Transport and communications 13·5%; Financial services 22%.
Exports: S$51·3 billion in 1985: Machinery and transport equipment 32·8%; Mineral fuels 25·7%; Crude materials (including rubber) 6·6%.
Monetary unit: Singapore dollar (S$). 1 dollar = 100 cents.
Denominations:
Coins 1, 5, 10, 20, 50 cents; 1 dollar.
Notes 1, 5, 10, 20, 25, 50, 100, 500, 1000, 10 000 dollars.
Exchange rate to £ sterling: 3·2823 (26 Jan. 1987).
Political history and government: A former British colony, with internal self-government from 3 June 1959. Singapore became a constituent state of the independent Federation of Malaysia, within the Commonwealth, on 16 Sept. 1963 but seceded and became a separate independent country on 9 Aug. 1965. The new state joined the Commonwealth on 16 Oct. 1965 and became a republic on 22 Dec. 1965. Legislative power rests with the unicameral Parliament, with 75 members elected by universal adult suffrage (voting being compulsory) from single-member constituencies for 5 years (subject to dissolution). The President is elected by Parliament for a 4-year term as constitutional Head of State. Effective executive authority rests with the Cabinet, led by the Prime Minister, which is appointed by the President and responsible to Parliament.
Length of roadways: 1643 miles *2644 km* (1983).
Length of railways: 16 miles *26 km* (1978).
Universities: 1.
Adult illiteracy: 14·0% (1985).
Expectation of life: 71 years average (1985).
Defence: Military service: 24–36 months; total armed forces 54 500 (1986); defence expenditure: 24·6% of total government expenditure in 1985–6.
Foreign tourists: 3 030 970 in 1985.

Solomon Islands

Population: 196 825 (census of 1980); 267 265 (estimate for 1985).
Area: 10 983 miles² *28 446 km²*.
Languages: English (official), Pidgin English (national) and 87 local (mainly Melanesian) languages.

Religion: mainly Christian (Anglican and Roman Catholic).
Capital city: Honiara, population 23 500 (1984 estimate).
Other principal towns: Gizo, Auki, Kirakira.
Highest point: Mt Makarakombou, 8028 ft *2447 m*.
Head of State: HM Queen Elizabeth II, represented by Sir Baddeley Devisi, GCMG, GCVO (b. 16 Oct. 1941), Governor-General.
Prime Minister: The Rt Hon. Sir Peter Kenilorea, KBE.
Climate: Warm season during north-west trade winds, Nov.–Apr.; cooler during south-east season, Apr.–Nov. In Honiara, average annual temperature is 27°C *80°F*, average annual rainfall about 2160 mm *85 in*.
Gross domestic product: SI$175 million in 1983.
Exports: SI$115 699 000 in 1984: Fish 24·9%; Copra 27·8%; Timber 26%; Cocoa 2·9%; Palm oil and kernels 16·5%.
Monetary unit: Solomon Islands dollar (SI$). 1 dollar = 100 cents.
Denominations:
Coins 1, 2, 5, 10, 20 cents; 1 dollar.
Notes 2, 5, 10, 20 dollars.
Exchange rate to £ sterling: 3·0258 (26 Jan. 1987).
Political history and government: The Northern Solomon Islands became a German protectorate in 1885 and the Southern Solomons a British protectorate in 1893. Germany ceded most of the Northern Solomons to the United Kingdom between 1898 and 1900. The combined territory was named the British Solomon Islands Protectorate. The first Chief Minister was appointed on 28 Aug. 1974. In June 1975 the territory was renamed the Solomon Islands, although retaining protectorate status. Full internal self-government was achieved on 2 Jan. 1976. After a constitutional conference on 6–16 Sept. 1977, Solomon Islands (as it was restyled) became independent, within the Commonwealth, on 7 July 1978, with the Chief Minister as the first Prime Minister.
Legislative power is vested in the unicameral National Parliament, with 38 members elected by universal adult suffrage for 4 years (subject to dissolution). The pre-independence Legislative Assembly became the first Parliament. Executive power is vested in the British monarch and is exercisable by the Governor-General, who is appointed for up to 5 years on the advice of Parliament and acts in almost all matters on the advice of the Cabinet. The Prime Minister is elected by and from members of Parliament. Other Ministers are appointed by the Governor-General, on the Prime Minister's recommendation, from members of Parliament. The Cabinet is responsible to Parliament. The country comprises seven provinces.
Length of roadways: 1425 miles *2300 km*.
Foreign tourists: 6790 in 1984.

Somalia

Official name: Jamhuuriyadda Dimuqraadiga Soomaaliya (Somali Democratic Republic).
Population: 5 980 000 (1986 estimate).
Area: 246 201 miles² *637 657 km²*.
Language: Somali, Arabic (both official); English, Italian.
Religions: Sunni Muslim; Christian minority.
Capital city: Muqdisho (Mogadishu or Mogadiscio), population 377 000 (1982 estimate).
Other principal towns (1982): Hargeisa 70 000; Kisimayu 70 000; Merca 60 000; Berbera 55 000.
Highest point: Surud Ad, 7894 ft *2406 m*.
Principal mountain range: Guban.
Principal rivers: Juba (Giuba), Shebelle (Scebeli).
Head of State: Maj-Gen Muhammad Siyad Barre (b. 1919), President and Prime Minister.
Climate: Hot and dry. Average temperature of 27°C *80°F*. Average maximum over 32°C *90°F* in interior and on Gulf of Aden. Cooler on Indian Ocean coast. Average rainfall less than 430 mm *17 in*. In Mogadishu, average maximum 28°C *83°F* (July, August) to 32°C *90°F* (April), minimum 23°C *73°F* (January, July, August) to

25°C *78°F* (April), rainiest month is July (20 days).
Labour force: 2 025 000 (1984 estimate): Agriculture, forestry and fishing 78%.
Gross domestic product: $492 million in 1975 (UN estimate).
Exports: 1423 million Somali shillings in 1983: Livestock 78·9%; Bananas 7·3%; Myrrh 6·3%; Petroleum products 3%.
Monetary unit: Somali shilling. 1 shilling = 100 centesimi.
Denominations:
Coins 1, 5, 10, 50 centesimi; 1 shilling.
Notes 5, 10, 20, 100 shillings.
Exchange rate to £ sterling: 168·08 (26 Jan. 1987).
Political history and government: Formed on 1 July 1960 as an independent country, called the Somali Republic, by a merger of the Trust Territory of Somaliland, under Italian protection, with British Somaliland (a protectorate until 26 June 1960). Following the assassination of the President on 15 Oct. 1969, the government was overthrown by a military *coup* on 21 Oct. 1969, when the constitution and political parties were abolished and the National Assembly dissolved. A Supreme Revolutionary Council (SRC) was established and the country's present name adopted on 22 Oct. 1969. The President of the SRC, Maj-Gen Muhammad Siyad Barrah, became Head of State. On 1 July 1976 the SRC was dissolved and its power transferred to the newly-formed Somali Revolutionary Socialist Party (SRSP). All members of the SRC became members of the ruling party's central committee and the President is the party's secretary-general.
A meeting of the SRSP on 20–25 Jan. 1979 produced a draft constitution, endorsed by the SRSP Central Committee on 20 May 1979. After approval by referendum on 25 Aug. 1979, the constitution was promulgated on 29 Aug. and came into force on 23 Sept. 1979. It defines the SRSP as the sole political party and the country's 'supreme authority'. Legislative power is vested in the People's Assembly, with six members appointed by the President and 171 elected by universal adult suffrage for 5 years (subject to dissolution). Elections to the Assembly were first held on 30 Dec. 1979 and its first session opened on 24 Jan. 1980. Executive power is vested in the President, nominated by the SRSP Central Committee and elected by the Assembly for 6 years. He appoints and leads the Council of Ministers. On 26 Jan. 1980 Gen Siyad Barrah was elected President. On 21 Oct. 1980 he declared a state of emergency and reinstituted the SRC, with extensive powers. The SRC's 17 members are all officers in the armed forces.
Length of roadways: 10 702 miles *17 233 km* (1971).
Universities: 1.
Adult illiteracy: 98·5% (males 97%; females 100%) in 1962 (UNESCO estimates); 40% (claimed after the 1974–75 literacy campaign).
Expectation of life: Males 39·4 years; females 42·6 years (UN estimates for 1970–75).
Defence: Military service voluntary; total armed forces 62 700 (1985); defence expenditure: 28% of total government expenditure in 1984.

South Africa

Official name: Republic of South Africa, or Republiek van Suid-Afrika.
Population: 31 305 607 (1983 estimate, including all the homelands).
Area: 471 445 miles² *1 221 037 km²* (excluding Walvis Bay, area 434 miles² *1124 km²*).
Languages: Afrikaans, English, Xhosa, Zulu, Sesuto (Sesotho), Tswana (Setswana), Sepedi.
Religions: Christian; Muslim and Hindu minorities.
Capital city: Administrative: Pretoria, population 547 280 (1985 census). Legislative: Cape Town (Kaapstad), population 854 503 (1980 census).
Other principal towns (1985): Johannesburg 1 359 725; Durban 447 856; Port Elizabeth 523 387; Kempton Park 249 768; Bloemfontein 232 044; Alberton 254 519; Benoni 215 431;

Pietermaritzburg 191516; Welkom 184271; Roodepoort 181891; East London 205372; Germiston 155282; Boksburg 162457.
Highest point: Injasuti, 11 182 ft *3408 m.*
Principal mountain range: Drakensberg.
Principal rivers: Orange (Oranje), 1300 miles *2092 km*; Limpopo; Vaal.
Head of State: Pieter Willem Botha (b. 12 Jan. 1916), State President.
Climate: Generally temperate (cool summers, mild winters). Average temperatures about 17°C *63°F.* In Cape Town, average maximum 17°C *63°F* (July) to 26°C *79°F* (February), minimum 7°C *45°F* (July) to 15°C *60°F* (January, February), rainiest month is July (10 days). In Johannesburg, average maximum 17°C *62°F* (June) to 25°C *78°F* (December, January), minimum 4°C *39°F* (June, July) to 14°C *58°F* (January, February), rainiest month is January (12 days). Absolute maximum temperature 51·56°C *124·8°F*, Main, 28 Jan. 1903; absolute minimum −14·7°C *5·5°F*, Carolina, 23 July 1926.
Labour force: 9 758 000 in 1985: Manufacturing 13·8%; Unemployed 6·4%.
Gross domestic product: 104 398 million rand in 1984–5: Mining and quarrying 15%; Manufacturing 21·5%; Trade 11·2%.
Exports: 25 319·9 million rand in 1984: Gold 46·1%; Mineral products 12%; Base metals and articles of base metal 9·5%; Pearls, precious and semi-precious stones 9·4%.
Monetary unit: Rand. 1 rand = 100 cents.
Denominations:
Coins 1, 2, 5, 10, 20, 50 cents; 1 rand.
Notes 2, 5, 10, 20, 50 rand.
Exchange rate to £ sterling: 3·159 (26 Jan. 1987).
Political history and government: After the Boer War of 1899–1902 two former Boer republics, the Transvaal and the Orange Free State, became part of the British Empire. On 31 May 1910 they were merged with the British territories of Natal and Cape Colony (now Cape Province) to form the Union of South Africa, a dominion under the British crown. Under the Statute of Westminster, passed by the British Parliament in December 1931 and accepted by South Africa in June 1934, the Union was recognized as an independent country within the Commonwealth. Following a referendum among white voters on 5 Oct. 1960, South Africa became a republic, outside the Commonwealth, on 31 May 1961. Under the initial republican constitution, legislative power was vested in a bicameral Parliament, made up exclusively of European (white) members holding office for 5 years (subject to dissolution). Under constitutional changes approved on 12 June 1980, the Senate was abolished from 1 Jan. 1981, leaving the House of Assembly as the sole legislative chamber. The House has 165 members directly elected by Europeans only. From 1 Jan. 1981 an additional eight members are chosen by the elected members while another four members are nominated by the President. Executive power is vested in the State President, elected by Parliament for a 7-year term as constitutional Head of State. He acts on the advice of the Executive Council (Cabinet), led by the Prime Minister, which is appointed by the President and responsible to Parliament. The constitutional changes introduced on 1 Jan. 1981 created the office of Vice State President (with a 7-year term) and established an advisory President's Council, with 56 non-African members (41 European, seven Coloured, seven Indian and one Chinese) nominated by the State President for a 5-year term. The Council, chaired by the Vice State President, was inaugurated on 3 Feb. 1981.
Each of the four provinces has an Administrator appointed by the President for 5 years and a provincial council elected (by whites only) for 5 years.
South Africa has granted independence to the Transkei (26 Oct. 1976), Bophuthatswana (6 Dec. 1977), Venda (13 Sept. 1979) and the Ciskei (4 Dec. 1981), African 'homelands' established by the government, but these acts have not received international recognition.
Length of roadways: 115036 miles *185 133 km*

(31 Mar. 1976).
Length of railways: 14 805 miles *23 821 km.*
Universities: 21.
Adult illiteracy: (1984) Whites 7%; Asians 29%; Coloureds 38%; Blacks 68%.
Expectation of life:
All races: Males 56·6 years; females 59·4 years (UN estimates for 1970–75).
For non-Africans (1959–61):
Asiatic: Males 57·70 years; females 59·57 years.
Coloured: Males 49·62 years; females 54·28 years.
White: Males 64·73 years; females 71·67 years.
Defence: Military service: 24 months; total armed forces 106 400 in 1985; defence expenditure: 15·1% of total government expenditure in 1985–6.
Foreign tourists: 792 387 in 1984.

Spain

Official name: The Kingdom of Spain.
*Population: 37 746 260 at the census of 1 Mar. 1981; 38 997 458 (1984 estimate).
*Area: 194 897 miles² *504 782 km²*.
Languages: Spanish (Castilian), Catalan, Basque, Galician.
Religion: Roman Catholic.
Capital city: Madrid, population 3 217 461 (1986 estimate).
Other principal towns (1986): Barcelona 1 756 905; Valencia 763 949; Sevilla 673 574; Zaragoza 592 666; Malaga 533 549; Bilbao 420 538; Las Palmas 379 693; Valladolid 335 374; Palma de Mallorca 313 376; Hospitalet 287 734; Cordoba 298 621.
Highest point: Mt Teide (Canary Is), 12 190 ft *3716 m.*
Principal mountain ranges: Pyrenees, Cordillera Cantábrica.
Principal rivers: Ebro (556 miles *895 km*), Duero (Douro), Tajo (Tagus), Guadiana, Guadalquivir.
Head of State: HM King Juan Carlos (b. 5 Jan. 1938).
Head of Government: Felipe Gonzalez (b. 5 Mar. 1942), President of the Government (Prime Minister).
Climate: Cool summers and rainy winters on north coast; hot summers and cold winters in interior; hot summers and mild winters on south coast. In Madrid, average maximum 8°C *47°F* (January) to 30°C *87°F* (July), minimum 0,5°C *33°F* (January) to 17°C *62°F* (July, August), rainiest month is March (11 days). In Barcelona, average maximum 13°C *56°F* (January) to 28°C *82°F* (August), minimum 5°C *42°F* (January) to 20°C *69°F* (July, August), rainiest months are April, May, October (each 8 days). Absolute maximum temperature 46,2°C *115 2°F*, Gualulcacin, 17 July 1943; absolute minimum −32,0°C −25·6°F, Estangento, 2 Feb. 1956.
Labour force: 16 280 000 in 1986: Industry 21%; Construction 6·1%; Services 42·3%; Unemployed 18%.
Gross domestic product: 18 875·9 billion pesetas in 1982: Agriculture, forestry and fishing 6·5%; Mining, manufacturing, electricity, gas and water 27·9%; Construction 7·6%; Trade 18·5%.
Exports: 4 104 143 million pesetas in 1985: Metal products 15·4%; Cars 8·8%; Machinery 11·8%; Refined petroleum and related products 8·2%.
Monetary unit: Spanish peseta. 1 peseta = 100 céntimos.
Denominations:
Coins 1, 2, 5, 10, 25, 50, 100 pesetas.
Notes 200, 500, 1000, 2000, 5000 pesetas.
Exchange rate to £ sterling: 196·7 (26 Jan. 1987).
Political history and government: In the civil war of 1936–39 the forces of the republic (established on 14 Apr. 1931) were defeated. Gen Francisco Franco, leader of the successful insurgent forces, acted as Head of State until his death on 20 Nov. 1975. The legislature, traditionally designated the *Cortes* (Courts), was revived in 1942 as a unicameral body, with strictly limited powers, named *Las Cortes Españolas*. In accordance with the 1947 Law of Succession, Prince Juan Carlos

right: **SOMALIA**
below: **SOUTH AFRICA**

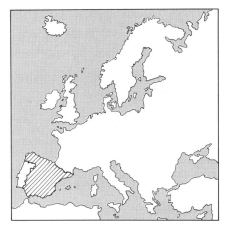

SPAIN

de Borbón, grandson of the last reigning monarch, became King on 22 Nov. 1975. The government's Political Reform Bill, passed by the *Cortes* on 18 Nov. 1976, was approved by a popular referendum on 15 Dec. 1976. This provided for a new bicameral *Cortes*, comprising a Congress of Deputies (350 elected members) and a Senate of 248 members (207 elected, 41 nominated by the King). Elections for the new *Cortes* were held on 15 June 1977. The old *Cortes* expired on 30 June 1977; the new legislature was inaugurated on 13 July and formally opened on 23 July 1977.
In 1978 a new constitution was approved by both Houses of the *Cortes* on 31 Oct., endorsed by a referendum on 6 Dec. and ratified by the King on 27 Dec. It entered into force on 29 Dec. 1978 and the *Cortes* was dissolved on 2 Jan. 1979. The constitution confirmed Spain as a parliamentary monarchy, with freedom for political parties, and it recognized and guaranteed the right of Spain's 'nationalities and regions' to autonomy. All the 'fundamental laws' of the Franco régime were repealed and the Roman Catholic Church was disestablished. The monarchy is hereditary, with the King having mainly formal prerogatives. Legislative power is vested in the bicameral *Cortes Generales*, comprising a Senate and a Congress of Deputies, both Houses elected by universal adult suffrage for 4 years (subject to dissolution). Members of the Congress are elected on the basis of proportional representation. For the elections of 1 Mar. 1979 the Congress had 350 seats and the Senate 208: 188 for continental Spain (4 for each of the 47 provinces), 5 for the Balearic islands, 11 for the Canary Islands (2 provinces) and 2 each for the African enclaves of Ceuta and Melilla. Executive power is held by the Council of Ministers, led by the President

276 Countries of the World

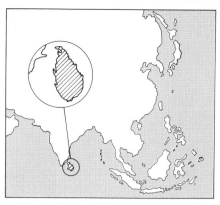

SRI LANKA

of the Government (Prime Minister), who is appointed by the King with the approval of the *Cortes*. Other Ministers are appointed on the Prime Minister's recommendation. The Government is responsible to the Congress. Spain comprises 50 provinces, each with its own Assembly (*Diputación Provincial*) and an appointed Civil Governor.
Length of roadways: 197978 miles *318 548 km* (1984).
Length of railways: 9617 miles *15 475 km*.
Universities: 33.
Adult illiteracy: 9·9% (males 5·7%; females 13·7%) in 1970.
Expectation of life: Males 72·5 years; females 78·6 years (1985).
Defence: Military service: 12 months; total armed forces 320000 (214000 conscripts) in 1985; defence expenditure: 10·7% of total government expenditure in 1983.
Foreign tourists: 43 235 363 in 1985.

*Figures refer to Metropolitan Spain, including the Canary Islands and Spanish North Africa (Ceuta and Melilla).

Sri Lanka

Official name: Sri Lanka Prajatantrika Samajawadi Janarajaya (Democratic Socialist Republic of Sri Lanka –'Exalted Ceylon').
Population: 15 599 000 (1984 estimate).
Area: 25 332 miles² *65 610 km²*.
Languages: Sinhala (official) 69%; Tamil 23%; English.
Religions (1981): Buddhist 69·3%; Hindu 15·5%; Muslim 7·6%; Christian 7·5%.
Capital city: Colombo, population 585 776 at 1981 census.
Other principal towns (1981): Dehiwela-Mt Lavinia 174 385; Moratuwa 135 610; Jaffna 118 215; Kotte 101 563; Kandy 101 281; Galle 77 183; Negombo 61 376; Trincomalee 44 913.
Highest point: Pidurutalagala, 8292 ft *2527 m*.
Principal rivers: Mahaweli Ganga (203 miles *327 km*), Kelani Ganga.
Head of State: Junius Richard Jayawardene (b. 17 Sept. 1906), President.
Prime Minister: Ranasinghe Premadasa (b. 23 June 1924).
Climate: Tropical, with average temperature of about 27°C *80°F*. Monsoon strikes the southwest of the island. In Colombo, average maximum 29°C *85°F* (June to December) to 31°C *88°F* (March, April); minimum 22°C *72°F* (December, January, February) to 25°C *78°F* (May); May and October rainiest (each 19 days).
Labour force: 5 015 060 in 1981: Agriculture, forestry and fishing 37·2%; Manufacturing 8·3%; Construction 2·5%; Trade 8·6%; Transport, storage and communications 4%; Community, social and personal services 11·9%; Unemployed 17·8%.
Gross domestic product: 147·5 billion rupees in 1984: Agriculture, forestry and fishing 24·3%; Manufacturing 16·5%; Construction 7·9%; Transport, storage and communications 10·5%; Trade 19·5%; Financial services 4·1%; Public administration 5·8%.
Exports: 36 541 million rupees in 1984: Tea 43%; Rubber 9%; Desiccated coconut 3·2%.

Monetary unit: Sri Lanka rupee. 1 rupee = 100 cents.
Denominations:
Coins 1, 2, 5, 10, 25, 50 cents; 1, 2, 5 rupees.
Notes 2, 5, 10, 20, 50, 100, 500, 1000 rupees.
Exchange rate to £ sterling: 43·58 (26 Jan. 1987).
Political history and government: Formerly, as Ceylon, a British dependency. It became independent, as a monarchy within the Commonwealth, on 4 Feb. 1948. The country's name and status were changed on 22 May 1972, when it became the Republic of Sri Lanka. Under the first republican constitution, the President was a non-executive Head of State and direction of the government was vested in the Cabinet. Legislative power was vested in the unicameral National State Assembly (formerly the House of Representatives), with 168 members elected for 6 years by universal adult suffrage. On 4 Oct. 1977 the Assembly adopted an amendment to the constitution to provide for a directly elected executive President. Under the amendment, signed into law on 20 Oct. 1977, the Prime Minister in office (J. R. Jayawardene) became President. It provided for the President to be Head of Government but also to appoint a Prime Minister. Jayawardene was sworn in as President for a 6-year term on 4 Feb. 1978 and was re-elected in 1982.
A new constitution was adopted by the Assembly on 16 Aug. 1978 and came into force on 7 Sept. 1978. The country's present name was introduced and the Assembly renamed Parliament. Future elections to Parliament are to be on the basis of proportional representation and Parliament is to have 196 members elected for 6 years (subject to dissolution). The President appoints the Prime Minister and other Ministers from among the members of Parliament. The President is not responsible to Parliament and may dissolve it. Sri Lanka comprises 24 administrative districts, each with a development council, first elected on 4 June 1981.
Length of roadways: 15 479 miles *24 911 km*.
Length of railways: 903 miles *1453 km*.
Universities: 6.
Adult illiteracy: 14% (males 9·2%; females 18·8%) in 1981.
Expectation of life: Males 64·8 years; females 66·9 years (1967).
Defence: Military service voluntary; total armed forces 21 560 (1985); defence expenditure: 5·1% of total government expenditure in 1984.
Foreign tourists: 317 734 in 1984.

Sudan

Official name: Al Jumhuriyat as-Sudan al-Dimuqratiya (the Democratic Republic of Sudan).
Population: 20 564 364 (1983 census).
Area: 967 500 miles² *2 505 813 km²*.
Languages: Arabic, Nilotic, others.
Religions: Muslim (in North), Animist (in South).
Capital city: El Khartum (Khartoum), population 476 218 at 1983 census.
Other principal towns (1983): Umm Durman (Omdurman) 526 287; El Khartum Bahri (Khartoum North) 341 146; Bur Sudan (Port Sudan) 206 727; Wadi Medani 141 065; El Obeid 140 024.
Highest point: Mt Kinyeti, 10 456 ft *3187 m*.
Principal mountain ranges: Darfur Highlands, Nubian Mts.
Principal rivers: Nile (the Blue Nile and White Nile join at Khartoum), 4145 miles *6670 km*.
Head of State: Ahmed El Merghani, President.
Climate: Hot and dry in desert areas of north (average maximum up to 44°C *111°F*); rainy and humid in tropical south. Average temperature about 21°C *70°F*. In Khartoum, average maximum 32°C *90°F* (January) to 42°C *107°F* (May), minimum 15°C *59°F* (January) to 26°C *79°F* (June); rainiest month is August (6 days). Absolute maximum 49,0°C *120·2°F*, Wadi Halfa, 7 and 8 June 1932, 9 and 13 June 1933, 19 June 1941; absolute minimum −0,8°C *30·6°F*, Zalingei, 6 Feb. 1957.

Labour force: 6 426 000 in 1984: Agriculture, forestry and fishing 74·5%.
Gross domestic product: £S6063 million in 1981–2: Agriculture, mining and manufacturing 41·8%; Government, household services, electricity and water 14·4%; Construction, commerce, hotels, finance and real estate 33·1%; Transport and communication 10·7%.
Exports: £S483·1 million in 1982: Animals 11·4%; Cotton 24·3%; Sorghum 22·3%; Groundnuts and groundnut products 12·3%; Sesame seed and sesame seed products 8·4%.
Monetary unit: Sudanese pound (£S). 1 pound = 100 piastras = 1000 millièmes.
Denominations:
Coins 1, 2, 5, 10 millièmes; 2, 5, 10 piastres.
Notes 25, 50 piastres; 1, 5, 10, 20 pounds.
Exchange rate to £ sterling: 3·82 (26 Jan. 1987).
Political history and government: An Anglo-Egyptian condominium from 19 Jan. 1899 until becoming an independent parliamentary republic on 1 Jan. 1956. On 25 May 1969 the civilian government was overthrown by army officers, under Col (promoted Maj-Gen) Ga'afar an-Numairi, who established a Revolutionary Command Council (RCC). Gen Numairi became Prime Minister on 28 Oct. 1969. On 13 Aug. 1971 the RCC promulgated a provisional constitution, proclaiming socialist principles. Gen Numairi was elected President (unopposed) in September 1971 and inaugurated for a 6-year term on 12 Oct. 1971. The RCC was dissolved and the Sudanese Socialist Union (SSU) established as the country's sole political party. A new definitive constitution was introduced on 8 May 1973. In March 1985 President Numairi was deposed while out of the country.
Legislative power is vested in the Legislative Assembly which was elected in April 1986. The assembly elected a Council of Five to head the state, led by the President. A Prime Minister is elected, according to the temporary constitution introduced by the assembly, for 4 years. At the end of this period a permanent constitution will be drawn up by the present elected assembly for a permanent democratic system in Sudan.
A transitional council has been formed to take over the governing of Southern Sudan until the constitutional conference is held to decide the future of the area.
Length of roadways: *c*. 31 070 miles *c. 50 000 km*.
Length of railways: 3418 miles *5500 km*.
Universities: 4 (plus the Khartoum branch of Cairo University).
Adult illiteracy: 85·3% (males 74·7%; females 96·3%) in 1966.
Expectation of life: Males 43·0 years; females 45·0 years (UN estimates for 1970–75).
Defence: Military service: conscription; total armed forces 56 600 (1985); defence expenditure: 13·1% of total government expenditure in 1984–5.

Suriname

Official name: Republiek Suriname (Republic of Suriname).
Population: 370 000 (1984 estimate).
Area: 63 037 miles² *163 265 km²*.
Languages: Dutch 37·1%; Hindustani 31·7%; Javanese 15·4%; Creole 13·8% (1964).
Religions: Christian 45·1%; Hindu 27·8%; Muslim 20·2% (1964).
Capital city: Paramaribo, population 103 738 (1971 census).
Other principal towns: Nieuw Nickerie, Nieuw Amsterdam.
Highest point: Julianatop, 4218 ft *1286 m*.
Principal mountain ranges: Wilhelmina Gebergte, Kayser Gebergte.
Principal rivers: Corantijn, Nickerie, Coppename, Saramacca, Suriname, Commewijne, Maroni (Marowijne).
Head of State: Lt-Col. Deysi Bouterse, Chairman of the National Military Council.
Climate: Sub-tropical, with fairly heavy rainfall and average temperatures of 21°C to 30°C *73°F* to *88°F*.
Labour force: 97 690 in 1980: Agriculture, forestry and fishing 7·7%; Mining 5·7%; Manu-

facturing 7·4%; Construction 4%; Trade 11·7%; Government services 38·9%; Unemployed 14·6%.
Gross domestic product: 2293 million Suriname guilders in 1983.
Exports: 765·1 million Suriname guilders in 1982: Alumina 53·8%; Aluminium 16·2%; Bauxite 6·8%; Rice 9·4%; Shrimps 7%; Wood and wood products 2·7%.
Monetary unit: Suriname gulden (guilder) or florin. 1 guilder = 100 cents.
Denominations:
  Coins 1, 5, 10, 25 cents; 1 guilder.
  Notes 1, 2½, 5, 10, 25, 100, 1000 guilders.
Exchange rate to £ sterling: 2·7275 (26 Jan. 1987).
Political history and government: Formerly a Dutch possession, with full internal autonomy from 29 Dec. 1954. Suriname became an independent republic on 25 Nov. 1975. The constitution vested legislative power in the *Staten* (Legislative Assembly) of 39 members, elected by universal adult suffrage for 4 years. The Assembly elected a constitutional President and Vice-President. Executive power was vested in the appointed Council of Ministers, led by the Prime Minister, which was responsible to the Assembly.

The government was overthrown in a *coup* on 25 Feb. 1980, when a National Military Council (NMC), comprising eight army officers, took power. The Cabinet resigned on the next day but the President remained in office. On 15 Mar. 1980 the NMC appointed a mainly civilian Cabinet, with Dr Henrik (Henk) Chin A Sen as Prime Minister. Elections to the *Staten*, planned for 27 Mar. 1980, were postponed until Oct. 1981, as originally due. On 15 Aug. 1980 the NMC dismissed the President and Dr Chin A Sen assumed this office while remaining Prime Minister. At the same time a state of emergency was declared and the constitution suspended. The *Staten* was replaced by an advisory assembly. On 20 Nov. 1980 Dr Chin A Sen became the country's first executive President and the office of Prime Minister was abolished. On 21 Dec. 1980 general elections were further postponed for 'at least two years'. In 1982 Dr Chin A Sen was dismissed by the NMC and in 1984 the subsequent Prime Minister was dismissed.

Suriname comprises nine districts.
Length of roadways: 5525 miles *8889 km.*
Length of railways: 104 miles *167 km.*
Universities: 1.
Adult illiteracy: 10% in 1985.
Expectation of life: Males 62·5 years; females 66·7 years (1963).
Defence: Total armed forces about 2000 (1985); defence expenditure: 5·4% of total government expenditure in 1985.
Foreign tourists: 66 096 in 1981.

Swaziland

Official name: The Kingdom of Swaziland.
Population: 494 534 (census of 25 Aug. 1976); 626 000 (estimate for 1984).
Area: 6704 miles² *17 363 km².*
Languages: English, Siswati.
Religions: Christian 60%, Animist.
Capital city: Mbabane, population 38 636 (1982).
Other principal towns (1976): Manzini 18 818; Havelock 4838; Mhlume 3921; Pigg's Peak 2192; Big Bend 2083.
Highest point: Emlembe, 6113 ft *1863 m.*
Principal mountain range: Lubombo.
Principal rivers: Usutu, Komati, Umbuluzi, Ingwavuma.
Head of State: HM King Mswati III.
Prime Minister: Mr Sotsha Dlamini.
Climate: Rainy season October to March. Annual average at Mbabane, in high veld, 1395 mm *55 in,* in low veld 635 mm *25 in.* Average temperatures 11°C *52°F* to 22°C *72°F* at Mbabane, 13°C *56°F* to 27°C *80°F* at Manzini, warmer on low veld.
Labour force: 131 145 aged 15 and over (census of 24 May 1966); 198 000 (mid-1970): Agriculture, forestry and fishing 81·0%; Services 12·7% (ILO estimates).

Gross domestic product: 554 million emalangeni in 1981: Agriculture, forestry and fishing (excluding government) 30% (agriculture 25%); Manufacturing 25%; Trade, restaurants and hotels 11%; Community, social and personal services 10%.
Exports: 323·7 million emalangeni (excluding re-exports) in 1983: Sugar 37·9%; Wood pulp 13·8%; Chemicals 13·2%.
*Monetary unit: Lilangeni (plural: emalangeni). 1 lilangeni = 100 cents.
Denominations:
  Coins 1, 2, 5, 10, 20, 50 cents; 1 lilangeni.
  Notes 1, 2, 5, 10, 20 emalangeni.
Exchange rate to £ sterling: 3·159 (26 Jan. 1987).
Political history and government: A former British protectorate, with internal self-government from 25 Apr. 1967 and full independence, within the Commonwealth, from 6 Sept. 1968. Swaziland is a monarchy, with executive authority vested in the King. He appoints a Cabinet, led by a Prime Minister. Under the independence constitution, legislative power was vested in a bicameral Parliament. On 12 Apr. 1973, in response to a motion passed by both Houses, the King repealed the constitution, suspended political activity and assumed all legislative, executive and judicial powers. On 24 Mar. 1977 the King announced the abolition of the parliamentary system and its replacement by traditional tribal communities called *tinkhundla.* A new constitution was promulgated on 13 Oct. 1978. The functions of the bicameral Parliament (*Libandla*), comprising a Senate (20 members) and a House of Assembly (50 members), are confined to debating government proposals and advising the King. No political parties are permitted. Elections were held on 27 Oct. 1978 to an 80-member electoral college which chose from its number 10 Senators and 40 members of the House. The King appointed a further 10 members to each chamber. The new Parliament opened on 19 Jan. 1979. Swaziland has 4 districts, each administered by an appointed District Commissioner.
Length of roadways: 1692 miles *2723 km* (1983).
Length of railways: 137 miles *220 km* (1983).
Universities: 1.
Adult illiteracy: males 68·7%; females 72·5% (1966).
Expectation of life: Males 41·8 years; females 45·0 years (UN estimates for 1970–75).
Defence: An army of 6250 (1982); defence expenditure: 6·4% of total government expenditure in 1983–4.
Foreign tourists: 122 905 in 1983.

* South African currency is also legal tender.

Sweden

Official name: Konungariket Sverige (Kingdom of Sweden).
Population: 8 342 621 (estimate for 1984).
Area: 173 654 miles² *449 793 km².*
Languages: Swedish; Finnish and Lapp in north.
Religion: Lutheran 95%.
Capital city: Stockholm ('log island'), population 1 420 198 in 1984.
Other principal towns (1984): Göteborg 669 151; Malmö 455 377; Uppsala 152 579; Norrköping 118 451; Västerås 117 658; Örebro 117 569; Linköping 115 600; Jönköping 107 031; Helsingborg 104 689.
Highest point: Kebnekaise, 6965 ft *2123 m.*
Principal mountain ranges: Norrland Mountains, Smaland Highlands.
Principal rivers: Ume (310 miles *499 km*), Torne (354 miles *569 km*), Angerman (279 miles *449 km*), Klar (304 miles *489 km*), Dal (323 miles *520 km*).
Head of State: King Carl XVI Gustaf (b. 30 Apr. 1946).
Prime Minister: Ingvar Carlsson (b. 9 Jan. 1934).
Climate: Summers mild and warm; winters long and cold in north, more moderate in south. In Stockholm, average maximum −0,5°C *31°F* (January, February) to 21°C *70°F* (July), minimum −5°C *22°F* (February) to 12°C *55°F* (July), rainiest month is August (10 days). Abso-

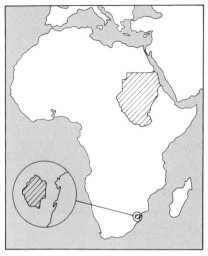

top: **SUDAN**
below: **SWAZILAND**

SURINAME

lute maximum temperature 38,0°C *100·4°F,* Ultuna, 9 July 1933; absolute minimum −53,3°C *−63·9°F,* Laxbacken, 13 Dec. 1941.
Labour force: 4 262 000 in 1985: Agriculture, forestry and fishing 4·3%; Mining and manufacturing 24·1%; Construction 6·0%; Trade, restaurants and hotels 11·9%; Communications 7·1%; Private services 15·2%; Public services 31·4%.
Gross domestic product: 861 billion kronor in 1985: Agriculture, forestry and fishing 3·7%; Mining and manufacturing 24·8%; Electricity, gas and waterworks 3·4%; Construction 8·1%; Private services 35·4%; Public services 24·6%.
Exports: 259 985 million kronor in 1985: Foodstuffs and beverages 2·8%; Raw materials 10·1%; Mineral fuels 4·9%; Manufactured goods 26%; Non-electrical machinery 14·9%; Electrical machinery 11·1%; Transport equipment 15·9%; Various finished goods 8·2%.
Monetary unit: Swedish krona (plural: kronor). 1 krona = 100 öre.
Denominations:
  Coins 10, 50 öre; 1, 5 kronor.
  Notes 5, 10, 50, 100, 500, 1000, 10 000 kronor.
Exchange rate to £ sterling: 9·965 (26 Jan. 1987).
Political history and government: Sweden has been a constitutional monarchy, traditionally neutral, since the constitution of 6 June 1809. Parliamentary government was adopted in 1917 and universal adult suffrage introduced in 1921. A revised constitution was introduced on 1 Jan. 1975. The King is Head of State but has very limited formal prerogatives. Legislative power is held by the Parliament (*Riksdag*), which has been unicameral since 1 Jan. 1971. It has 349 members elected by universal adult suffrage for 3 years, using proportional representation. Executive power is held by the Cabinet, led by the

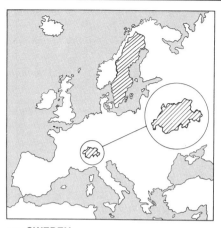

top: **SWEDEN**
encircled: **SWITZERLAND**

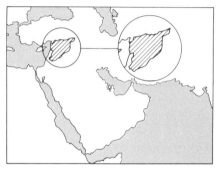

SYRIA

Prime Minister, which is responsible to the *Riksdag*. Under the 1975 constitution, the Prime Minister is nominated by the Speaker of the *Riksdag* and later confirmed in office by the whole House. After approval, the Prime Minister appoints other members of the Cabinet. Sweden is divided into 24 counties, each administered by a nominated governor.
Length of roadways: 108 323 miles *174 291 km* (1985).
Length of railways: 7497 miles *12 063 km* (1985).
Universities: 20.
Expectation of life: Males 73·08 years; females 79·13 years (1979–83).
Defence: Military service: Army and Navy 7½ to 15 months; Air Force 8 to 12 months; total armed forces 850 000 in 1985; defence expenditure: 7·8% of total government expenditure in 1985–6.
Foreign tourists: 3 060 000 in 1982.

Switzerland

Official name: Schweizerische Eidgenossenschaft (German), Confédération Suisse (French), Confederazione Svizzera (Italian): Swiss Confederation.
Population: 6 484 800 (1986).
Area: 15 943 miles² *41 293 km²*.
Languages: German 65%: French 18%; Italian 10%; Romansch 1%; Others 6%.
Religions: Roman Catholic 48%; Protestant 44%.
Capital city: Bern (Berne), population 300 505 (1985 estimate).
Other principal towns (1983): Zürich 834 777; Basel (Bâle) 362 548; Genève (Genf, Geneva) 376 351; Lausanne 257 212; Winterthur 106 818; St Gallen (Saint Gall) 124 320; Luzern (Lucerne) 158 350.
Highest point: Dufourspitze (Monte Rosa), 15 203 ft *4634 m* (first climbed 1855).
Principal mountain range: Alps.
Principal rivers: Rhein (Rhine) and Aare, Rhône, Inn, Ticino.
Head of State: Pierre Aubert (b. 1927), President for 1987.

Climate: Generally temperate, with wide variations due to altitude. Cooler in north, warm on southern slopes. In Zürich, average maximum 9°C *48°F* (January) to 30°C *86°F* (July), minimum −10°C *14°F* (January) to 10°C *51°F* (July), rainiest months are June and July (each 15 days). In Geneva, January coldest (−2°C *29°F* to 4°C *39°F*), July warmest (14°C *58°F* to 25°C *77°F*). Absolute maximum temperature 38,7°C *101·7°F*, Basel, 29 July 1947; absolute minimum −35,8°C *−34·4°F*, Jungfraujoch, 14 Feb. 1940.
Labour force: 3 170 900 in 1985: Agriculture 6·6%; Industry 38%; Services 55·4%.
Gross domestic product: 214 085 million Swiss francs in 1984.
Exports: 60 654 million Swiss francs in 1984: Metal manufactures 49·3%; Chemicals 21%; Textiles and clothing 7·1%; Foodstuffs 3·1%; Precious metal articles and jewellery 10·3%.
Monetary unit: Schweizer Franken (Swiss franc). 1 franc = 100 Rappen (centimes).
Denominations:
Coins 1, 2, 5, 10, 20, 50 centimes; 1, 2, 5 francs.
Notes 5, 10, 20, 50, 100, 500, 1000 francs.
Exchange rate to £ sterling: 2·34 (27 Jan. 1987).
Political history and government: Since 1815 Switzerland has been a neutral confederation of autonomous cantons. The present constitution, establishing a republican form of government, was adopted on 29 May 1874. The cantons hold all powers not specifically delegated to the federal authorities. On 1 Jan. 1979 a new canton, the first since 1815, was established when the Jura seceded from Bern. Switzerland now has 20 cantons and 6 half-cantons.
Legislative power is held by the bicameral Federal Assembly: a Council of States with 46 members representing the cantons (two for each canton and one for each half-canton), elected for 3 to 4 years; and the National Council with 200 members directly elected by universal adult suffrage for 4 years, using proportional representation. The two Houses have equal rights. A referendum on 7 Feb. 1971 approved women's suffrage in federal elections. Executive power is held by the Federal Council, which has 7 members (not more than one from any canton) elected for 4 years by a joint session of the Federal Assembly. Each member of the Council, which is responsible to the Assembly, has ministerial responsibility as head of a Federal Department. The Assembly elects one Councillor to be President of the Confederation (also presiding over the Council) for one calendar year at a time. Each canton has a constitution, an elected unicameral legislature and an executive.
Length of roadways: 41 357 miles *66 544 km* (1982).
Length of railways: 3124 miles *5027 km* (1985).
Universities: 7 (plus 2 technical universities).
Expectation of life: Males 70·29 years; females 76·22 years (1968–73).
Defence: Military service: 17 weeks recruit training, followed by reservist refresher training of three weeks per year for 8 out of 12 years, two weeks for 3 of 10 years, and one week for 2 of 8 years; total armed forces on mobilization: 625 000 in 1986; defence expenditure: 21·3% of total government expenditure in 1984.
Foreign tourists: 35 182 000 overnight stays in 1985.

Syria

Official name: Al-Jumhuriya al-'Arabiya as-Suriya (the Syrian Arab Republic).
Population: 9 934 000 (1984 estimate).
Area: 71 498 miles² *185 180 km²*.
Languages: Arabic (official); Kurdish; Armenian; Turkish; Circassian.
Religion: Muslim; Christian minority.
Capital city: Dimash'q (Damascus), population 1 112 214 (1981 census).
Other principal towns (1981): Halab (Aleppo) 985 413; Homs 346 871; Al Ladhiqiyah (Latakia) 196 791; Hama 177 208.
Highest point: Jabal ash-Shaikh (Mt Hermon), 9232 ft *2814 m*.

Principal mountain ranges: Ansariyah range, Jabal ar-Ruwā.
Principal rivers: Al Furat (Euphrates headwaters) (420 miles *676 km* out of 1400 miles *2253 km*), Asi (Orontes).
Head of State: Lt-Gen Hafiz al-Assad (b. 6 Oct. 1930), President.
Prime Minister: Dr Abdul Rauf al-Qasim (b. 1931).
Climate: Variable. Hot summers, mild winters and ample rainfall on coast. Inland it is arid with hot, dry summers and cold winters. In Damascus, average maximum 12°C *53°F* (January) to 37°C *99°F* (August), minimum 2°C *36°F* (January) to 18°C *64°F* (July, August), rainiest month is January (seven days).
Labour force: 2 063 080 1983: Agriculture, forestry and fishing 29·4%; Mining 13·5%; Construction 15·7%; Trade 10·2%; Transport, storage and communications 6·2%; Community, social and personal services 32·2%.
Gross domestic product: S£75 126 million in 1984: Agriculture, forestry and fishing 19·9%; Mining 8·1%; Manufacturing 8·7%; Construction 6·6%; Trade 23·3%; Transport, storage and communications 8·3%; Services 24·9%.
Exports: S£7274·8 in 1984: Cotton 18·7%; Other textile goods 5·1%; Crude petroleum 49·6%.
Monetary unit: Syrian pound (S£). 1 pound = 100 piastres.
Denominations:
Coins 2½, 5, 10, 25, 50 piastres; 1 pound.
Notes 1, 5, 10, 25, 50, 100, 500 pounds.
Exchange rate to £ sterling: 5·9974 (26 Jan. 1987).
Political history and government: Formerly part of Turkey's Ottoman Empire. Turkish forces were defeated in the First World War (1914–18). In 1920 Syria was occupied by French forces, in accordance with a League of Nations mandate. Nationalists proclaimed an independent republic on 16 Sept. 1941. The first elected parliament met on 17 Aug. 1943, French powers were transferred on 1 Jan. 1944 and full independence achieved on 12 Apr. 1946. Syria merged with Egypt to form the United Arab Republic, proclaimed on 1 Feb. 1958 and established on 21 Feb. 1958. Following a military *coup* in Syria on 28 Sept. 1961, the country resumed separate independence, under its present name, on 29 Sept. 1961. Left-wing army officers overthrew the government on 8 Mar. 1963 and formed the National Council of the Revolutionary Command (NCRC), which took over all executive and legislative authority. The NCRC installed a Cabinet dominated by the Arab Socialist Renaissance (Ba'ath) Party. This party has held power ever since. Lt-Gen Hafiz al-Assad became Prime Minister on 18 Nov. 1970 and assumed Presidential powers on 22 Feb. 1971. His position was approved by popular referendum on 12 Mar. 1971 and he was sworn in for a 7-year term as President on 14 Mar. 1971. Legislative power is held by the People's Council, originally appointed for two years on 16 Feb. 1971 to draft a permanent constitution. The constitution, proclaiming socialist principles, was approved by referendum on 12 Mar. 1973 and adopted two days later. It declares that the Ba'ath party is 'the leading party in the State and society'. The People's Council became a full legislature after election by universal adult suffrage on 25–26 Mar. 1973. For the elections of 1–2 Aug. 1977 the Council was increased to 195 members. Political power is held by the Progressive Front of National Unity, formed on 7 Mar. 1972 by a merger of the Ba'ath Party and four others. The Head of State is leader of the Ba'ath Party and President of the Front. Syria has 14 administrative districts.
Length of roadways: 10 383 miles *16 710 km*.
Length of railways: 995 miles *1601 km*.
Universities: 4.
Adult illiteracy: 60·0% (males 40·4%; females 80·0%) in 1970.
Expectation of life: Males 54·49 years; females 58·73 years (1970).
Defence: Military service: 30 months; total armed forces 402 500 (1985); defence expenditure: 31·5% of total government expenditure in 1984.

Foreign tourists: 976 030 in 1984.

Tanzania

Official name: United Republic of Tanzania (Jamhuri ya Muungano wa Tanzania).
Population: 21 062 000 (1984 estimate).
Area: 364 900 miles² *945 087 km²*.
Languages: English, Swahili.
Religions: Traditional beliefs, Christian, Muslim.
Capital city: Dodoma, population 45 703 (1978 census).
Other principal towns (1978): Dar es Salaam (former capital) 757 346; Zanzibar Town 110 669; Mwanza 110 611; Tanga 103 409; Mbeya 76 606; Morogoro 61 890; Arusha 55 281.
Highest point: Mount Kilimanjaro, 19 340 ft *5894 m*.
Principal mountain range: Southern Highlands.
Principal rivers: Pangani (Ruvu), Rufiji, Rovuma.
Head of State: Ndugu Ali Hassan Mwinyi, President.
Prime Minister: Joseph S. Warioba.
Climate: Varies with altitude. Tropical (hot and humid) on Zanzibar, and on the coast and plains. Cool and semi-temperate in the highlands. In Dar es Salaam, average maximum 28°C *83°F* to 31°C *88°F*, minimum 19°C *66°F* to 25°C *77°F*. In Zanzibar Town, average maximum 28°C *82°F* (July) to 33°C *91°F* (February, March), minimum 22°C *72°F* (July–September) to 25°C *77°F* (March–April), average annual rainfall 1575 mm *62 in*, April rainiest (16 days), July driest (four days).
Labour force: 5 747 096 (census of 26 Aug. 1967): Agriculture, forestry and fishing 91·6%.
Gross domestic product: 24 972 million shillings in 1984, Tanzania mainland only, at constant 1976 factor cost: Agriculture, forestry and fishing 46·2%; Manufacturing 4·7%; Trade 9·8%; Transport, storage and communications 6·6%; Financial services 11·3%; Community, social and personal services 19·3%.
Exports: 5748 million shillings in 1984, excluding trade with Kenya and Uganda: Coffee 38·6%; Raw cotton 12·4%; Diamonds 5·7%; Cashew nuts 7·6%; Tea 5·7%.
Monetary unit: Tanzanian shilling. 1 shilling = 100 cents.
Denominations:
Coins 5, 10, 20, 50 cents; 1, 5, 20 shillings.
Notes 10, 20, 100 shillings.
Exchange rate to £ sterling: 80·70 (26 Jan. 1987).
Political history and government: Tanganyika became a German protectorate in 1885. During the First World War (1914–18) the territory was occupied by British and Belgian forces. In 1919 the United Kingdom was granted a League of Nations mandate over Tanganyika. On 13 Dec. 1946 it became a United Nations Trust Territory under British administration. Tanganyika became an independent member of the Commonwealth on 9 Dec. 1961 and a republic on 9 Dec. 1962. Zanzibar, a sultanate under British protection since 1890, became an independent constitutional monarchy within the Commonwealth on 10 Dec. 1963. The Sultan was overthrown by revolution on 12 Jan. 1964 and the People's Republic of Zanzibar proclaimed. A new constitution was decreed on 24 Feb. 1964. The two republics merged on 26 Apr. 1964 to form the United Republic of Tanganyika and Zanzibar (renamed Tanzania on 29 Oct. 1964) and remained in the Commonwealth.

An interim constitution, declaring Tanzania a one-party state, was approved by the legislature on 5 July 1965 and received the President's assent three days later. Legislative power was vested in the unicameral National Assembly, with a term of five years (subject to dissolution). Executive power lies with the President, elected by popular vote for five years. He appoints a First Vice-President (who is Chairman of the Zanzibar Revolutionary Council), a Prime Minister and a Cabinet.

At a joint conference the ruling parties of Tanganyika and Zanzibar decided on 21 Jan. 1977 to merge into a single party, *Chama Cha Mapinduzi* (CCM or Revolutionary Party), formed on 5 Feb. 1977. The Party's leading decision-making organ is the National Executive, elected by party members.

On 25 Apr. 1977 the National Assembly approved a permanent constitution for Tanzania. On 26 Oct. 1980 elections were held for 111 seats (101 in Tanganyika, 10 in Zanzibar) in the 239-member Assembly. The remaining 128 members include 32 appointees from Zanzibar, 25 regional commissioners (one for each of the 20 administrative regions in Tanganyika, five for the two Zanzibar regions), the President of Zanzibar, 30 members nominated by the Head of State and 40 others (25 regional members and 15 representing state bodies) chosen by the Assembly's elected members.

Nyerere stepped down as President at the end of his term in 1985, and was succeeded by Ali Hassan Mwinyi, the sole candidate of the CCM Congress.

In Zanzibar, comprising the islands of Zanzibar and Pemba, a Revolutionary Council is responsible for internal government. On 13 Oct. 1979 this Council adopted a new constitution for the territory. A special session of the CCM approved the new Zanzibar constitution on 28 Dec. 1979 and legislation incorporating the necessary amendments to the Tanzanian constitution was approved on 2 Jan. 1980.
Length of roadways: 33 600 miles *54 000 km*.
Length of railways: 1616 miles *2600 km*.
Universities: 1.
Adult illiteracy: 54% in 1978.
Expectation of life: Males 46·4 years; females 49·7 years (UN estimates for 1970–75).
Defence: Military service voluntary; total armed forces 40 350 (1985); defence expenditure: 18·5% of total government expenditure in 1984–5.
Foreign tourists: 60 000 in 1985.

Thailand

Official name: Prathet Thai (Kingdom of Thailand), also called Prades Thai or Muang-Thai (Thai means free).
Population: 52 545 529 (1986).
Area: 198 457 miles² *514 000 km²*.
Language: Thai.
Religions: Buddhist, Muslim minority.
Capital city: Krungt'ep (Bangkok), population 5 446 708 (1986).
Other principal towns (1980): Chiang Mai 101 595; Nakhon Ratchasima 78 246; Khon Kaen 85 863; Udon Thani 71 142; Pitsanulok 79 942; Hat Yai 93 519.
Highest point: Doi Inthanon, 8452 ft *2576 m*.
Principal rivers: Mekong (2600 miles *4184 km*), Chao Pyha (154 miles *247 km*).
Head of State: HM King Bhumibol Adulyadej (b. 5 Dec. 1927).
Prime Minister: Gen Prem Tinsulanonda (b. 26 Aug. 1920).
Climate: Tropical monsoon climate (humid). Three seasons – hot, rainy and cool. Average temperature 29°C *85°F*. In Bangkok, average maximum 30°C *87°F* (November, December) to 35°C *95°F* (April), minimum 20°C *68°F* (December, January) to 25°C *77°F* (April, May), rainiest month is September (15 days). Absolute maximum temperature 44,1°C *111·4°F*, Mae Sariang, 25 Apr. 1958; absolute minimum 0,1°C *32·2°F*, Loey, 13 Jan. 1955.
Labour force: 25 183 500 in 1983: Agriculture, forestry and fishing 69·1%; Manufacturing 7·3%; Trade 8·7%; Services 10·1%.
Gross domestic product: 991 752 million baht in 1984: Agriculture 20%; Manufacturing 19·1%; Trade 18·7%; Services 25%.
Exports: 146 438 million baht in 1983: Rice 13·7%; Tapioca products 10·5%; Rubber 8%; Tin 3·6%; Maize 5·8%; Sugar 4·3%.
Monetary unit: Baht. 1 baht = 100 satangs.
Denominations:
Coins 25, 50 satangs; 1, 5 baht.
Notes 10, 20, 100, 500 baht.
Exchange rate to £ sterling: 39·37 (26 Jan. 1987).

TANZANIA

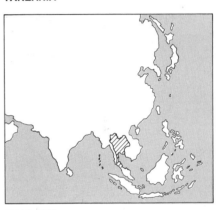

THAILAND

Political history and government: Thailand, called Siam before 1939, is a kingdom with an hereditary monarch as Head of State. The military régime established on 17 Nov. 1971 was forced to resign, following popular demonstrations, on 14 Oct. 1973. An interim government was formed and a new constitution, legalising political parties, was promulgated on 7 Oct. 1974. The constitutional government was overthrown on 6 Oct. 1976 by a military junta, the National Administrative Reform Council (NARC), which declared martial law, annulled the 1974 constitution, dissolved the bicameral National Assembly and banned political parties. A new constitution, promulgated on 22 Oct. 1976, provided for a National Administrative Reform Assembly (340 members appointed for 4 years by the King on 20 Nov. 1976). A new Prime Minister was appointed and the NARC became the Prime Minister's Advisory Council. On 20 Oct. 1977 a Revolutionary Council of military leaders (almost identical to the NARC) deposed the government, abrogated the 1976 constitution and abolished the Advisory Council. An interim constitution was promulgated on 9 Nov. 1977. It provided that the Revolutionary Council would become the National Policy Council (NPC) and that the Prime Minister would be appointed by the King on the advice of the NPC's chairman. General Kriangsak Chamanan, Supreme Commander of the Armed Forces and Secretary-General of the NPC, became Prime Minister on 11 Nov. 1977. Other Ministers were appointed by the King on the Prime Minister's recommendation. On 16 Nov. 1977 a National Legislative Assembly (NLA) of 360 members was nominated by the King on the advice of the NPC's chairman. On 23 Nov. the NLA opened and on 1 Dec. 1977 it appointed a 35-member committee to draft a new constitution.

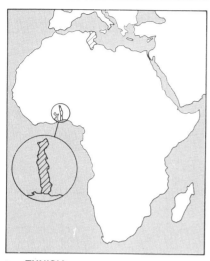

top: **TUNISIA**
encircled: **TOGO**

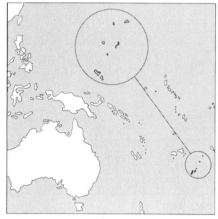

TONGA

A new constitution was approved by the NLA on 18 Dec. 1978 and promulgated on 22 Dec. 1978. Legislative power is vested in a bicameral National Assembly, comprising a House of Representatives (301 members elected for 4 years by universal adult suffrage) and a Senate (225 members appointed for 6 years by the King on the recommendation of the incumbent Prime Minister). The two chambers meet in joint session to appoint the Prime Minister and to debate motions of confidence. Elections to the House were held on 22 Apr. 1979. The nominated Senators were almost all military officers. On 11 May 1979 the Assembly invited Gen Kriangsak to continue as Prime Minister. After a new Cabinet was formed, the NPC was dissolved. Kriangsak resigned on 29 Feb. 1980. General Prem Tinsulanonda, Minister of Defence and Army Commander-in-Chief, was nominated by the Assembly to become Prime Minister, and was appointed by the King, on 3 Mar. 1980.

Thailand comprises 73 provinces, each headed by an appointed governor.
Length of roadways: 20 601 miles *33 148 km* (1983).
Length of railways: 2321 miles *3735 km* (1983).
Universities: 11 (plus 2 technical universities).
Adult illiteracy: 21·3% (males 12·7%; females 29·5%) in 1970.
Expectation of life: Males 53·6 years; females 58·7 years (1960).
Defence: Military service: 2 years; total armed forces 233 100 (1986); defence expenditure: 18·9% of total government expenditure in 1985–6.
Foreign tourists: 2 438 270 in 1985.

Togo

Official name: La République togolaise (the Togolese Republic).

Population: 3 030 000 (1985 estimate).
Area: 21 933 miles² *56 785 km²*.
Languages: French (official), Ewe, Kabiye.
Religions: Animist; Christian and Muslim minorities.
Capital city: Lomé, population 366 476 (1983 estimate).
Other principal towns (1 Jan. 1977): Sokodé 33 500; Palimé 25 500; Atakpamé 21 800; Bassari 17 500; Tsévié 15 900.
Highest point: 3018 ft *919 m*.
Principal rivers: Mono, Oti.
Head of State: Gen Gnassingbe Eyadéma (b. 26 Dec. 1937), President.
Climate: Equatorial (hot and humid). On coast, average temperatures 24°C *76°F* to 28°C *82°F*, higher inland (average 36°C *97°F* in drier north).
Labour force: 719 308 (excluding unemployed) aged 15 and over (1970 census); 859 000 (mid-1970): Agriculture, forestry and fishing 73·3%; Industry 10·9%; Services 15·8% (ILO estimates).
Gross domestic product: 133 829 million CFA francs in 1976: Agriculture, forestry and fishing 32%; Industry 11·9%; Trade, restaurants and hotels 22·3%.
Exports: 80 000 million francs CFA in 1984: Phosphates 50%; Cocoa beans 26%; Cotton 9%.
Monetary unit: France de la Communauté financière africaine.
Denominations:
   Coins 1, 2, 5, 10, 25, 50, 100, 500 CFA francs.
   Notes 50, 100, 500, 1000, 5000 CFA francs.
Exchange rate to £ sterling: 464·75 (26 Jan. 1987).
Political history and government: Formerly a United Nations Trust Territory under French administration, an independent republic since 27 Apr. 1960. An army *coup* on 13 Jan. 1967 deposed the President and established military rule under Lieut-Col (later Major-Gen) Etienne Gnassingbe Eyadéma, who suspended the constitution and dissolved the National Assembly. Eyadéma proclaimed himself President on 14 Apr. 1967. Political parties were banned and the President ruled by decree through an appointed Council of Ministers. On 29 Nov. 1969 the President established a single ruling party, the *Rassemblement du peuple togolais* (RPT). A congress of the RPT on 27–29 Nov. 1979 approved a new constitution for Togo. This provides for a one-party state, with legislative power vested in a 67-member National Assembly (elected for five years by universal adult suffrage) while executive power is held by the President, directly elected for seven years. The constitution was approved by referendum on 30 Dec. 1979, when President Eyadéma was re-elected (unopposed) and the new Assembly elected (from a single list of RPT candidates). On 13 Jan. 1980 the President proclaimed the 'Third Republic'. Togo is divided into four regions, each administered by an appointed Inspector.
Length of roadways: 4879 miles *7850 km* (1981).
Length of railways: 325 miles *525 km*.
Universities: 1.
Adult illiteracy: 84·1% (males 73·1%; females 92·9%) in 1970.
Expectation of life: Males 41·9 years; females 45·1 years (UN estimates for 1970–75).
Defence: Total armed forces 5080 (1985); defence expenditure: 8% of total government expenditure in 1985.
Foreign tourists: 126 300 in 1984.

Tonga

Official name: Pule'anga Fakatu'i 'o Tonga (Kingdom of Tonga).
Population: 96 448 (1984 mini-census).
Area: 270 miles² *699 km²*.
Languages: Tongan, English.
Religion: Christian, mainly Wesleyan.
Capital city: Nuku'alofa, population 27 740 (1984).
Highest point: Kao, 3380 ft *1030 m*.
Head of State: HM King Taufa'ahau Tupou IV, GCMG, GCVO, KBE (b. 4 July 1918).
Prime Minister: HRH Prince Fatafehi

Tu'ipelehake, KCMG, KBE (b. 7 Jan. 1922).
Climate: Warm and pleasant. Average annual temperature is 23°C *73°F*. Hot and humid from Jan. to March (32°C *90°F*). Average annual rainfall 1600 mm *63 in* on Tongatapu, 2080 mm *82 in* on Vava'u.
Labour force: 18 626 (excluding persons seeking work for the first time and 2809 other unemployed) at 1976 census: Agriculture, forestry and fishing 56·1%; Community, social and personal services 24·0%.
Gross domestic product: 86·3 million pa'anga in 1982–3.
Exports: 9 995 621 pa'anga in 1984.
Monetary unit: Pa'anga. 1 pa'anga = 100 seniti.
Denominations:
   Coins 1, 2, 5, 10, 20, 50 seniti; 1, 2 pa'anga.
   Notes 50 seniti; 1, 2, 5, 10 pa'anga.
Exchange rate to £ sterling: 2·2995 (26 Jan. 1987).
Political history and government: Tonga is a kingdom ruled by an hereditary monarch. It was under British protection from 18 May 1900 until becoming independent, within the Commonwealth, on 4 June 1970. The King is Head of State and Head of Government. He appoints, and presides over, a Privy Council which acts as the national Cabinet. Apart from the King, the Council includes six Ministers, led by the Prime Minister (currently the King's brother), and the Governors of two island groups. The unicameral Legislative Assembly comprises 23 members: the King, the Privy Council, seven hereditary nobles elected by their peers and seven representatives elected by literate adults (male voters must be tax-payers). Elected members hold office for three years. There are no political parties.
Length of roadways: 269 miles *433 km*.
Adult illiteracy: 0·4% (males 0·3%; females 0·5%) in 1976.
Expectation of life: 55·2 years (both sexes) in 1965.
Defence: Defence budget, 1972/73: 74 100 pa'anga.
Foreign tourists: 84 679 in 1984.

Trinidad and Tobago

Official name: The Republic of Trinidad and Tobago.
Population: 1 168 200 (1984).
Area: 1981 miles² *5130 km²*.
Languages: English (official), Hindi, French, Spanish.
Religions: Christian; Hindu and Moslem minorities.
Capital city: Port of Spain, population 58 400 (1985).
Other principal towns (1985): San Fernando 34 200; Arima 24 600.
Highest point: Cerro Aripo, 3085 ft *940 m*.
Principal mountain ranges: Northern and Southern, Central.
Principal rivers: Caroni, Ortoire, Oropuche.
Head of State: Ellis Emmanuel Innocent Clarke (b. 28 Dec. 1917), President.
Prime Minister: A. N. R. Robinson (b. 16 Dec. 1926).
Climate: Tropical, with an annual average temperature of 29°C *84°F*. The dry season is January to May.
Labour force: 465 800 in 1985: Petroleum, mining and quarrying 2·3%; Agriculture, forestry, fishing 6·4%; Manufacturing 10·6%; Construction 15·6%; Government services 16·8%; Unemployed 15·6%.
Gross domestic product: TT$18 971·9 million in 1985: Petroleum 24%; Manufacturing 6·7%; Agriculture 3·4%; Construction and quarrying 11%; Transportation 10·1%; Government services 15·3%.
Exports: TT$5301·2 million in 1984: Mineral fuel and lubricants 81·4%; Chemicals 10·9%; Manufactured goods 3·2%.
Monetary unit: Trinidad and Tobago dollar (TT$) 1 dollar = 100 cents.

Denominations:
Coins 1, 5, 10, 25, 50 cents; 1 dollar.
Notes 1, 5, 10, 20, 100 dollars.
Exchange rate to £ sterling: 5·5008 (26 Jan. 1987).
Political history and government: Formerly a British dependency. The colony's first Chief Minister, Dr Eric Williams, took office on 28 Oct. 1956. A new constitution was introduced, with Dr Williams as Premier, on 20 July 1959. Internal self-government was granted after elections on 4 Dec. 1961. Following a constitutional conference on 28 May–8 June 1962, Trinidad and Tobago became an independent member of the Commonwealth, with the Premier as Prime Minister, on 31 Aug. 1962. The country became a republic on 1 Aug. 1976. Dr Williams, Prime Minister since independence, died on 29 Mar. 1981.

Legislative power is vested in a bicameral Parliament, comprising a Senate with 31 members, appointed for up to five years by the President (16 on the advice of the Prime Minister, 6 on the advice of the Leader of the Opposition and 9 at the President's own discretion), and a House of Representatives (36 members elected by universal adult suffrage for five years). The President is a constitutional Head of State elected for five years by both Houses of Parliament. He appoints the Prime Minister to form a Cabinet from members of Parliament. The Cabinet has effective control of the government and is responsible to Parliament.
Length of roadways: 3216 miles *5175 km* (1984).
University: 1 (shared with Jamaica, Barbados and other Caribbean territories).
Adult illiteracy: 3·9% (males 2·7%; females 5·2%) in 1985.
Expectation of life: Males 64 years; females 68 years (1979).
Defence: Total armed forces: 2130 in 1985; defence expenditure: 3·2% of total government expenditure in 1984.
Foreign tourists: 191 470 in 1984.

Tunisia

Official name: Al-Jumhuriya at-Tunisiya (the Republic of Tunisia).
Population: 6 966 173 (1984 census).
Area: 63 400 miles² *164 150 km²*.
Languages: Arabic, French.
Religions: Muslim; Jewish and Christian minorities.
Capital city: Tunis, population 556 654 (1984).
Other principal towns (1984): Sfax (Safaqis) 231 911; Bizerte 94 509; Djerba 92 269; Gabes 92 259; Sousse 83 509; Kairouan 72 254; Gafsa 60 970.
Highest point: Djebel Chambi, 5066 ft *1544 m*.
Principal river: Medjerda (300 miles *482 km*).
Head of State: Habib Ben Ali Bourguiba (b. 3 Aug. 1903), President.
Prime Minister: Rashid Sfar (b. 11 Sept. 1933).
Climate: Temperate, with winter rain, on coast; hot and dry inland. In Tunis, August warmest (20°C *69°F* to 33°C *91°F*), January coolest (6°C *43°F* to 14°C *58°F*), December rainiest (14 days). Absolute maximum temperature 55,0°C *131·0°F*, Kébili, 7 Dec. 1931; absolute minimum −9,0°C *15·8°F*, Fort-Saint, 22 Dec. 1940.
Labour force: 1 810 000 in 1980: Agriculture, forestry and fishing 30·5%; Manufacturing 16·6%; Construction 8·7%; Trade, banking and insurance 15%; Unemployed 12·9%.
Gross domestic product: 6860 million dinars in 1985: Agriculture, forestry and fishing 18·2%; Manufacturing 12·7%; Services 27·7%.
Exports: 1399·1 million dinars in 1984: Petroleum derivatives 44·8%; Fertilizers 8·4%; Clothing and accessories 11·9%; Olive oil 4·1%; Phosphoric acid 5·7%.
Monetary unit: Tunisian dinar. 1 dinar = 1000 millimes.
Denominations:
Coins 1, 2, 5, 10, 20, 50, 100, 500 millimes.
Notes 500 millimes; 1, 5, 10, 20 dinars.
Exchange rate to £ sterling: 1·2481 (26 Jan. 1987).

Political history and government: Formerly a monarchy, ruled by the Bey of Tunis. A French protectorate from 1883 until independence on 20 Mar. 1956. The campaign for independence was led by the Neo-Destour Party (founded by Habib Bourguiba), since October 1964 called the *Parti Socialiste Destourien* (PSD), the Destourian (Constitutional) Socialist Party. Elections were held on 25 Mar. 1956 for a Constitutional Assembly, which met on 8 Apr. 1956 and appointed Bourguiba as Prime Minister two days later. On 25 July 1957 the Assembly deposed the Bey, abolished the monarchy and established a republic, with Bourguiba as President. A new constitution was promulgated on 1 June 1959. Legislative power is vested in the unicameral National Assembly, first elected on 8 Nov. 1959. The Assembly's members are elected by universal adult suffrage for five years. Executive power is held by the President, elected for five years by popular vote at the same time as the Assembly. On 3 Nov. 1974 President Bourguiba was re-elected for a fourth term of office but on 18 Mar. 1975 the Assembly proclaimed him 'President for life'. The President, who is Head of State and Head of Government, appoints a Council of Ministers, headed by a Prime Minister, which is responsible to him. From 1963 to 1981 the PSD was the only legal party. An 18-year ban on the Tunisian Communist Party was lifted on 18 July 1981. Elections were held on 1 Nov. 1981 for a new National Assembly, with 136 members chosen from 23 multi-member constituencies. Parties other than the PSD were permitted to contest the elections but none received the necessary 5% of the valid votes to achieve subsequent legal recognition.
Length of roadways: 14 730 miles *23 700 km* (1981).
Length of railways: 1328 miles *2136 km*.
Universities: 1.
Adult illiteracy: 62·0% (males 48·9%; females 72·2%) in 1975.
Expectation of life: Males 54·0 years; females 56·0 years (UN estimate for 1970–75).
Defence: Military service: 12 months, selective; total armed forces 35 100 (1986); defence expenditure: 8·3% of total government expenditure in 1981.
Foreign tourists: 1 500 000 in 1984.

Turkey

Official name: Türkiye Cumhuriyeti (Republic of Turkey).
Population: 51 420 757 (1985 census).
Area: 301 076 miles² *779 452 km²*.
Languages: Turkish 90·2%; Kurdish 6·9%; Arabic 1·2%; Zaza 0·5% (1965).
Religion: Muslim 98%.
Capital city: Ankara (Angora), population 3 462 880 in 1985.
Other principal towns (1985): Istanbul 5 858 558; Izmir (Smyrna) 2 316 843; Adana 1 757 102; Bursa 1 327 762; Konya 1 791 635.
Highest point: Büyük Ağridaği (Mt Ararat), 17 011 ft *5185 m*.
Principal mountain ranges: Armenian Plateau, Toros Dağlari (Taurus Mts), Kuzey Anadolu Dağlari.
Principal rivers: Firat (Euphrates), Dicle (Tigris), Kizilirmak (Halys), Sakarya.
Head of State: Gen Kenan Evren (b. 1918), President.
Prime Minister: Turgut Özal.
Climate: Hot, dry summers and cold, snowy winters in interior plateau; mild winters and warm summers on Mediterranean coast. In Ankara, average maximum 4°C *30°F* (January) to 30°C *87°F* (August), minimum −4°C *24°F* (January) to 15°C *59°F* (July, August), rainiest month is December (9 days). In Istanbul, average maximum 7°C *45°F* (January) to 27°C *81°F* (July, August), minimum 2°C *36°F* (January) to 19°C *66°F* (August), rainiest month is December (15 days). Absolute maximum temperature 46,2°C *115·2°F*, Diyarbakir, 21 July 1937; absolute minimum −43,2°C *−45·8°F*, Karaköse, 13 Jan. 1940.

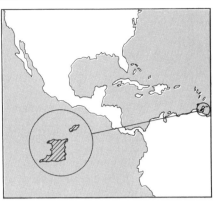

TRINIDAD AND TOBAGO

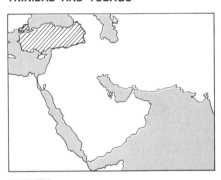

TURKEY

Labour force: 19 212 193 in 1980: Agriculture, forestry and fishing 57·8%; Manufacturing 10·3%; Trade 5·6%; Community, personal and social services 12·6%; Unemployed 3·4%.
Gross domestic product: 25 754·7 billion liras in 1985: Agriculture 17·4%; Industry 31·8%.
Exports: US$7·1 billion in 1984: Cotton 8·1%; Iron and steel 7·4%; Tobacco 3%; Textiles 14%; Fruit and peel 7·9%.
Monetary unit: Turkish lira. 1 lira = 100 kuruş.
Denominations:
Coins 25, 50 kuruş; 1, 2½, 5 liras.
Notes 5, 10, 20, 50, 100, 500, 1000, 5000, 10 000 liras.
Exchange rate to £ sterling: 1120·77 (26 Jan. 1987).
Political history and government: Formerly a monarchy, ruled by a Sultan. Following the disintegration of the Ottoman Empire after the First World War, power passed to the Grand National Assembly, which first met on 23 Apr. 1920. The Assembly approved a new constitution on 20 Jan. 1921, vesting executive and legislative authority in itself. It abolished the sultanate on 1 Nov. 1922 and declared Turkey a republic on 29 Oct. 1923. The armed forces overthrew the government on 27 May 1960, the Assembly was dissolved and political activities suspended until 12 Jan. 1961. A new constitution was approved by referendum on 9 June 1961 and took effect on 25 Oct. 1961. Legislative power was vested in the bicameral Grand National Assembly, comprising the Senate of the Republic (with, in 1980, 19 life senators plus 150 elected and 15 appointed members serving a six-year term) and the National Assembly (450 members elected by universal adult suffrage for four years). The Grand National Assembly elected one of its members to be President of the Republic for a single seven-year term. The President appointed the Prime Minister from among members of the legislature.

Following a period of severe political violence, martial law was proclaimed on 26 Dec. 1978 in 13 of Turkey's 67 provinces. This was later extended to other provinces. The President's term of office ended on 6 Apr. 1980 but, despite more than 100 ballots in the Grand National Assembly, no candidate gained enough support to succeed him. On 11–12 Sept. 1980 a military *coup* deposed the civilian government. Power was assumed by a five-member National Secur-

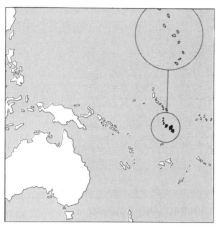

TUVALU

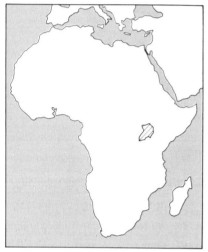

UGANDA

ity Council (NSC), led by the Chief of the General Staff, Gen Kenan Evren. Martial law was extended to the whole country and the Grand National Assembly dissolved. General Evren became Head of State and the NSC was sworn in on 18 Sept. A mainly civilian Council of Ministers was appointed on 21 Sept. The NSC adopted a provisional constitution, giving itself unlimited powers, on 27 Oct. 1980. All political parties were dissolved on 16 Oct. 1981. A Consultative Assembly of 160 members (40 nominated by the NSC and 120 selected from provincial governors' lists), appointed to draft a new constitution, opened on 23 Oct. 1981. In 1982 Evren was elected as president.
Length of roadways: 36853 miles *59 297 km* (1983).
Length of railways: 5204 miles *8373 km* (1983).
Universities: 26.
Adult illiteracy: 32·5% in 1980.
Expectation of life: Males 58·3 years; females 59·4 years (UN estimates for 1970–75).
Defence: Military service: 20 months; total armed forces 618 000 (475 000 conscripts) in 1986; defence expenditure: 15·6% of total government expenditure in 1985.
Foreign tourists: 2 800 000 in 1985.

Tuvalu

Population: 8299 (1985 mini-census).
Area: 9·5 miles² *24,6 km²*.
Languages: Tuvaluan, English.
Religion: Christian (Congregational 97%).
Capital city: Fongafale (in Funafuti atoll, population 2810 in 1985).
Other principal atolls: Nanumea, Niutau, Vaitupu.
Head of State: HM Queen Elizabeth II, represented by Sir (Fiatau) Penitala Teo, GCMG, ISO, MBE (b. 23 July 1911), Governor-General.

Prime Minister: The Rt. Hon. Dr Tomasi Puapua.
Climate: Warm and pleasant, with day temperatures between 27°C *80°F* and 32°C *90°F* and a minimum of about 21°C *70°F* at night. Average annual rainfall about 3050 mm *120 in.* Rainy season Dec.–Feb., dry Aug.–Oct.
Exports: A$36 766 in 1982: Copra 72·5%.
Monetary unit: Australian currency (*q.v.*).
Political history and government: Formerly known as the Ellice (Lagoon) Islands. In Sept. 1892 the group became a United Kingdom protectorate and was linked administratively with the Gilbert Islands. The Gilbert and Ellice Islands were annexed by the UK on 10 Nov. 1915, effective from 12 Jan. 1916, when the protectorate became a colony. The Gilbert and Ellice Islands Colony (GEIC) was later expanded to include other groups. A referendum was held in the Ellice Islands in Aug.–Sept. 1974, when over 90% of voters favoured separation from the GEIC. The Ellice Islands, under the old native name of Tuvalu ('eight standing together'), became a separate British dependency on 1 Oct. 1975. The 8 Ellice representatives in the GEIC House of Assembly became the first elected members of the new Tuvalu House of Assembly. They elected one of their number to be Chief Minister. Tuvalu's first separate elections were held on 29 Aug. 1977, when the number of elective seats in the House was increased from 8 to 12. Following a 4-day conference in London, a new constitution was finalized on 17 Feb. 1978. Afer 5 months of internal self-government, Tuvalu became independent on 1 Oct. 1978, with the Chief Minister as the first Prime Minister. Tuvalu is a 'special member' of the Commonwealth and is not represented at meetings of Heads of Government.
Tuvalu is a constitutional monarchy. Executive power is vested in the British monarch and is exercisable by the Governor-General, who is appointed on the recommendation of the Prime Minister and acts in almost all matters on the advice of the Cabinet. Legislative power is vested in the unicameral Parliament, with 12 members elected by universal adult suffrage for 4 years (subject to dissolution). The pre-independence House of Assembly became the first Parliament. The Cabinet is led by the Prime Minister, elected by and from members of Parliament. Other Ministers are appointed by the Governor-General, on the Prime Minister's recommendation, from members of Parliament. The Cabinet is responsible to Parliament. Each of the 8 inhabited atolls has an elected Island Council.
Expectation of life: Males 56·9 years; females 59·0 years (average for Kiribati and Tuvalu, 1958–62).

Uganda

Official name: The Republic of Uganda.
Population: 15 300 000 (1985 estimate).
Area: 91 134 miles² *236 036 km²*.
Languages: English (official), Luganda, Ateso, Runyankore.
Religions: Christian, Muslim, traditional beliefs.
Capital city: Kampala, population 454 974 (1981 estimate).
Other principal towns (1981): Jinja-Njeru 45 060; Mbale 28 039; Entebbe 20 472.
Highest point: Mount Stanley, 16 763 ft *5109 m* (first climbed 1900), on the border with Zaire.
Principal mountain range: Ruwenzori.
Principal rivers: Nile, Semliki.
Head of State: Yoweri Museveni, President.
Prime Minister: Dr Samson Kisekka.
Climate: Tropical, with an average temperature of 22°C *71°F*. There is a seasonal variation of only 11°C *20°F*.
Labour force: 6 086 000 in 1984: Agriculture, forestry and fishing 78·5%.
Gross domestic product: 6890 million shillings in 1982: Agriculture 52%; Manufacturing 6%; Other industries 7%; Services 35%.
Exports: 138 753 million shillings in 1984: Coffee 91·8%.

Monetary unit: Uganda shilling. 1 shilling = 100 cents.
Denominations:
  Coins 5, 10, 50 cents; 1 shilling.
  Notes 5, 10, 20, 50, 100, 500, 1000 shillings.
Exchange rate to £ sterling: Not available on 26 Jan. 1987.
Political history and government: Formerly a British dependency. The first Council of Ministers took office on 13 Apr. 1961 and the first Chief Minister was appointed on 2 July 1961. Uganda was granted internal self-government on 1 Mar. 1962, when the Chief Minister became Prime Minister. The leader of the Uganda People's Congress (UPC), Dr Milton Obote, became Prime Minister on 30 Apr. 1962. The country achieved independence, within the Commonwealth, on 9 Oct. 1962. Uganda became a republic, with a nominal President and Dr Obote continuing as executive Prime Minister, on 9 Oct. 1963. The constitution was suspended, and the President deposed, on 24 Feb. 1966. A provisional constitution, effective from 15 Apr. 1966, ended the former federal system and introduced an executive presidency, with Dr Obote as Head of State. A unitary republic was established on 8 Sept. 1967. After an assassination attempt against President Obote on 19 Dec. 1969, all parties other than the UPC were banned.
President Obote was deposed on 25 Jan. 1971 by an army *coup*, led by Major-Gen (later Field Marshal) Idi Amin Dada, who assumed full executive powers as Head of the Military Government and suspended political activity. The National Assembly was dissolved on 2 Feb. 1971, when Amin declared himself Head of State, took over legislative powers and suspended parts of the 1967 constitution. He was proclaimed President on 21 Feb. 1971 and ruled with the assistance of an appointed Council of Ministers. On 25 June 1976 the Defence Council appointed Amin 'President for Life'. No legislature was formed under Amin but a large advisory assembly, the National Consultative Forum, held its first meeting on 15–20 Jan. 1978.
After border fighting with Tanzanian forces in 1978, Ugandan troops captured the northern part of Tanzania. Amin announced Uganda's annexation of this territory on 1 Nov. 1978. Tanzania retaliated and its forces entered Uganda in Jan. 1979. The Ugandan capital fell to combined Tanzanian and Uganda National Liberation Front forces on 10–11 April 1979 and Amin's rule was overthrown. On 11 Apr. 1979 the UNLF formed a provisional government, the National Executive Committee (NEC), and on 13 Apr. it was sworn in. Lule became Chairman of the NEC and Head of State. On 8 May 1979 the new régime announced a two-year ban on political parties. The UNLF, the sole authorized political organization, formed a 30-member National Consultative Council (NCC) as a provisional parliament. On 20 June the NCC replaced President Lule by Godfrey Binaisa. In Sept. 1979 the UNLF nominated members of 33 district councils. On 3 Oct. these councils elected 61 members of an expanded NCC. Additional members were appointed from the Uganda National Liberation Army (UNLA). The new NCC, with 127 members, was inaugurated on 6 Oct. 1979.
On 12 May 1980 President Binaisa was relieved of his post when power was assumed by the UNLF's Military Commission, led by Paulo Muwanga. Muwanga stated that the new régime was an interim one and committed to general elections. On 22 May a three-man Presidential Commission was appointed. On 23 June it was reported that four political parties, including the UPC (led by ex-President Obote), would be allowed to contest the elections.
Voting took place on 10–11 Dec. 1980 for the 126 elective seats in a new National Assembly. Deputies to the Assembly, representing single-member constituencies, were elected by universal adult suffrage. The UPC gained a majority and, as the party's presidential candidate, Dr Obote was declared Head of State. He was sworn in on 15 Dec., when constitutional rule was restored.

In 1985 Obete was overthrown by an army coup, and Lt.-Gen. Tito Okello became president. He in turn was overthrown by Yoweri Museveni, whose National Resistance Army gained control of the country in 1986.
Length of roadways: 17 337 miles *27 901 km.*
Length of railways: 799 miles *1286 km.*
Universities: 1.
Adult illiteracy: 52% (1983).
Expectation of life: Males 48·3 years; females 51·7 years (UN estimates for 1970–75).
Defence: Total armed forces 18 000 (1985); defence expenditure: 17% of total government expenditure in 1983–4.
Foreign tourists: 12 786 in 1983.

The Union of Soviet Socialist Republics

Official name: Soyuz Sovyetskikh Sotsialisticheskikh Respublik (abbreviation in Cyrillic script is CCCP), sometimes shortened to Sovyetskiy Soyuz (Soviet Union).
Population: 262 436 227 (census of 17 Jan. 1979); 281 000 000 (1986 estimate).
Area: 8 649 540 miles² *22 402 200 km².* This official total includes two areas of ocean, the White Sea (34 750 miles² *90 000 km²*) and the Sea of Azov (14 400 miles² *37 300 km²*).
Languages (1970): Russian (official) 58·7%; Ukrainian 14·6%; Uzbek 3·8%; Byelorussian 3·2%; Tatar 2·4%; Kazakh 2·2%; over 130 languages in total.
Religions: No state religion. Christian with Jewish and Muslim minorities.
Capital city: Moskva (Moscow), population 8 642 000 (1985 estimate).
Other principal towns (1985): Leningrad 4 867 000; Kiev 2 448 000; Tashkent 2 030 000; Baku 1 693 000; Kharkov 1 554 000; Minsk 1 472 000; Gorky 1 399 000; Novosibirsk 1 393 000; Sverdlovsk 1 300 000; Kuibyshev 1 257 000; Tbilisi 1 158 000; Dnepropetrovsk 1 153 000; Yerevan 1 133 000; Odessa 1 126 000; Omsk 1 108 000; Chelyabinsk 1 096 000; Donetsk 1 073 000; Alma-Ata 1 068 000; Ufa 1 064 000; Perm 1 056 000; Kazan 1 047 000.
Highest point: Pik Kommunizma (Garmo, later Pik Stalin), 24 589 ft *7494 m* (first climbed 3 Sept. 1933).
Principal mountain ranges: Caucasus, Urals, Pamirs, Tien Shan.
Principal rivers: 14 rivers over 1000 miles *1609 km* in length (see pages 19–20).
Head of State: Andrei Gromyko, President of the Presidium of the Supreme Soviet of the USSR.
Head of Government: Mikhail Gorbachev, General Secretary of the Communist Party of the Soviet Union.
Climate: Great variations. Summers generally short and hot, winters long and cold. Very hot in central Asia, extremely cold in north-east Siberia. Average maximum and minimum temperatures for selected places:
Moscow: Average maximum −6°C *21°F* (January) to 24°C *76°F* (July). Average minimum −13°C *9°F* (January) to 13°C *55°F* (July). Rainiest months July, August (each 12 days).
Archangel: Average maximum −13°C *9°F* (January) to 18°C *64°F* (July). Average minimum −18°C *0°F* (February) to 10°C *51°F* (July). Rainiest month October (12 days).
Odessa: Average maximum −2°C *28°F* (January) to 26°C *79°F* (July). Average minimum −5°C *22°F* (January) to 18°C *65°F* (July, August). Rainiest months January and June (each 7 days).
Yakutsk: Average maximum −43°C *−45°F* (January) to 23°C *73°F* (July). Average minimum −47°C *−53°F* (January) to 12°C *54°F* (July). Rainiest months September, October, November (each 10 days).
Absolute maximum temperature 50,0°C *122·0°F*, Termez (Uzbekistan), July 1912; absolute minimum −71,1°C *−96·0°F*, Oymyakon, 1964.
Labour force: 129 474 000 in 'socialized' sector in 1984: Agriculture and forestry 19·5%; Indus-

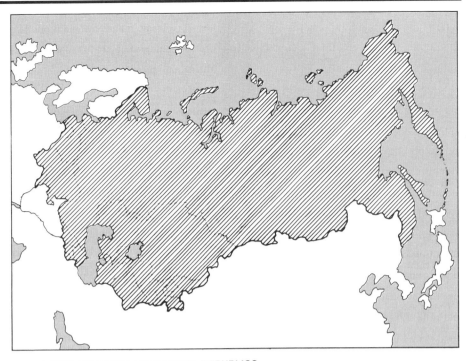

THE UNION OF SOVIET SOCIALIST REPUBLICS

try 29·3%; Transport 8·4%; Construction 8·8%; Distribution, supplies and catering 7·7%; Education 7·5%.
Net material product: 569·6 billion roubles in 1984: Agriculture 19·8%; Industry 46%; Construction 10·7%; Transport and communications 6%; Distribution and supply 17·6%.
Exports: 67 891 million roubles in 1983: Petroleum and petroleum products 41·6%; Machines and equipment 12·5%.
Monetary unit: Rubl' (ruble or rouble). 1 rouble = 100 kopeks.
Denominations:
  Coins 1, 2, 3, 5, 10, 20, 50 kopeks; 1 rouble.
  Notes 1, 3, 5, 10, 25, 50, 100 roubles.
Exchange rate to £ sterling: 0·9869 (26 Jan. 1987).
Political history and government: Formerly the Russian Empire, ruled by an hereditary Tsar (of the Romanov dynasty from 1613). Prompted by discontent with autocratic rule and the privation caused by the First World War, a revolution broke out on 27 Feb. (12 March New Style) 1917, causing the abdication of the last Tsar three days later and the establishment of a provisional government. During the following months Soviets (councils) were elected by some groups of industrial workers and peasants. A republic was proclaimed on 1 Sept. (14 Sept. NS) 1917. A political struggle developed between government supporters and the Bolshevik Party (founded in 1903 and called the Communist Party from 1919), which advocated the assumption of power by the Soviets. On 25 Oct. (7 Nov. NS) 1917 the Bolsheviks led an insurrection, arrested the provisional government and transferred power to the All-Russian Congress of Soviets. The Bolsheviks won only 175 out of 707 seats in the elections of 25–27 Nov. 1917 for the Constituent Assembly. The Assembly met on 18 Jan. 1918 but was forcibly dissolved by the Bolsheviks, who proclaimed a 'dictatorship of the proletariat'. On 31 Jan. 1918 Russia was proclaimed a Republic of Soviets. A constitution for the Russian Soviet Federative Socialist Republic (RSFSR) was adopted on 10 July 1918. Armed resistance to Communist rule developed into civil war (1917–22) but was eventually crushed. During the war other Soviet Republics were set up in the Ukraine, Byelorussia (White Russia) and Transcaucasia. These were merged with the RSFSR by a Treaty of Union, establishing the USSR, on 30 Dec. 1922. The USSR's first constitution was adopted on 6 July 1923. By splitting the territory of the

original four, two more Republics were added in 1925 and another in 1929. A new constitution was adopted on 5 Dec. 1936, when the number of Soviet Socialist Republics (SSRs) was raised from seven to eleven. On 31 Mar. 1940 territory ceded by Finland became part of the newly-formed Karelo-Finnish SSR. Territory ceded by Romania on 28 June 1940 became part of the new Moldavian SSR on 2 Aug. 1940. The three Baltic republics of Lithuania, Latvia and Estonia were annexed on 3–6 Aug. 1940, raising the number of Union Republics to 16. This was reduced to the present 15 on 16 July 1956, when the Karelo-Finnish SSR was merged with the RSFSR.

A new constitution took effect on 7 Oct. 1977. According to the constitution, the Communist Party is 'the leading and guiding force of Soviet society'. Early in 1978 new constitutions, modelled on that for the USSR, came into force in all 15 Union Republics.

The Soviet Union is formally a federal state comprising 15 Union (constituent) Republics of equal status, voluntarily linked and having the right to secede. Some of the 15 Union Republics contain Autonomous Republics and Autonomous Regions. The RSFSR also includes 10 National Areas. The highest organ of state power is the bicameral legislature, the Supreme Soviet of the USSR, comprising the Soviet (Council) of the Union, with 750 members elected from constituencies, and the Soviet (Council) of Nationalities, with 750 members (32 from each of the 15 Union Republics; 11 from each of the 20 Autonomous Republics; five from each of the eight Autonomous Regions; one from each of the 10 National Areas). Both houses have equal rights and powers and their terms run concurrently. Members are directly elected (from a single list of candidates) for five-year terms by universal adult suffrage. At a joint session the members elect the Presidium of the Supreme Soviet (39 members, including, as *ex officio* deputy chairmen, the 15 chairmen of the Supreme Soviets of the Union Republics) to be the legislature's permanent organ. The Chairman of the Presidium serves as Head of State. The Supreme Soviet also appoints the Council of Ministers (called People's Commissars until 16 Mar. 1946), headed by a Chairman, to form the executive and administrative branch of government, responsible to the Supreme Soviet.

Each of the 15 Union Republics has a constitution and state structure on the same pattern as the central government, with a

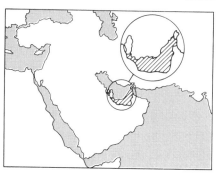

THE UNITED ARAB EMIRATES

unicameral Supreme Soviet and a Council of Ministers to deal with internal affairs. The Chairmen of the Councils of Ministers of the Union Republics are *ex officio* members of the USSR Council of Ministers. The Union Republics are entitled to maintain direct relations with foreign countries. Two of them, the Ukrainian and Byelorussian SSRs, are separately represented in the United Nations.

Throughout the whole country, real power is held by the highly centralized Communist Party of the Soviet Union (CPSU), the only legal party, which has an absolute monopoly of power in all political affairs and controls government at all levels. The Party had over 19 million members in 1981. Its highest authority is, in theory, the Party Congress, which should be convened at least every five years (the 27th Congress was held on 25 Feb.–6 Mar. 1986). The Congress elects the Central Committee (308 full members and 170 candidates, i.e. non-voting, members were chosen in 1986) which supervizes Party work and directs state policy. The Committee, which meets twice a year, elects a Political Bureau (Politburo), which is the Party's most powerful policy-making body. In 1987 the Politburo had 12 full members (including the General Secretary) and seven candidate members. Apart from the RSFSR, each Union Republic has its own Communist Party, with a Central Committee led by a First Secretary, but they are subsidiary to, and form an integral part of, the CPSU.

Length of roadways: 942 635 miles *1 516 700 km* (1984).
Length of railways: 92 000 miles *148 000 km* (1985).
Universities: 69.
Adult illiteracy: 0·2% in 1979.
Expectation of life: Males 64 years; females 73 years (1985).
Defence: Military service: Army and Air Force 2–3 years, Navy 5 years; total armed forces over 5 300 000 (Western estimate) in 1985; defence expenditure, 1983: official figure was 4·9% of total government expenditure in 1985, but Western estimates put the figure at several times this proportion.
Foreign tourists: 5 590 000 in 1980.

The United Arab Emirates

Official name: Al-Imarat Al-A'rabiya Al-Muttahida.
Population: 1 621 000 (1985 census).
Area: 35 575 miles² *92 100 km²*.
Language: Arabic.
Religion: Muslim.
Capital city: Abu Dhabi, population 670 000 (1985 estimate).
Other principal towns (1985): Dubai 419 000; Sharjah 269 000; Ras al Kaimah 116 000.
Highest point: Western Al-Hajar, 3900 ft *1189 m*.
Principal mountain range: Al-Hajar.
Head of State: Shaikh Zayed bin Sultan Al-Nahayan (b. 1918), President.
Prime Minister: Shaikh Rashid bin Sa'id Al-Maktoum (b. 1914).
Climate: Very hot and humid, with summer temperatures of over 38°C *100°F*; cooler in the eastern mountains.

Labour force: 600 000 (1985 estimate); Construction 30%; Trade, restaurants and hotels 15%; Community, social and personal services 30%.
Gross domestic product: 116 793 million dirhams in 1982: Agriculture, forestry and fishing 1%; Mining and quarrying 48·1%; Manufacturing 8·7%; Construction 9·4%; Trade 9%; Financial services 10%.
Exports: 52 902 million dirham in 1984: Oil 85%.
Monetary unit: UAE dirham. 1 dirham = 100 fils.
Denominations:
  Coins 1, 5, 10, 25, 50 fils; 1 dirham.
  Notes 1, 5, 10, 50, 100 dirhams.
Exchange rate to £ sterling: 5·599 (26 Jan. 1987).
Political history and government: Formerly the seven shaikhdoms of Trucial Oman (the Trucial States), under British protection. An independent federation (originally of six states), under a provisional constitution, since 2 Dec. 1971. The seventh, Ras al-Khaimah, joined the UAE on 11 Feb. 1972. The highest federal authority is the Supreme Council of the Union, comprising the hereditary rulers of the seven emirates (the rulers of Abu Dhabi and Dubai have the power of veto). From its seven members the Council elects a President and a Vice-President, each with a 5-year term. The President appoints a Prime Minister and a Union (Federal) Council of Ministers, responsible to the Supreme Council, to hold executive authority. The legislature is the Federal National Council, a consultative assembly (comprising 40 members appointed for two years by the rulers of the constituent emirates) which considers laws proposed by the Council of Ministers. The provisional constitution, originally in force for 5 years, was extended to 1981 by a decree of 28 Nov. 1976. There are no political parties. In local affairs each ruler has absolute power over his subjects.
Length of roadways: 1367 miles *2200 km* (1984).
Universities: 1.
Adult illiteracy: 43·7% (males 39·6%; females 55·8%) in 1975 (population aged 10 and over).
Expectation of life: Males 54·8 years; females 58·2 years (UN estimates for 1970–75, average for Bahrain, Qatar and the United Arab Emirates).
Defence: Military service voluntary; total armed forces 50 000 (1985); defence expenditure: 45% of total government expenditure in 1985.

The United States of America

Population: 227 658 000 (census of 1 Apr. 1980); 236 600 000 (1984 estimate).
Area: 3 615 122 miles² *9 363 123 km²*.
Language: English.
Religions: Protestant, Roman Catholic, Jewish, Orthodox (*see* p. 204).
Capital city: Washington, D.C., population 638 333 at 1980 census.
Other principal towns (1980): New York 7 071 639; Chicago 3 005 072; Los Angeles 2 966 850; Philadelphia 1 688 210; Houston 1 595 138; Detroit 1 203 339; Dallas 904 078; San Diego 875 538; Phoenix 789 704; Baltimore 786 775; San Antonio 785 882; Indianapolis 700 807; San Francisco 678 934; Memphis 646 356; Milwaukee 636 212; San Jose 629 442; Cleveland 573 822; Columbus 564 871; Boston 562 994; New Orleans 557 515; Jacksonville 540 920.
Head of State: Ronald Wilson Reagan (b. 6 Feb. 1911), President.
Climate: Its continental dimensions ensure extreme variety, ranging in temperature between the 56,7°C *134°F* recorded in Death Valley, California, on 10 July 1913, and the −60,0°C *−76°F* at Tanana, Alaska, in January 1886. Mean annual averages range between 24,7°C *76·6°F* at Key West, Florida, and −12,1°C *10·1°F* at Barrow, Alaska. Excluding Alaska and Hawaii, rainfall averages 736 mm *29 in* per year and ranges between 1412 mm *55·6 in* in Louisiana and 218 mm *8·6 in* in Nevada.

Climate in representative population centres are:
Anchorage, Alaska: Average daily high 18°C *65°F* July; −7°C *19°F* January. Average daily low −15°C *5°F* January; 9°C *49°F* July. Days with rain 15 in August; 4 in April.
San Francisco, Cal: Average daily high 20°C *69°F* September; 13°C *55°F* January. Average daily low 7°C *45°F* January; 13°C *55°F* September. Days with rain 11 in January–February; nil in July–August.
Washington, DC: Average daily high 30°C *87°F* July; 5°C *42°F* January. Average daily low −3°C *27°F* January; 20°C *68°F* July. Days with rain 12 in March, May; 8 in September–October.
Chicago, Illinois: Average daily high 27°C *81°F* July; 0°C *32°F* January. Average daily low −8°C *18°F* January; 19°C *66°F* July. Days with rain 12 in March, May; 9 in July–October.
Honolulu, Hawaii: Average daily high 28°C *83°F* August–September; 24°C *76°F* January–February. Average daily low 19°C *67°F* February–March; 23°C *74°F* September–October. Days with rain 15 in December; 11 in February, May.
New York, NY: Average daily high 28°C *82°F* July; 3°C *37°F* January. Average daily low −4°C *24°F* January–February; 19°C *66°F* July–August. Days with rain 12 in January, March, July; 9 in September–November.
Miami, Florida: Average daily high 31°C *88°F* July–August; 23°C *74°F* January. Average daily low 16°C *61°F* January–February; 24°C *76°F* July–August. Days with rain 18 in September; 6 in February.
Labour force: 115 005 000 aged 16 and over in 1984, excluding 1 697 000 in the armed forces and 8 539 000 unemployed: Agriculture, forestry and fishing 3·2%; Mining 0·9%; Construction 6·3%; Manufacturing 20%; Transportation and other public utilities 7%; Wholesale and retail trade 20·9%; Finance, insurance and real estate 6·4%; Professional and related services 20·1%; Other services 29·5%.
Gross domestic product: $3275·7 billion in 1983: Agriculture, forestry and fishing 2%; Manufacturing 21·1%; Trade 17%; Financial services 22·3%; Community, social and personal services 8·7%.
Exports: $217 888 million in 1984: Food and live animals 8·2%; Crude materials 5·1%; Machinery and transport equipment 54·7%; Chemicals 6·3%.
Monetary unit: US dollar ($). 1 dollar = 100 cents.
Denominations:
  Coins 1, 5, 10, 25, 50 cents; 1 dollar.
  Notes 1, 2, 5, 10, 20, 50, 100 dollars.
Exchange rate to £ sterling: 1·528 (26 Jan. 1987).
Length of roadways: 3 891 781 miles *6 261 876 km* (1984).
Length of railways: 147 049 miles *236 602 km*.
Universities: over 3000 (including colleges) in 1978.
Adult illiteracy: 1·0% (males 1·1%; females 1·0%) in 1969.
Expectation of life: Males 68·7 years; females 76·5 years (1975).
Defence: Military service voluntary; total armed forces 2 200 380 (1985); defence expenditure: 27·9% of total government expenditure in 1986.
Foreign tourists: 20 800 000 (including visits for study or transit) in 1984.

The United States of America ranks fourth in area (3 615 122 miles² *9 363 123 km²*), fourth in population (an estimated 229 807 000 in 1981) and first in economic production of all the countries in the world.

The area of the 48 coterminous states comprises 3 022 260 miles² *7 827 617 km²*. The principal mountain ranges are listed on p. 17. The highest point is Mount McKinley (20 320 ft *6194 m*) in Alaska.

There are eight US river systems involving rivers in excess of 1000 miles *1609 km* in length, of which by far the vastest is the Mississippi–Missouri (see page 19).

At the 1980 census the declared racial origins

THE FIFTY STATES OF THE UNITED STATES OF AMERICA
(in order of admission)

1.	Delaware	26.	Michigan
2.	Pennsylvania	27.	Florida
3.	New Jersey	28.	Texas
4.	Georgia	29.	Iowa
5.	Connecticut	30.	Wisconsin
6.	Massachusetts	31.	California
7.	Maryland	32.	Minnesota
8.	South Carolina	33.	Oregon
9.	New Hampshire	34.	Kansas
10.	Virginia	35.	West Virginia
11.	New York	36.	Nevada
12.	North Carolina	37.	Nebraska
13.	Rhode Island	38.	Colorado
14.	Vermont	39.	North Dakota
15.	Kentucky	40.	South Dakota
16.	Tennessee	41.	Montana
17.	Ohio	42.	Washington
18.	Louisiana	43.	Idaho
19.	Indiana	44.	Wyoming
20.	Mississippi	45.	Utah
21.	Illinois	46.	Oklahoma
22.	Alabama	47.	New Mexico
23.	Maine	48.	Arizona
24.	Missouri	49.	Alaska
25.	Arkansas	50.	Hawaii (see note)

Note: The state of Hawaii consists of a chain of more than 100 islands (including 8 large ones) stretching for about 1600 miles *2575 km*. The map shows the island of Hawaii (largest and easternmost of the group) but about 80% of the population are on the island of Oahu, which contains Honolulu and Pearl Harbor.

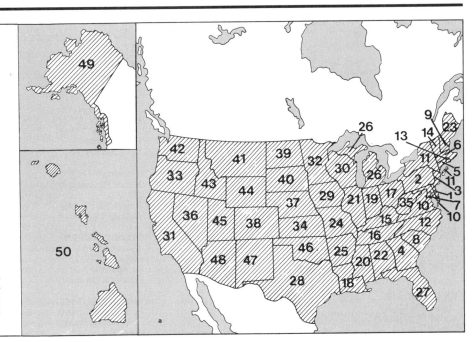

of the population were: White 83·2%; Black 11·7%; Indigenous 0·6%; Asian and Pacific Islander 1·5%; Other 3·0%. The population of foreign origin included at March 1972:

Jewish	6 460 000
Italian	8 764 000
German	25 543 000
British (UK)	29 548 000
Polish	5 105 000
Russian	2 188 000
Irish (Republic)	16 408 000
Spanish and Spanish origin	9 178 000
French	5 420 000

The principal religious denominations in 1984 were (in millions):

Roman Catholic	52·1
Baptist	25·8
Methodist	13·6
Lutheran	8·3
Jewish	5·7
Presbyterian	3·2
Protestant Episcopal Church	2·8
Eastern Orthodox	3·9
Mormon	3·7
United Church of Christ	1·7

The capital city is Washington, District of Columbia (DC). The District of Columbia (population 631 000, 1981 estimate) is the seat of the US Federal Government, comprising 69 miles² *179 km²* from west central Maryland on the Potomac River opposite Virginia. The site was chosen in October 1790 by President Washington and the Capitol corner stone laid by him on 18 Sept. 1793. Washington became the capital (Philadelphia 1790–1800) on 10 June 1800.

Historical note: Evidence from the most recent radiometric dating has backdated human habitation of North America to *c.* 35 000 BC. This occupation was probably achieved via the Bering Bridge (now the 55 mile *88,5 km* wide Bering Strait) from north-east Asia.

The continent derived its name from the Italian explorer Amerigo Vespucci (1454–1512), discoverer of the north-east South American coastal regions in 1498. The German cartographer Martin Waldseemüller named the New World 'Terra America' in his atlas published in St Dié, France, in April 1507.

The earliest European landing on present US territory was on 27 Mar. 1513 by the Spaniard Juan Ponce de León in Florida. The discovery of the US Pacific coast was by Juan R Cabrillo who landed from Mexico on 28 Sept. 1542, near San Diego, California. The oldest town of European origin is St Augustine, Florida,

founded on 8 Sept. 1565 on the site of Seloy by Pedro Menéndez de Avilés with 1500 Spanish colonists. The British exploration of what is now US territory began with Philip Amadas and Arthur Barlowe in Virginia in 1584. Henry Hudson sailed into New York harbour in September 1609. The Plymouth Pilgrims reached Cape Cod 54 days out from Plymouth, England, in the *Mayflower* (101 passengers and 48 crew) on 9 Nov. 1620. On 6 May 1626 Peter Minuit bought Manhattan island for some trinkets valued at $39. In 1664 the area was seized by the British and granted to Charles II's brother, the Duke of York, and the city of New Amsterdam was renamed New York.

By the 18th century there were 13 British colonies along the Atlantic seaboard of North America. The American revolution and the War of Independence (total battle deaths 4435) occupied the years 1763–83. The incident of the Boston Tea Party occurred on 16 Dec. 1773 and the Battle of Bunker Hill on 17 June 1775. The Declaration of Independence was made on 4 July 1776. This was recognized by Britain in March 1782. General George Washington was chosen President in February 1789 and the first US Congress was called on 4 Mar. 1789, when the US Constitution took effect. Washington took office on 30 Apr. 1789.

The War of 1812 between the US and Great Britain was declared by Congress on 18 June 1812, because Britain seized US ships running her blockade of France, impressed 2800 seamen and armed Indians who raided US territory. In

20th Century Presidents

Name	Dates of Birth and Death	Party	Dates in Office
Theodore Roosevelt	27 Oct. 1858 to 6 Jan. 1919	Republican	1901–09
William Howard Taft	15 Sept. 1857 to 8 Mar. 1930	Republican	1909–13
Thomas Woodrow Wilson	28 Dec. 1856 to 3 Feb. 1924	Democratic	1913–21
Warren Gamaliel Harding	2 Nov. 1865 to 2 Aug. 1923	Republican	1921–23
John Calvin Coolidge	4 July 1872 to 5 Jan. 1933	Republican	1923–29
Herbert Clark Hoover	10 Aug. 1874 to 20 Oct. 1964	Republican	1929–33
Franklin Delano Roosevelt	30 Jan. 1882 to 12 Apr. 1945	Democratic	1933–45
Harry S Truman	8 May 1884 to 26 Dec. 1972	Democratic	1945–53
Dwight David Eisenhower	14 Oct. 1890 to 28 Mar. 1969	Republican	1953–61
John Fitzgerald Kennedy	29 May 1917 to 22 Nov. 1963	Democratic	1961–63
Lyndon Baines Johnson	27 Aug. 1908 to 22 Jan. 1973	Democratic	1963–69
Richard Milhous Nixon	b. 9 Jan. 1913	Republican	1969–74
Gerald Rudolph Ford	b. 14 July 1913	Republican	1974–77
James Earl Carter	b. 1 Oct. 1924	Democratic	1977–81
Ronald Wilson Reagan	b. 6 Feb. 1911	Republican	1981–

Presidential Elections
US Presidential elections occur on the first Tuesday after the first Monday of November in every fourth year – these coincide with leap years. Election is not by popular majority but by majority of votes in the Electoral College which comprises 538 Electors divided between the States on the basis of one Elector for each of the 100 Senators (upper house) and the 435 Representatives (lower house) plus, since 1964, three Electors for the District of Columbia. Thus a Presidential election victory is achieved by securing at least 270 votes. Recent results have been:

Year	Republican	Democrat	Plurality
1944	99	432	Roosevelt (D) over Dewey (R) by 333
1948	189	303	Truman (D) over Dewey (R) by 114
1952	442	89	Eisenhower (R) over Stevenson (D) by 353
1956	457	73	Eisenhower (R) over Stevenson (D) by 384
1960	219	303	Kennedy over Nixon (R) by 84
1964	52	486	Johnson (D) over Goldwater (R) by 434
1968	301	191	Nixon (R) over Humphrey (D) by 110
1972	521	17	Nixon (R) over McGovern (D) by 504
1976	241	297	Carter (D) over Ford (R) by 56
1980	489	49	Reagan (R) over Carter (D) by 440

THE 50 STATES OF THE UNITED STATES OF AMERICA

Name, with date and order of (original) admission into the Union. Nicknames	Area (inc inland water). Pop. at 1980 Census (with rankings). Population density per mile² per km². State Capital. Admin. divisions	Major Cities (with population at 1 Apr. 1980)
ALABAMA (Ala) 14 Dec. 1819 (22nd) 'Heart of Dixie' 'Cotton State' 'Yellowhammer State'	51 998 miles² *134 623 km²* (29th) 3 893 888 (22nd) 74·9 *28,9* Montgomery 67 counties	Birmingham (284 413) Mobile (200 452) Montgomery (178 157) Huntsville (142 513) Tuscaloosa (75 143) Dothan (48 750) Gadsden (47 565)
ALASKA (Aleut, 'Great Land') 3 Jan. 1959 (49th) 'The Last Frontier' 'Land of the Midnight Sun'	591 004 miles² *1 530 109 km²* (1st) 401 851 (50th) 0·7 *0,3* Juneau* 19 election districts	Anchorage (173 017) Kenai Peninsula borough (25 282) Fairbanks (22 645) Juneau (19 528)
ARIZONA (Ariz) 14 Feb. 1912 (48th) 'Grand Canyon State' 'Apache State'	113 417 miles² *293 637 km²* (6th) 2 718 215 (29th) 23·9, *9,2* Phoenix 14 counties	Phoenix (764 911) Tucson (330 537) Mesa (152 453) Tempe (106 743) Glendale (96 988)
ARKANSAS (Ark) 15 June 1836 (25th) 'Land of Opportunity' 'Wonder State' 'Bear State'	53 187 miles² *137 701 km²* (27th) 2 286 435 (33rd) 43·9 *17* Little Rock 75 counties	Little Rock (158 461) Fort Smith (71 384) North Little Rock (64 419) Pine Bluff (56 576) Fayetteville (36 604) Hot Springs (35 166)
CALIFORNIA (Cal) 9 Sept. 1850 (31st) 'Golden State'	158 706 miles² *410 890 km²* (3rd) 23 667 902 (1st) 149·1 *57,6* Sacramento 58 counties	Los Angeles City (2 966 763) San Diego (875 504) San Francisco (678 974) San Jose (636 550) Long Beach (361 334) Oakland (339 288) Sacramento (275 741) Anaheim (221 847) Fresno (218 202) Santa Ana (203 713)
Sixteen other towns in California had a 1980 population of over 100 000: Riverside (170 876); Huntington Beach (170 505); Stockton (149 779); Glendale (139 060); Fremont (131 945); Torrance (131 497); Garden Grove (123 351); Pasadena (119 374); San Bernadino (118 057); Oxnard (108 195); Sunnyvale (106 618); Modesto (106 105); Bakersfield (105 611); Berkeley (103 328); Concord (103 251); Fullerton (102 034).		
COLORADO (Colo) 1 Aug. 1876 (38th) 'Centennial State'	104 090 miles² *269 489 km²* (8th) 2 889 964 (28th) 27·7 *10,7* Denver 63 counties	Denver (491 396) Colorado Springs (215 150) Aurora (158 588) Lakewood (112 848) Pueblo (101 686) Arvada (84 576) Boulder (76 658) Fort Collins (64 632)
CONNECTICUT (Conn) 9 Jan. 1788 (5th) 'Constitution State' 'Nutmeg State'	5018 miles² *12 992 km²* (48th) 3 107 576 (25th) 634·3 *245,0* Hartford 8 counties	Bridgeport (142 546) Hartford (136 392) New Haven (126 109) Waterbury (103 266) Stamford (102 453) Norwalk (77 767) New Britain (73 840)
DELAWARE (Del) 7 Dec. 1787 (1st) 'First State' 'Diamond State'	2044 miles² *5292 km²* (49th) 594 338 (47th) 290·8 *112,3* Dover 3 counties	Wilmington (70 195) Newark (25 247) Dover (23 512) Elsmere (6493) Milford (5358) Seaford (5256)
FLORIDA (Fla) 3 Mar. 1845 (27th) 'Sunshine State' 'Peninsula State'	58 664 miles² *151 881 km²* (22nd) 9 746 324 (7th) 180·1 *69,6* Tallahassee 67 counties	Jacksonville (540 898) Miami (346 931) Tampa (271 523) St Petersburg (236 898) Fort Lauderdale (153 256) Hialeah (145 254) Orlando (128 394) Hollywood (117 188)
GEORGIA (Ga) 2 Jan. 1788 (4th) 'Empire State of the South' 'Peach State'	58 910 miles² *152 518 km²* (21st) 5 464 265 (13th) 92·7 *36,8* Atlanta 159 counties	Atlanta (425 022) Columbus (169 441) Savannah (141 634) Macon (116 860) Albany (73 934) Augusta (47 532)

* On 4 Nov. 1976 Alaskan voters approved a proposal to move the state capital to Willow South.

1814 Maj-Gen Robert Ross burnt the Capitol and the White House in Washington. The war which inspired national unity cost only 2260 battle deaths. The Monroe Doctrine (the isolationism of the Americans from Europe) was declared on 2 Dec. 1823.

On 1 Nov. 1835 Texas proclaimed independence from Mexico. In the Alamo in San Antonio a US garrison was massacred (including Sen David Crockett) on 6 Mar. 1836.

The secession of States over the question of slave labour on cotton plantations began with South Carolina on 20 Dec. 1860. The Southern States of South Carolina, Georgia, Alabama, Mississippi, Louisiana and Florida formed the Confederate States of America on 8 Feb. 1861. War broke out on 12 Apr. 1861 with the bombardment of Fort Sumter in Charleston Harbor, South Carolina. The war culminated in the Battle of Gettysburg in July 1863 during which there was a total of 43 000 casualties. President Abraham Lincoln was assassinated on 14 Apr. 1865. Slavery was abolished by the adoption of the 13th Amendment (to the Constitution) on 18 Dec. 1865.

The total fatal casualties in the Civil War were *c.* 547 000 of which the Union forces (North) lost 140 400 in the field and the Confederates (South) 74 500 in battle and *c.* 28 500 in Union prisons. In 1867 the USA purchased Alaska from Russia. By 1890 the USA was in full possession of the continental territories which now comprise the 48 contiguous states (statehood being granted to all by 1912). Hawaii was annexed in 1898. The dates of the United States' entry into the World Wars of 1914–18 and 1939–45 respectively were 6 Apr. 1917 and 8 Dec. 1941. Alaska and Hawaii became the 49th and 50th states in 1959.

Government: The 1789 constitution established a federal republic in which extensive powers are reserved to the component states (originally 13, now 50).

At federal level, legislative power is held by the bicameral Congress of the United States. The upper house is the Senate, with 100 members (two from each state) elected by universal adult suffrage for six years (one-third retiring every two years). The second chamber is the House of Representatives, with 435 voting members directly elected from single-member constituencies for two years. The number of Representatives per state is determined periodically according to population but each state is entitled to at least one Representative. Since 1970 the District of Columbia has been represented by a non-voting delegate.

Federal executive power is vested in the President, who serves for a four-year term and (by a constitutional amendment ratified on 26 Feb. 1951) is limited to two terms in office. The President, with a Vice-President, is elected by an Electoral College composed of electors (themselves chosen by direct popular vote) from each state and the District of Columbia (see Presidential Elections in box above). Usually, the presidential candidate with a majority of popular votes in any state receives the whole of that state's Electoral College votes.

The President appoints a Cabinet which must be approved by the Senate. A presidential veto on legislative proposals may be overridden by a separate two-thirds vote in each house of the Congress.

Each state has a constitution modelled on the federal pattern, with its own legislature (all but one bicameral) and executive power held by a popularly elected Governor.

THE 50 STATES OF THE UNITED STATES OF AMERICA

Name, with date and order of (original) admission into the Union. Nicknames	Area (inc inland water). Pop. at 1980 Census (with rankings). Population density per mile² per km². State Capital. Admin. divisions	Major Cities (with population at 1 Apr. 1980)
HAWAII 21 Aug. 1959 (50th) 'Aloha State'	6471 miles² *16 753 km²* (47th) 964 691 (39th) 163·8 *63,3* Honolulu (on Oahu) 5 counties	Honolulu (365 048) Ewa (190 037) Koolaupoko (109 373) Wahiawa (41 562)
IDAHO 3 July 1890 (43rd) 'Gem State' 'Gem of the Mountains'	83 564 miles² *216 347 km²* (13th) 943 935 (41st) 11·3 *4,4* Boise City 44 counties, plus small part of Yellowstone Park	Boise City (102 451) Pocatello (46 340) Idaho Falls (39 590) Lewiston (27 986) Twin Falls (26 209) Nampa (25 112)
ILLINOIS (Ill) 3 Dec. 1818 (21st) 'Prairie State'	56 400 miles² *146 020 km²* (24th) 11 426 518 (5th) 203 *78,4* Springfield 102 counties	Chicago (3 005 072) Rockford (139 712) Peoria (124 160) Springfield (99 637) Decatur (94 081) Joliet (77 956) Evanston (73 706)
INDIANA (Ind) 11 Dec. 1816 (19th) 'Hoosier State'	36 185 miles² *93 683 km²* (38th) 5 490 224 (12th) 152·8 *59* Indianapolis 92 counties	Indianapolis (700 807) Fort Wayne (172 196) Gary (151 953) Evansville (130 496) South Bend (109 727) Hammond (93 714) Muncie (77 216)
IOWA (Ia) 28 Dec. 1846 (29th) 'Hawkeye State'	56 275 miles² *145 696 km²* (25th) 2 913 387 (27th) 51·7 *20,0* Des Moines 99 counties	Des Moines (191 003) Cedar Rapids (110 243) Davenport (103 264) Sioux City (82 003) Waterloo (75 985) Dubuque (62 321) Council Bluffs (56 449)
KANSAS (Kan) 29 Jan. 1861 (34th) 'Sunflower State' 'Jayhawk State'	82 277 miles² *213 015 km²* (14th) 2 364 236 (32nd) 28·8 *11,1* Topeka 105 counties	Wichita (279 272) Kansas City (161 087) Topeka (115 266) Overland Park (81 784) Lawrence (52 738) Salina (41 843)
KENTUCKY (Ky) (officially the Commonwealth of Kentucky) 1 June 1792 (15th) 'Bluegrass State'	40 409 miles² *104 619 km²* (37th) 3 660 777 (23rd) 92·3 *35,7* Frankfort 120 counties	Louisville (298 451) Lexington (204 165) Owensboro (54 450) Covington (49 013) Bowling Green (40 450) Paducah (29 315)
LOUISIANA (La) 30 Apr. 1812 (18th) 'Pelican State' 'Creole State' 'Sugar State' 'Bayou State'	52 453 miles² *135 800 km²* (31st) 4 203 972 (19th) 93·5 *36,1* Baton Rouge 64 parishes (counties)	New Orleans (557 482) Shreveport (205 815) Baton Rouge (219 486) Lafayette (81 961) Lake Charles (75 051)
MAINE (Me) 15 Mar. 1820 (23rd) 'Pine Tree State'	33 265 miles² *86 123 km²* (39th) 1 125 027 (38th) 36·3 *14* Augusta 16 counties	Portland (61 572) Lewiston (40 481) Bangor (31 643) Auburn (23 128)
MARYLAND (Md) 28 Apr. 1788 (7th) 'Old Line State' 'Free State'	10 460 miles² *27 081 km²* (42nd) 4 216 975 (18th) 428·7 *165,6* Annapolis 23 counties, plus the independent city of Baltimore	Baltimore (786 775) *Dundalk (85 377) *Towson (77 768) *Silver Spring (77 411) *Bethesda (71 621) *Wheaton (66 280)
MASSACHUSETTS (Mass) 6 Feb. 1788 (6th) 'Bay State' 'Old Colony State'	8284 miles² *21 447 km²* (45th) 5 737 037 (11th) 732 *282,7* Boston 14 counties	Boston (562 994) Worcester (161 799) Springfield (152 319) New Bedford (98 478) Cambridge (95 322)
MICHIGAN (Mich) 26 Jan. 1837 (26th) 'Wolverine State'	58 527 miles² *151 526 km²* (23rd) 9 262 078 (8th) 162·6 *62,8* Lansing 83 counties	Detroit (1 203 339) Grand Rapids (181 843) Warren (161 134) Flint (159 611) Lansing (130 414)

THE 50 STATES OF THE UNITED STATES OF AMERICA

Name, with date and order of (original) admission into the Union. Nicknames	Area (inc inland water). Pop. at 1980 Census (with rankings). Population density per mile² per km². State Capital. Admin. divisions	Major Cities (with population at 1 Apr. 1980)
MINNESOTA (Minn) 11 May 1858 (32nd) 'North Star State' 'Gopher State'	84 402 miles² *218 517 km²* (12th) 4 075 970 (21st) 51·4 *19,9* St Paul 87 counties	Minneapolis (370 951) St Paul (270 230) Duluth (92 811) Bloomington (81 831) Rochester (57 855)
MISSISSIPPI (Miss) 10 Dec. 1817 (20th) 'Magnolia State'	47 689 miles² *123 467 km²* (32nd) 2 520 638 (31st) 53 *20,5* Jackson 82 counties	Jackson (202 895) Biloxi (49 311) Meridian (46 577) Hattiesburg (40 829) Greenville (40 613)
MISSOURI (Mo) 10 Aug. 1821 (24th) 'Show Me State'	68 945 miles² *178 499 km²* (19th) 4 916 686 (15th) 71·3 *27,5* Jefferson City 114 counties, plus the independent city of St Louis	St Louis (453 085) Kansas City (448 159) Springfield (133 116) Independence (111 806) St Joseph (76 691) Columbia (62 061)
MONTANA (Mont) 8 Nov. 1889 (41st) 'Treasure State'	147 138 miles² *380 940 km²* (4th) 786 690 (44th) 5·3 *2,1* Helena 56 counties, plus small part of Yellowstone National Park	Billings (66 798) Great Falls (56 725) Missoula (37 205) Butte (33 388) Helena (23 938)
NEBRASKA (Nebr) 1 Mar. 1867 (37th) 'Cornhusker State' 'Beef State' 'Tree Planter's State'	77 355 miles² *200 272 km²* (15th) 1 569 825 (35th) 20·5 *7,9* Lincoln 93 counties	Omaha (311 681) Lincoln (171 932) Grand Island (33 180) North Platte (24 479) Fremont (23 979)
NEVADA (Nev) 31 Oct. 1864 (36th) 'Sagebrush State' 'Silver State' 'Battle Born State'	110 561 miles² *286 242 km²* (7th) 799 184 (43rd) 7·2 *2,8* Carson City 17 counties	Las Vegas (164 674) Reno (100 756) North Las Vegas (42 739) Sparks (40 780) Carson City (32 022)
NEW HAMPSHIRE (NH) 21 June 1788 (9th) 'Granite State'	9279 miles² *24 023 km²* (44th) 920 610 (42nd) 101·9 *39,4* Concord 10 counties	Manchester (90 936) Nashua (67 865) Concord (30 400) Portsmouth (26 254)
NEW JERSEY (NJ) 18 Dec. 1787 (3rd) 'Garden State'	7787 miles² *20 161 km²* (46th) 7 364 823 (9th) 986·2 *380,9* Trenton 21 counties	Newark (329 248) Jersey City (223 532) Paterson (137 970) Elizabeth (106 201) Trenton (92 124) Camden (102 551) Woodbridge (90 074)
NEW MEXICO (NM) 6 Jan. 1912 (47th) 'Land of Enchantment' 'Sunshine State'	121 335 miles² *314 136 km²* (5th) 1 302 894 (37th) 10·7 *4,1* Santa Fe 32 counties	Albuquerque (331 767) Santa Fe (48 899) Las Cruces (45 086) Roswell (39 676) Clovis (31 194)
NEW YORK (NY) 26 July 1788 (11th) 'Empire State'	49 108 miles² *127 141 km²* (30th) 17 557 288 (2nd) 367 *141,8* Albany 62 counties	New York City (7 071 030) Buffalo (357 870) Rochester (241 741) Yonkers (195 351) Syracuse (170 105) Albany (101 727) Utica (75 632) Niagara Falls (71 384)
NORTH CAROLINA (NC) 21 Nov. 1789 (12th) 'Tar Heel State' 'Old North State'	52 669 miles² *136 360 km²* (28th) 5 874 429 (10th) 111·5 *43,1* Raleigh 100 counties	Charlotte (314 447) Greensboro (155 642) Raleigh (149 771) Winston-Salem (131 885) Durham (100 831) High Point (64 107) Fayetteville (59 507)
NORTH DAKOTA (ND) 2 Nov. 1889 (39th) 'Sioux State' 'Flickertail State'	70 665 miles² *182 952 km²* (17th) 652 717 (46th) 9·4 *3,6* Bismarck 53 counties	Fargo (61 308) Bismarck (44 485) Grand Forks (43 765) Minot (32 843) Jamestown (16 280)

THE 50 STATES OF THE UNITED STATES OF AMERICA

Name, with date and order of (original) admission into the Union. Nicknames	Area (inc inland water). Pop. at 1980 Census (with rankings). Population density per mile² per km². State Capital. Admin. divisions	Major Cities (with population at 1 Apr. 1980)
OHIO 1 Mar. 1803 (17th) 'Buckeye State'	41 330 miles² *107 003 km²* (35th) 10 797 630 (6th) 263·2 *101,7* Columbus 88 counties	Cleveland (573 822) Columbus (564 871) Cincinnati (385 457) Toledo (354 635) Akron (237 177) Dayton (203 588) Youngstown (115 436) Canton (94 730)
OKLAHOMA (Okla) 16 Nov. 1907 (46th) 'Sooner State'	69 919 miles² *181 020 km²* (18th) 3 025 290 (26th) 43·2 *16,7* Oklahoma City 77 counties	Oklahoma City (403 213) Tulsa (360 919) Lawton (80 054) Norman (68 020) Enid (50 363) Midwest City (49 559)
OREGON (Ore) 14 Feb. 1859 (33rd) 'Beaver State'	97 073 miles² *251 322 km²* (10th) 2 633 105 (30th) 27·3 *10,5* Salem 36 counties	Portland (366 383) Eugene (105 624) Salem (89 233) Springfield (41 621)
PENNSYLVANIA (Pa) 12 Dec. 1787 (2nd) 'Keystone State'	45 308 miles² *117 302 km²* (33rd) 11 863 895 (4th) 264·3 *102,1* Harrisburg 67 counties	Philadelphia (1 688 210) Pittsburgh (423 938) Erie (119 123) Allentown (103 758) Scranton (88 117) Reading (78 686) Bethlehem (70 419)
RHODE ISLAND (RI) 29 May 1790 (13th) 'Little Rhody'	1214 miles² *3143 km²* (50th) 947 154 (40th) 903 *348,8* Providence 5 counties	Providence (156 804) Warwick (87 123) Cranston (71 992) Pawtucket (71 204) East Providence (50 980) Woonsocket (45 914) Newport (29 259)
SOUTH CAROLINA (SC) 23 May 1788 (8th) 'Palmetto State'	31 113 miles² *80 552 km²* (40th) 3 121 833 (24th) 100·3 *38,7* Columbia 46 counties	Columbia (99 296) Charleston (69 510) North Charleston (65 630) Greenville (58 242) Spartanburg (43 968)
SOUTH DAKOTA (SD) 2 Nov. 1889 (40th) 'Coyote State' 'Sunshine State'	77 116 miles² *199 653 km²* (16th) 690 178 (45th) 9·0 *3,5* Pierre 67 counties (64 county governments)	Sioux Falls (81 343) Rapid City (46 492) Aberdeen (25 956) Watertown (15 649) Brookings (14 951) Mitchell (13 916)
TENNESSEE (Tenn) 1 June 1796 (16th) 'Volunteer State'	42 144 miles² *109 111 km²* (34th) 4 591 120 (17th) 111·6 *43,1* Nashville 95 counties	Memphis (646 356) Nashville-Davidson (455 651) Knoxville (183 139) Chattanooga (169 565) Clarksville (54 777) Jackson (49 131)
TEXAS 29 Dec. 1845 (28th) 'Lone Star State'	266 807 miles² *690 763 km²* (2nd) 14 228 383 (3rd) 54·2 *20,9* Austin 254 counties	Houston (1 594 086) Dallas (904 078) San Antonio (785 410) El Paso (425 259) Fort Worth (385 141) Austin (345 496) Corpus Christi (231 999) Lubbock (173 979) Arlington (160 123) Amarillo (149 230) Garland (138 857) Beaumont (118 102) Pasadena (112 560)
UTAH 4 Jan. 1896 (45th) 'Beehive State'	84 899 miles² *219 804 km²* (11th) 1 461 037 (36th) 17·7 *6,8* Salt Lake City 29 counties	Salt Lake City (163 033) Provo (73 907) Ogden (64 407) Orem (52 399) Sandy City (51 022) Bountiful (32 877) Logan (26 844)
VERMONT (Vt) 4 Mar. 1791 (14th) 'Green Mountain State'	9614 miles² *24 891 km²* (43rd) 511 456 (48th) 55·1 *21,3* Montpelier 14 counties	Burlington (37 712) Rutland (18 436) Bennington (15 815) Essex (14 392) Colchester (12 629)

URUGUAY

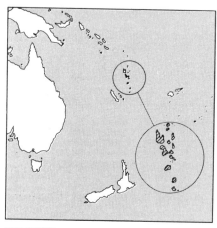

VANUATU

THE 50 STATES OF THE UNITED STATES OF AMERICA

Name, with date and order of (original) admission into the Union. Nicknames	Area (inc inland water). Pop. at 1980 Census (with rankings). Population density per mile² per km². State Capital. Admin. divisions	Major Cities (with population at 1 Apr. 1980)
VIRGINIA (Va) (officially called the Commonwealth of Virginia) 26 June 1788 (10th) 'The Old Dominion' 'Cavalier State'	40 767 miles² *105 546 km²* (36th) 5 346 818 (14th) 134·7 *52* Richmond 98 counties, plus 32 independent cities	Norfolk (266 979) Virginia Beach (262 199) Richmond (219 214) Newport News (144 903) Hampton (122 617) Chesapeake (114 226) Portsmouth (104 577) Alexandria (103 217) Roanoke (100 427) Lynchburg (66 743)
WASHINGTON (Wash) 11 Nov. 1889 (42nd) 'Evergreen State' 'Chinook State'	68 139 miles² *176 412 km²* (20th) 4 130 163 (20th) 62·0 *23,9* Olympia 39 counties	Seattle (493 846) Spokane (171 300) Tacoma (158 501) Bellevue (73 903) Everett (54 413) Yakima (49 826) Bellingham (45 794) Vancouver (42 834) Bremerton (36 208)
WEST VIRGINIA (W Va) 20 June 1863 (35th) 'Mountain State' 'Panhandle State'	24 282 miles² *62 866 km²* (41st) 1 949 644 (34th) 80·3 *31* Charleston 55 counties	Charleston (63 968) Huntingdon (63 684) Wheeling (43 070) Parkersburg (39 967) Morgantown (27 605) Weirton (24 763) Fairmont (23 863)
WISCONSIN (Wisc) 29 May 1848 (30th) 'Badger State'	56 153 miles² *145 380 km²* (26th) 4 705 335 (16th) 86·4 *33,4* Madison 72 counties	Milwaukee (636 212) Madison (170 616) Green Bay (87 899) Racine (85 725) Kenosha (77 685) West Allis (63 982) Appleton (59 032)
WYOMING (Wyo) 10 July 1890 (44th) 'Equality State'	97 809 miles² *253 228 km²* (9th) 469 557 (49th) 4·8 *1,9* Cheyenne 23 counties, plus most of Yellowstone National Park	Casper (51 016) Cheyenne (47 283) Laramie (24 410) Rock Springs (19 458) Sheridan (15 146) Green River (12 807)

* 1970 census figures

Uruguay

Official name: La República Oriental del Uruguay (the Eastern Republic of Uruguay).
Population: 2 921 798 (1985 census).
Area: 68 037 miles² *176 215 km²*.
Language: Spanish.
Religion: Roman Catholic.
Capital city: Montevideo, population 1 345 858 (1980 estimate).
Other principal towns (1975): Salto 71 000; Paysandú 61 000; Las Piedras 53 000; Rivera 49 000; Melo 38 000; Mercedes 35 000; Minas 35 000.
Highest point: Cerro de las Animas, 1643 ft *500 m*.
Principal mountain range: Sierra de las Animas.
Principal river: Uruguay (1000 miles *1609 km*).
Head of State: Julio María Sanguinetta, President.
Climate: Temperate (average 16°C *61°F*). Warm summers and mild winters. Moderate rain. In Montevideo, average maximum 14°C *58°F* (July) to 28°C *83°F* (January), minimum 6°C *43°F* (June, July, August) to 17°C *62°F* (January), rainiest months are August and December (each 7 days). Maximum recorded temperature 44°C *111·2°F*, Rivera, February 1953; minimum −7°C *19·4°F*, Paysandú, June 1945.
Labour force: 1 077 468 (excluding 17 131 seeking work for the first time) at 1975 census: Agriculture, forestry and fishing 17·6%; Manufacturing 20·8%; Trade, restaurants and hotels 13·6%; Community, social and personal services 31·9%.

Gross domestic product: 29 982 million new pesos in 1984, at constant 1978 prices: Agriculture, forestry and fishing 10·3%; Manufacturing 17·7%; Commerce 12·3%; Transport and storage 5%; Services 34·8%.
Exports: US$928·9,000 in 1984: Live animals and animal products 24·7%; Vegetable products 13·9%; Chemical products 3·3%; Skins and hides 15·8%; Textiles and textile products 30·3%.
Monetary unit: New Uruguayan peso. 1 new peso = 100 centésimos.
Denominations:
Coins: 1, 2, 5, 10 new pesos.
Notes: 50, 100, 500, 1000 new pesos.
Exchange rate to £ sterling: 270·68 (26 Jan. 1987).
Political history and government: A republic comprising 19 departments. A new constitution approved by plebiscite on 27 Nov. 1966 and taking effect on 1 Mar. 1967, provided that elections by universal adult suffrage be held every five years for a President, a Vice-President and a bicameral legislature, the General Assembly (Congress), comprising a Senate (30 elected members plus the Vice-President) and a 99-member Chamber of Representatives. Elections to both Houses were on the basis of proportional representation.

Executive power is held by the President, who appoints and leads the Council of Ministers. Juan María Bordaberry Arocena was elected President on 28 Nov. 1971 and took office on 1 Mar. 1972. The armed forces intervened on 8 Feb. 1973 to demand reforms and military participation in political affairs. On 13 Feb.

President Bordaberry accepted the military programme. On 27 June the President dissolved both Houses of Congress. On 19 Dec. 1973 he appointed a new legislature, a 25-member Council of State, headed by a President, to control the executive and draft plans for constitutional reform. On 12 June 1976 the President was deposed by the armed forces and replaced by the Vice-President. On 27 June the new régime established the Council of the Nation, with 46 members (the Council of State and 21 officers of the armed forces). On 14 July the Council of the Nation elected a new President, who took office for a five-year term on 1 Sept. 1976. A proposed constitution, which would have institutionalized the role of the armed forces within a 'restricted democracy', was rejected in a referendum on 30 Nov. 1980. A new President, appointed by the Council of State, took office on 1 Sept. 1981 for a 3½-year term, to prepare for elections and the return of civilian rule, and in Feb. 1985 the military regime stood down following the completion of the election in Nov. 1984.
Length of roadways: 32 300 miles *52 000 km*.
Length of railways: 1867 miles *3004 km*.
Universities: 1.
Adult illiteracy: 2·6% in 1978 for those between 10 and 44 years.
Expectation of life: Males 65·51 years; females 71·56 years (1963–64).
Defence: Military service voluntary; total armed forces 31 900 (1985); defence expenditure 11·1% of total government expenditure in 1984.
Foreign tourists: 1 035 000 in 1985.

Vanuatu

Official name: The Republic of Vanuatu.
Population: 135 558 (1985 estimate).
Area: 5700 miles² *14 763 km²*.
Languages: Bislama (ni-Vanuatu pidgin), English, French.
Religion: Christian.
Capital city: Port Vila, population 14 000 (1980 estimate).
Other principal town: Luganville (Santo).
Highest point: Mt Tabwebesana, 6195 ft *1888 m*.
Head of State: *Ati* George Sokomanu (né Kalkoa) MBE, President.
Prime Minister: Rev. Walter Hadye Lini, CBE (b. 1943).
Climate: Warm and generally pleasant. Southeast trade winds, May–Oct. Average annual rainfall from 1140 mm *45 in* in south to 6350 mm *250 in* in north. In Port Vila, average temperatures from 16°C *60°F* to 33°C *92°F*, average annual rainfall 2050 mm *81 in*.
Labour force: 51 130 in 1979: Agriculture, forestry and fishing 76·8%; Manufacturing 1·9%; Construction 2·2%; Trade 4·3%; Transport, storage and communications 2·6%; Community and social services 10·7%.
Gross national product: $50 million in 1978 (World Bank estimate).
Exports: 4300 million vatu in 1984: Copra 61·5%; Fish 16·5%; Timber 3·4%; Meat and meat products 3·3%.
Monetary unit: Vatu (formerly New Hebrides franc). 1 vatu = 100 centimes.
Denominations:
  Coins 1, 2, 5, 10, 20, 50 vatu.
  Notes 100, 500, 1000 vatu.
Exchange rate to £ sterling: 170 (26 Jan. 1987).
Political history and government: Formerly the Anglo-French Condominium of the New Hebrides. The United Kingdom and France established a joint administration on 20 Oct. 1906, each power being represented by a Resident Commissioner. The first elections under universal adult suffrage were held for two municipal councils on 16 Aug. 1975. To increase the territory's autonomy, the administration's Advisory Council, established in 1957, was replaced by a Representative Assembly of 42 members (including 29 popularly elected on 10 Nov. 1975). The Assembly's first full working session was delayed until 29 Nov. 1976. Later it was reduced to 39 members, all directly elected. The Assembly chose the territory's first Chief Minister on 5 Dec. 1977 and he formed a Council of Ministers, with powers of internal self-government, on 13 Jan. 1978. A conference ending on 19 Sept. 1979 adopted a constitution providing for the islands to become an independent republic. The constitution was signed by the Resident Commissioners on 5 Oct. and its terms were agreed on 23 Oct. by an exchange of notes between the British and French governments. Elections were held on 14 Nov. for a new Representative Assembly with increased powers. On 29 Nov. 1979 the Assembly elected the Rev. Walter Lini to be Chief Minister. On 30 July 1980 the New Hebrides became independent, as Vanuatu ('our land'), and joined the Commonwealth. The Assembly was renamed Parliament and Lini became Prime Minister.

Legislative power is vested in the unicameral Parliament, elected for a four-year term by universal adult suffrage, partly on the basis of proportional representation. The President is a constitutional Head of State elected for five years by an electoral college consisting of Parliament and the presidents of regional councils. The first President was the former Deputy Chief Minister, George Kalkoa, who was elected on 4 July 1980 and adopted the surname Sokomanu ('leader of thousands'). Executive power is vested in the Prime Minister, elected by and from members of Parliament. Other Ministers are appointed by the Prime Minister from among members of Parliament. The Council of Ministers is responsible to Parliament. The constitution also provides for a Council of Chiefs, composed of traditional tribal rulers, to safeguard Melanesian customs.

Length of roadways: 620 miles *1000 km*.
Foreign tourists: 25 000 in 1985.

The Vatican City

Official name: Stato della Città del Vaticano (State of the Vatican City).
Population: 1000 (1986 estimate).
Area: 108·7 acres *44 hectares*.
Languages: Italian, Latin.
Religion: Roman Catholic.
Head of State: Pope John Paul II (b. Karol Wojtyła, 18 May 1920).
Head of Government: Cardinal Agostino Casaroli (b. 24 Nov. 1914), Secretary of State.
Climate: See Italy for climate of Rome.
Monetary unit: Italian currency (*q.v.*).
Political history and government: An enclave in the city of Rome, established on 11 Feb. 1929 by the Lateran Treaty with Italy. The Vatican City is under the temporal jurisdiction of the Pope, the Supreme Pontiff elected for life by a conclave comprising members of the Sacred College of Cardinals. He appoints a Pontifical Commission, headed by the Secretary of State, to conduct the administrative affairs of the Vatican, which serves as the international headquarters, and administrative centre, of the worldwide Roman Catholic Church.

The Holy See (a term designating Rome as the Pope's own bishopric) is a distinct, pre-existing entity. Both entities, although united in the person of the Pope, are subjects of international law. The Holy See has diplomatic relations with foreign states on the basis of its religious status.

The 'Apostolic Constitution' (*Regimini Ecclesiae Universae*) published on 15 Aug. 1967, and effective from 1 Mar. 1968, reformed the Roman Curia, the Papal Court which acts as the central administrative body of the Church. The Vatican City remains an absolute monarchy, with legislative, executive and judicial power vested in the Pope. The College of Cardinals, whose members are created by the Pope, serves as the chief advisory body (at the end of 1984 there were 124 Cardinals). An Apostolic Letter of 21 Nov. 1970 decreed that, from 1 Jan. 1971, Cardinals reaching the age of 80 would lose the right to elect the Pope. On 5 Mar. 1973 the Pope announced that the number of Cardinals permitted to participate in the conclave would be limited to 120. Rules governing the conclave, issued on 13 Nov. 1975, included these limits and also stipulated that, to be successful, a candidate should normally have a two-thirds majority plus one vote.
Lengths of railways: 0·54 mile *0·86 km*.
Universities: There are 5 pontifical universities in Rome.

Venezuela

Official name: La República de Venezuela ('Little Venice').
Population: 17 316 741 (1985 estimate).
Area: 352 144 miles² *912 050 km²*.
Language: Spanish.
Religion: Roman Catholic.
Capital city: Santiago de León de los Caracas, population 2 944 000 (1980 estimate).
Other principal towns (1980): Maracaibo 901 000; Valencia 506 000; Barquisimeto 489 000; Maracay 344 000; Barcelona/Puerto La Cruz 275 000; San Cristóbal 272 000.
Highest point: La Pico Columna (Pico Bolívar), 16 427 ft *5007 m*.
Principal mountain ranges: Cordillera de Mérida, Sierra de Perijá, La Gran Sabana.
Principal river: Orinoco (1700 miles *2736 km*).
Head of State: Dr Jaime Lusinchi, President.
Climate: Varies with altitude from tropical in steamy lowlands to cool in highlands. Maximum recorded temperature 38°C *100·4°F*, minimum −6°C *21·2°F*. In Caracas, average temperature 20°C *69°F*, average maximum 20°C *75°F* (January) to 27°C *81°F* (April), minimum 13°C *56°F* (January, February) to 17°C *62°F* (May, June),

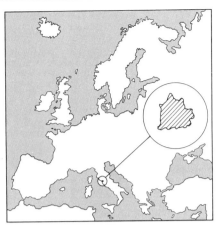

THE VATICAN CITY

VENEZUELA

rainiest months are July and August (each 15 days).
Labour force: 5 902 359 in 1985: Agriculture, forestry and fishing 12·8%; Manufacturing 13·7%; Construction 6·3%; Trade 17·8%; Transport, storage and communications 5·9%; Financial services 4·6%; Community, social and personal services 24·5%.
Gross domestic product: 348 454 million bolívares in 1984.
Exports: US$17 518,000 in 1981: Petroleum and petroleum products 92·8%.
Monetary unit: Bolívar. 1 bolívar = 100 céntimos.
Denominations:
  Coins 5, 12·5, 25, 50 céntimos; 1, 2, 5 bolívares.
  Notes 10, 20, 50, 100, 500 bolívares.
Exchange rate to £ sterling: 11·46 (26 Jan. 1987).
Political history and government: A federal republic of 20 states, two Federal Territories and a Federal District (containing the capital), each under an appointed Governor. The last military dictatorship was overthrown by popular revolt on 21–22 Jan. 1958, after which Venezuela returned to democratic rule. A new constitution was promulgated on 23 Jan. 1961. Legislative power is held by the bicameral National Congress, comprising a Senate (44 elected members plus ex-Presidents of the Republic) and a Chamber of Deputies (199 members). Executive authority rests with the President. Senators, Deputies and the President are all elected for 5 years by universal adult suffrage. Members of both houses of Congress, whose terms run

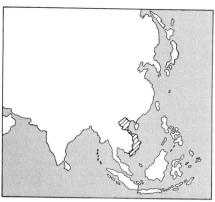

VIET-NAM

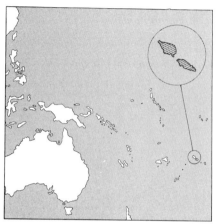

WESTERN SAMOA

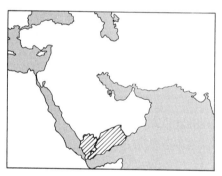

left: **THE YEMEN ARAB REPUBLIC**
right: **THE PEOPLE'S DEMOCRATIC REPUBLIC OF YEMEN**

concurrently with that of the President, are chosen partly by direct election and partly on the basis of proportional representation, with seats for minority parties. The President has wide powers and appoints a Council of Ministers to conduct the government. He may not have two consecutive terms of office.
Length of roadways: 39 186 miles *63 050 km.*
Length of railways: 152 miles *245 km.*
Universities: 14.
Adult illiteracy: 13·1% (males 11·6%; females 14·5%) in 1985.
Expectation of life: 66 years (1978).
Defence: Military service: 18 months, selective; total armed forces 49 000 (1985); defence expenditure: 6·1% of total government expenditure in 1984.
Foreign tourists: 201 600 in 1983.

Viet-Nam

Official name: Công hoa xã hôi chu nghia Viêt Nam (Socialist Republic of Viet-Nam).
Population: 61 950 000 (1986 estimate).
Area: 128 402 miles² *332 559 km².*

Language: Vietnamese.
Religions: Buddhist, Taoist, Confucian, Christian.
Capital city: Hã-nôi (Hanoi), population 2 674 400 (1983).
Other principal towns (1979): Ho Chi Minh City (formerly Saigon) 3 419 978 (including Cholon); Haiphong 1 279 067; Da-Nhang (Tourane) 492 194 (1973); Nha-trang 216 227 (1973); Qui-Nhon 213 757 (1973); Huê 209 043 (1973).
Highest point: Fan si Pan, 10 308 ft *3142 m.*
Principal rivers: Mekong (2600 miles *4184 km*), Songkoi (Red River), Songbo (Black River), Ma.
Head of State: Truong Chinh (formerly Dang Xuan Khu, b. 1908), Chairman of the Council of State.
Political Leader: Le Duan (b. 1908), First Secretary of the Central Committee of the Communist Party of Viet-Nam.
Prime Minister: Pham Van Dong (b. 1 Mar. 1906).
Climate: Hot and wet in the north, warm and humid in the south. The rainy monsoon season is from April or May to October. In Hanoi, average maximum temperature 20°C *68°F* (January) to 33°C *92°F* (June), minimum 13°C *56°F* to 25°C *78°F* (June, July, August); rainiest month August (16 days). In Ho Chi Minh City, average maximum 30°C *87°F* (November, December) to 35°C *95°F* (April), minimum 21°C *70°F* (January) to 24°C *76°F* (April, May); rainiest month July (23 days).
Labour force: 23 100 000 in 1984: Agriculture, forestry and fishing 68%.
Gross national product: 20 742 million dông in 1978.
Exports: $535 million in 1979 (unofficial estimate).
Monetary unit: Dông. 1 dông = 10 hào = 100 xu.
Denominations:
   Coins 1, 2, 5 xu.
   Notes 2, 5 xu; 1, 2, 5 hào; 1, 2, 5, 10, 20, 30, 50, 100 dông.

Exchange rate to £ sterling: 122·8 (26 Jan. 1987).
Political history and government: Formerly part of French Indo-China, Viet-Nam was occupied by Japanese forces, with French co-operation, in Sept. 1940. On 6 June 1941 nationalist and revolutionary groups, including the Communist Party of Indo-China, formed the *Viet-Nam Doc-Lap Dong Minh Hoi* (Revolutionary League for the Independence of Viet-Nam), known as the *Viet-Minh*, to overthrow French rule. On 9 Mar. 1945 French administrative control was ended by a Japanese *coup* against their nominal allies. After Japan's surrender in Aug. 1945, *Viet-Minh* forces entered Hanoi and formed a provisional government under Ho Chi Minh, leader of the Communist Party. On 2 Sept. 1945 the new régime proclaimed independence, as the Democratic Republic of Viet-Nam (DRV), with Ho as President. On 6 Mar. 1946, after French forces re-entered Viet-Nam, an agreement between France and the DRV recognized Viet-Nam as a 'free' state within the French Union. The DRV government continued to press for complete independence but negotiations broke down and full-scale hostilities began on 19 Dec. 1946. The war continued until cease-fire agreements were made on 20–21 July 1954. These provided that DRV forces should regroup north of latitude 17°N. Thus the DRV was confined to North Viet-Nam.
On 8 Mar. 1949, during the first Indo-China war, the French government made an agreement with anti-Communist elements for the establishment of the State of Viet-Nam, under Bao Dai, Emperor of Annam. Originally within the French Union, the State made an independence agreement with France on 4 June 1954. After the cease-fire agreements of 20–21 July 1954 French forces withdrew, leaving the State's jurisdiction confined to the zone south of latitude 17°N. Complete sovereignty was transferred by France on 29 Dec. 1954. Following a referendum, Bao Dai was deposed and the Republic of Viet-Nam proclaimed on 26 Oct. 1955. In 1959 an insurgent movement, supported by North

Viet-Nam, launched guerrilla warfare to overthrow the Republic. On 20 Dec. 1960 the insurgents formed the National Front for the Liberation of South Viet-Nam, known as the National Liberation Front (NLF). From 1961 the USA supported the Republic with troops, numbering over 500 000 by 1969. From 1964 regular forces from North Viet-Nam, numbering about 250 000 by 1975, moved south to support the NLF. On 10 June 1969 the NLF announced the formation of a Provisional Revolutionary Government (PRG) to administer 'liberated' areas. A 'peace' agreement on 27 Jan. 1973 led to the withdrawal of US forces but fighting continued until the Republic surrendered to the PRG on 30 Apr. 1975. The territory was renamed the Republic of South Viet-Nam.
Following the PRG victory, it was agreed to merge North and South Viet-Nam. Elections were held on 25 Apr. 1976 for a single National Assembly (for both North and South) of 492 members. The new Assembly met on 24 June and the country was reunited as the Socialist Republic of Viet-Nam on 2 July 1976.
On 18 Dec. 1980 the National Assembly adopted a new constitution. The highest state authority is the Assembly, a unicameral body elected by universal adult suffrage for five years. The Assembly elects from its members a Council of State to be its permanent organ, with a term of office corresponding to that of the Assembly. The Council's Chairman serves as Head of State. The highest administrative organ is the Council of Ministers, headed by a Prime Minister, which is elected by, and responsible to, the Assembly. A new National Assembly was elected on 26 Apr. 1981, when 496 members were chosen from 93 constituencies. The first Chairman of the Council of State was elected on 4 July 1981.
Political power is held by the Communist Party of Viet-Nam, described by the constitution as 'the only force leading the state and society'. The Party was established on 20 Dec. 1976 in succession to the *Dang Lao Dong Viet-Nam* (Viet-Nam Workers' Party), formed in 1951. The Party Congress of 14–20 Dec. 1976 elected a Central Committee (101 full members and 32 alternate members) to supervise Party work. The Central Committee elected a Political Bureau (Politburo), with 14 full and three alternate members, to direct its policy.
On 6 July 1976 representatives of the former DRV's Communist-led National Fatherland Front, the NLF and other groups met to organize a united Viet-Nam Fatherland Front, formally launched during a congress on 31 Jan.–4 Feb. 1977. The Front presents an approved list of candidates for elections to all representative bodies.
Viet-Nam comprises 37 provinces and three cities.
Length of roadways: 215 767 miles *347 243 km.*
Length of railways: 1616 miles *2600 km.*
Universities: 3.
Adult illiteracy: 16% (males 9·5%, females 21·7%) in 1979.
Expectation of life: Males 43·2 years; females 46·0 years (UN estimates for 1970–75).
Defence: Military service: 2 years minimum; total armed forces 1 027 000 (1985).

Western Samoa

Official name: The Independent State of Western Samoa (Samoa i Sisifo).
Population: 159 000 (1984 estimate).
Area: 1097 miles² *2842 km².*
Languages: Samoan, English.
Religions: Congregational, Roman Catholic, Methodist, Mormon.
Capital city: Apia, population 33 170 (1981 census).
Highest point: Mauga Silisli, 6094 ft *1857 m.*
Head of State: H H Malietoa Tanumafili II, CBE (b. 4 Jan. 1913).
Prime Minister: Va'ai Kolone.
Climate: Warm all the year round. Rainy season November to April. In Apia, average maximum 29°C *84°F* to 30°C *86°F*, minimum 23°C *74°F* to

24°C 76°F; rainiest month is January (22 days).
Labour force: 41 506 in 1981: Agriculture, forestry and fishing 60·4%; Construction 5·5%; Trade 4·4%; Government services 19·8%.
Gross domestic product: 30·3 million tala (at factor cost) in 1972: Agriculture, forestry and fishing (excluding government) 49·9% (agriculture 45·3%); Government services 21·6%.
Exports: 27·4 million tala in 1983: Copra 5·1%; Cocoa 16·8%; Taro and taamu 8·7%.
Monetary unit: Tala. 1 tala = 100 sene.
Denominations:
  Coins 1, 2, 5, 10, 20, 50 sene.
  Notes 1, 2, 10 tala.
Exchange rate to £ sterling: 3·22 (26 Jan. 1987).
Political history and government: The islands became a German protectorate in 1899. They were occupied by New Zealand forces during the First World War (1914–18). In 1919 New Zealand was granted a League of Nations mandate over the islands. In 1946 Western Samoa was made a United Nations Trust Territory, administered by New Zealand. An independence constitution, adopted by a Constitutional Convention on 28 Oct. 1960, was approved by a UN-supervised plebiscite in May 1961. The islands duly became independent on 1 Jan. 1962. The position of Head of State (*O le Ao o le Malo*) was held jointly by two tribal leaders, one of whom died on 5 Apr. 1963. The other remains Head of State for life, performing the duties of a constitutional monarch. In the absence of the Head of State, his functions are performed by a Council of Deputies. Future Heads of State will be elected for five years by the Legislative Assembly. The Assembly is a unicameral body of 47 members, including 45 Samoans elected by about 11 000 *matai* (elected clan chiefs) in 41 constituencies and two members popularly elected by voters (mainly Europeans) outside the *matai* system. Members hold office for three years (subject to dissolution). The country's first political party was formed by an anti-government group in Mar. 1979.

In most cases, executive power is held by the Cabinet, comprising a Prime Minister and 8 other members of the Assembly. The Prime Minister, appointed by the Head of State, must have the support of a majority in the Assembly. Cabinet decisions may be reviewed by the Executive Council, comprising the Head of State, the Prime Minister and some other Ministers.

Western Samoa joined the Commonwealth on 28 Aug. 1970.
Length of roadways: 1296 miles *2085 km*.
Adult illiteracy: 2·2% (males 2·2%; females 2·1%) in 1971.
Expectation of life: Males 60·8 years; females 65·2 years (1961–66).
Foreign tourists: 36 717 in 1983.

The Yemen Arab Republic

Official name: Al-Jamhuriya al-‘Arabiya al-Yamaniya.
Population: 7 161 851, excluding 1 395 123 working abroad (1981 census).
Area: 75 290 miles² *195 000 km²*.
Language: Arabic.
Religion: Muslim.
Capital city: Sana'a, population 277 817 (1981).
Other principal towns: Hodeida 126 386; Ta'iz 119 572.
Highest point: Jebel Hadhar, 12 336 ft *3760 m*.
Principal mountain range: Yemen Highlands.
Head of State: Col ‘Ali Abdullah Saleh (b. 1942), President.
Prime Minister: Maj. ‘Abd ul Aziz Abdulghani.
Climate: Very hot (up to 54°C *130°F*) and extremely humid on semi-desert coastal strip. Cooler on highlands inland (average maximum of 22°C *71°F* in June) with heavy rainfall and winter frost. Desert in the east.
Labour force: 1 127 572 in 1975: Agriculture 73·6%; Manufacturing 3%; Construction 4·7%; Trade 6·1%; Social services 7·6%; Unemployed 6·2%.
Gross domestic product: 12 949 million riyals in

1981–2: Agriculture, forestry and fishing 28·5%; Trade 8·8% Transport, storage and communications 17·5%; Government services 14·7%.
Exports: $217·5 million riyals in 1981: Biscuits 13·2%; Hides and skins 1%; Coffee 1%.
Monetary unit: Yemeni riyal. 1 riyal = 100 rials.
Exchange rate to £ sterling: 15·73 (26 Jan. 1987).
Political history and government: Formerly a monarchy, ruled by an hereditary Imam. Army officers staged a *coup* on 26–27 Sept. 1962, declared the Imam deposed and proclaimed a republic. Civil war broke out between royalist forces, supported by Saudi Arabia, and republicans, aided by Egyptian troops. The republicans gained the upper hand and Egyptian forces withdrew in 1967. A Republican Council, led by a Chairman, took power on 5 Nov. 1967 and announced a new constitution (which did not permit political parties) on 28 Dec. 1970. This provided for a unicameral legislature, the Consultative Council of 179 members (20 appointed by the Republican Council and 159 directly elected for 4 years by general franchise on 27 Feb.–18 Mar. 1971). On 13 June 1974 power was seized by army officers who suspended the constitution and established a Military Command Council. On 19 June 1974 the new régime published a provisional constitution which, for a transitional period, gave full legislative and executive authority to the Command Council, whose Chairman was granted the powers of Head of State. The Consultative Council was dissolved after the *coup*, later reinstated but dissolved again on 22 Oct 1975. The first Chairman of the Command Council, Lt-Col Ibrahim al-Hamadi, was assassinated on 11 Oct. 1977. The remaining three members of the Command Council formed a Presidential Council, under Lt-Col Ahmad Husain al-Ghashmi, and imposed martial law.

On 6 Feb. 1978 the Command Council issued a decree providing for the formation of a Constituent People's Assembly, with 99 members appointed by the Council for 2 to 3 years. The new Assembly first met on 25 Feb. 1978. On 22 Apr. it elected Ghashmi to be President for a 5-year term. The Command Council was then dissolved. President Ghashmi was assassinated on 24 June 1978 and the Assembly formed a four-man provisional Presidential Council. On 17 July 1978 the Assembly elected a member of the Presidential Council to be President and he was sworn in on 18 July. On 8 May 1979 the President signed a constitutional declaration which provided that the Assembly would be expanded to 159 members, with a two-year term of office. On the same day 60 new members were selected. The President rules with the assistance of an appointed Cabinet, led by a Prime Minister. Yemen comprises eleven provinces.
Length of roadways: 11 947 miles *19 223 km*.
Universities: 1.
Adult illiteracy: Males 70%; Females 75%.
Expectation of life: Males 45 years; females 50 years.
Defence: Military service: 3 years; total armed forces 36 600 (1986); defence expenditure: 29% of total government expenditure in 1984.
Foreign tourists: 42 235 in 1983.

The People's Democratic Republic of Yemen

Official name: Jumhuriyat al-Yaman al-Dimuqratiya ash-Sha'abiya.
Population: 2 225 000 (1984 estimate).
Area: 130 066 miles² *336 869 km²*.
Language: Arabic.
Religion: Muslim.
Capital city: Aden, population 264 326 (1981 estimate).
Other principal town: Al Mukalla, population 100 000.
Highest point: Qaured Audilla, 8200 ft *2499 m*.
Head of State: Heidar aı-Attas, acting President.
Climate: Summer extremely hot (temperatures over 54°C *130°F*) and humid. Very low rainfall (average less than 76 mm *3 in* per year). Winter can be very cold in high areas.

Labour force: 452 600 in 1981: Agriculture and fishing 45·2%; Industry 10·6%; Construction 7·5%; Transport 6·4%; Commerce 9·2%; Services 21·2%.
Gross domestic product: 320 million dinars in 1982: Agriculture, forestry and fishing 19·4%; Manufacturing 25·2%; Trade, restaurants and hotels 12·7%.
Exports: 222·9 million dinar in 1984: Petroleum products 95·9%.
Monetary unit: Yemeni dinar. 1 dinar = 1000 fils.
Denominations:
  Coins 1, 5, 25, 100, 250 fils.
  Notes 250, 500 fils; 1, 5, 10 dinars.
Exchange rate to £ sterling: 0·5243 (26 Jan. 1987).
Political history and government: Formerly the British colony of Aden and the Protectorate of South Arabia. Became independent, outside the Commonwealth, on 30 Nov. 1967 as the People's Republic of Southern Yemen. Power was held by a revolutionary movement, the National Liberation Front, renamed the National Front (NF). The interim legislative authority was the NF's Supreme General Command. On 22 June 1969 the country's first President was replaced by a Presidential Council. Salim Rubayyi ‘Ali became Chairman of the Council on 24 June 1969. A new constitution, adopted on 30 Nov. 1970, gave the country its present name and provided for the establishment of a unicameral legislature, the Supreme People's Council (SPC). A Provisional SPC, inaugurated on 14 May 1971, had 101 members, including 86 elected by the NF's General Command and 15 by trade unions. It was empowered to appoint members of the Presidential Council and the Cabinet. In Oct. 1975 the ruling NF merged with two smaller parties to form the United Political Organisation–National Front (UPO-NF).

On 26 June 1978 the Head of State, Rubayyi ‘Ali, was ousted from power and executed by opponents within the UPO-NF. The Prime Minister, ‘Ali Nasir Muhammad, became interim Head of State. It was announced on 28 June that the three parties within the UPO-NF had agreed to form a Marxist-Leninist ‘vanguard' party. The constituent congress of the new party, the Yemen Socialist Party (YSP), was held on 11–14 Oct. 1978. Constitutional amendments providing for a new form of legislature and the abolition of the Presidential Council were approved on 31 Oct. 1978. A 111-member People's Supreme Assembly (PSA), replacing the SPC, was elected on 16–18 Dec. At its first session, on 27 Dec. 1978, the PSA elected an 11-member Presidium (to replace the Presidential Council) and elected as Chairman of the Presidium (and thus as Head of State) ‘Abd al-Fattah Isma'il, Secretary-General of the YSP, the sole legal party. On 21 Apr. 1980 Isma'il relinquished his positions as Head of State and YSP leader, being replaced in both offices by the Prime Minister, previously Deputy Chairman of the PSA Presidium.

In Jan. 1986 a coup attempt developed into civil war and the government of ‘Ali Nasir Muhammad was overthrown.

The country, also called Democratic Yemen, is divided into 8 governorates.
Length of roadways: 1150 miles *1851 km*.
Universities: 1.
Adult illiteracy: 58·6% (males 41·4%; females 74·8%) in 1985.
Expectation of life: Males 40·6 years; females 42·4 years (UN estimates for 1970–75).
Defence: Military service: 2 years; total armed forces 27 500 (1985); defence expenditure: 55·1 million dinar in 1982.

Yugoslavia

Official name: Socijalistička Federativna Republika Jugoslavija (Socialist Federal Republic of Yugoslavia).
Population: 22 424 711 (census of 31 Mar. 1981); 23 123 000 (estimate for mid-1985).
Area: 98 766 miles² *255 804 km²*.

YUGOSLAVIA

Languages: Serbo-Croatian/Croato-Serbian, Slovenian, Macedonian.
Religions: Serbian Orthodox, Roman Catholic, Muslim, Macedonian Orthodox and smaller Protestant groups.
Capital city: Beograd (Belgrade), population 1 470 075 at 1981 census.
Other principal towns (1981): Zagreb 855 568; Skopje 504 932; Sarajevo 448 519; Ljubljana 305 211; Novi Sad 257 685; Priština 210 040; Titograd 132 290.
Highest point: Triglav, 9396 ft *2864 m*.
Principal mountain ranges: Slovene Alps, Dinaric Mts. Šar-Pindus and Rhodope ranges, Carpathian and Balkan Mts.
Principal rivers: Dunav (Danube) (1700 miles *2848 km* total length, in Yugoslavia 368 miles *588 km*) and tributaries (Drava, Sava (590 miles *945 km*), Morava), Vardar.
Head of State: Sinan Hasani (b. 1922), President of the Presidency of the SFRY for 1986–87.
Head of Government: Branko Mikulić (b. 1928), President of the Federal Executive Council.
Climate: Mediterranean climate on Adriatic coast (dry, warm summers; mild, rainy winters). Continental climate (cold winters) in hilly interior. In Belgrade, average maximum 3°C *37°F* (January) to 29°C *85°F* (July), minimum −3°C *27°F* (January, February) to 16°C *61°F* (July). Rainiest months are April, May, June, December (each 9 days). In Split, average maximum 14°C *57°F* (January) to 30°C *87°F* (July, August), minimum 4°C *39°F* (January, February) to 20°C *68°F* (July), rainiest month is December (11 days). Absolute maximum temperature 46,2°C *115·2°F*, Mostar, 31 July 1901; absolute minimum −37,8°C *−36·0°F*, Sjenica, 26 Jan. 1954.
Labour force: 9 358 671 in 1981: Agriculture, forestry and fishing 28·7%; Mining and manufacturing 23·6%; Trade 8·8%; Community, social and personal services 16·9%; Unemployed 6·2%.
Gross material product: 6 325 843 million dinar in 1984: Agriculture, forestry and fishing 14·4%; Manufacturing and mining 41·5%; Trade 19·3%; Transport and communications 7%.
Exports: 1 279 736 million dinar in 1984: Food and live animals 8·6%; Chemicals 9·7%; Basic manufactures 22·8%; Machinery and transport equipment 31%; Miscellaneous manufactures 17·9%.
Monetary unit: 1 dinar = 100 para.
Denominations:
Coins 5, 10, 20, 25, 50; 1, 2, 5, 10 dinars.
Notes 10, 20, 50, 100, 500, 1000 dinars.
Exchange rate to £ sterling: 674·79 (26 Jan. 1987).
Political history and government: Yugoslavia was formed by a merger of Serbia, Croatia, Slovenia, Montenegro and Bosnia-Herzegovina. A pact between Serbia and other South Slavs was signed on 20 July 1917 to unite all the territories in a unitary state under the Serbian monarchy. The Kingdom of Serbs, Croats and Slovenes was proclaimed on 1 Dec. 1918. It was renamed Yugoslavia on 3 Oct. 1929. The Kingdom was invaded by German and Italian forces on 6 Apr.

1941. Resistance was divided between royalists and Partisans, led by the Communist Party under Marshal Tito (*né* Josip Broz). Their rivalry led to civil war, won by the Partisans, who proclaimed the Federal People's Republic of Yugoslvia, with Tito as Prime Minister, on 29 Nov. 1945. A Soviet-type constitution, establishing a federation of 6 republics, was adopted on 31 Jan. 1946. Yugoslav leaders followed independent policies and the country was expelled from the Soviet-dominated Cominform in June 1948. At its 6th Congress, on 2–7 Nov. 1952, the Communist Party was renamed the League of Communists of Yugoslavia (LCY). A new constitution was adopted on 13 Jan. 1953 and Tito sworn in as President the next day.

Another constitution, promulgated on 7 Apr. 1963, introduced the country's present name. Since 29 July 1971 national leadership has been held by a Collective Presidency. Tito was elected 'President for life' on 16 May 1974. With his death, on 4 May 1980, the office of President was terminated.

The present constitution, which increased decentralization, was adopted on 21 Feb. 1974. Legislative power is vested in the bicameral Federal Assembly, comprising a Federal Chamber of 220 members (30 from each of the 6 republics and 20 each from the two autonomous provinces within Serbia) and a Chamber of Republics and Provinces, with 88 members (12 from each Republican Assembly and 8 from each Provincial Assembly). Members are elected for four years by communal assemblies which have been chosen by about 1 million delegates, themselves elected by universal adult suffrage, with voters grouped according to their place of work.

The Collective Presidency has nine members: the President of the Presidium of the LCY's Central Committee (*ex officio*) and eight others (one each from the republics and provinces) elected by the Federal Assembly for five years. The posts of President and Vice-President of the Collective Presidency rotate annually in a fixed sequence among the members. The Federal Assembly also elects the Federal Executive Council, led by a President and five Vice-Presidents (one from each of the six republics), for a four-year term as the administrative branch of government.

The only authorized political party is the LCY, which controls political life through the Socialist Alliance of the Working People of Yugoslavia. The LCY's highest authority is the Congress. The 13th Congress, held in 1986, elected a Central Committee of 163 members (equal number of members from each republic, and a corresponding number of members from the provinces and from the Army) to supervize the LCY's work. The Committee elected a Presidium of 23 members to direct its policy. Since the death of Tito, the President of the Presidium is chosen annually on a rotation basis among the republics and provinces. The Presidium had decided on 15 May 1979 that the post of Presidium Secretary (previously nominated by Tito) should be similarly filled by rotation, though for a two-year term.

Each constituent republic has its own government, with an indirectly elected assembly and an executive.
Length of roadways: 72 741 miles *117 041 km* (1983).
Length of railways: 5870 miles *9399 km*.
Universities: 19.
Adult illiteracy: 8·8% (males 3·4%; females 13·9%) in 1985.
Expectation of life: Males 67·7 years; females 73·2 years (1980–1).
Defence: Military service: 15 months (12 months for the sole supporter of the family); total armed forces 241 000 (154 000 conscripts) in 1985: defence expenditure: 30·4% of total government expenditure in 1984.
Foreign tourists: 7 224 000 in 1984.

Zaire

Official name: La République du Zaïre (the Republic of Zaire).
Population: 26 671 407 (1984 census).
Area: 905 365 miles² *2 344 885 km²*.
Languages: French (official), Lingala, Kiswahili, Tshiluba, Kikongo.
Religions: Animist, Roman Catholic, Protestant.
Capital city: Kinshasa (formerly Léopoldville), population 2 443 876 (1976).
Other principal towns (1976): Kananga (Luluabourg) 704 211; Lubumbashi (Elisabethville) 451 332; Mbuji-Mayi 382 632; Kisangani (Stanleyville) 339 210; Bukavu (Costermanville) 209 051.
Highest point: Ngaliema (Mt Stanley), 16 763 ft *5109 m* (first climbed 1900), on the border with Uganda.
Principal mountain ranges: Chaîne des Mitumba, Ruwenzori.
Principal rivers: Zaïre (Congo), Ubangi, Kasai.
Head of State: Lt-Gen Mobutu Sese Seko Kuku Ngbendu wa Za Banga (b. Joseph-Désiré Mobutu, 14 Oct. 1930), President.
Head of Government: Kengo wa Dondo, First State Commissioner.
Climate: Tropical. Hot and humid in Congo basin, cool in highlands. In Kinshasa, March and April hottest (22°C *71°F* to 32°C *89°F*), July coolest (18°C *64°F* to 27°C *81°F*) and driest, April and November rainiest (16 days each). Absolute maximum temperature 41,0°C *105·8°F* at Yahila; absolute minimum −1,5°C *29·3°F*, Sakania, 11 Jan. 1949.
Labour force: 13 145 000 in 1984: Agriculture, forestry and fishing 72%.
Gross domestic product: 31 295·9 million zaires in 1982: Agriculture 35·7%; Construction and public works 6%; Mining and metallurgy 11·5%; Commerce 21·3%; Services 18·5%.
Exports: 9925 million zaires in 1982: Copper 42·4%; Cobalt 9·7%; Zinc 2·3% Diamonds 4·4%; Crude petroleum 14·7%; Coffee 6·2% Industrial products 15·5%.
Monetary unit: Zaire. 1 zaire = 100 makuta (singular: likuta) = 10 000 sengi.
Denominations:
Coins 10 sengi; 1, 5 makuta.
Notes 10, 20, 50 makuta; 1, 5, 10 zaires.
Exchange rate to £ sterling: 121·093 (26 Jan. 1987).
Political history and government: Formerly the Belgian Congo, independent as the Republic of the Congo on 30 June 1960. Renamed the Democratic Republic of the Congo on 1 Aug. 1964. Power was seized on 24 Nov. 1965 by army officers, led by Maj-Gen (later Lt-Gen) Joseph-Désiré Mobutu (from January 1972 called Mobutu Sese Seko). The new régime, with Mobutu as President, was approved by Parliament on 28 Nov. 1965. A new constitution approved by referendum, was adopted on 24 June 1967. Mobutu was elected President by popular vote on 31 Oct.–1 Nov. 1970 and inaugurated for a 7-year term on 5 Dec. 1970. The country's present name was introduced on 27 Oct. 1971. A unicameral National Legislative Council of 244 members, led by Mobutu, was elected by acclamation for 5 years on 2 Nov. 1975. The President appoints and leads the National Executive Council, a cabinet of State Commissioners with departmental responsibilities. On 6 July 1977 the President appointed a First State Commissioner, equivalent to a Prime Minister. Direct elections for a new Legislative Council were held on 15–16 Oct. 1977, when 268 members were elected (from 2080 candidates) to serve a 5-year term. Mobutu was re-elected President (unopposed) and sworn in on 5 Dec. 1977.

Since 1970 the only authorized political party has been the *Mouvement populaire de la révolution* (MPR) or People's Revolutionary Movement. The highest policy-making body is the MPR's Political Bureau. In 1979 the Bureau had 38 members, including 20 appointed by the President and 18 elected (two from each region and two from Kinshasa). The Bureau has a 7-

member Permanent Committee. On 14 Feb. 1980 the Legislative Council approved constitutional changes, including the dissolution of the MPR's executive secretariat and the replacement of elected members of the MPR's Political Bureau, when their terms expired in 1982, by presidential nominees. A meeting of the Political Bureau on 31 July–4 Aug. 1980 agreed on the establishment of a central committee (114 members appointed by the President on 2 Sept.) and the creation of a new executive secretariat.

Zaire comprises eight regions, each headed by an appointed Commissioner, and the capital district of Kinshasa, under a Governor.
Length of roadways: 90 100 miles *145 000 km*.
Length of railways: 3264 miles *5252 km*.
Universities: 3.
Adult illiteracy: 84·6% (males 70·8%; females 97·2%) in 1955–58.
Expectation of life: Males 41·9 years; females 45·1 years (UN estimates for 1970–75).
Defence: Military service voluntary; total armed forces 26 000 (1985); defence expenditure: 6·6% of total government expenditure in 1982.
Foreign tourists: 24 000 in 1982.

Zambia

Official name: The Republic of Zambia.
Population: 5 661 801 (census of 1 Sept. 1980); 6 650 000 (1985 estimate).
Area: 290 586 miles² *752 614 km²*.
Languages: English (official), Nyanja, Bemba, Tonga, Lozi, Lunda, Luvale.
Religions: Roman Catholic, Protestant, Animist.
Capital city: Lusaka, population 538 469 (1980).
Other principal towns (1980): Kitwe 314 794; Ndola 282 439; Mufulira 149 778; Chingola 145 869; Kabwe 143 035.
Highest point: 6210 ft *1893 km*.
Principal mountain range: Muchinga Mts.
Principal rivers: Zambezi and tributaries (Kafue, Luangwa), Luapula.
Head of State: Dr Kenneth David Kaunda (b. 28 Apr. 1924), President.
Prime Minister: K. S. K. Musokotwane.
Climate: Hot season September–November, rainy season November–April, winter May–September. Day temperatures 27°C *80°F* to 38°C *100°F* in hot season, sharp fall at night. Average annual rainfall from 635 mm *25 in* in south to 1270 mm *50 in* in north. In Lusaka, average annual minimum 18°C *64°F*, maximum 31°C *88°F*, average rainfall 8382 mm *33 in*.
Labour force: 363 800 in 1983: Agriculture, forestry and fisheries 9·4%; Mining and quarrying 16·6%; Manufacturing 13·2%; Construction 11·6%; Transport and communications 7%.
Gross domestic product: 4290 million kwacha in 1984: Agriculture, forestry and fishing 16·3%; Mining and quarrying 15·5%; Manufacturing 23%; Trade 13·7%; Community and social services 18·7%.
Exports: US$866 million in 1986: Copper and other non-ferrous metals 96%.
Monetary unit: Zambian kwacha. 1 kwacha = 100 ngwee.
Denominations:
Coins 1, 2, 5, 10, 20, 50 ngwee.
Notes 50 ngwee; 1, 2, 5, 10, 20, 50 kwacha.
Exchange rate to £ sterling: 22·164 (26 Jan. 1987).
Political history and government: Formerly the British protectorate of Northern Rhodesia. On 24 Oct. (UN Day) 1964 the territory became an independent republic, as Zambia (named from the Zambezi river), and a member of the Commonwealth. A one-party state was proclaimed on 13 Dec. 1972 and inaugurated by a new constitution on 25 Aug. 1973. Legislative power is held by the unicameral National Assembly, with 135 members (10 nominated by the President and 125 elected for five years by universal adult suffrage). There is also an advisory House of Chiefs (27 members) to represent traditional tribal authorities. Executive power is held by the President, elected by popular vote at the same time as the Assembly.

He appoints a Cabinet, led by a Prime Minister, to conduct the administration. The sole authorized party is the United National Independence Party (UNIP), led by the President. The highest policy-making body is UNIP's Central Committee (25 members), to which the Cabinet is subordinate. Zambia is divided into 9 provinces, each administered by a member of the Central Committee.
Length of roadways: 22 627 miles *36 415 km* (31 Dec. 1979).
Length of railways: 748 miles *1204 km*.
Universities: 1.
Adult illiteracy: 52·4% (males 38·5%; females 65·4%) in 1969.
Expectation of life: Males 44·3 years; females 47·5 years (UN estimates for 1970–75).
Defence: Military service voluntary; total armed forces 15 500 (1984); defence expenditure, 1979: $388 million.
Foreign tourists: 100 000 approx. in 1985.

Zimbabwe

Population: 8 174 892 (1985 estimate).
Area: 150 804 miles² *390 580 km²*.
Languages: English (official), Sindebele, Chishona.
Religions: Tribal beliefs, Christian minority.
Capital city: Harare (Salisbury), population 656 000 (1982 census).
Other principal towns (1982): Bulawayo 414 000; Chitungwize 175 000; Gweru (Gwelo) 79 000; Mutara (Umtali) 70 000; Kwekwe (Que Que) 48 000; Kadoome (Gatooma) 45 000; Hwange (Wankie) 39 000; Masvingo (Fort Victoria) 31 000.
Highest point: Mount Inyangani, 8503 ft *2592 m*.
Principal mountain ranges: Enyanga, Melsetter.
Principal rivers: Zambezi and tributaries (Shangani, Umniati), Limpopo and tributaries (Umzingwani, Nuanetsi), Sabi and tributaries (Lundi, Odzi).
Head of State: Rev. Canaan Sodindo Banana (b. 5 Mar. 1936), President.
Prime Minister: Robert Gabriel Mugabe (b. 21 Feb. 1924).
Climate: Tropical, modified by altitude. Average temperature 18°C *65°F* to 24°C *75°F*. In Salisbury, average daily maximum 21°C *70°F* (June, July) to 28°C *83°F* (October), minimum 7°C *44°F* (June, July) to 15°C *60°F* (November–February), January rainiest (18 days).
Labour force: 2 177 860 in 1982: Unemployed 14·1%.
Gross domestic product: Z$5699 million in 1984: Agriculture and forestry 13·8%; Mining 9·3%; Manufacturing 27·5%; Construction 3·8%; Finance and insurance 5·4%; Distribution, hotels and restaurants 13·1%; Transport and communications 6·7%; Public administration and education 13·8%.
Exports: Z$1271 million in 1984: Food and live animals 13·2%; Tobacco 22·3%; Cotton lint 9·1%; Asbestos 5·8%; Ferro-alloys 12·2%; Nickel metal 5%.
Monetary unit: Zimbabwe dollar (Z$). 1 dollar = 100 cents.
Denominations:
Coins ½, 1, 2½, 5, 10, 20, 25 cents.
Notes 1, 2, 5, 10 dollars.
Exchange rate to £ sterling: 2·4975 (26 Jan. 1987).
Political history and government: The British South Africa Company was granted a Royal Charter over the territory on 29 Oct. 1889. On 12 Sept. 1923 Southern Rhodesia (as it was known) was transferred from the Company to the British Empire and became a colony. It was granted full self-government (except for African interests and some other matters) on 1 Oct. 1923. The colony became part of the Federation of Rhodesia and Nyasaland (the Central African Federation), proclaimed on 1 Aug. 1953. A new constitution, which removed most of the UK's legal controls (except for foreign affairs), was promulgated on 6 Dec. 1961 and made fully operative on 1 Nov. 1962. This constitution provided for a limited African franchise and

top: **ZAIRE**
centre: **ZAMBIA**
below: **ZIMBABWE**

could have led to ultimate majority rule. The Federation was dissolved on 31 Dec. 1963.

On 17 Dec. 1961 leaders of the banned National Democratic Party formed the Zimbabwe African People's Union (ZAPU), using the site of an ancient African ruin as the name of the whole country. The party split on 9 July 1963 and a breakaway group formed the Zimbabwe African National Union (ZANU) on 8 Aug. 1963.

Ian Smith became Prime Minister on 13 Apr. 1964. After Northern Rhodesia achieved independence as Zambia on 24 Oct. 1964, Southern Rhodesia became generally (although not officially) known as Rhodesia. A state of emergency was declared on 5 Nov. 1965 and Ian Smith made a unilateral declaration of independence (UDI) on 11 Nov. 1965. The Smith régime abrogated the 1961 constitution and proclaimed its own, naming the country Rhodesia. The British Government regarded UDI as unconstitutional and having no legal validity, and no other country formally recognized the territory's independence. A new constitution was approved by referendum on 20 June 1969, adopted on 29 Nov. 1969 and took effect on 2 Mar. 1970, when a republic was proclaimed.

Attempts to reach a constitutional settlement acceptable to all parties proved unsuccessful. ZAPU and ZANU had both taken up arms against the illegal régime and a full-scale guerrilla war was begun by African nationalists in Dec. 1972. After a meeting with the US Secretary of State on 19 Sept. 1976, Smith announced that his regime had agreed to proposals leading to majority rule within two years. On 9 Oct., in preparation for negotiations, ZAPU and the Mugabe faction of ZANU announced the formation of an alliance as the Patriotic Front (PF). In 1977 Smith began negotiations with three African parties within Rhodesia, although the main guerrilla groups (based in neighbouring countries) did not participate. An agreement was signed on 3 Mar. 1978 for an 'internal settlement' (not internationally recognized), providing for a transition to majority rule by 31 Dec. 1978. A transitional administration, comprising Europeans and Africans, was formed but the elections leading to majority rule were postponed.

A 'majority rule' constitution, changing the name of the country to Zimbabwe Rhodesia, was approved by the House of Assembly on 20 Jan. 1979. It vested legislative authority in a bicameral Parliament, comprising a 100-member House of Assembly (in which 72 seats were reserved for Africans and 28, including 20 directly elected, were to be held by Europeans for at least 10 years) and a Senate of 30 members.

The constitution, which included entrenched provisions safeguarding the position of whites, was approved by European voters in a referendum on 30 Jan. 1979. The new constitution was not accepted by the United Kingdom and the new régime did not gain international recognition.

At the meeting of Commonwealth heads of government in Lusaka, Zambia, on 1–7 Aug. 1979, agreement was reached on proposals for a fresh attempt to secure legal independence for the country. As a result, a constitutional conference was held in London from 10 Sept. to 15 Dec. 1979 between the British government, the Muzorewa régime, elected under the new constitution, and the PF. It was announced on 19 Oct. that all parties had agreed on the terms of a new constitution for an independent republic of Zimbabwe. On 15 Nov. agreement was reached on transitional arrangements for the pre-independence period, including the restoration of British rule and elections for a new government. The final agreement (covering constitutional, transitional and cease-fire arrangements) was signed on 21 Dec. 1979.

The independence constitution provided for the establishment of a republic under the name of Zimbabwe. Legislative power is vested in a bicameral Parliament, comprising a Senate (40 members), with delaying powers only, and a House of Assembly (100 members). Members of both houses serve a term of five years (subject to dissolution). Of the Senators, 14 are chosen by those members of the House elected by Africans; 10 are chosen by those members of the House elected by non-Africans; 10 are African chiefs elected by the Council of Chiefs (five from Mashonaland, five from Matabeleland); and six are appointed by the President on the advice of the Prime Minister. Members of the House are directly elected by adult suffrage in single-member constituencies: 80 by Africans and 20 by non-Africans. Executive power is vested in the President, a constitutional Head of State elected by Parliament for a six-year term, but is exercised in almost all cases on the advice of the Executive Council (Cabinet), led by the Prime Minister. The President appoints the Prime Minister and, on the latter's recommendation, other Ministers. The Executive Council is responsible to the House of Assembly.

On 2 Jan. 1980 the two parties in the PF announced that they would contest the elections to the new House of Assembly separately: as ZANU (PF), led by Mugabe, and as the Patriotic Front (ZAPU). The elections were again held in two stages: on 14 Feb. for non-African members and on 27–29 Feb. for African members. ZANU (PF) won an overall majority and Mugabe was appointed Prime Minister by the Governor. The 34 elective seats in the Senate were filled on 19 Mar. and the six nominated Senators appointed on 11 Apr. ZANU (PF)'s nominee for President was the sole candidate. Zimbabwe became legally independent, and a member of the Commonwealth, on 18 Apr. 1980, when the constitution entered into force and the President and Prime Minister were sworn in. The Emergency Powers Act of 1965 remained in force.

Length of roadways: 105 900 miles *170 400 km.*
Length of railways: 2110 miles *3394 km.*
Universities: 1.
Adult illiteracy: 95·3% (males 94·4%; females 96·3%) in 1962 (Africans only).
Expectation of life: Males 49·8 years; females 53·3 years (UN estimates for 1970–75). Europeans: Males 66·9 years; females 74·0 years (1961–63).
Defence: Military service selective; total armed forces 42 000 (1985); defence expenditure: 13·3% of total government expenditure in 1984–5.
Foreign tourists: 319 826 in 1985.

SOURCES

Population: Primarily *de facto* but for some countries the figures cover *de jure* population. *Source:* mainly UN, *Population and Vital Statistics Report.*

Area, Capital city and Principal towns: *Source:* national data; also UN, *Demographic Yearbook.*

Labour force: Figures refer to the total economically active population. The categorisation of the labour force is, in most cases, according to the International Standard Industrial Classification of all Economic Activities (ISIC). *Sources:* ILO, *Year Book of Labour Statistics* and *Labour Force Estimates and Projections, 1950–2000.*

Gross domestic product: Unless otherwise indicated, GDP is given in terms of purchasers' values (market prices), i.e. GDP at factor cost (producers' values) plus indirect taxes net of subsidies. Net domestic product is GDP less consumption (depreciation) of fixed capital. Gross national product (GNP) is GDP plus net income from abroad. National income is net national product, i.e. GNP less capital consumption. Net material product (NMP) comprises the net value of goods and 'material' services produced, i.e. gross output (including turnover taxes) minus intermediate material (including capital) consumption. Gross material product (GMP) is NMP plus consumption of fixed capital. *Source:* UN, *Yearbook of National Accounts Statistics* and *Monthly Bulletin of Statistics;* International Bank for Reconstruction and Development, *World Bank Atlas.*

Exports: Total merchandise exports, valued f.o.b. (free on board). *Source:* mainly UN, *Yearbook of International Trade Statistics.*

Exchange rate: In most cases the rate given is the mid-point quotation (i.e. half way between the buying and selling rates). *Sources: Financial Times.*

Length of roadways: *Source:* mainly International Road Federation, *World Road Statistics.*

Length of railways: *Source:* mainly *Railway Directory and Yearbook* (Railway Gazette International, IPC Transport Press).

Adult illiteracy: Unless otherwise stated, figures refer to persons aged 15 years and over. Literacy is defined as the ability to both read and write, so semi-literates are treated as illiterate. *Sources:* UNESCO, *Statistical Yearbook;* UN, *Demographic Yearbook.*

Expectation of life: *Source:* mainly UN, *Demographic Yearbook.*

Defence: *Source:* International Institute for Strategic Studies, *The Military Balance.*

Foreign tourists: Unless otherwise indicated, figures refer to visits for leisure or business and cover persons staying at least 24 hours or making at least one overnight stay. *Source:* UN, *Statistical Yearbook* (quoting World Tourism Organisation, Madrid).

INDEX

INDEX

INDEX

INDEX

INDEX